The New York Times
Twentieth Century in Review

THE COLD WAR
VOLUME I: 1918–1963

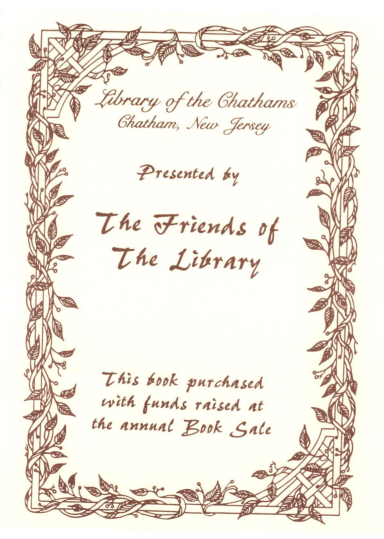

Other Titles in
The New York Times 20th Century in Review

The Gay Rights Movement

Forthcoming

Political Censorship
The Balkans

𝕿𝖍𝖊 𝕹𝖊𝖜 𝖄𝖔𝖗𝖐 𝕿𝖎𝖒𝖊𝖘
Twentieth Century in Review

THE COLD WAR
VOLUME I: 1918–1963

Editor
Francis J. Gavin

Introduction by Craig R. Whitney

FITZROY DEARBORN PUBLISHERS
CHICAGO · LONDON

For information write to:

FITZROY DEARBORN PUBLISHERS
919 North Michigan Avenue, Suite 760
Chicago IL 60611
USA

or

FITZROY DEARBORN PUBLISHERS
310 Regent Street
London W1B 3AX
England

British Library and Library of Congress Cataloging in Publication Data are available.

ISBN 1-57958-321-0

First published in the USA and UK 2001

Typeset by Print Means Inc., New York, New York

Printed by Edwards Brothers, Ann Arbor, Michigan

Cover Design by Peter Aristedes, Chicago Advertising and Design, Chicago, Illinois

CONTENTS

VOLUME I
1918–1963

VOLUME II
1964–1992

PREFACE

The unfolding of past events, whether in our own lives or the lives of great nations, can appear logical and almost predictable when viewed from the present. The cold war is a case in point. Political scientists make a compelling argument that the decades-long conflict between the United States and the Soviet Union (and to a lesser extent China) was, to use their terminology, "overdetermined." In other words, like a Greek tragedy, there was a certain inevitability to the clash and how it unfolded over time. These two giant, revolutionary states with competing ideologies and sprawling interests around the globe emerged from the ruins of World War II bound to quarrel. In retrospect, the Stalinization of Eastern Europe, the Marshall Plan and the formation of NATO, Sputnik and the space race, the intractable dispute over Berlin, and even the wars in Korea, Vietnam and Afghanistan appeared driven by unwritten but certain laws of modern international politics. Even the cold war's end seemed scripted, as the side with the bankrupt ideology eventually collapsed under its own weight.

Fortunately, tracing the cold war's development in the pages of The New York Times quickly cures one of this common but dangerous fallacy of historical determinism. These articles capture the immediacy, intensity and uncertainty of the conflict in a way no textbook can. Consider the dramatic events during the last week of October and first week of November 1956. On October 21, The New York Times led with the shocking headline, "Poles Report Firing on Russian Regiment to Prevent Its Entry From East Germany." Six days later the paper detailed the spread of the revolt in Hungary, and the Soviets appeared, at least momentarily, unprepared to intervene. But days later, a new event shared the headline—an Israeli attack into Egypt's Suez region that was supported by the British and French.

This was a key moment of the cold war. Reading these articles today, one cannot help but ask the sort of "what-if" questions that make the past come alive. How would the Soviets have responded to the revolts in Eastern Europe if the Suez debacle had never taken place? How did the American presidential election, only days away, complicate deliberations in Washington, Moscow, London, Paris, Cairo and Tel Aviv? We can never fully answer these types of questions, but the New York Times articles provide a hair-raising sense of the day-to-day, even hour-to-hour shifts that can alter international politics forever. Reading The Times from this period offers a greater sense of the contingency, the danger, the possibility of different outcomes, than most histories written decades later could ever hope to convey.

That does not mean these articles can replace historical analysis. In fact, the articles are primary historical documents, revealing the prejudices, concerns, fears and ideologies of their time. Not far beneath the surface of the typically calm and sure prose, one senses the fear in the coverage of the North Korean invasion of the South, worried awe in descriptions of the Sputnik launch, outrage at the downing of KAL Flight 007 and anticipation and hope in any article describing a superpower summit. At times, even the calm and sure prose disappears, as with the almost shrill use of the term "Red" to describe any communist, regardless of national origin, well into the 1960s. One is impressed by the effort of most New York Times writers to obtain Archimedean objectivity. Nevertheless a critical examination of these articles provides students of the past with a window into the mentalities of the day.

The New York Times 20th Century in Review: *The Cold War* is laid out in nine sections, beginning with the final days of World War I and ending 74 years later with President George Bush and President Boris Yeltsin declaring the formal end to the decades-long struggle. Though historians argue about when the cold war started, it is clear that America and Communist Russia were fascinated by each other years before their conflict began. This is why the first section, "Precursors to the Cold War: America and the Soviet Union Enter the World Stage," details U.S.-Russian relations before the cold war even started. The New York Times covered America's military involvement in the Russian civil war, as well as the Red scare within the United States. Throughout the 1930s, a certain myopia about the Soviet Union set in, both among elites in the country and The New York Times, and it is difficult to find articles detailing the horrors of Joseph Stalin's purges, collectivization and forced industrialization. But the paper did capture the growing specter of fascism and war in Europe and Asia. The spirit of cooperation and collaboration with "Uncle Joe," as Stalin was dubbed, throughout battles and wartime conferences is covered in great detail.

What is most interesting about the period following World War II is not that these two allies clashed so soon after the war's end, but that they cooperated for as long as they did. This transition is captured in Part II, "From Alliance to Acrimony: The Origins of the Cold War." Behind all the banner headlines proclaiming U.S.-Soviet wartime friendship, there were signs of trouble. On April 17, 1943, a small article appeared detailing Poland's request for an investigation into charges that the Soviets murdered Polish Army officers at Katyn Forest. Sixteen months later, the article on the Warsaw revolt could not hide the Soviet refusal to aid the hapless rebels. Hope persisted over reason at Yalta and even through Potsdam, as Americans and The New York Times convinced themselves that postwar cooperation could last. But speeches by two of the three wartime leaders—Stalin and Winston Churchill—during the winter months of 1946 dashed dwindling hopes. The next year saw the United States steel itself for the reality of the cold war with the Truman Doctrine, the Marshall Plan and the National Security Act.

Despite the charged rhetoric, the clash between the Soviets and Americans seemed unlikely to break out in a shooting war in 1946 and 1947. But the character of the conflict began to shift ominously in 1948, starting with the Prague coup in February and intensifying with the Soviet blockade of Berlin in April. This is captured in Part III, "The Cold War Intensifies." This risk of a hot war increased even further in the second half of 1949 through 1950, following the "fall" of China, the Soviet detonation of an atomic device, the start of McCarthyism and the North Korean invasion of the South. The United States was again at war, but a different kind of war from World War II, limited and far away, yet full of terrible danger. The unspeakable shock at the intervention of "Red" China in the Korean War and the traumatic civil-military conflict caused by President Harry S. Truman's firing of Gen. Douglas MacArthur shook the confidence of the country, a sentiment well captured in these articles. The reader can sense the growing desperation in the reports, as if there was a chance that the United States might stumble into a third world war that it could actually lose.

The election of the revered commander of D-Day as president of the United States, told in Part IV, "The Eisenhower Period," began the slow process of easing the desperate sense of panic. The year 1953 witnessed the death of Stalin, the armistice in Korea and the beginning of the end of McCarthyism. There were crises during this period, and the nuclear danger never seemed far away, but conflicts over Indochina, Guatemala, Lebanon and even the Taiwan Strait seemed unlikely to result in global war. There even appeared reason for hope, as the wartime allies managed to sign a treaty on Austria and both the Soviets and Americans traded various proposals to ease tensions. There were shocks, to be sure, including the Soviet crackdown in Hungary and the launching of Sputnik. But one had the sense that while cold war competition could last for decades longer, there was no reason to think it should lead inevitably to atomic Armageddon.

That growing sense of calm was ruptured on November 11, 1958, when Soviet Premier Nikita Khrushchev demanded an end to the four-power occupation of Berlin. This incident initiated the terrifying period chronicled in Part V, "The Great Crises: Berlin, Cuba and Elsewhere." Reading the articles from those years, one is hard put to determine what was real and what was theater. The "Kitchen" debates between Khrushchev and Vice-President Richard Nixon, the downing of an American U-2 reconnaissance plane, the failure of the Paris summit, the beginnings of the space race, the Bay of Pigs fiasco, the series of Soviet ultimatums on Berlin—these events were frightening, but weren't there large elements of posturing in both the American and Soviet positions? That these episodes in fact amounted to a real clash, the closest the Soviets and Americans came to war, was confirmed in the summer of 1961 by the disastrous Vienna summit and then reaffirmed with President John F. Kennedy's call for partial mobilization and Khrushchev's decision to build the Berlin Wall. The tension rose as H-bomb testing resumed and a war of nerves broke out over Berlin. The confrontation culminated in the Cuban Missile Crisis in October 1962, perhaps the most dangerous two weeks of the entire cold war.

The post-Missile-Crisis period, which should have seen decreased tension and increased American power, instead witnessed "Vietnam and American Retreat," covered in Part VI. Perhaps even more interesting than *what* events The Times covered during this period was *how* they were covered. The tone of the articles shifts, subtly and unmistakably, as doubts over the United States' policies in Southeast Asia mushroomed. While Vietnam dominated the coverage, The Times followed many other critical stories, including the six-day Arab-Israeli war, the Glassboro superpower summit, China's Cultural Revolution and the crushing of the Prague uprising by the Soviet Union.

Watergate dominates our memory of the Nixon and Ford period. But as Part VII, "Détente and Confrontation," reveals, it was also a time of extraordinary movement in world politics. In West Germany, Chancellor Willy Brandt ushered in "Ostpolitik" with the East. The Bretton Woods international monetary system was upended, the Middle East exploded into war again, and India and Pakistan fought a quick but costly conflict. America finally extricated itself from Vietnam, but not before suffering tens of thousands more casualties and rending the domestic political scene still further. But the cold war entered a mature, less dangerous phase, as President Richard Nixon visited China and pursued arms control with the Soviets. The danger of superpower war receded.

Or so it seemed. The presidency of Jimmy Carter initially marked a move away from the harsh rhetoric of the cold war toward the more uplifting theme of human rights. But as Part VIII, "Cold War II" reveals, it was too soon to call the bipolar conflict over. The New York Times chronicled the deteriorating superpower relations, culminating in the brutal Soviet invasion of Afghanistan. The 1980 election in the United States brought to power Ronald Reagan, a politician ideologically driven by a deep distrust of communism and a fervent belief in the need to strengthen America's defenses. The year 1983, like 1949, 1953 and 1962, marked one of the turning points of the cold war. Reagan denounced the Soviet Union as the "focus of evil" in the modern world and two weeks later laid out his Strategic Defense Initiative to the world. Grenada was invaded, the United States pursued controversial policies throughout Latin America, and NATO deployed intermediate-range nuclear missiles despite widespread protests in Western Europe. The Soviets and Americans traded increasingly harsh invectives, and the world was given a fictional account of what a thermonuclear war might look like through ABC's broadcast of "The Day After," one of the most watched programs in television history.

Historians will long debate what caused the stunning changes chronicled in the final section, "The End of the Cold War." But the articles included here convey two emotions felt universally during that period—great surprise and hope. The emergence of Mikhail Gorbachev as a new type of Soviet leader and his dramatic summits with Reagan at Geneva, Reykjavik, Washington and Moscow took the world by storm. But the real transformation of the cold war came later. In 1989, the most magical year of the cold war, Soviet soldiers left Afghanistan, Poland set free elections, Czechoslovakia chose dissident playwright Vaclav Havel as its president, and the terrible symbol of the East-West divide in Europe, the Berlin Wall, was torn down. There were setbacks and dangers along the way, as China's Communists ruthlessly put down protests and reactionary forces in Russia tried to halt the disintegration of the Soviet Union. But the suddenness and ease with which this terrible, decades-long conflict ended could never have been predicted.

I hope the articles I have selected will lure students of all ages into further exploring the history of the cold war, a terrifying conflict that dominated international politics and news coverage for almost half a century, and whose effects will be felt for years to come.

In closing, I would like to thank Andrew Erdmann of Harvard University and Shelly Reese of the University of Virginia for their help. I would like to offer particular thanks to the project's research assistant, Christopher Freise of the University of Virginia who provided indispensable assistance and advice on the book.

Dr. FRANCIS J. GAVIN

Francis J. Gavin is an assistant professor at the LBJ School of Public Affairs at the University of Texas at Austin. Previously, he was a John M. Olin Postdoctoral Fellow in National Security Affairs at Harvard University's Center for International Affairs and an International Security Fellow at Harvard's Center for Science and International Affairs. He has published scholarly articles in the "Journal of Cold War Studies," "Diplomatic History," the "Journal of European Integration History" and "Orbis," and his book, "Gold, Dollars and Power: Money, Security and the Politics of the U.S. Balance of Payments Deficit, 1958–1971," will be published in 2002.

INTRODUCTION

By Craig R. Whitney

Beyond a doubt, two world wars and the cold war that followed reshaped the world in the 20th century. European and Pacific powers with global colonial ambitions rose and fell, the Soviet Union rose and fell, China rose resurgent. But the overwhelming new fact at the beginning of the 21st century was the emergence of a single global power, the United States, so dominating that the French invented a new word to describe it: "hyperpower." And it was not American conquest in the two world wars, but the triumph of American, democratic, free-market economic values over Marxist totalitarianism in the cold war that created a state of affairs, in the Western world at least, not seen since the days of the Pax Romana.

There was much that was troubling in the victory. The 45-year-long struggle with the Soviet Union ended with that nation's demise, but that struggle helped magnify many smaller conflicts that remained unsettled long after the cold war was only a distant memory.

In another time, Cuba and the United States might have come to terms after Fidel Castro overthrew the corrupt dictatorship of Fulgencio Batista, even though Castro was a communist; in the cold war, the Cuban-Soviet alliance brought the world to the brink of nuclear cataclysm in 1962.

Korea and Vietnam were sundered into communist and noncommunist halves. In Korea, the United States and its United Nations allies fought a proxy war against the Soviet Union and a real one against Communist China. In Vietnam, American leaders saw communism as an attempt by China and the Soviet Union to extend their control to all of Southeast Asia. In another era, the United States might have supported Ho Chi Minh's determination to rid Vietnam of the vestiges of French colonialism; instead, a war in a small Asian country that should not have been of any strategic or economic significance to the United States cost 58,000 American and millions of Vietnamese and Cambodian lives. The American military, traumatized by its failure in Vietnam, gradually rebuilt itself, no longer as a citizens' army but as an all-professional force wary of involvement in overseas adventures unless victory and quick withdrawal could be assured in advance.

The Middle East pitted America and its ally Israel against the Soviet Union and its allies in the Arab world, with the global ideological struggle serving to prolong and worsen the underlying regional antagonism, until Egypt broke the pattern when Anwar Sadat went to Jerusalem in 1977. African countries struggling with ethnic problems left behind by colonialism became deadly battlegrounds for factions supported and armed by rival ideological camps, while India, often joined by countries that did not share its democratic values, led a movement that sought to remove its members from the fray through "nonalignment."

But the cold war also produced a historical transformation that no one living at the beginning of the 20th century would have thought possible: a free and united Europe from the Atlantic almost to the Urals, as Charles de Gaulle put it, with blood enemies like Germany, France, Britain, Italy and Austria all pursuing democratic values and building prosperity during a peace that lasted more than 50 years. With the Soviet Union armed to the teeth at their eastern doorstep, the Western Europeans, shielded, aided and encouraged to unite by the United States, buried their past differences to create the longest economic boom they had ever known, prolonged and protected by the American-led NATO alliance. The American strategic umbrella shielded Japan, Korea and Southeast Asian democracies as well, and once American antagonism with Communist China ended, a true "greater East Asian co-prosperity sphere"—quite unlike the one that a militarized Japan had tried to impose by force 50 years earlier—increased the standard of living and ensured the well-being of millions upon millions of Asian peoples.

Though the cold war did not begin until after the Western allies of World War II fell out with the Soviet Union, the clash of world views that underlay the conflict had begun decades earlier. It was an irony of history that Marxism, spawned by the Industrial Revolution, would first take root in Russia, the one large European country that had never been industrialized, while the world's biggest industrial giant, the United States, rooted Marxism out before it ever had a chance to sprout. "Bolsheviks" were sniffed out at Ellis Island in 1919 the way drug smugglers would be at John F. Kennedy airport many decades later, then detained and deported. "Deportation is the answer of the United States Government to the challenge of I.W.W. [Industrial Workers of the World] and Bolshevist agitators who come to this country with the avowed purpose of stirring up trouble in industry and social life," The Chicago Tribune reported then, and newspapers like The New York Times picked up the report and republished it without a negative word.

At the time, American troops were fighting the Bolsheviks in Siberia and in Murmansk in Russia's Arctic north in a brief attempt to roll back the "Reds," as Times headlines were already referring to the communists long before anybody ever dreamed there would be a cold war. The "Reds"—more than the "Huns" who had drawn the reluctant United States into Europe's struggles in World War I, even more than the Japanese whose ethnic cousins were interned in America during World War II—conjured up in the American mind a combination of both external and internal subversion.

It was not until 1933 that the United States extended diplomatic recognition to the Soviet Union. Hopes that formal diplomatic relations would contribute to the establishment of world peace were dashed when Joseph Stalin and Adolph Hitler joined forces in 1939 to divide up Eastern Europe. But when Germany turned its armies toward Moscow in 1941, it sealed its own doom and unwittingly assured the emergence of the United States and Russia after the war as global and military powers, each with a nuclear arsenal capable of annihilating much of the globe—the Damoclean sword that created this new state of hostilities called the cold war.

For most of the next few decades, Europe was the theater where danger that the cold war could turn hot seemed greatest. The fear arose after a frightening, systematic Soviet campaign of subversion and subjugation of the Eastern European countries that Stalin's armies had wrested from the Nazis. "Totalitarian regimes imposed upon free peoples, by direct or indirect aggression, undermine the foundations of international peace and hence the security of the United States," President Harry S. Truman warned in 1947 as Greece seemed about to go under in turn, and perhaps it would have if the United States had not come to its aid. The Truman Doctrine underlay the Berlin Airlift that kept the Russians from squeezing off West Berlin, an island of freedom 110 miles inside the Russian occupation zone in Germany, in 1948.

Perceiving Soviet threats to freedom in Western Europe as threats to the United States itself, Washington established the North Atlantic Treaty Organization (NATO) in 1949 and, through the Marshall Plan, provided economic aid to its prostrate Western European allies and West Germany, encouraging them to lay aside the antagonisms of the past and work together to build a prosperous future, as they did with the Common Market, later the European Union, starting in 1957. If the American strategic nuclear umbrella made Soviet attack on Western Europe unthinkable, so too did the fear of Soviet nuclear retaliation keep the Western allies from attempting to "roll back" Soviet control over Eastern Europe, even when subjugated peoples tried to rise up in revolt against it in East Germany in 1953, in Poland and Hungary in 1956, and in Czechoslovakia in 1968.

In Asia, after Communist forces aided and abetted by the Soviet Union won the civil war in China in 1949, bringing hundreds of millions more people under Marxist rule, application of the Truman Doctrine was more problematic. Secretary of State Dean Acheson would later be blamed for inviting North Korea to invade South Korea in 1950 by including

Japan but not Korea in the American Pacific defense perimeter in a speech in Washington early that year. But the United Nations, led by the United States, was able to come to South Korea's aid because the Soviet Union's delegate, Yakov A. Malik, was boycotting sessions of the Security Council to protest its refusal to throw out Nationalist China.

The North Korean invasion, Truman said, made it "plain beyond all doubt that Communism has passed beyond the use of subversion to conquer independent nations and will now use armed invasion and war." By "Communism" he meant not only the new Communist Chinese regime in Beijing but something else—a vast, creeping menace centrally directed from Moscow that was a threat to American interests all over the "free world" but also to Americans at home. Senator Joseph McCarthy and others exploited this nightmare vision to pursue ideological warfare against "un-American activities," whipping up an atmosphere that in the late 1940s and early 1950s sometimes verged on hysteria.

The Korean War brought American troops into direct combat in 1950, not with Russian but with Chinese forces, in a conflict that ended in stalemate but killed nearly 34,000 Americans. Not until 47 years after the conflict ended did the two Koreas finally begin to discuss peace, with American troops still stationed along the demilitarized zone between them, their presence regarded by both sides, in the end, as an indispensable guarantee of regional security and stability.

Communism made its way into the Western Hemisphere when the United States spurned Fidel Castro after his victory in 1959. Washington failed in an attempt to unseat him with the Bay of Pigs invasion in 1961, but in the following year, the Soviet leader Nikita Khrushchev had to back down in the Cuban Missile Crisis, the closest the world came to nuclear holocaust during all of the cold war. The Kennedy Administration's firm resistance to Khrushchev's attempt to challenge the Monroe Doctrine by sneaking nuclear-tipped missiles into America's own backyard prevailed over the Russians then, and never again did American troops or mercenaries try to topple Castro by force. Nonetheless, U.S. hostility toward his regime remained vigorous a decade after the cold war was over.

But below the nuclear threshold, elsewhere, in Asian, African and Caribbean countries where the legacy of European colonialism made Marxist ideas attractive to leaders seeking to rid themselves of foreign domination, the cold war could and often did turn deadly. In places like Congo, Mozambique and Angola, tens of thousands of people would die in what were to some extent proxy wars between the United States and the Soviet Union, who dared not fight with each other. In Latin America, until the 1980s, almost any military dictator seemed to look good to Washington as long as the Cuban contagion was kept from spreading to other places in the Western Hemisphere.

In Asia, United States policymakers completely misread the nature of Ho Chi Minh's struggle to complete the liberation of Vietnam from French colonial rule, with help from Communist China and the Soviet Union after 1954. In response, the United States tried to build South Vietnam into an anticommunist bulwark intended to keep the Chinese from rolling down the Southeast Asian peninsula to Singapore. That the Vietnamese had spent thousands of years fending off Chinese domination and considered the Chinese their hereditary enemies seemed irrelevant to American officials, including Secretary of State Dean Rusk, who said American involvement was necessary to stop "the steady extension of Communist power through force and threat."

The Vietnamese communists finally did win the independence they had sought and unified the country under their rule in 1975. Four years later, Vietnam was at war again—against China.

If Vietnam taught Americans that there were limits to what they could achieve in their global crusade against communism, Afghanistan taught Soviet leaders that there were limits to their global crusade to spread it. Moscow's attempt to impose a Communist regime in 1979 on a fractious Islamic nation with fearsomely difficult terrain quickly became the same kind of deadly and costly stalemate that had bogged down the United States in Vietnam.

The seemingly simple and stark certainties of the early cold war had by then given way to complexity. The Sino-Soviet alliance had turned into a Sino-Soviet ideological split, one that presidents Richard Nixon and Jimmy Carter quickly seized on to establish U.S. relations with Beijing and play a new "China card" against Moscow. And, starting with Nixon, American presidents began to engage Soviet leaders in negotiations aimed at putting a ceiling on the lethal nuclear arms race, producing the first strategic arms limitation agreement in 1972.

Weary of being forever on war footing, Germany and the other European allies began seeking détente with the Soviet Union on their own. But Soviet leaders inadvertently sowed the seeds of their own system's destruction in 1975 by embracing a historic European security accord in Helsinki. Leonid Brezhnev had sought an agreement in which the West would recognize Russia as a legitimate European continental power and regard Eastern Europe's borders behind the zone as inviolate. But growing dissident minorities in almost every Eastern European country and in the Soviet Union seized on the promises of human rights and democracy written into the Helsinki accords, demanding that they be observed and respected. And the United States, as a full party to the Helsinki Accord, loudly championed those rights.

By the late 1980s, a younger Soviet leader, Mikhail S. Gorbachev, recognized that the demand for freedom was legitimate. More than that, he saw that as economy and industry grew more complex, totalitarianism without freedom was incapable of competing on either economic or, ultimately, military grounds. Gorbachev saw the Soviet planned economy, and the military-industrial complex that depended on it, beginning to fall down around his ears. Meanwhile, Ronald Reagan, leading a resurgent American economy into the greatest military buildup since World War II, challenged him in Berlin, "Mr. Gorbachev, tear down this wall."

And on the night of November 9, 1989, the Wall, which had gone up on August 13, 1961, to keep the people of East Germany from running away from communism, did come down. Hungary had set the stage the previous summer, symbolically rolling up the barbed wire on its border with Austria, an opening quickly seized upon by tens of thousands of East Germans on vacation in Hungary. And when Gorbachev made it clear that Soviet tanks in East Germany would stay in their bases when East Germans took to the streets to demand the basic human freedoms so long denied them, the whole Eastern European Communist system began to unravel. By 1990, all of Eastern Europe except Yugoslavia had overthrown Communist rule, Germany was reunited, and the following year the Soviet Union was no more.

Could not just peaceful coexistence but real peace have been achieved decades earlier, if people like John Foster Dulles and Konrad Adenauer had been willing to accommodate Soviet strategic interests in Europe rather than pushing back against them? Stalin had offered in 1952 to withdraw Soviet occupation forces from a free and united Germany, but Adenauer had preferred to integrate West Germany into free Western Europe rather than run the risk of his country's becoming a "people's democracy" like those the Russians had imposed in the East. West Germany rearmed and joined the alliance, while Soviet forces remained in vastly superior numbers in East Germany and Eastern Europe. Spies from both sides of the Iron Curtain, using identical weapons of blackmail and subversion, played their deadly games of espionage. And steadily, the power and the influence of the United States grew in a global economy whose prosperity was protected by American strategic military might.

President Dwight D. Eisenhower himself had called, in his farewell address, for vigilance over a military-industrial complex that was given its own logic and momentum by the demands of the cold war, but nuclear arsenals on both sides expanded to incredible dimensions despite the 1972 arms limitation agreement.

But the conflict was not merely a figment of the fevered American imagination, nor was it a pretext for the projection of American economic imperialism, or for American military preponderance. The Soviet menace to freedom in Europe was real through many decades, and American firmness in resisting that threat, with the NATO allies, brought stability, peace and prosperity to Western countries in such measure that as soon as the Soviet Union collapsed, its former satellites clamored to join both the European Union and the NATO alliance.

The end of the cold war brought new problems. Old ethnic tensions that had been stifled under Communist rule or suppressed by the danger of escalation into global nuclear conflict produced conflict in the Balkans almost immediately, bringing about the violent disintegration of Yugoslavia and finally dragging NATO and the United States into their first war on the continent in 50 years—a bombing campaign that did not cost a single American life. Russian troops that had limped out of Afghanistan in 1989 were soon sent to fight against their own erstwhile compatriots in Chechnya, and the United States and its allies showed no inclination to try to stop the Russian attacks with military force. In Africa, when Hutu people began massacring Tutsis in Rwanda in 1994, the United States and its European allies declined to intervene to prevent a humanitarian catastrophe.

In 1990 and 1991, Western troops mobilized and fought a war in the Persian Gulf after Iraq, apparently under the impression that all the wraps were off now that the cold war was over, brazenly seized Kuwait. That conflict ended with Sadam Hussein still in power in Baghdad, leaving the cauldron of violence simmering for most of a decade. And, even without the cold war to fuel the conflict, Israel and its Arab neighbors remained divided over Jerusalem and Palestine in ways that seemed no less intractable than they had been when Moscow and Washington had squared off in opposing camps.

The cold war coda finally came in Europe with the downfall of Slobodan Milosevic in Yugoslavia at the end of 2000. By that time, in Asia, the United States was building a new economic and political relationship with its former adversaries in China in a new, global economy driven by technology and communication.

But the new era that brought American "hyperpower" also made the United States the scapegoat for all those who felt left out, victimized, or ignored in the new order of things. Terrorism would remain a grave threat to American interests, fueled by resentment long after the disappearance of the Communist powers who had encouraged anti-American guerrilla movements during the cold war.

Of all the challenges the United States faced, none was greater, perhaps, than that of figuring out how to bring prosperity and democracy to the third world African and Latin Americzan countries that had been denied well-being by the diversion of constructive economic resources to military ends, the greatest human sacrifice imposed by the cold war. Redeeming that sacrifice could well be the heaviest burden imposed by the victory.

Craig R. Whitney is an assistant managing editor of The New York Times. In his 30 years with the newspaper, he has served as bureau chief in Saigon, Bonn, Moscow and London and as Washington editor and foreign editor. He contributed heavily to the paper's coverage of the fall of communism in Europe in 1989 and 1990. His book, "Spy Trader," published by Times Books/Random House, profiles the East German lawyer and cold war go-between Wolfgang Vogel.

PART I

PRECURSORS TO THE COLD WAR:
AMERICA AND THE SOVIET UNION ENTER THE WORLD STAGE

January 4, 1918

ALLIES NOW MAY RECOGNIZE LENINE

*Attitude of Powers Modified as Result of
Peace Conference Failure.*

WILL MAKE POLICY CLEAR

*New British Ambassador "in Marked Sympathy with
Revolutionary Russia's Ideas."*

Special Cable to The New York Times.

LONDON, Friday, Jan. 4—The Daily Chronicle this morning says:

"In view of the developments in the peace negotiations between Russia and the Central Powers which appear to have broken down it is now understood that at least de facto recognition may be given by the Western Powers to the Lenine Government.

"A statement of the allied policy will shortly be sent to Russia, which will be of a democratic character. As a consequence and also on the same presumption regarding the course of events, Mr. Litvinof, who has been appointed Bolshevist Ambassador in London, may also receive de facto recognition and occupy the Russian Embassy in London. Sir George Buchanan, who is to retire shortly under the age limit, will also be replaced by a diplomat 'in marked sympathy with the ideas of revolutionary Russia.' "

"Sir George is leaving Petrograd for London immediately, having obtained Trotzky's permission to depart, along with a number of military and civil officers." The foregoing points are taken from a statement by a diplomatic correspondent of The Chronicle, who writes as follows:

"Circumstances obviously have changed in the last few hours as the result of the Bolshevist discovery of German duplicity. As our own correspondent expressed it, the German method has been to give with one hand and take away with the other. Now that the Russian Government is acutely aware of this, anything may happen.

"There are three alternatives. The Bolsheviki will give way or the Germans, or there will be a rupture of relations. The first is hardly likely in view of Trotzky's declaration. The second is possible, for the Germans are past masters in the art of specious compromise. But the third is most probable, since the Bolsheviki have exhibited a perspicacity which was hardly expected in this country. Russia is a land of boundless surprises, and we may quite possibly witness a revival of the war. If not in its most active form, it might be at least a sullenly defensive war, necessitating the keeping on the frontier of a considerable German force. It would at least prevent those pleasant and profitable commercial exchanges which Germany hopes for.

"Assuming such situation and consolidation of Bolshevist power—provided of course, failure to extract a peace does not wreck the Lenine regime—then recognition of that power as a de facto Government follows. Since that is so, a Socialist would be the logical representative of that Government. Maxim Litvinoff, who has been appointed by Trotzky, is, therefore, a likely enough occupant of Chesham Place. Fresh-colored, genial, large-minded, attached to England, where he has lived for nine years, and to English institutions—he has married an English wife—he has many friends.

"Naturally the question of our own embassy at Petrograd is raised. Sir George Buchanan, whose services, as well as his personal courage, cannot be too highly estimated, will, in the natural order of things, shortly retire, for he approaches the age limit. In his place would be sent probably a diplomat in marked sympathy with the ideas of revolutionary Russia.

"Be that as it may, we may expect shortly some new statement of policy in regard to Russia which, should it lean toward the latest developments of democracy, would undoubtedly strengthen the Allies' cause in Russia."

The Chronicle, discussing the situation editorially, says:

"The Governments of Britain, France, and the United States cannot be indifferent to what is happening, and they would be foolish if they let their case go by default for the sake of persisting in nonrecognition of the Bolshevist Government. There has been too much abdication of this sort on our part already. Formal recognition is always a many sided question, calling for circumspection and often for delay, but the practical recognition, which consists in maintaining active relations with as little friction as possible and with vigilant attention to practical issues, can never be embarked on too soon. The Allies did not embark on it soon enough."

As regards Buchanan's successor The Chronicle says: "What is wanted for the moment is not so much a new Ambassador as a Chargé d'Affaires of an unconventional type, a good, practical man, and at the same time a man acceptable to the de facto Government, to make the best of Anglo-Russian relations, whatever the internal Russian situation may be. Such a man may conceivably be found inside the ranks of the diplomatic service though he is likelier to be found outside."

The Chronicle continues: "The impending vacancies at our Paris and Washington Embassies are of another kind. They require to be filled at once by Ambassadors of the highest authority and ability, higher than any shown by the outgoing occupants of these posts. Much more is needed than the usual level of British Ambassadorial capacity, such as it has shown itself during the last two generations under the system of an aristocratic diplomatic service. The Government ought to go outside and from the ranks of politics, law, journalism, or business appoint men of thoroughly tried experience and capacity. We have many capable men who would be worthy and acceptable representatives of England at Washington, such as Viscount Grey, Earl Reading, and Austin Chamberlain. Britain has suffered too much in this country from incompetent Ambassadors appointed in the routine of a bad service. She cannot afford to follow that routine blindly in these crucial instances."

* * *

March 4, 1918

PEACE SIGNED, GERMAN ADVANCE ENDS; RUSSIA FORCED BY NEW TERMS TO CEDE LANDS TAKEN FROM TURKEY IN 3 WARS

TALK USELESS, ENVOYS SAID

Delay Would Only Make Things Worse—
Aviator Bombs Petrograd.

ANCIENT BORDER RESTORED

Regions of Batoum, Kars, and Karabagh, in Caucasus,
Are Given Up.

RUMANIA'S TURN NOW

Basis of Conditions Fixed by Central Powers
Agreed To by King Ferdinand.

BERLIN, March 3, (Via London)—"By reason of the signing of the peace treaty with Russia," says the official communication from headquarters tonight, "military movements in Great Russia have ceased."

PETROGRAD, March 3—The peace treaty with Germany has been signed.

The following message, addressed to Premier Lenine and Foreign Minister Trotzky, had been received yesterday at the Smolny Institute from the delegation at Brest-Litovsk:

As we anticipated, deliberations on a treaty of peace are absolutely useless, and could only make things worse in comparison with the ultimatum of Feb. 21. They might even assume the character of leading to the presentation of another ultimatum.

In view of this fact, and in consequence of the Germans' refusal to cease military action until peace is signed, we have resolved to sign the treaty without discussing its contents, and leave after we have attached our signatures. We, therefore, have requested a train, expecting to sign today and leave afterward.

The most serious feature of the new demands compared with those of Feb. 21 is the following:

To detach the regions of Karaband, Kars, and Batoum from Russian territory on the pretext of the right of peoples to self-determination.

AMSTERDAM, March 3—A dispatch from Brest-Litovsk filed yesterday says that fresh peace negotiations with Russia were opened at a plenary meeting under the chairmanship of Minister von Rosenberg, assistant to the Foreign Secretary.

As regards the regulation of political questions, the Chairman proposed that a common treaty should be concluded between the four Teutonic allies and Russia while economic compacts and legal questions should be dealt with partly in appendices to the main treaty and partly in supplementary treaties for each separate allied power.

The head of the Russian delegation expressed agreement with this plan, whereupon the actual negotiations were begun. The Chairman handed the Russian Chairman the draft of the main political treaty drawn up jointly by the Allies, and gave a detailed explanation of the individual treaty stipulations. The drafts for the economic and legal agreements, with a corresponding explanation, were likewise communicated. The Russian delegation reserved determination of its attitude to the individual points until the material in its entirety is laid before it. The negotiations were continued in the afternoon, and the next plenary sitting was fixed for this (Sunday) morning at 11 o'clock.

According to reports emanating from Poland, Leon Trotzky, the Bolshevist Foreign Minister, did not return to the peace conference at Brest-Litovsk because Germany objected to his continuance as a Russian delegate. It is stated that Trotzky's resignation will be forthcoming as a result.

Semi-official German and Austrian statements received here today set forth claims of forward steps toward peace between the Central Powers and Rumania.

The Berlin dispatch quotes a Bucharest message under today's date declaring that the Rumanians have accepted the basis for negotiations proposed by the Central Powers and will send representatives to deliberate upon the conclusion of peace.

The Vienna dispatch states that word has been received from Bucharest that the negotiations with the Rumanians are progressing favorably.

VIENNA, March 3, (via London)—The War Office today issued the following announcement:

The armistice with Rumania came to an end yesterday. The Rumanian Government declared itself ready to enter upon a great armistice preparatory to negotiations in connection with peace parleys on the basis of conditions fixed by the Central Powers.

THE NEW TERRITORY TAKEN.

Restores to Turkey Lands Lost Through Four Wars in 90 Years.

The territorial cessions in Transcaucasia which the Germans have now added to those previously demanded in Eastern Europe destroy the results of four wars waged by Russia against Turkey—1828–29, 1834–5, 1877–8, and the campaigns in Asia Minor of the present war. Batoum, a sea-port twenty miles north of the Turkish frontier, has one of the best harbors on the Black Sea, and has been the port of outlet for much of the petroleum and other products of Transcaucasia. The Government of which it was the capital was ceded to Russia after the war of 1878, and eight years later the city was strongly fortified by Russia as a base for future conflicts with Turkey.

The frontier province of which Kars is the capital, lying to the east of Batoum, was also part of the spoils of the war of 1878. Kars itself, a city strongly situated and occupying a strategic position, has been the scene of much bitter fighting in the wars between Turkey and Russia. It was captured in 1828 by the Russian armies, but restored to Turkey upon the conclusion of peace. Again, in the Crimean War, it was taken after a six months' siege, in which the Turkish army was commanded by the English General Williams, but again the treaty of peace forced Russia to give it up.

In the Russo-Turkish war of 1877–8 the Russian Army, after successes in the early Summer of 1877, besieged Kars in June, but after several weeks, during which there was desperate fighting and considerable glory to both sides, the siege was raised following the reinforcement of the Turkish Army. In October, however, the Turks, under Mukhtar Pasha, were defeated, and Kars was again besieged and stormed after a heroic defense on Nov. 11. This time both the town and the surrounding district were allowed to remain in Russian hands.

The region mentioned in the cable dispatches as Karaband is probably that of Karabagh, lying to the north of the Persian border in the southern part of the province of Yelizavetpol. The total area of the territories ceded is apparently about 18,000 to 20,000 square miles, and the population may be somewhat less than 1,000,000. The bulk of the inhabitants of these districts, as of the lands over the Turkish and Persian frontiers, are Armenians.

In addition to these territories which were in her possession at the outbreak of the war, Russia loses the fruits of a brilliant campaign conducted in Turkish Armenia under the leadership of the Grand Duke Nicholas Nikolaievitch in 1916.

Caucasian Campaign in This War.

Russia's offensive power in the early part of the war was occupied in Europe, and this permitted Turkey, whose troops were at that time preparing under German leadership the attack on the Suez Canal, which failed disastrously in February, 1915, and who had no other occupation than the defense of Mesopotamia against the British expedition from India, to take the initiative in Transcaucasia. While a Turkish raiding force crossed the Persian frontier to support the intrigues of the German diplomats in that country, a strong army set out from the fortress of Erzerum, fifty miles southwest of the Transcaucasian frontier, which was the centre of the strategic defense of Turkish Armenia, and moved against the Russian army in Kars. The operations culminated in a battle fought in December, 1914, at Sarikamysh, just inside the Russian border, in which the Turkish troops were disastrously defeated.

The necessity of defending the Dardanelles and Bagdad kept the Turks from making any further attempt during 1915, and the Russians were too busy on the German and Austrian fronts to make serious advances in Armenia, though a small expeditionary force landed at a Persian port on the Caspian drove the Turks pretty well out of Persia and foiled the machinations of the German agents in that country. The Caucasus front once more became active when the Grand Duke Nicholas was made Viceroy and Commander in Chief after being removed from command in Europe following the great retreat in the Summer and Fall. He spent the early part of the Winter in reorganizing the armies of the Caucasus, and in January, 1916, the Russians made a general advance. They were victorious in a number of battles, and finally, in the middle of February, stormed the forts around Erzerum and captured the city.

This victory, notable in itself, was particularly heartening to the Allies as coming at a time when they had almost forgot the taste of success. The Turkish forces driven out of Erzerum retreated westward toward Erzingan and southwest toward Mush and Bitlis. The Russians were close on their heels in the southern region and occupied Mush and Bitlis early in March. Meanwhile an army landed on the Black Sea coast captured the important port of Trebizond in April, and in July the city of Erzingan, where some of the Turkish armies had rallied, was occupied. Meanwhile a raiding force had been sent into the district of Urumiah, on the Turco-Persian border, and had cleared this of Turks, as well as inflicting losses on the Kurds of the mountains around Rowandiz.

This, however, marked the limit of the Russian advance. The troops were fighting in an extremely difficult country, with no good lines of communication, and had become scattered to a considerable extent in pursuing the Turks. Indeed, before the victory at Erzingan Mush and Bitlis had been retaken by the Turks; and attempts to establish connection with the British army in Mesopotamia failed, aside from the entry into the British camp of a squadron of Cossack raiders.

The failure of munitions caused by reactionary treachery in the Imperial Government, which hampered Brusiioff's offensive in Galicia, was apparently in evidence here, too, and the Grand Duke's armies were compelled to halt on a wide semi-circular front, 100 to 150 miles in Turkish territory. There have been no real military operations on this front since, though occasional reports have come through of the sporadic attempts made by the Turks to regain their lost ground.

The territory in the Caucasus taken from Russia by the treaty of peace is comprised within the heavy black lines shown in the map. As vaguely defined in the news from Petrograd this comprises the regions of Batoum, Kars, and Karaband, presumably Karabagh (Black Garden). The ceded territory was wrested from Turkey by Russia in three wars.

As early as last May A. F. Kerensky, then Minister of War, warned the Russians that they were in danger, if the army continued to retrograde in morale, of losing not only Armenia, which he declared they could not return to the mercies of the Turks and Kurds, but also some of the Caucasus. But apparently the troops here retained some of their fighting spirit, for as late as November the Russian troops around Erzingan were holding their own against desultory attacks.

Germany's Former Terms.

The territorial cessions and other terms demanded in Western Europe by the Germans, as made public by the Russian Government on Feb. 23, included the surrender of all of Courland, Poland, and Lithuania, except part of the Province of Grodno. "Russia renounces every claim to intervene in the internal affairs of these regions," said the official German demand as given out by the Russians. "Germany and Austria-Hungary have the intention to define further the fate of these regions, in agreement with their populations."

Livonia and Esthonia were further to be evacuated by the Russians and "occupied by German police until the date when the constitution of the respective countries shall guarantee their social security and political order."

Russia was also to stop her revolutionary crusade against Finland and the Ukraine (the frontiers of this latter country were left conveniently undefined) and to keep her warships in port until the conclusion of peace. But there was hardly a hint of the present demands in Transcaucasia in the clause: "Russia will do all in its power to secure for Turkey the orderly return of its Anatolian frontiers."

Other clauses provided for economic relations very favorable to Germany, and for the abandonment by Russia of "every propaganda and agitation, either on the part of the Government or on the part of persons supported by the Government, against members of the Quadruple Alliance and their political and military institutions, even in territories occupied by the Central Powers." There was added an indemnity, variously reported at $4,000,000,000 and $1,500,000,000.

Forty-eight hours were given for the acceptance of this proposal. A section of the Bolshevist Government wanted to fight, but Lenine forced the decision to surrender, which was announced to the Germans by wireless. At first, however, the Germans refused to recognize this promise, and continued the invasion of Russia with practically no opposition until the last two or three days, when their small advanced detachments were compelled to fall back on the main bodies.

* * *

July 21, 1918

EX-CZAR OF RUSSIA KILLED BY ORDER OF URAL SOVIET

Nicholas Shot on July 16 When It Was Feared That Czechoslovaks Might Seize Him.

WIFE AND HEIR IN SECURITY

Bolshevist Government Approves Act, Alleging Plot for a Counter-Revolution.

PRISONER'S PAPERS SEIZED

Former Emperor's Diary and Letters from Rasputin Soon to be Made Public.

LONDON, July 20—Nicholas Romanoff, ex-Czar of Russia, was shot July 16, according to a Russian announcement by wireless today.

The former Empress and Alexis Romanoff, the young heir, have been sent to a place of security.

The message announces that a counter-revolutionary conspiracy was discovered, with the object of wresting the ex-Emperor from the authority of the Soviet Council. In view of this fact and the approach of Czechoslovak bands, the President of the Ural Regional Council decided to execute the former ruler, and the decision was carried out on July 16.

The central executive body of the Bolshevist Government announces that it has important documents concerning the former Emperor's affairs, including his own diaries and letters from the monk Rasputin, who was killed shortly before the revolution. These will be published in the near future, the message declares.

The text of the Russian wireless message reads:

"At the first session of the Central Executive Committee, elected by the fifth Congress of the Councils, a message was made public that had been received by direct wire from the Ural Regional Council concerning the shooting of the ex-Czar Nicholas Romanoff.

"Recently Yekaterinburg, the capital of the Red Urals, was seriously threatened by the approach of Czechoslovak hands and a counter-revolutionary conspiracy was discovered which had as its object the wresting of the ex-Czar from the hands of the council's authority. In view of this fact, the President of the Ural Regional Council decided to shoot the ex-Czar, and the decision was carried out on July 16.

"The wife and the son of Nicholas Romanoff have been sent to a place of security.

"Documents concerning the conspiracy which was discovered have been forwarded to Moscow by a special messenger. It had been recently decided to bring the ex-Czar before a tribunal to be tried for his crimes against the people, and only later occurrences led to delay in adopting this course.

"The Presidency of the Central Executive Committee, having discussed the circumstances which compelled the Ural Regional Council to take its decision to shoot Nicholas Romanoff, decided as follows:

" 'The Russian Central Executive Committee, in the person of its President, accepts the decision of the Ural Regional Council as being regular.'

"The Central Executive Committee has now at its disposal extremely important documents concerning the affairs of Nicholas Romanoff—his diaries, which he kept almost up to his last days, the diaries of his wife and his children, and his correspondence, among which are the letters of Gregory Rasputin to the Romanoff family. These materials will be examined and published in the near future."

Execution Foreshadowed.

There have been rumors since June 24 that ex-Czar Nicholas of Russia had been assassinated. The first of these stated that he had been killed at Yekaterinburg by Red Guards. This report was denied later, but this denial was closely followed by a Geneva dispatch saying that Nicholas had been executed by the Bolsheviki after a trial at Yekaterinburg. This report seemed to be confirmed by advices to Washington from Stockholm.

The next report was what purported to be an intercepted wireless message from M. Tchitcherin, the Bolshevist Foreign Minister, in which it was stated that Nicholas was dead. Still another report was to the effect that he had been bayonetted by a guard while being taken from Yekaterinburg to Perm. Of all these reports there was no direct confirmation.

There seemingly is no question that yesterday's dispatch is authentic. It comes in the form of a Russian wireless dispatch, and, as the wireless plants of Russia are under the control of the Bolsheviki, it appears that it is an official version of the death of the former Emperor.

* * *

August 16, 1918

FIRST REGIMENT OF AMERICANS IN VLADIVOSTOK

Sent There from Manila, Landed Yesterday, and Another Is Following.

JAPANESE CHIEF ON THE WAY

Archangel Expedition Now 100 Miles from Vologda and the British Hold Baku.

BOLSHEVIKI FLEE MOSCOW

News That Entente Is Coming from East, North, and South Stirs All Russia.

Special to The New York Times.

WASHINGTON, Aug. 15—Coincident with the Tokio announcement that General Otani had on Monday left for Vladivostok to direct the operations of the Japanese Expeditionary Force in Siberia, formal announcement was authorized by Secretary Baker late this evening that the first American contingent of troops "is now arriving at Vladivostok."

This contingent is the 27th Regular Infantry Regiment of the United States Army. It is commanded by Colonel Henry D. Styer, a West Point graduate, who was at the Army War College in 1914 and is a seasoned infantry commander. The 27th, like the 31st Regiment of Infantry, which is also en route to Vladivostok, was sent from the Philippines, where both units have been serving since 1916. The arrived of the 31st has not yet been announced.

Neither of these regiments is at full war strength. They are on a peace footing. The 27th and 31st Regiments will be supplemented by other troops to be sent from the United States. Secretary Baker and General March, the Chief of Staff, have requested that the size of the Expeditionary Force be not mentioned at this time, but it can be stated with official sanction that the size of the expedition will not be in excess of 10,000 Americans.

Japan, it is understood, will send to Vladivostok an expeditionary force identical in size with that which the United States is forming.

Seek to Cut off Archangel Reds.

LONDON, Aug. 15—The allied Archangle expeditionary force has reached Pabereshskaia, 100 miles south of Archangle on the railroad toward Vologda, it is announced here.

Additional allied troops have been landed along the shore of Onega Bay, 100 miles southwest of Archangel, for the purpose of intercepting the Bolshevist forces which retired from Archangel.

Yet another allied detachment is pushing toward Kotlass, 260 miles south of Archangel, on the Dvina River.

South of the Volga River, Generals Alexieff and Denikine apparently are endeavoring to amalgamate their anti-Bolshevist forces with the army of the Czechoslovaks.

The Red forces, on retiring, are declared to have committed every form of atrocity upon the civilian population. They offered fairly determined resistance to the allied advance, and the progress of the expeditionary force was delayed.

British From Bagdad Reach Baku.

LONDON, Aug. 15—A British force from Northwestern Persia has reached the Caspian Sea and taken over a part of the defenses of Baku.

Whether the Allies will be able to hold Baku permanently in view of the difficulties of transporting supplies is too early to predict. However, if the British can hold their position a short time longer, which now seems likely, they probably will be able to cut off the enemy from an outlet to the sea, thus protecting the important oil fields of the Baku district.

It appears from the meagre information at hand in London that the British detachment voyaged by steamer from Enzelli, Russia, to Baku, demonstrates that the allied hold on the Caspian Sea already is fairly established. The allied naval forces now undoubtedly will endeavor to make secure their communications, and once this task is accomplished there will be hardly a possibility of the Central Powers gaining possession of the Baku oil fields.

The brief advices received here indicated that the Russian General Dokuchaieff was commanding at Baku.

The British advance through Persia from Bagdad was accomplished under the greatest difficulties. In the mountainous sections they were resisted by a few groups of tribesmen, but they quickly overcame this opposition. The British force crossed the Persian frontier and reached Enzelli, on the Caspian Sea, by way of Hamadan.

* * *

November 11, 1918

ARMISTICE SIGNED, END OF THE WAR!

WAR ENDS AT 6 O'CLOCK THIS MORNING

The State Department in Washington Made the Announcement at 2:45 o'Clock.

ARMISTICE WAS SIGNED IN FRANCE AT MIDNIGHT

Terms Include Withdrawal from Alsace-Lorraine, Disarming and Demobilization of Army and Navy, and Occupation of Strategic Naval and Military Points.

By The Associated Press.

WASHINGTON, Monday, Nov. 11, 2:48 A. M.—The armistice between Germany, on the one hand, and the allied Governments and the United States, on the other, has been signed.

The State Department announced at 2:45 o'clock this morning that Germany had signed.

The department's announcement simply said: "The armistice has been signed."

The world war will end this morning at 6 o'clock, Washington time, 11 o'clock Paris time.

The armistice was signed by the German representatives at midnight.

This announcement was made by the State Department at 2:50 o'clock this morning.

The announcement was made verbally by an official of the State Department in this form:

"The armistice has been signed. It was signed at 5 o'clock A. M., Paris time, [midnight, New York time,] and hostilities will cease at 11 o'clock this morning, Paris time, [6 o'clock, New York time.]

The terms of the armistice, it was announced, will not be made public until later. Military men here, however, regard it as certain that they include:

Immediate retirement of the German military forces from France, Belgium, and Alsace-Lorraine.

Disarming and demobilization of the German armies.

Occupation by the allied and American forces of such strategic points in Germany as will make impossible a renewal of hostilities.

Delivery of part of the German High Seas Fleet and a certain number of submarines to the allied and American naval forces.

Disarmament of all other German warships under supervision of the allied and American Navies, which will guard them.

Occupation of the principal German naval bases by sea forces of the victorious nations.

Release of allied and American soldiers, sailors, and civilians held prisoners in Germany without such reciprocal action by the associated Governments.

There was no information as to the circumstances under which the armistice was signed, but since the German courier did not reach German military headquarters until 10 o'clock yesterday morning, French time, it was generally assumed here that the German envoys within the French lines had been instructed by wireless to sign the terms.

Forty-seven hours had been required for the courier to reach the German headquarters, and unquestionably several hours were necessary for the examination of the terms and a decision.

It was regarded as possible, however, that the decision may have been made at Berlin and instructions transmitted from there by the new German Government.

Germany had until 11 o'clock this morning, French time, (6 o'clock, Washington time,) to accept. So hostilities will end at the hour set by Marshal Foch for a decision by Germany for peace or for continuation of the war.

The momentous news that the armistice had been signed was telephoned to the White House for transmission to the President a few minutes before it was given to the newspaper correspondents.

Later it was said that there would be no statement from the White House at this time.

* * *

January 5, 1919

AMERICANS PRESS FIGHTING IN RUSSIA

*Advance Artillery Near Kadish,
Although Bolsheviki Outnumber Them Three to One.*

BATTLE IN THE BITTER COLD

Victory Largely a Matter of Endurance—Our Men Well Fed and Clothed, Official Advices Say.

ARCHANGEL, Jan. 5, (Associated Press)—Fighting about the village of Kadish, which was recaptured by the American forces Dec. 30, is continuing. The American artillery has moved up slightly and is almost continually shelling the enemy. There have been numerous outpost encounters in the thick woods bordering on the Petrograd road.

The Bolshevist force outnumbers the Americans nearly three to one and is seeking to outflank them, but the American soldiers, though tired after five days and nights of fighting activity in the extreme cold, are bearing up splendidly. The battle is largely a question of endurance in the arctic weather.

Now and then in the course of the fighting the Americans encounter hidden machine-gun positions in the woods or along the road. One of these held out for five hours, until the Americans, advancing step by step or crawling in the snow, succeeded in flanking it.

There is some respite with darkness, which descends at 3 o'clock in the afternoon, but the shelling at night is making perilous the matter of the transport of munitions and provisions along the high-road in sleighs or on men's backs through the forest. The Russian peasant drivers of these sleighs, stricken with fear, in some instances turn and bolt in the wrong direction, only to be forced to proceed by American soldiers.

The American trench mortars are doing splendid work. On the Vologda Railway front the Bolshevist shelling continues. American patrols are encountering the enemy in the Onega sector, where it is considered probable that the American forces may withdraw from the exposed positions to one of the captured villages.

WASHINGTON, Jan. 4—An official report received from the Military Attaché with Ambassador Francis in Russia, announced today by General March, shows that the total deaths from all causes in the American forces in the Archangel region up to Nov. 25 were 86. Of these 9 were killed in action, 7 died of wounds, 3 were drowned, and 2 died as a result of accidents and 65 from disease.

Later official reports, General March said, showed that the military situation at Archangel was entirely in hand and that the troops were adequately fed and clothed for Winter campaigning in that section.

Assertions were made by Senator Townsend of Michigan in the United States Senate that reports had reached him of serious conditions, due to lack of food and clothing, existing among the American troops in North Russia.

* * *

February 10, 1919

54 FOREIGN REDS ON THE WAY EAST TO BE DEPORTED

*Train Passes Through Chicago
with Two Carloads of Alien Prisoners.*

ROUNDED UP IN FAR WEST

*Some Are from Seattle,
Where Bolsheviki and I. W. W. Started Big Strike.*

ARRESTS MADE QUIETLY

Immigration Officials Determined to Rid the Country of European Anarchists.

Special to The New York Times.

CHICAGO, Monday, Feb. 10—The Chicago Tribune this morning prints the following:

Deportation is the answer of the United States Government to the challenge of I. W. W. and Bolshevist agitators who come to this country with the avowed purpose of stirring up trouble in industry and social life.

The first Federal blow against the wave of Anarchism already launched on the Pacific Coast came to light yesterday when fifty-four labor agitators passed through Chicago in two heavily-guarded tourist sleepers bound for immediate deportation from an Atlantic port.

A motley company of I. W. W. troublemakers, bearded labor fanatics, and red flag supporters were huddled in crowded berths and propaganda-strewed compartments of the prison train, which slipped in and out of the city so quietly that few Federal officials were aware of its existence. As far as is known, no movement of the kind has ever before been attempted by the Government and the train blazed a trail which, immigration authorities agree, will entirely solve the greatest danger of an industrial unrest during the reconstruction period.

Three leaders of the Seattle uprising, one prominent Spokane agitator, a dangerous I. W. W. leader from Denver and five alien convicts arrested in Chicago, were among the prisoners gathered into the Federal net and now well on their way toward the land of their birth, after trial and conviction as undesirable citizens.

The remainder were alien labor agitators picked up by officers of the United States Immigration Service during a year of quiet campaigning in industrial centres of the Pacific coast.

They were guarded by fourteen heavily armed immigration officers, who paced up and down the length of the train from the time it reached the Chicago yards until it pulled from the city with clearance orders over all traffic. A. D. H. Jackson, chief of the Seattle office of the Immigration Service, was in command.

Dragnet Set Two Years Ago.

"The proceeding against enemies of this type is simple," declared an official with the train. "Just two hours before the Seattle strike was called we had gathered forty agitators into these cars with everything cleared away between them and the middle of the Atlantic Ocean. For more than a year the Immigration Service has been working quietly in all industrial centres, checking up on the strange aliens who appeared during war months and gathering evidence against I. W. W. leaders and trouble makers who call themselves Bolsheviki.

"When the evidence was compiled against this particular crew each case was brought to a Federal hearing, and all court findings sent to Washington, where they were reviewed by Secretary of Labor Wilson. The Secretary has the power to order this type of prisoner deported or released, and so far there has been little trouble in getting quick action.

"While labor circles were seething with trouble along the coast, our prison train slipped out for the Atlantic long before strike leaders were aware that some cherished members of their organization had left their midst. We picked up additions to the party in Spokane and one joined us from Denver.

Habeas Corpus Failed.

"The surprise seemed to take the wind from the sails of the agitators. Only one man rebelled when told of Uncle Sam's decision to rid the country of his presence. He got out a writ of habeas corpus against deportation, which was promptly quashed by a Federal Judge in Spokane. The courts have opened every facility and given every co-operation in this work."

When the prison train reached Chicago, red flags that waved from the cars on the first day's run, I. W. W. banners, and strike placards were piled on the littered tourist berths which held all of the earthly goods of the prisoners. One I. W. W. songbook, with its flaring red cover, was propped in a car window, but it was hastily removed when a big guard passed by and tapped on the glass. The prisoners seemed thoroughly cowed and convinced at last that Uncle Sam means business in dealing with their class.

"We let 'em howl and wave the red flag as much as they wanted to after we left Seattle," said a train guard, "and when they found that they could do it without causing anybody trouble, they quit and have been quiet ever since.

"Before we reached the State of Montana Mr. Jackson went through and told the prisoners that for their own good they had better remain quiet and not allow red stuff to show from the windows.

" 'The cowboys of this State don't like I. W. W.'s,' he told them. 'If they see you coming through with a lot of racket and find out who you are, they might let loose with some fireworks. These cowboys are mighty quick on the trigger hereabouts.'

"That was enough. The Bolshevist Army pulled in its banners and faded from sight as we passed through Montana towns."

Avoided Mob at Butte.

The one and only attempt at a mob delivery of the prisoners was frustrated by the foresight of the Federal officers. Before the prison train reached Butte, Mont., officers were warned that I. W. W. leaders in that city and Helena had learned of the deportations and were massing to deliver their comrades. The two cars, then attached to a regular train, were cut off at a junction and put into another train which made a wide detour, missing both Butte and Helena and striking the main line well to the east of the danger point, while the I. W. W. mob spread over Montana in a futile attempt at rescue.

One thousand men in a typical I. W. W. mob stormed the Butte station when the original train reached that point, according to reports received here by the guards. Three hundred members of the mob swept gatemen and police officers aside and insisted on searching the train. They were allowed to do so and left without causing further trouble when they found what had happened up the line.

Throughout the trip railroad men and Federal officers are co-operating to keep the route and running schedule secret. Chief Jackson has no fear of running into any additional trouble on the remainder of his journey. While in Chicago, his fourteen guards were placed in complete command of the train and although Federal officers and railroad men were notified of the movement, the immigration guards did not require assistance of any kind.

Only one woman, the wife of a Finnish agitator arrested in Spokane, was among the prisoners.

Handcuffs for All.

She hugged a car window and gloomily watched the guards as they paced their beats. In a forward compartment a blanket concealed fifty-four pairs of business-like handcuffs to be used in emergencies or when the prisoners leave their cars.

"The handcuffs helped convince these birds that they are not appreciated in America," remarked a stocky little guard who wore a civilian overcoat over his infantry uniform. He received his discharge just in time to serve in the first active campaign of Uncle Sam's war against the reds.

"We don't need the cuffs now," said the guard. "What we need is a number of good gags. This is a musical gang. They sing foreign songs for hours. Some of 'em wake up in the night to do it."

The majority of the prisoners will be sent back to Russian provinces. Some are Norwegians, some Scandinavians, and some Finns, according to their guards.

The five prisoners who were added to the party here are alien convicts who have been sentenced to deportation under the 1917 act for some time past. They are not connected with the I. W. W. or Bolshevist movement, as far as could be learned. One of the Chicago prisoners served a sentence in the House of Correction for failure to register.

Practically all of the prisoners have been in the United States more than a year, according to the Finn leader and spokesman of the party, who has been a Bolshevist representative in every city west of the Mississippi. He led a half-hearted cheer from his barred window yesterday and exhibited the tattered end of a red flag when he was sure no "quick trigger" cowboy lurked in the vicinity.

The immigration service bases its new policy of deportation on the immigration act passed by Congress in October, 1917.

* * *

June 29, 1919

PEACE SIGNED, ENDS THE GREAT WAR

ENEMY ENVOYS IN TRUCULENT SPIRIT

Say Afterward They Would Not Have Signed Had They Known They Were to Leave First by Different Way.

CHINA REFUSES TO SIGN, SMUTS MAKES PROTEST

These Events Somewhat Cloud the Great Occasion at Versailles—Wilson, Clemenceau, and Lloyd George Receive a Tremendous Ovation.

VERSAILLES, June 28, (Associated Press)—Germany and the allied and associated powers signed the peace terms here today in the same imperial hall where the Germans humbled the French so ignominiously forty-eight years ago.

This formally ended the world war, which lasted just thirty-seven days less than five years. Today, the day of peace, was the fifth anniversary of the murder of Archduke Francis Ferdinand by a Serbian student at Serajevo.

The peace was signed under circumstances which somewhat dimmed the expectations of those who had worked and fought during long years of war and months of negotiations for its achievement.

Absence of the Chinese delegates, who at the last moment were unable to reconcile themselves to the Shantung settlement, struck the first discordant note. A written protest which General Smuts lodged with his signature was another disappointment.

But bulking larger than these was the attitude of Germany and the German plenipotentiaries, which left them, as evident from the expression of M. Clemenceau, still outside of formal reconciliation and made the actual restoration to regular relations and intercourse with the allied nations dependent, not upon the signature of the "preliminaries of peace" today, but upon ratification by the National Assembly.

To M. Clemenceau's warning in his opening remarks that they would be expected, and held, to observe the treaty provisions loyally and completely the German delegates, through

Dr. Haniel von Haimhausen, replied after returning to the hotel that had they known that they would be treated on a different status after signing than the allied representatives, as shown by their separate exit before the general body of the conference, they never would have signed.

Under the circumstances the general tone of sentiment in the historic sitting was one rather of relief at the uncontrovertible end of hostilities than of complete satisfaction.

The ceremony had been planned deliberately to be austere, befitting the sufferings of almost five years, and the lack of impressiveness and picturesque color, of which many spectators, who had expected a magnificent State pageant, complained, was a matter of design, not merely omission.

The actual ceremony was far shorter than had been expected, in view of the number of signatures which were to be appended to the treaty and the two accompanying conventions, ending a bare forty-nine minutes after the hour set for the opening.

Premier Clemenceau called the session to order in the Hall of Mirrors at 3:10 P. M.

The signing began when Dr. Hermann Müller and Johannes Bell, the German signatories, affixed their names. Herr Müller signed at 3:13 o'clock and Herr Bell 3:13 o'clock.

President Wilson, the first of the allied delegates, signed a minute later. At 3:49 o'clock the momentous session was over.

The most dramatic moment connected with the signing came unexpectedly and spontaneously at the conclusion of the ceremony, when Premier Clemenceau, President Wilson and Premier Lloyd George descended from the Hall of Mirrors to the terrace at the rear of the palace, where thousands of spectators were massed.

Great Demonstration For Allied Leaders.

With the appearance of the three who had dominated the councils of the Allies there began a most remarkable demonstration. With cries of "Vive Clemenceau!" "Vive Wilson!" "Vive Lloyd George!" dense crowds swept forward from all parts of the spacious terrace. In an instant the three were surrounded by struggling, cheering masses of people, fighting among themselves for a chance to get near the statesmen.

It had been planned that all the allied delegates would walk across the terrace after signing, to see the great fountains play, but none of the others plenipotentiaries got further than the door.

President Wilson, M. Clemenceau and Mr. Lloyd George were caught in the living stream which fired across the great space and became part of the crowd themselves. Soldiers and the bodyguards struggled vainly to clear the way. The people jostled and struggled for a chance to touch the hands of the leaders of the Allies, all the while cheering madly.

Probably the least concerned for their personal safety were the three themselves. They went forward smilingly, as the crowd willed, bowing in response to the ovation, and here and there reaching out to shake an insistent hand as they passed on their way through the château grounds to watch the playing of the fountains—a part of the program which had been planned as a dignified State processional of all the plenipotentiaries.

Every available point of vantage in the palace and about the grounds was filled with thousands of people, who, less hardy than their comrades, had not been able to join the procession. No more picturesque setting could have been selected for this drama.

The return of President Wilson, M. Clemenceau, and Lloyd George toward the palace was a repetition of their outward journey of triumph. As they reached the château, however, they turned to the left instead of entering. The crowd was in doubt as to what was intended, but followed, cheering tumultuously.

Nearby a closed car was waiting and the three entered this and they drove from the grounds together amid a profusion of flowers which had been thrust through the open window.

All the diplomats and members of their parties who attended the ceremony of treaty signing wore conventional civilian clothes. Outside of this also there was a marked lack of gold lace and pageantry, with few of the fanciful uniforms of the Middle Ages, whose traditions and practices are so sternly condemned in the great, seal-covered document signed today.

One spot of color was made against the sombre background by the French Guards. A few selected members of the Guard were there, resplendent in red-plumed silver helmets and red, white and blue uniforms.

A group of allied Generals, including General Pershing, wore the scarlet sash of the Legion of Honor.

As a contrast with the Franco-German peace session of 1871, held in the same hall, there were present today grizzled French veterans of the Franco-Prussian war. They took the place of the Prussian guardsmen of the previous ceremony, and the Frenchmen today watched the ceremony with grim satisfaction.

The conditions of 1871 were exactly reversed. Today the disciples of Bismarck sat in the seats of the lowly, while the white marble statue of Minerva, Goddess of War, looked on. Overhead, on the frescoed ceiling, were scenes from France's ancient wars.

German Protest at the Last Minute.

Three incidents were emphasized by the smoothness with which the ceremony was conducted. The first of these was the failure of the Chinese delegation to sign. The second was the protest submitted by General Jan Christian Smuts, who declared the peace unsatisfactory.

The third, which was unknown to the general public, came from the Germans. When the program for the ceremony was shown to the German delegation, Herr von Haimhausen of the German delegation went to Colonel Henri, French liaison officer, and protested. He said:

"We cannot admit that the German delegates should enter the hall by a different door than the Entente delegates; nor that military honors should be withheld. Had we known there would be such arrangements before, the delegates would not have come."

After a conference with the French Foreign Ministry it was decided, as a compromise, to render military honors as the Germans left. Otherwise the program as originally arranged was not changed.

Secretary Lansing was the first of the American delegation to arrive at the palace, entering the building at 1:45 o'clock.

The Peace Treaty was deposited on the table at 2:10 o'clock by William Martin of the French Foreign Office. It was inclosed in a stamped leather case.

Premier Clemenceau entered the palace at 2:20 o'clock.

Detachments of fifteen soldiers each from the American, British and French forces entered just before 3 o'clock and took their places in embrasures of the windows, overlooking the château park, a few feet from Marshal Foch, seated with the French delegation at the peace table.

The American soldiers who saw the signing of the treaty were all attached to President Wilson's residence. They were: George W. Bender, Baltimore; Stanley Cohek, Chicopee, Mass.; George Bridgewater, Palestine, Texas; Harlan Hayes, Green City, Wis.; J. S. Horton, Lexington, Miss.; William R. Knox, Temple, Okla.; Albert E. Landreth, Portsmouth, Va.; Sergeant Sam Lane, Prosper, Texas; George Landance, Philadelphia; M. D. Mary, Havre, Mon.; Fred Quantz, Cleveland; Hubert Ridgeway, Mo.; Raymond Riley, Baltimore, and Frank Wilgus, Allentown, Penn.

With the thirty poilus and Tommies they were present as the real "artisans of peace" and stood within the enclosure reserved for plenipotentiaries and high officials of the conference as a visible sign of their rôle in bringing into being a new Europe.

Premier Clemenceau promptly stepped up to the French detachment and shook the hand of each man. The men had been selected from those who bore honorable wounds, and the Premier expressed his pleasure at seeing them there and his regret for the sufferings they had endured for their country.

Delegates of the minor powers made their way with difficulty through the crowd to their places at the table. Officers and civilians lined the walls and filled the aisles.

President Wilson entered the Hall of Mirrors at 2:50 o'clock. All the allied delegates were then seated except the Chinese, who did not attend.

The difficulty of seeing well from many parts of the hall militated against demonstrations on the arrival of the chief personages. Only a few persons saw President Wilson when he came in, and there was but a faint sound of applause for him.

An hour before the signing of the treaty those assembled in the hall had been urged to take their seats, but their eagerness to see the historic ceremony was so keen that they refused to remain seated, and crowded toward the centre of the hall, which is so long that a good view was impossible from a distance. Even with opera glasses, correspondents and others were unable to observe satisfactorily, as the seats were not elevated; consequently there was a general scramble for standing room.

German correspondents were ushered into the hall just before 3 o'clock and took standing room in a window at the rear of the correspondents' section.

When Premier Lloyd George arrived many delegates sought autographs from the members of the Council of Four, and they busied themselves for the next few minutes signing copies of the official program.

At 3 o'clock a hush fell over the hall, and the crowds shouted for the officials, who were standing, to sit down, so as not to block the view. The delegates showed some surprise at the disorder, which did not cease until all the spectators had seated themselves or found places against the walls.

Muller and Bell Show Great Composure.

At seven minutes past 3 Dr. Müller, German Secretary for Foreign Affairs, and Dr. Bell, Colonial Secretary, were shown into the hall, and quietly took their seats, the other delegates not rising.

They showed composure, and manifested none of the uneasiness which Count von Brockdorff-Rantzau, head of the German peace delegation, displayed when handed the treaty at Versailles.

Dr. Müller and Dr. Bell had driven early to Versailles by automobile from St. Cyr instead of taking the belt line railroad, as did the German delegates who came to receive the terms of peace on May 7. Their credentials had been approved in the morning.

In the allotment of seats in the ceremonial chamber places for the German delegates were on the side of the horseshoe table, where they touched elbows with Japanese plenipotentiaries on their right and the Brazilians on their left. Delegates from Ecuador, Peru, and Liberia faced the Germans across the narrow table.

M. Clemenceau, as President of the Conference, made this address:

"The session is open. The allied and associated powers on one side and the German reich on the other side have come to an agreement on the conditions of peace. The text has been completed, drafted, and the President of the Conference has stated in writing that the text that is about to be signed now is identical with the 200 copies that have been delivered to the German delegation.

"The signatures will be given now and they amount to a solemn undertaking faithfully and loyally to execute the conditions embodied by this treaty of peace. I now invite the delegates of the German reich to sign the treaty."

There was a tense pause for a moment. Then in response to M. Clemenceau's bidding the German delegates rose without a word and, escorted by William Martin, master of ceremonies, moved to the signatory title, where they placed upon the treaty the sign manuals which German Government leaders declared until recently would never be appended to this treaty.

They also signed a protocol covering changes in the document and the Polish undertaking.

It was too distant to see, even with glasses, the expression on the faces of the German plenipotentiaries during the ceremony, but observers among the officials say that the Germans fulfilled their roles without apparent indications of emotions such as marked Count von Brockdorff-Rantzau's dramatic declarations at the first meeting.

President First Leader to Sign.

When they regained their seats after signing, President Wilson immediately arose and, followed by the other American plenipotentiaries, moved around the sides of the horseshoe to the signature tables.

President Wilson, and not M. Clemenceau, thus had the honor of signing as first of the leaders of the world alliance, but the honor was due to the alphabet, not other considerations, as the signatures occur in the same French alphabetical order as the enumeration of the allied and associated powers in the prologue of the treaty—the same order which determined the seating of the delegations at the plenary sessions of the interallied conference.

Premier Lloyd George came next, after the American envoys, with the English delegation. The British dominions followed.

The representatives of the dominions signed in the following order: For Canada—Charles J. Doherty, Minister of Justice; Sir George Foster, Minister of Trade and Commerce, and Arthur L. Sifton, Minister of Customs. For Australia—Premier William M. Hughes and Sir Gilbert Cook, Minister for the Navy. For New Zealand—W. F. Massey, Prime Minister and Minister of Labor. For the Union of South Africa—Premier Louis Botha and Jan Christian Smuts, Minister of Defense. For India—Edwin S. Montagu, Secretary for India, and the Maharaja of Bikanir.

Surprise Over Smuts's Protest.

A murmur of surprise passed around the hall when it became known that General Smuts, representing South Africa, signed under protest and filed a document declaring that the peace was unsatisfactory.

He held that the indemnities stipulated could not be accepted without grave inury to the industrial revival of Europe. He declared that it would be to the interests of the allied powers to render the stipulations more tolerable and moderate.

General Smuts asserted that there were territorial settlements which he believed would need revision, and that guarantees were provided which he hoped would soon be found out of harmony with the new peaceful temper and unarmed state of the Central Powers. Punishments were also foreshadowed, he said, over which a calmer mood might yet prefer to pass the sponge of oblivion.

M. Clemenceau, with the French delegates, were the next in line for the signing, then came Baron Sailonji and the other Japanese delegates. The Italians came after the Japanese, and they, in turn, were followed by the representatives of the smaller powers.

During the attaching of the signatures of the great powers and the Germans a battery of moving picture machines and cameras clicked away so audibly that they could be heard above the general disorder.

At 3:45 the booming of cannon in celebration of the peace broke the monotony in the Hall of Mirrors, where the crowd had already tired of watching the signing.

China's failure to send her delegates to the ceremony created much comment. The vacant seats of the Chinese were noted early in the proceedings, but it was expected that the delegates would arrive later. Then the report was circulated officially that the Chinese would not sign without reservation on Shantung, and would issue a statement this evening on their position.

Some Confusion About Arrangements.

While the formal proceedings moved with system and complete adherence to program, the same cannot be said for other arrangements, which detracted markedly from the impressiveness of the event. So many spectators had, in one manner or another, gained access to the hall that the struggle for points of vantage at times approached the stage of a brawl, and the few officials intrusted with keeping order had the greatest difficulty in obtaining a semblance of it.

Cries of "Down in front!" which were probably never before heard at a gathering of similar importance, were addressed quite as often to officials of the Conference as to unofficial spectators. The stage for the ceremony was as crowded as the spectators' inclosures, giving a picture of crush and confusion. The plenipotentiaries and attachés, instead of arriving in delegations, formally introduced by ushers, as had been planned, drifted in individually as at the earlier sessions.

Among the American witnesses of the signing were Mrs. Wilson, accompanied by Miss Wilson and Mrs. Lansing, Mrs. House, Mrs. Wallace, Mrs. Scott, and several other wives of delegates and officials; Herbert Hoover, Bernard M. Baruch, Vance McCormick, John W. Davis, Ambassador to Great Britain; Hugh C. Wallace, Ambassador to France; Henry Morgenthau, and about seventy of the more important attaches of the Peace Commission.

The close of the ceremony came so quickly and quietly that it was scarcely noticed until it was all over. M. Clemenceau arose almost unremarked, and in a voice almost lost amid the confusion and the hum of conversation, which had sprung up while the minor delegates were signing, declared the conference closed and asked the allied and associated delegates to remain in their places for a few minutes—this to permit the German plenipotentiaries to leave the hall and the building before the general exodus.

None arose as they filed out, accompanied by their suite of secretaries and interpreters, just as all the plenipotentiaries had kept their seats when Dr. Müller and Dr. Bell entered. This was regarded as an answer to the action of Count von Brockdorff-Rantzau in reading his speech seated at the first meeting, but even more as an expression of sentiment at the German attitude toward the acceptance of peace.

Germans White-Faced as They Left.

Beyond the demonstration for the allied leaders the main interest of the people about the palace was centred in the arrival and departure of the Germans. Few people witnessed the arrival of the Germans, but, despite the precautions of the soldiers, great crowds gathered about the rear of the palace when the envoys from Berlin left after signing the treaty.

There was no audible demonstration against the Germans, but there was a distinct current of hostility evident among the crowd which jammed close to the cars. The Germans were white-faced and quite apparently suffering strong emotion, but whether it was fear, anger, or chagrin one could only surmise.

The scene around the palace had been an animated one from an early hour. All day yesterday workmen and officials were busy in the château putting final touches on the arrangements, but the Hall of Mirrors was not yet ready. Much remained to be done at the last moment.

The peace table—a huge hollow rectangle with its open side facing the windows in the hall—was, however, in place, its tawny yellow coverings blending with the rich browns, blues, and yellows of the antique hangings of the room and the rugs covering the dais. The mellow tints of the historical paintings in the arched roof of the long hall completed the picture.

Last minute changes were made today in the program to expedite the signing of the treaty. Two additional tables were placed beside the large one within the Hall of Mirrors. One of the new tables held the Rhine Convention and the other the protocol, containing changes in and interpretations of the treaty. The arrangement of the tables thus enabled three persons to be engaged simultaneously in affixing their signatures.

Most of the seventy-two plenipotentiaries had to write their names only twice, once on the treaty and once on the protocol. The convention covering the left bank of the Rhine and the treaties regarding the protection of minorities in Poland was signed only by delegates of the great powers.

Because of the size of the treaty and the fragile seals it bore, the plan to present it for signing to Premier Clemenceau, President Wilson, and Premier Lloyd George was given up.

A box of old fashioned goose quills, sharpened by the expert pen pointer of the French Foreign Office, was placed on each of the three tables for the use of plenipotentiaries who desired to observe the traditional formalities.

Tables for the secretaries were placed inside the table for the plenipotentiaries.

Chairs for the plenipotentiaries were drawn up around three sides of the table, which formed an open rectangle fully eighty feet long on its longer side. A chair for M. Clemenceau, President of the Peace Conference, was placed in the centre of the table facing the windows, with those for President Wilson and Premier Lloyd George on the right and left hand, respectively. The German delegates' seats were at the side of the table nearest the entrance which they could take after all the others had been seated.

This arrangement was made to permit the Germans to leave after the signature of the treaty before the allied delegations, not waiting for the procession of allied delegates to the terrace to witness the playing of the fountains.

Crowds Gathered Early.

This morning was cloudy, but just before midday the clouds began to break.

People began to gather early in the neighborhood of the palace. As the morning wore on the crowds kept increasing in size, but the vast spaces around the château swallowed them up at first.

By noon eleven regiments of French cavalry and infantry under command of General Brecard had taken positions along the approaches to the palace, while within the court on either side solid lines of infantry in horizon blue were drawn up at attention.

Hours before the time set for the ceremony an endless stream of automobiles began moving out of Paris up the cannon-lined hill of the Champs Elysées, past the Arc de Triomphe, and out through the shady Boils de Boulogne, carrying plenipotentiaries, officials, and guests to the ceremony. The thoroughfare was kept clear by pickets, dragoons, and mounted gendarmes.

In the meantime thousands of Parisians were packing regular and special trains upon the lines leading to Versailles and contending with residents of the town itself for places in the park where the famous fountains would mark the end of the ceremony.

Long before the ceremony began a line of gendarmes was thrown across the approaches. While theoretically only persons bearing passes could get through this line, the crowds gradually filtered into and finally filled the square.

Within this square hundreds of fortunate persons had taken up positions at the windows of every wing of the palace.

The automobiles, bearing delegates and secretaries, had reserved for their use the Avenue du Paris, the broad boulevard leading direct to the château's court of honor, French soldiers being ranged along the highway on both sides.

At the end of the court a guard of honor was drawn up to present arms as the leading plenipotentiaries passed, this guard comprising a company of Republican Guards in brilliant uniform. The entrance for the delegates was by the marble stairway to the "Queen's Apartments" and the Hall of Peace, giving access thence to the Hall of Mirrors.

This formality was not prescribed for the Germans, who had a separate route of entry, coming through the park and gaining the marble stairway through the ground floor.

*   *   *

SENATE DEFEATS TREATY, VOTE 49 TO 35

LACK 7 VOTES TO RATIFY

28 Republicans and 21 Democrats Support Lodge Reservations.

23 DEMOCRATS OPPOSE

12 Republicans Also Against Resolution—
Reconsideration Is Blocked.

PEACE DECLARATION URGED

Knox Move Waits Until Monday—Senators Look to Wilson for
Next Step.

Special to The New York Times.

WASHINGTON, March 19—The Senate this evening, for a second time, refused to ratify the treaty of peace with Germany, and sent it back to President Wilson.

By a vote of 49 to 35, seven short of the necessary two-thirds of the members present, the Senate rejected the Lodge resolution of ratification.

It then adopted a resolution, proposed by Senator Lodge, to return the treaty to the President, advising him formally that the Senate had failed to advise and consent to its ratification.

The resolution reads:

"That the Secretary of the Senate be instructed to return to the President the Treaty of Peace with Germany signed at Versailles on the twenty-eighth day of June, 1919, and respectfully inform the President that the Senate has failed to ratify said treaty, being unable to obtain the constitutional majority required therefor."

Following this action, Senator Robinson of Arkansas, a Democrat, moved to reconsider the vote by which ratification failed. A lively parliamentary battle followed, in which the Republican mild reservationists joined the Democrats in an effort to keep the Senate from creating a condition which prevented further action on the treaty at this time. A ruling by Senator Cummins, who was in the chair, and refusal of the mild reservationists to co-operate further with the Democrats unless they were assured that the second vote on the treaty would be taken at once, cut short Mr. Robinson's efforts.

The Senate adjourned to meet again Monday, after the treaty had been ordered to be returned to the President. As that will have been done by Monday, the motion to reconsider cannot be made again, Senator Lodge said after the voting, because the Senate cannot reconsider action on a question over which, by its own vote, it has relinquished control.

What President Wilson will do now is problematical. No statement is obtainable at the White House concerning the rejection of the treaty.

On the resolution of ratification fourteen more Democrats voted to accept the treaty with the Lodge reservation than on the occasion of the former vote, just four months ago. On November 19, when the Senate rejected the Lodge ratifying resolution by 41 to 51, but seven Democratic Senators voted to ratify: Gore, Myers, Owen, Pomerene, Shields, Smith of Georgia and Walsh of Massachusetts.

Today the following Democrats joined the seven: Ashurst, Beckham, Chamberlain, Fletcher, Henderson, Kendrick, King, Nugent, Phelan, Pittman, Ransdell, Smith, Thammell and Wolcott.

The roll call upon the Lodge resolution of ratification was as follows:

FOR THE RESOLUTION—49.

Republicans—28.

Ball,	Jones, Wash.,	Phipps,
Calder,	Kellogg,	Smooth,
Capper,	Kenyon,	Spencer,
Colt,	Keyes,	Sterling,
Curtis,	Lenroot,	Sutherland,
Dillingham,	Lodge,	Wadsworth,
Edge,	McLean,	Warren,
Elkins,	McNary,	Watson.
Frelinghuysen,	New,	
Hale,	Page,	

Democrats—21.

Ashurst,	King,	Ransdell,
Beckham,	Myers,	Smith, Gat.,
Chamberlain,	Nugent,	Smith, Md.,
Fletcher,	Owen,	Trammell,
Gore,	Phelan,	Walsh, Mass.,
Henderson,	Pittman,	Walsh, Mon.,
Kendrick,	Pomerene,	Wolcott.

AGAINST THE RESOLUTION—35.

Republicans—12.

Borah,	Gronna,	McCormick,
Brandegee,	Johnson, Cal.,	Moses,
Fernald,	Knox,	Norris,
France,	La Follette,	Sherman.

Democrats—23.

Comer,	Johnson, S.D.,	Simmons,
Culberson,	Kirby,	Smith, S. C.
Dial,	McKellar,	Stanley,
Gay,	Overman,	Swanson,
Glass,	Reed,	Thomas,
Harris,	Robinson,	Underwood,
Harrison,	Sheppard,	Williams.
Hitchcock,	Shields,	

Twelve Senators were absent or not voting. As a two-thirds vote was necessary to ratify, pairs were grouped in the ratio of two for ratification to one against. Senator Penrose, Republican, of Pennsylvania, was paired against ratification with Senators Harding, Republican, of Ohio and Nelson, Republican, of Minnesota, who were for ratification. Senator Fall, Republican, of New Mexico was paired against ratification with Senators Newberry. Republican, of Michigan and McCumber, Republican, of North Dakota, who were for ratification. Senator Poindexter, Republican, of Washington was paired against ratification with Senators Cummins, Republican, of Iowa and Townsend, Republican, of Michigan, who were for ratification. Senator Smith, Democrat, of Arizona was paired against ratification with Senators Gerry, Democrat, of Rhode Island and Jones, Democrat, of New Mexico, who were for ratification.

Interest in the vote on the resolution of ratification centred in the Democratic attitude, as it was clear that unless a considerable number of them refused longer to accept the views of President Wilson, there could be no ratification by the Senate. Long before the vote was taken today Senators knew that the Democrats would not bolt the President in sufficient numbers to provide the needed two-thirds.

Fight Over Reconsideration.

The Senate spent a listless day listening to speeches, but shortly after 8 P. M. a quorum call brought more than eighty Senators into the chamber, and the cry of "vote" was raised at once. The roll call on ratification was taken without more debate.

After Senator Cummins had announced from the chair that the resolution, having failed to receive the required two-thirds, was rejected, Senator Lodge at once presented his resolution to return the treaty to the President.

On this the vote was 47 to 37. Six Democratic Senators voted for it, Gore, Kirby, Reed, Shields, Walsh of Massachusetts and Williams.

Immediately after the adoption of this resolution Senator Robinson of Arkansas, under a prior arrangement with Republican mild reservationists, moved that the Senate reconsider the vote by which it had failed to adopt the resolution of ratification.

Senator Watson of Indiana moved to lay Mr. Robinson's motion on the table. This motion failed because mild reservationists voted with the Democrats to prevent the Robinson motion from being thus summarily disposed of. The vote was 34 to 43 against tabling the motion. The result in detail was:

FOR TABLING THE MOTION—34.

Republicans—31.

Borah,	Gronna,	Norris,
Brandegee,	Johnson, Cal.,	Page,
Calder,	Jones, Wash.,	Phipps,
Capper,	Kenyon,	Smoot,
Cummins,	Knox,	Spencer,
Curtis,	Lodge,	Sterling,

Dillingham,	La Follette,	Sutherland,
Elkins,	McCormick,	Wadsworth,
Fernald,	Moses,	Warren,
France,	New,	Watson.
Frelinghuysen,		

Democrats—3.

| Reed, | Shields, | Walsh, Mass. |

AGAINST TABLING MOTION—43.

Republicans—7.

Colt,	Kellogg,	Lenroot,
Edge,	Keyes,	McNary.
Hale,		

Democrats—36.

Ashurst,	Johnson, S. D.,	Ransdell,
Beckham,	Jones, N. M.,	Robinson,
Chamberlain,	Kendrick,	Sheppard,
Comer,	King,	Simmons,
Dial,	Kirby,	Smith, Ga.,
Fletcher,	McKellar,	Smith, Md.,
Gay,	Nugent,	Smith, S. C.,
Gerry,	Overman,	Stanley,
Harris,	Owen,	Swanson,
Harrison,	Phelan,	Trammell,
Henderson,	Pittman,	Walsh, Mon.,
Hitchcock,	Pomerene,	Wolcott.

Senator Robinson, having vanquished those who wanted to prevent him from discussing the motion to reconsider, began to urge its adoption, when he was again halted by Senator Brandegee, who made a point of order against the motion.

He argued that the Senate had disposed of the matter by adopting the Lodge resolution to send the treaty to the President. After considerable parliamentary wrangling and the citing of precedents, Senator Cummins ruled, though he said that he did so with some doubt in his mind as to the correctness of his opinion, that the Robinson motion was not in order.

An appeal from this decision was expected, but to the surprise of Republican Senators it was not taken.

Debate on Second Treaty Vote.

Senator Lodge said that if any Senators wished to vote again on the question of ratification, he did not wish to prevent them from doing so, provided the vote could be taken without any further debate. He said that he would ask unanimous consent that the vote be considered if Senators would agree in turn that the vote be taken at once.

That did not fit in with the plans of the Democratic Senators, who had hoped to leave the motion to reconsider pending until tomorrow or Monday.

The irreconcilables, who had won their victory and were not disposed to have it snatched from their grasp, also found the prospect of another vote not to their liking. Senators Borah and Brandegee pointed out that some Senators had left the chamber, and had even left Washington, as soon as possible after the vote on the resolution of ratification.

"I have no objection to voting on this question as long as the Secretary can call the roll," said Senator Borah. "But I do object to a vote and I will not permit one tonight, unless the Senators who thought they had settled something and left the Senate are protected in their absence."

Senator Brandegee observed that as it seemed to be necessary to take several votes in the Senate to decide when a matter was disposed of, he would not object to Mr. Lodge's request for unanimous consent to reconsider, provided that the absentees were covered by suitable pairs arranged on the spot.

Hitchcock Urged Cooling Off.

"I see nothing to be gained by voting again immediately upon a question which we have just voted upon once," said Senator Hitchcock. "My idea was for a day or two to let us cool off. Maybe in that time the matter could be arranged."

"I could think that after a year of debate we might ask for an end of this sort of thing," retorted Senator Lodge. "To keep this thing here just to fool with it for a day or two more is not to be thought of."

Senator Norris then suggested the absence of a quorum with a view to learning, he said, how many Senators had left the chamber. After the roll call Senator Curtis, the Republican whip, stated that the call disclosed that Senators Ball, Republican, of Delaware, Sherman, Republican, of Illinois, McLean, Republican, of Connecticut, and Thomas, Democrat, of Colorado, were absent and unpaired.

Senator Robinson then moved again that the Senate reconsider the vote of ratification, and at the same time to request the President to return to the Senate the Treaty and accompanying papers. This was a way of repealing the Lodge resolution adopted earlier, which was an obstacle to the motion to reconsider under Senator Cummins's ruling.

Senator Lodge made a point of order against the motion, but before the chair could rule Senator Robinson withdrew his motion. He did this on receipt of information from the mild reservationists that they would not support his motion unless he agreed that the second vote be taken immediately on ratification. The mild group's decision to stand by Senator Lodge's wish was reached at a hastily summoned conference just outside the door of the Senate chamber.

Senator Lodge once again asked unanimous consent that the Senate reconsider his vote, repeating his statement that he was unwilling to debar any Senator from voting again on ratification. But Senator Hitchcock observed that there was nothing to be gained and he objected.

The hope of the mild reservationists and of some Democrats was that when the Senate reconsidered the vote by which it had rejected the ratifying resolution some Democrats would change their votes and support ratification. A number of Democrats were urged to do this on the ground that having made their record of consistency on the first roll call they could afford for the sake of ratifying the treaty and bringing to an end the state of war to vote against the President.

Peace Declaration Move Waits.

Senator Knox then obtained the floor and moved that the Senate proceed to consider his resolution declaring the state of war between the United States and Germany at an end, by repealing the resolution declaring war, adopted in April, 1917.

Senator Lenroot said he agreed with Senator Knox that the Senate should soon consider that or some similar measure, but he urged that it be deferred.

Senator Lodge thereupon moved that the Senate adjourn until Monday, at which time, he said, the Knox resolution probably would be called up. This motion prevailed.

Before it reached the question of ratification the Senate adopted the Lodge amendment to the preamble of the resolution of ratification, providing that silent acquiescence in the Senate reservations by the European powers would signify their acceptance of them. It rejected, by a vote of 41 to 42, Senator Brandegee's amendment, providing that the President must deposit notice of ratification within ninety days after the Senate acted.

Lenroot Assails President.

Senator Lenroot delivered a speech in which he said that President Wilson on his Western tour called Article XI. of the League covenant his favorite and the heart of the instrument, while in his more recent pronouncements to Democratic Senators on reservations he has insisted that Article X. was the covenant's heart.

"The President's illness has affected either the President's recollection of his judgment," said Senator Lenroot. "Has President Wilson changed his mind, or has his mind changed him?"

Mr. Lenroot said that the President was willing to see the treaty defeated rather than remove from American boys the obligation to go into foreign wars. He assailed Senators who voted the Irish self-determination reservation into the ratifying resolution, declaring that they did it in an effort "to put somebody in a hole," and told the Democrats that if they insisted on taking the treaty into the political campaign they would "insure a tremendous Republican victory."

"The stubbornness of President Wilson is indefensible," he said. "We will meet you in the campaign as being for America first; you will meet us as being advocates of the surrender of Americanism. We will meet you as Americans; you will meet us as internationalists."

Senator Edge of New Jersey urged ratification of the treaty and said that today's vote would show how many of those who voted yesterday for the Irish reservation were really friends of Ireland.

Walsh of Montana Switches.

Senator Walsh of Montana, who previously voted against ratification with the Lodge reservations, and who through both fights on the treaty had stood consistently with President Wilson, announced that he would vote this time to ratify. Mr. Walsh said that he had come to believe that he and others had overestimated the importance of Article X. The peace of the world would, in his opinion, be safeguarded as well under Articles XI., XII., XV. and XVI. as under Article X.

In a carefully prepared analysis of the various reservations Mr. Walsh gave his opinion of each. His speech was received with the greatest attention by Democrats.

Some thought that his change might cause a stampede to the Lodge reservations. This impression was heightened in some quarters when Senator Ransdell of Louisiana, another staunch Administration Senator, arose immediately afterward and announced that he, too, had decided to vote for ratification.

Senator Myers of Montana, Senator Walsh's Democratic colleague, in stating that he would again vote for ratification with the Lodge reservations, as he did last November, declared that the Allies were trying to make a travesty of the Peace Treaty and the League covenant at the very outset by yielding to Germany on the question of the Kaiser's trial and the trials of other Germans held guilty of complicity in offenses against international law.

"As well try a horse thief before twelve other horse thieves or a bootlegger before a jury of bootleggers or bartenders as to make the grotesque and monstrous agreement that Germany shall try the war criminals," said Mr. Myers.

He declared also that the United States should not help Germany with money or food.

Senators Pomerene and Owen also spoke briefly, and then Senator Hoke Smith delivered a long set speech of which he had given notice yesterday.

Treaty "Gone," Lodge Declares.

After the session ended Senators of both parties united in declaring that in their opinion the treaty was now dead to stay dead. Senator Reed of Missouri, a Democrat, one of the irreconcilables whose fight helped kill the treaty, said many Democrats who favored the treaty had told him that they were through with it unless the President, in sending it back to the Senate, should express willingness to accept the Lodge reservations.

Senator Smith of Georgia said after the vote that he felt certain it would be impossible to get the Senate to give serious consideration to the treaty further as long as the same circumstances existed concerning reservations.

Senator Simmons of North Carolina, another Democrat, expressed a like view.

Senator Lodge said that the treaty was "gone." He declared that if the President should decide to send it once more to the Senate with another request that it be ratified, it would remain a long time in the Committee on Foreign Relations.

Senator Borah and the other irreconcilables were exceedingly well satisfied. They said that the Senate's action was but a forecast of what the country would do when the clearcut issue of ratification unqualified by any reservations or rejection was presented to it.

Senator Johnson of California, one of the irreconcilables, left at once to resume his western speaking tour against the league and in behalf of his own candidacy for the Republican nomination for President. Senator Borah will go soon, and Senator Reed is also about to begin a speaking tour.

* * *

March 20, 1920

AMERICA ISOLATED WITHOUT TREATY

Its Defeat, Washington Feels,
Will Add to Our Unpopularity Abroad.

STILL TECHNICALLY AT WAR

Hope Expressed That Wilson Will Take Steps to
Reestablish Relations.

Special to The New York Times.

WASHINGTON, March 19—In its international aspects the rejection of the Versailles Treaty by the Senate leaves the United States in an awkward position. America's isolation is now a reality. Not only is this Government not a member of the world league, designed to prevent future conflicts between nations, but it is also still at war with Germany.

A secondary effect of the Senate's action will be the withdrawal of the United States Government from participation in the arrangements now being discussed at Paris for the disposition of the Turkish Empire.

And this is not all. The feeling that has grown up in Europe on account of Senate opposition to the League of Nations is bound to be emphasized by today's action. President Wilson, who fought to have the League covenant accepted, is now in disfavor in France and Italy and is being criticised.

Recent expression in the European press has indicated that America itself was in disfavor. It might be going too far to say that the United States has lost the friendship of the world, but to say that the world's friendship has declined would not be far wrong.

Apparently nobody knows what course President Wilson will take now that the treaty has been rejected. If the Senate, as seems likely, follows its action of today by adopting Senator Knox's resolution declaring that a state of peace exists between the United States and Germany, the President is practically certain to ignore it. He holds that this is an act constitutionally vested in the Executive and that no action by Congress can compel him to follow any other course than that which he chooses.

There is a general opinion in administration circles that the President should act at once to end the anomalous condition of affairs that exist between the United States Government and the nations against which it declared war. He will be advised that negotiations for a peace should be entered into at once with Germany, Austria and Hungary, and at the same time the United States should begin exchanges with its late allies to obtain their assent to the protection of the rights guaranteed the United States in the treaties with the governments with which it was at war.

The United States has no diplomatic or consular officer, as such, in Germany, Austria or Hungary. It has "Commissioners," so called, at Berlin, Vienna and Budapest, but it can conduct no diplomatic relations or business relations with any of these countries until a treaty of peace has been formally ratified. In these circumstances American trade with the former Central Powers will be greatly handicapped. Great Britain, France, Italy, Japan and other allied powers are in a position to engage in the conduct of trade and commerce with Germany and Austria, but the United States is not.

It will take a long time to negotiate a treaty of peace with Germany. In the meantime American trade with that country must suffer to the extent that the former allies of the United States will be in position to build up trade relations.

The President has no power to proceed under the terms of the treaty, now that it is rejected. He must, if he takes any positive action, enter into new negotiations with Germany. To what extent the rejection of the treaty will affect the status of the American occupation of part of the Rhine provinces is something that only the future can determine. For the present the United States occupies that territory by virtue of the armistice of Nov. 11, 1918. The armistice terms are still in force as far as the United States Government is concerned. This Government could insist that it has the right to retain its armed forces on the Rhine, and it is not likely that the European powers would object. But it would not cause surprise if President Wilson decided to withdraw the American troops, taking the position that the rejection of the treaty did not justify him in keeping them there any longer.

* * *

April 6, 1921

MONROE DOCTRINE FOR ALL THE WORLD REPUBLICAN SENATORS' NEW POLICY; NO ALLIANCES, BUT A STAND FOR PEACE

SHAPING NEW DECLARATION

Senators' Program Is to Bar Any Association of Nations.

HARDING IS FOR CAUTION

Sees No Reason for Precipitate Action,
but Has Not Changed Views.

APPEAL BY VIVIANI FAILS

Envoy Is Told Pledge Will Not Be Given to
Protect France Especially.

Special to The New York Times.

WASHINGTON, April 5—Overshadowing all other subjects of public interest in Washington is the determination of the Republican leaders in the Senate to set up a new policy in international affairs. This policy is now in process of formulation. It literally "scraps" the League of Nations Covenant as far as the United States is concerned, it abandons any and all adherence to the rest of the Versailles Treaty and it refuses to ally the United States with any particular foreign Government.

In the view of leading Republican Senators this new policy is intended to keep the United States from entering any association of nations by whatever name it may be designated. In substance the new policy would place the United States on record as willing to interpose its influence whenever the peace of the world is again threatened, but it would assume this position independently of all other nations.

A Washington dispatch in today's issue of The New York Times gave an outline of these purposes. Today they were set forth in a definite way by one of those in a position to speak for the framers of the new policy. Senator New of Indiana, a member of the Committee on Foreign Relations, thus explained the policy in the following statement to the correspondent of The Times:

"It is the purpose to define a new national policy in world affairs. The attitude of the United States is equivalent to a declaration of a new world policy. It has its parallel in the Monroe Doctrine. The Monroe Doctrine related to the countries of this hemisphere. The proposed declaration defines the future attitude of the United States with reference to the peace of the world by whomever threatened.

"It is directed toward the interest of the preservation of civilization. It declares no direct alliance and countenances none. But it is notice to the world that the United States, determining for itself when and how it shall interpose, will stand ready to do its full part for the preservation of world peace whenever and by whomever assailed.

"In 1814 Napoleon sought to subjugate Europe and to conquer the world and all but succeeded in doing so. A century later it was the German Kaiser. Who can say but that a similar attempt may be made by some new Emperor or Kaiser in some other nation's behalf a century hence? The policy to be defined is general in its application, just as the Monroe Doctrine was general, even though both had their origin because of specific acts."

Knox Resolution to Define Aims.

This policy, according to present indications, is to be defined through the medium of Senator Knox's resolution, providing for a separate peace with Germany. There are indications which some persons are inclined to construe as showing a disposition on President Harding's part to have consideration of any such declaration postponed for a time.

While the President appears to be in no hurry, or, as he expressed it to some of those with whom he discussed his attitude, there was no occasion for precipitate action, everything that is apparent on the surface goes to show that he is in accord with the wishes of the majority of his party in the Senate in relation to the Knox resolution.

This new definition of American world policy by Republican leaders in the Senate was explained to René Viviani, special envoy of France, at the dinner given in his honor last night by Senator McCormick. Before the evening was over M. Viviani had been impressed with the intention of the Republicans to put through the Knox resolution and no doubt was left that it would be approved by President Harding.

The information he obtained had the additional force of having been communicated by the men who control the foreign policies of the Senate, for the other guests were Senator McCormick's fellow members of the Committee on Foreign Relations. In addition the company included Senator McKinley of Illinois, Colonel George Harvey and Stephane Lauzanne, editor of the Paris Matin.

Special Plea for France Failed.

The conversation between M. Viviani and the Senators consumed several hours. Perhaps the most dramatic period came when M. Viviani, explaining the desire of France for security from German aggression, pleaded that the Knox resolution should contain a definite mention of the danger of German aggression. He suggested that the resolution be so framed that it would commit the United States to interpose if the peace of Europe was again threatened by Germany. What he was told by Senator Knox and others left no doubt of the intention of the Republican leaders of the Senate, at least, to confine the declaration of policy to general terms which would leave this Government free to take any course it saw fit in the event of threatened war without binding it to France or any particular notion that might be in danger of being drawn into hostilities.

In this connection it was pointed out to M. Viviani that France had her Napoleon who had sought to conquer Europe. What if another Napoleon should rise in France and with his country behind him seek to dominate Europe or the world? it was asked. Would it not then be the duty of the United States to intervene against France, even on the side of Germany, if that nation was the immediate object of French aggression?

It was therefore considered to be the wiser policy, M. Viviani was told, to leave the United States free to determine her course in such an emergency should the peace of the world be threatened. The Wilson-Clemenceau treaty of alliance concluded at Paris in connection with the Versailles Treaty was unacceptable to the Senate, as M. Viviani already knew, and it would not be possible to have that body ratify an arrangement or declaration that would commit this Government to support any particular nation if hostilities were likely. Each case would have to be determined individually as it arose.

Before the conversation ended M. Viviani was made to feel that all hope of a special declaration by the United States in France's behalf which would furnish the security for which the French Government has pleaded had disappeared.

Polish Treaty Brought Up.

At one period of the discussion the refusal of the Senate to agree that the United States should be a party to the

League of Nations was brought up, and it was explained to M. Viviani that the American Government and people were set against any alliances which would not leave them free to determine in each individual case of threatened breach of the world's peace what America's course should be. Would not France feel that she, too, would want to be free in certain instances where she was apparently bound by the dictates of the League organization? was the implication of suggestions advanced.

M. Viviani was reminded that France and Poland had made a treaty of alliance. What would be France's course, he was asked, if the League of Nations should refuse to recognize this alliance? M. Viviani answered that France could then withdraw from the League. His answer pleased his hearers, all or nearly all of whom were in entire sympathy with the rejection of the League covenant.

M. Lauzanne, who served as interpreter for M. Viviani, made the remark that France had no fear except of God and the United States Senate, and the Senate was nearer to earth and appeared more active at present.

Senator Knox had another conference today with President Harding concerning his separate peace resolution and afterward consulted Representative Porter, Chairman of the Committee on Foreign Affairs. The Knox measure will require the sanction of the House, as well as the Senate, before it can be submitted to the President. A feeling of confidence that the resolution will be acted upon favorably by Congress prevails among those who support Mr. Knox's purposes.

Oppose Delaying Resolution.

The only delay that now seems to be in sight may come through a feeling that the adoption of the Knox resolution while the reparations controversy between the European Allies and Germany remains unadjusted would give aid and comfort to the German Government and serve to embarrass the Allies. This view is dismissed by the supporters of the resolution with the statement that the informal memorandum of Secretary Hughes to the German Government makes clear to Germany that the United States stands squarely with her former war associates in their attitude toward her.

The idea has been advanced that the Knox resolution should contain a pledge of support of the allied Governments in their present effort to compel Germany to acknowledge responsibility for the war and to promise to pay reparational damages to the extent of Germany's ability to pay. The supporters of the resolution are firmly opposed to that procedure. They contend that as Secretary Hughes has already made such declarations, it is not necessary to report them. The understanding exists that President Harding shares this view. He has indicated that he favored a policy of defining our foreign policy "piecemeal," which was interpreted to mean that, if any legislative declaration of the position outlined in the Hughes memorandum should be necessary, it should not be included in the Knox resolution.

Harding Is for Caution.

The President's coming message to Congress, it was learned authoritatively, will deal mainly with domestic problems but of necessity will touch upon foreign issues, as the President feels that the American people are entitled to know the situation and what progress is being made toward a solution of international matters. In his opinion, the domestic situation is necessarily connected with the international situation.

As far as the President is concerned no announcement is now feasible as to his attitude toward international affairs, particularly with regard to peace with Germany and Austria. His position, it was explained today, is that the Government's decisions on foreign questions will be prudent, having in mind America's rights and aspirations in the world.

The explanation was also made at the White House that with regard to the Knox resolution the President feels that there is no occasion for "precipitate" action by the United States. The President, however, it was made known, saw no particular reason for any marked reversal of his previous course in voting for the Knox resolution as a Senator and in approving it in his speech of acceptance.

*   *   *

May 31, 1921

SOVIETS BANKRUPT; LENIN ADMITS IT

Moscow Dispatch Quotes Him as Saying That Capitalism Must Be Unfettered.

URGES RECALL OF EXILES

Reported Proposal to Executive Committee Calls for Return of Constitutional Democrats.

RIGA, May 30 (Associated Press)—According to a direct Moscow dispatch received today from independent sources, Nikolai Lenin, the Soviet Russian Premier, declared yesterday that Communism was in complete bankruptcy and asked the presiding officers of the All-Russian Central Executive Committee to approve the unlimited return of capitalism and the recall to Russia of the Constitutional Democrats and other parties to aid in rebuilding the State.

The Moscow dispatch says that Lenin has submitted the following written proposition:

"Whereas, in the realization that Communism has come to complete bankruptcy, and in order to save the idea of communism for the future and find without too big a change of policy the way out of the abyss into which communism has thrust the country, it is recognized that unlimited freedom must be allowed capitalism, and that the Constitutional Democrats and Representatives of the 'Realpolitik' [practical politics] shall be summoned to resume the work of rebuilding the State."

The dispatch asserts that this proposition caused tremendous excitement, but does not say whether it was adopted.

The statements contained in the dispatch have not been carried in any official Bolshevist advices, nor has anything tending to confirm them been received from any other source.

The Russian Soviet Government has refused a proposal of an Anglo-Dutch-Belgian oil company for concessions in the Groznyi and Baku regions of the Caucasus. Up-to-date the Government has not granted a single concession, according to advices received here.

M. Lomoff, a member of the Russian Economic Council, speaking at the recent Economic Congress held in Moscow, said, according to Russian papers received here, that so far Russia had had no real bidders for concessions.

"Even the most valuable concessions, from the standpoint of Russia, could not be sufficiently advertised and brought to the attention of the capitalists under present conditions. Russia is too badly cut off from Western Europe now to be able to solve this difficult problem."

M. Lomoff mentioned several English and Canadian companies as having made bids for timber and pulp concessions in the north, but said nothing concerning Washington B. Vanderlip in this connection. Replying to a question, M. Lomoff said that no agreement had yet been signed with Mr. Vanderlip with regard to Kamchatka, because this question hinged on an American-Russian trade treaty.

M. Lomoff said Russia had refused offers from a number of German firms for coal and iron concessions and also from Frenchmen for the establishment of automobile plants in Petrograd.

* * *

August 13, 1921

LENIN ABANDONS STATE OWNERSHIP AS SOVIET POLICY

Official Decree Retains Control of Only a Few of the Big National Industries.

TO LEASE TO INDIVIDUALS

Payments for Postal, Railroads and Other Public Services Are Re-established.

BROWN MEETS LITVINOFF

He Demands Protection for American Food and for Personnel of Relief Bodies.

By WALTER DURANTY
Special Cable to The New York Times.

RIGA, Aug. 12—Lenin has thrown communism overboard. His signature appears in the official press of Moscow on Aug. 9, abandoning State ownership, with the exception of a "definite number of great industries of national importance"—such as were controlled by the State in France, England and Germany during the war—and re-establishing payment by individuals for railroads, postal and other public services.

The new economic policy embodied in the decree was adopted by unanimous vote by the Council of Commissars of the People after a long detailed discussion in which the views of the chief Russian political and labor union organizations were expressed at length. The decree enjoins the State henceforward to conduct only a definite number of great industries of national importance. The other industries and enterprises are to be leased to individuals, co-operative bodies and labor organizations.

The labor unions will be called on to help fix working conditions, the standard of living, and to arrange other details of the new industrial system.

Special efforts will be made to encourage small industries which are considered an important adjunct to State industry and agriculture. The Pan-Russian Economic Council will create commissions to fix working, living and payment conditions in leased enterprises and concessions.

The decree emphasizes the importance in the present juncture and during the translation period of wages in kind and collective remuneration—by which presumably is meant some scheme of profit sharing.

These points shall be decided with the help and guidance of the labor unions and executive councils, with the view of restoring industrial efficiency to the maximum. To improve the State's financial position, individuals will be made to pay for railroad, postal and other public services. Along these lines will be directed all coming labor union and administrative measures, in order to establish a new economic policy devoted to the purpose of fostering the maximum commodity production and individual development.

Revokes Free Public Services.

RIGA, Aug. 12 (Associated Press)—Formal decision to revoke free postal, railway, telegraph and tramway service in Soviet Russia, together with the abandonment of the free grant of tools and household goods to workmen, and the possibility of a gradual change to the monetary system instead of the exchange of goods, are announced in dispatches received here today from the Rosta News Agency, the official Soviet news disseminator at Moscow.

These important steps toward putting into effect Lenin's new policy, which are taken as indication that his plan is moving still further in the direction of the industrial and capitalistic systems of the rest of the world than was at first believed, are announced in decrees to the people's commissars, signed by Lenin.

Detailed instructions drafted by the Council of Commissars after a consultation with the various trade organizations show that only the big industries will remain under national management; the others will be left to the co-operatives and individuals, wages to be regulated by the trade unions.

The decision to charge for the postal, tramway and other services was made, says the Resta Agency, "to restore the value of the currency."

By another decree the Government organizations are instructed to secure payment for everything furnished workmen, except for food rations and medicine given those having cards. This is interpreted as meaning a great curtailment of the free ration list through strict limitation of cards to actual workmen, who will be subjected to collective rationing, factories or departments to receive a food supply based on their output, irrespective of the number of employees.

A message to the Riga Rundschau from Moscow states that the taxes in Russia will be payable in money.

Lenin Speeches Forecast Action.

Ever since Leonid Krassin for Soviet Russia and Sir Robert Horne for Great Britain signed on March 10 an agreement opening trade relations between the two countries, and, as it turned out by an interpretation of the document by English courts, a recognition of Soviet sovereignty, two questions have received indeterminate discussion: Would Lenin abandon his scheme for universal communism? Would he abandon communism in Russia, or limit its working there?

The terms of the Krassin-Horne Agreement forbade propaganda abroad, but propaganda still continued. Lenin said on several occasions that the present state of Russia made it impossible to proceed without the aid of capitalistic interests from abroad, but his propagandists interpreted his words to mean the abandonment of communism. On the eve of the American agreement to help feed the famished Russians, there was a rumor to the effect that the distribution of food would be through the old Samvors, or county organizations, which would be revived for that purpose, or through the co-operative associations, also to be revived. But later a representative of the Lenin Government stated that the distribution of food would be carried out through the Russian Government itself, which had no intention of yielding any of its prerogatives.

In every case in which the story has come that Lenin was about to yield to the exigencies of recognized and approved industrial and commercial usage and had abandoned or at least qualified either his ideas or his administration of communism, another story followed that he had made no such concessions to either the failure of his ideas and administration in Russia or their lack of welcome abroad.

The news printed this morning that he has now abandoned communism except in those large industries which other nations nationalized during the war, and hence for a time administered socialistically, may belong to the foregoing series of assertions to be followed by a dementi or it may be something new.

A speech Lenin made at the Bolshevist congress in April was interpreted to mean by his propagandists abroad that he had asserted that a return to capitalism would alone save Russia. What he actually said was that under certain conditions private ownership would be restored to the peasants, who would not otherwise deliver their crops to the Soviet—a trap, it was asserted, to get hold of the peasants' stores. And while Lenin continued to make similar speeches, his agents at Stockholm, Copenhagen, and even in London were trying to make business arrangements for him by old methods.

Then in an article in the Moscow Pravada of May 8 Lenin actually repeated what his propagandists had said in regard to his Bolshevist speech. In this article he presumed that the proletariat was opposed to private ownership and would with reluctance part with communism, for he wrote:

"Those who don't understand that it is necessary to begin with the improvement of the peasants and who interpret our measures as favoring the peasants and a renunciation of proletarian dictatorship are simply possessed of empty purses * * * At the present stage we must choose this alternative. Either we must prohibit every kind of private exchange of goods, which would be political and national suicide, or we must aid the development of capitalism in Russia while we are trying to transform it into State capitalism. This is economically possible and does not contradict the proletarian dictatorship. On the contrary, State capitalism is one stage in the advance of free capitalism."

In a speech before the third international congress at Moscow on July 11, Lenin again pleaded for his policy of limited private ownership and abortive capitalism from abroad, while reiterating his world-views to the following words:

"We must utilize this breathing space to prepare for the outbreak of the world revolution in all capitalist countries."

It will thus be said that the idea of limited communism for large industries (State capitalism) was the first put forward on May 8, while its transitory character is defined in the speech of July 11.

* * *

February 5, 1922

CONFERENCE FINISHES WORK, APPROVING TWO TREATIES; LEADERS OF ALL DELEGATONS HAIL BIG ACHIEVEMENTS; JAPAN AND CHINA FORMALLY SIGN THE SHANTUNG TREATY

LAST SESSION A BUSY ONE

Two Far Eastern Treaties and Many Resolutions Are Adopted.

SPEECHMAKING FOLLOWS

Heads of All the Delegations Express Gratification Over the Results Obtained.

'A NEW ERA,' SAYS BALFOUR

Portugal's Envoy Praises Our Leadership in Affairs of the World.

By ELMER DAVIS
Special to The New York Times.

WASHINGTON, Feb. 4—The work of the Conference for the Limitation of Armament was ended today, except for the signing of the treaties which it has produced, in a four-hour plenary session, the sixth since the conference met twelve weeks ago today.

The principal accomplishment of the session was the adoption of two treaties relating to Chinese affairs. The first covers the "open door," including the Root resolutions, pledging the powers to give China a chance to get on her feet and not to seek for themselves any unfair or special advantages, binds the signatories to respect Chinese neutrality and empowers any of the powers concerned, including China herself, to call a conference of all the signatories in case a situation arises "which in the opinion of any one of them" involves the application of the stipulations of the present treaty.

The second treaty deals with the Chinese tariff, and provides for the assembling at Shanghai as soon as possible of a commission, which shall revise the Chinese tariff so as to make it equivalent to 5 per cent. ad valorem, instead of about 3½ per cent. as at present. The treaty also provides for a special conference to take steps toward the abolition of the likin or internal customs in China and to authorize the levying of a surtax, in most instances 2½ percent., on Chinese imports as soon as it finds it advisable. A further revision is to be made in four years to adjust the specific duties fixed by the revising commission to the ad valorem rates, and thereafter revisions are to take place every seven years instead of every ten as heretofore. Senator Underwood, who presented the treaty to the conference, said that it might be expected to double the maritime customs revenue of China.

The conference also adopted a resolution providing for the establishment of a Board of Reference in Peking to consider questions arising from the application of the open door principles; approved a supplement to the four-power treaty, which removed the "homeland" of Japan from discussion by specifying Formosa, the Pescadores, the Japanese half of Sakhalin, and the mandated islands as the Japanese insular possessions, which are guaranteed by the treaty; adopted resolutions on the Chinese Eastern Railway; took note of the American, Japanese and French statement on Siberia, the Japanese, Chinese and American statement on the twenty-one demands, and a declaration by China that she would not alienate any of her territory; and finally heard a declaration by the five powers signatory to the naval treaty that they would regard it as a "breach of honor" to sell any of the warships designated for scrapping between the present and the date of ratification of the treaty.

Something like two hours after the conference ended, Japan and China signed the agreement embodying the settlement of the Shantung controversy. On Monday, after the signing of the other treaties, the conference will end with an address by President Harding.

Conference Achievements Lauded.

The formal session of today's conference completed its real work in two hours. Then two hours more were given over to speeches by members of the delegations, giving their estimate of the importance of what had been done.

Mr. Balfour, first of the speakers, declared that the delegates had felt that they were "consciously working in the service of mankind."

He went on:

"Cast your eyes back to only a few months ago, when a spirit of deep anxiety overshadowed the mind of every man who contemplated the state of public feeling in the great Pacific area. Already this feeling of mutual fear has given way to a feeling of very different character and confidence has taken the place of mistrust.

"The greatest step toward regularizing the relations of the powers in China has been taken by this conference. We have tried to lay the foundations of honest dealings between the powers in China and with China, and a nation which deliberately separates itself from the collective action we have taken here, that nation will not be able to plead ignorance of its obligations."

Discussing the three accomplishments of the conference, naval limitation, the four-power treaty and the Chinese agreements, he said that none of them could be considered without taking the others into account.

"With the diminution of armaments," he added, "there goes a great diminution in the likelihood of their ever being required. This conference is unique in history as the most successful attempt to promote peace."

Referring to the laying down of the naval reduction program by Secretary Hughes at the opening session on Nov. 12, he said:

"Everything turned on that first day. From that day on I had no doubt that we would achieve great results. We have accomplished almost all that anybody could hope for, and far more than experienced statesmen had ever dared expect."

Hughes's Estimate of Results.

Mr. Hughes, the last of the speakers, said that the measure of success that the conference had attained had been due first of all to the fact that it had "a definite and limited aim."

"We have not occupied ourselves," he went on, "in endeavoring to elucidate the obvious, but rather have set ourselves to removal of controversy and the reduction of armament in so far as possible.

"We have been successful because we have not been content with expressing pious hopes, but rather have devoted ourselves to the realization of those hopes. There has been talk of national interests. What we have sought is the realization of the highest national interest in making peace and for the removal of the causes of controversy."

From a somewhat different viewpoint the work of the conference was discussed by Baron Kijuro Shidehara, the Japanese Ambassador, who said that there had been no differences in the purpose of the delegations, and that the only variation had been in the methods by which the common purpose was pursued.

Discussing the Chinese question, he said:

"No one denies to China her sacred right to govern herself. No one stands in the way of China working out her own destiny. Japan believes she has made to China every possible concession compatible with reason, fairness and honor."

He disclaimed any desire for special Japanese privileges in China, pointing out that Japan had no reason to ask for anything but equality of opportunity in view of her special geographical position which gave her an easy access to Chinese markets. Her only special interest in China, he said, was to see that she could obtain raw materials from China, and sell her manufactured products in China, on equal terms with other nations.

"This conference," he concluded, "ushers into the world a new spirit of international friendship and understanding."

Sze Hails Shantung Agreement.

Alfred Sze, the Chinese Minister, who followed him, said that "much that seemed impossible has been accomplished," and that the Shantung agreement was "greatly conducive to concord and good understanding between the two nations."

Special interest was attracted by the eloquent address of Viscount d'Alte, the Portuguese Minister, who ranks next to Ambassador Jusserand in length of service in Washington. He reviewed the history of American participation in world affairs, first by war relief and then as a combatant in the German war, and ended with the declaration "America has justified her leadership of the world."

M. Albert Sarraut, for the French delegation; Senator Carlo Schanzer, for the Italian delegation; Baron de Cartier de Marchienne, the Belgian Ambassador, and Jonkheer van Blokland for the Dutch delegation also gave enthusiastic estimates of the importance of the work of the conference, and the spirit displayed. When Mr. Hughes concluded his speech, ending the session, Baron de Cartier stood up and led the applause.

In this, the more social part of the session, Mr. Balfour was deputed for the conference to express the gratitude of the delegates to the secretariat staff and to Mr. Camerlynck, the translator, and Mr. Hughes performed the same function for the technical advisers, the newspaper correspondents and the American Advisory Commission.

* * *

January 23, 1924

LENIN DIES OF CEREBRAL HEMORRHAGE; MOSCOW THRONGS OVERCOME WITH GRIEF; TROTSKY DEPARTS ILL, RADEK IN DISFAVOR

SOVIET CONGRESS IN TEARS

Mass Hysteria Only Averted by a Leader's Brusque Intervention.

BODY WILL LIE IN STATE

Is to Be Taken to Moscow Today From Village Where Premier Passed Away.

KREMLIN WALL HIS TOMB

Washington Expects No Immediate Change in the Policy of the Russian Government.

By WALTER DURANTY
By Wireless to The New York Times.

MOSCOW, Jan. 22—Nikolai Lenin died last night at 6:50 o'clock. The immediate cause of death was paralysis of the respiratory centres due to a cerebral hemorrhage.

For some time optimistic reports had been current as the effects of a previous lesion gradually cleared up, but Lenin's nearest friends, realizing the progress of the relentless malady, tried vainly to hope against hope.

At 11:20 o'clock this morning President Kalinin briefly opened the session of the All-Russian Soviet Congress and requested every one to stand. He had not slept all night and tears were streaming down his haggard face. A sudden wave of emotion—not a sound, but a strange stir—passed over the audience, none of whom knew what had happened. The music started to play the Soviet funeral march, but was instantly hushed as Kalinin murmured brokenly:

"I bring you terrible news about our dear comrade, Vladimir Ilyitch." [Nikolai Lenin was his pen name.]

High up in the gallery a woman uttered a low, wailing cry that was followed by a burst of sobs.

Kalinin Breaks the News.

"Yesterday," faltered Kalinin, "yesterday, he suffered a further stroke of paralysis and—" There was a long pause as if the speaker were unable to nerve himself to pronounce the fatal word; then, with an effort which shook his whole body, it came—"died."

The emotional Slav temperament reacted immediately. From all over the huge opera house came sobs and wailing, not loud nor shrill, but pitifully mournful, spreading and increasing. Kalinin could not speak. He tried vainly to motion for silence with his hands and for one appalling moment a dreadful outbreak of mass hysteria seemed certain. A tenth of a second later it could not have been averted, but Yunakidze, Secretary of the Russian Federal Union, thrust forward his powerful frame and with hand and voice demanded calm. Then Kalinin, stumbling, read out the official bulletin.

" 'Jan. 21 the condition of Vladimir Ilyitch suddenly underwent sharp aggravation. At 5:30 P. M. his breathing was interrupted and he lost consciousness. At 6:50 Vladimir Ilyitch died from paralysis of the respiratory centres.

" 'Dated 3:25 A. M., Jan. 22.

" 'Signed:

" 'Drs. OHUNK [Lenin's personal physician and chief of the Moscow Health Department, who gave Lenin first treatment when wounded Aug. 30, 1918.]

" 'SEMISKO [a close personal friend of Lenin, and Minister of the Health Department],

" 'FOERSTER,

" 'GTYE,

" 'OSIGOF,

" 'YEWISTRATOF.'

"We propose," continued Kalinin, "that the twenty-first day of January henceforth be set aside as a day of national mourning." By a tragic coincidence today—Jan. 9, old style, is a similar Bolshevist holiday in memory of Father Gapon's petitioners, massacred by the Czar's troops in the courtyard of the Winter Palace on "Bloody Sunday," 1905.

"Do you agree?" questioned Kalinin.

A confused sound, half sob, half sigh, was the only assent.

Whole Congress Gives Way to Grief.

Kalinin tried to tell the funeral arrangements, but broke down completely.

Kamenief and Zinovief, equally unnerved, and other members of the Presiding Committee had laid their heads on the table and cried like children. Even the daredevil Cossack leader Budyenny was weeping unrestrainedly, while the delegates in the body of the theatre stood motionless, sobbing, with tears coursing down their cheeks.

Finally Lashevitch, a member of the Central Executive Committee of the Communist Party and President of the Siberian Revolutionary Committee, stepped to the speakers' rostrum. His strong, square body in khaki uniform with dull red facings radiated calm as in a firm voice he announced that the members of the Presiding Committee and a group of senior delegates to the Congress would go tomorrow at 6 A. M. by special train to the village of Gorky, 28 versts from Moscow, where Lenin died, to bring back the body by train, reaching Moscow at 1 o'clock, and the delegation would escort it to the "House of Columns"—the former nobles' club in the centre of the city—where it would lie in the state until the funeral on Saturday in order that the population might "freely and without restriction" be permitted to pay their last respects to the dead leader.

So great was the continued emotion that no one on the presiding committee thought to give the order finally to play the Soviet funeral march until reminded from the audience.

Owing to a partial breakdown of wires, the result of a recent abnormal snowfall, it appears that the news of Lenin's fatal seisure did not reach Moscow until shortly after 8 o'clock last night. Lenin's wife, Nadjeduda Constantinova Krupshata, was with him at the end. Kalinin and other leaders left for Gorky about 9 o'clock, but the news was not known even in the Government offices until late at night.

Moscow Public Stunned.

The news of Lenin's death only became known to the general public by special fly sheet editions which appeared on the streets at 6 o'clock. It was snowing heavily and as usual on a Moscow holiday in Winter there were comparatively few people about. The flags decorating the public buildings are hung out from the facade rather than hoisted on a mast above, so the only half-masted red banner over the clock tower of the Kremlin and the flags on the foreign missions gave the sign of mourning.

Curiously enough the newsboys did not shout the tidings, but each speedily became the centre of a group asking "What is the news? Is it a telegram from abroad, or what?" At the first glimpse of the black bordered sheet someone cried: "Trotzky is dead!" That it seems was the impression of even several members of the presiding committee of the Soviet Congress last night when a few leaders left hurriedly in obvious perturbation, so little did any one expect the sudden end of Lenin.

As the news became known it produced literal stupefaction. The correspondent watched dozens of people seize the sheet and stare blankly at the huge headline. A spell of silent dismay that overspread one group after another was perhaps the most remarkable tribute to the dead leader, for these were not Communists or workers, but people of all sorts, poor and prosperous alike. The correspondent heard a well-dressed man say dazedly to a tattered beggar:

"Lenin is dead."

"Didn't you know that?" was the reply with an extraordinary mingling of scorn and pride. "All the city knows it—I knew this morning."

The fly sheet announced that a special committee had been appointed to make arrangements for the funeral, consisting of Djerjinsky, President Muralof, Military Governor of Moscow; Lashevitch, member of the Supreme War Council and President of the Siberian Revolutionary Committee; Voroshilof, Budenny's Chief of Staff, and also a member of the Supreme War Council; Molotoff, Zelinski and Yenakidze. Their first act was to order the closing of all theatres and places of amusement until the funeral.

Blood Vessel Burst in Brain.

An autopsy performed on Lenin's brain this afternoon showed it flooded with blood. The theory of the physicians is that the bursting of a small blood vessel produced almost complete paralysis of the respiratory system which was followed an hour later by an extensive lesion causing instant death.

The house where Lenin died has a tragic history. It is a broad, low mansion with columns in the Italian style in the centre. It was bought a score of years ago by Sava Morosof, self-made billionaire chief of the Russian textile trust. Morosof had liberal ideas, and after a bitter dispute in 1905 with his brothers, who opposed his plan for extended profit sharing with the employes, killed himself. The house stands in the centre of a wooded hilly park through which winds a mile and a half drive from the hamlet of Gorky—the first village in Russia, thanks to Lenin, to obtain electrification, upon which the Bolshevist leader laid such stress for Russia's future development.

Lenin will be buried in the Kremlin Wall in the Red Square where lie John Reed, Sverdlof, first President of the Soviet Republic, and other well-known figures of the Bolshevist revolution.

Sidelights on Lenin's Character.

Interesting sidelights on Lenin's character have been given to The New York Times correspondent by a young woman who worked for him as stenographer. In the dark days of 1918 when Soviet Russia was beleaguered on all sides by enemies, Lenin received the news that Trotsky had defeated the Czechoslovaks at Sviask, near Kasan, on the Volga. Lenin, she said, danced with glee like a child.

The first time she spoke with him was a little earlier when during an important meeting he noticed she kept looking up from her work to watch the man of whom she had heard so much but had never seen before. After the meeting Lenin came to her desk.

"Little Comrade," he said smiling, "here I am. We must shake hands because we are going to work together."

Much more recently the girl put the Council of Soviet Comissars' stamp in the wrong place above Lenin's signature. She did not like to confess her error, but when the document was sent back for correction she took it to Lenin and said: "You ought to have signed on the left under the stamp as well as here on the right."

Lenin looked at her with twinkling eyes and replied:

"I sign wherever and as often as necessary, my little comrade—to correct your mistakes."

Internal Effect in Russia.

What has been the internal effect in Russia of Lenin's death? Only today the Pravda prints a final furious attack by Stalin, the chief machine leader, upon Trotsky, Radek, Preobrajenski and other "insurgents." But the fact that the speech which was delivered three days ago was allowed to go abroad in the columns of the Pravda seems to show that the Bolsheviki are less worried about the split in their ranks than the machine's leaders would be willing to admit.

Nevertheless with Lenin dead and with Trotsky ill and his supporters blamed and even in some cases expelled from high positions, it is the general opinion that Lenin's death will unify and strengthen the Communist Party as nothing else could do. No one who knows them both doubts that Trotsky and Stalin will bury the hatchet over his grave.

Trotsky had a high fever all last week and left for the Caucasus Saturday. It is doubtful whether he will be able to return for the funeral, but his friends say there is no possible doubt of his loyalty.

Lenin's successor as President of the Russian Council of Commissars will be determined, it is stated, by the Congress of the Russian Soviet Federation, which is unlikely to meet before Monday. Rykov and Kamenef are the most probable candidates.

* * *

August 28, 1928

15 NATIONS SIGN PACT TO RENOUNCE WAR IN PARIS ROOM WHERE LEAGUE WAS BORN; BRIAND DEDICATES IT TO NATIONS' DEAD

KELLOGG IS DEEPLY MOVED

Tears in the Secretary's Eyes as He Listens to French Statesman.

STRESEMANN GETS OVATION

Delegates Within and Crowds Outside Warmly Applaud the Reich's Foreign Minister.

GERMAN FLAG IS DISPLAYED

Featured in Street Decorations— Soviet Emblem Amid Colors on Foreign Office.

By EDWIN L. JAMES
Special Cable to The New York Times.

PARIS, Aug. 27—In sumptuous setting but with simplicity of ceremony "the Pact of Paris" was signed in the Quai d'Orsay this afternoon.

In the crimson and gold Salle de l'Horloge of the French Foreign Office, the delegates of fifteen nations affixed their signatures to the Briand-Kellogg general treaty for the renunciation of war, which from now on will be known by its newer and simpler name.

It was a quarter to 4 o'clock when Dr. Gustav Stresemann, Foreign Minister of Germany, signed first for Germany and two minutes later that Secretary of State Frank B. Kellogg signed for the United States.

As in response to the roll-call the representatives of the thirteen other States affixed their signatures the rays of six great movie sunlights played over the room, that the sight might be seen by 500,000,000 humans represented there. Incidentally, they helped to raise the temperature of the overheated hall to give added zest to tea which was served in the gardens after the hour's ritual was over.

Two Only Uniforms American.

The motion pictures will show that in the gathering to consecrate peace there were but two uniforms. They were both American and worn by an Admiral and a naval Commander who accompanied Secretary Kellogg.

Tonight there will be delivered to the Governments at all the capitals of the world not represented today a formal invitation to adhere to the Pact of Paris by which the nations of the earth promise never to go to war again.

The American Secretary of State made no speech. To the general surprise of the assemblage, the spokesman of the United States had nothing to say about the treaty he presented to the world. Out of respect for the policy of silence which Mr. Kellogg had advocated there were no speeches except that of M. Briand, who presided. But what a speech he made! Eloquent he was and precise. Contrary to his habit he read his address, which meant that it had been prepared with care and calculation.

When he sat down, there was no longer room for doubt in anyone's mind of what Europe thinks the treaty means. It means, he said, the beautiful beginning of the work in which all the parties to the Pact of Paris must continue. If Secretary Kellogg still felt this afternoon as he did in Washington, his silence today incurred the risk of the rest of the world thinking that it betokened consent to M. Briand's words.

Briand Recalls Woodrow Wilson.

It would be a heartless man who did not feel that the spirit of Woodrow Wilson lived this afternoon in that great hall where a decade ago he gave the League of Nations to the world. If thoughts of him and his work were lacking in the minds of any one, M. Briand supplied the lack when he welcomed Mr. Kellogg into the room where "his illustrious predecessor, President Wilson, had sat."

Briand heaped praise on the League of Nations, "that powerful institution of organized peace," and he hoped the Pact of Paris would be of great benefit to it.

Queerly enough, by a last-minute change in the protocol, Secretary Kellogg sat on the left of M. Briand, whereas President Wilson had sat on the right of Premier Clemenceau. Dr. Stresemann sat today on the right of the Foreign Minister. This change was explained officially by the statement that the alphabetical rule had been followed, but the arrangement of other delegates scarcely confirms this.

Yet Mr. Kellogg's feelings could not have been keener had he sat in Woodrow Wilson's chair. In the midst of M. Briand's speech it was seen that emotion caused tears to trickle down the cheeks of the American Secretary of State.

The delegates had gathered in the office of M. Briand from 2:30 on. Sharply at 3 a Swiss Guard with a halberd led the way into the Salle de l'Horloge, the statesmen took their seats and two minutes after 3, M. Briand began to speak.

France's Peaceful Intentions.

Paying a tribute to "the greatest collective deed born of peace," the Foreign Minister expressed the hope that today's ceremony held in the capital of France would cause the peaceful intentions of France "at last to be understood by the world."

Turning first to Mr. Kellogg he said: "Sitting today among us in this very hall where his illustrious forerunner, President Wilson, had already brought to the work of peace such high conscience of the part played by his country, Mr. Kellogg can look with just feeling of pride on the progress that has been made in such a short time since the day when we both began to examine the means of carrying out this far-reaching diplomatic undertaking."

He next paid a tribute to Dr. Stresemann, praising the occasion which brought Germany to sign the Pact of Peace with her former enemies. Next came a tribute to the absent Sir Austen Chamberlain.

In stirring tones, M. Briand pointed out that this treaty, unlike most treaties, was not born of war. It was not to settle a conflict but to prevent conflicts.

"The League of Nations," he said, "deeply imbued with the same spirit, had likewise issued a declaration tending in fact to obtain eventually the same result as the new pact."

But, he remarked, the United States had no share in that, whereas today's treaty brought America's signature.

Turning again to the League, of which he is one of the leaders, the French Foreign Minister said:

"The League of Nations, a vast political undertaking of insurance against war and a powerful institution of organized peace, where there is room to welcome all fresh contributions to the common work, cannot but rejoice at the signing of an international contract whereby it is to benefit.

"Far from being inconsistent with any of its obligations, this new act, on the contrary, offers it a kind of general reinsurance. Thus those of its members who will soon be able to ask the League to register today's contract will rightly feel they are bringing it a precious token of their attachment and loyalty."

Purpose of the Treaty.

M. Briand declared that the new treaty branded as illegal war which had always been the attribute of sovereignty. The treaty, he said, aimed to abolish selfish and willful war. "Thus," he said, "shall the smaller nations henceforth enjoy real independence in international discussions." In the future, said M. Briand, the nation which went on the warpath ran the risk of bringing against it all the other nations.

Emphasizing the joint responsibility and interest of all nations in preventing war, he quoted President Coolidge's words: "An act of war in any part of the world is an act that injures the interests of my country."

Predicting that all nations would quickly become parties to the Pact of Paris to prevent war, M. Briand added:

"It will henceforth behoove us as a sacred duty to do all that can and must be done for that hope not to be disappointed. Peace is proclaimed. That is well; that is much. But it still remains necessary to organize it. In the solution of difficulties right and not might must prevail. That is to be the work of tomorrow."

In closing M. Briand said that all the nations represented had shed blood in the World War and he proposed to dedicate the Pact of Paris to all the dead of the great war. When he sat down a great burst of applause started. In fact, it began before he finished—when he turned to Dr. Stresemann as he said "all the dead of the great war."

Then Professor Camerlynk translated the speech into English. When he had done, it was apparent that the crowd expected to hear Secretary Kellogg. Murmurs of "l'Americain, l'Americain," ran around the hall. But instead M. Briand rose again and read the preamble and text of the treaty, after which, in response to the alphabetical roll-call, the delegates moved around a little stand in a recess of the big horseshoe table and put their signatures on the official copy of the Pact of Paris.

At three minutes to 4 it was all over. The Swiss Guard banged his halberd on the floor and the delegates filed out behind him through M. Briand's office into the gardens of the Quai d'Orsay Palace. After half an hour's conversation over tea and cake they scattered to their respective embassies.

They had condemned war as an ever hateful thing. Yet every country they represented was born of war.

Within forty-eight hours Mr. Kellogg will leave France on a ship of war with the Pact of Peace, the immediate future of which depends on the American Senate. In the hall where an American President pro- was rejected by the Senate, there was created today an opportunity for the Senate to approve another American plan which M. Briand, speaking for the assembled countries, said he hoped would be of great benefit to the League of Nations, born in this same Quai d'Orsay on the same sort of sunshiny day just about ten years ago.

Bold and outspoken we were then. Timid and silent we were today. Will a different beginning bring a different culmination?

* * *

January 24, 1929

SOVIET ARRESTS 150 FOR CIVIL WAR PLOT

Followers of Exiled Trotsky Are Accused of Preparing to Overthrow Government.

RED ARMY NAMED IN PLAN

Alleged Scheme Was to Rally Troops Round Old Chief—All Prisoners Held in Isolation.

Special Cable to The New York Times.

RIGA, Jan. 23—The Soviet police have arrested 150 adherents of Leon Trotsky, the former Minister of War now in exile in Russian Turkestan, according to an official announcement received here tonight from Moscow. Many of the arrests were in the capital but others were in various parts of the country.

All of the prisoners were confined in isolated cells. Among the more notable of them are Odivani, Voronsky, Pankratoff, Drobnis, Globus, Kavtaradze, Gaievsky and Greenstein.

Earlier reports from Moscow stated that arrests, made on a wide scale, had included non-Communists as well as dissident party members of the Trotsky Opposition in connection with a new alleged anti-Soviet plot. Quantities of literature condemned as subversive have been seized.

For a week there have been indications of a move of unusual importance against fractious Communists. It has been said that the Soviet authorities intended further repressive action against M. Trotsky himself as well as drastic general measures against heterogeneous malcontents both inside and outside the Communist party, all of whom were described as henchmen of Trotsky in his persistent opposition campaign or his non-party allies.

This evening the Soviet authorities instructed the daily papers of Moscow and all provincial newspapers to publish simultaneously an identical explanation of the present stage of the "war against Trotsky."

This explanation warns "waverers who stand at the crossroads" that the followers of M. Trotsky are preparing a "new civil war" and among other things are trying to gain the support of the Red Army.

There is said to be hope of rallying the troops round their old chief in his fight for a "return" of "straight Leninism."

The communiqué declares that during 1928 the Trotsky Opposition developed into an active anti-Soviet organization which is now making war against the Soviet Union itself and everything which the Soviet Government holds dear.

It adds that all anti-Soviet forces are rallying under the banner of M. Trotsky, who is accused of publishing anti-Soviet articles abroad and trying to turn hostile elements in other countries against the Soviet Union.

The communiqué concludes by asserting that ruthless war must be waged against the Trotsky counter-revolutionary organization.

* * *

December 6, 1931

SOVIET RUSSIA NOW AT A CRISIS IN HER FIVE-YEAR PROGRAM

Internal and Foreign Factors Which May Force Her to Make a Drastic Revision of Her Plans for Industrialization

By JOSEPH SHAPLEN

Announcement by the Amtorg Trading Corporation, Soviet commercial agency in the United States, that it has embarked upon a program of retrenchment in its operations and purchases, and dispatches from the Moscow correspondent of The New York Times revealing that the government may be forced to "revise" the Five-Year Plan are two of several indications of an advancing economic and financial crisis in Soviet Russia.

Hitherto, it has been the proud boast of Soviet spokesmen that Russia has remained untouched by the world depression, while industrial countries—the countries of so-called capitalism—have been feeling the severe stress of economic and financial dislocation. Economic facts now indicate that this conception of Russia's position is unfounded.

An examination of Soviet exports, imports, trade balance, gold reserve and foreign credits throw light on the reasons for the disquieting dispatches from Moscow and the widespread discussions in the European press concerning the Soviet Government's ability to pay its commercial debts, conservatively estimated at $450,000,000, and its credit stability in the immediate future.

Foreign Creditors of Russia.

That these discussions should now occupy so much space in the press of those countries which were among the first to establish commercial relations with Soviet Russia and have in the past been more generous than others in extending commercial credits to Moscow is in itself a significant reflection of recent Soviet economic changes. This is particularly true of the German press, which more than the press of any other country has urged the expansion of trade with Russia and in recent weeks has repeatedly, and in the face of official denials from representatives of the Soviet Government, returned to the subject of a possible Soviet moratorium on foreign obligations.

How the world depression has affected Soviet trade is indicated in a Moscow dispatch from the correspondent of The New York Times under date of Nov. 23. We learn from this dispatch that "the total export figures for the first nine months show that the Soviet Union exported 15,600,000 tons of goods with a value of $300,000,000 and imported 2,500,000 tons of goods at a cost of $405,000,000, leaving an adverse trade balance of $105,000,000," which is about nine times as large as the adverse trade balance of 1930. The same dispatch says that the same nine months' period last year "showed exports of 1,000,000 fewer tons, but the value was $70,000,000 greater, which shows what the world depression has done to Soviet trade."

A comparison of Soviet exports and imports for the last three years will serve to emphasize this change, and the implications it entails for the entire program of economic development embodied in the Five-Year Plan. The facts will become all the more apparent when we view the unfavorable trade balance in the light of Soviet commercial obligations abroad and the resources available to meet these obligations. For it need not be emphasized that Soviet credits abroad, so essential to the uninterrupted operation of industry under the Five-Year Plan in view of the disorganized condition of Russia's own internal market, depend in the main upon the Soviet Government's ability to meet its foreign obligations.

Value of Russian Exports.

Figures published by the Soviet Government early in September give the value of exports for the first six months of 1931 as $168,425,000, against $232,155,500 for the corresponding period last year. (For purposes of convenience in translating the figures into dollars the statistics are presented in round figures). In tonnage, last year's exports were 7,487,000 tons as compared with 8,241,000 tons in 1931. In other words, while exports for the first six months of this year exceeded last year's by 754,000 tons their value was $63,730,500 less. The figures for the first nine months of this year given in the dispatch from Walter Duranty to The New York Times bear out the unfavorable tendency of the trade balance.

While this tendency is to be ascribed fundamentally to the drop in world prices, a measure of responsibility falls upon the Soviet Government's policy of underselling by methods that can only be characterized as "dumping." By this policy, according to experts, the Soviet Government had succeeded in forcing down prices sharply on several commodities prominent on its export list, such as wheat, lumber, oil, furs.

The implications of the growing unfavorable trade balance of Russia assume more serious significance when coupled with the fact that world market prices reveal no upward tendency, and the measures contemplated by various countries to protect themselves against foreign dumping. The recent revolution in British tariff policy may be cited as an example. In this connection it must be remembered that about 50 per cent of Soviet exports go to England and Germany. Moreover, a rise in world market prices would be of no great advantage because of Russia's shortage of exportable goods, that is because of the breakdown in the export program of the Five-Year Plan itself.

Under the Five-Year Plan, Soviet exports were to increase in value 250 per cent by 1933 as compared with 1928. In 1930, two years after the launching of the plan, the increase was only 33 per cent, as against the increase of 75 to 80 per cent contemplated for this two-year period. In 1931, the third and "decisive" year of the Five-Year Plan, to use the Soviet Government's own characterization, even this lagging measure of increase is not being maintained, despite the rigorous restriction of the internal market.

With only about 65 per cent of the contemplated wheat collections extracted from the peasantry, according to official September figures, the prospects for continuing and increasing wheat exports are not very bright. Moscow dispatches and a close perusal of the Soviet press reveal that the collectives are now meeting the same difficulties with respect to surrendering their grain to the government at low fixed prices as were experienced from the individual peasants and the so-called "kulaks" in the past, and that the forcibly collectivized peasants have not changed their economic natures.

It has been estimated by some that the difficulties being raised by the collectives and the failure of crops in large regions of the Volga, Siberia and Urals will mean a loss to the Soviet Government this year of $75,000,000.

As regards industrial commodities for export purposes, indices for this year, with the exception of oil, show that production continues to lag considerably behind the Five-Year Plan. As Mr. Duranty cabled to The Times on Nov. 29, this year's total program of industrial production "will be only a fraction more than half accomplished and will be less than last year's." Mr. Duranty speaks also of "the failure of each branch of transportation, coal, iron and steel," pointing out that this reacts on the other branches and all four react on industry as a whole, especially new construction, where desperate efforts have been needed to keep within a month or six weeks of the schedules.

"New construction," he adds, "is further retarded by the decreased purchasing power abroad of Soviet exports, and certain cuts may be necessary in the rate of equipment, from both foreign and native sources, although it is asserted that the slowing down will not be greater than necessary to correspond with the delay on actual construction schedules."

The Question of Imports.

The natural corrective for the unfavorable trade balance would be a decrease in imports. But for the Soviet Government this would be fraught with serious danger, for any appreciable reduction in the imports of machinery and equipment would not only impede plants already in operation but bring to a standstill many now in process of completion. From competent observers on the spot we know how great is the wear and tear in Soviet plants owing to lack of skilled personnel and inability of the workers to handle the machinery with proper care. Failure to obtain from abroad the necessary spare parts and auxiliary equipment would quickly aggravate a situation already serious and further impede production now proceeding under increasing difficulties.

A few figures will show how difficult it is for the Soviet Government to curtail imports without jeopardizing the entire Five-Year program, subjecting industry to serious perturbations and thus further aggravating the crisis on the agricultural front.

For the first six months of 1931 the value of Soviet imports totaled $258,638,000, as against $277,840,500 for the corresponding period last year, a decrease of only about 7 per cent, despite the considerable fall in prices of metals, machinery and industrial equipment. In tonnage, the imports show an increase—1,603,000 tons for the first six months of this year, as shown in September figures, as against 1,390,000 for the corresponding period in 1930.

Official Soviet figures reveal an unfavorable trade balance of $355,450,000 for the period between Jan. 1, 1920, and June 30, 1931. Actually, these figures are too low, because until 1929 they did not include freight costs to the point of destination, foreign duties and other transportation expenditures.

How has the Soviet Government been covering this unfavorable trade balance? The coverage has been by foreign currencies received from abroad, tourist income and the sale of precious stones and art objects. In addition, and particularly until 1925, the Soviet Government exported considerable gold. Railway orders alone between 1921 and 1923 required the exportation of $100,000,000 in gold.

Financial Obligations.

Since the launching of the Five-Year Plan, however, the Soviet Government has incurred obligations abroad estimated in round figures at $450,000,000. With the unfavorable trade balance for the first nine months of this year totaling

The Times Wide World Photo.

Joseph Stalin. Dictator of Soviet Russia.

$105,000,000, with the chances of its improvement obviously negligible for reasons already stated, where is the Soviet Government to obtain the money to meet its obligations falling due in greater part before the end of 1932? Surely not from the reserves of the Soviet State Bank, for according to its statement as of Sept. 1, 1931, the reserves of the bank on that date were as follows:

Gold	$272,072,275
Precious metals	11,732,690
Foreign currencies	25,083,900
Notes due in foreign currencies	1,442,100
Total	$310,330,965

On Sept. 1, according to the official State bank statement, these reserves covered a circulation of 2,403,461,270 tchervontzi rubles and 2,467,800,000 rubles in treasury notes (nominally $2,450,000,000), which means a gold covering of the currency in circulation of 13 per cent, as against the legal requirement of 25 per cent.

It is obvious that under these circumstances any further export of gold would aggravate the inflation process which has been under way during the last two years (absolutely contrary to the provisions of the Five-Year Plan) and might well bring on a currency crisis.

It needs to be added that the aforementioned statement of gold reserves of the Soviet State Bank does not reflect fully the seriousness of the situation, for from the total must be deducted $50,000,000 exported in May-June of this year to the Deutsche Bank in Berlin as collateral on obligations.

It is probable that but for the world depression the crisis of the Five-Year Plan would not have asserted itself so soon and with such force, for in formulating the plan the Bolsheviki allowed for a decline in world price levels of 13 to 17 per cent during the five-year period. But already in 1930 their export calculations began to suffer severe dislocation. By retrenchment of internal consumption and curtailment of elementary needs of the population, the Soviet Government managed to fulfill its export program for that year: an increase in export tonnage of 51.9 per cent. The sharp fall in prices, however, brought an increase in the value of this increased tonnage of only 12.2 per cent. With imports for 1930 increased by 47.5 per cent, the year 1930 closed with a passive trade balance of $11,250,000, as against an active balance of $21,500,000 for 1929.

Viewed from the perspective of this development, the figures for 1931 began to assume most disquieting proportions: an adverse trade balance of $105,000,000 for the first nine months of the year in the face of a declining export yield, the danger of any appreciable curtailment of imports and an impoverished gold reserve, which, under the maximum Soviet gold production, cannot be amplified much beyond $40,000,000 a year.

In addition to the general fall in price levels, Soviet export calculations have suffered a shock from the decline of the British pound, since Soviet payments in Germany and the United States must be made in gold values. Hence the recent efforts of the Soviet Government to obtain an extension of its notes and commercial credits. As one of the reasons for the retrenchment of its operations in the United States, the Amtorg has cited the refusal of American firms to improve their commercial credits to the Soviet Government.

It need hardly be stated that those countries which have hitherto extended modest credits to Moscow were animated entirely by commercial considerations. The fact is that under the pressure of economic developments, both inside and outside of Soviet Russia, there is now in progress a process of revaluation of Soviet economic prospects. Hence the growing reluctance of American firms to enter into a modification of credit conditions as required by the Soviet Government, and the insistence of the French upon a trade arrangement on the basis of a balancing of Soviet exports and imports—an arrangement which can be of no value to the Soviet Government. German industrialists who hitherto have been most insistent in their demands for the development of Russo-German trade and have obtained from their government credits for Soviet Russia totaling some 1,000,000,000 marks ($238,000,000), now find that the German Government refuses to grant additional credits.

Debts Can Be Put Off.

Were Soviet Russia faced with the necessity of making substantial payments within the next few months a proclamation of a moratorium could hardly be avoided. But half of the Soviet commercial debt abroad, or some $225,000,000, is due to Germany. The payments due in the next few months are relatively small. Before the end of this year Soviet Russia must pay only 93,000,000 marks ($22,134,000). Large payments, totaling some 400,000,000 marks ($95,200,000), will fall due in 1932. Of this sum, 133,000,000 marks ($31,654,000) falls due in the first six months of the new year and the rest in the latter part of 1932. According to the Berliner Tageblatt, which is responsible for these figures, a portion of these payments may be extended into 1933.

This does not take into consideration obligations to other countries, most of which are of a short-term character. The Amtorg's obligations in the United States are estimated at from $75,000,000 to $80,000,000 falling due in 1931 and 1932. It is significant of the general attitude of American business toward the Soviet Government's ability to meet these obligations that the rate of discount on Amtorg paper has been 3 per cent per month plus ½ per cent interest.

This is the situation which, combined with the failures in the development of the Five-Year Plan, the discouraging export prospects and the other elements already mentioned, is fundamentally responsible for the dispatches from Moscow.

* * *

October 9, 1932

STALIN NOT A DICTATOR, PROF. WARD DECLARES

Educator, Back From Russia, Says Masses Have Increasing Share in Control.

The government of Soviet Russia is not a personal dictatorship of Josef Stalin, Professor Harry F. Ward of Union Theological Seminary, chairman of the American Civil Liberties Union, told more than 200 guests at a luncheon in his honor at the Hotel Woodstock yesterday. He has just returned from a prolonged stay in Russia.

Stalin, he said, has a great deal of influence because of his ability to manipulate the party machinery and "because of his common sense."

"He is close to the common people," said Professor Ward, "and he senses what, in between the too-fast pace of the lefts and the too-slow pace of the rights, will go over."

The machinery of the Communist set-up, he said, prevents personal ambition. He quoted young Communists to the effect that "Stalin is where he is because he goes where we want to go; if he did not the machinery would operate against him as against any one else."

He said that the masses were having an increasing part in controlling their affairs, in formulating policies as well as executing them. The development in Russia, he said, is toward the democratic factor, with the word "democracy" being used with pride today where it was only mentioned with a sneer as recently as 1924, when he made his last visit there.

He added that there is much more room today for the expression of public and private opinion there.

"With an expanding economic life," he said, "it is inevitable that the area of freedom should grow under the Soviets. It is equally inevitable that with a contracting economic life and increasing insecurity under the capitalist system the area of freedom should shrink. Traditional liberties become increasingly dangerous, and are therefore denied."

Professor Ward was introduced by Amos Pinchot, brother of Governor Pinchot of Pennsylvania and a member of the board of directors of the Civil Liberties Union.

*   *   *

November 18, 1933

UNITED STATES RECOGNIZES SOVIET, EXACTING PLEDGE ON PROPAGANDA; BULLITT NAMED FIRST AMBASSADOR

PRESIDENT REVEALS PACT

Reads to Press Letters in Which He and Litvinoff Bind Nations.

FREE WORSHIP CONCEDED

Russia Also Agrees to Allow Americans Own Counsel if Brought to Trial.

WORLD PEACE IS STRESSED

Russo-American Claims Will Be Adjusted Through Regular Diplomatic Channels.

By WALTER DURANTY
Special to The New York Times.

WASHINGTON, Nov. 17—Official relations between the United States and the Soviet were established at ten minutes before midnight yesterday. Or, to express it more simply, the United States recognized the U. S. S. R. at that hour after sixteen years and nine days of the Soviet Government's existence. The fact of the establishment of relations was announced this afternoon by President Roosevelt, but historically speaking the date was 11:50 P. M., Nov. 16.

The undertakings of the two governments were set forth in eleven letters and a memorandum exchanged between the President and Maxim Litvinoff, Soviet Commissar for Foreign Affairs, covering agreements and concessions completed in ten days of negotiation.

Subject to the approval of the Soviet Government, William C. Bullitt of Philadelphia, special assistant to the Secretary of State, was designated to be the first American Ambassador to the U. S. S. R.

The pact, read to the press by Mr. Roosevelt at his press conference this afternoon, covers propaganda, freedom of worship, protection of nationals and debts and claims.

Anti-Propaganda Pledge.

The United States receives the most complete pledge against Bolshevist propaganda that has even been made by the Soviet Government, and includes "organizations in

receipt of any financial assistance from it" as well as persons or organizations under the jurisdiction or control of the government. Complete freedom of worship is assured Americans, as well as assurance against discrimination because of "ecclesiastical status."

To Americans is accorded "the right to be represented by counsel of their choice" if brought to trial in the U. S. S. R., which represented perhaps the most definite concession that M. Litvinoff made. The President made reciprocal pledges except regarding religion, which the Soviet did not desire.

Debts and claims were left to be thrashed out later for "a final settlement of the claims and counter-claims" between the governments "and the claims of their nationals." Claims arising out of the military occupation of Siberia by American forces, or assistance to military forces in Siberia after 1917, were waived, but the Murmansk occupation was not mentioned.

One may surmise that the article relating to propaganda was drawn up after the most careful consideration by the Americans of the propaganda treaties or clauses between the Soviet and Latvia and the Soviet and Afghanistan, or both, but it goes further than either of these two, and might almost be termed a diplomatic victory of high order.

The question of religious freedom has great political importance and is treated with corresponding detail. Americans are allowed everything they can want in this respect, but it is worth noting that M. Litvinoff takes the opportunity of "slipping something over" in a quiet way by quoting the laws of the Soviet Union to show that many of the reports upon the restriction of religious liberty in that country have been exaggerated.

The American side, however, scores a tactical success in M. Litvinoff's admission that "no persons having ecclesiastical status" shall be refused visas to enter the U. S. S. R. on that account.

With regard to the protection of American nationals, President Roosevelt has succeeded in obtaining one sentence which will have a considerable reverberation and cause no small heartburning in Downing Street, London, namely:

"Americans shall have the right" (if brought to trial in the U. S. S. R.) to "be represented by counsel of their choice." That sounds like something rather different from the circumstances of the Metro-Vickers trial, not to mention the earlier Shakta trial in which three Germans were involved.

In the matter of debts and claims, the honors are more evenly divided than appears at first sight. The important phrase here is "preparatory to a final settlement of the claims and counter-claims between the two governments" in the first paragraph of M. Litvinoff's letter, which to a certain extent detracts from the apparent importance of the waiving of immediate claims by the Soviet.

M. Litvinoff stated that there would be no mixed claims commission to adjust various Russo-American claims. They will all be handled through regular diplomatic channels.

It is also within the bounds of possibility that some more far-reaching agreements, at least with regard to the private debts, may be arrived at shortly, although they do not form part of the documents published today.

It is not surprising that the Russians agreed to waive a claim against the effects of the American Expeditionary Force in Siberia, because both in fact and intent it was far from damaging to Soviet interests. But here, too, what looks like an American victory is somewhat modified by the point that there is no reference to the American Expeditionary Force in Murmansk, which undoubtedly will provide the basis for a Soviet claim, according to the Alabama precedent.

Speaking by and large, it is probable that claims and counter-claims, so far as the two governments are concerned, and not impossibly the pre-revolution debts as well, will more or less cancel each other, whereas the American claims for money or property of American nationals seized by the Soviet will fall in another category.

President Reads Treaty.

There must have been 200 newspaper men in the circular study of the Chief Executive when he made his historic announcement, and the way he did it gave an interesting illustration of the character of Franklin D. Roosevelt, his sense of drama—I hope the word "showmanship" is not "lèse-majesté"—and his profound knowledge of psychology. Every one present was on tiptoe waiting for news about the result of the negotiations with M. Litvinoff.

Mr. Roosevelt smiled pleasantly at the crowd, cast an affectionate eye round the walls at his splendid collection of colored prints of old New England scenes and stated in a conversational tone that he had gratifying news from the iron and steel industry about the working of their NRA code. This he thought was important news, and it seemed, too, that there were encouraging reports along the same line from the textile industry.

It was a genuine "coup de théâtre," and there was something like a gasp of suspense from his hearers.

Reporters are supposed to be toughened by their profession against surprises but, speaking personally at least, there was one of them who was startled. And the President knew it and got the full flavor of that moment of thrill.

Then quietly and calmly he proceeded to read the preamble to what is tantamount to an American-Soviet treaty.

The preamble consists of a letter from the President to the Commissar stating:

"I am very happy to inform you that as a result of our conversations, the Government of the United States has decided to establish normal diplomatic relations with the Government of the Union of Soviet Socialist Republics and to exchange Ambassadors.

"I trust that the relations now established between our peoples may forever remain normal and friendly, and that our nations henceforth may cooperate for their mutual benefit and for the preservation of the peace of the world."

Formal recognition was followed immediately by the designation of Mr. Bullitt as Ambassador to Russia. Hard on the heels of this announcement came publication by the State Department of the correspondence terminating the tenuous hold of representatives of the old Kerensky régime on the Russian diplomatic and consular service in this country.

No Russian Ambassador to the United States has been designated, but it is taken for granted that an announcement will be made in the very near future.

At the National Press Club this evening, while President Roosevelt was speeding toward Warm Springs, Ga., for a Thanksgiving holiday, M. Litvinoff in a brief speech and in reply to questions reviewed the negotiations for the benefit of Washington newspaper correspondents.

It is worth noting that the final phrase in the President's letter is "for the preservation of the peace of the world."

That is no formal insertion. Indeed there is hardly a word or line in the whole exchange of letters which does not merit the most careful scrutiny and attention.

M. Litvinoff replied in almost the same phrasing, and he, too, stressed the preservation of world peace which, as I cabled from Moscow, was the keynote of the first official Soviet reaction to the news of the President's message to Kalinin.

The letters cover four points of vital moment and are listed, one may presume, in the order of their importance. I venture that presumption because if ever there has been a conference in world history, and historically this conference may be found to rank among the most decisive, which really did "proceed according to plan," at least according to President Roosevelt's plan, it is this one.

You can hardly call it "an open covenant openly arrived at," that is to say, not so far as the last three words are concerned, but as a piece of "State planning," to employ the phrase familiar in Moscow and not unknown in Washington, it stands unique in post-war international events.

Put briefly, the points are propaganda, freedom of worship, protection of nationals and the question of debts and claims.

Right here there is to be noticed a most interesting point. As to propaganda, M. Litvinoff's letter comes first, expressing what the Soviet undertakes in this matter. The President's letter follows, recording, registering, and approving the said undertaking.

In the case of protection of nations, M. Litvinoff announces that certain steps shall be taken and the President assents, after which M. Litvinoff adds a short note of explanation upon the somewhat obscure question of economic espionage, which he clarifies. Once more M. Litvinoff leads in the matter of debts and claims and the President takes note of and records what he says.

To discuss the four points in detail, the propaganda letter of the Commissar contains four articles which admirably illustrate upon what a fair and reciprocal footing these negotiations have been conducted. Because, although all four articles are apparently undertakings by the Soviet, the first two are specifically things in which the United States is interested, whereas the two latter are things in which the Soviet is interested.

President Accepts Terms.

The fourth article is reminiscent of a clause in the Franco-Soviet non-aggression pact which referred primarily to "White Russian," or Nationalist Georgian and Ukrainian anti-Bolshevist organization.

The President's reply recapitulates the four articles, but adds significantly "it will be the fixed policy of the Executive of the United States within the limits of the powers conferred by the Constitution and laws of the United States to adhere reciprocally to the engagements above expressed."

The agreement was described in informed circles as including every concession the Soviet Government has ever made singly to any other country. The significant thing is that in this case the concessions are lumped into one vastly important international document—and were made prior to recognition.

To sum up, it would seem to me, with a certain knowledge of both countries, that this is one of the best and fairest international agreements I have ever read because it has a solid basis of mutual understanding and respect.

If one wants to estimate the "horse trade," I should say M. Litvinoff has got perhaps a shade the worst of it, but, on the other hand, to vary the metaphor, M. Litvinoff is taking home a pretty fat turkey for Thanksgiving.

And don't forget that there is no mention of future credits and business in these documents, save rather vague allusions to consular conventions, and so forth. It is absurd to suppose that such subjects have not been discussed and may lead to great mutual benefits.

There are other points of international and political interest which have perhaps been covered. The negotiations have taken ten days, and, without being oversanguine, it may happen that, in view of the gravity of the issues involved in this moment of international confusion, general perplexity and danger, too, some future historian will term them "ten days that steadied the world."

* * *

April 28, 1937

SENATE AND HOUSE REACH AGREEMENT ON NEUTRALITY BILL

Act to Replace Expiring Law Gives President Discretion on 'Cash-and-Carry' Policy

VOTE TOMORROW PLANNED

House Committee Reports a 'War Profits' Measure That Omits Draft of Labor

By HAROLD B. HINTON
Special to The New York Times.

WASHINGTON, April 27—Agreement on neutrality legislation to replace the law that expires by limitation at midnight Saturday was reached late today by the conference committee appointed by the Senate and the House to iron out the differences in the two resolutions the respective chambers had passed.

Leaders planned to rush the compromise measure through both houses on Thursday and to send it by airplane to President Roosevelt on Friday or Saturday for his signature.

The President will be at sea by that time on his fishing vacation trip, but he has indicated his willingness to sign the measure so that there will be no gap in the country's neutrality legislation, first adopted in the Summer of 1935.

The mechanics of transmitting the engrossed resolution, duly attested by Vice President John N. Garner and Speaker William B. Bankhead of Alabama, will present no great difficulty, as the Navy Department always keeps flying boats available to take and bring back official mail and documents to and from the President when he is at sea.

Provisions of Existing Law

The existing neutrality law provides that the United States will permit no exportation of arms, ammunition or implements of war to any belligerent or to any faction in civil strife. It also prohibits loans to such belligerents or factions.

American nationals are warned in the law that they may travel on vessels registered under a belligerent flag only at their own risk. American republics, when at war with a non-American power and not cooperating in such war with a non-American power, are exempt from the provisions of the act.

The legislation that the conferees agreed upon today would extend the scope of the existing law in the following respects:

1. Trade with belligerents or factions could be placed on a "cash and carry" basis by the President, if he found such a step necessary to preserve the peace and neutrality of the United States, so that some foreign government or individual would accept all right, title and interest in commodities destined for a belligerent before the shipment left the United States.

This discretion was permitted to cover the contingency of a war between two small nations which in no way endangered the peace or neutrality of the United States. The life of this section would be limited to two years.

2. Travel by American nationals aboard belligerent vessels would be declared illegal, with such exceptions and under such regulations as the President might prescribe. This exception was intended to cover necessary travel by military officers, government couriers, newspaper correspondents and so forth.

3. American merchant vessels could be prohibited from transporting to belligerents such commodities other than arms, ammunition or implements of war, which they are absolutely prohibited from transporting, as the President might proclaim. This feature was intended to permit the President to ban American transportation of any goods that might be declared contraband by any of the belligerents.

4. American merchantmen engaged in trade with belligerents would be forbidden to be armed.

5. The President would be directed to include in the arms embargo the usual lethal weapons that he proclaimed April 16, 1936, "but not to include raw materials or other articles or materials not of the same general character as those enumerated" in that proclamation. This was intended to limit the arms sections to primary contraband.

6. Contributions to belligerents, factions or "asserted governments" (this language was intended to cover the Insurgent forces in Spain, which have been recognized as a government by Italy and Germany), would be banned, with the exception that contributions to and solicitations for medical aid, food or clothing intended to relieve human suffering might be permissible by or to non-partisan welfare organizations such as the Red Cross, with the approval and under the regulations of the President.

Provision on Canada Modified

A House provision, intended to exempt normal trade with Canada from the full operation of the law in the event that Great Britain was at war and Canada should be considered to be a belligerent as well, was slightly modified by the conferees.

The new language would authorize the President to control exports to belligerents in American vessels "except under such limitations and exceptions as the President may prescribe as to lakes, rivers and inland waterways bordering on the United States, and as to transportation on or over lands bordering on the United States."

The conferees expected that there would be no difficulty in putting the compromise measure through the House.

The Munitions Committee bloc in the Senate, headed by Senator Gerald P. Nye of North Dakota, may object to the degree of discretion that is left to the President in some instances, and conservatives may object that not enough discretion has been left in the resolution, but Senator Key Pittman of Nevada, chairman of the Senate Foreign Relations Committee, said that he had "every reason to believe there would be no attempted filibuster."

In the meantime, the House Military Affairs Committee, by a vote of 21 to 2, recommended passage of a "war profits" bill that would give the President wide powers to control the economic life of the country in time of war.

The committee has been considering for a month, in executive session, the so-called American Legion bill on this subject, but it modified that project materially before reporting a measure today.

The measure it recommended would give the President power in time of war to license all industry and commerce, to fix prices, salaries, rents, and so forth, and to proclaim priorities in delivery.

The recommended bill, however, would omit the controversial sections dealing with the power to draft labor and management into the civilian employ of the government, and to take over national resources and public services.

Chairman Stresses Change

"There is no draft of anything nor any conscription of labor," Representative Lister Hill of Alabama, chairman of the committee, explained. "That would sovietize or communize the country and might disrupt production in time of war. If you scramble this thing during wartime, how are you going to unscramble it afterward?"

The taxing feature of the American Legion bill, which would have levied 95 per cent of all profits of individuals or corporations above an average of the three years prior to the declaration of war, was also deleted, and the following provisions substituted:

"Section 9. (A) During any war in which the United States is engaged, there shall be in effect a system of taxation which, without preventing a fair, normal return to labor, management and invested capital, such return to be fixed by Congress, shall absorb all surplus profits above such return.

"(B) Whenever Congress shall declare war, the Secretary of the Treasury shall within thirty days thereafter recommend to the Congress a plan of taxation (retroactive or otherwise) making effective the provisions of subsection (A).

"(C) To this end, the Secretary of the Treasury is hereby authorized and directed, upon the enactment of this act, to cause a continuing study to be made from year to year, with such investigations and accumulation of data as may be necessary, which would be the basis in formulating a plan of taxation as outlined by subsection (A) to be transmitted to the Congress upon a declaration of war."

The new tax section was the work of a subcommittee appointed to study that controversial feature of the proposed legislation. Senator Nye and his colleagues of the Munitions Committee have introduced a bill that would tax away all so-called war profits, and there are other projects almost as drastic pending.

A bill substantially like the one reported today passed the House two years ago, after introduction by the late Representative John McSwain of South Carolina.

Organized labor has expressed great opposition to the labor draft portions of the Legion bill, on the ground that the powers proposed to be exercised by the President might be used for strike-breaking or other activities by a conservative administration.

*   *   *

March 1, 1938

SOVIET TRIAL DELAY URGED BY U.S. GROUP

Message Asks Postponement to Allow Arrival in Moscow of Body of Observers

DANGER TO JUSTICE SEEN

Will Irwin, Villard and Holmes Among Signers—Hearing Is Scheduled for Tomorrow

A request that the trial of Alexei Rykoff, Nikolai Bukharin and nineteen others on charges of treason, murder and conspiracy be postponed for six weeks to permit the arrival in Moscow of an international committee to witness and report on the trial was addressed yesterday to the Soviet Government by a group of prominent Americans, including Will Irwin, Oswald Garrison Villard and John Haynes Holmes.

The request was sent to the Soviet Government in a telegram addressed to Soviet Ambassador Alexander Troyanovsky for transmission to Moscow.

Speaking as "friends of the Russian people," those who signed the telegram pointed out that "the vital interests of world peace and international democracy require that the fullest possible light be cast upon the grave questions raised in the indictment in the latest and most comprehensive of the series of Moscow trials" and declared that "the Soviet Government should not be averse to exhibiting a decent respect for the opinion of mankind" by granting the request for a postponement of the trial, which is scheduled to begin tomorrow.

Effect on Justice Cited

"Nothing could be more harmful to the interests of the Soviet Government itself and make more difficult if not impossible the position of the true friends of democracy in their efforts to be of service to the Russian people in the present critical international situation and in the fight against fascism than another demonstration trial that would further shake the faith of civilized mankind in Soviet justice," the telegram sent through Ambassador Troyanovsky declared.

"By accepting our proposal the Soviet Government would give a demonstration of good faith, the effects of which would be conducive to the promotion of the high purposes by which this telegram is motivated."

The telegram added that the composition of the committee that would go to Moscow "will be announced immediately upon the acceptance of our proposal by your government."

Included among the signers of the telegram, in addition to Mr. Irwin, Mr. Villard and Mr. Holmes, were Reinhold Niebuhr, professor at Union Theological Seminary; Lincoln Colcord, Harry Laidler, director of the League for Industrial Democracy; Mary Fox, secretary of the league, and Gerhardt Seger, former Social Democratic member of the German Reichstag.

Marks Fourth Major Trial

The Rykoff-Bukharin trial is the fourth of a series since the assassination of Sergei M. Kiroff in December, 1934, that has attracted world-wide attention both because of the prominence of the accused and the political significance attached to the proceedings. The trials have marked high points in the uninterrupted purges ushered in with the Kiroff assassination. The known number of victims of these purges, compiled from official Soviet reports and news dispatches, exceeds 1,200. The purges began with a speech by Joseph Stalin demanding that enemies of the Soviet Union be "mercilessly exterminated." Among those exterminated, awaiting trial or under arrest are virtually all the prominent members of the Bolshevist old guard who took leading or important parts in the October Revolution.

Previous demonstration trials that produced volumes of sensational testimony involving accusations similar to those now confronting Mr. Rykoff, Mr. Bukharin and their fellow-defendants were:

1. The Zinovieff-Kameneff trial of August, 1936, which resulted in the execution of sixteen defendants, including Gregory Zinovieff and Leo Kameneff among a group of outstanding Bolsheviki.

Radek Escaped Execution

2. The Radek-Piatakoff trial of January, 1937, which sent thirteen of seventeen defendants to death, including Piatakoff, former assistant commissar of heavy industries, and L. Serebriakoff, former assistant commissar of communications. Others executed occupied positions of high importance in the Soviet economic and administrative machine. Karl Radek, Soviet Russia's most prominent publicist and authority on international affairs, and Gregory Sokolnikoff, former Ambassador to Great Britain, escaped execution with two others when their sentences were commuted to imprisonment.

3. The Tukhachevsky trial of June, 1937, which sent eight high-ranking military officials, described collectively as the brains of the Soviet Army, before a firing squad. Heading the group was Marshal Mikhail Tukhachevsky, vice commissar of defense. Several other military and naval officials have fallen victims of the terror since the Tukhachevsky trial.

Among other groups of old Bolsheviki who have suffered death or imprisonment since the Kiroff assassination are many Caucasian Bolsheviki, including Budu Mdivani and Nestor Lakoba. Bolshevist leaders put to death more recently included Leo M. Karakhan, former Vice Commissar of Foreign Affairs, and Avel S. Yenukidze, at one time Stalin's political mentor and close associate, who was until 1935 secretary of the Central Executive Committee of Soviets and occupied under Lenin a position of influence in the Soviet hierarchy.

All Branches Affected

The purge has affected all branches of the Soviet regime, including the Communist party, Communist Youth League, the administrative, political and economic machines, the army, navy, aviation service, educational institutions and the press. It not only has involved the centers of the Soviet regime in Moscow and Leningrad but has extended far and wide into all the regions and republics composing the Soviet Union.

The names of Mr. Rykoff and Mr. Bukharin were implicated in the Zinovieff-Kameneff trial, but a month later they were exonerated of any guilt in the accusations faced by the defendants in that trial, including the charge of complicity in the Kiroff assassination. A Moscow cable to The New York Times dated Sept. 9, 1936, declared that "an investigation developed no evidence warranting their trial and the cases have been closed."

In accordance with the result of this investigation, Mr. Rykoff was permitted to remain in his post as Commissar of Communications and Mr. Bukharin continued as editor of Izvestia, official organ of the Soviet Government.

Following the Radek-Piatakoff trial, however, Mr. Rykoff and Mr. Bukharin were arrested. In April came the arrest of Henry G. Yagoda, former head of the secret police, who is one of the prominent defendants in the trial scheduled for tomorrow. The fate of the prisoners remained a mystery until the announcement in Moscow on Sunday that they would be tried and the publication of the indictment.

Similar mystery has surrounded the fate and whereabouts of Christian G. Rakovsky, former Ambassador to France, also a defendant. Like Mr. Rykoff and Mr. Bukharin, Mr. Rakovsky had fallen into disfavor, was expelled from the Community party, rehabilitated and reinstated in his position as a party member. He, too, was again arrested after the Radek-Piatakoff trial.

Fate Remains Unknown

In March, 1937, Valery I. Mezhlauk, then Commissar of Heavy Industry, made an address in Moscow, reported in cables to The New York Times, in which he declared that Mr. Rykoff and Mr. Bukharin "have been strenuously resisting official efforts to draw from them admissions that they participated in or even knew of the campaign of sabotage and terrorism" of which they were suspected during the Radek-Piatakoff trial. Several months later, Mr. Mezhlauk himself was removed from office, together with his brother. More recently there have been unconfirmed reports that they have been executed. Their fate remains unknown.

One of the most puzzling points in the indictments against the group headed by Mr. Rykoff and Mr. Bukharin is the charge that the accused had helped plan the death of Maxim Gorky. Mr. Gorky died on June 18, 1936, of pneumonia. His death had aroused much regret among former Oppositionists in the Russian Communist party for the reason that, as a close friend of Stalin's, he was known to have exercised a softening influence upon the Soviet dictator in the direction of moderation in the treatment of members of the Opposition.

Significant in this connection was the fact that the Zinovieff-Kameneff trial, which ushered in the series of demonstration trials of old Bolsheviki, was not embarked upon by Stalin until after Mr. Gorky's death. Mr. Gorky was known to have taken a strong stand against utilizing the Kiroff assassination as an excuse for extermination of the Opposition.

*　*　*

October 1, 1938

CZECH RULERS BOW, BUT UNDER PROTEST

*Nation Must Be Preserved, the Premier Tells Country—
He Calls Terms Dictated*

By G. E. R. GEDYE
Wireless to The New York Times.

PRAGUE, Czechoslovakia, Sept. 30—"Under protest to the world"—so run the headlines in nearly all newspapers tonight—the Czechoslovak Government bowed today to the dictated terms from Munich. The official announcement states that the government of the republic decided at the meeting of the Cabinet at midday under President Eduard Benes to accept the Munich decisions of the four great powers.

The announcement continues:

"This it did in the consciousness that the nation must be preserved and no other decision was possible today. At the moment of taking this decision the Czechoslovak Government protests the action of the four great powers, which was entirely one-sided and taken without Czechoslovakia's participation."

After preparation by only one brief official broadcast and while newspapers were still forbidden to publish anything, the full catastrophe was made known to the nation at 5 P. M. by radio by Premier Jan Syrovy. In conveying to the nation these heart-breaking tidings General Syrovy said that Munich's dictated terms had to be accepted in order to avoid the useless massacre of the population.

Addressing his hearers as "citizens and soldiers," General Syrovy recalled how during the World War he had helped far from the Fatherland to create a national Czechoslovak Army.

"You know how my comrades in arms readily sacrificed their lives for the nation," he said. "Now as then it is a question of the life of the nation. As soldier and Premier, I must think first of the lives of millions of hard-working citizens, men, women and children."

Then in a voice deeply moved with emotion General Syrovy said:

"I am passing through the saddest moment of my life, for I am fulfilling a most painful duty, a duty which for me is worse than death. But because I have fought and because I know what are the conditions essential to winning a war, I must tell you frankly, as my duty as responsible army commander bids me, that the forces arrayed against us at this moment oblige us to recognize their superiority and act accordingly.

"It is my aim to preserve the life of the nation—it is a duty inherited from our fathers who lived a harder life than we, because their life was not free.

"Only Possible Road"

"This mission we must fulfill with love in our hearts but with clear understanding in our heads. Our task in this fateful hour was to consider everything and to decide which way would lead us to this objective.

"As a soldier conscious of my responsibility, I tell you this way must be the way of peace, because we wish to face a new life with unweakened national forces.

"Before making up my mind to utter these words, I considered everything and am convinced that the road we are taking is the only possible one.

"In Munich four European powers decided to summon us to accept new frontiers which separate us from the German-populated districts of our State. We were confronted with a choice between desperate and hopeless defense, which would have meant the sacrifice of our whole younger generation, their children and their wives, and acceptance of the conditions imposed on us under pressure and without war, which in their mercilessness are unexampled in history.

"We wanted to contribute to the maintenance of peace, indeed, but never in the manner that has now been forced upon us.

"We were abandoned. We stood entirely alone. All the States of Europe, including our neighbors to the north and south, stand today under arms. We were a fortress besieged by forces far stronger than ours.

Considered All Courses

"Moved to the depths of their beings, all your leaders considered, together with the army chiefs and the President of the Republic, every possibility still open. We have recognized that, in the choice between the reduction of our frontiers and the death of our nation, it is our sacred duty to preserve the life of our people in order to emerge unweakened from this terrible period that our nation may arise again, as it has done so often in the past.

"At this tragic moment we must all give thanks to our army for its readiness to preserve the nation from destruction. To yield to four great powers and enormous military superiority is not dishonorable.

"We shall fulfill the conditions imposed on us by force. We call on our nation and people to overcome their bitterness, disillusionment and pain and help secure a future within our new frontiers.

"We all stand aboard the same ship. Every one must help bring it, damaged though it is, into the harbor of peace. The most important thing is that there should be no disunion within our ranks.

"There are many around us hoping to exploit your indignation for their own ends. Beware of foreign agents who seek to create disunion. We have already arrested many such agents-provocateurs. Do not be misled or deceived by others.

There are smaller States than ours that lead healthy existences and are capable of resistance. We shall be within narrow frontiers, but we shall be all together in one family.

"There will be many obstacles gone that formerly existed to the proper conduct of our State. Our army will stand guard over the nation as before, and with your help we shall succeed in resurrecting the State within our new frontiers.

"We depend on you. Trust us!"

Speakers Lament "Betrayal"

There followed an exhortation by General Ludwig Jan Krecji, commander in chief of the army. Then the strains of the Czechoslovak national anthem came with infinite pathos very slowly over the ether.

The scheduled radio program was immediately canceled as a sign of national mourning. Thenceforth one heard only warnings at intervals to the public to keep calm and beware of Nazi agents-provocateurs who hoped to incite the people to revolution and make this excuse for German invasion of the remainder of Czechoslovakia.

There were also many moving speeches by patriotic men on Czechoslovakia's great national tragedy. Most of them referred to "France's betrayal of us to Germany, aided by Britain."

As the news of the national disaster and humiliation was broadcast from loudspeakers, which at the beginning of the crisis had been installed in all principal streets, Prague became a city hushed by grief. One saw persons standing with tears in their eyes, unable to trust themselves to speak. Those who did speak never spoke above a whisper. From the moment of the announcement that the blow had fallen there was not a face that bore a smile even for an instant.

Only a week ago this city sent out its fathers and sons to face tremendous odds in defense of the country. At that time, with death from the skies threatening throughout every perilous moment of lightning mobilization, crowds in the pitch-dark streets kept up their courage. Today, with the knowledge that they had been deprived, not by foes, but by friends, of their impregnable system of fortifications, into which had gone millions of crowns and thousands of hours of labor, they were moved to a grief on which it was painful to intrude. On every face was written the consciousness of belonging to a martyred nation.

Noisy Reaction Follows

"It is a heartbreaking fact," writes the Prager Tageblatt, "that the four-power group which has made its first action the dismemberment of Czechoslovakia includes three powers in whose ranks Czechoslovak legionnaires fought during the war and in the interests of two of which during the succeeding twenty years Czechoslovakia has modeled her policy, often at great cost to herself."

To the first stunned silence of the masses succeeded a noisy reaction. Crowds formed in Vaclavske Namesti, headed by national flags, and as on the night of the overthrow of the Hodza Cabinet set off across the river for the hill on which Hradschin Palace is situated. They sang the national anthem, shouting: "Rather death than peace with dishonor"; "Give us arms to defend ourselves"; "We demand a people's government."

The Communist party after long deliberations today had issued orders for no demonstrations against the government, and the maintenance of strict party discipline so that the Germans might have no excuse for further encroachment. Nevertheless there were shouts—either spontaneous or instigated by agents-provocateurs—to call on the Soviet for help.

Before the statue of King Wenceslaus dense crowds assembled and listened to moving and pathetic speeches by impromptu speakers who minced no words concerning Britain's "double dealing" and "France's treachery."

To the disaster of the actual terms imposed on Czechoslovakia was added the humiliation of her treatment in Munich and Prague. The writer learned in official circles that when the Czech Minister to Berlin, Dr. V. Mastny, tried to see the British and French delegations before the final decision was taken yesterday he was turned away from the door. After all was over the British called him in and handed him the terms for the partition of his country. He said he wished to make a few observations. He was told curtly he could spare himself the trouble.

No answer was required from Czechoslovakia, Dr. Mastny was informed—only prompt obedience. Then came the slight here. It was not the two diplomats, whom the Czechs call the "intriguing duo," Basil C. Newton of Britain and Victor Leopold de Lacroix of France, who delivered the Munich decision, but the German chargé d'affaires, who went posthaste at 6:30 this morning to Foreign Minister Kamil Krofta to bear the tidings of the agreement.

Fears for Non-Henleinists

Wenzel Jaksch, leader of the German Social Democrats, told the writer that he feared Czechoslovakia might refuse to receive the German democratic and German-Jewish refugees from the Sudeten areas, who would only add to the large number of unemployed that will be created by the partition of Czechoslovakia and the seizure of most of her industries, natural resources and essential communications under the Munich decision.

"I am going," he said, "to appeal with all the force at my command to Chamberlain to recognize this enormous responsibility toward a people placed in deadly peril by the 'solution' he and Daladier have seen fit to impose on this country. If he remains deaf to my pleas nothing but massacre and torture await hundreds of thousands of Democrats and Jews in the Sudeten districts. Already there are more than 100,000 refugees in a destitute condition in the interior of the country. The number will be trebled once the full extent of this disaster is known. Just as the Nazi horrors in Austria were worse than those in Germany so will the terror in the Sudeten area exceed anything which even the Austrians have known."

Commenting on the national crisis tonight's Ceske Slovo states:

"Czechoslovaks at least can hold their heads erect. No one in the world can accuse us of cowardice. We might be happy if we could say the same for others. We have suffered worse treatment even than this and we have arisen again. Henceforth we trust no one but ourselves. Let us rest firm and happy in the knowledge that we remain a brave and unconquered nation. We have been defeated, but by lies and superior strength. It was a well-thought-out lie to say that the minorities in our State were a danger to peace. That danger was brought in from Germany in the form of agitation and arms, but the world's common sense had broken down the propaganda campaign and we have been left alone.

"Our State will be smaller but our nation far greater than before."

Narodni Listy comments:

"Our people, good-hearted, trustful and peace-loving, have again been led up to Golgotha to buy European peace with its sacrifices. The history of the Czechs is almost an uninterrupted tragedy, but the nation has and maintains the will to live."

*   *   *

October 1, 1938

BRITAIN AND GERMANY MAKE ANTI-WAR PACT; HITLER GETS LESS THAN HIS SUDETEN DEMANDS

PEACE AID PLEDGED

Hitler and Chamberlain Voice Their Nations' Will Never to Fight

DEMOBILIZATION FORESEEN

Four Zones Reich Will Occupy Only Half of Sudeten Area—Chief Forts Not Included

Prime Minister Chamberlain and Chancellor Hitler, at a final conference at Munich yesterday, agreed that: "We regard the agreement signed last night and the Anglo-German naval agreement as symbolic of the desire of our two peoples never to go to war with one another again." Terms imposed on Czechoslovakia were found to be milder than Hitler's Godesberg plan. They provided immediate occupation of about half of the Sudeten area, the rest to be allotted by the International Commission or to be subject to plebiscite.

Poland delivered an ultimatum to Prague demanding the cession of the Teschen district, setting 6 A. M. New York time as the limit for reply. Hungary prepared to make a two-point demand for cessions.

Czechoslovakia accepted the Munich terms and Premier Syrovy, announcing "We have been abandoned," made a protest to the world. General Krejci told the army to obey orders.

The first of the German troops crossed the Czechoslovak border from Austria an hour after midnight, or 7 P. M. Friday New York time. Large concentrations were made for the further occupation. The International Commission began sessions in Berlin on the evacuation and allocation of territory.

Mr. Chamberlain met a great demonstration when he arrived in London, and a similar one was accorded to Premier Daladier when he reached Paris.

Premier Mussolini was hailed on his journey through Italy and in Rome by vast crowds rejoicing over peace.

Britain and Germany Agree

By FREDERICK T. BIRCHALL
Wireless to The New York Times.

MUNICH, Germany, Sept. 30—The whole aspect of European relations has been changed by developments today following the signature of the four-power agreement over Czechoslovakia in the early hours of this morning.

The Czechs have consented to the agreement, but far transcending their acceptance in importance to the world at large are the results of an intimate conversation between Chancellor Adolf Hitler and Prime Minister Neville Chamberlain in Herr Hitler's private apartments just before the departure of the British delegation.

These results were made known in the following joint communiqué issued after the conversation:

We, the German Fuehrer and Chancellor and the British Prime Minister, have had a further meeting today and are agreed in recognizing the question of Anglo-German relations as of the first importance of the two countries and for Europe.

We regard the agreement signed last night and the Anglo-German naval agreement as symbolic of the desire of our two peoples never to go to war with one another again.

We are resolved that the method of consultation shall be the method adopted to deal with any other questions that may concern our two countries, and we are determined to continue our efforts to remove probable sources of difference and thus contribute to assure the peace of Europe.

Never has a simpler document been issued in history with consequences more far-reaching or more pregnant with hope. If the two men who issued it stick to their resolves the peace of Europe seems assured for a generation at least.

In an interview with American and British correspondents at which he announced this accord Mr. Chamberlain declared that he hoped it would lead to a general European demobilization.

He said that there was in fact a general impression here that as far as Germany was concerned Chancellor Hitler would order immediate demobilization in the Reich as soon as he was convinced that the Czechoslovak Government genuinely desired and was in a position to carry out the terms of the four-power evacuation plan.

A more careful examination of this plan and last night's agreement than were possible early this morning when it was handed out greatly modifies the first impression that it gives the Germans all their own way. There are large conces-sions, but they show only in the details. This is especially notable when the evacuation is considered in the light of maps that were not available last night at the same time as copies of the plan.

Czechs here find that the agreement in fact is a great improvement on the German demands embodied in the Godesburg memorandum.

The Godesberg document envisaged complete military occupation of the whole Sudeten German area and certain contiguous districts also not previously regarded as German, the whole territory to be evacuated being, in fact, arbitrarily determined by the Reich.

The new agreement provides for the evacuation over a period of ten days of certain areas already determined by the four powers or to be determined by the international boundary commission set up by the conference.

Members of the Commission

The members of this commission are Baron Ernst von Weizsaecker, Secretary of State in the German Foreign Office, and Sir Nevile Henderson, André François-Poncet, Bernardo Attolico and Dr. Vostech Mastny, respectively the British, French and Italian Ambassadors and Czech Minister to Berlin. They are being assisted by experts. Sir Nevile has the aid of Frank Ashton-Gatkin of the Runciman mission. On this commission, it will be noted, the British, French and Czech Governments together have a majority.

The commission will also determine the plebiscite areas, which in the Godesberg memorandum were determined by the Reich and were considered by the Czechoslovak Government to have been so adjusted as to insure a German majority in every district.

Under the Godesberg memorandum, also, the plebiscite areas were to have been occupied by German troops immediately; under the four-power plan all plebiscite areas will be occupied by an international force, the composition of which will be decided by the International Boundary Commission.

Instead of demanding that the entire Sudeten area should be occupied by German troops tomorrow [Oct. 1] as set forth in the Godesberg memorandum, Herr Hitler for the sake of agreement contented himself with what amounts to little more than a symbolic or token occupation on that day.

Territory Number One, as it is called, which is to be occupied first, is a stretch roughly seventy kilometers [43.5 miles] long and only fifteen kilometers [9.3 miles] deep at its widest point. It is adjacent to the former Austrian frontier and contains neither Czech fortifications nor Czech troops. The limit of the German advance is a line running roughly from Feuenbach via Boehm-Krumau to Kaplitz and thence straight to the frontier.

The Germans are entitled under the agreement to march into this district any time after midnight tonight. Mr. Chamberlain said today, however, that he had reason to believe that the occupation would not begin until tomorrow night. This would give the international commission time to supervise the withdrawal. It is expected to travel tomorrow morning from Berlin to the area to be evacuated.

[The first German troops actually marched across the Czechoslovak border into this district at 1 o'clock this morning (7 P. M. Friday, Eastern standard time), The Associated Press reported.]

The agreement envisages the progressive evacuation by Oct. 7 of four districts that together comprise a little more than half the Sudeten area and total substantially less than the districts marked for immediate occupation on the Godesberg map. They do not include the so-called Czech Maginot Line or any of the chief border fortifications.

The rest of the evacuation program is equally moderate. District Number Two, to be occupied Oct. 2 and 3, is a small corner on the northern Czech frontier. The limit of the German advance is a straight line running roughly through Bodenbach, Tetraten and Reichenberg to the frontier.

District Number Three, to be occupied Oct. 3, 4 and 5, is the turbulent Asch and Eger section. The line marking the limit of the German advance runs from Waldmunchen via Karden to Oberleutensdorf.

District Number Four, to be occupied Oct. 6 and 7, is a small salient also on the northern frontier. The German advance line will run through Grulich and Zoptau via Freudenthal and Jaegerndorf.

The rest of the predominantly German territory to be occupied by Oct. 10 will be determined by the international boundary commission. Apparently the agreement includes no territories beyond those conceded by the Czechoslovak Government at the request of the British and French.

The sole criticism aimed at the accord here today was that the Czech Government had not had a chance to make suggestions of its own but could only accept or refuse. The answer to this was, of course, the necessity for reaching an agreement before tomorrow.

On the other hand, it can no longer be said that the transfer is being made under pressure of force. The arrangements for the evacuation and occupation, the determination of boundaries, the holding of plebiscites and the settlement of all questions arising from the transfer are in the hands of the international commission.

Huber Masaryk of the Czechoslovak Foreign Office and Mr. Ashton-Gatkin left Munich for Prague by air at 6 o'clock this morning carrying the agreement.

An Unexpected Transformation

It was raining in Munich today, with heavy clouds and a low ceiling that must have made Mr. Chamberlain's air journey back to London anything but enjoyable in its initial stages, at least. But in another sense, rarely has the diplomatic sky shone blue with brighter promise after the blackest of threatened thunderstorms. It is a transformation as unexpected as it has been sudden.

The change leaves everybody satisfied and everybody optimistic again. Herr Hitler is undoubtedly happy, for this morning's Anglo-German pledge of future intentions fulfills his dream of again establishing good relations with Britain and aspirations he has cherished from the outset of his political career. They are frankly expounded in his book "Mein Kampf," and he has never lost sight of them.

The British are pleased, for it removes from them the menace of war with the only great power with which it was conceivable Britain might have to go to war. The strong British faction that has regarded German friendly cooperation as the only means of insuring the British Empire's future will be particularly happy.

The people at large will be overjoyed, for it removes the menace from the air, the new realization of which had left them stunned and horror-stricken during the last week. The trenches in Hyde Park can now be filled and the turf relaid. Mr. Chamberlain is returning to London with a reputation never attained by any British statesman since Pitt.

The German people will be in seventh heaven when the full significance of the new accord comes home to them. This is what they wanted and always have wanted and they will be quick to realize it.

Already the newspapers are proclaiming the accord in their largest type in black and red: "Germany and England—Never Again in a War With Each Other."

Women weeping from sheer joy pelted Mr. Chamberlain with flowers when he left his hotel for the airfield this afternoon and crowded around his motor car just to touch him as he stepped in. To them Adolf Hitler, who has brought this about, has become more than a god.

The thoughtful see in this more than a mere political accord, for such friendship, if it develops along the right lines, may prove the one thing needed and at the same time possible to make life in Germany more tolerable.

Nazism, with some aspirations in its make-up that the outside world has grudgingly recognized as commendable, has needed most a friendly restraining influence upon its excesses. It is just possible that this new tie may prove the soft brake upon intolerance—not immediately, but as time goes on.

The interview at which the accord was reached occurred between two men unable to speak a common language. Herr Hitler knows no English, and Mr. Chamberlain a little rudimentary German, for in his childhood he had a German nurse. But it is a German of scant use in such a conversation as was held this morning.

The only other person present was Dr. Paul Schmidt, the German Foreign Office interpreter, who is a marvel both in the matter of precise interpretation and memory.

On Chamberlain's Initiative

The meeting was held on Mr. Chamberlain's initiative. He had called to say good-bye. The conversation lasted an hour and a half. The accord was announced by the Prime Minister himself later in the simplest and most casual fashion. Returning to his hotel, he sent out word that he would receive the British and American correspondents before his departure.

They found him sitting at a desk drinking a cup of coffee and smoking a cigar. He said to them:

"I have always been of the opinion that if we could find a peaceful solution of the Czechoslovak question it would open the way generally to appeasement of Europe. This morning I had a further talk with the Fuehrer and Chancellor and we both signed this declaration."

He then handed out the joint communiqué, adding that the Prague Government had accepted the terms of last night's agreement. That decision, he said, had been communicated to him by the British Minister in Prague.

Replying to questions, Mr. Chamberlain said that at this morning's meeting only Dr. Schmidt, the interpreter, had been present besides Herr Hitler and himself. Premier Edouard Daladier of France had not been there; the agreement reached was an Anglo-German agreement.

All of the principal foreign participants in the four-power conference left Munich today. At 7:30 A. M. Premier Benito Mussolini's special train departed for Rome. M. Daladier and the French delegation took off by plane about noon.

Before his departure the French Premier conversed at length with Field Marshal Hermann Goering, who urged upon him that the four-power agreement with Czechoslovakia opened the way toward a Franco-German understanding.

A factor toward such an understanding may be the impression left by Herr Hitler on M. Daladier, who met him for the first time.

"That," said the French Premier in a conversation afterward, "is a man with whom one can make politics."

The British delegation, which had been the last to arrive in Munich, was also the last to leave today. It departed amid a tremendous ovation. Both at the hotel and air field crowds waited in the rain to cheer Mr. Chamberlain. Men thronged about him to shake his hand and women pressed flowers on him.

Daladier Urges Reich Amity

MUNICH, Sept. 30—Premier Edouard Daladier of France, before taking off for Paris from Oberweisenfeld Airdrome today, declared in a statement to DNR, official German news agency, that the French and German people "must come to a cordial understanding."

"I have had the pleasure personally to establish that no feeling of hate or enmity of any kind prevails in Germany against France," he said.

"Be assured that the French, on their part, feel no hostility toward Germany."

Crowds gathered around M. Daladier's hotel during the morning and gave him repeated ovations. When he appeared at a window cheers and "Heils" arose.

* * *

January 31, 1939

TROTSKY BANISHED AS MENACE TO SOVIET UNITY, SAYS HIGH RUSSIAN OFFICIAL ARRIVING AT BERLIN

KOVNO, Lithuania, Jan. 30—Late advices from semi-official sources in Moscow said that the Communist party had decided that because of Leon Trotsky's continued meddling with internal party affairs, it would be necessary to remove him from Soviety territory in order to preserve national unity.

It was understood that his family would be allowed to accompany him on the condition that be would never attempt to return to Moscow.

BERLIN, Jan. 30 (Jewish Telegraphic Agency)—Leon Trotsky has been banished from Russia, according to a leading Soviet official who has arrived in Berlin from Moscow.

He said the decision to exile Trotsky was taken by the Politbureau, the most important branch of the Soviet government. Of the ten members five voted for Trotsky's banishment, one abstained from voting and four voted against it.

Those who voted against Trotsky's exile, he said, were Kalinin, Rykof, Bucharin and Tomsky. The resolution was proposed by Joseph Stalin, Trotsky's principal foe.

After the decision was reached, according to this official, the Angora Government was approached for an arrangement to admit Trotsky to Constantinople. Mustapha Kemal Pasha, however, had informed Stalin, he said, that the admission of Trotsky to Constantinople would involve many delicate problems. He would, however, agree to admit the exile to Angora provided Trotsky were kept strictly within the grounds of the Soviet Embassy and when visiting the city be accompanied by guards.

The Soviet official further said that rumors prevalent in Moscow indicated that Trotsky had been seen in Tiflis on his way to Belgium, whence he would be transported to Constantinople.

CONSTANTINOPLE, Jan. 30—Leon Trotsky is expected to take shelter in Constantinople or Angora soon. The Turkish Government has agreed to allow his entry.

MOSCOW, Jan. 30—The Soviet Government has declined thus far to issue an authoritative statement on the whereabouts of M. Trotsky.

Rumors that the exiled leader has been banished from Russia spread rapidly through Moscow today.

* * *

August 22, 1939

GERMANY AND RUSSIA AGREE ON NON-AGGRESSION

GERMANS ELATED

Amity Treaty With Soviet Lifts Fear—
Negotiations in Moscow Tomorrow

ACT ON POLAND THURSDAY

That Day Reported in Berlin to Be Set for
'Solution' of Present Dispute

By OTTO D. TOLISCHUS
Wireless to The New York Times.

BERLIN, Tuesday, Aug. 22—Chancellor Adolf Hitler threw another bombshell into the camp of those trying to halt him when it was officially announced here last night that Germany and Soviet Russia had agreed to conclude a non-aggression pact and that Foreign Minister Joachim von Ribbentrop, author of the anti-Comintern pact, would arrive in Moscow Wednesday to "conclude the negotiations."

This announcement, distributed throughout the country by extra editions of newspapers, was hailed here with supreme elation as a great diplomatic victory over Britain because it was taken to mean the end of the Anglo-French-Russian alliance negotiations and the collapse of Britain's "encirclement" policy, lifting from German minds the specter of the Russian steamroller in case of a new war.

It is still too early to judge the implications of this new coup, repeatedly predicted in these dispatches because it affects the alignment of many powers, particularly Japan. But one immediate significance revealed itself when German quarters spread the rumor that Herr Hitler was also determined to force a solution this week of the Polish-German conflict, which started over Danzig and now involves the fate of Poland and the issue of a new world war. A German solution will be sought by diplomacy if possible; if not, by the German Army.

Thursday as the Day

According to usually well-informed sources, the German General Staff has orders to be ready for immediate military action by Thursday, and these, perhaps, are not unintentional revelations. This information is taken as a German warning that unless diplomacy finds a way out of the deadlock by that time Herr Hitler is determined to break the deadlock by force of arms.

Before the Russo-German non-aggression pact was announced, some circles were still inclined to regard this threat as merely another move in the "war of nerves," and Polish circles in particular characterized it as "bluff." But the Russian pact, which completely isolates Poland in the east and holds over her the menace of a new partition between her mighty neighbors, puts a different light on matters, and this threat is also backed up by troop concentrations on both sides of the entire German-Polish frontier.

On the German side East Prussia—where most able-bodied men up to 55 are mobilized—is virtually an armed camp. Considerable troop concentrations are also reported in Pomerania, Silesia and Slovakia. According to the best military opinion, these troops are still insufficient for an invasion of Poland, but they are rapidly being increased and preparations are being made to rush flying divisions to their aid.

Some bombing squadrons and tank contingents—the latter painted black with a white cross for identification—are passing through Berlin itself, heading east, and trucks and automobiles are being concentrated at strategic points to move troops quickly. Extensive Polish troop concentrations, admitted in Warsaw, now take big headlines in the German press.

For Decision on Poland

The entire German press with inspired unanimity took the stand yesterday that the decision regarding Poland was at hand. The semi-official news service, Dienst aus Deutschland, said:

"The impression prevails in Wilhelmstrasse as well that a decision is ripening quickly."

And though that service said that "all competent authorities anticipate this decision with great calm, based on confidence that the Fuehrer's policy will be successful and will again bring home to the German people a gain as peaceful as it will be substantial," other publications emphasized that Germany would not shrink from any alternative. They pointed to the expansion of Germany's military might and her excellent strategic position created by the Westwall, which in pages of pictures and description was again presented as a death trap to all French and British soldiers.

At the same time all German quarters and publications continued to emphasize that only immediate Polish acceptance of the German demands, which now aim at complete revision of eastern borders to remove all the "injustices of Versailles," can save the situation, and they continued to hammer at London to persuade the Poles to accept.

"It is now up to London"—that is the stand of Wilhelmstrasse, which while preparing for emergencies to the extent of establishing a special night service, yet holds that diplomacy still has a chance and also hints that many moves are also under way behind the scenes. What these moves may be, aside from the new Russo-German pact, are not revealed, but a few of the visible or prospective ones are as follows:

Josef Lipski, Polish Ambassador to Germany, took a plane for Warsaw yesterday to consult his government, presumably on the Russo-German pact, but whether he also took a message from the German Government was not disclosed.

Franz von Papen, Herr Hitler's special Ambassador in particularly delicate situations, was received by the Chancellor at Berchtesgaden yesterday and entrusted with a secret mission on which Herr von Papen left immediately by plane for an undisclosed destination—assumed to be London, but it may be Rome.

Today, presumably after the British Cabinet meeting, Ambassador Sir Neville Henderson is scheduled to go to Salzburg, and no pretense is being made in such a case that he would merely go to attend motor races.

In addition, diplomatic quarters paid serious attention to a rumor current here that Premier Mussolini of Italy had made an offer to London to remain neutral if Britain remained neutral in a purely Polish-German conflict. That rumor may form the basis of a report abroad that Bernardo Attolico, Italian Ambassador, has brought to Herr Hitler a "negative" answer from Signor Mussolini, which was hotly denied here as another "British lie manoeuvre."

Whether these diplomatic moves will produce a solution remains to be seen, but it is a fact that the new crisis is developing so much like an oft-rehearsed and now almost hackneyed stage play that nobody is quite able to take it seriously and inevitably looks forward to diplomatic intervention that will again "save peace in our time" and give Germany what she wants. And in that confidence may lurk danger.

Meanwhile, the German press spreads the Russo-German pact in huge headlines across the front page, together with Polish troop movements, which are declared to be an intolerable provocation to a big power like Germany, as well as further charges about Polish atrocities that must be halted and halted immediately.

In German military circles an isolated Poland is not considered a major military obstacle, especially since the Westwall permits Germany to throw the major part of her massed army against the country. They give Poland not more than a fortnight before she would be overrun.

For that reason Germany confidently expects today that Poland will throw up her hands and yield and therewith Eastern Europe and all its riches will soon be opened to German organizing efficiency, bringing Herr Hitler's dream of empire close to reality.

As regards the new German-Russian agreement, it actually merely revitalizes and strengthens the already existing Russo-German Treaty of Rapallo and the Pact of Berlin, which provide for the neutrality of one partner in case the other is attacked. The terms of the new agreement apparently are still to be fixed, but if Germany has her way the non-aggression pact will be unconditional, and the new Russo-German trade agreement, announced yesterday, suggests that Russian neutrality might even be friendly neutrality.

As a feat in appeasement Herr Hitler's "appeasement" of Joseph Stalin is unique, considering the former National Socialist campaign against bolshevism. The only question diplomats are asking now is: "Has Stalin also succeeded in appeasing Hitler?"

* * *

August 22, 1939

LONDON STAGGERED

*Nazi-Soviet Pact Blow Is Received in
Anger and Stupefaction*

TALK OF POLES YIELDING

*British Seen Facing Peril of a Reich Dominant in Europe—
Cabinet Will Meet Today*

By FERDINAND KUHN Jr.
Special Cable to The New York Times.

LONDON, Aug. 21—The deadliest high explosives could not have caused more damage in London than the news late tonight that the Nazi and Soviet Governments had agreed on a non-aggression pact behind the backs of the British and French military missions in Moscow.

Anger and stupefaction were the first reactions here. They were all the more intense because neither of the Western governments appeared to have had any inkling of what was impending. It will take some time for the smoke to clear away, but when it does the diplomatic picture may well be changed beyond all recognition.

First impressions were that the Russian-German pact would complete the encirclement of Poland by showing that Russian help would not be forthcoming in the event of invasion and that it would make continuance of the three-power talks in Moscow difficult if not impossible. Moreover, the news conjured up the specter, always dreaded in this country, of Germany and Russia, as allies, dividing the Baltic States and Eastern Europe between them.

Nazi Triumph of First Rank

Such speculation may prove to be too highly colored, but there could be no doubt tonight that Britain had suffered a humiliation of the first order and that German diplomacy had won one of its biggest triumphs. It remains to be seen how the anti-aggression "front" will survive this bombshell, especially in view of Russia's close relations with Turkey and her long frontier with Rumania.

Prime Minister Chamberlain and his Ministerial colleagues will feel the full shock of the news from Berlin when they meet tomorrow afternoon in a full-fledged Cabinet meeting originally intended to cope with the danger of a German invasion of Poland. All day today there had been signs of a swiftly developing crisis, with ominous reports from Berlin, Prague, Vienna, Bratislava and other cities of vast numbers of German troops on the move eastward.

It had been intended that after the Cabinet meeting Viscount Halifax, the Foreign Secretary, might make a statement over the radio repeating once more and in most detailed terms that Britain would fight in fulfillment of her pledges whenever the Poles felt that their independence was threatened. The general idea was not only to repeat the explicit terms of the British guarantee but also to recall Mr. Chamberlain's warning of last year that Britain would fight any attempt to "dominate Europe by force."

Believe Poles May Bow Now

It was not known tonight whether this speech would be made or whether its contents would be altered because of the German-Soviet development. Certainly the British feel that the ground has been cut from under their feet, but still more from under the Poles. Unofficially it is thought here that the Poles may yield quickly now without any "pressure" from any one or anything except the force of the sudden event that has made their position untenable.

If this happens the threat of immediate war hanging over Europe may be averted for a time, but the ultimate reckoning for Britain and France may be heavier than they ever expected. For a Germany that controls Poland will indeed be the dominant power in Europe, and the British will be up against a danger that they have not experienced since the days of Napoleon.

The effect of tonight's shock upon the Conservative Ministers is unpredictable in its extent or duration. Most of them have a strong anti-Communist bias, which they have smothered in the past few months because they needed Russian help and because they genuinely believed Russia's self-interest would prevent her from linking up with Germany. Even if the non-aggression pact turns out to be a most innocuous document, all the old suspicions are bound to be revived and they cannot fail to influence British policy.

Mr. Chamberlain's personal bitterness against Chancellor Hitler after the invasion of Czecho-Slovakia is believed to have played a part in the astonishing revolution of British foreign policy that followed. He is hardly likely to feel less deceived and humiliated by the Russians now, and he may have a hard time controlling his feelings about Russian "tactics."

Arthur Greenwood, deputy leader of the Labor party in the House of Commons, was among Mr. Chamberlain's late visitors this evening. He left Downing Street, however, before the German radio had announced the news of the pact, and in a talk with reporters later he gave no indication that Mr. Chamberlain had had the slightest idea of what was about to be announced from Berlin.

Some Expect General Election

Indeed, some political observers felt tonight that Mr. Chamberlain might call a general election very quickly if the immediate danger of war should disappear in the next few days. An unexpected card has been placed in Mr. Chamberlain's hands, with unexpected embarrassments for the Opposition parties.

The Prime Minister can go before the voters as a man who yielded to the Opposition and began alliance negotiations with Russia, even to the extent of sending a military mission to Moscow. He can win Conservative sympathies by appearing as a man who has been cruelly "let down." He can put the blame for any diplomatic disasters upon the Russians and if he chooses he can appeal to the strong anti-Communist streak that exists not only among British Conservatives but in the ranks of the trade-union movement as well.

The Opposition, of course, can blame Mr. Chamberlain for "dawdling" over the Russian alliance and for inviting the retribution that fell on his head tonight. But in such a campaign there would be few who would bet against Mr. Chamberlain's being returned with a big majority.

Earlier today news of the Soviet-German trade treaty had given the British a disagreeable foretaste of what was coming—if they could have guessed it. Officials were careful not to comment publicly for fear of jeopardizing the Anglo-Russian atmosphere and the newspapers generally followed suit by not emphasizing the agreement or commenting on it editorially.

Nevertheless, there were mutterings about Russian "blackmail" and "trickery" in concluding such an agreement at a time of crisis. Supposing that Mr. Chamberlain would make such an agreement with Germany now, it was suggested, what a howl would go up from Russia and from Russian sympathizers elsewhere that the Prime Minister was attempting a new "appeasement."

Yet, as the crisis atmosphere deepened throughout the day, there was still no sign of shaken nerves in government quarters or among the British public.

The outlook seemed serious, but the British attitude was one of sheer unbelief that any man could rush the Continent into war in the face of the most explicit warnings ever given in peacetime by one great power to another. As one official described it, "Hitler is not only drifting to the edge of the dam but he is rowing as hard as he can toward it; there is no sign he wants to pull back or that he could do so if he wanted to."

Nazis Buying in London

Britain seemed to be calm and ready and in deadly earnest, except for one disclosure that certain departments of the government were not yet contemplating war. This was detailed news of large German purchases of copper, rubber and other commodities here in the last few days for delivery before Sept. 1.

Since the beginning of August the Germans have bought 17,000 tons of rubber here at a cost of £1,300,000 and 8,000 tons of copper at a cost of £360,000 and also substantial quantities of tin and lead. Although these purchases have reduced the visible stocks of rubber here to 50,000 tons, or only 67 per cent of the amount at the end of 1936, and the stocks of copper to 28,000 tons, or 61 per cent of the 1936 total, the government made no move to prevent these shipments of essential war materials to a potential enemy.

Today Germans were busy here buying large quantities of shellac and other gums used for varnish and picric acid. The explanation, it was said, is that there no mechanism for checking exports except war legislation, and that in any case Germany's purchases here have depleted her precious stock of foreign exchange.

The British may try to minimize the humiliation they have just suffered in the Russian-German pact move; they are sure to take the line publicly that their guarantee to Poland remains in full force. After all, they gave the guarantee on March 31, before Mr. Chamberlain even thought of bolstering it by a formal alliance with Russia, although the British Government and the Poles alike believed the Russians would help in the event of war.

Nevertheless, the guarantee can hardly be the same again after tonight's announcement. Germany appears to have won a stunning triumph and it will be for Britain, France and Poland to adjust themselves to it in the next few days as best they can.

* * *

September 1, 1939

GERMAN ARMY ATTACKS POLAND; CITIES BOMBED, PORT BLOCKADED; DANZIG IS ACCEPTED INTO REICH

HITLER GIVES WORD

In a Proclamation He Accuses Warsaw of Appeal to Arms

FOREIGNERS ARE WARNED

They Remain in Poland at Own Risk—Nazis to Shoot at Any Planes Flying Over Reich

By OTTO D. TOLISCHUS
Special Cable to The New York Times.

BERLIN, Friday, Sept. 1—Charging that Germany had been attacked, Chancellor Hitler at 5:11 o'clock this morning issued a proclamation to the army declaring that from now on force will be met with force and calling on the armed forces "to fulfill their duty to the end."

The text of the proclamation reads:

To the defense forces:

The Polish nation refused my efforts for a peaceful regulation of neighborly relations; instead it has appealed to weapons.

Germans in Poland are persecuted with a bloody terror and are driven from their homes. The series of border violations, which are unbearable to a great power, prove that the Poles no longer are willing to respect the German frontier. In order to put an end to this frantic activity no other means is left to me now than to meet force with force.

"Battle for Honor"

German defense forces will carry on the battle for the honor of the living rights of the reawakened German people with firm determination.

I expect every German soldier, in view of the great tradition of eternal German soldiery, to do his duty until the end.

Remember always in all situations you are the representatives of National Socialist Greater Germany! Long live our people and our Reich!

Berlin, Sept. 1, 1939.

ADOLF HITLER.

The commander-in-chief of the air force issued a decree effective immediately prohibiting the passage of any airplanes over German territory excepting those of the Reich air force or the government.

This morning the naval authorities ordered all German mercantile ships in the Baltic Sea not to run to Danzig or Polish ports.

Anti-air raid defenses were mobilized throughout the country early this morning.

A formal declaration of war against Poland had not yet been declared up to 8 o'clock [3 A. M. New York time] this morning and the question of whether the two countries are in a state of active belligerency is still open.

Reichstag Will Meet Today

Foreign correspondents at an official conference at the Reich Press Ministry at 8:30 o'clock [3:30 A. M. New York time] were told that they would receive every opportunity to facilitate the transmission of dispatches. Wireless stations have been instructed to speed up communications and the Ministry is installing additional batteries of telephones.

The Reichstag has been summoned to meet at 10 o'clock [5 A. M. New York time] to receive a more formal declaration from Herr Hitler.

The Hitler army order is interpreted as providing, for the time being, armed defense of the German frontiers against aggression. The action is also suspected of forcing international diplomatic action.

The Germans announced that foreigners remain in Polish territory at their own risk.

Flying over Polish territory as well as the maritime areas is forbidden by the German authorities and any violators will be shot down.

When Herr Hitler made his announcement Berlin's streets were still deserted except for the conventional early traffic, and there were no outward signs that the nation was finding itself in the first stages of war.

The government area was completely deserted, and the two guards doing sentry duty in front of the Chancellery remained their usual mute symbol of authority. It was only when official placards containing the orders to the populace began to appear on the billboards that early workers became aware of the situation.

* * *

June 11, 1940

ITALY AT WAR, READY TO ATTACK

DUCE GIVES SIGNAL

Announces War on the 'Plutocratic' Nations of the West

ASSURES 5 NEUTRALS

Bid Is Made to Russia, But Rome Has No Pledge of Aid

By HERBERT L. MATTHEWS
By Telephone to The New York Times.

ROME, Tuesday, June 11—Italy declared war on Great Britain and France yesterday afternoon, to take effect at one minute past midnight. The land, air and sea forces of the Italian Empire were already in motion.

It is a war, as Premier Benito Mussolini announced to the people from his balcony at the Palazzo Venezia at 6 in the evening, against the "plutocratic and reactionary democracies of the West." For the moment that does not include the United States, but few Italians believe that they will see the war to a finish without having the Americans against them.

Signor Mussolini expressly excluded Turkey, Switzerland, Yugoslavia, Greece and Egypt as enemies unless they attacked Italy or the Italian possessions.

Turkey provides the burning question of the day. Italians are absolutely convinced that the Turks will not move against them and will not honor their agreement with the Allies. It is hoped to confine Italian activity to France, Great Britain and the Mediterranean and to keep the Balkans tranquil. If that can be done, Italians think, the Turks will remain quiet.

Soviet Action Discounted

Russia has washed her hands of the struggle. The Italians know that any disturbance in the Balkans will immediately bring her in; but as long as the struggle is confined to the west and south the Soviet will do nothing either to hinder or help. This was told to your correspondent a few hours ago by a very authoritative source.

It was emphasized there were no agreements about furnishing material or anything else, nor any threats or promises.

The Italian Ambassador, Augusto Rosso, left in the morning for Moscow and Ivan Gorelkin, Soviet Ambassador, is coming back to Rome, thus ending a long period without such representation. The Italians were anxious to restore full diplomatic relations in this critical period, according to this writer's informant, and the Russians agreed, but without compromising themselves.

It thus appears that Premier Mussolini has embarked on this dangerous venture without really knowing what Soviet Russia will do in the long run.

President Roosevelt's speech clearly has come too late. There was nothing that the United States could do to halt this conflict, the Italians say. Whatever brake Mr. Roosevelt may have exercised was overcome by the momentum of the whole Fascist policy. Once it was set in motion, nothing could stop it.

The Italians do not believe that the United States can affect the issue, whatever it does. They are sure American help cannot assume large proportions for many weeks, before which they believe the war will be over.

Ever since the beginning of the war Signor Mussolini had said that when he came out on the balcony of the Palazzo Venezia the people of Italy would be speaking. From that moment it was known that when he spoke Italy would already be at war. So when the word finally went around to gather in the Piazza Venezia and all the squares of Italian cities and towns, no one could doubt what the announcement would be.

The first resolute words that were spoken ended the long and nerve-wracking period of suspense, with its dramatic ups and downs, its days of hope and pessimism, but its always rising tension.

Long ago your correspondent was able to say that Italy would be at war before June 20, probably between June 10 and 20. Sometimes it seemed that it was coming sooner, but never was there any hope that Italy would stay out of the war indefinitely.

The pressure from the United States appeared to be having effect. In Moscow Soviet spokesmen referred to Italy in strong terms that seemed to indicate Russia was also trying to restrain Signor Mussolini. But American pressure had to be ignored and the Soviet was really offering no objections, except to involvement of the Balkans.

As far as France was concerned, it is now clear that the elimination of former Premier Edouard Daladier from the Cabinet, far from being a conciliatory gesture to Italy, was the last act of defiance. M. Daladier, it is stated here on high authority, was working with Pierre Laval, former French Premier, to capitulate and make a separate peace, or at least to make generous proposals to Italy. His ejection means that France has chosen to fight it out to the end.

King Victor Emmanuel, one must presume, was not restraining Premier Mussolini and has put himself at the head of his nation. Immediately after the great gathering in the Piazza Venezia, the crowd surged up the Quirinal Hill to the palace, where the King awaited them, wearing his field uniform. As he stood on the balcony and saluted, the crowd shouted, "Savoia!" again and again.

Already the Premier had spoken of Victor Emmanuel as "His Majesty the King and Emperor, who has always interpreted the soul of his Fatherland." With those words ended any doubts that might have been held about the King's feelings or actions. He has never thwarted any of the plans or desires of Signor Mussolini.

Missions First to Learn

The diplomatic missions were probably the first to realize that Italy was entering the war, for they received notification early in the morning that the Sicilian Straits had been closed with floating mines during the night. Thus the Mediterranean is already a sea of danger, for the currents are strong through those straits and some of the mines are being carried away.

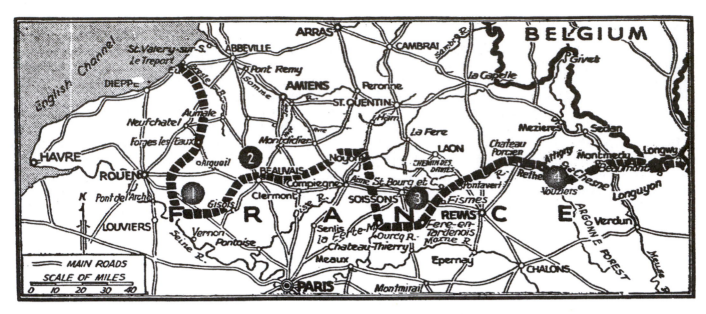

On the western end of the line the Germans pushed a wedge to the Seine southeast of Rouen (1) and struck mighty blows in the region of Beauvais (2). In the center they reached the Ourcq River below Soissons (3). To the east they crossed the Aisne at two points near Vouziers (4).

Italy's announcement of her entry into the war was accompanied by no attack anywhere. One report had Italian troops invading the French Riviera (1), but this was unsupported. Rome's troops landed at two Italian-owned points on the Yugoslav coast: Zara (2) and Lagosta (3). In Albania (4) Italian military preparations were accelerated.

For the moment that is the only act of hostility that is known with certainty to have taken place. All the wild reports about every place from Corsica to Jibuti, French Somaliland, are still in the realm of potentialities rather than facts. Real hostilities were to begin at midnight, but, of course, the armed forces were already under way when the Premier spoke. In actual fact, since fighting is impractical in the dark, it was expected the first attack would begin with dawn.

The war fever began to grip Rome in the morning and mounted steadily as the news of the great gathering in the Piazza Venezia was passed around. There were still some who hoped it was merely connected with the fact that the day was Navy Day, but that belief was gradually dissipated, more by instinct than through any certain knowledge.

Rumors began to fly early in the afternoon—that Corfu had been taken, a landing made in Tunisia, that Jibuti and Malta had fallen and the Italian troops were on the march into France. Those trying to check on the open secret that the liners Rex, Conte di Savoia and Augustus, which were supposed to sail on specified dates, were being used as troop ships, found the Italian Line offices closed and other sources of information equally uninformative.

U.S. Liner Reaches Leghorn

The American export liner Exochorda has got through to Leghorn and should be in Genoa by tonight, but her passage through the Mediterranean may well be perilous, as both Leghorn and Genoa are within easy bombing distance of France and Corsica. About 200 Americans have planned to sail on the Exochorda from Genoa.

The first official information of what was coming appeared in the Ministry of War's announcement that the blackout regulations were to go into effect. Evening newspapers throughout Italy carried the regulations and they were broadcast. Only a "partial blackout" was ordered, in that streets were to be dimly lighted and automobiles to use blue lights.

Then Rome began to hum and buzz with unusual activity. Troops marched through, converging on the Piazza Venezia. Fascist party men went from shop to shop along the Corso Umberto and other main avenues leading into the Piazza Venezia, ordering the stores to close at 5 o'clock.

Gradually the huge piazza became dense with persons knowing that a great historic moment had come for Italy. By 6 o'clock fully 100,000 men and women were packed in the open square and the converging streets.

Many thousands of new posters were scattered over the already covered walls of Rome's houses. They helped to stir feelings a little, but posters have become commonplace in recent weeks.

All Ordered to Listen

Then the radio began announcing that at 6 o'clock Signor Mussolini would speak and all citizens were to gather in the main square of every city, town and village, where loudspeakers had been set up connected with installations of the Rome radio stations. Dozens of times during the afternoon an announcer came to the microphone to make that same report. In between martial music was played.

At 5:40 the microphones were turned over to an announcer in the Palazzo Venezia. Listeners everywhere could hear the cries of the huge crowd, which knew now that it was to listen to the most fateful words that had been heard in Italy since 1915.

Already the evening newspapers in every city had spread the news. Rome's Lavoro Fascista, for instance, was clear enough with its huge headlines and a photograph of the Premier in uniform.

In the Piazza Venezia itself the excitement was rising to a high pitch. Each individual spread his own emotions and was, in turn, caught up in a sensation of mass hysteria that always accompanies such a moment in history. Shouts became screams, and the excess of feeling had to be shown in action as well as by voice. Waves of movement seemed to ripple up and down the surface of the vast crowd. Persons pushed and nudged each other, jumped up and down and turned around meaninglessly.

On the radio a German was speaking to the listeners in the Reich, telling them how "the whole Italian people speaks to us, the German people." The Germans in Rome were there, too, he said, right under the balcony of the Palazzo Venezia.

At 6 o'clock precisely the Premier appeared on his balcony in his Blackshirt militia uniform, setting off the already aroused emotions of the people as if with an electric charge. Never did he appear more dominating, more sure of himself. Never has his voice been so clear and strong.

At another window stood the Foreign Minister, Count Ciano, in the uniform of an airman. He, like Ettore Muti, Secretary-General of the Fascist party, is doubtless going to join his squadron, the "Disperata," which he led in the Ethiopian war. Because Signor Muti was away, his substitute, Pietro Capoferri, called for the traditional cheer: "Viva Il Duce!"

Despite the loudspeakers, Signor Mussolini's words could not be heard on the outer edges of the square. There one found a surprisingly light-hearted attitude, in some cases, toward the grave news he was going to impart. Those who heard well, however, responded with enthusiasm.

The announcement that the declaration of war had been handed to the Allies' ambassadors was cheered tremendously. The mention of the King brought out the greatest enthusiasm of all, except near the end, when the Premier said "We will conquer!" Then the response was deafening.

"Proletarian and Fascist Italy is for the third time on her feet," he cried, "strong, proud and more compact than ever. There is but one categorical watchword binding to all; it has already penetrated and fired the hearts of all from the Alps to the Indian Ocean: Conquer! And we will conquer—to give finally a long period of peace with justice to Italy, to Europe and to the world.

"People of Italy, rush to your arms and show your tenacity, your courage and your valor!"

At 6:20 P. M. it was over. The Premier was called out to his balcony again five or six times, and then the crowd marched off toward the Quirinal Palace, bearing their placards, some of which had single words, like "Tunisia, Jibuti, Corsica, Suez, Malta, Cyprus." These are the war aims of Fascist Italy, plus one other, expressed this way on one of the placards: "We don't give a damn for the democracies."

* * *

June 11, 1940

STAB IN BACK, SAYS ROOSEVELT

OUR HELP PLEDGED

President Offers Our Full Material Aid to Allies' Cause

AMERICA IN DANGER

Fate Hangs on Training and Arms, He Says at Charlottesville

By FELIX BELAIR Jr.
Special to The New York Times.

CHARLOTTESVILLE, Va., June 10—"On this 10th day of June, 1940, the hand that held the dagger has struck it into the back of its neighbor." In these words tonight President Roosevelt condemned the decision of Premier Mussolini which took Italy into the war on the side of Germany.

The remark was interpolated by the President in an address at the graduation exercises of the University of Virginia here. There could be no missing the depth of his feeling, since he put into the words all the emphasis at his command.

Italy's intervention was denounced furthermore as a definite threat to the way of life and the trade and commerce of the Americas. This government, he said, would give all material aid to France and Great Britain as "opponents of force."

The Chief Executive of the United States spoke to the nation and to the world only a few hours after Premier Mussolini announced his decision to join hands with Chancellor Hitler and unleashed his fascist legions against France and Great Britain. More details were revealed by Mr. Roosevelt of his correspondence with the Italian dictator in an effort to keep Italy at peace and to prevent the spread of war to the Mediterranean basin.

"To the Regret of Humanity"

"Unfortunately—unfortunately, to the regret of all of us and to the regret of humanity—the chief of the Italian Government was unwilling to accept the procedure suggested, and he has made no counter proposal," the President said.

And a moment later:

"The Government of Italy has now chosen to preserve what it terms its freedom of action and to fulfill what it states are its promises to Germany. In so doing it has manifested disregard for the rights and security of other nations, disregard for the lives of the peoples of those nations which are directly threatened by the spread of this war, and has evidenced its unwillingness to find the means, through pacific negotiation, for the satisfaction of what it believes are its legitimate aspirations."

The President bespoke the prayers and hopes of this nation for those peoples beyond the seas who were battling for their freedom.

"In our American unity," he said, "we will pursue two obvious and simultaneous courses: we will extend to the opponents of force the material resources of this nation and at the same time we will harness and speed up the use of those resources in order that we ourselves in the Americas may have equipment and training equal to the task of any emergency and every defense."

The latter utterance was the President's only reference to plans for compulsory universal military training for which he already has expressed sympathy and which have been gaining in popularity during the past fortnight. He had withheld release of his address until after hearing Premier Mussolini's war declaration and revised the text accordingly.

After characterizing an America isolated from a world dominated by the policy of force as a prison into which its liberty loving people would be thrust by the defeat of France and Great Britain, the President said this country must now concern itself with how to prevent the building of that prison and the incarceration of its population.

"Let us not hesitate—all of us," he added, "to proclaim certain truths. Overwhelmingly we, as a nation, and this applies to all the other American nations, we are convinced that military and naval victory for the gods of Force and Hate would endanger the institutions of democracy in the Western World; and that equally, therefore, the whole of our sympathies lie with those nations which are giving their life blood in combat against these forces.

"Once more the future of the nation and of the American people is at stake," the President said. "The program unfolds swiftly and into it will fit the responsibility and the opportunity of every man and woman to preserve our heritage in days of peril."

To do otherwise was to entertain "the now obvious delusion that we of the United States can safely permit the United States to become a lone island in a world dominated by the philosophy of force."

While such an island might be the "dream" of those who continue to talk and vote as isolationists, the Chief Executive continued, it was to him and the overwhelming majority of Americans "a helpless nightmare of a people without freedom, a people lodged in prison, handcuffed, hungry, and fed through the bars from day to day by contemptuous, unpitying masters of other continents."

Mr. Roosevelt said the Italian dictator told him several months ago of his intention to limit the spread of war in the Mediterranean region and to maintain the peace of more than 200,000,000 people.

He replied to Signor Mussolini that this aim of the Italian Government met with a sympathetic response in this country and made it clear that if Italy became involved in the war there was no telling "how much greater the extension of the war might eventually become."

Later on, according to the President, he offered the good offices of the White House in bringing before the French and British Governments any proposals from the Italian Government that might lay a basis for peaceable negotiations looking to Italy's remaining at peace.

The President said he told the Italian Chief of State that while this government could not assume responsibility for any such proposals outlining Italy's aspirations or for resulting agreements reached with France and Great Britain, he would ask the latter for assurances that they would faithfully execute such agreements.

Mr. Roosevelt said he proposed to seek further assurance from France and Britain that Italy's voice in any subsequent peace conference would have the same authority as if the Italians had taken part in the war as belligerents.

Calls for Full Speed Ahead, Now

The situation today called for "full speed ahead," without hindrance or detours, the President said, both in material aid to the Allies and in complete rearmament.

It was in a setting of academic splendor that the President became the first Chief Executive since Cleveland to address a University of Virginia graduating class. Behind him sat the faculty of the university and distinguished guests. The President himself faced the microphone in his crimson hood.

Before him in somber black were nearly 500 grim-faced undergraduates. When Mr. Roosevelt gave deliberate emphasis to this nation's sympathies with those who were staking their lives in the fight for freedom overseas, they broke into the wildest applause, cheering and rebel yells.

As the President neared the end of his speech the cheering became general and members of the faculty stamped their feet and applauded. Wherever Mr. Roosevelt mentioned this nation's determination to preserve free institutions and liberties and to perpetuate democracy within our borders, those on the platform and in the audience forgot academic decorum in spontaneous approbation.

The address was delivered not only to the graduation class of the university here but to the many other classes throughout the years. Thus, he spoke, Mr. Roosevelt said, to a cross-section of the nation as a whole.

Rain drove the exercises indoors. The crowd that jammed the university gymnasium responded with enthusiasm when he said:

"The whole of our sympathies lie with those nations which are giving their life blood in combat."

Accompanied by Mrs. Roosevelt, Brig. Gen. Edwin M. Watson, his secretary and military aide, and Captain Daniel J. Callaghan, naval aide, the president drove through rain drenched, crowded streets from the train side to reach the memorial gymnasium. Cheers greeted him as he appeared on the rear platform on his special train and again when he drew up to the gymnasium door.

John Lloyd Newcomb, president of the university, was on hand to greet Mr. Roosevelt as he detrained. And somewhere in the gymnasium audience of 497 graduates was the Chief Executive's son, Franklin D. Roosevelt Jr., at whose insistence the President left Washington early in the afternoon to be on hand.

President Roosevelt did not amplify the statement that "we will extend to the opponents of force the material resources of this nation." There was little doubt among observers, however, that he contemplated a more direct form of assistance that has been available to the Allies under the cash-and-carry provisions of the Neutrality Act.

Heretofore the Federal Government has not aided the Allies as a government, all sales of airplanes and other implements of war having gone through the medium of private corporations. Even in the "trade-in" program whereby the government is facilitating shipment of planes, guns and munitions presently in Federal hands, the assistance has been forwarded, technically, through sales by corporations.

Neutrality Law Change Hinted

The Hague Convention forbidding sales of arms and munitions to a belligerent government by a neutral is held not to apply to the "trade-in" program. It apparently was the President's intention in his address to call for a more direct form of assistance to France and Great Britain, possibly through modification of the Neutrality Act.

As soon as he had completed his address, Mr. Roosevelt went directly to his train, which left for Washington after he had conferred with Washington officials by portable telephone. On his arrival he also had talked with Washington.

* * *

August 21, 1940

TROTSKY, WOUNDED BY 'FRIEND' IN HOME, IS BELIEVED DYING

Exiled Soviet Leader Struck With Axe by Supposedly Ardent Supporter

GUARDS SUBDUE ATTACKER

They Accuse Russian Secret Police—Victim's Chances Called One in Ten

By The United Press

MEXICO CITY, Aug. 20—Leon Trotsky was struck many times in the head with an axe today by a man who called at his suburban home "so frequently he seemed to be one of the family," and physicians at the Green Cross Emergency Hospital said the exiled Communist leader might not live through the night.

AGAIN ATTACKED
Leon Trotsky as he appeared at a press conference at Coyoacan on Aug. 7 when he charged that "Stalin and the Russian secret police" had ordered the May 24 attempt on his life.

Mr. Trotsky was operated upon and immediately placed in an oxygen tent. The surgeons said it was too early to determine the results of the operation. They said the most serious wound was one that pierced the skull and entered the brain, causing a hemorrhage. The operating surgeon added that the chances are "90 to 10 that he cannot live."

The 60-year-old former Soviet War Commissar's assailant was tentatively identified as Frank Jackson, was later found to be Jacques Monard van den Dreschd, 36 years old, said to have been born in Persia.

Guards at Mr. Trotsky's home who rushed into the study and overpowered van den Dreschd when they heard the famous exile scream, said the assailant probably was a member of the OGPU (Russian Secret police).

Intimate of Trotsky Home

Considered to be an ardent Trotsky supporter, van den Dreschd, who told police he was a journalist and had been educated in Paris, had been admitted to and given the run of the heavily-guarded Coyoacan home for more than eight months.

"He called so frequently he seemed to be one of the family," said one of the guards.

The guards said a woman, whom they believed to be an American, and who had posed as van den Dreschd's wife, also had gained a close friendship with Mr. Trotsky.

Great patches of blood stained the floor of the study after the attack. Mr. Trotsky, according to the police who were called by the guards, apparently struggled desperately with his assailant. The receiver on the telephone in the room had been unhooked, which was taken to indicate that he probably had tried to signal for help.

Mrs. Trotsky followed the guards into the study, screaming, "Let him live! Let him live!" She accompanied him to the hospital and remained secluded there during the operation.

The pickaxe used by van den Dreschd had a stocky wooden handle about a foot long. It appeared hardly ever to have been used before. The axe itself was of steel, with a sharply pointed pick at one end and a forked hammer claw on the other, such as is used to pull nails.

The steel head measured about seven or eight inches from tip to tip.

Van den Dreschd, who also was taken to the hospital with head injuries suffered when the guards subdued him, was described as about six feet tall with short, slipped black hair. He wears glasses.

He was questioned by secret police while lying on a cot.

Van den Dreschd, whose good command of the English language made some of the guards think he might be American, won a place in Mr. Trotsky's most intimate circle of friends, and so he was admitted to the former Commissar's study.

Police Chief General Manuel Nuñez said van den Dreschd told him he had known Mr. Trotsky for a long time and "would give my life's blood" for him. Lately, however, he appeared to have differed violently with Mr. Trotsky's views and his management of the Fourth Internationale.

The clash of opinions was believed to have precipitated the attack.

The assault occurred between 4:30 and 5:30 P. M.

After the operation on her husband, Mrs. Trotsky was seen, wearing a sterilized white robe, silently holding her husband's hand in the bleak operating room. She had been with Mr. Trotsky virtually every moment since he was attacked. The exile was conscious for a time before the operation and talked with police officials, but they said he had no statement to make.

Secret police found van den Dreschd's blood-stained raincoat in the study, with a new ornate dagger between eight and ten inches long hidden in a secret pocket. The dagger apparently never had been used.

When the guards rushed into the room, they found the man then known as Jackson with a pistol in his hand but he had not used it. Head Guard Harold Robbins disarmed him and beat him over the head with the butt of the gun.

"Jackson thought he could do a quiet job," Robbins said, "and would use the gun if necessary to shoot his way out, but apparently he lost his courage after hitting him (Trotsky) with the instrument."

Since an attack upon him last May, Mr. Trotsky's villa has been transformed into a veritable fortress with three-gun pill boxes mounted on a fifteen-foot-high brick wall. The entrance is barred by a steel door, and the entire place is policed by guards.

Mr. Trotsky, in a recent interview, expressed fear that a second attempt on his life might be made at the height of the German blitzkrieg against Great Britain.

Had Narrow Escape in May

Leon Trotsky narrowly escaped death on May 24 this year when a salvo of machine-gun bullets swept through the bedroom of his home on the outskirts of Mexico City. He and his wife escaped unharmed, but Robert Sheldon Harte of New York, 25-year-old guard, was kidnapped and later found dead in a farmhouse.

Mr. Trotsky accused Joseph Stalin, Soviet dictator, of instigating the assassination plot against him. The Mexican police have not been able to find the attackers.

A few weeks after the assassination attempt Diego Rivera, Mexican painter in whose house Mr. Trotsky formerly had lived, fled from Mexico and asserted in this country that a group of Stalinite and Nazi agitators had attempted to assassinate him three days after the attempt on Mr. Trotsky.

The police investigation of the attempt against the life of the former Russian leader developed that twenty-one men had taken part in the attack, and that it apparently was directed by the Mexican Communist party.

Mr. Trotsky has been an exile from Russia since Mr. Stalin came into power. The two men were the two contenders for the succession to Nicolai Lenin, co-leader with Mr. Trotsky of the Russian revolution, but Mr. Stalin gradually worked himself into a position of power and eased the other out.

After brief stays in Turkey, France, Sweden and Norway, the exile came to Mexico in 1937 and lived with the Riveras. Two years later he and the painter disagreed over their views on the world revolution, which had always been advocated by Mr. Trotsky, and the former Russian leader left the Rivera home.

*　*　*

August 22, 1940

TROTSKY DIES OF HIS WOUNDS; ASKS REVOLUTION GO FORWARD

Assassin Says He Broke With Victim After Exile Asked Him to Carry Out Acts of Sabotage in Russia

---

By ARNALDO CORTESI
Special Cable to The New York Times.

MEXICO CITY, Aug. 21—After twenty-six hours of an extraordinarily tenacious fight for life, Leon Trotsky died at 7:25 P. M. today of wounds inflicted upon his head with a pickaxe by an assailant in his home yesterday.

Mrs. Trotsky was with him to the last. Two of his secretaries also were present.

Almost his last words, whispered to his secretary, were:

"Please say to our friends I am sure of the victory of the Fourth International. Go forward!"

The 60-year-old exile's losing struggle for existence continued all last night and all day today with alternate ups and downs. He rallied somewhat at the middle of the day but by evening it was evident the end was near.

The assassin, Jacques Mornard van den Dreschd, for months an intimate of the Trotsky household, had a declaration written in French on his person when he was arrested yesterday. Police said today that in it he told of having quarreled with his leader when Mr. Trotsky tried to induce him to go to Russia to perform acts of sabotage.

The declaration adds that the writer decided to kill Mr. Trotsky because the latter did everything in his power to prevent van den Dreschd from marrying Sylvia Ageloff of Brooklyn, who had introduced the two men to each other.

Miss Ageloff, who is held as a witness, is said to have met van den Dreschd two years ago in Paris, and it was through her that he was able to win Mr. Trotsky's confidence, for her sister, Ruth, was Mr. Trotsky's secretary in 1937.

Questioned by police, she declared she introduced "Frank Jackson," as she knew him, to Mr. Trotsky in perfect good faith not knowing he had any designs on the former Soviet War Commissar's life.

She was so remorseful that she threatened to commit suicide if Mr. Trotsky died. She revealed that "Jackson" always seemed plentifully supplied with money and told police he once gave her $3,000 saying it was left him by his mother when she died.

The assassin, who entered Mexico posing as a Canadian, Frank Jackson, now is said to have been born in Teheran, Iran, son of a Belgian diplomat. Police say many letters in English, French and Russian were found in his hotel room.

With remarkable fortitude, Mr. Trotsky, despite his very severe wound, was able to grapple with his assailant and then run from the room in which he was attacked, shouting for help. He did not collapse until his wife and his guards had rushed to his aid. For some time he retained full lucidity of mind and was able to make a few statements.

Along the same corridor in the hospital, only two doors away, lay his assailant. Police guard the door of his room for fear that if there was an organized attempt on Mr. Trotsky's life, the organizers may murder "Jackson" to prevent his testifying.

The devotion of Mrs. Trotsky filled every one who saw her with pity. This small, white-haired, retiring woman was the first to run to her husband's aid when he called for help and to grapple with his assailant. She did not leave Mr. Trotsky's bedside for a single minute.

Joseph Hansen, one of Mr. Trotsky's American secretaries, issued the following written account of the attack on his chief:

"Trotsky knew the assassin, Frank Jackson, personally for more than six months. Jackson enjoyed Trotsky's confidence because of his connection with Trotsky's movement in France and the United States. Jackson visited the house frequently. At no time did we have the least ground to suspect he was an agent of the GPU (Russian secret police).

"He entered the house on Aug. 20 at 5:30 o'clock. He met Mr. Trotsky in the patio near the chicken yard, where he told Trotsky he had written an article on which he wished his advice. Trotsky agreed as a matter of course and walked with him to the dining room, where they met Mrs. Trotsky. Jackson asked Mrs. Trotsky for a glass of water, explaining his throat was dry. She offered him tea, since she and Trotsky had just finished their afternoon tea. He refused, taking only water.

"Trotsky then invited Jackson into the study but without previously notifying his secretaries. The first indication of something wrong was the sound of terrible cries and a violent struggle in Trotsky's study. Secretary-guards at first thought an accident had occurred. The two who were closest immediately left their posts and rushed to the dining room next to Trotsky's study. Here they met Trotsky coming from the study with blood streaming down his face. One of the guards immediately attacked the assassin, who stood with a gun in his hand, and the other helped Trotsky recline on the dining-room floor.

"The assassin apparently struck Trotsky from behind with a miner's pick or alpenstock—the point penetrating into the brain. Instead of dropping unconscious as the assassin had evidently planned, Trotsky still retained consciousness and struggled with the assailant. As he lay bleeding on the floor later, he described the struggle to Mrs. Trotsky and Secretary Hansen. He told Hansen: 'Jackson shot me with a revolver. I am seriously wounded. I feel that this time it is the end.'

"Hansen tried to convince him it was only a surface wound and could not have been caused by a revolver, because nobody heard a shot, but Trotsky replied: 'No, I feel here (pointing to his heart) that this time they have succeeded.'

"Later in the ambulance he again talked with Hansen, declaring: 'Jackson was either a member of the GPU or a Fascist—most likely a member of the GPO.' In the hospital just before he lost consciousness he called Hansen to his side and asked him if he had a note book to jot down the following declaration:

" 'I am close to death from the blow of a political assassin who struck me in my room. I struggled with him. He had entered the room to talk about French statistics. He struck me. Please say to our friends—I am sure of the victory of the Fourth International. Go forward!' "

Mr. Hansen added on his own initiative that "Jackson" was in Paris at the time of the disappearance of Rudolph Clement, former secretary to Mr. Trotsky, whose murdered body was found floating in the Seine without hands or legs. Mr. Hansen thought it possible he took a leading role in the assault on the Trotsky house on May 24, when an armed band gained entrance and machine-gunned the Trotskys' bedroom.

The secretary suggests van den Dreschd persuaded Robert Sheldon Harte to open the door for the assailants on this occasion, and because Harte, a guard, could have identified the betrayer, he was kidnapped and killed. This would explain why "Jackson" went to the United States immediately after May 24, it was said.

During the last weeks, when everything had quieted down, he returned to Mexico under orders from the Russian secret police to complete his job, Mr. Hansen continued. He added that the Russian police evidently had some strong hold over "Jackson." During his struggle with the guards, he cried out several times: "They have imprisoned my mother." Mr. Hansen suggests that van den Dreschd was threatened with the death of relatives in Russia or elsewhere.

The secretary ended by accusing three Left Wing Mexican newspapers, "as agents of the OGPU," of carrying out "moral preparation for the May 24 assault," which he says was nothing more than preparation for the final fatal attack.

Denies Miss Ageloff Knew Trotsky

Monte Ageloff, a brother of Miss Sylvia Ageloff, said yesterday that, so far as he knew, his sister never knew Leon Trotsky and that no members of his family were members of the Communist party.

He and his father, Samuel, and his brother, Allan, have a real estate office at 191 Joralemon Street, Brooklyn. He said his sister had gone to Mexico about a month ago. She is about 30 years old, he added, and lives with two other sisters, Ruth and Hilda, in an old-fashioned walk-up apartment house at 50 Livingston Street, Brooklyn.

U. S. GROUP ACCUSES STALIN

Head of Trotskyite Party Charges Soviet Chief Instigated Attack

Joseph Stalin instigated the attack on Leon Trotsky in Mexico City on Tuesday, James P. Cannon, national secretary of the Socialist Workers party, 116 University Place, charged in a statement made public yesterday.

Mr. Cannon said he was informed over the telephone by Joseph Hansen, secretary to Mr. Trotsky, that Mr. Trotsky's last words before losing consciousness were: "I will not survive this attack. Stalin has finally accomplished the task he attempted unsuccessfully before." Mr. Cannon declared:

"We accuse Stalin before the world as the real organizer of this crime. Stalin, whose regime has enmeshed the Soviet Union in the perils of the capitalist war, thinks that in this way he can silence the voice of Trotsky, which has been the steadfast and eloquent voice of working class internationalism throughout these decades of Stalinist reaction and degeneration in the Soviet Union and in the Communist parties throughout the world.

"The fight for Trotsky's ideas will go on whatever the fate that awaits this titanic figure in the history of man's struggle for liberation. This we of the Fourth International pledge to Stalin and to the rulers of the capitalist world, who have shared their violent hatred of the man who, with Lenin, stood as the living symbol of the world workers' revolution."

The Socialist Workers party announced that it is planning to hold the funeral of Mr. Trotsky in this city. Arrangements were being sought in telephone conversations with Mexico City to transport the body of the murdered leader to New York for this purpose.

"We plan to hold the funeral here," said Mr. Cannon, "to give the working people of New York an opportunity to show their reverence for the memory of this great leader and their hatred and contempt for Stalinism."

*   *   *

June 22, 1941

HITLER BEGINS WAR ON RUSSIA, WITH ARMIES ON MARCH FROM ARCTIC TO THE BLACK SEA; DAMASCUS FALLS; U.S. OUSTS ROME CONSULS

BAD FAITH CHARGED

Goebbels Reads Attack on Soviet— Ribbentrop Announces War

BALTIC MADE ISSUE

Finns and Rumanians Are Called Allies in Plan of Assault

By C. BROOKS PETERS

By Telephone to The New York Times.

BERLIN, Sunday, June 22—As dawn broke over Europe today the legions of National Socialist Germany began their long-rumored invasion of Communist Soviet Russia. The non-aggression and amity pact between the two countries, signed in August, 1939, forgotten, the German attack began along a tremendous front, extending from the Arctic regions to the Black Sea. Marching with the forces of Germany are also the troops of Finland and Rumania.

Adolf Hitler, in a proclamation to the German people read over a national hook-up by Propaganda Minister Dr. Joseph Goebbels at 5:30 this morning, termed the military action begun this morning the largest in the history of the world. It was necessary, he added, because in spite of his unceasing efforts to preserve peace in this area, it had definitely been proved that Russia was in a coalition with England to ruin Germany by prolonging the war.

Saw Stalemate in West

Herr Hitler, in his proclamation as reported here, made one vitally interesting statement, namely, that the supreme German military command did not feel itself able to force a decisive victory in the West—apparently on the British Isles—when large Russian troop concentrations were on the Reich's borders in the East.

The Russian troop concentrations in the East began in August, 1940, Herr Hitler asserted. "Thus, there occurred the effect intended by the Soviet-British cooperation," he added, "namely, the binding of such powerful German forces in the East that a radical conclusion of the war in the West, particularly as regards aircraft, could no longer be vouched for by the German High Command.

[The German radio announced early today that documentary proof would shortly be given of a secret British-Russian alliance, made behind Germany's back.]

Designed "to Save Reich"

The German action, Herr Hitler explained to his fellow-National Socialists, is designed to save the Reich and with it all Europe from the machinations of the Jewish-Anglo-Saxon warmongers.

The German Foreign Minister, Joachim von Ribbentrop, followed Dr. Goebbels on the air with a declaration of the Reich Government read before the foreign correspondents in the Foreign Office. Herr von Ribbentrop said he received V. G. Dekanosoff, the Russian Ambassador, this morning and informed him that in spite of the Russian-German non-aggression pact of Aug. 23, 1939, and an amity pact of Sept. 28, 1939, Russia had betrayed the trust that the Reich had placed in her.

"Contrary to all engagements which they had undertaken and in absolute contradiction to their solemn declarations, the Soviet Union had turned against Germany," the Reich note asserted. "They have first not only continued, but even since the outbreak of war intensified their subversive activities against Germany in Europe. They have second, in a continually increasing measure, developed their foreign policy in a tendency hostile to Germany, and they have third massed their entire forces on the German frontier ready for action."

The Soviet Government, it was charged, had violated its treaties and broken its agreements with Germany. This was characterized as evidence that Moscow's "hatred of National Socialism was stronger than its political wisdom." Recalling the enmity between bolshevism and nazism, it was asserted that Bolshevist Moscow was "about to stab National Socialist Germany in the back" while the latter was "engaged in a struggle for existence."

"Germany has no intention of remaining inactive in the face of this grave threat to her Eastern frontier," it was proclaimed. "The Fuehrer has therefore ordered the German forces to oppose this menace with all the might at their disposal. In the coming struggle the German people are fully aware that they are called upon not only to defend their native land but to save the entire civilized world from the deadly dangers of bolshevism and clear the way for true social progress in Europe."

Continuing his allegations, Herr von Ribbentrop declared that the German High Command had repeatedly directed the attention of the German Foreign Office to the steadily increasing menace of the Russian Army to Germany. These communications from the High Command will be published in detail, it was declared.

All doubts of the aggressive intention of the Russian concentration were dispelled, it was declared, by the news that the Russian general mobilization was complete and that 160 divisions were concentrated facing Germany.

This apprehension was heightened, it was stated, by news from England concerning the negotiations of Sir Stafford Cripps with a view to establishing closer collaboration between Britain and the Soviet Union and the appeal of Lord Beaverbrook to support Russia in her forthcoming conflict.

Proclamation Heard Here

The announcements made in Berlin were heard here by short-wave listening stations of both the Columbia and National Broadcasting Systems.

Adolf Hitler's proclamation was followed by a statement containing a formal declaration of war by the Nazi Foreign Minister, Joachim von Ribbentrop.

Berlin announced that the German Army was on the march, and that "German troops all along the Russian border from the Baltic to the Balkans are moving into their last-minute positions."

A London broadcast by the British Broadcasting Corporation, however, formally denied that report.

"It can be definitely stated," said the BBC, "that no actual troop movements on the part of either Germany or Russia have as yet taken place."

The only word from Moscow, received several hours after the German announcement, was a London report of a statement issued in the Russian capital declaring that the Soviet and Great Britain were now "in full accord" on the international situation.

Herr Hitler's proclamation, read by Dr. Goebbels at 5:30 A. M., Berlin time, included a vicious attack on the Reich's former associate in European policy, and a charge that Russia had acted in concert with Britain and the United States to "throttle" the Reich.

Finland and Rumania were hailed in the Hitler proclamation as German allies and clear intimation was given that invasion of Russia already might have begun.

"In this very moment," said Herr Hitler's statement, addressed "to the German people" "a marching of German armies is taking place which has no precedent."

Charging against Russia a whole series of border violations, the Hitler proclamation asserted that Soviet planes "again and again" had crossed the Reich's frontiers.

He added that the German people could no longer look peacefully upon these developments.

"I have therefore today decided to give the fate of the German people and the Reich and of Europe into the hands of our soldiers," the announcement from Herr Hitler continued.

Joined by Rumania

The statement indicated that Rumania, in association with Germany, might stand ready to attempt the recapture of Bessarabia, seized by Stalin's legions earlier in the war.

Herr Hitler declared that German and Rumanian soldiers united under Premier Ion Antonescu, stood ready "from the river of the Danube to the shores of the Black Sea."

"The task is to safeguard Europe and thus to save all," the proclamation set forth.

The phrase was seen as a return by Herr Hitler to his assertion, frequently made in earlier years, that Germany stood as Europe's bulwark against bolshevism.

Heavy concentrations of Nazi troops have been reported for several weeks along the borders of partitioned Poland, in apparent readiness for such a stroke. Finland, now referred to as an associate by Herr Hitler's proclamation, recently announced advanced degrees of army mobilization.

Herr Hitler's proclamation denounced the Russian occupation of the Baltic State of Lithuania, annexed to the Soviet Union with Estonia and Latvia after Mr. Stalin's troops had been permitted to occupy bases there.

Germany, he said, never intended to occupy that Baltic country—an intimation that the Soviet Union had made a pretext of such a desire on the part of the Reich as a basis for action.

"Russia," he said, "always put out the lying statement that she was protecting these [the Baltic] countries."

Herr Hitler's proclamation gave an official German version of British relations with Russia, designed, he charged, to prevent the realization of European peace, which he, himself, desired.

Foreign Minister von Ribbentrop's statement declared that Germany, at the time of the announcement, already was taking what he called "military measures of defense" in the Russian situation and that he had so informed the Russian Ambassador in Berlin.

The phrase used recalled that German description of the preliminary phases of the attack on Poland—"counter-attack with pursuit."

Neither Dr. Goebbels's reading of Herr Hitler's proclamation nor the formal statement by Herr von Ribbentrop, which immediately followed on the German radio, gave details of demands reported to have been made on Russia by the Reich.

Included in these, it had been reported earlier, were claims on the Ukraine and the Caucasus for wheat and oil. Since the demands were launched, Russia had been reported organizing elaborate "war games" in these southern areas.

Herr Hitler last night asserted that, in these, the Soviet had mobilized 160 divisions.

He blamed Russia also for causing Germany the necessity of intervention in the Near East, charging that the Soviet "organized the putsch" in Yugoslavia—after the Yugoslav Government had agreed to Axis terms.

In addition, Herr Hitler's proclamation, according to unofficial translation made here, blamed Russian "penetration" into Rumania, as well as the British guarantee of Greece, for placing "new large areas in the war."

* * *

December 8, 1941

JAPAN WARS ON U. S. AND BRITAIN; MAKES SUDDEN ATTACK ON HAWAII; HEAVY FIGHTING AT SEA REPORTED

GUAM BOMBED; ARMY SHIP IS SUNK

U. S. Fliers Head North From Manila—Battleship Oklahoma Set Afire by Torpedo Planes at Honolulu

104 SOLDIERS KILLED AT FIELD IN HAWAII

President Fears 'Very Heavy Losses' on Oahu—Churchill Notifies Japan That a State of War Exists

By FRANK L. KLUCKHOHN
Special to The New York Times.

WASHINGTON, Monday, Dec. 8—Sudden and unexpected attacks on Pearl Harbor, Honolulu, and other United States possessions in the Pacific early yesterday by the Japanese air force and navy plunged the United States and Japan into active war.

The initial attack in Hawaii, apparently launched by torpedo-carrying bombers and submarines, caused widespread damage and death. It was quickly followed by others. There were unconfirmed reports that German raiders participated in the attacks.

Guam also was assaulted from the air, as were Davao, on the island of Mindanao, and Camp John Hay, in Northern Luzon, both in the Philippines. Lieut. Gen. Douglas MacArthur, commanding the United States Army of the Far East, reported there was little damage, however.

[Japanese parachute troops had been landed in the Philippines and native Japanese had seized some communities, Royal Arch Gunnison said in a broadcast from Manila today to WOR-Mutual. He reported without detail that "in the naval war the ABCD fleets under American command appeared to be successful" against Japanese invasions.]

Japanese submarines, ranging out over the Pacific, sank an American transport carrying lumber 1,300 miles from San Francisco, and distress signals were heard from a freighter 700 miles from that city.

The War Department reported that 104 soldiers died and 300 were wounded as a result of the attack on Hickam Field, Hawaii. The National Broadcasting Company reported from Honolulu that the battleship Oklahoma was afire. [Domei, Japanese news agency, reported the Oklahoma sunk.]

Nation Placed on Full War Basis

The news of these surprise attacks fell like a bombshell on Washington. President Roosevelt immediately ordered the country and the Army and Navy onto a full war footing. He arranged at a White House conference last night to address a joint session of Congress at noon today, presumably to ask for declaration of a formal state of war.

This was disclosed after a long special Cabinet meeting, which was joined later by Congressional leaders. These leaders predicted "action" within a day.

After leaving the White House conference Attorney General Francis Biddle said that "a resolution" would be introduced in Congress tomorrow. He would not amplify or affirm that it would be for a declaration of war.

Congress probably will "act" within the day, and he will call the Senate Foreign Relations Committee for this purpose, Chairman Tom Connally announced.

[A United Press dispatch from London this morning said that Prime Minister Churchill had notified Japan that a state of war existed.]

As the reports of heavy fighting flashed into the White House, London reported semi-officially that the British Empire would carry out Prime Minister Winston Churchill's pledge to give the United States full support in case of hostilities with Japan. The President and Mr. Churchill talked by transatlantic telephone.

This was followed by a statement in London from the Netherland Government in Exile that it considered a state of war to exist between the Netherlands and Japan. Canada, Australia and Costa Rica took similar action.

Landing Made in Malaya

A Singapore communiqué disclosed that Japanese troops had landed in Northern Malaya and that Singapore had been bombed.

The President told those at last night's White House meeting that "doubtless very heavy losses" were sustained by the Navy and also by the Army on the island of Oahu [Honolulu]. It was impossible to obtain confirmation or denial of reports that the battleships Oklahoma and West Virginia had been damaged or sunk at Pearl Harbor, together with six or seven destroyers, and that 350 United States airplanes had been caught on the ground.

The White House took over control of the bulletins, and the Navy Department therefore, said it could not discuss the matter or answer any questions how the Japanese were able to penetrate the Hawaiian defenses or appear without previous knowledge of their presence in those waters.

Administration circles forecast that the United States soon might be involved in a world-wide war, with Germany supporting Japan, an Axis partner. The German official radio tonight attacked the United States and supported Japan.

Axis diplomats here expressed complete surprise that the Japanese had attacked. But the impression gained from their attitude was that they believed it represented a victory for the Nazi attempt to divert lease-lend aid from Britain, which has been a Berlin objective ever since the legislation was passed and began to be implemented.

Secretary of the Treasury Henry Morgenthau Jr. announced that his department had invoked the Trading With the Enemy Act, placing an absolute United States embargo on Japan.

Robert P. Patterson, Under-Secretary of War, called on the nation to put production on a twenty-four-hour basis.

A nation-wide round-up of Japanese nationals was ordered by Attorney General Biddle through cooperation by the FBI and local police forces.

Action was taken to protect defense plants, especially in California, where Japanese are particularly numerous. Orders were issued by the Civil Aeronautics Authority to ground most private aircraft except those on scheduled lines.

Fleet Puts Out to Sea From Hawaii

The Navy last night swept out to sea from its bombed base at Pearl Harbor after Secretary of State Cordell Hull, following a final conference with Japanese "peace envoys" here, asserted that Japan's had been a "treacherous" attack. Neither the War nor the Navy Department had been able to communicate with its commanders in Manila.

Secretary of War Henry L. Stimson ordered the entire United States Army to be in uniform by today. Secretary Frank Knox followed suit for the Navy. They did so after President Roosevelt had instructed the Navy and Army to expect all previously prepared orders for defense immediately.

United States naval craft are expected to operate out of Singapore as soon as possible in protecting the vital rubber and tin shipments necessary to our national defense program.

Despite these preliminary defense moves, however, it was clear that further detailed discussions would soon take place between officials of the United States, Great Britain, China, the Netherlands and Australia to devise a total scheme of limiting the activities of the Japanese Fleet.

Immediate steps will be taken also to meet the increased menace to China's lifeline, the Burma Road. Reliable information indicates that the Japanese are preparing a large-scale assault on the road in the hope of cutting off American supplies before the Allies can transport sufficient forces into defensive positions.

Censorship was established on all messages leaving the United States by cable and radio.

In Tokyo United States Ambassador Joseph C. Grew obtained a reply to Secretary Hull's early message, according to dispatches from the Japanese capital.

The attack on Pearl Harbor and Honolulu began "at dawn," according to Stephen Early, Presidential secretary. Because of time difference, the first news of the bombing was released in Washington at 2:22 P. M. Subsequently it was announced at the White House that another wave of bombers and dive bombers had come over Oahu Island, on which Honolulu is situated, to be met by anti-aircraft fire again.

An attack on Guam, tiny island outpost, subsequently was announced. The White House at first said that Manila also had been attacked but, after failure to reach Army and Navy commanders there, President Roosevelt expressed the "hope" that no such attack had occurred. Broadcasts from Manila bore out this hope.

The Japanese took over the Shanghai Bund. Japanese airplanes patrolling over the city dropped some bombs, reportedly sinking the British gunboat Peterel.

Hawaii Attacked Without Warning

Reports from Hawaii indicated that Honolulu had no warning of the attack. Japanese bombers, with the red circle of the Rising Sun of Japan on their wings, suddenly appeared, escorted by fighters. Flying high, they suddenly dive-bombed, attacking Pearl Harbor, the great Navy base, the Army's Hickam Field and Ford Island. At least one torpedo plane was seen to launch a torpedo at warships in Pearl Harbor.

A report from Admiral C. C. Bloch, commander of the naval district at Hawaii, expressed the belief that "there has been heavy damage done in Hawaii and there has been heavy loss of life."

This was subsequently confirmed by Governor Joseph B. Poindexter of Hawaii in a telephone conversation with President Roosevelt. The Governor also said that there were heavy casualties in the city of Honolulu.

At the White House it was officially said that the sinking of the Army transport carrying lumber and the distress signal from another Army ship "indicate Japanese submarines are strung out over that area." Heavy smoke was seen from Ford Island near Honolulu.

In the raids on Hawaii Japanese planes were shot down, one bomber hitting and bursting into flames just behind a post-office on the Island of Oahu. It was reported without confirmation that six Japanese planes and four submarines were destroyed.

The second attack on Honolulu and its surrounding bases occurred just as President Roosevelt was talking to Governor Poindexter at 6 o'clock last evening.

There was no official confirmation of United Press reports from Honolulu that parachute troops had been sighted off Pearl Harbor.

Many Japanese and former Japanese who are now American citizens are in residence in Hawaii.

Saburo Kurusu, special Japanese envoy who has been conducting "peace" negotiations while Japan was preparing for this attack, and Ambassador Kichisaburo Nomura called at the State Department at 2:05 P. M. after asking for the appointment at 1 P. M. They arrived shortly before Secretary Hull had received news Japan had started a war without warning. Mrs. Roosevelt revealed in her broadcast last night that the Japanese Ambassador was with the President when word of the attacks was received.

The two envoys handed a document to Mr. Hull, who kept them waiting about fifteen minutes. Upon reading it, he turned to his visitors to exclaim that it was "crowded with infamous falsehoods and distortions."

President Roosevelt ordered war bulletins released at the White House as rapidly as they were received. A sentence or two was added to the story of the surprise attack every few minutes for several hours.

Cabinet members arrived promptly at 8:30 last evening for their meeting in the White House Oval Room. President Roosevelt had been closeted with Harry L. Hopkins in the Oval Room since receiving the first news. He had conferred with Secretaries Stimson and Knox by telephone and also with General George C. Marshall, Chief of Staff. Admiral Harold R. Stark, Chief of Naval Operations, was too busy to talk to the President even by telephone.

The first to arrive was Secretary of Commerce Jesse H. Jones. Secretary Knox came last. Secretary Hull was accompanied by two bodyguards.

Congressional leaders joining the Cabinet in the oval room at 9 P. M. included Senator Hiram Johnson of California, hitherto an isolationist and for long the ranking minority member of the Senate Foreign Relations Committee.

Others present were Speaker Rayburn, Representative Jere Cooper of Tennessee, representing Representative John W. McCormack, the House Majority Leader, who was not able to reach Washington in time for the conference; Chairman Sol Bloom of the House Foreign Affairs Committee and Representative Charles A. Eaton, ranking minority member; Vice President Wallace, who flew here from New York; Senator Allen W. Barkley, majority leader; Senator McNary and Senator Warren R. Austin, ranking minority member of the Foreign Relations Committee.

Cheering crowds lined Pennsylvania Avenue to see them arrive, another evidence of the national determination to defeat Japan and her Axis allies which every official is confident will dominate the country from this moment forth.

Senator W. Lee O'Daniel of Texas, of hillbilly band and hot biscuits fame, added a touch of inadvertent comedy to the scene when he arrived uninvited. He said he had come to "try to learn a few things" and "to make sure Texas is represented at this conference," thus ignoring the presence of Senator Connally.

Senator Barkley, who arrived in Washington by automobile about 7 P. M., said he did not find out about the Japanese attack until nearly 6 o'clock.

The formal positions of the United States and Japanese Governments toward the war were officially set forth by the release at the White House of the text of President Roosevelt's message of yesterday to Emperor Hirohito and by the Japanese document handed Ambassador Grew in Tokyo.

President Voiced Hope for Peace

The President's message expressed a "fervent hope for peace" and outlined the dangers of the situation.

"We have hoped that a peace of the Pacific could be consummated in such a way that the nationalities of many diverse peoples may exist side by side without fear of invasion," the President told the Emperor.

The President, recalling that the United States had been directly responsible for bringing Japan into contact with the outside world, said that in seeking peace in the Pacific "I am certain that it will be clear to Your Majesty, as it is to me, that

* * * both Japan and the United States should agree to eliminate any form of military threat."

The Japanese document, despite the obviously carefully prepared attack on American bases, insisted that:

"On the other hand, the American Government, always holding fast to theories in disregard of realities and refusing to yield an inch on its impractical principles, caused undue delay in the [peace] negotiations."

Late last night, the United States Government announced that all American republics had been informed of the "treacherous attack" by Japan. It was stated that "very heartening messages of support" were being received in return.

The State Department statement on this matter said:

"All the American republics have been informed by the Government of the United States of the treacherous attack by Japan upon the United States. Immediately upon receipt of word of the attacks on Hawaii and other American territory, wires were dispatched to the American diplomatic missions, instructing them to inform the Foreign Offices at once. This government is receiving very heartening messages of support from the other American republics."

Senator Connally, as head of the powerful Foreign Relations Committee, predicted that world-wide war involving this nation probably depended on European developments within the next few days, according to The United Press.

Connally Promises Reply to "Treachery"

As Roland Young, committee clerk, took to Senator Connally's apartment drafts of the war declaration of April 2, 1917, Mr. Connally said:

"Professing a desire for peace and under the pretext that she coveted amicable relations with us, Japan stealthily concealed under her robe a dagger of assassination and villainy. She attacked us when the two nations were legally at peace.

"With rare and tolerant patience our government has striven to adjust our differences with Japan.

"Japan has now declared war upon the United States and on Great Britain. We shall resist this cruel and unjustifiable assault with naval power and all the resources of our country. We shall wreak the vengeance of justice on these violators of peace, these assassins who attack without warning and these betrayers of treaty obligations and responsibilities of international law.

"Let the Japanese Ambassador go back to his masters and tell them that the United States answers Japan's challenge with steel-throated cannon and a sharp sword of retribution. We shall repay this dastardly treachery with multiplied bombs from the air and heaviest and accurate shells from the sea."

Late last night American officers at the Mexican border were detaining all Japanese attempting to enter or leave the United States, according to a United Press dispatch from San Diego.

New York City, Chicago and other police forces acted to control Japanese nationals and with regard to consulates.

James L. Fly, chairman of the Federal Communications Commission and the Defense Communications Board, said further activity by amateur radio stations would be permitted only upon special governmental authorization.

He said he has been in constant touch with heads of all important communications companies with relation to execution of pre-existing plans for cooperation during any emergency.

*　*　*

December 12, 1941

U.S. NOW AT WAR
WITH GERMANY AND ITALY

WAR OPENED ON US

Congress Acts Quickly as President Meets Hitler Challenge

A GRIM UNANIMITY

Message Warns Nation Foes Aim to Enslave This Hemisphere

By FRANK L. KLUCKHOHN
Special to The New York Times.

WASHINGTON, Dec. 11—The United States declared war today on Germany and Italy, Japan's Axis partners. This nation acted swiftly after Germany formally declared war on us and Italy followed the German lead. Thus, President Roosevelt told Congress in his message, the long-known and the long-expected has taken place.

"The forces endeavoring to enslave the entire world now are moving toward this hemisphere," he said.

"Never before has there been a greater challenge to life, liberty and civilization."

Delay, the President said, invites great danger. But he added:

"Rapid and united effort by all of the peoples of the world who are determined to remain free will insure a world victory of the forces of justice and righteousness over the forces of savagery and barbarism."

For the first time in its history the United States finds itself at war against powers in both the Atlantic and the Pacific.

Quick and Unanimous Answer

Congress acted not only rapidly but without a dissenting vote to meet the Axis challenge. Within two and three-quarters hours after the reading of Mr. Roosevelt's message was started in the Senate and House at 12:26 P. M., the President had signed the declarations against Germany and Italy. Seventy-two hours previously the Japanese attack on Hawaii had brought about the declaration of war against the other Axis partner.

Congress also quickly completed legislation to allow selectees and National Guardsmen to serve outside the Western Hemisphere and set the term of service in the nation's forces until six months after the termination of the war.

In the Senate the vote was 88 to 0 for war against Germany and 90 to 0 for war against Italy. The vote in the House was 393 to 0 for war against Germany and 399 to 0 for war against Italy. The larger Congressional vote against Italy was attributable to the fact that some members reached the floor too late to vote on the declaration against Germany.

In the House, Miss Jeannette Rankin, Republican, of Montana, who cast the lone dissenting vote on Monday against declaring war on Japan, today voted a non-committal "present" with regard to Germany and Italy.

Ignoring Hitler's declarations before the Reichstag today regarding American policy, and Mussolini's to a crowd before the Palazzo di Venezia in Rome, Congress adopted identical resolutions against Germany and Italy. It merely noted that their governments had thrust war upon the United States.

Grim Mood in Congress

Congress acted in a grim mood, but without excitement. Not only on the floors of the Senate and House, but in the galleries the grim mood prevailed. President Roosevelt, busy at the White House directing the battle and production effort as Commander in Chief, did not appear to read his message, as he did when war was declared upon Japan.

There was a deeply solemn undernote as the members assembled at noon. Senator Walsh, chairman of the Senate Naval Affairs Committee, had announced that the naval casualty lists resulting from the Japanese bombing of Pearl Harbor Sunday had arrived, and that families would be notified by the Navy Department as soon as possible.

Tonight the State Department called newspaper offices to announce that the Hungarian Government had broken off diplomatic relations with the United States. Notice was given to the United States Minister to Budapest at 8 P. M., Budapest time [2 P. M. Eastern standard time], by the Hungarian Prime Minister. The State Department's announcement said:

"The Hungarian Prime Minister at 8 P. M. informed the American Minister that in view of the solidarity of the Central European States, which he compared with the solidarity of the States of the Western Hemisphere, Hungary was obliged to break diplomatic relations with the United States. He said this was not with the intention of declaring war on this country."

The declarations against Germany and Italy pledged all the resources of United States, manpower, material and production "to bring the conflict to a successful termination." After signing that against Germany at 3:05 P. M., and that against Italy at 3:06 P. M., before the same group of congressional leaders who on Monday saw him sign the declaration against Japan, President Roosevelt remarked:

"I've always heard things came in threes. Here they are."

Senator Glass of Virginia, who was Secretary of the Treasury in the last World War, told Mr. Roosevelt that "some men in the Senate Foreign Relations Committee wanted to soften the resolutions so as not to hurt the feelings of civilians in the Axis countries."

"I said, 'Hell, we not only want to hurt their feelings but we want to kill them,' " the Virginian remarked.

Associated Press Wirephotos

Left: The President set his signature to the act against Germany. Center: He checked the time with Senator Tom Connally. Right: After that he pronounced the United States officially at war with Italy.

As a result of the ending of peace by Germany and the United States which has existed, at least formally, for twenty-three years, the United States is at war with Germany, Italy, Japan and Manchukuo and Hungary has suspended diplomatic relations.

Among the countries at war with one or all of the Axis powers are Great Britain, Canada, Australia, New Zealand, South Africa, the Soviet Union, China, the Netherlands Government and its East Indies possessions; the refugee governments of France, Belgium, Poland, Greece, Yugoslavia, Czechoslovakia and Norway; and these others in the Western Hemisphere: Panama, Nicaragua, El Salvador, Honduras, Haiti, the Dominican Republic, Cuba and Guatemala.

Announcement was made early in the day that the President would send a message to Congress. This was soon after Hans Thomsen, German chargé d'affaires, delivered the Nazi dictator's declaration of war to the State Department at 8:15 A. M. and after the Italian declaration was delivered to George Wadsworth, American chargé d'affaires in Rome.

Stephen Early, Presidential secretary, told reporters that "as expected," Germany had declared war and "Italy had goose-stepped along, apparently following orders."

After the declaration against Germany was voted the commotion in the House gallery was so great that Speaker Rayburn suspended proceedings until all the visitors who wished to depart had done so. About three-quarters of those in the galleries then left.

Viscount Halifax, the British Ambassador, sat in the front row of the Senate diplomatic gallery with Lady Halifax, Dr. A. Loudon, the Netherlands Minister, and Henrik de Kaufmann, the Danish Minister.

They saw the Senate vote the resolution for war against Germany in five minutes after the start of the President's message, time taken up largely with recording the vote. The House, with a larger roll-call, took twelve minutes to record its unanimous vote. Both houses acted in more leisurely fashion with regard to Italy. The Senate took another thirteen minutes, and the House completed action in another twenty minutes.

The signing ceremony was equally simple and rapid. Congressional leaders did not reach the White House until a minute after 3 P. M. Those present were Vice President Wallace, Senate Majority Leader Barkley, Chairman Connally of the Senate Foreign Relations Committee, Senate Minority Leader McNary and Senators Austin and Glass. From the House came Speaker Rayburn, Majority Leader McCormick, Chairman Bloom of the Foreign Affairs Committee, Minority Leader Martin and Representatives Eaton of New Jersey and Luther Johnson of Texas.

Earlier in the day the President sent telegrams to Representative Martin, as chairman of the Republican National Committee, and to Edward J. Flynn, chairman of the Democratic National Committee, thanking them for the patriotic action of both major parties in eschewing partisan politics and thus promoting unity.

PART II

FROM ALLIANCE TO ACRIMONY: THE ORIGINS OF THE COLD WAR

ROOSEVELT, CHURCHILL MAP 1943 WAR STRATEGY

LEADERS GO BY AIR

Aim at 'Unconditional Surrender' by Axis, President Says

MILITARY AIDES TALK

French Chiefs Declare Groups Will Unite to Liberate Nation

By DREW MIDDLETON
Special Cable to The New York Times.

CASABLANCA, French Morocco, Jan. 24 (Delayed)— President Roosevelt and Prime Minister Churchill today concluded a momentous ten-day conference in which they planned Allied offensives of 1943 aimed at what the President called the "unconditional surrender" of the Axis powers.

The President flew 5,000 miles across the Atlantic with his Chiefs of Staff to confer with Mr. Churchill and British military, naval and air chieftains in a sun-splashed villa within sound of Atlantic breakers. Every phase of the global war was discussed in conferences lasting from morning until midnight. Both war leaders emphasized that the conference was wholly successful and that complete agreement had been reached on great military enterprises to be undertaken by the United Nations this year.

General Henri Honoré Giraud, High Commissioner for French North Africa, and General Charles de Gaulle, leader of Fighting France, met at the conference and found themselves in accord on the primary task of liberating France from German domination. President Roosevelt predicted that French soldiers, sailors and airmen would fight beside the Allied armies in the liberation of France.

Stalin Kept Informed

The President and Mr. Churchill expressed regret for Premier Joseph Stalin's inability to leave the Russian offensive, which he is directing personally, but emphasized that all results of the conferences had been reported to the Soviet leader. [Generalissimo Chiang Kai-shek was similarly advised, The Associated Press reported.]

Assurance of future world peace will come only as a result of the total elimination of German and Japanese war power, the President declared. He borrowed a phrase from General Grant's famous letter to the Confederate commander at Forts Donelson and Henry—"unconditional surrender"—to describe the only terms on which the United Nations would accept the conclusion of the war.

He emphasized, however, that this did not mean the destruction of the populace of Germany, Japan and Italy, but the end of a philosophy based on the conquest and subjugation of other peoples in those countries.

Sitting side by side in the bright sunlight on the grassy lawn of the villa, the President and the Prime Minister reviewed the work of the conference, in which the Chiefs of Staff conferred two or three times a day, reporting at intervals to them.

The President saw three objectives before the United Nations in 1943.

The first of these is maintenance of the initiative won in the closing days of 1942, its extension to other theatres and an increase in those in which the Allies now hold the upper hand.

Second, the dispatch of all possible aid to the Russian offensive must be maintained with the double objective of whittling down German manpower and continuing the attrition of German munitions and material on the Russian front.

Third, Mr. Roosevelt called for assistance for the Chinese armies, now in their sixth year of war, with Japanese domination ended forever.

Both Leaders Satisfied

To gain these objectives the military and political leaders of the United Nations are determined to pool all their resources, military and economic, in 1943 to maintain the initiative wherever it is now held and to seek every opportunity to bring the enemy to battle on terms as unfavorable as those now prevailing in Tunisia.

Both leaders were extremely satisfied at the successful conclusion of the fourth meeting between them since the beginning of the war. Cooperation between the American and British Chiefs of Staff was described by Mr. Roosevelt as the closest possible, with the military leaders living together and working as personal friends more than as allies.

President Roosevelt predicted that the war would proceed according to schedule, with every indication that 1943 would be an even better year for the United Nations than 1942.

The conference, which probably made more important decisions than any other called by the United Nations, was held in a lush tropical setting in conditions of greatest secrecy. The President's villa was shaded by palm trees, with Bougainvillaea climbing on trellises around the house, and oranges nodding on trees in the yard. A swimming pool in the back yard had been turned into an air raid shelter, but no

German planes approached Casablanca during the conferences, and if any had come they would have been greeted by squadrons of British and United States fighter planes flying guard over the region.

Talks Closely Guarded

Many acres of the resort were enclosed in two lines of barbed wire, on which tin cans were hung. If any one had been foolhardy enough to approach these lines he would have been riddled by bullets from machine guns or bayoneted by some of the hundreds of American infantrymen who stood helmeted atop roofs or patrolled the shady walks around the area.

Both the President and the Prime Minister seemed confident and satisfied when they appeared at the noon press conference today. The President wore a worn gray suit and the Prime Minister was dapper in a gray pin-stripe suit topped by a somewhat battered gray Homburg hat. The sunshine winked in a jeweled "V" and an American Distinguished Service Order bar in his lapel buttonhole.

The two unmilitary-looking men, who lead half of the strongest coalition in history, were accompanied by General de Gaulle and General Giraud. For the benefit of camera men the two generals shook hands.

"A historic moment," President Roosevelt commented.

The sun beat fiercely on the group. Mr. Churchill asked the President, "Don't you want a hat?"

"I was born without a hat," Mr. Roosevelt replied.

While the President and the Prime Minister talked, guards silhouetted on near-by rooftops never relaxed their vigil and tight formations of fighters roared overhead.

Mr. Roosevelt revealed that the Allied victories in North Africa had made his fourth meeting with Mr. Churchill necessary. The situation had been reviewed in the meeting and plans made for the next steps in 1943, he said.

Both he and Mr. Churchill expressed deep regret for Premier Joseph Stalin's inability to leave the Russian offensive which he is directing personally, but emphasized that all the results of the conferences between the President, the Prime Minister and their Chiefs of Staff committees had been reported to the Soviet leader.

Mr. Churchill agreed with Mr. Roosevelt that the conference was unprecedented in history. Describing himself again as the President's ardent lieutenant, Mr. Churchill declared they worked together as partners and friends and described their cooperation as one of the sinews of war of the Allied powers.

The Prime Minister began to speak slowly, but gradually raised his voice as he described the frustration of the enemy by the men Adolf Hitler had called incompetents and drunkards. This brought a laugh. Mr. Churchill beamed.

The events in North Africa have altered the whole strategic aspect of the war, making the Germans and Italians fight under conditions of great difficulty, he declared. He described General Field Marshal Erwin Rommel as a fugitive from Libya and Egypt now trying to pass himself off as the liberator of Tunis. But he reminded the correspondents that General Sir Bernard

L. Montgomery was hot on Marshal Rommel's trail and that everywhere that Mary went the lamb was sure to go.

Purpose Is Unconquerable

Design, purpose and an unconquerable will lie behind all that is being done by Britain and America, the Prime Minister said solemnly. These will be applied to enforce unconditional surrender upon the criminals who plunged the world into the war, he concluded.

Both the President and Mr. Churchill seemed hopeful on the results of the de Gaulle-Giraud meeting, in which the two French leaders found themselves in "entire agreement" on the end to be achieved, which is the liberation of France and defeat of the enemy. Yet although a joint communiqué issued by the two generals said this could be achieved only by union in war on all Frenchmen fighting side by side. It gave no clue as to how the present difficulty in the North African political situation is to be adjusted.

It is felt, however, that the conference between the generals and their talks with Mr. Churchill and Mr. Roosevelt has cleared the way for an agreement of some sort between Generals Giraud and de Gaulle on the political aspects of their crusade for the liberation of France. The mere fact that they were seen talking together and were photographed shaking hands should do much to unite the French all over North Africa and to emphasize that a union of General de Gaulle's followers with the other factions must be carried out swiftly if the French are to bulk large in the United Nations' war plans.

First Flight of President

Mr. Roosevelt, the first President to leave the United States in wartime, became the first to inspect United States troops in the field since Abraham Lincoln when he reviewed armored and infantry units in a day snatched from the long series of arduous conferences. Riding in a jeep, the President inspected camps, talked with dozens of men and officers and ate "chow" with the soldiers.

"We had a darn good lunch," he said. "I wish the people back home could see the troops and their equipment. They have the most modern weapons we can turn out. The men are in good health and high spirits and I found the officers and men most efficient. Their morale is splendid and I know they will keep it up. Tell the folks back home that I am mighty proud of them."

The President visited Port Lyautey, scene of heavy fighting during the American landing, and placed wreaths on the graves of American and French soldiers buried there. He also directed that a wreath be placed on the grave of Edward Baudry, Canadian Broadcasting Company war correspondent, who was killed by a Spanish anti-aircraft bullet on a flight to cover the conference.

Among the happy features of his visit were talks the President had while here with two of his sons, Lieut. Col. Elliott Roosevelt, who is with the Allied Air Force, and Lieutenant Franklin D. Roosevelt Jr., who is on duty with the Navy.

Mr. Roosevelt had one other break from the conferences. This came when he dined with the Sultan of Morocco, Sidi Mohammed, at "a delightful party." According to the President, they got along extremely well and he found the Sultan deeply interested in the welfare of his people.

The President flew to Africa in two aircraft, switching from one to the other at a point on the journey. It was his first flight since his historic trip from Albany to Chicago in 1932 when he accepted the presidential nomination. He was accompanied by Mr. Hopkins on the flight, the first ever made by a President of the United States.

[The President flew by Chopper to a point in North Africa, then changed to a four-motored bomber especially fitted for comfort, The United Press reported.]

Service Chiefs in Talks

The United States Chiefs of Staff, General George C. Marshall of the Army, Admiral Ernest J. King of the Navy and Lieut. Gen. Henry H. Arnold of the Air Forces, preceded the President and already had begun conferences with their British "opposite numbers," General Sir Alan Brooke, Chief of the Imperial General Staff, Admiral Sir Dudley Pound, Chief of the Naval Staff, and Air Chief Marshal Sir Charles F. A. Portal, Chief of the Air Staff, when the rest of the party arrived. W. Averell Harriman, United States Lend-Lease Expediter, joined the conference from London.

The Chiefs of Staff were assisted by Lieut. Gen. Brehon B. Somervell, chief of the United States Services of Supply; Field Marshal Sir John Dill, chairman of the British military mission to the United States; Lord Louis Mountbatten, chief of the operational command, and Lieut. Gen. Sir Hastings Ismay, Chief of Staff to Mr. Churchill as Defense Minister.

Conferences took place two or three times daily, with constant reports going to the President and the Prime Minister.

The Prime Minister, who arrived first at the rendezvous, was accompanied by Lord Leathers British Minister of War Transport. The President had just settled in his spacious white villa when Mr. Hopkins ushered in Mr. Churchill and the first of their many conferences began. It lasted through dinner and continued until 3 o'clock the next morning.

The Chiefs of Staff, the President and the Prime Minister conferred with Allied military and political leaders from all over the African theatres. Lieut. Gen. Dwight D. Eisenhower, commander of Allied operations; his deputy, Lieut. Gen. Mark W. Clark, and General Sir Harold R. L. G. Alexander, Commander in Chief of the Middle East forces, represented the ground troops. Admiral of the Elect Sir Andrew Browne Cunningham, Allied naval Commander in Chief in North Africa, gave the naval views on what Mr. Churchill described as the great events impending, while Major Gen. Carl A. Spaatz, chief of Allied air operations, Air Marshal Sir Arthur William Tedder, vice chief of the air staff, and Lieut. Gen. Frank M. Andrews, United States Middle East commander, discussed the air situation.

Not the least interesting of these conferences were those between Mr. Churchill, Mr. Roosevelt, Harold Macmillan, British Resident Minister in North Africa and Robert D. Murphy, civil affairs officer on General Eisenhower's staff, in which the tangled political situation was reviewed.

It is impossible to assess the value of the conference as yet, but it may be said that its close probably heralded the end of the long lull in Tunisia. Both Mr. Churchill and Mr. Roosevelt give every indication that the Allies' watchword is "get on with the job." The Casablanca "unconditional surrender" conference was a directors' meeting of one-half of the mighty coalition now definitely on the offensive.

Two chief results of the conference appear to be, first, full admission that the Allies intend to press home the present strategic advantage during their campaigns in 1943, and, second, the fact that Generals de Gaulle and Giraud have been brought together in a meeting that, if barren of definite political agreement at least showed France and French North Africa that they have agreed in principle and are ready to work together.

The President's use of General Grant's famous defy "unconditional surrender" gives the key to the Allies political strategy in the closing months of the war and indicates that, although many may be shown to the Axis peoples, none will be shown to their leaders.

This warning should do much to hush the German propaganda that claims that events in North Africa show that the Allies have been willing to cooperate with "Quislings" here and may be expected to do so again when the Continent is invaded.

There is no doubt that the conference was the most important of the four held by the two leaders, for this time they were not occupied by expedients to gain time or hold the enemy in check, but to fashion a crushing offensive against the Axis.

Although the meeting took place in Africa, it is unwise to believe that the Mediterranean is the only war theatre that will figure largely in the war news in the next six months. Every front was reviewed and discussed in the conferences and plans were made for new operations, and above all for maintenance of the precious initiative.

* * *

January 27, 1943

THE OFFICIAL COMMUNIQUE

By The Associated Press

CASABLANCA, French Morocco, Jan. 26—Following is the text of the official communiqué on the conference of President Roosevelt and Prime Minister Churchill:

The President of the United States and the Prime Minister of Great Britain have been in conference near Casablanca since Jan. 14.

They were accompanied by the combined Chiefs of Staff of the two countries; namely,

FOR THE UNITED STATES:

General George C. Marshall, Chief of Staff of the United States Army; Admiral Ernest J. King, Commander in Chief of the United States Navy; Lieut. Gen. H. H. Arnold, commanding the United States Army Air Forces, and

FOR GREAT BRITAIN:

Admiral of the Fleet Sir Dudley Pound, First Sea Lord; General Sir Alan Brooke, Chief of the Imperial General Staff, and Air Chief Marshal Sir Charles Portal, Chief of the Air Staff.

These were assisted by:

Lieut. Gen. B. B. Somervell, Commanding General of the Services of Supply, United States Army; Field Marshal Sir John Dill, head of the British Joint Staff Mission in Washington; Vice Admiral Lord Louis Mountbatten, Chief of Combined Operations; Lieut. Gen. Sir Hastings Ismay, Chief of Staff to the Office of the Minister of Defense, together with a number of staff officers of both countries.

They have received visits from Mr. Murphy [Robert Murphy, United States Minister in French North Africa] and Mr. Macmillan [Harold Macmillan, British Resident Minister for Allied Headquarters in North Africa]; from Lieut. Gen. Dwight D. Eisenhower, Commander in Chief of the Allied Expeditionary Force in North Africa; from Admiral of the Fleet Sir Andrew Cunningham, naval commander of the Allied Expeditionary Force in North Africa; from Major Gen. Carl Spaatz, air commander of the Allied Expeditionary Force in North Africa; from Lieut. Gen. Mark W. Clark, United States Army [commander of the United States Fifth Army in Tunisia], and, from Middle East Headquarters, from General Sir Harold Alexander, Air Chief Marshal Sir Arthur Tedder and Lieut. Gen. F. M. Andrews, United States Army.

The President was accompanied by Harry Hopkins [chairman of the British-American Munitions Assignment Board] and was joined by W. Averell Harriman [United States defense expediter in England].

With the Prime Minister was Lord Leathers, British Minister of War Transport.

For ten days the combined staffs have been in constant session, meeting two or three times a day and recording progress at intervals to the President and Prime Minister.

The entire field of the war was surveyed theatre by theatre throughout the world, and all resources were marshaled for a more intense prosecution of the war by sea, land, and air.

Nothing like this prolonged discussion between two allies has ever taken place before. Complete agreement was reached between the leaders of the two countries and their respective staffs upon war plans and enterprises to be undertaken during the campaigns of 1943 against Germany, Italy and Japan with a view to drawing the utmost advantage from the markedly favorable turn of events at the close of 1942.

Premier Stalin was cordially invited to meet the President and Prime Minister, in which case the meeting would have been held very much farther to the east. He was unable to leave Russia at this time on account of the great offensive which he himself, as Commander in Chief, is directing.

The President and Prime Minister realized up to the full the enormous weight of the war which Russia is successfully bearing along her whole land front, and their prime object has been to draw as much weight as possible off the Russian armies by engaging the enemy as heavily as possible at the best selected points.

Premier Stalin has been fully informed of the military proposals.

The President and Prime Minister have been in communication with Generalissimo Chiang Kai-shek. They have apprised him of the measures which they are undertaking to assist him in China's magnificent and unrelaxing struggle for the common cause.

The occasion of the meeting between the President and Prime Minister made it opportune to invite General Giraud [General Henri Honoré Giraud, High Commissioner of French Africa] to confer with the Combined Chiefs of Staff and to arrange for a meeting between him and General de Gaulle [General Charles de Gaulle, Fighting French Commander]. The two generals have been in close consultation.

The President and Prime Minister and their combined staffs, having completed their plans for the offensive campaigns of 1943, have now separated in order to put them into active and concerted execution.

* * *

April 17, 1943

POLES ASK INQUIRY IN SOVIET 'MURDERS'

List 15,000 Prisoners Missing After Nazis Charge Discovery of 10,000 Bodies in Graves

RED CROSS IS SUGGESTED

Spokesman Says Russia Has Thwarted All Efforts to Obtain Information

---

Wireless to The New York Times.

LONDON, April 16—Following German reports of the discovery of the corpses of 10,000 Polish officers who were Soviet war prisoners massacred by the Russians near Smolensk in 1940—the Polish War Minister, Lieut. Gen. Marjan Kukiel stated tonight that the Polish Government had suggested an impartial investigation by a Red Cross commission on the spot.

The Polish communiqué stated that Red Star, the official organ of the Red Army, reported on the first anniversary of the Russian invasion of Poland that 10,000 officers had been taken prisoner among the 181,000 prisoners.

According to the information of the Polish Government three prisoner camps were set up—at Kozielsk, east of Smolensk, with 4,500 officers; at Starobyelsk, near Kharkov, with 3,800 men, and at Ostashkovo, near Kalinin, with 380 officers.

At the beginning of 1940 the Soviet authorities informed the prisoners that they were able to return to their families in Poland. Sixty to three hundred men were allowed daily to proceed west toward Smolensk. Starting in April, 1940, the camps were gradually liquidated and in June 400 men were deported to Griazoviec in Central Russia.

With the conclusion of the Polish-Soviet pact of July, 1941, the Polish Government claimed these officers for the Polish Army formed on Russian territory. At the end of August a group of officers arrived from Griazoviec, but none of the others appeared. In other words, 8,300 officers, 7,000 noncommissioned officers and privates could not be found.

Pleas Reported Ignored

Polish Ambassador Stanislaw Kot repeated the request, but it remained unanswered. Premier Wladyslaw Sikorski, during the Moscow visit of December, 1941, asked Premier Joseph Stalin personally what had happened to the officers and received the answer that they would be released.

Lists of all the officers were presented to the Soviet Government, but none of the officers listed was sent to the Polish Army. Nearly 15,000 men simply disappeared.

Polish circles here insist that in order to counteract German propaganda aimed at sowing distrust, the Allies and Russia allow an impartial mission to fully investigate the disquieting affair.

The Berlin radio in broadcast heard in London tonight announced that the German Government had invited international Red Cross officials to inspect the mass graves at Katyn in the Smolensk area.

List 2,000,000 Hostages Held

WASHINGTON, April 16 (U.P.)—The National Catholic Welfare Conference charged today that Russia is holding 2,000,000 Poles "as virtual hostages" in an attempt to force the Polish Government to agree to Soviet claims on prewar Polish territory.

A report by the conference's news service said Russia was engaged in "a campaign to coerce the government of Poland into recognizing Russian sovereignty over territories of Eastern Poland seized by Russia during the German-Russian invasion in 1939 and 1940."

Recently the Soviet Government decreed that all Poles deported to Russia after the invasion are to be considered Russian citizens, the report said, adding that Russia had "resorted to the disruption of Polish relief activities and to the confiscation of relief supplies sent to the unfortunate Polish people in Russia from the United States."

* * *

December 4, 1943

ROOSEVELT, STALIN, CHURCHILL AGREE ON PLANS FOR WAR ON GERMANY IN TALKS AT TEHERAN

DECISIONS VARIED

Moscow Radio Asserts Political Problems Were Settled

PARLEY NOW IS OVER

Axis Reports Predict an Appeal to Germans to Quit Hitler

By JAMES B. RESTON
By Cable to The New York Times.

LONDON, Saturday, Dec. 4—The Moscow radio announced early this morning that President Roosevelt, prime Minister Churchill and Premier Stalin had met in Teheran, Iran, "a few days ago" to discuss questions relating to the war and the post-war period. "A few days ago," the Moscow radio said shortly after midnight, "a conference of the leaders of the three Allied nations—President Roosevelt, Prime Minister Churchill and Premier Stalin—took place at Teheran.

"Military and diplomatic representatives also took part. The questions discussed at the conference related to the war against Germany and also to a range of political questions. Decisions were taken which will be published later."

[An Associated Press dispatch from London quoted the Soviet monitor as saying that full details of the conference might be announced between noon and 2 P. M., Eastern war time today, basing this prediction on the usual routine of the Moscow radio when announcing future broadcasts.]

The radio announcement, which came as a surprise to official quarters in London, said nothing about the present location of Mr. Roosevelt and Mr. Churchill, who held a five-day meeting with Generalissimo Chiang Kai-shek last week and made plans for the defeat of the Japanese and the dismemberment of their empire.

Details Are Awaited

Early this morning the Moscow radio had not indicated the nature of political and military discussions that took place in the Iranian capital, but it was generally assumed they dealt with the coordination of military plans for the final assault on Hitlerite Germany and with the unification of political plans for making peace with Germany on the basis of "unconditional surrender."

Official information that has come back to London since the Prime Minister left the capital has been extremely limited and indeed until the Moscow radio made its announcement the German radio was the main source of reports on the movements of the three leaders. It was, however, generally expected in London that the three leaders would in the course of their discussions decide to appeal to the German people over the heads of their Government to surrender or take the consequences of the air war in the west and an invasion of Russian armies from the east.

Stalin Crosses Own Border

While Mr. Churchill and Mr. Roosevelt had had seven previous conferences on the war, this was the first among the three leaders, and so far as is known it marked the first time that Mr. Stalin had left the Soviet Union since the revolution in 1917. The meeting was foreshadowed after the Quebec conference when Mr. Churchill told the House of Commons he "hoped" to meet with Mr. Roosevelt and Mr. Stalin before the first of the year.

The Prime Minister had met Premier Stalin once before in the autumn of 1942, when he journeyed to Moscow to explain to him why it was impossible for the United States and Britain to invade the continent of Europe from the west that year.

Previous to that conference the United States and Britain had undertaken to concern themselves with the "urgent tasks" of creating a second front in 1942, and it is now known that the first Stalin-Churchill meeting was unsatisfactory to Mr. Stalin for military reasons. There are reasons for believing, however, that in Teheran very little if anything remained to be settled on the question of the second front except perhaps that of coordination of attacks on Germany from the east and west.

In addition to the coordination of military plans for a decisive phase of the war in Europe, it is generally believed by observers in London that the Teheran agenda covered a variety of questions that were either discussed briefly or shelved entirely by Secretary of State Cordell Hull, British Foreign Minister Anthony Eden and Foreign Commissar Vyachesalaff M. Molotoff when they met in Moscow last month.

Among the first of these questions was the status of the Polish Government, with which Premier Stalin broke diplomatic relations early this year. Since Britain went to war with Germany under the terms of the treaty alliance with Poland and since the Russian armies in their great westward sweep are now approaching the former Russo-Polish frontier, the Governments of both the United States and Britain have been hopeful that this Russo-Polish breach might be repaired.

Premier Stalin has already stated in a letter to The New York Times that he wished to see a "strong, independent Poland," and efforts have been made by London to try to get Mr. Stalin not only to renew diplomatic relations with Poland but, it is believed, to make Poland a party to the Russo-Czech twenty-year treaty alliance that will be signed within a few days.

It is assumed that the long-range question of the future Germany also was on the Teheran agenda for discussion and the question naturally arises as to whether the principle of "punishing" the aggressor would be applied to Germany as severely as it was applied to Japan in the Cairo declaration.

Whatever else the Allies may have agreed to coordinate at Teheran they did not coordinate their announcements about the fact that meetings were being held. The fact that the meetings were imminent was reported first in American newspapers. The fact that the North African conference with Generalissimo Chiang Kai-shek had ended was reported prematurely by a Reuter correspondent in Lisbon. Senator Tom Connally, chairman of the Senate Foreign Relations Committee, shared with the German radio the honor of "breaking" prematurely the fact that Mr. Stalin, Mr. Roosevelt and Mr. Churchill were in session and now this morning the Moscow radio, without pre-arrangement with London and Washington, announced that the conference had ended. Thus everybody "scooped" everybody else, which makes everybody even, although it makes nobody happy.

Axis Voices Concern

Before the Moscow broadcast today Axis sources continued to voice apprehension over the results of the parley.

Typical of their laborious attempts to anticipate the official announcements of the conference was the following comment in the Angriff:

"It seems that we are again to be asked to capitulate as a favor to the enemy. But we will again turn a deaf ear to this friendly invitation. The war criminals could have saved themselves a long trip."

The German telegraph service, picking up this same theme, which is general in the German press and radio, said "the [Allied] discussions are expected to result in a kind of ultimatum for the capitulation of the German people and its allies. The German people, however, know that their enemies try to hide their own weakness and difficulties behind every new propaganda bluff. This war of nerves is the enemy's last resort.

"The Russian drive has failed, the Allies have been unable to produce more than a slow-motion offensive in Italy, and the bombing in the west has failed to undermine either German morale or German production."

Elsewhere in the German press, however, correspondents do not support this official bravado. A remarkable article in Wednesday's Voelkisher Beobachter, for example, complains bitterly:

"Those people who spoke with deep sympathy about the people of bombed London have nothing else to say about bombed Berlin except, 'Well, you started it. Remember Warsaw, Rotterdam, London and Coventry? What you are now getting is only what you deserve.'"

Similarly Axis satellites are not either dismissing the "Big Three" conference lightly or attempting to speak like Germans of "the trumpets of Jericho which will leave the walls unmoved." They are admitting openly that the conference will have "great significance" no matter what it does.

* * *

June 6, 1944

ALLIED ARMIES LAND IN FRANCE IN THE HAVRE-CHERBOURG AREA; GREAT INVASION IS UNDER WAY

EISENHOWER ACTS

U.S., British, Canadian Troops Backed by Sea, Air Forces

MONTGOMERY LEADS

Nazis Say Their Shock Units Are Battling Our Parachutists

COMMUNIQUE NO. 1 ON ALLIED INVASION

By Broadcast to The New York Times.
LONDON, Tuesday, June 6—The Supreme Headquarters of the Allied Expeditionary Force issued this communiqué this morning:

"Under the command of General Eisenhower, Allied naval forces, supported by strong air forces, began landing Allied armies this morning on the northern coast of France."

By RAYMOND DANIELL
By Cable to The New York Times.
SUPREME HEADQUARTERS ALLIED EXPEDITIONARY FORCES, Tuesday, June 6—The invasion of Europe from the west has begun.

In the gray light of a summer dawn Gen. Dwight D. Eisenhower threw his great Anglo-American force into action today for the liberation of the Continent. The spearhead of attack was an Army group commanded by Gen. Sir Bernard L. Montgomery and comprising troops of the United States, Britain and Canada.

General Eisenhower's first communiqué was terse and calculated to give little information to the enemy. It said merely that "Allied naval forces supported by strong air forces began landing Allied armies this morning on the northern coast of France."

After the first communiqué was released it was announced that the Allied landing was in Normandy.

Caen Battle Reported

German broadcasts, beginning at 6:30 A. M., London time, [12:30 A. M. Eastern war time] gave first word of the assault. [The Associated Press said General Eisenhower, for the sake of surprise, deliberately let the Germans have the "first word."]

The German DNB agency said the Allied invasion operations began with the landing of airborne troops in the area of the mouth of the Seine River.

[Berlin said the "center of gravity" of the fierce fighting was at Caen, thirty miles southwest of Havre and sixty-five miles southeast of Cherbourg, The Associated Press reported. Caen is ten miles inland from the sea, at the base of the seventy-five-mile-wide Normandy Peninsula, and fighting there might indicate the Allies' seizing of a beachhead.]

[DNB said in a broadcast just before 10 A. M. (4 A. M.

Eastern war time) that the Anglo-American troops had been reinforced at dawn at the mouth of the Seine River in the Havre area.]

[An Allied correspondent broadcasting from Supreme Headquarters, according to the Columbia Broadcasting System, said this morning that "German tanks are moving up the roads toward the beachhead" in France.]

The German accounts told of Nazi shock troops thrown in to meet Allied airborne units and parachutists. The first attacks ranged from Cherbourg to Havre, the Germans said.

[United States battleships and planes took part in the bombardment of the French coast, Allied Headquarters announced, according to Reuter.]

The weather was not particularly favorable for the Allies. There was a heavy chop in the Channel and the skies were overcast. Whether the enemy was taken by surprise was not known yet.

Eisenhower's Orders to Troops

Not until the attack began was it made known officially that General Montgomery was in command of the Army group, including American troops. The hero of El Alamein hitherto had been referred to as the senior British Field Commander.

In his order of the day, made public at the same time as the first communiqué, General Eisenhower told his forces that they were about to embark on a "great crusade."

The eyes of the world are upon you, he said, and the "hopes and prayers of liberty-loving people everywhere march with you." The order, which reflected a full appreciation of the mighty task ahead and yet reflected the calm, sober confidence that permeates these headquarters, was distributed to assault elements after their embarkation. It was read by the commanders to all other troops in the Allied Expeditionary Force.

The news that has been so long and so eagerly awaited broke as war-weary Londoners were going to work. Hardly any of them knew what was happening, for there had been no disclosure of the news that the invasion had started in the British Broadcasting Corporation's 7 o'clock broadcast.

Even the masses of planes roaring overhead did not give the secret away, for the people of this country have grown accustomed to seeing huge armadas of aircraft flying out in their almost daily attacks against German-held Europe.

Details of how the assault developed are still lacking. It is known that the huge armada of Allied landing craft that crept to the French coast in darkness was preceded by mine sweepers whose task was to sweep the Channel of German mine fields and submarine obstructions.

Big Allied warships closed in and engaged the enemy's shore batteries.

Airborne troops landed simultaneously behind the Nazis' coast defenses.

Triphibious Strategy

Not only were the troops of the United States, Canada and Britain united in a single fighting team, but their huge land, sea and air forces operated as a perfectly integrated machine.

Today provided the first example in northwest Europe of "triphibious strategy" in which Navy and Air Forces first help the Army gain a foothold on enemy territory as the Army goes about the grim business of seizing airports and harbors for development of the attack.

Soon after his first communiqué and order of the day were published General Eisenhower broadcast a message to the underground movement of Europe, warning its members to stand fast and continue passive resistance but not to endanger lives "until I give you the signal to rise and strike the enemy."

In the coastal area where the Allies have landed little help is expected at the outset from French patriots because the Germans have been at pains to remove from there all but old men, women and children.

However, there was indication in General Eisenhower's broadcast that the Army of France would fight under the United Nations banner, for he said:

"Citizens of France, I am proud to have again under my command the armed forces of France."

Announcement of the great "triphibious" attack was undramatic in its setting. Correspondents assigned to the Supreme Allied Headquarters were summoned by telephone just as the official German news agency, DNB, was broadcasting the fact that the invasion had begun. To maintain the initiative in battle it was necessary to surrender the initiative in the war of words.

In a room, the walls of which were plastered with maps, the correspondents gathered at pine tables and listened to officers lay down the law on censorship and fill in the background of the manner in which the soldiers of Britain and America and all fighting services of the countries had been welded into one fighting unit.

Nazi Reports of Action

German broadcasts at 9 o'clock, London time, said:

"Combined landing operations of the Anglo-Americans, which were launched both from sea and air against the European west coast early today, extended over the whole coastal sector between Havre and Cherbourg.

"The main centers of air landing attacks are in the whole of Normandy as well as at the most important river mouths in the Seine Bight. Amphibious operations on a large scale were simultaneously begun between the Seine estuary and the mouth of Vire River, thirty miles south of Cherbourg.

"In addition to the numerous landing craft of various types, light naval craft of the Allies are being employed in considerable numbers," the Germans went on.

"Off the Seine estuary six heavy naval units and twenty destroyers were made out.

"German coastal batteries engaged (Allied) naval craft off shore.

"Considerable parts of the parachute formations that had to carry out the initial attack on western Europe against massed defense at the river mouth and near most important airfields on Normandy Peninsula already have been wiped out.

"According to preliminary reports the First British Parachute Division may already be considered badly mauled."

* * *

July 22, 1944

MONETARY PARLEY AGREES ON TERMS OF WORLD BANK

By RUSSELL PORTER
Special to The New York Times.

BRETTON WOODS, N. H., July 21—The United Nations Monetary and Financial Conference reached an agreement today on a plan for an $8,800,000,000 International Bank of Reconstruction and Development to guarantee post-war international investments. The total capital of the world bank is the same as the aggregate of the international monetary fund to stabilize currencies which was accepted last week. Thus two vital parts of the post-war program to try to insure world peace and prosperity have been accepted, with some reservations, by all the forty-four United and Associated Nations participating in the conference, subject to the approval of the Congress of the United States and the executive and legislative branches of other Governments.

In order to reach an agreement, the United States delegation had to abandon its position that the subscriptions to the bank, which represent each country's risks in guaranteeing international loans, should be the same as the quotas in the fund, which represent a country's rights to acquire foreign exchange with which to buy goods in the world market.

However, it is the opinion of the United States delegation, after receiving the advice of its four members of Congress, two Republicans and two Democrats, and its one banker member, Edward E. Brown, president of the First National Bank of Chicago, that the fund and bank agreements have been provided with sufficient safeguards for United States interests to warrant Congressional approval.

Fund Adoption Unanimous

Like the fund agreement, which the conference adopted yesterday, the bank agreement received a unanimous vote of acceptance, subject to general reservations by all the participating delegations to the effect that they were not "recommending" it but merely "submitting" it to their home Governments for approval or rejection.

The United States agreed to increase its subscription to the bank to $3,175,000,000, or $425,000,000 more than its $2,750,000,000 quota in the fund. Thus the American share of the risk will be more than 36 percent instead of one-third as proposed by our delegates when the Bretton Woods conference opened.

At that time the idea was to have a $9,000,000,000 bank for the forty-four participating nations, with about $1,000,000,000 reserved for enemy and neutral countries when they are admitted after the war. Roughly the same reserve is now envisaged, so that the ultimate capital of the bank should be about $9,800,000,000.

Only two other countries agreed to increase their bank subscriptions over their fund quotas. These were China, which went up from $550,000,000 to $600,000,000, and Canada, from $300,000,000 to $325,000,000.

Russia won her fight for a substantially smaller share in the Bank's risks than she received in the fund's benefits, which in her case are expected to be substantial in the rehabilitation of her war-devastated cities, factories and homes, whereas for most other countries which do not have her State-controlled economy the fund's principal functions are expected to be in the field of currency stabilization.

Russian Bank Subscription

The Russian subscription to the Bank is $900,000,000, or $300,000,000 less than her $1,200,000,000 quota in the fund.

During last week's controversy over the fund quotas, Russia won her demand to have her quota raised from $850,000,000 to $1,200,000,000.

Great Britain accepted a bank subscription of $1,300,000,000, the same as her fund quota. Thus she is the second largest risk—taken in the Bank, as well as the second largest contributor to the fund.

France agreed to a bank subscription of $450,000,000, the same as her fund quota. However, she still wants a larger quota in the fund, arguing that national prestige entitles her to a higher rating than Russia or China.

India agreed to a $400,000,000 bank subscription equal to her fund quota. The Netherlands did the same with $250,000,000.

Other countries which accepted the same bank subscriptions as fund quotas were Australia, Belgium, Czechoslovakia, Iceland, Liberia, Luxembourg, New Zealand, Norway, the Philippines, Poland and South Africa.

Twenty-six countries besides Russia won lower bank subscriptions than their fund quotas. They were Egypt, Ethiopia, Greece, Iran, Iraq, Yugoslavia and the nineteen Latin-American republics participating in the conference.

Latin-American Concession

The Latin-American group, led by Luis Machado, personal representative of President-elect Grau of Cuba, held a caucus preceding the final conference meeting on the bank and agreed to the United States' request for larger Latin-American subscriptions than the group had previously offered.

Originally, the Latin-American group said that it did not want to assume any substantial part of the risks of the bank and would not make anything but "token" subscriptions. Later, after getting the concession that "equitable" consideration would be given by the bank directors to loans for exploitation of the natural resources of undeveloped countries, it offered to subscribe 60 per cent of its fund quotas.

The Latin Americans agreed today to bank subscriptions averaging 70 per cent of their aggregate fund quotas. This meant a group increase of $40,000,000.

Mr. Machado said that the Latin American group did this in order to show its solidarity with the United States in post-war relations. He added that the Latin Americans realized that the bank would probably give priority to loans for reconstruction of devastated Europe, but nevertheless did not ask for any "quid pro quo" on behalf of those countries which want loans for industrialization and modernization of their agricultural plant.

Subscription Issues Backed

The bank plan was adopted by the conference at a closed plenary session after reports by special committees on subscriptions and other issues had been approved by the commission dealing with the bank.

Aside from the general reservations made by all delegations, Russia and Australia were the only countries which asked that specific reservations to the bank agreement be entered. The Russian delegation made a reservation that it would like a more specific pledge than the bank agreement contained to the effect that lower interest and commission rates would be fixed for loans for the restoration and reconstruction of war-devastated properties.

The Australian delegation said that its instructions from its home Government did not permit it to sign the agreement at this time.

The conference accepted the "conservative" one-to-one ratio of assets to guarantees, meaning that the bank cannot guarantee at any one time more than its capital assets available for that purpose.

Statement by Russians

Explaining the reasons for Russia's reservations and pledging his country's cooperation in this and future international conferences to establish post-war peace and prosperity, M. S. Stepanov, chairman of the Russian delegation, said:

"The Soviet Union, whose foreign trade is conducted by the state, will assume its proper place in the solution of these problems.

"Occupation by the Hitlerites and transformation of many democratic countries into battlefields has brought disaster to them. Among these countries the Soviet Union occupies a special position. The Hitlerite barbarians were especially ferocious in looting and plundering the temporarily occupied Soviet territories.

"Consequently industry and agriculture have been ruined over a considerable part of the U.S.S.R., and hundreds of cities and thousands of other populated places destroyed. The Hitlerite Huns have also caused very great damage to other countries. However, international economic collaboration between the freedom-loving peoples will help the liberated countries to restore and rebuild their economic structure.

"Like other forms of international collaboration, economic collaboration and particularly collaboration in monetary and financial spheres, requires mutual understanding, mutual respect for the interests of the participating nations and the sovereign rights of their States. The international monetary fund should in all its activity be guided by the above principles. The conference has prepared such provisions for the fund which would meet these sound requirements for effective international collaboration.

Import of Conference Cited

"The work of the conference has been successfully accomplished although we had to deal with many questions of a difficult nature. This conference will be regarded as one of the the important efforts of the United Nations to solve the post-war economic problems of the world.

"The delegation of the U.S.S.R. has made some reservations regarding the draft agreement on the fund which were mentioned by the reporting delegate. I have to state, of course, that the approval of the draft agreement at this conference, as has been indicated in the invitation of the Government of the United States to this conference, should not be regarded as approval of the draft in whole or in any of its parts on behalf of the U.S.S.R. Government.

"The U.S.S.R. delegation deems it its duty to submit the draft agreement on the fund prepared by this conference for the consideration of the U.S.S.R. Government, reserving the full right of the U.S.S.R. Government to make a free and independent study of the draft and to decide all questions connected therewith.

"Our conference, which aims to secure post-war international collaboration among freedom-loving peoples in monetary and financial spheres, is a new contribution to the mutual efforts of the United and Associated Nations which are destined to achieve our mutual goal, everlasting peace and world prosperity."

*   *   *

August 11, 1944

LONDON POLES SEEN FAILING IN MOSCOW

Mikolajczyk Hopeful of Later Accord,
but His Departure Is Viewed as Error

By W. H. LAWRENCE
By Wireless to The New York Times.

MOSCOW, Aug. 10—Premier Stanislaw Mikolajczyk and other representatives of the London Polish Government in exile left Moscow by plane for London early today to lay before M. Mikolajczyk's Cabinet the inconclusive results of their Moscow discussions with Premier Joseph Stalin, Foreign Commissar Vyachesloff M. Molotoff and the leaders of the new Polish Committee of National Liberation.

While M. Mikolajczyk, at an early morning press conference, appeared hopeful that he would soon return to Warsaw for further and final conferences with Polish Committee of Liberation representatives, some well-informed persons here thought the London Polish Government, which has missed a lot of buses, had just missed another.

This school of thought contended that M. Mikolajczyk should have exercised the broad grant of authority given to him by his Cabinet before his departure from London and continued the conversations here or in Poland until they had reached definite results and an agreement that M. Mikolajczyk could accept had been hammered out.

Rival Group Is Honored

As far as the Polish situation is concerned, the most significant item in this morning's Moscow newspapers was a communiqué relating the high honors given to the departing Lublin-bound Poles at the Soviet and Polish flag-draped Moscow airport yesterday morning, when a guard of honor stood at attention while a band played the national anthem of Poland and the Soviet Union.

This demonstration honored Boleslaw Berut, head of the National Council; Edward B. Osubka-Morawski, chairman, and Foreign Affairs Minister; Wincenty Witos, leader of the People's party; Col. Gen. Michal Rola-Zymierski, Director of National Defense, and other officials of the Polish Committee of Liberation, which by agreement has been entrusted with administering the Polish territory liberated by the Red and Polish armies. Andrei Vishinsky, Vice Commissar of Foreign Affairs, headed the Soviet delegation at the airport to see them off, and pictures of M. Berut and M. Osubka-Morawski appeared on the front pages of all papers today.

There has been no editorial comment in the Soviet press thus far on the negotiations between the London and Lublin groups of Poles, and the only reference to Mr. Mikolajczyk in today's press was a brief front-page announcement that he and his associates had "paid a farewell visit" last night to Marshal Stalin and Mr. Molotoff.

United States Ambassador W. Averell Harriman bade farewell to M. Mikolajczyk at the Soviet guest house just before the Premier went to the airport. There was no turnout of high Russian officials at the airport, since the two Governments have not maintained diplomatic relations for more than a year.

Poles in London Pessimistic

By Wireless to The New York Times.

LONDON, Aug. 10—Pessimism on the part of the Poles in London on the possibility of reaching a satisfactory agreement on Russo-Polish relations was apparent today, though official silence was being maintained on what some Poles here had no hesitation in describing as a "breakdown" in the Moscow negotiations.

The return of Premier Stanislaw Milolajczyk within a few days is expected and Polish officials are intent on maintaining their silence until he has had a chance to place before his Government the proposals discussed with the Soviet-sponsored Polish Committee of National Liberation.

The fact that M. Mikolajczyk failed to come to an agreement with Premier Stalin on this trip, although his mission possessed virtually unlimited authority from his Government, was viewed in unofficial Polish circles as an unhappy augury for the future. These sources said the only limitation of M. Mikolajczyk's authority in the Moscow talks was that he could not sign anything to deprive Poland on her independence. He would not have returned without an agreement, they added, unless this was the issue at stake.

These sources were admittedly none too hopeful for the success of the mission even before it began and they said that when the news of M. Mikolajczyk's first meeting with the Committee of National Liberation was announced they were sure it had failed. If Marshal Stalin and the Polish leader had seen eye to eye, they reasoned, there would have been no need for discussions with the committee's representatives.

M. Mikolajczyk went to Moscow prepared to offer some seats in the Polish Government to members of the Russian-backed committee. While there is no knowledge in London of the proposals the Premier is bringing back, one informed Pole said, "apparently the committee has made a similar offer and is willing to accept some Poles here in a government formed by the committee."

Underground Chief Honored

An official decree appointing Tomasz Arciszewski, 60-year-old Socialist leader who arrived in London only two weeks ago, as President-designate of Poland, was published in the official Polish Gazette today.

The bearded patriarch of the Polish Socialist party was active in the underground until he left Warsaw on July 18 after his nomination as President-designate by the Polish Council of National Unity, the underground Polish Parliament.

The Gazette also contained letters from President Wladislaw Raczkiewicz to Gen. Kazimierz Sosnkowski, confirming the Polish Government's decision to relieve him of his post as President-designate, to which he was named by President Raczkiewicz in Paris after the fall of Poland. General Sosnkowski also has been Commander in Chief of Polish armed forces since the death of Gen. Wladislaw Sikorski and it was decided some months ago that the President-designate should not hold either an Army or a Government post.

Held Not a Post-War Question

Special to The New York Times.

WASHINGTON, Aug. 10—The Polish question that has been under discussion in Moscow is regarded here as a current political problem that will have no place in the forthcoming exploratory conversations here on a security organization for the post-war world, Edward R. Stettinius Jr., Acting Secretary of State, said at a press conference today.

The security conference, he explained, is designed to plan for an instrument that will deal with future conflicts.

Mr. Stettinius spoke in response to questions, which also elicited the information that the question of borders is not expected to arise in the exploratory conversations either.

Asked about the problem of the military occupation of Germany, Mr. Stettinius pointed out that that would be dealt with by Secretary of State Cordell Hull, our army authorities and the European Advisory Commission.

He could throw no light on the discussions between the Soviet Government and the Polish Government in Exile, as official reports have not yet been received from Ambassador W. Averell Harriman on the conversations of the last few days. Mr. Harriman has reported to the department since the negotiations began, but official communications require some time in transmission from Moscow.

In general, Mr. Harriman was hopeful of the success of these negotiations.

* * *

August 11, 1944

POLES IN WARSAW APPEAL FOR HELP

Underground Forces Say They Face Extermination if Aid Is Not Sent Speedily

LONDON, Aug. 10 (U.P.)—Polish underground troops fighting the Germans in Warsaw issued a desperate appeal for help today and said they faced "total extermination" unless immediate and large-scale aid was received.

The daily communiqué received from Warsaw by Polish headquarters here said General Bor's patriots had been forced to evacuate the west-central district of Wola and Theatre Square, in the heart of the city, after heavy fighting. Polish authorities here were alarmed and feared that Bor's men would be forced to retreat into a trap where they would be cut to pieces by superior forces of Germans.

A German military spokesman in Berlin, according to a Transocean agency broadcast, admitted for the first time that Bor's forces had "initially scored a number of successes in an uprising attempt," but claimed the Polish capital "again is firmly in German hands."

The German spokesman said a radio SOS message from General Bor to Soviet forces outside Warsaw had "led to no result."

A two-star Polish staff officer here said he believed General Bor was now making a "last hopeless stand."

Poles' Plight Is Desperate

After reporting the loss of the Wola and Theatre Square areas, General Bor's communiqué said the German advance in the Bielany district of northwest Warsaw had been "temporarily held" but indicated his forces would not be able to hold out much longer. He has reported them as short of arms and ammunition since the underground campaign against the Germans opened on Aug. 1.

In a new message to Premier Stanislaw Mikolajczyk, General Kazimierz Sosnkowski and other members of the Polish Government-in-Exile here, General Bor said:

"For nine days heavy fighting for the liberation of Warsaw has been going on. The heroism of the Polish home army and the gallantry of the Warsaw population have been unsurpassed up to now. In this heroic effort to free our capital we have been left to our own fate. This is felt more keenly because since our struggle started Soviet and German forces have been deadlocked on the eastern outskirts of Warsaw.

"If our bloody efforts shall not be in vain, if the soldiers and population shall be permitted to live on, if our forces and the civilians can be saved from total extermination, immediate help must be sent by supplying us with ammunition and weapons on a large scale and by bombarding the enemy positions. This appeal is urgent. That is what the people of Warsaw and all Poland firmly insist upon."

Red Paper Sees a Bluff

MOSCOW, Aug. 10 (U.P.)—The first press reference to the insurrection in Warsaw was contained in today's Soviet newspapers in a dispatch datelined London and quoting The Daily Worker. It said:

"Tales about battles in Warsaw, in the opinion of certain circles, are a bluff intended to achieve a two-fold aim: First, should Warsaw be liberated in the next few days, the London reactionaries will hold that they, and not the Red Army, were responsible for the liberation; second, should final liberation be delayed some time, they will shout that the Red Army abandoned the Polish underground army to its fate when the latter tried to achieve collaboration."

* * *

December 3, 1944

MOSCOW REVEALS MORE OF ITS FOREIGN POLICY

France, Represented by De Gaulle,
Is To Figure in New European Line-Up

By RAYMOND DANIELL
By Wireless to The New York Times.

LONDON, Dec. 2—Gen. Charles de Gaulle has gone to the Kremlin at Premier Stalin's invitation. No doubt he will take the opportunity of finding out at first hand how far France can go with her western neighbors without offending the Russians, who have shown a not surprising degree of hypersensitivity about the formation of a so-called "western bloc," which the British are busily fostering on the fringe of Europe nearest them.

Prime Minister Churchill's trip to Paris was interpreted as a symbolic resurgence of the Entente Cordiale. That was the underlying meaning of his expressions of friendship for France, his faith in her future and of the admission of France to the European Advisory Council. All this was gratifying enough to the French after the frustrations of the past four years, but to have it followed by an invitation to their national leader to go to Moscow to talk things over was gratifying, to say the least, because it was a tangible proof to the cold, hungry and confused people that high-sounding

phrases about the return of France to her place as a great power might really mean something.

Tragic Lesson for France

For France has learned the tragic lesson that has been driven into the minds of Frenchmen twice in one generation: once, in 1917, when Russian resistance collapsed and France almost succumbed to the weight of German arms suddenly freed to be hurled against her, and again in 1940, when, after the failure of the western powers to reach an agreement with Russia, France found herself helpless against a Germany that, for the moment, was secure militarily in the East.

There is a strong possibility, therefore, that French foreign policy will return to the twin pillars upon which it rested prior to 1914. Georges Bidault, French Foreign Minister, who accompanied General de Gaulle to Moscow, said in a recent interview:

"France's understanding of Russia's conceptions and her spiritual and geographical proximity to the Anglo-Saxon countries have put her into a position in which she could usefully contribute to reducing the possibilities of friction between the east and the west. France, therefore, must look toward her friends in the west as well as in the east."

In view of the anxieties caused in this country by exaggerated reports of the power and influence of the French Communist party in that liberated country, these words, if not the sequence of ideals, found a ready welcome.

But it remains to be seen whether Moscow will be as receptive to the idea of a Franco-British alliance as the British are to a restoration of the traditional relations of France and Russia. The recent propaganda line from Moscow has tended to indicate that, while the Russians approve of regionalism in eastern Europe, they regard it as a manifestation of capitalist sin in the west.

British Views in Diplomacy

In that, Russians, in the British view, are not very different from their American allies. Recent expressions in the United States, where Pan-American unity has for a long time been a cardinal part of American policy, have indicated a tendency toward the belief that all great powers ought to enter a world organization without tails to their kites.

But this war has made Great Britain especially conscious of her size in relation to her partners in the grand alliance. Naturally, this country wants to augment its own voice in the councils of the nations, and it is coming to the conclusion that even though it speaks for its whole scattered empire, which is by no means assured, there will be an inequality in the concentration of power among them at any given place.

In the nineteenth century Pax Britannica served as an antidote to war because of this nation's unchallengeable sea power. It had a mighty fleet and it had impregnable bases from which that fleet could operate, but it could prevent aggression only where it straddled a potential enemy's lines of communication.

Air power, rockets, buzz-bombs and the blitzkrieg technique have taught the British that there is no security for them on their island once war breaks out on the Continent, and they are looking for allies near home, the establishment of bases on the Continent, the mobilization of an unchallengeable force on the side of law and order—their side—to make war unattractive to a potential aggressor.

A Quest for Allies

To put it bluntly, the British are willing that Russia should be top dog in eastern Europe provided they are permitted to occupy a similar role in the west. In attempting to establish a close economic and military alliance with Belgium, the Netherlands and France, they hold that they are organizing a "cordon sanitaire" against a resurgent Nazi Germany, just as the Russians by their treaty with Czechoslovakia and their insistence upon a friendly government in Poland are protecting themselves against future German aggression.

Moscow's objections to a British alliance with the small powers of western Europe seem especially unrealistic to the people here in the light of the attitude of the Soviet Union toward its own neighbors.

The Russians have made their own deal with Eduard Benes of Czechoslovakia and the British have accepted it as a private contract within the scope of their own twenty-year treaty of friendship with the Soviet Union, and they are willing to accept it within the framework of the world organization as it was envisaged at Dumbarton Oaks.

The absorption of the Baltic States and the partition of Poland were not at first easy for the average man to swallow, although the Government recognized their inevitability. The recent behavior of Poland's exiles in London, however, has made it somewhat easier for the ordinary Englishman to accept the idea that Russian demands are reasonable and the attitude of the exiled Government untenable.

For a long time the rift between Poland and Russia was a source of grave embarrassment to Britain, but the shelving of former Premier Stanislaw Mikolajczyk, who in the minds of the public here stood for reconciliation with the Soviet Union, has alienated public opinion from the exiled Government. The general feeling here now is that the London Government of Premier Tomasz Arciszewski has little chance of surviving and that its members have an even smaller chance of playing any effective part in shaping Poland's future.

When the Polish Government lost M. Mikolajczyk and embarked on its present course, it is felt here, it yielded its claim to leadership to a rival government more willing to work with the great power to whose forces it must look for liberation from the Nazi terror.

The British are ready to recognize the Russian claim to what has been considered Polish territory up to the Curzon Line and to sympathize with Soviet insistence on the friendly government of a reconstituted nation that has been carved up so often. The British, however, look askance at what appears to them to be a Russian determination to solve the Soviet Union's own strategic problems unilaterally while objecting to British plans to organize a similar sphere of influence in the west.

Fruits of Cooperation

British and American arms cleared France of the enemy, but the people here know that it could not have been done so quickly if the Red Army had not first torn the "guts" out of the Wehrmacht, as Mr. Churchill phrased it, and they are willing to give credit where credit is due. But the Russians' success in ridding their own country of the German invaders would not have been possible without Anglo-American air power, the British Navy and the constant threat of an Allied invasion of Europe from the west.

* * *

January 1, 1945

LUBLIN POLISH GROUP NAMES ITSELF PROVISIONAL REGIME

By W. H. LAWRENCE
By Cable to The New York Times.

MOSCOW, Dec. 31—The Polish Provisional Government was formed today, with Boleslaw Berut named President. Edward B. Osubka-Morawski was nominated Prime Minister and Minister of Foreign Affairs. The decision to create a Provisional Government was made at a special meeting of 105 members of the Polish National Council representing the underground and resistance movements, who have decided to break forever with the Polish Government in exile now in London.

The new Government will present a thorny diplomatic problem for the United Nations, all of whom except the Soviet Union recognize the London Government as the legitimate Polish regime. Prompt recognition is expected, however, from the Soviet Union, for the Polish National Council has already received authority to carry on the civil administration in the areas liberated by the Red Army.

Gen. Charles de Gaulle's Provisional Government may be the next, as Christian Fouchet, delegate to the Lublin Committee, was the only foreign diplomat other than the Soviet counselor present at today's meeting.

M. Berut made it clear amid cheers today that he hoped the new Government would soon be able to establish close and friendly relations with the United States and Great Britain, but well-informed sources here do not regard Anglo-American recognition as imminent.

The Socialist and Peasant parties have five portfolios in the new Government, the Workers' party has four and two were given to the Democratic party. The Minister of Defense and Commander in Chief, Gen. Michael Rola-Zymierski, is not a member of any party.

* * *

February 13, 1945

BIG 3 DOOM NAZISM AND REICH MILITARISM

YALTA PARLEY ENDS

Unified Blows at Reich,
Policing Spheres and Reparations Shaped

FRANCE TO GET ROLE

Broader Polish, Yugoslav Regimes Guaranteed—
Curzon Line Adopted

By LANSING WARREN
Special to The New York Times.

WASHINGTON, Feb. 12—Allied decisions sealing the doom of Nazi Germany and German militarism, coordinating military plans for Germany's occupation and control and maintaining order and establishing popular Governments in liberated countries were signed yesterday by President Roosevelt, Marshal Stalin and Prime Minister Churchill near Yalta in the Crimea, the White House announced today.

The conference, held in the summer palace of former Czar Nicholas II on the Black Sea shore, also called for a United Nations security conference in San Francisco on April 25.

The parleys, hitherto shrouded in secrecy except for a brief outline of the agenda issued Feb. 7, were held day and night from Feb. 4 until the final signatures were affixed. The announcement did not refer to President Roosevelt's future movements except that he had left the Crimea.

Main Points of Accord

Major decisions of the conference include:

(1) Plans for new blows at the heart of Germany from the east, west, north and south.

(2) Agreement for occupation by the three Allies, each of a separate zone, as Germany is invaded, and an invitation to France to take over a zone and participate as a fourth member of the Control Commission.

(3) Reparations in kind to be paid by Germany for damages, to be set by an Allied commission. The reparations commission, which will establish the type and amount of payments by Germany, will have its headquarters in Moscow. [Secretary of State Stettinius and Ambassador Harriman arrived in Moscow Monday.]

(4) Settlement of questions left undecided at the conference at Dumbarton Oaks and decision to call a United Nations conference at San Francisco April 25 to prepare the charter for a general international organization to maintain peace and security.

(5) Specific agreements to widen the scope of the present Governments in Poland and Yugoslavia and an understanding to keep order and establish Governments in liberated countries conforming to the popular will and the principles of the Atlantic Charter.

"Blows . . . from the east, west, north and south"

(6) A general declaration of determination to maintain Allied unity for peace.

German People Apart

The statement announced common policies for enforcing unconditional surrender and imposing Nazi Germany's doom. The document draws a distinction between the Nazi system, laws and institutions, the German General Staff and its militarism, which will be relentlessly wiped out, and the German people.

"It is not our purpose," it declared, "to destroy the people of Germany, but only when nazism and militarism have been extirpated will there be hope for a decent life for Germans, and a place for them in the comity of nations."

Until this conference the Allies had laid down no iron-clad program for the control and complete reorganization of Germany. Military plans will be made known only "as we execute them," said the statement, and the surrender terms "not until the final defeat has been accomplished."

Coordinated administration and control has been provided in a central Control Commission, which will be established with headquarters in Berlin. Part of its work will be to insist on the destruction of all German military equipment, elimination or control of all German industry that could be used for military production, the punishment of war criminals and the wiping out of all Nazi institutions from the German economic and cultural life.

The document mentioned no discussion of plans in the Far Eastern theatre of the war or any understanding with the Soviet Union for entry into the war against Japan, but the fact that the date for the United Nations conference, April 25,

Prime Minister Churchill, President Roosevelt and Marshal Stalin on the grounds of Livadia Palace.

comes one day after the date determining of a renewal of the Russo-Japanese agreement was remarked as significant.

That San Francisco had been chosen as the site for the next security conference of the United Nations, along with the date, aroused considerable interest here because of the city's remoteness from the European theatre of war and its position nearer the Far Eastern theatre.

New Cabinet Indicated

Special dispositions with regard to Poland include the widening of the present Provisional Government to include other democratic leaders in Poland and abroad.

The agreement sets the Polish eastern boundary, with a few alterations in favor of Poland, along the Curzon Line and recognizes that Poland must acquire substantial territory in the north and west but leaves these decisions to the peace conference. This is the first official mention to confirm the Allies' contemplation of a general peace conference.

With regard to the conflict for power in Yugoslavia the Allies have agreed that Marshal Tito and Dr. Ivan Subasitch shall set up the Government they have proposed but to include former members of the Parliament who did not collaborate with the enemy.

These Governments, it is provided, will be succeeded by those formed in conformity with desires expressed in popular elections and in the spirit of the Atlantic Charter. The state-

ment does not deal specifically with the situation in Greece or other countries but declares that the conference also made a general review of other Balkan questions.

Fascism to Be Uprooted

In a declaration on the liberated areas, the Allies announced the intention of consulting in the interests of the liberated peoples and to cooperate in rebuilding the national economic life in these countries. Vestiges of nazism and fascism are to be destroyed, and the Allies will cooperate to establish internal peace, carry relief and form interim governments broadly representative in the Axis satellite states as well as in liberated Allied countries.

An important feature of the international security discussions was contained in the announcements that the three powers had reached agreement on the disputed question of voting procedure, which prevented completion of the work at Dumbarton Oaks. No indication of the solution was given.

The three Chiefs of State were assisted by their Foreign Ministers, chiefs of military staffs and numerous other experts, as was the case in the previous three-power meetings. Besides Secretary of State Edward R. Stettinius Jr., President Roosevelt was accompanied by Harry L. Hopkins, his special assistant, and Justice James F. Byrnes, Director of the Office of War Mobilization and Reconversion.

Other United States delegates included W. Averell Harriman, Ambassador to the Soviet Union; H. Freeman Matthews, the State Department's Director of European Affairs; Alger Hiss, Deputy Director of Special Political Affairs, and Charles E. Bohlen, assistant to the Secretary of State.

Throughout the conference President Roosevelt occupied apartments in the former palace of the Czars. Marshal Stalin and Prime Minister Churchill were housed in separate establishments near by.

Three women were with the delegations. Though they did not participate in the discussions, they were received as conference guests. They were Mrs. Anna Boettiger, daughter of President and Mrs. Roosevelt; Mrs. Sarah Oliver, daughter of Prime Minister and Mrs. Churchill, and Kathleen Harriman, daughter of the Ambassador to Moscow.

President Roosevelt's party also included Edward J. Flynn of New York, who did not attend conference meetings but was invited as a personal friend when Mr. Roosevelt learned that he was planning a visit to Moscow.

Leahy Also in Party

Others in the President's personal party were Admiral William D. Leahy, chief of staff to the President; Mr. Byrnes, Vice Admirals Ross T. McIntyre and Wilson Brown, Maj. Gen. Edwin M. Watson and Stephen Early, the President's secretary.

President Roosevelt, whose movements have been obscured by censorship for more than three weeks, left Washington for the Crimea conference almost immediately after his inauguration ceremonies, on Jan. 20. The details of the voyage were not made public, but it was revealed that the President met Prime Minister Churchill on the island of Malta, which the British and American delegations reached Feb. 2. President Roosevelt and Mr. Churchill made a prolonged exchange of views and there were formal discussions between the British and United States military chiefs of staff.

President Roosevelt left Malta the night of Feb. 2, going by air direct to Yalta, where he was met by Foreign Commissar Vyacheslaff M. Molotoff, who extended greetings for Marshal Stalin.

The Presidential party proceeded along the Black Sea shore two miles southwest to Livadia, where stands the magnificent Summer Palace.

Meetings began the next day on the arrival of Marshal Stalin, who flew from his headquarters on the Russian front, where the Silesian offensive was just getting under way. The delegates met either in committees or as a group. Besides daily meetings of the three heads of Governments and the Foreign Secretaries, separate meetings of the Foreign Secretaries and their advisers were held daily.

The Foreign Secretaries arranged for regular conferences every three or four months. The meetings will be held in rotation in the three capitals, the first to be called in London after the San Francisco meeting.

At the close of the conference President Roosevelt presented to Marshal Stalin a number of decorations awarded by the United States to military men in the Red Army. Those to be decorated will receive the rank of Commander in the Legion of Merit. They include Marshal Alexander M. Vasilevsky, Chief of the General Staff of the Red Army; Air Chief Marshal Alexander A. Novikoff, commanding general of the Red Air Forces; Gen. A. K. Repin, Chief of the Soviet Military Mission to the United States; Lieutenant General Brendal, Lieutenant Colonel Krolenko, Major General Levanovich, Major General Slavin, Deputy Chief of the Red Army Staff, and Colonel Byaz.

The decorations were given in recognition of distinguished services in connection with their cooperation in American Air Force shuttle-bombing operations in Germany.

The first news of the historic consultation at Yalta was issued at the White House by Jonathan Daniels, administrative assistant to the President, who opened his announcement to the impatient correspondents with the statement: "This is it."

Announcement of the Allied report on the conference made in the Senate was greeted with cheers, which continued while the upper house adjourned.

* * *

February 14, 1945

HULL WILL ATTEND SECURITY PARLEY

May Head the United Nations Session in San Francisco— Vandenberg a Delegate

Special to The New York Times.

WASHINGTON, Feb. 13—Secretary Stettinius will be chairman of the United States delegation to the United Nations conference on drafting a world security plan on the basis of the Dumbarton Oaks proposals, which will convene at San Francisco on April 25.

The delegation will include Cordell Hull, former Secretary of State, who will serve as its senior adviser; four members of Congress, and two others. The latter six are:

Senator Tom Connally, Democrat, of Texas, chairman of the Committee on Foreign Relations; Senator Arthur H. Vandenberg, Republican, of Michigan, author of the resolution proposing an immediate agreement by the Allies for keeping Germany and Japan permanently demilitarized; Representative Sol Bloom, Democrat, of New York, chairman of the House Committee on Foreign Affairs; Representative Charles A. Eaton, Republican, of New Jersey, ranking minority member of the House Committee; Commander Harold Stassen, former Governor of Minnesota and a strong advocate of international collaboration for peace, and Dean Virginia Gildersleeve of Barnard College.

The designation of Mr. Hull indicated that the former Secretary, who has been a patient at the Naval Hospital at Bethesda, Md., would be able to leave the hospital before the meeting date of the conference.

It also projected the possibility that he would be chairman of the conference, inasmuch as President Roosevelt in accepting his resignation as Secretary of State referred to him as the father of the United Nations and expressed the hope that he would serve as chairman of the conference, which even then was being planned.

Mr. Hull exercised a guiding hand in the Dumbarton Oaks conference, at which Mr. Stettinius presided.

The selection of members of Congress was made in recognition of the part which the Senate would play in approving the charter of the security organization to be drafted at San Francisco.

In that respect the delegation is similar to the one appointed for the Inter-American Conference, which will convene in Mexico City on Feb. 21. Furthermore, the same pattern has been followed in the appointment of a woman member of the delegation. Representative Edith Nourse Rogers, Republican, of Massachusetts, is a member of the delegation to the Mexico City conference.

In addition, the Congressional representation on both delegations is drawn from both major parties, while at the same time the persons chosen are friendly to the concept of international collaboration for peace.

President Roosevelt, Prime Minister Churchill and Premier Stalin during the Crimean meeting at Yalta cabled to Mr. Hull their wishes for "speedy recovery." The message, sent by Secretary Stettinius, said:

"I have been instructed to transmit the following message to you on behalf of the undersigned who were guests of the Prime Minister this evening at dinner:

" 'We have missed you at this conference and send to you our affectionate greetings. We wish for you a speedy recovery in order that all of us may have the benefit of association with you again.

" 'Signed: Roosevelt, Stalin, Churchill, Molotoff, Eden, Stettinius.' "

Mr. Hull replied as follows:

"I am in receipt of your cable of Feb. 11 transmitting a most cordial message of greeting from President Roosevelt, Prime Minister Churchill, Marshal Stalin, Mr. Eden, Mr. Molotov and yourself. Please convey my grateful appreciation to each of them, together with my fervent wish for the fullest measure of success in their immense undertaking now and in the future."

Senator Connally, when informed of his selection as a delegate, said:

"The President recognizes the functions of the Senate and his action indicates his desire to have the utmost cooperation between the Senate and the executive. I feel that the members of the Senate designated by the President as members of the delegation to the United Nations conference will cooperate with the executive department in striving to secure the best possible organization for world peace and security."

* * *

March 1, 1945

PROPHECY OF PEACE

President Hopeful for Future, Thinks Arms Cuts May Come Later

HAILS YALTA PLANS

*But Says Some of These Are Secret Now—
To Attend World Parley*

By JOHN H. CRIDER
Special to The New York Times.

WASHINGTON, Feb. 28—President Roosevelt returned to the White House today, making clear his determination to play an active personal role in the implementation of the steps toward an enduring peace taken in concert with Prime Minister Churchill and Marshal Stalin at the Yalta conference.

He had traveled 14,000 miles in his absence of five weeks, in which he met for a second time with the British and Russian leaders to map the final strategy of the war and discuss the coming peace.

Looking tanned and refreshed after his post-Yalta "vacation" aboard a cruiser returning across the Atlantic, Mr. Roosevelt had not been back in the White House more than a few hours when it was announced that he would make a report to a special joint session of Congress tomorrow on the Crimea conference.

The White House also confirmed that he planned to play host to the United Nations delegates at the security conference to be held at San Francisco in April.

When the President appears in the well of the House at 12:30 P. M. tomorrow for his historic address to both houses of Congress, it will mark the first time that he has reported directly to Congress, following his meetings with Prime Minister Churchill and Marshal Stalin, although on Christmas Eve of 1943, after his return from the Teheran conference, he delivered a radio message from his Hyde Park home in which he discussed broad outlines of that conference and announced the appointment of Gen. Dwight D. Eisenhower to head the Allied drive on Germany from the west.

It will be the first time the President has appeared in person on Capitol Hill since he delivered the State of the Union message on Jan. 7, 1943. The President's address is expected to be broadcast by all radio networks and short-waved overseas.

First official word of the President's return came at 10:30 o'clock this morning at a news conference held by Jonathan Daniels, an administrative assistant to the President, at which he categorically denied rumors that the President's health had been impaired, stating that he had "never seen him (the President) looking better."

Although it was not known exactly how long the President would speak to Congress tomorrow, Mr. Roosevelt had told associates he expected to talk from forty-five minutes to an hour. An early draft of his address had run to about 4,900 words, but this was expected to be trimmed down to around 4,500 words.

The President, who appeared to be responding to strong pressure from the public and from immediate advisers to take Congress into his confidence regarding the agreements reached at Yalta, will be following the example of Prime Minister Churchill, whose current report to Parliament on the same matters may still be continuing on the day the President speaks.

Return of activity at the White House was immediately reflected in a rekindling of activity in other parts of the capital, where there has been a marked lethargy during the President's absence.

Legislation Had Been Slowed

Even at the Capitol, where major legislation has been under consideration, Administration programs were felt to be hampered by the President's absence. Twice while away he communicated his views to Congressional leaders, once regarding the George bill and again during consideration of manpower legislation by the Senate Military Affairs Committee.

The President's appearance before the joint session tomorrow was regarded as the high point in an intensive program on the part of the Administration to avoid mistakes by the Wilson Administration in the peacemaking following the last war, when a suspicious Congress rode roughshod over some of President Wilson's major commitments at the Versailles Conference.

It was believed that Mr. Roosevelt would not have undertaken to address Congress if he were not, in fact, in as good health and spirits as his aides declared him to be.

Another evidence of Mr. Roosevelt's heartiness was his drive in a heavy rain and sleet storm at noon to Arlington Cemetery to take part in the burial services for his secretary, friend and military aide, Major Gen. Edwin M. Watson, who died Feb. 20 at sea while on the return voyage from the Crimea.

After lunch the President went from the Executive Mansion to his office and worked until 5:45 at an accumulation of official routine and in polishing up his address to Congress.

President Looks to Arms Cuts

WASHINGTON, Feb. 28 (AP)—President Roosevelt has hopes that such a secure peace will follow the war that the Allies can gradually cut down their armaments.

His hopes extend even to the day—fifty or sixty years from now, he says—when a spirit of peace may embrace Germany and Japan.

The President's report to Congress on his victory-and-peace mission to the Crimea tomorrow will not tell all. Some understandings reached at the Big Three meetings on the Black Sea were secret, he said. Whether these involved political or military arrangements, or both, was part of the secrecy.

It is no secret that the President exhibited the strongest kind of hope for an increasingly better world to grow out of this war.

He told a small news conference aboard the cruiser which brought him home that the Yalta Conference, wherein Germany's downfall and lasting peace were topics, was one of a series of steps toward this better world.

To reporters of The Associated Press, The United Press and The International News Service, Mr. Roosevelt commented:

That the American public and press were quite right in saying with virtual unanimity that the parley was a great achievement.

This comment demonstrated that, despite his five weeks of travel away from the White House, he had been supplied reports on the American scene.

Concerning Japan, the United States was respecting Russia's neutrality, Mr. Roosevelt told his seagoing news conference. He said that he did not know whether Russia would be asked to enter any discussion of Pacific problems before the defeat of Germany.

President Recalls History

Looking fifty to sixty years in the future, Mr. Roosevelt saw a chance that even Japan and Germany might become respectable nations some day. He dipped into his recollections of history to recall that Japan became militaristic less than ninety years ago and that Germany turned to the sword after 1890.

They could go the other way just as rapidly, he said, in effect. But he stressed that they must purge themselves before they were even to be thought of as members of an international organization to keep the peace.

"Do you think," he was asked, "that Germany and Japan should ever in the foreseeable future be permitted to rearm?"

No, he replied.

The President said that he had no plans for a Pacific war council this year with Mr. Churchill and Generalissimo Chiang Kai-shek. Nor did he have in mind a talk with General Charles de Gaulle, although he said he would be glad to see the French leader at any time.

The Chief Executive made the point that America did not seem to realize that there would be a long, hard battle to subdue Japan. People blew hot and cold on the subject, he said, and he stressed a need for industrial emphasis on the Pacific war once Germany had capitulated.

There was no single accomplishment of the Crimean conference that stood out above the others, Mr. Roosevelt declared. He said progress was made all along the line, just as there had been progress toward an improved world every few months since the war began.

"Do you believe," a reporter asked, "that the conference can be the foundation for world-wide peace for more than the generation of the men who are building that peace?"

While that could not be answered categorically, he said, the conference did look ahead over a great many years, over a period as long as humanity could be expected to believe in the principles espoused by the United Nations. It looked at the human race, he added, and not with any idea it would end in fifty years.

In addition, the President said, the conference dealt at length on problems presented by small countries with static economies and living standards and on means of helping them. This was on the premise that a nation that was not moving forward and bettering her standards was a more potential war danger than one which was advancing.

Aides praised the manner in which Mr. Roosevelt presided as chairman and moderator at the big conference. They said he was able to produce agreements in several fields in which the principals originally did not see eye to eye.

Two instances apparently were the decisions on voting procedure of the projected United Nations Council and on a new governmental and territorial set-up for Poland. Mr. Roosevelt did not discuss these points with newsmen, however.

Of all the leading advisers who accompanied Mr. Roosevelt to the parley, only his personal chief of staff, Admiral William D. Leahy, and his naval aide, Vice Admiral Wilson Brown, returned with him. The others left the party at various points and on various missions.

Samuel I. Rosenman, Presidential counsel, joined the President at Algiers to help prepare while crossing the Atlantic the President's report to Congress and to discuss civilian supplies for liberated areas. Mr. Rosenman already had gone to Europe to survey supply requirements.

Mrs. John Boettiger, the Chief Executive's daughter, made the entire trip, but not in an official capacity. She took care of minor details, such as deciding who would dine with her father.

* * *

March 31, 1945

COX SEES PROMISE OF A LONG PEACE AS PUNISHED WORLD COMES TO SENSES

Says in Interview at Miami That Wilson's Blueprints Are Being Used to Build Structure of New League of Nations

MIAMI, Fla., March 30 (AP)—James M. Cox, who carried the banner for the League of Nations in the Presidential campaign of 1920, saw today a promise of "long continued and perhaps permanent international peace."

He sounded the cheerful note in one of his rare interviews, granted to The Associated Press because tomorrow is his seventy-fifth birthday.

The former Governor of Ohio is observing the anniversary at a time when the end of the war is approaching and the course of events is becoming reminiscent of 1920, when he became the Democratic nominee for President and fought for the league envisioned by Woodrow Wilson.

"A new age opens before us," he declared. "That shouldn't be alarming. Every generation has a new world to face. We confront swifter change than in past times, but we have better means of adjusting ourselves. Man's life has been an age-long struggle to rise to larger stature. Some have succeeded in the adjustment and have gone forward progressively. Others have missed the mark and vanished from the race.

"A constant evolution has been going on. It has taken ages to develop our civilization and there are ages yet to go. All this tells us we must be patient, yet everlastingly at the present pressing task.

Says Future Is Promising

"We enter into the strange new day in the midst of widespread grief and desolation, yet with every prospect of new and better things ahead. There is promise of long continued and perhaps permanent international peace. The world has been punished and in a chastened spirit has come to its senses at last.

"We shall have the benefits of scientific achievements. The mysteries of nature are one by one being solved and the material way of life, if we manage well, will be easier and happier. We have won many battles against disease and shall win many more. Because of this, we shall be a happier people, for health brings happiness. A healthy body, moreover, promotes that wholesome state of mind which begets understanding and harmony among men and nations."

Mr. Cox was asked whether the present war could have been avoided.

"This war did not need to be," he replied. "The conviction of that fact will grow as we demonstrate that an outlaw nation cannot run at large, and that disputes can be settled without resort to war. Time will reveal even more clearly than it has already done that the conspiracy which wrecked the project for peace after the first World War was the most tragic and sinful chapter in our history.

"I sometimes hear it said that in the coming cooperation of nations for peace, the errors of Woodrow Wilson will be avoided. The whole structure that is being built now is laid out from the blueprints embedded in the mind and soul of that martyred president. There will be changes in detail, but not in principle.

Defends League of Nations

"Time brings its compensations. The wisest of men is the county coroner who gets the last look at things. Those who would cast discredit on Woodrow Wilson are only trying to cover up their own guilt in the conspiracy of 1919. If there still be active now some remains of the sinister movement of that time, it must be because an enduring peace will expose the wrong which they accomplished then. If a League of Nations succeeds today, it would have succeeded had these political plotters given it the chance a quarter of a century ago.

"But enough of the past. The wisdom which the past has taught warns us that the path to peace is too sacred to be befouled by personal or partisan spite. The evils of today come from the neglects of yesterday. Our tomorrow will be what we make it today."

In connection with domestic affairs, Mr. Cox said "there is a disquieting situation."

"We Americans seem to run too much to extremes," he commented. "We have two forms of radicalism as we had in prohibition. Then we went from the open, uncontrolled, disgraceful saloon to the menacing gansterism under prohibition. In time the pendulum struck center.

"Right now we have the radical reactionary on the one hand who can see little virtue in progressive economic and social policy.

"On the other hand, there seems to be forming a sort of cult in this country which appears to believe that we are going backward if we don't have a new reform every day.

"If we can only develop a sense of balance in this country, our conditions will be very much more reassuring."

* * *

April 13, 1945

PRESIDENT ROOSEVELT IS DEAD

END COMES SUDDENLY AT WARM SPRINGS

Even His Family Unaware of Condition as Cerebral Stroke Brings Death to Nation's Leader at 63

ALL CABINET MEMBERS TO KEEP POSTS

Funeral to Be at White House Tomorrow, With Burial at Hyde Park Home—Impact of News Tremendous

---

By ARTHUR KROCK
Special to The New York Times.

WASHINGTON, April 12—Franklin Delano Roosevelt, War President of the United States and the only Chief Executive in history who was chosen for more than two terms, died suddenly and unexpectedly at 4:35 P. M. today at Warm Springs, Ga., and the White House announced his death at 5:48 o'clock. He was 63.

The President, stricken by a cerebral hemorrhage, passed from unconsciousness to death on the eighty-third day of his fourth term and in an hour of high triumph. The armies and fleets under his direction as Commander in Chief were at the gates of Berlin and the shores of Japan's home islands as Mr. Roosevelt died, and the cause he represented and led was nearing the conclusive phase of success.

Less than two hours after the official announcement, Harry S. Truman of Missouri, the Vice President, took the oath as the thirty-second President. The oath was administered by the Chief Justice of the United States, Harlan F. Stone, in a one-minute ceremony at the White House. Mr. Truman immediately let it be known that Mr. Roosevelt's Cabinet is remaining in office at his request, and that he had authorized Secretary of State Edward R. Stettinius Jr. to proceed with plans for the United Nations Conference on international organization at San Francisco, scheduled to begin April 25. A report was circulated that he leans somewhat to the idea of a coalition Cabinet, but this is unsubstantiated.

Funeral Tomorrow Afternoon

It was disclosed by the White House that funeral services for Mr. Roosevelt would take place at 4 P. M. (E. W. T.) Satur-

day in the East Room of the Executive Mansion. The Rev. Angus Dun, Episcopal Bishop of Washington; the Rev. Howard S. Wilkinson of St. Thomas's Church in Washington and the Rev. John G. McGee of St. John's in Washington will conduct the services.

The body will be interred at Hyde Park, N. Y., Sunday, with the Rev. George W. Anthony of St. James Church officiating. The time has not yet been fixed.

Jonathan Daniels, White House secretary, said Mr. Roosevelt's body would not lie in state. He added that, in view of the limited size of the East Room, which holds only about 200 persons, the list of those attending the funeral services would be limited to high Government officials, representatives of the membership of both houses of Congress, heads of foreign missions, and friends of the family.

President Truman, in his first official pronouncement, pledged prosecution of the war to a successful conclusion. His statement, issued for him at the White House by press secretary Jonathan Daniels, said:

"The world may be sure that we will prosecute the war on both fronts, East and West, with all the vigor we possess to a successful conclusion."

News of Death Stuns Capital

The impact of the news of the President's death on the capital was tremendous. Although rumor and a marked change in Mr. Roosevelt's appearance and manner had brought anxiety to many regarding his health, and there had been increasing speculation as to the effects his death would have on the national and world situation, the fact stunned the Government and the citizens of the capital.

It was not long, however, before the wheels of Government began once more to turn. Mr. Stettinius, the first of the late President's Ministers to arrive at the White House, summoned the Cabinet to meet at once. Mr. Truman, his face gray and drawn, responded to the first summons given to any outside Mr. Roosevelt's family and official intimates by rushing from the Capitol.

Mrs. Roosevelt had immediately given voice to the spirit that animated the entire Government, once the first shock of the news had passed. She cabled to her four sons, all on active service:

"He did his job to the end as he would want you to do. Bless you all and all our love. Mother."

Those who have served with the late President in peace and in war accepted that as their obligation. The comment of members of Congress unanimously reflected this spirit. Those who supported or opposed Mr. Roosevelt during his long and controversial years as President did not deviate in this. And all hailed him as the greatest leader of his time.

No President of the United States has died in circumstances so triumphant and yet so grave. The War of the States had been won by the Union when Abraham Lincoln was assassinated, and though the shadow of post-war problems hung heavy and dark, the nation's troubles were internal. World War II, which the United States entered in Mr.

Harry S. Truman being sworn in by Chief Justice Harlan F. Stone in the Cabinet Room of the executive offices in the White House. Watching the solemn ceremony are, left to right: Secretary of Labor Frances Perkins, Secretary of War Henry L. Stimson, Secretary of Commerce Henry A. Wallace, War Production Board Chairman J. A. Krug, Secretary of the Navy James Forrestal, Secretary of Agriculture Claude R. Wickard, unidentified person, Attorney General Francis Biddle, Secretary of State Edward R. Stettinius Jr., Mrs. Truman, Secretary of the Interior Harold L. Ickes, Speaker Sam Rayburn, War Mobilization Director Fred M. Vinson, Representative Joseph W. Martin Jr., House minority leader; Representative Robert Ramspeck and Representative John W. McCormack, House majority leader.

Roosevelt's third term, still was being waged at the time of his death, and in the Far East the enemy's resistance was still formidable. The United States and its chief allies, as victory nears, were struggling to resolve differences of international policy on political and economic issues that have arisen and will arise. And the late President's great objective—a league of nations that will be formed and be able to keep the peace—was meeting obstacles on its way to attainment.

Mr. Roosevelt died also in a position unique insofar as the history of American statesmen reveals. He was regarded by millions as indispensable to winning the war and making a just and lasting peace. On the basis of this opinion, they elected him to a fourth term in 1944. He was regarded by those same millions as the one American qualified to deal successfully and effectively with the leaders of other nations—particularly Prime Minister Winston Churchill and Marshal Joseph Stalin—and this was another reason for his re-election.

Yet the constitutional transition to the Presidency of Mr. Truman was accomplished without a visible sign of anxiety or fear on the part of any of those responsible for waging war and negotiating peace under the Chief Executive. Though the democratic process has never had a greater shock, the human and official machines withstood it, once the first wave of grief had passed for a leader who was crushed by the burdens of war.

President Truman entered upon the duties imposed by destiny with a modest and calm, and yet a resolute, manner. Those who were with him through the late afternoon and evening were deeply impressed with his approach to the task.

"He is conscious of limitations greater than he has," said one. "But for the time being that is not a bad thing for the country."

How unexpected was President Roosevelt's death despite the obvious physical decline of the last few months is attested by the circumstance that no member of his family was with him at Warm Springs, no high-ranking associate or long-time intimate, and that his personal physician, Rear Admiral Ross McIntyre, was in Washington, totally unprepared for the news.

Personal Physician Surprised

The Admiral, in answer to questions from the press today, said "this came out of a clear sky," that no operations had been performed recently on Mr. Roosevelt and that there had never been the slightest indication of cerebral hemorrhage. His optimistic reports of the late President's health, he declared, had been completely justified by the known tests.

This ease of mind is borne out by the fact that Mrs. Roosevelt was attending a meeting of the Thrift Club near Dupont Circle when Stephen Early, the President's secretary, telephoned her to come to the White House as soon as possible. Mrs. John Boettiger, the only daughter of the family, was visiting her slightly ailing son at the Naval Hospital at Bethesda, Md., some miles away.

While these simple offices were being performed by those nearest and dearest, the President lay in the faint from which he never roused. A lesser human being would have been prostrated by the sudden and calamitous tidings, but Mrs. Roosevelt entered at once upon her responsibilities, sent off her message to her sons and told Mr. Early and Admiral McIntire, "I am more sorry for the people of the country and the world than I am for us." When Mr. Truman arrived and asked what he could do for her, Mrs. Roosevelt rejoined calmly, "Tell us what we can do. Is there any way we can help you?"

Flag at Capitol Lowered

As soon as the news became a certainty the White House flag was lowered to half-staff—the first time marking the death of an occupant since Warren G. Harding died at the Palace Hotel in San Francisco, Aug. 2, 1923, following a heart attack that succeeded pneumonia. The flag over the Capitol was lowered at 6:30 P. M. Between these two manifestations of the blow that had befallen the nation and the world, the news had spread throughout the city and respectful crowds gathered on the Lafayette Square pavement across from the executive mansion. They made no demonstration. But the men's hats were off, and the tears that were shed were not to be seen only on the cheeks of women. Some Presidents have been held in lukewarm esteem here, and some have been disliked by the local population, but Mr. Roosevelt held a high place in the rare affections of the capital.

The spoken tributes paid by members of Congress, a body with which the late President had many encounters, also testified to the extraordinary impression Mr. Roosevelt made on his times and the unparalleled position in the world he had attained. The comment of Senator Robert A. Taft of Ohio, a constant adversary on policy, was typical. "The greatest figure of our time," he called him, who had been removed "at the very climax of his career," who died "a hero of the war, for he literally worked himself to death in the service of the American people." And Senator Arthur H. Vandenberg of Michigan, another Republican and frequent critic, said that the late President has "left an imperishable imprint on the history of America and of the world."

More Than Mere Words

These were not mere words, uttered in conformity to the rule of "nil nisi bonum." Mr. Roosevelt's political opponents did what they could to retire him to private life, and their concern over his long tenure was real and grew as the tenure increased. But ever since his fourth-term victory in 1944 they have felt sincerely that it would be best for the country if he were spared to finish the great enterprises of war and peace which the country had commissioned him to carry through.

And when they called his death a national and international tragedy they meant it.

But this tribute paid, this anxiety expressed, they and the late President's political supporters and official aides turned their hearts and minds again to the tasks before the nation. No one said "On to Berlin and Tokyo!" For Americans do not speak dramatically. But that is what every one meant, and it was the gist of what President Truman said and did after the homely ceremony that made him the head of the State.

When the dignitaries were assembled with Mr. Truman for this solemn purpose, there was a slight delay until his wife and daughter should arrive. Then the Chief Justice, using a Bible borrowed from Mr. Roosevelt's office and speaking from memory, read the oath and the new President repeated it after him. Then he and Mrs. Truman called on Mrs. Roosevelt and, as the President said, went "home to bed."

He wore a gray suit, a white shirt and a polka-dot tie. His face was grave but his lips were firm and his voice was strong. He said through Mr. Early that his effort will be "to carry on as he believed the President would have done." And he arranged to meet with the Army and Navy chiefs tomorrow, to assure them as tonight he did the people that his purpose is to continue the conduct of the war with the utmost vigor and to the earliest possible and successful conclusion.

While these simple but dignified processes of democracy were in motion, preparations were being made to render fit respect to the memory of the dead President. It was decided that Mrs. Roosevelt, their daughter and other members of the family should fly to Warm Springs to accompany the remains to Washington, arriving Saturday.

Meanwhile, it was announced that the nation-wide series of Jefferson Day dinners have been canceled, and similar honors of observance will be paid at the Capitol, throughout the United States and at many places in the world that looked to Mr. Roosevelt as its leader from darkness to the light.

* * *

April 24, 1945

POLISH ISSUE STILL UNSOLVED; TRUMAN, MOLOTOFF CONFER

Russian, Eden and Stettinius Hold Repeated Meetings and Secretary Reports Often to White House— Soong at Night Session

By LANSING WARREN
Special to The New York Times.

WASHINGTON, April 23—After two meetings of President Truman and Foreign Commissar V. M. Molotoff and three conferences of the Big Three Foreign Secretaries, it appeared today that the deadlock on the Polish question remained. Consultation is taking place here before the opening of the San Francisco Conference. Another meeting of the Foreign Secretaries was held tonight. It ended at 11:30 P. M. with the issues still unsettled.

Half an hour after the night session started, T. V. Soong, Acting Prime Minister of China, joined the conference. It was the first meeting of the high Sino-Russian officials.

The White House stated late today that Mr. Molotoff would consult his Government on the Polish issue and that the discussions would be continued by the British, United States and Soviet Foreign Secretaries at San Francisco.

The situation was complicated during the day by a memorandum presented by the Polish exiled government in London to the British and United States Governments expressing regret at not being invited to the United Nations conference.

The London Poles expressed their desire to cooperate in establishing good relations between Poland and Russia and reminded the Allies of the need for free elections. This appeal follows the signature by the Russian Government of an accord of mutual assistance with the Provisional (Lublin) Government of Poland, which the Soviet Government wishes to represent the Poles at San Francisco despite the agreement in Crimea for reorganization to include other Polish groups.

As the situation stands on the eve of the conference the Soviet Union continues to press for an invitation to be extended to the Lublin Polish Government. The exiled Poles in London have made a bid for inclusion of at least resistance leaders in that Government and are desirous of an invitation for themselves. The British and the United States Governments, who have recognized only the London Poles, are asking for reorganization of the Lublin Government before an invitation can be issued.

President Truman, said the White House statement, has twice received Mr. Molotoff during his short stay in Washington. Secretary of State Edward R. Stettinius Jr. has conferred with Mr. Molotoff and Anthony Eden, British Secretary for Foreign Affairs, on the Polish situation.

"In view of the limited time at their disposal in Washington prior to the opening of the San Francisco conference on Wednesday, and in order to permit Mr. Molotoff to consult with his Government following these conversations," said the statement, "the discussions in regard to the Polish situation will be continued by the three Foreign Secretaries at San Francisco."

The Foreign Secretaries of the Big Three powers sat down for a final conference about 9 o'clock at night. Secretary Stettinius appeared to be in a much more confident mood. Mr. Molotoff was accompanied by the largest delegation that he has brought to any of the meetings.

A half hour after the conference opened, Mr. Soong joined the session. His presence was construed as a prelude to cooperation of the Four Powers sponsoring the San Francisco Conference.

The final hours were spent in technical arrangements for the San Francisco meeting.

Dr. Soong went immediately to the air field after the consultation and was followed by Secretary Stettinius and his associates. Secretary Eden said that his plane would leave in the morning. Mr. Molotoff departed by plane at 2:30 A. M.

The consultations during the day failed to reach agreement, owing, it was said, to the inability of the Foreign Commissar to make commitments without reference to his Government.

The White House statement said, however, that they discussed "other matters connected with the San Francisco conference."

Early in the day Mr. Stettinius, Mr. Molotoff and Mr. Eden conferred at the State Department for more than two hours. They were assisted by advisers and experts.

The British delegation consisted of Mr. Eden, Sir Alexander Cadogan, Permanent Secretary of the British Foreign Office; Sir Archibald Clark-Kerr, Ambassador to Moscow, and Major Arthur Bierse, assistant to Mr. Eden.

The Russian delegation included Mr. Molotoff, Andrei Gromyko, Ambassador to the United States; A. A. Scholey, Counselor of the Soviet Enabassy in London, and Boris Feedorovich Potserol, senior assistant to Mr. Molotoff.

American officials present included Secretary Stettinius and Joseph C. Grew, Under-Secretary of State; James C. Dunn, assistant secretary of State; W. Averell Harriman, Ambassador to Moscow; Charles G. Bohlen, State Department expert on Russia, and Eldridge Durbrow, director of the Division of Eastern European Affairs.

Mr. Eden arrived early and consulted with Mr. Stettinius for a few minutes before the arrival of Mr. Molotoff, and remained a few minutes after the conference adjourned.

No one would make any statement. Mr. Stettinius did say that the consultation would be continued. Mr. Molotoff merely saluted press questioners and left without speaking. Asked if there would be further conferences, Ambassador Gromyko replied:

"I do not know."

Secretary Stettinius accompanied Mr. Eden to the door on the main floor of the building and went immediately to the White House to report to President Truman. After that conference, he declared:

"I can't say anything now."

Secretary Stettinius held another conference with Mr. Eden and Mr. Molotoff was expected. He did not, however, arrive, and the Big Three meeting was deferred to 9 o'clock tonight.

At 5:31 P. M. Mr. Molotoff, accompanied by Ambassador Gromyko and other Russian experts, called for his second consultation with President Truman at the White House. They made the trip both ways to and from the Blair-Lee House, on the other side of Pennsylvania Avenue from the White House, in two large limousines, escorted by a dozen motorcycle police.

Present at this meeting were apparently Admiral Leahy and Ambassador Harriman, who had entered the White House from the side entrance. Mr. Molotoff was received by George Summerlin, Protocol officer, who led him into the President's office. The conference lasted about 24 minutes. It was shortly after this meeting that the White House made a statement on the Polish issue.

Throughout the day the atmosphere at the State Department and the White House appeared to be tense. All the participants in the gatherings were more than usually uncommunicative.

Leaving the White House all the principal personages refered news men to the Secretary of State, but Mr. Stettinius during his many hasty exits and entrances at the White House and State Department kept repeating:

"I can't say anything now."

* * *

May 1, 1945

RUSSIANS FLY VICTORY FLAG ON REICHSTAG

STALIN HAILS EVENT

Interior Ministry Won—Tiergarten Region of Berlin Is Besieged

TOLL OF NAZIS SOARS

1,800,000 Captured or Killed in 4 Months—Baltic Port Seized

By The Associated Press

LONDON, Tuesday, May 1—Red Army troops, storming the blazing administrative heart of Berlin, captured the gutted shell of the German Reichstag yesterday, running up the Russian victory flag over the Nazi monument in a sweep that threatened to split the last defenders of the German capital.

The fall of all Berlin appeared imminent. The Russians stepped up their struggle for the city to unprecedented proportions in a possible bid to win the entire city today while Moscow celebrates May Day.

Soviet troops were within a mile of tearing the capital into two isolated pockets, each less than nine square miles. They had won the Ministry of the Interior, near the Reichstag; were laying siege to Hitler's underground fortress in the Tiergarten, were at Berlin's triumphal arch, the Brandenburg Gate, and were across the Spree River from Berlin's cathedral.

Stalin Issues May Day Order

German broadcasts admitted that the ten-day battle for the devastated capital was as good as lost, while Premier Stalin, in a May Day order of the day, said that the war was approaching its end and declared: "The last assault is on."

Marshal Stalin said that 1,800,000 Germans had been killed or captured during the last three to four months of fighting on the eastern front. His announcement meant that 11,540,000 German casualties had been inflicted by the Red Army in less than four years of war.

As 9,000 more German troops surrendered in Berlin, raising to 65,500 the toll of enemy dead and captured in four days, north of the dying capital Red Army troops, rolling out mile-an-hour gains across Mecklenburg Province, seized the Baltic port of Greifswald and smashed within forty-two miles of Rostock. The port of Swinemuende was isolated.

Far to the south, Gen. Andrei I. Yeremenko's Fourth Ukrainian Army captured Moravska-Ostrava, the "Pittsburgh of Czechoslovakia," while cavalrymen of the Second Ukrainian Army plunged through the Morava River Valley toward a junction that would roll up a German salient in eastern Moravia.

The capture of the famous Reichstag building, which was wrecked by fire in February, 1933, four weeks after Hitler had assumed power, and was used by the Nazis as a pretext for seizing dictatorial powers, was announced in Moscow's nightly war bulletin.

Marshal Gregory K. Zhukoff's First White Russian Army captured Germany's legislative chambers after they had stormed over the Moltke River bridge from Mosbit and seized the Ministry of the Interior.

Sweeping across the barricades in wide Koenigsplatz they broke into the Reichstag and "hoisted the banner of victory," Moscow said.

Heinrich Himmler's Ministry of the Interior lies north of the famous Kroll Opera House, used by the German Parliament after the burning of the Reichstag. Here, little more than a month before his attack on the Soviet Union, Hitler told the Nazi assembly:

"Germany can no longer be subjugated. She is so strong that no combination of Powers could ever successfully prevail against her."

But as the Russians raised their flag over the Reichstag, Marshal Stalin said that the days of Hitler's Germany were counted.

The Russian's, standing at the Brandenburg Gate and across the street from the American Embassy, were battling into the eastern end of the Tiergarten, where Hitler and Propaganda Minister Goebbels have been reported directing Berlin's defense from a fortified underground headquarters.

Along with the Reichstag and the Ministry of the Interior, Marshal Zhukoff's troops captured 200 city blocks in the heart of the capital. The central post office, on the east bank of the Spree opposite the Dom (cathedral) also was seized by troops battling into the center from Alexanderplatz. The fall of these buildings placed Red Army assault forces at either end of mile-long Unter den Linden.

Only a mile separated Marshal Zhukoff's troops at the Reichstag from those who, advancing into the central district from the south, had captured Anhalter rail depot Sunday. A junction in the center of Berlin would split the fanatical German defenders into a nine-square-mile pocket to the north—in the area of Wedding Gesundbrunnen and Humboldthain—and another pocket southwest of the Teirgarten.

In the latter area, Marshal Ivan S. Koneff's First Ukrainian troops captured several blocks of buildings in the city district of Wilmersdorf and won the Westkreuz Metropolitan Railway junction, four miles southwest of the Reichstag.

The mile-long area between Marshal Zhukoff's two prongs is packed with all Germany's major administrative buildings, including Hitler's great Reich Chancellery.

Meanwhile, Marshal Rokossovaky's Second White Russian Army rolled forward from twenty to twenty-three miles across the North German Plains on a great 100-mile front in conjunction with elements of Marshal Zhukoff's army due north of Berlin.

Tearing through faltering defenses, Marshal Rokossovsky's troops shattered the entire enemy line based on the Stralsund-Berlin railroad, and with the capture of Greifswald, Soviet troops rolled within eighteen miles southeast of Stralsund.

In Germany's southern region, General Yeremenko's troops toppled the Slovak road center of Zilina along with Moravska-Ostrava, forty-eight miles to the northwest. Long under Soviet artillery fire, Moravska-Ostrava, third city of Czechoslovakia, guards the northern roads into Moravia.

At the same time, Marshal Rodion Y. Malinovsky's Second Ukrainians advanced to within sixty-two miles of a link-up by smashing forward through the Morava River Valley from the south along a twenty-five-mile front. Marshal Malinovsky's troops gained six miles and captured Ivanovice, twenty miles southwest of the Morava Valley stronghold of Olomouc.

* * *

May 3, 1945

BERLIN FALLS TO RUSSIANS, 70,000 GIVE UP

EPIC SIEGE IS OVER

Shell of German Capital Yielded to Red Army by Beaten Nazis

343,000 LOST BY FOE

Baltic Link With British Is Near as Rostock and Warnemuende Fall

By The Associated Press

LONDON, Thursday, May 3—Berlin, greatest city of the European Continent, fell yesterday afternoon to the Russians as 70,000 German troops laid down their arms in the surrender that Adolf Hitler had said never would come.

The Soviet triumph, after twelve days of history's deadliest street fighting, was announced last night by Premier Stalin in an Order of the Day and in the Soviet communiqué broadcast from Moscow this morning.

Marshal Stalin first issued an Order of the Day announcing destruction of the German Ninth Army trapped southeast of Berlin, with the capture of 120,000 of its men and the slaughter of at least 60,000.

Rostock and Warnemuende Fall

A second Order announced the capture of Germany's big Baltic ports of Rostock and Warnemuende in a forty-four-mile drive by the Second White Russian Army.

Then Marshal Stalin proclaimed the fall of Berlin. It capitulated at 3 P.M., Moscow time, and by 9 P.M. 70,000 of its staggering defenders had been rounded up and counted by the Russians.

The New York Times (British Official via U.S. Signal Corps Radiotelephoto)

Left: Representative of Col. Gen. Heinrich von Vietinghoff-Scheel affixing signature to the document in royal palace at Caserta as his aide looks on. Right: Lieut. Gen. W. D. Morgan, British Army, placing his name on the articles. Standing behind him are (left to right) Air Vice Marshal George Baker, Chief of Staff to the Allied Mediterranean Air Forces; Maj. Gen. A. P. Kislenko and Lieut. M. Vraevsky, both representing Russia, and Maj. Gen. Lyman L. Lemnitzer, American deputy chief of staff in the Mediterranean.

[The defense of Berlin cost the Germans 343,000 men killed or captured, according to Soviet casualty figures, The United Press reported.]

For the conquest of Berlin his proclamation called for the top Moscow victory salute of twenty-four salvos from 324 cannon in tribute to the armies that took Berlin, the First White Russian and the First Ukrainian.

Those armies, commanded by Marshals Gregory K. Zhukoff and Ivan S. Koneff, had jumped across the Oder River sixteen days previously and on April 21 had fought into Berlin. They encircled the sprawling city, which already had been wrecked by American and British bombers, and tore the remains to bits in some of the bitterest big-scale street fighting of all time.

End of Six-Year Empire

Thus fell the once mighty capital, which Marshal Stalin described as "the center of German imperialism and heart of German aggression" and Hitler had proclaimed as the seat of his "thousand-year Reich" empire—the empire that in less than six years died as it had been born, in blood and suffering

The greatest city ever to fall in battle, Berlin lay a 341-square-mile monument to the death of millions and to the diseased ambition of one man, Adolf Hitler.

How many persons died there will never be known with accuracy, but before the war that greatest of continental cities had a population of 4,335,000, and only Monday night the Russians announced that the fanatical Nazi defenders were killing many of the civilians with their fire.

The fury of that defense was everything that Hitler had said it would be, and even Wednesday afternoon his dwindling cohorts had contended over the Hamburg radio that resistance in Berlin was "not yet broken," even while admitting that the garrison had been ripped into isolated pockets.

The finale came in the innermost heart of the city, in the government district that had been Hitler's pride and in the pill-boxes and underground fortifications of the once-attractive Tiergarten.

The Russians announced few details of the last day of the German capital, which by one day missed falling on the traditional Soviet May Day holiday.

But during the days of siege and isolation, both they and the Germans had told of a gigantic, never-waning conflict that raged in the air, on the rooftops, in houses and in the streets, and in cellars and the extensive subway tunnels—a conflict that progressed yard by yard as Nazi fanatics shot any person who even mentioned the words "surrender" or "retreat."

Yet surrender they did at last, to Red Army men who had fought across a continent, 1,560 miles from the ruins of Stalingrad, since the Nazi tide reached the flood at that Volga city in January, 1943.

Whatever feebly flickering hopes the ragged, hollow-eyed survivors of Berlin may have had of miraculous last-minute salvation were snuffed out when Marshal Stalin announced the destruction of the German Ninth Army, which had been encircled for a week southeast of Berlin and had tried in vain to break back into the capital.

Then came the strategically important, but less dramatic, advance of the Second White Russians along the Baltic coast, taking Rostock and seven other towns. This placed the Russians only twenty-nine miles from the British, who took the Baltic ports of Luebeck and Wismar.

Remaining to the Germans north of the ashes of Berlin was only a twisting, virtually indefensible strip on the Mecklenburg plain about thirty miles wide and steadily narrowing.

The Russian march west from Stralsund and northwest from Demmin swept up Warnemuende, seven miles north of Rostock; Ribnitz, Marlow and Bodden, east of Rostock, and Teterow and Laage, on the main road southeast of Rostock.

A wide and solid link-up of the eastern and western Allies all the way north to the Baltic appeared imminent.

Far to the south, other Soviet armies were swinging westward through Czechoslovakia toward Prague in a converging drive toward the western Allies that would shred yet another developing pocket of Nazi resistance.

*   *   *

May 3, 1945

WAR IN ITALY ENDS

Last Enemy Force Gives Up Just 20 Months After Landings

DEFEAT IS COMPLETE

Unconditional Surrender Opens 'Back Door' to German Bastion

By VIRGINIA LEE WARREN
By Wireless to The New York Times.

ADVANCED ALLIED HEADQUARTERS, Italy, May 2— Twenty months after the Allies' troops first set foot on Italian soil the war for Italy ended at noon today, when hostilities ceased under the unconditional surrender signed by the Germans last Sunday afternoon at Allied Headquarters in Caserta.

The terms, revealed only today, cover all land, sea and air forces, estimated at almost 1,000,000 men. They apply to all northern Italy to the Isonzo River in the northeast and to the Austrian provinces of Vorarlberg, Tyrol and Salzburg and portions of Carinthia and Styria.

The surrender of the Austrian provinces swept away most of the area that the Germans had claimed that they would use for a redoubt. It also greatly lessened the chances for any last-ditch stand on the Continent. The portion of Italy not included in the surrender lies along the Yugoslav border and takes in the Istrian Peninsula, already in the hands of Yugoslav Partisans.

Germans Must Disarm

Soon after noon today the German command's radio ordered its forces still trying frenziedly to flee into the Alps before the Fifth and Eighth Armies to lay down their arms. The unconditional-surrender terms call for the "immediate immobilization and disarmament of the enemy's ground, sea and air forces."

The Germans gave up just twenty-one days after the Eighth Army and fourteen days after the Fifth Army had begun the spring offensive that swept over every important city in northern Italy, brought in more than 160,000 prisoners and sealed off all the major Alpine passes. The surrender of Col. Gen. Heinrich von Vietinghoff-Seheel, the German Commander in Chief in the southwest and Commander in Chief of Army Group C, marked the first time in this war that Germany had formally acknowledged the loss of a country that she had dominated. Even Field Marshal Sir Harold R. L. G. Alexander, the Allies' commander in this theatre, had said that Italy might well be the last battlefield.

The instrument of surrender was signed in the former summer palace of the Neapolitan Kings in Caserta by one German representative on behalf of von Vietinghoff Scheel and by another on behalf of Obergruppenfuehrer Karl Wolff, supreme commander of the Elite Guard and police and general plenipotentiary of the German Army in Italy. The two Germans then returned by a secret route to von Vietinghoff's headquarters high in the Alps. On the following day came the announcement by Gen. Mark W. Clark, the Allies ground commander, that the military power of Germany in Italy had virtually ceased.

Main Points Listed

The text of the surrender instrument has not been given out, but the five main points are these:

(1) The German Commander in Chief's unconditional surrender of all forces under his command or control on land, at sea or in the air, to the Allies' Supreme Commander in the Mediterranean theatre.

(2) The cessation of all hostilities on land, at sea and in the fair by the enemy forces at noon, Greenwich mean time, on May 2, 1945.

(3) The immediate immobilization and disarmament of the enemy's ground, sea and air forces.

(4) The obligation of the German Commander in Chief in the southwest to carry out any further orders issued by the Allies' Supreme Commander.

(5) Disobedience of orders or noncompliance with them to be dealt with in accordance with the accepted laws and usages of war.

"The instrument of surrender stipulates that it is independent of, without prejudice to, and will be superseded by any general instrument of surrender imposed by or on behalf of the United Nations and applicable to Germany and the German armed forces as a whole," the Allies announced.

Remnants of twenty-two German and six Italian Fascist divisions are affected by the order. The surrender of the southern Austrian provinces turns over to the Allies such important cities as Salzburg and Innsbruck and gives them controls of territory within ten miles of Berchtesgaden. But it is the winning of Italy on the Allies' terms that means most to the thousands of American and British soldiers who saw their comrades fall at the Volturno River and Anzio and Cassino; and those who lived through those bloody ordeals felt that they had survived only to endure an Italian Valley Forge high in the cruel Apennines on a "forgotten front."

[The territory covered in the surrender is that commanded by the two Germans who surrendered, it was explained in Washington. Thus it covers northern Italy and those parts of the Austrian Alps that extend to the Munich area, which is under another command. It does not include Berchtesgaden because the town is in Germany.]

To the troops Marshal Alexander addressed a special order of the day paying tribute to them. General Clark and Gen. Joseph T. McNarney, deputy commander, also praised the troops.

It may now be revealed that intimations toward surrender were made to the Allies before the Fifteenth Army Group came down out of the Apennines and up from the mud flats of the Comaochio lagoon to drive across the Po Valley, but the Allies were interested only in unconditional terms. When it became apparent a few days ago that, even if the Germans could flee over the Alps, they would land in the arms of the American Seventh Army, the Yugoslav Partisans or the French Forces converging on Italy from the north, east and west, the German commanders got word through to Marshal Alexander that they were ready to negotiate.

Last Saturday two German officers in civilian clothes flew down to Caserta, reaching there at 4 P. M. By 2 P. M. on the following day, the documents were ready for signatures after consultations with the heads of state and Chiefs of Staff of the United States, Britain and Russia in which they had fully agreed on the terms. All three nations had representatives to witness the signing of the documents. Lieut. Gen. W. D. Morgan, Chief of Staff of Allied Headquarters, signed as Marshal Alexander's representative.

30 Miles From Austria

ROME, May 2 (AP)—Before the surrender was announced the Allies' armies were reported to be within thirty miles of the Austrian border.

British armored spearheads dashed toward the Austrian border beyond captured Udine, northeast of Venice. New Zealand troops joined Yugoslav forces that penetrated into Italy along the Isonzo River, fourteen miles northwest Trieste at the head of the Adriatic Sea.

The Yugoslavs announced the complete occupation of Trieste Gorizia and Monfalcone, sealing off the Istrian Peninsula south of Trieste. A convoy of thirty enemy ships, including the 1,500-ton hospital ship Freyburg, surrendered quickly off the Istrian Peninsula when two Hurricanes flew over them at noon yesterday. The convoy included landing craft and launches.

Aerial reconnaissance showed that German troops fleeing into Austria from northeastern Italy were destroying bridges, blasting roads and wrecking airfields.

The American Thirty-fourth Division, driving west from Milan, captured Santhia, forty-eight miles from Milan, after having crossed the Ticino River and occupied Novara, twenty-seven miles west of Milan. Brazilian troops joined with other Fifth Army units in Alessandria.

On the west coast American troops pushing beyond Noli were within fifty miles of the French Riviera frontier.

*　　*　　*

May 8, 1945

THE WAR IN EUROPE IS ENDED!

GERMANS CAPITULATE ON ALL FRONTS

*American, Russian and French Generals Accept Surrender in
Eisenhower Headquarters, a Reims School*

REICH CHIEF OF STAFF ASKS FOR MERCY

*Doenitz Orders All Military Forces of Germany To Drop Arms—
Troops in Norway Give Up—
Churchill and Truman on Radio Today*

By EDWARD KENNEDY
Associated Press Correspondent

REIMS, France, May 7—Germany surrendered unconditionally to the Western Allies and the Soviet Union at 2:41 A. M. French time today. [This was at 8:41 P. M., Eastern Wartime Sunday.]

The surrender took place at a little red schoolhouse that is the headquarters of Gen. Dwight D. Eisenhower.

The surrender, which brought the war in Europe to a formal end after five years, eight months and six days of bloodshed and destruction, was signed for Germany by Col. Gen. Gustav Jodl. General Jodl is the new Chief of Staff of the German Army.

The surrender was signed for the Supreme Allied Command by Lieut. Gen. Walter Bedell Smith, Chief of Staff for General Eisenhower.

It was also signed by Gen. Ivan Susloparoff for the Soviet Union and by Gen. Francois Sevez for France.

[The official Allied announcement will be made at 9 o'clock Tuesday morning when President Truman will broadcast a statement and Prime Minister Churchill will issue a V-E Day proclamation. Gen. Charles de Gaulle also will address the French at the same time.]

General Eisenhower was not present at the signing, but immediately afterward General Jodl and his fellow delegate, Gen. Admiral Hans Georg Friedeburg, were received by the Supreme Commander.

Germans Say They Understand Terms

They were asked sternly if they understood the surrender terms imposed upon Germany and if they would be carried out by Germany.

They answered Yes.

Germany, which began the war with a ruthless attack upon Poland, followed by successive aggressions and brutality in internment camps, surrendered with an appeal to the victors for mercy toward the German people and armed forces.

After having signed the full surrender, General Jodl said he wanted to speak and received leave to do so.

"With this signature," he said in soft-spoken German, "the German people and armed forces are for better or worse delivered into the victors' hands."

"In this war, which has lasted more than five years, both have achieved and suffered more than perhaps any other people in the world."

LONDON, May 7 (AP)—Complete victory in Europe was won by the Allies today with the unconditional surrender of Germany.

[The first announcement that Germany had capitulated came at 8:09 A. M., Eastern Wartime, when German Foreign Minister Count Lutz Schwerin von Krosigk stated in a broadcast over the Flensburg radio that Grand Admiral Karl Doenitz, new Chancellor of Germany, had ordered the unconditional surrender of all German armed forces.

[In this broadcast announcing the German surrender, Count Schwerin von Krosigk called upon the Germans "to stand loyally by the obligations we have undertaken."

["Then we may hope that the atmosphere of hatred which today surrounds Germany all over the world will give place to a spirit of reconciliation among the nations, without which the world cannot recover," he added. "Then we may hope that our freedom will be restored to us, without which no nation can lead a bearable and dignified existence."]

Germany's formal capitulation marked the official end of war in Europe, but it did not silence all the guns, for battles went on in Czechoslovakia.

Boehme Says Troops Were Unbeaten

In Norway, however, Gen. Franz Boehme, German Commander in Chief, broadcast an Order of the Day over the Oslo radio tonight commanding his troops to lay down their arms in obedience to Count Schwerin von Krosigk's "announcement of unconditional surrender of all German fighting troops."

The Norwegian garrison surrendered at the order of Boehme, who said that the capitulation "hits us very hard because we are unbeaten and in full possession of our strength in Norway and no enemy has dared to attack us."

"In spite of all that," he added, "in the interests of all that is German we also shall have to obey the dictate of our enemies. We hope that in the future we shall have to deal with men on the other side who respect a soldier's honor * * * clench your teeth and keep discipline and order. Obey your superiors. Remain what you have been up to now—decent German soldiers who love their people and homeland more than anything in the world."

He said he also "expected" that the Norwegian population "will keep the discipline with respect to the Germans that the German soldiers in Norway always kept toward the Norwegians."

Under the terms of the capitulation, the Germans will march across the border into internment in Sweden.

The Swedish Telegraph Agency in a broadcast said an Allied naval force of forty-eight ships had been sighted at the entrance of Oslo Fjord and a landing was expected "at any moment."

Sevez Says Negotiators Differed

By Wireless to The New York Times.

PARIS, May 7—There was one official voice on the surrender heard in Paris tonight or rather it will be heard when the Figaro appears tomorrow morning. That was the voice of General Sevez who, in spite of the complete lack of other official confirmation of German's capitulation, told a reporter for the Figaro that it was he who had signed the capitulation for France.

General Sevez said that the discussion went on all afternoon and late into the night. German General Friedeberg seemed crushed by the emotional effect of the surrender, General Sevez said.

"Sometimes we were separated from the Germans and discussed questions among the Allies," he declared. "Sometimes the Germans took places facing us. Each point discussed led to further discussion.

"We were seated behind a narrow school table. General Smith had General [Lieut. Gen. Sir Frederick E.] Morgan and me at his right while General Susloparoff was at his left. When the Germans came in, we were already seated. All three Germans bowed before us without a word.

"Repeatedly the Germans went to a telephone booth connected directly with Doenitz. We did the same to talk with our superiors. Only General Smith remained in direct contact with General Eisenhower, whose residence was at Reims.

"When the capitulation was signed General Eisenhower received the three Germans. It was finished at 2:40 o'clock Monday morning. I was called by telephone by General Eisenhower who put a plane at my disposal to take me to Reims. Soon afterward I arrived in the small schoolhouse where the offices of the Supreme Command were."

General Sevez, who is Assistant Chief of Staff of the French Army, said he was called because the French Chief of Staff, Gen. Alphonse-Pierre Juin, was in San Francisco.

Surrender of Criminals Required

By Wireless to The New York Times.

LONDON, May 7—The terms made ready for Germany by the European Advisory Commission are believed first of all to call for the disarmament of all forces, the surrender of war criminals and complete obedience to the orders of Allied Military Government authorities for restoring order in Germany.

At a time to be jointly decided by the Allies, the Allied Control Commission, composed of the Commanders in Chief of the British, American, Soviet and French forces in Germany, will take charge of the Reich.

The permanent shape of the future Reich is not expected to be decided until the peace conference is held, perhaps two years hence, but some adjustments of the German border in favor of Poland and the Soviet Union may take place in the interim.

One question that may be settled promptly is that of drafting labor from Germany to rebuild the devastated European countries. More than 10,000,000 men may soon be in Allied captivity and until peace has been signed they will remain prisoners of war and can be sent to work wherever they are needed.

The British and American forces will soon have captured more Germans than the total number of men in their own forces and consideration must be given to the reallocation of these prisoners.

* * *

June 8, 1945

HOUSE VOTES BY 345 TO 18 FOR BRETTON WOODS PACTS

Republicans Are Only Opponents of Bill but 138 of Party Support It—Truman, Morgenthau Hail Non-Partisan Victory

By C. P. TRUSSELL
Special to The New York Times.

WASHINGTON, June 7—The House erased party lines today to approve by a vote of 345 to 18 participation by the United States in the International Monetary Fund and Bank for Reconstruction and Development in accordance with the agreements reached by forty-four United Nations at Bretton Woods last summer.

The eighteen members who voted "No" were all Republicans, but 138 other Republicans joined with 205 Democrats, a Progressive and a member of the American Labor party in support of the legislation.

Voting against the bill, which now goes to the Senate where its passage is expected generally, were Representatives Buffett of Nebraska, Olevenger, Jones and Smith of Ohio; Ellis of West Virginia, Gwynne of Iowa, Knutson and O'Hara of Minnesota; Lemke of North Dakota, Mason and Sumner of Illinois, Reed of New York, Rich of Pennsylvania, Rizley and Schwabe of Oklahoma, Robsion of Kentucky, Schwabe of Missouri and Scrivner of Kansas.

At his first-opportunity, as he opened this afternoon's news conference, President Truman hailed the House action and said he was exceedingly happy over the vote. He declared that the overwhelming nonpartisan support given this program for stabilizing international currencies and cooperating in post-war economic reconstruction led him to believe that the Congress would really be in favor of the coming peace treaties.

Henry Morgenthau Jr., Secretary of the Treasury, said:

"The House of Representatives, in voting overwhelming approval of the Bretton Woods legislation, has spoken forcefully for the principle of international cooperation. The action will engender a feeling of great confidence throughout the world at a time when it is important that we concentrate our efforts upon the achievement of world security and peace.

"It is particularly encouraging to observe that Democrats and Republicans worked together for the passage of the legislation and that the vote represented a strong majority in each party. The American people and the peoples of the world will welcome this evidence of statesmanship in world affairs. It presages an era of world cooperation which will lead to prosperity for all."

Had Urged Quick Passage

As debate on the legislation opened on Tuesday, the President, in a letter to Representative Brent Spence, Banking and Currency Committee chairman, had said its prompt enactment was of paramount importance in the establishment of a sound economic foundation for lasting peace. He praised the committee's action in reporting the measure to the House, after two months of hearings and study, by a vote of 23 to 3, and then added:

"Let us hope and pray that the example set by your committee on the Bretton Woods legislation will become a pattern for American participation in international economic and security cooperation."

The House sent the bill to the Senate in the form in which its Banking Committee reported it. Two attempts, by Miss Jessie Sumner of Illinois, to change the program drastically and prevent its conforming to the Bretton Woods agreement, were beaten back by margins ranging from 6 to 1 to 11 to 1.

When the House met at noon there was pending a proposal by Miss Sumner that approval be given to United States participation only in the $9,100,000,000 International Bank for Reconstruction and Development. Under the agreements, membership in the bank is contingent on participation in the proposed $8,800,000,000 International Monetary Fund. By this particular action Miss Sumner sought to put the House on record.

Sumner Motion Beaten Badly

The roll was called and the motion was defeated by a vote of 325 to 29, all of the supporting votes being cast by Republicans, but with 121 Republicans voting against it. Ten of the twenty-nine Republicans who voted with Miss Sumner voted later for passage of the legislation unamended. They were Representatives Bennett and Cole of Missouri; Bishop, Johnson and Vursell of Illinois; Brehm and Jenkins of Ohio; Curtis of Nebraska; Hoffman of Michigan and Rees of Kansas. Representative O'Konski of Wisconsin voted present.

Hearings on the House bill are scheduled to begin before the Senate Banking and Currency Committee on Tuesday. While it was predicted in some quarters that the legislation would be changed by the Senate committee or the Senate itself, it was believed that it would not be altered to any extent which would pull it out of line with the Bretton Woods agreements.

The proposed International Monetary Fund, under the program, would be operated chiefly through short-term aid in stabilizing international currencies. The projected bank would provide long-term economic reconstruction loans. While the amendments written into the original draft of the legislation by the House committee would make no change in the forty-four-nation agreements, they provide an American interpretation of the role of the two agencies.

To guide the United States representatives on the fund and the bank there would be a five-member advisory council of department heads and other Federal officials to consult with them and report to the Congress every two years.

* * *

June 8, 1945

VETO ROW IS ENDED AS RUSSIA YIELDS

DEADLOCK IS ENDED

Stalin Alters His Stand in 'Interest of Success of the Conference'

YALTA FORMULA IS UPHELD

Small Nations Are Expected to Agree on Big 5 Solution Proposed by Stettinius

By JAMES B. RESTON
Special to The New York Times.

SAN FRANCISCO, June 7—The Soviet Government agreed tonight to allow freedom of discussion in the World Security Council, thereby ending "the battle of the veto" and assuring the success of the United Nations Conference.

After a démarche by Harry Hopkins in Moscow, proposed by Secretary of State Stettinius and approved by President Truman, Marshal Stalin instructed his delegation here to abandon its previous request for a veto over discussion of international disputes in the security council and to show a "conciliatory attitude" in "the interests of the success of the conference."

As a result of this decision, the six most critical days of the conference have ended, but while the right of discussion is now assured, the five-power veto as suggested by the late President Roosevelt at Yalta has not been "softened." In some ways, compared with the United States' original interpretation, it has been "hardened." What has been "softened" is not the veto but the conference opposition to it.

Carrying out the instructions from Marshal Stalin, the head of the Russian delegation, Andrei A. Gromyko, went to American headquarters at 1 P. M. today and conferred with Secretary Stettinius, then explained to a Big Five meeting at 3 P. M. that his Government wished to make four amendments in its unyielding note of Friday.

These amendments did not meet the original American position in its entirety. For example, the Russians still propose, and the other four now approve, that whenever there is a dispute in the Security Council over whether a decision should require the unanimity of the five permanent members, the vote on this matter should carry the right of veto.

There was, however, really only one point at issue among the five major powers. This was whether one nation had the right to veto a decision as to whether a dispute should be brought before the Security Council and discussed.

American View Prevails

The technical committee of the Big Five, in its paper of May 26, said that no country should have this right of veto over discussion. The Russian note of Friday, revising the technical committee's interpretation, said that the veto should apply to this right of discussion. Thus the point at issue was the principle of free discussion. Our delegation, strongly supported by Britain, France and China, did not waver in their support of this principle, and the Russian Government has now agreed to accept their view.

The question now is what the conference will do. Originally the veto problem was not a dispute among the Big Five but between them on the one hand and the small and middle nations on the other. Every present indication, however, is that the original controversy has been overwhelmed by the Big Five dispute and that the other nations will now, admittedly after some complaining, accept tonight's Big Five interpretation which will go before the conference committees tomorrow.

The reaction of the conference steering committee was favorable this evening. Mr. Stettinius read to the heads of all delegations a statement emphasizing that the Big Five had finally agreed to support two principles: The principle of free discussion and the principle of the unanimity of the five permanent members of the Security Council on all questions requiring "action."

This statement, ending the six-day deadlock over the veto, was well received. The truth is that the Russians have, by their tactics, produced the votes, if not the whole-hearted support, of the small powers for a Big Five veto over virtually every decision in the Security Council, except a decision on the right of the Council to take up a case and hear discussion on it.

When the conference started six weeks ago, there was strong pressure on the Big Five to reduce the veto power. An aggressive Soviet diplomacy early in the conference whittled this demand down to a general request to abandon the veto over decisions to "investigate" disputes. It was this demand for the right of "free investigation" that resulted in the Russian demand for the right to veto "free discussion," and the crisis over this has been just serious enough to persuade the small powers to take the "discussion" and forget about the rest.

Mr. Stettinius' statement on the veto agreement emphasized that the Big Five were not changing but sustaining the Security Council voting formula suggested by Mr. Roosevelt and accepted by Marshal Stalin and Prime Minister Churchill at Yalta.

Under the terms of the Big Five agreement, the Secretary said, unanimity of the permanent members of the Council is required, as provided by the Yalta agreement, in all decisions relating to enforcement action and, except as to parties to disputes, in all decisions for peaceful settlement. But this requirement of unanimity, he added, does not apply to the right of any nation to bring a dispute before the Council, and no individual member of the Council can alone prevent a consideration and discussion by the Council of a dispute or situation thus brought to its attention.

Delay in Drafting Seen

"The successful conclusion of discussions on this matter among the four sponsoring powers and France," the Stettinius statement asserted, "offers a new and heartening proof of the will and ability of the Allied nations which have fought side by side in the war to construct, upon the strong foundation."

The chances are, however, that it will still take two weeks of discussion and drafting and translating before the final text of the Security Charter can be completed. The debate over the veto provisions may be long, though they probably will not change a word either in the draft of the Yalta voting text or in the interpretation. But the drafting alone is an intricate job and it may take nearly a week between completion of the document and final approval in the capitals of the fifty States represented at the conference.

It is perhaps worth while to emphasize what the Big Five settlement does not do as well as what it does. It does not affect the right of the Big Five to sit in judgment on themselves. It does not take away the individual right of each of the five to veto a decision to take any kind of enforcement action such as sending troops against an aggressor, or making a military demonstration against a potential aggressor, or cutting off trade with a dangerous power, or breaking diplomatic relations with an aggressor nation.

Moreover, this agreement of tonight does not affect the veto on a wide range of topics which come under the heading of "peaceful procedures" for settling a dispute. For example, under the agreement, all five, unless they are parties to the dispute, retain their right to veto the following:

(A) Whether a matter should be investigated;

(B) Whether a dispute or situation is of such a nature that its continuation is likely to threaten the peace;

(C) Whether the Council should call on the parties to settle a dispute by means of their own choice;

(D) Whether, if the dispute is referred to the Council, a recommendation should be made as to methods and procedures of settlement;

(E) Whether the Council should make such recommendations before the dispute is referred to it;

(F) What should be the nature of this recommendation;

(G) Whether the legal aspect of the dispute should be referred to the court for advice;

(H) Whether a regional agency should be asked to concern itself with the dispute, and

(I) Whether the dispute should be referred to the General Assembly.

The Big Five agreement does, however, take the veto away on five things:

First, the Big Five had agreed before this note that the veto could not, as it could under the Dumbarton Oaks proposals, paralyze action against an aggressor by regional agencies such as the Pan-American security system.

Second, they also agreed that the veto would not operate to prevent alliances directed against a revival of German aggression from operating or remaining in force even if the security council took the necessary measures to prevent that aggression.

Third, the new agreement did emphasize that the veto could not be applied against a nation that wished to take a case before the Council and could not prevent any nation from discussing that case. This does not mean that anyone with a dispute could merely go into the Security Council and start talking about it. What it does mean is that when the Council is asked to hear a case, it decides on this as a "procedural matter" and all procedural matters in the Security Council are decided by any seven of the eleven members of the Council. Unless those seven votes were attained, the case could not be heard, but no one nation could prevent discussion of the case merely by applying its veto.

Fourth, the Big Five agreement stipulated that the veto could not be applied to the election of judges in the International Court of Justice.

Fifth, the new agreement also directs that the five permanent members should not have a veto over decisions contained in Section D of Chapter 6 of the new charter. This section deals with procedure in the Security Council, with such things as the following:

Decisions to hold meetings away from the permanent seat of the organization, to set up special agencies to deal with specific problems, to adopt its own rules of procedures, to invite non-members to sit on the Security Council when they are parties to a dispute, and to elect its own president.

U. S. Backing for Soviet Likely

Now that the controversy is moving from the realm of the Big Five to the realm of the other nations, it is reasonably certain that there will be some attempt to take away the veto on the right to investigate a dispute. But the Russians have made it clear that they will not have that, and after the last six days, they can count on not only the other sponsor powers but also the active efforts of the United States to seek the votes of the Latin American powers in favor of the present Big Five agreement.

The American delegates have stood together on the principle of free discussion throughout this controversy, despite considerable pressure to yield. In the Sunday night meeting of the delegation and after talks with the other sponsors and representatives of the British Dominions, there was unanimity for going direct to Marshal Stalin with the question.

Accordingly, Mr. Stettinious expressed to President Truman the sentiment of the delegation and the critical nature of the dispute, and Ambassador Averell Harriman and Mr. Hopkins were instructed to impress on Marshal Stalin the importance of the principles involved and the inability of the United States to go back on the promise of free discussion which it had already made in public statements.

Mr. Hopkins carried out these instructions before he left Moscow and was able to advise the President this morning that Marshal Stalin had acceded to our request. Thus, the small nations have the right of discussion, the American delegation is pleased with the accomplishment and the Russians are pleased that the others are happy.

* * *

June 10, 1945

YUGOSLAVS ACCEPT ANGLO-U.S. POLICING OF TRIESTE REGION

Alexander to Control Western Venezia Giulia and Lines to Austria Under Accord

2,000 TITO MEN TO REMAIN

Others to Be Out by Tuesday—Agreement Holds Final Settlement Not Prejudiced

By BERTRAM D. HULEN
Special to The New York Times.

WASHINGTON, June 9—A temporary military administration of the Italian Province of Venezia Giulia, including Trieste, under Allied control has been agreed on by the United States, Britain and Yugoslavia, the State Department announced today.

Military details are to be worked out by Marshal Tito, Premier of Yugoslavia, and Field Marshal Sir Harold R. L. G. Alexander. The agreement "in no way prejudices or affects" the ultimate disposition of western Venezia Giulia or Marshal Tito's claim to Trieste.

The agreement was regarded as one putting an end to conditions that reached disturbing proportions when Yugoslav troops sought to control the territory by armed might. The situation posed for the British and Americans loss of control of supply lines into Austria, and their opposition led Marshal Tito to abandon his plan.

Communications Protected

The agreement gives Marshal Alexander control of the whole western territory of Venezia Giulia, including Trieste, and vital communications, railways and roads leading into Austria.

Marshal Tito consented to withdraw from the area within seventy-two hours all but 2,000 of his troops, who will occupy a district designated by Marshal Alexander and that will be controlled through his administrative services. A small Yugoslav mission will be attached to his headquarters as observers.

Any Yugoslav irregulars in the area under Allied control will either give their arms to Allied military authorities and disband or withdraw from the area.

Furthermore, the Yugoslav Government has agreed to return residents of the area whom it arrested or deported, except those who were Yugoslav nationals in 1939. It is also required to make restitution of property it has confiscated or removed.

The area under control of the Supreme Allied Commander was defined as "the portion of the territory of Venezia Giulia west of a line which includes Trieste, the railways and roads from there to Austria via Gorizia, Caporetto, and Tarvisio, Pola and the anchorages on the west coast of Istria." [The line north of Trieste roughly follows the Isonzo River.]

Marshal Alexander was empowered to govern the areas west of the line, Pola and other areas on the west coast of Istria that he might deem necessary for the occupation. It was stipulated that use would be made of any smooth-working Yugoslav civil administration already set up.

10,000 Demonstrate in Trieste

By Wireless to The New York Times.

LONDON, June 9—The British-United States-Yugoslav agreement which was signed in Belgrade was said today to satisfy every principle held by the Western Allies in demanding that Marshal Tito's troops evacuate the Venezia Giulia area of Italy.

The line from which Yugoslav troops were to be withdrawn was drawn north from Trieste through Gorizia to Villach, on the Austrian frontier.

The regular Yugoslav troops are to be withdrawn from Marshal Alexander's areas by 8 A. M. Tuesday.

The Yugoslav Foreign Minister, Ivan Subasitch, expressed confidence that the military staffs would meet soon and reach a "full mutual understanding."

A crowd of about 10,000 citizens thronged the main square of Trieste last night in a demonstration apparently intended to show Soviet observers that the population wants Trieste to become Yugoslav.

* * *

July 21, 1945

TRUMAN SAYS WE WANT NO TERRITORY, ASK ONLY PEACE AND WORLD PROSPERITY WITH 'MANKIND'S GREATEST AGE' AS GOAL

PARLEY AIM HINTED

Amid Potsdam Secrecy President Sets Line of U. S. Diplomacy

JAPAN INCLUDED IN IMPORT

Speech Keyed to Flag-Raising at Control Office—
Stalin and Churchill Confer

By RAYMOND DANIELL
By Wireless to The New York Times.

BERLIN, July 20—In a speech couched in the plain language of the average man, President Truman renounced today territorial or monetary gain as the war or peace aims of the United States.

He said that America was waging war solely to bring peace and prosperity to "the world as a whole" and he declared that it was his plan to harness the machine that had vanquished Nazi Germany to the cause of peace and thus insure "the greatest age in the history of mankind."

His speech, delivered when the flag that flew over the Capitol when the Japanese bombed Pearl Harbor was raised over the headquarters of the United States Group Control Council here, was more than the platitudinous expression of an orator at a patriotic ceremony. Coming, as it did, in the midst of the tripartite conference, where the deliberations the leaders of the three victorious nations in Europe are cloaked in secrecy, it took on the aspect an official declaration of national policy.

THE PRESIDENT'S SPEECH

The text of the speech:

General Eisenhower, Officers and Men:

This is an historic occasion. We have conclusively proven that free people can successfully look after the affairs of the world.

We are here today to raise the flag of victory over the capital of our greatest adversary. In doing that we must remember that in raising that flag we are raising it in the name of the people the United States who are looking forward to a better world, a peaceful world, a world in which all people will have the opportunity to enjoy the good things of life, and not just a few at the top.

Let us not forget that we are fighting for peace and for the welfare of mankind. We are not fighting for conquest. There is not one piece of territory or one thing of a monetary nature that we want out of this war.

We want peace and prosperity for the world as a whole. We want to see the time come when we can do the things in peace that we have been able to do in war.

If we can put this tremendous machine of ours, which has made victory possible, to work for peace, we can look forward to the greatest age in the history of mankind. That is what we propose to do.

Clue to Policy Sought

This was the first such pronouncement made by any head of a state since the conference that is expected to settle the face of Europe for generations began.

While the speech, which took only 1 minute 50 seconds to deliver, was lacking in details of how its lofty ideal was to be achieved, it was a statement that will be studied carefully in the chancelleries of Europe and Asia and at the firesides at home as a clear statement of the line United States diplomacy is taking in this congress of victors, where ancient fears and rivalries of the Old World challenge the practical idealism of the new, and hitherto isolated, world across the sea.

President Truman's pronouncement was not limited to Europe. Since it was not, and since the United States is engaged in what was a global war until Germany surrendered, it was assumed that he meant that the United States had no more designs on the lands of other nations in the Pacific than in Europe. This, at least, was the plain import of his words, and those who know him best say that he speaks his mind after he has made it up.

What might easily have been a routine patriotic display— and a day hardly passes without one in Berlin—was turned into a historic occasion by the President's simple, homely declaration of the faith that sent millions of American boys into battle far from home for a belief that few of them could express.

It was a reaffirmation of the principles for which Britain went to war in 1939 and for which one after another little European country committed what seemed national suicide rather than abandon them.

It was a simple ceremony at which Mr. Truman spoke; it was over in less than seven minutes. However, it overshadowed in importance anything that has emanated from that guarded enclosure of villas where Mr. Truman, Prime Minister Churchill and Premier Stalin, on whose shoulders rests the heavy responsibility of preserving the peace their countrymen have won at such bitter cost, have been wrestling with problems that had never been solved by their predecessors at Vienna or Versailles or, for that matter, anywhere in this world.

The flag hoisted to the top of the pole over Group Control headquarters, which before Germany's surrender was headquarters for the air defense of central Germany, was the same as that raised over Rome, first enemy capital to fall to the western Allies' arms. After Japan has accepted unconditional surrender, it will fly over Tokyo.

The scene of today's ceremony was a cobbled barrack square. The white-painted flagpole was in the center. At its base was a bed of hydrangeas.

Gathered in the square were a band and a battalion of the Fifty-first Armored Infantry of the Second Armored Division, part of the American occupying force in Berlin.

Into the enclosure made by bomb-damaged buildings the President and his party entered about 2 P. M. With Mr. Truman were Gen. Dwight D. Eisenhower, Gen. Omar N. Bradley, Gen. George S. Patton Jr. in lacquered helmet, riding breeches and boots; Lieut. Gen. Lucius D. Clay and Secretary of War Henry L. Stimson. Mr. Truman wore a brown double-breasted suit and a gray hat. Mr. Stimson was dressed in gray. They were the only ones in civilian clothes in that line of men before the bare flagpole.

Old Glory Over Berlin

As they took their places the band played "Hail to the Chief" and then, with the troops at Present Arms and the band playing the national anthem, Old Glory, held by Corp. Wilbur Richard of Portland, Ind., was hauled slowly and reverently to the top of the pole by Corp. Frederick D'Angelo of Wilmerding, Pa. Corp. Abraham Liberman of Cambridge, Mass., and Charles Magnifico of Jersey City, white-helmeted members of the color guard, stood at salute at the base of the staff.

There was not much news from the Potsdam compound, where the delegates of the three major powers are meeting. Foreign Secretary Anthony Eden, who was reported to have recovered from the indisposition that kept him from President Truman's state dinner last night, returned to his place on the committee of Foreign Secretaries, which plans the agenda for the discussion by the heads of state.

It was disclosed belatedly, after the British press had been speculating whether British-Russian relations had cooled, that Prime Minister Churchill had dined alone with Premier Stalin Wednesday night and spent several hours with him, accompanied only by interpreters.

The Prime Minister entertained Secretary of State James F. Byrnes and Lord Cherwell at luncheon today.

Reich Control Reported Discussed

BERLIN, July 20 (U.P.)—It was understood that the Big Three at their meetings up to tonight had confined themselves largely to political and economic problems.

[A United Press dispatch from Wiesbaden said that it was reported authoritatively that the Big Three at their first meetings discussed the problem of controlling Germany. It was added that they were understood to be in almost complete accord. Among those called in to discuss Germany, it was said, were General Clay, who is chief of the American Group Control Commission; Robert Murphy, General Eisenhower's political adviser, and General Bradley.]

Vice Admiral Emory S. Land, War Shipping Administrator, arrived in Potsdam yesterday. He had been summoned from Washington by the President.

Truman Scans Pacific War

BERLIN, July 20 (AP)—With Admiral William D. Leahy, Presidential Chief of Staff, and other military advisers, President Truman went over hourly reports today from the Pacific battlefront, using maps similar to those in the map room at the White House.

* * *

August 7, 1945

FIRST ATOMIC BOMB DROPPED ON JAPAN; MISSILE IS EQUAL TO 20,000 TONS OF TNT; TRUMAN WARNS FOE OF A 'RAIN OF RUIN'

NEW AGE USHERED

Day of Atomic Energy Hailed by President, Revealing Weapon

HIROSHIMA IS TARGET

'Impenetrable' Cloud of Dust Hides City
After Single Bomb Strikes

By SIDNEY SHALETT
Special to The New York Times.

WASHINGTON, Aug. 6—The White House and War Department announced today that an atomic bomb possessing more power than 20,000 tons of TNT, a destructive force equal to the load of 2,000 B-29's and more than 2,000 times the blast power of what previously was the world's most devastating bomb, had been dropped on Japan.

The New York Times (U.S. Air Force)

Hiroshima, a city of 318,000 on Honshu, one of the main enemy homeland islands as it was seen on a reconnaissance flight before the attack.

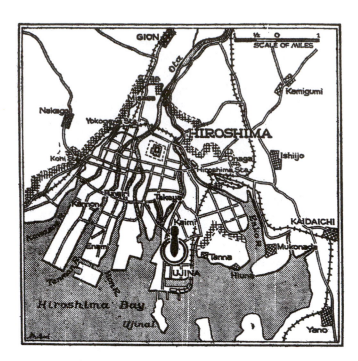

The symbol on the map indicates the approximate spot, north of the docks, where the new explosive that wiped out 60 per cent of Hiroshima was dropped.

The announcement, first given to the world in utmost solemnity by President Truman, made it plain that one of the scientific landmarks of the century had been passed, and that the "age of atomic energy," which can be a tremendous force for the advancement of civilization as well as for destruction, was at hand.

At 10:45 o'clock this morning, a statement by the President was issued at the White House that sixteen hours earlier—about the time that citizens on the Eastern seaboard were sitting down to Sunday suppers—an American plane had dropped the single atomic bomb on the Japanese city of Hiroshima, an important army center.

Japanese Solemnly Warned

What happened at Hiroshima is not yet known. The War Department said it "as yet was unable to make an accurate report" because "an impenetrable cloud of dust and smoke" masked the target area from reconnaissance planes. The Secretary of War will release the story "as soon as accurate details of the results of the bombing become available."

But in a statement vividly describing the results of the first test of the atomic bomb in New Mexico, the War Department told how an immense steel tower had been "vaporized" by the tremendous explosion, how a 40,000-foot cloud rushed into the sky, and two observers were knocked down at a point 10,000 yards away. And President Truman solemnly warned:

"It was to spare the Japanese people from utter destruction that the ultimatum of July 26 was issued at Postdam. Their leaders promptly rejected that ultimatum. If they do not now accept our terms, they may expect a rain of ruin from the air the like of which has never been seen on this earth."

Most Closely Guarded Secret

The President referred to the joint statement issued by the heads of the American, British and Chinese Governments, in which terms of surrender were outlined to the Japanese and warning given that rejection would mean complete destruction of Japan's power to make war.

[The atomic bomb weighs about 400 pounds and is capable of utterly destroying a town, a representative of the British Ministry of Aircraft Production said in London, the United Press reported.]

What is this terrible new weapon, which the War Department also calls the "Cosmic Bomb"? It is the harnessing of the energy of the atom, which is the basic power of the universe. As President Truman said, "The force from which the sun draws its power has been loosed against those who brought war to the Far East."

"Atomic fission"—in other words, the scientists' long-held dream of splitting the atom—is the secret of the atomic bomb. Uranium, a rare, heavy metallic element, which is radioactive and akin to radium, is the source essential to its production. Secretary of War Henry L. Stimson, in a statement closely following that of the President, promised that "steps have been taken, and continue to be taken, to assure us of adequate supplies of this mineral."

The imagination-sweeping experiment in harnessing the power of the atom has been the most closely guarded secret of the war. America to date has spent nearly $2,000,000,000 in advancing its research. Since 1939, American, British and Canadian scientists have worked on it. The experiments have been conducted in the United States, both for reasons of achieving concentrated efficiency and for security; the consequences of having the material fall into the hands of the enemy, in case Great Britain should have been successfully invaded, were too awful for the Allies to risk.

All along, it has been a race with the enemy. Ironically enough, Germany started the experiments, but we finished them. Germany made the mistake of expelling, because she was a "non-Aryan," a woman scientist who held one of the keys to the mystery, and she made her knowledge available to those who brought it to the United States. Germany never quite mastered the riddle, and the United States, Secretary Stimson declared, is "convinced that Japan will not be in a position to use an atomic bomb in this war."

A Sobering Awareness of Power

Not the slightest spirit of braggadocio is discernable either in the wording of the official announcements or in the mien of the officials who gave out the news. There was an element of elation in the realization that we had perfected this devastating weapon for employment against an enemy who started the war and has told us she would rather be destroyed than surrender, but it was grim elation. There was sobering awareness of the tremendous responsibility involved.

Secretary Stimson said that this new weapon "should prove a tremendous aid in the shortening of the war against Japan," and there were other responsible officials who privately thought that this was an extreme understatement, and that Japan might find herself unable to stay in the war under the coming rain of atom bombs.

It was obvious that officials at the highest levels made the important decision to release news of the atomic bomb because of the psychological effect it may have in forcing Japan to surrender. However, there are some officials who feel privately it might have been well to keep this completely secret. Their opinion can be summed up in the comment by one spokesman: "Why bother with psychological warfare against an enemy that already is beaten and hasn't sense enough to quit and save herself from utter doom?"

The first news came from President Truman's office. Newsmen were summoned and the historic statement from the Chief Executive, who still is on the high seas, was given to them.

"That bomb," Mr. Truman said, "had more power than 20,000 tons of TNT. It had more than 2,000 times the blast power of the British 'Grand Slam,' which is the largest bomb (22,000 pounds) ever yet used in the history of warfare."

Explosive Charge Is Small

No details were given on the plane that carried the bomb. Nor was it stated whether the bomb was large or small. The President, however, said the explosive charge was "exceedingly small." It is known that tremendous force is packed into tiny quantities of the element that constitutes these bombs. Scientists, looking to the peacetime uses of atomic power, envisage submarines, ocean liners and planes traveling around the world on a few pounds of the element. Yet, for various reasons the bomb used against Japan could have been extremely large.

Hiroshima, first city on earth to be the target of the "Cosmic Bomb," is a city of 318,000, which is—or was—a major quartermaster depot and port of embarkation for the Japanese. In addition to large military supply depots, it manufactured ordnance, mainly large guns and tanks, and machine tools and aircraft-ordnance parts.

President Truman grimly told the Japanese that "the end is not yet."

"In their present form these bombs are now in production," he said "and even more powerful forms are in development."

He sketched the story of how the late President Roosevelt and Prime Minister Churchill agreed that it was wise to concentrate research in America, and how great, secret cities sprang up in this country, where, at one time, 125,000 men and women labored to harness the atom. Even today more than 65,000 workers are employed.

"What has been done," he said, is the greatest achievement of organized science in history.

"We are now prepared to obliterate more rapidly and completely every productive enterprise the Japanese have above ground in any city. We shall destroy their docks, their factories and their communications. Let there be no mistake; we shall completely destroy Japan's power to make war."

The President emphasized that the atomic discoveries were so important, both for the war and for the peace, that he would recommend to Congress that it consider promptly establishing "an appropriate commission to control the production and use of atomic power within the United States."

"I shall give further consideration and make further recommendations to the Congress as to how atomic power can become a powerful and forceful influence toward the maintenance of world peace," he said.

Secretary Stimson called the atomic bomb "the culmination of years of herculean effort on the part of science and industry, working in cooperation with the military authorities." He promised that "improvements will be forthcoming shortly which will increase by several fold the present effectiveness."

"But more important for the long-range implications of this new weapon," he said, "is the possibility that another scale of magnitude will be developed after considerable research and development. The scientists are confident that over a period of many years atomic bombs may well be developed which will be very much more powerful than the atomic bombs now at hand."

Investigation Started in 1939

It was late in 1939 that President Roosevelt appointed a commission to investigate use of atomic energy for military purposes. Until then only small-scale research with Navy funds had taken place. The program went into high gear.

By the end of 1941 the project was put under direction of a group of eminent American scientists in the Office of Scientific Research and Development, under Dr. Vannevar Bush, who reported, directly to Mr. Roosevelt. The President also appointed a General Policy Group, consisting of former Vice President Henry A. Wallace, Secretary Stimson, Gen. George C. Marshall, Dr. James B. Conant, president of

Harvard, and Dr. Bush. In June, 1942, this group recommended vast expansion of the work and transfer of the major part of the program to the War Department.

Maj. Gen. Leslie R. Groves, a native of Albany, N. Y., and a 48-year-old graduate of the 1918 class at West Point, was appointed by Mr. Stimson to take complete executive charge of the program. General Groves, an engineer, holding the permanent Army rank of lieutenant colonel, received the highest praise from the War Department for the way he "fitted together the multifarious pieces of the vast country-wide jigsaw," and at the same time, organized the virtually air-tight security system that kept the project a secret.

A military policy committee also was appointed, consisting of Dr. Bush, chairman; Dr. Conant, Lieut. Gen. Wilhelm D. Styer and Rear Admiral William R. Purnell.

In December, 1942, the decision was made to proceed with construction of large-scale plants. Two are situated at the Clinton Engineer Works in Tennessee and a third at the Hanford Engineer Works in the State of Washington.

These plants were amazing phenomena in themselves. They grew into large, self-sustaining cities, employing thousands upon thousands of workers. Yet, so close was the secrecy that not only were the citizens of the area kept in darkness about the nature of the project, but the workers themselves had only the sketchiest ideas—if any—as to what they were doing. This was accomplished, Mr. Stimson said, by "compartmentalizing" the work so "that no one has been given more information than was absolutely necessary to his particular job."

The Tennessee reservation consists of 59,000 acres, eighteen miles west of Knoxville; it is known as Oak Ridge and has become a modern small city of 78,000, fifth largest in Tennessee.

In the State of Washington the Government has 430,000 acres in an isolated area, fifteen miles northwest of Pasco. The settlement there, which now has a population of 17,000, consisting of plant operators and their immediate families, is known as Richland.

A special laboratory also has been set up near Santa Fe, N. M., under direction of Dr. J. Robert Oppenheimer of the University of California. Dr. Oppenheimer also supervised the first test of the atomic bomb on July 16, 1945. This took place in a remote section of the New Mexico desert lands, with a group of eminent scientists gathered, frankly fearful to witness the results of the invention, which might turn out to be either the salvation or the Frankenstein's monster of the world.

Mr. Stimson also gave full credit to the many industrial corporations and educational institutions which worked with the War Department in bringing this titanic undertaking to fruition.

In August, 1943, a combined policy committee was appointed, consisting of Secretary Stimson, Drs. Bush and Conant for the United States; the late Field Marshal Sir John Dill (now replaced by Field Marshal Sir Henry Maitland Wilson) and Col. J. J. Llewellin (since replaced by Sir Ronald Campbell), for the United Kingdom, and C. D. Howe for Canada.

"Atomic fission holds great promise for sweeping developments by which our civilization may be enriched when peace comes, but the overriding necessities of war have precluded the full exploration of peacetime applications of this new knowledge," Mr. Stimson said. "However, it appears inevitable that many useful contributions to the well-being of mankind will ultimately flow from these discoveries when the world situation makes it possible for science and industry to concentrate on these aspects."

Although warning that many economic factors will have to be considered "before we can say to what extent atomic energy will supplement coal, oil and water as fundamental sources of power," Mr. Stimson acknowledged that "we are at the threshold of a new industrial art which will take many years and much expenditure of money to develop."

The Secretary of War disclosed that he had appointed an interim committee to study post-war control and development of atomic energy. Mr. Stimson is serving as chairman, and other members include James F. Byrnes, Secretary of State; Ralph A. Bard, former Under-Secretary of the Navy; William L. Clayton, Assistant Secretary of State; Dr. Bush, Dr. Conant, Dr. Carl T. Compton, chief of the Office of Field Service in OSRD and president of Massachusetts Institute of Technology, and George L. Harrison, special consultant to the Secretary of War and president of the New York Life Insurance Company. Mr. Harrison is alternate chairman of the committee.

The committee also has the assistance of an advisory group of some of the country's leading physicists, including Dr. Oppenheimer, Dr. E. O. Lawrence, Dr. A. H. Compton and Dr. Enrico Fermi.

The War Department gave this supplementary background on the development of the atomic bomb:

"The series of discoveries which led to development of the atomic bomb started at the turn of the century when radioactivity became known to science. Prior to 1939 the scientific work in this field was world-wide, but more particularly so in the United States, the United Kingdom, Germany, France, Italy and Denmark. One of Denmark's great scientists, Dr. Neils Bohr, a Nobel Prize winner, was whisked from the grasp of the Nazis in his occupied homeland and later assisted in developing the atomic bomb.

"It is known that Germany worked desperately to solve the problem of controlling atomic energy."

* * *

ATOM BOMBS MADE IN 3 HIDDEN 'CITIES'

Secrecy on Weapon So Great
That Not Even Workers Knew of Their Product

By JAY WALZ
Special to The New York Times.

WASHINGTON, Aug. 6—The War Department revealed today how three "hidden cities" with a total population of 100,000 inhabitants sprang into being as a result of the $2,000,000,000 atomic bomb project, how they did their work without knowing what it was all about, and how they kept the biggest secret of the war.

One of these, Oak Ridge, situated where only oak and pine trees had dotted small farms before, is today the fifth largest city in Tennessee. Its population of 75,000 persons has thirteen supermarkets, nine drug stores and seven theatres.

A second town of 7,000 was built for reasons of isolation and security on a New Mexico mesa. The third, named Richland Village, houses 17,000 men, women and children on remote banks of the Columbia River in the State of Washington.

None of the people, who came to these developments from homes all the way from Maine to California, had the slightest idea of what they were making in the gigantic Government plants they saw all around them.

Oak Ridge, the most remarkable of the towns and heart of the entire project, was operated under the camouflaged name of Manhattan Engineer District, a title selected by Maj. Gen. Leslie L. Groves, director of the vast program. Only a few top ranking scientists, engineers and Army officers knew what the "District" was doing and fewer still realized the full implications.

The manager of one plant, for example, was kept completely isolated from other plants where different processes and methods were used. Work was so compartmentalized that each worker knew only his own job, and had no inkling of how his part fitted into the whole.

Some of the men, it was told today, could not be sure they were actually producing anything. They would see huge quantities of material going into the plants, but nothing came out. "This created an atmosphere of unreality," said a War Department statement, "in which giant plants operated feverishly day and night to produce nothing that could be seen or touched."

Oak Ridge is the residential center for the workers in one division of the Manhattan Engineer District, known as the Clinton Engineer Works, which covers a huge Government reservation of 59,000 acres. Oak Ridge, itself, spreads over eight square miles. It accommodates 10,000 family units, has dormitories for 13,000 residents, 5,000 trailers and huts and barracks for more than 16,000 other inhabitants.

*　*　*

SOVIET DECLARES WAR ON JAPAN; ATTACKS MANCHURIA, TOKYO SAYS; ATOM BOMB LOOSED ON NAGASAKI

2D BIG AERIAL BLOW

Japanese Port Is Target in Devastating New Midday Assault

RESULT CALLED GOOD

Foe Asserts Hiroshima Toll Is 'Uncountable'—Assails 'Atrocity'

By W. H. LAWREICE
By Wireless to The New York Times.

GUAM, Thursday, Aug. 9—Gen. Carl A. Spaatz announced today that a second atomic bomb had been dropped, this time on the city of Nagasaki, and that crew members reported "good results."

The second use of the new and terrifying secret weapon which wiped out more than 60 per cent of the city of Hiroshima and, according to the Japanese radio, killed nearly every resident of that town occurred at noon today, Japanese time. The target today was an important industrial and shipping area with a population of about 253,000.

The great bomb, which harnesses the power of the universe to destroy the enemy by concussion, blast and fire, was dropped on the second enemy city about seven hours after the Japanese had received a political "roundhouse punch" in the form of a declaration of war by the Soviet Union.

Vital Transshipment Point

GUAM, Thursday, Aug. 9 (AP)—Nagasaki is vitally important as a port for transshipment of military supplies and the embarkation of troops in support of Japan's operations in China, Formosa, Southeast Asia and the Southwest Pacific. It was highly important as a major shipbuilding and repair center for both naval and merchantmen.

The city also included industrial surburbs of Inase and Akunoura on the western side of the harbor, and Urakami. The combined area is nearly double Hiroshima's.

Nagasaki, although only two-thirds as large as Hiroshima in population, is considered more important industrially. With a population now estimated at 253,000, its twelve square miles are jam-packed with the eave-to-eave buildings that won it the name of "sea of roofs."

General Spaatz' communiqué reporting the bombing did not say whether one or more than one "mighty atom" was dropped.

Hiroshima a 'City of Dead'

The Tokyo radio yesterday described Hiroshima as a city of ruins and dead "too numerous to be counted," and put forth the claim that the use of the atomic bomb was a violation of international law.

The broadcast, made in French and directed to Europe, came several hours after Tokyo had directed a report to the

Western Hemisphere for consumption in America asserting that "practically all living things, human and animal, were literally seared to death" Monday, when the single bomb was dropped on the southern Honshu city.

The two broadcasts, recorded by the Federal Communications Commission, stressed the terrible effect of the bomb on life and property.

European listeners were told that "as a consequence of the use of the new bomb against the town of Hiroshima on Aug. 6, most of the town has been completely destroyed and there are numerous dead and wounded among the population."

[The United States Strategic Air Forces reported yesterday that 60 per cent of the city had been destroyed.]

"The destructive power of these bombs is in describable," the broadcast continued, "and the cruel sight resulting from the attack is so impressive that one cannot distinguish between men and women killed by the fire. The corpses are too numerous to be counted.

"The destructive power of this new bomb spreads over a large area. People who were outdoors at the time of the explosion were burned alive by high temperature while those who were indoors were crushed by falling buildings."

Authorities still were "unable to obtain a definite check-up on the extent of the casualties" and "authorities were having their hands full in giving every available relief possible under the circumstances," the broadcast continued.

In the destruction of property even emergency medical facilities were burned out, Tokyo said, and relief squads were rushed into the area from all surrounding districts.

The Tokyo radio also reported that the Asahi Shimbun had made "a strong editorial appeal" to the people of Japan to remain calm in facing the use of the new type bomb and renew pledges to continue to fight.

[A special meeting of the Japanese Cabinet was called at the residence of Premier Kantaro Suzuki to hear a preliminary report on the damage, The United Press said.]

A Propaganda Front

Voice broadcasts and wireless transmissions aimed at North America and Europe during the day apparently were trying to establish a propaganda point that the bombings should be stopped.

For example, a Tokyo English language broadcast to North America, accusing American leaders of fomenting an "atrocity campaign" in order "to create the impression that the Japanese are cruel people," as preparation for intensive Allied bombing of Japan, took up the subject of atomic bombing, and described it as "useless cruelty" that "may have given the United States war leaders guilty consciences."

"They may be afraid that their illegal and useless and needless bombing may eventually bring a protest from the American people unless some means of hardening them can be provided," the broadcast continued.

The broadcast to the United States went on to ask: "How will the United States war leaders justify their degradation, not only in the eyes of the other peoples but also in the eyes of the American people? How will these righteous-thinking American people feel about the way their war leaders are perpetuating their crime against man and God?

"Will they condone the whole thing on the ground that everything is fair in love and war or will they rise in anger and denounce this blot on the honor and tradition and prestige of the American people?"

The broadcast said that "authorized quarters in Tokyo made the following statement on Aug. 8 with regard to the United States disregard for humanity:

"International law lays down the principle that belligerent nations are not entitled to unlimited choice in the means by which to destroy their opponents.

"This is made clear by Article 22 of The Hague Convention. Consequently, any attack by such means against open towns and defenseless citizens are unforgivable actions. The United States ought to remember that at the beginning of the fighting in China it protested to Japan on numerous occasions in the name of humanity against smaller raids carried out by Japan."

[Article 22 of The Hague Convention of 1907 Respecting the Laws and Customs of War on Land states: "The right of belligerents to adopt means of injuring the enemy is not unlimited."]

The Tokyo announcer used the French phrase "villes demilitarises," or "open towns," although Hiroshima was known to be a quartermaster depot and a garrison town of considerable military importance.

The description of the havoc followed the line offered earlier in the broadcast to the United States, the "disastrous ruin" that struck the city, crushed houses and buildings, and "all of the dead and injured were burned beyond recognition," said the broadcast.

*   *   *

August 11, 1945

JAPAN OFFERS TO SURRENDER; U. S. MAY LET EMPEROR REMAIN; MASTER RECONVERSION PLAN SET

CABINET BACKS BID

Domei Says Ministers Unanimously Voted to Sue for Peace

ASKS QUICK ANSWER

Reports Emperor Issued Orders After Appeal to Soviet Failed

The Japanese Government's decision to sue for peace was voted unanimously by the full Cabinet, including the War and Navy Ministers, at a meeting that lasted from Thursday until dawn Friday, Domei, the Japanese news agency, reported last night.

Domei said earlier that the Japanese Government had addressed a message to the Swiss and Swedish Governments for transmission to the United States, Great Britain, China and the Soviet Union accepting the Potsdam ultimatum on the understanding that Emperor Hirohito's sovereignty was not questioned, the Federal Communications Commission reported.

Domei, quoting the message, said at 7:35 A. M. [EWT]:

"In obedience to the gracious command of His Majesty the Emperor, who, ever anxious to enhance the cause of world peace, desires earnestly to bring about an early termination of hostilities with a view of saving mankind from the calamities to be imposed upon them by further continuation of the war, the Japanese Government asked several weeks ago the Soviet Government, with which neutral relations then prevailed, to render good offices in restoring peace vis-a-vis the enemy powers.

Claims Peace Move Failed

"Unfortunately, these efforts in the interest of peace having failed, the Japanese Government, in conformity with the august wish of His Majesty to restore the general peace and desiring to put an end to the untold sufferings engendered by the war as quickly as possible, have decided upon the following:

"The Japanese Government are ready to accept the terms enumerated in the joint declaration which was issued at Potsdam on July 26, 1945, by the heads of the Governments of the United States, Great Britain and China and later subscribed to by the Soviet Government with the understanding that the said declaration does not comprise any demand which prejudices the prerogatives of His Majesty as a sovereign ruler.

"The Japanese Government hope sincerely that this * * *"

At this point the transmission was interrupted. Domei waited a moment and then said, "Stand by."

The FCC then reported that Domei's carrier wave went off the air, but American monitors still stood by.

Another Domei transmitter, beamed to Europe, said in English at this time, 7:51 A. M. [EWT] that "it is authoritatively learned that the Japanese Government decided to accept the three-power proclamation of Potsdam of July 26 as described by the Soviet Union."

The Domei transmitter aimed at Europe sent a jumbled passage after the sentence ending "* * * as described by the Soviet Union," and then began sending the following, the FCC reported:

"Acceptance of the Potsdam proclamation as communicated to these Governments through the Swiss and Swedish Governments was expressed by authoritative quarters here today. These quarters recalled a broadcast addressed to Japan on July 27 by Captain Zacharias, who professed to be the spokesman for the Washington Government, in which he said that Japan's acceptance of Allied peace terms will make it possible to apply the Atlantic Charter to Japan and therefore the Japanese nation will be free to adopt a form of Government of their own choosing.

Says Emperor Made Decision

"The same quarters stressed that the decision by the Japanese Government to accept the peace terms, as set forth in the Potsdam proclamation under extremely difficult circumstances, has been due to the august wish of His Majesty, the Emperor, who was anxious to forward the cause of world peace as well as the welfare of His Majesty's subjects.

"These quarters further stressed that whether in war or in peace it is the immutable conviction of the entire Japanese nation firmly to uphold Japan's national . . . "

The FCC said that this transmission then broke off.

The FCC monitors, listening into Japanese voice and wireless emissions, said that no further reference was heard about the surrender offer since the original transmission to North America and the subsequent transmission to Europe broke off, up to 9:15 A. M. [EWT].

At that time a Domei transmitter sending Romanized Japanese to the Orient carried repeats of reports on the fighting and general news put out overnight by the Japanese.

The Tokyo shortwave voice transmitter repeated the Imperial Headquarters communiqué on the fighting on the new Russians fronts, repeated the text of a protest on the atom bomb and similar items, among them an account of President Truman's speech.

The Tokyo home and empire radio, which has not been heard mentioning the offer, continued to broadcast routine stories.

Original Message Concluded

Then at 9:33 A. M. [EWT] Domei transmitted a one-sentence conclusion to the text of its purported message, repeating the first part.

The concluding sentence read in full:

"The Japanese Government hope sincerely that this understanding is warranted and desire keenly that an explicit indication to that effect will be speedily forthcoming."

Immediately after Domei transmitted the conclusion of the message text, it directed a message to Europe substantially repeating the transmission it had made earlier to that area.

The later transmission, however, clarified the opening statement to show the Japanese saying that "authoritative quarters" in Tokyo had expressed the "conviction" that the Allied Governments had "no ground" on which to oppose the Japanese acceptance of the Potsdam proclamation.

The dispatch, as before, then went on to refer to the broadcast by Captain Zacharias of July 27.

While the Japanese propaganda agencies did not mention the surrender offer, as such, to home audiences in Japan, Hiroshi Shimomura, president of the Japanese Board of Information, did issue a formal statement to the Japanese people yesterday afternoon (Tokyo time) in which he said that the Russian declaration of war and the United States' use of a "new type of bomb" had made the Japanese "recognize the fact that the situation at present is at its worst."

He called upon the Japanese people, nevertheless, to give their best efforts at home and on the battlefield "to defend the last line and to build up racial honor in the just defense of our nation."

This statement by Mr. Shimomura followed an unusual audience that, the Tokyo radio reported Thursday, he had had with Emperor Hirohito.

Some three hours before Domei had transmitted the Japanese offer to accept the terms of the Potsdam ultimatum, Japanese War Minister Gen. Korechika Anami issued an appeal to Japanese troops to "fight to the last" against the Soviet Union.

According to the Domei report, General Anami said:

"I declare to the entire forces: Russia has finally taken up arms against us. Regardless how colored her declaration may be, her ambition to invade and seize greater east Asia is very clear.

"Such is the state of affairs. What is there to say but that we will give our all to carry through toward the successful consummation of this holy war for the defense of our divine land. I firmly believe that in fighting to the end, even if we may be forced to exist on grass and sleep in the fields, there is life in death.

"This is the spirit of serving the nation with seven lives—that is, Kusunoki Masashige's spirit, and the faith of Hojo Tokimune that life springs from nonexistence, indestructibility from destruction.

"I call upon every member of the entire army to exert every effort to manifestation of the Nanko [Kusunoki Masashige] spirit and destroy the enemy with Tokimune's faith. Aug. 10, 1945, Signed: Minister of War."

Calls for More Crops

President Kotaro Sengoku of the Wartime Agricultural Corps also issued a proclamation to Japanese farmers to increase food production "for their own sake regardless of the future condition of affairs," Domei reported.

Domei quoted Sengoku's proclamation as follows:

"The situation has taken a sudden change and our imperial land is now faced with a grave crisis. My faith is firm that the Government will do its utmost for the country and the people by taking appropriate measures to cope with the crisis.

"At this time, the farming people should hold fast to their unwavering structure and quietly devote their efforts to their work. It is absolutely necessary to devote efforts to increased production of food for their own sake regardless of the future condition of affairs.

"It is my desire that every farmer concentrate his efforts toward the carrying out of increased production. Particularly as the responsibility of the farmers and farming villages will increase, the prefectural agricultural associations are called upon to intensify the concentration of the efforts of the farmers under their jurisdiction and take appropriate measures to enable united operation regardless of conditions."

Meanwhile, trading on the Japanese Stock Exchange in Tokyo was suspended "under orders of the finance ministry," Domei said. The order applies to operations "throughout its main office and agencies," said the Domei dispatch.

Peace Committee Reported

CHUNGKING, China, Aug. 10 (U.P.)—Informed Chinese circles reported tonight that Emperor Hirohito had formed a "peace committee" consisting of members of the royal family and high present and former Government officials, which met Friday morning and decided to offer to surrender.

The committee was reported to have included the Emperor's two brothers, Prince Chichibu and Prince Takamatsu; former Premiers Prince Fumimaru Konoye, Hideki Tojo, Baron Kiichiro Hiranuma and Koki Hirota, the present Premier and Ministers of War, Navy and Foreign Affairs.

* * *

September 18, 1945

ITALY'S PEACE PACT HELD UP; BIG 5 MINISTERS IN IMPASSE

By HERBERT L. MATTHEWS
By Wireless to The New York Times.

LONDON, Sept. 17—The Council of Ministers of the five great Powers announced tonight its inability to prepare a draft of the peace treaty for Italy during this visit to London of the Foreign Secretaries. The draft will have to be submitted to the council at its next session, which will probably take place some three or four weeks after this session ends. This means that many hopes—especially those of the United States delegation—have been dashed against the extraordinary complexities and conflicting views of the great Powers. The Italian peace treaty seemed simple and easy from 3,000 miles away in Washington.

But that was before the demands, rivalries, conflicting ideologies and power politics in its crudest and strongest forms swirled around the green baize table in Lancaster House and made a confused and hapless mess out of all the good intentions. The best that the Foreign Ministers could do has been to work on directives to their deputies and experts, who will then prepare a draft treaty for Italy.

They could not—through accident today—even take up the Yugoslav and Italian claims regarding their common frontier, which was to have been discussed. Vice Premier Edvard Kardelj, chief Yugoslav delegate, was late in arriving after a stormy air voyage and was not well enough to appear, so that the discussion will take place tomorrow morning.

Today's session was confined to minor questions, with little progress being made. There were two meetings, one this morning headed by the British Foreign Secretary, Ernest Bevin, and the other this afternoon, with Foreign Commissar Vyacheslaff Molotoff presiding. The latter meeting, according to one who was present, was largely a monologue by Mr. Molotoff, but it must be remembered that everything said at the council has to be translated into two other languages—in this case, English and French—which means that at best Mr. Molotoff could talk for only twenty minutes every hour.

What he said has been kept secret, but there is one very important thing about it that is not secret.

It can be taken as certain now that the Russians are meeting stronger opposition from the other Powers, especially from the United States and Great Britain, than in any international conference since they became one of the United Nations. They have made great demands since this council started, but there is no evidence yet that they are getting more than the other Powers consider is due to them.

Representatives of the British Dominions were present to speak for their Governments, and the Italian Foreign Secretary, Alcide de Gasperi, was all ready with his statement and plea. Your correspondent saw him his evening and found him discouraged but determined to present his case in as friendly and dignified a manner as possible.

He would not state in advance what it would be, for both he and Ambassador Count Nicolo Carandini feel that they must pay respect to their juridical situation as members of a Government living under an armistice and, hence, still theoretically enemies of the United Nations.

Italians Somewhat Relieved

The Yugoslavs, being allies and members of the United Nations, have no such restrictions and are stating their case freely and widely.

The Italians seemed somewhat relieved that the Foreign Ministers had failed in their efforts to draw up a draft peace treaty during these talks, for it has been obvious that any treaty made in the present atmosphere would have been harsh. At the same time, it is felt, "as Premier Ferruccio Parri has made clear," that the Italian Government cannot go on indefinitely under the armistice. Signor Parri is known to feel that elections cannot be held until Italy is free, and he has also made it clear that his Government will not sign what they would consider an unjust peace.

In an interview that the Premier gave in Rome to the Giornale del Mattino he attacked the Yugoslav claims made in a document printed in Monday morning's New York Times, and he made it clear that the Italians would ask for the so-called "Wilson Line," which the World War I President decided in 1919 to be a fair compromise. That line more or less bisects the Istrian Peninsula.

Signor Parri attacked the line established by Allied military forces during the war, known as the Morgan Line, which gives virtually all Istria to the Yugoslavs but leaves Trieste to the Italians. According to tomorrow morning's London Times, the British will favor a compromise between those two lines.

The British are primarily concerned with keeping the great Adriatic port of Trieste out of hands that might be considered Russian or Russian dominated, but whatever they and the Americans feel, their case is based upon what they consider solid factual ethnical reasons.

From that viewpoint, Signor de Gasperi tomorrow morning will be speaking for the United States and Britain as well as Italy. Where he and his country seem bound to lose out is in the fact that what would be for the Anglo-Saxon Powers a compromise between two lines is pure loss to the Italians, who will have only the consolation of knowing that it could have been worse.

So far as general principles are concerned, there will be an effort at least to get recognition for what Italy has done in the past two years of co-belligerency on the Allied side. It is hoped that some interim document can be agreed upon, even if tentatively, to replace the onerous armistice.

For it is obvious from tonight's communiqué that months must pass before there can be a peace treaty and perhaps many months. Here is what the last and most important paragraph of the communiqué says:

"The Council thereupon decided to postpone until tomorrow morning the hearing of views from the invited Governments upon the Italo-Yugoslav frontier question and continue its consideration of the directive which will guide the deputies in their preparation of a draft peace treaty with Italy. This draft is to be submitted to the Council at its second session."

This means that the Foreign Secretaries of the five great powers who started their meeting so hopefully here last Tuesday will have been able to give their deputies only general instructions on the lines they are to follow in preparing the draft peace treaty. The next session of the Council will, at best, be in mid-October, and more likely November. At that time the Ministers will then have to begin further series of discussions like those now being held. When or if they decide upon a draft treaty, it must be submitted to all the countries interested—and they are many—and probably to the general peace conference.

That is why months must pass before Italy can have her peace treaty and be admitted to the United Nations Organization—unless some interim arrangement is worked out to give her a tentative status. Meanwhile, this particular session of Ministers will presumably be free after tomorrow to go on to other subjects.

The treaty with Bulgaria is supposed to be the next subject on the agenda, but it is obvious that no preparations have been made to offer any possibility of drawing up a draft treaty now.

It was obviously not even possible to prepare thoroughly for the Italian treaty in advance. Efforts were made to do so, but it is known, for instance, that Washington received its copy of the British memorandum on the draft treaty for Italy a few weeks before the conference opened, but the American delegation was surprised when it was presented, according to a reliable source.

*   *   *

October 19, 1945

TRUMAN ASKS WORLD CHIEFS TO END THE POLITICAL IMPASSE

May Be Acting to Prepare Meeting of Big 3 or Big 5—President Denies Knowledge About Mysterious Gromyko Trip

By BERTRAM D. HULEN
Special to The New York Times.

WASHINGTON, Oct. 18—President Truman has entered into correspondence with the leaders of the other members of the Big Five, as well as the nations interested in the Far East, in an effort to resolve the problems that led to the impasse at the London meetings of the Council of Foreign Ministers. These involved European questions and the Far East.

In making this known today at his press conference in response to questions, Mr. Truman admitted that there was a situation at present. He had received recently a communication from Generalissimo Joseph Stalin, he said, but it was a formal reply on an earlier matter and, he added, it had nothing to do with the present situation.

At the same time the President described as a good plan the view of Generalissimo Chiang Kai-shek that the Japanese people should be permitted to decide whether they should retain or get rid of their Emperor. He had not known of such a plan, in response to a question, but he thought it was a good plan.

In announcing that he had taken the initiative in the matter of exchanges of communications among the world's leaders, President Truman said he was sure the problems would be worked out. No meeting of the Big Three was in contemplation, he added.

However, in opinion here, if the exchanges develop satisfactorily and reach a point where personal conversations will be more advantageous and will have every prospect of success, a meeting on the top level may be held. The present exchanges, it was observed, could point in the direction of a Big Three or Big Five meeting eventually.

In addition to the Big Five President Truman is approaching the Netherlands, Australia, New Zealand and the Philippines, who are interested in the Advisory Commission on the Far East, which will hold its organization meeting here next Tuesday. Russia has not as yet accepted an invitation to participate.

However, the chief hope for a successful solution of the many problems lies in a direct appeal to Generalissimo Stalin. It was apparent today that he had not yet replied to any communication the President may have sent him.

In diplomatic circles the view was expressed that Russia might be re-examining her foreign policy in the light of the meeting of Foreign Ministers and our rejection of her demand for a four-power control commission in Tokyo.

In this connection mystery still surrounds the dramatic turn-about flights of Andrei A. Gromyko, the Soviet Ambassador. President Truman said he did not know why the Ambassador made the brief visit and wished he did. It seems to be interesting to everybody, he added. He assumed that the Ambassador had come here briefly on personal business.

The subsequent intimation by the Ambassador in London that he had left a communication with the State Department yielded nothing here. The department made a thorough search of its offices and quizzed its personnel without result.

Speculates on Failure

The situation requiring the exchanges between the chiefs of State was described today by Hugh R. Wilson, former Ambassador to Germany and a professional diplomat of long experience, who is now adviser on foreign affairs to the Republican National Committee.

"The conference of Foreign Ministers in London," he said in an address before the DAR, "met under conditions which made it practically impossible to succeed and thereby caused irritation among the most powerful members of the United Nations.

The method—or lack of it—that had worked with the Big Three, with full powers and under pressure of military necessity, failed when the pressure had been lifted and when men without full powers were in discussion. All the differences that had been passed over and held in abeyance under the pressure of necessity for unity during the prosecution of the war sprang into glaring light.

"What had been foreseen as a meeting to draft treaties of peace for the defeated powers, starting with Italy, turned into a meeting overwhelmingly occupied by the attempt to establish a peace between the principal members of the United Nations."

Mr. Wilson set forth the desires of the Soviet Union as follows:

"1. The Soviet Union desires unrestricted handling on its part of the states of Eastern Europe. America insistence on something approximating a Bill of Rights for the people of those states was made clear and unequivocal.

"2. The Soviet Union desires a share in the control of Japan. Our Government has suggested a share by the Russians in the political advice to be given to General MacArthur.

"3. The Soviet Union desires large funds for rehabilitation. An American position has not yet been taken in respect to this problem.

"4. The atomic bomb. The revelation of its secret is earnestly desired by the Russians."

Gromyko Heightens Mystery

LONDON, Oct. 18 (UPI)—Soviet Ambassador Gromyko, back in London after a mysterious twenty-four-hour trip to Washington, refused to say today whether he had carried a letter from Premier Stalin to President Truman, but added, "The State Department may have something to say on it."

"There is nothing mysterious about my flight to America," Mr. Gromyko said. "I had business to transact, and having completed it, I returned at once."

Mr. Gromyko thought it probable that he would remain in London for the duration of the United Nations Executive

Committee meetings, but he would not say whether he intended to report to Moscow in the near future.

* * *

October 19, 1945

GERMANS INDICTED IN MASSACRE OF 11,000 POLES IN KATYN FOREST

With Russians Scheduled to Prosecute Case, Accused Are Expected to Recall Former Charge That Red Army Killed Victims

Special to The New York Times.

BERLIN, Oct. 18—An indictment returned today before the International Tribunal holds the Germans responsible for the slaughter of 11,000 Polish officers in the Katyn forest near Smolensk.

This is but one of the many war crimes for which the majority of the German war leaders awaiting trial at Nuremberg will have to answer, but it is likely to prove by far the most controversial issue of the whole trial.

For the Germans have charged that the massacre was perpetrated by the Russians themselves before the German attack on the Soviet Union and the defence can hardly be expected to miss the opportunity to challenge the Russian prosecutors for proof of the charge.

The discovery of the bodies in mass graves in the Katyn Forest and its announcement by Germany marked one of the diplomatic crises of the war. The Polish Government in Exile in London immediately appealed to the International Red Cross to investigate and fix the responsibility. The Russians retorted by declaring this an unfriendly action by an ally and ultimately severed relations with the London Poles.

Later the Russians held a public exhumation of the bodies but the results were inconclusive.

Now for the first time the whole issue is thrown before a legal tribunal bound by the rules of evidence applying to military tribunals. Since it has been agreed that the Russian prosecutor, R. A. Rudenko, shall have charge of the presentation of proof relating to war crimes committed east of a line running north and south through the center of Berlin, it will fall to the lot of the Russians to prove their own charge that the Germans slaughtered the Poles and buried them in the Katyn forest.

It is an issue that the Germans are almost sure to challenge with all the documentation at their disposal.

The fate of these Polish officers was a mystery to Polish leaders for a long time before their bodies were found. It is said that the late former Premier, Gen. Wladislaw Sikorski, on his first visit to Moscow at Christmastime in 1941, asked Premier Stalin about what had happened to them, and at first received satisfactory assurances regarding their safety.

Much of the proof of what really happened in the Katyn forest will devolve upon the date upon which these Polish officers were slaughtered; for if the crime was committed after the date when the Germans overran their last resting place it could not possibly have been committed by the Russians.

The Germans overran the Katyn Forest in July, 1941.

* * *

November 16, 1945

3 NATIONS OFFER ATOM BOMB TO UNO ON RECIPROCAL BASIS, INSPECTIONS AS SAFEGUARDS

It Would Take Over World's Basic Scientific Knowledge, Promote Use of Energy

By FELIX BELAIR Jr.
Special to The New York Times.

WASHINGTON, Nov. 15—President Truman and Prime Ministers Attlee of Great Britain and W. L. Mackenzie King of Canada expressed their willingness in a joint statement today to share, on a reciprocal basis with other United Nations, detailed information on the practical application of atomic energy "just as soon as effective enforceable safeguards against its use for destructive purposes can be devised." Inspection of nations is one of the provisions.

To this end and for extension and consolidation of the authority of the United Nations Organization as an instrument for world peace they proposed the creation within the organization of a new commission to formulate recommendations to eliminate the use of atomic energy for destructive purposes and to promote its widest use for industrial and humanitarian purposes.

Meanwhile the three atomic-energy custodians said they were "not convinced that the spreading of the specialized information regarding the practical application of atomic energy, before it is possible to devise effective, reciprocal and enforceable safeguards acceptable to all nations, would contribute to a constructive solution of the problem of the atomic bomb."

"Opposite Effect" Possible

"On the contrary," they said in the joint communiqué, "we think it might have the opposite effect."

Thus after five days of continued conferences the three leaders combined a concrete program for sharing their knowledge of atomic force with a strong appeal to all nations to contribute toward strengthening of the United Nations Organization to the end of banishing the scourge of war from the earth forever.

"Faced with the terrible realities of the application of science to destruction, every nation will realize more urgently than before the overwhelming need to maintain the rule of law among nations and to banish the scourge of war from the earth," the communiqué concluded.

Left to right, front row: Prime Minister Attlee, President Truman and Prime Minister King. Rear row: T. L. Rowan, secretary to Mr. Attlee; Dr. Vannevar Bush, United States expert; Maj. Gen. E. I. C. Jacob, British expert; Representative Charles A. Eaton, Senator Brien McMahon, Canadian Ambassador Lester B. Pearson, Secretary of State James F. Byrnes, Representative Sol Bloom and Admiral William D. Leahy at the White House yesterday.

"This can only be brought about by giving wholehearted support to the United Nations Organization, and by consolidating and extending its authority, thus creating conditions of mutual trust in which all peoples will be free to devote themselves to the arts of peace. It is our firm resolve to work without reservation to achieve these ends."

As had been anticipated, the communiqué contained no direct reference to the Soviet Union or the keen desire here and in London for a more wholehearted cooperative spirit on the part of the Soviet in their annual councils, such as that of the Big Five Foreign Ministers. That nation was unmistakably in the minds of all three leaders, however, when they proposed to make available all atomic energy information for purposes of peace to the world, and said:

"We trust that other nations will adopt the same policy, thereby creating an atmosphere of reciprocal confidence in which political agreement and cooperation will flourish."

However this gesture of cooperation with the Soviet Government may be received in Moscow, it evoked no enthusiasm from representatives from that government here. Embassy officials had no comment to make for publication on their attitude toward the communiqué, but they were known to be expecting a more substantial offer than the communiqué conveyed.

President Truman read the joint communiqué to assembled reporters a few minutes after 11 A. M. today while Prime Ministers Attlee and King, seated at his right and left, listened silently. It was evident that none of the principals had had his normal quota of sleep last night following the White House final working session that continued past midnight.

Mr. Truman read with a hoarse voice, and the two Ministers slumped in their chairs, looking up occasionally to reveal blood-shot eyes. All of them had continued working with their own staffs after the agreement on the communique was reached last night, and the President prefaced his reading of the statement by telling reporters they would have to reserve any questions on the document until a later date when he said they would be more familiar with it.

In the background, as the President read the statement for the three conferees, were Senators and Representatives directly concerned with legislation to control atomic energy domestically, as well as research and experimentation in that field. Standing quietly and alone over to one side stood Dr.

Vannevar Bush, Director of the Office of Scientific Research and Development.

Specific Proposals

In addition to recommending establishment of a UNO commission to formulate recommendations, the United States, British and Canadian leaders called for specific proposals dealing with the following phases of the control problem:

(a) For extending between all nations the exchange of basic scientific information for peaceful ends.

(b) For control of atomic energy to the extent necessary to insure its use only for peaceful purposes.

(c) For the elimination from national armaments of atomic weapons adaptable to mass destruction.

(d) For effective safeguards by way of inspection and other means to protect complying States against the hazards of violations and evasions.

It was suggested in connection with the work of the commission that it should proceed by separate stages, "the successful completion of each one of which will develop the necessary confidence of the world before the next stage is undertaken."

It was specifically suggested that the commission might well devote its attention first to a wide exchange of scientists and scientific information on atomic energy and, as a second stage, the development of full knowledge concerning natural resources of raw materials.

The heads of the three Governments had said in the communiqué that they believed "the fruits of scientific research should be made available to all nations," since freedom of investigation and free interchange of ideas were essential to the progress of knowledge. Then it said that in pursuance of this policy the basic scientific information to development of atomic energy for peaceful purposes already had been made available to the world.

Statement Is Questioned

This statement was challenged elsewhere in the Federal establishment, however, and Dr. Vannevar Bush was quoted as saying that while considerable basic information had been made available, the statement was not, strictly speaking, accurate.

Whatever the validity of the challenge from this highly placed official, it was considered an extremely important one in view of another pertinent passage in the communiqué that "the military exploitation of atomic energy depends, in large part, upon the same methods and processes as would be required for industrial uses."

In all, the agreed-on declaration by the three leaders embraced nine interrelated principles, the first of which was a recognition that the application of recent scientific discoveries to the methods and practice of war has placed at the disposal of mankind means of destruction hitherto unknown "against which there can be no adequate military defense, and in the employment of which no single nation can have a monopoly."

A second point accepted the responsibility of the United States, Britain and Canada to take the initiative in international action to prevent use of atomic energy for destructive purposes and its channeling to peaceful and humanitrian ends. Then the principals declared their awareness that "the only complete protection for the civilized world from the destructive use of scientific knowledge lies in the prevention of war."

They said no system of safeguards could of itself provide an effective guarantee against atomic weapons by a nation bent on aggression and recognized that weapons equally destructive as atomic energy might yet be devised.

No Demands on Russia

Plainly a compromise or meeting of minds between President Truman and Prime Minister Attlee, the document was important for what it did not say as well for what it did. It contained no request of Russia to clarify its post-war territorial and other aspirations in eastern Europe, that delicate subject being left for diplomatic inquiry.

Prime Minister Attlee returned to the White House for further discussions with President Truman this afternoon, and although nothing was learned officially of the nature of his conversation, it was assumed that it dealt with the necessary diplomatic implementation of the document with others of the United Nations.

Secretary of State James F. Byrnes immediately communicated the text of the agreed declaration to Russia, China and France as members of the Foreign Ministers Council and later in the day to other members of the United Nations. The British Foreign Office meanwhile had sent out texts of the documents to their diplomatic representatives in all foreign capitals with which it had friendly relations.

Secretary Byrnes, it was learned, will devote a large part of an address that he is making tomorrow night at Charleston, S.C., to the subject of atomic energy in international relations and the agreed declaration issued today in the framing of which he was an active participant. The Secretary had planned originally to discuss world trade but altered his plans in the light of today's communiqué. The address will be broadcast at 8 P.M. over the National Broadcasting network.

Prime Minister Attlee will call on President Truman briefly again tomorrow morning to bid him goodbye before leaving on an afternoon train for Ottawa with Prime Minister King.

* * *

December 25, 1945

BIG 3 END IMPASSE ON PEACE TREATIES; GIVE FRANCE ROLE, FIX 21-NATION PARLEY; POPE SEES MENACE IN TOTALITARIANISM

COMPROMISE MADE

Russia Wins Diplomatic Victory as Big 3 Will Dominate Drafting

CONFERENCE BY MAY 1

Only Nations That Fought Will Be Invited to Take Part— Stalin Host at Dinner

By BROOKS ATKINSON
By Cable to The New York Times.

MOSCOW, Dec. 24—If the Governments of France and China agree, only members of the Foreign Ministers Council who were signatories to the surrender terms for Italy, Rumania, Bulgaria, Hungary and Finland will participate in the preparation of the respective peace treaties, according to an announcement this evening by the three Foreign Secretaries now meeting in Moscow. The announcement says specifically:

"The terms of the peace treaties with Italy will be drafted by the Foreign Ministers of the United Kingdom, United States, Soviet Union and France. The terms of the peace treaties with Rumania, Bulgaria and Hungary by the Foreign Ministers of the Soviet Union, United States and United Kingdom. The peace treaty for Finland by the Foreign Ministers of the Soviet Union and United Kingdom."

Draft to Precede Parley

After the peace treaties have been drafted the Council of Foreign Ministers will convoke a large conference that will include "all members of the United Nations that actively waged war with a substantial military force against European enemy states." The peace conference will be held no later than May 1, 1946.

After the conclusion of the general conference "and upon consideration of its recommendations the states signatory to the terms of armistice with Italy, Rumania, Bulgaria, Hungary and Finland—France being regarded as such for purposes of the peace treaty with Italy—will draw up the final texts of the peace treaties."

The final texts will be signed by representatives of the states represented at the conference which are at war with the enemy states in question. "The texts of the respective peace treaties will then be submitted to other United Nations which are at war with the enemy states in question," the communiqué says.

Deputies to Resume Work

Deputies of the Foreign Ministers Council in London, who have been held up in the work of drafting peace treaties since the collapse of the London meeting, will be instructed to resume their work on the basis of understandings reached on questions discussed at the London meeting. The peace treaties will come into force immediately after they are ratified by the respective Allied states. The peace treaties are also subject to ratification by the enemy states in question.

All these proposals are subject to agreement by France and China, who are members of the Foreign Ministers Council. Tonight's statement concludes by saying that the present conversations are continuing in a friendly spirit on other matters and "it is hoped that a communiqué covering the work of the conference may be issued within a day or two."

Tonight's proposals appear to represent a combination of Russian and United States points of view on this subject as they were revealed in the London Council meeting. At that time the Soviet Union maintained that peace treaties with Italy, Bulgaria, Rumania, Hungary and Finland should be drafted only by the Foreign Secretaries of nations that actually waged war on these countries. Mr. Byrnes proposed a general peace conference of all members of the United Nations that actively waged war against European enemy States.

Tonight's communication states that the following countries will be invited to attend such a general peace conference in addition to the Big Five: Australia, Belgium, White Russian Soviet Socialist Republic, Brazil, Canada, Czechoslovakia, Ethiopia, Greece, India, the Netherlands, New Zealand, Norway, Poland, the Union of South Africa, Yugoslavia and the Ukranian Soviet Socialist Republic.

This is the first concrete news that has been released about the current session of the Foreign Ministers, and it is regarded as a good indication that a large measure of agreement has been reached. It shows willingness on both sides to consider the other viewpoint. It is hoped that the final communiqué will disclose other agreements that bear out the attitude of optimism that has grown up about the Big Three conference in the past few days.

Present indications are that the current conference will be concluded tomorrow or Wednesday. The full conference had a four-hour session this afternoon in Spiridonovka House. Premier Stalin was host at a dinner in the Kremlin tonight, at which eleven members of the American delegation and an equal number of the British delegation met with the Russian hosts. Such dinners are usually regarded as the final social gathering of such conferences.

Today the general consensus is that the Big Three conference has been worth while and has removed obstacles that had grown up in collaboration during the past two and a half months. It is believed that it will be possible now to resume the work of international affairs and of the United Nations Organization with a fair measure of success. Many grave problems remain; others are bound to arise in the course of time, but the recent log jam has now been broken.

The work has been easier than at the London conference. The Russians have been excellent hosts. Tonight's communiqués on the tangled subject of the peace treaties is regarded as proof that the conference was able to achieve reasonable agreement on at least one subject that sharply divided the Foreign Ministers of the Big Three early in October.

Called Soviet Diplomatic Victory

MOSCOW, Dec. 24 (U.P.)—The effect of the accord is that Russia has won a diplomatic victory in that the Big Three will dominate the peace terms, preparing both preliminary drafts and final texts.

Well-informed quarters here remained most optimistic regarding the general success of the Moscow conference. But some cautiously said that the program was of limited extent and indicated that no startling agreements might be announced on big problems, such as atomic energy control.

Stalin Host to Byrnes, Bevin

MOSCOW, Dec. 24 (AP)—Generalissimo Stalin was host at an official dinner in the Kremlin tonight for United States Secretary of State Byrnes, British Foreign Secretary Bevin and twenty other American and British guests. For Mr. Byrnes and Mr. Bevin it was the high point of their Moscow visit, which has been marked by friendliness that went beyond the traditional Russian courtesy to guests.

It was Premier Stalin's first big official dinner as host to foreigners since his return from an extended vacation near the Black Sea.

While it was Christmas Eve to a large part of the world, the date was not observed in the Soviet Union, where, following the old calendar, the Russian Orthodox Church celebrates the Nativity on Jan. 7. At the Spasso House, however, United States Ambassador W. Averell Harriman planned an elaborate Christmas Eve party to take place after the Kremlin dinner.

It is customary at such dinners for Premier Stalin to sit with the senior ranking visiting guest on his right. In this case it would be Mr. Byrnes. Mr. Bevin as junior in office to Mr. Byrnes would be seated at Generalissimo Stalin's left.

* * *

January 1, 1946

HISTORY TEACHING IN JAPAN BROUGHT UNDER ALLIED BAN

By BURTON CRANE
By Wireless to The New York Times.

TOKYO, Dec. 31—The suspension of teaching of Japanese history, geography and morals by Japanese schools was ordered today by Allied Headquarters. Textbooks and teachers' manuals, the Education Ministry was told, must be collected and destroyed and the pulp used to make new books from which militaristic ideas are eliminated.

Current-events programs tied to radio news periods will substitute for three subjects with which Japan's military clique indoctrinated school children. The open-discussion method is planned wherever possible, students debating what is happening to Japan and to the rest of the world.

The Japanese Education Ministry is preparing to have textbooks on the three subjects rewritten, and temporary substitutes, probably in pamphlet form, are planned for next spring.

The order covered fifty textbooks and teachers' manuals from which, Allied Headquarters discovered, excisions would be impracticable. It also rescinds all regulations telling teachers how to present the three subjects.

Brig. Gen. Ken R. Dyke, chief of the Civilian Information and Education Section, revealed the plans for rewriting history textbooks, giving the greatest latitude possible to free speech. "I see no reason why the Japanese should not have pro-Japanese histories," he said. "All nations relate history from their own viewpoints. As long as Japanese scholars put the early 'history' where it belongs, under the category of folklore, and as long as they do not indulge in misstatements of fact, they will be allowed to write 'Japanese' history.

"I would like to see the Japanese establish something like a Rockefeller Institute, from which experts might obtain grants making possible an intensive rewrite job, divided according to their abilities and possibly according to historical periods in which they have specialized. That would expedite the replacing of objectionable material. If the aid of eminent British and American historians is desired for such an effort, I'm sure it would be available.

"Whatever method is used in rewriting, as soon as the material reaches 'semi-final' form, we plan to make it available for a series of movies with full dramatization of each important incident so the Japanese people generally as well as school children can see and understand their true history for the first time.

"History is the most important, but large sections of [Japan's] geography is devoted to justification of Japan's territorial ambitions. Moreover, large chunks have been rendered obsolete recently.

"Japan's morals are of course, generally excellent."

One paragraph of Gen. Douglas MacArthur's directive told the Japanese to submit a plan for a substitute school program to present "fundamental social, economic and political truths and relating them to the world and to the students' life."

Asked who would determine economic truths, General Dyke laughed, and replied:

"This is one of those phrases that sound all right when read quickly but which turn your stomach when read slowly. Here is the method we shall follow. We will invite the Japanese to name experts in each subject. As usual, this section will be obliged to reject 70 per cent of the suggested names, but eventually we will get a suitable panel of reasonably liberal men. These will work out the general lines for presentation of a substitute program with our assistance and advice."

The directive requires the banned textbooks to be collected in the Tokyo, Osaka, Kyoto and Kobe areas not later than the beginning of the spring term. Not later than April, the order requires a detailed report covering the collection in other areas, including the total of volumes collected together with places where they are stored.

* * *

January 1, 1946

HIROHITO DISCLAIMS DIVINITY

DEITY IDEA BLASTED

Emperor Asks Japanese to Build New Nation Based on Peace

REJECTS NOTIONS OF OLD

Denies His People Are Above Others and Swears to Liberty for Masses

By LINDESAY PARROTT
By Wireless to The New York Times.

TOKYO, Tuesday, Jan. 1—Emperor Hirohito in a New Year's message to his people today proclaimed that the notion of his own divinity—buttressed by the Japanese Constitution and law—was a matter of "legends and myths." He called on the nation to eliminate its evils of the past and to work united to found a new and peaceful Japan.

The message, the first to the Japanese public by the Emperor since he announced, more than four months ago, the nation's defeat and surrender, took the form and had the force of an imperial rescript, the most binding command to his subjects that the Japanese system of religion and jurisprudence had been able to devise.

In more than one way it was a historic document, one that will rank in Japanese annals with the declarations of Hirohito's grandfather, Emperor Meiji, establishing a modern Japan at the end of its feudal period. Hirohito evidently felt as much for his rescript opened with Meiji's most famous assertion of principles at the opening of his reign on March 14, 1868.

Refers to Mutual Trust

"The ties between us and our people," Hirohito continued, according to the official translation, "have always stood upon mutual trust and affection. They do not depend upon mere legends and myths. They are not predicated on the false conception that the Emperor is divine and that the Japanese people are superior to the other races and fated to rule the world."

The Japanese language version added a phrase that the English translation by Allied headquarters slurred: "The Tenno [Emperor] is not a living god."

[This wording follows closely that of Gen. Douglas MacArthur's order of Dec. 15 abolishing Shinto as the national religion. That order, in addition to barring "the doctrine that the Emperor of Japan is superior to the heads of other states because of ancestry, descent or special origin," prohibited "the doctrine that the people of Japan are superior to the people of other lands."]

This was the first time a Japanese Emperor had ever sent a New Year's rescript to the nation, Japanese sources said, and one of the few occasions in recent decades when the people as a whole had been addressed on the broadest national topics by their ancestral ruler. Rescripts in general are enactments of measures passed by the Parliaments.

Reaffirms Meiji Oath

In his denial of his divinity the man whom the Japanese Constitution calls "sacred and inviolable" made two pledges.

The first was to take anew the charter oath of Emperor Meiji, with its pledge of free assembly and government according to public opinion, its promise to discard old usages and its gift of "justice and equity" to "all common people" as well as the governing class. The second was a new assertion: "We stand by the people and we wish always to share with them in their moments of joys and sorrows."

From his subjects the Emperor asked two efforts: unity and work. If Japan united in a resolve to seek civilization in peace, the rescript said, a bright future would crown not only Japan but also all humanity.

These words were strong for a man who, according to some reports—more believed, apparently, abroad than here—had been hesitating on the verge of abdication or for a monarch who had seen his country defeated, occupied and bankrupt while his own traditional privileges were still at the discretion of Japan's conquerors.

Emperor Defines Aim

Opening his "greeting" to the New Year with a repetition of Meiji's oath and his pledge to reaffirm it, Hirohito told his subjects his aim was to restore the country to its own feet and that they must "proceed unflinchingly toward the elimination of misguided practices of past." By keeping in close touch with the people's desires, he said, "we will construct a new Japan through thoroughly being pacific."

The rescript recognized the troubles through which the nation was passing, but the ruler, who according to Japanese belief is descended directly from the Sun Goddess Amaterasu, warned that he was "deeply concerned" lest, as a result, they wander into revolutionary paths.

[Hirohito, in speaking of restlessness in Japan, referred for the first time to the nation's defeat.]

Whether Hirohito wrote the message is, of course, not known, though its tone was markedly unlike that of the old "palace guard" who in the past was closest to the throne. The text was handed to Japanese papers through the Imperial Household offices for release this morning and copies were sent to Allied Headquarters for translation and transmission to the rest of the world.

Whoever wrote the document touched on one of the sorest subjects in Japan's internal situation: the ordinary citizen's growing distrust of the Shidehara Government and its general unwillingness to raise a hand to carry out Government orders, as exemplified in the recent almost total omission to deliver public rice collections.

"Our Government should make every effort to alleviate their [the Japanese people's] trials and tribulations," the rescript said.

MacArthur Pledges Freedom

TOKYO, Jan. 1 (U.P.)—General MacArthur, in a New Year's statement to the Japanese people today promised they would have freedom they had never known before.

"It is necessary for the masses of Japan to awaken to the fact that they now have the power to govern, and what is done must be done by themselves," he said.

* * *

January 20, 1946

IRAN ASKS COUNCIL TO PROBE MEDDLING CHARGED TO SOVIET

Files Plea Seeking Settlement of Azerbaijan Issue and Withdrawal of Troops

NEGOTIATION EFFORT CITED

Syria and Lebanon Urge Recall of British-French Forces— Early UNO Tests Posed

By JAMES B. RESTON

By Wireless to The New York Times.

LONDON, Jan. 19—Iran formally charged the Soviet Union tonight with interfering in her internal affairs and asked the Security Council of the United Nations Organization to investigate the dispute and recommend appropriate terms of settlement.

Coincidentally, Syria and Lebanon demanded "an early and complete withdrawal" of British and French troops from the Levant States but did not, as in the case of Iran, ask the UNO to take action in the matter.

Thus on the ninth day of the first session of the General Assembly the security organization was confronted with charges against three members of the Big Five, which have special rights and responsibilities in the primary task of keeping the peace.

The demands of Syria and Lebanon were contained in speeches delivered before the sixteenth plenary session, but Iran's request was presented in a formal note by the head of the Iranian delegation, Seyed Hassan Taqizadeh, to the Acting Secretary General of the Assembly, Gladwyn Jebb of Britain.

TEXT OF IRAN'S NOTE

The text of the note, which was immediately sent to the eleven members of the Security Council, including the Soviet Union, follows:

Sir:

Owing to interference by the Soviet Union, through the medium of their officials and armed forces, in the internal affairs of Iran, a situation has arisen which may lead to international friction.

In accordance with Article 23 of the Charter of the United Nations, the Iranian Government have repeatedly tried to negotiate with the Government of the Soviet Union but have met with no success.

Accordingly, the Iranian delegation to the General Assembly of the United Nations, on behalf of the Iranian Government, have the honor to request you, in accordance with the terms of Article 35 (Paragraph 1) of the Charter, to bring the matter to the attention of the Security Council so that the Council may investigate the situation and recommend appropriate terms of settlement.

The Iranian delegation is prepared to assist the Security Council by furnishing a full statement of the facts which have given rise to the present situation, together with a copy of the relevant treaty which binds the parties concerned.

I have the honor to be, Sir, your obedient servant,

S. H. TAQIZADEH,

Head of the Iranian Delegation.

Early Consideration Unlikely

The Security Council is expected to hold its second meeting early next week, but it is unlikely that the Iranian request will be considered fully for several days. At its first meeting the Council approved agenda that contained consideration of the Big Three's atomic energy resolution and recommendations about the office of Secretary General. These matters will probably be discussed before the Iranian question arises.

[A hint of an armed rising by tribesmen against the Provincial Government of Bakhtiari, in south central Iran, was contained in a protest to Teheran against the Governor, according to a Soviet Tass agency report cited by a Columbia Broadcasting System correspondent in Moscow.]

The Security Council may have to take several affirmative votes before getting to the substance of the Soviet-Iranian dispute. For example, seven of the eleven members of the Council may have to approve placing it on the agenda, and they may have to vote whether to investigate the case as the Iranian note requests.

On these questions the Soviet Union would not have a vote, since it is a party to the dispute and none of the great powers would have the right of veto, but if the Council decided to take any action against the Soviet Union to remove Russian troops from Iran, Moscow would have the power to veto such action.

The Iranian Government made two specific charges against the Soviet Union. First, it said, Russian troops are interfering with the Iranian Government's rights to manage its affairs. Second, it charged, the Soviet Union is helping dissident elements who are trying to establish an independent stay in the Iranian Province of Azerbaijan.

The Russians deny both charges. They say that their troops are in Iran with the written approval of the Iranian Government, that their officials and troops are not assisting the "separatists" in Azerbaijan and that they intend to withdraw their troops on March 2 in accordance with the terms of the agreement.

1942 Treaty Introduced

The basis of the Iranian argument is the British-Soviet-Iranian treaty of Jan. 29, 1942. Under Article 1 of this treaty Britain and the Soviet Union undertook to respect the territorial integrity, political independence and sovereignty of Iran.

Under Article 4 they were permitted to maintain troops in Iran on the understanding that this would not be a military occupation and would disturb the normal life and administration of the country as little as possible.

Under Article 5 they were obligated to remove their troops six months after the end of hostilities with Germany and her associates.

The Iranian case as prepared here and as ready for presentation to the Security Council charges that the Russians have broken all these agreements. In the first place, the Iranians say, the Russians are interfering with the territorial integrity and political independence of Iran because Iranian officials are not free even to go into the Russian-occupied area.

Secondly, they maintain, the Russians are interfering with the normal life of the country by refusing to allow the courts to operate, by restricting the freedom of action of Iranian officials and by refusing to allow Iranian troops to take action against what the Iranian Government considers a "rebel movement" in Azerbaijan.

Thirdly, the Teheran Government insists, the Soviet troops should have left in November. This date is six months after the close of the European war. Iranian officials here argue that since the Soviet Union was not in the war against Japan when the Anglo-Soviet-Iranian agreement was signed in 1942 they should have left six months after the close of the war with Germany—Nov. 7—instead of six months after the termination of hostilities with Japan—March 2.

Russians Are Silent

The Russians would say nothing tonight about the appeal or the substance of the dispute. They stood on the statement that they would get out by March 2 as agreed and that they were not interfering with the normal life of Iran any more than was necessary to avoid bloodshed and carry out their military tasks.

The Iranian communication to the acting Secretary General of the United Nations referred to a section of the Charter that Secretary of State James F. Byrnes had mentioned in the hope of keeping this dispute out of the current meeting. This was Article 33, which obligates members of the security organization to seek a solution to their problems by negotiation or arbitration before bringing them before the United Nations.

The Iranian case prepared for presentation to the Security Council notes that the Iranian Government attempted to negotiate with Russian officials in northern Iran and even offered to send its Premier to Moscow to discuss the problem but was not able to get Russian permission to do either.

Consequently, the Iranian delegation decided, in accordance with Paragraph 1 of Article 35 of the Charter, to bring the matter to the attention of the Council. This article asserts that any member of the United Nations may bring to the attention of the Security Council any dispute or situation that may lead to international friction.

The Iranian communication was worded to coincide with the precise language of the Charter. It asked the Council to investigate the situation, as the Council is authorized to do in Article 34, and recommend appropriate terms of settlement, as the Council may do under Article 37 if it finds the dispute likely to endanger the maintenance of peace and security.

The consensus here is that the Council, if it decides to deal with the case, will not do more than recommend that the two parties make another attempt to settle it themselves or that if it decides to investigate, the matter may drag on until after March 2, when the Russians have agreed to get out.

There is great interest in the case among the delegates not only because of the substance of the dispute but also because it is considered a test case for the organization.

The case of the Syrians and Lebanese against British and French troops in the Levant is not taken nearly so seriously here, partly because the General Assembly was asked merely to note it and not to take action on it. In presenting the case, the head of the Syrian delegation, Faiz al-Khoury, said that the British and French had made an agreement on their troops in the Levant without even discussing it with the states concerned, and argued that their self-appointed role of custodians of security in the Levant was out of keeping with the principles and purposes of the Charter.

"The Syrian Government, acting on a motion passed by the Syrian Parliament," he concluded, "has requested the Syrian delegation to bring this matter to the attention of the United Nations, demanding an early and complete withdrawal of foreign troops."

NEW IRANIAN RISING HINTED
Bakhtiari Tribes Charge Abuses, Moscow Report Says

LONDON, Jan. 19 (U.P.)—A Moscow broadcast said today that tribesmen of Bakhtiari had protested to Teheran against their Provincial Government, hinting at a rising against it "with all our forces."

The Moscow broadcast, by a Columbia Broadcasting System correspondent, quoting Tass, was the first sign that the Government of Iran, plagued by the autonomous movement in Azerbaijan Province, might face another crisis.

The Bakhtiari tribesmen already have sent to Teheran a blunt protest against their Governor, Morteza Kuli Khan Sam Sam, the broadcast quoted Tass as having said.

The news agency said the tribesmen, in the message to the Government, contended that they should not be considered rebels "if they defended their lives and property with all forces."

Foreign Aid to Governor Hinted

LONDON, Jan. 19 (Reuter)—Moscow newspaper reports of a new Iranian trouble spot suggested that the Bakhtiari

Governor enjoyed foreign protection, a broadcast said. According to the Moscow reports, it is rumored in Isfahan that "a highly placed foreign representative has intervened in favor of the Governor and is said to have threatened that foreign troops would be brought into the area if the tribesmen should oppose the Governor."

From Baghdad there were indications that the Iranian conflict might soon extend across the frontier to Iraq. A Kurdish delegation has gone to Baghdad to demand district and village self-government and other local reforms. According to reports, the delegation has told the Government that if it does not meet the demands Iraqi Kurds will formally institute relations with the Kurdish Liberation Committee in the Soviet-controlled territory of northwest Iran.

* * *

February 10, 1946

STALIN SETS A HUGE OUTPUT NEAR OURS IN 5-YEAR PLAN; EXPECTS TO LEAD IN SCIENCE

LAYS WARS TO CAPITALISM

He Promises to End Rationing Soon, After Stressing Ability to Stand Recent Blows

By The Associated Press

LONDON, Feb. 9—Premier Joseph Stalin announced tonight a new Five-Year Plan for the Soviet Union with huge production boosts "to guarantee our country against any eventuality," and asserted that the present capitalistic world economy sets the stage for war.

He predicted, too, that Soviet scientists could "not only catch up with but also surpass those abroad."

Premier Stalin set goals for steel, pig iron, coal and oil production close to the output of the United States which he said might require three new Five-Year Plans, if not more.

In a pre-election speech, broadcast by the Moscow radio, the Premier promised that "soon rationing will end," and that the Russian worker's standard of living would be raised.

Blames Capitalism for War

Declaring that the war was "the inevitable result of the development of the world economic and political forces on the basis of monopoly capitalism," he asserted:

"Perhaps the catastrophe of war could have been avoided if the possibility of periodic redistribution of raw materials and markets between the countries existed in accordance with their economic needs, in the way of coordinated and peaceful decisions.

"But this is impossible under the present capitalistic development of world economy. Thus, as a result of the first crisis in the development of the capitalistic world economy,

the first World War arose. The second World War arose as a result of the second crisis."

Premier Stalin, making his first speech since Sept. 2, spoke on the eve of elections for the Supreme Soviet in the district where he is a candidate for re-election.

He called for an industrial output of 50,000,000 tons of pig iron a year, 60,000,000 tons of steel, 500,000,000 tons of coal, and 60,000,000 tons of oil. When these goals are reached, "only then can we consider our country guaranteed against any eventuality," he said.

[The Statesman's Yearbook of 1945 said Russia's estimated production in 1941 was 18,000,000 tons of pig iron, 22,000,000 tons of steel, 191,000,000 tons of coal, and 38,000,000 tons of oil. The American Iron and Steel Institute gives United States production of pig iron in 1944 as 61,007,000 tons and steel as 89,641,000 tons. The United States Bureau of Mines reported United States production of coal and coke in 1944 as 683,700,000 tons.]

Hails Socialist Economy

By BROOKS ATKINSON
By Wireless to The New York Times.

MOSCOW, Feb. 9—Premier Stalin in the first part of his speech before the electors assembled in the Bolshoi Theatre represented World War II as proving the triumph of Russia's socialist economy. Early in the speech he said:

"It would be incorrect to think that the war arose accidentally or as the result of the fault of some of the statesmen. Although these faults did exist, the war arose in reality as the inevitable result of the development of the world economic and political forces on the basis of monopoly capitalism."

He emphasized that Marxists have repeatedly declared the capitalistic system of world economy contained elements of crises and war. Since the development of capitalistic countries was unbalanced, some lacking raw materials and markets, the world was split into conflicting groups.

After the Axis powers had invaded and annexed the remnants of the bourgeois democracies of Western Europe, Premier Stalin said, the entrance of the Soviet Union into the war could not but strengthen the anti-Fascist and liberating character of the war. He recognized the part that coalition of the democratic countries played in the victory.

Premier Stalin said the victory now made possible a check-up of the qualities of the leaders of the Allies. The war proved the triumph of the socialist system, gave proof of its vitality, he added.

Some foreign press representatives before the war, Premier Stalin went on, had said the Soviet system was a house of cards held together by the Cheka and would collapse quickly. But now, he said, none questioned the vitality of the Soviet system; in fact, he declared it more vital than any non-Soviet system.

Premier Stalin also declared that the victory proved the triumph of the Soviet system of states of many nations, which foreign press representatives had regarded as an artificial structure.

Recalls Sneers at Army

On the Red Army the Generalissimo said that six years ago many foreigners had repeatedly declared that the Soviet forces were badly equipped and led, had a low morale and would be adequate on defense but unable to take an offensive. Now, he continued, everyone recognized that the Red Army was equal to its task and that the war had proved it to be no colossus with feet of clay. No one should forget, he said, that the Red Army defeated the German Army, which had been the terror of Europe.

It would be a mistake to think victory was attained without preparation or that preparation was a matter of only a couple of years or that victory was a result only of courage, Premier Stalin declared. Modern armies need special training, equipment, supplies and industries, he added.

"Can it be said," he inquired, "that, before its entry into the second World War, our country already possessed the minimum supplies necessary for satisfying in the main all these requirements? I think we can give an affirmative answer."

The Premier said it would be proper to regard the three five-year plans as preparation for the situation the Soviet Union faced in 1941.

The speech lasted just less than one hour. Premier Stalin spoke in a conversational tone and without bombast, grouping his words unemotionally and often repeating statements interrupted by applause. He was applauded for five minutes when introduced. The audience applauded most enthusiastically when he announced that food rationing could soon be abandoned.

* * *

February 10, 1946

TEXT OF PREMIER STALIN'S ELECTION SPEECH BROADCAST BY MOSCOW RADIO

LONDON, Feb. 9 (AP)—The text of Premier Stalin's talk as recorded by the Soviet monitor from a Moscow radio broadcast:

Comrades: Eight years have elapsed since the last elections. This is a period rich in events of a decisive character. The first four years passed in strenuous work of the Soviet people in the fulfillment of the Third Five-Year Plan.

During the past four years the events of the struggle against the German and Japanese aggressors developed—the events of the Second World War. Doubtless the war was the main event of that period.

It would be incorrect to think that the war arose accidentally or as the result of the fault of some of the statesmen. Although these faults did exist, the war arose in reality as the inevitable result of the development of the world economic and political forces on the basis of monopoly capitalism.

Our Marxists declare that the capitalist system of world economy conceals elements of crisis and war, that the development of world capitalism does not follow a steady and even course forward, but proceeds through crises and catas-trophes. The uneven development of the capitalist countries leads in time to sharp disturbances in their relations, and the group of countries which consider themselves inadequately provided with raw materials and export markets try usually to change this situation and to change the position in their favor by means of armed force.

As a result of these factors, the capitalist world is sent into two hostile camps and war follows.

Perhaps the catastrophe of war could have been avoided if the possibility of periodic redistribution of raw materials and markets between the countries existed in accordance with their economic needs, in the way of coordinated and peaceful decisions. But this is impossible under the present capitalist development of world economy.

Causes of 2 World Wars

Thus, as a result of the first crisis in the development of the capitalist world economy, the First World War arose. The Second World War arose as a result of the second crisis.

This does not mean, of course, that the Second World War was a copy of the first. On the contrary, the Second World War is radically different from the first in its character. It must be kept in mind that the main Fascist States—Germany, Japan and Italy—before attacking the Allied countries had abolished at home the last remnants of the bourgeois democratic liberties, had established a cruel terrorist regime, had trampled under foot the principles of sovereignty and freedom of the small nations, declared the policy of seizure of other peoples' lands as their own policy, declared for the whole world to hear that they strove for world domination and spread of the Fascist regime throughout the world.

Thereby, in the seizure of Czechoslovakia and the central part of China, the Axis states had shown that they were prepared to carry out their threats at the expense of the enslavement of all the freedom-loving people.

In view of this circumstance the Second World War against the Axis powers, as distinct from the First World War, assumed from the very beginning an anti-Fascist liberating character, having also as one of its aims the re-establishment of democratic liberties.

The entry of the Soviet Union into the war against the Axis powers could only strengthen and did strengthen the anti-Fascist and liberating character of the Second World War. On this basis was established the anti-Fascist coalition of the Soviet Union, the United States of America, Great Britain and other freedom-loving countries, which subsequently played a decisive part in the rout of the armed forces of the Axis powers.

Origin of World War II

What about the origin and character of the Second World War? In my opinion, everybody now recognizes that the war against fascism was not, nor could it be, an accident in the life of the peoples; that the war turned into a war of the peoples for their existence; that precisely for this reason it could not be a speedy war, a "lightning war."

As far as our country is concerned, this war was the most cruel and hard of all wars ever experienced in the history of our motherland. But the war has not only been a curse; it was at the same time a hard school of trial and a testing of all the people's forces. The war was with us at the rear and at the front.

For us this was an excellent school of experience, heroism, honesty and devotion. [A few words inaudible.] This war has shown many of our Soviet people in their real light and thus helped to judge them as they deserve.

These were the "positive" sides of the war. For us it has a great importance, because thus we had an opportunity to pass judgment on our party and our people.

During the war we were obliged to judge the activities of the representatives of our party, to analyze them and to draw the necessary conclusions. So our conclusions, which will be drawn now, will be certainly right. And so, what is the balance of the war; what are our conclusions?

There is one general conclusion, and on this basis all other conclusions can be drawn. The general balance of the war lies in the fact that even before the war was begun the enemy lost the war and we, together with our allies, were the victors. We have achieved a complete victory over the enemies.

But this conclusion is too general and we cannot stop there. Obviously, to smash the enemy in such a conflict as the second World War—in a war as never occurred before in the history of mankind—was to achieve a historic world victory. However, in order to understand the great historic importance of our victory, it is necessary to go further.

Now victory means, first of all, that our Soviet social system has won, that the Soviet social system has successfully stood the test in the fire of war and has proved its complete vitality.

As is well known the assertion often has been made in the foreign press that the Soviet social system is a risky experiment, doomed to failure, that the Soviet system is a house of cards, without roots in real life, and imposed on the people by the organs of the Cheka [secret police] and that it would be sufficient [two words inaudible] for this whole house of cards to smash.

Now we can say that the war has refuted all the assertions of the foreign press as without foundation. The war has shown that the Soviet social system is a truly popular system, issued from the depths of the people and enjoying its mighty support. The Soviet social system is a form of the organization of society that is fully capable of life and stable. Moreover, the point now is not whether the Soviet social system is or is not capable of life [some words inaudible] none of the skeptics any longer dares to come out with doubts as to whether the Soviet social system is capable of life or not.

Hails Soviet Social System

The point is that the Soviet social system has proved to be more capable of life and more stable than a non-Soviet social system, that the Soviet social system is a better form of organization of society than any non-Soviet social system.

The assertion has been made in the foreign press that the multi-national state represents an artificial structure, and in the case of any complications the disintegration of the Soviet Union is inevitable, that the Soviet Union would meet the fate of Austro-Hungary. Now we can say that the war has proved these statements of the foreign press false and devoid of any foundation.

The war has shown that the Soviet multi-national state system has successfully stood the test, has grown still stronger during the war and has proved a completely vital state system. Now we can say that the analogy with Austro-Hungary cannot be substantiated, since our multi-national state has grown up, not on a bourgeois foundation, which fosters feelings of national mistrust and national animosity, but on a Soviet foundation, which, on the contrary, promotes the feeling of friendship and fraternal collaboration between the peoples of our state.

Moreover, after this war no one dared any more to deny the vitality of the Soviet state system. Now it is no longer a question of the vitality of the Soviet state system, since there can be no doubt of its vitality any more. The point now is that the Soviet state system has proved an example of a multi-national state system where the national problem and the problem of collaboration among nations are solved better than any other multi-national state.

Third, our victory implies that it was the Soviet armed forces that won. Our Red Army had won. The Red Army heroically withstood all the adversities of the war, routed completely the armies of our enemies and emerged victoriously from the war.

World's Misgivings Recalled

This is recognized by everybody—friend and foe. The Red Army was equal to its great task. But the matter did not stand like this some six years ago in the prewar period. Many recognized authorities in the art of war abroad stated frequently that the condition of the Red Army filled them with great misgivings, that the Red Army was badly armed and had not the requisite commanders, that its morale left much to be desired, that it might perhaps serve for defense but would be useless for an offensive, and that in the event of a blow from the German troops the Red Army would fall to pieces like a colossus with feet of clay.

Such statements were made, not only in Germany but also in France, Britain and America. Now we can say that the war has made these statements look ridiculous. The war has shown that the Red Army was not a colossus with feet of clay but a first-class modern army with completely up-to-date armament, most experienced commanders and high morale and combat qualities.

One should not forget that the Red Army is that same army which routed completely the German Army—the terror of all the armies of peace-loving states. It should be noted that there are fewer and fewer critics of the Red Army. And in addition the foreign press begins to publish more and more frequently statements about the high qualities of the Red Army and the skill of its soldiers and commanders.

This is understandable after the victories at Moscow and Stalingrad, and of course Kursk and Belgorod, Kiev and Kirovograd, Minsk and Bobruisk, Leningrad and Tallin on the Vistula and Niemen, the Danube and the Oder, at Vienna and Berlin. After all this it is impossible not to recognize that the Red Army is a first-class army, which could teach others quite a lot.

This is how we understand concretely our country's victory over its enemies. This is a rough summary of the war. It would be a mistake to think that one could win such an historic victory without preparing the whole country beforehand for active defense. It would be no less erroneous to assume that this preparation could be carried out in a short time, three or four years.

It would be even more erroneous to think that we had won a victory only thanks to the courage of our troops. It is impossible to win a victory without courage, but courage alone is not enough to finish the job and overpower an enemy that possesses a large army, first-class armament, well-trained officer cadres and fairly well-organized supplies.

To be able to meet the blow from such an enemy, to counter it and later to inflict on him a crushing defeat, it was necessary to have, in addition to the unprecedented bravery of our troops, completely modern armament in sufficient quantities and well-organized supplies, also in sufficient quantities. But this in turn demands the possession in sufficient quantities of such things as metals, equipment and tools for enterprises, fuel for the work of the enterprises, transport, clothing, etc.

Can it be said that, before its entry into the Second World War, our country already possessed the minimum supplies necessary for satisfying in the main all these requirements? I think we can give an affirmative answer. The preparation of this enormous task involved the carrying out of three Five-Year Plans of national economic development. It is precisely these three Five-Year Plans that helped to create these material positions.

Recalls Defense Preparations

In this respect our country before the Second World War, say in 1940, was several times better off than in 1913 before the First World War. What material possibilities were at the disposal of our country on the eve of the Second World War? In order better to understand this, I will give you a brief report on the activity of the Communist party in the preparation of our country for active defense.

If we take the data available for 1940 and compare them with those of 1913, the eve of the First World War, we see the following picture:

In 1913 our country produced 4,220,000 tons of pig iron, 4,230,000 tons of steel, 29,000,000 tons of coal, 9,000,000 tons of oil, 21,600,000 tons of marketed grain, 740,000 tons of raw cotton—such were the material resources of our country with which it entered the First World War.

This was the economic base of old Russia, the basis which it could use to conduct the war. As for the year 1940, in that year our country produced 15,000,000 tons of pig iron, almost four times as much as in 1913; 18,300,000 tons of steel, four and one-half times more than in 1913; 166,000,000 tons of coal, five and one-half times more than in 1913; 31,000,000 tons of oil, three and one-half times more than in 1913; 38,000,000 tons of marketed grain, 17,000,000 tons more than in 1913; 2,700,000 tons of raw cotton, three and one-half times more than in 1913.

Such were the material resources with which our country entered the second World war.

This was the economic base of the Soviet Union, the base which it could use to conduct the war. As you see, the difference is colossal. Such an unprecedented development in production cannot be considered the simple and ordinary development of a country from backwardness to progress. It was a leap into an advanced country, from an agrarian country into an industrial one.

These historic transformations were achieved in the period of the three Five-Year Plans, starting from 1928—the first year of the first Five-Year Plan. Before that, we had to occupy ourselves with the restoration of industry that had been destroyed and with healing the wounds of the first World War and the civil war.

If we take into consideration the fact that the first Five-Year Plan was completed in four years, and that the execution of the third Five-Year Plan was interrupted by the war in its fourth year, it appears that the transformation of our country from an agrarian into an industrial country required only thirteen years.

Thirteen years is an incredibly short period for the realization of such a gigantic task. This, indeed, explains the fact that the publication of these figures aroused disputes in the foreign press. Friends decided that a miracle had taken place. Foes declared that the Five-Year Plans were Bolshevik propaganda and inventions of the Cheka. But since miracles do not exist in this world, and our Cheka is not so powerful that it could abolish the laws of social development, public opinion in Europe had to reconcile itself to the fact.

The point now is: What was the policy by the aid of which the Communist party succeeded in securing these material resources in our country in such a short period?

First of all, it was by the aid of the Soviet policy of industrialization of the country. The Soviet method radically differs from the capitalist method of industrialization. In capitalist countries industrialization usually starts with light industry, since light industry requires smaller investments and the turnover of capital is quicker, and it is easier to obtain profits than in heavy industry.

Lengthy Process Involved

Only after a considerable time has elapsed, in which light industry accumulates profits and concentrates them in banks, only then comes the turn of heavy industry, and a gradual transfer of accumulated capital into heavy industry starts creating the conditions for its development.

But this is a lengthy process, requiring a long period of time, several decades, during which one has to wait for the development of the light industry [some words inaudible].

It is clear that the Communist party could not take this path. The party knew that war was approaching, that it was impossible to defend the country without heavy industry, that it was necessary to begin the development of heavy industry as quickly as possible, and that to be too late in this task meant to lose. The party remembered Lenin's word that without heavy industry it would be impossible to safeguard the independence of our country, that without it the Soviet system could perish.

Therefore, in our country the Communist party reversed the usual path of industrialization and began the industrialization of our country with the development of heavy industry. This was very hard but not impossible to achieve. A great help in this task for us was the nationalization of industry and banking, enabling us to transfer money speedily into heavy industry.

It would have been impossible to achieve, without this, the transformation of our country into an industrial country in so short a period of time.

Second, a factor in carrying out our policy was the collectivization of the rural economy. Here our aim was to give to the country more bread, more cotton. And it was necessary to change from small-scale peasant economy to large-scale agricultural economy, for only the large-scale farm is in a position to apply new, modern technique and to use all its achievements to increase production.

It was necessary to make large-scale agricultural economy a collectivist one. The Communist party could not adopt the capitalist method of developing the rural economy, not only because of reasons implicit in our principles but also because the capitalist type represents a slow development and implies a ruination of the peasants.

That is why the Communist party embarked on the road of the collectivization of the rural economy through uniting individual peasant properties into a new form—a "kolkhoz." This collectivization proved itself a beneficial experience, not only because it did not involve the ruination of peasants but also, and in particular, because it gave the chance of covering the whole country—within a few years—with a net of large-scale collective farms.

Without collectivization we would not have been able to eliminate the age-old backwardness of our agriculture in so short a period of time. It cannot be said that the party's policy did not meet with resistance in this respect. Not only backward people, who always resist everything new, but also many others of the party systematically held back the party and tried in all sorts of ways to drag it on to the usual, capitalist line of development.

These were machinations of Trotskyites and Rightists, participating in the sabotage of the measures of our government [a few words missing].

Party Always in the Lead

The further merit of the party consists in the fact it "was not sleeping over the chestnuts" and was following the road once entered. It did not adjust itself to the stragglers and at all times kept its leadership.

There can be no doubt that only thanks to this firmness and grit did the Communist party come out on top, not only in industrialization but in the collectivization of agriculture as well.

The question now arises, was the Communist party able to utilize correctly all these material conditions to increase war production and to supply the Red Army with the necessary equipment. I think that it was able to do so, and to do so with the maximum success. If one does not count the first year of the war, when the transfer of the industry to the east retarded the full swing of mass production, then, in the course of the three main years of the war, the party was able to achieve successes which gave it the possibility not only to supply the front with sufficient quantities of artillery, machine guns, rifles, planes, tanks [some words inaudible] our equipment being not only not inferior in quality to the German but on the whole being superior to the German.

Our tank industry in the last three years at least produced on the average over 30,000 tanks, self-propelled guns and armored cars per year. It is also known that our aircraft industry produced in the same period about 40,000 planes per year. It is also known that our artillery industry produced annually in the same period about 120,000 guns of all calibers, about 450,000 light and heavy machine guns, over 3,000,000 rifles and about 2,000,000 automatic rifles.

Huge Munitions Production

It is also known that our mortar industry in the period 1942-1944 produced on the average about 100,000 mortars per year. It is obvious that in the same time a corresponding quantity of artillery shells, various kinds of mines, air bombs, and rifle and machine-gun ammunition was also produced.

It is known that in 1944 alone more than 240,000,000 shells, bombs and mines were produced and more than 7,400,000,000 cartridges.

Such is the general picture of the supplies for the Red Army in regard to equipment and ammunition. As you see, it does not resemble the picture which the supplies of our armies presented during the First World War, when the front experienced a chronic shortage of artillery and shells, when the Army fought without tanks, and when one rifle was issued for every three soldiers.

Regarding supplying the Red Army with food and uniforms, it is generally known that the front not only did experience no shortage in this respect, but even had the necessary reserves.

That is how the matter stands with regard to the work of the Communist party of our country during the period before the outbreak of the war and during the war.

Party's Immediate Plans

Now a few words on the plans for the work of the Communist party in the near future. As is known, these plans are confirmed in the very near future. The fundamental task of the new Five-Year Plan consists in restoring the areas of the country which have suffered, restoring the pre-war level in industry and agriculture, and then exceeding this level by more or less considerable amounts.

Apart from the fact that in the very near future the rationing system will be abolished, special attention will be focused on expanding the production of goods for mass consumption, on raising the standard of life of the working people by consistent and systematic reduction of the cost of all goods, and on wide scale construction of all kinds of scientific research institutes to enable science to develop its forces.

I have no doubt that if we render the necessary assistance to our scientists they will be able not only to overtake but also in the very near future to surpass the achievements of science outside the boundaries of our country. As far as plans for a longer period are concerned, the party intends to organize a new mighty upsurge of national economy, which will enable us to increase the level of our production, for instance, three-fold as compared with the pre-war level.

To achieve this we must endeavor to see that our industry produces 50,000,000 tons of pig iron per year, 60,000,000 tons of steel, 500,000,00 tons of coal and 60,000,000 tons of oil.

Only under such conditions will our country be insured against any eventuality. Perhaps three new Five-Year Plans will be required to achieve this, if not more. But it can be done and we must do it.

Such is my brief account of the work of the Communist party in recent past and its plan of work for the future. It is up to you to judge whether the party has worked and is working correctly, and whether it could not have worked better.

Some say that victors should not be judged, that they should not be criticized or checked. This is not correct. Victors can and must be judged, they can and must be criticized and checked.

This is good, not only for the cause but also for the victors themselves. Why? Because there will be less conceit and more modesty. I consider that the election campaign is the judgment of the electors on the Communist party as being the party of the rulers. The results of the elections will signify the verdict of the electors. Our party would not be worth much if it were afraid to face this verdict. The Communist party is not afraid to receive the verdict of the electors.

New Unity Is Stressed

In the election struggle, the Communist party does not come forward alone; it enters the elections together with the non-party people. In former days Communists had an attitude of a certain mistrust towards non-party persons. This is explained by the fact that the "non-party" banner frequently masked certain bourgeois groupings, who did not find it advantageous to present themselves to the electors without a mask. Such groupings existed. There was such a state of affairs in the past but now times have changed.

Non-party people are now separated from the bourgeoisie by a barrier which is called the Soviet social system. This very same barrier unites the non-party people with the Communists into one common collective of Soviet peoples.

Living in one common collective, they fought together for the strengthening of the might of our country. Together they fought and shed their blood at the fronts for the sake of the freedom and greatness of our motherland. Together they forged and created the victories over the enemies of our countries. The sole difference between them is that some of them are members of the party and others are not. But this difference is only a formal one.

What is important is that both Communists and non-party people are fulfilling one common task. Therefore, the block of Communists and non-party persons is in my view a natural and common cause.

In conclusion, permit me to express my gratitude for the confidence which you have shown me in nominating me as candidate for Deputy to the Supreme Soviet. I will try to justify this confidence.

* * *

March 6, 1946

BRITON SPEAKS OUT

Calls for Association of U. S., British to Stem Russian Expansion

APPEASEMENT IS OPPOSED

'Iron Curtain' Dividing Europe Is Not What We Fought For, Churchill Says at Fulton, Mo.

By HAROLD B. HINTON
Special to The New York Times.

FULTON, Mo., March 5—A fraternal association between the British Empire and the United States was advocated here today by Winston Churchill to stem "the expansive and proselytizing tendencies" of the Soviet Union.

Introduced by President Truman at Westminster College, Great Britain's wartime Prime Minister asserted that a mere balance of power in the world today would be too narrow a margin and would only offer "temptations to a trial of strength."

On the contrary, he added that the English-speaking peoples must maintain an overwhelming preponderance of power on their side until "the highroads of the future will be clear, not only for us but for all, not only for our time but for a century to come."

Says Curtain Divides Europe

Mr. Churchill painted a dark picture of post-war Europe, on which "an iron curtain has descended across the Continent" from Stettin in the Baltic to Trieste in the Adriatic.

Warsaw, Berlin, Prague, Vienna, Budapest, Belgrade, Sofia and Bucharest are all being subjected to increasing pressure and control from Moscow, he said, adding:

"This is certainly not the liberated Europe we fought to build up. Nor is it one which contains the essentials of permanent peace."

Even in front of the "iron curtain," he asserted, Italy was hampered in its efforts to return to a normal national existence by "Communist-trained Marshal Tito's claims to former, Italian territory," and the re-establishment of a strong France was impeded by fifth columns working "in complete unity and absolute obedience to the directions they receive from the Communist center."

He strongly intimated a parallel between the present position of the Soviet Union with that of Germany in 1935, when, he said, "Germany might have been saved from the awful fate which has overtaken her and we might all have been spared the miseries Hitler let loose upon mankind without a single shot being fired."

But time is running short, he warned, if the world is not "to try to learn again, for a third time, in a school of war incomparably more rigorous than that from which we have just been released."

His words, he continued, were not offered in the belief that war with the Soviet Union was inevitable or imminent. He expressed the view that Russia does not desire war, but cautioned that Moscow does desire the fruits of war and the indefinite expansion of its power and policies.

Appeasement Is Opposed

The difficulties of the Western democracies, he said, will not be removed by closing their eyes to them, by waiting to see what happens, or by a policy of appeasement.

Expressing admiration and regard for Marshal Stalin, Mr. Churchill asserted that the English-speaking peoples understood Russia's need to secure her western frontiers against renewed German aggression and welcomed Russia into her rightful place among the leading countries of the world.

From his experience with them, he said that he learned that Russians admired nothing so much as strength, and that they had no respect for military weakness.

Given an overwhelming show of strength on the side of upholding the principles of the United Nations Organization, Mr. Churchill asserted, the Soviet Union would be prepared to come to a settlement of outstanding differences with the Western world.

He suggested that the secret of the atomic bomb be kept in the hands of the United States, Great Britain and Canada, because "it would be imprudent and wrong" to confide it to the UNO, while that organization was "still in its infancy."

He said that no one in the world had slept less well because the atomic secret was in its present custody, but the people of the world would not rest so soundly if that secret were possessed by "some Communist or neo-Fascist State."

He also called for immediate establishment of a UNO air force, to be made up of a number of squadrons from member countries capable of supplying them. These squadrons would be trained and equipped at home, but would be stationed abroad. They would not be required to go into action against their own country, but would otherwise be at the orders of the UNO.

Although he expressed confidence in the ultimate ability of the UNO to preserve the peace of the world, Mr. Churchill said that it must become "a true temple of peace" and not "merely a cockpit in the power of Babel."

Comparing its inception with that of the League of Nations, he regretted that he could not "see or feel the same confidence or even the same hopes in the haggard world at this time."

The fraternal association he advocated between the British Empire and the United States would include interchange of officers and cadets among the military schools of the associates, similarity of weapons and training manuals, common war plans, joint use of all naval and air bases and intimate relationships among high military advisers.

With this potential strength behind them, he said, the English-speaking peoples could reach "now, in 1946, a good understanding on all points with Russia."

The special relationships of the type he urged, Mr. Churchill argued, would be fully consistent with loyalty to the UNO.

He recalled the special relations between the United States and Canada, the United States and the other American republics, and the twenty-year treaty between Great Britain and Russia (he interjected that "I agree with Mr. Bevin [British Foreign Minister] that it might well be a fifty-year treaty") as examples of international cooperation which serve to buttress, not undermine, the peace of the world.

The United States now stands at the pinnacle of world power, Mr. Churchill asserted, and shares with the other English-speaking peoples what he described as the over-all strategic concept of "the safety and welfare, the freedom and progress of all the homes and families of all the men and women in all the lands."

For the United States to ignore or fritter away its "clear and shining" opportunity would be to "bring upon us all the long reproaches of the after-time," he added.

Turning to the Far East, Mr. Churchill called the outlook there "anxious," especially in Manchuria, despite the aspects of the Yalta agreement, to which he was a party.

He defended the agreement on the ground that the war with Germany was then expected to last until the autumn of 1945, with the war against Japan calculated to endure eighteen months after that.

Mr. Churchill gave his listeners the impression that he and President Roosevelt would not have dealt so generously with Marshal Stalin, had they realized that collapse of the Axis was near at hand.

War and tyranny were the twin evils Mr. Churchill saw threatening the world today. He looked for the hunger and distress now afflicting so much of the world to pass fairly quickly, and for "the inauguration and enjoyment of an age of plenty."

"Nothing can stand in the way of such an outcome," he said, except "human folly or sub-human crime."

Mr. Churchill described himself as a "private visitor" with no official mission or status of any kind, and as a man whose early private ambitions had been satisfied beyond his wildest dreams.

He said that Mr. Truman had granted him full liberty "to give you my true and faithful counsel in these anxious and baffling times."

In his introduction the President said that he and Mr. Churchill both believed in freedom of speech, adding:

"I know he will have something constructive to say."

When Mr. Truman later took the platform to acknowledge the doctorate of laws which Westminster conferred on him, as well as on Mr. Churchill, he told the audience that it was "your moral duty and mine, to see that the Charter of the United Nations is implemented as the law of the land and the law of the world."

The President, however, made no direct reference to the "fraternal association" Mr. Churchill suggested.

"We are either headed for complete destruction or are facing the greatest age in history," Mr. Truman said, adding:

"It is up to you to decide, and up to me to see that we follow that path toward that great age and not toward destruction.

"The release of atomic energy has given us a force which means the happiness and welfare of every human being on earth or the destruction of civilization.

"I prefer to think we have the ability, the moral stamina and the energy to see that the great age comes about, not destruction."

Churchill Drops Serious Note

When it came Mr. Churchill's turn to thank Dr. Franc Lewis McCluer, the faculty and trustees of Westminister College for the honor they conferred on him, he dropped the serious tenor of his earlier address and made the following remarks:

"Mr. President, President McCluer, Members of the Faculty: I am not sure that I may say fellow-members of the faculty. I am most grateful, and through you to the authorities of the State of Missouri and to the college authorities, for their great kindness in that conferring upon me another of these degrees, which I value so highly and, as I was saying only the other day at Miami, which have a double attraction to me, that they do not require any preliminary examinations.

"I value very much this token of good-will which comes from this center of education in the very heart of the United States and in the State which is so dear to the heart of the President of this great country.

"I also thank you all here for the great patience, indulgence, kindness and attention to listen to what I had to say, for I am quite sure it will have been right and wise to say at this juncture. I am very glad to have had this opportunity and am grateful to all who have come here and assisted me to discharge my task.

"I am, of course, unswerving in my allegiance to my own king and country, but I can never feel entirely a foreigner in the United States which is my motherland and where my ancestors, forebears on that side of the family for five generations, have lived.

"I was, however, a little puzzled the other day when one branch of the Sons of the Revolution invited me to become a member, on the grounds that my forebears undoubtedly fought in Washington's armies.

"I felt on the whole that I was on both sides then, and therefore I should adopt as far as possible an unbiased attitude. But I may justly tell you how proud is my love for this great and mighty nation and empire of the United States."

This was a gala day in Fulton and Jefferson City, the State Capital, where the President and Mr. Churchill left their train. In both towns the motor cavalcade drove slowly around the principal streets, which were lined with spectators.

Police estimated that the normal population of 8,000 turned out in Fulton and was augmented by some 20,000 visitors who had come from as far distant as St. Louis.

Dr. McCluer entertained the President and Mr. Churchill with the members of their immediate party at luncheon in his home on the campus before the ceremonies.

The President and Mr. Churchill marched into the gymnasium at the end of the long academic procession. Mr. Truman wore the hood indicating the honorary doctorate of laws conferred on him last summer by the University of Kansas City, while Mr. Churchill wore a scarlet hood indicating an Oxford degree.

Mr. Churchill's speech was received with marked applause in the passages where it dealt with the responsibility of this country to see that another World War was avoided, but the proposal for "fraternal association" brought only moderate handclapping.

Churchill, Truman in St. Louis

ST. LOUIS, March 5 (AP)—The train carrying the President and Mr. Churchill from Fulton stopped here tonight, and Mr. Truman appeared on the near platform clad in striped pajamas with a topcoat over his shoulders. He smiled to the crowd, and Mr. Churchill appeared at his side.

Someone called out, "Where is your cigar, Winnie?" and Mr. Churchill, without his usual cigar, waved and called: "God bless you all."

Then he turned and with the President re-entered the train.

Mr. Truman will leave the train at Columbus, Ohio, where he is scheduled to speak tomorrow.

* * *

March 26, 1946

IRAN AN OLD TARGET OF BRITAIN, RUSSIA

Persia Long Caught in Clash of Two Powers' Interests—Oil Rivalry a Factor

1664 SAW FIRST QUARREL

Cossack Incursion Described by Historian—Britain Got Fuel Concession in 1901

By W. H. LAWRENCE

The latest Iranian-Soviet issue, scheduled to come before the United Nations' Security Council today, was preceded by a history of Persian-Russian quarrels over special economic advantages going back to 1664.

Problems of trade rivalry between the British Empire and Russia have been a source of constant embarrassment through the years to the small, potentially rich but economically and politically backward Middle Eastern country.

As the Security Council members look at it, the problem raised by Iran's complaint, supported by the British and United States Governments, concerns the rules of fair play among nations, subscribed to by the powers that adopted the United Nations Charter. It involves the retention of Red Army forces beyond the March 2 deadline for their withdrawal and thus an implicit threat of force to gain economic advantages for the Soviet Union.

The question of treaty violation and of a possible violation of the Charter transforms the Iranian case from a mere quarrel between Iran and Russia, or Russia and Britain, with the Iranians caught in the middle, to a problem demanding international attention.

Friendly Neighbors Sought

At the root of the dispute is the contest for economic supremacy in Iran. Involved, too, is the insistence by the Soviet Union that Governments that border it must be "loyal." There are some who believe that the Russians want political dominance as well as economic concessions so a road for them to the south and the Persian Gulf ports would be easy.

Iran has only 628,000 square miles and a population of about 15,000,000, of whom 3,000,000 are nomads. The country is of great strategic importance to Britain since it lies on its lifeline of empire, and furnishes, through its oil developments, fuel, important for war and peace, and sorely needed foreign exchange.

Iran is of great importance to the Russians, too, since the country is a gateway to and from the south and, during the recent war, was the bridge along which lend-lease shipments totaling more than 4,160,000 long tons moved from the Western Hemisphere alone. Many persons once feared it might be the meeting place for the Germans and Japanese in their effort to conquer the world.

The present issue is, from the economic point of view, concerned chiefly with oil and the demand of the Russians that they receive important concessions in the undeveloped northern provinces.

This proposal, revealed in the Soviet press in October, 1944, marked the first time the Soviet Government had indicated a desire to use its money and effort to develop economic properties in foreign countries and was thus, in part, a reversal of the Soviet policy of utilizing all its energies and resources for internal development.

The Iranian Government refused to consider the Soviet proposals as well as new oil concessions wanted by American or British companies. Because the British have a virtual monopoly in the current Iranian production of about 10,000,000 tons of oil annually, the Soviet Government regarded the Iranian refusal as an unfriendly act.

Iran was at the time occupied by Red Army, British and United States forces. The British and the Russians had gone in jointly in September, 1941, to depose Riza Shah Pahlevi and install his son, Mohammed Riza Pahlevi, because Iran had been overrun by Axis agents and it was feared Adolf Hitler would try to move against the Soviet Union from the south.

That occupation by the British and the Russians was formalized in the British-Soviet-Iranian treaty in January, 1942, which respected the political and territorial integrity of Iran and provided that foreign troops would leave within six months after hostilities ceased.

American troops were evacuated by Jan. 1 and the British had left by March 2, 1946, the deadline, but many Soviet forces remained. On Sunday the Moscow radio announced new withdrawals of forces and said the Red Army would be entirely out of Iran within five or six weeks barring unforeseen developments.

Margret Boveri's "Minaret and Pipeline, Yesterday and Today in the Near East," records that the "Russians appeared in Persia for the first time in 1664" and that "quarrels broke out immediately."

"The Russian mission, consisting of 800 men, had been received with the greatest hospitality in Ispahan and lodged in a vast palace," the book continued. "Then it was discovered that in reality these men were disguised merchants who alleged themselves to be diplomatic envoys in order to escape taxation. The Shah was furious, and the Russians were treated with contempt. This in its turn angered the Russians and they organized a Cossack invasion of the Caspian Province of Mazenderan. This was the first Russian attempt upon Persian territory."

A cardinal principle of Russian foreign policy always has been the desire for warm-water ports. The Persian Gulf was vital to the Russians in the recent war when the Dardanelles was closed by German occupation of the Balkans and the Murmansk route was dangerous and costly.

British pre-eminence in the development of Iran's oil dates back to 1901, when William Knox D'Arcy obtained an exclusive sixty-six-year concession for oil throughout Persia except the five northern provinces. The price he paid has been put at about $20,000.

Russian rights to oil development concessions in the northern provinces were conceded by the British in a 1907 agreement, in which the Czar recognized the southern part of Iran as an exclusive British sphere. This settlement continued in force until the end of the first World War and until the Russian revolution installed the Communist Government, which was opposed by British and United States armies and financial interests. During this period of foreign intervention British troops established a military protectorate in Iran. They were not withdrawn until 1921.

In 1921 the Iranian and Soviet Governments signed an agreement providing for nullification of Russian oil concessions on condition they would not be transferred to other powers. Moscow recently accused the Iranians of violating this agreement.

One clause of that agreement has been mentioned by Generalissimo Stalin and other Soviet leaders as justification for the continued retention of Soviet forces in Iran, but this interpretation of the treaty has been assailed as inaccurate by British and United States leaders.

* * *

March 26, 1946

TRUMAN, GREETING UNO, PLEDGES U. S. SUPPORT; BYRNES WARNS NO NATION MUST BY-PASS LAW; IRAN CASE UP TODAY; STALIN SPEAKS OF ACCORD

COUNCIL IN SESSION

The Security Body Hears U. S. Officials, Dewey Demand World Unity

AGGRESSION SCORED

No Delay of Iran Issue Is Likely Until Soviet Explains Events

By JAMES B. RESTON

The Old World that twice in a generation summoned the United States to the field of battle came to the New World yesterday in search of peace.

Seven months after a war in which they lost more than 15,000,000 men, the eleven nations on the United Nations Security Council met for the first time at their new interim headquarters at Hunter College in the Bronx in an effort to preserve the peace that they had sacrificed so much to gain.

President Truman welcomed them with a promise and a warning. The promise was that this time the United States would support the principles of collective security. The warning was that unless the rest of the United Nations lived up to their name, they would not have a home anywhere in the world.

Treaty Breakers Scored

These observations, which topped the program after the Soviet delegate had consented to a plan that postponed the

Iranian discussion until today, were delivered on behalf of the President by Secretary of State James F. Byrnes, who made a few remarks of his own about nations who take the law into their own hands. For the benefit of those who are mainly interested in maintaining the present status quo, Mr. Byrnes observed that the United Nations Charter was never intended to sanctify ancient privilege, and for the benefit of those who are determined to change the status quo in accordance with their own ideas, he declared that no country was justified in by-passing the UNO and using force or the threat of force except in defense of the law.

Just to make it unanimous, so far as the United States official welcoming party was concerned, Gov. Thomas E. Dewey intimated to the delegates that these sentiments were in no way a monopoly of the present Democratic Administration, but went for the Republican party as well. Mr. Dewey was the Presidential nominee of that party in 1944. Mayor William O'Dwyer and James J. Lyons, Bronx President, also welcomed the eleven members of the Council.

Iran's Plea Up Today

Most of the 600 persons who managed to get into the renovated Hunter College gymnasium for the opening session here were probably wondering during the speeches of welcome whether or when Iran's appeal to the Council against the presence of Red Army troops in that country was going to come up, but actually this question had been decided in private talks downtown before the delegates reached the chamber.

It was suggested to the Soviet delegate on the Council, Andrei A. Gromyko, that maybe it would not be wise to start the Council meeting off with an argument, and therefore, he was asked to agree to limit yesterday's session to the ceremonies and to shelve Iran until today.

Some of the men who participated in the discussions on this subject got the impression that Mr. Gromyko was under pretty strict instructions to bring the matter up at once, but this problem was met by agreeing that there should be no mention of the agenda for the forthcoming session. Instead, it was decided that there should be speeches and nothing more.

The Russian Ambassador, who favors carrying out his government's instructions without too much improvisation, finally consented, but unless something unforeseen happens— which sometimes occurs in Iranian politics—Mr. Gromyko will press for adjournment of the meeting at 11 o'clock this morning when the Council convenes.

There is a possibility that Mr. Gromyko will be able to persuade the Council in a few days that his Government and the Government of Premier Ahmad Ghavam in Iran have made progress in reaching an agreement for the withdrawal of Red Army troops from Iran. There is, however, very little possibility that he will be able to convince his colleagues this morning that the Council should rise before the Iranian case is clarified.

They want to know what they are being asked to postpone. They want to know what has happened since the fifth session of the Security Council in London last Jan. 30, when they

Secretary of State James F. Byrnes reading Mr. Truman's message yesterday. Seated (left to right), Dr. Pedro Leao Velloso, Brazil; Trygve Lie, Secretary General; and Dr. Quo Tai-chi, China. Behind Mr. Lie is Governor Dewey and behind Dr. Quo is Mayor O'Dwyer.

agreed to let Iran and the Soviet Union negotiate further on their problems.

Specifically, they want to know why the Soviet troops did not get out of Iran by March 2, 1946, as they were obliged to do under the Anglo-Russian-Iranian agreement of 1942, and as the Russian Vice Foreign Minister, Andrei Y. Vishinsky told the Security Council in London they would do.

Also, they want to know whether the Red Army troops, as Mr. Vishinsky testified in London, are still refusing to allow Iranian troops and officials to move freely inside Iran, and whether, in any agreement that may have been reached between the Teheran and Moscow Governments, the Soviet Union has lived up to its treaty obligation under the Charter not to use force or the threat of force.

The Soviet argument in this case is that they not only are negotiating with the Iranian Government but are making progress in these negotiations. In support of this contention, Mr. Gromyko could submit as evidence the statements of the Iranian Premier, who has indicated that as a result of the negotiations, he is confident that the Russian troops will be withdrawn.

Also, the Russians point out that under Article 33 of the Charter, members of the UNO are obligated to settle their differences by negotiation, mediation or arbitration before bringing them to the Security Council, and they insist that since they are negotiating with the Iranians and making progress in these negotiations they should be permitted to continue doing so without further intervention by the Council.

The opposition to this argument rests primarily on the decision of the Security Council when it reached a decision on the case last January, and on the recent appeal by Iran to the Council. In January, while agreeing to turn the case over to further negotiations between Teheran and Moscow, the Council ended its resolution by requesting that the parties "inform the Council of any results achieved in such negotiations," and by insisting on the Council's right at "any time to request information on the progress of negotiations."

In view of these provisions, and in view of the fact that the Iranian Government on March 18 charged the Soviet Union with violating its agreement to get out, interfering in the internal affairs of Iran, breaking the treaty provisions of the Charter and endangering international peace and security, the Council at the very least will demand to know whether these charges still stand and what the situation is.

Nobody mentioned Iran at yesterday's meeting, but what Secretary Byrnes said on behalf of the President and what he said as the head of the executive department in charge of our foreign policy certainly had a bearing on the past, present and future of the Iranian case.

After Dr. Quo Tai-chi, the chairman of the Council, had expressed his gratitude that the United Nations had been located in the land of "freedom and equality," Mr. Byrnes made it quite clear that the United States expected the other members of the United Nations to settle their disputes in the Security Council Chamber.

"Nations, like individuals," he said, "should do their best to adjust their disputes without resort to litigation. But no nation has the right to take the law into its own hands. If disputes cannot be settled by friendly negotiations, they must be brought before the Security Council."

With an obvious reference to both the British and the Russians, who, during the London meeting of the Council, complained that their honor was involved in charges brought before the Council, Mr. Byrnes pointed out that questions of honor between individuals were no longer left to the test of dueling pistols, and questions of honor among nations, therefore, he insisted, could not be left to the ordeal of battle.

Governor Dewey was even more direct in his welcome. Without mentioning directly what happened in the previous twenty-three meetings of the Security Council, he drew attention to certain developments and habits in those meetings. The Security Council, he observed, could be used for propaganda purposes to stir up unrest and confusion in the world; it could be misused in a spirit of maneuver in the hope that by clever tactics one or another nation could be put in a false light.

"But any nation that sits on the Council or comes before it in such a spirit," the Governor said directly, "commits a crime against humanity."

To the Council, of course, Mr. Dewey was not only the Governor of the State of New York, but the Presidential nominee and present titular head of a political party that had contributed greatly to the defeat of the League of Nations after the last war.

Mr. Dewey, recognizing this, took the opportunity of dispelling any doubts about where he or his party stood on the question of America's support of the United Nations. He said that when the wartime coalition pledged itself at Dumbarton Oaks and the San Francisco conference to transform itself into a coalition for peace, that pledge had the support of both great political parties in the United States. What was true then, he added, was also true today.

Mayor O'Dwyer, whose municipal duties have evidently prevented him from taking a very active part in the arrival of this new institution in the city, assured the delegates yesterday that he was glad to see them, and so did the President of the Bronx, Mr. Lyons, who went Mr. O'Dwyer one better by suggesting that maybe the UNO ought to stay here in the Bronx permanently.

It would be stretching a point to say that yesterday's events were equal in spirit to the great occasion. The setting was superb. What had looked like any normal gymnasium less than three weeks ago had been transformed by American technical genius into a dignified, comfortable and functional room capable of seating nearly 600 persons.

But the speeches were read and having been read, they were followed, as in London, by long and dreary translations, which admittedly were necessary but which broke the tempo and allowed the audience to relax into private conversation.

Here was indeed, what Mr. Byrnes described as "a moment of great importance in the history of the world." Around the great semicircular table sat the representatives of eleven nations who had lost more than 25,000,000 men in two wars within a single generation. They were meeting for the first time, in the New World. They were meeting at the end of a war in which fighting together they had meet and conquered the greatest threat to civilization in the history of man. They were gather on a last-chance venture to prove that man is not unteachable.

And yet their was no greatness to the meeting. Despite the setting, despite the aid of lighting effects that would have done justice to any theater in Manhattan, it did not quite come off. The new theme in the Council is that its deliberations should not be dramatic, as they were at London, but deliberative and even dull, and this was certainly the note struck in the first meeting in the United Sates.

* * *

March 26, 1946

BRITISH M.P.'S GOING TO IRAN TO GAUGE FREEDOM OF ACTION

By Herbert L. Matthews
By Cable to The New York Times.

LONDON, March 25—The inevitable second thoughts today put a damper on the enthusiasm here over Moscow's announced intention to withdraw Soviet troops from Iran. This was not because the importance of that concession had been overrated but because the Russians had not yet replied to the British note of March 3 or to subsequent representations about the presence of Soviet troops in Iran in violation of the British-Soviet-Iran 1942 treaty. Neither has there been any confirma-

tion from the British charge d'affairs in Teheran or Moscow of a Red Army withdrawal. Foreign Under-Secretary Hector McNeil underlined in the Commons another point of British dissatisfaction when he said:

"The Foreign Secretary regrets the present campaign carried on against this country by the Soviet press and radio. It is difficult to reconcile the tone and intention of the Soviet propaganda with the spirit of the Anglo-Soviet treaty of alliance for post-war collaboration and mutual assistance of 1942. The Government will neglect no means, by which misunderstanding may be removed and our policy made plain to the people and Government of Russia."

Absence of Reply Noted

Mr. McNeil also put on the record that Foreign Secretary Ernest Bevin had not received any reply from Moscow about Iran.

Mr. McNeil announced that a Parliamentary group would visit Iran. When a Member asked whether the group would have the fullest freedom of movement, particularly in northern Iran, the Under-Secretary replied that he would be surprised if there were any unreasonable barriers but that the House had better wait.

Mr. McNeil added that he meant barriers from the Iranian Government.

The two-man British Parliamentary delegation is scheduled to fly from London to Teheran tomorrow to inquire into what is going on in Iran. It is made up of Michael Foot, Labor Member for Devonport, and Brig. A. H. Head, Conservative, from Carshalton, Surrey. Both are leading younger members of Parliament. They agreed to go when they received assurances that they could travel freely in the Russian-occupied zone.

The question of Azerbaijan [where a Russian-supported regime declared its autonomy] is one of many that are keeping the British skeptical about the Russian announcement.

What worries the British most of all is the price Iran may have paid for the promise of withdrawal. Information of this is awaited most keenly.

The British have never considered oil concessions as of primary importance in this matter. It is only one factor, and not a very important one, in their view. In any event, no informed person here believes it is the cause of what has happened in Iran; it is merely a manifestation of the power politics being played for the Middle East, it is believed here.

Moreover, it is asserted that Premier Ahmad Ghavam cannot grant any oil concessions. By Iranian law there can be no concession until Iran is clear of foreign troops. To change this law the Majlis [Parliament] must act, but the Majlis cannot be assembled until there is a new election and elections cannot be legally held until foreign troops quit Iran. Everything is thus tied up with the withdrawal of the Soviet troops.

It is no exaggeration to say that the British will believe the Russian promise when the last soldier has gone. As one spokesman put it, if the Soviet Union could make a binding treaty and follow it up with a solemn official promise to withdraw its troops by March 2, and still not do so, how can they expect the British to believe a unilateral pronouncement now?

This was another way of saying that the Russian treaty violation had profoundly shaken British trust and that this had been the most serious aspect of the Iranian affair.

Some Britons, like some Americans, believe that straight talks with Premier Stalin might help. Vernon Bartlett, Independent Member of Parliament, asked Prime Minister Attlee whether he would consider such a meeting. The Prime Minister replied that he was always ready to do so but "since the Security Council of the UNO is now holding a meeting in New York I don't think it would be advisable to make a proposal of such far-reaching importance to Marshal [Generaliasimo] Stalin at the present time."

That emphasis on the UNO was calculated. The British not only base their entire foreign policy on the UNO in general but see in it their only hope for answers to the riddles they are asking about Iran.

Iranians Shun Treaty Issues

Although members of the Iranian delegation declined last night to comment on yesterday's opening session of the Security Council at Hunter College, other delegates close to the Iranian situation said that the nation's delegation had received no new instructions from Teheran.

From these delegates it was learned that the Iranian delegation was not concerned with whether any treaty had been violated. Teheran's position, these delegates said, is that Iran is willing to collaborate in any arrangement that will improve relations between Iran and the Soviet Union short of compromising the fundamental question, which they declared was the evacuation of Russian troops.

* * *

April 6, 1946

BYRNES ASKS 4-POWER TALKS APRIL 25 BY MINISTERS TO SPEED PEACE PACTS; SOVIET AND IRAN ANNOUNCE AGREEMENT

BIG ISSUES SETTLED

Joint Oil Company Will Be Organized if New Parliament Approves

ALL TROOPS WILL LEAVE

Question of Azerbaijan Is Left to Settlement by Teheran by 'Peaceful' Methods

By GENE CURRIVAN
By Wireless to The New York Times.

TEHERAN, Iran, April 5—The Soviet and Iranian Governments have reached complete agreement on all matters concerning them, according to a joint communiqué issued today by Premier Ahmad Ghavam and Ivan C. Sadchikov, Soviet Ambassador, after discussions that lasted until 4 A. M.

The agreement reached was threefold. It embraced the evacuation of the Red Army, the formation of an oil company, with the proviso that the next Parliament approves, and approach to a settlement of the Azerbaijan autonomy problem.

Text of Communiqué

The communiqué read as follows:

Negotiations begun in Moscow between the Prime Minister of Iran and Soviet authorities were continued in Teheran after his return and the arrival of the Soviet Ambassador. These negotiations ended fifth Farvardin 1325 [April 4, 1946] and a complete agreement was reached on all questions.

Red Army troops will evacuate all Iranian territory within one and one-half months from Sunday, March 24, 1946.

An agreement for the formation of a joint Irano-Soviet oil company and its terms will be submitted to the fifteenth Majlis for its approval within seven months after March 24.

With regard to Azerbaijan, since it is an internal Iranian affair, peaceful arrangements will be made between the Government and the people of Azerbaijan for the carrying out of improvements in accordance with existing laws and in a benevolent spirit toward the people of Azerbaijan.

What was announced today was not a pact or treaty between the two countries but a declaration than an agreement had been reached on outstanding problems.

The point that is bound to cause some concern here and abroad is the agreement to form a Soviet-Iranian oil company. It has been the general belief that the question of oil could not be discussed while foreign troops occupied the country.

Firouz Explains Ruling

The accepted interpretation of the constitution is that any Government official who discussed this matter with foreign representatives would be liable to eight years imprisonment.

At a press conference today Prince Mozzafar Firouz, Propaganda Minister, disposed of this apprehension by saying that the law prohibited only the granting of oil concessions while the country was occupied and did not prevent the formation of an oil company with Iranian and Soviet money as is planned for this one.

Furthermore, he said, the broad outlines alone of the company have been agreed upon and no details have been worked out yet. The question of the controlling interest also has not been decided, Prince Firouz said.

Before the company can be formed, he added, it must be approved by the Majlis and that cannot be elected until all Russians are out of the country.

With Premier Ghavam's present popularity and influence it is unlikely that he will get a Majlis that would oppose him on major matters. The largest party here is left-wing Tudeh and that has been supporting him all along.

Amity With Soviet Seen

Amplifying the announcement of the agreement, Prince Firouz said that the negotiations that ended so satisfactorily this morning had been continued in spite of discussion of the Iranian question by the Security Council.

"As a result of these negotiations between the two countries all outstanding questions have been settled on a basis of complete reciprocity and good will," Prince Firouz declared. "I inform you gentlemen of the satisfaction with which the Iranian Government and people interpret this happy event, which we hope will bring about a new era in relations between the Iranian and Russian peoples.

"It is to be noted with special satisfaction that the policy of the Imperial Government to maintain the best relations with the great powers, our allies and neighbors, especially Britain and the United States, has been crowned with complete success by realizing the same good and friendly relations with our great northern ally and neighbor.

"I believe this event is of paramount importance and will be welcomed by all our allies as a great contribution toward international peace and concord."

Prince Firouz said that the agreement had received the unanimous approval of the Cabinet.

If this agreement is carried out to the letter, Iran should soon be able to function like a normal country for a change. All indications are that her major troubles are over.

Russians Join in Rejoicing

TEHERAN, Iran, April 5 (AP)—There was general rejoicing and relief here tonight over the developments today.

Representatives of the Russian Embassy, who have carefully avoided contacts with foreign newsmen for several months, dined and danced tonight in the hotel where newsmen have established a "press center." Word went around that the Soviet press attaché was planning a party for foreign correspondents.

Meanwhile, heavy Russian artillery, tanks and armored vehicles by the score moved north across the Russian-Iranian frontier at Astara today. "They definitely are moving out," a foreign military observer said.

Discussing another trouble spot, Prince Firouz said that the reports about fighting between Kurdish tribesmen and Iranian troops in the west were "greatly exaggerated" and that the "situation is under control." He added, however, that Iranian reinforcements had been sent to the area "to meet any eventuality."

He also disclosed that a brother of former Premier Sāid Zia ed-Din Taratatri named Moussain, had been arrested on charges of "subversive activities against the Government." These were the same charges leveled against Sāid Zia, a right wing leader, when he was arrested on orders from Premier Ghavam. Pince Firouz said investigation of the charges against Sāid Zia was continuing.

Iraqi Kurds Doubt Revolt

BAGHDAD, Iraq, April 4 (Delayed) (AP)—Majid Bey Mustafa, Kurdish leader and member of the Iraqi Parliament, said today he believed that the report of the proclamation of a new Kurdish State with headquarters at Mosul was "completely untrue" and declared the United Nations should investigate conditions among the Kurds.

Five other Kurdish spokesmen, including Ali Kamal, a former Parliament member, also said they did not believe the report.

[A former Kurdish member of Iran's Parliament said in Hamadan, Iran, Monday that "Kurds of Iran, Turkey, Iraq and Syria, meeting at Mehabad (Saujbulagh), have proclaimed a new and greater Kurdish State" centered at the Iraq oil city of Mosul and headed by Mullah Mustafa of the Barzani Tribe.]

The Iraq Kurdish leaders said they believed it was illogical that such headquarters would be set up in an oil city, a possible source of trouble, and that the choice of Mullah Mustafa as chief was also illogical.

* * *

June 15, 1946

U. S. WILL TELL ATOM SECRET, DESTROY BOMBS, IF U. N. ESTABLISHES CONTROLS WITHOUT A VETO

BARUCH URGES PACT

Favors Rule by a Treaty to Outlaw New Missile, Bar Atomic Race

ASKS DIRE PENALTIES

Speech at First Sitting of U.N. Board Sees the World at Crossroads

By W. H. LAWRENCE

The United States formally offered yesterday to give up its store of atomic bombs and turn over all the secrets of harnessing atomic energy for peaceful means to an international Atomic Development Authority in which no nation could wield a veto power.

Bernard M. Baruch, elder statesman and a key figure in two World Wars, outlined the program in a forceful and eloquent speech in which the world was warned that its choice was a simple one, "world peace or world destruction."

The American offer highlighted the first meeting of the United Nations Atomic Energy Commission at Hunter College in the Bronx. The Commission consists of representatives of the United States, the United Kingdom, the Soviet Union, Canada, France, China, Poland, Australia, the Netherlands, Egypt, Mexico and Brazil.

Under U. N. Auspices

Mr. Baruch's plan was a bold bid to outlaw atomic energy as a means of mass destruction and thus avert a mad armament race among the nations of the world.

The United States representative on the commission proposed instead that an authority to be established by treaty under auspices of the United Nations and ratified by all peaceful nations should receive exclusive control over raw materials and the production of atomic energy under a system by which nations would be speedily punished for any violation of the international pact. This treaty would renounce the use of the atom bomb in war and limit the development of atomic energy to peaceful means.

Stressing the paramount importance of the problem, Mr. Baruch said:

"There is a famine throughout the world today. It starves men's bodies. But there is a greater famine—the hunger of men's spirit. That starvation can be cured by the conquest of fear and the substitution of hope, from which springs faith— faith in each other; faith that we want to work together toward salvation, and determination that those who threaten the peace and safety shall be punished."

Essential Rules Enumerated

The white-haired Mr. Baruch, whom President Wilson called "Dr. Facts," went directly to the heart of a great political issue, the veto power, in outlining the safeguards that this country regards as essential to set up before it gives up its monopoly, the possession of atomic bombs and the knowledge how such weapons are made.

It is essential to world security, Mr. Baruch said, that there should be immediate, certain and serious penalties for any nation that committed any of the following violations of international atomic control:

(1) Illegal possession or use of an atomic bomb.

(2) Illegal possession, or separation, of atomic material suitable for use in an atomic bomb.

(3) Seizure of any plant or other property belonging to or licensed by the authority.

(4) Willful interference with the activities of the authority.

(5) Creation or operation of dangerous projects in a manner contrary to, or in the absence of, a license granted by the international control body.

"It would be a deception, to which I am unwilling to lend myself, were I not to say to you and to our people that the matter of punishment lies at the very heart of our present security system," Mr. Baruch said. He added:

"There must be no veto to protect those who violate their solemn agreements not to develop or use atomic energy for destructive purposes. The bomb does not wait upon debate. To delay may be to die. The time between violation and preventive action or punishment would be all too short for extended discussion as to the course to be followed."

The United States, he said, is ready to stop the manufacture of atomic bombs, to dispose of existing bombs either by destroying them or turning them over to the international authority for policing purposes and to give the control body the full "know-how" on atomic energy "when an adequate system for the control of atomic energy, including the renunciation of the bomb as a weapon, has been agreed upon and put into effective operation and condign punishments set up for violations of the rules of control which are to be stigmatized as international crimes."

Calling for "an international law with teeth in it," Mr. Baruch said the world wanted not "pious hopes" but a program "of enforceable sanctions." Mere words, he added, are not sufficient to warrant the relinquishment by the United States of the atomic bomb secrets.

"It must have a guarantee of safety not only against the offenders in the atomic area but against the illegal users if other weapons—bacteriological, biological, gas—perhaps— why not? against war itself," Mr. Baruch declared.

Because Mr. Baruch's policy statement had not been distributed until Thursday afternoon, none of the delegates replied categorically to it. They listened with great interest as he outlined the position of the United States Government, which had full Administration backing. Informally, they expressed their appreciation for the contribution Mr. Baruch had made.

Next Meeting Wednesday

Pending instructions from their Governments, the delegates decided to put off full-scale discussion of the whole problem and of Mr. Baruch's proposal until Wednesday at 3 P. M.

Yesterday's session was begun with a welcoming address by Trygve Lie, Secretary General of the United Nations, who promised Mr. Baruch's selection as temporary chairman. After Mr. Baruch had spoken, the commission decided to rotate the chairmanship monthly on an alphabetical basis. Dr. H. V. Evatt, Australia's Minister of External Affairs, assumed the chair.

Mr. Lie said he did not share the views of those who despaired of the future and doubted the ability of man to control a power "which at one single stroke might destroy more than many generations can build."

"It cannot be beyond the resources of the human mind, which has made such enormous strides in this technical development to control it, to prevent its abuse and to use it for the good of all," the Secretary General said.

A message of greeting came also from President Truman and was read by Mr. Baruch. It said:

"I ask you as the American representative on the United Nations Atomic Energy Commission to express to the members my sense of the extraordinary importance of the work in which they are about to engage. Nothing concerns the whole world more than the achievement of the purpose that brings them together. I speak for my fellow-Americans in wishing them godspeed."

In his 4,000-word policy statement Mr. Baruch did not go into details of how the proposed authority would be constituted, how it would be financed or how it would obtain ownership and control of raw materials everywhere in the world and the American atomic-bomb producing plants.

Nor did he offer details of the kind of punishment that would be dealt to any violator of the proposed international agreement.

In general, his recommendations followed the policy proposed by a special State Department committee headed by Under-Secretary of State Dean Acheson and David E. Lilienthal, chairman of the Tennessee Valley Authority.

Implicit in Mr. Baruch's statement offering the United States' secrets to a world authority under specific conditions was that we would give up not only the "know-how" of harnessing the energy stored in the bomb but also the means of detonating it so the authority would know how to ban detonants.

To the proposed control authority, as suggested by Mr. Baruch, would be entrusted all phases of the development and use of atomic energy, starting with raw material and including managerial control or ownership of all atomic energy activities potentially dangerous to world security, the power to control, inspect and license all other atomic energy without regard to where it is situated and the duty of fostering the beneficial uses of atomic energy.

It would also carry on an extensive research program into all phases of atomic energy so the organization would be better equipped to comprehend and detect possible misuses.

In spelling out the authority's operations, Mr. Baruch advocated that because its operations "are intrinsically dangerous to security" the facilities and stockpiles should be distributed throughout the world."

* * *

June 15, 1946

BARUCH'S SPEECH AT OPENING SESSION OF U. N. ATOMIC ENERGY COMMISSION

The text of Bernard M. Baruch's address before the Atomic Energy Commission of the United Nations follows:

My fellow-members of the United Nations Atomic Energy Commission, and my fellow-citizens of the world:

We are here to make a choice between the quick and the dead.

That is our business.

Behind the black portent of the new atomic age lies a hope which, seized upon with faith, can work our salvation. If we fail, then we have damned every man to be the slave of fear. Let us not deceive ourselves: We must elect world peace or world destruction.

Science has torn from nature a secret so vast in its potentialities that our minds cower from the terror it creates. Yet terror is not enough to inhibit the use of the atomic bomb. The terror created by weapons has never stopped man from employing them. For each new weapon a defense has been produced, in time. But now we face a condition in which adequate defense does not exist.

Will of Mankind Invoked

Science, which gave us this dread power, shows that it can be made a giant help to humanity, but science does not show us how to prevent its baleful use. So we have been appointed to obviate that peril by finding a meeting of the minds and the hearts of our peoples. Only in the will of mankind lies the answer.

It is to express this will and make it effective that we have been assembled. We must provide the mechanism to assure that atomic energy is used for peaceful purposes and preclude its use in war. To that end, we must provide immediate, swift and sure punishment of those who violate the agreements that are reached by the nations. Penalization is essential if peace is to be more than a feverish interlude between wars. And, too, the United Nations can prescribe individual responsibility and punishment on the principles applied at Nuremberg by the Union of Soviet Socialist Republics, the United Kingdom, France and the United States—a formula certain to benefit the world's future.

In this crisis we represent not only our governments but, in a larger way, we represent the peoples of the world. We must remember that the peoples do not belong to the governments, but that the governments belong to the peoples. We must answer their demands; we must answer the world's longing for peace and security.

In that desire the United States shares ardently and hopefully. The search of science for the absolute weapon has reached fruition in this country. But she stands ready to proscribe and destroy this instrument—to lift its use from death to life—if the world will join in a pact to that end.

In our success lies the promise of a new life, freed from the heart-stopping fears that now beset the world. The beginning of victory for the great ideals for which millions have bled and died lies in building a workable plan. Now we approach fulfillment of the aspirations of mankind. At the end of the road lies the fairer, better, surer life we crave and mean to have.

Peace Key to Democracy

Only by a lasting peace are liberties and democracies strengthened and deepened. War is their enemy. And it will not do to believe that any of us can escape war's devastation. Victor, vanquished and neutrals alike are affected physically, economically and morally.

Against the degradation of war we can erect a safeguard. That is the guerdon for which we reach. Within the scope of the formula we outline here, there will be3 found, to those who seek it, the essential elements of our purpose. Others will see only emptiness. Each of us carries his own mirror in which is reflected hope—or determined desperation—courage or cowardice.

There is famine throughout the world today. It starves men's bodies. But there is a greater famine—the hunger of men's spirit. That starvation can be cured by the conquest of fear, and the substitution of hope, from which springs faith—faith in each other; faith that we want to work together toward salvation; and determination that those who threaten the peace and safety shall be punished.

The peoples of these democracies gathered here have a particular concern with our answer, for their peoples hate war. They will have a heavy exaction to make of those who

Bernard M. Baruch (center) as he was appointed temporary chairman by Secretary General Trygve Lie at first session of the United Nations Atomic Energy Commission. On the left is Sir Alexander Cadogan, United Kingdom delegate on the Security Council.

fail to provide an escape. They are not afraid of an internationalism that protects; they are unwilling to be fobbed off by mouthings about narrow sovereignty, which is today's phrase for yesterday's isolation.

The basis of a sound foreign policy, in this new age, for all the nations here gathered, is that: anything that happens, no matter where or how, which menaces the peace of the world, or the economic stability, concerns each and all of us.

That, roughly, may be said to be the central theme of the United Nations. It is with that thought we begin consideration of the most important subject that can engage mankind—life itself.

Let there be no quibbling about the duty and the responsibility of this group and of the Governments we represent. I was moved, in the afternoon of my life, to add my effort to gain the world's quest, by the broad mandate under which we were created. The resolution of the General Assembly, passed Jan. 24, 1946, in London reads:

Section V. Terms of Reference of the Commission

The Commission shall proceed with the utmost dispatch and inquire into all phases of the problem, and make such recommendations from time to time with respect to them as it finds possible. In particular, the Commission shall make specific proposals:

A. For extending between all nations the exchange of basic scientific information for peaceful ends;

B. For control of atomic energy to the extent necessary to insure its use only for peaceful purposes;

C. For the elimination from national armaments of atomic weapons and of all other major weapons adaptable to mass destruction;

D. For effective safeguards by way of inspection and other means to protect complying states against the hazards of violations and evasions.

The work of the Commission should proceed by separate stages, the successful completion of each of which will develop the necessary confidence of the world before the next stage is undertaken.

Our mandate rests, in text and in spirit, upon the outcome of the conference in Moscow of Messrs. Molotov of the Union of Soviet Socialist Republics, Bevin of the United Kingdom, and Byrnes of the United States of America. The three Foreign Ministers, on Dec. 27, 1945, proposed the establishment of this body.

Their action was animated by a preceding conference in Washington, on Nov. 15, 1945, when the President of the United States, associated with Mr. Attlee, Prime Minister of the United Kingdom, and Mr. Mackenzie King, Prime Minister of Canada, stated that international control of the whole field of atomic energy was immediately essential. They proposed the formation of this body. In examining that source, the Agreed Declaration, it will be found that the fathers of the concept recognized the final means of world salvation—the abolition of war. Solemnly they wrote:

"We are aware that the only complete protection for the civilized world from the destructive use of scientific knowledge lies in the prevention of war. No system of safeguards that can be devised will of itself provide an effective guarantee against production of atomic weapons by a nation bent on aggression. Nor can we ignore the possibility of the development of other weapons, or of new methods of warfare, which may constitute as great a threat to civilization as the military use of atomic energy."

Through the historical approach I have outlined, we find ourselves here to test if man can produce, through his will and faith, the miracle of peace, just as he has, through science and skill, the miracle of the atom.

Scope of Proposed Power

The United States proposes the creation of an International Atomic Development Authority, to which should be entrusted all phases of the development and use of atomic energy, starting with the raw material and including:

(1) Managerial control or ownership of all atomic energy activities potentially dangerous to world security.

(2) Power to control, inspect and license all other atomic activities.

(3) The duty of fostering the beneficial uses of atomic energy.

(4) Research and development responsibilities of an affirmative character intended to put the Authority in the forefront of atomic knowledge and thus to enable it to comprehend, and therefore to detect, misuse of atomic energy. To be effective, the Authority must itself be the world's leader in the field of atomic knowledge and development and thus supplement its legal authority with the great power inherent in possession of leadership in knowledge.

I offer this as a basis for beginning our discussion.

But, I think, the peoples we serve would not believe—and without faith nothing counts—that a treaty merely outlawing possession or use of the atomic bomb constitutes effective fulfillment of the instructions to this commission. Previous failures have been recorded in trying the method of simple renunciation, unsupported by effective guarantees of security and armament limitation. No one would have faith in that approach alone.

Now, if ever, is the time to act for the common good. Public opinion supports a world movement toward security. If I read the signs aright, the peoples want a program, not composed merely of pious thoughts, but of enforceable sanctions—an international law with teeth in it.

We of this nation, desirous of helping to bring peace to the world and realizing the heavy obligations upon us, arising from our possession of the means for producing the bomb and from the fact that it is part of our armament, are prepared to make our full contribution toward effective control of atomic energy.

Proposals for Regulation

When an adequate system for control of atomic energy, including the renunciation of the bomb as a weapon, has been agreed upon and put into effective operation and condign punishments set up for violations of the rules of control which are to be stigmatized as international crimes, we propose that:

(1) Manufacture of atomic bombs shall stop,

(2) Existing bombs shall be disposed of pursuant to the terms of the treaty, and

(3) The Authority shall be in possession of full information as to the know-how for the production of atomic energy.

Let me repeat, so as to avoid misunderstanding: My country is ready to make its full contribution toward the end we seek, subject, of course, to our constitutional processes, and to an adequate system of control becoming fully effective, as we finally work it out.

Now as to violations: in the agreement, penalties of as serious a nature as the nations may wish and as immediate and certain in their execution as possible, should be fixed for:

(1) Illegal possession or use of an atomic bomb;

(2) Illegal possession, or separation, of atomic material suitable for use in an atomic bomb;

(3) Seizure of any plant or other property belonging to or licensed by the Authority;

(4) Willful interference with the activities of the Authority;

(5) Creation or operation of dangerous projects in a manner contrary to, or in the absence of, a license granted by the international control body.

It would be a deception, to which I am unwilling to lend myself, were I not to say to you, and to our peoples, that the matter of punishment lies at the very heart of our present security system. It might as well be admitted, here and now, that the subject goes straight to the veto power contained in the Charter of the United Nations so far as it relates to the field of atomic energy. The Charter permits penalization only by concurrence of each of the five great powers—Union of Soviet Socialist Republics, the United Kingdom, China, France and the United States.

Specific Veto Suggested

I want to make very plain that I am concerned here with the veto power only as it affects this particular problem. There must be no veto to protect those who violate their solemn agreements not to develop or use atomic energy for destructive purposes.

The bomb does not wait upon debate. To delay may be to die. The time between violation and preventive action or punishment would be all too short for extended discussion as to the course to be followed.

As matters now stand, several years may be necessary for another country to produce a bomb, de novo. However, once the basic information is generally known, and the authority has established producing plants for peaceful purposes in the several countries, an illegal seizure of such a plant might permit a malevolent nation to produce a bomb in twelve months, and if preceded by secret preparation and necessary facilities perhaps even in a much shorter time.

The time required—the advance warning given of the possible use of a bomb—can only be generally estimated, but obviously will depend upon many factors, including the success with which the Authority has been able to introduce elements of safety in the design of its plants and the degree to which illegal and secret preparation for the military use of atomic energy will have been eliminated. Presumably no nation would think of starting a war with only one bomb.

This shows how imperative speed is in detecting and penalizing violations.

The process of prevention and penalization—a problem of profound statecraft is, as I read it, implicit in the Moscow statement, signed by the Union of Soviet Socialist Republics, the United States and the United Kingdom a few months ago.

Guarantee Is Essential

But before a country is ready to relinquish any winning weapons, it must have more than words to reassure it. It must have a guarantee of safety, not only against the offenders in the atomic area, but against the illegal users of other weapons—bacteriological, biological, gas—perhaps—why not?—against war itself.

In the elimination of war lies our solution, for only then will nations cease to compete with one another in the production and use of dread "secret" weapons which are evaluated solely by their capacity to kill. This devilish program takes us back not merely to the Dark Ages, but from cosmos to chaos. If we succeed in finding a suitable way to control atomic weapons, it is reasonable to hope that we may also preclude the use of other weapons adaptable to mass destruction. When a man learns to say "A" he can, if he chooses, learn the rest of the alphabet, too.

Let this be anchored in our minds:

Peace is never long preserved by weight of metal or by an armament race. Peace can be made tranquil and secure only by understanding and agreement fortified by sanctions. We must embrace international cooperation or international disintegration.

Science has taught us how to put the atom to work. But to make it work for good instead of for evil lies in the domain dealing with the principles of human duty. We are now facing a problem more of ethics than of physics.

The solution will require apparent sacrifice in pride and in position, but better pain as the price of peace than death as the price of war.

Fundamental Plan Outlined

I now submit the following measures as representing the fundamental features of a plan which would give effect to certain of the conclusions which I have epitomized.

(1) General—The Authority should set up a thorough plan for control of the field of atomic energy, through various forms of ownership, dominion, licenses, operation, inspection, research and management by competent personnel. After this is provided for, there should be as little interference as may be with the economic plans and the present private, corporate and state relationships in the several countries involved.

(2) Raw Materials—The Authority should have as one of its earliest purposes to obtain and maintain complete and accurate information on world supplies of uranium and thorium and to bring them under its dominion. The precise pattern of control for various types of deposits of such materials will have to depend upon the geological, mining, refining and economic facts involved in different situations.

The Authority should conduct continuous surveys so that it will have the most complete knowledge of the world geology of uranium and thorium. Only after all current information on world sources of uranium and thorium is known to us all can equitable plans be made for their production, refining and distribution.

(3) Primary Production Plants—The Authority should exercise complete managerial control of the production of fissionable materials. This means that it should control and operate all plants producing fissionable materials in dangerous quantities and must own and control the product of these plants.

Research Monopoly Urged

(4) Atomic Explosives—The Authority should be given sole and exclusive right to conduct research in the field of atomic explosives. Research activities in the field of atomic explosives are essential in order that the Authority may keep in the forefront of knowledge in the field of atomic energy and fulfill the objective of preventing illicit manufacture of bombs. Only by maintaining its position as the best informed agency will the Authority be able to determine the line between intrinsically dangerous and non-dangerous activities.

(5) Strategic Distribution of Activities and Materials—The activities entrusted exclusively to the Authority, because they are intrinsically dangerous to security, should be distributed throughout the world. Similarly, stockpiles of raw materials and fissionable materials should not be centralized.

(6) Non-Dangerous Activities—A function of the Authority should be promotion of the peacetime benefits of atomic energy.

Atomic research (except in explosives), the use of research reactors, the production of radioactive tracers by means of non-dangerous reactors, the use of such tracers and to some extent the production of power should be open to nations and their citizens under reasonable licensing arrangements from the Authority. Denatured materials, whose use we know also requires suitable safeguards, should be furnished for such purposes by the Authority under lease or other arrangement. Denaturing seems to have been overestimated by the public as a safety measure.

(7) Definition of Dangerous and Non-Dangerous Activities—Although a reasonable dividing line can be drawn between dangerous and non-dangerous activities, it is not hard and fast. Provision should, therefore, be made to assure constant re-examination of the questions, and to permit revision of the dividing line as changing conditions and new discoveries may require.

(8) Operations of Dangerous Activities—Any plant dealing with uranium or thorium after it once reaches the potential of dangerous use must be not only subject to the most rigorous and competent inspection by the Authority, but its actual operation shall be under the management, supervision and control of the Authority.

(9) Inspection—By assigning intrinsically dangerous activities exclusively to the Authority, the difficulties of inspection are reduced. If the Authority is the only agency which may lawfully conduct dangerous activities, then visible operation by others than the Authority will constitute an unambiguous danger signal. Inspection will also occur in connection with the licensing functions of the Authority.

(10) Freedom of Access—Adequate ingress and egress for all qualified representatives of the Authority must be assured. Many of the inspection activities of the Authority should grow out of, and be incidental to, its other functions. Important measures of inspection will be associated with the tight control of raw materials, for this is a keystone of the plan. The continuing activities of prospecting, survey and research in relation to raw materials will be designed not only to serve the affirmative development functions of the Authority, but also to assure that no surreptitious operations are conducted in the raw materials field by nations or their citizens.

(11) Personnel—The personnel of the Authority should be recruited on a basis of proven competence, but also so far as possible on an international basis.

(12) Progress by Stages—A primary step in the creation of the system of control is the setting forth in comprehensive terms of the functions, responsibilities, powers and limitations of the Authority. Once a charter for the Authority has been adopted, the Authority and the system of control for which it will be responsible will require time to become fully organized and effective. The plan of control will, therefore, have to come into effect in successive stages. These should be specifically fixed in the charter or means should be otherwise set forth in the charter for transitions from one stage to another, as contemplated in the resolution of the United Nations Assembly which created this commission.

(13) Disclosures—In the deliberations of the United Nations Commission on Atomic Energy, the United States is prepared to make available the information essential to a reasonable understanding of the proposals which it advocates. Further disclosures must be dependent, in the interests of all, upon the effective ratification of the treaty. When the Authority is actually created, the United States will join the other nations in making available the further information essential to that organization for the performance of its function. As the successive stages of international control are reached, the United States will be prepared to yield, to the extent required by each stage, national control of activities in this field to the Authority.

(14) International Control—There will be questions about the extent of control to be allowed to national bodies, when the Authority is established. Purely national authorities for control and development of atomic energy should to the extent necessary for the effective operation of the Authority be subordinate to it. This is neither an endorsement nor a disapproval of the creation of national authorities. The Commission should evolve a clear demarcation of the scope of duties and responsibilities of such national authorities.

Broad Criticism Invited

And now I end. I have submitted an outline for present discussion. Our consideration will be broadened by the criticism of the United States proposals and by the plans of the other nations, which, it is to be hoped, will be submitted at their early convenience. I and my associates of the United States delegation will make available to each member of this body books and pamphlets, including the Acheson-Lilienthal report recently made by the United States Department of State, and the McMahon Committee Monograph No. 1 entitled "Essential Information on Atomic Energy" relating to the McMahon bill recently passed by the United States Senate, which may prove of value in assessing the situation.

All of us are consecrated to making an end of gloom and hopelessness. It will not be an easy job. The way is long and thorny, but supremely worth traveling. All of us want to stand erect with our faces to the sun, instead of being forced to burrow into the earth like rats.

The pattern of salvation must be worked out by all for all.

The light at the end of the tunnel is dim, but our path seems to grow brighter as we actually begin our journey. We cannot yet light the way to the end. However, we hope the suggestions of my Government will be illuminating.

Lincoln's Words Paraphrased

Let us keep in mind the exhortation of Abraham Lincoln, whose words, uttered at a moment of shattering national peril, form a complete text for our deliberation. I quote, paraphrasing slightly:

"We cannot escape history. We of this meeting will be remembered in spite of ourselves. No personal significance or insignificance can spare one or another of us. The fiery trial through which we are passing will light us down in honor or dishonor to the latest generation.

"We say we are for peace. The world will not forget that we say this. We know how to save peace. The world knows that we do. We, even we here, hold the power and have the responsibility.

"We shall nobly save, or meanly lose, the last, best hope of earth. The way is plain, peaceful, generous, just—a way which, if followed, the world will forever applaud."

My thanks for your attention.

* * *

POLISH VOTE HEAVY; RED VICTORY LIKELY

Government Majority Expected to Win on Issue of One House of Parliament

---

By W. H. LAWRENCE
By Wireless to The New York Times.

WARSAW, June 30—An estimated 80 per cent of the 10,600,000 eligible Polish voters participated today in the national referendum—the first elections in Poland in eleven years—which were reported unusually free of violence except for disturbances in former German territory recently taken over by Poland. Well-informed observers believe the left-wing group in the present Polish regime has succeeded in winning approval for a one-house Parliament. No official figures were available at a late hour tonight, but it was considered probable that Stanislaw Mikolajczyk, Agriculture Minister and leader of the Peasant party, has failed to win a test of strength with his left-wing opponents. He opposed the single house parliamentary system.

Up to a late hour tonight Warsaw had heard of reports of violence during the day in East Prussia and in Silesia. Two persons were said to have been wounded at Allenstein, in East Prussia, as a result of a terrorist raid.

The reports were not so clear on what happened at Stagowidy, in the Stettin area, where it was said armed bandits seized a polling booth and destroyed the first ballots cast. Subsequently, however, it was reported that Government forces reoccupied the voting station, and balloting was resumed.

There was no dispute between the left-wing group and Mikolajczyk supporters on the two other referendum questions—approval of the present regime's industrial and agricultural reforms and establishment of the western Polish border on the Oder River and the Neisse.

Beginning at 7 A. M. and led by President Boleslaw Bierut, the voters in cities, towns, villages and country school districts flocked to the polls. Many were in large groups. Some were driven in trucks, including those supplied by UNRRA, and others walked.

In Warsaw, at least, there was no evidence of Soviet troops.

In devastated, rubble-strewn Warsaw, the most damaged city in Europe, election officials estimated that 360,000 would vote during the twelve-hour period, and they said that the vote of more than 60 per cent had been cast by 4:30 P. M. In Silesia, former German territory, 85 per cent were said to have voted by 6 P. M.

Among Government officials as well as foreign observers there was surprise at the quiet prevailing on election day.

The general belief that Mr. Mikolajczyk would lose his fight to defeat the one-house parliamentary proposal naturally led to conjecture concerning what effect this might have on Poland's political future and that of Poland itself. More cautious observers were not inclined to draw definite conclusions until the precise majority for one house was clearly established by the final official returns.

It also was difficult to assay Mr. Mikolajczyk's personal strength since his name was not on the ballot.

The left-wing Government group controlled a vast majority of polling communications, including the press and radio, and this made it difficult, if not impossible, for people in many parts of Poland to realize that Mr. Mikolajczyk opposed Proposition No. 1 and the reasons for his stand.

The voting was favored by a bright warm day in Warsaw, which brought the crowds out early. The polls opened at 7 A. M., and in this predominantly Catholic country many citizens voted before mass. They seemed cheerful and eager as they stood in line to cast their vote. Even the President waited twenty minutes at Warsaw Polling Place 22, a few blocks off the main street, before walking up to a second floor voting room through an entrance gaily decorated with a gilded Polish eagle and the red and white bunting of the Polish national colors.

In all, there were 11,046 voting places throughout the country, of which 183 were in Warsaw. A few meager returns may be expected tonight, but official and final results may not come for several days and are not required to be submitted for twelve days.

* * *

U. S. PROTESTS PICKETS IN RUMANIA, OPPOSITION CHARGES VOTING FRAUDS

By The Associated Press

BUCHAREST, Rumania, Wednesday, Nov. 20—Brig. Gen. Courtland Van Rensselaer Schuyler, head of the United States military mission to Rumania, protested to the Rumanian Government last night against the picketing of the American mission office by supporters of Premier Petru Groza's Communist-dominated Government.

The pickets ranged themselves around the mission building where approximately 5,000 Rumanian citizens, who said they had not been able to register for yesterday's parliamentary elections, came to complain.

Subsequently, the Ministry of the Interior announced that 90 to 95 per cent of Rumania's registered voters had participated in the balloting. In a communiqué broadcast over the Bucharest radio the Ministry also promised that the results would be announced this morning.

This Government announcement came after three opposition parties—the National Liberal, National Peasant and Independent Socialist—had protested in two notes to the Allied Control Commission, the Government and the United States mission against what they charged were irregularities at many voting stations in Bucharest.

The Government also charged the Opposition groups with irregularities. Government reports from the Tarava

Marb district said two members of the Communist party were killed in a polling booth skirmish. The opposition also was accused of having attacked and occupied for a time the Galac Prefecture.

Reports indicated that the voting was heavy. Because of the number of persons waiting to vote, balloting continued until late last evening in Bucharest.

The capital was relatively quiet during the election, although there were reports that vendors of opposition newspapers had been beaten up in several localities and taken to the hospital. Government supporters encircled the National Peasant and National Liberal headquarters and besieged their newspaper offices.

In their protest, the three opposition parties said that in some places in the capital voters and poll watchers were not allowed access to the polls. There also were complaints that the names of many persons were omitted from the voting register.

Cordons of troops were assigned to keep order within a radius of 500 meters (almost a third of a mile) of each polling booth in the country. In Bucharest alone there were 240 such booths.

The Opposition press last night was allowed, after some delay, to print the text of British and United States notes delivered last Saturday to the Government protesting the conduct of the election campaign.

8,000,000 Are Registered

Almost 8,000,000 persons, including women for the first time, were registered. The principal issue was whether to retain in office Premier Groza's six-party bloc, which favors more cordial relations with Russia and establishment of a Communistic society. The Opposition, in general, favors the retention of a middle-class capitalistic regime.

Government supporters pointed to the historic fact that no Rumanian Government ever had lost an election. The Government bloc is composed of the Communists, Social Democrats, Ploughman's Front (M. Groza's own party, National Popular party), Dissident Peasants and Dissident Liberals.

One-man and splinter parties, however, accounted for at least thirty-three different party symbols on the ballot. Because of the nation's high degree of illiteracy the voters made their selection by marking the party symbol of their choice.

48 Foreign Writers Present

Interior Minister Teohari Georgeoru, Communist, apparently kept his promise that there would be no widespread political arrests on the eve of the election. Government officials conceded last week that some 200 Opposition leaders had been thrown into jail, but indications were that these arrests had occurred at least ten days ago.

Approximately forty-eight foreign correspondents were on hand for the election. American correspondents rejected an invitation by the Ministry of Information to participate in an officially conducted tour of the polling places. The Americans said they would prefer to cover the voting on their own, even if this meant that they would not be admitted to voting places.

Correspondents of other nationalities, including the British, accepted the invitation. [Kenneth Matthews, Balkan correspondent of the British Broadcasting Corporation, who was to cover the election, was refused a visa by Soviet authorities, the British radio reported in a broadcast recorded by the Columbia Broadcasting System.]

U. S., British Notes Rejected

Special to The New York Times.

WASHINGTON, Nov. 19—Rumania entered upon the balloting in her general election today with both the United States and Great Britain unsuccessful in their last-minute efforts to obtain assurances of free and equitable voting conditions.

Dean Acheson, Acting Secretary of State, announced this morning that a reply had been received to the final United States appeal late last week that Opposition parties be allowed to participate in the election. He said no progress had been made through the exchange of notes. Britain, which made a similar appeal, received a reply that was described in London as negative.

In the reply to the United States, which was delivered yesterday by Foreign Minister George Tatarescu to Burton Y. Berry, the American political representative in Bucharest, the Rumanian Government reiterated views expressed in a note on Nov. 2. At that time it rejected the United States appeal as an interference in its internal affairs and as not reflecting the views of the Big Three, since the Soviet Union had made no representations.

The note delivered yesterday then went on to assure the United States that the democratic principles of freedom and justice that Washington had invoked would remain the constant guide for action in Rumania.

In the course of a series of exchanges in recent weeks on the elections, Rumania had promised at one time to act with the rights of the Opposition parties in mind. The United States' final appeal last week was an effort to hold her to that promise. However, it was considered premature today to say whether the withdrawal of Mr. Berry might be considered, should the election be found to have been highly irregular.

An unofficial translation of the latest note from M. Tatarescu, as made by the Rumanian Foreign Office, follows:

"I have the honor to acknowledge the receipt of your note of Nov. 15, 1946. The Rumanian Government, after having examined its contents most carefully, considered it necessary to reassert in reply its view set forth in its note of Nov. 2 and wishes to assure the United States Government that the democratic principles of freedom and justice invoked in your note are and will remain the constant guidance of its action in the present general elections as well as in the achievement of the great reforms destined to reorganize the basic establishments of the Rumanian State."

* * *

December 22, 1946

POLES GIVE BRITISH SHARP 'NO' ON VOTE

Warsaw Note Says London Has Failed in Deed and Spirit to Live Up to Yalta Pact

By SYDNEY GRUSON
Special to The New York Times.

WARSAW, Dec. 21—The Polish Government has told Great Britain that it will not enter into "further debates" about the forthcoming elections. It also rejected Britain's note of Nov. 22 and accused her of failing to fulfill her Potsdam and Yalta obligations to Poland "in deed or spirit."

The sharp-toned note was presented by Zygmunt Modzelewski, Vice Minister of Foreign Affairs, to the British Ambassador, Maj. Victor Cavendish-Bentinck, last Thursday. The United States as well as Britain had sought assurances on Nov. 22 that all parties would obtain equal opportunity in the elections.

The Poles will reject the American note as well in the answer to be delivered to Ambassador Bliss Lane next week. But the answer to the United States will be couched in milder terms than those used to the British, who were told, in effect, to "mind your own business."

Old Grievances Aired Again

A long list of detailed charges against Britain, covering all the old grievances that have been the subject of numerous exchanges between the two countries, was contained in the latest blast from the Poles. One charge was that Britain still tolerated and financed the activities of the old Polish Government in London, "although they are plotting the third World War."

The Poles declared they had acted entirely in conformity with the Potsdam and Yalta resolutions and that Polish sovereignty excluded consideration of opinions that Britain had no right to try to "impose."

The British Government's attempts to justify its actions toward the London Poles, some of whom "are considered to be advisers of the British Government," were insufficient, the Polish note said. It added that "the right of asylum should be available only to individuals, and not to organizations trying to act as governments."

The establishment of the resettlement corps for former Polish soldiers under British command contravened Britain's obligations to place them under Polish command, the note said. "The soldiers have become the object of international barter, instead of returning home with their arms, as they deserved."

The Poles said that Britain's delay in recognizing the Polish provisional government had enabled the London émigré government to dispose of Polish state funds, archives and heirlooms. They protested against the retention by Britain of Polish gold and warships and stated that the return of the gold "would have enabled the present Government to speed up the rate of the nation's recovery."

The note charged that a campaign to advise Poles against returning home was financed "not only from British State funds but also from British finance sources," despite Britain's obligation under Potsdam to assist in the speediest repatriation. It also complained against the British decision of last August reducing the quotas of Germans to be accepted into the British zone of Germany from the former eastern territories of the Reich. These quotas, the note concluded, were now of "insignificant numbers."

British Deny Validity of Charges

Special to The New York Times.

LONDON, Dec. 21—British official quarters denied tonight the validity of the points raised in the Polish reply on free elections, and contended, moreover, that they dodged the issue.

It was insisted that precise assurances of free and unfettered balloting had been given in Potsdam, no matter what interpretation the Polish Government now seeks to place on those undertakings.

Warsaw's assertion that publication of the electoral law fulfills its obligations was regarded as irrelevant, since the question of equal campaign facilities under that law still remains. All the information received by the British indicates that the democratic parties are struggling against Government-imposed disabilities that are becoming more formidable as the date of elections draws near.

As for the Polish charges against Britain, this point-by-point reply is given in Whitehall:

(1) The British Government withdrew recognition of the former Polish Government in London in 1945. Its former members enjoy no diplomatic privileges and those still here have only the rights of private residents of this country.

(2) The Polish armed forces are being dissolved under an orderly plan that has been fully publicized, but Britain is pledged not to force any unwilling soldiers to return to Poland.

Polish Dilatoriness Charged

(3) Virtually all Polish assets have been handed over to the Polish Government.

(4) Settlement of the Polish gold question has been made in an agreement not yet ratified by the British Government. It is felt that the gold is the property of the Polish people, and that until a government has been confirmed by a free democratic election it cannot be safely returned.

(5) The question of Polish war ships is still under consideration.

(6) Delay in the repatriation of Poles willing to return is owing to the failure of the Polish Government to provide an adequate number of screening officers. It was the Polish Government itself that had insisted on such screening process. The British are prepared to repatriate 10,000 a month, but the Warsaw Polish officers do not clear nearly that number. The belief here is that the Polish Government would rather not have these men returned before the elections.

(7) The agreement to permit German-Poles to enter the British zone in Germany has had to be modified because of the pressure of well-known adverse circumstances there.

Whether the Foreign Office would send a new note to Warsaw had not been decided here tonight.

* * *

December 22, 1946

GUERRILLA BATTLES RAGE IN INDO-CHINA

*Hanoi Fight Goes On, Viet Nam Units Attack in Many Towns—
Blum Seeks Peace Course*

By The Associated Press

PARIS, Dec. 21—Full scale guerrilla warfare raged today in major cities and towns of northern Indo-China as French troops battled the Viet Namese in bloody street fighting that reached its greatest intensity in the flaming native quarter of Hanoi.

The tree-shaded avenues of Hanoi, capital of the Province of Tongking and of the Viet Nam Republic, were cut by barricades and trenches. Many houses in the Viet Namese section were burning. Rifle firing and the clatter of patrolling French armor and planes were continuous.

A dispatch from Hanoi said that military casualties in that city from the ranks of the French troops and guerrillas totaled about thirty killed and eighty wounded as of Friday night.

[With its Overseas Territories Minister flying to Indo-China Sunday, the Blum Government of France still sought a means of restoring peace and avoiding an all-out effort for reconquest that might be crucial for the French Empire and in home affairs.]

In Paris, a Viet Nam spokesman, M. Maio, told the newspaper France-Soir that, "if the hostilities continue, Indo-China is lost."

"We will destroy everything and we will die," he continued fiercely. "There will be a permanent state of war."

If Viet Nam did not get satisfaction from a first-hand investigation by Premier Leon Blum's Government, he asserted, an appeal would be taken to the United Nations, and meanwhile the Viet Namese would fight.

A French communiqué describing the situation as of early today, gave a picture of continuing street battles and widespread fighting after two nights and days of terror, in which several cases of the murder and kidnapping of Europeans were reported in Hanoi dispatches.

The communiqué, from the French Command in Saigon, said Viet Namese snipers were still firing from housetops in Hanoi and that their forces, aided by native Tu Ye militiamen, still held the postoffice building. Earlier the French regained a hospital.

The Viet Namese were hurling "violent attacks" against the French forces at Bacninh and at Phulangthuong, about thirty miles north of Hanoi, but the French command had the situation "in hand," the communiqué stated. Fighting was going on in Namdinh, fifty miles south of Hanoi.

Marius Moutet, France's Minister for Overseas Territory, postponed until tomorrow night his scheduled departure for Saigon as fog closed in over Paris, grounding the plane that was to carry him and other members of his mission to the scene of the fighting.

Moutet Will Speed Efforts

M. Moutet had promised to be back in Paris within two weeks to give the National Assembly a first-hand report on the situation, deferring until then a full-dress parliamentary debate on Indo-China, a subject intertwined with France's financial and political crisis.

Premier Blum, obviously worried, told a party group that he still hoped the situation was not as serious as the reports seemed to indicate.

The communiqué said French troops, suffering heavy losses, had advanced in two sectors of northern Indo-China but lost a small garrison at Vinh, 155 miles south of Hanoi and on the coastal rail line leading to Saigon.

The small French detachment at Vinh capitulated after an ultimatum by the Viet Namese, but only after demanding and receiving guarantees for protection of French lives and property, the communiqué said.

The French were subject to a fierce attack at Tourane, almost 400 miles south of Hanoi on the same rail line, but managed to retain both the town and the airport. Heavy losses were suffered by both sides, the communiqué said.

Unofficial estimates said Viet Namese forces numbered 30,000, but it was pointed out that this could be swelled by thousands of natives. Under terms of the Viet Nam agreement with France the native republic was to have 10,000 troops.

A neutral source in Paris said French forces in Indo-China probably numbered 65,000. They were believed to have 10,000 to 15,000 in the north, confined chiefly to main cities. They were well equipped with British, French and American material, including light armor. A French Air Force squadron of Spitfires has been patrolling in Tongking.

French Paratroops May Go

PARIS, Dec. 21 (Reuters)—French Twenty-fifth Airborne Division paratroops were reported from Algiers today to be ready to leave Bone, Algeria, for Indo-China.

Vice Admiral Georges Thierry d'Argenlieu, High Commissioner for Indo-China, left Tunis by air today for Hanoi.

M. Moutet, leaving for Saigon tomorrow, is determined to visit Hanoi. He hopes to see Dr. Ho Chi Minh, President of the Viet Nam Republic, who fled from Hanoi, although there is no certainty about Dr. Ho's present whereabouts.

M. Moutet also intends to go on to Nanking to see Generalissimo Chiang Kai-shek, a personal friend, to insure China's neutrality.

* * *

January 8, 1947

MARSHALL REPORT ON CHINA CALLS LIBERALS ONLY HOPE

By BERTRAM D. HULEN
Special to The New York Times.

WASHINGTON, Jan. 7—Gen. George C. Marshall, special envoy to China, whose appointment as Secretary of State was announced tonight, declared in a statement issued through the State Department today that the salvation of China "would be the assumption of leadership by the liberals in the Government and in the minority parties."

His statement, which called these liberals "a splendid group of men, but who as yet lack the political power to exercise a controlling influence," was in the form of a review of the situation before his departure for the United States to succeed Secretary of State James F. Byrnes. The statement was regarded as an appeal for a genuinely liberal movement to save China from the extremists of the Nationalists and Communists.

Whether General Marshall's report, buttressed by his new official stature, would result in jarring the Chinese into the adoption of a sane, democratic and constitutional program was a matter of conjecture.

The statement was in the nature of a report to the American people. General Marshall went candidly into the many phases of the Chinese problem.

The special envoy declared that efforts to bring about peace in China had been frustrated by "extremist elements of both sides." He spared neither the Communists who, he said, would not hesitate to wreck China to gain their own political ends nor a "dominant group of reactionaries" in the Kuomintang, which he described as the first among "the most important factors" responsible for the breakdown of the negotiations between the Communists and the Nationalist Government.

Further, he deplored the "dominating influence of the military" upon the civil government.

He also condemned the propaganda of both sides with its "deliberate misrepresentation and abuse" of the United States, tactics about which he had found it difficult to remain silent. He described the Communist propaganda as "vicious," that of the Nationalist Government only as having contained "numerous misrepresentations."

Yet he refused to be completely discouraged, instead suggesting that "now that the form for a democratic government has been laid down by the newly adopted Constitution, political measures will be the best."

Between the dominant reactionary groups in the Government and the irreconcilable Communists, he maintained, "lies the problem of how peace and well-being are to be brought to the long suffering and presently inarticulate mass of the people of China."

In describing his efforts to get both sides together, he expressed the hope that the Government would offer a "genuine welcome" to all groups, including the Communists in the proposed reorganization.

* * *

March 13, 1947

TRUMAN ACTS TO SAVE NATIONS FROM RED RULE; ASKS 400 MILLION TO AID GREECE AND TURKEY; CONGRESS FIGHT LIKELY BUT APPROVAL IS SEEN

NEW POLICY SET UP

President Blunt in Plea to Combat 'Coercion' as World Peril

PLANS TO SEND MEN

Goods and Skills Needed as Well as Money, He Tells Congress

By FELIX BELAIR Jr.
Special to The New York Times.

WASHINGTON, March 12—President Truman outlined a new foreign policy for the United States today. In a historic message to Congress, he proposed that this country intervene wherever necessary throughout the world to prevent the subjection of free peoples to Communist-inspired totalitarian regimes at the expense of their national integrity and importance.

In a request for $400,000,000 to bolster the hard-pressed Greek and Turkish Governments against Communist pressure, the President said the constant coercion and intimidation of free peoples by political infiltration amid poverty and strife undermined the foundations of world peace and threatened the security of the United States.

Although the President refrained from mentioning the Soviet Union by name, there could be no mistaking his identification of the Communist state as the source of much of the unrest throughout the world. He said that, in violation of the Yalta Agreement, the people of Poland, Rumania and Bulgaria had been subjected to totalitarian regimes against their will and that there had been similar developments in other countries.

Cardinal Points of Departure

As the Senate and House of Representatives sat grim-faced but apparently determined on the course recommended by the Chief Executive, Mr. Truman made these cardinal points of departure from traditional American foreign policy:

"I believe that it must be the policy of the United States to support free peoples who are resisting attempted subjugation by armed minorities or by outside pressures.

"I believe that we must assist free peoples to work out their own destinies in their own way.

"I believe that our help should be primarily through economic and financial aid which is essential to economic stability and orderly political processes."

In addition to the $400,000,000, to be expended before June 30, 1948, the President asked Congress to authorize the detail of American civilian and military personnel to Greece and Turkey, upon the request of those countries. The proposed personnel would supervise the use of material and financial assistance and would train Greek and Turkish personnel in special skills.

Lest efforts be made to cast him in the role of champion of things as they are, the President recognized that the world was not static and that the status quo was not sacred. But he warned that if we allowed changes in the status quo in violation of the United Nations Charter through such subterfuges as political infiltration, we would be helping to destroy the Charter itself.

Aware of Broad Implications

President Truman said he was fully aware of the "broad implications involved" if the United States went to the assistance of Greece and Turkey. He said that, while our aid to free peoples striving to maintain their independence should be primarily financial and economic, he reminded Congress that the fundamental issues involved were no different from those for which we fought a war with Germany and Japan.

The standing ovation that marked the close of the President's address was echoing through the Capitol corridors as he left the building to motor to the National Airport, where he left by plane for Key West, Fla., for a four-day rest on orders of his personal physician, Brig. Gen. Wallace Graham.

The President appeared tired from the ordeal of his personal appearance before the joint session, but evidently satisfied that the specific recommendations of his message, with its delineation of the implications of a new policy, had temporarily discharged the obligation of the Executive. It was the turn of Congress to make the next move.

That move was not long in the making. Senator Arthur H. Vandenberg, chairman of the Foreign Relations Committee, called a meeting of his group for tomorrow morning to consider the President's proposals. The House Foreign Affairs Committee was to consider the kindred $350,000,000 appropriation for destitution relief in liberated countries.

In the sharp and conflicting reaction to the President's program, many voices were raised on each side of the Capitol in approval and in criticism. However, there was little doubt that the vast majority in both houses would reflect the wishes of their leaders and go down the line for the new policy and the added financial responsibility it implied.

Would Bar Any Coercion

Apparently conscious of the advance demands by Senator Vandenberg and others that he set forth the full implications of his recommendations, President Truman explained that one of the primary objectives of our foreign policy had been the creation of conditions in which this and other nations would work out a way of life free from coercion by outside influences.

It was to insure the peaceful development of nations, free from coercion, that the United States had taken a leading role in the establishment of the United Nations, Mr. Truman went on. And the United Nations was designed to provide a lasting freedom and independence for all its members.

But these objectives could not be attained, said the President, "unless we are willing to help free peoples to maintain their free institutions and their national integrity against aggressive movements that seek to impose upon them totalitarian regimes."

Anticipating criticism, not long in developing, that his proposals to lend $250,000,000 to Greece and $150,000,000 to Turkey would "by-pass the United Nations," Mr. Truman explained that, while the possibility of United Nations aid had been considered, the urgency and immediacy were such that the United Nations was not in a position to assist effectively.

The President made it clear that the responsibilities he asked Congress to face squarely had developed suddenly because of the inability of Great Britain to extend help to either the Greek or Turkish Government after March 31. He said the British withdrawal by March 31 foreshadowed the imposition of totalitarian regimes by force in both countries unless the United States stepped in to support the existing Governments.

The President reiterated that it was a serious course on which he was asking Congress to embark. But he said he would not ask it except that the alternative was much more serious. The United States contributed $341,000,000,000 toward the winning of World War II, the President recalled.

Although there was a note of apology for the present Greek Government, which the President conceded had made mistakes, it was described as a freely elected one.

The Greek Government, he said, represents 85 per cent of the members of the Greek Parliament. He recalled that 692 American observers had been present in Greece when the Parliament was elected and had certified that the election represented a fair expression of the views of the Greek people.

Although the President did not specify the allocation of the $400,000,000, it has been generally understood that the Administration intends to use $250,000,000 for Greece and $150,000,000 for Turkey. He asked further authority to permit the speediest and most effective translation of the funds into "needed commodities, supplies and equipment," which was taken to refer to the supply of surplus war equipment to the Greek Army out of United States Army supplies in Europe.

* * *

March 23, 1947

PRESIDENT ORDERS INQUIRY ON DISLOYAL JOBHOLDERS; COMMUNISTS FIRST TARGET

FBI WILL AID STUDY

In Unprecedented Step Heads of Departments Must Back 'Purge'

REVIEW BOARD IS CREATED

It Will Hear Final Appeals of All Workers or Applicants Marked For Job Elimination

By WALTER H. WAGGONER
Special to The New York Times.

WASHINGTON, March 22—President Truman, by executive decree, ordered into effect today an elaborate and unprecedented program of security and precautions against Federal employment of any person who, on "reasonable grounds," can be judged disloyal.

The Presidential Order called for an immediate investigation of the loyalty and intentions of every person entering civilian employment in any department or agency of the Executive Branch of the Government.

Present job holders who have not already been checked for loyalty will be scrutinized by the Federal Bureau of Investigation, and their fate will rest on the decision of department heads held "personally responsible" for the character of their subordinates.

Although they were not singled out in the order, Communists and Communist sympathizers would be the first targets of the President's prescribed loyalty standards, it was indicated.

There have been repeated allegations in Congress that Communists held Federal posts, and many attacks have been made on the Administration for not ridding itself of them.

Charges Made By House Group

The House Civil Service Committee charged this week that only nine persons had been discharged from Government jobs as Communists since July 1, and promised a "full-scale investigation" of additional suspected employees.

Mr. Truman called for this sweeping program on the recommendation of his six-agency Temporary Commission on Employe Loyalty, which he named by Executive Order on last Nov. 25.

The President received the Commission's thirty-eight-page report on Feb. 20. Its publication had been held up, according to Charles G. Ross, White House press secretary, so that Mr. Truman could "study it and give time for the preparation of an Executive Order which carries out and implements the recommendations of the Commission."

Introducing his order, the President stated that every Government employe "is endowed with a measure of trusteeship over the democratic processes which are the heart and sinew of the United States."

It was of vital importance that all Federal employes be of "complete and unswerving loyalty" to this country, he continued, adding that the presence of any disloyal or subversive persons "constitutes a threat to our democratic processes."

Major Provisions of Order

Other major provisions of the ruling, in summary form, are as follows:

1. A "central master index" will be compiled of the records of all persons who have undergone loyalty checks by any agency or department since Sept. 1, 1939.

2. An over-all "Loyalty Review Board" will be set up in the Civil Service Commission, consisting of three "impartial" officers or employes of the commission. The board will review cases as an authority of final appeal for employes recommended for dismissal on grounds of disloyalty.

3. One or more three-member loyalty boards will be named by the head of each department or agency to hear cases within the agency itself.

4. The Attorney General will list all "totalitarian, fascist, communist or subversive" groups and organizations, and those which have a policy of "advocating or approving the commission of acts of force or violence to deny other persons their rights" under the Constitution, or "seeking to alter the form of government of the United States by unconstitutional means."

5. Should "derogatory information" with regard to loyalty standards of any job applicant be uncovered, a "full field investigation," utilizing all the Government's resources, will be conducted.

Maximum Protection Sought

"Maximum protection must be afforded the United States against infiltration of disloyal persons into the ranks of its employes," said the President, "and equal protection from unfounded accusations of disloyalty must be afforded the loyal employes of the Government."

The President's program, although ordered into effect immediately, requires funds, which have not yet been appropriated. It is widely felt, however, that if Congress will authorize any additional expenditures, a loyalty program such as the President has set forth will be provided with funds.

In the meantime Mr. Truman instructed the Secretaries of War and Navy and of the Treasury, so far as the Treasury Department relates to the Coast Guard, to continue to enforce and maintain "the highest standards of loyalty within the armed services."

Files to be Made Available

The government's total resources will be mobilized to carry out the President's ruling. In addition, investigation of a job applicant may include reference to the files of the FBI, the Civil Service Commission, military and naval intelligence authorities, any other "appropriate government investigative or intelligence agency," the House Committee on Un-American Activities, and state and local law enforcement agencies.

Also considered as potential sources of information relating to a person's loyalty are the schools and colleges attended by the applicant, his former employers, references given on his application, and any other source not specified or excluded in the order.

Names of persons giving information about an applicant or employe under investigation may be withheld under the terms of the order. The investigating agency must, however, supply sufficient information to enable the department involved to make "an adequate evaluation" of the statements.

The investigator must also advise the agency requesting the information in writing that "it is essential to the protection of the informants or to the investigation of other cases that the names of the informants not be revealed."

Condemned Activities Listed

The specific "activities and associations" condemned in the President's program are:

Sabotage, espionage, or trying or preparing for either;

Knowingly associating with spies or saboteurs;

Treason or sedition, or the advocacy of either;

Advocacy of revolution, force, or violence to change the constitutional form of the American Government;

Intentional, unauthorized disclosure to any person, "under circumstances which may indicate disloyalty to the United States," of documents or information of a confidential or nonpublic character obtained by the person making the disclosure as a result of his Government position;

Performing his duties, whatever they are, or in any way acting in a manner which better serves the interests of a foreign Government than the United States;

Membership in or affiliation with any of the groups designated by the Attorney General as "totalitarian, Fascist, Communist, or subversive."

The first step in eliminating present employes suspected of disloyalty will be the submission to the FBI of the personnel rolls of all departments or agencies covered by the order.

The FBI will then check each name against its records of persons against whom there is already a body of evidence pointing to disloyalty. Suggestions of disloyalty by any employes will be returned to the department.

Departments will make their own investigations of suspected employes or request investigation by the Civil Service Commission.

Job applicants will be investigated first by the Civil Service Commission if they are entering positions which it covers, or, if they are not, by the department or agency in which they are seeking employment.

*　*　*

April 7, 1947

DE GAULLE SAYS U. S. HAS ALLY IN FRANCE

In Event 'New Tyranny' Faces World, Both Nations Will Be on Same Side, He Pledges

By HAROLD CALLENDER
Special to The New York Times.

PARIS, April 6—Speaking in Strasbourg today, former President de Gaulle said that "if a new tyranny should ever menace all or part of the world, we may be certain that the United States and France would be together to oppose it."

"May this solid certainty strengthen everywhere the minds and hearts of men who are free and intend to remain so," he added in an address to celebrate the liberation of Alsace. His audience included the United States Ambassador, Jefferson Caffery.

M. de Gaulle, whose return to politics with a speech in Bruneval a week ago alarmed his opponents, led up to that final sentence of his short speech today by saying that there existed between the United States and France a similarity of ideals that had created "a kind of moral bond that is truly unusual and that nothing has been able to break."

It was for this reason, he said, that whenever justice in the world was violated, the conscience of France and of America awakened in unison, and "our two democracies" responded alike "when they had to defend menaced liberty."

This joint action took place, continued M. de Gaulle in both world wars when France joined Britain and when the United States went to the rescue of Europe, "wholly menaced by the same peril," and of Asia.

The Americans who fell in liberating Alsace, said M. de Gaulle, bore testimony to "the great movement that drew their country to the aid of those who fought against oppression."

The mystery of whether M. de Gaulle would talk politics this afternoon was maintained to the last moment. The French news agency reported at noon that M. de Gaulle's aides still professed ignorance on that point. To many, the "politics" seemed somewhat obscure even after his speech had been made.

M. de Gaulle's final sentence, quoted at the beginning of this dispatch, could not have been uttered by his Communist opponents. They have loudly contended that President Truman's speech on Greece had revealed the United States as a reactionary and imperialistic power seeking to crush democracy in small nations.

Nor could that sentence have found a place in the speech M. de Gaulle delivered in Bar-le-Duc last July, when he depicted both Russia and the United States as expansionist powers, between which a Europe led by Britain and France should maintain a balance.

Shift of Opinion Is Seen

Since every word in each speech of M. de Gaulle is carefully weighed in advance, the question inevitably asked here was whether he had abandoned the essentially neutral attitude toward the United States and Russia that he displayed in July and the attitude that characterized French policy during his regime, and since.

M. de Gaulle's mention of a possible future menace to freedom far exceeded the requirements of his major theme—the role of the United States in the liberation of Alsace. Hence his final sentence seemed to some to point in the same direction as Mr. Truman's speech to Congress, which no French leader has fully endorsed so far.

Moderate and conservative commentators have been saying since Mr. Truman's speech that France must soon choose between Russia and the United States. But the official policy has been to avoid this choice. The policy of lining up with the United States and Britain probably would have its internal counterpart in a Government without the Communists. Both the Socialists and the Catholic Popular Republicans consider such a Government impossible.

At any rate, M. de Gaulle did comply with Premier Ramadier's request to avoid internal politics at this unveiling of the inscription commemorating the United States soldiers who fell in liberating Alsace.

After Ambassador Caffery had thanked Strasbourg and Alsace and spoken of French-American friendship, M. de Gaulle began his address to the crowd filling the cathedral square. M. de Gaulle sent a telegram to Gen. Dwight D. Eisenhower paying tribute to the United States armies.

As tomorrow is a national holiday, it is expected that a large part of the crowd that poured into Strasbourg for today's ceremony will remain to hear M. de Gaulle make then what is widely advertised as an important speech on domestic politics.

* * *

April 8, 1947

SOVIET CHARGES U. S. HURTS U. N. BY PLAN FOR GREECE, TURKEY

Gromyko in Security Council Asks for a Commission to Supervise Help to Athens

CALLS ANKARA INSINCERE

He Asserts It Deserves No Aid—Urges the Atom Bomb Be Destroyed Ahead of Control

By THOMAS J. HAMILTON
Special to The New York Times.

LAKE SUCCESS, N. Y., April 7—Andrei A. Gromyko, Soviet Deputy Foreign Minister, charged today that the United States aid program for Greece constituted intervention in Greek internal affairs. He demanded that the United Nations Security Council establish a commission to see to it that United States help for Greece was administered exclusively for the benefit of the Greek people.

Although he praised the courage of the Greek people in fighting the Axis, he pointed out to the Security Council that Turkey did not enter the war on the side of the Allies until a few days before VE-Day. He asserted that Turkey had "profiteered" during the war by selling raw materials to Germany and was not entitled to assistance.

The Soviet Union's formal reply to the Truman proposals was delivered before an audience that jammed the Security Council chamber. Mr. Gromyko accused the United States of having seriously undermined the authority of the United Nations, and of having produced distrust among its members.

Done in Professorial Way

Mr. Gromyko, who was wearing a sober blue suit, made his 2,500-word statement in the manner of a professor reading a dissertation. However, he warmed up afterward when Warren R. Austin, the United States representative, formally proposed that the Security Council direct its Balkan frontier commission to keep representatives in the area, while it was drafting its report.

This, Mr. Gromyko asserted, was an attempt to put up a "screen" bearing the initials "U. N." to "hide the activities of the United States, which are not in the interests of the United Nations, if only because they constitute an effort to intervene in the internal affairs of Greece."

Mr. Gromyko's criticisms of the United States program were supported by the representatives of Bulgaria and Yugoslavia, which, though not members of the Security Council, were admitted to the discussions because the Balkan commission is investigating incidents on Greece's northern frontier.

On the other hand, Australia endorsed the statement by Mr. Austin of March 28, which notified the Security Council of the American program. Vasili Dendramis, the Greek representative, contented himself with thanking the representatives of the United States, Australia and the Soviet Union for their tribute to the heroism of the Greek people during the war.

All in all, today was the most spectacular day in Mr. Gromyko's career, and the overflow audience stayed on almost until the final wrangling over the date when the Security Council would consider the clashing United States and Soviet proposals.

Interestingly enough, Mr. Gromyko made his statement before the Conventional Arms Commission in the morning in Russian, but used English for his full-dress declaration to the Security Council in the afternoon. He reverted to Russian for extemporaneous remarks, indicating that he uses English only when time permits him to make advance preparation.

For the first time in Security Council history, Soviet attachés had copies of the Security Council declaration available for newspapermen, and even handed them out before he began speaking, with a "hold for release" embargo.

Although not so large, the audience at the meeting of the Security Council's Commission on Conventional Armaments this morning followed his remarks with equally close attention. Attacking the "artificial obstacles" that, he said, were being placed in the way of disarmament by Great Britain and the United States, the Soviet spokesman reiterated his demand for an international convention to outlaw the atomic bomb immediately, without waiting for the establishment of international control and inspection.

The same men are members of the two agencies, and after a luncheon recess, both delegates and public, including ninety West Point cadets, returned to the chamber to hear Mr. Gromyko on the general question of the Truman proposals.

Mr. Austin, who has yet to mention that the United States program provides any military equipment for either Greece or Turkey, had said in his speech of notification that the Truman program for Greece was intended to meet an "emergency" situation, and that he hoped the United Nations would be able to carry out a long-time program of reconstruction.

Technically, Mr. Austin had spoken merely regarding the Greek charges that resulted in the present commission's being sent to the Balkans, and Mr. Gromyko was the first speaker recognized today on that subject. The Soviet representative lost no time in attacking the United States contention that the Truman proposals would strengthen the United Nations. He charged that the United States had by-passed the organization and had only informed it of its plans post-factum.

Gromyko Asks Cooperation

Emphasizing that cooperation was necessary to strengthen international confidence in the United Nations—which, he said, was still lacking—Mr. Gromyko contended that the United States should have appealed to the Security Council against the "allegedly existing threat" of outside intervention in Greece.

Despite Mr. Austin's silence on the subject, Mr. Gromyko showed that he was fully aware of Administration disclosures to Congress that all of the $150,000,000 intended for Turkey, and half the $250,000,000 for Greece, would be used to equip and train their armies.

He charged, in fact, that "the major portion" of the appropriation for Greece was for military purposes, and that civilian and military instructors would be sent to both countries, although, according to reports from Washington, no United States experts are to be sent to Turkey.

Sending troops or even instructors to any country is an interference in its internal affairs and a serious blow to its independence, said Mr. Gromyko, who declared that because of their bravery during the war the Greek people deserved better treatment from the United States.

Mr. Gromyko charged that Mr. Austin had attempted "artificially" to link up the United States program with the United Nations by proposing that the Security Council investigating commission remain in the Balkans to keep a watch on the frontiers.

The very fact that the commission was still there, he contended, was a reason to wait until it had submitted its report. Afterward, he said, the Security Council could take the nec-

essary measures. He charged that the United States had ignored both the report of the commission and the future decision of the Council.

Briton Supports Austin

No other speakers were listed to follow Mr. Gromyko's address, but Sir Alexander Cadogan, British representative, then asked to be recognized and gave the British Government's endorsement to Mr. Austin's previous suggestion that the Balkan commission keep a sub-commission in the area, first, while it was drawing up its report in Geneva, and, secondly, until the Security Council acted on its report.

Sir Alexander argued that it would be "ridiculous" if the commission failed to have available the latest information when it prepared its report, and he spoke guardedly of the possibility of "a major incident involving foreign intervention in the next few weeks." The British representative, who was referring apparently to rumors that the impending withdrawal of British troops might be followed by an attack on Greece's northern frontiers, contended that nobody who had the interests of the Greek people "sincerely at heart" would object.

The difficulty was that neither Mr. Austin nor Sir Alexander had a draft of the resolution ready to submit. After the Syrian representative, Faris El Khouri, had argued that it was premature for the Council to order the establishment of a sub-commission now, Col. W. R. Hodgson, Australian representative, gave the first endorsement of the United States program by another member of the Security Council.

Colonel Hodgson, who omitted any mention of the Turkish program, said that Australians, having fought alongside the Greeks, knew their courage, and he declared that the Greeks had asked help from the one ally who was in a position to help them.

The United States, far from by-passing the United Nations, has done just the opposite, said the Australian representative, who pointed out that under the Vandenberg amendment to the Turkey-Greece program, the Security Council would have the right to call on the United States to withdraw.

Mr. Austin, who has not mentioned the Vandenberg amendment to the Council since it has not yet been adopted by Congress, meanwhile had been drafting his resolution, which he submitted as follows:

"Resolved, that during the absence of the commission from the area in which it has conducted its investigation, the commission shall maintain in the area concerned a subsidiary group composed of a representative of each of the members of the commission."

France Amends Resolution

This language was so comprehensive that it apparently would have authorized the establishment of a permanent Balkans commission. Alexandre Parodi, French representative, then stressed that it was essential to show that the step was of a temporary nature, and suggested the substitution of

"Resolved, that pending a new decision by the Security Council" for the introductory clause.

This change was accepted by Mr. Austin, but Mr. Gromyko, renewing his attack on the "artificial" effort to link up the commission's work with the United States program, declared again that the latter raised "a different and wider question."

Indicating his suspicion that the resolution was intended to establish a permanent border agency, he insisted that if the commission left any representatives they would be there as representatives of their governments, not as "Mr. Smith or Mr. Brown."

Boyan Athanassov of Bulgaria and Stane Krasovec of Yugoslavia supported Mr. Gromyko's criticisms of the Greek Government and the United States program.

The debate will be resumed when the Council meets at 10:30 A. M. Thursday.

* * *

June 6, 1947

MARSHALL PLEADS FOR EUROPEAN UNITY

AS 'CURE' FOR ILLS

Only Then Can Our Aid Be Integrated, Says the Secretary

HITS 'PIECEMEAL' BASIS

He Tells Harvard Alumni Our Policy is Not Set Against 'Any Country or Doctrine'

By FRANK L. KLUCKHOHN
Special to The New York Times.

CAMBRIDGE, Mass., June 5—The countries of Europe were called upon today by the Secretary of State, George C. Marshall, to get together and decide upon their needs for economic rehabilitation so that further United States aid could be provided upon an integrated instead of a "piecemeal" basis. This was important to make possible a real "cure" of Europe's critical economic difficulties, he asserted in an address to Harvard alumni this afternoon after he had received the honorary degree of Doctor of Laws at this morning's commencement exercises.

General Marshall supported President Truman's statements in Washington earlier today that United States aid abroad was necessary. He declared that Europe "must have substantial additional help or face economic, social and political deterioration of a very grave character."

"There must be some agreement among the countries of Europe as to the requirements of the situation," he warned, adding that no American aid would be given to "any government which maneuvers to block the recovery of other countries." The Secretary emphasized that governments or parties or groups, seeking to make political capital by perpetuating human misery, would encounter "the opposition of the United States."

General Marshall was the recipient of several ovations as he participated in Harvard's first fully normal post-war graduation exercises. The first came when he moved to the platform before Memorial Church in the procession of 2,185 undergraduates, graduate students and the honor group who were to receive degrees. The second ovation came when James B. Conant, president, conferred an honorary degree upon him.

The biggest ovations came just before and after he spoke, with applause interlarded when the Secretary said American help would be withheld from those making capital of trouble in Europe.

General Marshall was one of the last to speak this afternoon. Gen. Omar N. Bradley, administrator of veterans' affairs, who also received a Doctor of Laws degree, had asserted that the expenditure of $12,000,000,000 for veterans' education was a good investment for the United States and Dr. Conant had called for the raising of $90,000,000 to increase Harvard's activities.

"Friendly Aid" Stressed

After asserting that no "assured peace" or political stability was possible without the aid of the United States in effecting a return to normal economic health in the world, General Marshall said that "the initiative, I think, should come from Europe." This country should restrict itself to "friendly aid" in the drafting of a European program and later in supporting this program "as far as it may be practical for us to do so," he added.

He held it to be essential that several and, if possible, all European states should effect what he termed a "joint" program. It would be neither "fitting nor efficacious" for us to draw up a unilateral program and then foist it upon possibly unwilling governments and nations, said the General.

Economic rehabilitation in Europe would require "a much longer time and greater effort" than had been officially foreseen, he continued. Then he stressed that the United States was willing to give "full cooperation" to countries willing to assist in steps toward European recovery, and denied that the policy of the United States was directed against "any country or doctrine."

For American Understanding

In a few brief words after his prepared talk, Secretary Marshall said that he regarded full understanding by the American people of foreign problems and the aims of American policy to be of high importance.

He already had expressed the fear that the enormous complexity of problems and the mass of facts available were confusing people.

The dislocation of the entire fabric of European economy through the breaking up of commercial ties and the elimination of private banks, insurance companies and the loss of capital, probably was even more serious than the destruction of physical property of all sorts and the losses in manpower, he explained.

The Secretary said that one important factor leading to the threat of a complete "breakdown" in Europe was the fact that the cities were no longer producing much that the farmers wanted and that, as a result, the farmers were making little effort to raise enough to feed the cities. Thus, with city people short of food and fuel, he added, "the Governments are forced to use their foreign money and credits for necessities instead of reconstruction."

The Secretary, who was presented to the Harvard alumni by Gov. Robert F. Bradford, returned to Washington by air after the ceremonies.

General Bradley, in the uniform of a full general with four rows of ribbons, devoted himself largely to one facet of the country's program, his own.

"In the United States, of the 2,300,000 students in colleges, 1,200,000 are veterans, getting their education mostly at Government expense," he said. "Within twenty months after the close of the war the American people had already invested nearly $2,500,000,000 in the (educational) program. By the time it is completed, the program may have cost a total of $12,000,000,000, or barely enough to have run the war for several weeks."

"There are times when it may be more dangerous to spend too little than to spend too much." General Bradley continued. "For example, if ever we should expose our people to sickness, our resources to waste, our economy to depression and our nation to aggression in a panicky effort to save dollars, we may some day have to ask ourselves if such savings were worth the cost.

"If we offer youth a fair chance to make its way in the nation we need not fear political deflection to either the left or right. We cannot meet the challenge of rival ideologies with labels and reaction. We must offer these young veterans progress and the opportunity for constant self-betterment throughout their busy lives."

General Bradley obtained a laugh from his audience when, referring to his honorary degree, he said:

"Like thousands of other veterans, I appear to be getting my education as a result of the GI bill."

* * *

June 27, 1947

BARUCH DOUBTS RUSSIAN WAR, BUT URGES MOBILIZATION PLAN

By ANTHONY LEVIERO
Special to The New York Times.

WASHINGTON, June 26—Bernard M. Baruch urged today enactment of a sixteen-point, work-or-fight mobilization program which he said would enable this country to cope with an emergency without repeating the preparedness errors of the two World Wars.

Speaking at the graduation exercises of the Industrial College of the Armed Forces, the adviser of Presidents put universal military training at "the apex of the pyramid."

Mr. Baruch said that he saw no immediate threat of war with Russia. He asserted, however, that he found "irritations," which he did not fear would become "explosions," then added:

"But in the cold war that is being waged against us, we must always remember that their objective is our unrest. We can guard against that by a firm belief in ourselves, under the magnificent flowering of our century and a half of national life."

Russian Failure Predicted

Mr. Baruch said that Russia would be disappointed if she expected the United States to suffer an economic collapse.

"We shall continue long after their experiment has failed," he asserted as he denounced Russian sympathizers who were trying to change the American way of life.

Mr. Baruch said that he doubted that Great Britain's "great experiment" would succeed. He questioned whether Britain could go on with collectivism, socialism and regimentation without endangering the principles for which she fought alongside this country.

Presented as "father and master of economic mobilization" by Brig. Gen. E. B. McKinley, college commandant, Mr. Baruch read an outline of action drawn up by the War Industries Board of World War I, of which he was chairman. President Wilson had accepted it, he added, "as the mandate of our existence."

That formula of thirty years ago was still good, Mr. Baruch asserted, and yet he added, the early errors of World War I were repeated in World War II.

"Faltering step by faltering step we moved towards controls," Mr. Baruch said, "but those controls were never sufficient and far-reaching enough. If they had been applied immediately, many lives would have been saved, our casualties lowered and billions saved. Despite warnings of graver danger, the English and French made even more mistakes.

"Also, as a result of piecemeal price control, we are now faced with inflation which, next to human slaughter, maiming and destruction, is the worst consequence of war. It creates lack of confidence of men in themselves and in their government.

"If, from the beginning, there had been an effective overall price control law including everything—regulation and control of all prices, wages, rents and food—there would have been a quicker ending of the war, a lessened cost, and less dissatisfaction among all classes.

"But after having granted favors to one class, group after group fought for favors, until we found ourselves upon economic stilts. Then restrictions were removed while peace was still distant."

In addition to his sixteen points, he endorsed the pending bill for uniform hemispheric armament and training to "make South, Central and North America a complete unit."

Would Be Ready for War

Instead of leaving mobilization to Executive action, Mr. Baruch proposed that his "minimum program" should be "placed upon the statute books, ready to function, should war come." The points of his plan were as follows:

"Mobilize the full might of America—militarily, economically and spiritually.

"Have universal military training.

"All men and women subject to mobilization with a work-or-fight clause. The same applies to all professions, science, callings, crafts, industrial and agricultural efforts, including labor of all kinds. In other words, there should be a pool of all our manpower—brains and brawn—ready to be tapped at any moment for war purposes.

"An industrial plan ready to go into effect with full control of production, distribution and prices, with the power of allocation, priority and even exclusion for everything. The wisdom with which we organize our resources, men, money and materials will make for the greatest of all—winning morale.

Would End War Profits

"Taking unfair profits out of war and preventing inflation through an over-all price regulation, tax and savings program. There must be only enough profit to keep our economy and production going. That cannot be done by favoring any one segment of our society.

"While we must keep our civilian structure alive, skeletonize by restricting materials and manpower for unnecessary wants. In the last war too much went for wants rather than needs.

"An organization to export materials in demand by other nations and to buy the things our nation needs or desires to keep from enemy hands.

"Accumulation of critical imports.

"Retention of war plants, particularly synthetic rubber plants.

"Intensified scientific research.

"A standard form of contract set up now.

"An Intelligence Service enlarged far beyond what now exists.

"Information and propaganda organized, gone over and continually improved to be ready when action demands.

"Until some effective international guarantee of security has been established, as envisioned Woodrow Wilson and Franklin Roosevelt, or resort to war eliminated, we cannot disregard the dangers inherent in developing mass housing in cities. Surveys must be made of underground industrial establishments, refuge for civilians and dispersal of populations.

"These organizations should be planned in considerable detail and gone over every three or six months by the National Resources Board. Competent men should be trained to fill the key positions. The Chiefs of Staff should make recommendations to the Resources Board for such changes as they deem wise and necessary. Setting up of industrial and social machinery should not be left to M-Day.

"All organizations continually posed to the proper Congressional committees, keeping them in touch with defense plans. The American people must be taken into fullest confidence. They will do anything required of them if they are told why. Do not try to fool them."

* * *

July 3, 1947

PARIS PARLEY ENDS WITH EUROPE SPLIT; MOLOTOV, BALKING, WARNS ON BLOCS; BRITAIN AND FRANCE TO PUSH AID PLAN

BEVIN IS DEFIANT

Says Britain 'Has Faced Threats Before'— Sees 'Travesty of Facts'

BIDAULT PLEDGES HELP

Denies Marshall's Program Would Subjugate Europe— To Ask Others to Join

By HAROLD CALLENDER
Special to The New York Times.

PARIS, July 2—The complete failure of the conference of Foreign Ministers of the three big European powers on United States aid to Europe was formally recorded today. With it the splitting of Europe into two separate blocs headed in different directions became conclusive and virtually official.

The break-up of the conference resulted from Soviet Foreign Minister Molotov's refusal, despite British and French pleas, to budge one inch from his rigid opposition to any common constructive action by European countries as a response to United States Secretary of State Marshall's proposal of United States aid on that condition. His refusal took the form of a final rejection of a compromise French proposal for such action.

British Foreign Secretary Bevin and French Foreign Minister Bidault then announced together for the first time, that their Governments would go on without the Soviet Union to rally other countries around the Marshall proposal. They said their Governments would seek to obtain quickly a continental response in the form of a program of self help among the European nations as the first step toward justifying United States aid.

Bevin, Bidault Meet Today

Mr. Molotov and his delegation of eighty-nine are expected to depart for Moscow tomorrow. Mr. Bevin will remain for a meeting tomorrow morning with M. Bidault, which will be a resumption of their two-power conference held before Mr. Molotov's arrival.

Within a few days these two powers are expected to invite all Europe except the Soviet Union and Spain—the leading Communist and Fascist states—to join in this kind of collective acceptance of the Marshall proposal.

Thus a Western European bloc, long the bugaboo of the Communists and of Moscow, seemed to take shape suddenly and as the inevitable consequence of the words spoken here by Mr. Molotov, who even today professed to deprecate this development.

"This is the Western bloc," said a high French official tonight. "We enter it without excessive joy but as a necessity. It was inevitable. I do not think the reaction within France will be as grave as some had anticipated."

Suggest Rift in Soviet Bloc

Mr. Bevin likewise disliked this splitting of Europe into two camps but he held that it had been forced by the Soviet Union.

British officials said tonight they hoped the line of division might run somewhat farther East than the line hitherto drawn. They thought it was not at all sure that on the issue of the Marshall plan either Poland or Czechoslovakia would stick to the Moscow line that credits in dollars were a menace to the sovereignty or independence of half-starving European states.

These two eastern European countries, usually regarded as Soviet satellites, already have indicated their desire to accept and profit by the Marshall proposal.

The British remarked that Mr. Molotov, in giving examples of the countries upon which he said pressure from the West would be brought, himself had mentioned Poland and Czechoslovakia, which the British regard as the most independent-minded of the so-called satellites.

After having accused Britain and France of dividing Europe "into two groups of states and creating new difficulties in their mutual relations" Mr. Molotov made what Mr. Bevin interpreted as a threat against the two Western powers.

"The Soviet Government considers it necessary to caution the Governments of Great Britain and France against the consequences of such an action which would be directed not toward the unification of the efforts of the countries of Europe in the task of their economic rehabilitation after the war but would lead to opposite results, which have nothing in common with the real interests of the peoples of Europe," said Mr. Molotov.

To this Mr. Bevin quickly replied that he regretted that Mr. Molotov had threatened "that if we continued this beneficent work we must face grave consequences." Mr. Bevin then said:

"My country has faced grave consequences and threats before. It is not the sort of prospect which will deter us from doing what we consider our duty."

Finality of Split Noted

There was a quality of finality about this split and in these words that had not characterized such interchanges in any of the previous Foreign Ministers' conferences, plain though the talking was on more than one occasion.

A moment earlier Mr. Bevin had replied to Mr. Molotov's aspersions on the Western world in general in a manner much like that of Secretary of State Marshall in his speech in Washington yesterday.

"Molotov's remarks were based upon a complete travesty of the facts and a complete misrepresentation of everything the British Government had submitted," said Mr. Bevin. "I suppose the method is to go on repeating these misrepresentations, in the hope that someone will at last believe them."

Both Mr. Bevin and M. Bidault had a strong suspicion that the Soviet Union would say no to any proposal, however framed, that involved close cooperation in production and exchange between the capitalistic or semi-capitalistic states of democratic western Europe and the states that are more or less directly and completely under Soviet domination. But they felt that for the historic record they must not themselves precipitate this division of Europe, even though it were inevitable.

For this reason Mr. Bevin had approved M. Bidault's attempt at a revised Western proposal yesterday, although French officials, eager to indicate M. Bidault had acted independently, had erroneously said last night that there was no such prior approval, and although Mr. Bevin all along had been less patient than M. Bidault toward Mr. Molotov.

Mr. Bevin and M. Bidault likewise were fully aware that if the Soviet Union said yes and qualified for United States aid, the approval of such aid by Congress probably would be less prompt and less generous to say the least. Some had reported that Congress in that case might not even grant the aid.

Dilemma of Westerners

Hence Mr. Bevin and M. Bidault were obliged on the one hand to try to avoid a sharper split of Europe and on the other hand to consider Congressional reaction regarding aid that was indispensable to their own and other countries. Their conciliation of the Soviet Union seemed to risk the loss or reduction of the aid they sought.

Some suggested that if the Kremlin had been clever it would have accepted the British and French proposal intact and thus gambled on the chance that the Soviet Union's presence among the European applicants would lead Congress to refuse any substantial aid to Europe.

The reasons that the Kremlin did not venture to take this chance are believed here to be that it feared there would be in any case enough United States aid to undermine the solidarity of the Soviet bloc of hitherto fairly obedient states. The Kremlin was said to fear this would produce in Europe a measure of recovery under capitalist auspices that would offer an embarrassing contrast to that measure the Soviet Union has been able to produce within its own borders under different auspices and by different methods.

The Kremlin presumably might have gambled on the assumption that such a capitalist triumph was ruled out by the historic determinism that Moscow spokesmen profess to feel sure will soon wreck the United States in an economic slump.

Mr. Molotov's apparent fear of the power of the dollar, reiterated the last four days in Paris, was regarded as hardly sustaining the likewise reiterated predictions of a slump in the United States that have flowed from the Moscow radio and filled the columns in the Western Communist press.

After a night's reflection and presumably a telephone call to the Kremlin, Mr. Molotov opened today's meeting by saying he had examined the French proposal of yesterday. This had suggested an organization to study European resources and needs and only afterward an inquiry regarding "the possibility of receiving American economic aid." Mr. Molotov has urged the reverse order.

Mr. Molotov said the Marshall proposal had inspired the French and British Governments to desire to create an organism above the European countries that would interfere in their internal affairs and give directions regarding their economic development. The French and British desire, he said, to insure a predominant position for themselves in the Steering Committee they proposed. The smaller European countries would become controlled states, he argued, and so lose their independence to satisfy the desires of a few great powers.

The French plan, he said, proposed United States aid should be dependent upon the obedience shown by the European countries to this committee. Mr. Molotov then argued this would lead to pressure upon Poland to deliver coal, even if at the expense of other Polish industries; upon Czechoslovakia to increase her food production to the deteriment of her industries; upon Norway to abandon the development of her steel industry in the interest of foreign trusts.

Rejects French Proposal

How could the small countries defend their sovereignty against the great ones in such a situation? asked Mr. Molotov. He answered his own rhetorical question by a negative.

Therefore, the Soviet Union cannot share the French enthusiasm for aid from foreign sources, said Mr. Molotov. He contended the decisive part in European recovery was not that of United States aid as the French plan had indicated, but internal measures taken by each country.

Mr. Molotov objected that the French plan proposed to use German resources although the reparations demands of victims of German aggression had not been met. He complained that nothing had been done to establish a central German Government and that in the Western zones a policy of federalism tended to separate those parts of Germany from the rest.

United States credits, Mr. Molotov added, would serve not to reconstruct the European economy but to oppose one part of Europe to another part to the advantage of the powers that wanted to dominate other countries.

Replying, M. Bidault expressed disappointment at Mr. Molotov's speech and warned the Soviet Union against any action that would divide Europe into two groups. France, he said, has done her utmost to avoid such a division and disclaims any responsibility for it.

M. Bidault replied to each of Mr. Molotov's arguments, saying the French plan proposed guarantees against the infringement of the sovereignty of any state and that all Poland, Czechoslovakia and others were asked to do was to say what they could furnish to Europe in exchange for United States aid.

The decisive role of the United States was compared by M. Bidault with that played by the few thousand men coming up at the crucial final stage at the battles of Marengo and Waterloo. He said a decision regarding Germany was left, as now, to the commanders in chief.

Bidault to Continue Study

"In the name of my Government, I add that France is determined, and her Government feels obliged, to continue the study of the prospects offered by the suggestions of Secretary Marshall," M. Bidault continued. "This will be done with all those willing to collaborate. I hope no refusal is final and that consequently the work will not be that of a reduced Europe."

Mr. Bevin, who was chairman today, made only a short speech. He said he had seen in the Marshall proposal a way to serve quickly the rehabilitation and independence of Europe, not a way to undermine Europe; a way to make Europe free, not to further the domination of any state.

It has not proved possible, he added, for all three powers at this conference to give the lead to cooperation "but Britain will continue to strive for the unity of Europe and for its independence and independence of its internal units."

An article to appear in the Communist newspaper Humanite tomorrow will say that the British and French refused to change their plan because it doubtless had been suggested by the United States. "The hour is grave," the writer, Pierre Herve, will add, "Will Bidault agree to German recovery, to abandon our demands for reparations, to make of France an Atlantic bridgehead and to follow that policy which disintegrates Europe, divides it into two blocs and serves the designs of the warlike?"

* * *

July 12, 1947

MARSHALL VOICES U. S. PERTURBATION ON EUROPEAN SPLIT

In Grave Session With Senate Group,
He Says Scope of His Plan Still Is Undetermined

KEEPS FAITH IN PROGRAM

Sees It Not Inconceivable That Soviet May Yet Join—
First Liaison Parley Is Secret

By WILLIAM S. WHITE
Special to The New York Times.

WASHINGTON, July 11—In a long, grave conference today Secretary of State Marshall put before the Senate Foreign Relations Committee this Government's anxious view of a continent breaking in two by the total withdrawal of the Soviet block from joint efforts at Europe's rehabilitation.

General Marshall was before the committee for almost two hours, in conditions of secrecy not approached in such Congressional executive sessions since the war. It was the initial meeting in a strong new liaison arranged between Capitol Hill and the State Department.

It was the first opportunity the Secretary had had to discuss with the Senators in detail the Marshall plan for aiding the reconstruction of Europe, a plan of helping Europe to help herself, since he had laid it down in his Harvard University speech of June 5.

Officially, nothing was given out after General Marshall's appearance; the "stop" placed upon direct information was the most complete since hostilities were ended.

To Avoid Interference

The indications were that this was decided on to avoid even the suggestion of United States interference with the Conference on European Economic Cooperation, limited now to Western powers, opening tomorrow in Paris with the Marshall formula as its base.

In spite of this extraordinary reticence, however, these were among the impressions known to have been left among the Secretary's Senatorial consultants:

(1) The Administration was most worried about the East-West division in Europe, deepened during the day by the refusal of Finland, the last of the eight States in the Soviet arc, to take a seat at Paris.

(2) The situation at the moment was developing so rapidly that no one could tell today just how broad, or how narrow, an area might eventually be encompassed in the Marshall plan when it reached its more active phase. The United States simply had to be prepared, in this connection, for whatever might develop.

(3) When the Administration brought that plan to Congress to ask for funds, it would be one for rehabilitation and not relief, and European self-help would be its central aspect. [General Marshall told the Senators that, at this time, he saw no need for legislation to put the European recovery program into effect and said the plan might not be ready until early next year, The United Press reported.]

(4) The United States was going ahead with the strongest faith in the plan, with or without Russia, and it was not inconceivable that once it was in operation, and the Russians saw that it cast no threat to Moscow, Soviet participation might yet come about.

Inquiries disclosed a rising belief in the Senate that a special session of Congress in the fall was likely to deal with the European rehabilitation problem, in spite of the fact that President Truman has stated that he sees no present necessity for such a session.

Talk Circles the Globe

It was being pointed out at the Capitol, in both Republican and Democratic quarters, that Mr. Truman had not foreclosed the possibility of calling Congress back should the need arise.

Some Senators were talking in terms of a recommendation to the Republican leaders that they not actually adjourn Congress in late July until next January, as is now planned, but simply arrange for a sixty-day recess.

This is not probable, but it is possible that adjournment might be taken in such a way as to permit Senator Arthur H. Vandenberg, Republican, of Michigan, chairman of the Foreign Relations Committee and Senate President pro tem, and House Speaker Joseph W. Martin Jr., Republican, of Massachusetts, to summon Congress independently of the President.

Secretary Marshall's conference with Senator Vandenberg and his colleagues, around the long oval table of the Foreign Relations Committee room, brought the most widely ranging discussion of foreign affairs in which the General has yet participated.

The talk circled the globe, quite apart from the matter of the Marshall plan. The Far East came up for discussion, and in particular the position of affairs in China.

As to the Paris conference opening tomorrow, Secretary Marshall and the White House maintained silence, so far as any public expressions were concerned.

The refusal of the Soviet satellite states to participate brought no surprise, even though Norman Armour, Assistant Secretary of State for Political Affairs Abroad, had appealed earlier this week to them, and to Russia, to join in the conference.

* * *

July 27, 1947

UNIFICATION SIGNED

President Acts in Plane Just Before Take-Off for Mother's Home

CONFIRMATION IS SPEEDY

Senate Upholds Nomination by Truman, by Voice Vote, Just Before Quitting

By BERTRAM D. HULEN
Special to The New York Times.

WASHINGTON, Sunday, July 27—President Truman signed in dramatic circumstances yesterday the history-making legislation unifying the nation's armed forces. Immediately afterward he nominated the Secretary of the Navy, James Forrestal of New York, to head the program as Secretary of Defense.

The nomination had been expected in Capitol Hill circles, and the Senate's Armed Services Committee unanimously endorsed Mr. Truman's proposal within two hours of its arrival from the White House. And, in executive session, just before adjournment early this morning, the Senate, by voice vote, confirmed the nomination of Mr. Forrestal. He thus became the nation's first Secretary of Defense.

Mr. Truman signed the armed services merger legislation in the Presidential plane, The Sacred Cow, at the National Airport, delaying for that purpose by 17 minutes his departure on a hurriedly arranged flight to the bedside of his dying mother, Mrs. Martha E. Truman, in Grandview, Mo.

The measure had been signed a few minutes before by Senator Arthur H. Vandenberg of Michigan, President pro tem of the Senate, and Joseph W. Martin Jr. of Massachusetts, Speaker of the House. It was rushed to the President under police escort by Carl A. Loeffler, secretary of the Senate; Leslie Biffle, secretary to the Senate minority, and Harry C. Burke, clerk of the Senate Enrolled Bills Committee.

Six pens were used in signing the measure. Mr. Truman directed that they be given to Mr. Forrestal, Robert P. Patterson, who has just retired as Secretary of War; Kenneth C. Royall, the new Secretary of War; W. Stuart Symington, Assistant Secretary of War for Air; Senator Chan Gurney of South Dakota, chairman of the Senate Armed Services Committee, who piloted the legislation through the Senate, and Clark M. Clifford, special counsel to the President.

Mr. Forrestal had no immediate comment to make and the Navy Department said he would not be available over the week-end. But he scheduled a news conference for 11 o'clock Monday morning.

Quiet and determined, Mr. Forrestal is the only member of the late President Roosevelt's Cabinet who remains in the Cabinet of Mr. Truman. He came here in 1940 as an administrative assistant to President Roosevelt. Two months later he was appointed Under-Secretary of the Navy, a post created out of the war necessity. He became Secretary of the Navy upon the death of Frank Knox in May, 1944.

A native of Beacon, N. Y., and 55 years of age, Mr. Forrestal was president of Dillon, Read & Co. in New York when he was called to public service seven years ago. A graduate of Princeton in 1915, he served as a lieutenant, junior grade, in the Naval Air Service in the first World War.

Scope of New Act

The act under which he will administer the armed forces is designed to preserve the independence of the Army, the Navy and the new Air Force. Each will have its own department under a secretary. The aim is to coordinate the striking power of the nation, promote efficiency and economy, and integrate domestic, foreign and military policies.

The service secretaries do not have Cabinet rank, that being reserved for the Secretary of Defense. He will establish general policies and programs, and exercise general direction.

The legislation further provided for a National Security Council consisting of the heads of the units making up the new national military establishment. Its meetings will be presided over by the President and it will assess, appraise and recommend problems entering into American military power. Under the council will be a Central Intelligence Agency.

The Department of the Army will include land, combat and service forces, and such aviation and water transport as is deemed organic.

The Department of the Navy will include combat and service units. It will retain the Naval Aviation Service intact.

The Marine Corps for the first time is assigned by law to the Navy.

The new department of the Air Force will have transferred to it the Army Air Force, the Air Corps, U.S.A., and the General Air Force (Air Force Combat Command).

Standing behind the combined structure will be a War Council to advise the Secretary of Defense on broad police matters, the joint chiefs of staff, a munitions board for coordinating industrial plans, research and development, and other subsidiary organizations.

The primary functions and responsibilities of the three armed services were spelled out in detail by President Truman in an executive order that was issued from the White House after his departure for Missouri.

At the same time Gen. Dwight D. Eisenhower, Army chief of staff, sent to all Army commanders throughout the world a message saying "there will be no change in the official status of the Army with respect to the Air Force until specific orders are issued setting it up as an autonomous agency." He especially urged good relations between the three armed forces as of "paramount importance" and "a keystone of Army policy."

Gen. A. A. Vandegrift, commandant of the Marine Corps, said in a statement that it was the duty of every marine "to carry out not only the letter but the spirit of the unification law." The corps will continue in its mission under unification, he declared, adding "that is all we ever asked."

Admiral Chester W. Nimitz, chief of Naval operations, in a dispatch to the Navy personnel, said such differences of opinion as were expressed in the Naval service in the past with respect to the merits of the new organization were resolved by the President's approval of the act.

"The personnel of the Navy and all of its components will apply themselves wholeheartedly and with the fullest spirit of cooperation to the implementation of its provisions," he promised.

*   *   *

July 27, 1947

INTERNAL DEFENSE DUE TO BE UNIFIED

Commander of 'Home Theatre' Would Have Staff From the Army, Navy, Air Forces

By ANTHONY LEVIERO
Special to The New York Times.

WASHINGTON, July 26—As a result of unification of the armed forces, it was learned today, the War Department has conceived the eventual establishment of a single defense commander for the whole of this country.

Under this concept, the continental United States would be organized as a home theatre in case of attack, and the commander would be under the immediate direction of the joint chiefs of staff. He would have a combined Army-Navy-Air Force staff.

The home theatre commander would be the generalissimo of all task forces assigned by each of the armed services. In other words, according to the Army concept, he would have a unified command on the pattern of Gen. Douglas MacArthur's in Japan and Gen. Lucius D. Clay's in Germany.

In the event of an attack, the home theatre commander would organize the defense and conduct operations. The scope of his responsibilities would be defined by the joint chiefs of staff, but he would be spared all administrative responsibilities, except those essential to his mission.

Eventually, it was said, the same principle might be extended to the lower commands in the critical areas of this country, thus a single commander might be put over the ground, sea, and air elements in each of the commands now held down separately by the services in their respective geographical areas. These are the field army areas, air defense commands and sea frontiers.

Whether the supreme commander would be established in the near future or only when an emergency impended was not learned.

The desirability of having coinciding geographical areas was considered. The Army and the Air Force agreed as to their own jurisdiction that this would be desirable though not absolutely necessary. It was stressed that the application of unified command in overseas areas was based on control of forces and not of geographical areas.

There is wide variance between present sea frontiers and ground and air units; as between the latter two, the differences are not as great.

Acceptance of the War Department plan is contingent on the approval of the new Secretary of Defense authorized in the unification bill. It was expected, however, that the plan will be approved, as it is an application of unified command envisaged in the measure and practiced successfully in the recent war.

In any event, it was learned, the plan has been agreed on in principle by Gen. Dwight D. Eisenhower, Army Chief of Staff, and Gen. Carl Spaatz, who will be Chief of Staff of the new independent Air Forces.

Agreement Called Considerable

From authoritative sources it was also established that the War department and the Army Air Forces had achieved an extraordinary degree of harmony and agreement during the last six months in a mutual study of the problems which would arise after their separation.

Mutual acceptance of the idea of a single commander of home defense was only one of a great many phases of national security on which the War Department and the AAF came to an understanding, at least on broad lines.

Despite the apparently affirmative and salutary tone of the mutual study, officials at a high level declined to permit disclosure of the high-ranking conferees or official attribution of conclusions and recommendations. They said that they believed that this should not be done until the new Secretary of Defense was informed of the negotiations.

In the long study leading in effect to an amicable divorce agreement, the War Department and the Army Air Forces canvassed every division of the general staff and of the air staff and of the various special staffs and technical services. Problems were sought and the answers given. Every arm and service received the opportunity to outline its problems and recommend solutions.

For his part, General Spaatz, it was learned, directed his staff to plan the immediate future of the Air Force in accordance with the agreed principles.

It was acknowledged by highly placed officers that there were some disagreements, but virtually only in details, and that there would be few, if any, difficult problems to pass up to the Secretary of Defense for decision. As far as could be ascertained, no disagreement had reached the proportions of a dispute.

Differ on Medical Plans

The two services did not see eye to eye, it was said, on the medical service. The AAF insisted on its own complete service, while the Army sought to keep a virtual monopoly in this field through its Medical Corps. In recent weeks, however, there was a softening of the Army attitude, and Air Force medical officers are confident of an amicable settlement of the issue.

Apart from the emancipation of the Air Force, a possibly radical change as a result of unification was indicated in the Army. One source stated that three reorganization plans were under consideration, and that one of these might mean the abolition of the Army Ground Forces staff.

If such a change occurred, some of the AGF functions might be assigned to the War Department General Staff, which might also undergo alterations as the unifying principle begins to permeate downward from the top Secretary.

The contemplated Army changes were linked to the idea of establishing the single defense commander with a strictly operational role and without any training or administrative responsibilities. What the alternative plans were was not learned. It was suggested in one quarter, however, that the AGF staff could be "streamlined" in accord with the new concept.

As presently phrased, the directive in Army regulations to Gen. Jacob L. Devers, AGF commander, states that he would carry planned operations for home defense "in conjunction with" designated naval and Air Force commanders. It was said that the phrase "in conjunction with" meant neither unified command nor a joint staff.

General Devers has command of the six field armies, but he also is charged with training and administrative functions and the operation of service schools and replacement facilities, responsibilities which might have to be stripped down in building up a joint operational staff.

Fears among ground officers that unification might weaken the doctrine of close support of ground forces by tactical air units were termed groundless by competent Air Force officers. In perpetuation of the wartime principle of unified command, they said that a theatre or task force commander would have over-all control of all elements, including air units assigned by direction of the joint chiefs of staff.

It was recognized that the top commander could be drawn from the Army, Navy or Air Force, depending on which had the predominant role in a given area or operation.

Agreement was reached that the Army would be responsible for the conduct of operations by airborne troops, and that the Army would train, equip and organize the ground troops used in such operations. It was also agreed that the Army would control the supporting air units, but the Air Force would train, organize and equip its own personnel and units.

The Air Force has responsibility for research and development of guided missiles, and it was agreed that this arrangement would remain undisturbed. In this field, which promises fantastic weapons, each department specifies its own needs and expenditures.

The new department of the Army, it was learned, will relinquish the task of formulating policies on psychological warfare. It was believed that this role should be transferred out of the general staff upward to the joint chiefs of staff, or even higher, perhaps to one of the several agencies created in the unification bill.

The Air Force would get equality with the Army and Navy in the field of intelligence. The two departments said that they felt that no single agency could furnish all forms of intelligence for all the Government's departments. This was believed to reflect concern that the Central Intelligence Agency, created by the President and carried forward in unification, might interpret its powers too sweepingly.

The conferees reasserted the orthodox principle that intelligence was a function of command, and that no commander could adequately discharge his duty if he were deprived of the means of gaining knowledge about the enemy.

As far as could be established, the two services believed the top intelligence agency should devote itself primarily to the evaluation rather than the collection function. Holding that this agency should go far beyond the scope of military intelligence, they suggested that it should coordinate and collate national policy intelligence collected by all Government departments. That would mean drawing conclusions from military, economic, industrial, political, and counter-subversive data.

Those who studied the problem said that this country's greatest danger today arose not from the failure to analyze and interpret available information to best advantage but from the failure to collect enough intelligence by which this country could arrive at accurate conclusions about the dangers that might confront it.

An Army point of view on medical service suggested that a single such service be established in one of the armed forces to serve the entire national defense establishment. But a number of other proposals of equal weight were offered, including separate medical corps for each department. One suggestion was that over a period of years all general hospitals might be centralized in one department.

Single Service Opposed

The Air Force, with its special field of aviation medicine, and the Navy, with needs peculiar to the conditions of its operations, would never agree to a single medical corps, their spokesmen asserted.

The Air Force is holding out for independent services not only on the ground that each department must practice and develop special fields of medicine but must cover all other fields if it is to attract competent physicians and surgeons and assure them full careers.

Under the Air Force plan each department would operate the general hospitals in areas in which it has predominant interest and would accept patients in these hospitals from other departments.

The conferees of the two services were said to have approached their work with a determination to correct weaknesses in the national defense system which were discovered in the recent war. They also said that it was no reflection on the leaders who prosecuted the war to acknowledge that mistakes were made. The defects found, they added, were as follows:

Foreign and military policy was not always coordinated; the machinery to adjust the civilian economy to military requirements was inadequate; the first plan to mobilize material resources, manpower and productive capacity was inadequate and gaps occurred in matching programs for material and personnel with strategic plans.

Also coordination between the Army and Navy was inadequate; there was a failure to coordinate thoroughly the military and other war budgets, and within and between the military services, there was duplication of procurement and poor planning of material requirements.

* * *

October 6, 1947

REDS OF 9 NATIONS REVIVE COMINTERN TO FIGHT U. S. 'IMPERIALIST HEGEMONY'

BELGRADE IS SEAT

New Information Bureau Will Seek to Unify Strategy of Reds

SOCIALIST RIGHT WING HIT

Attlee, Ramadier, Renner and Others Are Accused as 'Traitors' to Workers

---

By SYDNEY GRUSON
Special to The New York Times.

WARSAW, Poland, Oct. 5—The leaders of world communism proclaimed today what amounted to the re-establishment of the Communist International [Comintern] to combat what they called United States "dollar imperialism."

A manifesto issued after a secret meeting in Poland declared that the world was split in two and called on Europe to align itself on the side of the "Soviet Union and other democratic countries," against "the camp of imperialism and anti-democratic forces whose chief aim is the establishment of a world-wide American imperialist hegemony."

The wording of the manifesto also indicated that the establishment of the "Information Bureau" was a measure directed against the Marshall plan in western Europe.

Nine Nations Represented

A communiqué on the meeting said that party chieftains of nine European countries had decided to establish an "Information Bureau" in Belgrade, Yugoslavia, charged with "organizing the exchange of experience and in case of necessity coordinating the activities of Communist parties on the basis of common agreement."

The communiqué was accompanied by a long manifesto charging the United States with attempting to enslave the world through dollar imperialism and warmongering. It also bitterly attacked the "Rightist Socialists" who it said were leading their countries to "vassal-like dependence on the United States."

The manifesto recorded as "traitors" to the working class Prime Minister Attlee and Foreign Secretary Bevin of Britain, Léon Blum and Premier Paul Ramadier of France, Dr. Kurt Schumacher, Socialist leader in Germany, President Karl Renner and Adolf Schaerf of Austria, and Giuseppe Saragat, Socialist leader in Italy.

Stalin's Advisers Present

The eighteen delegates to the conference were led by Col. Gen. Andrei A. Zhdanov and Georgi M. Malenkov of the Soviet Union, two of Prime Minister Stalin's closest advisors. Other delegates were Edward Kardelj and Milovan Dilas of Yugoslavia, Vulko Chervenkov and V. Poptomov of Bulgaria, Anna Pauker and George Gheorgiu-Dej of Rumania, M. Farkasz and Joseph Revai of Hungary, Vice Premier Wadislaw Gomulka and H. Minc of Poland, Jacques Duclos and Etienne Fajon of France, R. Slansky and S. Basztovanski of Czechoslovakia and Luigi Longo and Eugenio Reale of Italy.

The communiqué gave no details of the conference itself but it is believed to have taken place in a Silesian resort town from Sept. 21 to Sept. 28.

No word of the presence in Poland of General Zhdanov and Mr. Malenkov has been allowed to leak out, although the press reported at various times in the last two weeks that one or another of the others were paying a short visit to Warsaw.

M. Duclos, in fact, made a fairly widely publicized trip around western Poland at the Polish Communist party's invitation ostensibly to review the industrialization of that territory.

The "Information Bureau" will be composed of two delegates from the Central Committees of the Communist parties in the nine countries. According to the communiqué, the bureau will issue a bi-monthly press bulletin in Russian and French.

Implying that hitherto Communist parties of the nine countries had acted entirely independently, a resolution adopted by the conference said this lack of "common bonds" between the parties was a "grave deficiency in the present situation."

"Experience has shown that this division between Communist parties is incorrect and harmful," a preamble to the resolution stated. "The requirement for an exchange of experience and voluntary coordination of actions of the separate parties has become particularly necessary now in the conditions of the post-war international situation and when the disunity of the Communist parties may lead to damage for the working class."

Besides reshaping the Comintern in a new form the meeting of Communist leaders appeared to imply the end of their attempts to rule European Socialist Governments made up of men who refused 100 per cent allegiance to them. Mr. Bevin came in for particular attention in the manifesto as the most consistent and arduous spokesman of imperialistic British foreign policy.

He and the others were said to hide behind a mask of democracy and Socialist phraseology while serving as the faithful "toadies of the imperialists." They were said to be disrupting the ranks of labor and poisoning the conscience of the labor movement.

In the manifesto the United States was singled out as the cause of most of the evil in the world today—the directing force of the anti-Communist group of nations.

The United States is becoming more aggressive, militarily, economically and ideologically because the forces of "socialism and democracy" are strengthening while the forces of capitalism grow weaker during the present "universal crisis of capitalism," the manifesto added.

The United States and Britain fought the war simply to eliminate Germany and Japan as competitors in the world markets while the Soviet Union and its friends wanted only lasting cooperation between the nations of Europe, the liquidation of fascism and the prevention of renewed aggression by Germany, it declared.

The manifesto said the Marshall plan was a façade behind which the United States was working the European end of a world-wide plot for which the former German and Japanese capitalists were being enlisted on the side of the United States.

The holding of the meeting in Poland, the choice of Belgrade as the seat of what all observers here were agreed would be the central planning committee of international Communist activities and the wording of the resolution all pointed up that every effort has been made to indicate that this was not a Moscow dictated maneuver.

The wording of the resolution also was aimed at indicating that this was to be a free association of all participants, with each carrying equal weight in the deliberations of the bureau.

* * *

October 22, 1947

MENJOU TESTIFIES COMMUNISTS TAINT THE FILM INDUSTRY

Actor Says 'Mission to Moscow' and 'North Star' Were Films Carrying Propaganda

HEARING EJECTS LAWYER

Screen Critic Asserts 44 of 100 Broadway Plays in 1936-46 Aided Communist Line

By ANTHONY LEVIERO
Special to The New York Times.

WASHINGTON, Oct. 21—Adolphe Menjou and two other witnesses depicted today the Hollywood motion-picture community as being deeply tainted and split by communism but increasingly alert to the dangers.

The veteran screen actor was the first witness of the second day of hearings by the House Un-American Activities Committee on Communist infiltration of the motion-picture industry.

John Charles Moffitt, motion-picture critic of Esquire Magazine and a former screen writer, while devoting most of his testimony to Communist activities in Hollywood, declared that "Broadway is practically dominated by Communists."

Mr. Moffitt said that Hollywood had made a fine record in fighting communism, that it sometimes slipped, "but it has a better record than Broadway."

Criticizes Broadway Plays

He asserted that forty-four plays out of 100 produced on Broadway between 1936 and 1946 furthered the Communist party line and that thirty-two others favored that line.

As Mr. Menjou took the stand in the caucus room of the old House Office Building the committee formally received in evidence the testimony he had given in Hollywood. In that testimony he said that the movie capital was "one of the main centers of Communist activity in America" and that the "masters of Moscow" were seeking to use American films subversively in an effort to overthrow the United States Government.

Mr. Menjou appeared today under a blaze of kleig lights and the admiring glances of most of a large audience, although it was evident that some visitors from Hollywood were hostile to him.

The session today had the elements of a lively Hollywood script. It had humor, anger, glamor, climactic action and cheers for the star as well as his supporting cast of two.

Ousted for Interruption

The major point of tension came when Charles J. Katz of Los Angeles, a lawyer, demanded the privilege of cross-examining a witness who was naming names of alleged Communists. A policeman and a committee investigator seized him by the arms and shoved him out of the room, marched him to an elevator and did not let him go until he was on the street, two flights below.

Mr. Menjou talked in great detail and with much knowledge of the past and present exponents of Marxism. He explained that he began the study of the subject as a doughboy of the Fifth Division in World War I when he was stationed in the birthplace of Karl Marx in Germany.

In diction as impeccable as his attire, he warned with great earnestness against the dangers of Red philosophy. But he also made his audience laugh, as when he said:

"I'd move to the state of Texas if they (the Communists) come over here, because I think the Texans would kill them on sight."

At the close of the session Paul V. McNutt, counsel for the Motion Picture Producers Association, held a press conference in which he asserted the industry insisted that there was no Communist propaganda in its pictures. He stated: "As I listened to the evidence the last two days, even the most damning evidence shows that they are 98 per cent pure and that is as good as Ivory soap."

Mr. McNutt, a former Governor of Indiana and former High Commissioner of the Philippines, called on the committee to furnish a list of allegedly tainted pictures, saying that the industry was ready to defend them. He declared that Representative J. Parnell Thomas, committee chairman, had turned down several requests for the list.

He said also that as a lawyer he would advise the industry to avoid concerted action to compile a blacklist of Communist writers, directors and other studio employes with the idea of denying employment to them.

Such action, he asserted, was without warrant of law and was not in accord with an announced policy of Congress or rulings of the Supreme Court and, therefore, would involve the producers in serious legal difficulties.

Hollywood films, he declared, spoke for themselves and the American public was capable of judging them.

Witnesses yesterday and today, however, mentioned films which they believed carried Communist propaganda. Mr. Menjou assailed two, "Mission to Moscow," based on the book by Joseph E. Davies, former Ambassador to Moscow, and "North Star," a film written by Lillian Hellman.

"I think it was a thoroughly dishonest picture," Mr. Menjou said of "Mission to Moscow."

"If it was based on Mr. Davies' book it should have portrayed the Moscow treason trials and Vishinsky's part in it."

Of "North Star" he said that it depicted the German attack on Russia and "that it would have been better unmade."

He added:

"Fortunately both films were unsuccessful. The better the entertainment the more dangerous it is."

Mr. Menjou urged the industry to produce some anti-Communist films, predicting they would be an "enormous success." He suggested that one could be about the recent Communist sweep of Bulgaria by Dimitrov and of Petkov's execution there.

"I am not here to smear," said Mr. Menjou upon taking the witness chair. "I am here to defend the industry that I spent the greater part of my life in. I'm here to defend the producers and the motion picture industry."

"I might also say," interjected Mr. Thomas, "that we are not here to smear the industry or the people working in it. We're here to get the facts and only the facts."

When asked by Robert E. Stripling, committee counsel, if he had any evidence of Communist infiltration of motion pictures, Mr. Menjou mentioned the two films. He stated that the red propaganda was not so obvious as "vote for Stalin" and the public would not see the hammer and sickle in it. It was much more subtle, he added, evident in brief sequences.

He asserted that the committee investigation and the Motion Picture Alliance for the Preservation of American Ideals were already preventing "a great amount of subtle and sly propaganda" from getting into films.

In reply to a question, Mr. Menjou said he could not positively identify Communists, but that "I know a great many people who act like Communists." Among these he numbered John Cromwell, a director.

Sam Wood, the producer, said yesterday that Mr. Cromwell was trying to lead the Screen Directors Guild "into the red river."

"Mr. Cromwell, in his own home, said that capitalism was through in America and that I would live to see the end of it," Mr. Menjou testified. "That is a strange statement from a man who earns more than $250,000 a year and who owns a large amount of real estate in Hollywood."

Mr. Menjou handed to Mr. Stripling a photostat of what he said was the Communist membership card of Herbert Sorrell, head of the Conference of Studio Unions. He testified that the photostat showed that Sorrell used the name Herbert K. Stewart on the card. He did not explain how he obtained the photostat, but Mr. Stripling was familiar with it and stated that the name "Stewart" was the maiden name of Sorrell's mother.

Mr. Menjou referred to the "very disastrous" year-long studio strike in Hollywood, saying it was a jurisdictional dispute "which could have been settled but Sorrell didn't want to settle it."

The actor urged the public to read several books which he named to become fully aware of the dangers of communism. He mentioned the Max Eastman "condensation" of Marx's "Das Kapital," William Z. Foster's "Towards a Soviet America," T. S. Eliot's "The Dark Side of the Moon" and the anonymous "Pattern for World Revolution."

The Pittsburgh-born actor declared that he disagreed with those who believed that Russia was relaxing its opposition to religion. The Communist party, he continued, would never relax in this respect because "they're anti-God," although the people of Russia "are deeply, deeply religious and are crying for religion."

Mr. Thomas asked if the witness agreed with those who asserted the committee inquiry was an attempt at movie censorship and control of the industry.

The New York Times (by Tames)

Adolphe Menjou (right) checking a transcript of earlier testimony with Robert E. Stripling, committee investigator, before appearing at the House Un-American activities hearing yesterday.

"I don't see how anybody can say that who has the intelligence of a louse," responded Mr. Menjou.

Mr. Menjou closed his testimony with a plea for universal military training. The audience loudly clapped hands until he left the room.

Mr. Katz, one of the attorneys for nineteen Hollywood writers subpoenaed to appear next week, was rushed out of the room during the testimony of Mr. Moffitt.

Mr. Moffitt declared that Communist members of the Story Analysts Guild, by preparing "very bad synopses of stories" offered by non-Communist writers, were able to defeat the efforts of these writers to get their scripts produced. Those he accused were: "Frances Millington, head of the story or reading department at Paramount"; "Simone Maise"; "Bernie Gordon"; "Dave Robison of Warner Brothers"; "Thomas Chatham" with or formerly of Warners; "Michael Uris of Enterprise"; "Jesse Burns" and "Lona Packer of MGM."

"I represent a number of those persons," exclaimed Mr. Katz, heading toward the committee. "You said you want a fair hearing and cross-examination. . . ."

His words were lost in the hubbub as Mr. Thomas banged his gavel and ordered him ejected. In the corridor Mr. Katz said he wished to know of any instance where a story was suppressed by the story analysts, but before he could say more he was pushed into the elevator.

A few minutes later Bartley C. Crum, another lawyer, stood up and indignantly demanded, "We ask the same right accorded to Howard Hughes." He referred to the practice before the Senate War Investigating Committee of permitting Mr. Hughes, the aviation industrialist, to submit questions to be put to witnesses.

A committee investigator ran to seize Mr. Crum and a policeman headed for him, too. But Mr. Crum sat down, a few more words were exchanged and the hearing resumed.

Mr. Moffitt began to say that the incidents reminded him of how the gallery tried to dominate the sessions of the Commune during the French Revolution.

"If you are referring to what is taking place I don't even want you to refer to it," Mr. Thomas said sharply.

Mr. Moffitt said the trade paper, Hollywood Reporter, had asked the following writers whether they were not Communists and had party cards bearing the numbers following their names, but that they had not replied: Dalton Trumbo, 36,805; Ring Lardner Jr., 25,109; Richard Collins, 11,148; Harold Buchman, 46,802; Lester Cole, 46,805; Henry Myer, 25,065; William Palmer, no number; Gordon Kahn, 48,294; Harry Rhaf, 25,113; Harold J. Salemson, no number; and John Wexley, no number.

The committee did not press the Broadway phase of the inquiry and Chairman Thomas said later that he had no present intentions of inquiring in that direction.

Rupert Hughes, a screen writer, testified that John Howard Lawson, another writer, was a leading Communist in the movie colony. He accused Mr. Lawson of trying "to make it [the Screen Writers Guild] an instrument of Communist power." Later he said it was absolutely under Communist domination but that democratic elements "are trying to take it back."

Mr. Hughes told of an instance when Warner Brothers paid him $15,000 for a 5,000-word plot attacking communism, but an agent told him every theater showing it would be attacked with "stinkpots." It was never produced, he added.

Mr. Moffitt told of an instance when, he said, Mr. Lawson advised a meeting of writers assumed to be Communists that they should avoid trying to make a whole film communistic, as the producers would recognize it and kill it. Mr. Lawson suggested only about five minutes of Communist propaganda, Mr. Moffitt added, and to put this in the most expensive parts of the film so that it could not be removed without expensive retakes and rebuilding of sets.

*　*　*

December 31, 1947

KING OF RUMANIA ABDICATES; 'PEOPLE'S REPUBLIC' SET UP

Michael Quits Suddenly—
Presidium Is Chosen to Rule Provisionally

By W. H. LAWRENCE
Special to The New York Times.

BUCHAREST, Rumania, Dec. 30—King Michael of Rumania abdicated today and the Communist-dominated Government immediately proclaimed a "People's Republic."

Michael, last surviving monarch behind the Iron Curtain, made his decision to quit the throne suddenly, and the decision was announced by radio to the Rumanian people without warning at 6 o'clock this evening. Why he had abdicated was not announced.

The King returned to Rumania only nine days ago from his first trip abroad since the war. He was then apparently determined to fight for retention of his throne and for Communist permission to marry Princess Anne of Bourbon-Parma, to whom he became engaged while attending the wedding of Princess Elizabeth in London.

[A Government official said, according to The Associated Press, that Michael was free to live in Rumania and marry Princess Anne. Other agency dispatches reported that Michael had been arrested, that he had gone to Turkey on his way to Switzerland, and that he was still in Bucharest.]

The Communist sweep in Eastern Europe is now complete, and the bloc of Poland, Czechoslovakia, Hungary, Yugoslavia, Albania, Bulgaria and Rumania is under the influence of Communist governments subservient to the Soviet Union, without even the handicap of passive resistance such as King Michael put up.

While Michael is undoubtedly beloved by his people, it is a certain fact that as of late tonight there have been no publicly known demonstrations against his removal, and the Government radio has reported demonstrations by Communists in favor of his leaving the throne. It is equally true, of course, that Juliu Maniu, Opposition leader, now serving a life sentence, had a great hold on the affections of the Rumanian people, but he went to jail without a single popular demonstration in his favor and against the Government.

The Rumanian Parliament received the King's abdication in a specially convoked session at 5:15 P. M. and immediately elected a five-member Presidium headed by Mihai Sadoveanu, President of Parliament and a novelist. Parliament will meet again at 10 o'clock tomorrow morning, and it is probable that M. Sadoveanu will be named Provisional President of the Republic.

Michael's abdication decree said that because of the great political, economic and social changes effected in Rumania since the war, the institution of the monarchy no longer corresponded to the present conditions of state and thus represented a serious obstacle to the country's future development.

Michael, who took the throne for the second time in 1940, when his father, King Carol, was forced to abdicate by Field Marshal Ion Antonescu, pro-Nazi dictator, renounced the throne not only for himself but for all members of his family. He declared that the Rumanian people were free to choose their own future form of government.

The Government of Premier Petru Groza followed immediately with the proclamation of a "People's Republic," declaring that the removal of the monarchy opened great opportunities for the advancement of popular democracy and for increasing the welfare of workers, peasants and intellectuals.

Heading the new republic provisionally as members of the presidium, in addition to M. Sadoveanu, are Ion Miculi, Gheorghe Ster, Nicolai Parhon, and Stefan Voitec, who until today was Minister of Education. M. Sadoveanu was elected to Parliament as an Independent, and M. Voitec is a Social Democrat. The others are Communists.

As soon as the King had abdicated and the Presidium had been chosen, the Groza Government offered its resignation en masse. The presidium reappointed all the present members of the Government with the exception of M. Voitec, who renounced his portfolio to become a member of the presidium. His post as Minister of Education was assumed temporarily by a fellow-Social Democrat, Lotar Radaceanu, Minister of Labor and Social Security.

The King's decision obviously came with great speed. Members of his Court, who had been questioned as recently as midday, offered no information of the potential development and it was felt then that the King would, as usual receive all members of the foreign diplomatic corps on New Year's Day.

When or if Michael will leave Rumania was not disclosed tonight. Efforts to establish contact with members of his staff by telephone or in person were unavailing, but more news may be forthcoming after tomorrow's sitting of Parliament.

* * *

December 31, 1947

WALLACE OFFERS OWN PLAN TO HELP EUROPE RECOVERY

He Asks U. N. Control of 5-Year Program, No Communist Ban, Moscow Share in Ruhr Rule

ACCEPTS U. S. REDS' HELP

Says 'Industrial Giants' Rig Prices, Run Old Parties— Sees Liberals 'Intimidated'

Special to The New York Times.

MILWAUKEE, Wis., Dec. 30—A seven-point "Wallace plan" to replace the Marshall plan for the recovery of Europe and calling, among other things, for the placing of Germany's Ruhr valley under control of the Big Four, was proposed by Henry A. Wallace, third party Presidential candidate, in a speech here tonight.

Describing the Marshall plan as "a plan based on world division and conflict," Mr. Wallace said that his own program for European recovery was "based on world unity and friendship" and would be administered from the framework of the United Nations and "not by unilateral action by the United States."

Mr. Wallace said he was proposing the placing of Germany's industrial heartland, the Ruhr valley, under international control of the Big Four "in order that its resources may be made available in the reconstruction of Europe and to guarantee that Germany shall never again be in a position to threaten the security of its neighbors or the peace of the world."

The rest of Mr. Wallace's program for European recovery called for:

1. A proposal from the United States to the United Nations for the establishment of a United Nations reconstruction fund modeled after the United Nations Relief and Rehabilitation Administration.

2. Administration of the fund by an agency of the United Nations established for the purpose.

3. Financing of the fund by "contributions appropriated by our Congress and other nations possessed of the means in an amount sufficient to finance an over-all five-year plan."

4. Priority in allocation of funds "to those nations which suffered most severely from Axis aggression; allocations to be based solely on these considerations of merit and need, without regard to the character of the politics and social institutions of the recipient nations."

5. Allocation of funds by the U. N. agency to be made "with scrupulous respect for the national sovereignty of all beneficiary countries, with no political or economic conditions attached to loans or grants." The U. N. agency "must not make aid conditional upon conformity by any nation with an over-all economic plan," he said.

6. No moneys to be made available for the financing or purchase of military supplies, armaments "or war preparations." "We propose a plan," Mr. Wallace said, "that will effectuate the fine words spoken by Secretary Marshall at Harvard last June—not a plan whose deeds contradict those words."

Referring to the present stalemate between the United States and Russia, Mr. Wallace said:

"The Russians certainly are not blameless for the cold war. But even if we should accept every charge made against the Russians, it does not excuse an American policy which runs contrary to American principles.

"We must reaffirm our faith in the United Nations. It cannot succeed if the most powerful nation in the world destroys confidence in the principle of world organization and operates in direct violation of that principle. We can't talk the language of one world and use our economic and political power to split that one world in two."

Mr. Wallace asserted that "millions upon millions of Americans fear to speak out against policies they know are dangerous." He charged that the nation had been "intimidated by the current campaign which brands every progressive idea as 'communistic.' "

He added:

"The progressive principles of Abraham Lincoln and Theodore Roosevelt can no longer be found in the Republican party. Nor can the progressive principles of Jefferson, Jackson, Wilson and Franklin Roosevelt be found in the Democratic party's leadership in the executive branch." He added that "a handful" of Democratic Congressmen "are still true to the progressive faith of Roosevelt."

"Important members of both the old parties," Mr. Wallace charged, "are whooping it up for war with Russia."

Turning to the home front, Mr. Wallace laid much of the country's ills to "a relative handful of wealthy men," who, he said, were "directing" the affairs of the nation.

"Industrial and financial giants control both parties," he declared.

Mr. Wallace said he never really understood "the machinations of these key giants" until "I had to actually sit in the chair of Herbert Hoover and Jesse Jones as Secretary of Commerce."

He asserted that high prices and profits today "were planned that way" by men who oppose democratic planning for peace and abundance.

In a press conference earlier today Mr. Wallace said that he would not repudiate Communist party support.

"I would think," he said, "that they (Communists) would vote for me, because I am eager for peace with Russia. Like the Quakers and Methodists, they want peace.

"I am eager for the support of everyone who wants peace. I don't care who they are."

He added, however, that he hoped the Communists would "have a heart and not come out and pass resolutions for me."

Asked if he believed that American Communists were Russian agents, Mr. Wallace replied, "I don't know." He said that he had asked American Communists the same question and that most of them seemed to be "poor, lonesome souls who have no contact with Russia."

"I wouldn't back anyone who advocated overthrow of the Government by violence," he added.

Communist party members took part actively in the sale of tickets for Mr. Wallace's speech here. Ticket charges ranged from 50 cents to a $2 top.

He was greeted on his arrival here by a group headed by John F. Gminski, chairman of the Wisconsin Citizens for Wallace Committee. Gminski recently was ousted from the Democratic unit of the Twenty-fourth Ward on charges of Communist sympathies.

PART III

THE COLD WAR INTENSIFIES

February 10, 1948

U.S. FINANCED NAZIS, SAYS SOVIET REPLY ON 1939 DOCUMENTS

WEST IS CASTIGATED

Appeasement by Britain and France Attacked as War Factor

HISTORY-FAKING CHARGED

Soviet Complains Munich Was Not Covered—
Says It Too Will Publish Records

By The United Press

MOSCOW, Feb. 9—The Soviet Union, replying to publication of secret Russian-German diplomatic documents by the United States State Department, charged tonight that the United States, Great Britain and France had made World War II possible by financing Adolf Hitler's war industry and appeasing Germany.

The Soviet Information Bureau issued the reply in a 6,000-word statement entitled "Falsifiers of History—A Historical Note."

Russia complained that the documents published by the United States gave only the German side of the picture. The true reason for their publication, the statement said, was "to present a distorted picture of events, to heap lies on the Soviet Union, to slander it and undermine the international influence of the Soviet Union as a truly democratic and stanch fighter against aggressive and anti-democratic forces."

The statement also said that this was a Presidential election year in the United States, and that "United States ruling circles" had used the documents "to undermine, by means of their campaign of slander against the Soviet Union, progressive elements in their own country who advocate better relations with the Soviet Union."

Documents to Be Released

The Soviet Information Bureau, whose statement was issued by order of the Council of Ministers, said it would release soon secret documents, alleged to have been concealed by the Western powers, "concerning the relations between Hitler Germany and the Governments of Great Britain, the United States and France."

The bureau said that documents captured by Soviet troops would be published to put Russian-German relations in their true perspective and prove that the responsibility for World War II rested on the Western powers. Russia said that although it was the United States that had published the captured German documents, the British and French Governments had given their approval and "by doing so those Governments have assumed full responsibility for the consequences."

Going on to attack the pre-war policies of the three big Western Allies, Russia said they had helped German imperialism to prepare for World War II. "A golden rain of American dollars" nurtured Hitler's war industry, the Russian reply said, and Britain and France appeased Germany diplomatically.

"What would have happened if the United States had not financed German heavy industry, and Britain and France had not rejected collective security, but on the other hand had organized resistance to the German aggressors?" the reply asked.

Pre-War Policies Assailed

"The result would have been that the Hitlerites would have lacked armaments, the Hitlerite annexation policy would have been caught against collective security and the Hitlerite chances of unleashing a second world war would have been reduced to a minimum.

"If, in spite of unfavorable conditions, the Hitlerites had still ventured to unleash the second World War, they would have been defeated in the first year.

"Unfortunately this did not happen because of the ruinous policy that was pursued by the United States, Britain and France in the course of the whole pre-war period.

"It is they who are guilty of allowing the Hitlerites to unleash with some measure of success a war that lasted nearly six years and took millions of human lives."

This statement charged that such American financial powers as du Pont, Morgan, Rockefeller and Lamont, and Standard Oil and the British Imperial Chemical Trust had played a part in financing Hilter. It singled out John Foster Dulles, Allen Welsh Dulles and James V. Forrestal regarding what were described as their connections with German capitalists.

This was the first stage, the stage of United States responsibility for Hilterite aggression, the document said. The second stage was the policy of appeasement and the renunciation of the collective security that was sought by Russia, the statement declared.

In the period before the war, the statement added, the Soviet Union pleaded through the League of Nations for collective security, but was blocked by the British and French.

Anti-Soviet Aim Charged

The Western powers did not believe that fostering Hitlerite aggression was dangerous because they planned to direct it eastward toward Russia, the statement charged.

"It should be clear to everyone that it was this policy of the British and French ruling circles, as expressed in their renunciation of collective security, in their refusal to resist German aggression, in their connivance with Hitler Germany's aggressive demands, that led to the second World War," it was stated.

The documents of which the Russians complained were published by the State Department on Jan. 21. They had been found by the Ninth Division of the United States First Army in the Harz Mountains of Germany in April, 1945. They covered the course of Russian-German relations from April, 1939, up to the time Germany attacked Russia on June 21, 1941.

They indicated, from the German side, that Russia had made the first move to better the long bitter relations between the two countries. They continued on through the dramatic conclusion of a German-Russian non-aggression treaty on Aug. 23, 1939, nine days before Germany attacked Poland, the division of Poland and discussions on splitting up Europe into spheres of influence.

The Soviet Information Bureau said today that the documents had been published "in collaboration" with Britain. The bureau added that as far back as the summer of 1946 the United States, Britain and France had agreed to publish material captured from German Foreign Office archives of the United States and Britain.

"Noteworthy in this connection is the fact that the published collection contains only the materials relating to the period 1939-1941," the Soviet Information Bureau stated.

"Materials relating to the preceding year and in particular to the Munich period have not been included by the Department of State in the collection and thus have been concealed from world public opinion.

"This action is certainly not accidental but pursues aims that have nothing to do with the objective and honest treatment of historical truth.

"In order to justify in some way before world public opinion the unilateral publication of this collection of unverified and arbitrarily picked out records made by Hiliterites officials, the British and American press circulated an explanation according to which the Russians rejected the proposal of the West to publish jointly a full account of the Nazi diplomacy.

In connection with the charge that American dollars helped Germany to build up her war industry the Soviet statement declared:

"The fakers of history would like to forget all this as they try to evade responsibility for their policy that unleashed the second World War and led to a war disaster without parallel in history and cost mankind millions upon millions of victims."

In 1938, soon after Hitler had attained power, Britain, France, Germany and Italy, at the initiative of Britain, "came to terms with German-Italian fascism, which even at that time did not try to conceal its aggressive intentions," the statement said.

It must not be forgotten, the statement continued, that "the first and foremost prerequisite of Hitlerite aggression was provided by the resurgence and modernization of German heavy industry, and this became possible only as a result of the financial support of ruling circles of the United States of America."

The statement said that the 1933 "pact of accord and cooperation" signed in Rome by Britain, France, Germany and Italy meant renunciation of the policy of strengthening peace-loving nations against aggressive states, and that thus "Great Britain and France dealt a blow to the cause of peace and security."

German-Polish Pact Cited

In 1934, the Russian reply stated, Britain and France helped Hitler to take advantage of Poland's then anti-Russian policy and this resulted in the conclusion of a German-Polish pact, "the first serious breach in the edifice of collective security."

To "confuse the reader and at the same time to slander the Soviet Government," the statement went on, "an American journalist asserts that the Soviet Government was opposed to collective security and that Maxim Litvinov was dismissed and replaced by Vyacheslav Molotov in the post of Foreign Affairs because he had been pursuing a policy of consolidating collective security."

"It is clear," the Soviet reply said, "that Litvinov did not pursue any policy of his own but the policy of the Soviet Government. On the other hand, everybody knows what a struggle for collective security was waged by the Soviet Government and its representatives, including Litvinov, throughout the pre-war period.

"As regards the appointment of Molotov to the post of Foreign Affairs, it is quite clear that in a complex situation, when Fascist aggressors were preparing the second World War, when Great Britain and France, aided by the United States, were plainly abetting the aggressors and spurring them on to start the war against the Soviet Union, it was necessary to have in such a responsible post as that of Foreign Commissar a political leader with greater experience and greater popularity in the country than Litvinov.

"The historical truth, as can be seen from all this, consists in that Hitlerite aggression became possible firstly because the United States helped Germany to establish within a short period of time a war-economic base for German aggression, and thus provided this aggression with arms, and secondly because the traducing of collective security disorganized the ranks of the peace-loving countries, disrupted the united front of these countries against aggression, paved the road for German aggression and helped Hitler to unleash the second World War."

Protest in 1945 Reported

MOSCOW, Feb. 9 (AP)—The Soviet Information Bureau's statement asserted that the Russians had approached the British in 1945 and insisted that the Soviet Union should be represented in a study of the captured documents.

"The Soviet Government," the statement added, "held that publication of such documents without careful, objective verification * * * could only lead to a worsening of relations between the member states of the anti-Hitlerite coalition. The

British Foreign Office, however, declined the Soviet proposal on grounds that the Soviet Government had prematurely raised the question of exchanging copies of captured Hitlerite documents."

Russia's statement also said:

"The Soviet Government possesses important documents that were captured by Soviet troops during the smash-up of Hitlerite Germany; publication of these documents will help present the true picture of how Hitler's aggression and the second World War were in reality prepared and developed."

The Soviet declaration dealt extensively with events following World War I, paying special attention to the Dawes reparations plan for Germany.

The statement went into the naval agreement reached in London by Nazi Foreign Minister Joachim von Ribbentrop. The Russians asserted that Germany thereby was allowed to build up her navy and added that "this action encountered no opposition on the part of England, France or the United States."

*   *   *

February 25, 1948

SOVIET IN U. N. HITS ERP AS U. S. WEAPON

Russian Extols Soviet System While Scoring Marshall Plan as Method of Expansion

---

Special to The New York Times.

LAKE SUCCESS, N. Y., Feb. 24—The Soviet Union today blasted the Marshall Plan as an "American weapon for economic and political expansion" designed to split Europe and give this country control over the economies of Western European countries.

The Russian attack on United States policy was delivered here by Dr. Amazasp A. Arutiunian in a two-and-a-quarter-hour recital during which the Russian economist alternately extolled the advantages of the Soviet system of planned economy and criticized the damaging and unstable effects that he insisted were the outcome of capitalism.

Speaking before the Economic and Social Council, the Soviet delegate contended that the United States had attained its top position in world trade at the expense of other nations. This country, he argued, has pursued a policy of "grabbing markets" from economically weakened nations, created a "dollar famine" and hampered post-war recovery.

The United States' own financial "instability," inflation and monetary fluctuations, he charged, have been brought on largely by heavy American expenditures for armaments.

Briton Sees No Proofs

In reply to the charges, Christopher Mayhew, British delegate, criticized the Soviet delegate for failing to produce pertinent data to support his claims. Of the thirty-three figures cited to show the superiority of the Soviet collective system, twenty-nine, he contended, were mere percentages showing increases over previous years. Such estimates, Mr. Mayhew added, cannot be compared with the production records of other countries since they give no "absolute" production figures or statistics.

Mr. Mayhew also denied Russian claims that United States pressure was being exerted to halt the nationalization of British industry.

"There has been no pressure exerted whatsoever," Mr. Mayhew insisted, and he went on to show that of the list of industries that the British Government announced would be nationalized, all but two—iron and steel—had been taken over. These too, he added, will be nationalized in the future.

The bulky Soviet statement—available only in Russian—had been long awaited by the Council members as the first official commentary on the United Nations world economic survey, which was released here recently and which indicated the top position attained by the United States in production, trade and other economic potential.

The 1,000-line Soviet statement was devoted largely, however, to detailed descriptions of the success of Russian rehabilitation and improved economic conditions, which, Dr. Arutiunian said, have been attained by the new "popular democratic governments" in the eastern European states of Albania, Yugoslavia, Hungary, Poland, Czechoslovakia, Rumania and Bulgaria. Economic reconstruction of these countries—all members of the Soviet bloc—is proceeding at a faster pace than that of many Western powers, he said.

Needs Russian Translators

United Nations economists said that a more detailed picture of Soviet conditions could have been included in the world survey if the economic department had a staff equipped to translate the Russian documents. The additional information given by Dr. Arutiunian, these officials added, gave an idea of the percentage of Soviet advances domestically but no basis in tonnage of agricultural or other production for comparison with the economies of other member nations.

According to Dr. Arutiunian, the targets of Russia's first post-war plan have been fulfilled 100 per cent. In the war-devastated areas of the Soviet Union, he estimated, steel and coal production in 1947 was 35 to 19 per cent higher than in 1946. Wages of workers in 1947 increased 23 per cent over the previous year; grain production reached pre-war levels, and the state was able to allot an increasing sum to education and medical assistance. There has also been an increase of 23 per cent, he said, in the production of consumer goods, which should answer foreign criticisms that insufficient attention is given to the needs of Soviet citizens, he said.

"By the Marshall Plan," he concluded, "ruling American classes mean to create a bloc in Western Europe which will make these countries the wheels of the American chariot of capitalism."

*   *   *

February 26, 1948

BENES BOWS TO COMMUNISTS, GOTTWALD FORMS CABINET; ONE SLAIN IN PRAGUE PROTEST

REDS FORCE ISSUE

Thousands of Workers Threaten to Walk Out if President Resists

POLICE CURB OPPOSITION

Beat Back Group of Students Attempting to Gain Palace to Protest New Cabinet

By ALBION ROSS
Special to The New York Times.

PRAGUE, Feb. 25—President Eduard Benes gave Communist Premier Klement Gottwald permission this afternoon to install a Communist dominated Czechoslovak Government of the type found in other Eastern European countries now considered satellites of the Soviet Union.

The President accepted the program after an exchange of letters between him and the presidium of the Communist party. In his letter M. Benes insisted upon a parliamentary government representative of all parties in the National Front. The Communists replied that the government would be representative but they barred the leaders of the three parties whose ministers had resigned from the Government last week.

Today the chiefs of the Communist-controlled General Confederation of Labor ordered a general strike if the President refused to bow to the demands of the Communist party. Factory and office workers councils ordered out into the main square of Prague 50,000 to 100,000 members to demonstrate for a strike or to express support for the President if he accepted the Communist program.

Police Kill One Student

At least one person was killed and several were wounded when the police fired on a procession of 1,500 students marching to ask President Benes not to install the new government. The police beat the students with rifle butts and blocked off every route to the Hradcany castle toward which they were marching.

After a long discussion with the President at the castle on the Communist victory, the Premier told the workers they must "be faithful to the President" and that the President had decided for the will of the people on something that was certainly not entirely in accord with his own wish.

The presidency agreed to a perfectly constitutional solution of the Government crisis. The new Cabinet installed by Premier Gottwald will have a parliamentary majority made up of Communists, at least part of the Social Democrats and a group of men from the parties whose ministers resigned Friday in a protest against what they described as efforts to set up a police state.

Communists Rule Courts Now

In the new cabinet both the Ministry of the Interior, controlling the police, and the Ministry of Justice, controlling the courts, will be held by Communists.

The Cabinet will have thirteen Communists, four Social Democrats, two men who split off from the Czech National Socialist party, two who split off from the People's party and one who left the Slovak Democratic party.

Two members of the Cabinet, Jan Masaryk, remaining as Minister of Foreign Affairs, and Gen. Ludwig Svoboda, remaining as Minister of War, are without party affiliations.

In the former Cabinet were nine Communists, four Czech National Socialists, three Social Democrats, four People's party members, four Slovak Democrats and two nonpartisan members. In the new Cabinet five ministers have no official party connection.

Two Social Democrat Ministers, Vaclav Majer, Minister of Food, and Frantisek Thymes, Deputy Premier, resigned before the new Government was formed. The former president of the Social Democratic party, Bohumil Lausmann, made his peace with the victors after having signed a pro-Communist agreement with Zdenek Fierlinger, ousted and now reinstalled president of that party. M. Lausmann will be a deputy premier. His party, however, was badly split and the present Leftist-dominated organization is regarded as a puppet organization.

The Communists made a great show of force to attain their objectives. The city was thick with four and eight men police patrols armed with automatic rifles, marching single file as if going into battle. The armed militia of the nationalized factories was readied.

After the President's submission to the Communists, these armed "workers guards" were summoned to what the national radio called a "triumphal march" to old town square.

Communists Suggest Strike

Throughout the country Communist-organized action committees had taken over the ministries, Government offices and installations of all sorts. Every effort was made to give the impression that if the President refused the Communists' demands and tried to enforce his decision the result would be civil war.

The decision of the President has not halted the rush of events toward another form of state and society. M. Gottwald ordered the Communist party and other followers to form new revolutionary action committees at once.

The official radio announced tonight the formation of new action committees to take over the offices of the director of Prague University. Another action committee was formed to take over the direction of the student organization, which student elections showed to be overwhelmingly opposed to the Communists. Everywhere civil servants and officials were being expelled and sent on leave with pay until authorities decided their fate.

Editors of many leading Prague and other newspapers were expelled from the Association of Journalists. This automatically barred them from any journalistic activity in Czechoslovakia.

Almost all former ministers were expelled from the Association of the National Revolution, the organization that grouped those who participated in the liberation of the country from the Germans. Many of them had been leaders in that struggle.

Arrests were made. Seven high functionaries were arrested in the Ministry of Justice. A committee set up in the name of the Czech National Socialist party started expelling members from that party. A similar group was operating in the People's party. About fifty students are understood to be under arrest for disturbing the peace after their demonstration.

Their leaders had hoped to get peacefully to the castle by marching. The police considered their shouting of slogans such as "Remember the seventeenth of November," which is the date of the student martyrs of the occupation as a provocation and apparently resented constant appeals to save the Masaryk republic.

Legally the situation today is such that an election could oust the Gottwald Government. The three parties whose Ministers resigned Friday, and whose resignation the President finally accepted today, still exist.

"Reactionaries" to Be Curbed

However, orders issued by the Action Committee for Greater Prague were a good indication of how much chance the Opposition was going to have to carry on an election campaign. The orders provided that in plants, offices and all public buildings no meetings of "reactionary elements" were to be permitted.

The production of leaflets or any other printed matter against the Gottwald Government or "the people" was prohibited. The circulation of any such material also was prohibited.

Such leaflets, posters or other propaganda material will be confiscated immediately and turned over to the police, along with those guilty of having circulated it.

The Greater Prague Action Committee also directed that all persons in public life and all members of the national committees who displayed differences with the Gottwald Government should be immediately replaced with persons nominated by action committees.

These actions today followed President Benes' letter to the Communists yesterday, which was released to the official news agency last night but was not made public until this morning.

It requested Premier Gottwald to negotiate and "not allow a prolongation of the split in the nation into two quarreling parts."

The President said he insisted "on a parliamentary democracy, adding that he had "built my political work on these principles and cannot—without betraying myself—act otherwise."

"The present crisis of democracy here, too, cannot be overcome but through democratic and parliamentary means," he declared. "I thus do not overlook your demands. I regard all our political parties as associated in the National Front. As

bearers of political responsibility we have accepted the principle of the National Front and this proved to be successful up to the recent time when the crisis began.

"This crisis, however, according to my opinion, does not deny the principle in itself. I am convinced that on this principle, even in the future, the necessary cooperation of all can be achieved. All disputes can be solved for the benefit of the nation and the common state of the Czechs and the Slovaks."

The President repeated his previous promise that only a Cabinet with M. Gottwald as its head would be permitted since the Communists were the largest single party. He added:

"It is clear to me that socialism is the way of life desired by the overwhelming part of our nation. At the same time I believe that with socialism a certain measure of freedom and unity is possible. These are vital principals of all our national life."

The Communist reply to this said in effect two things. It constituted a refusal to negotiate with the leaders of the parties whose ministers had resigned. It stated that the Cabinet would consist of representatives of parties who were not approved by their party central committees as well as representatives of the "big nation-wide organizations."

This latter plan is a departure from government by elected party representatives and the adoption of a quite different principle. Since the members of the "nation-wide organizations" also vote for parties, such organizations through participation in government would reinforce any political party with which they might be affiliated.

The Communist letter stated with regard to the Czech National Socialist party, the People's party and the Slovak Democratic parties:

"Recent events undisputably proved that these three parties no longer represent the interests of the working people of the cities and countryside; that their leaders have betrayed the fundamental ideas of the people's democracy and the National Front, as they have been stated in the Kosice Government program and that they have assumed the position of opposition undermining the structure of the state.

Says Reforms Were Blocked

"This was shown again and again in the Government, in Parliament, in the press of those parties and in actions that, with menacing levity, were organized by their central secretariats against the interests of the working people, against the security of the state, against the alliance of the republic, against state finance, against nationalized industries and against urgent agricultural reform."

Taking up the charge of foreign seditious connections the Communists told the President:

"These parties even got in touch with foreign circles hostile to our people's democratic order and our alliances and in collaboration with these hostile foreign elements they attempted the disruption of the present form of the republic.

"This constantly increasing activity was crowned by an effort to break up the Government, an attempt that, as it was proved, should have been accompanied by actions aiming at a putsch."

* * *

April 2, 1948

CLAY HALTS TRAINS

Gives Up Ground Links Temporarily— Soviet Increases Barriers
CANAL BARGES STOPPED
Britons Force the Russians Out of a Road Blockade Set Up in Their Sector

By The Associated Press

BERLIN, April 1—The United States began flying food into Berlin today to thwart a Soviet squeeze aimed at forcing its wartime Western Allies out of this former German capital.

[A Berlin dispatch to The New York Times said that Soviet fighter planes had "buzzed" every United States military passenger craft flying in and out of Berlin but otherwise had not molested them.]

The Russians put swiftly into effect a calculated program of travel and transport restrictions to this isolated Allied outpost deep in the Soviet zone. The restrictions were:

(1) Halting of all military trains between Berlin and the Western zones, cutting off normal military supply channels.
(2) Stopping British barge traffic to the four-power capital.
(3) Instituting rigorous examinations of traffic on the Autobahn, only highway linking the city with the West.
(4) Turning back one rail coach occupied by civilians of several nationalities.

For several hours the Russians maintained a traffic-snarling inspection along the edges of their Berlin sector but later they removed the barriers.

Clay Cancels U. S. Train

But the air was free, and Gen. Lucius D. Clay, the United States commander, announced he would use it to supply the 8,575 United States military personnel and civilians in the city. He canceled military train service to Berlin which could not be pushed through the Soviet cordon without inviting a clash, and called on air power to win the political battle for Berlin.

[The British reported that 400 soldiers had forced the Russians to retire from a roadblock they had established illegally in the British sector by having set up counter blocks, another dispatch to The New York Times said.]

At stake in the dispute was the question of prestige in the cold war between the East and the West. If the Russians succeeded in dislodging the Western Allies from the former German capital, their stock would rise, and the hopes of the supporters of the Western powers in all Germany and Europe would sag.

Tonight a United States official said United States planes had flown 15,000 pounds of food into Berlin in the first few hours after the Clay order.

The four-power agreement laying out air corridors over the Soviet zone to Berlin does not restrict the number of flights.

No Restrictions on Planes

The United States Air Force based in Wiesbaden will be able to fly in any number of planes with supplies, and the only apparent way the Russians can interfere is to attempt to force or shoot them down. It seemed apparent any such attempt would bring serious international incidents.

The Tempelhof Airdrome in Berlin is in the United States sector and the Russians could interfere with it only by sending armed forces across United States occupied territory in the city.

The British also announced two extra flights into Berlin as a temporary measure.

Dispatches from Hamburg said the tense situation had given Germans living along the 400 miles of frontier in the British zone a case of jitters.

The British verified reports that Russian border posts had been strengthened by the addition of ten or a dozen men at each place, presumably to bolster the guard against border crossers. Persons crossing from the Soviet zone said there was widespread requisitioning of quarters for troops near the border.

All three Western Allied commanders rejected Soviet demands that Russian authority be obtained for freight shipments out of Berlin, that their inspectors be allowed to board military trains to examine personally the papers of passengers and that a somewhat similar Soviet check be made on incoming freight shipments.

United States supply officers thereupon went into conference with Brig. Gen. C. K. Bailey, Chief of Staff, to iron out the difficulties created by the Soviet action. Air Force officials said they hoped to move all the passenger and freight traffic normally handled by train. Officials said there were enough supplies in the city for a "considerable time."

Late today Maj. Gen. N. C. D. Brownjohn, Deputy British Military Governor, went into a conference with Lieut. Gen. G. S. Lukjantschenko, Soviet Chief of Staff. General Brownjohn asked for the conference last night when he refused to submit to the Russian orders for tightened restrictions.

Afterward a spokesman said the atmosphere of the hour conference was "not hostile, but firm enough." He added that General Brownjohn does not feel optimistic that anything will come of it.

Despite the strained atmosphere there were no reports of incidents between the Russians and the personnel of the other Allies during the day. The Russians assigned some of their best troops to the checkpoints in Berlin, on the Autobahn and on the railroad where Berlin-bound traffic was halted.

The Russians were not stopping any of the thirty-two trains a day sent over the line to carry food, coal and other supplies to the Berlin German.

Passengers on the Autobahn, especially those in uniform, who had Russian translations of their travel permits and proper identification documents also apparently were getting through without difficulty after inspection.

The last military train to reach Berlin was a French train from Paris. It reached here at 5:20 P. M. The French train commander had not received orders to bar Russian inspectors.

A large number of Germans whose papers were considered insufficient by the Russians were held at Marienborn.

The British Inland Water Transport Office in Hamburg said German barges carrying food to the British in Berlin along the Mittelland Canal were stopped.

In mid-morning, when the Russians began imposing travel restrictions within Berlin, they also showed special interest in trucks.

The New York Times

The Russians rigorously examined traffic on the Autobahn or superhighway leading west into Berlin, with Nowawea (1) as the main check point. They also turned back all military trains between Berlin and the Western zones at Marienborn (2), and halted British barge traffic in the Mittelland Canal and the Elbe to the north (3). The United States flew food into the city from Air Force headquarters at Wiesbaden (4), landing it at Tempelhof airfield (A on inset); the British were using Gatow airfield (B). Soviet troops who established a road block just within the British sector (C) withdrew after 400 British soldiers had established counter-blocks.

Soviet Planes Active

By DELBERT CLARK
Special to The New York Times.

BERLIN, April 1—Soviet fighter planes rose today to "buzz" every United States military passenger plane flying the agreed route into and out of Berlin, but did not otherwise molest them. United States, British and French authorities suspended today all rail traffic between their zones and Berlin rather than submit to detailed search by Soviet troops at the zone frontier.

General Clay, Gen. Sir Brian Robertson and Gen. Joseph-Pierre Koenig, United States, British and French zone commanders, respectively, conferred for an hour this morning with the chiefs of military missions of several Western European countries accredited to the Allied Control Council. No communiqué was issued but informants said no conclusion had been reached.

General Clay spent the afternoon in a conference with key United States officials.

It appeared clear today that the new Soviet policy, while designed to make it more difficult for the Westerners to remain in Berlin, had an important secondary motive. This was to halt the flow of merchandise and capital equipment out of their sector of Berlin to the Western zones.

As tension between the former Allies has increased, so this flow has increased until the Russians decided to do something about it.

The only explanation of the Russians' latest action is that they wish to force the Western allies out of Berlin. If they really mean business there is little question they eventually will be able to do so despite Western protestations of intentions to remain.

The fact that the Russians control most of the Berlin electricity and water supply alone gives them a whip hand. The Western powers in Berlin are as much on an island as if they were in the middle of the Pacific—and they know it.

British Block Russians

By EDWARD A. MORROW
Special to The New York Times.

BERLIN, April 1—Approximately 400 British soldiers today scored their first victory for the Western allies over the Russian in this city's war of nerves. A Soviet squad of soldiers who had established a military post and roadblock at a crossroads 100 yards within the British sector this morning withdrew shortly before midnight across the Soviet border.

The Soviet retreat from their illegally maintained roadblock was made after the British troops, supported by a squadron of British armored motor cars, had established three counter roadblocks, leaving but one road open to the Russians—the one leading back to the Soviet zone. The British roadblocks interfered much more seriously with Russian traffic in and out of the city than the Russian roadblock did to the British traffic.

Led by six officers, the Soviet contingent halted three British vehicles and arrested the drivers, as well as two British wives and a United States Military Government officer. All persons arrested were released this afternoon.

Told by the British that they were in the British sector, the Russians refused to leave their post. They said they had received instructions to establish a road block near Gross Glienecke, which overlooks the British-controlled Gatow airport and controls traffic from the West to the airfield. They added they could not leave without the permission of Maj. Gen. A. G. Kotikov, Soviet commandant in Berlin.

British Blockade Roads

Within the space of a few hours British troops moved on the scene with armored cars and immediately set up their road blocks.

At the same time Maj. Gen. E. O. Herbert, commandant of the British troops, sent a strong protest to General Kotikov, requesting the withdrawal of the Russian troops, which followed later.

The United States official picked up by the Russians was Ellyson G. Outten of Norfolk, Va. He said he had been courteously treated.

* * *

April 2, 1948

U. S. FLIES FOOD INTO BERLIN AS RUSSIANS BLOCK TRAFFIC; BRITISH FOIL SOVIET SALLY

EXPERTS SAY U. S. HAS RIGHT TO OPERATE TRAINS TO BERLIN

Base Opinion on Four-Power Agreements—Vague Wording Causes Confusion on Course—Americans to Stay

By JAMES RESTON
Special to The New York Times.

WASHINGTON, April 1—The United States has a legal basis for running its supply trains through the Soviet zone into Berlin, but, as usual, the Big Four documents covering the case are vague and open to various contradictory interpretations.

That's the unhappy tentative conclusion the legal experts here have reached after a quick survey of all the Allied documents available on the regulations governing the four-power occupation of the former German capital.

The United States case, according to officials at the State Department, is as follows:

(1) On Nov. 14, 1944, the European Advisory Commission, composed of representatives of the United States, the Soviet Union and Great Britain, agreed that an inter-Allied governing authority should be established in Berlin. This agreement did not say anything about the right of transport through the Soviet zone of Eastern Germany into the United States, British and French sectors of Berlin, but the official view here is that it assumed the right of passage.

(2) On June 5, 1945, the United States, the Soviet Union, Britain and France issued a declaration that included the general instrument of Germany's surrender, and the arrangements for administering that country under an Allied Control Council.

This agreement stated that "the administration of the 'greater Berlin' area will be directed by an inter-Allied governing authority, which will operate under the general authority of the Control Council * * *"

Again this document did not make specific provision for the Western powers to have free access into their sectors of Berlin. However, the official view here is that the fact of establishing the joint control council and defining the geographical sectors of the capital would have been meaningless unless the right of passage to and from the zones were intended.

Other Documents Cited

(3) Beyond these two general commitments, officials at the State Department cite numerous official agreements between the Western powers and the Soviet Union on the specific question of transporting officials and supplies through the Soviet zone into Berlin.

For example, the four-power Transport Directorate, sitting in Berlin, on various occasions reached agreements about the precise lines over which United States trains were to pass, the documents that were to be carried by personnel traveling on these trains, the points at which the trains were to stop, etc.

Likewise the four-power Air Directorate, which, like the Transport Directorate, was a subcommittee under the Allied Council in Berlin, clearly agreed on the air lanes through which United States planes were to pass, the height at which they were to fly, the ways in which they were to be marked, etc.

These decisions were later referred to and approved by the Allied Coordinating Committee, which serves directly under the four commanders on the Control Council, and as late as last summer, the Transport Directorate reached a new decision about an alternate rail route over which empty freight cars were to pass.

Here, however, is the loophole under which the Russians are apparently acting: The Allied statement of June 5, 1945, stipulated that the Control Council should act unanimously on matters affecting Germany as a whole, but in the event of disagreement, it left each of the four commanders in chief free to operate as he wished in his own zone.

Thus, the United States and Britain, when they were unable to get the Russians to carry out the Potsdam Agreement to treat Germany as "an economic unit," exerted the right to act as they pleased in their own zones.

Whether the agreements reached in the Air and Transport Directorates supersede the right of each Government to do as it pleases in its own zone is a question that could occupy a good prosecutor like Andrei Y. Vishinsky for months, and that is a prospect that is not viewed with equanimity here.

Meanwhile, the moral aspects of the question, and the practical problems raised by the Soviet action, are occupying United States officials far more than the legalities of the case. Washington officials are agreed on these points:

(1) The Soviet Union is trying to make the Western Allies withdraw from Berlin.

(2) Its intent is to organize Berlin as a political center under its control and proclaim it as the capital of all Germany. This would do three things: It would increase the Russian prestige; it would lower that of the Western Allies if they had to with-

draw, and it would give the Russians a free hand to communize Berlin, which, even under Hitler, did not take so easily or happily to strict regimentation.

(3) The United States' intent is to stay on in Berlin. Officials of the State Department said today that the actions of the Soviet had not changed the United States' policy on this central point.

Puzzled on Procedure

Just how this operation is to be carried out if the trains really are stopped for good, however, is not so clear in Washington. At the Defense Department it was said that there are about 9,000 United States soldiers, officials and dependents in Berlin, but that more than 2,000,000 Germans in the three Western sectors of the capital were dependent on shipments of supplies from the United States, British and French zones.

Carrying supplies by air, even for the 9,000 United States citizens and soldiers in Berlin, would be extremely difficult for the Air Force as it is now established, but the transport planes are available in this country to do the job, and can be organized into a shuttle service if necessary.

In the last analysis, however, one of the important aspects of the incident is that it will increase the support of this Administration for Congressional action on rearmament, the draft, and universal military training.

Representative Hale Boggs, Democrat, of Louisiana, told the House that the Soviet action was "a challenge to Congress to pass selective service immediately and bring our military force to its full authorized strength."

"I cannot imagine a greater threat to peace," he concluded.

* * *

May 1, 1948

AMERICAS' CHARTER SIGNED IN BOGOTA

Hemisphere Organization Made Firm in Parley Wind-Up— Economic Pact Tomorrow

By MILTON BRACKER
Special to The New York Times.

BOGOTA, Colombia, April 30—In the dwelling that was the home here in the Eighteen Twenties of Simon Bolivar, South America's liberator, the twenty-one American nations symbolically concluded today pacts that effectively give them jointly a new constitution.

Foremost among the documents concluded as a result of the month's labors of the Inter-American Conference was the treaty-charter of the Organization of the American States.

This treaty gives organic status, as a regional grouping under the United Nations, to the fifty-eight-year-old Pan American Union.

Also in the measures signed in the Bolivar home was a resolution emphasizing that totalitarianism in any form, and

particularly international communism, is not wanted in the Western Hemisphere.

The delegates signed two treaties, two conventions that have virtual treaty status and a variety of resolutions, including—besides that against communism—one looking to the ending of colonial control by any European nation in American hemisphere territory.

A third treaty, covering basic economic cooperation, is scheduled to be signed Sunday, assuming that a die-hard Mexican position on expropriation does not cause further delay.

Hence the actual formal closing of the conference will come with a plenary session opening at 10 A. M. Sunday.

A leading United States delegate said during the afternoon's signing ceremony that he had heard the Mexicans were considering reopening this topic of expropriations—an issue that had caused the sharpest debate in the conference's Economic Commission.

But the general impression is that this last tangle will be resolved so that the economic treaty and the final act of the conference—embodying everything done since the opening on March 30—can be signed.

Because the signing ceremony took place with this city still under martial law and memories of the bloody outbreak of April 9 still fresh, the anti-Communist resolution stood out.

In regard to that period of revolt and rioting that followed the assassination of Dr. Jorge Eleicar Gaitan, Colombian Liberal party leader, the United States remains on record in the words of Secretary of State Marshall as convinced the outbreak was an international phenomenon, rather than simply a local disturbance.

The ceremony in the Bolivar house found seven Foreign Ministers and fourteen chief delegates of other rank seated around the rim of an old dining room facing a large table. The only other officials in the room were former President Eduardo Santos of Colombia, Dr. Alberto Lleras Camargo, director general of the Pan American Union, and Alfonso Garcia Robles, representing the United Nations.

The ceremony began just after 4 P. M. After speeches by Dr. Eduardo Zuleta Angel, Foreign Minister of Colombia and presiding officer of the conference, and former President Ramón Betancourt of Venezuela, the roll was called in the order of conference procedure.

Five Sign for United States

A band in the patio played the national anthem of each delegation as its members went up to sign.

The United States was fifth in the order. The senior delegates now here all signed—Norman Armour, Assistant Secretary of State; William D. Pawley, former Ambassador to Brazil; Walter J. Donnelly, Ambassador to Venezuela; Paul C. Daniels, Ambassador to Honduras, and Willard L. Beaulac, Ambassador to Colombia.

Bogota's electric power went off and lights went out, bringing a momentary use of candles, between the signings of Chile and Cuba. The power was restored in time for the United States signature. The Colombian Army has announced that the 9 P. M. curfew would remain at least through tomorrow.

At a plenary session of the conference this forenoon in the damaged Capitolio, the delegates formally voted approval of the agreements, which in general have in common an integration with Article 52 of the United Nations Charter on regional arrangements.

So far as collective defense goes, the conference in effect gave affirmation to the procedures of the treaty of Rio de Janeiro of 1947.

The Charter of the Organization of the American States was known during drafting stage as the organic pact. In eighteen chapters and 112 articles it formally bands the republics of the hemisphere into a new body, lays down the rights and duties of the states and outlines their principles, polices and organization.

It reconstitutes the governing board of the Pan American Union as the Permanent Council of the organization, dependent now directly on the Governments through their Foreign Ministers.

The second treaty signed bears the name of the Pact of Bogota. It is basically a consolidation of twenty years' work on Pacific settlement and details methods of arbitration, conciliation and mediation.

The United States filed two reservations to this pact. The first disapproves of the submitting of political as well as legal disputes to the International Court of Justice at The Hague. The second opposes a provision whereby an alien is prohibited from getting diplomatic assistance where his case is in the courts of the nation wherein he is an alien.

A major accord was the declaration on diplomatic relations, which effectively provides that continuance of such relations does not imply approval of the internal policies of one state by another—notably in reference to a revolutionary change of government. This measure may open the way to United States recognition of the present regime in Nicaragua.

The United States abstained on the colonial resolution. This proclaims it as the just aspiration of the American states to rid the hemisphere of colonies. It establishes a new organization to meet in Havana in September to consider ways and means. Despite its abstention, the United States is expected to be represented in this group.

Also signed without the United States was an inter-American charter of social guarantees, comprising a detailed statement of the rights of labor. The United States submitted a reservation supporting the principle of international action in behalf of labor, but declaring itself not bound by the statement of this inter-American charter.

Most of the personnel of the United States delegation still here will leave tomorrow morning by plane for Washington. Messrs. Armour, Donnelly, Daniels and Pawley are remaining to get the economic wrinkles ironed out and to sign the final act on Sunday.

* * *

May 15, 1948

ZIONISTS PROCLAIM NEW STATE OF ISRAEL; TRUMAN RECOGNIZES IT AND HOPES FOR PEACE; TEL AVIV IS BOMBED, EGYPT ORDERS INVASION

THE JEWS REJOICE

Some Weep as Quest for Statehood Ends— White Paper Dies

HELP OF U. N. ASKED

New Regime Holds Out Hand to Arabs— U. S. Gesture Acclaimed

By GENE CURRIVAN
Special to The New York Times.

TEL AVIV, Palestine, Saturday, May 15—The Jewish state, the world's newest sovereignty, to be known as the State of Israel, came into being in Palestine at midnight upon termination of the British mandate.

Recognition of the state by the United States, which had opposed its establishment at this time, came as a complete surprise to the people, who were tense and ready for the threatened invasion by Arab forces and appealed for help by the United Nations.

In one of the most hopeful periods of their troubled history the Jewish people here gave a sigh of relief and took a new hold on life when they learned that the greatest national power had accepted them into the international fraternity.

Ceremony Simple and Solemn

The declaration of the new state by David Ben-Gurion, chairman of the National Council and the first Premier of reborn Israel, was delivered during a simple and solemn ceremony at 4 P. M., and new life was instilled into his people, but from without there was the rumbling of guns, a flashback to other declarations of independence that had not been easily achieved.

The first action of the new Government was to revoke the Palestine White Paper of 1939, which restricted Jewish immigration and land purchase.

In the proclamation of the new state the Government appealed to the United Nations "to assist the Jewish people in the building of its state and to admit Israel into the family of nations."

The proclamation added:

"We offer peace and amity to all neighboring states and their peoples, and invite them to cooperate with the independent Jewish nation for the common good of all. The State of Israel is ready to contribute its full share to the peaceful progress and reconstitution of the Middle East."

World Jews Asked to Aid

The statement appealed to Jews throughout the world to assist in the task of immigration and development and in the "struggle for the fulfillment of the dream of generations—the redemption of Israel."

Plans for the ceremony had been laid with great secrecy. None but the hundred or more invited guests and journalists was aware of the meeting until it started, and even the guests learned of the site only ten minutes before. It was held in the Tel Aviv Museum of Art, a white, modern-design two-story building. Above it flew the Star of David, which is the state's flag, and below, on the sidewalk, was a guard of honor of the Haganah, the army of the Jewish Agency for Palestine.

As photographers' bulbs flashed and movie cameras ground out reels of the scene, great crowds gathered and cheered the Ministers and other members of the Government as they entered the building. The security arrangements were perfect. Sten guns were brandished in every direction and even the roofs bristled with them.

The setting for the reading of the proclamation was a dropped gallery whose hall held paintings by prominent Jewish artists. Many of them depicted the sufferings and joys of the people of the Diaspora, the dispersal of the Jews.

The thirteen Ministers of the Government Council sat at a long dais beneath the photograph of Theodor Herzl, who in 1897 envisaged a Jewish state. Vertical pale blue and white flags of the state hung on both sides. To the left of the ministers and below them sat other members of the national administration. There are thirty-seven in all, but some were unable to get here from Jerusalem.

At 4 P. M. sharp the assemblage rose and sang the Hatikvah, the national anthem. The participants seemed to sing with unusual gusto and inspiration. The voices had hardly subsided when the squat, white-haired chairman, Mr. Ben-Gurion, started to read the proclamation, which in a few hours was to transform most of those present from persons without a country to proud nationals. When he pronounced the words "We hereby proclaim the establishment of the Jewish state in Palestine, to be called Israel," there was thunderous applause and not a few damp eyes.

After the proclamation had been read and the end of the White Paper and of its land laws pronounced, Mr. Ben-Gurion signed the document and was followed by all the other members of the administration, some by proxy. The last to sign was Moshe Shertok, the new Foreign Minister and the Jewish Agency's delegate to the United Nations. He was roundly applauded and almost mobbed by photographers.

The ceremony ended with everyone standing silently while the orchestral strains of the Hatikvah filled the room. Outside, the fever of nationalism was spreading with fond embraces, warm handshakes and kisses. Street vendors were selling flags, crowds gathered to read posted bulletins, and newspapers were being sold everywhere.

As the sabbath had started, there was not the degree of public rejoicing that there would have been any other day.

The proclamation was to have been read at 11 P. M. but was advanced to 4 because of the sabbath. Mr. Shertok explained that the proclamation had to be made yesterday because the mandate was to end at midnight and the Zionists did not want a split second to intervene between that time and the formal establishment of the state.

In the preamble to the declaration of independence the history of the Jewish people was traced briefly from its birth in the Land of Israel to this day. The preamble touched on the more modern highlights, including Herzl's vision of a state, acknowledgment of the Jewish national homeland by the Balfour Declaration in 1917 and its reaffirmation by the League of Nations mandate and by the United Nations General Assembly resolution of Nov. 29, 1947.

It asserted that this recognition by the United Nations of the right of the Jewish people to establish an independent state could not be revoked and added that it was the "self-evident right of the Jewish people to be a nation, as all other nations, in its own sovereign state."

The proclamation stated that as of midnight the National Council would act as a Provisional State Council and that its executive organ, the National Administration, would constitute a provisional government until elected bodies could be set up before Oct. 1.

Israel, the proclamation went on, will be open to immigration by Jews from all countries "of their dispersion." She will develop the country for the benefit of all its inhabitants, it added, and will be based on precepts of liberty, justice and peace taught by the Hebrew prophets.

The new state, according to the proclamation, will uphold the "social and political equality of all its citizens without distinction of race, creed or sex" and "will guarantee full freedom of conscience, worship, education and culture."

The statement pledged safeguarding of the sanctity and inviolability of shrines and holy places of all religions. It also contained a promise to uphold the principles of the United Nations.

There was great cheering and drinking of toasts in this blacked-out city when word was received that the United States had recognized the provincial Government. The effect on the people, especially those drinking late in Tel Aviv's coffee houses, was electric. They even ran into the blackness of the streets shouting, cheering and toasting the United States.

*　　*　　*

June 8, 1948

WEST TO MAINTAIN TROOPS IN GERMANY TILL PEACE IS SAFE

U. S. a Party to Pledge Given in Six-Power Proposals for Western Zones' Regime

FEDERAL FORM SUGGESTED

International Authority in Ruhr, Including Germans, Asked—Paris Holds Key to Plan

By HERBERT L. MATTHEWS
Special to The New York Times.

LONDON, June 7—The United States, along with Great Britain and France, guarantees to keep military forces in Germany "until the peace of Europe is secured," it was revealed today, when the recommendations of the six-power conference on Western Germany were published as a second and final communiqué. The conference, which lasted six weeks and was held in London, ended on June 1.

France won this security pledge and also some important concessions covering the economic control of the Ruhr. There is to be an International Authority, composed of the United States, Britain, France, the Benelux countries and Germany, to direct the distribution of Ruhr coal, coke and steel and to supervise trade and investments so as to prevent discrimination against any foreign power.

The fate of these recommendations now lies in the hands of the French National Assembly. Information received here indicates that the hopes of acceptance are better than would appear outwardly. It is believed that the publication of today's communiqué will help the French Government to prevail, as it will prove that there has been a genuine compromise and that the United States and Britain went a long way to meet the French demands.

No Problems Like France's

The United States, Britain and the Benelux countries (Belgium, the Netherlands and Luxembourg) are certain to accept the recommendations, as their representatives at the conference were at all times in touch with their Governments and these countries have no political problem like France's. In any event, the recommendations can take effect without Benelux sanction.

If France rejects the recommendations, the whole Western German situation will have to be reviewed. No three-power meeting is planned in such a contingency. It is more likely that the United States and Britain would go ahead as much as possible on their own, without France.

There is no timetable in the recommendations, as certain dates are tacitly understood as goals. First would come acceptance of the recommendations by the Governments concerned. Then the Military Governors of the three western zones of Germany would hold a joint meeting with the German Minister-Presidents of their zones. This should take place by June 15.

The Minister-Presidents would then be authorized to convene a constituent assembly to prepare a constitution. Each German state will decide for itself the procedure and regulations for choosing the members of the constituent assembly. It was agreed during the conference that Sept. 1 should be aimed at as the date for convening the assembly.

Federal Form Is Objective

The constitution is to provide a framework for "a federal form of government which adequately protects the rights of the respective states and which at the same time provides for adequate central authority and which guarantees the rights and freedoms of the individual."

If the Military Governors are satisfied with the fulfillment of these requirements, the proposed constitution will be submitted for ratification to the people of Western Germany. If all goes well, Western Germany will have a government in the spring of 1949.

Thus the occupying powers have control all along, and this is even more obvious in the vital clauses on security. In fact, the opening sentences, if accepted, would represent the most important commitment on Western European security yet taken.

"The United States, United Kingdom and French delegations reiterated the firm views of their Governments that there could not be any general withdrawal of their forces from Germany until the peace of Europe is secured and without prior consultation," the communiqué reads. "It was further recommended that the Governments concerned should consult if any of them should consider that there was a danger of resurgence of German military power or of the adoption by Germany of a policy of aggression."

British and American sources here refused or were unable to define the key phrase of this passage: "until the peace of Europe is secured." But all agreed that it meant a long time. A peace treaty with Western Germany would not necessarily mean peace an Europe.

There are other clauses intended to calm French fears of a resurgent Germany. Disarmament and demilitarization will be supervised by a new "military security board" and there will be a system of inspection to make sure that even when there is a general withdrawal of occupation forces, Germany cannot again become a military menace. "Key areas" would continue to be occupied—a point insisted upon by France.

At the end of the main communiqué a long annex gives a statement of principles concerning the proposed International Authority for the Ruhr. It guarantees deliveries of coal, coke and steel, about which France is worried, and also protects the position of the Benelux countries.

Voting on the International Authority is so arranged that the United States and Britain, by voting solidly, can always have a majority over France and the Benelux countries. There are fifteen votes, but the United States and Britain each control three of their own and one each for their respective German zones.

Moreover, Gen. Lucius D. Clay, the United States Military Governor in Germany, is considered to have won a victory with the insertion of clauses tying the actions of the International Authority to the Organization for European Economic Cooperation, in which the Military Governors represent their zones, and placing implementation of the findings of the International Authority under the Military Governors. This implementation is tied to "any agreements relative to the provision of financial assistance to Germany"—and it is the United States that furnishes such assistance.

At the same time the International Authority has a good deal more than mere advisory powers and, aside from getting guarantees of coal, coke and steel deliveries, France can feel reassured about the length and strictness of the control over the heavy industries of the Ruhr.

The communiqué reiterates the old but now almost hopeless assertion that the door is always open to eventual four-power agreement on the German problem. However, the Western states are in fact bracing themselves for a sharp Soviet reaction.

Sir William Strang, Permanent Under-Secretary of the British Foreign Office, who presided over the six-power conference, went to the Soviet Embassy this morning and presented to Ambassador Georgi N. Zarubin a copy of the communiqué in advance of its publication. In Berlin another copy was handed to Marshal Vassily D. Sokolovsky, Soviet Commander in Chief in Germany. In both cases care was taken to add nothing orally or otherwise to the text of the communiqué.

It is realized that the six-power action offers the Soviet Union an excuse to put the squeeze on Berlin again or even to absorb the eastern zone of Germany into Russian territory. This was a calculated risk.

* * *

June 17, 1948

RUSSIANS WALK OUT OF BERLIN MEETING

Say There Will Be No More Sessions of Four-Power Body—
U. S. Determined to Stay

By EDWARD A. MORROW
Special to The New York Times.

BERLIN, June 16—The Soviet Union snapped the last link in four-power government in Germany tonight when its representatives stalked out of a meeting of the Berlin Kommandatura.

Earlier in the day the Soviet-sponsored People's Congress Council assumed the aspect of a provisional government of Germany. It sent three demands to the Western powers, insisting on the scrapping of the proposed Western state, the withdrawal of occupation troops and the calling of a Big Four peace conference.

The Russians' action in the Kommandatura, which closely resembled their walkout at the Allied Control Council meeting March 20, in effect has completely divided Berlin into Eastern and Western camps.

Col. Frank L. Howley, United States commandant, said while he felt the Soviet step marked the end of the Kommandatura "any joker who thinks the United States, Britain and France are going to be dealt out of Berlin has another guess coming."

The Soviet action occurred a few minutes after Colonel Howley had decided at 11:20 o'clock that he could turn over the other items on the agenda to his deputy, W. T. Babcock. Colonel Howley had obtained permission from the chairman, Brig. Gen. Jean Ganeval, to leave the meeting, which began at 10 o'clock this morning. The United States commandant said he had had "more than my quota of conference for the day."

Col. Alexis Yelizarov, deputy to Soviet Commandant Maj. Gen. Alexander G. Kotikov, who was absent because of illness, declared he considered Colonel Howley's departure "rude" and led the unusually large Soviet delegation out of the room.

Observers pointed out that it was not the first time any of the commandants had left a meeting and allowed their deputies to continue the discussions.

As General Ganeval called to the departing delegation that the date for the next meeting had not been set, Colonel Yelizarow was understood to have replied that "there will not be any next meeting."

While Colonel Howley said he felt the Soviet step meant the end of meetings of the Kommandatura, other observers noted that the Russians had left the issue hanging in the air in the same fashion as they had the question of Control Council meetings.

A British spokesman declared: "We did not get the impression that there would not be another future meeting. The withdrawal appeared to be impromptu."

Whether there is another meeting, observers from all three Western Powers agreed that little constructive work could be expected on a quadripartite basis. Four items on today's agenda ended without agreement. These included a British proposal calling for unrestricted parcel post service for Germans, a French proposal defining standards for socialization of this city's industry and two Soviet papers. One of the latter accused the United States and British of trying to split the city by allowing city representatives to discuss trade with the bizonal area and the other charged United States officials with prohibiting Germans from working in the Soviet sector.

The Kommandatura meeting did achieve one major agreement. A French proposal to raise the food rations for Berliners was approved by all four powers, after Soviet modifications had been accepted.

The French proposal was an answer to the unilateral action announced by the Russians a fortnight ago increasing the number of hot meals to be distributed in their sector.

Arguing that a distribution of food only to workers in specified industries was not broad enough, the French proposed that rations for housewives and children be increased. The Russians proposed a moderate increase for workers and all four powers agreed that all categories of ration-card holders should receive increases ranging from 100 to 250 calories a day.

After several other items had been brought up under other business, including a half-hour Soviet tirade accusing United States officials of splitting the Berlin trade unions, Colonel Yelizarov proposed again to go through the Soviet fourteen-point program for improving conditions in Berlin.

It was at this point that Colonel Howley, according to Soviet observers, said he "had to get some sleep."

After the Soviet delegation quickly followed his departure, General Ganevel remarked to the rest of the group that he had considered Colonel Howley's departure correct and adjourned the meeting. It is now up to the commandants' chiefs of staff to arrange another meeting, if such is to be held. The Chiefs of Staff at the Control Council level have not found it necessary to convene the council once since that body's meeting broke up.

*   *   *

June 17, 1948

TENSION IN EUROPE

*Insecurity Said to Be Principal Basis
for the Present Situation Overseas*

By HANSON W. BALDWIN

The Russian "squeeze" on Berlin grew somewhat tighter yesterday, as the French political crisis—in part a product of the six-power agreement for the consolidation of western Germany—deepened.

This new crisis in two countries—and crisis is perhaps too strong a word—is not unexpected. It must be viewed against the perspective of Europe—against the Soviet acceptance of a Danubian conference, against the lack of any significant overt Communist moves in Italy since the election, against a situation in Greece that has improved for the democracies, deteriorated for communism.

So viewed, it does not reflect, as yet, any significant general change in Russian policy; neither does it mean unalterable Russian determination to persist in past tactics.

Rather it represents the fever chart of an ill patient; periodically until the patient recovers—or dies—we must expect increases in temperature.

The present rise on the fever chart of Europe is not, however, a general one; so far it is limited to Germany and France. Yet neither situation should give too much cause for alarm.

The Soviet tactics in Berlin represents a continuation of the needling process that failed to force the Western powers out of Berlin before the Italian elections. They also represent a preliminary Soviet reply to the six-power program for Western Germany.

France is more feverish, ironically enough, chiefly because of Germany. The French have had a military inferiority complex ever since the Franco-Prussian War, and increasingly since World War II. And not without reason; the might of Germany had impressed itself upon the French consciousness in three great wars in seventy years.

Today, the mere specter—though far removed—of the revival of German military power is enough to shake the "throne" of any French statesman. Nor is the French problem of security limited to fear of Germany alone. The Soviet Union now looms like a colossus, its military shadow cast across Europe. Gone with the wind are the great French armies of yesterday; today France maintains about eight or nine divisions, only one or two of them well equipped, some of them out of the country.

Insecurity Grips Europe

This, then, is the real reason for the present excitement in Western Europe—a lack of security. The same insecurity has been the basis of most of the preceding crises of the past eighteen months, but this time the fear is not bred by economic insecurity or by fear of Communist action from within the state, but by fear of military action from without the state.

No matter how little basis in reason or logic there may be for such a fear today, it is a fear, bred in emotional experience, that will be very difficult to eradicate.

Yet the problem, reduced to the simplest possible terms, is still the same problem the United States has confronted since the war. The problem in the case of Germany is to restore that country to sufficient strength economically to take her off the back of the United States taxpayer and to enable her to resume her self-supporting place in a sound economy of Europe without restoring her military might. The problem in the case of France is to secure her against aggression from either Germany or the Soviet Union.

Initially the problem is economic and political; ultimately it is military—in the one case, to prevent the renaissance of German armed strength, in the other to restore French armed strength. Both are difficult.

Yet, if France could build up fifty to seventy-five well-equipped divisions, plus a good air fleet, much of her present feeling of insecurity would disappear. Such a goal obviously must be a long-term one. The United States can furnish military aid to France, but there is no such vast quantity of surplus war material available as most people imagine.

The United States Army has stock for the initial equipment of twenty divisions, but modern items, such as recoilless guns, new antitank guns, etc., are lacking. The present United States military program, now being approved by Congress, will require funds and manufacturing facilities for considerable military equipment.

If the United States is to add to that by manufacturing equipment for France and other European countries, the cost factor intervenes, for its own national defense program and the European Recovery Program already mean staggering expenditures.

There is no quick and easy way by which France can receive equipment for fifty or more divisions; therefore, the problem of physical security for France and some economic security for Germany is a long-term one.

But a political guarantee could immediately change the whole picture in Europe and, since much of Europe's crisis fever is psychological, could immediately reduce that fever.

The United States must assure France in the strongest terms possible by tangible and intangible means that it stands behind her. The United States also must make this clear to the Soviet Union.

If the United States stand is unequivocal and explicit; if the United States makes it clear beyond any shadow of doubt that it will use all its great might against a recrudescence of German militarism or against Communist aggression, the fever will ebb—and not only temporarily.

The Congressional committees that may have to compromise the differences between Senate and House versions of the draft bill ought to heed the words of Secretary of Defense Forrestal:

"If I were writing this bill," he testified May 3, "I would have included a provision authorizing the deferment of persons engaged in scientific and technical study, in research and so on."

The omission of specific and mandatory provisions of this nature is the greatest danger of the present draft law. The whole question of scientific and technical students, doctors and dentists ought to be carefully handled lest the United States repeat the mistakes of World War II when the draft became a dragnet and not really selective service.

* * *

June 19, 1948

NEW GERMAN MARK TO BE INTRODUCED IN WEST TOMORROW

Former Currency Is Scrapped by Three Allied Powers—
Berlin Is Excluded

VALUE TO BE SET LATER

Russian Commander Accuses 3 Other Powers of 'Lying' on
Reasons for Changes

By JACK RAYMOND
Special to The New York Times.

FRANKFORT ON THE MAIN, Germany, June 18—The three Western Allies announced today that a new form of German currency, to be called the Deutsche mark, would be issued Sunday to replace the Reichsmark, used since the inflation days of 1923 and now virtually worthless. They said the conversion rate would be announced later.

At the same time they banned the import and export of Reichsmarks into the Western zones, but ordered no special customs guards placed at the zonal borders.

Thus they effectively separated the economy of the Western zones from that of the Soviet zone. The Western sectors of Berlin were not included in the currency reform, but special precautions will be taken to continue sending supplies to those sectors.

Halt in East-West Trade Seen

Western Allied officials here admitted that trade between the Western and Eastern zones would be suspended. Jack Bennett, financial adviser to Gen. Lucius D. Clay, United States Military Governor, said "it is likely that the Soviet Military Administration will be called upon to work out a new trade agreement to restore a barter-like exchange of goods between the East and the West."

[The Russians announced in Berlin that all railway and road traffic from the Western zones had been halted to prevent the influx of Reichsmarks into the Soviet zone. United States guards on the only highway leading from the West to Berlin said Russian soldiers had halted all Western Allied personnel trying to reach the former German capital, The Associated Press reported early Saturday.

[Soviet Commander Marshal Vassily D. Sokolovsky denounced the currency reform program in a statement Saturday, saying that the Western powers were "lying" about the reasons for the action, The Associated Press also said.]

Backing the new money will be the "productive capacity of Western Germany and the Marshall Plan," the Western powers said, since Germany has no gold or silver resources.

They conceded that considerable unemployment, lasting about six months, could be expected as the immediate reaction to the monetary reform program.

Sunday, all Germans will be permitted to turn in to the food ration offices in which they registered 60 Reichsmarks. In return they will get 40 Deutschemarks, with 20 more due them within two months.

Next Saturday all their Reichsmark holdings must be registered and new money will be issued subsequently at a conversion rate yet to be announced.

Wages and Prices Frozen

Meanwhile wages and prices are to remain the same. A series of bizonal laws, presumably to be duplicated in the French zone, was approved over Communist-Socialist opposition in the Bizonal Economic Council this morning. The laws give Dr. Ludwig Erhard, Bizonal Economies Minister "dictatorial" powers to raise and lower prices of certain commodities as he sees fit in the next few months.

A one-week moratorium has been placed on all debts. Like wages, however, they are to be paid in the new currency. While the Reichsmark is to be invalidated, small coins of the denomination of one pfennig and less and one-half mark notes will be retained in use temporarily, at one-tenth of their original value.

At a press conference Western Allied financial experts expressed as much curiosity about the possible effects on the average German worker as their questioners. These officials said they expected large quantities of hoarded goods and huge stocks of new imports, such as tobacco, to be released shortly. This, they said, would help crack the market and give the German worker a chance to buy something with his money—quite impossible to do with Reichsmarks.

Although they were supposed to be secret, the new currency measures leaked out during the week and by this morning regular black market centers were in an uproar. For a few hours cigarettes were selling for eighteen Reichsmarks apiece. Then the trade stopped as the combination of rumors and real news provoked barriers of suspicion.

Regular retail shops either have been closed or their owners have refused to sell anything for more than a week.

Mr. Bennett revealed that the new money had been printed in the United States and shipped here last January. He said this was done in the hope that it would be available for quadripartite currency reform. He said there was no likelihood of a four-power measure now.

Sokolovsky Bars Money Dealings

BERLIN, Saturday, June 19 (AP)—Marshal Vassily D. Sokolovsky, Soviet commander in Germany, denounced the currency reform for Western Germany today in a 2,000-word proclamation to the German people.

He accused the United States, Britain and France of completing the splitting of Germany and forbade importation of the new currency into the Soviet zone.

Marshal Sokolovsky accused the three Western occupying powers of "lying" about the reasons for their currency action. He charged they had prepared the plan "secretly" and "against the will and interests of the German people."

He also forbade importation of the new Deutsche marks into Berlin—which the Western powers do not intend to do—because he said the city "is located in the Soviet occupation zone of Germany and is economically part of the Soviet zone."

The Russian commander decreed that Germans in the Soviet zone and Berlin who dealt in new or old money from the West would be punished for "damaging the economy."

* * *

June 20, 1948

WEST TURNS TO AIR AS SOVIET CUTS OFF BERLIN LAND LINKS

British Fly Planes to Europe to Handle Transport—
Rail and Road Travel Halted

RUSSIAN GUARD INCREASED

Berlin Assembly Rejects Tie to East—
People's Council Claims Right to Rule

By DREW MIDDLETON
Special to The New York Times.

BERLIN, June 19—The United States and British Military Governments countered the Soviet Military Administration's land blockade of Berlin with air power today as the Russians strove to complete the isolation of this city and bring the whole of the Soviet zone behind the "iron curtain."

Within Berlin itself there were two important developments. The City Assembly, led by stout-hearted parliamentary democrats, flatly rejected a Soviet bid for the inclusion of Berlin in the Eastern zone.

This was matched on the Soviet side by the People's Council, which, in an appeal to all Germans, classified itself as the only representative of the German people and asked them to rally against the West.

Employing the start of currency reform in the Western Zones as an excuse, the Russians have halted all travel by automobile or passenger train, by an American, Briton or Frenchman or German into their zone and into Berlin.

To enforce the new ban on all eastbound traffic, Marshal Vassily D. Sokolovsky, commanding the Soviet forces in Germany, reinforced the Soviet Army's frontier guards all along the ragged line that forms the frontier between the British zone on the west and the United States zone on the southwest and south.

British Post Armored Cars

The Russian concentration appeared to be especially strong at Helmstedt, where the superhighway to Berlin from the British zone crosses into the Russian area.

Looking across the frontier the Russians could see the silhouettes of a dozen armored cars the British had brought to the frontier to help handle the long lines of travelers in cars, trucks and wagons and on foot who sought to move eastward.

All entry into the Soviet zone was barred. Two diplomats, one Swiss and the other Dutch, who tried to drive eastward were turned back to mingle with the hundreds of Germans who milled uncertainly in the area west of the control point.

Railroad traffic, which fuels and to a considerable extent feeds Berlin, was moving eastward, however, although the Russians turned back a number of freight cars on the usual excuse that they were so old as to be "unsafe."

No military freight cars bound for Berlin are expected to reach the Soviet inspection point on the railroad at Marienborn until Monday or Tuesday, however. When they do the Western powers will get a further insight into the Soviet intentions.

The inspection at Marienborn was, if anything, stiffer than it has been since it was instituted a week ago, British official sources said.

The British joined United States officials in turning to air power to answer Russian manpower. Transport aircraft flew to the Royal Air Force field at Bueckeburg near Minden from Britain this morning and as long as the Soviet ban lasts all British personnel will be flown to and from Berlin.

The United States Army Air Transport Service, greatly augmented since the United States Military Government passenger train service ended April 1, proceeded normally. Reserve pools of transport planes in addition to those now in use are available in the United States zone.

The superhighway linking Berlin with the West was closed to East-bound traffic at 5 o'clock this morning but West-bound traffic proceeded normally. By 10 A. M. the United States Army check point had halted and turned back ten United States vehicles enroute for Berlin.

German passenger train service from Berlin to the Western zones also was halted. No passenger trains were scheduled to enter the Soviet zone from the West.

According to official United States sources barge traffic on the waterways is being maintained. A United States barge entered the Soviet zone with a cargo of food after having been cleared by Soviet authorities.

Berliners Express Concern

Within Berlin itself there is new emphasis from the Russian side on inclusion of the city's Western sectors into the Soviet zone. Berliners halt United States personnel on the street to ask if Marshal Sokolovsky was correct in persistently coupling the Soviet zone and Berlin in the statement he issued early this morning attacking the Western measures for currency reform.

Spurred by the horrors of currency reform conjured in their fertile imaginations, the Communists put their campaign for the establishment of Berlin as the capital of a prospective Russian-dominated Reich into high gear.

The Executive Committee of the Soviet-sponsored Socialist Unity party issued a long statement appealing to the Germans to unite against the "splitters of Germany" and warned that the time would come when a big democratic people's movement under the leadership of the People's Council would make an end of the protectorate government in "Frankfort on the Main."

The German economic commission for the Soviet zone published a similar statement, in which unemployment, industrial doldrums and a fall in the standard of living all were pictured as the results of the currency reform in the West.

The belief among the Germans with some contact with the Soviet Military Administration is that currency reform for the Soviet zone will be announced sooner than the first of month, when it was generally expected.

In the view of senior United States and British Military Government officials the currency reform in the West has served the Russians well by giving them an excuse for measures that go far beyond the expected control action and tighten the Soviet Military Administration's grip on Berlin.

The next step—as no one believes it is far off—will be the intensification of the Russian economic blockade and resulting shortages of fuel and food in the Western sectors of the city. The Russians hope to effect the withdrawal of the United States, British and French forces here through indirect pressure exerted by the hungry people of those sectors.

* * *

June 24, 1948

RUSSIANS BAR FOOD TO WESTERN BERLIN IN CURRENCY FIGHT

Complete Railroad Blockade After U. S., Britain, France Introduce New Marks

ELECTRICITY IMPORTS CUT

Communist Disorders Delay City Assembly as Members Reject Russian Control

By DREW MIDDLETON
Special to The New York Times.

BERLIN, Thursday, June 24—All railroad traffic between the Western zones and Berlin, over which most of the city's fuel and a large part of its food are transported, has been halted by the Soviet Military Administration and the blockade of the city except by air is now complete.

This Soviet action followed an announcement yesterday by the three Western powers that they would introduce the new Western Deutsche mark into Berlin in an apparent answer to Russian currency reform.

The Soviet Administration also took direct action against the industries of the Western sectors. It ordered the complete stoppage of imports of electric power in these sectors. Approximately 50 per cent of the present power consumption is imported from the Zschornowitz plant.

Thus the final stages of the battle for Berlin were set in a day that was marked by a Communist-led disorder delaying the meeting of the City Assembly for more than two hours and resulting in injuries to several officials.

The Russian blockade on railway freight and passenger service from the Western zones to Berlin was announced this morning by the Soviet-licensed news service ADN. The news service report said it had resulted from "technical trouble" with the tracks.

Tie to Currency Was Seen

Maj. Gen. Paul Kvshnin, chief of the transportation division of the Soviet Military Administration, issued the order to end all passenger and freight traffic, which is believed to be directly connected with Russian efforts through currency reform to put an economic squeeze on the Germans in the Western sectors.

For two weeks the Russians have subjected Western rail traffic to increasingly severe restrictions, but until last night some traffic always had been able to move.

The new Soviet step was foreshadowed by Dr. Heinrich Rau, head of the economic commission in the Soviet zone, who predicted that Soviet measures for winning financial control of Berlin would cause "severe difficulties" for the people of the Western sectors.

"If the Western sectors are not supplied by air they will encounter very serious economic difficulties," Dr. Rau said.

Americans Supplied by Air

At present United States forces and civilian employes in the city are being supplied by air and British passenger travel is by transport plane. But the supply of food and fuel by air for the 2,750,000 Germans in the three Western sectors would be almost impossible.

The Soviet Military Administration plans city-wide demonstrations against the Western powers and their currency reform by Communist flying squads, similar to the action groups that sped the fall of democracy in Czechoslovakia, a United States security organization said.

Youthful members of the Communist-led Socialist Unity party have been organized into flying squads. These will demonstrate outside the food offices when the Berliners of the Western sectors begin to change their Reichsmarks for the new Western currency tomorrow and Saturday.

The object will be to drive the Germans away, prevent the conversion of Reichsmarks and maintain the Soviet-backed marks with their identification stamps as the people's principal currency.

This plan, produced by the political strategists of the Soviet Military Administration, reveals Russian doubts as to the ability of their new currency to circulate on an equal basis with the Western-sponsored money.

In this city, now riven financially as well as politically between the East and the West, the control of the contents of Hans Schmidt's pocketbook has become the principal objective of the world's four greatest powers.

The Western powers' decision to introduce the new Deutsche mark into Berlin was seen as a challenge to the Russian currency reform, and the assumption that Berlin was ruled by the Soviet Military Administration, as expressed by Marshal Vassily D. Sokolovsky, Soviet commander, Tuesday night.

The Western powers' reply to the Soviet currency reform was the blunt rebuttal of Marshal Sokolovsky's assertation that Berlin belonged to the Russians. So was the letter written to him by Gen. Sir Brian Robertson, British Military Governor.

It is believed that the Soviet currency reform, which begins today, will be accompanied by the establishment of a Russian military cordon around the Soviet part of the city to prevent the entrance of Germans from the Western sectors.

It is probable that the Russian action will be met by a similar one on the Western side. Troops of the Sixteenth Infantry, a constabulary squadron and military police battalions were confined to their barracks late yesterday and told to remain on the alert.

The tripartite declaration on the introduction of currency reform into the Western sectors emphasized that the step was the result of the "arbitrary" action taken by Marshal Sokolovsky Tuesday night "in total disregard" of Berlin's status is an enclave occupied by four powers and the agreements reached by these powers on the management of money and banking in the city.

The Russians also have refused to recognize the prerogatives of the Kommandatura as the supreme law-making body of the city, the Western powers' announcement said.

Orders have been issued that the laws on currency reform published by the Russians will not apply in the Western sectors, the declaration added. Throughout the three Western sectors all banks and shops, save food and drug stores, were closed and all debts were suspended.

The conversion of Reichsmarks now held by Germans for the new Deutsche mark will begin at 7 o'clock tomorrow morning. Through Saturday the people of the Western sectors will be able to convert a nominal amount of Reichsmarks at the rate of one for one and will be asked to surrender and report all old currency holdings.

The concurrent circulation of new Eastern and Western currencies depends on Russian cooperation and "circumstances will compel them to cooperate," according to Sir Eric Coates, British financial adviser.

Sir Eric echoed the opinions of other Western financial experts who believe that in a test between two currencies the Western one will drive out the Eastern if it is allowed in the Soviet sectors.

Sir Eric declared it would be possible to detach the banks in the Western sectors from the City Bank of Berlin.

His optimism must be contrasted with the evident Russian intention expressed by Dr. Rau of establishing "very severe" measures to protect the economy of the Soviet zone from Western money.

The ban on electricity imports apparently was one of those measures.

United States Military Government utility officials said this power cut was "not too serious in summertime" but would mean great hardship in the winter.

There are enough power plants in the Western sectors to meet 60 per cent of the present load but these would not be able to operate without incoming coal. The coal stockpile position of these plants is poor since the Russians have been hampering inbound shipments. Most of the shipments that have been coming in have gone to the plant in the Soviet sector.

Dr. Rau said frankly he did not believe the Western powers would be able to feed the people of their zones since food supplies in the Soviet zone would not be purchasable save with Russian zone currency.

* * *

June 27, 1948

CHURCHILL LIKENS BERLIN TO MUNICH; VOWS AID TO BEVIN

He Tells Audience of 100,000 Russia Has Made Up Her Mind to Drive Allies From City

RESOLUTE COURSE URGED

War Chief Says It Is Not Only Best but Sole Chance of Averting Another War

By BENJAMIN WELLES
Special to The New York Times.

LUTON, England, June 26—In vigorous but measured terms Winston Churchill told an audience of 100,000 here today that the issues raised by the present situation in Berlin were "as grave as those we now know were at stake at Munich ten years ago."

Britain's war leader and chief of the Opposition Conservative party took occasion at a monster rally here to pledge to the Labor Government the Conservative party's support in the present crisis between the Western powers and the Soviet Union over Germany.

"There can be no doubt," Mr. Churchill declared, that the "Communist Government of Russia has made up its mind to drive us and France and all the other Allies out and turn the Russian zone in Germany into one of its satellite states under the rule of totalitarian terrorism."

All should have learned by now, Mr. Churchill said, that there is no safety "in yielding to dictators—whether Nazi or Communist." He urged a "firm and resolute course" as "not only the best but the only" chance of preventing a third world war and he pleaded his support for the Government "in the stand which, with all their devotion to the cause of peace, they have felt bound to make."

Otherwise, however, Mr. Churchill left no doubt in the minds of his listeners that on virtually all other questions, domestic and foreign, the Conservative party was ready to engage the Socialist-Labor Government and party in battle for political control of the country at the "first opportunity afforded us."

Hits Domestic Policies

A huge crowd, for several hours before the meeting, had strolled with evident enjoyment through the vast estate in the grounds of which Mr. Churchill spoke. They enjoyed watching a gymkhana and open-air dancing and listened to a girls' choir and a local brass band. They also laughed and cheered at the former Prime Minister's repeated sallies at the expense of the Labor Government.

Ranging in his field of attack from the Government's domestic policies, which he termed inadequate and mismanaged, to "imperial and overseas affairs," Mr. Churchill charged that Britain at present was "dependent on that great republic of the United States for our safety and for our daily bread."

The Socialist Government, he said, has allowed widespread growth of communism and internecine strife in India, Burma and Malaya through its lack of force and its inept administration.

"It does not matter where you look in the world," he said, "you will see how grievously the name and prestige of Britain has fallen."

Asserting that by every conceivable test the Conservative party now had a "substantial" majority in the British Isles, Mr. Churchill said that time was working for the Conservatives and he prophesied the end of the Socialist rule at the next general elections.

"In a new Parliament lies the only way to make England herself again a part of the British Empire and a name for all its people," he said.

Recalls Bevin's Pledge

LUTON, June 26 (AP)—Winston Churchill today warned Britain to sheer away from appeasement in the Berlin crisis with Russia.

"We are all naturally anxious about what is happening in Berlin," he said. "Last month, on May 4, Mr. Bevin said in Parliament that 'we are in Berlin as of right. It is our intention to stay there.'

"It is certain that he would not have said that without having made sure that the United States is equally resolved."

"The only hope of peace is to be strong," Mr. Churchill asserted, "to act with other great, freedom-loving nations and to make it plain to the aggressor while time remains, that we should bring the world against him, and defend ourselves and our cause by every means should he strike a felon's blow."

Mr. Churchill said that the United States provided an excellent example of the strength to be found in bi-partisan and multi-partisan direction of foreign policy.

"The Americans are actually involved in a Presidential election, and yet in the midst of all that struggle and party divisions they preserve what is called bi-partisan conduct of foreign affairs, far above party. The Government and their opposition work together through their leading men in foreign policy.

"Both sides are prepared to vote generous subsidies to Europe and especially to Britain. Both sides are supporting strong and effective defenses. And all this in the middle of vehement and bitter party politics."

* * *

June 27, 1948

COMMUNISTS MENACE SOUTH ASIA; UNIFIED BLOW AT RESOURCES SEEN

By The Associated Press

SINGAPORE, June 26—The flood of communism is spilling south from China over the rich lands of Southeast

Asia. Senior British officials assert that the Communists have launched a major offensive in the area.

[Violence reached a day of climax in Malaya where nine persons were killed and native Communists demanded that all Europeans leave the Peninsula, Reuters reported.]

An Associated Press survey shows that Communists are openly bidding for power in Malaya and Burma, and are trying to infiltrate into positions of influence in Indo-China and Indonesia. Even in conservative Siam an increase in Communist activity is reported.

Information from Southeast Asia's capitals and from British officials indicates that the Communist aims are twofold:

(1) To slow the flow of rubber, tin, oil and other strategic raw materials into recovery factories and defense stockpiles of the United States and Western Europe;

(2) To lay the foundation for an eventual strike for full political control.

Orders for the Communist offensive are believed by authorities to have come from elsewhere in Asia, but not from Russia or China.

"D-Day" in Malaya was seven weeks ago.

British officials say that the new terrorist campaign in Malaya definitely is not the spontaneous outburst of peasants in a period of unrest, but is directed from a central headquarters—presumably a South Asian Comintern about which little is known.

This is the picture, country by country, as reported by Associated Press correspondents:

INDONESIA

Qualified sources believe that the Communists count Indonesia as one of their most promising fields for winning supporters.

The Republicans have steadily lost influence since the Dutch military offensive last summer which drove Republican forces out of the richest sections of Java and Sumatra.

So far the Indonesian Communist party has been insignificant numerically, but it has aligned with the Labor party, the Socialist Party (a Left-Wing splinter group) and youth groups in a "Peoples' Democratic Front." Recent recognition of the Republic by the Soviet Union and outspoken Soviet support for the Indonesians at Lake Success have increased the front's influence among non-Communists.

INDO-CHINA

Well-informed sources believe that Indo-China is the second place upon which the Communists are counting strongly.

About 120,000 French and French colonial troops have frustrated Viet Namese hopes for independence but have not yet been able actually to defeat the Viet Namese.

Communist influence already is strong in Viet Nam. Only 10 or 20 per cent of the Viet Nam revolutionary rank and file are Communists. But the top leadership is avowedly Communist. It includes three Comintern veterans, President Ho Chi Minh, Nguyen Giap and Tran Van Giau.

MALAYA

The first Communist target in Southeast Asia is Malaya, the world's greatest producer of natural rubber. There, guerrilla warfare already is under way. British officials say there is direct evidence that it is Communist-directed.

Terrorist attacks by small Communist bands against estates, mines and Chinese Kuomintang leaders have averaged more than one a day. At least twenty-four Chinese and Europeans have been killed in these attacks.

The Communists control an army of up to 5,000 trained guerrillas who operated under Allied officers against the Japanese during the war. In addition, they control several dozen killer gangs, numbering from ten to twenty-four each, whose specific task is the assassination of Europeans and Chinese in key positions on rubber estates and tin mines.

BURMA

Open fighting has been reported for months between Communist guerrillas and forces of the Leftist Government. Before Britain granted Burma independence in January, the Communists were among the loudest advocates of immediate independence. Once it was granted, they turned against the new independent Government.

SIAM

Police Chief Chartrakarn Kosol said there had been increased Communist activity in Bangkok, including secret meetings and increased Left-Wing labor activity. Although relatively calm, Siam fears it may be next on the Communist list.

A Russian Embassy was established at Bangkok last year. There has been speculation it might become the nerve center for Communist activity in all Southeast Asia.

*   *   *

June 29, 1948

COMINFORM DENOUNCES TITO, CHARGING HE LEANS TO WEST; HIS EXPULSION THREATENED

SOVIET RIFT BARED

Yugoslav Leaders' Acts Termed 'Hateful' and 'Slanderous' of Russia

VIEWS HELD TROTSKYIST

Belgrade Accused of Retreat From Leninism and Straying From Cominform Fold

By The Associated Press

PRAGUE, June 28—The Communist Information Bureau denounced today Marshal Tito's leadership of Yugoslav Communists. The international Communist organization declared that Belgrade's Premier and other top members of the party must hew to the Moscow line or get out.

The Yugoslav leaders were accused by the Moscow-blessed bureau of pursuing a hateful and slanderous policy toward Russia and of leaning toward Western methods.

The blast came in a 3,000-word statement adopted at a meeting in Rumania this month of the Cominform, a meeting at which Yugoslav Communists, among the Cominform's founders, were not represented. The statement was published here today. According to the statement, the Yugoslav Communist leaders had placed themselves outside the Cominform ranks.

Marshal Tito and his top aides were accused of retreating from Marxism-Leninism by "undertaking an entirely wrong policy on the principal question of foreign and internal politics."

Confidence in Party Expressed

The statement called for "either a true return to Marxist policy or a change of Communist leaders in Yugoslavia."

One section of the declaration indicated that Marshal Tito and his chiefs might get a chance to change their ways before final action was taken. It said:

"The aim of * * * sound elements of the Communist party of Yugoslavia is to force their present leaders to confess openly and honestly their faults and correct them; to part from nationalism, to return to internationalism and in every way to fix the united Socialist front against imperialism; or, if the present leaders of the Communist party of Yugoslavia prove unable to do this task, to change them and to raise from below a new internationalistic leadership of the Communist party of Yugoslavia. The Information Bureau does not doubt that the Communist party can fulfill this task."

Kardelj Among Four Named

Singled out for criticism were Marshal Tito, Vice Premier Edvard Kardelj, a founder of the Cominform; Milovan Djilas, Minister for Montenegro, a Yugoslav state, and Col. Gen. Alexander Rankovitch, who as Minister of the Interior has bossed Yugoslavia's police force.

There was speculation that such a blast would have been issued only after specific action had been taken against Marshal Tito, but there was no confirmation of this. Dispatches from Belgrade said Marshal Tito was believed to be at his summer home in Bled.

Col. Gen. Andrei A. Zhdanov, a member of the Soviet Union Communist Politburo and often rated one of the three most powerful men in Russia, attended the Cominform meeting and signed its official statement. As published in Rude Pravo, official newspaper of the Czechoslovak Communist party, the statement said that the Yugoslav Communist leaders had "created a hateful policy in relation to the Soviet Union and to the All-Communist Union of Bolsheviks."

An "undignified policy of underestimating Soviet military specialists was allowed" by the Yugoslavs and members of the Russian Army were discredited by them, it said.

Russian "private specialists" in Yugoslavia were put under guard of the organs of state security and were watched, the statement added. It said that the Soviet Union's delegate to the Cominform in Belgrade also had been under surveillance.

The Cominform contended that a slander propaganda campaign "borrowed from the arsenal of counter-revolutionary Trotskyism" had been conducted against Russia. This campaign, it said, pictured Russia as "degenerate."

"All these facts," the statement said, "prove that the leading persons in the Communist party of Yugoslavia took a standpoint unworthy of Communists."

In wooing Western states, Yugoslavia's leaders, according to the declaration, strove toward a capitalist ideology. The statement said:

"Yugoslav leaders, orienting themselves badly in the international situation and frightened by extortionate threats of the imperialists, think that by a series of concessions to imperialistic states they can gain the favor of these states to make an agreement with them about the independence of Yugoslavia and gradually to implant in the Yugoslav people the orientation of these states; that is, an orientation of capitalism."

The statement said that the accused Yugoslavs had begun to identify Russia's foreign policy "with that of the imperialistic powers" and to treat Russia "in the same manner as they treat the bourgeois states."

Inside Yugoslavia, the statement went on, Communist leaders "are retreating from positions of the working class and are parting from the Marxist theory of class war." The declaration said "capitalist elements in their country are growing," and added:

"The Cominform believes that the present leadership of the Yugoslav Communist party is revising the Marxist-Lenin theory of the Communist party. Whereas this theory says that the Communist party stands for the leading and guarding strength in a country, in Yugoslavia the People's Front, not the Communist party, is considered the main, principal strength. This means devaluating the Communist party."

The statement condemned the "purging and arresting" of two Yugoslav Communists "because they had dared to criticize the anti-Soviet conceptions of the leaders and to express themselves for the friendship of Yugoslavia with the Soviet Union."

Sreten Zujovitch was dismissed last month as Finance Minister and Andrija Hebrang as Minister of Light Industry in a Government shake-up.

According to the statement, Yugoslav delegates "refused to defend their actions before the Cominform and to listen to criticism and reproaches from other Communist parties." It went on: "This may be considered as a violation of equality among Communist parties and as calling for creation of a privileged attitude of the Yugoslav Communist party in the Cominform."

The Cominform was set up by Russia and eight other Eastern European nations last year. Its headquarters is in Belgrade.

Marshal Tito long has been regarded as one of the staunchest leaders of communism outside the Soviet Union. He catapulted to the head of Yugoslavia's Government from command of that country's wartime partisans. He has had many conferences in the Kremlin. His Government once was described by Senator Styles Bridges of New Hampshire as "a Red puppet dancing to Joe Stalin's tune."

* * *

August 18, 1948

ALGER HISS ADMITS KNOWING CHAMBERS; MEET FACE TO FACE

Ex-Official States He Knew Spy Accuser in 1934 and 1935 as 'George Crosley'

IN CONFRONTATION HERE

He Again Denies All Charges—Thomas Accuses Truman of Trying to Conceal Data

By C. P. TRUSSELL
Special to The New York Times.

WASHINGTON, Aug. 17—Alger Hiss, former State Department official and now president of the Carnegie Foundation for International Peace, admitted today, according to Representative Richard M. Nixon, that he knew the man who has accused him of being a leader in a pre-war Communist "underground" in Washington, but knew him as "George Crosley."

The accuser is Whittaker Chambers, a senior editor of Time magazine, who faced Mr. Hiss this afternoon in a room at the Commodore Hotel in New York. It was the first time the two had been brought face to face since Mr. Chambers, on Aug. 3, told the House Committee on Un-American Activities that there had been such a Communist group, the purpose of which was to put at key posts in the Government either Communists or fellow travelers.

Up to this afternoon's meeting, details of which were given by telephone tonight by Representative Nixon, California Republican, who is a committee member, Mr. Hiss had denied that he ever had known Mr. Chambers, by that name or as "Carl," the pseudonym which Mr. Chambers said he employed while active as a courier for the Communist ring in 1934 and 1935. Mr. Chambers, according to Mr. Nixon, said he did not recall having used the name "George Crosley."

[According to the Associated Press, Mr. Nixon said that Mr. Hiss denied again all the accusations Mr. Chambers made against him in the committee's open hearings.]

Did Not Identify Photograph

In the face of declarations by Mr. Chambers that he had known Mr. Hiss so well that when he quit the Communist party in 1937, he went to the home of Mr. Hiss in Georgetown (an old residential section of Washington) and implored him to "break loose" from the Communist crowd, Mr. Hiss had also testified that he could not identify a photograph of Mr. Chambers taken when he was on the witness stand.

"Leaks" from secret closed sessions of the committee while Mr. Hiss and Mr. Chambers were under earlier questioning had it that Mr. Chambers described furniture, paintings on the walls and other objects of the Hiss home.

Until today's face-to-face meeting the diametrically conflicting stories of Mr. Hiss and Mr. Chambers had prompted the committee even to think of resorting to a "lie detector." Mr. Chambers was reported to be willing to take such a test.

Yesterday, when Mr. Hiss was brought to Washington for another checking of his testimony against what Mr. Chambers had said at a closed session of inquiry in New York last week, he was admittedly asked whether he would submit to a "lie detector" examination.

The initial reaction of Mr. Hiss, it was reported later, was that such an instrument might record emotional stress rather than making a true measurement of veracity. He was reported to have promised to give his decision tomorrow on whether he would submit to such a test.

Presses for a Showdown

The committee did not wait. As emphasized by Mr. Nixon, there remained a question of whether there might have been, in Mr. Hiss's insistent declarations that he had never known or even seen Mr. Chambers, a case of mistaken identity.

It was concluded that the only way this gap between sworn declaration and fact could be closed was to have the men face each other.

Mr. Nixon stated that Mr. Hiss in stating that he recognized Mr. Chambers as a man he had known as "George Crosley," said that his acquaintance with him was in 1934 and 1935.

"These developments," Mr. Nixon declared, "make it all the more necessary that public hearings of the committee pursue these leads."

Public hearings of the House Committee were suspended officially today until Sept. 7. But Aug. 25 had been set yesterday as a "day of confrontation" for Mr. Hiss and Mr. Chambers when they would appear before the committee under oath with each in jeopardy of possible perjury fines up to $10,000 and/or long imprisonment.

The secret trip to New York was made today by Representative J. Parnell Thomas, committee chairman, and two other members, Mr. Nixon and Representative John McDowell, Republican, of Pennsylvania. Accompanying them were Robert E. Stripling, chief investigator for the committee, and a battery of five other investigators.

The trip followed a charge by Mr. Thomas that President Truman had attempted to "conceal" information concerning Communist espionage within the Federal Government.

Mr. Thomas charged also that noncooperation by the Executive branch had obstructed his committee's efforts to "learn the truth" about the spy rings cited at recent hearings, but that the investigation would be pressed forward regardless.

When its public hearings resume next month, the chairman declared, the committee would "bring into full focus the operations of still another espionage ring which secured some of our most vital information."

"This question of communism and all of its ramifications against the Government and the people cannot be dismissed by 'red herring' charges, even if they come from the President of the United States," Mr. Thomas added.

His assertions were in a formal statement which he read to reporters at the close of an executive meeting of the committee.

As this meeting was in progress the controversy between the Senate (Ferguson) investigating sub-committee and Attorney General Tom C. Clark, also over a withholding of Government records from Congressional investigation, grew more intense.

The Attorney General, in a letter to Senator Ferguson Sunday, said that the Congressional hearings were detrimental to the efforts of the Department of Justice to obtain a sound basis for espionage prosecutions.

Senator Ferguson countered, in new correspondence today, that the Justice Department had approved the hearings before they started.

This evening, in a continuation of this exchange, Mr. Clark denied that such approval had been given and termed Senator Ferguson's latest letter "inaccurate" at various points.

Other developments today included these:

The House committee, learning of the sudden death in New Hampshire yesterday of Harry Dexter White, who had been accused in spy ring testimony of having provided information that was forwarded to Russia, said its plans for future investigation would not be changed "in the slightest degree."

In appearing voluntarily Friday to pronounce "unqualifiedly false" the charges against him, Mr. White had advised the committee in a note to the chairman that he had had a heart attack and requested a recess after each hour of questioning.

As a result of the "leaks" from the committee there was a threat by an irate member to force it to "investigate itself." This member, who sought to remain anonymous for the present, alleged that "someone," on the committee or on its staff, had violated "an oath of secrecy."

In the latest exchange between the Attorney General and Senator Ferguson, Senator Ferguson contended that such care had been taken in avoiding conflict with Justice Department investigations that no action had been taken by the committee until after the New York grand jury had returned its indictments against twelve top leaders of the American Communist party.

The committee was concentrating on how William W. Remington, a Commerce Department official, had been able to hold three key posts in the Government service while he was under investigation as an accused provider of secret information being sent to Russia.

Senator Ferguson asserted that the only information his committee wanted from the Government files was straight-out employment records as they were made out for Mr. Remington and others.

He asked that the Attorney General reconsider his continued refusals to turn over these records. He suggested that he and Mr. Clark "sit down" together and explore the situation. Mr. Clark replied:

"You may be sure I will be glad to 'sit down' with you, as your letter suggests, and explore this or any other question, with a view to assuring that the future handling of this situation will promote the national interest."

States Basis of Identification

Mr. Hiss said last night at a press conference here that he had identified Mr. Chambers as a man he had known as George Crosley solely on the basis of testimony given by Mr. Chambers.

"As far as I am concerned, he is Crosley," he added, "and I told the committee so."

In reply to questions, Mr. Hiss repeated emphatically his denials that he was or ever had been a Communist. He added that he was not sympathetic in any way toward communism.

The press conference was held in the apartment of Mr. Hiss at 22 East Eighth Street.

Mr. Hiss declared that he did not desire to engage in any public controversy with the committee. He remarked, however, that there seemed to be "something funny" about its action in "moving up" from Aug. 25 the session at which he and Mr. Chambers were to confront each other.

Mr. Hiss also remarked that after yesterday's session he had "noted the conjunction of time" between the summons to him to face Mr. Chambers and the death of Harry Dexter White, another key figure in the committee's inquiry.

It was after reading accounts of secret testimony given by Mr. Chambers before the committee, he asserted, that he thought of the person he had known fifteen years ago as George Crosley. The Chambers testimony, he added, revealed a wide knowledge of an apartment Mr. Hiss had occupied in Washington and of his personal affairs.

Mr. Hiss said he had known Mr. Crosley as a free-lance journalist who came to him in search of material for articles when he was counsel to the Senate Munitions Committee. He arranged, he stated, for Mr. Crosley to sublet his Washington apartment for the summer, he having bought a house in Georgetown, and also gave him an old automobile, since he had bought a new one. Later he saw Mr. Crosley, he said, but never received any of the rent.

"Crosley never paid one cent on the apartment," Mr. Hiss declared, "and in addition to that he touched me for $30 or $40. Furthermore, I never saw any of the articles."

Observing that the loan was not repaid, Mr. Hiss asserted that he had regarded the free-lance writer as a "dead-beat."

Mr. Chambers denied yesterday, Mr. Hiss asserted, that he ever had been known to him as Crosley, and when asked by how he had come to live in the apartment, replied:

"Alger, we were both Communists."

* * *

October 9, 1948

BRITON WARNS U. S.

Declares Weapon Alone Lies Between Freedom and Red Domination

HINTS NEED OF SHOWDOWN

Sees No Hope for a Russian Shift— Fears 'Remorselessly Approaching' 3d War

By HERBERT L. MATTHEWS
Special to The New York Times.

LLANDUDNO, Wales, Oct. 9—In the strongest speech he has made since the end of World War II Winston Churchill today urged the United States not to destroy its atom bomb stocks and warned the Western World that only those bombs stood between freedom and Communist domination.

The Conservative party leader and wartime Prime Minister rose to a towering and fervent spate of eloquence in expressing his conviction that there was no hope that the Soviet rulers would change their policies and that the only possibility of peace lay in strength.

Mr. Churchill has never made a speech of more dire prophecy on "what seems to be a remorselessly approaching third world war." The use of that phrase followed his regretful opinion that the United Nations had "been reduced to a mere cockpit in which the representatives of mighty nations and ancient states hurl reproaches, taunts and recriminations at one another."

He hinted that the Western powers should use the advantage given to them by their unique possession of the atomic bomb "to bring matters to a head and make a final settlement."

"The Western nations will be far more likely to reach a lasting settlement without bloodshed if they formulate their just demands while they have the atomic power and before the Russian Communists have got it, too," he said.

Although he called upon the Western nations to "act," nowhere did he indicate that he was thinking in terms of a preventive war.

"The old pilot," as someone called him a few days ago, brought the hitherto somnolent annual conference of the Conservative party in this Welsh seaside resort to an end this afternoon in a blaze of excitement for everyone knew that these were words that would echo around the world and they believed that the Americans would pay more heed to Mr. Churchill than to Foreign Secretary Bevin.

This was Mr. Churchill's first speech since before the Berlin negotiations broke down and today he spoke his mind on that issue too. He saw it as "a situation which may at any time precipitate a hideous world struggle" and added that if he had been responsible it would never have developed in that way.

Deplores Troop Withdrawal

Mr. Churchill declared that the gulf that was opening between Asiatic Communist Russia and the Western democracies, large and small, was already brutally obvious to the victorious British War Cabinet of the national coalition even before Hitler destroyed himself and the Germans laid down their arms.

The British and American Governments should not have withdrawn their forces so quickly from Germany, he asserted. Hinting at an apparent disagreement with President Roosevelt, Mr. Churchill said it would have been wiser for the British armies to take Berlin and for the United States armies to enter Prague, as, he said, they could have done.

Now, said Mr. Churchill, no one must be encouraged by false hopes or formulas because "the fundamental danger and antagonisms will still remain."

He stressed that the Kremlin leaders particularly "dread the friendship of the free civilized world as much as they would its hostility" since it would mean the end of their power and goals.

"Therefore," said Mr. Churchill, in what was to prove one of the key passages of his speech, "while patience should always be practiced to the utmost limits which our safety allows, we should not delude ourselves with the vain expectation of a change of heart in the ruling forces of Communist Russia.

"Neither should we be under any delusion about the foundations of peace. It is my belief, and I say it with deep sorrow, that at the present time the only sure foundation of peace and of the prevention of actual war rests upon strength.

Bomb As Peace Guarantee

"If it were not for the stocks of atomic bombs now in the trusteeship of the United States there would be no means of stopping the subjugation of Western Europe by Communist machinations, backed by Russian armies and enforced by political police * * *.

"I hope that the Western nations, and particularly our own country and the United States, will not fall into the same deadly trap twice over.

"Of one thing I am quite sure; that if the United States were to consent, in reliance upon any paper agreement, to destroy the stocks of atomic bombs which they have accumulated they would be guilty of murdering human freedom and committing suicide themselves.

"I hope you will give full consideration to my words. I have not always been wrong."

These words were constantly interrupted by great applause.

In discussing Berlin, Mr. Churchill won applause by saying that the Conservatives would support the Labor Government "in not being bullied, bulldozed and black-mailed out of Berlin, whatever the consequences may be."

While also calling for support of the Government's rearmament and recruiting campaigns, Mr. Churchill said:

"I have no confidence in the military arrangements and preparations of the Socialist Government or in the men who now come forward to lead national movement."

This, after all, was a speech to a party convention, and while Mr. Churchill is a dominating world figure whose words today were broadcast throughout the United States, he is also a party leader. Hence much of his speech was directed toward stirring his followers to work for the party's return to power in the general elections of 1950.

As a plea to Wales, for instance, which has only a few Conservative M.P.'s and generally is solidly Labor and Liberal, Mr. Churchill pledged the Conservatives to make provision for a Cabinet Minister especially responsible for Wales.

He asserted that the conservatives "represent today, without doubt or question, a considerable majority of the British electorate." This confidence in victory in 1950 has indeed dominated the annual conference that ended today.

*   *   *

November 4, 1948

TRUMAN WINS WITH 304 ELECTORAL VOTES; DEMOCRATS CONTROL SENATE AND HOUSE; EUROPE SEES FOREIGN POLICY CONTINUING

OHIO POLL DECIDES

It Clinches for President in Race Called Miracle of Electioneering

NO RECORD BALLOT IS SEEN

Dedicating Himself to Peace, Prosperity, Truman Says He Wants to Deserve Honor

By ARTHUR KROCK

The State of Ohio, "mother of Republican Presidents," furnished the electoral bloc early yesterday forenoon which assured to President Harry S. Truman a four-year term in his own right as Chief Executive of the United States. Until this late accounting of votes cast in Tuesday's general election put Ohio firmly in Mr. Truman's column, after it had fluctuated throughout the night, he was certain of but 254 electoral votes, which were twelve less than the 266 required.

The historic role played by Ohio was only one of the dramatic and extraordinary phases of the election of 1948. The President, opposed by the extreme right and left wings of the Democratic party, won a minimum of 304 electoral votes as against 189 acquired by his Republican opponent, Gov. Thomas E. Dewey of New York; carried a Democratic majority in Congress along with him after the Republicans had held this for two years; and gained victory through a multi-sectional combination of states that did not include New York, New Jersey, Pennsylvania and four of the Southern states in normal Democratic territory.

Miracle of Electioneering Seen

In the political history of the United States this achievement by Mr. Truman will be set down as a miracle of electioneering for which there are few if any parallels. His victory made him the undisputed national leader of the Democratic party, which,

though bitterly divided for the past few years, has acknowledged none since the death of Franklin D. Roosevelt, whom Mr. Truman succeeded from the office of Vice President.

When it was assured that he would have Ohio's electors and hence the majority he needed, and Governor Dewey had wired his congratulations and publicly conceded defeat, the President dedicated his official future to world peace and domestic prosperity and said to his brother, J. Vivian Truman, simply: "I just want to deserve the honor."

No Record Vote Indicated

In the result, unexpected by nearly everyone who qualified as a judge of elections except the President himself, there were these other attendant circumstances:

1. The popular vote, expected to reach 51,000,000 or 52,000,000 and thus break the record poll of about 49,548,000 in the Presidential contest of 1940, will probably be far short of the 1940 total.

2. It is possible that Mr. Truman's plurality over Mr. Dewey will not exceed 2,000,000 and may be less than that, which is smaller than the electoral division of 304 to 189 would ordinarily indicate. But this can be partly attributed to the fact that two splinter Democratic tickets were in the field—the States' Rights Democratic headed by Gov. J. Strom Thurmond of South Carolina, and the Progressives headed by Henry A. Wallace, which will poll almost 2,000,000 votes more than probably would have gone in large measure to the national Democratic ticket in normal circumstances.

3. To the vote cast for Mr. Wallace can be traced definitely the failure of the President to carry only one state, New York, with forty-seven electors.

4. California, after see-sawing all Tuesday night and yesterday morning as in 1916, and as Ohio did this year, ended in the Truman column as it did in Woodrow Wilson's contest with Charles E. Hughes thirty-two years ago. But then California made the drama of victory for Wilson: this year Ohio had taken the laurels by an hour or two.

5. The winning combination of states for Mr. Truman bore some resemblance to Wilson's in 1916, but there were notable exceptions, such as Iowa and Illinois which the President carried Tuesday in his group of twenty-eight states. His popular and electoral majority differed from Wilson's also in that it was supplied by an unusual combination of large popular blocks with grievances against the Republican Eightieth Congress which the President had accentuated—such as union labor—contented farmers in normal Republican territory who like the current price levels and did not want to take a chance on a new regime in which they might decline, and urban consumers who, though disturbed over prices, were more disturbed over emotional issues like "civil rights" and Palestine.

6. In the wake of the President's attacks on the record of the Eightieth Congress, centering on tax reduction and the Taft-Hartley Act, a minimum of 258 Democrats were returned to the House of Representatives (the last one had 185) and a minimum of fifty-four to the Senate which, when

it recessed, contained only forty-five. The Republicans in the House exchanged 243 for 167 with more losses in sight, and, in the Senate, forty-two members for fifty-one. The fly in this ointment, however, is that under the Democratic label in Congress are two bitterly divided wings of the party which has been unable to cooperate very often for years.

Missouri Maintains Record

7. Missouri, Mr. Truman's home state, maintained the record it has had since 1994 of being on the winning side of every Presidential contest. But Maryland, which had a much longer lien on that record, lost it Tuesday by giving its electors to Governor Dewey.

8. For the first time since the death of President Roosevelt, the United States will have a Vice President and the Senate a President in the person of Alben W. Barkley, now a member of the Senate from Kentucky, the present minority and former majority leader. And Representative Sam Rayburn of Texas will be restored to the Speaker's dais in the Eighty-first Congress.

9. More than fifty members of Congress who helped to make the Taft-Hartley Act into law over Mr. Truman's veto were defeated for re-election. This will likely be reflected in the President's labor legislative policy which he will doubtless present to the Eighty-first Congress.

10. In contests for Governor, Democrats defeated Republican incumbents in eight States, were ejected in one and may be in another—Washington—a net gain of six or seven. The major parties each had twenty-four Governors on election day.

Truman Carries 28 States

The President's victory was so complete and so surprising to almost everyone except himself that analyses of the reasons will recur for years and began yesterday as soon as Ohio's decision was known. But, assuming that California will stay in his column, it was enough for his opponents temporarily to realize that Mr. Truman carried twenty-eight states, in addition to the other victories to which he led his party, and Mr. Dewey sixteen, as follows:

Truman—Arizona, Arkansas, California, Colorado, Florida, Georgia, Idaho, Illinois, Iowa, Kentucky, Massachusetts, Minnesota, Missouri, Montana, Nevada, New Mexico, North Carolina, Ohio, Oklahoma, Rhode Island, Tennessee, Texas, Utah, Virginia, Washington, West Virginia, Wisconsin, Wyoming.

Dewey—Connecticut, Delaware, Indiana, Kansas, Maine, Maryland, Michigan, Nebraska, New Hampshire, New Jersey, New York, North Dakota, Oregon, Pennsylvania, South Dakota, Vermont.

Mr. Wallace carried no state. Governor Thurmond got the 38 electors of Alabama, Louisiana, Mississippi and South Carolina, while 2 of Tennessee's 12 electoral votes are pledged to him, but are in dispute.

It was plain from the above division that the inter-sectional combination of voting groups effected by President Roosevelt after 1932 and held by him in sufficient numbers to maintain victory through the election of 1944 has been renewed as a national majority by Mr. Truman, for the time being at any rate. This pattern was not many minutes old when Governor Dewey, summoning a press conference, said that he would never again seek the Presidency. It was his third try—twice as the Republican nominee (1944 and 1948) and once (1940) as an unsuccessful candidate for the nomination.

During the long hours of Tuesday night and yesterday morning, when it seemed possible that the Presidential contest might be carried into the next House of Representatives, many persons were deeply disturbed over the possible effects of this on the international situation and the pressing problems of the domestic economy that underlie it. But, with the decision of Ohio and California, and the establishment of the new complexion of Congress, these fears subsided in a feeling that the continuity of the American Government was one of the most definite results of the general election of 1948.

* * *

December 16, 1948

HISS INDICTED FOR PERJURY IN COMMUNIST SPY INQUIRY; NEW JURY TO MEET TODAY

TWO COUNTS IN BILL

Turning Over of State Papers to Spy Courier in 1938 Is Alleged

HEARINGS TO BE CONTINUED

Conviction Could Mean Ten Years in Prison— Accused Persists in Denial

By RUSSELL PORTER

Alger Hiss, former State Department official, was indicted by a Federal grand jury yesterday on two counts of perjury.

The grand jury charged that Mr. Hiss lied when he testified before it that neither he nor his wife ever turned over any State Department documents to Whittaker Chambers, self-styled courier for a Communist spy ring, and that he never saw Mr. Chambers after Jan. 1, 1937.

After examining the evidence presented to it, the grand jury held that Mr. Hiss saw Mr. Chambers in February and March, 1938, and turned over to him "secret, confidential and restricted" documents and other papers in violation of Federal law.

Mr. Hiss denied last night that he had committed perjury. In a statement issued through the office of his lawyer, Edward C. McLean, the defendant said:

"My testimony before the grand jury was entirely truthful."

Arraignment Today Probable

United States Attorney John F. X. McGohey told reporters that Mr. Hiss would be notified through his attorney to appear in Federal court for arraignment, probably this morning.

If convicted, Mr. Hiss would be subject to penalties of five years in prison and $2,000 fine on each of the two counts in the indictment.

The indictment was handed up to Federal Judge John W. Clancy by the same special grand jury that recently indicted twelve American Communist leaders on charges of conspiracy to "teach and advocate" the forcible overthrow of the United States Government.

This grand jury has been sitting for eighteen months and yesterday was the last day of its existence. It was recalled two weeks ago to investigate new charges made by Mr. Chambers in defending himself against a $75,000 libel suit brought by Mr. Hiss.

Mr. Chambers original charges against Mr. Hiss before the House Committee on Un-American Activities did not charge espionage, but alleged that Mr. Hiss and his brother, Donald, also a former State Department official, were members of a pre-war Communist underground "apparatus" in Washington.

Papers Shown in Libel Case

After Mr. Chambers repeated his charges on the radio without Congressional privilege and was sued for libel, he produced in a Baltimore court a number of documents to support his charges. Then he turned over to House Committee investigators a number of microfilm copies of additional documents, which he took from a hollowed-out pumpkin on his farm near Baltimore the night of Dec. 2.

Mr. Chambers then charged that Mr. Hiss had turned over to him at various times, particularly in early 1938, various State Department documents for transmission to a Soviet spy ring.

The grand jury met nine days in the last two weeks on the new Chambers revelations. Among the witnesses were Mr. Chambers, Mr. Hiss, his wife, Priscilla, his brother Donald, and several other persons named by Mr. Chambers. Mr. Chambers and Mr. Hiss have been before the Grand Jury every day.

Yesterday Mr. Hiss and Mr. Chambers left the grand jury room on the fourteenth floor of the Federal Court Building about the same time, shortly before the indictment was handed up. As usual Mr. Chambers slipped down a back stairway to a lower floor to avoid reporters, and Mr. Hiss walked out to the corridor where reporters were waiting.

When Mr. Hiss took an elevator from the fourteenth floor, however, it stopped at the eleventh floor to take on Mr. Chambers. The latter turned his back on Mr. Hiss, and the two rode downstairs without saying a word.

Then, at 5:37 P. M., the grand jury filed out of its room into elevators that took the eighteen members present down to Judge Clancy's court room on the third floor.

Judge Clancy took his seat on the bench at 5:45 o'clock. Thomas J. Denegan, special assistant to the Attorney General, who has been presenting the evidence, announced that the grand jury was ready to make its report.

Jerome Blumauer, acting foreman of the jury, a plastics manufacturer, of 205 West Eighty-eighth Streets then handed up the indictment to Judge Clancey.

Jury's Work Is Praised

Mr. McGohey and Mr. Donegan both commended the grand jury for the amount of time they had devoted to their duties in the last eighteen months.

At the suggestion of one of the jurors, Mr. Donegan read a statement from the jury that it had been unable to complete its investigation of all the matters that had come before it, and that unfinished matters would receive the attention of a successor grand jury that will be impaneled today.

Judge Clancy then discharged the grand jury with the thanks of the court, saying that in recognition of its unusually arduous work its members would be released from grand jury duty for the next five years if they wished.

Copies of the indictment were made public by Mr. McGohey after court adjourned. Mr. McGohey pointed out that the indictment showed that Mr. Hiss had made his allegedly false statements under oath at yesterday's session of the grand jury. He said the Government had the two witnesses needed to prove its case and would produce them in court when the case was tried.

He declined to say whether the statute of limitations barred prosecution of the alleged abstraction of the documents from State Department files.

Mr. McGohey said the new grand jury would start work right away, continuing the investigation of Communist espionage charges. The new grand jury, he said, will be briefed on the testimony taken by the old one. If necessary, he added, some of the same witnesses who have testified before the old jury will be called before the new one.

A panel of 100 persons from whom the new grand jury will be selected report at 10:30 A. M. today to Judge Clancy. The panel includes business executives, merchants, salesmen, consultants, housewives and authors. Twenty-three members will be selected and sworn in by Judge Clancy.

Kilpatrick on the Panel

John Reed Kilpatrick president of the Madison Square Garden Corporation, and Harry Scherman, book publisher, of the Book of the Month Club, are on the panel.

In addition to the Chambers charges, the new grand jury will look into charges made by Miss Elizabeth T. Bentley, a former Communist agent, before the House committee. Abraham George Silverman, a former Government economist, named by Miss Bentley, was on the grand jury floor yesterday. So was Henry Julian Wadleigh, former Government economist, named by Mr. Chambers.

Mr. Chambers told reporters yesterday that when he talked in 1939 with A. A. Berle Jr., former assistant Secretary of State, he gave Mr. Berle the names of Communist members of the Washington underground "apparatus," and also the name of Col. Boris Bykov, alleged head of one of the Soviet spy rings to whom Mr. Chambers gave information.

He also said he had named a Washington dentist believed to be in active contact with the Soviet spies, a metallurgist with a high laboratory position in the United States Steel Corporation, and a civilian employee of the Aberdeen, Md., proving grounds. He said he had urgently warned Mr. Berle of the need for getting this man out of Aberdeen promptly.

Mr. Berle has said that the information given by Mr. Chambers in 1939 was not as specific as that which he has given this year.

Attorney General Tom Clark said last night that he was "not surprised" at the indictment. Mr. Clark, who was attending a dinner at the Waldorf-Astoria Hotel, predicted Mr. Hiss would be brought to trial some time next month.

He was asked whether the indictment would affect President Truman's characterization of the House committee's investigation as a "red herring."

"I don't think it will alter it," Mr. Clark replied.

In Washington, Representative R. M. Nixon of California, a member of the House committee, said the indictment was a vindication of the committee's activities. He said the committee would continue with the investigation of other leads, including facts given by Mr. Chambers regarding others besides Mr. Hiss.

"Despite criticism from all sources from the President down," said Mr. Nixon, "the indictment establishes beyond doubt the justification for committees of Congress investigating in this field."

* * *

December 16, 1948

THEFT OF NORDEN BOMB SIGHT FOR RUSSIA IN 1938 REPORTED

*House Committee Hears Aberdeen Employe Stole
Formulae—Hiss Case 'Closed,' Group
Presses Widening Espionage Inquiry*

By C. P. TRUSSELL
Special to The New York Times.
WASHINGTON, Dec. 15—Secret mathematical formulae vital to duplication of bomb sights and believed to concern the famed Norden sight were stolen and delivered to Russia in 1938, reports reaching the House Committee on Un-American Activities indicated today as it pursued its spy hunt.

This disclosure came among developments such as follows:

With the indictment by a special Federal grand jury in New York of Alger Hiss, former State Department official, on two counts alleging perjury in the Hiss-Chambers case, the committee set out to run down new leads. Spokesmen said the "Hiss phase" was now closed so far as the committee was concerned.

These spokesmen recalled, however, that Whittaker Chambers, confessed prewar courier for a Communist underground and principal witness against Mr. Hiss, had made accusations that reached to other departments and areas, including the new case of bomb-sight espionage at the Army's testing ground at Aberdeen, Md. They said the committee would continue through all ramifications for spy charges. They contended that the grand jury action thus far had proved the value of Congressional investigations.

Representative Karl E. Mundt, acting committee chairman, observed:

"In conclusion may I express the hope that nobody will ever again refer to this case as a 'red herring.'"

His reference was to an opinion expressed repeatedly by President Truman and stated again at his latest news conference last week.

The House committee reached for a new witness, but missed by a matter of minutes. He had checked out of a Washington hotel shortly before a committee investigator arrived with a subpoena.

There was a possibility that he would be found and questioned tomorrow. It was emphasized that he was not an espionage "suspect," but a man who "was in position" to give valuable information concerning the "elite" pre-war underground for which Mr. Chambers testified he was a courier.

The typewriter on which, according to testimony by Mr. Chambers, many secret State Department documents were copied after temporary removal from files for delivery to Soviet agents, probably has been found. It is believed to be in the hands of the Federal Bureau of Investigation or the New York Grand Jury.

It was asserted in responsible quarters that a finding of the typewriter itself might not be essential to identification of the person or persons who did the actual typing, because of other evidence gathered and presumably delivered to the New York Grand Jury as late as yesterday.

This evidence was described as being "extremely important," perhaps the "most conclusive" in the long controversy between Mr. Hiss and Mr. Chambers. It concerned, it was reported, examination by experts of the type-face of copies of State Department documents which Mr. Chambers swore he had received, compared with other typing from the same machine.

1939 Warning Recalled

A civilian employe of the Aberdeen Proving Ground who is alleged to have released bombsight secrets in 1938 to the Communist underground, for which Mr. Chambers swore he was a courier, was said to be still in the employ of the Government, presently on sick leave. The FBI, committee members said, have his name and address. They added that he was also "within the jurisdiction of the committee" for questioning at any time.

In New York today, according to dispatches, Mr. Chambers told reporters that in 1939 he had told Adolf A. Berle Jr., then Assistant Secretary of State, that removal of a certain civilian employe from the Aberdeen establishment was "an urgent necessity." This, Mr. Chambers said, was about a year after he had broken with the Communist party.

According to information received by committee members, the case involved the Norden bomb-sight which was one of the country's military secrets. From 1931, when a working model astonished military observers, until 1944, the secrecy surrounding it was held to be comparable to that which has surrounded the atomic bomb.

In 1941, in the trial of sixteen accused as Nazi spies in New York, it was alleged by the prosecution that the secrets of the Norden instrument, which some fliers said could put a bomb into a pickle barrel from three miles up, had gone to Germany in 1938.

During World War II there was much controversy as to whether this secret instrument had been lend-leased to the Allies. Until 1944 it was denied officially that anyone but the United States had the secret. In 1946, however, the Navy disclosed that it secretly trained 140 Russian airmen in this country in 1944 under lend-lease, and that 188 Navy patrol bombers, 100 of them equipped with the Norden bomb-sight, were transferred to Russia.

The House committee decided to make public all, except four, of the other documents allegedly pilfered from State Department files and found, ten years later, copied in microfilm in a pumpkin on Mr. Chambers' Maryland farm, or in exhibits produced by him in defense of a $75,000 libel suit filed by Mr. Hiss. The contents of these documents are scheduled to be released, starting with newspapers tomorrow afternoon.

The four to be withheld, according to Mr. Mundt, were considered by the State Department to be even at this late date, dangerous, if published, to national or international interest.

* * *

April 4, 1949

12 NATIONS TO SIGN ATLANTIC ALLIANCE AT CAPITAL TODAY

President Will Be at Ceremony to Hail Policy of Mutual Aid for Western Countries

WORLD BROADCASTS SET

Secretary of State Acheson to Open Historic Assembly of Ministers at 3 P. M.

By JAMES RESTON
Special to The New York Times.

WASHINGTON, April 3—The North Atlantic treaty, ending the military isolation of the United States as the United Nations and the European Recovery Program ended its political and economic isolation, will be signed at the State Department auditorium on Constitution Avenue here tomorrow afternoon.

Secretary of State Acheson, who as an Assistant Secretary and later as Under-Secretary of State helped devise the United Nations, the ERP, and the Truman Doctrine policies, will open the ceremonies at 3 P. M. and sign for the United States.

President Truman will make a short speech at the close of the ceremony, welcoming the policy of mutual assistance among the members of the North Atlantic community.

The Foreign Secretaries and nations signing the treaty, in the order of signature, will be as follows: Paul-Henri Spaak, Belgium; Lester B. Pearson, Canada; Gustav Rasmussen, Denmark; Robert Schuman, France; Bjarni Benediktsson, Iceland; Count Carlo Sforza, Italy; Joseph Bech, Luxembourg; Dr. Dirk U. Stikker, the Netherlands; Halvard M. Lange, Norway; José Caeiro da Matta, Portugal; Ernest Bevin, United Kingdom; and Dean G. Acheson, United States.

Seven Ratifications Required

The ceremonies, including the speeches of the President and the Foreign Ministers, will be broadcast beginning at 2:45 P. M., EST to the nation by all radio and television networks and to the world in forty-three languages in the largest arrangement of shortwave facilities ever assembled.

The terms of the pact will be presented to the United States Senate as a treaty soon after it is signed by the various Governments. It will not be ratified by the President until two-thirds of those present and voting in the Senate approve its terms, and it will not come into force until ratifications have been deposited here by seven nations, the United States, Britain, Canada, France, the Netherlands, Belgium and Luxembourg.

For Canada, Denmark, Norway, and Iceland, this will be the first multilateral mutual assistance treaty in peacetime. The United States made a brief treaty of alliance with France late in the eighteenth century, a commitment to defend Panama early in this century, and, in 1947, a mutual assistance engagement with the other nations of the Western Hemisphere.

But even for Britain, France, and the other members of the Brussels alliance, this intercontinental treaty is unprecedented in scope.

Though no immediate commitment will be involved by tomorrow's signature, the treaty, when properly ratified, will commit its signatories to consider an armed attack on one of them as an armed attack on all. And in consequence of this commitment each signatory will agree, under its own constitutional processes, to take forthwith "such action as it deems necessary, including the use of armed force, to restore and maintain the security of the North Atlantic area."

There has been not the slightest tendency on the part of any of the nations that will sign the pact tomorrow to hesitate as a result of the opposition of the Soviet Union to the pact.

The Foreign Ministers held a final meeting on Saturday to take a last look at the text. One delegation had a question about the punctuation of the treaty, and the Portuguese Foreign Minister raised a technical question about the relationship between the pact and Portugal's defensive understanding with Franco Spain.

This point was passed, however, without implying any connection whatsoever between Generalissimo Franco and the pact, and no other questions about the text were raised.

For the first time since the negotiations on this pact started late last summer, there was some talk on Capitol Hill tonight about the possibility of a reservation being written into the treaty by the United States Senate.

Though Secretary Acheson has stated specifically that ratification of the pact by the United States does not bind this country to supply arms to other members of the alliance, several influential members of the Senate believe that this point should be expressly stated in a written reservation appended to the Senate's consent to ratification.

Such a reservation would not be an expression of the Senate's opposition to such an arms program, but its sponsors want to emphazise that the United States is not, by signing the treaty, promising to deliver arms. The view of the State Department is that such a reservation is unnecessary.

The Truman Administration plans a limited arms program (between $1,000,000,000 and $1,800,000,000), which will be sent to Congress for the consideration and majority approval of both Houses. This program, which will also include all other military assistance programs in which the United States is involved, will be before the Senate when the North Atlantic treaty comes up for detailed study.

* * *

June 17, 1949

TRUMAN DECLARES HYSTERIA OVER REDS SWEEPS THE NATION

Situation Brought About by Spy Trials and Loyalty Inquiries Similar to Others in Past

CITES 1790S' SEDITION ACT

Excitement Will Die as It Has Before, He Holds— Judges College Stir Unwarranted

By ANTHONY LEVIERO
Special to The New York Times.

WASHINGTON, June 16—This country is experiencing a wave of hysteria as a result of current spy trials and loyalty inquiries, President Truman suggested today, but he asserted emphatically that we were not going to hell.

The President likened the current situation created by the conflict with communism to the troubled atmosphere engendered in the early days of the Republic by the alien and sedition laws. He also recalled what he characterized as the crazy activities of the Ku Klux Klan after World War I, and said that every great crisis brought a period of public hysteria.

The present feeling would subside as similar situations had died out after past periods of stress, Mr. Truman contended.

The Chief Executive did express confidence, however, that the hysteria had no part of his Executive Department in its grip. He gave assurance that if this ever happened he would root it out.

The country had not gone to hell in the Washington-Adams-Jefferson era and it would not now, President Truman asserted.

The views of the Chief Executive were elicited during his weekly news conference which today took longer than usual as correspondents tried to inquire into the whole wide range of the espionage-loyalty field.

Noteworthy in the long discussion was the coolness the President indicated toward J. Edgar Hoover, who for many years has been the director of the Federal Bureau of Investigation.

For instance, when he was asked whether Mr. Hoover had his confidence, the President replied obliquely that Mr. Hoover had done a good job. He denied, however, that the FBI chief had submitted his resignation.

In summary form, some other views expressed by Mr. Truman were:

No comment to a suggestion that an inquiry on the scale of the Roberts Pearl Harbor investigation be made of the FBI and its practices.

Contempt for an investigation of school textbooks undertaken by the House Committee on Un-American Activities.

President's Views Implied

While he has withheld confidential loyalty reports from Congressional committees, Mr. Truman said he would not attempt to do this with the judiciary where, as in the Judith Coplon spy case, the requirement was a fair trial.

The President's views were mostly implied rather than explicit. That was because they were not voluntary declarative statements but answers to questions. His meaning was none the less clear. In the detailed report that follows, the questions are given verbatim and in the order in which they occurred, while the President's answers are given indirectly, as required by White House rules.

The discussion was started by Frederic W. Collins of The Providence Journal with this question:

"Mr. President, my paper has suggested editorially that you appoint a special commission, something like the Roberts Pearl Harbor committee, to make a thorough inquiry into FBI practices and to make a report to you not for publication—a quiet, closed study of the FBI."

Did you ever hear of anything like that in Washington, the President answered, laughing. The allusion to the fanfare of inquiries on Capitol Hill was obvious.

"Do you think such a study might be valuable?" came back Mr. Collins.

No comment, replied Mr. Truman.

Questions on other topics followed and then came this one:

"The House Un-American Activities Committee has suggested that schools and colleges send in a list of their school books, and California University has asked for an oath from its faculty. Do you see in these developments any threat to educational freedom in this country?"

Mr. Truman said he thought the question was pretty well answered in a cartoon in the Washington Post this morning. The cartoon by Herbert L. Block ridiculed the inquiry.

"Mr. President, an awful lot of fine people are being branded as Communists, Reds, subversives and what not these days at any number of trials, hearings, the situation in the Army and things of that sort. Do you have any word of counsel you could give on this rash of branding people?"

Yes, yes, he had given it once before, said Mr. Truman. He suggested that the reporters read the history of the Alien and Sedition Acts in the Seventeen Nineties, under almost exactly the same situation. They would be surprised at how parallel the cases are when they had read how they came out.

Questions on two other topics ensued as newsmen went after their particular stories and then came this follow-up question:

"Mr. President, regarding the alien and sedition laws, how can we apply their lesson to the problem of today?"

Just continue to read your history through the Jefferson Administration and you will find out that the hysteria subsided and that the country did not go to hell at all, and it isn't going to now, Mr. Truman replied.

[The Alien and Sedition Acts had their origins in two main causes: The possibility of war with France developed and three Alien Acts were passed by Congress to deal with naturalization, deportation, imprisonment or banishment of aliens. While they were rarely applied they scared many Frenchmen into leaving this country. The Sedition Act was inspired by the violent partisanships of the press of the times. In the face of strong public opinion, the law was used relatively few times by the Federalists against Jeffersonian Republican editors.]

"Mr. President, the first thing Jefferson did was to release eleven newspaper publishers from prison," observed a reporter.

Jefferson made a mistake on that, Mr. Truman said, but not seriously. He laughed. Then he went on to say that Jefferson not only had done that but had released a Federal judge, if he was not mistaken.

"What was that date?"

It began in John Adams' Administration and went over into Jefferson's—it was in the Seventeen Nineties, Seventeen Ninety-sevens and Seventeen Ninety-eights, he thought, said Mr. Truman.

"Do you think hysteria is causing this, and that it is fit for a country that is as strong and powerful as this country?"

Such things happened after every great crisis, after every great war, Mr. Truman replied. It had happened after the first World War, he went on, when the Ku Klux Klan went out to clean up the country. They tried to do crazy things. Out in Indiana they tried to clean up and they made a mess of things.

"Are you confident that no part of your executive branch is gripped by this hysteria?"

He was, and he would clean it out if it were, the Chief Executive said.

"In the case of Gordon Clapp [chairman of the Tennessee Valley Authority characterized as "unemployable" by the Army] you stepped in quickly to straighten that out. Do you intend to step in if an executive is involved in one of these cases?"

Certainly, he always did that, that was not new at all, said Mr. Truman.

"Did J. Edgar Hoover submit his resignation?" He had not, said Mr. Truman.

"Do you confer with Mr. Hoover from time to time?"

He makes reports from time to time and he conferred with him through the Attorney General, the President responded.

"Mr. President, there has been a lot of smoke around Mr. Hoover for the last several days; could you go further and clear that situation up?"

There was nothing for him to clear up, the President said.

"There is no idea that Mr. Hoover has any intention of resigning?"

He had never heard of it, he had just answered that, and he knew nothing about it, Mr. Truman said.

"Does Hoover have your confidence?"

Says Hoover Has Done Good Job

Hoover has done a good job, was the answer.

"You said last week that all these investigations just amounted to a lot of headline hunting."

That was all, Mr. Truman answered before the reporter finished the question with this: "Does that include Hoover?"

You could make your own assay on that situation as well as he could, the President said.

"Is your Administration giving any thought to providing protection to Executive papers?"

Every effort had been made to protect them, the President replied, but it was not the policy of the Executive to interfere with the judiciary when it is trying to give a person a fair trial.

"Would it be helpful if there were a law on the subject?"

That would relieve the executive from having to make a decision, was Mr. Truman's opinion.

"Do you think it might be a good thing to clear out of the files of the FBI all unsubstantiated allegations that persons are Reds, subversives and things like that?"

No comment, Mr. Truman said.

*   *   *

August 6, 1949

U. S. PUTS SOLE BLAME ON CHIANG REGIME FOR COLLAPSE, HOLDS MORE AID FUTILE; ACHESON BIDS REDS AVOID AGGRESSION

WHITE PAPER BLUNT

Stresses That Chinese Nationalists Failed to Utilize Past Help

ACHESON BARS DEFEATISM

Warns Communists to Shun Imperialism From Moscow— Wedemeyer Report Issued

By HAROLD B. HINTON
Special to The New York Times.

WASHINGTON, Aug. 5—The Chinese National Government is on the verge of collapse solely because of the military, political and economic incapacity of the Kuomintang's leaders, the State Department found in a China White Paper made public today.

Secretary of State Dean Acheson, both in transmitting the report to President Truman and in oral comment on the document, rejected the theory that greater aid from the United States could have enabled Generalissimo Chiang Kai-shek and his lieutenants to defeat the Chinese Communists by force.

Mr. Acheson declared in his letter of transmittal to Mr. Truman that if the Chinese Communist regime should lend itself "to the aims of Soviet Russian imperialism and attempt to engage in aggression against China's neighbors, we and the other members of the United Nations would be confronted by a situation violative of the principles of the United Nations Charter and threatening international peace and security."

U. S. Assistance Is Cited

In a prepared statement after release of the White Paper, Mr. Acheson said that the National Government of China "has been unable to rally its people and has been driven out of extensive and important portions of the country, despite very extensive assistance from the United States and advice from eminent American representatives which subsequent events proved to be sound."

The White Paper included the controversial report on China made to President Truman by Lieut. Gen. Albert C. Wedemeyer in 1947. In his report General Wedemeyer recommended that Manchuria be placed under a guardianship or United Nations trusteeship of the United States, China, the Soviet Union, France and Britain, that this country continue economic aid to China under certain controls and that China reform her military establishment and accept supervision of her field forces.

Secretary Acheson said that the voluminous record (more than 1,000 pages) with the official title, "United States Relations with China," had been made public at this time so that the public of the United States could understand fully the background of "the situation in China, which will test to the full our unity of purpose, our ingenuity and our adherence to the basic principles which have, for half a century, governed our policy toward China."

U. S. to Review Policy

The Secretary repeated that a complete review of United States policy in the Far East would be undertaken immediately, with the cooperation of the National Security Council, the National Military Establishment, the Treasury, the Economic Cooperation Administration, the Senate Foreign Relations Committee and the House Foreign Affairs Committee.

Raymond B. Fosdick, former president of the Rockefeller Foundation, who has been retained as a consultant for this review, along with Dr. Everett Case, president of Colgate University, will report to the State Department on Monday to begin the study, Mr. Acheson said. Other outside assistance may be sought, he added, in an effort "to bring to bear the united wisdom and resourcefulness of our Government in meeting the present situation and by future developments in Asia and the Far East."

Pending adoption of a long-range national policy toward that area of the world, Mr. Acheson said in a statement issued at a press conference, the State Department would be guided by the following basic principles, which he considers still valid:

1. Encouragement of the development of China as an independent and stable nation "able to play a role in world affairs suitable for a great and free people."
2. Support of the creation in China of economic and political conditions to safeguard basic rights and liberties, and to progressively develop the economic and social well-being of its people.
3. Opposition to the subjection of China to any foreign power or to a regime acting in the interest of a foreign power, as well as the dismemberment of China by a foreign power, openly or clandestinely.
4. Consultation with other interested powers on measures contributing to the security and welfare of the peoples of the Far East as a whole.
5. Support of efforts by the United Nations to maintain peace and security in the Far East.

Bars Defeatist Attitude

Mr. Acheson described the Chinese Communists as serving the imperialist interests of a foreign power, but conceded they had been able to persuade large numbers of Chinese that they had been acting in their interest. He indicated his belief that they would ultimately fail, saying that he did not "share the defeatist attitude which some current comments reflect."

"The United States, for its part," he said, "will be prepared to work with the people of China and of every other country in Asia to preserve and to promote their true interest, developed as they choose and not as dictated by any foreign imperialism."

Most of the information contained in the White Paper had been communicated in confidence to the Senate Foreign Relations Committee and the House Foreign Affairs Committee by Secretary of State George C. Marshall in February, 1948, Mr. Acheson said.

The bulk of the book is taken up by documents dealing with developments since V-J Day, although there is an introductory chapter giving the highlights of Sino-American relations from 1844 to 1943—from the signature of the Treaty of Wanghai through the open-door policy of Secretary of State John Hay and the support of China against Japanese aggression to the repeal of the Chinese exclusion acts.

As early as Sept. 22, 1944, Gen. Joseph W. Stilwell was complaining to General Marshall, the Chief of Staff, that Generalissimo Chiang believed that the war in the Pacific was nearly over and would be won without great Chinese expenditure of effort.

General Stilwell described the Generalissimo's policy as one of "grabbing for loans and post-war aid, for the purpose of maintaining his present position, based on one-party government, a reactionary policy, or the suppression of democratic ideas with the active aid of his gestapo."

Reports from a number of foreign service officers in the field, before and after General Stilwell's complaint, tended to confirm his estimate of the situation.

Maj. Gen. Patrick J. Hurley arrived in China about this time as President Roosevelt's personal representative, with the rank of ambassador. His mission was to get the National armies and the Communists to unite in fighting against the Japanese, instead of immobilizing large portions of their combat troops to watch each other.

"The defeat of Japan is, of course, the primary objective," he reported in December, "but we should all understand that if an agreement is not reached between the two great military establishments of China, civil war will in all probability ensue."

Hurley Sought Accord

General Hurley undertook, on instruction from President Roosevelt, to act as intermediary between Generalissimo Chiang and the Communist leaders in Yenan, including Mao Tse-tung and Gen. Chou En-lai, who stayed part of the time in Chungking as Communist representative. As fast as he could get one side to agree to a plan for unification, the other would impose new reservations, and he resigned the mission, in the belief it was hopeless, on Nov. 26, 1945.

Meanwhile, a secret agreement had been reached between Premier Stalin, President Roosevelt and Prime Minister Winston Churchill at the Yalta conference in February, 1945. The White Paper devotes a chapter to this meeting, at which Mr. Stalin agreed to throw the Soviet Union into the war against Japan, in return for extensive concessions in Manchuria.

"In general the Russian conditions were conceded," the White Paper comments. "It should be remembered that at this time the atomic bomb was anything but an assured reality; the potentialities of the Japanese Kwantung Army in Manchuria seemed large; and the price in American lives in the military

The New York Times (by George Tames)

Secretary of State Dean Acheson in his office with an open volume of the White Paper.

campaign up the island ladder to the Japanese home islands was assuming ghastly proportions.

"Obviously, military necessity dictated that Russia enter the war against Japan prior to the mounting of Operation Olympic (the planned assault upon Kyushu) roughly scheduled for Nov. 1, 1945, in order to contain Japanese forces in Manchuria and prevent their transfer to the Japanese home islands."

The commentary conceded that it was unfortunate the commitments undertaken in the name of China were not made known to the Chinese Government.

"President Roosevelt and Marshal Stalin, however, based this reticence on the already well known and growing danger of leaks to the Japanese from Chinese sources due to the debilitating and suppurative effects of the war," it is explained. "Here again military exigency was the governing consideration. At no point did President Roosevelt consider that he was compromising vital Chinese interests."

After V-J day, President Truman sent General Marshall to China in another effort to unify the country and avoid civil war. By that time, General Wedemeyer, who had succeeded General Stillwell in command of U. S. forces in the China theater, was reporting that Generalissimo Chiang intended to defeat the Chinese Communists in Manchuria before he consolidated his own position in North China—an operation that General Wedemeyer considered impossible.

General Marshall found China's economic and financial condition becoming rapidly weaker through inflation, administrative inefficiency and corruption, despite the fact the Government came out of the war with official reserves in excess of $400,000,000, with as much held in foreign exchange assets by Chinese citizens.

Cease-Fire Obtained

By January, 1946, he had obtained a cease-fire agreement from both the National armies and the Communist forces, and had sent out field teams to supervise execution of the agreement. Distrust on both sides fanned by breaches of the truce by both sides gradually led to a resumption of active hostilities, and General Marshall was recalled to the United States at the end of 1946 to become Secretary of State in a few weeks.

"There was a point beyond which American mediation could not go," the White Paper says. "Peace and stability in China must, in the final analysis, be achieved by the efforts of the Chinese themselves."

Before he left China, General Marshall recommended that Dr. John Leighton Stuart, president of Yenching University, be named as United States Ambassador to China. Dr. Stuart is now en route to the United States for consultations, after having been detained in Nanking for several weeks by the Chinese Communist forces.

Ambassador Stuart's reports continued to record inability of the National Government to deal with the worsening situation. After Generalissimo Chiang withdrew in favor of Vice President Li Tsung-jen, he reported that the Generalissimo still was interfering in governmental affairs to the embarrassment of his successor.

At home, Secretary Marshall advised President Truman, in the summer of 1947, to send General Wedemeyer on a fact-finding mission to China and Korea. In his final report, the General found his previous estimates of the military incapacity of the National Government's strategists still valid, and recommended that Manchuria be placed under a guardianship or United Nations trusteeship of the Soviet Union, Great Britain, China, France and the United States until the government was strong enough to establish control.

Because of this recommendation, the report was suppressed in Washington. It was considered that a proposal smacking of dismemberment would be fatal to Chinese morale at that period. The report is published for the first time as an annex to the White Paper.

General Wedemeyer recommended, in addition, that United States aid to China be continued, but under certain stipulations. These included political and military reforms, effective use of Chinese resources in a program of economic reconstruction and acceptance of American advisers in military and economic fields to assure that the United States aid was employed effectively.

In the military field, he urged that the National Government reduce its military budget and increase the efficiency of its military establishment through urgently required reforms; that it develop, with United States advice, a sound supply and maintenance program.

Role in Japan Ruled Out

He also recommended that it be permitted to buy military supplies and equipment from the United States; that it obtain ammunition immediately; that it complete quickly its plan for eight and one-third air groups and expanded air transport service; that it drop plans to participate in the occupation of Japan; and that it accept advice and supervision in its field forces, training centers and logistical agencies.

Before leaving China, General Wedemeyer was invited to address on Aug. 22, 1947, a joint meeting of the State Council and the Ministers of the National Government. He was highly critical of the Government and apparently aroused sharp resentment among many of his listeners.

The tragic sequence of events related by the documents in the White Paper concludes on a note consistent with its general theme. A report of April 23, 1949, from the United States Embassy in Nanking is quoted as follows:

"The ridiculously easy Communist crossing of the Yangtze was made possible by defections at key points, disagreements in the high command, and the failure of the air force to give effective support."

* * *

September 23, 1949

YUGOSLAVIA SPLITS WITH SOVIET AT U. N.

Once-Solid Bloc Is Deserted in Russians' Fight on Debate on Human Rights Cases

By A. M. ROSENTHAL

Yugoslavia split publicly yesterday with the once solid Soviet bloc by deserting Russia's fight against United Nations General Assembly debate on the religious trials and human rights cases in Bulgaria, Rumania and Hungary.

[In Belgrade a Yugoslav leader described Soviet foreign policy in a manner regarded as an attempt to inform Governments at the United Nations of the dangers implicit in the Yugoslav-Russian conflict.]

The Yugoslav defection brought with it the Assembly's first open airing of the fight among the one-time partners in the Communist Information Bureau. Belgrade accused its neighbors of having violated treaties—and heard Poland charge Yugoslavia with having lined up on the side of the West.

The Cominform struggle came out during an Assembly session at Flushing Meadow on the adoption of an agenda for the coming months. Despite Russian opposition, the Assembly decided to go ahead with debate on the trials and on other controversies that the Soviet Union wanted to keep off the agenda—the Balkans, Korea and the Little Assembly.

The first agenda item fought by the Soviet group was the one reading "observance in Bulgaria, Hungary and Rumania of human rights and fundamental freedoms." Jan

Drohojowski of Poland said that the General, or steering, Committee already had approved the item but that it was up to the Assembly to upset the actions of that "rubber stamp committee."

Czechoslovakia supported Poland and then Yugoslavia took the floor. The speaker for Belgrade was Dr. Ales Bebler, Deputy Foreign Minister, once a pillar of the Soviet group in the Assembly. He spoke in French, earnestly and briefly.

Dr. Bebler said that the three countries involved were neighbors of Yugoslavia and that at one time his country would in principle have opposed inclusion of the item in the agenda. But he charged that all three had violated treaties to which Yugoslavia was a partner and that therefore he would abstain on the vote.

Manuilsky Is "Amazed"

As soon as Dr. Bebler sat down, Dmitri Z. Manuilsky of the Ukraine walked slowly to the rostrum. He said that the Yugoslav's speech had nothing to do with the issue, that he was "amazed" at it and that it was a mere "camouflage" for an "unfriendly" attitude toward Rumania, Bulgaria and Hungary. On the ballot 38 countries voted for inclusion of the item, 5 against, and Yugoslavia was one of 11 abstaining.

Later Dr. Juliusz Katz-Suchy of Poland commented that the United States and Britain were being aided by some "old and some new" countries, a reference to Yugoslavia.

The Assembly went on to vote overwhelmingly to have full debate on the Balkan situation, the extension of the Interim Committee (Little Assembly), Korea and creation of a United Nations guard force. On these issues, Yugoslavia voted with the Soviet Union, but toward the end of the session Dr. Bebler voted with the majority to defeat a Russian effort to postpone debate on a report of the International Law Commission.

The agenda, as finally approved, contained sixty-eight items. The original list had seventy-three but several were amalgamated. Other proposals were withdrawn, including an Argentine item calling for a conference to revise the United Nations Charter.

The Assembly also approved creation of a special political committee to handle the debate on Korea, the religious trials, the Little Assembly, atomic energy and other items. The regular Political and Security Committee will deal with Palestine, the former Italian colonies, Indonesia and the Balkans.

* * *

September 24, 1949

ATOM BLAST IN RUSSIA DISCLOSED; TRUMAN AGAIN ASKS U. N. CONTROL; VISHINSKY PROPOSES A PEACE PACT

U. S. REACTION FIRM

President Does Not Say Soviet Union Has an Atomic Bomb

PICKS WORDS CAREFULLY

But He Implies Our Absolute Dominance in New Weapons Has Virtually Ended

By ANTHONY LEVIERO
Special to The New York Times.

WASHINGTON, Sept. 23—President Truman announced this morning that an atomic explosion had occurred in Russia within recent weeks. This statement implied that the absolute dominance of the United States in atomic weapons had virtually ended.

"We have evidence that within recent weeks an atomic explosion occurred in the U.S.S.R.," President Truman said.

These words stood out in red-letter vividness in a brief undramatic statement in which the Chief Executive said that the United States always had taken into account the probability that other nations would develop "this new force."

He pleaded once again for adoption of the system of international control of atomic energy promulgated by the United States and supported by the large majority of countries now assembled in the United Nations General Assembly at Flushing Meadow.

McMahon Reveals News

Mr. Truman announced the discovery to the Cabinet, assembled in the White House at 11 A. M. for the usual Friday meeting. Simultaneously on Capitol Hill Senator Brien McMahon, Democrat, of Connecticut, stood before the members of the Joint Congressional Atomic Energy Committee and gave them the news, which Mr. Truman had passed on to him at 3:15 P. M. yesterday.

White House correspondents had their usual conference with Charles C. Ross, the President's secretary, at 10:30 A. M. It was routine, but as they filed out his secretary, Miss Myrtle Bergheim, advised them not to go away. A moment before 11 A. M. Miss Bergheim entered the press room and said: "Press!"

The news men filed into Mr. Ross' office. He said he wished the door closed, and a secret service man took his post there. Then Mr. Ross said that he would pass out an announcement and that nobody was to leave the room until everyone present had a copy. Then he began passing around the President's mimeographed statement.

Tass Correspondent Attends

One of the first reporters to scan his copy exclaimed, "Russia has the atomic bomb!" There was a wild rush through the door and to the telephones in the near-by press room. One of the news men who sprinted out was the correspondent of Tass, the official Soviet news agency.

"The President has just given it to the Cabinet," said Mr. Ross as they went.

Thus the President did not personally appear, and there was no opportunity then or later to put questions to him.

Secretary of Defense Louis Johnson came out of the Cabinet meeting soon afterward. He began shaking his head as the questions came. Reporters literally clutched his arms as he headed for his limousine.

"Have we made any change in the disposition of our forces since this happened?" This question was asked twice.

"No," Mr. Johnson finally said.

"Does the Cabinet know any more about this than is contained in the President's statement?"

"The Cabinet knows all about it," Mr. Johnson replied to this. "It was fully informed."

"Do you have reason to believe this was the first atomic explosion in Russia?" asked another reporter.

This time Mr. Johnson smilingly shook his head, negatively.

"Don't overplay it," returned Mr. Johnson, departing. In the circumstances this parting word was cryptic.

"Privately as well as publicly, high civilian and military officials were calm and reassuring. In no quarter was there any hint of dismay. Tonight the soft-spoken Gen. Omar N. Bradley, chairman of the Joint Chiefs of Staff, expressed the official tone and demeanor in this statement:

"The calmer the American people take this the better. We have anticipated it for four years and it calls for no change in our basic defense plan."

Acheson Mentions 'Weapon'

President Truman did not say that Russia had an atomic bomb. Only Secretary of State Dean Acheson, who was at the United Nations General Assembly in New York, went so far as to say he assumed that a "weapon" had caused the explosion. Other Cabinet members and lower officials neither privately nor publicly would go behind Mr. Truman's phrase—"an atomic explosion occurred"—to indicate precisely what had caused it.

Mr. Truman's use of that phrase was studied and premeditated, it was learned, and led certain officials to suggest that Russia might have been getting to the point of testing a bomb that might be neither so practicable nor so effective as that of the United States. There was also some doubt that Russia had been able to begin stockpiling numbers of the so-called absolute weapon, as the United States has been doing since the explosion over Hiroshima.

Nevertheless it was obvious that the force and the magnitude of the explosion had been comparable to the deadly effect of the United States atomic bombs, else its positive detection and evaluation by this country would not have been possible.

The Russian development, consequently, was bound to have a profound effect, ultimately, on international relations, and particularly on the balance of power between the democracies and Russia and her satellites. It appeared to have reduced this country's absolute dominance in atomic weapons to a relative superiority that would gradually diminish.

Four Years After

Today's announcement from President Truman came a little more than four years after the historic moment on Aug. 6, 1945, when he announced that one atomic bomb had erased one Japanese city.

President Truman, it was understood, will not alter his firm determination that the atomic bomb and its custody must remain in the hands of civilian officials—the Atomic Energy Commission. While the bombs are stored by the commission, it was said that the procedure for their immediate transfer to the military in case of emergency has been carefully worked out.

Congress received the news with demands that the United States should try once more in the United Nations to win approval of the atomic-control plan presented there by Bernard M. Baruch and obstructed by Russia and her allies. Other expressions on Capitol Hill reflected a confidence in the capability of United States military leaders to deal with the problem posed by probable Russian possession of atomic bombs.

Guarded, carefully considered views expressed privately by high, responsible officials in the Administration were to the effect that the development increased the insecurity of the United States "by a very small degree." Nevertheless they were concerned that the people in the United States should realize that there no longer was anything like total security, that it was better not to continue to take refuge in the false security that monopoly possession of the atomic bomb had created.

A military interpretation was that the explosion did not indicate a major improvement in Russian military potential. In support of this view, it was said that one experimental explosion did not mean that Russia had achieved mass production of the bomb. Also, while the United States has had a four-year head start in atomic bomb stockpiling, Russia will be hindered by her inferiority in know-how, raw materials, engineering facilities and electric power.

On the side of the United States, the discovery was expected to have a unifying effect—to bring about a keener appreciation of what should be done for national security without regard to partisanship. In the armed forces it was believed it would tend to diminish the fierce interservice rivalry currently dividing the Navy and the Air Force.

The news was expected to give added weight to Air Force strategists who contend that another war would be fought with massive, strategic air power, with the atomic bomb as the supreme weapon, and that the main avenues to the targets would be over the North Pole.

No Change in Policy

While airpower theories might get new stress it was indicated there would be no change in the fundamental policy that there should be a balance of ground, air and naval power, employed as a unified team in their respective and traditional roles.

Discovery of the Russian explosion was a feat of United States intelligence operations. The achievement was credited both to scientific means—secret, delicate instruments able to detect atomic irradiation at great distances—and undercover activities.

Information about the time and the location of the explosion was carefully guarded. Inquiries indicated that it had occurred deep in Russia, perhaps nearer the Far East than Europe.

As to time, Mr. Truman said it had occurred within "recent weeks" and it was confirmed that this meant after the Blair House conference he had called in mid-July to consider whether there should be closed cooperation with Britain and Canada in the atomic field.

French Foreign Minister Robert Schumann told the Assembly yesterday that it would be useless to reopen the debate on international atomic control and disarmament until a "real spirit of confidence" had got the upper hand in international relations.

The United States delegation, it is understood, is in general agreement. Secretary Acheson, in his address to the Assembly Wednesday, said that the United States was ready to discuss any proposal advanced in good faith.

Detection of the explosion, in the achievement of which the Russians were said to have been aided by German physicists, was only the beginning of a momentous problem. Many experts—scientific, military, political—participated in analyzing and evaluating it, and then in deciding what should be said and done about it.

The task of evaluation took days. Painstaking work was done on the data collected, probably by high-flying aircraft with Geiger counters and other instruments, and also by far-flung detection ground bases equipped with seismographs and secret devices.

As often happened during wartime, the problem then arose: was it more important from an intelligence standpoint to make no disclosure so Russia could not measure how much we knew, or was it more important to tell the United States public? The decision was that the public should know.

How much would be told was a problem that had not been settled yet at 4 P. M. yesterday, when Mr. Truman held his weekly press conference.

* * *

February 1, 1950

TRUMAN ORDERS HYDROGEN BOMB BUILT FOR SECURITY PENDING AN ATOMIC PACT; CONGRESS HAILS STEP; BOARD BEGINS JOB

HISTORIC DECISION

President Says He Must Defend Nation Against Possible Aggressor

SOVIET 'EXPLOSION' CITED

His Ruling Wins Bipartisan Support on Capitol Hill— No Fund Request Due Now

By ANTHONY LEVIERO
Special to The New York Times.

WASHINGTON, Jan. 31—President Truman announced today that he had ordered the Atomic Energy Commission to produce the hydrogen bomb.

The Chief Executive acted in his role of Commander in Chief of the Armed forces, ordering an improved weapon for national security. Thus, from the domestic standpoint, he removed the question of producing the super-weapon as an issue that might be argued on moral grounds.

As for international statecraft, Mr. Truman, by treating the hydrogen bomb as an addition to the American armory, also removed it as an issue that might be interpreted as an advanced threat or inducement in seeking international control of atomic weapons.

Nevertheless, Mr. Truman said that his perseverance in providing for national defense would be matched by his efforts to seek international control of atomic weapons.

New Phase of Atomic Age

In his announcement, Mr. Truman regarded the hydrogen bomb as a progressive outgrowth of United States production of the uranium-plutonium atomic bomb. He put it this way: the commission was "to continue its work on all forms of atomic weapons, including the so-called hydrogen or super-bomb."

His use of the word "continue" was understood to imply that with national security the over-riding consideration, the chief factor guiding his decision was whether it was practicable to make the weapon. Scientists have said that it is.

In effect, the President's decision, which won wide acclaim in Congress, marked the advent of a new phase of the atomic age and a surge ahead of Russia in the race to retain military ascendancy:

The bombs that visited destruction on Hiroshima and Nagasaki split the atom. The new bomb would fuse atoms instead, but with a power 100 to 1,000 times greater than the improved fission bombs that have been developed since the Japanese cities were struck.

The President's Statement

The President made his decision known in the following brief statement:

"It is part of my responsibility as Commander in Chief of the armed forces to see to it that our country is able to defend itself against any possible aggressor. Accordingly, I have directed the Atomic Energy Commission to continue its work on all forms of atomic weapons, including the so-called hydrogen or super-bomb. Like all other work in the field of atomic weapons, it is being and will be carried forward on a basis consistent with the over-all objectives of our program for peace and security.

"This we shall continue to do until a satisfactory plan for international control of atomic energy is achieved. We shall also continue to examine all those factors that affect our program for peace and this country's security."

On Capitol Hill when news of the Chief Executive's decision was received there, Republicans and Democrats joined in approving it. This bipartisanship boded well for Congressional backing of the new project, though it was said in informed quarters that Mr. Truman would not request funds for it at this time.

The Joint Congressional Committee on Atomic Energy held a previously scheduled meeting about an hour after the President's statement came out, and its chairman, Senator Brien McMahon, Democrat, of Connecticut, said that it had approved Mr. Truman's decision. He added that the committee would now proceed with meetings in which the implementation of the hydrogen bomb program would be studied.

Louis Johnson, Secretary of Defense, who had been in Mr. Truman's office today, would say no more than that "the President's statement speaks for itself." The view of the professional soldier was expressed by an anonymous but high-ranking officer speaking in the absence of Gen. Omar N. Bradley, Chairman of the Joint Chiefs of Staff. He said:

"This is one of the gravest decisions the United States has ever had to make, but it had to be done."

Mr. Truman was as undramatic in making his announcement as he was last Sept. 23 when he disclosed that Russia had achieved an atomic explosion—a development that clearly showed that our absolute dominance in atomic weapons was virtually ended. The President was not in his office when the historic statement came out. He was lunching at Blair House, the official residence.

It was 1:55 P. M. when Miss Genevieve Irish of the White House staff walked through the lobby of the Executive Offices and into the press room, crying "press."

White House reporters hurried into the office of Charles G. Ross, the press secretary. He requested that none should leave the room until each had a copy of the mimeographed statement that he held in his hands. He does not make such a request unless the subject is momentous.

Truman Preferred Secrecy

Mr. Truman's decision was a direct result of the discovery in September of the Russian explosion. After it was established beyond doubt that the Soviet Union had accomplished atomic fission, he called in David E. Lilienthal, chairman of the Atomic Energy Commission, and asked what should be done about holding this country's lead in atomic weapons.

Mr. Lilienthal, who is to resign about Feb. 15, was reported to have reminded the President of the possibility of producing the hydrogen super-bomb and asked if he wished to go head with it. Thereupon Mr. Truman sought the advice of Mr. Lilienthal as well as of the three other leading officials concerned—Mr. Johnson, General Bradley and Dean Acheson, Secretary of State.

It was learned that the President would have produced the hydrogen bomb in secrecy, as most military weapons have been in the past, except for the great debate over it that erupted last November and has continued since.

Mr. Truman was represented as feeling that while the new weapon was particularly destructive, this country should have kept its development secret so as to retain the element of surprise as an additional measure of security.

The President sought to discourage discussion of the new type of bomb after Senator Edwin C. Johnson, Democrat, of Colorado, said in a television broadcast that this country was making considerable progress in developing an atomic bomb 1,000 times deadlier than the one dropped on Nagasaki.

J. Howard McGrath, Attorney General, and Senator McMahon were called to the White House on Nov. 25 and urged by Mr. Truman to prevent leaks on data so vital to national security.

Informed sources characterized as ludicrous published estimates that it would take $2,000,000,000 to $4,000,000,000 to produce the hydrogen bomb. The figure would be nearer $200,000,000, it was said, since this country's vast, well-developed atomic plants and "know-how" would be used in its production. In this respect, it was added, the United States retained a great advantage over Russia.

Because the work could be undertaken by the Atomic Energy Commission with its present resources, officials said no new funds would be needed immediately. The work could be carried on with present appropriations and plants until advanced stages were reached.

*   *   *

February 4, 1950

BRITISH JAIL ATOM SCIENTIST AS A SPY AFTER TIP BY F. B. I.; HE KNEW OF HYDROGEN BOMB

TWO CHARGES MADE

First Alleges Betrayal of Information in U. S., 2d Site Not Named

COURT HEARING IS BRIEF

Klaus Fuchs, a Ministry Aide, Is Remanded in Custody to Reappear on Friday

By BENJAMIN WELLES
Special to The New York Times.

LONDON, Feb. 3—A senior British scientist who has worked on atomic projects in the United States and Britain was charged here today with having betrayed atomic research secrets.

The accused was Dr. Klaus Emil Julius Fuchs, aged 38, employed at the main British atomic research center. He was arrested yesterday on information passed on to the British Government by the United States Federal Bureau of Investigation.

One of the two charges leveled against him in the Bow Street Magistrate's Court was that "on a day in February, 1945, in the United States" he "communicated to a person unknown information relating to atomic research which was calculated to be, or might be, directly or indirectly useful to an enemy."

The second identical charge placed the date of the alleged offense in 1947 but made no mention of where it had taken place.

The action against Dr. Fuchs was taken under the Official Secrets Act. The penalty on conviction under the act is penal servitude for three to fourteen years.

Earlier Case Recalled

In a similar case another British atomic scientist, Dr. Alan Nunn May, was sentenced to ten years imprisonment in 1946.

German-born, Dr. Fuchs acquired British nationality in 1942. He has been employed at the Harwell atomic research establishment, from where he was summoned yesterday to the headquarters in London of the Ministry of Supply, which controls atomic research. There he was arrested.

Dr. Fuchs declined to make any answer to the charges.

Police officers testified that on his arrest Dr. Fuchs had asked immediately to see his superior, M. W. Perrin, Deputy Controller of Atomic Energy at the Ministry of Supply. When Mr. Perrin entered the office Dr. Fuchs was reported to have said to him:

"Do you realize the effect of this at Harwell?" (Atomic energy research establishment where Dr. Fuchs was employed.)

Mr. Perrin was said to have replied that he thought he understood.

Otherwise the court proceedings were brief. The presiding magistrate, Sir Laurence Dunne, set hearing for Feb. 10.

At the United States Embassy it was learned that no request for Dr. Fuchs' apprehension had been made through embassy channels.

British Government agencies declined to comment on the case or even to discuss the scientist's biographical background.

In United States 3 Years

It was learned, however, that Dr. Fuchs had been in the United States on atomic energy matters in 1943 and had stayed until 1946, when he returned to the Ministry of Supply. On his return he became head of the Ministry's Theoretical Physics Division.

Last September he was a member of the British delegation to the Anglo-American-Canadian talks here on hazards and safety factors connected with atomic piles "and other related matters." These talks did not include atomic weapons.

Members of the United States Atomic Commission's reactor safeguard committee who took part were Drs. Edward Teller, chairman; Manson Benedict; Joseph W. Kennedy, Abel Wolman and John A. Wheeler. Dr. Frederic de Hoffmann and Comdr. Joseph M. Dunford of the United States informed Senators, was to harden Congressional opinion against the Atomic Energy Commission also took part.

There is a feeling that the arrest of Dr. Fuchs may embarrass the British Government on the eve of the tri-power talks scheduled to be held here Feb. 9 to 12 to discuss a greater exchange of atomic information among Britain, the United States and Canada.

While Britain is not believed to have access to the same degree of atomic information as the United States, she has announced her intention of building atomic weapons at the earliest possible time.

Britain's atomic installations officially reported are an atomic research "university" at Harwell, a former Royal Air Force field near an isolated village on the Berkshire Downs; a research center at Didcot, Berkshire; a uranium smelting factory at Springfields, Lancashire, and a bulk plutonium production center at Sellafield in Cumberland.

Remanded Till Friday

LONDON, Feb. 3 (UP)—Dr. Fuchs' appearance in court was brief.

Prosecutor Christmas Humphreys asked that he be required only to give formal evidence of Dr. Fuchs' arrest, and that Dr. Fuchs then be remanded for one week.

The only witness was Comdr. Leonard Burt of the special branch of Scotland Yard—the section that deals with espionage.

Commander Burt said that at 3:30 P. M. yesterday, with a Scotland Yard inspector, he called on Dr. Fuchs and told him that he was a police officer and had come to arrest him.

"I told him the nature of the charge and I cautioned him," Commander Burt told the court—in Britain arresting officers must warn that anything a defendant says may be used against him.

"He made no reply."

"Do you want to ask any questions?" said the magistrate.

"No," Dr. Fuchs replied quietly.

"Do you want the court to do anything about legal representation for you?" the magistrate asked.

"I don't know of anybody," Dr. Fuchs replied.

"Fuchs is a man of means," the prosecutor interposed. "I do not wish to be faced next Friday with a request for legal aid—which would mean further delay."

"Will you bear that in mind?" said the magistrate. "This case will be taken next Friday. If you wish legal representation, any person you desire will be informed and you will be put in charge with him. But the case will be taken next Friday morning, and I shall not listen to any representations unless they are of a very extraordinary nature that will justify a further remand."

The police agreed to give Dr. Fuchs his money and eyeglasses and he was ordered to Brixton for one week.

*   *   *

March 15, 1950

MISS KENYON CITES PATRIOTIC RECORD TO REFUTE CHARGES

Denies at Senate Hearing She Has or Ever Has Had Tie of Any Kind With Communism

M'CARTHY NAMES 4 MORE

Says Dr. Shapley, J. S. Service, Prof. F. L. Schuman and an Ex-Diplomat Are Pro-Reds

By WILLIAM S. WHITE
Special to The New York Times.

WASHINGTON, March 14—Dorothy Kenyon, a former member of this country's mission to the United Nations, denied under oath today "any connection of any kind with communism or its adherents."

Repudiating at a Senate investigation charges made against her by Senator Joseph R. McCarthy, Republican of Wisconsin, Miss Kenyon offered documentary evidence that in 1939 she had publicly denounced the Stalin-Hitler pact and that as recently as 1949 she had been violently attacked by Soviet propaganda.

Miss Kenyon appeared this afternoon before the inquiry, which is being conducted by a Senate Foreign Relations subcommittee, in the absence of her accuser, Senator McCarthy. In the morning session the Wisconsin Senator had attacked five more persons and had handed in the names of twenty-five others for "further investigation."

The five assailed by Senator McCarthy this morning were Gustavo Duran, former State Department official; Dr. Harlow Shapley, Harvard astronomer; Dr. Frederick L. Schuman of Williams College; John Stewart Service, State Department official, and an unidentified man, who, the Senator said, was formerly connected with the State Department.

Recalls White Committee Service

Miss Kenyon testified that she was publicly urging American aid for Britain and France against the Nazis before the German invasion of Russia, while the Communists were then demanding isolation from the war, and that she had been one of the original members of William Allen White's Committee to Defend America by Aiding the Allies.

The only Republican subcommittee member present, Senator Bourke B. Hickenlooper of Iowa, declared from the bench that there was not "the least evidence," or "the least belief" on his part, that she had been "in any way subversive or disloyal."

Mr. Hickenlooper argued, however, over the sardonic cries of the Democrats, that in his interpretation Senator McCarthy had not charged her with subversion.

The Democrats retorted that the Senate resolution ordering the investigation, on the basis of Senator McCarthy's original accusations that "at least fifty-seven Communists" were or recently had been in the State Department, directed an investigation of those charged with being "disloyal." If Mr. McCarthy was not charging disloyalty, they said, he could not have brought the case before the subcommittee's forum.

McCarthy's Charges Cited

They pointed also to the fact that Senator McCarthy, in testifying last week, had asserted that Miss Kenyon had been "affiliated with at least twenty-eight Communist front organizations" and that her "Communist activities" were "deep rooted" and extended "back through the years."

Miss Kenyon, who termed herself "an independent, liberal, Rooseveltian Democrat," conceded that her name might have been used, "even at times with my consent, in connection with organizations that later proved to be subversive but which at the time seemed to be engaged in activities or dedicated to objectives that I could and did approve."

But never, she swore, had she been knowingly identified with any organization, or person, holding subversive views.

She acknowledged, in a long cross-examination by Senator Hickenlooper, that she had been in one way or another associated at one time with some of the organizations on Senator McCarthy's list that had perhaps later been declared subversive by the House Committee on Un-American Activities or the Attorney General.

It was possible, she said, that she had been a "sucker," a word attributed to her in a newspaper interview, as to some of the organizations that had used her name. It was also possible, she said, that her interest in "little people and civil liberties" had made "enemies" for her.

Miss Kenyon, dressed in black and wearing a black hat, by implication offered to submit to cross-examination by Senator McCarthy himself, saying that she was "ready to answer the questions the members of this subcommittee, or anyone permitted by the subcommittee, may care to ask."

Mr. McCarthy, however, did not attend the afternoon session at which Miss Kenyon was heard.

He left at the noon recess, having previously stated that he could attend no afternoon sessions. He refused the demand of the subcommittee chairman, Senator Millard E. Tydings, Democrat, of Maryland, that he submit at once the names of the eighty-one "cases" of doubtful loyalty or habits who, he had stated, were or had been in the State Department.

In this charge, made on the Senate floor in February, Mr. McCarthy distinguished them from the fifty-seven persons he asserted actually were Communists.

Mr. Tydings said that this was a "baffling" refusal. He contended that the subcommittee could not proceed to demand or subpoena the State Department and other loyalty files of accused persons until Mr. McCarthy gave the names.

Senator McCarthy retorted that Mr. Tydings already had "plenty to go on," with the names already put in the record and with the twenty-five additional names that he had handed up privately this morning. He would provide the names of the eighty-one "cases" mentioned, he said, as soon as he had "time to document them."

His new accusations asserted that:

1. Mr. Duran, a State Department official who resigned in October, 1946, engaged in Soviet activities in the Spanish civil war, according to American military intelligence. Mr. McCarthy said Mr. Duran was now an official of the United Nations. The office of the United Nations Secretary General, Trygve Lie, had declined to give information about Mr. Duran, Mr. McCarthy asserted, but the available data indicated that he was now working in the International Refugee Organization program.

2. Dr. Shapley, appointed to a United Nations post by the State Department, had been connected with Communist front organizations.

3. A former State Department official, whose name he withheld, was reported in the Washington police files to be homosexual and had been allowed to resign from the State Department in 1948 only to find employment in a "most sensitive" place, the Central Intelligence Agency. Mr. McCarthy gave this name privately to the subcommittee. It was an "important" case, he asserted, because perverts were officially considered to be security risks because they were "subject to blackmail."

4. Mr. Service, a State Department official, and now a member of the United States diplomatic mission in Calcutta, India, "where he is helping determine the all-important policy of our Government toward India," was a "bad security risk." He said Mr. Service had "Communist affiliations."

5. Professor Schuman, "a highly placed lecturer with the Department of State," and a consultant on Far Eastern Affairs, was a sponsor of Communist fronts.

Mr. McCarthy charged that Mr. Duran, on the authority of American military intelligence reports known to the State

The New York Times (by George Tames)

Dorothy Kenyon before Senate Foreign Relations subcommittee in Washington yesterday.

Department, had been active during the Spanish civil war in "secret Soviet operations in the Spanish Republican Army," and had been a "regional head of the Spanish counterpart" of the Russian secret police.

Mr. Duran, Mr. McCarthy went on, after resigning from the State Department "under intense Congressional pressure" in 1946, had gone to the United Nations with what was indicated by "a confidential report" to have been the backing of "a member of the present Presidential Cabinet."

Senator McCarthy put in exhibits indicating that Col. Wendell G. Johnson, United States military attaché in Madrid, on June 4, 1946, had sent to the State Department and other agencies a report stating, on the authority of an anti-Franco Spaniard, that Mr. Duran as commanding officer of an international brigade in Spain had ordered the execution of two men without justification.

In December of 1943, Mr. McCarthy testified, Lieut. Edward J. Ruff, assistant United States military attaché in the Dominican Republic, had officially declared himself convinced that Mr. Duran was a Communist.

The Senator offered a Dec. 21, 1943, memorandum signed with the typed name of Spruille Braden, then Ambassador to Cuba, backing Mr. Duran for State Department foreign service work and calling him "not a Communist but a liberal of the highest type."

Finally, he quoted excerpts from a book by Indalecio Prieto, former Minister of Defense for the Spanish Republic, to the effect that Soviet agents had forced Mr. Duran upon him to be an official of the Spanish "S. I. M.," which the Senator termed a secret police group.

Shapley Appointment Noted

Of Mr. Shapley, Senator McCarthy testified that he had been appointed to the National Commission for the United Nations Educational, Scientific and Cultural Organization by the "predecessor" of Secretary of State Dean Acheson, Gen. George C. Marshall.

Dr. Shapley had not been dismissed by Secretary Acheson, Mr. McCarthy went on, although he had been "prominent in the affairs" of the "Scientific and Cultural Conference for World Peace" held in New York in 1949 and "denounced by Mr. Acheson himself as 'a sounding board for communistic propaganda.' "

As to Mr. Service, Senator McCarthy told the subcommittee that he had information that the Loyalty Appeals Board of the Civil Service Commission ten days ago had returned to the State Department "the file of Mr. Service with the report that they did not feel they could give him clearance."

Mr. Service's "Communist affiliations," Mr. McCarthy testified, were "well known," but, after four or five investigations concerning his loyalty, he remained "one of the small, potent group of 'untouchables' who year after year formulate and carry out the plans for the Department of State."

The Senator asserted that Mr. Service and five others interested in the magazine Amerasia had been arrested in 1945 on charges of espionage for the "theft" of secret Government papers but had not been prosecuted.

Amerasia, Mr. McCarthy continued, shortly had opened attacks upon the then Under Secretary of State Joseph C. Grew, leading to his dismissal in favor of Mr. Acheson, because Mr. Grew had wanted to take a hard line in prosecuting the espionage charges.

Mr. Grew, the Senator added, also had opposed "the clique which favored scuttling Chiang Kai-shek and allowing the Communist element in China to take over."

Mr. McCarthy's main charge against Dr. Schuman was that he was "one of the closest collaborators in and sponsors of Communist-front organizations in America," and that if he was not "a card-holding member of the Communist party the difference is so slight that it is unimportant."

Mr. McCarthy testified that Dr. Schuman also had supported Henry A. Wallace for President in 1948 and had been associated in one way or another with the following organizations, all of which, the Senator said, had been cited as subversive by the Attorney General or the House or California State un-American activities committees:

American Committee for the Protection of Foreign Born, American Council on Soviet Relations, American League for Peace and Democracy, American Russian Institute, American Slav Congress, Civil Rights Congress, Committee for Boycott Against Japanese Aggression, Friends of the Soviet Union, African Aid Committee, National Conference of American Policy in China and the Far East.

Senator Hickenlooper's cross-examination of Miss Kenyon was prolonged but level in tone.

Mr. Hickenlooper went to many of the organizations that Miss Kenyon herself had mentioned in her prepared statement. Often, her response was that she could not recall any such association. Again, she said, here and there, that perhaps she had made a speech before one of them.

Once or twice, when Senator Hickenlooper handed her a photocopy of a letterhead of an organization, she observed that she was "in good company" at the time.

Miss Kenyon conceded that in a recent speech in Troy, N. Y., she had stated that the then current perjury trial of Alger Hiss, the former State Department official, was "a product of hysteria created by the House Committee on Un-American Activities." She still stood on that opinion, she said in effect.

She testified also that in the same speech she had said that "in the present temper of the country" it was doubtful that Hiss could obtain a fair trial and that there was "not a shred" of direct evidence against him save from Whittaker Chambers and from "documents that went back to Mr. Chambers."

In saying that he saw no evidence of disloyalty on her part, Senator Hickenlooper told Miss Kenyon that he thought Senator McCarthy had meant only to "suggest that your membership in organizations at least later termed subversive was a matter for concern so far as security risks go in the State Department."

Miss Kenyon retorted that she was "trying to keep her temper," but that Mr. McCarthy had charged her with "a great deal more than that."

Miss Kenyon in Flat Denial

What the State Department should do, she added, in her case, or any case, was to "look at the record in the round and all the activities of the subject." To brand any organization subversive short of a court hearing she asserted, was in itself a "violation of civil rights," as was "guilt by association."

Miss Kenyon, in her direct statement denying Senator McCarthy's charges, declared that she had had no warning that they were coming and that they had "seriously jeopardized, if not destroyed," the professional and personal reputation she had acquired in a lifetime.

Her answer to Mr. McCarthy was summarized in this passage:

"I am not and never have been a Communist. I am not and never have been a fellow-traveler. I am not and never have been a supporter of, or member of, or a sympathizer with any organization known to me to be, or suspected by me of being, controlled or dominated by Communists.

"As emphatically and unreservedly as possible, I deny any connection of any kind or character with communism or its adherents. If this leaves anything unsaid to indicate my total and complete detestation of that political philosophy, it is impossible for me to express my sentiments. I mean my denial to be all-inclusive."

She testified that in 1940 she was in the forefront of an effort in the American Labor party to keep it from "Communist domination" and that when this effort had failed she had left the party.

As a final item in her defense, her counsel read into the record a statement signed by thirteen New York lawyers, including John W. Davis, a former Presidential candidate, and Robert P. Patterson, a former Secretary of War, asserting of their "own knowledge" that she "never had the slightest sympathy with communism in any of its forms."

* * *

April 28, 1950

HOOVER PROPOSES REORGANIZING U. N. TO OUST RUSSIANS

As an Alternative, He Calls for a United Stand by Peoples Who Cherish Freedom

WOULD EASE PERIL TO US

In Address to Publishers Here Ex-President Urges Nation to Scan Soviet Record

By RUSSELL PORTER

Herbert Hoover proposed last night that the United Nations be "reorganized without the Communist nations in it."

"If that is impractical," said the former President in a nation-wide radio broadcast, "then a definite new united front should be organized of those people who disavow communism, who stand for morals and religion, and who love freedom."

He called for definite "mobilization" against "the police state and human slavery," against "Red agnosticism" and against "Red imperialism."

Mr. Hoover spoke at the Bureau of Advertising dinner closing the three-day, sixty-fourth annual convention of the American Newspaper Publishers Association. The dinner was held in the Waldorf-Astoria Hotel.

About 1,800 members and guests of the association attended. It was announced that the dinner was the largest ever held in the Waldorf-Astoria.

Receives Frequent Applause

The audience stood up, applauded and cheered Mr. Hoover warmly both at the beginning and the end of his speech. They interrupted frequently with applause, especially when he outlined his proposal for reconstituting the United Nations.

Disavowing any intent toward military alliance, Mr. Hoover explained his plan as one to "redeem" the United Nations for its original purpose on the basis of "moral and spiritual cooperation" for peace.

A "phalanx" of free-world nations could come closer to a working relationship with the Communist world, he said, than the United States alone, and would lessen the danger to the American people.

"By collective action," he added, "we could much more effectively keep conspiring agents and bribers out of all our borders and our laboratories."

He said his program would constitute "total diplomacy" and would be "logical and practical."

"All this may give pain to some people," he conceded. "But by their cries ye shall know them."

Mr. Hoover counseled the American people to take "a cold and objective look" at the record before going any further with the present policy concerning Soviet Russia.

"We are becoming more and more isolated as the sole contender in this cold war," he declared. "We are steadily losing ground because the non-Communist states are being picked off one by one or are compromising with the Communists."

He said the United States needed to know "who are with us" and "who we can depend on" in the cold war.

Recalls 1941 Warning

Recalling that in 1941 he had warned the American people that collaboration with Stalin to bring freedom to mankind was a "gargantuan" jest, he said last night:

"I used the wrong adjective, I should have said tragic."

Instead of liberty having been expanded, he found a dozen nations and 600,000,000 human beings had been "enslaved."

Moreover, in the last twelve years, he said, Russia has violated more than thirty-five "solemnly signed agreements." He cited "about a dozen" provisions of the United Nations Charter that had been "violated either in spirit or in letter by Soviet Russia."

"The Kremlin," he said, "has reduced the United Nations to a propaganda forum for the smearing of free peoples. It [the U. N.] has been defeated as a preservative of peace and goodwill."

The "cold war," as it has been conducted, he said, has proved "expensive and dangerous" to this country. There has resulted a "belated" realization that "this is not one world but two worlds."

"The one-world idea," he remarked, "seems to be lost in those secret files."

Mr. Hoover said the American people appeared to be in a "fog" as a result of "cold war" reverses, but he did not feel "disheartened."

"We have the greatest organ of education known to man— a free press," he reminded. Then, looking at the newspaper men massed in front of him, he added:

"You can dissolve much of our confusions and frustrations."

* * *

June 26, 1950

SETBACK FOR INVADERS REPORTED

COUNTER-ATTACK ON

Line Drives North at Foe After Invader Is 15 Miles From Seoul

BOMBS FALL ON CAPITAL

Evacuation of American Wives and Children Begins Under Cover of U. S. Aircraft

By The Associated Press

SEOUL, Korea, Monday, June 26—South Korean troops today launched a counter-attack and reportedly drove the invaders from the Communist North backward five miles on a front twenty-five miles north of Seoul.

Defense Stiffens

Special to The New York Times.

SEOUL, Korea, Monday, June 26—Twenty-four hours after they had launched their unprovoked attack upon the Republic of Korea, Communists of North Korea were reported to be in retreat in some sectors.

In the center of the line that stretches across the Thirty-eighth Parallel the Communists were being held, although at one point along the Uijongbu road they were only fifteen miles from the capital city of Seoul. [The United Press said the South Koreans were reported to have stopped heavy tank attacks in this area.]

This morning, according to the South Korean Office of Public Information, South Korean troops pushing northward captured Haeju, capital of Hwanghae Province, which is one mile north of the border and sixty-five miles northwest of Seoul, taking ten anti-aircraft pieces and ten trucks.

Some reports asserted that Red troops at Chumunjin, on the east coast seven miles south of the parallel, seemed to be gradually retreating.

[The Associated Press reported that a United States Mustang fighter had been attacked over Seoul by a Russian-made plane, presumably North Korean. Ten persons having lunch at the United States Embassy said the Mustang drove off the Russian craft, but a United States military adviser stated that the Mustang took evasive action and shook off the Russian plane. The Korean police said that six civilians were killed by two bombs dropped by the plane. It was the first aerial attack on Seoul since the Communist invasion began.

[An aerial engagement between an American fighter plane and a Soviet-built aircraft was reported by the United States Ambassador in Korea to have taken place over Inchon, where American women and children were being placed aboard evacuation ships. The Americans were receiving protection from a "heavy air cover" of United States planes operating from bases in Japan.]

Last night the official news round-up declared that Red forces estimated at 50,000 were continuing to penetrate and had captured Kaesong, Pochon, and southern territories west of the Imjin River, using tanks and armored infantry and help by guerrillas.

At that time, said the statement, one Red division was attacking Ongjin Peninsula and another division, with heavy artillery, was attacking Chunchon.

People's Army units, said the announcement, had landed at widely separated points along the east coast, where they had been joined by guerrillas, and succeeded in cutting the highway to Samchock, South Korea's largest east coast coal mine five miles south of the border, which stretches 125 miles across Korea.

Meanwhile Seoul, which is only thirty-eight miles south of the border, was being menaced by a Communist force of approximately 3,000, which was attacking Moonsan, only sixteen miles to the north.

Four Korean Divisions

Still another division was reported assaulting defense lines on Taeok Mountain, two miles south of the parallel.

Last night's announcement said that four South Korean divisions were already engaging the enemy and that three more were being brought up into closer reserve positions.

There have been no reports of North Korean tanks able to break through for independent action. At Pochon, ten Red tanks were destroyed.

Sihn Sung Mo, the acting Premier, has asked John J. Muccio, the United States Ambassador, to appeal to the United States for airplanes and more arms from Okinawa or Japan.

The curfew tonight began at 9 o'clock, instead of at midnight, as is normal. The prisons, which contain many political prisoners, are heavily guarded, and every city corner is being guarded by alert police armed with carbines.

There are now approximately 2,000 Americans in Korea.

The Communist offensive started at dawn yesterday at several points along the Thirty-eighth Parallel. Kaesong, a city forty-five miles north of here, was taken by the Reds at 9:30 A. M. and another column pushed through to Changdan, twenty miles north of Seoul.

Regiment Lands on Coast

Meanwhile a force estimated at one regiment with ten tanks landed on the east coast and fighting was begun in the west, on the Ongjin Peninsula. In the east, the Reds attacked at Chunchon and Kangnung.

All privately owned buses and trucks in Seoul were commandeered by the military police for emergency use. Army jeeps equipped with loudspeakers toured the streets, telling soldiers: "Join your units immediately."

A Cabinet statement warned the people to disregard alarmist rumors adding: "The Republican Army is fervently counter-attacking. The world now knows who is the aggressor in this strategic conflict. We will persevere no matter how great the sacrifice and individual losses."

The Communist drive on Seoul was made under fierce artillery fire. The attackers were also supported with tanks.

The South Korean police and Army were both making active preparations within Seoul for any emergency. Traffic has been cut off here. Thus far, Communist air activity has been slight.

One Soviet-made Yak fighter reconnoitered over Seoul and Kimpo Airport yesterday morning.

The reconnaissance was followed by a raid by five Soviet-type fighters that strafed the Kimpo Airport and the Seoul railroad station. A gasoline tank on the airfield was hit and three persons were injured at the railroad station.

[Reports from Tokyo said that a United States C-54 was fired on at the time but whether this was a civil or military plane was not known. Reports said there were no casualties and that damage to the plane was slight.]

The North Korean dawn attack was followed after five hours by a broadcast from the Soviet-controlled Pyongyang radio, which laid the blame for the surprise attack on an offensive supposed to have been made by the South Koreans along the Thirty-eighth Parallel.

"The People's Republican Army," the broadcast said, repulsed South Korean invading forces at the northern border town of Yongyang. The broadcast added:

"The People's Republic [North Korea] wished to remind the South Korean puppet regime that unless the puppets immediately suspend their adventurous military actions, the People's Republic will be obliged to resort to decisive counter-measures."

Russian Tankmen Reported

SEOUL, Monday, June 26 (AP)—Sihn Sung Mo, Defense Minister as well as Acting Premier, said he had received word that ten of twenty Northern tanks captured north of Seoul had Russian crewmen.

He did not make clear whether he meant that the captured tanks were fully manned by Russians or might have contained only one Russian each. There also was a possibility of confused identities.

Col. W. H. S. Wright, acting chief of the United States Military Advisory Group in Korea, returned from Tokyo early Monday in an unescorted United States Navy plane. His first try had been turned back when North Korean Russian-made Yak planes bombed and strafed Seoul's Kimpo airfield Sunday afternoon.

A Southern spokesman said that 1,000 guerrilla invaders had been completely surrounded near Samchock, coastal town twenty miles inside South Korea. He said that Southern troops were moving to the relief of Kaesong, southern town on the border, which was the first to fall in the Northern invasion at dawn Sunday.

The large town of Chunchon, near the east coast sixty miles from Seoul, was surrounded by an entire Red division with heavy artillery.

Four groups of Red guerrillas and armored troops landed at widely separated points on the east coast and cut the coastal highway south of Kangnon, which is twenty miles below the border, the advisory group reported.

The South Korean Government announced that one of its coast guard vessels sank a Russian ship off Chumunjin, on the east coast.

The South Korean gunboat Bakdusan (Whitehead Mountain) reported that it had encountered another Soviet ship of about 500 tons on the east coast north of Pusan and had chased it northward. The 173-foot Bakdusan is the largest vessel in the South Korean Navy.

A Southern Government spokesman said that eight additional vessels were moving southward and being engaged by South Korean ships. He did not identify these eight by nationality.

Rhee Said to Wish to Move

TOKYO, Monday, June 26 (AP)—An unconfirmed report circulated here today that South Korean President Syngman Rhee wanted to move his Government from Seoul to Taejon, ninety air-miles south-southeast.

According to this report, Ambassador John J. Muccio was trying to persuade Dr. Rhee to keep the Republic's seat of Government at Seoul.

Evacuation Is Started

The evacuation of about 1,000 American women and children from Korea to two freighters in the harbor at Inchon, eighteen miles west of the capital, was taking place "under heavy air cover" of United States fighter planes from bases in Japan, United States Ambassador John J. Muccio said last night (Monday, Korea time) in a telephone conversation with The New York Times.

Mr. Muccio said that while the embarkation of the women and children was in progress, a Soviet-built Yak fighter plane and a United States Air Force P-61 Black Widow fighter had engaged in a dogfight over the harbor. The planes disappeared still dueling behind clouds, he added.

Apparently recovering from the initial shock of the surprise North Korean attack, Mr. Muccio declared, South Korean military forces appeared to be stiffening their resistance all along the line.

"There has been a surprising lack of guerrilla activity and a complete absence of sabotage by North Korean agents here," Mr. Muccio added.

Heavy rains and low clouds over South Korea during the opening phases of the assault, he said, had deprived the invaders of strong air support.

"The attack might have been much more serious," he added, "if they had been able to get more planes into the air."

He said that no estimates of casualties in the first twenty-four hours of fighting had been announced by the Korean Army. He added: "There have been no Americans injured."

He indicated that the embarkation of the women and children would be completed at about 1 A. M., Monday, New York time.

Mr. Muccio said he intended to remain at his post.

* * *

June 26, 1950

U. N. CALLS FOR CEASE FIRE IN KOREA; DEMANDS NORTH WITHDRAW TROOPS

RED NORTH 'GUILTY'

Security Council Acts Swiftly at U. S. Call to End Hostilities

VOTE 9-0, RUSSIA ABSENT

Yugoslav Abstains—Decision Begins Charter Steps to Stop Communist-Led Aggression

By A. M. ROSENTHAL
Special to The New York Times.

LAKE SUCCESS, June 25—The United Nations Security Council found North Korea guilty today of breaking the peace, demanded that the Communist Government pull back its troops at once and called for an immediate cease-fire throughout Korea.

Ten members of the Council—the Soviet Union stayed away—rushed to Lake Success for an emergency meeting, requested by the United States, and acted swiftly on one of the bluntest resolutions ever presented in the United Nations.

Nine of those countries voted for the resolution handed in by the United States. There were no countries voting against it; Yugoslavia raised a hand in abstention.

The resolution carried with it the clear implication that the United Nations would move to take stronger measures if North Korea flouted the Council. United States spokesmen said the motion was put forward under Chapter 7 of the United Nations Charter, the "last resort" charter, which permits the Security Council to invoke sanctions, blockade and even military action.

Question of Obedience

The key question debated in the delegates lounge after the meeting was: Would North Korea obey. Many delegates believed that the Northern Koreans would follow the Soviet line and announce that any action taken by the Security Council with the participation of the Nationalist Chinese was entirely illegal.

But even as the delegates were filing out of the Council chamber, the United Nations was taking steps to make sure the words of the resolution got through to authorities of North Korea and the Republic of Korea to the south.

Copies of the resolution were dispatched by commercial cable and radio to North and South Korean capitals. And as backstop, the Voice of America, the British Broadcasting Corporation and All-India Radio were asked to broadcast the resolution, beamed to Korea.

The next phase for the United Nations is waiting—two days of waiting. The Security Council will meet again at 3 P. M. Tuesday; and it hopes to have a new report and possibly recommendations from its seven-member, on-the-spot Commission on Korea.

It was a report from that Commission that provided the basis for the action of the Council in denouncing the Northern Government and asking for withdrawal and cease-fire.

Trygve Lie Receives Dispatch

At 10:30 this morning, Secretary General Trygve Lie received a brief dispatch from the Commission telling of attacks from the North and warning that full-scale war was shaping up. The Commission stated that there had been no confirmation of a published report that North Korea had formally declared war.

[President Truman said in Kansas City before his return to Washington on Sunday that he knew of no declaration of war. Press reports received over Saturday night from Seoul had said the North Korean radio broadcast such a declaration.]

By the time Mr. Lie received the dispatch, delegates were speeding back from week-ends in the country and were on their way to Lake Success for the extraordinary meeting of the Council. All through the night and the early morning, telephone calls had gone out to the delegates, summoning them.

The first step toward the meeting was taken by Ernest A. Gross, acting chief of the United States delegation. At 3 A. M., after hours of consultation with top-level State Department figures in Washington, Mr. Gross telephoned Mr. Lie, told him the United States judged North Korea to be an aggressor, and asked for the Security Council to be convened today.

From that point, the word went to Sir Benegal N. Rau of India, this month's chairman of the Council, who agreed to call the meeting. Secretariat workers were roused and got busy, phoning all delegations on the Security Council. The Soviet delegation got a call, of course.

The normal hush of Lake Success—most Sundays see just a few maintenance workers and skeleton-staff clerks on the job—was broken about 8 A. M. Five hours later the first diplomats showed up at the delegates' lounge.

When the Council came to order at 2:32 P. M., Sir Benegal gave the floor first to Mr. Lie. The Secretary General made a bluntly worded statement:

"The report received by me from other sources in Korea make it plain that military actions have been undertaken by Northern Korean forces.

"The present situation is a serious one and is a threat to international peace. I consider it the clear duty of the Security Council to take the steps necessary to re-establish peace in that area."

Mr. Gross presented the United States case then. He told of the news of the fighting in Korea, said the assault was

The New York Times (by Patrick Burns)

Dr. John M. Chang, Korean Ambassador to the United States, with Secretary General Trygve Lie of the U. N. at Lake Success yesterday.

launched by the North as an "unprovoked attack." It was a breach of the peace and act of aggression, he said.

"This is clearly a threat to international peace and security," he added.

The United States delegate reviewed a few milestones in the United Nations activity in Korea—the establishment of the Commission, the holding of elections in South Korea, the General Assembly resolution declaring the Republic of Korea to be the lawful Government of the country.

Korean Envoy to U. S. Speaks

Mr. Gross presented his resolution. Sir Benegal invited Dr. John Myun Chang, Korean Ambassador to Washington, to speak. The Ambassador said that the invasion was an "all-out effort."

"Its objective is to destroy my Government and to bring my country under the domination of the Communist-supported puppet regime of the North," Dr. Chang went on.

"However," the armed forces of our country are meeting the attack with fortitude and bravery.

"Our people are determined to resist the invaders and lay down their lives in order that a free and independent democratic Korea might survive."

Delegates from various member nations spoke up in favor of the United States resolution. One by one, the representatives of Britain, France, China, Ecuador, Cuba and Egypt echoed the same theme: The fighting in Korea was the fault of the Northern regime, it was an act of aggression, a breach of the peace and a threat to the rest of the world.

There was an hour-long time-out for delegates to assemble in an office provided by Mr. Lie and work out drafting changes in the resolution.

The Security Council convened again at 5:30 P. M. and Norway voiced support of the resolution as amended.

Attention turned at that point to Djuro Nincitch, the alternate delegate from Yugoslavia, who had been having a difficult day. He was in and out of the Council room during the afternoon, busy on the telephone with his chief, Dr. Ales Bebler, who was away in the country.

Mr. Nincitch told the Council that aggression from any side was untenable. But in Korea, he went on, there seemed to be lack of precise information that could enable the Council to pin responsibility.

The thing for the Council to do, said the delegate for Marshal Tito's Government, was to call for a cease fire, not blame anybody, not ask for withdrawal of the Northern troops and set out on an investigation that would bring in the facts needed for a final decision.

Mr. Nincitch presented a resolution to that effect and saw it defeated. Only Yugoslavia voted for her proposal. Norway, India and Egypt abstained. The United States, Britain, France, China, Ecuador and Cuba voted no.

Revision of Resolution

The delegates' amendment work on the United States resolution resulted in several changes. The United States had asked for a cease fire directed solely at North Korea. The amended version called for a general cease fire, but retained the accusation clause and the provision that North Korea retire its forces to the Thirty-eighth Parallel, the dividing line between North and South.

In the original version, the United States spoke of an armed invasion of the Republic. The amended resolution spoke of an armed attack on the Republic by forces from the North. In all cases, the United States accepted the amendments.

In addition to the immediate demands for cessation and withdrawal, the resolution called on all members of the United Nations to avoid giving assistance to North Korea. As one delegate said: "We are not talking there about assistance from Lower Slabodia."

As for the United Nations Commission on Korea, now in Seoul, the resolution directed it to observe the withdrawal of the North Korean forces—"if it can," was the mental reservation of most persons here—and to keep the Security Council informed.

Among after-the-meeting statements, Dr. Chang, the Korean Ambassador, said the resolution was a symbol of the feeling of the people of the world, but that he would have hoped for something stronger, more direct.

Mr. Gross said Warren R. Austin, chief United States delegate, was flying here from Vermont and would be in charge of the "next development department." Mr. Gross said any further steps that would be recommended by the United States in case of non-compliance would be decided on "at the highest level."

The resolution itself, Mr. Gross commented, was a clear indication that the Security Council understood the gravity of the situation. A reassuring factor, he called that, and added:

"In the past it has not always been true that the United Nations has acted as quickly and as vigorously."

* * *

June 28, 1950

TRUMAN ORDERS U. S. AIR, NAVY UNITS TO FIGHT IN AID OF KOREA; U. N. COUNCIL SUPPORTS HIM; OUR FLIERS IN ACTION; FLEET GUARDS FORMOSA

BID MADE TO RUSSIA

President Asks Moscow to Act to Terminate Fighting in Korea

CHIANG TOLD TO HALT

U.S. Directs Him to Stop Blows at Reds—Will Reinforce Manila

By ANTHONY LEVIERO
Special to The New York Times.

WASHINGTON, June 27—President Truman announced today that he had ordered United States air and naval forces to fight with South Korea's Army. He said this country took the action, as a member of the United Nations, to enforce the cease-fire order issued by the Security Council Sunday night.

Then acting independently of the United Nations, in a move to assure this country's security, the Chief Executive ordered Vice Admiral Arthur D. Struble to form a protective cordon around Formosa to prevent its invasion by Communist Chinese forces.

Along with these fateful decisions, Mr. Truman also ordered an increase of our forces based in the Philippine Republic, as well as more speedy military assistance to that country and to the French and Vietnam forces that are fighting Communist armies in Indo-China.

After he had started these moves that might mean a decided turn toward peace or a general war, the President sent Ambassador Alan G. Kirk to the Russian Foreign Office in Moscow to request the Soviet Union to use its good offices to end the hostilities. This was an obvious proffer of an opportunity for Russia to end the crisis before her own forces might get involved.

Door Opened for Russia

In the capital this was regarded as being at once a possible face-saving device for Russia in a showdown crisis and a feeler to determine her intentions.

The decisions amounted to a showdown in the "cold war" with Russia, in which this country has at last decided to begin shooting in a limited area. Yet all the decisions followed a carefully worked out formula of action within the framework of the United Nations, as well as unilateral moves that avoided any direct provocation of the Soviet Union.

Mr. Truman based the decision to fight for the South Koreans entirely on the Security Council resolution which called upon all members of the United Nations to help carry it out. And at the Pentagon it was explained that our air and naval forces would fight only below the Thirty-eighth Parallel line that divides South Korea from the Russian-sponsored North Korea.

"The Security Council called upon all members of the United Nations to render every assistance to the United Nations in the execution of this resolution," Mr. Truman stated. "In these circumstances I have ordered United States air and sea forces to give the Korean Government troops cover and support."

Russia Is Not Mentioned

Mr. Truman carefully avoided mentioning Russia in his statement. He pivoted today's great shift in United States foreign policy on a conclusion that the "cold war" had passed from an uneasy passive stage to "armed invasion and war." He blamed "communism."

"The attack upon Korea makes it plain beyond all doubt that communism has passed beyond the use of subversion to conquer independent nations and will now use armed invasion and war," he said. "It has defied the orders of the Security Council of the United Nations issued to preserve international peace and security. In these circumstances the occupation of Formosa by Communist forces would be a direct threat to the security of the Pacific area and to United States forces performing their lawful and necessary functions in that area."

President Truman took the unusual action of virtually ordering the Chinese National Government to cease its air and sea operations against the Chinese mainland. He tersely stated that the Seventh Fleet "will see that this is done," adding that the future status of Formosa would have to await peace in the Pacific, or a peace settlement with Japan, or United Nations action.

In many major speeches Mr. Truman has not hesitated to name Russia as the country that had obstructed peace efforts in the United Nations through her use of the veto or the boycotting of its meetings.

In military parlance, the term "cover and support" used by Mr. Truman as missions for our forces means that they would seek to destroy any North Korea air, ground or sea forces, as well as their installations, that are encountered below the Thirty-eighth Parallel. They would do the same in support of any counter-offensive that the South Korea forces might be able to mount.

Thus the complexion of the Korean situation was changed overnight. Yesterday officials were inclined to see South Korea, with her small, poorly equipped forces, as good as lost. It was acknowledged, as President Syngman Rhee of South Korea had complained, that aid in the form of munitions and supplies was "too little and too late."

Victory Is Seen for South

Today the view was that American air and naval forces could assure overwhelming superiority to South Korea and bring victory, unless, of course, Russia similarly aided North Korea.

The decisions were made last night in Blair House and before the night was over the coded action orders were being radioed to Gen. Douglas MacArthur in Tokyo and to other per-tinent places. The formula encompassing all the action, it was learned authoritatively, began to take shape Sunday night in the first Blair House conference and it was custom-tailored for the resolution that the United States representative was directed to introduce in the Security Council meeting that night.

The correlated diplomatic action in Moscow was announced this afternoon by the State Department. Ambassador Kirk delivered a note, the text of which was not published.

Lincoln White, State Department press officer said:

"The Embassy asked that the Soviet Government use its influence with the North Korean authorities for the withdrawal of the invading forces and the cessation of hostilities."

President Truman was gratified with markedly good reaction that followed news of his decisions. There was typical bipartisan support as in other great emergencies that have faced the country, and Mr. Truman was particularly pleased with the message he received from Gov. Thomas E. Dewey of New York, his opponent in the Presidential race of 1948. He promptly sent a grateful reply. As one White House official expressed it, "there was a wonderful closing of ranks."

The unity on the political front was more than matched among the high civilian and military leaders of the nation who made the recommendations for action. Mr. Truman, before he even left his home in Independence, Mo., on Sunday to cope with the crisis, had formed a determination to do something drastic, something that would be neither appeasement nor merely passive. Both Defense and State Department officials, it was learned, worked with great harmony and easy agreement on the recommendations that were drawn up to meet his basic requirements.

Secretary of State Dean Acheson was said to have been a strong hand in working out the diplomatic requirements, both as to Moscow and the Security Council, and in urging the use of force. Those at the fateful council with the President in his home at Blair House last night were the same that met with him Sunday, after his hurried return from Independence.

They were Mr. Acheson, Philip C. Jessup, Ambassador at Large, John D. Hickerson, Assistant Secretary of State for United Nations Affairs, and Dean Rusk, Deputy Under Secretary of State; Louis Johnson, Secretary of Defense; Gen. Omar N. Bradley, chairman of the Joint Chiefs of Staff; Gen. J. Lawton Collins, Army Chief of Staff; Gen. Hoyt S. Vandenberg, Chief of Staff of the Air Force; Admiral Forrest P. Sherman, Chief of Naval Operations; Frank C. Pace Jr., Secretary of the Army; Thomas K. Finletter Secretary of the Air Force; and Francis P. Matthews, Secretary of the Navy.

The proposed actions—air and naval support for South Korea to enforce the United Nations resolution and the decision on Formosa establishing unilaterally a line of United States defense in the Western Pacific—were already familiar. Mr. Truman canvassed the situation once again from every possible angle and then made his decisions. That, in brief, was the story of the meeting as told by one familiar with it.

This morning Secretary Johnson, Stephen T. Early, the Deputy Secretary of Defense, and Generals Bradley and Collins went to the President's office before 10 A. M. and apparently reported that the orders had gone out.

Then in mid-morning, before the announcement was made to the world, Mr. Truman summoned Congressional leaders and members of the committees dealing with foreign affairs in the Senate and the House. There were Republicans and Democrats, including Speaker Sam Rayburn, Senator W. Scott Lucas, the Senate Majority Leader, and Senator Tom Connally, chairman of the Senate Foreign Relations Committee, and John Kee, his opposite number in the House.

Secretary Johnson said, as the President's statement indicated, that none of our ground troops would be committee in the Korean conflict.

President Truman, as if to inspire confidence and calm in public, walked instead of drove to Blair House.

He lunched with his Cabinet. Eight were present, Maurice J. Tobin, Secretary of Labor, being out of town.

* * *

June 28, 1950

STATEMENT ON KOREA

By The Associated Press

WASHINGTON, June 27—The text of President Truman's statement today on Korea:

In Korea the Government forces, which were armed to prevent border raids and to preserve internal security, were attacked by invading forces from North Korea. The Security Council of the United Nations called upon the invading troops to cease hostilities and to withdraw to the Thirty-eighth Parallel. This they have not done, but on the contrary have pressed the attack. The Security Council called upon all members of the United Nations to render every assistance to the United Nations in the execution of this resolution.

In these circumstances I have ordered United States air and sea forces to give the Korean Government troops cover and support.

The attack upon Korea makes it plain beyond all doubt that communism has passed beyond the use of subversion to conquer independent nations and will now use armed invasion and war.

It has defied the orders of the Security Council of the United Nations issued to preserve international peace and security. In these circumstances the occupation of Formosa by Communist forces would be a direct threat to the security of the Pacific area and to United States forces performing their lawful and necessary functions in that area.

Accordingly I have ordered the Seventh Fleet to prevent any attack on Formosa. As a corollary of this action I am calling upon the Chinese Government on Formosa to cease all air and sea operations against the mainland. The Seventh Fleet will see that this is done. The determination of the future status of Formosa must await the restoration of security in the Pacific, a peace settlement with Japan, or consideration by the United Nations.

I have also directed that United States forces in the Philippines be strengthened and that military assistance to the Philippine Government be accelerated.

I have similarly directed acceleration in the furnishing of military assistance to the forces of France and the associated states in Indo-China and the dispatch of a military mission to provide close working relations with those forces.

I know that all members of the United Nations will consider carefully the consequences of this latest aggression in Korea in defiance of the Charter of the United Nations. A return to the rule of force in international affairs would have far-reaching effects. The United States will continue to uphold the rule of law.

I have instructed Ambassador Austin, as the representative of the United States to the Security Council, to report these steps to the Council.

* * *

September 4, 1950

REDS PUSH WITHIN 10 MILES OF TAEGU, APPROACH POHANG IN RENEWED DRIVE; DEFENDERS COUNTER AT MANY POINTS

U. S. TANKS MOVE UP

Prepare to Retaliate in North, Where Enemy Infiltrates Lines

M'ARTHUR IS OPTIMISTIC

Commander Says Attack of Foe Has Failed to Produce 'Weak Spots' in U. N. Positions

---

By LINDESAY PARROTT
Special to The New York Times.

TOKYO, Monday, Sept. 4—Fighting savagely against the Communist general offensive all along the United Nations perimeter in Korea, United States and South Korean troops today were counter-attacking or preparing counter-attacks. They sought to regain ground lost in the onslaught Friday against positions along the Naktong River line and yesterday in the northern sector from the Naktong to the east coast.

The severest fighting raged in the north, where yesterday afternoon the invaders struck against the hinge of the United States and South Korean lines northeast of Waegwan. Attacking in division strength under a heavy barrage of artillery and mortar fire, the Reds had forced a withdrawal of 6,000 yards at one point on the same ground where a fortnight ago they attempted to seize the key city of Taegu down the "bowling alley" road south from Kunwi.

At the deepest penetration, their advance parties approached to within ten miles of Taegu last evening, infiltrating behind thinly held lines of the United States First Cavalry Division. This morning, however, United States tanks were rumbling up the road to strike back.

Cavalry in Counter-Attack

On the left, Gen. Douglas MacArthur's communiqué said early this morning, other regiments of the cavalry division were counter-attacking against heavy enemy resistance to retake positions with a blow against the right flank of the enemy wedge.

Thus far, General MacArthur said, the coordinated Communist offensive, although it made gains in the south, center and east, "failed to produce desired weak spots in the United Nations line."

The defense ring had been bent under the pressure of an enemy with most of his reserves now in the line. The defenders had yielded ground again, but the Communists thus far had failed to score a break-through as they sought to sweep behind Allied advance positions and take the key bases of Taegu and Pusan. This was the picture that headquarters announcements and front-line reports both drew.

Meanwhile yesterday and this morning the United States Twenty-fifth Division on the south had almost restored the positions lost in Friday's enemy drive, and marines of the First Provisional Brigade were flattening the Communist bulge across the Naktong River near Yongsan, advancing a mile to three miles in a five-pronged drive south and west of the city.

Two Old Battlegrounds Chosen

An Eighth Army communiqué at 10:35 o'clock this morning said that the enemy at 7 A. M. had launched a new "heavy" attack against the Twenty-fifth Division, but reserve elements succeeded in restoring positions, relieving units that had been isolated.

For yesterday's attacks the Communists chose two old battlegrounds—the "bowling alley" northeast of Taegu and the barren hilly area northwest of Pohang. It was here a fortnight ago that the invaders struck through the mountains and through Kigye toward Pohang, the seaport and advanced United States airstrip. Yesterday, in the renewed attack, they made what an Eighth Army communiqué called their greatest gain of the day against the South Korean divisions, forcing back the defenders "several thousand yards."

Simultaneously infiltrators again had thrown a roadblock across the Pohang-Yongchon highway south of Kigye—one of the arteries over which supplies can move to the defenders in the north, a tactic they have employed more than once, sacrificing their guerrilla infiltrators eventually for the temporary harassment of Allied rear communications while they launched a drive in the front.

From south to north, official reports and accounts of eyewitnesses at the front gave a picture of see-saw fighting that had brought in reserves on both sides as the Communists struck what some thought was their decisive blow to overrun the Korean peninsula before United Nations strength could be accumulated to drive them back of the Thirty-eighth Parallel. United States troops were on the offensive in the southern zone—the invaders elsewhere.

On the Twenty-fifth Division front, from the south coast north to the Nam River, General MacArthur's headquarters early this morning said there was "no significant action." Earlier reports of the Eighth Army in Korea indicated that the enemy attack was limited largely to attempts to extricate groups cut off in the United Nations rear or by those groups to break out.

Two Divisions Badly Mauled

Two enemy divisions that made the attack Friday had been badly mauled, and there were some indications that the strongest remaining forces were being withdrawn to the north of the Nam. The Eighth Army reported that the "situation was well under control, with front-line positions almost completely restored and enemy groups in the rear areas contained." Here the invaders' drive to take Masan and menace the vital Pusan area seemed definitely to have broken down.

North along the Naktong River from its junction with the Nam to positions just west of Yongsan, there was fierce fighting. Here the Communists had punched their deepest salient into the Naktong River line, bastion of the United Nations defense in Korea, and they were struggling determinedly to hold it.

Here Marines of the First Provisional Brigade were fighting over ground that they had taken last month when they flattened out the invaders' earlier penetration across the river. Now they had a bulge of twelve miles wide and twelve miles deep to eliminate between the big bend of the Naktong and Changnyong to the north.

[A Second Division spokesman said Monday that United States infantrymen had recaptured Lake Upo, in the area west of Changnyong, according to The Associated Press. The United Press reported that the Second Division had driven Red troops from Changnyong.]

Working with infantrymen of the United States Second Division and armed with Patton tanks—the heaviest armor yet put into the war by the Allies, and the United States answer to the Soviet-made SU-34's—the Marines were striking in a five-pronged drive west and south of Yongsan. According to the most recent reports, issued this morning, they had gained about one mile westward and three miles south along the Yongsan-Masan road.

United States heavy tanks had given a good account of themselves in encounters with Russian armor, knocking out at least three, probably more, according to front-line reports. But on some sections of the front, rain, coming after the long Korean dry spell, somewhat hampered the massive Allied effort of the Air Force, Navy and Marine Corps planes flying in close support of the ground troops.

There were no reports of action opposite Hyonpung, where the Communists drove their first salient across the Naktong River in advance of their general offensive. On the right of the First Cavalry Division to the north, however, troopers moving forward in attack aimed to capture hills from which it would be possible for them to strike toward the Communist advance down the Kunwi "bowling alley" and the tough fighting developing.

It was in the "bowling alley" area itself that the Heaviest combat raged yesterday. Here the Communists yesterday afternoon launched an hour's barrage of guns and mortars. Then, first with one regiment and later with three, they flung the attack toward the south down the Kunwi-Taegu road, forcing back the defenders.

The highway is a two-lane black-top one, best in Korea, a country not distinguished for its modern roads. It is up this road on which heavy United States tanks and guns can move with ease. But it runs through a narrow valley flanked by sharp hills, and these the Communists are again using to facilitate their infiltration tactics.

The invaders, it appeared, were trying to drive a wedge between the United States and South Korean defenders who cooperated in the biggest combined operation of the war last month to throw back their first onslaught here. Front-line reports indicated that they had by-passed the ruined village of Tabu and again were back in the so-called walled city near Kasan.

Last night an Eighth Army communiqué said that on this northwest corner of the perimeter some of the lost positions had been restored.

The Eighth Army this morning reported that the South Korean Third Division was "under heavy pressure" near Pohang after withdrawals of 1,000 to 6,000 yards. Two enemy divisions, presumably the Fifth and Twelfth, were in the attack, utilizing the numerical superiority that the invaders have enjoyed since the start of the war. The emphasis of the attack was toward Pohang itself and the Pohang-Yongchon road.

There were scanty reports of the fighting in the center of the northern front where invaders earlier had been driving down the Uisong-Sinnyong road. A headquarters communiqué yesterday afternoon said that Korean Republican units had made small gains in local actions, straightening lines and reducing enemy pockets.

Intelligence reports indicated that the North Korean Fifteenth Division, which recently had been moved eastward to the vicinity of Komang, in position to strike either down the Uisong road or toward Pohang, again had been shifted back to the center of the line. Whether it was now preparing to join the hobbling early drive was obscure, as was the meaning of its movement back and forth.

But an intelligence spokesman said that the North Korean divisions, which live on the country, have been finding little food and forage since the front had become more stabilized after their big initial drive. Some of these movements behind the lines, it was believed, may constitute attempts by the invaders to find new areas for their troops to loot.

Around Kigye exact positions were obscure although the North Koreans apparently again had driven through the ruined settlement with the crossing of mountain trails and were again occupying the hill to the south overlooking passes toward Pohang. Here unidentified United States elements have been backing South Korean lines, with unconfirmed reports of heavy tanks in action in the flatter coastal region as the first Communist drive into Pohang was blocked.

[The United Press reported that the Reds drove back United States and South Korean defenders about a mile to take Angang, which put them in a position to block Pohang's supply routes.]

The communiqué said that "friendly units" were counter-attacking south of Kigye, to wipe out the roadblock there established by enemy forces characterized as "small"—perhaps organized guerrillas who have been in comparative force in the hilly region along the east coast since the early part of the war, possibly under command of regular North Korean Communist security troops used for such purposes.

Virtually unopposed, the Air Force yesterday again had a record day in Korea, flying more than 600 missions, highest total of the war to date. The majority of the strikes were made in support of ground troops, both in the south and in the area south of Kunwi, where yesterday afternoon F-80 jets struck at the enemy on the "bowling alley" front. One squadron of Mustangs alone flew ninety missions yesterday before returning to its bases in Japan, refueling and rearming in Korea between its strikes.

South Koreans Raid Island

SOMEWHERE IN KOREA, Sept. 3 (AP)—A South Korean naval spokesman said today that South Korean Marines raided Pigum Island, off Mokpo, on the southwestern tip of the peninsula.

1,000 Transmitters Said To Jam 'Voice'

WASHINGTON, Sept 3 (UP)—Moscow is using "at least 1,000" jamming transmitters to keep the Russian people from hearing Voice of America broadcasts that carry the "war of truth" behind the Iron Curtain, State Department officials estimated today.

Listening posts abroad have identified the location of 250 powerful, long-range Soviet transmitters that allow an average of only 30 per cent of the Voice's programs to penetrate into the Soviet Union.

The Russians also have developed a smaller "local" transmitter that tosses squeals, howls and "wolf calls" at the United States broadcasts. Most of these, estimated to number 750, are located in the Moscow area.

* * *

September 10, 1950

MORE U. S. TROOPS FOR EUROPE ORDERED BY THE PRESIDENT; ALLIES IN KOREA BRACE LINES

RISE 'SUBSTANTIAL'

Truman Bases Action on Recommendations Made by Bradley

ATLANTIC MOVES AWAITED

Eisenhower Proposed as Head of Combined Army— Taft Backs Bigger Force

By PAUL P. KENNEDY
Special to The New York Times.

WASHINGTON, Sept. 9—President Truman approved today proposals for "substantial increases" in the strength of United States forces in Western Europe. The approval was based on recommendations of the Joint Chiefs of Staff and concurred in by the Secretaries of State and Defense, the President added.

The extent of the increases will be worked out in coordination with the other North Atlantic pact nations, Mr. Truman said in a short formal statement.

Today's Presidential action followed closely upon recommendations by Congressmen for an increase in United States military strength to bolster Western Europe against possible Soviet aggression.

Senator Henry Cabot Lodge Jr., Republican of Massachusetts, proposed yesterday an increase in the United States military strength to a point where thirty ground divisions would be available for fighting. He told the Senate that the United States might be called upon to furnish twenty divisions to bolster the defense of Europe.

Statement by President

The President's statement approving an increase in United States military forces in Western Europe follows:

"On the basis of recommendations of the Joint Chiefs of Staff, concurred in by the Secretaries of State and Defense, I have today approved substantial increases in the strength of the United States forces to be stationed in Western Europe in the interest of the defense of that area.

"The extent of these increases and the timing thereof will be worked out in close coordination with our North Atlantic Treaty partners. A basic element in the implementation of this decision is the degree to which our friends match our actions in this regard.

"Firm programs for the development of their forces will be expected to keep full step with the dispatch of additional United States forces to Europe. Our plans are based on the sincere expectations that our efforts will be met with similar action on their part. The purpose of this measure is to increase the effectiveness of our collective defense efforts and thereby insure the maintenance of peace."

May Be Discussed Here

The President's action was interpreted as one of the final touches to a pattern that had been shaping up here for several days regarding United States future policy on Western European defense. It is expected that the completed outline will be taken to New York next week by Secretary of State Dean Acheson for discussion at the Western Big Three foreign ministers conference and the North Atlantic Council meeting.

Only one item, the subject of considerable speculation here, is missing thus far and that is the possibility that an American would be named to head a unified European command. A highly reliable source said yesterday that an American would be acceptable to Europe if he were advanced. This source emphasized, however, that the job should be considered on the basis of the candidate's merits rather than his nationality.

The name most prominently mentioned here and published today as a likely choice was that of Gen. Dwight D. Eisenhower.

General Eisenhower, who has repeatedly said he would respond to a call to duty, recently offered his services in any capacity. Persons advocating his selection as a supreme commander point out that he is known and liked in Europe. They say he has already proved his ability to weld the fighting forces of many nations into an effective team.

Others being mentioned for the position include Gen. Omar N. Bradley, Chairman of the Joint Chiefs of Staff, and Gen. George C. Marshall, Chief of Staff in World War II and now president of the American Red Cross.

As matters stand it appears probable that the United States representation at the coming meetings in New York will advocate as part of a basic Western European defense plan:

1. An increase in United States military strength, with the increase to be matched by the Atlantic Pact nations.
2. An increase by Britain of her forces on the Continent and the possible dispatch of some Canadian troops.
3. The formation and arming of a West German contingent to be integrated into a West European army. This contingent would be fully equipped by the United States and would have its own officers.

Some authorities here argue that this plan or something closely resembling it must be adopted to give real meaning to an over-all defense of the West.

They contend this is particularly true of West Germany, where there is a pronounced reluctance to plan for any sort of an individual defense but an equally pronounced receptiveness to enter into a common defense program.

Taft to Back Lodge Plan

Senator Robert A. Taft, Republican of Ohio, said today that he would support Senator Lodge's move to bring United States fighting strength up to thirty divisions, or about 500,000 men. He said, however, he would be slow in sending troops to Europe until a unified defense plan had been worked out and European countries pledged troops of their own.

"There is still no final plan for defending western Europe," he commented. "Until there is such a plan, we won't be able to tell what the European countries are going to do for themselves. I'm willing to send more troops to Europe but I want to know first what is needed."

A United States official has estimated that the Russians now have 170 divisions in their own country and twenty-seven in eastern Germany. Fifteen of the latter are armored divisions, he said. This is in addition to sizable forces in the satellite countries.

Defense officials here, of course, will not disclose the number of United States troops in Western Europe. However, reports published in July placed the number at about 110,000. This is exclusive of naval forces.

*   *   *

September 15, 1950

U. N. FORCES LAND BEHIND COMMUNISTS IN KOREA; SEIZE INCHON, PORT OF SEOUL; MOVE INLAND; U. S. WILL PRESS FOR A JAPANESE PEACE TREATY

---

3 LANDINGS MADE

Allies Strike at Western Port and Two Points North of Pohang

4TH PUSH REPORTED

Units of U. S. Marines Join Blow
Behind the Front Lines of Foe

By The Associated Press

TOKYO, Friday, Sept. 15—United Nations invasion forces landed today at Inchon, the port city for Seoul on Korea's west coast—150 miles behind the 130,000-man North Korean Army at the fighting front.

Covered by planes and warships, United States troops stormed ashore on the island of Wolmi, linked to Inchon by a causeway. South Korean Marines landed at Inchon.

In a simultaneous operation other United States forces landed immediately behind the Communist lines on the east coast. They made two landings—one two miles northeast of Communist-held Pohang, the other at Yongdok, more than twenty-five miles north of Pohang.

[Sources in Washington said the United States forces involved were units of the Second Marine Division.]

The west coast invasion, preceded by cruiser and destroyer bombardments and sweeping carrier plane strikes, swung the United Nations to the offensive for the first time since the Reds began the war last June 25.

Close to 38th Parallel

The invasion at Inchon, putting United Nations forces close to the Thirty-eighth Parallel which the North Koreans crossed June 25, was announced by the South Korean Commander in Chief, Maj. Gen. Chung il Kwon.

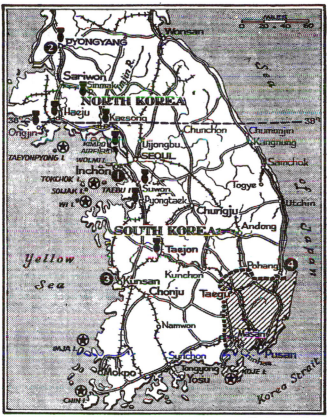

The New York Times

United States and South Korean forces landed at Inchon (1) and drove inland, while other South Korean troops landed near Pohang (4) and at another point on the east coast about twenty-five miles north of Pohang. A fourth landing was reported made at Kunsan (3) on the west coast. Earlier, United Nations naval planes had battered targets from Pyongyang (2) and southward (points are indicated by bomb devices). South Koreans already hold islands marked by stars. The diagonally shaded area is the United Nation's southern beachhead.

He said that heavy pressure was quickly exerted by the invasion forces on the Communists near Kimpo airfield, Seoul's big air base. Kimpo is twelve miles northwest of Seoul and ten miles north of Inchon.

A report from Pusan said that still other United Nations forces had gone ashore at Kunsan, a west coast city 100 miles south of Seoul. The report came from Chin Soo, South Korean National Assemblyman, who said a warship bombardment had supported the landing.

One thousand South Korean commandos went ashore on the east coast near Pohang, striking at a coastal road that would bar the way to any retreat by the North Korean forces defending the port. The commandos quickly called for air support.

A big United States battleship was reported Thursday to be off the east coast in the Pohang-Yongdok sector.

Invasion Follows Naval Attack

The North Koreans had been expecting an invasion at Inchon since Rear Adm. John M. Hoskins, commander of Task Force 77, sent British and United States cruisers and destroyers close in to bombard Inchon Wednesday. The targets included Wolmi Island.

While their shells hit the area, carrier planes for the second straight day ranged 210 miles from Kunsan to Pyongyang, capital city of the North Koreans, hitting at airfields.

B-29's coordinated these blows, blowing up an underground arsenal north of Pyongyang and severing rail lines from Pyongyang for 100 miles south to Seoul and for 200 miles southeast to Kumchon.

[Gen. Douglas MacArthur's headquarters announced at noon today, Friday, that United Nations forces were again in the walled city of Kasan, ten miles north of Taegu, from which they had been forced to retreat last weeks, The United Press reported.]

The Pyongyang radio broadcast claimed shore guns had sunk three destroyers and four landing craft Wednesday. United States officials in Washington quickly said the three destroyers had suffered superficial damage and denied that any ships had been sunk.

The South Korean announcement of the invasion had been preceded by assurances of Lieut. Gen. Walton H. Walker, United Nations field commander in Korea, that an offensive could be expected soon.

Invasion Is Called Sound

TOKYO, Friday, Sept. 15 (UP)—From a military strategy viewpoint, the United Nations invasion of North Korea today was a sound operation because:

1. It drove into the Communist army's heart and it transferred the main front to the vital center of the Korean Republic.
2. It left the bulk of the North Korean army along the southeastern perimeter without any visible means of supply and support from North Korea.
3. It presented the Communists with a two-front war at a time when they already were reeling from heavy losses in the south.
4. It aimed a high powered wedge at the only good communications route running from north to south in Korea.
5. It saved Allied lives because it gave the United Nations a military foothold in the north that would have been slow and costly to gain by fighting through rugged hills between Taegu and Seoul.

Gen. Douglas MacArthur hit the North Korean Communists with the same punch that made him famous in World War II and the landing at Inchon bore the general's trademark.

Hit them where they are light and cut them off was General MacArthur's strategic creed when he fought the Japanese from New Guinea through the Philippines from 1942 to 1945.

The amphibious landings were commanded by Rear Admiral James Doyle, veteran of many South Pacific landings. They were supported by Task Force 77, commanded by Rear Admiral E. C. Ewen, whose planes had raked the west central part of Korea for two days to soften up the enemy. Heavy cruisers and destroyers of the Seventh Fleet commanded by Vice Admiral Arthur D. Struble also were in on the action, smashing shore targets with their big guns.

Contrary to usual military practices, the landing was made early in the afternoon because of the widely fluctuating tides, which rise nearly thirty feet. The assault craft rode in on the low tide at 1:15 P. M. The tide was at a low of seven inches at the time and it was scheduled to reach a high of twenty-nine feet, eleven inches at 7:20 P. M.

* * *

October 7, 1950

SOUTH KOREA TROOPS CROSS 38TH PARALLEL IN NEW AREA; WEST REASSURES RED CHINA

FOE HIT IN CENTER

Push Northward Widens and Jabs Main Defense Line of Communists

AIR STRIKES AID DRIVE

U. S. Pilots Work on Apparent Enemy Build-Up at Wonsan—Marine Sector Active

By LINDESAY PARROTT
Special to The New York Times.

TOKYO, Saturday, Oct. 7—South Korean Republican troops in force crossed the Thirty-eighth Parallel at a new point yesterday. Reports from Korea today said that they were striking at sections of the defense line prepared by the North Korean Communist People's Army above the old artificial border between North and South Korea.

The thrust across the Parallel, the reports said, was made by the Republican Sixth Division striking north from Chunchon in the mountainous region of Central Korea. The Sixth Division had passed the Pukhan River and moved about three miles north of the Parallel to capture the town of Chichon.

This put the South Koreans on the road to Hwachon, one of the bastions of the Communist line across the peninsula. Chichon, about eight miles from Hwachon, is a main highway crossing.

[Field reports said that elements of the South Korean Sixth Division had entered Hwachon, The Associated Press reported.]

Progress Up East Coast

Troops of the South Korean Third and Capital Divisions widened and deepened the salient they had already driven over the Parallel on the East Coast and moved to within about twenty-five miles of the important seaport and rail center of Wonsan.

An overnight communiqué from Gen. Douglas MacArthur's headquarters said the Republican Sixth Division had cleared enemy resistance from Chunchon and "advanced north." Chunchon had kept Republican troops busy several days mopping up stubborn enemy resistance.

Headquarters announcements here, starting yesterday, seemed to have eliminated mention of the whereabouts of United States Divisions in Korea, some of which had been reported moving up to the Thirty-eighth Parallel for a possible United Nations drive into the Communist-held territory as implicitly sanctioned by the General Assembly's Political and Security Committee at Lake Success.

A headquarters spokesman acknowledged United Nations forces were in movement and regrouping.

Action North of Seoul

But the only outfit named was a regiment of the United States First Marine Division, which as of yesterday morning was moving beyond Uijongbu, north of Seoul, and "still fighting."

[The Marines, according to The Associated Press, continued advances north from Uijongbu. United States units in this sector were about fifteen miles south of the Parallel. The United Press said the South Korean Eighth Division was attacking Saturday north from the Uijongbu area within a mile of the Parallel.

[British and Australian troops joined the Americans in the area Friday, the dispatches said.]

The deepest advance into Communist territory again was made yesterday by the Republican Third Division, which has pushed up the road along the east coast all the way from Pohang, the farthest limit of the Communist invasion.

Brushing aside resistance by an enemy force of possibly battalion strength in the vicinity of Changjon, the Third Division rolled northward beyond Tongchon.

[After taking Tongchon, the division had moved five miles along the coast Saturday morning and was in the town of Kojo, said a United Press dispatch.]

Somewhere between Tongchon and Wonsan, the Communists have been reported digging in with remnants of their Fifth, Twelfth and Fifteenth Divisions possibly reinforced by fresh troops from the Red capital at Pyongyang.

The Third Division, therefore, was probably nearing a main hub of enemy resistance on the east coast.

The advance was supported by fighters of the United States Fifth Air Force striking with rockets and the deadly jellied gasoline ahead of the Republicans. The Air Force said jet F-80's and F-51 Mustangs "struck in some force against Communists" concentrating near Wonsan.

The United States fighter pilots also hit rail and highway lines from Pyongyang to Wonsan and thence south.

The ground attack inward from the east coast was made by elements of the South Korean Capital Division, which had crossed the Parallel behind spearheads of the Third. Pushing north to the vicinity of Hwangpo, Capital Division troops swung inland to protect their left flank.

They moved southwest toward a possible junction with South Korean Sixth Division units thrusting twelve miles to Yongdae and then an additional fifteen miles to Inje and Yachon. [Front reports said Capital Division troops had occupied these villages.]

The advance was made against developing Communist resistance as the South Koreans neared what were believed to be the main Red defense lines. The enemy fought stubbornly before Capital Division men broke through at Yongdae, the MacArthur communiqué said.

Later reports said a concentration of about 2,000 enemy troops held up the advance southwest of Yongdae before it was overcome.

As the South Koreans broadened their advance the United States Air Force continued to strike at two main targets, Red communications and military bases to the north and positions along the Communist defense cordon from Wonsan through Hwachon, Kumhwa Chorwon. F-80 jets struck and and destroyed four buildings in Chorwon. Flames that followed a rocket hit apparently were from a fuel dump, pilots said.

Enemy troops concentrating near Kumhwa were attacked by accurate rocket fire with "good results." F-80's hit a factory in Kumhwa. Fighters and light bombers attacked railroad lines near Wonsan.

For a second successive day, Superforts attacked the Kan Arsenal north of Pyongyang and battered railway and highway bridges on routes to the Red capital.

Enemy Columns Spotted in North

TOKYO, Saturday, Oct. 7 (UP)—United States fliers over Korea north of the Thirty-eighth Parallel, reported two enemy tank convoys moving down from Northwestern and Northeastern Korea. Marine fighter-bombers ripped into one of the columns in attacks Friday night.

Reports transmitted from Kimpo Airfield near Seoul said a huge enemy convoy reported last Tuesday stretching over an estimated 100 miles below the Manchurian border now was reported by United States Air Force reconnaissance pilots to have been broken up into smaller units north of Pyongyang.

The pilot of a B-26 reported a convoy of Red tanks north of Pyongyang. He returned to Kimpo and took Marine fighter-bombers back to the area where they knocked out four tanks and six trucks.

Far East Air Forces reconnaissance pilots reported a thirty-tank column from Manchuria moving southward over poor roads toward the east coast port of Wonsan.

Group Back at Pohang Strip

UNITED STATES FIFTH AIR FORCE HEADQUARTERS, Korea, Saturday, Oct. 7 (UP)—The Thirty-fifth Fighter-Bomber Group of the Fifth Air Force returned today to Pohang Airstrip, from which it had been driven in mid-August by the North Korean Communists.

* * *

October 31, 1950

CHINESE RED UNIT HELPS FOE DRIVE ALLIES BACK IN KOREA; INVADERS ADVANCING IN TIBET

SOUTH KOREANS HIT

Attacking Peiping Force Said to Be in at Least Regimental Strength

7TH DIVISION MOVES AHEAD

Advance Units More Than 50 Miles From Landing Beach— Others Going Ashore

By LINDESAY PARROTT
Special to The New York Times.

TOKYO, Tuesday, Oct. 31—Communist troops identified by a spokesman of the United States Army's Tenth Corps as soldiers of the Chinese Red Army launched today a strong counter-attack against the South Korean Republican divisions on the east coast of Korea fifty miles below the Manchurian border.

Although details were lacking, unofficial reports indicated that the Chinese Communists were at least in regimental strength and possibly numbered as much as one division.

This morning's attack was reported to have cut the communications of advance guards of the Republican Capital Division, which has been pushing in from the east coast toward Pujon Reservoir. This is in the mountainous section of Korea south of the headwaters of the Yalu River, which marks the boundary line between Korea and Manchuria.

[Officers of the Republican Sixth Division, according to The Associated Press, said that a force of more than 10,000, most of them Chinese, had cut up the South Koreans.]

Reports said also that the Communist troops had placed a roadblock across the coastal highway twelve miles north of the large industrial city of Hamhung. Prisoners said that they had been ordered to take Hamhung by Nov. 1.

Extent of Commitment Uncertain

It was yet uncertain whether the reported appearance of Chinese troops in force meant that the Communist Government of Mao Tse-tung had decided to intervene formally in the Korean war as United Nations forces neared the sensitive international boundary.

Previous reports that Chinese soldiers had been captured on the west coast were met by headquarters comment that intervention, which might have been most effective when the United Nations forces were compressed into the narrow perimeter around Pusan, now would be too late to reverse the situation unless a huge-scale commitment was made.

Meanwhile two United States divisions, making up Maj. Gen. Edward M. Almond's Tenth Corps, with a strength of about 50,000 men, landed in the east coast in the past week.

The United States First Marine Division for the last few days has been moving up to the Hamhung-Hungnam area after its landing last Thursday at Wonsan. The Marines are now understood to be concentrated around the twin cities, and General Almond has announced that their mission was to drive to the Manchurian border.

The United States Seventh Infantry Division was also confronting the Communists in the east coast area after landing at Iwon on Sunday. Reports yesterday said that advance elements of the division's Seventeenth Regimental Combat Team were more than fifty miles northwest of the landing beach, on narrow country roads.

Exact positions were not announced, but the regiment presumably was behind the South Korean troops moving on Pungsan to north and east of the Republicans, under attack near Pujon Reservoir. Other troops of the Seventh Division and heavy equipment were still coming ashore from Navy transports on the Iwon beaches.

Elements of Fortieth Corps

Reports of the Chinese Communist counter-attack followed repeated assertions by South Korean Army leaders that their men for several days had been facing elements of the Chinese Fortieth Corps, which supposedly had been concentrated along the Yalu River border.

Airmen flying patrols close to the frontier had reported seeing no concentrations of Chinese troops, and headquarters spokesmen insisted that there was no indication to date of any mass intervention.

South Korean reports, however, have stated that the Chinese had had as many as 125,000 men in the border area. They added that Chou En-lai, Chinese Foreign Minister, had asserted that China would not stand idly by to watch the wreckage of the North Korean Communist regime by United Nations armies.

The Tenth Corps' reports, it was understood, were based on the capture of about twenty prisoners in the area of the South Korean Capital Division.

The unit from which the prisoners came was not identified, but front-line reports said it had launched a heavy attack on the South Koreans, driving into the Republican advance and making a penetration of several miles south of Pujon Reservoir before being contained.

A Marine Corps spokesman said that Chinese Communist prisoners taken in an attack yesterday afternoon had identified the unit from which they came as the 376th Artillery Division of the Chinese Red Army. The Tenth Corps office asserted, however, that there was no evidence of more than one regiment of Chinese in the area.

It has been said here that the Chinese Army in Manchuria included many native Koreans or men of the Korean race resident north of the border. Two divisions of such soldiers were transferred to the North Korean Army after the close of the Chinese Civil War and became the nucleus of the North Korean forces that crossed the Thirty-eighth Parallel last June in the attempt to overrun the peninsula.

The Chinese, it has been said, have been particularly concerned with the attack toward the Yalu River in its central and upper course because of the series of dams that, although power installations on the Korean side, provide hydroelectric energy for industry in the Mukden area as well as the now generally wrecked North Korean factories.

Meanwhile, on other sectors of the Korean front, official reports said that enemy resistance was hardening and that the Communists in some areas again were staging local offensives.

Some sources here believed that this stiffening resistance and the reports of a Chinese counter-offensive indicated a breakdown of the plan to permit South Koreans and possibly other non-American United Nations troops to drive to the Manchurian border while United States forces remained outside some "buffer area" south of the Yalu.

The United States, with seven divisions available in the theatre, probably had the only force strong enough to insure victory against the tough, reinforced North Korean resistance.

Only small advances were reported yesterday on any section of the front, and the United Nations drive appeared definitely to have been slowed down after its rapid thrusts following the fall of Pyongyang.

Indications that the North Korean Communist Government still was attempting to enforce orders of Premier Kim Il Sung to fight to the end against the United Nations "aggresssion" came from a weak broadcasting station that called itself Sinuiju radio. Apparently it was operating from Sinuiju, a city just across from the Chinese settlement of Antung, near the mouth of the Yalu.

The radio said that national mobilization for war of all men and women in North Korea had been put into effect. At the same time reports from Korea said that Communist guerrillas seem to have adopted a policy of organized terrorism behind the United Nations lines.

* * *

November 6, 1950

M'ARTHUR SAYS 'ALIEN' REDS HAVE REOPENED KOREAN WAR; SEES 'GRAVEST' ISSUE RAISED

U. N. CHIEF IS STERN

Calls Intervention One of 'Most Offensive Acts' of Lawlessness

BIG ENEMY TRAP AVERTED

General Declares Troops Move Into Korea From Manchuria, Beyond Reach of His Army

By LINDESAY PARROTT
Special to The New York Times.

TOKYO, Monday, Nov. 6—Gen. Douglas MacArthur, in a special communiqué he issued this morning as Commander in Chief of the United Nations forces in Korea, charged "the Communists" with "one of the most offensive acts of international lawlessness of historic record" by intervening in and in effect renewing the Korean war after the thorough defeat of the North Korean armies.

Without notice of belligerency, General MacArthur charged, the Communists had moved "alien" forces across the Yalu River, the international boundary between North Korea and Manchuria, and massed "a great concentration" in the "privileged sanctuary" of Chinese territory across the border. Their intention, the United Nations commander said, was to lay a trap for destruction of the United Nations forces that had shattered and were pursuing remnants of the North Korean Army—an outcome that was averted only by the skillful maneuvers of the commander in the field.

Mission to Destroy Foe

"Our present mission is limited to the destruction of those forces now arrayed against us in North Korea," General MacArthur said. But he indicated that the Communists' massing of reserves in presumably neutral territory with the intent of further armed intervention might not forever command immunity.

"Whether and to what extent these reserves will be moved forward to reinforce units now committed remains to be seen and is a matter of the gravest international significance," the statement said.

General MacArthur's statement, in which perhaps significantly he spoke as United Nations Commander in Chief, made no direct mention of Chinese Communist troops in North Korea. But it came at a time when other sources indicated that United States forces were now in effect involved in a large-scale undeclared war with Chinese soldiers of Mao Tse-tung.

[At Lake Success a United States spokesman expressed doubt that a formal complaint to the United Nations would be made on the basis of General MacArthur's statement alone. The United States delegation will transmit the MacArthur communication to the Security Council.]

Two Red Divisions Identified

While General MacArthur stated only that "alien Communist forces" had moved across the Yalu River, a spokesman for the United States Eighth Army in Korea identified two Chinese Communist divisions in combat on the critical western sector of the Korean front.

Other sources indicated that as many as five divisions might be massing in the west, not only for defense of the Yalu River power plants, which are important to Chinese industry, but for a drive in strength to recapture the former Korean Communist capital at Pyongyang.

Yesterday Chinese and North Korean troops threw a series of savage attacks against the United Nations positions along the Chongchon River, about forty miles north of the former capital. Their fight, front-line reports said, much more closely resembled an attempt to find a weak spot and score a breakthrough southward than it did a movement to defend the Yalu hydro-electric stations, the nearest of which is more than fifty miles away and which, despite unchallenged

United Nations control of the air, has been inconsistently spared by Allied bombers.

General MacArthur's statement, only the eleventh he has issued since the war began over his own signature as general of the United States Army and Commander in Chief of the United Nations forces, was the first formal recognition at this headquarters of the mass intervention by Chinese troops, which last week sprung a surprise counter-attack against South Korean divisions racing for the Manchurian frontier.

Headquarters in Doubt

Hitherto intelligence spokesmen here had declined to acknowledge that actual Chinese Army organizations were in combat and implied that the Chinese might be "volunteers" of Korean ancestry stiffening the North Koreans for defensive counter-attacks rather than troops assigned to a full-scale counter-offensive.

The United Nations commander said that last week the Korean war had been brought to a "practical end"; that 135,000 North Korean prisoners had been taken and total losses of 335,000 inflicted, "representing a fair estimate of North Korean total military strength" and that "the defeat of the North Koreans and destruction of their armies was thereby decisive."

"In the face of this victory of United Nations arms the Communists committed one of the most offensive acts of international lawlessness of historic record by moving without any notice of belligerency elements of alien Communist forces across the Yalu River into North Korea and massing a great concentration of possible reinforcing divisions with adequate supply behind the privileged sanctuary of the adjacent Manchurian border," General MacArthur continued.

There was a possibility at that time of a "great military reverse," General MacArthur said. He added that the "potential danger was avoided with minimum losses only by the timely detection and skillfull maneuvering of the United Nations commander responsible for that sector"—presumably Lieut. Gen. Walton H. Walker, commander of the United States Eighth Army.

As a result of the trap laid by the Communists—some here call it an attempt at a new Pearl Harbor—General MacArthur said that the enemy had brought a fresh army into the field. These are Chinese troops who, according to front-line accounts, have new Russian-made tanks, artillery, multiple rocket-launchers and even a potential air force of Yaks and jet-propelled fighters.

Behind these Chinese combat forces and reorganized remnants of the North Korean Army are possible "large alien reserves," General MacArthur said. In the present situation these can be massed at will behind the Manchurian border and moved across the frontier as required. But they and their supply trains remain immune from attack until the boundary is actually crossed. Both the reserves and the supply concentrations are "beyond the limits of our present sphere of military action," General MacArthur pointed out.

* * *

January 16, 1951

TRUMAN SUBMITS A 71½ BILLION CRISIS BUDGET; ASKS 16 BILLION TAX RISE, 61 BILLION FOR ARMS; ALLIES DRIVE IN WEST KOREA, QUIT WONJU AREA

A PEACETIME HIGH

Arms and Foreign Aid Take 69% of Total—Fair Deal Included

IT IS TIED TO DEFENSE

Sentiment in Congress Accepts Military Cost, Is Cool to Others

By JOHN D. MORRIS
Special to The New York Times.

WASHINGTON, Jan. 15—President Truman laid before Congress today a budget calling for $71,594,000,000 of expenditures in the fiscal year beginning next July 1 to meet what his accompanying message called "the compelling demands" of national security "in a period of grave danger."

He said that the budget, by far the largest in peacetime history, reflected this country's determination to achieve a twofold goal:

First, to strengthen itself and its allies sufficiently to deter further Communist aggression.

Second, to create reserves of trained manpower and industrial capacity to permit immediate mobilization of "all our power," if that should become necessary.

The President estimated receipts at $55,138,000,000 for a prospective deficit of $16,456,000,000 and indicated that he would soon request a tax increase of at least that amount.

Gives Revised 1951 Figures

"At this time," he asserted, "sound public finance and fiscal policy require that we balance the budget. I shall shortly submit to the Congress recommendations for new revenue legislation."

The new budget, setting forth in detail the Administration's program for the 1952 fiscal year and giving revised estimates of expenditures and receipts in the 1951 fiscal year, which ends next June 30, was presented to the House of Representatives and Senate by messenger shortly after they convened today.

Congressional comment indicated a general disposition to provide any funds necessary for the defense program, but there was widespread complaint that the President had failed to economize sufficiently in nondefense fields.

Bitter battles were predicted over Mr. Truman's renewal of many Fair Deal proposals, particularly one for the establishment of a Fair Employment Practices Commission, an issue that caused some Southern Democrats to bolt the party in last year's elections.

The President briefed reporters at a budget "seminar" on Saturday with the understanding that any information was to be withheld from publication until today.

Revenue Record Set in 1949

In reply to questions at that time, he said he might ask Congress for a tax increase of as much as $20,000,000,000, retroactive to Jan. 1; that the Marshall Plan would have to be continued beyond June 30 of 1952, and that he intended to continue pressing for his civil rights program.

On the expenditure side, the budget represented a 78 per cent increase over the 1951 total of $47,210,000,000, the previous peacetime record. Under the biggest wartime budget $98,703,000,000 was spent in 1945.

Prospective receipts were far above any other year, either in peace or war, even without allowing for further tax increases.

The $55,138,000,000 revenue estimated for the 1952 fiscal year compares with the current fiscal year's peacetime record, an estimated $44,512,000,000. The all-time record, established in 1945, was $44,762,000,000.

In his budget message, President Truman emphasized that military and international programs accounted directly for 69 per cent of the expenditures proposed for the 1952 fiscal year. Together, they comprised $48,900,000,000 of the budget total.

The President noted that the budget also contained "expenditures for programs which will maintain and develop our national strength over the long run, keeping in mind that the present emergency may be of long duration and we must, therefore, be prepared for crises in the more distant as well as in the immediate future."

He thus keyed to the defense program a number of previously recommended Fair Deal measures and reiterated his requests for enactment of legislation necessary to carry them out.

They included compulsory health insurance, aid to education, a Fair Employment Practice Act, expansion of Social Security and a farm program along lines proposed by Charles F. Brannan, Secretary of Agriculture.

Funds for all of them except the Brannan plan were budgeted. There was no explanation of the one omission.

The President also recommended anew and budgeted funds for a dozen other items requiring legislation, including authority to construct defense plants, higher postal rates, a St. Lawrence Seaway and power project, loans for Indians, defense housing incentives and extension of authority to control exports, rents, prices, wages and the distribution of materials.

Free Service Insurance Asked

One new proposal was for revision of the service men's life insurance system to provide automatically and free of charge an indemnity of $10,000 to survivors of all who die in military service. He suggested that this be supplemented by a voluntary insurance program, limited to veterans whose insurability at standard rates has been impaired by military service.

Another new recommendation was for a $1,000,000,000 increase in the lending authority of the Export-Import Bank to meet "the increased need for undertakings to expand output of defense materials."

Mr. Truman laid great emphasis on the necessity for "strict economy" in nondefense spending and contended that he had tailored the budget accordingly. In substantiation he issued a special table comparing defense and nondefense outlays and instructed the Budget Bureau to prepare a list of 133 specific items that had been reduced below 1951 levels.

The special table showed a decrease of $1,082,000,000 in expenditures exclusive of "major national security programs." The security programs, totaling $52,510,000,000 for 1952 as compared with $27,044,000,000 for 1951, were listed as military services, international security, atomic energy, defense production and controls, civil defense, maritime activities, defense housing and community facilities and dispersal of Federal agencies.

Military Outlay 'Tentative'

The same table listed automatic reductions netting $761,000,000 in expenditures fixed by law, such as veterans' benefits and farm price supports. The actual nondefense economies claimed were thus reduced to $321,000,000. Tapering off of the veterans' educational program alone accounted for about $800,000,000 of automatic reductions. This was partly offset by increases in other nondefense outlays fixed by law.

Of the thirteen major functional categories contained in the budget itself, ten showed higher expenditures for the new fiscal year. The three showing declines were transportation and communication, housing and community development and veterans' services and benefits.

The President emphasized, however, that "the entire Government is being redirected to meet the compelling demands of national security, and each functional category includes activities which support, directly or indirectly, the defense effort."

It was consequently difficult to separate defense from nondefense expenditures.

Far the biggest budget category was military services, expenditures being estimated at $41,421,000,000 as compared with $20,994,000,000 for 1951. Even this, the President said, was "tentative" and subject to substantial adjustment as the defense program progressed.

Outlays for international security and foreign relations were likewise tentative. Like the military budget, the international category contained no detailed breakdown of outlays for specific programs. The total was listed at $7,461,000,000 as compared with $4,726,000,000 in the current year.

Atomic Budget Expanded

Increases over current-year expenditures were also listed for finance, commerce and industry, labor, natural resources, agriculture and agricultural resources, education and general research, social security, health and welfare; general government, and interest.

Considerable stress was placed on the national defense nature of many items included in such categories.

The atomic energy program, for example, was covered under the natural resources classification, and the President budgeted $1,277,000,000 for it. This represents an increase of $469,000,000 over 1951.

Outlays in 1951, Mr. Truman said, provided enlargement of production capacity for atomic materials and weapons. The 1952 increases will provide also for "the investigation and development of new and improved weapons," he reported.

In addition, he said, they will allow for continuing development of new designs of nuclear reactors, including those for production of fissionable material, the generation of power and the propulsion of ships and aircraft.

Also listed under natural resources were defense-connected programs for discovery and development of mineral resources and production of electric power, likewise calling for higher expenditures than in 1951.

For the Tennessee Valley Authority alone, the President budgeted $236,000,000, an increase of $65,000,000 over the current year. He also called for immediate redevelopment of Niagara power facilities, enabled by a recent treaty with Canada.

Holds Public Works Necessary

He said that the only major new public works projects provided in the budget were "those directly necessary to the defense effort." The principal reductions in that connection were $57,000,000 for flood control and $90,000,000 for irrigation projects. The public roads program was held close to the 1951 level.

While actual expenditures to meet all of the Government's requirements in the 1952 fiscal year were estimated at $71,594,000,000 President Truman asked Congress for a total of $83,505,000,000 in new spending and lending authority. The extra $11,911,000,000 consists mainly of appropriations of funds that will not be disbursed until 1953 or later.

The principal item is an appropriation of another $10,000,000,000 sought for the military services to supplement the current year's spending authority.

Although his budget message appeared to leave no doubt that he would call on Congress for a tax increase of at least $16,456,000,000, the amount of prospective deficit, President Truman refused to be pinned to that figure at his question-and-answer session with reporters.

Contends U. S. Can Carry Load

He said it might be more and it might be less, depending on conditions existing when he submits a special tax message expected special within a few weeks.

Finally, however, he conceded that the request would be for $16,000,000,000 to $20,000,000,000 and declared that he wanted the increase made retroactive to Jan. 1.

Reminded that some Congressional leaders felt that the national economy would be unable to withstand such a heavy tax load, the President said simply that he did not agree with them.

As a matter of fact, the President disclosed, the exact amount of new taxes to be requested has not yet been deter-

mined. He added, however, that he had made it perfectly plain that he did not see any sense in increasing the national debt.

Prospects of as much as $15,000,000,000 in new tax requirements prompted new speculation over the possibility of a Federal sales tax to augment other levies.

Asked if such a levy was under consideration, President Truman said that all possible sources of revenue were being studied.

A $15,000,000,000 tax increase would be almost twice the size of any previous one. Together, the two revenue bills enacted last year were designed to produce $7,700,000,000 annually. The biggest single tax-increase bill to date was a $7,000,000,000 measure enacted in 1942.

Besides the indicated increases in regular taxes, the President's renewed request for compulsory health insurance entailed $275,000,000 of additional social security levies. The social security taxes are administered apart from the budget through separate payroll deductions shared by employers and employes.

For the period preparatory to setting up a health insurance system, Mr. Truman proposed an extra payroll tax of one-half of 1 per cent, to be shared equally by employers and employes.

In dealing with other aspects of his welfare program, President Truman again budgeted $300,000,000 for grants to states for operating expenses of elementary and secondary schools, but did not take a stand on the issue of aid to parochial school students for transportation and other auxiliary services. A national controversy over that question killed the aid-to-education bill in the last Congress.

Last year the President also recommended aid to college students, but omitted that proposal from the new budget "pending reconsideration of the kind of program that will best fit into Selective Service policies and general manpower requirements."

Also Disability Insurance

In urging expansion of social security, Mr. Truman deplored the fact that self-employed farmers, many public employes, members of the armed forces and others still were not covered by old age and survivors' insurance.

He also renewed recommendations for disability insurance and for liberalization of the unemployment insurance program.

Grants to states for strengthening public health services were likewise requested anew, with $5,000,000 budgeted for the first-year cost. At the same time, the President called for prompt enactment of legislation to help increase enrollment in medical and related schools. He budgeted $25,000,000 for nursing school scholarships and grants to states for vocational training of practical nurses.

Mr. Truman's estimate of receipts from regular taxes anticipated rapid expansion of the national economy. It was based on forecasts that total individual income would average $245,000,000,000. The 1951 budget was based on an annual rate of $221,000,000,000. The rate during the fourth quarter of the calendar year 1950 is estimated at $233,400,000,000.

Despite the resulting increases in tax collections, supplemented by the imposition of higher rates in 1950, Mr. Truman forecast that the national debt would rise to $276,000,000,000 by June 30 of 1952 unless taxes were further increased. It now stands at about $256,000,000,000.

*   *   *

March 30, 1951

3 IN ATOM SPY CASE ARE FOUND GUILTY; MAXIMUM IS DEATH

Woman and 2 Men Convicted of Wartime Espionage in Behalf of Soviet Union

JURY SPLIT FOR A WHILE

One Member Was Not Sure at First About One Defendant— Sentencing Next Thursday

By WILLIAM R. CONKLIN

Possible death sentences moved closer to three defendants in the nation's first atomic spy trial when a Federal Court jury found all three guilty of espionage for Soviet Russia at 11 o'clock yesterday morning.

Though the jury was aware that death was a maximum penalty, it made no recommendation for leniency. Judge Irving R. Kaufman was prepared to receive such a recommendation, but had told the jury in his charge that it would not be binding upon him. Judge Kaufman will sentence the three at 10:30 o'clock next Thursday.

The convicted spies are Julius Rosenberg, 32 years old, an electrical engineer; his wife, Ethel, 35, and Morton Sobell, 34, an electronics expert. United States Attorney Irving H. Saypol, Government prosecutor, said David Greenglass, 29, would be brought up for sentencing at the same time.

Greenglass, a brother of Mrs. Rosenberg, was a key Government witness against the woman and her husband at the trial, which began on March 6. He had confessed his part in the spy plot.

Fifth Defendant a Fugitive

The indictment is still pending against a fifth defendant, Anatoli A. Yakovlev, former Russian vice consul here. Yakovlev has been a fugitive since he left New York with his family on Dec. 27, 1946, bound for Russia.

Rosenberg and his wife, who lived at 10 Monroe Street in Knickerbocker Village, are parents of two sons, Michael, 8, and Robert, 4. Sobell and his wife, Helen, have a daughter, Sydney, 11, and a son, Mark, 18 months. Greenglass and his wife, Ruth, are the parents of two small children. Mrs. Greenglass was named as a co-conspirator but not as a co-defendant.

The jury of eleven men and one woman had received the case at 4:53 o'clock Wednesday afternoon. After deliberating for several hours, they spent the night in a midtown hotel and resumed deliberations at 9:50 o'clock yesterday morning.

When they announced at 11 o'clock that they had reached a verdict, they had considered the evidence for seven hours and forty-two minutes.

Judge Kaufman, it was reported, has not yet decided on what punishment he will inflict. Harry Gold, a Government witness against the Rosenbergs and Sobel, got a thirty-year sentence in Philadelphia after confessing his part in the same spy conspiracy. The heavy sentence was imposed despite a plea for leniency by the Department of Justice, which considered Gold a cooperative witness.

The "Hold-Out" Juror

Juror No. 7, Harold H. Axley, was reported as the lone juror who had not been convinced of the guilt of one of the three defendants. A Bronx restaurant man, Mr. Axley refused to discuss the case when reached at his home, 350 East 207th Street, the Bronx. However, he would not deny that he had been the "hold-out" juror.

Courtroom rumor had it that one juror had not been convinced of the guilt of Sobell before the final verdict was reached. Late Wednesday night the jury had reported that it had agreed on two defendants, but had disagreed on a third. The jury did not identify either the single defendant or the other two.

Counsel for all three defendants announced that they would appeal after sentencing. Emanuel H. Bloch, attorney for the Rosenbergs, said:

"Despite the verdict, Mr. and Mrs. Rosenberg have authorized me to say that they are innocent of the crime of which they were convicted. They will appeal to the highest courts of this land, and they always will maintain their innocence. I think they thought that in this political climate it was almost impossible to overcome a charge of this kind."

Harold M. Phillips, 76-year-old attorney who joined Edward Kuntz in defending Sobell, announced that he also would appeal.

"Our client will carry his fight to the highest court, confident that his innocence will be established and that justice will be done," Mr. Phillips said.

Of the three defendants, Sobell seemed hardest hit by the verdict. His counsel had hoped that the jury would find him less implicated than the Rosenbergs, and the jury split on Wednesday night had fortified their hope. All three defendants took the guilty verdict stoically without changing expression.

On leaving the United States Courthouse in Foley Square, Rosenberg declined to comment on his conviction. He was taken, handcuffed, to the Federal House of Detention on West Street. Sobell, also handcuffed, went to the City Prison adjoining the Criminal Courts Building. Mrs. Rosenberg was unfettered, and went to the House of Detention for Women, 10 Greenwich Avenue. All three will remain in cells until sentenced next week.

Judge Kaufman, who will be 41 in June, thanked the jury for its verdict.

"You have my deepest gratitude for the conscientious and industrious way in which you went about deliberating in this case," the judge said. "This case is important to the Government of the United States.

"My own opinion is that your verdict is a correct verdict, and what I was particularly pleased about was the time which you took to deliberate in this case. I must say that as an individual. I cannot be happy because it is a sad day for America.

Judge Thanks Attorneys

"The thought that citizens of our country would lend themselves to the destruction of their own country by the most destructive weapon known to man is so shocking that I can't find words to describe this loathsome offense. I say a great tribute is due to the Federal Bureau of Investigation and to J. Edgar Hoover for the splendid job they have done in this case."

Judge Kaufman thanked the defense attorneys for "demeaning themselves as attorneys should." On the Government side he commended Mr. Saypol; Myles J. Lane, Mr. Saypol's chief assistant; Roy M. Cohn and James Kilsheimer, Assistant United States Attorneys, and Special Agents Harrington and Norton of the F. B. I., who worked on the case.

"The conviction of defendants in a criminal case is no occasion for exultation," Mr. Saypol said. "The conviction of these defendants is an occasion for sober reflection."

"It is not possible for a great nation to be free from traitors. But this case shows that it is possible to reach them and ultimately bring them to the bar for punishment.

"Lord Acton said: 'Eternal vigilance is the price of freedom.' This case has merely adapted that saying to the atomic age.

"The jury's verdict, mature and reflected upon, is a ringing answer of our democratic society to those who would destroy it. First, because a full, fair, open and complete trial in sound American tradition was given to a group of people who represented perhaps the sharpest secret eyes of our enemies.

"They were given every opportunity, as you the jury know, to present every defense. I myself would fight at all times for their right to defend themselves freely and vigorously.

"Second, the verdict is a warning that our democratic society, while maintaining its freedom, can nevertheless fight back against treasonable activities. The case has ramifications so wide that they involve the very question of whether or when the devastation of atomic war may fall upon this world."

With the conviction of the Rosenbergs and Sobell, the F. B. I. believes that others who have engaged in espionage may be prompted to confess their activities.

Deterrent Against Spying Seen

The Government agency also feels that the convictions will be a substantial deterrent to anyone tempted to spy for a foreign power. In recent years Mr. Saypol has obtained more than a dozen convictions, with sentences of twenty-five years or more, in counterfeiting cases. The United States Secret Service has informed the Department of Justice that counterfeiting is now a rare crime in the Southern district of New York.

The New York Times

Julius Rosenberg and his wife, Ethel, leaving the courthouse. In background are United States marshals.

The Federal prosecutor would not say what recommendation he would make for punishment of the three convicted as spies. It is expected, however, that he will ask the death penalty as one proportionate to the crime of stealing the atom bomb secret in 1945 from the United States for Soviet Russia.

American authorities believe that this information made it possible for Russia to explode several atomic bombs five to ten years earlier than independent research would have made possible. President Truman announced on Sept. 23, 1949, that the Russians had effected "an atomic explosion."

The trial took fifteen court days instead of the eight weeks that had been forecast when it began on March 6. The Rosenbergs were two of the four defense witnesses. Sobell did not take the witness stand.

The Rosenbergs consistently claimed constitutional privilege against self-incrimination in refusing to answer questions on their Communist party membership and associations. Judge Kaufman upheld their refusals to answer.

The Government contended that common membership in the Communist party provided the motive for the three to engage in spying for Russia. Several of the Government's twenty-two witnesses testified that the Rosenbergs and Sobell were Communists.

Government experts testified that the sketch and twelve-page description of the atom bomb made by Greenglass in January, 1945, contained sufficient information to divulge the secret. Harry Gold testified that he delivered this data to Yakovlev for transmission to Soviet Russia.

Testimony on the structure and function of the atom bomb remains impounded by Judge Kaufman to prevent circulation of the information. The trial judge directed the stenographers not to transcribe this portion of the testimony, at the request of the Atomic Energy Commission.

* * *

April 5, 1951

TROOPS FOR EUROPE BACKED BY SENATE; HOUSE ASKED TO ACT

Upper Chamber Invites Lower, 45 to 41 to Concur
After Deciding Long-Fought Issue

RETAINS ADVISORY CURB

Approves Sending 4 Divisions but Says Congress
Should Pass on Further Force

By WILLIAM S. WHITE
Special to The New York Times.

WASHINGTON, April 4—The Senate approved today a policy of assigning American ground troops to the international force being raised in Europe for the common defense of the western world.

It endorsed the designation of General of the Army Dwight D. Eisenhower as the supreme commander of that force.

It specifically affirmed President Truman's plans to send four divisions to Europe, to stand with two already there.

It admonished him, however, to dispatch no more than those four divisions without the further approval of Congress.

All this the Senate accomplished, after three months of debate and consideration, in adopting by 69 to 21 a simple resolution expressing the "sense" or opinion of its members.

This resolution is a finished legislative product. It approves for the first time in peace in the history of the United States the commitment of its ground forces to an international army.

Once it had been approved, however, the Senate then passed, but this time by the narrow vote of 45 to 41, exactly the same declarations, though this time in the form of a concurrent resolution, which now must go to the House of Representatives for its action.

Alteration by House Possible

Every point of substance in the issue at hand was precisely the same. The concurrent resolution, however, involved the addition of two words to a Senate recommendation that consideration be given to bringing other nations into the Western defensive alliance. The simple Senate resolution had mentioned West Germany and Spain. The other one added Greece and Turkey.

Neither document would do more than assert the right of Congress to pass on troop commitments beyond the four divisions. Neither would have the force of law.

The second, or concurrent, resolution, however, conceivably could be altered in the House of Representatives into a form that would have the force of law. If passed there in such an altered form and then in the Senate and not successfully vetoed by him it would become a mandatory direction upon the President that would put any further troop movements in the ultimate control of Congress.

For this reason, the Administration's chief foreign policy spokesman, Senator Tom Connally, Democrat of Texas, and all his closest associates stood to the end against the concurrent resolution, in an effort to keep the issue out of the House.

Approval Provision Attacked

Those who accomplished this second approach were Senators against any commitment of troops to Europe, Senators acting in the belief simply that both Houses ought to participate, Senators hoping that in the House a legal mandate could be put up on the President.

The day's final voting therefore was as full of complications as it was harshly contested.

Those like Senator Connally who were seeking to give the President, General Eisenhower and the other military authorities the greatest possible control were not altogether happy even with the simple Senate declaration, though it approved the heart of the project, the dispatch of the four divisions.

They tried to the end to knock out the requirement for Congressional approval of any further American reinforcements of General Eisenhower's command.

They attempted this and failed by 59 to 29 in objecting to an automatic action that made the concurrent resolution read precisely as did the simple resolution just passed.

Their lost objective was to knock out of the second text what they had twice been unable to knock out of the first—the phrase "Congressional approval."

In the most decisive of all ballots, that approving the simple resolution and thus a dispatch of troops, which now may shortly be begun, forty-two Democrats and twenty-seven Republicans prevailed over nineteen Republicans and two Democrats.

Of these two Democrats, one, Senator J. William Fulbright of Arkansas, voted against the project, he announced, not because he did not "wholeheartedly" endorse it, but because he believed that even the moral restrictions being placed about the President were unconstitutional. The other Democratic dissenter, Senator Allen J. Ellender of Louisiana, had indicated simply that he was against the whole troop enterprise.

In the efforts of the Administration's backers to keep "Congressional approval" out of the concurrent resolution, the losers were twenty-four Democrats and five Republicans. These latter were Senators James Duff of Pennsylvania, Irving M. Ives of New York, Henry Cabot Lodge Jr. of Massachusetts, Leverett Saltonstall of Massachusetts and Charles W. Tobey of New Hampshire.

The winners were forty Republicans and nineteen Democrats.

Before this the Administration's foreign policy leaders had lost in a collateral attempt, though one not directly connected to the troop issue, to defeat a Senate declaration that "consideration" ought to be given to bringing Franco Spain and West Germany into the Western defensive alliance.

Inclusion of Four Countries Asked

This proposal, by Senator Joseph R. McCarthy, Republican of Wisconsin, prevailed by 48 to 41 and later was altered to include Greece and Turkey. The Administration forces based their declared objection to it primarily on the ground that it tended toward extending the alliance for which the troops are actually to be sent, the North Atlantic Treaty. Spain, West Germany, Greece and Turkey are not members.

The Administration had won an overwhelming Senate approval not only for the dispatch of the four divisions, the only American commitment in sight at the present time. It had won also the Senate's acceptance of the general proposition that American troop contributions must amount to the country's "fair share."

The Republicans—and some Democrats—who had accused President Truman of attempting to act all alone in committing troops had raised at minimum a strong psychological barrier against anything of that sort.

"The Important Thing" Noted

Senator Connally, however, in closing the debate asserted that the result ought to be viewed in the light mainly of building up the defensive strength of Western Europe.

"The important thing," he said, "is that the Senate has emphatically and explicitly approved the assignment of four additional divisions of ground troops to General Eisenhower's command and has given the general himself a vote of confidence.

"Certainly, if there was ever any doubt on the part of our friends—or potential enemies—that the United States would not be willing to implement the North Atlantic Treaty with ground troops, that doubt has now been dispelled.

"Four divisions was what the [United States] Joint Chiefs of Staff recommended, and that is what the Senate has approved.

"The course of world events is uncertain, but it is my view that there will be no world war this year. The Russians will not defy the free nations of the world.

"The strength of the free nations, which is the best preventive of war, is steadily increasing, and this resolution will be helpful in that direction."

Some of those who had engaged Mr. Connally and the Administration most desperately in the long debate that had gone before joined him in helping to roll up a big vote for the four divisions.

One of those was Senator Robert A. Taft of Ohio, the Senate Republican leader on domestic policy, though Senator Kenneth S. Wherry of Nebraska, the Republican floor leader, stayed in opposition, with the hard core of the party's Old Guard to the end.

Recalling that he had challenged, and still challenged, the President's right to dispatch troops without the assent of Congress, Senator Taft nevertheless declared that the sort of "Congressional approval" demanded for the future had at least strongly asserted that view.

Recalling also that he had supported vain Senate efforts to put a direction by law upon the President, Mr. Taft nevertheless said of the simple resolution at hand:

"I hope very much we can secure as universal approval for this resolution as we could hope to obtain."

Among those who voted against the troop project in all its aspects, Senator Everett M. Dirksen, Republican of Illinois, asserted that the American public was "being sold a bill of goods" as he asserted it had by those who before World War II urged aid for the Western Allies.

In this, Mr. Dirksen compared the Committee to Defend America by Aiding the Allies, which was headed by the late William Allen White, to the present Committee on the Present Danger, which supports military aid to Western Europe.

Twelve members of the Committee on the Present Danger, Senator Dirksen asserted, were members of the old Committee to Defend America by Aiding the Allies.

"All of them," he went on, "are there, including my old friend Bob Patterson, former Secretary of War; Robert E. Sherwood, who wrote Roosevelt's memoirs; Barry Bingham [president of The Louisville Courier-Journal]; Julius Ochs Adler, publisher of The New York Times." [General Adler is vice president and general manager of The New York Times. Its president and publisher is Arthur Hays Sulzberger.]

* * *

April 6, 1951

M'ARTHUR WANTS CHIANG ARMY USED ON CHINA MAINLAND

In Sharp Digression From U.S. Policy,
He Views 2d Front Diversion as Logical

GIVES WARNING ON EUROPE

Reply to House Minority Chief Says Fate Depends on Asia—
U. N. Drive in Korea Gains

By ANTHONY LEVIERO
Special to The New York Times.

WASHINGTON, April 5—General of the Army Douglas MacArthur favors a Nationalist second front on China's mainland and is convinced that the fate of Europe will be decided in the war against communism in Asia.

The United Nations commander's latest and sharpest digression from Administration Far Eastern policy was expressed in a letter read in the House of Representatives today by Minority Leader Joseph W. Martin Jr. of Massachusetts.

Representative Martin introduced the letter in a speech lashing the Administration for making contradictory statements on the nature of the peril facing the nation and for failing to establish a second front with Generalissimo Chiang Kai-shek's troops on Formosa.

[The United Nations offensive on Thursday pushed deeper into North Korea, with elements of four United States and two South Korean divisions and of a British Brigade across the Thirty-eighth Parallel on a seventeen-mile front.]

Fighting Europe's War Now

General MacArthur struck at the very basis of the Administration's concept of how the tide of Communist imperialism is to be rolled back and defeated. With barbed words he asserted that he was fighting Europe's war with arms in the Far East while Europe's diplomats continued to fight communism with words. If the war in the Far East is lost, then the fall of Europe is "inevitable," General MacArthur asserted.

General MacArthur's opinion clashes completely with the Administration's concept that civilization, as it has developed in free countries, can survive only if Europe is held as the main bastion against the Soviet tide. Furthermore, the Administration regards the Korean war as a comparatively small one that is being fought with the aim of avoiding a third world war.

General MacArthur asserted that "the Communist conspirators have elected to make their play for global conquest" in Asia. While the Administration is concerned about the great manpower potential of the Orient, it is even more concerned over the possibility of losing Europe's great industrial productivity to Soviet Russia.

To Ease Korea Pressure

Mr. Martin had referred in a letter to the general to the opening of "a second Asiatic front to relieve the pressure on our forces in Korea," using 800,000 anti-Communist Chinese troops, which, he said, were under Generalissimo Chiang's control on Formosa.

General MacArthur's letter, latest in a series of digressions from Administration policy that began last August, follows:

"I am most grateful for your note of the 8th forwarding me a copy of your address of Feb. 12. The latter I have read with much interest, and find that with the passage of years you have certainly lost none of your old-time punch.

"My views and recommendations with respect to the situation created by Red China's entry into war against us in Korea have been submitted to Washington in most complete detail. Generally, these views are well known and clearly understood, as they follow the conventional pattern of meeting force with maximum counter-force as we have never failed to do in the past. Your view with respect to the utilization of the Chinese forces in Formosa is in conflict with neither logic nor this tradition.

"It seems strangely difficult for some to realize that here in Asia is where the Communist conspirators have elected to make their play for global conquest, and that we have joined the issue thus raised on the battlefield; that here we fight Europe's war with arms, while the diplomats there still fight it with words; that if we lose the war to communism in Asia the fall of Europe is inevitable; win it, and Europe most probably would avoid war yet preserve freedom. As you point out, we must win. There is no substitute for victory."

Suggested Formosa Occupation

In a message to the Veterans of Foreign Wars last August General MacArthur suggested United States occupation of Formosa, in conflict with the policy merely to neutralize that strategic island until its status is settled. He withdrew the message, as President Truman requested, but not before it received world-wide distribution.

On March 24, General MacArthur invited the Commander in Chief of the Chinese and North Korean forces to confer with him in the field to end the war, a proposal that was rejected. His statement, made without prior consultation with Washington, disturbed officials here and, elsewhere, and afterward it was reported that the Joint Chiefs of Staff had instructed General MacArthur to clear all future statements of a political nature with Washington.

In his speech during the debate on the universal military training and service bill, Mr. Martin declared "it is high time that the Administration and the Pentagon came clean with the Congress and with the American people." He referred to the statement by Speaker Sam Rayburn yesterday implying that Russian troops were massing in Manchuria and that the beginning of World War III might be near.

Then Mr. Martin recalled that Senator Tom Connally, Texas Democrat, had said about the same time in the Senate that he believed "there will be no world war this year."

Mr. Martin said he did not know whether the world was on the brink of another war and added:

"But I do know this—because of adherence to policies long since proven disastrous our State Department today is blocking the use of the fullest resources available to us. I refer to the failure to employ the 800,000 anti-Communist Chinese troops on Formosa under the command of Generalissimo Chiang Kai-shek."

* * *

April 11, 1951

TRUMAN RELIEVES M'ARTHUR OF ALL HIS POSTS; FINDS HIM UNABLE TO BACK U. S.-U. N. POLICIES; RIDGWAY NAMED TO FAR EASTERN COMMANDS

PRESIDENT MOVES

Van Fleet Is Named to Command 8th Army in Drastic Shift

VIOLATIONS ARE CITED

White House Statement Quotes Directives and Implies Breaches

By W. H. LAWRENCE
Special to The New York Times.

WASHINGTON, Wednesday, April 11—President Truman early today relieved General of the Army Douglas MacArthur of all his commands in the Far East and appointed Lieut. Gen. Matthew B. Ridgway as his successor.

The President said he had relieved General MacArthur "with deep regret" because he had concluded that the Far Eastern Commander "is unable" to give his wholehearted support to the policies of the United States Government and of the United Nations in matters pertaining to his official duties.

General MacArthur, in a message to House Minority Leader Joseph W. Martin Jr. of Massachusetts, made public by Mr. Martin last Thursday, had publicly challenged the President's foreign policy, urging that the United States concentrate on Asia instead of Europe and use Generalissimo Chiang Kai-shek's Formosa-based troops to open a second front on the mainland of China.

The change in command is effective at once. General Ridgway, who has been in command of the Eighth Army in Korea since the death in December of Gen. Walton H. Walker, assumes all of General MacArthur's titles—Supreme Commander, United Nations Forces in Korea, Supreme Commander for Allied Powers, Japan, Commander-in-Chief, Far East, and Commanding General U. S. Army, Far East.

Commanded in Greece

The Eighth Army command will pass to Lieut. Gen. James A. Van Fleet whose most recent important command was as head of the American military mission in Greece, when that country was repelling a Communist-directed guerrilla attack under the Truman doctrine.

In ousting General MacArthur for his public disagreement with American policy designed to localize the Asiatic war, the President said:

"Full and vigorous debate on matters of national policy is a vital element in the Constitutional system of our free democracy.

"It is fundamental, however, that military commanders must be governed by the policies and directives issued to them in the manner provided by our laws and Constitution. In time of crisis this consideration is particularly compelling.

"General MacArthur's place in history as one of our greatest commanders is fully established. The nation owes him a debt of gratitude for the distinguished and exceptional service which he has rendered his country in posts of great responsibility. For that reason, I repeat my regret at the necessity for the action I feel compelled to take in his case."

The White House made the announcement of the relieving of General MacArthur at a hastily summoned press conference at 1 A. M. White House Press Secretary Joseph Short said that the announcement had been timed to coincide with delivery of the order to General MacArthur from the President which was dispatched over regular Army telecommunication. The hour in Tokyo was 3 P. M. Wednesday.

General MacArthur was told by the President to turn over all his commands at once to General Ridgway. The President added authority for General MacArthur "to have issued such orders as are necessary to complete desired travel to such place as you select." The General has not been in the United States for approximately fifteen years.

The order to General Ridgway to assume General MacArthur's commands was signed by Defense Secretary George C. Marshall, who added:

"It is realized that your presence is Korea in the immediate future is highly important, but we are sure you can make the proper distribution of your time until you can turn over active command of the Eighth Army to its new commander. For this purpose, Lieut. Gen. James A. Van Fleet is en route to report to you for such duties as you may direct."

Violations Indicated

In making public the order relieving General MacArthur the White House also released secret documents that had been sent as instructions to General MacArthur and that, it was indicated, the General had violated, leading to his dismissal.

The secret classification on these documents was removed by direction of the President in order that the public might be given the background leading to the President's action.

The first, under date of Dec. 6, 1950, and sent by the Joint Chiefs of Staff to General MacArthur and all other United States Army commanders, said that the President had directed, among other things, the following:

"No speech, press release or other public statement concerning foreign policy should be released until it has received clearance from the Department of State.

"No speech, press release or other public statement concerning military policy should be released until it has received clearance from the Department of Defense.

"In addition to the copies submitted to the Department of State or Defense for clearance, advance copies of speeches and press releases concerning foreign policy or military policy should be submitted to the White House for information.

"The purpose of this memorandum is not to curtail the flow of information to the American people, but rather to insure that the information made public is accurate and fully in accord with the policies of the United States Government."

Another Directive Cited

That same document included another Presidential directive to Defense Secretary Marshall and Secretary of State Dean Acheson. The President told them that all officials overseas, including both military commanders and diplomatic representatives, should exercise "extreme caution" in all their public statements, should clear all except routine statements with their departments and should "refrain from direct communication on military or foreign policy with newspapers, magazines, or other publicity media in the United States.

General MacArthur had, of course, violated this directive several times since it was issued.

"The second document in the White House dossier dated March 20 and addressed to General MacArthur from the Joint Chiefs of Staff advised him that the State Department was planning a Presidential announcement in the near future that the United Nations was prepared to discuss condition of settlement in Korea now that the bulk of South Korea had been cleared of aggressors.

"Strong United Nations feeling persists that further diplomatic efforts toward settlement should be made before any advance with major forces north of the Thirty-eighth Parallel," the March 20 directive said.

"Time will be required to determine diplomatic reactions and permit new negotiations that may develop. Recognizing that [the Thirty-eighth] Parallel has no military significance, State [Department] has asked J. C. S. (Joint Chiefs, of Staff) what authority you should have to permit sufficient freedom of action for next few weeks to provide security for United Nations forces and maintain contact with enemy. Your recommendations desired."

MacArthur Statement on Korea

The next document in the White House release was the text of General MacArthur's statement on Korea as it appeared in The New York Times of March 25. The implication was obvious that the only source the White House had for this declaration was The Times and that it had not arrived by cable from General MacArthur in advance as his military superiors had directed. It was in that statement that the general reported that South Korea had been substantially cleared of all organized Communist forces, that the enemy was suffering heavily from United Nations action and that General

MacArthur announced his readiness to confer at any time with the enemy commander-in-chief in the field "in an earnest effort to find any military means whereby the realization of the political objectives of the United Nations in Korea, to which no nation may justly take exception, might be accomplished without further bloodshed."

On March 24 the Joint Chiefs of Staff in a message marked "Personal for MacArthur" told the Far Eastern Commander that Mr. Truman had again called his attention to the Dec. 6 directive for advance clearance of statements bearing on foreign or military policy. Referring to the general's most recent statement the Joint Chiefs of Staff added that "any further statements by you must be coordinated as prescribed" in the December instructions.

"The President has also directed that in the event Communist military leaders request an armistice in the field you immediately report that fact to the J. C. S. for instructions," the March 24 instruction said.

The next document dated Jan. 4 also addressed from the Joint Chiefs to General MacArthur said that the problem of arming additional Republic of Korea troops was under consideration. It detailed the problems of armament supplies and shortages. The J. C. S. said that it appeared that the South Korean forces could be increased by from 200,000 to 300,000 men armed with rifles, automatic rifles, carbines and submachine guns.

The message added, however, that if these troops were organized into new divisions they would be relatively ineffective due to lack of artillery and other supporting weapons. The Joint Chiefs added, therefore, that it was probable that only about 75,000 more South Koreans can be effectively utilized immediately," with an ultimate build-up to 100,000.

General Asked for Comment

This message asked General MacArthur for his comments and recommendations as to how many additional South Korean troops could be employed profitably, how long it would take to organize and train them, whether they should be added to existing divisions or added to new ones and "other points in connection with current problems."

General MacArthur's answer dated Jan. 6 was interpreted by Mr. Short to reporters as a recommendation against the arming of additional South Koreans.

The White House press release gave the general's answer in full. Noting the shortages of available arms from the United States, General MacArthur suggested "it is possible that the over-all interests of the United States will be better served by making these weapons available to increase the security of Japan rather than arming additional R. O. K. forces."

"In view of the probable restricted size of the battlefield in which we may operate in the near future, and the high priority of N. P. R. J. (National Police Reserve of Japan) requirements the value of attempting to organize, train and arm additional R. O. K. forces in the immediate future appears questionable," said General MacArthur in his Jan. 6 message at a time when United Nations forces were in full retreat as a result of the unexpected intervention of Chinese Communist forces into the Korean war in late November.

"It is considered that the short-range requirements can best be met by utilizing available manpower to replace losses in existing R. O. K. units rather than creating new organizations. The long-range requirements for or desirability of arming additional R. O. K. pers. [personnel] appears to be dependent primarily upon determination of the future U. S. Mil. [military] position with respect to both the Korean campaign on the generally critical situation in the Far East."

The Final Document

The final document was General MacArthur's letter to Republican Leader Martin. In parentheses the White House noted that this statement of foreign and military policy had been obtained from the Congressional Record of April 5, 1951 although it was dated March 20, 1951 and had not come to the White House for review between the date of its writing and the time Representative Martin chose to make it public.

The implication was more than clear that this was the letter in which General MacArthur wrote himself out of a job.

There had been no indication when the White House closed up for the day at about 6 P. M. yesterday that any announcement was impending.

The only development that could be said to give a hint of the President's attitude was the abrupt cancelation of an appointment arranged by Erle Cocke Jr., American Legion commander, with Mr. Truman.

The interview was called off as soon as Mr. Cocke announced publicly his strong support of General MacArthur's proposal to use Generalissimo Chiang Kai-shek's Formosa-based troops to open a second front against the Chinese Communists on the mainland of China. Mr. Cocke also backed the Far Eastern commander's demand for authority to bomb Communist bases in Manchuria.

The White House stood on its dignity in discussing the Cocke incident. Joseph Short, Presidential Press Secretary, said that the Legion head had telephoned yesterday, reporting that he had just returned from Rome "and wanted to see the President before making any statement to the press."

"A couple of hours later there appeared on the news tickers interviews by Mr. Cocke in which he informed reporters what he was going to tell the President," Mr. Short added. "At that point, it seemed unnecessary for him to have the appointment. The appointment was canceled."

But Mr. Short's statement left an area of doubt as to whether Mr. Cocke was being left off the White House calling list because he had backed General MacArthur's policy or simply because he had offended the President by talking in advance of an appointment he had requested. He had accompanied the request with the voluntary statement that he wanted to see the President before he made any statements.

* * *

April 18, 1951

M'ARTHUR IS HAILED BY SAN FRANCISCO; GREAT CROWDS ROAR HERO'S GREETING; BRADLEY OPPOSES WIDENING KOREA WAR

GENERAL CHEERFUL

Throng Pushes to Ramp Ahead of Dignitaries for Own Welcome

HE EXPRESSES HIS THANKS

Says He and Wife Have Looked Toward Moment for Years— 17 Guns Boom Salute

By LAWRENCE E. DAVIES
Special to The New York Times.

SAN FRANCISCO, April 17—General of the Army Douglas MacArthur came home tonight to a hero's welcome.

A crowd of several thousand cheered when Lieut. Col. Anthony Story piloted the General's Constellation plane, the Bataan, to earth at San Francisco International Airport.

The plane landed at 8:29 P. M. [11:29 Eastern standard time].

Seven minutes later General MacArthur stepped from the plane to end a fourteen-year absence covering a fateful period in his life and the nation's.

"Mrs. MacArthur and myself," he said, "have thought and thought of this moment for years. Now that it has come the marvelous hospitality of your great city is more wonderful even than we had ever anticipated. Thank you all so much."

As the general rode in triumph to his quarters in the St. Francis Hotel after the reception at the airport the traffic jam, miles in length, became one of the greatest in the history of San Francisco.

Largest Since Roosevelt

It was larger than that occurring during any recent Presidential visit. The nearest in density and determination of the people to retain their place of vantage was the visit of President Roosevelt here in 1937.

The Police Department threw twenty radio patrol cars, thirty-nine motor-cycle officers and 150 beat men into the effort to control the crowd.

Protocol went by the boards as, despite police precautions, crowds pushed in against the ramp at the airport and put on a tumultuous reception of their own for a smiling, waving General.

Preceding him as the plane drew to a stop was Mrs. MacArthur herself, a laughing, purple-clad woman who came down the gangway on the arm of Colonel Story.

On the Mainland Again

Her husband appeared through the doorway behind her and walked the fourteen steps down the gangay. This descent put him on the United States mainland for the first time since he had sailed out of this port in 1937 to help the Philippines build up their pre-war constabulary.

Here the best laid reception plans of civil and military authorities went awry.

Mayor Elmer E. Robinson of San Francisco, chairman of the municipal reception committee, stepped forward to grasp General MacArthur's hand and bid him welcome.

"I'm happy to be here," the distinguished guest said.

The original schedule was kept to this extent—the five official welcomers were able to get in their handshakes. Following Mayor Robinson, who had urged the General to make this his first continental stop on his flight to Washington to address a joint session of Congress, were these military leaders:

Lieut. Gen. Albert C. Wedemeyer, Commander of the Sixth Army, who stepped forward as the top Army officer in the area and as the personal representative of General of the Army George C. Marshall, Secretary of Defense; Vice Admiral George E. Murray, Commander of the Western Sea Frontier, and Maj. Gen. William E. Hall, Commander of the Fourth Air Force.

Salute Finally Sounds

By this time, even while General MacArthur waited on the bottom step of the gangway, the first of two 75-mm. cannons taken to the airport to boom out a salute, was to have been fired.

But crowds of well-wishers surged in to shake the hands of the General without a command, and the plans were automatically changed. General MacArthur stopped to wave and smile to dozens of newspaper, newsreel and television camera men. Some one thrust a huge bouquet of red roses into the arms of his wife, Jean, who continued to wear a broad smile.

Finally the reception committee was able to get the General under way through the pushing crowd of officials and newspaper men and he advanced about twenty paces.

Here, while tumult continued, the first cannon boomed out. Every five seconds the cannons were fired until they had given the visitor the seventeen-gun salute prescribed for a five-star general.

The reception seemed out of control of the planners even now. General MacArthur did snap to attention, however, as drummers and buglers of the fifty-eight-piece band of the Sixth Army, led by Chief Warrant Officer Nathan A. Cammack, played four ruffles and flourishes. This was followed with "The General's March."

Greeted by His Men

Meanwhile, the honor guard, in regimental parade finery, with its campaign ribbons and medals, its red scarves, white gloves and helmet liners, had presented arms.

Capt. Preston H. Blum, a veteran of many Pacific campaigns, had assembled his guard of four platoons of the Thirtieth Engineers Base Topographical Battalion from Fort Winfield Scott long before the General was due in from Honolulu. At least 30 per cent of the men, he said, had served in various MacArthur campaigns in World War II.

"This is quite an honor," Captain Blum remarked. "They just picked us out and gave us the job."

General MacArthur was to have decided, after the band selections, whether he was to inspect the guard.

But he was in a happy mood and permitted himself to be pushed along before the front line of the guardsmen and back again, at a sharp pace, while Mayor Robinson and the other greeters waited behind, looking as if they were uncertain whether their guest would be back again.

The smiling General soon reappeared, without any sign that only last week he had been shorn of all his commands in the Far East by President Truman because of public disagreement with the Administration's high policy in Asia.

Soon there were cries, "He's going to make a speech."

General MacArthur did indeed mount a gangway and delivered himself of his brief message of appreciation for a stirring welcome.

It was the first time a crowd on the United States mainland—numbering in this case perhaps 10,000—had had the opportunity to say "well done" to the Pacific war hero for his World War II victories and his accomplishments of the last six years in the occupation of Japan.

To some onlookers the welcome represented simply that; to others the event was an emphatic expression of confidence in the MacArthur pattern for fighting communism in the Far East.

The home-coming program was shortened and simplified at General MacArthur's request. Nevertheless, the Army, placing itself under civilian orders in the welcome arrangements, brought forth its traditional ceremony of pomp and color for the last of the victorious World War II generals to come back home.

The Sixth Army Band played selections from "South Pacific" while the official motorcade to roll the sixteen miles to the St. Francis Hotel in San Francisco was being made ready. Then it swung into "California, Here I Come" as General MacArthur entered an open car with Gov. Earl Warren and Mayor Robinson.

Mrs. MacArthur, carrying her roses, rode with Mrs. Warren and Mrs. Robinson.

Maj. Gen. Courtney Whitney, for years General MacArthur's secretary, rode with the co-chairmen of San Francisco's Citizens Committee, John F. Neylan and Henry Boyen.

Others who came in with the General were Col. Sidney Huff, his senior aide, and Mrs. Huff, an Australian who was seeing America for the first time; Col. Charles Canada, his physician and Sgt. Francisco Valbuena, the General's cabin attendant.

Sight for Arthur

It was also the first glimpse of the mainland for young Arthur, who had a half-smile as he walked down the gangway behind his mother and followed his father on his rounds.

One of the toughest jobs of the reception was handled by Cpl. William C. Dillon of Charleston, S. C., who had waited with five-star general's flag to serve as General MacArthur's orderly at the inspection. Corporal Dillon kept up the fast pace set by the general with the crowd's help, and the flag sometimes swayed precariously.

General MacArthur's drive to San Francisco, which usually takes not more than thirty minutes, was extended well beyond the hour mark as the cavalcade of official cars attempted to force their way through the crowd-jammed streets.

The first mile of the journey took more than ten minutes and the two miles from South San Francisco, the peninsula's steel center, to Brisbane, two miles away, required five minutes.

The next five miles of the drive to the San Mateo County line required ten minutes and then the cavalcade of cars slowed to a snail's pace as it entered the San Francisco residential district.

The deeper the cavalcade penetrated into downtown San Francisco the more difficult was progress. The two blocks from Nineteenth and Mission Streets and Twenty-second Street required five minutes, according to the log of the Police Department's traffic division.

Despite the delay, several thousand persons waited patiently at the Powell Street entrance of the St. Francis Hotel for a glimpse of the General and members of his party.

Ninety minutes after the General left the airport he still had not reached his hotel. He was hemmed in by crowds at Eighth and Market Streets on the fringe of San Francisco's downtown district, at 10:15 P. M., with the most densely packed streets still to be traversed.

General MacArthur switched from the closed sedan he entered at the airport to an open car at Bayshore Boulevard and Alemany Boulevard as he entered the most crowded areas.

The snowballing reception that caused the motorcade to stop at almost every street corner after reaching the Market Street area carried General MacArthur to the hotel at 10:45, almost an hour and three-quarters after leaving the airfield. Earlier estimates of a crowd of 200,000 were revised upward as high as a half million.

A tired but seemingly well satisfied general retired to his suite, and soon the maitre d'hôtel was on hand with supper menus.

It was indicated to reporters and photographers in the sixth-floor corridors that the party hoped to retire as early as possible to be in shape for another strenuous day.

* * *

April 20, 1951

M'ARTHUR CALLS ASIA POLICY 'BLIND TO REALITY'; SAYS JOINT CHIEFS SHARED VIEWS ON STRATEGY; CHEERED BY CONGRESS; HERE FOR PARADE TODAY

LANDS AT IDLEWILD

General Is Welcomed by Mayor—Million Line Route to His Hotel

17-GUN SALUTE FIRED

Impellitteri Calls the Turnout Only 'Sample' of City's Reception

By WILLIAM R. CONKLIN

General of the Army Douglas MacArthur got a substantial foretaste last night of the welcome awaiting him today when more than 1,000,000 New Yorkers greeted him after he landed at 9:16 P. M. from his Constellation Bataan at New York International Airport in Idlewild, Queens.

In a voice husky with weariness, the tall five-star General said:

"I cannot tell you how heart-warming is this very special welcome. When we reach the City of New York, we know we have come home. Good night."

These words were addressed to about 1,000 members of the official welcoming party at the airport. General MacArthur, accompanied by Mrs. MacArthur and their son, Arthur, 13 years old, had still to see the nocturnal outpouring of New Yorkers who stayed up to welcome him. Chief Inspector August Flath of the Police Department said "more than one million" persons lined the 17½-mile route from the airfield to the Waldorf-Astoria Hotel.

Welcome to Begin at 11 A. M.

With fair weather predicted for today it seemed likely that 5,000,000 would see General MacArthur on his official welcome beginning at 11 o'clock this morning. His schedule calls for a morning visit to Central Park, a noontime parade up Broadway from the Battery to City Hall, the official reception there and a luncheon given by the city at the Waldorf-Astoria at 2 P. M. Seven thousand of the city's 18,400 policemen will be used in the arrangements for the parade.

The party arrived at the Waldorf at 11:37 last night to mark the end of a day that had begun with a noontime address by the General to both houses of Congress. He made two additional speeches in Washington before leaving that city at 8 P. M. When the flickering on-off navigation lights of his airplane came over Idlewild last night it marked the end of a 10,000-mile flight that had begun last Sunday (Monday, Tokyo time) in Tokyo. Before leaving the airport General MacArthur faced a three-tiered press gallery and said:

"I have traveled 10,000 miles in the last eight days to find out who truly rules the United States. I found out. It is you, the press."

En route here the general received enthusiastic welcomes at stops in Honolulu, San Francisco and Washington. Grover

A. Whalen, chairman of the Mayor's Reception Committee, cautioned welcomers before the General arrived against "roughing him up."

"There was confusion and disorder in the other cities," Mr. Whalen said. "We want New York to be the only city where that does not happen. If you find the police restrictions are severe, it is so that General MacArthur will not be mauled."

1,100 Police on Duty

With 1,100 police assigned last night, there was no trace of disorder at the airport or along the route through Queens to the Waldorf. In an aside to General MacArthur at the airport Mr. Whalen told the soldier-statesman not to worry about being rushed by the press. Pointing to the stands, he added:

"We've got them chained out there."

Mayor Impellitteri told the general that his airport reception was "only a sampling of the biggest, the best, and the warmest reception which will demonstrate that the people of our city hold you in the highest esteem."

Mrs. Impellitteri gave Mrs. MacArthur a large bouquet of American Beauty roses. Young Arthur MacArthur, asked to speak over the radio in honor of his first glimpse of New York, piped up:

"I thank you. Hello."

Mrs. MacArthur, wearing a purple frock, a black sealskin jacket and a small hat, said:

"It is a great pleasure to be here. Thank you so much."

As the General's foot touched earth at the airport the first gun of a seventeen-gun salute was fired by a battery of four 75s. The First Army Band played "Old Soldiers Never Die," "The Army Blue and Gray" and "Anchors Away," among other airs. General MacArthur inspected the First Army Honor Guard on the airfield. He wore his famous peaked cap, and a long beige trenchcoat buttoned to the throat.

The General's big silvery airplane was first sighted over the airport at 9:10 P. M., its red and green navigation lights blinking as Col. Anthony Story, the pilot, circled the field before landing on Runway 22. Using two of its four engines, the Bataan taxied a mile and a half to a spot directly in front of the press hangar. At precisely 9:25 o'clock Mrs. MacArthur and their son preceded the General down a bunting-draped gangway from the airplane.

Rides With Mayor and Whalen

After inspecting the Honor Guard and the band, General MacArthur took his place in the right rear of an open car. Mayor Impellitteri sat on his left and Mr. Whalen shared the front seat with a uniformed police driver.

The motorcade moved off the airport at 9:45 o'clock bound for Van Wyck Expressway, Queens Boulevard, the Queensborough Bridge and the Waldorf-Astoria. Moving at about eight miles an hour, it took one hour and fifty minutes to reach the hotel. On the way out the same trip had taken fifty minutes.

The party arrived in the street-level entrance to the Waldorf Towers at 11:36 P. M.

Stepping slowly from the open car, firmly supported by Mr. Whalen, the General appeared close to exhaustion. His lips were set in a tight line and he walked quickly through police lines twenty paces to a revolving door leading to the elevator that was waiting to whisk him to the thirty-seventh floor suite.

With a tired grin and a weary shake of his head, he greeted a newspaper man he had known in Japan and Korea. He paused as if to say something, but permitted himself to be pushed along by Mr. Whalen.

Mrs. MacArthur, appearing tired but happy, said she was "very glad" to be back in New York. In response to a reporter's question, Arthur said he liked New York "fine."

The mother and son posed patiently for a battery of photographers before passing through the revolving door.

The MacArthurs were whisked to their suite and well-wishers were turned away to give the distinguished visitors an opportunity to rest up for the ordeal of today's gigantic reception.

10,000 to Parade to City Hall

The honor guard and band of the First Army will march in today's parade of 10,000 from the Battery to City Hall. Contingents from the Air Force, Navy and Marine Corps also will march and more than 500 officers and men from Mitchel Air Force Base in Hempstead, L. I., will join the parade with their 581st Air Force Band.

Many business concerns have given their employes two-hour lunch periods for today so they can participate in the reception. A survey by the Commerce and Industry Association showed that only a few companies had released their employes for the entire afternoon. The double lunch hours were centered between 10:30 A. M. and 2 P. M. to cover the time that General MacArthur would be moving through the city.

Joseph P. Ryan, president of the International Longshoremen's Association, A. F. L., said 40,000 harbor workers here and in New Jersey would stop work from noon to 7 P. M. to honor the hero of the Pacific. Many of these men, he said, would march with the 5,000 veterans in this morning's parade.

With one exception, every established market in Wall Street will shut down trading for the welcome parade. Because Friday is the only notice day for regular delivery under the No. 6 domestic raw sugar contract—a domestic sugar contract providing for delivery of sugar alongside ship—the New York Coffee and Sugar Exchange has announced that it will be unable to close completely. However, so far as possible, employes will be given time off to see the parade.

The New York Stock Exchange and the New York Curb Exchange will close from 11 A. M. to 1 P. M.

The Cotton Exchange and the Wool Associates on the Cotton Exchange will knock off for the day at noon. The usual closing hour is 3 P. M.

The Cocoa Exchange will be closed from 11 A. M. to 1:30 P. M.

The New York Produce Exchange, which trades in cotton-seed oil and soybean oil futures, will suspend operations from 11:45 A. M. to 1:30 P. M.

Even the unorganized market in securities is closing down. The District No. 13 committee for the over-the-counter trade has made the suggestion that, in view of the difficulty of trading and making deliveries at the height of the parade, members should refrain from trying to do either between 11 A. M. and 1 P. M. There is little doubt that this suggestion will be followed.

*   *   *

April 20, 1951

GENERAL IS FIRM

*Denies Warmongering, Sees an Effort Made
to 'Distort' His Position*

VICTORY CALLED AIM

*MacArthur Ends Army Career
by 'Fading Away' Like the Old Soldier*

By WILLIAM S. WHITE
Special to The New York Times.

WASHINGTON, April 19—General of the Army Douglas MacArthur laid before Congress and the country today his side in his controversy with President Truman over military policy in Asia.

Before a joint meeting of the Senate and House of Representatives, he presented himself as an officer who had been broken for trying, as he saw best, to bring the Korean war to an end in victory, and convinced that he still was right.

Recalling the military ballad that "old soldiers never die, they just fade away," he told Congress in the last, emotional moment of his speech:

"And like the old soldier of that ballad, I now close my military career and just fade away, an old soldier who tried to do his duty as God gave him the light to see that duty. Good-by."

His Major Points Listed

He had just called for actions in support of United Nations troops fighting in Korea that would be the precise opposites of the deepest commitments President Truman had made. Generally supporting the views of a powerful Republican Congressional bloc, headed by Senator Robert A. Taft of Ohio, General MacArthur demanded:

Holding Formosa, the Chinese Nationalist island stronghold of Generalissimo Chiang Kai-shek, at all cost.

Bombing the marshaling areas on the China mainland from which the Chinese Communists are sending their troops down into the Korean battle line.

Tightening the economic blockade and a complete naval blockade of the Communist China mainland.

Using against the Communists the Formosa-based troops of Generalissimo Chiang, with the "logistical support" of the United States—meaning that their transportation and supply would be an American function.

Says Joint Chiefs Share Views

He asserted it was his "understanding" that his views in the past were "fully shared" by the President's own highest military advisers, the Joint Chiefs of Staff, so far as they involved blockade, "air reconnaissance" over Communist China and "removal of restrictions" on the Chinese Nationalist forces on Formosa.

He did not say that the Joint Chiefs had agreed with him about bombing the Communist Chinese buildup on the mainland, or about holding Formosa.

President Truman countered indirectly. The White House authorized a Defense Department spokesman to say that Mr. Truman's dismissal of General MacArthur was based "upon the unanimous recommendations of the President's principal civilian and military advisers including the Joint Chiefs of Staff."

It was for such views as he expressed, and a refusal to accept the contrary conceptions of the Administration, that Mr. Truman relieved General MacArthur from his high Far East command on the ground that he might provoke a third world war.

Speaking before millions who listened and watched over radio and television, General MacArthur, by implication, said that the President was "blind" to the realities in Asia and expressed the fear that Mr. Truman was ready to appease or even to surrender to communism in that area of the world. He declared that efforts had been made to "distort" his own position. He said by the plainest implication that he had been falsely represented by the President as a warmonger.

General MacArthur's appearance, in the blinding beams of a dozen floodlights and in a place where ordinarily only the heads of state may come to present their cases, visibly and profoundly shook the Democrats.

They seemed, for the most part, to be standing firm in support of the President on the great issue, in personal conviction as well as in the political necessities of the moment. They had, however, whatever their public statements, only one watchword to pass among themselves. This was to hold fast against the storm.

Republicans Are Jubilant

The Republicans, jubilant in all their orthodox ranks, raised roaring shouts of approval as the general proceeded through his justification of his own acts and his indictment of the President's military policy in the Far East.

Not even for them, however, was this a perfect day, for all of its splendor of booming bands for the hero of the Pacific war.

For General MacArthur, although he agreed with them that more military effort was essential in Asia, and that there

Senators, Representatives and military men applauding General of the Army Douglas MacArthur before he began his address to the joint meeting yesterday. At the right, in front row is the General's son, Arthur, standing beside Maj. Gen. Courtney Whitney, the General's secretary.

was no reason to suppose that this would provoke full war with the Soviet Union, nevertheless struck at two of their cardinal points.

He wholly rejected the long-held argument of some Republican leaders that the Chinese Communists should be regarded as hardly more than hired, or ideological, mercenaries of the Soviet Union. The fact, the general said, was that the Chinese Communists had little interest in ideologies and were simply a nation seeking imperial conquest, though their ambitions fitted into those of the Russians.

Again, he asserted that American military intervention in Korea, which the Republicans have been calling "Truman's War," was an act soundly taken, even though he, as high commander in the Far East, had not been told of it in advance.

At this, the Democrats, most of whom had been sitting somewhat painfully while the Republicans were throwing up a great din against the vaulted roof of the House chamber, took comfort of their own and lustily applauded.

The partial concurrence that he indicated between himself and the Joint Chiefs led instantly to Congressional demands for a clarification of precisely where the difference in views lay.

There was every prospect that full disclosures of the secret opinions of the Joint Chiefs would be forced in one or more Congressional investigations now being planned.

General of the Army Omar N. Bradley, chairman of the Joint Chiefs of Staff, would make only this comment:

"I thought it was a very fine speech. But as to details, you have to study those things word by word."

The following statement was issued by a Defense Department spokesman:

"The Senate Armed Services and Foreign Relations Committees have scheduled hearings to begin early next week on the whole Far Eastern question. There will be no statements from the Defense Department prior to that time."

However, the spokesman issued the additional statement, saying that the Joint Chiefs of Staff had participated in the "unanimous" recommendation to remove General MacArthur from his commands.

The general, as he ended his address and turned with moist eyes to grasp the hands of the presiding officers, Vice President Alben W. Barkley and Speaker Sam Rayburn, raised a dozen political speculations as to possible Republican Presidential candidates in 1952.

His farewell, many were quick to note, was the farewell of a soldier. It was quite clear that as a speaker on foreign policy he was far from done.

Striding down from the dais, erect and stern at first, he suddenly smiled widely, waved to his wife, who sat far above in the galleries, then, pointedly, waved to the Republican side of the House. He did not make any gesture toward the Democrats across the aisle.

Cries of "God Bless MacArthur" rose from spectators working their way down the high stairs from the galleries. In at least one House Office Building room, where stenographers and other Congressional employees were gathered, men and women were weeping.

This was the one constant in this day of the return of General MacArthur to the seat of American Power—a wave of emotionalism almost as papable as the thin moisture of the cloudy, if stirring, day.

General MacArthur, after leaving the Capitol, made three other public appearances—before a convention of the Daughters of the American Revolution, at the Washington Monument and at a meeting of the American Society of Newspaper Editors.

One of his aides earlier had called off the latter appointment, explaining that the general, weary from his day, was asleep in his hotel suite. But General MacArthur, upon awakening, went to the editors' meeting and chatted with them briefly.

At the monument grounds, a seventeen-gun salute rang out and an honor guard from all the military services stood at the present arms.

The White House led the Administration generally in declining any comment on what General MacArthur had to say. It was a great deal, a speech requiring forty minutes to deliver.

The scene in Congress was opened by the assembly of the House at its usual time, 12 o'clock noon. At 12:13 Mrs. MacArthur entered the galleries, and the House rose and cheered her.

At 12:18 the general's young son, Arthur, came in with a line of officers who had served under the MacArthur command. They sat in the chairs that ordinarily are placed for the President's Cabinet in joint sessions. This time no Cabinet officer was there.

Then, at 12:20 P. M., the floodlights sprang up and in marched the members of the Senate.

At 12:31, under special escort by a group of Senators and Representatives and preceded by the House Doorkeeper, William F. Miller, General MacArthur marched down the center aisle.

"Mr. Speaker!" Mr. Miller said, "General of the Army Douglas MacArthur!"

Advocates 'No Partisan Cause'

"Members of the Congress," Mr. Rayburn said, when General MacArthur had taken his place before the microphones, "I deem it a high privilege, and I take great pleasure in presenting to you General of the Army Douglas MacArthur." There was a demonstration from the floor for a minute or two.

General MacArthur, in a rather low, pleasant voice, began at once to read, his hands shaking slightly as he turned the pages of his manuscript. His expert delivery plainly impressed the politicians who sat before him.

He said at the outset that he was advocating no "partisan cause," and that he was speaking, "in the fading twilight of life, with but one purpose in mind: to serve my country."

Disclaiming any "rancor or bitterness," he nevertheless at once closed with those who held that military commitments to Asia must be subordinated to military commitments in Europe.

There had to be enough American strength on both fronts of the world, he said, and the contrary notion was "defeatism."

He put the position, as he saw it, that weakness in Asia would mean the loss of Europe, and the other way around as well.

World War II had so altered matters, he asserted, taking here a line advocated by Senator Taft and former President Herbert Hoover, that the Pacific, under the shelter of American air and sea power, had become a "protective shield" for the whole Western Hemisphere.

The island chain held by this and friendly countries, he added, could "dominate every Asiatic port from Vladivostok to Singapore" with sea-air power, so that there could be no thrust from the Pacific against us.

Thus, he added, "under no circumstances" must Formosa be permitted to fall, for its loss might throw the American defensive frontier back to California, Oregon and Washington State.

General MacArthur strongly praised the "leadership" of Generalissimo Chiang and asserted that, driven back now to Formosa, he had installed an "enlightened" administration that refuted "malicious gossip" against his earlier administration on the China mainland.

He hit once at those "abroad," presumably meaning the British, who had criticized his conduct of the Korean campaign, then declared, in substance, in a shaken voice, that he had been denied all that was essential to victory in Korea.

He had received no reinforcements, the general said. He had not been permitted to destroy (by bombing) the Chinese Communist build-up bases.

"Constantly," he added, he called for "new political decisions" that were essential to permit him to act adequately in the new situation created by the intervention in Korea of the Chinese Communists.

These decisions never came, he asserted, and his "anguish" grew over the attrition in Korea.

"Why, my soldiers asked me," General MacArthur said, "surrender military advantages to an enemy in the field? I could not answer.

"Some say to avoid spread of the conflict into an all-out war with China. Others, to avoid Soviet intervention. Neither explanation seems valid, for China is already engaging with the maximum power it can commit, and the Soviet will not necessarily mesh its action with our moves.

"Like a cobra, any new enemy will most likely strike whenever it feels that the relativity of military and other potentialities is in its favor on a world-wide basis."

General MacArthur sharply disclaimed any intention, as charged to him by the Democrats, to use American ground forces in China. "No man in his right mind" would advocate that, he asserted.

While strongly denying that he had any plan that might greatly expand the Korean war, he nevertheless struck out at the theory of holding actions and asserted:

"In war there is no substitute for victory."

* * *

May 11, 1951

PHILIPPINES DOOMS 6 TOP COMMUNISTS

9 Others Get Life Sentences for Murder, Armed Rebellion— 11 Receive Lesser Terms

By The United Press

MANILA, May 11—A Philippine court today sentenced six top Communist leaders to death and nine others to life imprisonment for murders, robberies and armed rebellion aimed at overthrowing the Philippine Government.

Eleven others received lesser prison, jail and reform school sentences—including a four-month sentence for one defendant convicted only of belonging to the Communist party—in the unprecedented six-month Politburo trial.

One woman defendant was sentenced to death and another to life imprisonment. Of the twenty-nine brought to trial, among them the highest ranking Communists in the Philippines, two women and one man were acquitted. Prison terms ranged from four months to seventeen years.

Judge Oscar Castelo of the Court of First Instance, facing the defendants in the heavily guarded courtroom in the war-ruined walled city, found them guilty, as principals or accomplices, of the "complex charge of rebellion with multiple murder, arsons and robberies."

The evidence "conclusively established" that the Communist party in the Philippines was patterned after that in Russia, Judge Castelo said in declaring it an "illegal association."

Its armed forces, the H. M. B. (Hukbong Mapagpalaya Nang Bayan—or Hukbalahaps) "are in an armed revolution to overthrow the Government of the Philippines" and replace it with a Communist form of government, he declared.

Among the terrorist acts cited by the Court was the ambush killing of Mrs. Manuel Quezon, widow of the President, in Nueva Ecija province in 1949, and the Camp Makabulos massacre last year.

"Were cases of this nature allowed to pass without condemnation and heavy punishment * * * the lives of mankind would constantly be imperilled and there would be no security in this country for its peace and tranquility would be upset and the authority of the Government seriously impaired," the Judge said.

The defendants took their sentencing quietly and seemed not to notice the heavily armed guards surrounding the courtroom to prevent a possible rescue attempt by Communist bands.

Those sentenced to death were Federico Maclang, 37, alleged chief of the organizational bureau of the party; Ramon Espiritu, 45, labor leader; Miss Iluminada Calonje, 24, alleged head of the Communist courier department; Cenon Bungay, a ranking Huk commander; Onofre Mangila, alleged member of the party's Central Committee, and Magno Bueno, military instructor in the Huk's Stalin University.

* * *

June 8, 1951

BRITISH HUNT 2 MISSING DIPLOMATS RANKED AS HIGH AND TRUSTED AIDES

Special to The New York Times.

LONDON, June 7—The Foreign Office disclosed today that two missing diplomats, being sought on the Continent in the belief that they planned to make their way to Russia, were two high and trusted Foreign Office officials, both of whom had served in the British Embassy in Washington.

They are Donald Duart MacLean and Guy Francis de Moncy Burgess, both of whom have been absent without leave since May 25. It was announced today that they had been suspended since June 1 and it was disclosed unofficially that efforts were being made to find them in Paris.

[Secretary of State Dean Acheson, replying to a question in Washington, agreed it would be "quite a serious matter" if the two men should "prove to be Soviet sympathizers." In Paris the French Sûreté confirmed that a search for the two men had been going on for more than a week and added that it seemed as if they had left France and already might be behind the Iron Curtain.]

The mystery was heightened tonight when the Foreign Office acknowledged that telegrams from Paris purporting to be from the two men had been received by their families within the last twenty-four hours. However, the authenticity of the messages had not been established and it was affirmed that the missing men had not communicated with the British Embassy in Paris.

The Foreign Office spokesman said there was no reason to suspect that the two men had taken any important documents with them but he added that both had passports with diplomatic visas.

Mr. MacLean, 38 years old, is a son of Lady Gwendolene Margaret MacLean and the late Sir Donald MacLean, a prominent Liberal who was Minister of Education in the National Government of 1931. The missing man's brother Alan, until his recent appointment as information officer to the British delegation to the United Nations, was private secretary to Sir Gladwin Jebb, Britain's permanent representative of the United Nations.

Mr. MacLean joined the Foreign Office in 1935 and served at the British Embassy in Washington from 1944 to 1948. Recently he had been serving as head of the American Department of the Foreign Office.

In 1940 Mr. MacLean received Foreign Office permission to marry Melinda Marling, an American, and they have two sons. His mother, Lady MacLean, was under medical care today suffering from shock at her son's mysterious disappearance.

Mr. Burgess, who went to the British Embassy in Washington in 1950, had returned recently to this country on leave. Previously he had served in the Foreign Office's Far Eastern section as a specialist on China and Chinese affairs.

For a time he was private secretary to Hector McNeil during the latter's tenure as Minister of State at the Foreign Office. During the war Mr. Burgess, who is 40 years old, served as official spokesman for the Foreign Office on many occasions as a member of its news department.

In the Foreign Office, Mr. Burgess, a graduate of Eton, was known as a close student of the writings of Lenin and Premier Stalin. Friends said that he used his knowledge to confound the Russians and that some of the most effective British replies to the Soviet Union had been based on advice from him.

* * *

September 2, 1951

U. S. SIGNS NEW PACT TO ASSURE DEFENSE OF SOUTH PACIFIC

Australia and New Zealand Accept Accord as Prelude to Treaty With Japan

WIDER ARRANGEMENT DUE

Latest Document Is Believed Forerunner of an 'Atlantic' Plan Covering Orient

---

By JAMES RESTON
Special to The New York Times.

SAN FRANCISCO, Sept. 1—The United States, Australia and New Zealand signed today a treaty of mutual defense extending United States security commitments from the Arctic and the Mediterranean deep into the Southwest Pacific.

The treaty, binding the three countries to recognize that an armed attack on any one of them would be "dangerous" to all, is expected to become part of a future Pacific-wide security system designed to block further expansion by the Communist nations.

Secretary of State Dean Acheson signed for the United States in a colorful ceremony at the ancient Spanish garrison, The Presidio in San Francisco Bay. Percy C. Spender, Australian Ambassador to the United States and Sir Carl Berendsen, New Zealand Ambassador, also signed the document, which must be ratified by the United States Senate.

Other Commitments by U. S.

In addition to its security commitments in defense of its own occupation forces in Germany, Japan, and Austria, and its world-wide United Nations obligations to oppose aggressors, the United States now has binding commitments to the other American republics under the Rio Treaty, to the members of the North Atlantic Treaty stretching from the North Cape to the shores of Africa, and to the Philippines, which signed another Security Pact with the United States Thursday.

Moreover, two other security arrangements are now in the process of negotiation: the addition of Greece and Turkey to the North Atlantic pact, expected to take place in Ottawa this month, and a military arrangement with Japan, which will be completed after the signing of the Japanese peace treaty.

The Tripartite pact was an essential preliminary to the approval by Australia and New Zealand of the Japanese peace treaty. Both these powers were apprehensive about the lack of more restraints in the United States "treaty of reconciliation" for Japan and sought a mutual defense arrangement with the United States as insurance against the revival of Japanese aggression.

Article 4 Is Key Clause

The key clause in the treaty is Article 4, which reads as follows:

"Each party recognizes that an armed attack in the Pacific area on any of the parties would be dangerous to its own peace and safety and declares that it would act to meet the common danger in accordance with its constitutional processes * * * "

An armed attack is defined in Article 5 as any such attack "on the metropolitan territory of any of the parties, or on the island territories under its jurisdiction in the Pacific or on its armed forces, public vessels or aircraft in the Pacific."

The working of the key clause in the pact, however, is much less specific than the obligations assumed by the nation-members of the North Atlantic Treaty.

The Atlantic pact states specifically that "the parties agree that an armed attack against one or more of them in Europe or North America shall be considered an attack against them all." No such clear statement of principle is contained in the tripartite.

Both pacts leave open the question of how to react to an armed attack in the constitutional domain of each country, but the North Atlantic Treaty sets a specific goal to be achieved. It states that each party should take "such action as it deems necessary, including the use of armed force, to restore and maintain the security of the North Atlantic area."

The United States-Australian-New Zealand treaty does not contain any such clear obligation to use force until peace is restored and maintained throughout the area.

However, the new treaty does define its purpose in the preamble. It states that by signing the treaty the representatives of the three nations desire to coordinate their efforts for collective defense, and "to declare publicly and formally their sense of unity so that no potential aggressor could be under the illusion that any of them stand alone in the Pacific area."

The treaty does not establish any detailed international machinery to carry out its purposes, though this may be done in the future. It merely creates a "council" consisting of the foreign secretaries of the three countries or their deputies to "consider matters concerning the implementation of this treaty."

Wider Treaty Indicated

In fact the wording of the document makes it clear that the pact is regarded officially as the forerunner of a wider and perhaps definitive Pacific accord. Such a pact, to include Britain, France, the Netherlands and Japan, has been the subject of vague discussion for the last year.

Article 8 of the Tripartite treaty says the present document will stand "pending the development of a more comprehensive system of regional security in the Pacific area."

Mr. Acheson mentioned specifically the prospect of wider security arrangements in the Pacific. The tripartite pact together with the United States-Philippines Mutual Defense Treaty "and the post-treaty arrangements between the United States and Japan," should form "the basis for peace in the Pacific," he said.

The Secretary of State added that the treaty merely formalized the ties that had existed among the three English-speaking nations over a long period of time.

"It affirms the well-established principle that the security of an individual nation is inevitably bound to the security of its partners in the free world; that our common desire for peace is coupled with a strong resolve to resist aggression," Mr. Acheson continued.

Ambassador Spender, former Foreign Minister of Australia, emphasized that the treaty was not directed against any nation. This was apparently an allusion to Communist charges that the pact was anti-Soviet and aggressive in its purpose.

The treaty was conceived not in hostility against anyone but in a devout dedication to the cause of peace, Mr. Spender said.

Spender Warns All Aggressors

"We announce to the world that if any nation, no matter who that nation may be, engages in aggression against any one of us, we will stand fast together and, in accordance with our respective constitutional processes, act together to repel that aggression," he said.

The New Zealand Ambassador gave a somewhat wider interpretation of the Tripartite pact than either of his colleagues, saying:

"We believe, and our acts and our policies have implemented that belief, that a true democracy must be willing to serve wherever democracy needs to be defended. And accordingly, this treaty does not restrict itself to its parties alone; it contemplates close and constant consultation with others of like interests or in like peril.

"By creating an area of stability in the Pacific this treaty may be expected to reduce world tensions and thus to prove a reinforcement of, and a contribution to, the general system of international security which is today slowly, but we hope surely, being erected," he added.

In addition to Mr. Acheson those who signed for the United States were Ambassador John Foster Dulles, who negotiated the pact; Senators Alexander Wiley, Republican of Wisconsin, ranking minority member of the Senate Foreign Relations Committee; John J. Sparkman, Democrat of Alabama; H. Alexander Smith, Republican of New Jersey, and Bourke Hickenlooper, Republican of Iowa, as well as Representatives Walter Judd, Republican of Minnesota, and Abraham Ribicoff, Democrat of Connecticut.

* * *

September 9, 1951

PEACE TREATY WITH JAPAN SIGNED; GROMYKO WARNS STEP RISKS WAR; U. S. AND TOKYO IN SECURITY PACT

REDS QUIT PARLEY

48 Other Nations Join With Tokyo in Ending State of Warfare

ACHESON HAILS ACCORD

Expresses Regret at Absence of Some Powers but Calls Pact Act of Greatness

---

By JAMES RESTON
Special to The New York Times.

SAN FRANCISCO, Sept. 8—Twenty years almost to the day after the Manchurian incident started her people on a generation of aggression, Japan signed this morning a treaty of peace with forty-eight nations of the non-Communist world.

The treaty conference formally ended at 11:54 A. M. [2:54 P. M., Eastern daylight time.]

The Communist world, which lies like a great crescent around what remains of the once mighty Japanese empire, boycotted the final ceremony in the big San Francisco Opera House.

Andrei A. Gromyko, Soviet Deputy Foreign Minister, who sought to impose a much more severe treaty on Japan, did, however, call a press conference to state his decision on the signature. This he did in the form of a warning that was almost a threat.

Stage Set for the Signing

By the time this ominous statement had been issued, the Japanese flag had been put in its place on the stage of the great hall, and the final details had been arranged for the signing of a bilateral security treaty giving Japan the protection of United States troops in the four main Japanese islands.

The peace treaty terms would do these things, among others:

1. Take away Japan's overseas empire, amounting to 45 per cent of all the territory she owned on Pearl Harbor Day, and reduce her to the four main islands of Honshu, Kokkaido, Kyushu and Shikoko. This would return her to the territorial status she held in 1854, when Commodore Matthew C. Perry of the United States introduced Japan to the modern world.

2. Obligate Japan to abide by the purposes and principles of the United Nations Charter in her intercourse with other nations.

3. Force Japan to pay limited reparations claims to the nations she damaged so badly in the war of 1941-45, particularly in Southeast Asia, and thus re-establish, under different circumstances the opportunity to resume commercial relations in her former "co-prosperity sphere."

4. Authorize Japan to sign separate treaties with those countries that did not attend this conference, and give her a choice of which China she wished to recognize—Nationalist China or Communist China.

5. Give her an opportunity to regain the Ryukyus and Bonin Islands, which include the major United States military base at Okinawa, provided she lives up to the terms of the treaty and proves to be a reliable partner in the defense of the Pacific.

Quick Ratification Seen

These terms will come into effect when they are ratified by the United States Senate and by a simple majority of the following states that signed the document: Australia, Canada, Ceylon, France, Indonesia, the Netherlands, New Zealand, Pakistan, the Philippines, and Britain.

Senator Ernest W. McFarland of Arizona, majority leader, said that an effort would be made to ratify the treaty before the Senate adjourns this autumn.

Though there was a sense of anxiety in the Opera House as a result of the Communist block's hostile attitude toward the treaty, and a sense of regret that India and China, which form so large a part of the world-neighborhood occupied by Japan, were not present, the conference seemed to agree that no better treaty could have been achieved by further delay.

Profound fears were expressed by this conference about the revival of Japanese aggression, about the failure to provide more reparations for Japan's neighbors in the co-misery sphere of Southeast Asia, and about the possible revival of unfair Japanese commercial competition in the markets of the world.

These were minor themes, however. The major theme was pronounced by the conference president, Secretary of State Dean Acheson, who scored something of a personal triumph here this week and who received a standing ovation at the close of the conference.

"What you have seen this morning is something unique in history," Mr. Acheson said. "You have seen an act of greatness of spirit, a true act * * * which is in accordance with the fundamental moral principles of the great spiritual teachers and leaders of all nations and of all religions."

Japanese Flag Flies

Mr. Acheson spoke these words extemporaneously from the high rostrum of the Opera House stage. Behind him, standing out against a black back-drop, were the flags of the fifty-two nations, including Japan's "rising sun," which has flown in strange company since the days of Theodore Roosevelt and the Treaty of Portsmouth.

"We regret that there are some who were unable or unwilling to join our meeting, and others, we regret, who came here but were unable or unwilling to join in this great constructive effort," Mr. Acheson said.

"But what we have done here we have done both for ourselves and for those who did not come here, because we have made a great peace for all peoples, not merely those here but for all peoples throughout the world."

On Mr. Acheson's left sat Herbert Morrison, British Foreign Secretary, who ended his vacation in time to get here last night, after the battle was over, and on Mr. Acheson's right sat Dr. Warren Kelchner, Secretary General of the Conference.

Mr. Acheson's description of the treaty as an instrument devoid of any meanness whatsoever, was perhaps not entirely in keeping with many misgivings held by some of the delegations, but his note of warning to the Japanese was undoubtedly popular.

The obstacles that remain before Japan, in her path toward equality, honor and friendship in the world can be removed if Japan acts toward other peoples with understanding, generosity and kindness, Secretary Acheson said.

Mr. Morrison, whose country was a co-sponsor of the treaty, gave the same theme a Labor party twist in his belated hail and farewell to the conference.

Morrison Warns on Labor

"Many of my countrymen were disturbed by the exceptional combination in pre-war Japan of a high degree of technical industrial efficiency with low labor standards, discouragement to trades unionism, and social reaction," he said. "That was not good. It would be a grave matter if it held sway in the future."

As soon as Mr. Morrison finished his address, the secretary general of the conference began calling the nations for signature. Each chief delegate, when called, walked to a modernistic yellow table, signed for his country, pocketed the gold pen, provided free by enterprising manufacturers thereof, and departed to the applause of the multitude.

When the United States was called, Mr. Acheson descended from the rostrum and joined Ambassador Dulles, and various senators and representatives, some of whose support for the secretary in the past had been at least negligible. There everybody smiled appropriately for the television gentlemen, and looked deceptively like one big happy family.

Senator Alexander Wiley, Republican of Wisconsin, a MacArthur man, represented the minority party, and Senator

John J. Sparkman, Democrat of Alabama, represented Senator Tom Connally, Democrat of Texas, who is running for re-election. Messrs. Acheson and Dulles, who also had something to do with the treaty, were loudly applauded when they got their golden pens.

Japanese Sign Last

Japan signed last. Aging Premier Shigeru Yoshida strode to the yellow table in a frock coat, wing collar and other appropriate haberdashery. He was accompanied by various members of his delegation, all of whom maintained an air of great dignity and punctuated each act with formal bows.

Considering the rush with which the conference was arranged and the terms of its reference and the attacks of its opponents, the events went off with less difficulty than was anticipated.

Geography, economics and politics being what they are, however, the conference certainly did not remove the dark misgivings of the delegates about the absence of India and the hostility of Communist China and the Soviet Union.

That they could make peace treaties by themselves but not peace the delegates were well aware, and the worst of it was that the determination of Japan's neighbors to obstruct the coming of peace seemed greater at the end of the conference than at the beginning.

* * *

November 29, 1951

FIGHTING VIRTUALLY HALTED ON MOST OF KOREAN FRONT; OFFICIAL CEASE-FIRE DENIED

VAN FLEET IS WARY

But U. N. Commanders Are Ordered to Shun Aggressive Action

SOME RED ATTACKS MADE

*Onslaughts in the East-Central Area Repulsed—
Three MIG's Shot Down, 4 Damaged*

By MURRAY SCHUMACH
Special to The New York Times.

TOKYO, Thursday, Nov. 29—An informal cease-fire seemed to be in effect yesterday along most of the Korean war front. Gen. James A. Van Fleet, Eighth Army commander, indicated he had not issued a cease-fire order, and a spokesman for General Matthew B. Ridgway's headquarters here supported the denial. But it was apparent that word had gone out to commanding officers at the front to refrain from taking aggressive action.

Whether these instructions to the United Nations officers not to fire unless fired upon were written or oral was not known here this morning.

Apparently, many Allied commanding officers were telling their troops along the western front that a temporary cease-fire was in effect and that the men were not to shoot except when attacked.

Typical Instruction

Typical of the interpretations placed upon the situation by officers along the western front was the instruction from one officer to the men of his unit: "There will be no firing except in self-defense or in defense of the main line of resistance. There has been a temporary cease-fire and I don't want to hear anything going off around here—.45's or anything."

General Van Fleet tried last evening to put a damper on reports that he had ordered a halt to aggressive action.

In a statement denying that a cease-fire existed in Korea, General Van Fleet insisted the Eighth Army would "safeguard itself against surprise and fulfill its mission," which was "to repel Communist aggression."

This, however, did not deny that an order had gone to all field commanders to halt aggressive action. At the front, even patrols were being curtailed.

At General Ridgway's United Nations Command headquarters the general's official spokesman denied that the Eighth Army had issued an order to refrain from aggressive action. The spokesman said General Van Fleet's statement was to be construed as meaning the war was still on, with no holds barred.

Communist Thrusts Blocked

The news from the front showed no attacks by United Nations troops except to repel thrusts by the Communist enemy. Official reports from Eighth Army headquarters bore out the dispatches.

In the North Korean skies, the war was still being fought in earnest late yesterday. In a clash between Communist and Allied jet fliers, United Nations pilots shot down three of the Reds' MIG's and damaged four.

One United States F-86 Sabre jet was lost in the fight. The aerial victory was the third in as many days bringing the total claimed score to seven MIG's destroyed and nine others damaged, against a loss of two Allied planes.

Details of regimental and battalion attacks by the Reds, made public today by Eighth Army headquarters in Korea, noted that a Communist regimental attack was made northwest of the Punchbowl, north of Inje, on the east-central front. It was in three phases, beginning shortly after nightfall and ended shortly after midnight.

The Communist battalion assault mentioned, continued for three hours northwest of Yanggu. This action was an attempt by the enemy to seize high ground. In the face of stiff Allied resistance, the Communists withdrew.

The Far East Air Forces had a part in tactical operations during the night, striking at enemy front-line positions with radar-controlled drops of air-bursting bombs from B-26's, despite overcast conditions.

Fifth Air Force's report on activities during the day said Allied fliers completed about 600 sorties, during which they killed or wounded about 160 enemy soldiers. In interdiction attacks Fifth Air Force cut Communist rail lines at more than 100 places, mostly from Kunu to Sunchon and from Sinanju to Sukchon.

United Nations naval units also were operating on the principle that the war was still on. Shells from the big guns of the warships blasted enemy positions along the east and west coasts.

On the ground, a paradoxial situation seemed to have developed. Along the Western front Communist soldiers were sipping tea within sight of Allied troops after playing volley ball in the open. The Communists along the east central front were very much at war. The Reds' company-size thrusts increasing to regimental strength, brought out heavy counter-fire from United Nations artillery.

Red Command Lag Possible

There was some indication that it might be proving difficult for top Communist officers to halt field actions by telling the troop commanders of the beginning of the thirty-day period during which the demarcation line drawn at Panmunjom could become a permanent cease fire line if an armistice was reached.

At Eighth Army headquarters General Van Fleet, to discourage premature conclusions about a de facto cease-fire, said:

"There is as of this date 28 November, 1951, no cease-fire in Korea. There is hope, but that hope must not be sabotaged by wishful thinking."

Censors were instructed to delete all direct quotations attributed to United Nations officers in Korea having to do with any order to have troops fire only when fired upon. However the censors permitted speculation by correspondents on the possibility that General Van Fleet's statement gave tacit support to this theory by saying the United Nations troops' mission was "to repel Communist aggression."

General Van Fleet's statement went on:

"There has been some speculation concerning the import of the military demarcation line agreement announced by the United Nations and Communist delegates.

"In the twenty-four hours following the announcement, questions have been raised regarding the future operations of the Eighth Army. The facts are these:

"The mission of the Eighth Army and attached ground forces in Korea is to repel Communist aggression in this theatre. The fact that a military demarcation line has been determined is but one of the points on the agenda. Until such time as an agreement is reached on all points which will insure an armistice in Korea, the Eighth Army will take any steps deemed necessary to safeguard itself against surprise and to fulfill its mission."

The United Nations Command truce delegation's camp at Munsan issued a statement of its own to this same effect. The delegation, through its spokesman Brig. Gen. William P. Nuckols, said:

"The United Nations Command delegation's position throughout the armistice talks from July 10 to date has been unmistakably clear and is without any reservation whatsoever on the question of the continuation of hostilities until a full military armistice is reached.

"The position last July was that the fighting would continue until some final agreement was reached on all agenda items. That is the United Nations Command delegation's position as of tonight. The Communists have been told repeatedly that any cease-fire will result from and follow a full military armistice agreement and this cease-fire will not precede the agreement."

Some Firing Likely to Keep Up

SEOUL, Korea, Nov. 29 (AP)—An Allied briefing officer at headquarters described the situation today in this way:

"We anticipate we will refrain from general offensive action during the thirty-day period"—while the truce teams seek agreement on a full armistice. "But we still expect to receive some artillery and mortar fire off and on."

"During the past twenty-four hours," the officer added, "the enemy has acted in two ways depending on where he was—both as if he thought the war was over, and as if he didn't think the war was over."

*   *   *

October 3, 1952

BRITAIN'S FIRST ATOMIC TEST IS SUCCESSFUL OFF AUSTRALIA

Cloud From the Explosion in Monte Bello Islands Unlike Those in U. S.

By Reuters

MELBOURNE, Australia, Friday, Oct. 3—Britain's first atomic weapon was successfully exploded at 8 A. M. today, West Australia time [7 P. M. Thursday, Eastern Standard time] in the Monte Bello Islands, fifty miles off the Northwest Australian coast.

The explosion sent a ragged cloud 6,000 feet into the air within a minute after the blast, a correspondent reported from Rough Range, Northwest Australia.

He said the cloud, which was a mile wide at the base, was totally unlike the familiar mushroom stem of the American atomic explosions.

Three minutes after the explosion, it was a mile wide at its center and the shape at the top was that of a ragged letter "Z."

The top edge was a grotesquely shaped gray mass of cloud.

The flash of the detonation as seen by the newspaper men from their hilltop vantage point was about as bright as the top segment of a setting sun. The blast had none of the earmarks of an underwater explosion. A tower detonation was definitely indicated.

Bearings taken by observers placed the position of the explosion as north of Hermite Island, possibly on Flag Island, which is the center of the 45-mile prohibited atomic zone.

It was Britain's first atomic explosion, making her the third nation in the world known to have a working atomic weapon.

The big blast came more than seven years after the fateful day in July, 1945, on which the United States exploded its first atomic bomb in the New Mexico desert. In the interval the United States had dropped two atomic bombs in wartime and conducted a long series of atomic weapon tests at proving grounds in the Pacific and the United States. Atomic explosions also had been traced to Russia.

Britain's test was conducted in utmost secrecy. An area of about 23,500 square miles around the bleak Monte Bello islands was declared a restricted zone as early as last May. The region was patrolled by naval squadrons. The movements of equipment and personnel during the weeks leading up to the test were veiled by strict censorship.

Observers reported that they felt no ground shock wave but a heavy air pressure pulse smacked the Australian mainland points nearest to the test islands, 4 minutes 15 seconds after the weapon's flash.

At the same time newspaper men heard a report like a crack of thunder followed by a prolonged rumble like a train going through a tunnel.

The air and the sound shock were sufficiently intense to make them feel a slight pain in the ears, they reported.

There was nothing about the appearance of the initial flash or the boiling cloud that followed to indicate that this first British atomic explosion was not anything but a standard atomic bomb, the only difference was the peculiar shape of the cloud.

The flash was far less intense than had been expected by the newspaper men on the hill, a coast peak, about sixty-five miles from the center of the prohibited testing area.

They were surprised that the effect of the bomb was barely felt on the mainland.

Commander of the Monte Bello operation was Rear Admiral David Torlesse, 50, director of air equipment for the British Admiralty from 1946 to 1948.

The scientific director was Dr. William George Penney, 43, since 1946 chief superintendent of armament research at the British Ministry of Supply.

His closest associate was Dr. O. M. Solandt, 43, Canadian guided missiles expert.

Prof. T. W. Titterton, atomic scientist who was at the first atomic explosion in the New Mexico desert and was the British Commonwealth observer at the Bikini atom test, also took part.

*   *   *

October 12, 1952

EISENHOWER FOR REPUDIATION OF YALTA TO GIVE POLAND HOPE

By W. H. LAWRENCE
Special to The New York Times.

DENVER, Oct. 11—Gen. Dwight D. Eisenhower today called for formal repudiation by the United States of the 1945 Yalta agreement with the Soviet Union to give the people of Poland hope that we "will work continually yet peacefully, until the courageous patriots of Poland are again masters of their own destiny."

He conferred this morning at his Brown Palace Hotel headquarters with a group of Polish leaders and then issued a formal statement marking Pulaski Day, the anniversary of the death of Gen. Casimir Pulaski, who came from Europe to join American revolutionaries fighting for their independence in 1776 and was killed in battle. The statement said:

"It is my great privilege to send fervent greetings to American citizens of Polish descent, on this anniversary of the death of their great Polish patriot, Gen. Casimir Pulaski.

"Pulaski, a Pole, realized that the independence of the United States was closely linked with his most earnest desire, the independence of his beloved Poland. He was therefore glad and proud to fight and die for the freedom of the United States.

'Brilliant Leadership' Cited

"In his struggle for the cause of our independence, Pulaski's brilliant leadership and courage at Brandywine, Charleston and Savannah were emulated in World War II by the Polish heroes of Monte Cassino, Arnheim and other battlefields in their fight for the liberation of Europe, under the leadership of my friends, General Anders and General Maczek.

"In our own country the traditional love of freedom of the Polish people and their readiness to sacrifice for it have been, time and again, manifested in peace and war among those millions of our citizens descended from the same blood as Pulaski.

"On this memorable day we pray for the independence of Poland, now captive under Communist domination. The platform of the Republican party pledged repudiation of the Yalta Agreement which, through its unilateral violation by the Soviet government, has resulted in the enslavement of Poland.

Polish Heroes Praised

"Thus we will give hope to the people of Poland and to all the American friends of Poland, whether or not of Polish origin, and the assurance that their liberty is forever in our minds.

"There must be strong and united support in the free world against all forms of Communist aggression and the American people will not forget the debt they owe to General Pulaski and to the Polish people. We must work continually, yet peacefully, until the courageous patriots of Poland are once again the masters of their own destiny."

In a statement on Oct. 5, when a Pulaski parade was held in New York, General Eisenhower praised "Polish heroes" for their defense of "human liberty all over the world."

James C. Hagerty, press secretary to General Eisenhower, said that the meeting with the Polish group was the only political activity of any kind planned during the week-end, which has been set aside for complete rest and relaxation.

Speech Deletion Confirmed

Meanwhile, with the publication of the information elsewhere, it now is possible to report that General Eisenhower confirmed in an off-the-record talk with newsmen on Oct. 5 that he had deleted from his Milwaukee speech a defense of General of the Army George C. Marshall after telling a Marshall critic, Senator Joseph R. McCarthy of Wisconsin, that he intended to deliver it.

The question came up during a talk with General Eisenhower after there had been some controversy over a dispatch published in The New York Times, Oct. 4, saying that the Marshall paragraph had been eliminated from the text after Senator McCarthy suggested that there were better places than his home state to make that speech.

The Associated Press subsequently published an anonymous denial of this story, quoting a top aide of General Eisenhower as asserting that Senator McCarthy saw only the final text of the Republican nominee's speech.

At first General Eisenhower denied to newsmen that he had taken out the Marshall reference at Senator McCarthy's request. But later, when reminded of the details of his conversation with the Senator, he said that his reasons for taking the reference out were substantially those advanced by the Wisconsin Republican.

General Eisenhower also indicated that he had been urged not to refer to General Marshall by Gov. Walter Kohler of Wisconsin who was, he pointed out, his host in the state.

The Republican nominee said that he had decided that since he already had defended General Marshall there was no point in repeating his defense, especially in Milwaukee.

Plays Golf With Old Friends

The Republican presidential nominee spent about half the morning at his hotel headquarters and then went out to the Cherry Hills Country Club to loaf, have lunch and play some golf with some old friends.

Other members of the foursome were Cliff Roberts of New York, Palmer Hoyt, publisher of The Denver Post, and John Culbreth of Denver. It was a bright sunny day and ideal for golfing or campaigning.

The nominee plans to attend church tomorrow at the Corona Presbyterian Church, which is near the home of his mother-in-law, Mrs. John S. Doud, and then probably will go out to Cherry Hills again in the afternoon.

Mrs. Eisenhower and Mrs. Doud, who do not like to fly, are aboard the Eisenhower campaign special, which is making its way to New Orleans, where the nominee will reboard it Monday night.

On Monday morning, the Republican nominee and his party will be off by air early for a series of speeches in Casper and Cheyenne, Wyo., during the morning; Tulsa and Oklahoma City, Okla., during the afternoon, with a major speech planned at night in New Orleans.

In the three days of next week, he will be making his major bid to carry Louisiana and Texas, where both Democratic Governors, Robert F. Kennon and Allan Shivers, have bolted the national ticket to back him.

He will work through Texas on Tuesday and Wednesday morning. On Wednesday afternoon he will fly to Shreveport, La., and on into Memphis and Knoxville, Tenn., en route to New York, which he will reach late that night.

Opposes Break with Russia

DENVER, Oct. 11 (AP)—General Eisenhower is opposed to suggestions that the United States break off diplomatic relations with the Soviet Union.

"There is an old Army axiom—never lose contact with your enemy," he told correspondents several days ago aboard his Presidential campaign train. "So I can't see anything to be gained by breaking off relations."

The question was presented last Sunday, after the Russians had requested the withdrawal of George F. Kennan, American Ambassador to Moscow. One of the General's backers, Senator William F. Knowland of California, who was then aboard the train, sent a telegram to Secretary of State Dean Acheson, urging that the United States, in retaliation, tell Moscow that Soviet Ambassador Georgi N. Zarubin was not welcome in Washington either.

In his talk with the political reporters, which was off the record at the time, General Eisenhower said, "I think it's better to keep someone there."

* * *

October 19, 1952

VISHINSKY UPHOLDS COMMUNIST STAND ON KOREA CAPTIVES

Tells U.N. Assembly That U.S. Uses Repatriation Question to Prolong War for Profit

REPEATS OLD ARMS PLAN

Stress on Reds' Oct. 8 Offer on Prisoners Held Possible Loophole to Renew Talks

By THOMAS J. HAMILTON
Special to The New York Times.

UNITED NATIONS, N. Y., Oct. 18—Andrei Y. Vishinsky, Soviet Foreign Minister, gave his full support today to the stand taken by Communist negotiators in Panmunjom for the repatriation of all prisoners of the Korean war, whether they want to go back or not. He asserted that this issue had been used as a pretext to support "a decision of the ruling circles of the United States" to "prosecute their shameless war against the Korean people."

"The American billionaires who are raking in tremendous profits from this war are not at all interested in having it come to an end," Mr. Vishinsky told the assembly in an hour and a quarter speech.

His speech, mainly a repetition of Soviet propaganda themes over the last three years and more, included the familiar assertion that financial and industrial magnates of the United States "thirst for a new war so that they may rake in millions of blood-spattered dollars."

Speech Called Rambling

However, Mr. Vishinsky also found occasion to repeat the theme of the "peaceful co-existence" of Communist and capitalistic countries. It was a rambling, badly organized speech, which at first glance seemed to bang the door on the possibility of an armistice in Korea.

The Soviet Foreign Minister described the United States stand against repatriation of prisoners against their will as meaning that some would go home and others would be kept in captivity. For good measure, he endorsed the armistice proposal submitted yesterday by Poland—it was made originally by the Soviet Union early in the Korean war—which would provide for the withdrawal of all foreign troops from Korea within two or three months, and which had previously been rejected by the United States.

However, Mr. Vishinsky went out of his way to emphasize a final offer by the Communist negotiators, made Oct. 8, after they had been notified that the United States, as the agent of the United Nations, had decided to suspend the talks.

Although this letter appears on the surface to be merely a repetition of the previous Communist position, or nearly so, sources close to the Soviet delegation drew it to the special attention of correspondents, and it may indicate that the Soviet Union has not closed the door to some kind of bargain.

The United Nations, as its final offer before the suspension of negotiations, had submitted three alternative suggestions on the procedure by which prisoners of war should have a choice after an armistice either to go home or stay where they were.

In reply the Communists said they would accept the proposal that Red Cross representatives should visit prisoners after "they had been turned over on both sides" to explain that "their return home had been guaranteed," that they should not fight again, and so forth. The letter then added:

"Following this a classification of prisoners of war shall be conducted in accordance with their nationality and domicile, as proposed by our side. Repatriation shall take place immediately after the classification. Exchange, visit, classification and repatriation of prisoners of war can be conducted under the supervision of control groups composed of representatives of neutral countries."

Some suggested the word "domicile" might be used as a loophole for North Korean prisoners who could claim South Korean residency if they did not want to go back. The very

lack of precision in this letter may be significant, it is believed.

For the basic reason for the refusal of the Communists to agree to voluntary repatriation has been their fear that half of the prisoners or more would choose not to go home, which would, of course, mean a severe loss of face.

It seems evident that if the Communists should ever decide to accept the United Nations position, they would attempt to cover it up by insisting that they had not given way on the basic principle and that they had merely accepted a slightly different line of procedure. According to dispatches from Tokyo, they in fact informed the United Nations that only "method and procedure" were involved in their Oct. 8 reply.

Indeed, if they were making a concession they did it so subtly that it was not noticed by the United Nations' negotiators. The United States, in a special report today to the Assembly on the entire course of the negotiations, said that the three alternative proposals had been rejected and that "no constructive proposals have been forthcoming from the Communists either since this rejection or in the more than six months prior to it."

Soviet Reply Indicated

"The months of meetings have been used for purely propaganda purposes by the Communists," said the report, and it appears very possible that Mr. Vishinsky brought up the question today for that purpose only.

However, members of the United Nations are clearly eager to end the war if this can be done on "just terms," as Secretary of State Dean Acheson demanded in his speech to the Assembly yesterday. Some delegates said they were very eager to have a further explanation of what Mr. Vishinsky actually had in mind. No further developments are expected from Mr. Vishinsky until the Political and Security Committee starts debating the Korean question.

Korea, according to a recommendation by Secretary General Trygv Lie, is third on the list of items to be considered by the committee. Mr. Vishinsky said nothing today about a tentative Soviet move earlier this week to have the committee take up Korea before the United States elections, but this may be revived when the Assembly reaches the committee meets early next week.

Meanwhile, a long message from the North Koreans was received today at the United Nations. It is known that this contains their version of the armistice negotiations, but nothing further has been disclosed.

In addition to endorsing the Polish proposal regarding the Korean armistice, Mr. Vishinsky gave his whole-hearted endorsement to another section of it that called for the prohibition of atomic weapons, a one-third reduction in the armed forces of the five great powers, a big five peace pact, and so forth.

This did not surprise the delegates for the Polish proposal was merely a repetition of a Soviet proposal in the General Assembly last year, which was itself merely a grab-bag for proposals previously made by the Soviet Union. The surprising thing was Mr. Vishinsky introduced no proposals of his own, and merely said "me-too" to a Soviet satellite.

Mr. Vishinsky placed most of the blame for "aggressive" United States policy, the "North Atlantic bloc," Korea and so forth on President Truman and Mr. Acheson, but declared that Gen. Dwight D. Eisenhower, Republican Presidential candidate, and John Foster Dulles, his principal foreign policy advisor, as well as the President and Mr. Acheson, had praised the doctrine of "deterrent strength" as much as they could.

In developing his theme that United States industry was being militarized, Mr. Vishinsky said he had to "make some allowance" for his campaign "electioneering," but that "even General Eisenhower" had said that "our economy is a war economy; our prosperity is a war prosperity."

The opening debate will continue on Monday, but only three speakers have been listed, since many delegates want to wait until after the United States election.

* * *

November 1, 1952

GENERAL ASSAILS ISOLATIONISM, DISAVOWS MCCARTHY METHODS

By JAMES RESTON
Special to The New York Times.

CHICAGO, Oct. 31—Gen. Dwight D. Eisenhower took a stand before a roaring Chicago Stadium crowd here tonight against both isolationism and McCarthyism. In his first speech in Chicago since he won the Republican Presidential nomination from the Middle West's favorite Senator, Robert A. Taft of Ohio, the nominee asserted:

"I have long insisted and do now insist that isolationism in America is dead as a political issue."

Referring to President Truman and Gov. Adlai E. Stevenson of Illinois as "my Siamese-twin opponents," and to the President as the "senior member of that partnership," the Republican nominee rejected Democratic charges that he had been changed by his conservative associates in the four months since the Republican nominating convention.

"They know I have not changed," he said, "they know my fundamental belief in Americanism. They know that I am steadfast in my basic conviction that peace is America's greatest need, and that peace for America is inseparable from peace for the world * * * They know that I have always rejected in the domestic scene the doctrines of the extremists. I denounce reaction just as I reject socialism."

Fairness Is Pledged

Though the nominee made no reference to the speech that Senator Joseph R. McCarthy, Republican of Wisconsin, made in this city several days ago, attacking Governor Stevenson and his associates, he left no doubt about where he stood in the controversy over the methods to be used in dealing with the Communist menace in the United States.

"There has been considerable concern—and rightfully so," he said, "about methods to be used in rooting communism out of our Government. There are those who believe that any means are justified by the end of rooting out communism.

"There are those who believe that the preservation of democracy and the preservation of the soul of freedom in this country can and must be accomplished with decency and fairness and due process of law."

Then, without referring to Senator McCarthy, the Republican nominee added:

"I belong to this second school. But at the same time, I say to you that no differences in theory can excuse any failure to see that Communist contamination inside our Government is stamped out."

In his attempt to win the twenty-seven electoral votes of this state, which President Truman carried by a margin of 33,612 in 1948, General Eisenhower flew in here today from New York. He will return to Manhattan tomorrow morning.

He toured the city this afternoon, making one speech at the Western Electric plant in Cicero shortly after noon, to a crowd of about 30,000 and then placed a wreath on a monument to a Negro soldier on the South Side of Chicago late in the afternoon.

At this later ceremony a small crowd of between 3,000 and 4,000 greeted him with respect but little enthusiasm. Everywhere else, however, he was given an example of the usual boisterousness and friendliness of the Republican Middle West.

Just how many people actually turned out to wave and cry out to the General this afternoon was anybody's guess.

The police, whose record in this election for accuracy in estimating crowds is not impressive, varied in their guesses today, between 200,000 and 500,000, but in any event a lot of people were on hand and seemed to bear out the assertion of former Senator C. Wayland Brooks of Illinois, who was on hand, that there are still a lot of Republicans in Cook County, Ill.

Charges Truman Runs Drive

Both the nominee and his staff showed some signs of weariness at the end of the long campaign tonight, although he managed to retain his natural good humor throughout the day.

"This has been some campaign!" the General said. "The present incumbent and his protégé have assailed me with the greatest collection of flimflamming accusations made in any campaign.

"In case you have had any doubt, the opposition is being directed by the senior member of that partnership, President Truman. He told a back platform crowd in Manly, Iowa, the other morning that he was the man who was running the Democratic campaign for President."

General Eisenhower said that the "true issues" of the campaign were so clear that they were "terrifying" to the opposition. He defined the main issues as "Korea, communism, corruption and prosperity based on peace."

On Korea, the nominee repeated his statement that he was going to the battlefield if he was elected for the obvious reason of trying to find out for himself what was being done there. This time, however, he added:

"I have no magic military wand to bring that war to an end. But I know that on the spot I can learn something that will be helpful in serving the American people in the cause of peace."

He also described his plan to go to Korea as "one practical step in working out a plan to stop our casualties and to help bring the war to an honorable end."

The Republican candidate condemned the Truman Administration for what he called its "pretzel-shaped evasions" on the issue of communism. He observed that even though it was deplorable, there was, after all, nothing extraordinary in the fact that Moscow should exert its mightiest efforts to try to penetrate the military secrets of America, that it should try to subvert American officials or that they should try to spread disruption and disunity in the United States.

"What is extraordinary," he declared, "is that the present Administration continues to pretend that none of these things have been so—that everything that has happened, every stolen secret, every disloyal official, is, they say, just an unfortunate, almost insignificant accident."

General Eisenhower said that it would be possible to make some allowance for the Democrats if they had had the honesty or the common sense or both to admit that they had been deceived and to show a stern purpose of preventing similar subversion in the future.

On what he called the third major issue of the campaign—corruption—General Eisenhower said that he had been shocked to discover on his return home last June from Western Europe how prevalent corruption in governmental positions had become. The American people, he said, were virtually accepting as part of their daily life a corruption headline in their newspapers.

Vilification Charged

He was met by a few hundred party workers when he arrived at the official Civil Aeronautics Administration section of the Chicago Airport after a flight from New York.

He drove from there in an open car to Cicero where he made his first speech in front of the Western Electric plant with a huge crowd blocking all traffic from sidewalk to sidewalk and with several thousand of people calling to him from the windows of the great industrial factory.

In this community, which is heavily populated by Czechoslovak Americans, General Eisenhower took occasion to condemn the record of the Administration in allowing Czechoslovakia to be overcome by the U.S.S.R.

The General observed that Governor Stevenson had said in Chicago at the beginning of the campaign, in "smoothly flowing words" that he was going to conduct a campaign that would "educate and elevate the American people."

Now, however, he said, the Democrats had stopped trying to defend their record and had allowed the campaign to descend into a series of charges and vilifications against the Republican party.

General Eisenhower reassured the workers that every single member of the "crusade" was pledged to the idea that at the first sign of any approaching depression the full power of private industry, of local and state government and of the Federal Government would be mobilized to see that never again would the nation have to suffer the consequences of mass unemployment.

He also observed that he and his associates were committed to the expansion and improvement of the present social security program, and more than that, that they were committed to do something about stopping inflation.

One of the major objectives in the candidate's visit to this city today was to try to persuade at least some of the Negro voters in Chicago's teeming South Side that they have nothing to fear in terms of their economic or social outlook from a Republican victory.

In the 1948 election some 90,000 Negroes in this city voted for President Truman and this was some 60,000 more than the President's margin over Gov. Thomas E. Dewey of New York in the contest for Illinois' electoral votes.

However, there was little in the mild reception that he received when he and his party arrived at the "Victory Monument" to indicate that the Negro voters on the South Side would support him in any great numbers next Tuesday.

There was some talk about General Eisenhower flying on from here tomorrow—an open day on his schedule—to California for a big political rally there, but this idea was abandoned and he is scheduled to return to New York to rest over the week-end before leaving again for Boston where he will wind up his campaign Monday night.

* * *

November 5, 1952

EISENHOWER WINS IN A LANDSLIDE; TAKES NEW YORK; IVES ELECTED; REPUBLICANS GAIN IN CONGRESS

RACE IS CONCEDED

Virginia and Florida Go to the General as Do Illinois and Ohio

SWEEP IS NATION-WIDE

Victor Calls for Unity and Thanks Governor for Pledging Support

By ARTHUR KROCK

Gen. Dwight D. Eisenhower was elected President of the United States yesterday in an electoral vote landslide and with an emphatic popular majority that probably will give his party a small margin of control in the House of Representatives but may leave the Senate as it is—forty-nine Democrats, forty-seven Republicans and one independent.

Dwight D. Eisenhower   Richard M. Nixon

Senator Richard M. Nixon of California was elected Vice President.

The Democratic Presidential candidate, Gov. Adlai E. Stevenson of Illinois, shortly after midnight conceded his defeat by a record turnout of American voters.

At 4 A. M. today the Republican candidate had carried states with a total of 431 electors, or 165 more than the 266 required for the selection of a President. The Democratic candidate seemed sure of 69, with 31 doubtful in Kentucky, Louisiana and Tennessee.

General Eisenhower's landslide victory, both in electoral and popular votes, was nation-wide in its pattern, extending from New England—where Massachusetts and Rhode Island broke their Democratic voting habits of many years—down the Eastern seaboard to Maryland, Virginia and Florida and westward to almost every state between the coasts, including California.

General Wins Illinois

The Republican candidate took Illinois, Governor Stevenson's home state. In South Carolina, though he lost its electors on a technicality, he won a majority of the voters. And, completing the first successful Republican invasion of the States of the former Confederacy, the General carried Texas and broke the one-party system in the South.

The personal popularity that enabled him to defeat Senator Robert A. Taft of Ohio in the Republican primaries in Texas, and present him with the issue on which he defeated the Senator for the Republican nomination, crushed the regular Democratic organization of Texas that was led by Speaker Sam Rayburn of the House of Representatives and had the blessing of former Vice President John N. Garner.

The tide that bore General Eisenhower to the White House, though it did not give him a comfortable working majority in either the national House or the Senate (the Democrats may still nominally control the machinery of that branch), probably increased the number of Republican governors beyond the present twenty-five.

"My fellow citizens have made their choice and I gladly accept it," said Governor Stevenson at 1:46 A. M., Eastern standard time, and he asked all citizens to unite behind the President-elect. The defeated candidate said he had sent a telegram of congratulation to General Eisenhower.

At 2:05 A. M., from the Grand Ballroom of the Commodore Hotel, General Eisenhower said he recognized the weight of his new responsibilities and that he would not give "short weight" in their execution. He also urged "unity" and announced he had sent a telegram of thanks to the Democratic candidate for his promise of support.

The issues of the unusually vigorous campaign that was waged by the candidates of the two major parties, with President Truman advocating Governor Stevenson's election, in a speaking tour throughout the country, as an endorsement of the record of his administration and that of the late President Roosevelt, were these:

• General Eisenhower asserted that it was "time for a change" from the twenty-year tenure of the Democrats in the White House, with control of Congress for all but two years in that period, the third longest in American history. Governor Stevenson promised to "refresh" his party and the Government and said that would be all the "change" the critical world situation justified.

• General Eisenhower forcefully attacked revelations of official corruption in the Truman Administration and charged first negligence and then tolerance of the infiltration of Communist agents in the Government. Governor Stevenson denounced both but defended the Administration as having done its full duty in the circumstances.

• General Eisenhower demanded a "new look" at the war in Korea and promised to make an inspection trip to the peninsula if he were elected. He charged that more South Koreans could and should have been trained to man the front lines "where our boys do not belong." Governor Stevenson and the President denounced this as a "cheap trick," and as an injury to the chances for an armistice in the Korean war.

• Governor Stevenson and the President assailed General Eisenhower because he declined to denounce Senator Joseph R. McCarthy of Wisconsin and other Republican Senators for "character assassination" and "isolationism." They also accused him of having "surrendered" to Senator Robert A. Taft of Ohio, whom he defeated for the Republican nomination, and of abandoning his "principles" in domestic and foreign policy thereby.

Fitzpatrick Concedes State

The great majority of the voters sustained General Eisenhower's position on all these issues. Their desire for a "change" rather than a "refreshment" of the Administration was noted by Paul E. Fitzpatrick, Democratic State Chairman of New York, when at 11 P. M. yesterday, he conceded the state to the Republicans.

This was thirteen minutes after Arthur E. Summerfield, Republican National Chairman, had asserted that General Eisenhower had been elected by a "landslide" that also carried majorities in both branches of Congress.

In states where the issues of corruption and Communist infiltration had been actively debated, the voting majority also sustained the General.

And, by the defeat for re-election in Connecticut of Senator William Benton, who has made a career of attacking Senator McCarthy; the re-election of Mr. McCarthy by a huge margin in Wisconsin; and the re-election of Senator William E. Jenner of Indiana, the voting majority indicated approval of the objectives of what the Democrats and independents have assailed as McCarthysim.

Effect of Korea Issue

There is no way of estimating the effect on yesterday's voters of the angry argument over the Korean war between the two Presidential candidates, with President Truman rising to heights of bitterness hitherto unscaled even by him in his denunciation of General Eisenhower's criticism of the Administration's pre-war policies in the Far East and the General's promise to go to the scene of the war, if elected.

But ever since General Eisenhower made the promise, it had been evident that the Democrats were alarmed about its vote-getting potential for the Republican candidate. Therefore, it is reasonable to conclude that on this issue, which became the central one of the final phase of the campaign, the voting majority preferred the position taken by General Eisenhower.

On the over-all issue of the record of the Roosevelt-Truman Administrations, including the New Deal and Fair Deal programs, that the President insisted was "all Stevenson had to run on," the result of the election will be taken by the Republicans as repudiation of Mr. Truman.

This undoubtedly will be the basis of the proposals to Congress that President-elect Eisenhower will make and that Congress will sustain, if it is controlled by the Republicans.

At midnight that control seemed possible but not certain. The Democrats lost two Senate seats to the Republicans in Connecticut—those of Mr. Benton and the late Brien McMahon—and that of Herbert R. O'Connor in Maryland.

The Republicans held the seats of Senator H. Alexander Smith of New Jersey, John W. Bricker of Ohio, and Irving M. Ives of New York, in addition to those of Messrs. McCarthy and Jenner. But final returns may disclose that the Democrats have taken the seat held by Senator Henry Cabot Lodge Jr. of Massachusetts by electing Representative John F. Kennedy to his place.

Since the Republicans must make a net gain of two to organize the Senate (that is to elect the chairman of its committees and its officers), and Senator Wayne Morse of Oregon, elected as a Republican, has resigned from the party and may vote on organization with the Democrats, the issue of party control of the Senate was in doubt and may be until Senator Morse decides on his course in that body.

The campaign just ended was unusual in many ways in addition to the fact that no retiring President ever had taken the stump with the intensity and activity Mr. Truman did in defense of his record.

The Republican and Democratic nominees both were reluctant candidates and powerful pressures had to be exerted on both before General Eisenhower would consent to seek the nomination and Governor Stevenson would agree to be drafted by his party convention.

Once nominated, however, each fought as hard as the most ambitious politician to whom a Presidential nomination has come as the consequence of unremitting efforts to acquire it.

General Eisenhower was persuaded to resign as Supreme Commander of the North Atlantic Treaty Organization by assurances that, if he agreed to accept the Republican nomination, he would be chosen by acclamation and elected easily.

Instead, he was obliged to wage a hard battle against Senator Taft that for a time split the Republican party wide open. And though it appeared at last midnight that his electoral and popular majorities would be large, the apparent strength of Mr. Stevenson was such that the General had to put everything he had into the campaign.

Governor Stevenson refused until the Democratic convention had been in session for three days to give the slightest encouragement to those who wanted to draft him.

He said and did a number of things calculated to discourage the effort, including a statement to the Illinois delegation that he was "temperamentally" and otherwise "unfit" to be President.

And, though he was the first Presidential candidate truly drafted in modern American history, the pattern was spoiled by the fact that he got delegate votes on the first two ballots in contest (though against his will and command) with Averell Harriman, Senator Estes Kefauver of Tennessee and Senator Richard B. Russell of Georgia.

Like the other reluctant candidate, however, Governor Stevenson fought as hard as he could to be elected. Beginning with a speech of acceptance that forecast a campaign on the highest level, he was soon trading blows—high ones and low ones—with General Eisenhower.

In the echelon of winners under the General the more conspicuous were:

Senator Harry F. Byrd, Democrat of Virginia, whose state endorsed his refusal to support Mr. Stevenson; Gov. Thomas E. Dewey, Republican of New York, who was among the early Eisenhower drafters and was most active in the successful campaign to carry the state; Senator McCarthy, who was made a national issue.

*   *   *

November 11, 1952

VISHINSKY DIMS TRUCE HOPE, SAYS SOVIET 'WILL NOT BUDGE'

Special to The New York Times.

UNITED NATIONS, N. Y., Nov. 10—Andrei Y. Vishinsky, Soviet Foreign Minister, announced today that the Soviet Union "will not budge" from its position that all Communist prisoners of war in Korea must be returned, whether they choose to be or not.

Mr. Vishinsky's bitter statement, which took two hours and thirty-two minutes to deliver to the Political and Security Committee of the General Assembly, appeared to have destroyed virtually all hope of a compromise, at least as far as the Soviet Union was concerned.

Among other things, he termed "unacceptable" a Mexican proposal, under which those prisoners not wishing to go back would be given asylum in countries other than their own until a permanent Korean settlement had been reached at a general political conference.

Peruvian Plan 'Unsatisfactory'

Mr. Vishinsky used the milder term "unsatisfactory" for a Peruvian proposal, under which the Assembly would create a five-nation committee to help return the prisoners, with those unwilling to be repatriated to remain in a neutralized zone under the committee's protection.

Dr. Luis Padilla Nervo, author of the Mexican resolution, said afterward that, although a fuller study of Mr. Vishinsky's speech might reveal grounds for encouragement, he had not noticed any while listening to it. The Mexican representative added that the speech had convinced him that it would not be worthwhile to proceed with the proposal for a compromise that many delegates had been examining in the last few weeks.

Essentially, this plan would call for an Assembly resolution accepting the principle laid down in the Geneva prisoner-of-war convention of 1949, which provides for the immediate repatriation, with virtually no exceptions, of all prisoners, and says nothing concerning the wishes of those who do not want to be returned.

The New York Times (by Patrick A. Burns)

ADAMANT RUSSIAN: Soviet Foreign Minister Andrei Y. Vishinsky addressing U. N. Political and Security Committee yesterday when he said that Russia would insist that all Korean prisoners of war be sent home. Listening to him are British Foreign Secretary Anthony Eden, center, and United States Secretary of State Dean Acheson. Seated behind them, left to right, are Ernest A. Gross, Selwyn Lloyd and Andrei A. Gromyko.

At the same time, however, the proposed resolution would leave the actual repatriation to a commission that, from its membership, could be depended upon not to send back any prisoners who did not want to go back and certainly would not use force to that end.

Peruvian More Hopeful

Dr. Victor A. Belaunde, author of the Peruvian resolution, was more hopeful tonight than Dr. Padilla Nervo, and said he planned another speech in the Political and Security Committee—which will not meet again before the latter part of the week—in which he hoped to overcome Mr. Vishinsky's objections.

The first public suggestion of the compromise plan came from Paul Martin of Canada in a speech in the committee a few days ago. Lester B. Pearson, Canadian Secretary for External Affairs and president of the Assembly, said he believed the attempt to "isolate and solve" the prisoner issue along these lines should be continued.

Mr. Pearson, observing that the twenty-one-nation resolution was concerned with "broad principles," said he hoped the proposal would make it possible to solve the issue before general Korean problems were taken up.

A number of Asian delegates have been attempting to work out a compromise along these lines, but L. N. Palar of Indonesia said he did not intend to present any resolution until some authoritative word had been received in the Assembly regarding the views of Gen. Dwight D. Eisenhower, the United States President-elect.

The Indian delegation also is working on the same basic idea, and the Indian Government, which has been in touch over the past few days with the Government of Communist China, is thought to have been asking the latter's views.

Mme. Pandit's Talk Awaited

It is assumed that the Indian delegation will not submit the resolution unless the Peiping Government agrees to the basic idea, and for this reason the Assembly speech tomorrow by Mme. Vijaya Lakshmi Pandit is awaited with special attention.

A spokesman for the United States delegation said Mr. Vishinsky's speech had been entirely negative, and had thrown no light on how to avoid forcible repatriation.

Mr. Vishinsky introduced a new draft of the resolution he had introduced Oct. 29. It was the same as its predecessor except for two additions:

First, it named the countries that would be members of the proposed commission: The United States, Britain, France, the Soviet, Communist China, India, Burma, Switzerland, Czechoslovakia, North Korea and South Korea.

Second, it specified that the commission, in addition to its efforts to bring about a settlement of the Korean question, should include in its work "the extending of all possible assistance to the repatriation of all prisoners of war by both sides."

Mr. Vishinsky brought forward a new argument against allowing prisoners to decide whether they wished to return: As soldiers they do not have the right to decide whether they want to go home any more than they have a right to decide whether they want to fight.

* * *

November 12, 1952

EDEN URGES ENEMY YIELD ON CAPTIVES TO END KOREA WAR

Asks Communists to Support Forcible Repatriation Ban— Offers 4-Point Plan

SUGGESTS POST-WAR TALK

Briton Endorses Schuman View That U. N. Lacks Authority in Colonial Disputes

---

By THOMAS J. HAMILTON
Special to The New York Times.

UNITED NATIONS, N. Y., Nov. 11—Anthony Eden, British Foreign Secretary, appealed today to the Soviet Union, Communist China and North Korea to accept the principle that "after an armistice [in Korea] a prisoner of war may not be either forcibly detained or forcibly repatriated."

Mr. Eden, who was the last of the Big Four foreign ministers to speak in the United Nations General Assembly's opening debate, said that he wished to state as simply as possible the four principles that he believed should prevail in the Korean armistice negotiations.

He did not mention a twenty-one-nation resolution, of which Britain was a sponsor, endorsing the stand taken by United Nations negotiators in Panmunjom, and implied that this would be laid aside for the time being, at least, if there appeared to be any prospect that the Communists would agree to a settlement along the lines he indicated.

Eden Offers Four Principles

Mr. Eden's four principles, which marked another attempt to find out whether any possibility of an agreement was hidden beneath the bitter rhetoric voiced yesterday by Andrei Y. Vishinsky, Soviet Foreign Minister, were as follows:

1. That every prisoner of war had the right, on the conclusion of an armistice, to be released.
2. That every prisoner of war had the right to be speedily repatriated.
3. That there was a duty on the detaining side to provide facilities for such repatriation.
4. That the detaining side had no right to use force in connection with the disposal of prisoners of war.

Mr. Eden pointed out that the three alternative proposals submitted by United Nations negotiators last month were in accordance with the four principles amplifying his basic principle, and added that "we would examine any method, any procedure which can ensure that these principles would be carried out."

"Is it possible to make a fairer offer than that?" Mr. Eden asked. At the same time he offered an assurance to the Soviet Union that Britain would agree to a political conference after an armistice, which would take up "reconstruction and stability in Korea" and then would "go on to a settlement of those other problems which we must solve to secure a lasting peace in the Far East."

Briton's Statement Conciliatory

Mr. Eden's statement, which was conciliatory in tone, is believed to have been addressed particularly to the Asian and Arab states, most of which have refrained thus far from stating their position on the Korean armistice question.

At the same time, however, he sided with France in denying the jurisdiction of the United Nations over the complaints against the French administration of Tunisia and Morocco that the Asians and Arabs had placed before the Assembly, and served notice that Britain was not giving up her colonies.

Mr. Eden emphasized that peoples of the non-self-governing territories "need the help which the colonial powers are able to give them, until they can stand on their own feet," and said the colonial powers had established law and respect for human rights, "replacing the rule of the jungle and the despot."

Britain regards her colonial duties as "a solemn trust," Mr. Eden said. He emphasized the benefits of British rule and declared:

"We are asked by some here to give up this work. Let me make our position clear; nothing will induce us to do so * * *.

"The Charter of the United Nations * * * represents the highest common factor of agreement between the nations, as to the powers which they are willing to pool for common purposes. If we attempt to stretch the meaning of the Charter and extend the areas in which the United Nations has jurisdiction, we run grave risks—unless we can carry all our fellow members with us—of weakening the very structure of the United Nations * * *.

"It was never intended to be an agency for controlling the domestic policies of its various members or for intervening between them and the territories for which they are internationally responsible."

Mr. Eden included in his speech a discussion of numerous issues, including the failure of the Big Four to reach agreement on a treaty for Austria, economic problems, disarmament and so forth.

Although he used moderate language, Mr. Eden gave an effective reply to the latest accusations by Mr. Vishinsky against the United Nations action in Korea. Mr. Eden said that the absence of any "aggression or imperialist purpose" had been demonstrated by the acceptance of the Soviet proposal for armistice discussions, "though the military position was at that time overwhelmingly in our favor."

Eden's Promise Interpreted

Mr. Eden's promise regarding the convening of a political conference after an armistice also was interpreted as an attempt to persuade the Soviet Union to agree to an armistice.

A considerable number of delegates are inclined to take Mr. Vishinsky's speech yesterday at face value and to conclude that the Soviet Union will not agree to any armistice agreement that does not provide for the return of all prisoners, without exception.

These delegates are now basing their hopes on Communist China, rather than the Soviet Union. Since India appears to be the only non-Communist country that has any reliable contacts with the Peiping Government, they are waiting for the Indian delegation to say what proposal, if any, stands a chance of acceptance.

However, Mme. Vijaya Lakshmi Pandit, head of the Indian delegation, who spoke this morning before Mr. Eden, made no suggestion except to urge that delegates of Communist China should be seated in the United Nations.

Dr. Luis Padilla Nervo of Mexico suggested that the Political and Security Committee should draw up a statement outlining the suggested settlement and ask the Peiping Government to state its views before the committee attempted to approve a resolution.

* * *

November 17, 1952

EXPERIMENTS FOR HYDROGEN BOMB HELD SUCCESSFULLY AT ENIWETOK; LEAKS ABOUT BLAST UNDER INQUIRY

FLASH IS DESCRIBED

Letter From Task Force Navigator Says Light Equaled 'Ten Suns'

3 ASSERT ATOLL VANISHED

Many at Scene Nov. 1 Believed That a Hydrogen Bomb Had Been Set Off

---

By The United Press

WASHINGTON, Nov. 16—The recent test explosion at Eniwetok was a devastating blast, according to composite eyewitness reports sent back by service men who evidently believed that a hydrogen bomb had been set off.

Service men's letters disclosed that "the bomb" had been transported to San Francisco under heavy guard, where it was loaded on a Navy vessel and placed in a special compartment. The door was welded shut and heavy chains were welded across the door.

Federal Bureau of Investigation agents accompanied "the bomb" aboard ship, and there were more civilian and security personnel aboard than sailors. There was a moment's anxiety when the ship's electronics gear picked up what was thought to be an unidentified submarine, but one letter writer said "nothing came of it."

The ship carried "the bomb" directly to the test island, apparently an atoll some thirty-five miles from Eniwetok in the Marshall group, where most United States atomic tests are held.

The test island apparently was about three miles long and somewhere between one-quarter of a mile and one mile wide, although the description of the island varied in the letters.

Vessels Scattered in Area

Vessels of the task force were scattered in an area around the island with the closest stationed about thirty miles from the center of the explosion, the letters said. Several ships apparently were thirty-five miles away. There was no indication whether land observers were closer to the scene.

But the letters clearly showed that the explosion took place on Nov. 1 with zero hour at 7:15 A. M., Eniwetok time.

Aboard the ships the men had donned protective clothing and had been instructed to turn their backs to the island ten seconds before the blast, close their eyes and cover their faces with their arms.

At 7:14 A. M. a voice over the loudspeaker of each ship started counting the seconds. During that time, one observer wrote home, everything was quiet. He said:

"In those last few minutes, especially when they were counting off the seconds, we all grew real tense and silence was so perfect you could hear a pin drop. In those last few seconds, I think everything I've been told ran through my mind. And in the last second, I said a silent prayer."

For six seconds after zero there was silence, no movement, no flash in the sky.

The first sign of the explosion came to the men aboard ship in the form of a flash many times brighter than the sun, followed by a wave of heat across their backs. Although the men had their backs turned with their arms across their dark glasses, the blinding light was not kept out.

"It would take at least ten suns" to equal the light of the explosion from a distance of thirty-five miles, a navigator wrote.

Ten seconds after zero, the men on ship started turning around to face the direction of the blast.

"I could hardly believe my eyes," one wrote. "A flame about two miles wide was shooting five miles into the air. This lasted for about 7.2 seconds. Then we saw thousands of tons of earth being thrown straight into the sky. Then a cloud began to form about twenty seconds after the shot."

"You would swear," another sailor wrote, "that the whole world was on fire. It was really something I'll never forget."

At least three eyewitnesses reported that the test island on which the bomb had been exploded disappeared after the blast.

"About fifteen minutes after shot time, the island on which the bomb had been set off from started to burn and it turned a brilliant red. It burned for about six hours. During this time it was gradually becoming smaller," one man wrote. "Within six hours an island that had once had palm trees and coconuts had now nothing. A mile wide island had disappeared."

PART IV

THE EISENHOWER PERIOD

January 16, 1953

TRUMAN, IN ADIEU, HOPEFUL OF PEACE AND SOVIET CHANGE

PRESIDENT ON AIR

Sees Shift by Russians, Perhaps of Own Will or Internal Trouble

TAKES PRIDE IN HIS RECORD

He Declares That 'I Have Tried to Give It Everything That Was in Me'

By PAUL P. KENNEDY
Special to The New York Times.

WASHINGTON, Jan. 15—Harry S. Truman bade his official farewell tonight to the American people, whose national destinies he has had a large share in directing for almost eight years as President of the United States.

His official leave-taking was in a half-hour radio and television chat at 10:30 P. M. from his office in the west wing of the White House. It was to be his last public address before he leaves office next Tuesday.

It was a nostalgic farewell, but not a sad one. He offered his best wishes to his successor, Gen. Dwight D. Eisenhower. He held out high hopes for a better and more peaceful world in the future. He saw an inevitable change in the Soviet regime.

The President asserted a restrained pride in the record of his stewardship. He said he would leave the White House with no regrets.

"I have tried to give it everything that was in me," he said, and he repeatedly expressed gratitude to the American people for their support and asked them to give that same support to his successor. "He will have mine and I want you to give him yours," the President said.

Cooperation Praised

Early in his talk President Truman praised General Eisenhower and his associates for their cooperation in arranging an orderly transition of Administrations.

Such an orderly transfer from one party to another has never taken place before in our history, Mr. Truman said. "I think a real precedent has been set."

He reviewed briefly what he obviously considered the most vital events of his tenure of office, a majority of them relating to the East-West conflict and the strengthening of the Western world.

"As the free world grows stronger, more united, more attractive to men on both sides of the Iron Curtain—and as the Soviet hopes for easy expansion are blocked—then there will have to come a time of change in the Soviet world," the President said.

"Nobody can say for sure," he continued, "when that is going to be or exactly how it will come about, whether by revolution, or trouble in the satellite states, or by a change inside the Kremlin.

"Whether the Communist rulers shift their policies of their own free will—or whether the changes comes about some other way—I have not a doubt in the world that the change will occur."

Tonight's talk was perhaps the most personal speech the President had made. The talk was based on a first draft he himself wrote Sunday night in his study in the White House.

As Mr. Truman reached the end of his talk, his wife and daughter, Margaret, moved to either side of the President. Like Mr. Truman at that moment, as he said he was grateful for the support of the American people, they were solemn. But as the glaring lights went out and the camera lens turned away, all three broke into smiles.

Members of the White House staff and friends were in the room. Among them were Mrs. Joseph Short, secretary to the President and widow of Mr. Truman's press secretary; Dr. Howard A. Rusk, associate editor of The New York Times, and his daughter, and Mrs. Florence Mahoney, a friend of Mrs. Truman and her two sons, one of whom was an Air Force lieutenant.

The President tonight repeated an assertion made in recent press interviews, that he considered his decision to oppose Communist invasion of Korea as the most important in his time as president.

Flying back from his home in Independence, Mo., that June day in 1950, the President said, he "turned the problem over in his mind in many ways, but my thoughts kept coming back to the Nineteen Thirties—to Manchuria, Ethiopia—the Rhineland—Austria—and finally to Munich.

"Here was history repeating itself," the President said. "Here was another probing action, another testing action. If we let the Republic of Korea go under, some other country would be next, and then another. And all the time the courage and confidence of the free world would be ebbing away, just as it did in the Nineteen Thirties. And the United Nations would go the way of the League of Nations."

The decision, he said, was a difficult one because he was a soldier in World War I and knew what a soldier went through.

"I knew well the anguish that mothers and fathers and families go through," he said. "So I knew what was ahead if we acted in Korea."

The most heartening fact following that decision, Mr. Truman said, was that the American people clearly had agreed with the President's action.

Portions of his talk apparently were based on his recent message to Congress in which he warned Premier Stalin about following the concepts of men who had formed their ideas before the atomic age.

The President said tonight that he received occasional letters from impatient persons asking why the atomic bomb was not used to stop the Korean conflict. Such an idea, he said, is repugnant to the American people.

"The whole purpose of what we are doing is to prevent World War III," he said.

The President said he supposed that history would remember his term of office as "the years when the 'cold war' began to overshadow our lives."

"But when history says that my term of office saw the beginning of the 'cold war,' " the President asserted, it will also say that in those eight years we have set the course that can win it.

"We have averted World War III up to now and we may already have succeeded in establishing conditions which can keep that war from happening as far ahead as man can see."

The President recounted other things that history would record of his Administration, and one of them, he said, was "that we in America have learned how to attain real prosperity for our people." He pointed to increased employment, bigger and better distribution of incomes in all groups, safety in bank deposits and "a tremendous awakening of the American conscience on the great issues of civil rights."

"So, as I empty the drawers of this desk and as Mrs. Truman and I leave the White House," President Truman said, "we have no regret. We feel we have done our best in the public service. I hope and believe we have contributed to the welfare of this nation and to the peace of the world."

*   *   *

March 6, 1953

STALIN DIES AFTER 29-YEAR RULE; HIS SUCCESSOR NOT ANNOUNCED; U.S. WATCHFUL, EISENHOWER SAYS

PREMIER ILL 4 DAYS

Announcement of Death Made by Top Soviet and Party Chiefs

STROKE PROVES FATAL

Leaders Issue an Appeal to People for Unity and Vigilance

By HARRISON E. SALISBURY
Special to The New York Times.

MOSCOW, Friday, March 6—Premier Joseph Stalin died at 9:50 P. M. yesterday [1:50 P. M. Thursday, Eastern standard time] in the Kremlin at the age of 73, it was announced officially this morning. He had been in power twenty-nine years.

The announcement was made in the name of the Central Commitees of the Communist party, the Council of Ministers and the Presidium of the Supreme Soviet.

Calling on the Soviet people to rally firmly around the party and the Government, the announcement asked them to display unity and the highest political vigilance "in the struggle against internal and external foes." [No announcement was made of a successor to Premier Stalin.]

The Soviet leader's death from general circulatory and respiratory deficiency occurred just short of four days after he had been stricken with a brain hemorrhage in his Kremlin apartment.

Accompanying the death announcement was a final medical certificate issued by a group of ten physicians, headed by Health Minister A. F. Tretyakov, who cared for Mr. Stalin in his last illness under the direct and closest supervision of the Central Committee and the Council of Ministers.

Pulse Rate Was High

The medical certificate revealed that in the last hours Mr. Stalin's condition grew worse rapidly, with repeated heavy and sharp circulatory and heart collapses. His breathing grew superficial and sharply irregular. His pulse rate rose to 140 to 150 a minute and at 9:50 P. M., "because of a growing circulatory and respiratory insufficiency, J. V. Stalin died."

[The news of Mr. Stalin's death was withheld by Soviet officials for more than six hours.]

Pravda appeared this morning with broad black borders around its front page, which was devoted entirely to Mr. Stalin. The layout included a large photograph of the Premier, the announcement by the Government, the medical bulletins and the announcement of the formation of a funeral commission headed by Nikita S. Khruschchev, secretary of the Central Committee of the party.

Other members of the commission are Lazar M. Kaganovich, Premier Stalin's brother-in-law; Nikolai M. Shvernik, President of the Soviet Union; Alexander M. Vasilevsky, War Minister; N. U. Pegov, an alternate member of the Presidium; P. A. Artemyev, commander of the Moscow military district, and M. A. Yasnov, chairman of the city of Moscow.

Pravda's announcement said Mr. Stalin's body would lie in state in the Hall of Columns.

His death brought to an end the career of one of the great figures of modern times—a man whose name stands second to none as the organizer and builder of the great state structure the world knows as the Soviet Union.

[The United Press said members of Mr. Stalin's family and his closest associates in the Presidium and Central Committee were at his bedside.]

The Soviet leader began his life in the simple mountain village of Gori deep in poverty-stricken Georgia. He rose to head the greatest Russian state that has ever existed. For nearly thirty years, Mr. Stalin was at the helm of the country. No other statesman of modern times has led his nation for a longer period.

This morning's official announcement declared that the Government and party would strengthen "the defense, capacity and might of the Soviet state" in every manner, and in "every way" strengthen the Soviet Army, Navy and organs of intelligence "with a view to constantly raising our preparedness for a decisive rebuff to any aggressor."

The declaration comprised an important statement of policy, both external and internal. With regard to foreign relations, it declared that the party and Government stood by an inflexible policy of securing and strengthening peace, of struggle against the preparation and unleashing of a new war, and for a policy of "international collaboration and development of businesslike connections with all countries."

Friendship for China Cited

The second foreign policy point was the declaration of firm support for "proletarian internationalism," for the development of brotherly friendship with [Communist] China, with the workers of all countries of the "people's democracy" and with the workers of capitalist and colonial countries fighting "for peace, democracy and socialism."

The announcement of Mr. Stalin's death was made to the Soviet people by radio early this morning. The announcement was early enough so that persons going to work had heard the news before leaving their homes.

This correspondence circled the Kremlin several times during the evening and early morning. The great red flag flew as usual over the Supreme Soviet Presidium building behind Lenin's Tomb.

Lights blazed late as they always do in many Kremlin office buildings. Sentry guards paced their posts at the Great Kremlin Gate.

The city was quiet and sleeping, and in Red Square all was serene. The guards stood their duty at Lenin's Tomb, but otherwise the great central square was deserted, as it always is in the hours just before daylight.

The last medical bulletin before the announcement of Mr. Stalin's death was issued shortly before 9 o'clock last night, reporting his condition as of 4 P. M. yesterday. It said his condition had grown worse despite every method of therapy employed by Soviet physicians.

The bulletin revealed that, at 8 o'clock yesterday morning, there occurred a sharp heart circulatory collapse, which was corrected by "extraordinary curative measures."

A second "heavy collapse" occurred at 11:30 A. M., which "was eliminated with difficulty."

Pravda, organ of the Central Committee of the Communist party, and Izvestia, organ of the Soviet Government, called on the Soviet people yesterday to rally around the party and the Government in "these difficult days" and to display what Izvestia characterized as "heightened revolutionary vigilance." Pravda also demanded from all Soviet citizens "stanchness of spirit and vigilance."

Pravda's editorial appeal to the populace was read repeatedly over the radio. It was also read and discussed in factories, shops and offices throughout the country. Pravda had clearly sounded the theme of the day—vigilance and unity.

Last night's medical bulletin on the Premier's condition declared that an electrocardiogram taken at 11 A. M., showed "sharp disturbances in blood circulation in the coronary arteries of the heart with lesions in the back wall of the heart." An electrocardiogram taken on Monday had not established these changes, the bulletin said.

After measures taken to liquidate the 11:30 A. M. collapse, the condition was eased to some extent, although the "patient's general condition continued extremely grave," the bulletin asserted.

At 4 P. M., Mr. Stalin's blood pressure stood at 160 over 120, the bulletin said, with his pulse rate 120 a minute and his respiration 36 times a minute. His temperature stood at 37.6 centigrade (99.68 degrees Fahrenheit), slightly lower than in a 2 A. M. bulletin.

The bulletin noted that the white blood corpuscle count stood at 21,000. At 2 A. M. the white blood corpuscle count was 17,000.

The bulletin said the principal objective of the struggle now being waged with Mr. Stalin's illness was an effort to curb the interruptions in respiration and in blood circulation, particularly coronary circulation.

Every device and treatment known to modern medicine was employed by a team of ten top Soviet specialists, headed by the country's new Health Minister, A. F. Tretyakov, and directed closely by the highest bodies of the party and Government— the Central Committee and the Council of Ministers.

The medical bulletin issued at 7 o'clock yesterday morning, giving his condition as of 2 A. M., was the second issued since Mr. Stalin's stroke Sunday night. It carried a most detailed account of the progress of the illness and the measures taken to combat it. The communiqué showed that, despite every treatment thus far employed, Mr. Stalin's breathing and heart functions continued to be sharply impaired. He lay unconscious.

Penicillin had been administered to Mr. Stalin. Other treatments mentioned in the communiqué were directly concerned with the fight to maintain and regularize his breathing and heart functions. These included the use of oxygen to supplement his oxygen deficiency, and camphor and caffeine to stimulate the heart. Strophantine and glucose also were introduced, and medical leeches applied as a means of bringing down his blood pressure.

In its call to the people to rally in unity and in vigilance around the party and Government, Pravda declared that the qualities now needed were "unity and cohesion, stanchness of spirit and vigilance," and called on all citizens to stand firm behind Mr. Stalin's goal—"building communism in our country."

Pravda called its editorial "Great Unity of the Party and People." Izvestia called its editorial "Unity and Solidarity of the Soviet People."

Izvestia said that in these times "there is no doubt" that all citizens will "multiply their strength in the struggle for a successful fulfillment of the tasks of Communist construction and will ceaselessly raise their revolutionary vigilance and even more closely rally their ranks around the Central Committee of the party and the Soviet Government."

Throngs of Muscovites made their way to Red Square this morning and stood in silent tribute to their lost leader.

The Hall of Columns where Mr. Stalin's body will lie in state is one of the most beautiful buildings in Moscow and one of the architectural jewels of Europe.

The building is ordinarily used as the house of Soviet trade unions, but is often employed for important state functions. It was here that Lenin's body lay in state in January, 1924, and it is here that many great thinkers of the Soviet world have lain in the last hours before their burial.

The central hall of the building is dominated by twenty-four beautiful marble columns reaching three stories to the ceiling. The room is hung with great chrystal chandeliers.

The Hall of Columns was erected in the mid-nineteenth century as a club for Moscow noblemen.

The outside of the hall, which is located in the heart of the city only a few hundred yards from Red Square, was decorated just after dawn today with heavy black-bordered red Soviet flags, which are used here as a symbol of mourning.

A great forty-foot portrait of Mr. Stalin in his gray generalissimo's uniform was erected on the front of the building. It was framed in heavy gilt.

In this famous hall Mr. Stalin's body will lie in state so that millions of Soviet citizens can throng past the bier and pay their last respects.

* * *

March 7, 1953

MALENKOV IS NAMED NEW SOVIET PREMIER; WIDE CHANGES DISCLOSED TO AVOID 'PANIC'; THRONGS PASS STALIN BIER; RITES MONDAY

FOUR TO HELP RULE

Beria, Molotov, Bulganin and Kaganovich Are Deputy Premiers

TEN-MAN PRESIDIUM

Molotov Is Again Foreign Minister—Vishinsky Demoted to U. N.

By HARRISON E. SALISBURY
Special to The New York Times.

MOSCOW, March 6—Georgi Maximilianovich Malenkov was named head of the Soviet government tonight in place of the late Joseph Stalin in a series of changes in the Soviet leadership.

Mr. Malenkov has assumed post of Chairman of the Council of Ministers, which was held by Stalin.

At the same time he was named as first in the list of the Presidium of the Central Committee of the Communist party, which is composed of ten members and four alternates.

Standing beside him in the chief and most responsible posts of Government and party in this reorganized structure are four veteran Soviet leaders and co-workers of Stalin— Lavrenti P. Beria, Vyacheslav M. Molotov, Nikolai A. Bulganin and Lazar M. Kaganovich. Those four become the First Deputy Chairmen of the Council of Ministers and with Mr. Malenkov constitute its Presidium.

The announcement over the Moscow radio at 11:30 o'clock tonight was made in the name of the Central Committee of the Communist party, the Council of Ministers and the Presidium of the Supreme Soviet.

Changes to Avoid 'Panic'

The changes in the directing bodies of the Government were made, it was announced, with the purpose of maintaining uninterrupted and correct leadership and avoiding "any kind of disarray and panic."

The announcement said the changes would secure the nation from any kind of interruption in directing the activity of state and party organs and "unconditionally secure" the successful carrying into effect of party and Government policies both internally and abroad.

The chief impression given by the Government both in tonight's announcement and in the proclamation of Stalin's death was one of firmness and the highest political vigilance, a sense of the rallying together of party and Government forces to withstand any threats from within or from without.

The Government was acting with the greatest resolution and with marked vigor. Mr. Malenkov lost no time in demonstrating his will and determination to prove a worthy custodian of the policies of monolithic unity and steel resolution that marked the leadership of Stalin.

Without any question, the most important feature of the announcement was the placing of Mr. Malenkov at the helm of the Soviet State. He long has been one of Stalin's closest associates and only a year ago last January, on the occasion of the award to him of the Order of Lenin on his fiftieth birthday, he was called by Pravda Stalin's "coadviser."

Tonight Mr. Malenkov became the man who is picking up the torch of the Soviet State and the Communist party and leading the Government and party forward along the pathway laid out by Stalin.

The 51-year-old Malenkov thus becomes the custodian of the tradition of revolutionary Soviet leaders begun by Lenin and Stalin.

Molotov Gets Back Old Job

At the same time, it was announced, several veteran Stalinist colleagues—in particular Mr. Beria, Mr. Molotov and Marshal Bulganin—would assume direct charge of vital ministries.

Thus Mr. Beria becomes head of the Ministry of Internal Affairs, in which is combined the former ministries of Internal Affairs and State Security.

Mr. Molotov becomes once more the Foreign Minister, succeeding Andrei Y. Vishinsky, who becomes his First Deputy and permanent Soviet Representative at the United Nations. Jacob A. Malik also was named a First Deputy Minister, and V. Zuznetsov, former head of the trade unions, becomes Deputy Foreign Affairs Minister.

Marshal Bulganin resumes his former post as head of the War Ministry and has as his first deputies, Marshal Alexander M. Vassilevsky, who has been acting as War Minister, and Marshal Georgi A. Zhukov, famous Soviet commander in World War II.

Marshal Klimenti E. Voroshilov, Stalin's old civil war associate and close friend since the days when they fought together at Staritsyn, becomes President of the Presidium of the Supreme Soviet in place of Nikolai M. Shvernik, who is recommended to resume his old post as head of Soviet trade unions.

Nikolai M. Pegor, who was one of the Communist party's secretaries, was named as Secretary of the Presidium of the Supreme Soviet. Alexander F. Gorkin, who has held the secretary's post, becomes Deputy Secretary.

The Ministries of Foreign and Internal Trade were united with Anastas Mikoyan as Minister. Mr. Mikoyan's chief deputy will be I. G. Kabanov, who recently has been head of state supply and formerly was electrical minister. T. T. Kumykyn, who formerly was Minister of Foreign Trade, and V. G. Zhavoronkov were named as his deputies.

The Government announced that the Supreme Soviet, which is the highest legislative body in the Soviet Union, had been summoned to meet on March 14 to ratify the changes in Government.

Power Is Concentrated

The first and most important change in the party structure was the announcement of a new Presidium of the Central Committee, which comprises ten members and four alternates. This Presidium replaces the Presidium of twenty-five members and eleven candidate members named last October.

The new party Presidium comprises Malenkov, Beria, Molotov, Voroshilov, Khrushchev, Bulganin, Kaganovich, Mikoyon, Saburov and Pervukhin. The alternates are Shvernik, Ponamarenkro, L. G. Melnikov, who is the party leader in the Ukraine, and M. Bagirov, the leader in Azerbaijan.

In place of the ten-member secretariat of the party, which was named last October, a new three-member secretariat was named. The new secretariat comprises Semyon D. Ignatiev, Peter N. Pospelov and N. N. Shatalin.

Mr. Ignatiev, who was elected last October to the Presidium of the Central Committee, formerly was the Central Committee representative for Uzbekistan. He is a prominent new leading member of the central party and Government apparatus. Only last month he was elected to the Moscow City Soviet, having been nominated by workers of the former Ministry of State Security. In tonight's list of appointments, all the chief positions in the Government went to men whose names have been known for years as the closest collaborators of Stalin. The most interesting change was the concentration into a more compact body.

* * *

April 7, 1953

U. N. AND KOREAN FOE AGREE ON VOLUNTARY REPATRIATION OF ALL AILING WAR CAPTIVES

A WIDER EXCHANGE

Accord May Set Pattern for Settlement of Last Issue Barring Truce

ENEMY MAKES CONCESSION

Allies, in Accepting Communist Proposal, Ruled Out Any Forced Returns

By The United Press

TOKYO, Tuesday, April 7—The United Nations and the Communists agreed today to voluntary repatriation of all sick and wounded Korean war prisoners, including those with minor disabilities.

It was a major concession by the Reds. If they are willing to apply the same principle to all prisoners the way will be clear for resumption of full-scale armistice negotiations and a possible early end of the Korean war.

United Nations officers disclosed the Communist agreement after morning and afternoon meetings of liaison teams at the truce village of Panmunjom, Korea.

Another meeting will be held at 11 A. M. tomorrow [9 P. M. Tuesday, Eastern standard time].

The United Nations earlier today agreed to a Communist proposal for exchanging sick and wounded prisoners, including those with minor ailments, on the firm condition that none be sent home against their will. Surprisingly, the Communists agreed almost immediately.

However, North Korean Maj. Gen. Lee Sang Cho said his side wanted to make clear that it reserved the right to ask for neutral nation custody of those prisoners held by the United Nations who would not be sent directly home.

Based on Geneva Convention

It did not appear that would present any obstacle. The neutral nation idea is contained in the Geneva Convention, which both sides have asked to be used as a basis for agreement.

General Lee said the United Nations "must not" use the voluntary repatriation principle "as a pretext for obstructing the repatriation of sick and injured prisoners who are willing to be repatriated."

The warning was in line with the Communist refusal to believe that any of their former soldiers would oppose repatriation.

Rear Admiral John C. Daniel, head of the United Nations liaison team, asked the Communists for an immediate exchange of information on the numbers of prisoners to be exchanged, according to nationality.

General Lee turned this down. He proposed instead immediate discussion of the machinery of exchange.

Under the plan offered by the Communists, all seriously sick and wounded prisoners would be returned to their homelands if they want to go.

Other prisoners who were expected to recover within a year or whose mental or physical health would be improved by a transfer would be handed over for neutral custody.

* * *

April 25, 1953

MacArthur Sees Key to Peace in Threat to Bomb Red China

By HAROLD B. HINTON
Special to The New York Times.

WASHINGTON, April 24—General of the Army Douglas MacArthur believes that a warning to the Kremlin of the power of the United States to destroy the industrial base of Communist China and cut its armies off from Soviet supplies might bring not only a settlement of the Korean war but of "all other pending global issues."

His views were in a letter to Senator Harry F. Byrd, Democrat of Virginia, who had asked for his comments on testimony before the Senate Armed Services subcommittee investigating ammunition shortages in Korea. Senator Byrd made the letter public today. Senator Byrd's letter was dated April 13 and General MacArthur's April 19.

"The Soviet is not blind to the dangers which actually confront it in the Far East in the present situation," General MacArthur wrote. "We still possess the potential to destroy Red China's flimsy industrial base and sever her tenuous supply lines from the Soviet.

"This would deny her the resource to support modern war and sustain large military forces in the field. This in turn would weaken the Communist Government of China and threaten the Soviet's present hold upon Asia.

"A warning of action of this sort provides the leverage to induce the Soviet to bring the Korean struggle to an end without further bloodshed. It would dread risking the eventuality of a Red China débâcle, and such a hazard might well settle the Korean war and all other pending global issues on equitable terms just as soon as it realizes we have the will and the means to bring them to a prompt and definite determination."

The testimony to which Senator Byrd asked General MacArthur's reaction was given by Frank Pace Jr., former Secretary of the Army. Mr. Pace said that General MacArthur, then commander in chief in the Far East, believed in the autumn of 1950 that the Korean fighting would be over in a few weeks.

Mr. Pace ascribed part of the responsibility for tardiness in new production of ammunition to this feeling of optimism. General MacArthur denied that in the early months of the conflict any "such optimism existed, either at the front or elsewhere." He said also:

"The labored effort made by the former Secretary of the Army to create without the slightest foundation of realism some sort of relationship between me and the ammunition shortage in Korea during the last two years since I left there is completely fantastic."

At the White House there was no comment on whether General MacArthur's plan for ending the Korean war and all other global issues was the same as that he gave to President Eisenhower last December.

Starting with the summer months of 1950, when the Eighth Army was first committed to the Korean battlefield, General MacArthur declared in his letter, there were desperate ammunition shortages, these shortages covering the period when the United Nations forces were driven back to a small beachhead surrounding Pusan.

Walker Exploit 'Amazing'

"As I recall," General MacArthur wrote, "General Walker at one stage was down to five rounds per gun. His heroically successful efforts under unparalled shortages of all sorts constituted an amazing military exploit."

The reference was to Lieut. Gen. Walton H. Walker, then commander of the Eighth Army, who was later killed in a jeep accident.

The Inchon landing in September turned the tide, General MacArthur continued, adding that that operation was "only grudgingly approved on my desperate insistence over the most serious professional doubts from higher authority."

With Pyongyang, the North Korean capital, captured and the North Korean armed forces in rout, General MacArthur asserted, "the inertia of our diplomacy" was responsible for failing swiftly to restore peace and unity to Korea.

He himself, he stated, did not believe the Chinese Communist commanders would intervene in Korea (large contingents entered the fight late in November, 1950) because of the risk they would run of having their forces cut off from supplies and annihilated.

He criticized the State Department's listening posts abroad and the Central Intelligence Agency for failing to get advance information of the intention of the Chinese Communists to enter the war.

General MacArthur declared that his recommendations to bomb military installations north of the Yalu, to blockade the coast of China and to employ Chinese Nationalist troops from Formosa, although approved by the Joint Chiefs of Staff on Jan. 12, 1951, were pigeonholed "somewhere between the offices of the Secretary of Defense (then General of the Army George C. Marshall), the Secretary of State (then Dean Acheson) and the President (Mr. Truman)."

"The overriding deficiency incident to our conduct of the war in Korea was not the shortage of ammunition or other matériel," the letter stated, "but in the lack of the will for victory, which has profoundly influenced both our strategic concepts in the field and our supporting action at home."

One of those who commented on General MacArthur's plan for ending the Korean war and bringing full peace was Senator Richard B. Russell, Democrat of Georgia, former chairman of the Armed Services Committee and now its ranking minority member. He said that "we need a new approach on the Korean war, but I am not willing to go that far."

Senator Russell presided over the hearings two years ago when General MacArthur, having been dismissed from his Far Eastern command by President Truman, expounded, behind closed doors, the strategic concepts he had brought back with him from Tokyo.

* * *

Associated Press Radiophoto

RIOT IN EAST BERLIN: A Soviet armored car and jeep moving through the thousands of catcalling demonstrators who jammed Unter den Linden in yesterday's anti-Communist outburst.

June 18, 1953

SOVIET TANKS FIGHT RIOTS IN BERLIN

MARTIAL LAW IS SET

Toll Placed at 16 Dead, at Least 119 Wounded—
Pro-Red Driven West

By WALTER SULLIVAN
Special to The New York Times.

BERLIN, June 17—Soviet tanks, troops and armored cars moved into East Berlin and martial law was declared this afternoon after 20,000 to 50,000 rioting workers had threatened to swamp the local police and seize the East German Government.

Three or four persons were reported to have been killed and at least fifty wounded, about half of them seriously. They either were hit by gunfire or were run down by the Russian trucks and tanks used to scatter rioters.

[An Associated Press dispatch from Berlin early Thursday placed the number of demonstrators killed at sixteen and quoted a Red Cross official as having said that 119 injured persons received treatment in West Berlin hospitals.]

Once the Soviet troops had gone into action, the more serious riots subsided and by mid-afternoon downtown East Berlin was clear of crowds except on Potsdamerplatz, where sporadic disorders continued into the evening.

The day's outbreak was a sequel to demonstrations by construction workers yesterday against the increase in work norms. Yesterday's demonstration, in which at least 5,000 were said to have been involved, grew into a broad anti-Communist protest that called for the resignation of the East German Government and free elections.

Today's demonstration, which included a call for a general strike, was urged last night by loudspeaker trucks. Soviet troops began moving into the city at 6:30 A.M.

Wounded Taken to West Berlin

Most of those wounded during the day were brought to West Berlin. Police trucks at times rode herd on stone-throwing crowds.

After martial law had been declared, Soviet soldiers drove trucks zigzagging wildly up and down Unter den Linden in front of the massive new Soviet Embassy building. To drive people from the streets they leaped from their trucks every now and then, firing bursts from their machine pistols into the air.

Hundreds of Russian soldiers watched as several demonstrators tore a Red flag from atop Brandenberg Gate where it had flown ever since the capture of Berlin as a symbol of the Soviet victory in the fight for the city. Shortly thereafter, two youths hoisted the black, red and gold flag of the German Republic.

Otto Nuschke, one of East Germany's Deputy Premiers, was turned out of his limousine, manhandled and driven across the border into the United States sector of Berlin. The bearded, portly Herr Nuschke, who is 70 years old, was a member of Parliament under the Weimar Republic and is head of the Christian Democratic faction in East Germany. Police officials said he was being held in an undisclosed place in West Berlin.

Eastern Police Enrage Workers

The workers, enraged by counter-attacks of the People's Police who drove them from the approaches to the principal ministries on Leipzigerstrasse, poured down streets like flooding streams of lava toward the border between the Soviet and United States sectors of Berlin.

At the corner of Zimmerstrasse, which forms the boundary of the Soviet and Western sectors, and Friedrichstrasse they tore up both United States and Soviet boundary markers. They ripped a Red flag from a border control shack and burned it as a crowd of onlookers cheered. They then set the shack itself afire.

The fury of the demonstrators was shown by a mason who rushed from the burning building with a new typewriter in his hands. He threw it to the ground with all his might, then pulled a mason's hammer from his pocket and pounded it to pieces.

Thousands of dissidents poured into the center of the city from neighboring districts and joined the fighting. Some columns marching through the streets consisted of men with briefcases, and women with shopping bags, with only a few workers among them.

Loudspeaker trucks toured West Berlin streets urging workers there to join their brethren in fighting the East German regime. Rias, official United States radio station, however, advised demonstrators not to fight the Russian soldiers but to concentrate on Germans.

The order instituting martial law was signed by Maj. Gen. P. T. Dibrowa, military commandant of the Soviet sector of Berlin. It said that as of 1 P. M. all demonstrations and other assemblies of more than three persons would be forbidden in public buildings as well as on the streets.

It established a curfew from 9 P. M. to 5 A. M. and said those who violated these orders would be subject to martial law.

At 4 P. M. Premier Otto Grotewohl issued a special proclamation attributing the outbreak to "Fascist and other reactionary elements in West Berlin." He said agents of "foreign powers" were backing the rioters.

[The United States, British and French commandants replied in a communiqué that "neither the Allied authorities nor the West Berlin authorities have, in any manner whatsoever, either directly or indirectly, incited or fostered such demonstrations," The Associated Press reported.]

Grotewohl Concedes Dissent

Herr Grotewohl acknowledged that construction workers had laid down their tools yesterday in a strike for a reduction of the working norms, which were raised 10 per cent last month. This question "has been disposed of since the Government canceled this measure," he added.

Hence he implied that the building workers no longer were responsible for the disorders. Nevertheless building sites were deserted during today's rioting. Herr Grotewohl urged the populace and in particular the workers and "technical intelligentsia" to cooperate with the Government in restoring order.

"Those to blame for the riots will have to answer for themselves and will be severely punished," he said. "Workers and all honest citizens are requested to seize the provokers and hand them over to state organs."

[An Associated Press dispatch said the East German Government radio announced shortly before midnight that the first mass arrests of "provocateurs" had been made. The broadcast said they had been seized from among the 3,000 men employed at the nationalized Bergmann-Borsig heavy machinery factory in the Soviet sector. The exact number arrested was not disclosed. All the plant employees had taken part in the general strike.]

As the mood of the crowds became uglier the Commandants of Berlin's three Western sectors mobilized all their troops in their barracks.

The British assigned troop units to various points along the border between the two parts of the city. The British military police also cordoned off parts of Potsdamerplatz, which continued into evening as the center of the rioting.

In Leipzigerstrasse, on the Soviet side of the square, several Russian tanks were drawn up in front of the ministries building, which formerly was Hitler's Reich air ministry.

The East German Government ordered its police yesterday to keep away from the demonstrators, but today it was obvious that the crowd was bent on storming the Government buildings.

Driven back from Government headquarters, the workers turned to less heavily guarded structures. They attacked the People's Police headquarters, but were driven back from the doorsteps by water jets and rifle fire.

They overturned several police vans, set them afire and moved on.

They were reported to have set afire the building of the official Communist party paper, Neues Deutschland, though from outside it appeared undamaged.

The attempt to storm the Politburo offices on Lothringerstrasse was met by an advance of Russian soldiers with fixed bayonets.

One of East Berlin's largest Government stores on the sectoral boundary at Potsdamerplatz was set afire by the rioters and for a long time West Berlin firemen stood by a few yards away, not wishing to cross the line into the Soviet sector. Finally they extinguished the fire.

The rioters apparently cut the power cables for both the elevated and subway systems, bringing them to a halt. Some looting was reported after shop windows had been smashed. Rumors that East German workers in other cities were demonstrating circulated in the city and led some to believe that radical changes in government would be necessary to bring the workers back to the factories.

Nevertheless, it was not clear tonight how large a proportion of the heavy industrial workers—normally the Communists' elite—were in the revolt. Likewise, so far, East German troops and the People's Police appeared to have remained loyal.

Russians Use Entire Division

BERLIN, June 17 (AP)—An entire Russian armored division was thrown into East Berlin tonight to crush the German workers' rebellion and general strike.

Nobody in particular called the general strike. It just mushroomed. No East German unions backed it. They are all Communist-officered, and to strike in the Soviet zone is as criminal as to cast a dissenting vote in the Red Parliament.

* * *

June 18, 1953

KOREAN ANTI-RED P. O. W.'S FREED BY RHEE IN DEFIANCE OF THE U. N.

25,000 FLEE CAMPS

President Accepts Full Responsibility for Act—Truce in Balance

By LINDESAY PARROTT
Special to The New York Times.

TOKYO, Thursday, June 18—The South Korean Government, breaking loose from United Nations control, today ordered the release of all the North Korean anti-Communist prisoners held in stockades south of the Thirty-eighth Parallel.

The order was issued by President Syngman Rhee, long bitterly opposed to an armistice in the Korean War on any terms other than unification of the peninsula. The North Korean prisoners in four camps near Pusan rioted early in the morning and broke free from behind the barbed wire barriers.

[Subsequently, Gen. Mark W. Clark's United Nations headquarters announced that 25,000 North Korean anti-Red prisoners had broken out, evidently with the aid of the South Korean guards. The United States troops, taking over, had to use tear gas and rifle-fire, and nine of the prisoners were killed. A South Korean Government broadcast from Seoul asserted the Republic would oppose anyone who tried to block the release.

[All rest and recreation leaves of United States soldiers in the Korean theatre had been canceled, said an Associated Press dispatch.]

American troops stepped into the breach with tear gas but did not open fire. About 980 of the prisoners who escaped had been recaptured near the camps.

New Guards at Camp

The Prisoner of War Command said order had been restored in all camps and new troops—presumably American—were standing by in case of new revolts among the men who faced return to their former masters or long continued captivity after an armistice.

The cleavage between the United Nations Command and the Seoul Government appeared to be complete. United Nations officers in Korea said units of American troops had been detached to search for and recapture the escaped prisoners. In Pusan, local authorities issued a directive to Korean citizens to feed and shelter any of the escapees who might seek refuge.

This afternoon, just after Dr. Rhee's announcement, the South Korean Cabinet went into an emergency session with their leader at the Presidential Mansion. It was believed the Koreans meant further to chart their course before Dr. Rhee met again with United States representatives, who have been urging him to accept the United Nations armistice terms rather than face a possible collapse of the Republic in an attempt to "go it alone."

No confirmation came from either official or United Nations sources that all 32,000 anti-Communist prisoners had been or would be freed.

Perhaps the most hopeful chance that Dr. Rhee's action might not lead to a complete rupture of the truce negotiations was the fact that no Chinese captives, as far as is known, were involved. At some stages of the truce talks the Communists appeared far more interested in the return of all the Chinese captives than in the far more numerous North Koreans and it had been suggested that under certain circumstances the return of the northerners even might be waived. If this remains the enemy attitude, a truce might yet be saved, some observers believed.

The prisoner development came as the armistice negotiators at Panmunjom reportedly put the final touch to a truce—reaching agreement on the demarcation line from which both armies would retire, after a cease-fire.

The South Korean revolt now raised the critical question whether an armistice could be concluded, particularly in view of frequent Communist propaganda assertions that the South Korean refusal to accept the truce terms was American inspired.

Dr. Rhee made the announcement of his order just before noon after previous instructions had been passed to all Korean prison guard officers by Lieut. Gen. Won Yung Duk, Provost Marshal of the South Korean Army. The Korean President in a defiant statement asserted he acted on his own responsibility and, in effect, cut loose from the United Nations Command to follow his own and an evidently predetermined line.

"I have ordered on my own responsibility the release of anti-Communist prisoners this day, June 18, 1953," Dr. Rhee said in his formal statement.

"The reason why I did this without full consultation with the United Nations Command and other authorities concerned is too obvious to explain."

Officials Asked to Aid

The President added that police officers and Governors of all South Korean provinces had been ordered to care for the released prisoners to their best ability, and he added: "We trust all our people and our friends will cooperate in this so there will be no unnecessary misunderstanding anywhere."

As the Koreans staged their revolt, the fate of an armistice now appeared to depend on the Communist reaction. Up to this afternoon no move had come from the enemy armistice delegation at Panmunjom in connection with the mass escapes and Dr. Rhee's defiance of the Allied command.

There was little doubt, however, that the Chinese North Koreans at least would lodge a strong protest, perhaps demanding that the United Nations recapture the fugitive prisoners and turn them over as the price of an armistice. At worst the Communists might break off the truce negotiations, finally asserting that the United Nations Command was unable or unwilling to carry out the agreed terms in the face of South Korean opposition.

It has frequently been asserted by Communist propagandists that the Americans, while negotiating for an armistice, actually have been fomenting South Korean defiance in order to continue the war.

The North Korean armistice delegates, who, from their headquarters in Kaesong, constantly monitor radio news from the outside world, undoubtedly are well aware of the development. Their attitude is expected to be made known when the next plenary armistice session is held—perhaps tomorrow. The negotiations were in adjournment today after a brief session yesterday, but they are subject to resumption at any time by a call from either side.

The breakout came at camps No. 6 at Namsan, No. 7 at Masan, No. 9 at Pusan and No. 5 at Sangmudai. All prisoners in those camps are anti-Communist North Koreans.

* * *

July 27, 1953

TRUCE IS SIGNED, ENDING THE FIGHTING IN KOREA

CEREMONY IS BRIEF

Halt in 3-Year Conflict for a Political Parley Due at 9 A. M. Today

By LINDESAY PARROTT
Special to The New York Times.

TOKYO, Monday, July 27—Communist and United Nations delegates in Panmunjom signed an armistice at 10:01 A. M. today [9:01 P. M., Sunday, Eastern daylight time]. Under the truce terms, hostilities in the three-year old Korean war are to cease at 10 o'clock tonight [9 A. M., Monday, Eastern daylight time].

[President Syngman Rhee of South Korea promised in a statement at Seoul Monday to observe the armistice "for a limited time" while a political conference tried to unify Korea by peaceful means, The United Press said.]

The historic document was signed in a roadside hall the Communists built specially for the occasion. The ceremony, attended by representatives of sixteen members of the United Nations, took precisely eleven minutes. Then the respective delegations walked from the meeting place without a word or handshake between them.

The matter-of-fact procedure underlined what spokesmen of both sides emphasized: That though the shooting would cease within twelve hours after the signing, only an uneasy armed truce and political difficulties, perhaps even greater than those of the armistice negotiations, were ahead.

Signers Are Expressionless

The representatives of the two sides were expressionless as they put their names to a pile of documents, providing for an exchange of prisoners, establishment of a neutral zone for the cease-fire and a later political conference that would attempt to settle the tragic Korean questions, unsolved by three years of fighting that caused hundreds of thousands of casualties.

According to the latest figures, revealed July 21 by the Department of Defense, the United States has suffered a total of 139,272 casualties. This included 24,965 dead, 101,368 wounded, 2,938 captured, 8,476 missing and 1,525 previously reported captured or missing, but since returned to military control.

Early this afternoon the Allied part in conclusion of the armistice agreement was completed at advance headquarters near Munsan, where Gen. Mark W. Clark, United Nations commander, put his name to the documents previously signed at Panmunjom.

General Clark signed in the presence of some of his high-ranking officers, Vice Admiral Robert P. Briscoe, commander of the naval forces in the Far East; Gen. Otto P. Weyland, head of the Far East Air Forces; Gen. Maxwell D. Taylor, Eighth Army commander; Lieut. Gen. Samuel Anderson of the Fifth Air Force, and Vice Admiral J. J. Clark, heading the Seventh Fleet.

Also present at Munsan was Maj. Gen. Choi Duk Shin, former South Korean representative on General Choi, who walked out of the United Nations armistice team the meetings at Panmunjom last May, also had boycotted the ceremony there this morning. As a result, no South Korean representative signed the truce, which South Korea will observe, at least temporarily, but did not approve.

Almost simultaneously, General Clark's headquarters in Tokyo released a message the general had written in advance of the armistice—a grim warning that the mere military armistice would not permit the United Nations to relax its vigilance against communism.

"I must tell you as emphatically as I can," said the statement, addressed to all members of the United Nations Command, "that this does not mean immediate or even early withdrawal from Korea. The conflict will not be over until the Governments concerned have reached a firm political settlement."

General Taylor, at Eighth Army headquarters in Korea, echoed General Clark's views and warning.

"There is no strong feeling that our problems here are over, nor that the armistice is an occasion for unrestrained rejoicing," he said.

For the United Nations, the documents were signed at Panmunjom by Lieut. Gen. William K. Harrison Jr. For the Communists, the signer was Lieut. Gen. Nam Il of North Korea, a Russian-trained school teacher who donned a military uniform after the outbreak of the Korean war.

Each Signs Nine Times

Seated at separate tables, each put his name nine times to nine copies of the armistice agreement in English, Korean and Chinese.

On General Harrison's table stood a miniature flag of the United Nations. The North Korean flag decorated the Communists place in the meeting house. On a central table lay piled copies of the agreement, bound in stiff blue cardboard covers. Aides passed them in turn to the two signers.

Pooled dispatches over Army communications from Panmunjom said General Harrison signed the first copy of the agreement at 10:01 A. M. General Nam put his signature to the final copy at 10:11 o'clock, ending the brief ceremony.

Because of what General Clark called unreasonable restrictions demanded by the Communists, the top military leaders of the opposing armies did not appear at the session. The enemy, it was revealed, had demanded that if Marshal Kim Il Sung, North Korean Premier and Commander in Chief and Gen. Peng Teh-huai, commander of the Chinese Communist troops in Korea, came to Panmunjom, all correspondents and all representatives of South Korea would be barred from the neutral zone. General Clark refused.

Following signing of the truce documents by General Clark, the agreement was scheduled to be sent to Marshal Kim and General Peng. Their names probably will be affixed in their secret headquarters near the bombed out North Korean capital of Pyongyang.

The United Nations delegation appeared on the scene at 9:30 o'clock this morning, alighting from helicopters that had brought them from Munsan, and filing past a guard of honor representing all units and services fighting on the peninsula.

Allied Observers Present

General Harrison was accompanied by his fellow American delegates, Rear Admiral John C. Daniel, Brig. Gen. R. N. Osborne and aides. The observers from the United Nations members lined the Allied section of the hall.

There were representatives of Turkey, Thailand, the Netherlands, France, the United Kingdom and the Commonwealth countries, Colombia, Belgium, Denmark, Luxembourg, Ethiopia, Philippines and Norway.

The Communists came to Panmunjom in a fleet of jeeps thirty-five correspondents of Iron Curtain countries accompanying them. Altogether, it was calculated that there were 130 press and radio correspondents and photographers of many nations in the hall.

Outside the thin wooden walls there was the mutter of artillery fire—a grim reminder that even as the truce was being signed men were still dying on near-by hills and the fight would continue for twelve more hours.

As the delegates settled in seats, aides took the bound copies of the armistice agreement from the central table and passed them to their chiefs. Marine Col. James C. Murray, one of the few Americans present today who saw the start of the truce negotiations two years ago, handed the documents to General Harrison and pointed out to him the place where he should sign. Both General Harrison and General Nam used a single fountain pen.

Lieut. Col. H. M. Orden of the liaison officers group blotted General Harrison's signatures and returned the documents, one by one, to the central table, from where they were passed to General Nam by a North Korean colonel, You Ju.

At no point in the armistice negotiations have the delegates given each other greetings beyond a possible silent nod. The procedure was the same today.

At one point General Harrison whispered briefly to Colonel Orden and an interpreter, Lieut. Kenneth Wu. There was a click of cameras and the grinding of newsreels. Otherwise, only the distant artillery broke the silence.

At 10:10 A. M. General Harrison finished, and General Nam one minute later. The North Korean general glanced at his watch, rose and strode quickly from the hall, without a glance at the United Nations table.

General Harrison strolled out in more leisurely fashion. To correspondents who asked him for comment, he replied: "You know I don't do that."

But he smiled and posed for pictures, saluted the honor guard and greeted some United Nations representatives before he climbed into a helicopter to fly back to Munsan at 10:27 A. M.

Inside the hall, the signed documents remained on the central table, watched by security guards and liaison officers, who remained for a brief meeting with interpreters. Presumably they were arranging the later signing of the armistice by the high commanders.

Seventy-two hours after the signature of the armistice, the troops will withdraw one and a quarter miles from the fighting line, and a neutral zone will be established between the armies.

Within a few days the first of returning United Nations war prisoners might be expected to trickle in. They are expected to reach their homes probably next month.

General Clark flew to Korea late yesterday afternoon to play his part in the revamped signing ceremonies.

The armistice negotiations were closing on the same note of scarcely veiled hostility and accusations of bad faith with which they began more than two years ago. General Clark, landing in Korea, made it clear he also had scant hope the truce would go far to solve the tangled problems of a divided Korea.

"A long and difficult road still lies ahead," he warned. "There are no short cuts. If we are to honor the great sacrifices which have been made in the name of freedom, if we are to achieve peace, if we are to uphold the principles of freedom, justice and human dignity we must continue our efforts toward peace and we must be ready to defend these principles whenever and wherever they are challenged."

Persons close to Dr. Rhee said his major interest today centered on a political conference that is to follow the truce, with the armistice for the time being regarded as an accomplished fact despite his former stubborn opposition to the cease-fire.

Thus far, there was little knowledge here just what the conference will do and even how it will be constituted. The armistice agreement itself states only that the commanders in the field "recommend to the Governments concerned" that the meeting be held to negotiate a withdrawal of foreign troops from Korea, a peaceful settlement of the Korean question, "etcetera."

No mention was made of what Governments would be included or of the question of unification of Korea, which

Dr. Rhee demands. Neither is the word "etcetera," on which the Communists insisted during the truce negotiations, further defined.

The Communists, it has been suggested, meant to bring in under that word such questions as Chinese Communist admission to the United Nations and the status of the Chinese Nationalist regime on Formosa.

Dr. Rhee, on the other hand, has stated that unification of Korea will be the conference's immediate task, and he is understood to have been disappointed over the supposed failure of the United States to clarify further conversations to that effect he held with Walter S. Robertson, Assistant Secretary of State for Far Eastern Affairs.

* * *

August 20, 1953

SOVIET ANNOUNCES A TEST EXPLOSION OF HYDROGEN BOMB

Powerful Weapon Detonated, Moscow Reveals— Blast Set at Aug. 12 by U. S.

By HARRISON E. SALISBURY
Special to The New York Times.

MOSCOW, Thursday, Aug. 20—The Soviet Government announced today that it had carried out an experimental explosion of a hydrogen bomb "within the last few days."

The announcement said the experimental explosion had disclosed that the hydrogen bomb had a force much greater than that of an atomic bomb. It said the weapon was "one of a variety of hydrogen bombs."

"Because of the existence in the hydrogen bomb of a powerful thermonuclear reaction, the explosion was of great strength," it continued. "The test showed that the power of the hydrogen bomb is many times greater than the power of the atomic bomb."

[The United States Atomic Energy Commission announced early Thursday that the Soviet Union had conducted an atomic test Aug. 12. It added that the test had involved both fission and thermonuclear reactions. President Eisenhower, informed in Denver of the Soviet announcement, had no comment.]

The Soviet statement gave no more details of the explosion, but added that the Soviet Government wished to emphasize that it was standing firm on its previous proposals for forbidding the use of atomic and other weapons of mass destruction within the framework of the United Nations and for strict international control of this prohibition.

Refers to Foreign Reaction

The Soviet statement asserted that in some countries, following Premier Malenkov's announcement of Aug. 8 that the United States no longer possessed a monopoly on the hydrogen bomb, efforts had been made to utilize the Soviet statement with a view to increasing the arms race.

The statement said "the Soviet Government regards it as essential to declare that there is not and was not any reason for such alarm."

The statement was published on page 2 of Pravda and other newspapers in the upper right-hand corner under a two-column headline, which said: "Government announcement about the test of the hydrogen bomb in the Soviet Union." There were no details about the results of the experimental explosion beyond the statement that it was of a force much greater than that of an ordinary atomic bomb and that it had been conducted "within the last few days" in the Soviet Union.

The statement was plainly intended to place once more in the forefront of international consideration the question of effective barring of the use of atomic, hydrogen and other mass-destruction weapons.

The fact that the statement reiterated the long-standing Russian position that such controls should be effected through the United Nations suggested that the Soviet Union would raise the question there soon.

U. S. Had Test Last Year

It has been reported that the United States last year had a hydrogen bomb explosion test, but there has been no official statement about its nature.

The phrase "one of a variety of hydrogen bombs" is similar to the phraseology employed two years ago when the Soviet first announced that an experimental atomic bomb had been exploded.

There was no doubt that the Soviet revelation that a hydrogen bomb test had been conducted in the Soviet Union would have far-reaching repercussions. Since explosions of atomic and hydrogen weapons are readily detected in all parts of the world because of the rapid diffusion of radiation effects, it was presumed that the United States now has evidence to support the correctness of the Soviet statement.

TEXT OF SOVIET STATEMENT

MOSCOW, Thursday, Aug. 20 (Reuters)—Following is the test of the hydrogen bomb statement published today by Pravda, official organ of the Soviet Communist party.

Within the last few days an explosion of one of a variety of hydrogen bombs was carried out for experimental purposes.

Because of the existence in the hydrogen bomb of a mighty thermonuclear reaction, the explosion was of great strength.

The test showed that the power of the hydrogen bomb is many times greater than the power of the atomic bomb.

It is known that the Soviet Union has for several years possessed the atomic weapon and made several tests with this weapon.

As follows from the speech of the Chairman of the Council of Ministers of the U. S. S. R., O. Malenkov, on Aug. 8 at the fifth session of the Supreme Soviet, the Soviet Union has taken possession of the secret of the production of the hydrogen bomb.

This information of the Soviet Government caused a great deal of reaction abroad.

Some foreign circles who had laid their stake on their policy of the monopoly of the United States in the possession of the atomic bomb, and later of the hydrogen bomb, aspired to intimidate people by the fact that the Soviet Union possessed the secret of the production of the hydrogen weapon, and, in connection with this, cause alarm, using it with the aim of intensifying the armaments drive.

The Soviet Government regards it as essential to declare that there is not and was not any reason for alarm. In accordance with the unchanging policy of the Soviet Union directed to the strengthening of peace and the security of nations, the Soviet Government repeatedly offered to the governments of other countries the carrying out of a considerable reduction of armaments and the forbidding of the use of the atomic and other kinds of weapons of mass destruction, establishing within the framework of the United Nations strict international control of this prohibition.

The Soviet Government solemnly stands on this position at the present time.

* * *

August 20, 1953

ROYALISTS OUST MOSSADEGH; 300 DIE IN IRANIAN FIGHTING

ARMY SEIZES HELM

Ex-Premier and Cabinet Flee Mobs—Zahedi Pledges Reforms

By KENNETH LOVE
Special to The New York Times.

TEHERAN, Iran, Aug. 19—Iranians loyal to Shah Mohammed Riza Pahlevi, including Teheran civilians, soldiers and rural tribesmen, swept Premier Mohammed Mossadegh out of power today in a revolution and apparently had seized at least temporary control of the country.

More than 300 persons were killed and 100 wounded during the fighting, which raged at key Government buildings. Two hundred were estimated to have died in the fierce last-stand battle at Dr. Mossadegh's heavily fortified home.

The nine-hour uprising placed Maj. Gen. Fazollah Zahedi at the helm of the nation after a twenty-eight-month rule by Dr. Mossadegh. General Zahedi, who had been in hiding for months, was appointed Premier Thursday by a royal decree but the Shah left the country Sunday, when Premier Mossadegh thwarted delivery of a second decree dismissing him.

The end came for the Mossadegh Government after a pitched tank and rifle battle in Kokh Avenue, where the former Premier's home stands, 100 yards from the Shah's Winter Palace. When the Premier's household guard was overwhelmed in the final rush of Royalist troops the home was found vacant. Dr. Mossadegh's personal bodyguard was dead.

Tanks Duel in Streets

The report in the streets was that Dr. Mossadegh himself had escaped. Dr. Mossadegh's defenders put up a stubborn battle during which Sherman tanks mounting 75 mm. cannon dueled at close quarters for nearly two hours.

The Army, which appeared to have been won for Dr. Mossadegh's side Sunday, turned on its top officers today. Dr. Mossadegh's Chief of Staff, Taghi Riahi, and other top officers fled long before the day was over.

General Zahedi broadcast his triumph in a tumultuous scene at Radio Teheran, which had been captured by Royalist forces at 2:20 P. M.

With the radio building swarming with yelling soldiers, General Zahedi broadcast the program he said his Government intended follow. Points in the program included:

• Re-establishment of a rule of law and re-establishment of public security.

• Elevation of the standard of living and a reduction in the cost of living.

• Mechanization of agriculture and formation of cooperative societies for the peasants.

• Raising workers' wages.

• Provision of free medical treatment.

• An extensive asphalt road-building program.

• Restoration of individual freedom and freedom of assembly.

He declared that he would rule until the Majlis Parliament had resumed its legislative functions.

The troops and police that took part in the overthrow were led by huge mobs shouting for the return of the Shah. They attacked key Government establishments in the city, burned the office of the pro-Government newspaper, Bakhtar-e-Emruz and of two Communist newspapers, of several pro-Government party offices and shouted for the death of Dr. Mossadegh. They also besieged the Foreign Ministry, Police Headquarters and Army General Staff Headquarters.

Virtually all armed forces in the city, except a few units defending Government buildings and Dr. Mossadegh's own household guards, joined the mobs in the attacks.

The first rush of Royalist troops and civilians was beaten off by heavy small-arms fire from the windows of the Police Headquarters. Casualties among the attackers, who arrived in six Army trucks, were reported to have been heavy there. Similar scenes were repeated at the other vital Government centers.

Eight truckloads of soldiers and five tanks rumbling into the city presumably under command of officers loyal to the Government gave their equipment to the first mob they encountered. The tanks came from the Abbas Abad garrison north of the city, a few miles from where General Zahedi may have been hiding in the foothills of the Elburz Mountains.

In the streets, the soldiers centered their attacks on civilians wearing white shirts, considered a trademark of Tudeh (Communist) party members.

Two thousand yelling partisans of the Shah demonstrated before the Soviet Embassy in Churchill Avenue. They were accompanied by a tank, but departed without attacking the Russians, who had slammed shut the heavy iron gates. The Embassy occupies an eight-square-block compound surrounded by a twelve-foot-high wall.

The street revolution began last night when police and soldiers shouting "Long live the Shah" and "Death to Mossadegh" smashed into pro-Government rioters. The rioters were Tudeh partisans and Pan-Iranists, who had often fought each other though both at this time were supporting Dr. Mossadegh. The troops beat the rioters unmercifully, forcing them to repeat their slogans at bayonet point.

Troops' Action Was the Spark

After last night's fighting, the soldiers and police returned to their barracks only to join the pro-Shah crowds this morning. Apparently the boldness of the troops in shouting for the Shah last night had given courage to the populace. Except for one small pro-Shah demonstration yesterday morning no voice previously had been raised in his behalf.

Anti-Shah mobs on Monday battered, sawed and threw down all the statutes in the city of the Shah and of his late father, Riza Shah.

A declaration signed by General Zahedi had been circulated among army cadres ordering the troops not to obey the illegal Mossadegh Government on pain of severe punishment. The declaration reproduced the general's signed commands in his own hand.

Gen. Mohammed Daftari, who is a nephew of Dr. Mossadegh, was reported at 1:30 P. M. to have taken over as chief of police in Teheran and military governor of the area by appointment of General Zahedi.

Immediately after capturing the telegraph office at 1:30 P. M. the rebels sent messages throughout Iran reporting the government overturn. They then captured the offices of the Press and Propaganda Department and marched on Radio Teheran which had been playing only recorded music in place of its customary news broadcasts. It was taken at 2:20 P. M.

Mossadegh's Furniture Sold

After Dr. Mossadegh's home finally had been stormed, the victorious mob hauled his furniture into the street and auctioned it to passers-by at low prices. A new electric refrigerator was offered for 300 tomans (about $36).

Dr. Mossadegh's home had been fortified with machine-gun nests on the roof and a high defensive wall outside his bedroom window.

Dr. Mossadegh's Cabinet was meeting at his home before the attack and at least some of them escaped with him.

In the assault on the Mossadegh home, the attackers captured Col. Ezatollah Mumtaz, who had betrayed the Royalists to Dr. Mossadegh Saturday night. They literally tore him to pieces.

General Zahedi moved swiftly to nail down the victory against counterblows. A curfew was imposed, beginning at 8 P. M., to last until 5 A. M. All stores except grocery, butcher and bakery shops were ordered to remain closed until further notice and assembly in the streets was forbidden.

General Zahedi also released all political prisoners, including at least thirty-one arrested by Dr. Mossadegh since the attempt to remove him Saturday, and about twenty arrested in connection with the kidnap murder in April of the national police chief, Mahmoud Afshartous. Dr. Mossadegh had attempted to use the Afshartous affair to discredit all opposition.

*   *   *

MOSCOW REPORTS NEW ATOM BOMBS BUT SUGGESTS BAN

Urges Prohibition on Weapons of Mass Destruction— U. S. Policy Is Again Attacked

By The Associated Press

MOSCOW, Friday, Sept. 18—The Soviet Union announced today that it had successfully tested some "new types" of atomic bombs in recent weeks.

It added that it hoped that a ban would be placed on all types of mass-destruction weapons and was looking into prospects for peaceful use of atomic energy in industry.

[In Washington, the Atomic Energy Commission said the 3Soviet statement confirmed a United States announcement of Aug. 31 on such explosions. Other sources suggested that the Moscow statement might have been timed to support Soviet proposals in the United Nations for atomic control and disarmament.]

A dispatch from the Soviet news agency Tass published in the Government newspaper Izvestia said the successful experiments had taken place.

It said that although the Soviet Union was able to give attention to the production of atomic weapons, the nation also followed a policy of strengthening peace and trying to reach agreement with other countries on the prohibition of atomic and hydrogen bombs and other kinds of weapons for mass destruction.

Details Are Lacking

No details were given about the "new types" tested.

The announcement on Page 2 of Izvestia said:

"In the last few weeks, in accordance with the plans of scientific research work in the sphere of atomic energy in the Soviet Union, there were carried out trials of some new types of atomic bombs. The trials were carried out successfully.

They fully confirmed the calculations and suggestions of scientists, engineers and constructors.

"It is quite clear up to this time, responsible circles of the United States reject the persistent proposals of the Soviet Union about the prohibition of atomic weapons. Therefore the Soviet Union, beginning with the demands of its own security, is able to give attention to the production of atomic weapons."

The Tass statement continued:

"But together with this, the Soviet Union will further follow its policy of strengthening peace between the peoples by trying to achieve agreement with other countries on the absolute prohibition of atomic-hydrogen and other kinds of weapons for mass destruction, for the considerable reduction of armaments and the establishment of strict international control, for the realization of these conditions.

"With this in view, the Soviet Union is carrying out the task of employing atomic energy for industrial purposes. The Soviet Union considers its most important task to insure that atomic energy is put to the service of peaceful programs."

U. S. Sees Its Report Confirmed

Special to The New York Times.

WASHINGTON, Sept. 17—The Atomic Energy Commission said tonight that the Soviet announcement of testing "new types" of atomic bombs was confirmation of an Aug. 31 United States announcement of such explosions.

A commission spokesman issued the following statement:

"The Tass report confirms the information released by the Atomic Energy Commission on Aug. 31 when it was stated that the explosion [of Aug. 23, 1953] was in the same range of energy release as our recent Nevada tests and would appear to be part of a series."

The commission spokesman tonight declined to elaborate, but it was recalled that in its earlier comment the commission had said that "if this proves to be the fact, no further announcements will be made unless intelligence indicates information of greater interest."

Last spring a series of eleven tests was carried out at the Las Vegas proving grounds by the commission. The largest blast in the Nevada tests was about two and a half times as potent as the bomb that hit Hiroshima during World War II.

With the usual secrecy prevailing here on atomic matters, there was no interpretation advanced as to the meaning of the phrase "new types" of atomic bombs.

There was interest in the timing of the Moscow news. One suggestion was that perhaps Andrei Y. Vishinsky, Soviet delegate to the United Nations, was preparing to advance some proposal regarding atomic control and disarmament at the General Assembly session now under way. Mr. Vishinsky has not yet spoken in the general debate, where his speeches are often used to advance key Soviet proposals.

The wording of tonight's commission statement would indicate that the Soviet explosions "of the last few weeks" were merely a continuation of the tests mentioned in the Aug. 31 statement. At that time the commission said a fission explosion, implying a conventional atomic weapon as contrasted with a hydrogen bomb, had taken place somewhere in the Soviet Union on Aug. 23.

Previously the commission reported that the Soviet Union had conducted tests involving both fission and thermonuclear hydrogen reactions last Aug. 12. The conventional uranium bombs produce their energy from the fission or splitting of atoms, while the hydrogen bombs derive their force from the fusion of hydrogen atoms to produce helium.

The United States has previously made five announcements concerning atomic explosions in the Soviet Union, the first being on Sept. 22, 1949.

* * *

November 12, 1953

U. N. VOTES TO HEAR ATROCITY CHARGES AGAINST REDS, 53-5

Soviet Bloc Unable to Bar Korea Case—Indian, Not Voting, Cites Prisoner Role

U. S. DELEGATION PLEASED

Had Feared Asian and African Abstentions—Bad Effect on Peace Talks Discerned

By THOMAS J. HAMILTON
Special to The New York Times.

UNITED NATIONS, N.Y., Nov. 11—Despite strong opposition by the Soviet bloc, the United Nations General Assembly decided today to place on its agenda a United States complaint on Communist atrocities in the Korean war.

The wording of the item is: "Question of atrocities committed by North Korean and Chinese Communist forces against United Nations prisoners of war in Korea."

The United States delegation has not yet submitted a memorandum detailing its charges, but a Defense Department report, made public Oct. 29, said nearly 30,000 prisoners, including 6,113 Americans, had been massacred or tortured.

[In Korea, the prisoner "explanations" and preliminary peace conference talks showed no evident progress.]

Fifty-three of the sixty member nations voted for an Assembly hearing on the United States charges, the five members of the Soviet bloc voted against, and India and Guatemala abstained. The vote gave great satisfaction to the United States delegation, which had feared that a number of Asian and Arab delegates would abstain.

Indian Stand Explained

V. K. Krishna Menon told the Assembly India's abstention should not be considered as expressing opposition to freedom of discussion or a "lack of revulsion" against atrocities, who-ever committed them. He expressed doubt that a debate or "acrimonious discussion" at this stage would facilitate a Korean settlement.

However, Mr. Menon said the basic reason was the belief that since India was chairman of the Neutral Nations Repatriation Commission it would be "totally improper" for her to participate in the discussion of "a matter which may well go before the [Korean] political conference." He said that in matters concerned with prisoners, "our objectivity should not be challenged in any way at all."

Dr. Salah Eddine Tarazi of Syria then said that although he had voted for inclusion of the item, this did not prejudge his attitude on the merits of the question. Leo Mates of Yugoslavia and Dr. Sudjarwo of Indonesia said they had voted for inclusion because of their belief in Assembly discussion. Mr. Mates said he doubted whether "mutual recriminations" were a good way of solving world problems and Dr. Sudjarwo appealed for moderation in the debate.

Under a procedure recommended by the Assembly's steering committee and approved today without a vote, the Assembly itself will debate the question instead of referring it to the Political and Security Committee, which is behind in its work. The debate may begin late next week.

Henry Cabot Lodge Jr., United States representative, gave four reasons for including the item on the agenda:

1. The atrocities were committed by forces engaged in aggression.
2. They were committed against the forces of the United Nations and those of South Korea, which the aggressors were trying to conquer.
3. They grossly violate principles of common humanity and decency.
4. These forces still stand, fully armed, in North Korea, and "we must recognize, in the midst of our prayers and labors for genuine peace, that this story of inhuman warfare is not brought out of a forgotten past but bears directly on the pressing problems of the present."

Vishinsky Charges 'Lies'

Andrei Y. Vishinsky, Soviet representative, then repeated his previous assertion that the charges were based on "a falsification of fact" and "flagrant lies." He said they were "designed to frustrate a peaceful settlement of the Korean question, foment war hysteria and forestall any reduction of international tension."

Mr. Vishinsky based his assertions on what he called the "provocative noise" raised by the United States press and radio, as well as on statements by United States officials.

The Soviet representative, despite an interruption by Mr. Lodge, repeated his previous assertion that the charges actually were based on those made in 1951 by Col. James M. Hanley, then attached to the Eighth Army. The Russian complained that United States representatives at Panmunjom were creating as many difficulties as possible to "thwart the holding of the political conference." He also repeated his

long-standing contention that South Korea had invaded North Korea.

* * *

December 11, 1953

VIETMINH RENEWS PEACE TALK OFFER

'Ready to Negotiate,' Red Radio Says as New Moves Impend in Vietnam Political Crisis

Special to The New York Times.

SAIGON, Vietnam, Dec. 10—The Communist Vietminh radio renewed today offers to negotiate a peace in Indo-China. A peace feeler was put out recently by Ho Chi Minh, Vietminh leader, in an interview with a Swedish newspaper.

"If the French Government is sincere and if it desires negotiations to end the war, our people and our Government are ready to negotiate," the broadcast said.

Observers here noted that the broadcast emphasized Vietminh aims of Indo-Chinese Independence of France and peace and made no mention of communism. It was thought here that the phrasing was designed to obtain backing for the Vietminh peace initiative among the people of Vietnam, one of the states of Indo-China. However, nowhere in the broadcast were any specific proposals made.

'Until Total Victory'

The radio maintained that Vietminh's policy had always been one that sought independence and peace and denied that Ho Chi Minh's offer was the result of any deterioration in the Vietminh's military position.

"If the French colonialists remain blind, our people are resolved to carry on resistance until total victory," the broadcast said. It added that military prospects were improving constantly for the Vietminh while France was being crushed more and more each day by greater and greater losses in men and money.

The latest Vietminh statement was made while the latent political crisis in the Vietnamese Government appeared to be taking an important turn. Premier Nguyen Van Tam, who has been under nationalist pressure for months, will see Chief of State Bao Dai tomorrow. He is expected to ask Bao Dai to shake up the Cabinet so as to include some representatives of the ultra nationalist elements here. The Government would then make a strong effort to increase its popular support against Vietminh inroads and will examine seriously Vietminh peace offers.

No Reaction From Paris

Special to The New York Times.

PARIS, Dec. 10—There was no reaction here today to the Vietminh broadcast reviewing an offer to negotiate a peace in Indo-China. However, the Cabinet declared shortly after a Stockholm newspaper interview with Ho Chi Minh that it would examine any Vietminh offers if they were made "in an official manner." Presumably today's broadcast will be considered to be no more "official" than was the interview.

Previous to this Cabinet statement Premier Joseph Laniel had said on two occasions before Parliament that the French Government was not necessarily seeking an unconditional surrender of the Vietminh and would consider an end to the fighting by diplomatic means.

The French have committed themselves to take no action on the peace front without the agreement and cooperation of Vietnam, Laos and Cambodia, the governments of which they recognize as the only legitimate ones in Indo-China.

Fortress Reinforced

HANOI, Vietnam, Dec. 10 (Reuters)—The French High Command said today it had rushed 136 planeloads of reinforcements, arms and supplies to Dienbienphu as 12,000 Communist-led Vietminh rebels closed in on the mountain fortress.

French bombers and fighters splattered Tuangiao, keypoint of the 316th Vietminh Division, with napalm (jellied gasoline) bombs, explosives and bullets yesterday as the reinforcements were being flown in.

In other action, French-Laotian forces yesterday captured the rebel stronghold of Muongngo, about seventy miles northeast of the Laos capital of Luang Prabang.

It was reported yesterday that the 316th Division had split into two columns and was moving from the north toward Dienbienphu and Laichau, capital of the Thai country.

Several hundred civilians have been flown out of Laichau, but a French High Command spokesman said French Union forces would defend the strategic area in northwest Indo-China.

* * *

January 13, 1954

DULLES SETS GOAL OF INSTANT REBUFF TO STOP AGGRESSOR

Aims at Prompt Retaliation at Sites of 'Own Choosing,' Not Local Defense

DEALS WITH REDS BARRED

Secretary, Honored at Dinner Here, Explains Adaptation of Military, Foreign Policy

John Foster Dulles, Secretary of State, said last night that the nation's military and foreign policy was being adapted to a basic decision: To confront any aggressor with "a great capacity to retaliate, instantly, by means and at places of our own choosing." The decision was made by the National Security Council, he said.

President Eisenhower's program seeks more effective and less costly security in cooperation with the allies of the United States "by placing more reliance on community deterrent power, and less dependence on local defensive power," Mr. Dulles said.

Speaking at a dinner given in his honor by the Council on Foreign Relations at the Hotel Pierre, Secretary Dulles promised continued efforts at negotiations with the Soviet Union on such issues as atomic energy, Germany, Austria and Korea.

But with the Berlin conference of the Big Four foreign ministers less than two weeks off, Secretary Dulles pledged there would be "no plan for a partnership division of world power with those who suppress freedom."

Dulles Hopeful on Peace

Mr. Dulles foresaw hope of peace because "there are limits to the power of any rules indefinitely to suppress the human spirit." He reported signs that Soviet leaders were bending to their people's desire for more food, more household goods and more economic freedom.

The Secretary's speech, entitled "The Evolution of Foreign Policy," had been heralded by the State Department as a major statement. The address, which pulled together a review of the Eisenhower course, was broadcast nationally over the Du Mont television network and rebroadcast later by the Mutual and National Broadcasting Company radio systems.

Many pre-Eisenhower foreign policies were "good," Mr. Dulles said. He cited aid to Greece and Turkey, the European Recovery Program, the Berlin airlift, United Nations resistance to attack in Korea and the building up of American and Western European armed strength.

But these were emergency actions, imposed on us by our enemies, Mr. Dulles said, and they were costly. He pictured new planning by President Eisenhower and his National Security Council, recognizing that there was no local defense that alone would contain the mighty land power of the Communist world.

"A potential aggressor must know that he cannot always prescribe battle conditions that suit him," Mr. Dulles said. "The way to deter aggression is for the free community to be willing and able to respond vigorously at places and with means of its own choosing."

Mr. Dulles' report tied in with President Eisenhower's notice in his State of the Union message last Thursday that atomic weapons might be used "against an aggressor if they are needed to preserve our freedom." There also had been earlier administration warnings that Communist aggression in Korea or open Chinese Communist aggression in Indo-China might evoke military reactions beyond these areas.

Out of the new planning, the Chiefs of Staff will be able to make a selection of military means instead of a "multiplication of means," Mr. Dulles said. This will make it possible "to get, and share, more security at less cost," he added.

With the Korean war ended, and armed forces no longer largely committed to the Asian mainland, a "strategic reserve" can be set up, Mr. Dulles continued.

The revised "long haul" build-up adopted for the North Atlantic Treaty Organization will avoid exhausting members' economic strength, he went on.

Secretary Dulles vowed confidence that "peace will soon have the indispensable foundation" of that European Defense Community," bringing in West Germany, and expressed hope for "a political community thereafter."

The Secretary said the new concepts of collective security would enable limiting foreign aid to "situations where it clearly contributes to military strength," such as Indo-China. With exceptions for continuing technical assistance and specific disaster relief, he forecast that economic aid would be trimmed in favor of seeking more trade and investments.

About 400 persons attended the dinner, which resumed a tradition of banquets by the Council on Foreign Relations in honor of Secretaries of State, interrupted in recent years by inability to make arrangements. John I. McCloy, the council's chairman, presided.

* * *

March 1, 1954

DULLES CONFIDENT OF LATINS' AMITY

In Caracas for Hemisphere Talk,
He Finds Atmosphere Warmer Than in Berlin

By PAUL P. KENNEDY
Special to The New York Times.

CARACAS, Venezuela, Feb. 28—John Foster Dulles, Secretary of State, heading the United States delegation to the tenth Inter-American Conference, arrived late this afternoon.

He immediately gave assurance that the numerous hemispheric problems would be approached in traditional friendship. He is convinced, he said, that the conference climate will be warmer than that of the recent Berlin meeting of the Big Four foreign ministers.

The Secretary arrived with a large part of the delegation aboard the Presidential plane Columbine. In an informal press talk at near-by Maiquetia Airport, he said he realized that many problems confronted the conference, but he was confident that the delegations of the conferring states would approach them as friends.

Noting that he had recently returned from Berlin, Mr. Dulles commented: "I know that the climate here, not only physically but also in terms of our conference, will be much more temperate than that of Berlin."

Later, Mr. Dulles left with Fletcher Warren, United States Ambassador, for the fifteen-mile drive to the United States Embassy, where he will reside for the duration of the talks.

Mr. Dulles was at a disadvantage because of the lack of time to prepare himself for the delicate and complicated matters on the agenda. He returned to Washington from the Big Four conference only ten days ago, and spent several days on

Capitol Hill informing Congress of that meeting and the coming Geneva parley on Far Eastern problems. As a result it was late this week before he could devote his thoughts exclusively to this conference.

While political issues, particularly the United States fight to push through an anti-Communist resolution, are likely to provide most of the fireworks at the talks the overriding issue will be economics.

The conference opens tomorrow morning in sprawling University City, a Government project so new that hundreds of workmen late today were clambering over the conference building.

There is no generally accepted estimate on the duration of the talks. It is known, however, that the United States delegation hopes to wind them up in three weeks. The Latin-American delegations think this is unrealistic and are talking in terms of four to six weeks. Twenty nations are represented, Costa Rica being absent.

Flies From Washington

WASHINGTON, Feb. 28 (AP)— John Foster Dulles, Secretary of State, took off this morning for the Inter-American Conference at Caracas, Venezuela.

He said he expected to stay a week or ten days at the conference. Seeing him off at the airport were Under Secretary of State Walter Bedell Smith, Manuel Tello, Mexican Ambassador and Roberto Heurcematte Panama's Ambassador.

* * *

March 17, 1954

ATOM SMASHER SETS RECORD; JAPAN GETS RADIOACTIVE FISH

Nuclear Downpour Hit Ship During Test at Bikini—
U. S. Inquiry Asked

By LINDESAY PARROTT
Special to The New York Times.

TOKYO, Wednesday, March 17—The Japanese police attempted to find and remove from public sale today some 12,000 pounds of fish landed from a vessel showered with radioactive ash during the recent atomic tests at Bikini Atoll.

Some already has been recovered and tested by officials of the Japanese Government's Science Research Institute, and was reported to be dangerous to human life.

Japan instructed her embassy in Washington today to make a formal inquiry to the United States. Twenty-three fishermen were burned by the atomic particles on March 1.

Geiger counters showed that the fish—mostly shark and tuna—had a "radioactive count of 7.5 millimeters." Such a degree of radioactivity was reported sufficient to be fatal to any person who remained for eight hours within thirty yards of the contaminated fish.

The sale of fish from Yaezu, where the vessel had landed south of here, was embargoed this morning at the central Tokyo market and the police believed that none had been sold here. Some tuna from the craft, however, was shipped to Osaka and Nagoya. Some was impounded there but it was feared some might have been sold to the public before the police were able to notify merchants of the ban.

The incident headlined this morning's Japanese press and already is the subject of an inquiry in the Diet (Parliament). It seemed likely that it would become a new focus of spreading anti-American feeling here.

[Reuters reported that all twenty-three of the fishermen aboard the vessel had been hospitalized on officials orders and that five had been put on the danger list. Their ship, the ninety-nine-ton Fukuryu Maru, will be burned at sea.]

Sections of the Tokyo press today asked whether the injury to the Japanese fishermen was the fault of the United States or flatly asserted that it was.

The Foreign Vice Minister, Akira Kodaki, told a Diet committee that the Japanese Government had received notification that tests would be made as early as September last year.

There apparently was some doubt, however, whether the warning was passed on to fishermen or whether the crews of Japanese sampans simply disregarded such notification.

Tatsujiro Torii, vice chief of the Maritime Safety Board—the coast guard—said no advance warning had been received through the Foreign Office.

The exact position of the ship when it was deluged with ashes also was an issue. Accurate navigation seldom is the strong point of Japanese fishing captains, and it therefore is uncertain whether the ship was inside the "closed area" of 200 miles around Eniwetok.

The log of the vessel reportedly showed it was about eighty miles off Bikini when the incident occurred, which, according to Japanese reports, would be outside the danger zone.

Reports of the incident here caused a minor panic among Tokyo housewives this morning. At an early hour when most shopping is done the fish stores were deserted in many areas. Some housewives gingerly buried in back yards the fish they had bought yesterday for today's meals—fish being the mainstay of the Japanese diet.

The Sanitation Department issued a warning that all fish must be washed in several rinses of water. About 2,000,000 pounds were distributed yesterday at the central market and through retailers, and some, according to the warning, may be radioactive.

Authorities at Yaezu buried in a deep trench the fish that had been landed from the suspect vessel and not already sold. Authorities in Tokyo, Osaka and Nagoya warned markets not to receive fish from the ports from which any vessels in the Bikini area had operated.

* * *

April 5, 1954

INDO-CHINA BATTLE SLACKENS AS FOE REGROUPS FORCES

Vietminh Is Believed Unable to Maintain All-Out Effort Against Dienbienphu

NEW LULL IS PREDICTED

Rebel Chief Withholds Pledge on Evacuation of Wounded by Mercy Planes Today

By TILLMAN DURDIN
Special to The New York Times.

HANOI, Vietnam, April 4—The Vietminh assault on Dienbienphu slackened today. It is believed possible that the Communist-led forces are unable to maintain the all-out effort against the French-held fortress and that their attack has entered a phase of diminished activity.

Vietminh thrusts against the stronghold last night and today were weaker than before and the weight of the Communist shelling has been reduced. All attacks were thrown back by the French Union defenders.

[The Associated Press said Vietminh forces began pulling back from the eastern and southeastern defenses of the fortress. The dispatch quoted a French spokesman as having said it was doubtful the Communists would be able to mount another heavy assault within the next twelve hours. However, a French High Command spokesman said the withdrawal was only about 400 to 500 yards, the dispatch added.]

It is considered possible in Hanoi that the Vietminh forces at Dienbienphu may be re-forming their battered battalions and accumulating supplies for another series of mass attacks.

Ambulance Planes Due

The French wounded are a problem and military quarters here were not hopeful that the Vietminh command would refrain from firing on ambulance planes scheduled to go in Monday for the injured.

No reply had been received by noon today to last night's radio message from Gen. Henri-Eugene Navarre, the French Commander in Chief, to Gen. Vo Nguyen Giap, the Vietminh commander, announcing that the planes were to be sent and that a group of international observers, including correspondents, would watch the operation from a separate plane flying above Dienbienphu.

Detailed arrangements were being made at Dienbienphu over the week-end to insure that French troops would cease fire except in sectors where they were being attacked. French bombings are scheduled to cease as the ambulance planes arrive.

Last night Vietminh attacks were launched as darkness fell. Three different points were hit: one in the northern part of the strong point that constitutes the northwestern sector of the central defense complex, two others in the southwestern part of the strong point that forms the southwestern sector of the central complex.

The northwest point had been an objective of Vietminh attacks during the two preceding nights, while Communist troops struck at the two points on the southwestern perimeter for the first time.

French Repel Attacks

Five hours of violent fighting, often at close quarters, went on before the French got the upper hand.

By midnight enemy troops had been hurled back from the footholds they managed to gain. In the southwest battle area the French this morning counted the bodies of 200 Vietminh dead.

French air attacks yesterday and last night were especially heavy. Jellied gasoline was again used on a large scale and fighter bombers dropped 1000-pound delayed-action missiles on Vietminh artillery positions.

The obviously tiring Vietminh forces appear to have lost the momentum of their earlier efforts this week. One informed source here today said the Vietminh killed totaled at least 4,000 for the last five nights and four days of fighting and this could mean more than 10,000 total casualties.

Vietminh forces still hold almost half of the northeast strong point of the French central defenses and one point in the northwest corner of the northwest strong point. French military sources here say that the Vietminh failed to obtain the objectives marked out for the week's phase of the Dienbienphu battle.

It is believed the Vietminh command had planned to take most of the eastern half of the French central positions and gain footholds elsewhere. If it turns out that a new period of diminished activity has settled over Dienbienphu, the Vietminh forces may for the next week or so engage in only harassing infantry attacks and artillery shellings.

It is generally believed in military quarters here that the Communists will make a third mass assault, if not immediately then in a week or so. Messages from the French Dienbienphu commander, Col. Christian de Castries, say the morale of the defenders remains high, though they are tired. Colonel de Castries has been nominated for brigadier general for his defense of Dienbienphu.

Meanwhile the Delta war continues. Nightly sabotage is being committed by Vietminh troops on the Hanoi-Haiphong railway and highway, but the French are managing to maintain operations for a period of time every day.

* * *

April 7, 1954

U. S. URGES ALLIES TO BACK WARNING TO CHINESE REDS

Asks Britain, France, Thailand, Australia, New Zealand and Philippines to Join in Move

DULLES TALKS TO ENVOYS

Diplomatic Circles in Paris Call Indo-China Step Good Gamble, Others Fear It

By WALTER H. WAGGONER
Special to The New York Times.

WASHINGTON, April 6—The first step toward possible "united action" against Chinese Communist intervention in Indo-China has been taken by the United States.

The State Department has suggested to six other allies, European and Asian, that they join in a common warning against further aggression by Communist China in any part of Southeast Asia.

The countries that have received this proposal, in talks here extending over the last several days, are Britain, France, Australia, New Zealand, the Philippines and Thailand.

The State Department answered "no comment" when asked about reports of the proposed joint declaration, but other diplomatic sources left no doubt that the suggestion had been made.

Henry Suydam, State Department news chief, declined to discuss reports of the proposed action, which have come from London, Paris and Canberra, Australia, but he confirmed that John Foster Dulles, Secretary of State, had consulted as recently as yesterday with diplomatic representatives of the six other governments "on the general situation confronting Southeast Asia."

[Diplomatic circles in Paris viewed the Dulles proposal on Indo-China as a justifiable gamble. Other quarters in France were alarmed. Only light action was reported from besieged Dienbienphu.]

Dulles Speech Here Cited

The proposal for a joint declaration followed Mr. Dulles' statement in New York March 29 that the "imposition" of the Communist political system on Southeast Asia "by whatever means, would be a grave threat to the whole free community."

"The United States feels that the possibility should not be passively accepted, but should be met by united action," the Secretary declared.

And yesterday, further setting the stage for some kind of joint effort, Mr. Dulles told the House Foreign Affairs Committee that the Chinese Communists were "coming awfully close" to a new aggression in Indo-China.

As indications mounted in support of Mr. Dulles' warning of "united action," diplomatic sources began to wonder whether United States policy might not have taken a new turn since last Feb. 10.

On that day, facing a news conference, President Eisenhower said that no one could be more bitterly opposed than he to United States involvement in a hot war in Indo-China. He said so far as it was humanly possible, he would make certain that it did not happen.

At the same meeting, the President later said he could not conceive of a greater tragedy for the United States than to get heavily involved, particularly with large units, in an all-out war in that region.

But on the basis of statements and communiqués going back more than two years, the United States and its Western Allies have long held the threat of counter-attack over Peiping should the Chinese Communists openly enter the Indo-China conflict.

The most recent was Mr. Dulles' speech of last Jan. 12, when he reiterated his warning in St. Louis last September that, "if there were open Red Chinese Army aggression [in Indo-China], that would have 'grave consequences which might not be confined to Indo-China.' "

There have also been these other suggestions that the Allies would act in unison against Chinese Communist intervention in Indo-China, or any other weak spot in Southeast Asia.

A Western Big Three foreign ministers' communiqué, issued here last July 14, declared that "an armistice in Korea must not result in jeopardizing the restoration or the safeguarding of peace in any other part of Asia," and that the fight of the three Associated States of Indo-China against "aggressive communism is essential to the free world."

In May, 1952, while the Truman Administration was still in power, Mr. Dulles asked an audience in Paris, in words very much like those he has used more positively since he became Secretary of State, whether it was not time for the Chinese Communists to know that if they sent their forces into Indo-China, "we will not be content to meet their armed forces at the point they select for their aggression but with retaliatory action of our own choosing."

And in January, 1952, during the United Nations General Assembly meeting in Paris, John Sherman Cooper, a United States delegate, served notice that any further Communist aggression in Southeast Asia "would, in the view of my Government, be a matter of grave concern which would require the most urgent and earnest consideration by the United Nations."

That statement of intentions promptly got the support of the British and French delegations.

* * *

April 8, 1954

PRESIDENT WARNS OF CHAIN DISASTER IF INDO-CHINA GOES

Says Result of Such a Loss to the Free World in Asia Would Be Incalculable

JOINT NOTICE IS PRESSED

Dulles Declares Admonition to Peiping Might Obviate Need for 'Action' Later

By ANTHONY LEVIERO
Special to The New York Times.

WASHINGTON, April 7—President Eisenhower said today that a Communist conquest of Indo-China would set off throughout Asia a chain reaction of disaster for the free world.

The consequences would be incalculable, the President said. In his news conference he spoke calmly but gravely about the crisis of the Indo-China war.

General Eisenhower said it was too early to report on results of the United States current efforts to marshal allies for united action to cope with the crisis.

While the war and negotiations with allies were still in a delicate stage, the President declined to say whether the United States would seek United Nations action or, as a last resort, go it alone to save Indo-China.

Dulles Reviews Policy Again

Meanwhile John Foster Dulles, Secretary of State, asserted that if the free nations demonstrated their united will, "it will diminish the need for united action." He reviewed foreign policy at a meeting of Republican women.

"I believe that, in general, most of our great problems come from not making sufficiently clear in advance what the dangers are to a potential aggressor," said Mr. Dulles.

[The Peiping radio declared Thursday that Secretary of State Dulles "lied and slanderously charged that China intervened in the Indo-China war," an Associated Press dispatch from Tokyo said. The broadcast charged Mr. Dulles "attempted to use this vile method to deceive and hoodwink world public opinion, cover up the crime of active United States intervention in the Indo-China war and create a pretext for the United States to extend its intervention there."]

Most of the twenty-five minutes of General Eisenhower's news conference was devoted to questions about the Indo-China war.

In his discussion the President spoke with the same sense of urgency that Secretary Dulles has been giving to the Indo-China problem in recent weeks. A few days ago the Secretary of State declared in a Congressional hearing that the overt actions of Communist China in the Indo-China war came close to the point of inviting instant and massive retaliation under this country's concept of protecting its vital interests.

Secret Talks Continue

The stress of this country's present policy was on mobilizing a ten-nation coalition for united action against the Communist forces that threatened to overcome Indo-China. Negotiations toward this goal were going on secretly with Britain, France, Australia, New Zealand, the Philippines, Thailand and the Associated States of Indo-China—Vietnam, Laos and Cambodia.

The negotiations were being pressed intensely, for the Administration was pessimistic about the possibilities of reaching a satisfactory settlement while France alone carried the main burden of the fighting.

President Eisenhower said he did not think the chances were good for negotiating a settlement with the Communists at the forthcoming conference on Far East problems in Geneva.

He reiterated this country's willingness to go as far as prudence would allow in seeking settlement of any world problem by conciliation or negotiated agreement. But he firmly said the United States would not overstep the safety line of its security by making any agreement with Communists that did not rest on a foundation of fact and deed.

President Eisenhower made in effect a geopolitical survey of the consequences of defeat.

Already about 450,000,000 persons have fallen under Communist dictatorship in Asia, and the free world cannot afford more losses of that kind, the President said.

The loss of Indo-China would lead to the loss of Burma, of Thailand, in fact of all of the great peninsula on which they are situated he said. With these countries would be lost tin, and tungsten and rubber and other materials needed by the free world, the President declared.

In the next consequence the strategic geography would go bad, he said. The whole island defense chain of Japan, Formosa and the Philippines would be turned or flanked, and this would also project the threat down into Australia and New Zealand, General Eisenhower went on.

The President noted one economic consequence. Japan must have the Indo-China region as a trading area, he said. If deprived of that trading area Japan will be compelled to turn in only one direction—the vast Communist empire of Red China or Manchuria, he added.

Thus in the span of exactly eight weeks the President was expressing a sharply revised viewpoint that took account of the possibility of intervention by the United States along with its allies if that were necessary to save Indo-China.

In seeking a special united front to deal with the threat to Indo-China the Administration was hopeful that the sheer weight of the arrangement would tend to bring about a solution by peaceful means.

On Feb. 10 President Eisenhower said that no one could be more bitterly opposed than he to getting the United States involved in a hot war in Indo-China. He also said he could conceive of no greater tragedy for this country than to get heavily involved there in an all-out war, especially with large units.

The President was asked if he agreed with Senator Joseph F. Kennedy, Democrat of Massachusetts, that Indo-China's independence should be guaranteed to justify an all-out effort there.

General Eisenhower said he always had tried to insist, in many years of talking with different Governments, on the principle that no outside country could be helpful to another if it did something that local people did not want.

President Eisenhower added that he did not know whether the Associated States of Indo-China wanted independence in the same sense that the United States was independent.

But the President went on to say that the aspirations of the peoples of the Far East must be met or else in the long run there could be no answer to the unrest there.

Advance notice to "potential aggressors" that their efforts were "doomed to failure," would greatly reduce the ultimate need for collective action or participation by governments alarmed by the grave developments in Indo-China, Mr. Dulles told the Republican women.

"With united will created it will diminish the need for united action," said Mr. Dulles. "But there should be, I hope, a willingness to have united action if the events should be such as to require that. I don't believe that things will go that far, particularly if we can create a unity of will which would make it apparent that the ambitious efforts of the Chinese Communists to dominate all of Southeast Asia and the Western Pacific are doomed to failure because it will encounter a united opposition so strong that it could not be overcome."

On Capitol Hill Roger M. Kyes, Deputy Defense Secretary, and Admiral Arthur W. Radford, Chairman of the Joint Chiefs of Staff, met with a bipartisan group of Senate leaders.

They were the Republican leader, William F. Knowland of California, and Leverett Saltonstall, Republican of Massachusetts, chairman of the Armed Services Committee, Lyndon Johnson, Democrat of Texas, the minority leader, and Richard B. Russell of Georgia, ranking minority member of the Armed Services group.

Some time after the meeting Senator Knowland confirmed that Indo-China had been the subject of discussion. "All I can say is that it was to keep us abreast of developments," he said.

* * *

May 8, 1954

DIENBIENPHU IS LOST AFTER 55 DAYS; NO WORD OF DE CASTRIES AND HIS MEN

ASSAULT SUCCEEDS

Fort Falls After 20-Hour Fight—Last Strong Point Is Silent

Special to The New York Times.

PARIS, May 7—The fall of Dienbienphu was announced today by Premier Joseph Laniel.

The news of the worst military defeat that the French have suffered since the Indo-China war began in December, 1946, came suddenly.

It was received with confused emotion. The heroic defense of Dienbienphu, besieged for fifty-five days, had been followed in screaming headlines since March 13, when the Vietminh launched its first attack—as if for the first time in more than seven years the public had fully realized that the country was fighting an enormously bloody and costly war.

M. Laniel told the Assembly that the heroic stronghold had been taken after twenty hours of fighting and continuous alertness for the last two months. He could not issue any information on the fate of the commander, Brig. Gen. Christian de Castries, or of the defenders or the wounded who have wasted underground for several weeks.

Final Concentration

All that he knew, the Premier said, was that the southern resistance point called Isabelle was still defended under the command of Col. André Lalande. French artillery with some tanks were concentrated at that center.

[Contact with the Isabelle outpost had been lost according to an Associated Press dispatch from Saigon.]

"The Vietminh now are only a few meters away" were the last words heard from General de Castries over the radio-telephone, the French Cabinet was told. The last dispatch received from the battle was that the central strong point had been submerged.

For the defenders of Dienbienphu there was French pride in their heroism and sadness for their fate. There was also some grim anger against those who had engulfed them in defeat and, if not anger, at least unkindly feelings for those responsible for French political and military policy.

Before last March the name of Dienbienphu, now solidly entrenched in French military annals, was unknown here but not in Indo-China, where it had some importance.

The Vietminh had taken Dienbienphu, a peaceful community of 9,000 persons, who grew rice and poppy for opium, in February, 1953, and used it to help launch operations against Laos in the following April.

French Seizure Nov. 21

Last November when a Vietminh column was spotted heading northwest in the Thai country to the French base of Laichau, the French decided to evacuate Laichau and seize Dienbienphu, using parachutists from the Tonkin area.

A successful operation was launched Nov. 21 and after the Laichau garrison moved in the French began daily efforts to strengthen it by building underground fortifications, improving the airfield and setting up barbed wire.

The establishment of the Dienbienphu base had strategic and political reasons. Close to the Laotian border, it helped fend off Vietminh attacks southward into Laos and against the capital of Luang Prabang by threatening the Vietminh rear and blocking supply lines.

The fact that the Vietminh withdrew from Laos and did not attack Luang Prabang is attributed to French control of Dienbienphu. The French also wished to remain in the Thai tribal country to encourage and help the Thai guerrillas hostile to the Vietminh.

Finally, Dienbienphu, because of its geographical position, was expected to require a large Vietminh force to attack it, thus relieving pressure on French defenses in the much more vital Tonkin delta area.

This is precisely what happened. The French garrison numbered 10,000 to 12,00 men, about 5,000 of whom were Vietnamese. The French Foreign Legion, which included a strong proportion of Germans, was also an important element.

There were also colonial troops, consisting of Tunisians, Algerians and Moroccans and a battalion of Thais, totaling perhaps 800 men. The great majority of officers were French. Against this force the Vietminh concentrated four divisions of about 40,000 men. On March 13, what the French Cabinet a few days ago compared to the World War I battle of Verdun was on with a massive Vietminh attack. It was thrown back with losses to the enemy estimated at from 5,000 to 8,000 men out of action. The second attack was launched March 30 and little by little, despite heavy Vietminh casualties, the French began to be squeezed into a smaller and smaller area of resistance.

'Asphyxiation' Tactics Used

From then until last night the Vietminh bit off progressively more and more applying what was called here asphyxiation tactics. Supply air drops became more and more difficult as the area of the airfield in French hands became smaller and smaller.

Early this morning only a single 105-mm howitzer out of 12 was in condition for firing and in the central redoubt only one 55-mm gun was working. Ammunition was very low.

Comparison with Verdun was apt in some respects. In neither case was a vital military position at stake, but in both national honor was intensely involved. But every Frenchman consolingly knows a victory was won at Verdun despite the terrible loss of lives. At Dienbienphu there was nothing left at the end but the defender's courage.

A later dispatch said that General de Castries told Hanoi headquarters before the telephone went silent that he had instructed all able-bodied men to try to get to the southern resistance center of Isabelle, which was then holding out. As far as he was concerned, he was saying, "We are not giving up."

* * *

June 28, 1954

PRESIDENT OF GUATEMALA OUSTED BY ANTI-COMMUNIST ARMY JUNTA; NEW RULERS OPPOSE REBEL CHIEF

ARBENZ IS DEPOSED

U. S. Is Asked to Help End the Bloodshed as Regime Shifts

By PAUL P. KENNEDY
Special to The New York Times.

GUATEMALA, June 27—The regime of President Jacobo Arbenz Guzman came to an end tonight. He agreed to step down in favor of a military junta.

The decision was forced by the army after an all-day meeting of its chiefs. Three colonels visited the National Palace and forced the President to agree to step down. His personal safety and that of his family were guaranteed.

The officers who visited the President were Lieut. Col. Carlos Sarti, head of the Supreme Council of Defense; Col. Enrique Parinello and Col. Carlos Enrique Diaz, Chief of Staff.

The Army chiefs agreed that one of the junta's first acts would be to move against the Communists. They also agreed to seize Col. Jaime Rosenberg, chief of the Civil Guard, and Col. Rogelio Cruz Wer, chief of police.

[The United Press reported the State Department announced it had received word that Col. Carlos Enrique Diaz, to whom Colonel Arbenz turned over the Government, had declared he would take steps to end the fighting in Guatemala. The new Guatemalan leader is an outspoken anti-Communist.]

[Luis Coronado Lira, secretary general of the rebels' provisional government, said the next bulletin of his group would give its official reaction. Speaking personally, he said, "we are fighting a system, not a man," and hence the replacement of Colonel Diaz for Colonel Arbenz was not important.]

[If the new regime wishes to comply with the conditions set in a recent rebel broadcast and take Colonel Arbenz in custody, he added, the way to a cease-fire may be cleared. He said the fall of the President was a step forward of final triumph for Colonel Castillo Armas.]

The President was reported to have been extremely angry when informed that the present situation could not continue. This occurred at 4 P. M today. Two hours later the radio announced that the President would address the nation at 9 P. M.

The four-year regime of the man who rose from second lieutenant to colonel and then to the Presidency ended after a day crammed with events, in which John E. Peurifoy, United States Ambassador, figured largely.

Mr. Peurifoy was called to the palace at the request of Foreign Minister Guillermo Toriello at 11 A. M. Señor Toriello asked whether the United States would use its offices to help stop bloodshed if a military junta should take over the Government. He said the only restriction would be that Col. Carlos Castillo Armas, leader of the revolt that began ten days ago, would not be allowed to come to power.

The Ambassador replied that he had no control over the situation, but would do all in his power to bring about peace.

He was then asked whether he would meet with Señor Toriello again in the afternoon or at night. He replied that he would. Señor Toriello then said he would resign if he thought it would help the situation.

Ambassador Peurifoy had hardly returned to the Embassy when he was called by Colonel Diaz and asked if he would attend a meeting of the five ranking Army colonels at Colonel Diaz' home.

Mr. Peurifoy went to see Colonel Diaz at 12:30 P. M. and remained until 3:15 P. M. At the meeting he was asked if the United States would assist in stopping the fighting if a three-man military junta took over.

He was also asked whether the United States would guarantee to recognize Colonel Diaz if he took over the Presidency and whether President Arbenz could remain as a member of the junta.

* * *

July 21, 1954

INDOCHINA ARMISTICE IS SIGNED

LONG WAR ENDING

2 Accords Completed—One on Cambodia Due Later Today

By THOMAS J. HAMILTON
Special to The New York Times.

GENEVA, Wednesday, July 21—Armistice agreements bringing the fighting in Vietnam and Laos to a halt were signed this morning by representatives of the French and Communist Vietnam forces.

A French spokesman said the armistice would take effect forty-eight hours later.

The signing ceremony, witnessed by representatives of the nine delegations participating in the Far Eastern conference here, began at 3:42 A. M. (9:12, P. M. Tuesday, Eastern daylight time). It brought to a close the eight-year struggle for Indochina.

The armistice in Cambodia will not be signed until later this morning. The Far Eastern conference will hold its final session this afternoon to complete work on the political settlement. Under it Laos and Cambodia will be neutralized and elections to create a unified government in Vietnam will be held within two years from the date of the armistice.

Pierre Mendès-France, French Premier, who had set July 20 as his deadline to obtain an armistice or resign, had missed it by a few hours. He canceled a radio speech to the

French people and went to bed before the two agreements were signed at the Palais des Nations, former headquarters of the League of Nations, where conference sessions have been held since the Indochina negotiations began last May.

Rebels Get Northern Part

Under the Vietnamese agreement, Vietnam is to be divided into two parts, about equal in area and population between the Communist-led Vietminh rebels who will hold northern Vietnam, north of a line along the Seventeenth Parallel, and the French-sponsored Government of Bao Dai.

The partition line thus is far enough north to preserve Huo, the ancient capital of Annam; Tourane, an important port and naval and air base, and the only major highway leading to Laos from the coast.

The French will not give up Hanoi and Haipong, in the Red River delta area, in the north, for approximately a year, which will give them time to evacuate personnel of the French expeditionary force in the territory remaining to them in the delta plus civilians fearing persecution by the Communists.

Under the armistice agreements, the Communists recognize the Governments of Laos and Cambodia. However, regrouping areas for Communist troops were authorized in Laos. The forces of the Communist "resistance government" in Laos will be concentrated in two provinces near the frontier with Vietminh territory. [Some sources identified the two provinces as Samneua and Phongsaly.]

The Cambodian delegation held out against the provision, and prolonged sessions of the "drafting committee" of the Vietminh and Cambodian representatives were necessary before an agreement could be reached early this morning. By that time it was too late to put the armistice in final form so that it could be signed along with the Vietnamese and Laotian agreements.

These were signed by Brig. Gen. Henri Delteil, representative of Gen. Paul Ely, French Commander in Chief in Indochina, and by Col. Ta Quang Buu, the Vietminh's Vice Minister of Defense.

Gen. Walter Bedell Smith, Under Secretary of State, who returned recently to take over the chairmanship of the United States delegation, took no part in the whirlwind diplomatic activity yesterday and this morning that resulted in agreement. A spokesman had said that the United States, not being a belligerent, was not primarily concerned. However, the delegation was represented by an observer at the ceremony.

Smith Issues Statement

General Smith issued the following statement:

"The United States delegation is very pleased with the important progress that has been made tonight toward ending the bloodshed in Indochina. As soon as we have had an opportunity to examine the final texts of the agreements reached by the belligerents, the United States delegation will express its views with regard to them."

"Meanwhile, we share the fervent hopes of millions throughout the world that an important step has been taken toward a lasting peace in Southeast Asia, which will establish the right of the peoples of that area to determine their own future"

Supervision of the three armistice agreements is entrusted to supervisory commissions composed of India, Canada and Poland. Each commission will operate by majority rule, except in important issues that "might lead to a resumption of hostilities."

Unanimous decisions will be required for these, meaning that Communist Poland will have a veto. However, the agreements provide that such cases shall be reported to the nine conference participants—France, Britain, the United States, the Soviet Union, Communist China, Vietnam, Laos, Cambodia and the Vietminh—which will take it up at a meeting of Ambassadors.

The Hanoi-Haiphong area in the north, as well as four or five regroupment areas south of the partition line for the Vietminh forces, are to be evacuated over a period of 300 days. The agreement provides that prisoners of war and civil internees captured in any circumstances will be freed within thirty days from the agreement's entry into force.

While the Laotian and Cambodian Governments will remain in control, they are to be neutralized, with their armed forces limited to those necessary for self-defense. These provisions will prevent the United States from supplying military instructors or equipment, and the two nations' only real protection will be the realization by the Communists that an armed attack may precipitate intervention by the United States.

Georges Bidault, Foreign Minister in the Government of former Premier Joseph Laniel, which fell because of its stand in the Geneva talks, had opposed any political settlement at this time. M. Mendès-France had sought to avoid fixing a date for Vietnamese elections, fearing that if they were held soon the Vietminh would gain control of the entire country.

The Communists, who had insisted originally that elections be held within six months, finally agreed that they be within two years. They will be supervised by India, Canada and Poland.

Reds to Stay in Laos

Moreover, the Communists will not evacuate all of Laos, although it had been the Western contention that the Communist forces in both Laos and Cambodia were Vietnamese rebel invaders and that both nations should be preserved intact.

The three key figures in the final stage of the conference—Premier Mendès-France, Anthony Eden, British Foreign Secretary, and Vyacheslav M. Molotov, Soviet Foreign Minister—met last night to discuss the situation. Shortly before midnight they called in Tep Phan, Cambodian Foreign Minister, and Pham Van Dong, Deputy Premier and acting Foreign Minister of the Vietminh, in hopes of reaching an agreement on Cambodia's objections to the "pockets" in its teirritory for Communist troops.

General Smith has been confined by an attack of lumbago, which was better yesterday. He stayed in his hotel while Mr. Eden, M. Mendès-France and Mr. Molotov—and to a lesser extent Chou En-lai, Premier of Communist China, and Pham Van Dong—engaged in whirlwind diplomatic activity.

Throughout the day's busy exchanges, General Smith was studying the tentative texts of the various agreements, which were understood to be nine in all. He had told the conference on his return that if it reached agreements that the United States could "respect," the United States in accordance with the United Nations Charter, would issue a unilateral statement that it would not seek to overturn them by force. A United States spokesman's only further comment was that if his Government found it could not "respect" the agreements, it might dissociate itself from them.

* * *

August 20, 1954

CONGRESS PASSES SOFTENED VERSION OF COMMUNIST BAN

Strips Party of Legal Rights—
Does Not Make It Crime Just to Be a Member

TAINTED UNIONS CURBED

Only 2 Votes Cast Against Bill—G. O. P. Leaders Predict Eisenhower Will Sign It

By C. P. TRUSSELL
Special to The New York Times.

WASHINGTON, Aug. 19—A modified bill to outlaw the Communist party in the United States was approved by both houses of Congress today, with only two votes against it.

It was thereupon sent to the White House for the President's signature.

The Senate approved the measure, 79 to 0, after it had been redrafted by a Senate-House of Representatives conference to remove a provision offered by Senator Hubert H. Humphrey, Democrat of Minnesota, making it a crime to belong to the Communist party.

The House approved the bill, officially called the Communist Control Act of 1954, shortly afterward by a vote of 265 to 2.

While the measure in its final form came closer to Administration specifications than a previous version overwhelmingly approved by the Senate, the question of a Presidential veto remained. Republican leaders, however, predicted with confidence that President Eisenhower would sign the measure.

Determined Administration opposition had developed against earlier drafts on the grounds they would nullify existing anti-Communist laws and conflict with the Administration's program to end the threat of Communist party subversion.

The Party Is Ostracized

The bill deprives the Communist party of "any of the rights, privileges and immunities attendant upon legal bodies." The party would thus be ostracized in this country and deprived of all legal rights, including that of a place on the ballot.

This development removed what had appeared to be the largest stumbling block to the adjournment of Congress. The House approved the $5,243,575,795 foreign aid appropriations bill, last of the session's money measures, and the Senate later completed Congressional action on it.

This left the Administration's Social Security bill as the only remaining hurdle to completing Congress' work. A conference committee has been unable to break a deadlock on the measure, which calls for broader coverage, higher benefits and taxes and other changes in the old age and survivors insurance program.

Congress, by its decision on the anti-Communist legislation declared, in effect, that it believed no existing Communist control law would be injured and that, at last, a direct step was being made to brand the Communist party as an outlaw.

However, in Senate-House conference adjustments of the differences between the two legislative branches, adopted unanimously, the legislators dropped a plan to make mere membership in the Communist party an automatic felony distinguishable by fines ranging to $10,000 and imprisonment up to five years.

Instead, members of the party and their willing collaborators in what was found legally to be a conspiracy to overthrow the Government of the United States by force and violence would be denied citizenship rights.

These would include holding of Federal posts, being employed in defense plants, making contracts protected by law, banking money, and possibly running for elective office.

Those who were found to be Communists would be required to register as such at the Department of Justice under the Internal Security Act. Failure to register might draw, on conviction, up to ten years in prison or $10,000 in fines or both.

The registration provision of the Internal Security Act of 1950 has been under court test by the Communist party for more than a year. A Federal District Court decision has upheld it. The case is now before a Circuit Court of Appeals, and probably will go to the Supreme Court for a final decision a year hence. Meanwhile, the registration provision has been unenforceable.

The Senate's unanimous vote approving the bill followed nearly three hours of debate this morning.

The House conducted no debate at all today. The two dissenters were Representatives Abraham J. Multer, Democrat of Brooklyn, and Usher L. Buddick, Republican of North Dakota.

Bill Called Fascistic

Mr. Multer said he had voted against the bill because "putting any group out of business in this way is basically wrong in principle; it is the way a Fascist would use, the totalitarian way."

Mr. Burdick said: "I am against any form of tyranny over the mind of man. I am for freedom of speech, freedom of the press. I am opposed to silence from fear, instead of reason."

The bill, which started out as an Administration measure to restrict Communist-infiltrated labor unions, also provides that any labor organization found by Government authorities to be dominated by Communists shall be stripped of all its rights under the National Labor Relations law.

This means that a union so labeled could be certified as a collective bargaining agent.

At the outset, the bill, managed on the floor by Senator John Marshall Butler, Republican of Maryland, faced opposition from members who saw in it a danger to all organized labor. They contended that labor already had cleaned its own house of Communist-dominated units.

Later the measure developed into a bitter political fight between Democrats and Republicans, with both sides seeking to fortify their positions for the coming Congressional elections.

There were, in addition, other factors, highly political, that motivated the Democrats when they surprised Congress last week with their move to outlaw the Communist party.

For many months Republicans in key places had accused the Democrats of "being soft" on communism. Senator Joseph R. McCarthy, Republican of Wisconsin, accused the Democrats of "twenty years of treason."

Former President Herbert Hoover laid Communist gains through the years at the Democratic door. Others picked up the cry and a major campaign issue was in the making.

Senator Humphrey offered the initial amendment to outlaw the Communist party and to make felons of its willing members and outside helpers. He was joined at first by Senator John F. Kennedy, Democrat of Massachusetts and Senator Wayne Morse, Independent of Oregon. Sixteen other Democrats clamored for added sponsorship.

The Democrats asserted that the Republicans, claiming full credit for fighting the Reds, had only plucked at branches of the tree and had not struck at the roots.

The result was the procession of bandwagon and bipartisan votes for outlawing the Communist party in each of the several forms the legislation appeared.

The House at first decided to strike at the party but not at its members except through existing laws. The Senate voted twice to bring the members into the picture and the House yielded. Then the conference compromise came early today, even without a formal meeting of the Senate and House conferees.

Senator Humphrey told the Senate today that he would agree to the compromise.

"Although it is not as strong a blow as Hubert Humphrey would like to have struck," he said, "it still outlaws the party by taking from it its rights and privileges. It will strengthen the Smith Act [of 1940, under which more than eighty Communist leaders have been convicted] that outlaws conspiracy to overthrow the Government.

"These rats are not going to get out of this trap. We have slammed the door on them, and if this law is not strong enough to do the whole job, I will come back next year to help make it stronger, if I am re-elected."

The Smith Act makes it a crime to conspire to teach overthrow of the Government by force. This was the law under which top Communist party leaders have been tried and convicted.

Widespread Debate Stirred

Debate on the most controversial part of the bill—to make it a crime to belong to the Communist party, omitted in the amended version—was not confined to Capitol Hill. Those in favor of the anti-Communist proscriptions contended that the prospective law would strengthen the Administration's hand, not weaken it, in rooting out subversion.

It was argued that its provisions would speed up prosecutions long stymied in legal technicalities, and that it would strike at the roots of Communist conspiracy.

Despite the almost unanimous character of the Congressional voting, there was considerable opposition to the amended version. Some said that it was too stern, and some that it was too weak, representing little more than a re-enactment of the four year-old Internal Security law which is still under court review.

Seldom, Capitol veterans said, had a major measure been made so apparently acceptable to a strongly opposing Executive Branch with so few words. Only two brief amendments were made by the conferees to the bill passed by the Senate and House. They contained thirty-seven words and struck out provisions that offended the Administration.

One change, "to save" the Internal Security Act, made Communists subject to its penalties instead of those of the Subversive Activities Control Act.

Originally it was provided that whoever knowingly and willingly became or remained a member of the Communist party or any other organization having its conspiratorial purposes would face a fine or a prison term or both.

Under a twenty-five-word change of language, a person found by the Subversive Activities Control Board to be a Communist conspirator would be deprived of certain citizenship rights and be required to register under the Internal Security Act. If he refused to register he would face possible fines up to $10,000 or ten years in prison or both.

The second, twelve-word change emphasized that a member of the Communist party or a Communist-front organization be shown to have had knowledge of the conspiratorial purpose and objectives of what he had signed up with before being exposed to the penalties of the law.

Kefauver Criticizes Measure

Thus far there have been no Communist registrations under the Internal Security Act. The party has declared that it would not register.

In spite of the unanimous vote in the Senate, that branch and its crowded galleries heard much criticism of the measure.

"Nobody in the history of this country has ever before been outlawed for his political beliefs. * * * You cannot destroy ideas by passing laws against them," said Senator Estes Kefauver, Democrat of Tennessee.

Senator Morse accused the conferees of "ducking and weaving" as boxers do, in an effort to make the legislation acceptable to the Administration.

"The fact remains," he asserted, "that you've got a watered-down bill here. We are running out on the Humphrey amendment which the Senate supported with an 85-to-0 vote when it was first presented.

"The only way to defeat this conspiracy to overthrow our Government is to reach the conspirators, the members, not their organizations that can appear and disappear at will," Senator Morse added. "This is a matter for the courts to handle for a calling of the conspirators to the bar of justice, and not a transferring of the business to the Subversive Activities Control Board.

"My record for the protection of the rights of all humans is known. But I am not for the protection of those who have set out to destroy those rights in the United States and throughout the free world."

The House also sent to the White House a bill under which convicted Communists would lose their citizenship. This was in response to a declaration by President Eisenhower in his State of the Union Message in January that when an American accepted the purposes and discipline of the Communist conspiracy he transferred his allegiance and was no longer entitled to citizenship.

* * *

August 25, 1954

EISENHOWER SIGNS RED CONTROL BILL, CITING PROTECTION

Says People Are Determined to Guard Against Plot by 'a Political Party'

By JOSEPH. A. LOFTUS
Special to The New York Times.

DENVER, Aug. 24—A bill to destroy the Communist party as a political and legal entry in the United States became law today.

President Eisenhower approved it with the declaration that the American people are determined to protect themselves against any organization that purports to be a political party while "actually a conspiracy dedicated to the violent overthrow of our entire form of Government."

Though the law does not make membership in the party a crime, as the Senate at first voted to do, it does impose legal, political, and economic penalties on party members and takes away the rights, privileges and immunities that legal bodies ordinarily have under the Federal Government.

Labor organizations found to be Communist-controlled will be stripped of their rights under the Taft-Hartley law; that is, they cannot bring complaints against employers or

other unions or get their names on a ballot to win or protect representation rights.

Five New Anti-Red Laws

This made five new anti-subversion laws placed on the statute books in recent days, with three more to be added. The President said he would approve them soon.

The law approved today goes further than the Administration had proposed. In the closing days of the session, the Senate voted to make party membership a crime. The Administration regarded that as unwise from a practical standpoint. The bill then was tailored a little closer to Administration specifications, although the possibility of a veto remained.

Whatever misgivings the President may have about these stiff provisions, he was cautious in expressing them. He said in a statement that "the full impact of these clauses upon the enforcement of the laws by which we are now fighting the Communist conspiracy in this country will require further careful study."

"I am satisfied, however," he declared, "that they were not intended to impair or abrogate any portion of the Internal Security Act or the criminal statutes under which the leaders of the Communist party are now being prosecuted and that they may prove helpful in several respects."

After signing the bill, President Eisenhower stepped outside the Lowry Air Force Base headquarters, where he makes his office, and spoke for the camera and sound men for a few minutes. He was asked about his speech to the country the night before.

The President said he was generally satisfied with the way the speech had gone off, but thought it had been too much to try to do in thirty minutes. He ought to have been more selective in his subject matter, he said. He thought his argument would have been better if he had not tried to cover so much ground.

The President did not speak last night from a text, but from cue cards, which were simply topical headings. Reporters, however, were able to write stories in advance on the basis of information supplied by James C. Hagerty, White House press secretary.

Mr. Hagerty, talking to the press, was using largely his own words, so advance stories were limited to indirect discourse, except for a part dealing with taxes. The President, using his own words in the broadcast, softened the political appeal, as well as some other parts, and added words of encouragement about Europe.

The President appeared in a cheerful mood today.

"When are you going to get some vacation?" he was asked.

"Oh, well," the President replied, "this is better than Washington."

* * *

August 31, 1954

FRENCH KILL E. D. C. TREATY, 319-264

BLOW DEALT NATO

*Washington Policy Also Upset—
Assembly in Uproar After Vote*

By HAROLD CALLENDER
Special to The New York Times.

PARIS, Aug. 30—The European Defense Community treaty, designed to rearm West Germany within a European army, was rejected by the French National Assembly today by a vote of 319 to 281.

This action was a blow to the North Atlantic Treaty Organization, which for two years has based its planning on the assumption of adding twelve German divisions to its European defense forces by virtue of this treaty.

It also was a blow to United States policy in Europe. Washington had counted on the treaty to increase Western defenses and to help strengthen West Europe politically and economically. This would have been accomplished through a long-term partnership of France, West Germany and their neighbors in the defense community, as well as in the European Coal and Steel Community.

The Assembly's vote took the form of adoption of a motion to adjourn the debate on the treaty sine die (without naming a day for resumption). This decision was accepted on all sides as tantamount to a rejection of the treaty and it was so understood by those voting on the motion.

Treaty Prepared in 1932

The action of the Assembly seemed to mark the end of the treaty, which was negotiated from October, 1950, was signed on May, 1952, and has been ratified by four of the signatory states—West Germany, Belgium, the Netherlands and Luxembourg. Italy, a fifth member, was expected soon to ratify it.

The signer of the treaty was Robert Schuman, former Foreign Minister. René Pleven, former Premier, was the author of the first draft.

The Assembly's vote incidentally rejected the Bonn peace contract with the Western Allies, granting approximate sovereignty to West Germany, since this treaty was included in the ratification measure under discussion. But the real issue was the defense community treaty. The application of the Bonn contract by Britain and the United States, with the tacit or explicit approval of France, was taken for granted.

The Assembly, tense after a three-day debate on the defense community treaty, broke into an uproar when the vote was announced.

The victorious opponents of the treaty sang the "Marseillaise," French national anthem. Pro-treaty deputies shouted "to Moscow" to express their view that the vote had been a victory for the Soviet Union, which had actively opposed the treaty.

Communists Are Jubilant

The jubilant Communists—without whose ninety-five votes the result would have been the opposite—sang the "Internationale."

The only speaker to make himself heard for a moment before the final adjournment was former Premier Paul Reynaud. Alluding to the cutting-off of the debate by the motion to postpone all discussion of the treaty, he said:

"For the first time in the history of the French Parliament, a treaty has been rejected without a word in its defense spoken by its author or its signer."

After the vote Premier Pierre Mendès-France said in a statement to the press that he had long warned "our friends and allies" that there was no majority for the defense community treaty in the Assembly, but that contrary reports had been credited abroad, notably at the Brussels conference of foreign ministers last week.

"I regret that our partners at Brussels and our Anglo-Saxon allies were mistaken about the sentiments of the National Assembly which have just been expressed in almost the same majority that I had predicted," the Premier said.

M. Mendès-France said the debate proved a great majority of the Assembly was attached to "the Western alliance" and that it was within that framework that "new solutions should be studied rapidly." He added that "this time we shall not lose three years," and said he hoped that very soon "our allies and the countries with the same interests as France will face clear decisions."

In addressing the Assembly, the Premier was not clear about these "clear decisions" to come. He declined to indicate how he would propose to rearm the West Germans—which he agreed had to be done—if the defense community treaty were killed. He defined there was only one alternative to the method of the treaty—that of taking West Germany into the North Atlantic Treaty Organization. He contended there were "several" methods but that the time had not come to "enumerate them all."

This multiplicity of methods of arming the Germans apparently has not yet been perceived in Washington. And in London the British Government made it clear a few days ago that it thought the best method was that of the treaty the French Assembly has now rejected.

Pro-treaty Frenchmen have argued that there are only two methods—to include the Germans in a European army or to let them have a national army either as members or non-members of the Atlantic alliance.

The Premier has talked of a third method: Arming the Germans under the control of the six European states that signed the treaty, plus Britain. But his critics doubt the West Germans will accept under this or other auspices the controls they accepted in the defense community treaty.

A distinguished French supporter of the European army plan said tonight that the Assembly had voted for a German national army with a general staff and probably Nazi generals, and that this had been done while the Government had taken a neutral stand and the debate was cut off.

Premier Mendès-France is prepared to go along with Washington and London in granting sovereignty to West Germany, although he promised to get first the approval of the Assembly.

He also has said he would discuss with Washington, London and the six states that were involved in the European army project what the next step would be regarding West German rearmament.

Coal-Steel Pool Affected

He said he would make proposals. He did not define them but some of his associates have sought a way of rearming the Germans under controls but without admitting West Germany into the North Atlantic Treaty Organization.

It is regarded as probable that the Premier will visit Washington in September and will then discuss with President Eisenhower and Secretary of State John Foster Dulles, the outlook for Western defense and European unity in the light of the negative action of the French Assembly.

The Premier probably is right in saying that this action of the Assembly was not directed against the Atlantic alliance though it was directed against a defensive plan on which that alliance had long relied—and long had waited on France's decision.

The Assembly's vote was mainly against West German rearmament and against the "Little Europe" of six nations the defense community treaty represents.

The result will be a setback for Dr. Konrad Adenauer, Chancellor of West Germany. The Bonn Chancellor has based his whole policy on this form of European unity and this method of avoiding a German national army—which the French Assembly now seems to have called into existence against the will of that German leader.

The Assembly's action may prove to be a setback for the European Coal and Steel Community, which was formed to prevent the growth of an aggressive German heavy industry on a national basis just as the defense community treaty was to prevent a German national army. For the French Assembly seems to have turned against the supranational principle upon which the Coal and Steel Community was founded.

The vote of the Assembly resulted from a series of parliamentary and political maneuvers that took place outside the chamber while the debate was going on or suspended.

Three types of maneuver developed.

One, by the pre-treaty ministers, was to persuade the Premier to resume negotiations with the foreign ministers of the other signatory states, which were broken off in Brussels Aug. 28. The Premier agreed to do so if the Assembly voted a motion approving what he had done in Brussels last week.

A second maneuver, by the pro-treaty deputies, was designed to force M. Mendès-France into a new negotiation while condemning him for the last one—which proved not to be a successful way of getting him to try again.

A third maneuver was intended to kill the treaty by moving an indefinite adjournment of the debate.

The Premier, while saying it pained him to do so, took a strictly neutral position. He had agreed to resume negotiations if the Assembly endorsed his terms and his previous conduct. But he was not satisfied with a motion from M. Pleven's group, the Democratic and Social Resistance Union, that would have sent him to a new conference on the basis of his own protocol for revision of the treaty, presumably because it was not a full vote of confidence in what he had done.

The Premier suggested both motions be withdrawn so the debate could go on—the motion for adjournment and the motion for new negotiations. The author of the second motion, Alfred Chupin, declined to withdraw his. There was then nothing left for the Assembly but to vote on both motions, beginning with that for adjournment, which had priority.

In favor of the motion for adjournment—that is, against the treaty—82-year-old Edouard Herriot, former Premier and Honorary Speaker of the Assembly, spoke for nearly an hour. His hands were trembling as he fingered documents and his voice was quaking as he told the Assembly the defense community treaty would mean "the end of France." He argued that the treaty discriminated against France in favor of Germany. He opposed new negotiations on the treaty but seemed to urge new negotiations with the Soviet Union.

After M. Herriot had mingled erroneous statements about the treaty with reminiscences of his political heyday in the Nineteen Twenties, when he said he had made a successful rapprochement with the Soviet Union, Christian Pineau, a Socialist, contended the motion for adjournment was strictly a procedural issue. In spite of this, nobody seemed to have any doubt that the Assembly was voting to reject the treaty or to continue the debate.

Hopes for Delay Are Held

Until the final hour there seemed a chance for a suspension of the debate pending a new negotiation. The Premier had said he was willing to negotiate again on his terms and the pro-treaty forces seemed willing also, since they had abandoned hope of getting a majority for the treaty as it stood.

It was this absence of a majority for the treaty, which both sides now acknowledged, that took away the enthusiasm for a debate on an issue that appeared to many to have been settled long before the vote.

But if the other motion had carried and new negotiations begun, the result almost certainly would have been a treaty shorn of its supranational character. It might have provided a framework, however, in which more substantial contents could have been put in years to come. Such was about the maximum for which the pro-treaty leaders could hope and they seemed to realize it.

Some argue that a majority for the treaty would have been possible if M. Mendès-France had taken the lead instead of following the Assembly. But to do this he would have had to be an ardent believer in the treaty, which he was not. Perhaps he also would have had to come into office sooner. He said tonight that there might have been a majority for the treaty eighteen months ago but that for many months the trend had been the other way.

It was the great error of United States leaders to be unaware of this trend, according to the Premier. He recently remarked that United States officials thought they could size up the French Assembly better than he could. When Mr. Dulles visited Paris in July, M. Mendès-France told him there was no majority for the treaty but Mr. Dulles replied that he had been otherwise informed.

* * *

August 31, 1954

PRESIDENT RULES OUT ISOLATION

TWIN PERILS CITED

*Eisenhower Tells Legion Withdrawal or
a War Would Lead to Ruin*

By PAUL P. KENNEDY
Special to The New York Times.

WASHINGTON, Aug. 30—President Eisenhower told the American Legion today that while there might be disappointment in progress of the European Defense Community treaty there must be no slackening of efforts toward it.

[In Des Moines, President Eisenhower described the rejection by the French Parliament of E. D. C. as a "major setback" in the fight against international communism but said the free world still was overwhelmingly strong, compared to the Iron Curtain countries. "All that "this free world needs to be safe," he added, "is a united approach to the problem of security and defense."]

"Neither the ups nor downs" of world developments justify complacency," the President said and "the free world must build on its successes and be spurred to new endeavor by its setbacks."

War and isolationism were to be shunned, the President said. "To follow the path of isolationism," he declared, "would surrender most of the free world to Communist despotism and ultimately forfeit our own security. Deliberately to choose the road to war would suddenly place in jeopardy the civilization which we are determined to preserve."

"We shall not be sidetracked into either of these dead ends," the President declared.

Pact Necessities Stressed

The President, tanned and relaxed, spoke to about 7,000 American Legion members and visitors here at the thirty-sixth national convention, which formally got under way this morning. In a speech largely devoted to foreign policy, the President emphasized the urgency of alliances within the free world. He made a point, however, of what he termed "the principle of united freedom" in which allied nations severally maintained freedoms of action as sovereign countries.

In practical terms, he explained, this meant "that we are not committed to giving any of our partners a veto over our actions, nor do we have a veto over their actions."

The President added in apparent assurance to our Allies, "we must, therefore, guard against the dangerous assumption that other nations, as our allies, are bound to do what we want. They have never bound themselves in this sense, nor have we bound ourselves to do what they want."

The President spoke in the National Armory where newsreel and television lights, the near capacity crowd and lack of cooling or ventilation sent the temperature up to steamy levels.

Other speakers at the session made these points:

• Admiral Arthur W. Radford, Chairman of the Joint Chiefs of Staff, voiced an opinion, as did President Eisenhower, that our reserve forces were inadequate. Today, Admiral Radford said, our reserve forces are not adequate to meet the needs of our national security."

• Cardinal Spellman of New York said that the recent Geneva conference, if it meant anything at all, meant "taps for the buried hopes of freedom in Southeast Asia! Taps for the newly betrayed millions of Indochinese who must now learn the awful facts of slavery from their eager Communist masters!"

• Mme. Chiang Kai-shek told the Legion that as long as the Formosa "footstool" remained free the Chinese people had a sanctuary of freedom to which eyes on the mainland turn. She said China some day would be free and so would the world.

• Gov. John Davis Lodge of Connecticut warned that the fight against totalitarianism was never ending. "Though we have overcome the world's dictators and would-be warlords * * * in open conflict, we have discovered * * * that a decisive battle on one front may yet leave the forces of oppression free to ignite fires of dissent in other quarters of the world," Governor Lodge said.

• Arthur J. Connell, National Commander, in his annual report charged that the American Medical Association had "opened a flank attack" on the Legion. He said an educational program had been initiated to counteract this. Mr. Connell previously had criticized the A. M. A. for its medical outlook on veterans.

• Lewis K. Gough, past national commander, speaking some time prior to the President, said, "It becomes increasingly evident that the United Nations no longer can claim to be an instrument for suppressing war and aggression."

U. N. Failures Are Noted

The President said that the United Nations, while it had accomplished much in the cause of peace, "clearly it has often failed to fulfill our hopes." This however, was "no reason to weaken our support," he said with emphasis. There was no discernable audience reaction to his comments on the United Nations.

The President received perhaps the loudest and most prolonged applause during a section of his speech dealing with the military reserves, a subject for years of strong Legion policy.

"Establishment of an adequate reserve—an objective for which the American Legion and other patriotic organizations have vainly fought for a generation—will be a number one item submitted to the Congress next year," the President said.

The Republic, he went on, has for 150 years prided itself on refusal to maintain a large standing army. "We have relied, instead, upon the civilian soldier," he said, "but we have done so without being fair either to the private citizen or to the security of the nation."

"We have failed miserably to maintain that strong, ready military reserve in which we have believed for 150 years," he added saying the reserve "must" be built and maintained and "wishful thinking and political timidity must no longer bar a program so absolutely essential to our defense."

While the President said a reserve program would be submitted to the next Congress, he did not go into detail as to what it might propose.

Two Plans Being Weighed

Generally, there have been two recent basic studies of the reserve program. One was by the National Security Training Commission, headed by Maj. Gen. Julius Ochs Adler.

This commission recommended a program of training 18-year-olds concurrently with the drafting of older youths for active duty. It submitted its report to President Eisenhower last December and at that time suggested an early start with at least 100,000 young men entering the training corps during 1955. Each would undergo six months training, it proposed, and then be transferred to the reserve for seven and one-half years.

This report was referred by the President to the Office of Defense Mobilization, which made a further study of the problem in relation to the over-all manpower picture.

The Defense Department then evolved its reserve program which has been put before the National Security Council. As outlined by Dr. John A. Hannah before he quit as Assistant Secretary of Defense for Manpower and Personnel, the Defense Department program calls for a ready reserve of more than 3,000,000 who could be called by the services to Federal duty immediately.

In addition, Dr. Hannah said, it calls for another pool of 750,000 men who would be called up one by one through Selective Service. Moreover, he said, it would mean the draft of 300,000 men a year at the rate of 25,000 a month.

There was high optimism among the delegates that as a result of the President's remarks a Legion program to get action on Universal Military Training next year would meet with success. Pre-convention speakers had urged the Legion to prepare a program to submit to Congress and not await White House action.

Early in his talk the President spoke of a bi-partisan approach to foreign problems and reiterated it several times during the twenty-seven-minute speech. In an elaboration of his prepared remarks he commented that "stability in our national purposes obviously cannot be obtained if there is to be marked change—or if the world is to fear a marked change—with every veering of partisan political winds."

Discussing efforts toward peace the President said "no responsible individual—no political party wants war. No matter how deep may be our differences in other fields, in this we are all Americans, nothing else."

Many listeners interpreted this remark on the spirit of bi-partisanship as a salve to the hurts caused by Republican barbs on "twenty years of treason" under Democratic Administrations.

"The only treasonable party we have is the Communist conspiracy—happily very small," he said.

Earlier with marked emphasis the President praised the Foreign Service officers, referring to them as "loyal and effective."

"With a few highly publicized exceptions, we have been fortunate in the high competence, professional ability, and devotion of these officers upon whom we must depend in our delicate and difficult negotiations with other nations and in assuring the world of our peaceful purposes," the President declared.

On the subject of subversion, he said that the battle against Communist conspiracy was continuing and that during the past nineteen months "the rate of convictions and deportations secured by the F. B. I. and the Department of Justice has been stepped up," continuing:

"And of this you may be sure: As we continue this battle we shall not impair the constitutional safeguards protecting our liberties. Our nation is too strong to give way to hysterical fear which, under the guise of preserving our institutions, would undermine the principles upon which they rest." He received a round of applause when he added, "I know the American Legion will support this wise, traditionally American approach."

The President, dressed in a light gray, single-breasted suit, appeared in the auditorium six minutes before he went on the air.

As he stepped to the podium President Eisenhower wore a blue Legion cap with "Abilene, Kansas" in gold lettering. Following the speech, Commander Connell stepped forward and pinned the Legion's Distinguished Service Medal on the President.

Adenauer Sends Greeting

Aside from the speeches there was little business transacted at this first session of the convention, which concludes Thursday.

Early in the session Commander Connell read the convention a cable received from Dr. Konrad Adenauer, Chancellor of the Federal Republic of Germany. Dr. Adenauer, who was unable to keep a speaking engagement at the convention, apologized for his absence but said "I should like to communicate to you at least in this way my cordial greetings and wishes."

The cablegram added, "Will you please tell the members of the American Legion that the German people feel closely bound to the American people by our common cultural heritage, our faith in democracy and human freedom, and by our will to preserve and defend those values."

Legion politics bubbling behind the scenes were moving Seaborn P. Collins Jr. closer to election as national commander.

The 41-year-old building contractor of Las Cruces, N. M., and World War II transport pilot, appeared almost certain of election when one of his two opponents, W. C. Daniel of Danville, Va., withdrew in favor of him. J. Addington Wagner of Battle Creek, Mich., remained in the race.

Cardinal Spellman in the tone and subject matter of his speech left little room for optimism and it was received in silence except at one point, when he commented he had warned before that it was "better to have protection and not need it than need it and not have it."

He was particularly skeptical of the results of the Geneva conference last July in which a cease-fire was agreed upon for Indochina.

"If we view the Geneva guarantee of independence for Laos, Cambodia and South Vietnam with a large measure of disbelief," Cardinal Spellman said, "it is only because we remember how Poland's hopes, and the hopes of all the other countries now in the Soviet orbit were shamelessly betrayed."

"There is no reason for believing that the partition of Vietnam will have any different effect than the partition of Korea," he continued. "Indeed, hardly was the ink dry on the Geneva Pact when the Communist leader of North Vietnam, Ho Chi Minh, boastfully proclaimed that within six months he expected to bring the independent states of Laos, Cambodia and South Vietnam under Communist control."

We have failed "tragically," the speaker declared, to realize that communism has a world plan and it has been following a carefully set up timetable for the achievement of that plan."

The final act of the first day of the convention was the commander's dinner tonight at which Madame Chiang was the principal speaker.

Madame Chiang, the first woman in Legion history to deliver the main address at one of its banquets, said the mainland of China had been lost through infiltration. It had been lost also, she declared, "by a campaign of smears and lies" and by "skillfully creating a schism between China and her natural Allies."

"What no other country in modern times has been able to do—to enslave the China mainland—Soviet Russia has done, and the Bear did it from inside China by corrupting the minds and souls of those who became its puppets—the Chinese Communists," she declared.

She said that the Chinese Nationalist Republic would continue its fight for a free China. "Conquerors have come and conquerors have gone, but our way of life has withstood them and will continue to withstand the present brutal masters who seek to continue enslaving our nation," she said.

The convention activities tomorrow will center on the traditional parade which is to begin at 2 P. M. and likely continue past midnight. The convention committee says 75,000 persons will march. Estimates of the number of spectators range up to 500,000.

* * *

September 4, 1954

CHINESE REDS SHELL 2 QUEMOY ISLANDS

By The Associated Press

TAIPEI, Formosa, Saturday, Sept. 4—Chinese Communist artillery bombarded two Nationalist-held islands off the China coast for more than five hours yesterday.

A Nationalist Government communiqué said about 5,000 shells had been fired at Quemoy and Little Quemoy. Casualties were listed as light—three killed, two seriously wounded and five slightly wounded.

[A Peiping radio broadcast heard in Tokyo Saturday said Chinese Communist artillery had sunk a Nationalist gunboat and damaged two others and military installations on Quemoy Island, The United Press said.]

The attack immediately raised speculation here whether it presaged an attempt to seize the two islands or was for political purposes only. Unofficial quarters regarded it mostly as an effort to inject disharmony into the Southeast Asia security conference that opens in Manila Monday.

Quemoy Island, a Nationalist strongpoint, is seven miles east of Amoy, Red-held island city just off the Chinese mainland. Little Quemoy is five miles east of Amoy. The Nationalist and Red holdings thus are within easy artillery range of one another.

Yesterday's attack was described in the Nationalist communiqué as the heaviest since the Communists tried unsuccessfully to seize Quemoy in October 1949. The Reds suffered heavy losses in that assault.

The artillery attack began about 3 P. M. Nationalist artillery immediately responded. Five hours and fifteen minutes later the Red guns fell silent, the communiqué said, "under our heavy artillery pressure." Quemoy is 100 miles west of the Chinese Nationalist stronghold of Formosa.

Most of the enemy shells fell into the sea, the communiqué asserted. It referred to the attack as a "bandit challenge which had been reckoned as probable."

The Nationalist Government did not seem too concerned about the possibility of a Communist attempt to capture Quemoy.

"If the bandits try to invade Quemoy," the communiqué said, "it would be most welcome by our troops, whose memory of their big victory in October, 1949, is still green.

"We also suppose the Communist bandits have not forgotten their big defeat. Our troops, whose morale is high and confidence unbounded, are prepared to give them another thrashing."

Yesterday's action followed a raid on Quemoy by a handful of Communists the night of Aug. 23, when they captured one Nationalist soldier.

* * *

September 28, 1954

COMMITTEE URGES M'CARTHY CENSURE; UPHOLDS 2 CHARGES, CRITICAL ON ALL; MOST SENATORS SEEM TO BACK REPORT

ACTION UNANIMOUS

Verdict Given on Counts of Abusing Zwicker, Contempt of Inquiry

By ANTHONY LEVIERO
Special to The New York Times.

WASHINGTON, Sept. 27—A special Senate committee unanimously recommended today that the Senate censure Senator Joseph R. McCarthy.

It said the Wisconsin Republican Senator should be rebuked for contempt of a Senate Elections subcommittee and for abuse of five fellow Senators and Brig. Gen. Ralph W. Zwicker.

The committee of three Republicans and three Democrats headed by Senator Arthur V. Watkins, Republican of Utah, recommended censure on two of five main categories of charges, which embodied thirteen specifications.

It called Mr. McCarthy's actions "contemptuous, contumacious and denunciatory," "highly improper" and "reprehensible." It also said Senator McCarthy had committed "grave error" and had "manifested a high degree of irresponsibility."

While it did not recommend censure on two categories, the committee severely criticized Mr. McCarthy, finding cause for sharp comment on every charge. On the remaining category involving abuses of colleagues in the Senate, the committee noted that much of this section had been placed under another section referring to the Elections subcommittee.

Benefits of Doubts Given

The committee did not vote censure on the two categories of charges relating to Senator McCarthy's solicitation and use of confidential data. The committee gave him the benefit of doubts, "mitigating circumstances" and the "charitable" interpretation of the "ambiguity of the statements" he made about a two-and-one quarter-page document from Army Intelligence files.

Following are the five categories of charges against Senator McCarthy and the committee findings.

Category I—That Senator McCarthy showed contempt of a Senate-Elections subcommittee in 1951 and 1952 and abused its members in refusing its repeated invitation to answer accusations filed against him. Verdict: Senator McCarthy should be censured.

Category II—That he incited Federal employees to give him confidential or classified documents. Verdict: Critical but Senator McCarthy should receive the benefit of "doubts" as to intent and not be censured.

Category III—That he unlawfully used and failed to return an Army Intelligence document containing classified Federal Bureau of Investigation information and might have violated the espionage law. Verdict: He showed "grave error" but should not be censured because of "mitigating circumstances."

Category IV—That he abused fellow Senators, including Elections subcommittee members and Senator Ralph E. Flanders, Republican of Vermont, author of the censure resolution. Verdict: Censurable as found in initial count but not for abuse of Senator Flanders, which had been provoked by Senator Flanders' action.

Category V—That Senator McCarthy abused Brig. Gen. Ralph W. Zwicker in denouncing him as "unfit to wear the uniform." Verdict: Should be censured.

Defense Is Rebutted

Virtually every phase of Senator McCarthy's defense, whether based on law, fact, the Constitution, Senate rule or Senate precedent, was rebutted by the Senate committee in its report.

The Senate will convene on Nov. 8 to debate and vote on the disciplinary action, based on a pending resolution of censure sponsored by Senator Flanders.

Censure would carry no punitive penalties, unless the Senate decided to go further by depriving Mr. McCarthy of his two committee chairmanships or entertained a move to expel him from the Senate. There was no intimation today that either of these steps was being considered.

All through its analysis of the evidence and of the charges, the special committee pleaded for the orderly and constitutional processes of Government.

The committee's severest indictment of Mr. McCarthy came after it had examined his attitude toward the Senate Elections subcommittee that had investigated his finances in 1951 and 1952.

"It is the opinion of the select committee that when the personal honor and official conduct of a Senator of the United States are in question before a duly constituted committee of the Senate, the Senator involved owes a duty to himself, his state and to the Senate, to appear promptly and cooperate fully when called by a Senate committee charged with the responsibility of inquiry," the Watkins Committee asserted.

"This must be the rule if the dignity, honor, authority and power of the Senate are to be respected and maintained. This duty could not and was not fulfilled by questioning the authority and jurisdiction of the subcommittee, by accusing its members of the dishonest expenditure of public funds, or even by charging that the committee was permitting itself to be used to serve the cause of communism.

"When persons in high places fail to set and meet high standards, the people lose faith. If our people lose faith, our form of Government cannot long endure."

Asserts Congress' Right

Along with its analysis of the conduct of Senator McCarthy, the Watkins committee:

• Asserted the right of Congress to obtain information, including secret information, from the Executive Branch of the Government, cautioning that the document security system should not become an "iron curtain" that prevented Congressional access to such data. This was stated as a prerogative of the Legislative Branch in the abstract, however, for the committee made no criticism of the Executive Branch.

• Said that, by the same token, Congress would expose itself to "equally sound criticism" if it failed to adapt itself to the reasonable regulations of the President and Executive agencies.

• Warned that Senator McCarthy's invitation to Federal employees to bring him information, which the committee said could be interpreted to mean confidential or classified data, could expose such employees who brought him information to "risk of effective penalties."

• Exposed a loophole in the Espionage Act. With respect to the charge that Senator McCarthy incited Federal employees to violate the Espionage Act by bringing him classified data, the committee said that the law did not "define who is entitled to receive information relating to the national defense." Hence the committee concluded that Senator McCarthy, as chairman of the Government Operations Committee and of its Permanent Investigations subcommittee, was not a person "not entitled to receive" information about national defense.

• Recommended that Senate leaders and ranking committee members of both parties confer with representatives of the Executive Branch to clarify procedures whereby Congress could obtain the confidential data it needed.

The other members of the committee were Senators Edwin C. Johnson, of Colorado, vice chairman; John C. Stennis of Mississippi and Sam J. Ervin Jr. of North Carolina, Democrats, and Frank Carlson of Kansas and Francis Case of South Dakota, Republicans.

On the Election Subcommittee

The committee devoted twenty-six pages to the report of Mr. McCarthy's conduct toward the committee. It divided the issue into thirteen legal questions and decided them all against Mr. McCarthy.

Senator McCarthy was accused of having refused repeated invitations to appear before the subcommittee. He contended that the committee had never been validated, that it had exceeded its authority by investigating his affairs before he entered the Senate, and that in its expenditures the subcommittee had been "guilty of stealing just as clearly as though the members engaged in picking the pockets of the taxpayers."

The Watkins committee asserted that Mr. McCarthy's reply to one request to appear from Senator Thomas C. Hennings, Democrat of Missouri, was "contumacious" and that other letters replying to invitations to appear were "clearly contemptuous, disregarding entirely his ability to cooperate, ridiculing

the subcommittee, accusing these committee officers of the Senate with dishonesty and impugning their motives, and making it impossible for them to proceed in orderly fashion, or to complete their duties."

"It is our opinion," the committee said, referring to the Elections subcommittee investigation, "that the failure of Senator McCarthy to explain to the Senate these matters: (1) Whether funds collected to fight communism were diverted to other purposes inuring to his personal advantage; (2) whether certain of his official activities were motivated by self-interest; and (3) whether certain of his activities in Senatorial campaigns involved violations of the law; was conduct contumacious toward the Senate and injurious to its effectiveness, dignity responsibilities, processes and prestige."

For "convenience" in discussions the committee merged with Category I its consideration of that part of Category IV relating to Mr. McCarthy's abuse of the Elections subcommittee members and found him censurable for it.

The members specified were Senators Guy M. Gillette of Iowa, A. S. Mike Monroney of Oklahoma and Carl Hayden of Arizona, Democrats, and Robert C. Hendrickson of New Jersey, Republican.

The committee was particularly concerned by Senator McCarthy's denunciation of Senator Hendrickson as "a living miracle without brains or guts."

"His public statement with reference to Senator Hendrickson was vulgar and insulting," the committee declared.

Among the legal arguments rejected by the Watkins Committee was Senator McCarthy's contentions that his actions during a previous Congress could not be investigated, and that his re-election of 1952 cleared him of any charges of prior misconduct.

The committee said the point that the Senate was a "continuing body" had often been upheld and needed little discussion.

As for the defense that re-election purged preceding actions, the committee said:

"Some of the questions, notably the use for private purposes of funds contributed for fighting communism, were not raised until after the election. The people of Wisconsin could pass only upon what was known to them.

"Nor do we believe that the re-election of Senator McCarthy by the people of Wisconsin in the fall of 1953 pardons his conduct toward the Subcommittee on Privileges and Elections. That charge is that Senator McCarthy was guilty of contempt of the Senate or a Senatorial committee.

"Necessarily this is a matter for the Senate and the Senate alone."

For General Zwicker, a soldier decorated for gallantry in action, this was a day of vindication. The committee found Senator McCarthy's treatment of him as "reprehensible" and censurable.

The Watkins committee found nothing to criticize in the soldier's conduct when he appeared before Senator McCarthy in New York last Feb. 18. On that occasion the general pleaded that a Presidential directive prohibited him from giving certain information about Maj. Irving Peress, a dentist denounced by Senator McCarthy as a "Fifth Amendment Communist."

Fails to Find 'Arrogance'

Moreover, the committee said, it had failed to detect any "arrogance" in General Zwicker, as Mr. McCarthy had charged, when the general was cross-examined in the investigation on the very matters that Senator McCarthy had raised in New York. The committee asserted that Senator McCarthy had subjected the general to an "unfair" examination, using "long hypothetical questions," and questions that were "not clear even upon careful inspection and reflection."

"Senator McCarthy knew that General Zwicker was a loyal and outstanding officer who had devoted his life to the service of his country," the committee said, "that General Zwicker was cooperative and helpful to the staff of the [McCarthy] subcommittee in giving information with reference to Major Peress, that General Zwicker opposed the Peress promotion and opposed the giving to him of an honorable discharge, and that he was testifying under the restrictions of lawful executive orders.

"Under these circumstances, the conduct of Senator McCarthy toward General Zwicker in reprimanding and ridiculing him, in holding him up to public scorn and contumely, and in disclosing the proceedings of the executive session [of the New York hearing] in violation of the rules of his own committee, was inexcusable."

Sees No 'Wrongful Intent'

The Watkins committee said under Category II that it had concluded not to recommend censure on the charge that he had incited Federal employees to bring him information.

"The select committee," said the report, "is convinced that the invitation so made, affirmed and reasserted by Senator McCarthy was motivated by a sense of official duty and not uttered as the fruit of evil design or wrongful intent."

The committee had found, however, that his televised appeal for data was susceptible of being construed to mean secret defense data as well as unclassified information. The committee commented it felt justified in giving Senator McCarthy the benefit of the latter or "more charitable construction."

It warned Federal employees they risked prosecution if they followed his advice by handing over classified information. And the committee criticized Senator McCarthy for not "expressly excluding" classified information in the televised

incident of the Army-McCarthy hearings, asserting that without this exclusion Senator McCarthy "tends to create a disruption of the orderly and constitutional functioning of the Executive and Legislative Branches of the Government, which tends to bring both into disrepute. Such conduct cannot be condoned and is deemed improper."

The Category III charges that Senator McCarthy made unlawful use of the mysterious intelligence document containing F. B. I. data likewise were not found censurable. The committee said, however, that Senator McCarthy had "committed grave error" in offering to make its contents public.

Before the Watkins committee Senator McCarthy declared that certain deletions in the document had made it unclassified and he demanded again that it be made public. But the committee agreed with the opinion of Attorney General Herbert Brownell Jr. that the paper did contain national security information.

The pending resolution of censure contains forty-six charges against Senator McCarthy, many of them duplicating, but the Watkins committee decided to hold hearings only on thirteen divided into five categories. Today the committee reported its reasons for eliminating most of them.

All of the charges were listed as well as the reasons given for ignoring them. For instance, the committee said that even if fully supposrted some charges would not be censurable. Some were deemed "to vague and uncertain," some would have required more time to investigate than the committee could afford under the terms of the resolution requiring a report before the Senate finally adjourned for this session.

McCarthy Comment Quoted

CHICAGO, Sept. 27 (AP)—The Chicago Tribune said tonight Senator McCarthy had made this comment of the committee's recommendation that he be censured by the Senate:

"If the Senate upholds this report and all its implications, it will have gone a long way toward abdication of its constitutional right to investigate wrong doings in the Executive departments.

"I do not care whether I am censured or not, but I will fight against establishing a precedent which will curb investigative power and assist any Administration in power to cover up its misdeeds."

The Tribune said in a dispatch from Washington that Mr. McCarthy made the statement at the Bethesda (Md.) Naval Hospital, where he was undergoing treatment for a chronic sinus condition.

*　*　*

October 3, 1954

LONDON CONFEREES SETTLE ALL DIFFERENCES ON ARMING AND GERMANS' SOVEREIGNTY

BONN ENDS CRISIS

Adenauer Promises Not to Build Atomic or Chemical Weapons

By DREW MIDDLETON
Special to The New York Times.

LONDON, Sunday, Oct. 3— All outstanding differences on the arming of West Germany and on the Federal Republic's sovereignty were resolved early this morning when the nine-power conference completed its deliberations.

The foreign ministers will meet again later in the day to approve and sign a final protocol for the conference, which will reveal the historic decisions taken during the five-day meeting.

A communique said that methods had been found to resolve the difficulties over the control of armaments.

These difficulties arose from the French desire for strict restrictions on West German armament industries and they were solved largely by a voluntary renunciation of German rights to the production of atomic bacteriological or chemical weapons, jet bombers and fighters and guided missiles—in other words, all unconventional weapons.

Agreement was reached on other outstanding issues, the communique added. United States Secretary of State John Foster Dulles, British Foreign Secretary Anthony Eden, Chancellor Konrad Adenauer of West Germany and the French Premier, Pierre Mendès-France, completed their work on German sovereignty, the communique said.

To Liquidate Occupation

It is expected that a declaration of intent pledging the Allies to the liquidation of the occupation of Germany, once agreement on their reserved powers has been worked out, will be part of the protocol to be signed tomorrow.

Paul-Henri Spaak, Belgian Foreign Minister, as he left the conference, said that of the nine powers in the conference "the most generous was England and that is a great victory for England."

Before the final protocol is signed the ministers will also approve the report of a working group on armaments control. A draft of this report, resolving differences on this issue between France and the eight other powers—the United States, Britain, Canada, Italy, West Germany, Belgium, the Netherlands and Luxembourg—has been approved in principle.

The "serious crisis" over control of West German armaments manufacture was met by a series of concessions, the most important of which was volunteered by Dr. Adenauer, according to an authoritative United States source.

As a result of yesterday's agreement in principle it is believed that the conference will salvage a large part of what United States policy sought through the European Defense Community treaty.

French Ratification Seen

It is now expected that West Germany's admission to the North Atlantic Treaty Organization will be ratified by the French National Assembly and that the armament of the Federal Republic can begin soon after the first of the year.

In the interval an expanded and revised Brussels Treaty Organization, backed by British military power to a hitherto unheard of degree, and including West Germany and Italy, will take shape as the core of European political and military unity.

Although West German sovereignty must await the completion of the detailed redrafting of the Bonn conventions, the United States, Britain and France will issue in the near future a declaration of intent to liquidate the occupation and will instruct their High Commissioners not to use their powers save in consultation with the Federal Government.

The arming of West Germany under the North Atlantic Treaty Organization, which was the objective of the conference, has almost been overshadowed in the eyes of United States diplomats by the "invaluable" asset of a powerful British military commitment to the defense of Europe.

The German concession, which broke the stalemate, was accompanied by a voluntary declaration by Dr. Adenauer that the Federal Republic had no intention whatsoever of building any atomic, biological or chemical weapons.

In support of his European approach, Dr. Adenauer added that West Germany would agree to restrictions on production of heavy weapons, tanks, heavy artillery and submarines if the other continental members of the Brussels Treaty Organization would accept similar restrictions.

With the support of Belgium and the Netherlands this proposal won general acceptance and this ended the argument over control of such weapons by delimiting the geographical areas in which they could be manufactured. The idea of geographic restrictions has now been dropped.

Members of the United States delegation are ascribing the success of the conference, first to Mr. Eden's offer of a British commitment on Wednesday, and, second, to Dr. Adenauer's move yesterday.

European diplomats who have read the European Defense Community treaty point out, however, that Dr. Adenauer's concessions equal just about what West Germany had originally surrendered under Article 107, Annexes one and two, of that treaty.

The French delegation was less satisfied than the German with the results of yesterday's sessions, two of which were restricted to a Minister and one adviser from each of the nine nations. But M. Mendès-France will support the compromise solution before the French Assembly, authoritative French sources said.

M. Mendès-France, who has been suffering from a heavy cold all week, left the Conference last evening and is in bed.

At the final meeting of the day, which began at 10 P. M., the French delegation was led by Rene Massigli, the Ambassador in London and Roland de Moustier, secretary of the French Ministry of Foreign Affairs.

The conflict that stalled the conference Friday was between a French plan for control of arms manufacture through an international agency with the widest powers to plan and guide production programs and to let contracts, and a less elaborate plan submitted by M. Spaak.

As a result of yesterday's compromise the arms production of the continental members of the expanded Brussels Treaty Organization—West Germany, Italy, the Netherlands, Belgium, Luxembourg and France—will be controlled by the council of the Brussels Treaty Organization.

M. Spaak appeared at the first session yesterday with various amendments to his plan intended to meet French objections to it and to bring his proposals and those of M. Mendès-France closer together.

But it was not until Dr. Adenauer's statement that the situation began to improve. The Chancellor's surrender on the issue of the manufacture of weapons does not involve small arms, machine guns, mortars and light artillery.

Although the possibility of last minute snags is acknowledged by all diplomats, agreements in principle now have been reached on a new European structure.

This does not include all the elements of the European Defense Community Treaty rejected by the French National Assembly on Aug. 30 but this drawback is more than offset, in the American view, by the active participation of Britain, which was not a member of the European Defense Community.

Strength of Bonn Forces

West Germany will be armed under the North Atlantic Treaty Organization. The strength of the forces contributed by the Federal Republic will be those envisaged under the European Defense Community treaty: twelve army divisions, an air force of about 1,000 planes and a small navy for coastal defense.

Control of these forces will be delegated to Gen. Alfred M. Gruenther, Supreme Allied Commander in Europe whose responsibilities will be widened when the NATO ministerial council meets in Paris later this month. This council also will fix the minimum forces to be contributed by the Germans while the Brussels Treaty Organization will set the maximum figures.

The United States delegation anticipates that the admission of West Germany to NATO will have to be presented to the Senate as a protocol to the North Atlantic Treaty. This process probably also will have to be carried out in other NATO capitals. But although there are some doubts about M. Mendès-France's ability to win approval of the French National Assembly before the first of the year, the Germans are jubilantly counting on starting their defense contribution early in the new year.

One of the real achievements of the conference, in the view of the United States delegation, has been the expansion of the Brussels Treaty Organization, which will provide a hard core in Europe for NATO in the form of an organization that includes a sovereign armed West Germany.

Although the Brussels Treaty Organization does not include some of the supranational aspects of the European Defense Community treaty, it does fit United States objectives in Europe to a large extent.

It is pointed out that action by its council can be taken by less than a unanimous vote on important matters and that by accepting this Britain has surrendered some of her cherished independence of action.

The British pledge of four divisions and a tactical air force to continental defense is regarded by the United States delegation as "the major contribution" to the success of the conference. The pledge is to the Brussels Treaty Organization, which has a fixed lifetime of forty-four years more and after that may be extended indefinitely.

One United States delegate said that this British action represented far more than Mr. Dulles expected to get when he came to London last Sunday.

The background to the British action and Dr. Adenauer's contribution is the willingness of the United States to continue support of any structure that promises European political and military unity. There are many ends to be tied up before the work of the conference is completed, the delegates agree.

For instance, the Bonn Conventions, under which West German sovereignty was to be established, will have to be revised and amended to meet the new situation.

The important aspects of these amendments are the reservation to the three occupation powers of their rights in Berlin, on the writing of a German peace treaty and the unification of the country and the stationing of their forces in Germany for the defense of Europe.

* * *

October 7, 1954

MOLOTOV PROPOSES BIG 4 CONFERENCE TO UNIFY GERMANY

Implies He Might Consider the Allies' Plan for Free Nation-Wide Elections

ASKS EXIT OF ALL TROOPS

Bid, Made in the Soviet Zone, Seen as Move to Stall Bonn Armament Accord

By M. S. HANDLER
Special to The New York Times.

BONN, Germany, Oct. 6—The Soviet Union proposed tonight an immediate four-power conference to reunify, neutralize and evacuate Germany.

Vyacheslav M. Molotov, Soviet Foreign Minister, who made the proposal, hinted that he was prepared to discuss the British-French-United States demand for free, unfettered elections.

He announced the new proposals at an East Berlin rally on the eve of the fifth anniversary of the founding of the Communist German Democratic Republic.

The proposals constituted the principal elements of the Soviet Government's new political and diplomatic offensive against the decision to arm West Germany—a decision that was first embodied in the defunct European Defense Community treaty and then carried over into last Sunday's nine-power agreement in London.

A two-fold aim was suspected in the Soviet Government's shift on the German question. The first was to lower the price of Germany's reunification. However, in making this offer Mr. Molotov warned the West Germans that they would forego forever the reunification of their country if they entered into a Western alliance.

Political Disturbance Sought

The second aim seemed to be to create such a political disturbance in West Germany that the United States, Britain and France would be obliged to go into another four-power conference. If Mr. Molotov's proposals were accepted at such a conference the Western defensive system in Europe would have to be dismantled and ultimately the United States would be expelled from Western Europe.

Mr. Molotov was flanked by the Communist rulers of West Germany and European Soviet satellite states when he spoke.

"The Soviet Government declares today that it proposes anew to the government of the United States, Britain and France to conclude an agreement on the withdrawal of the occupation troops from both East and West Germany and to solve this question immediately without delay," he said.

Mr. Molotov added that the failure of the European army project made it possible to "bring nearer to each other the points of view of the four powers on free all-German elections."

"For its part the Soviet Government expresses readiness to discuss the proposals made at the Berlin conference by the participants, as well as possible new proposals on the question of free all-German elections," he said.

At the Berlin conference early this year the Western Big Three insisted on free all-German elections as a precondition for organizing the regime of a reunified Germany.

Mr. Molotov's statements on voting therefore mean that the Soviet Government is prepared to re-examine the proposals of the Western powers that Mr. Molotov had rejected in Berlin or examine new proposals along the same lines.

Mr. Molotov hinted broadly that as a result of the defeat of the European Defense Community treaty, the Soviet Government was prepared to abandon its stand against free elections.

Mr. Molotov accompanied his overture, addressed ostensibly to the West Germans, with predictions of dire consequences if they refused to heed his advice. He said that if the nine-power London agreement to arm West Germany were carried out "the restoration of German unity would become impossible and there would be dangerous consequences for the peace of Europe."

The nature of the first of these consequences was clear: the permanent partition of Germany into two states, one allied to the West and the other to the East. The Soviet Foreign Minister did not elaborate on what he meant by "dangerous consequences for the peace in Europe."

In contrast to his warning about a rejection of his plan, Mr. Molotov said that if the Soviet proposals were accepted, they "would not only improve the lot of all Germans but also create better conditions for a rapprochment between East and West Germany and thereby indicate a willingness to lessen international tensions."

The Soviet Foreign Minister insisted that the basic problem for the German people was reunification and a peace treaty in agreement with the principles of the Potsdam Agreement. That agreement, signed in 1945, divided Germany into zones and provided for the control of Germany under a Council of Foreign Ministers.

The reference to the Potsdam agreement was made in passing and Mr. Molotov did not appear to lay great stress on this point.

Mr. Molotov repeatedly warned the West Germans that acceptance of the London nine-power agreement would remove the possibility of reuniting Germany. He asserted that the London negotiations were alien to the problem of German sovereignty.

He declared any plans to remilitarize Germany would be a threat to peace in Europe. Instead of emphasizing rearmament, the German people should concentrate their attention on reunifying their country, he repeated time and again.

Mr. Molotov reiterated the proposals made by Andrei Y. Vishinsky, chief Soviet delegate in the United Nations, for a package deal on disarmament and a ban on nuclear weapons, but the Soviet Foreign Minister added:

"However, one cannot propose a plan for restricting armaments and banning atomic weapons and at the same time pursue the remilitarization of West Germany. The one is not compatible with the other."

East Hailed, West Assailed

Mr. Molotov's speech was compounded of the usual elements found in Soviet speeches—long passages of praise for friends, diatribes against the enemy and finally, buried, a kernel of compromise.

He lavished praise on the East German regime, attacked Chancellor Konrad Adenauer but conceded that trade relations with West Germany had improved, said international tensions had declined somewhat but accused the Western powers of trying to create a war machine against the Soviet Union.

Mr. Molotov offered reunification at a fairly low price. Spelled out in detail the new Molotov plan held forth the hope to the Germans that they could reunify their country and choose any regime they desired on the basis of free elections. The price tag attached was that a reunified Germany must stand clear of any "entangling" alliances.

This type of solution was already well on the way to becoming a real issue in Germany. The Social Democratic party has plumped for a modified version of this solution. It has opposed the attempt to arm West Germany or integrate it in a Western alliance until every effort to negotiate a settlement with Moscow had been exhausted.

Some in Bonn Favor Talks

The Right-Wing and moderate politicians of Chancellor Adenauer's own coalition have been speaking openly of the necessity of talking with the Soviet Union on the problem of reunification.

The West German Bundestag will debate the London nine-power agreement tomorrow. Dr. Adenauer received a cool reception yesterday when he reported to the lower house on the results of the London conference. Mr. Molotov's offer will hang like a thick black cloud over the Bundestag when it convenes tomorrow.

The immediate impact of the Soviet proposal may not be immediately apparent in tomorrow's debate. The parties will take some time to digest the meaning and implications of the Soviet overture.

But judging by the private reactions of officials, both German and foreign, in Bonn tonight it was quite apparent that the Soviet proposal, coming at this time, had been a rude shock.

* * *

October 23, 1954

ATLANTIC COUNCIL APPROVES NEW EUROPEAN UNION TIES

Also Agrees Supreme Commander Should Have New Power—Links Its Members to 3-Nation Pledge to Protect Berlin

---

By THOMAS F. BRADY
Special to The New York Times.

PARIS, Oct. 22—The North Atlantic Council put together today the design for bringing to life the new Western European Union and adding the strength of a sovereign West Germany to the North Atlantic alliance.

The steps the council took were:

1. To approve the provisions of the Brussels Treaty linking the Western European Union and the North Atlantic Treaty Organization.
2. To agree on a protocol to the North Atlantic Treaty inviting West Germany to join the alliance.
3. To adopt a resolution strengthening the powers of the Supreme Allied Commander in Europe and reinforcing the collective military system.
4. To associate all fourteen Atlantic alliance powers with a declaration made in London by Britain, France and the United States calling the West German Federal Republic "the only freely and legitimately constituted" government in Germany and affirming that "they will treat any attack against Berlin from any quarter as an attack upon their forces and themselves."

The day's work, accomplished in a ninety-minute session broken by a one-hour recess, involved the consideration and approval of documents totaling more than 30,000 words.

The Council took note of documents approved earlier in the week by the foreign ministers of Britain, France, the United States and Germany granting West German sovereignty and formally ending the occupation.

It also considered all the documents approved at a nine-power meeting yesterday on the establishment of the Western European Union. That meeting was attended by the United States and Canada and the seven countries in the prospective union: France, Britain, the Netherlands, Luxembourg, Belgium, West Germany and Italy.

The resolution to strengthen the powers of the Supreme Allied Commander, Gen. Alfred M. Gruenther of the United States, would give him control over Allied supplies and logistic reserves on the Continent and the authority to direct where reserve supply dumps should be established. This, coupled with a new Atlantic pact plan for financing such dumps in rear areas, would give the Supreme Commander the power to prevent what had been called "a private war" by any member of the alliance.

Concession to French Seen

The resolution also recommended the integration of national forces into the Allied command at the level of the army group—a unit of at least 200,000 men—or at the level of the army—a unit of at least 100,000 men. It authorized the Supreme Commander to integrate smaller units into the Allied system where military efficiency permitted.

The latter provision is regarded as a concession to the French desire for low-level integration as a means of breaking up German forces. It is not expected to become operative, however, because Supreme Headquarters already has reported to the Council that integration below the army level is inefficient and that integration at the army group level is preferable.

The declaration on Berlin was designed to obviate any possible Soviet claim that the granting of sovereignty to West Germany would automatically terminate the partition of Berlin and necessitate the withdrawal of Allied troops.

The session culminated the work begun a little more than three weeks ago at the nine-power conference in London. John Foster Dulles, United States Secretary of State, called the achievement "an amazing demonstration of the ability of the statesmen here in Europe to distinguish between matters that were of primary importance and matters that were only of secondary importance."

Eden Praises Aid of U. S.

Sir Anthony Eden, British Foreign Secretary, paid tribute to the United States for "the ever-present background of continued helpfulness" and "the unselfish sharing of the burdens of this continent in these post-war years."

Dr. Konrad Adenauer, West German Chancellor and Foreign Minister, was admitted to the Atlantic council session as an observer.

When the business of the session was completed, the Council formed itself into a temporary committee of fifteen so that the West German Chancellor could be heard without setting a precedent.

He said the German people felt deeply the importance of the occasion and expressed their gratitude for the work that had been done to achieve the new alliance.

* * *

October 24, 1954

PROTOCOLS TO ARM BONN SIGNED; ADENAUER YIELDS ON THE SAAR; SOVIET ASKS FOUR-POWER PARLEY

15 NATIONS LINKED

Mendes-France Assents After a Last-Minute Victory in Paris

By HAROLD CALLENDER
Special to The New York Times.

PARIS, Oct. 23—The status of West Germany was changed today, and with it the face of Western Europe, through the signing by fifteen nations of protocols to three treaties.

A French-German agreement on the Saar, reached at what was almost literally the last moment, led the French Premier, Pierre Mendès-France, to sign all the protocols that he would otherwise have refused to sign.

When these protocols are ratified, which now seems certain in view of the French success on the Saar issue, the Bonn Republic will no longer be an occupied country but a sovereign and equal member of two Western alliances and a contributor to their military strength.

It will enter simultaneously the North Atlantic Treaty and the new Brussels Treaty Organization called the Western European Union. It will supply twelve divisions to the closely linked armies of the fifteen nations that will then belong to these two groups.

It will take its place as one of the major Western states, with a voice in their diplomatic relations with the Soviet Union as well as in their defense system.

Problem Is 6 Years Old

The problem of winning West Germany for the free world, with which statesmen have grappled desperately for about six years, will have been solved so far as treaties can solve it. The Bonn Republic will have "chosen freedom" in preference to the proffered alternative of a unified Germany nominally neutral but moving inevitably into the Soviet orbit.

Discussion with Moscow on the peace of Europe, which always centers in the German problem, can then take place on a new basis, since the unification of Germany in the manner so far proposed by Moscow will have been ruled out by West Germany itself—and West Germany is by far the greater of the two states into which the country is divided.

This is the result of four years of intensive and often embittered Western diplomacy, which began in September, 1930, when Dean Acheson, then United States Secretary of State, shocked the French by proposing to create ten West German divisions.

This addition to Western defenses was deemed urgent because of the Korean invasion the previous June, which had alarmed Washington regarding the immediate security of Europe as well as of Asia.

It did not appear urgent to the French, who feared and opposed any rearmament of Germans for reasons any student of recent history can cite. It took four years to persuade the French that the menace today was farther east, and that Germans must help safeguard the West—assuming they are now persuaded.

This French fear of turning any Germans into soldiers led to a long series of delays and conditions. One condition, thought up only last year, was a settlement of the Saar question.

At times in the last few days it looked as if this dispute might wreck or long defer the elaborate program drafted in London three weeks ago to settle the German problem. Close bargaining went on until midday today. But finally the West German Chancellor, Dr. Konrad Adenauer, agreed to most of the French demands.

The Saar will therefore remain detached from Germany and attached economically to France pending a peace treaty with Germany, when and if there is one. The industrial area will have a kind of "European status" under the guardianship of the Western European Union if the Saarlanders accept this in a popular referendum, which the French think they will do.

On the other hand, the pro-German parties, hitherto barred from Saar politics as enemies of the existing statute, will be free to campaign against the statute in the referendum and to take part in the elections to be held after its ratification. But they will not be free to agitate against it once it is adopted.

Dr. Adenauer made another notable concession to French fears. In a formal declaration that went into the record with the protocols, the Chancellor, on behalf of the Bonn Republic, understood that it would "never have recourse to force to achieve the reunification of Germany or the modification of the present frontiers of the German Federal Republic."

The Chancellor has been among the first to understand the French fears of German rearmament and to seek to allay them, believing this was as much in the interest of Germany as of France.

In the traditional Clock Room of the French Foreign Office, the foreign ministers of the United States, Britain, France and West Germany signed the protocol to the Bonn peace contract giving West Germany approximately full sovereignty. Under it Allied troops will remain by virtue of a convention giving West Germany's consent.

In the same gilded chamber, the foreign ministers of Britain, France, Belgium, the Netherlands and Luxembourg then signed the protocol inviting West Germany and Italy into the Brussels Treaty and additional protocols providing

WESTERN MINISTERS APPROVE PACT: This was scene as Britain, France, United States and West Germany signed agreement on Germany's sovereignty. At table are, from left, Chancellor Konrad Adenauer of Bonn Republic; Secretary of State Dulles; French Premier Pierre Mendès-France, and Sir Anthony Eden, British Foreign Secretary.

for an agency to inspect forces and armaments of the seven eventual members of that treaty.

Shortly afterward, in the Palais de Chaillot, where the North Atlantic Council had met, the foreign ministers of the fourteen members of this alliance signed an invitation to West Germany to join it. These ministers had adopted, along with the invitation, a resolution increasing the powers of the Supreme Commander of North Atlantic forces in Europe to permit him to integrate West German forces into his command and to exercise greater controls over the disposition and supplying of all his forces.

Thus there will be, both in the maximums for forces in the Brussels Treaty and in the additional controls of the Supreme Commander, limitations on both the size and the freedom of action of the new West German Army somewhat like those that would have been imposed in the defeated European Defense Community treaty. For the whole system, European and North Atlantic, authorized by today's signatures, was developed rapidly as a substitute for the defense community treaty, which was rejected by the French National Assembly Aug. 30.

These limitations apply to all the armies coming under the two treaties, since they cannot be discriminatory. But actually they were designed by assiduous planners to meet French

fears that once armed, whether in a European Army or not, the Germans might kick over the traces and use their troops for such national ends as those that Dr. Adenauer has undertaken that they will not seek by force.

Thus elaborate rules and devices have been created as safeguards against possible hostile or independent actions by a nation admitted into the Western alliance to strengthen it against a potential Soviet danger.

Nevertheless, the decisions formalized today represented a diplomatic victory for Dr. Adenauer in that they gave West Germany its sovereignty, including the right to arm, and brought it into the Western line-up, where he wanted it to be to remove any temptation for it to be drawn into an Eastern alliance.

They were a victory also for M. Mendès-France in that he not only contributed to the defeat of the European Defense Community treaty but promptly joined with the British and West German leaders in building a substitute acceptable even to the United States, which had long tended to hold that there could be no adequate substitute.

The French Premier maneuvered adroitly to give the appearance of a success to the French concession of admitting West Germany into the North Atlantic alliance—concession to which the French assembly had explicitly expressed its opposition and which it has not yet accepted, though it is expected to do so.

For M. Mendès-France partly covered up this concession by his triumph in getting Dr. Adenauer's agreement to surrender West German claims to the Saar for an indefinite period.

The French press these days has been full of the Saar problem and has said little about the entry of West Germany into NATO. Few Frenchmen know or care much about the Saar, but most of them are pleased by a diplomatic victory that other Foreign Ministers had long sought in vain.

Today's decisions represented a victory for Britain, too, for her Foreign Secretary, Sir Anthony Eden, had taken the first step toward them. After the defeat of the defense community plan he visited European capitals to propose bringing West Germany into the Brussels pact and NATO alike. He also persuaded his Government to agree to a commitment to keep troops on the Continent subject to the will of a majority of the seven Brussels Treaty nations.

Although today's operation was a European one, the result may be described as a victory for United States policy, for the United States took the initiative toward arming the West Germans and has long been busy seeking to insure by treaties that they should be tied inseparably with the West as a preliminary to any possible negotiations with Moscow on Germany.

* * *

April 17, 1955

ASIA-AFRICA TALKS START TOMORROW

Peace Held Aim of 29-Nation Parley—India Would Bar Formosa Issue in Sessions

By ROBERT ALDEN
Special to The New York Times.

BANDUNG, Indonesia, April 16—The stage was set today for Monday's opening session of the Asian-African conference.

Delegates representing 1,400,000,000 people—five-eighths of the world's population—have arrived in Indonesia for the conference.

As dusk was settling over Bandung's airfield, Prime Minister Jawaharal Nehru of India stepped from his plane and picked his way through rain puddles caused by a sudden cloudburst.

Mr. Nehru, as he arrived, indicated the Formosa question should not be brought up in the conference sessions. Indian delegates, however, are expected to seek a solution in informal talks outside the formal sessions.

Behind Mr. Nehru was U Nu, Prime Minister of Burma, with a bandana wrapped around his head in the manner of his country.

Pushed back by the crush of official greeters, Boy Scouts and shouting cameramen, was V. Krishna Menon, India's representative in the United Nations. He wore a white robe of homespun cloth that hung to his knees, and he carried a stick as he went around the puddles in sandals. Neglected in the wake of the two Prime Ministers, he seemed almost relieved when someone greeted him.

Egyptian Premier Greeted

Earlier the tall and immaculately uniformed Lieut. Col. Gamal Abdel Nasser, Premier of Egypt, had received the handshakes of Dr. Ali Sastroamidjojo, Premier of Indonesia, and the youthful Prince Norodom Sihanouk of Cambodia, who recently abdicated the throne of his country in favor of his father.

It was a colorful procession of leaders from two vast and often neglected continents who were now stepping into the focus of world attention. Their professed mission was to see that peace would prevail in the world.

One of the international figures who stepped off at the Bandung airport was Thailand's Foreign Minister, Prince Wan Waithayakon. The prince, a familiar figure at the United Nations, serve as one of the chairmen of the Geneva Conference on Asiatic Affairs and as a chairman of the recent Bangkok Conference, which implemented the Southeast Asia Collective Defense Treaty.

He expressed the hope that all would go well at the present conference and that it would make a substantial contribution to world peace and security and the economic well-being of the region.

Other delegations arriving today to attend the twenty-nine-nation meeting included those from Japan, Libya, the Sudan, Liberia and Ethiopia.

There were some uneasy moments during the day. Awkward silences appeared, for example, when Prince Norodom and the Indonesian Premier sat chatting in the airport tearoom. The prince is not altogether at home in English and exchanges on such commonplace subjects as the weather were sometimes strained.

There was another awkward moment when the Sudanese, Liberian and Ethiopian delegations stepped out of the same plane. Dr. Ali had difficulty sorting out just who was who, but in a moment or two everyone smiled pleasantly.

The conference is scheduled to get under way at 9 A. M. Monday with an address of welcome by President Sukarno of Indonesia. There will follow a series of twenty-minute speeches by each of the twenty-nine principal delegates to the conference. That will mean about ten hours of speeches, which should carry over into the second day. An agenda proposed by the five sponsoring powers—Indonesia, India, Ceylon, Burma and Pakistan—will also have to be voted upon, and a series of committees will be set up.

The conference is scheduled to conclude its work next Sunday, but an Indian member of the joint secretariat said today it would not surprise him if an additional day were needed to draft a final communiqué.

At the opening day's session all diplomatic missions to Indonesia, including that of the United States, will be invited, and Ambassador Hugh S. Cumming Jr. is now en route to Bandung from Jakarta to act as an observer at that session.

Chou En-lai Arrives

BANDUNG, Sunday, April 17 (Reuters)—Chou En-lai, Premier and Foreign Minister of Communist China, arrived in Bandung today to head his country's delegation to the conference.

* * *

April 24, 1955

CHOU ASKS FOR U. S. TALKS ON EASING FORMOSA CRISIS; WASHINGTON SETS TERMS

MOVE AT PARLEY

Premier Says Peiping Does Not Want War With This Country

By TILLMAN DURDIN
Special to The New York Times.

BANDUNG, Indonesia, April 23—Chou En-lai announced here today that Communist China was prepared to negotiate directly with the United States over Formosa and Far East questions in general.

A statement to this effect was released by the Premier of Communist China at the headquarters of the Asian-African conference. It came as the climax of a week of talk by Mr. Chou of peace and nonaggression and caused a sensation in conference quarters.

Prior to his public announcement, Mr. Chou disclosed at a luncheon his intention to propose United States-Red China talks.

He attended the luncheon with Dr. Ali Sastroamidjojo; Premier of Indonesia; Sir John Kotelawala, Prime Minister of Ceylon; Jawaharlal Nehru, Prime Minister of India; Brig. Gen. Carlos P. Romulo, chief delegate of the Philippines; Prince Wan Waithayakon, Foreign Minister of Thailand; Mohammed Ali, Prime Minister of Pakistan, and U Nu, Premier of Burma.

The luncheon was the materialization of a plan of Sir John, made public earlier this week, for convening the eight Asian leaders to discuss the possibility of a Formosa peace settlement.

'Friendly' to U. S. People

The eight officials returned from the luncheon to the conference headquarters at 4 P. M. and would say only that Mr. Chou would have an announcement. They then entered a closed meeting of the conference's political committee.

Two hours later the Chinese Premier and Foreign Minister sent a member of his delegation out of the meeting into the conference hall to pass his statement to correspondents.

The statement said:

"The Chinese people are friendly to the American people. The Chinese people do not want to have war with the United States of America. The Chinese Government is willing to sit down and enter into negotiations with the United States Government to dismiss the question of relaxing tension in the Far East and especially the question of relaxing tension in the Taiwan [Formosa] area."

The spokesman was reluctant to elaborate on the statement. However, he said the announcement meant "direct bilateral talks" and not a multipower conference of the type proposed for Formosa negotiations recently by the Soviet Union.

He said there was no plan to transmit the statement officially to Washington and added it would be circulated by the press and thus reach the United States Government.

General Romulo said the Chou government was not the product of discussions and a joint decision at the luncheon. He said the luncheon was marked by light conversation and afterward, at a brief talk between the eight men, Mr. Chou had stated his intention to make the announcement.

The Philippine official said he had been noncommittal since he had not been empowered by his Government to discuss Formosa. Prince Wan reportedly manifested a similar reaction but the Premiers of the Colombo powers voiced approval. The Colombo powers, so named because of a meeting at that Ceylon city in 1954, are India, Pakistan, Burma, Indonesia and Ceylon.

The announcement immediately became the top subject in conference circles. Most delegations felt the Red Chinese offer was a good move and opened up the possibility of a peaceful settlement of the Formosa issue. There were, however, dissents from this view among officials wary of Communist maneuvers.

The statement brought Mr. Chou's peace campaign here to its high point. It won for the Chinese Communists and the neutralists, headed by India, the dominant position in the conference atmosphere that had been established by the anti-Communist delegations.

Mr. Chou had timed his announcement astutely to come as the conference, now scheduled to terminate tomorrow evening, entered its final phase. He drew support among delegates by creating the feeling that a Formosa settlement might after all come from an Asian-African move.

Move Is Assessed

Observers here asserted that Mr. Chou's move could be mainly propaganda designed to appeal to Asian sentiment favoring an Asian solution of Asian problems and aimed at putting the United States in the position of accepting or rejecting an Asian initiative.

The United States has had few supporters here for a policy of fighting over the offshore China islands of Quemoy and Matsu and to this added to the favourable impact of Mr. Chou's gesture.

A source close to the Chinese Communist delegation said Peiping might agree to having Nationalist Chinese officials attend a Formosa conference as observed. The source admitted prospects were slim for a final Formosa settlement, but that a Red China-United States meeting might at least reach some arrangement that would diminish the likelihood of war.

Meanwhile, subcommittees engaged in drafting declarations of such subjects as racialism, colonialism, promotion of peace, Indochina, destructive uses of atomic energy and disarmament advanced to a stage today that permitted plans for closing the conference tomorrow evening.

The day was marked by continued clashes over the colonialism issue between the neutralist and Communist powers that wanted no allusions to the colonialist aspects of communism and the anti-Communist states that insisted on phrasing encompassing Communist domination and methods of infiltration and subversion.

It was during sessions of the committee of chief delegates discussing world peace that Mr. Chou engaged in extensive elaboration of Communist China's peaceful and friendly intentions toward other nations. He stated that all the world's problems could be settled peacefully, including his country's differences with the United States.

He dwelt at length on Peiping's desire to live in peace with Asian neighbors and made particular mention of Japan, the Philippines, Thailand, Laos and Cambodia.

Mr. Chou assured Prince Wan of Thailand that he could be "absolutely certain" Communist China would not attack Thailand and said although Peiping had no relations with Thailand he was eager to negotiate an agreement with Bangkok settling the question of the dual nationality of the 3,000,000 Thailand Chinese.

Similar Assurances Given

He gave similar assurances to Cambodia, Laos, the Philippines and Japan. He said at a dinner party last night he had emphasized Communist China's nonaggression aims to General Romulo and had asked him to transmit these promises to the Philippines President, Ramon Magsaysay.

The Communist Chinese Premier paid a tribute to Ichiro Hatoyama as the elected leader of the Japanese people and invited neighboring nations to send inspection teams to Communist China's borders to ascertain that no aggressive preparations were being made against them.

He said if neighboring peoples felt Communist China was not treating them correctly their complaints should be brought to him, and they would be settled.

Mr. Chou had a seven-point program for peace. The points covered respect for international boundaries, abstention from aggression and military threats, noninterference by one nation in the internal affairs of another, recognition of the equality of races and nations, respect for the rights of people to choose their own way of life and their own political and economic systems, a curb on nuclear and bacteriological weapons and an arms truce combined with peaceful use of atomic energy and the reduction of armaments by the great powers.

He offered the program as a change from his five principles of coexistence, but defended these by saying that Prime Minister Sir Anthony Eden of Britain, according to information given him by Mr. Nehru, had expressed approval of the principles. He said he would be delighted to join Sir Anthony in a statement on the principles.

The Five Principles

The five principles are respect for the national sovereignty and integrity of all nations, renunciation of intervention or interference in the territory or internal affairs of other nations, mutual cooperation for the promotion of mutual interest, recognition of the equality of races and nations, large and small, and non-aggression.

Mr. Chou denied charges of Communist aggression through infiltration and subversion.

He warned nations against joining regional groupings against Communist China. These, he said, would cause China to seek the support of likeminded nations and thus tensions would be increased.

General Romulo of the Philippines and Dr. Fadhil al-Jamali of Iraq made vigorous rejoinders to Mr. Nehru's condemnation yesterday of Asian and African nations for joining defense pacts. Dr. Jamali said there were only two ways of facing a threat of aggression—by preparation to resist and passiveness—and stated he unhesitatingly chose the former. He said it would require impressive evidence of a Communist change of heart in this respect to justify Western nations in abandoning a policy of "peace through strength."

General Romulo answered Mr. Nehru's criticisms of the Manila pact by declaring it was purely defensive.

* * *

May 14, 1955

WARSAW NATIONS APPROVE TREATY

8 in East Europe to Sign Pact Today—Unified Military Command Endorsed

By CLIFTON DANIEL
Special to The New York Times.

WARSAW, May 13—After sitting for only eight hours in three days the Warsaw conference of the East European Communist states came to a quick end today. At a thirty-minute session the delegates representing eight governments approved the final text of a military treaty that they will sign tomorrow.

They also give their formal approval to a decision to establish a unified command for the military forces that they will contribute to the new alliance.

Tomorrow the treaty will be signed at a formal ceremony here and the structure of the new command will be announced, probably along with the name of the commander in chief.

Once the eight chiefs of government have put their signatures to the pact, Vyacheslav M. Molotov, the Soviet Foreign Minister, is expected to leave Warsaw for Vienna. There he will meet the Foreign Ministers of France, Britain and the United States.

The time of the Soviet Foreign Minister's departure has not been announced, but he has agreed to be in the Austrian capital for informal talks with Secretary of State Dulles, Foreign Secretary Harold Macmillan and Foreign Minister Antoine Pinay tomorrow. The four ministers will sign the Austrian state treaty Sunday.

Genuine Issue Lacking

After the Warsaw treaty signing ceremony a mass meeting will be held on one of the main squares here, an organized demonstration in favor of the decisions of the Warsaw conference.

The brevity of the working sessions of the Warsaw conference, which started Wednesday, showed that there was no real issue to be resolved here.

As long ago as last Dec. 2 the eight powers—the Soviet Union, Poland, Czechoslovakia, Hungary, Rumania, Bulgaria, Albania and East Germany—proclaimed at the end of a conference in Moscow their intention to conclude a new pact in case the Western powers' Paris agreements for arming West Germany were ratified.

While the Soviet Union was exerting serious diplomatic efforts to prevent ratification, preliminary negotiations on the terms of the new Eastern alliance proceeded. The pact was all but ready for signature before the Warsaw conference convened.

The purpose of the conference obviously was only to proclaim the alliance with a flourish of publicity. Most of the four sittings were taken up with speeches by the senior delegates, all chiefs of Government. The most important of them, Premier Nikolai A. Bulganin of the Soviet Union, told the other delegates that they would have to face the fact that the Paris agreements would take effect.

The "treaty of friendship, co-operation and aid" that the eight will sign tomorrow will create an Eastern counterpart of the North Atlantic Treaty Organization, whose council sat recently in Paris.

Pact to Be Left Open

The treaty not only will provide for mutual assistance in the case of military aggression against one of the signatories but also will contain clauses on political, social and economic co-operation.

The pact will be left open to adherence by non-Communist Governments. This feature is being offered as proof that the Eastern powers do not wish to create a new military bloc but rather a universal security system open to all.

If such a system ever is established, the treaty will say, the alliance formed at Warsaw will be dissolved.

Like the NATO countries, the eight Communist states will not commit their entire armed forces to the joint command but will contribute only specified contingents.

There already exists a network of treaties among the eight Governments represented here. However, the delegates have declared that they do not constitute a sufficient safeguard against the "revival of German militarism."

* * *

May 15, 1955

SOVIET ACCEPTS WEST'S BID TO TOP-LEVEL BIG 4 PARLEY; AUSTRIA GETS PACT TODAY

TREATY APPROVED

Foreign Ministers Omit Clause on War Guilt, Back Neutrality

By JOHN MacCORMAC
Special to The New York Times.

VIENNA, May 14—The Big Four foreign ministers approved tonight the Austrian state treaty after having deleted from its preamble the clause implying Austrian war guilt.

They will sign the treaty in a formal sitting tomorrow.

The treaty mentioned but did not decide what form Austrian neutrality would take in the future and whether it and Austria's inviolability would be guaranteed by the four occupation powers.

Vyacheslav M. Molotov, Soviet Foreign Minister, proposed that the Governments of the U.S.S.R., the United States, the United Kingdom and the French Republic hereby declare that the Soviet Union, the United States, Great Britain and France shall respect and observe a statement of Austrian permanent neutrality of the kind observed by Switzerland in its relations with other cities.

The three Western foreign ministers said they had no objection to this in principle, but that they would prefer to await the form and text of Austria's declaration of neutrality. Austrian Foreign Minister Leopold Figl then declared that he had with him a proposal for Austria's neutrality. It was distributed to the four foreign delegations.

Austria's Neutrality Stand

The proposal takes the form of a resolution of the Austrian National Council asking the federal Government to submit to it a constitutional law to declare Austria's perpetual neutrality.

As a result, Austria, according to the resolution, would join no military alliances and would not permit the establishment of military bases of foreign states on her territory.

Austria would declare her desire to observe the principles laid down in the United Nations Charter for her relations with other states. She would take steps to achieve admission to the United Nations.

She would inform all states with which she has diplomatic relations of her declaration of neutrality and request its recognition. She would do this after her state treaty takes effect and her territory has been evacuated by the occupation armies.

Mr. Molotov read five paragraphs of the Moscow understanding of April 15 in which Austria undertook to declare her neutrality and agreed not to join military alliances or permit the establishment of military bases on her soil. He cited the Austrians' promise to ask for a guarantee of neutrality.

It is also expected that Austria in due course will ask for some form of guarantee of inviolability of her territory.

Secretary of State Dulles proposed that United States Ambassador Llewellyn E. Thompson Jr. sign the state treaty tomorrow along with himself, and the other foreign ministers agreed this procedure should be adopted in their own case.

The war guilt clause dropped from the preamble of the state treaty on Herr Figl's proposal read:

"Whereas following this annexation Austria as an integral part of Hitlerite Germany participated in the war against the Allied and the associated powers and other United Nations and whereas Germany made use for this purpose of Austrian territory troops and material resources and Austria cannot avoid certain responsibility arising from this participation in the war."

Diplomats Greet Molotov

Mr. Molotov arrived at the Russian military and civil airport at Voslau at 2:30 P. M. in a two-engine Soviet plane. He was greeted by Foreign Minister Figl, Soviet Ambassador Ivan I. Ilyichev, V. C. Vigaya Ragavan, Indian Charge d'Affaires in Vienna, and Ambassadors of the Soviet satellites.

Behind an earthwork could be seen the tails of two Russian MIG-17's. But the only Russian soldiers in sight were those who operated the ground-control station for the airport. This consisted of a table draped with a modern Russian cover with a glaring design. The table rested on a costly Persian rug spread on the grass and bore three Russian field telephones. Four Russian officers manned these while two others, undisturbed by the glare of camera flash bulbs, played a careful game of chess.

But despite the presence of two men of the M. V. D. type in plain clothes who kept their right hands in their pockets, security was provided by Austrian, not Russian, police. There was also an honor guard of gendarmerie, commanded appropriately enough by Major Ferdinand Kaes. Major Kaes was being attacked by a section of the Vienna press a few months ago for having been the first officer of the Austrian Army to get in contact with the advancing Soviet forces on April 2, 1945, in an effort to save Vienna from bombardment.

Figl Hails the Signing

"When you meet the other foreign ministers tomorrow to sign the state treaty," Herr Figl said to Mr. Molotov, "you will fill not only Austria but the whole world with hopeful pleasure. You come with the other foreign ministers as a real liberator."

Mr. Molotov, small, gray and as precise as ever, read a prepared statement in Russian that said:

"Negotiations took place in Moscow a month ago with the Austrian Government with which preparations for the conclusion of the Austrian state treaty came to an end.

"Now also complete agreement has been reached with the Governments of the United States, Great Britain and France. Thus Austria becomes an independent sovereign state."

The route along which Mr. Molotov proceeded from the airfield to Vienna was dotted with gendarmes and lined with people, some of whom waved red flags. Although, or perhaps because, the route lay through the Russian-occupied part of Lower Austria, enthusiasm seemed less in degree than that with which United States Secretary of State Dulles was greeted yesterday as he drove from Tulln Airfield to the capital.

* * *

July 10, 1955

NINE NOTED SCIENTISTS URGE WAR BAN

Warning on Nuclear Peril Was Signed by Einstein

By PETER D. WHITNEY
Special to The New York Times.

LONDON, July 9—Nine eminent scientists, including the late Albert Einstein, have appealed to the nations to forswear war because the hydrogen bomb threatens "the continued existence of mankind."

Bertrand Russell, British mathematician and philosopher, revealed today that Einstein subscribed to the appeal in a letter that reached London the day the physicist died in Princeton, N. J., April 18.

The appeal called on other scientists, in both the Communist and non-Communist worlds, to join in a conference. Its object would be to drive home to the average man the "very real danger of the extermination of the human race by dust and rain from radioactive clouds."

Among the signers were seven Nobel Prize winners. One of them, Prof. Leopold Infeld of Warsaw University, is behind the Iron Curtain. Another, Prof. Frédéric Joliot-Curie of France, is well known as a Communist sympathizer.

The American signers, besides Einstein, were Prof. Percy W. Bridgman, physicist of Harvard, and Prof. Hermann J. Muller, geneticist of Indiana University, both Nobel Prize winners.

Lord Russell today sent copies of the statement to President Eisenhower, Premier Nikolai A. Bulganin of the Soviet Union, Prime Minister Eden of Britain, President René Coty of France, Mao Tse-tung, Chinese Communist leader, and Prime Minister Louis S. St. Laurent of Canada—the heads of countries that have acquired or will eventually acquire nuclear armaments.

Lord Russell said the campaign by the scientists grew out of a broadcast he gave here last Dec. 23 on the nuclear peril. He received many letters of congratulation, among them one from Professor Joliot-Curie.

"I was pleased, because he is not only an eminent scientist but a noted Communist," Lord Russell said at a press conference today. The letter encouraged him to try to bridge differences between the Communist and anti-Communist worlds by an appeal to the scientists, "who understand the great danger."

Lord Russell was a pacifist in World War I, but in 1949 he said he would prefer a third war with atomic bombs to world domination by the Soviet Union. He made clear today his views had changed only in that he considered nuclear weapons had made the atomic bomb "like bows and arrows."

He said he wrote to Einstein suggesting that scientists "do something dramatic" and got wholehearted approval. The ailing physicist nominated Lord Russell to be "dictator of the enterprise" and signed the letter when it was sent to him before the others.

The letter was sent to eighteen scientists, of whom seven more agreed. Others were unwilling to sign because they held official posts but they were sympathetic. Prof. Dimitry V. Skobeltzyn of Moscow gave a friendly but noncommittal reply. Others, including China's Prof. Li Sze-Kuang, did not answer.

Professor Joliot-Curie's letter, last to arrive, contained a reservation limiting the ban on war to its use "as means of settling differences between states." This was construed by Lord Russell as intended by Professor Joliot-Curie to preserve the right of internal revolution.

Professor Muller also entered a reservation making plain that disarmament should not be solely in nuclear weapons but a balanced reduction "of all armaments."

Asked if he did not fear that his campaign might be exploited by the Communists, Lord Russell said he was sure he could prevent that.

"Their line is to prohibit the bomb," he said. "I am not in favor of prohibition, but of making it quite clear what will happen if it is used."

The scientists' appeal says the hope for safety by prohibition is "illusory." It argues that both sides would consider agreements no longer binding when war broke out and would set to work to manufacture hydrogen bombs. The only solution, it declared, is the abolition of war itself.

The significance of the adherence by Professor Joliot-Curie and Professor Infeld to a statement so thoroughly at variance with the Communist line of the last ten years was being discussed today.

Lord Russell said the statement meant that all nine signers dissented from the official estimates put forward in the United States of the limited danger of radioactivity. He said he thought "some" of these had been "not strictly accurate."

The statement declared that "the best authorities are unanimous in saying that a war with H-bombs might quite possibly put an end to the human race."

"Here, then," the statement declared, "is the problem which we present to you, stark and dreadful, and inescapable: shall we put an end to the human race: or shall mankind renounce war?"

* * *

July 22, 1955

EISENHOWER CALLS UPON SOVIET TO EXCHANGE ARMS BLUEPRINTS; ASKS MUTUAL AERIAL INSPECTION

ACTION NOW URGED

President Says Accord Would Ease Fears—3 Others Offer Plans

By ELIE ABEL
Special to The New York Times.

GENEVA, July 21—President Eisenhower proposed here today that the Soviet Union and the United States exchange complete blueprints of their military establishments and open both countries to unlimited aerial inspection by each other's planes.

The President addressed his dramatic proposal directly to the leaders of the Soviet Union at the afternoon session of the Big Four heads of government in the Palace of Nations, their fifth formal meeting. Turning to Marshal Nikolai A. Bulganin, Soviet Premier, and Nikita S. Khrushchev, First Secretary of the Soviet Communist party, President Eisenhower said:

"Our two great countries admittedly possess new and terrible weapons in quantities which do give rise in other parts of the world or reciprocally to the fears and dangers of surprise attack.

"I propose therefore that we take a practical step, that we begin an arrangement very quickly, as between ourselves—immediately."

President Outlines Steps

He then outlined these steps for lessening the danger that one of the two powers would attack the other and plunge the world into war:

• Each should give the other a complete blueprint of its military establishments "from one end of our countries to the other," he said.

• Each should allow the other's reconnaissance planes to "make all the pictures you choose and take them to your own country to study," he added. This step would "convince the world that we are providing as between ourselves against the possibility of a great surprise attack, thus lessening danger and relaxing tensions."

This was the heart of the President's proposal. It was not only controversial in itself but the method by which it was presented caused considerable discussion in Geneva late tonight.

It was reported that the five key paragraphs had been delivered extempore. Several high United States officials indicated the text they had seen beforehand did not contain the two-point plan.

There were various explanations, none of them official. One was that the aerial inspection idea had been in the President's mind for some time and that he decided to break it out after an opening speech by Marshal Bulganin, who presided at today's meeting.

Another theory was that the President fully intended to make these points but did not want to risk their leaking out by having the text in the hands of delegation clerks before he delivered the speech.

[A dispatch from Washington late Thursday night said the Joint Chiefs of Staff, with the approval of Charles E. Wilson, Secretary of Defense, had made the basic decision to exchange military data with the Soviet Union.]

At any rate the President's plan that the United States and the Soviet Union act immediately without waiting for a general disarmament agreement was received with enthusiasm by Edgar Faure, French Premier, and endorsed also by Sir Anthony Eden, British Prime Minister.

Whether Marshal Bulganin had anything to say about President Eisenhower's proposal was today's minor mystery in Geneva. British and United States spokesman said he had listened in silence. Leonid F. Ilyichev, Soviet spokesman said, but did not attribute the statement to his Premier, that the "frank declaration" on disarmament made around the great four-sided table this afternoon by all four heads of government would have "a great significance for the examination of this point in the future."

Pierre Baraduc, French spokesman was alone in reporting that Marshal Bulganin had described President Eisenhower's speech as a "sincere statement" that would have a "wide effect" and provided a "good augury" for a discussion of the disarmament question.

The French Premier said skepticism was the principal enemy of disarmament. If the peoples of the world could have listened to President Eisenhower they would have realized that July 21 was the day of the great change when the Geneva conference saw its first "victory over skepticism," M. Faure declared.

Sir Anthony, though more reserved, said had been deeply moved by the President's sincerity and hailed the proposal as a far-reaching one. The Prime Minister said that if adopted it would make a striking contribution to confidence among nations.

Four Proposals Presented

President Eisenhower's proposal was one of four presented or restated at today's session.

M. Faure elaborated the plan he outlined for the first time at a news conference in Paris, July 13, and repeated in his opening statement in Geneva Monday for arms reduction under budgetary controls and application of the money thus saved to an international fund for assistance to the underdeveloped areas.

He advocated making public, as means of building confidence in the world, the military levels of all countries and the amounts they were spending on armaments. Such a policy would banish the shadows surrounding arms levels before their reduction, M. Faure suggested.

Sir Anthony put before the conference a plan he described as modest and experimental for the establishment of a demil-

itarized belt for an agreed distance on either side of the Iron Curtain. A mixed inspection team drawn from the East and the West would supervise compliance in the area.

The Prime Minister emphasized there was no conflict between this plan and the proposals he made yesterday for reduction of forces and the creation of a demilitarized area in Germany. He said the plan remained dependent on the reunification of Germany.

Marshal Bulganin produced a plan of his own, identical in its general provisions with the Soviet disarmament proposal of May 10 before the United Nations Disarmament Subcommittee in London.

A feature of the Bulganian proposal today was a provision that the Soviet Union, the United States, Britain and France pledge themselves not to use nuclear weapons, except when the United Nations Security Council had established that an act of aggression had taken place. This was presented by Marshal Bulganin as an interim measure pending the conclusion of an international convention to reduce armaments and prohibit atomic weapons.

M. Faure proposed—and the other heads of government agreed—that the foreign ministers study all four proposals and prepare a directive for a conference of their own in the autumn, at which actual negotiation would be attempted now that the issues had been defined.

The foreign ministers, who met separately in the morning, are at work now on a similar directive to deal with the interlocked questions of European security and German reunification.

Foreign Chiefs Ask Delay

They were scheduled to report back to the heads of government this afternoon but decided to ask that the deadline be set back twenty-four hours.

The delegations were uncertain tonight whether tomorrow's heads-of-government meeting would deal with the directive on German reunity and European security, the disarmament question or the final item on the Big Four agenda—the improvement of East-West contacts.

The shape of tomorrow's afternoon meeting will be determined by the progress of the foreign ministers at their morning session.

The Big Four also agreed at the conclusion of their meeting today that the foreign ministers should draw up procedures for acquainting the United Nations Subcommittee on Disarmament with the substance of the Geneva discussions and the various new approaches outlined here.

The outlook was for a foreign ministers conference in October, with Geneva again the meeting place.

The precise form of the United States proposals on disarmament was a surprise to many diplomats otherwise well acquainted with Western strategy, although it had been clear for several days that President Eisenhower was preparing to say something new on this subject.

Perhaps the most important clue was the arrival here yesterday of Harold E. Stassen, the President's special assistant on disarmament problems; Nelson A. Rockefeller, White House adviser on psychological warfare, along with Admiral Arthur W. Radford, chairman of Joint Chiefs of Staff, and Robert B. Anderson, Deputy Secretary of Defense.

Gen. Alfred M. Gruenther, Supreme Allied Commander in Europe, also appeared at Ville Creux de Genthod, where the President has set up his Geneva White House.

Admiral Radford and Mr. Anderson had been standing by in Paris since last Sunday until the President summoned them. Mr. Stassen and Mr. Rockefeller reached Paris last Thursday.

The impact of the President's speech was spectacular. He did not pretend that a sound and reliable inspection plan would be easy to work out, emphasizing that the United States so far had been unable to develop a foolproof scientific alarm system and so far as he knew no other nation had succeeded in this effort.

His direct appeal to the Soviet leaders was depicted by President Eisenhower as the product of "searching my heart and mind for something that I could say here that could convince everyone of the great sincerity of the United States in approaching this problem of disarmament."

Whether or not it impressed Marshal Bulganin and Mr. Khrushchev, the President's plea captured popular interest, overshadowing the three other proposals.

*   *   *

September 20, 1955

PERON'S REGIME IS OVERTHROWN; JUNTA WILL MEET WITH REBELS; CROWDS HAIL FALL OF DICTATOR

PEACE IS SOUGHT

Government Orders Its Forces to End Fight—Port Is Shelled

By EDWARD A. MORROW
Special to The New York Times.

BUENOS AIRES, Tuesday, Sept 20—The Government of President Juan D. Perón fell last night.

A four-man junta of army generals assumed command of the forces that had fought unsuccessfully to keep General Perón in power. He had been master of Argentina since Oct. 17, 1945, and its President for nine years.

[A loyalist military junta told the rebels that General Perón had officially resigned the Presidency, The Associated Press reported.]

The junta quickly entered into negotiations to end the four-day civil war. Army and Navy units had joined in the rebellion and forced the resignation of the President, the Cabinet and other authorities.

Among those who tended their "irrevocable" resignations was the Minister of the Army, Gen. Franklin Lucero. On June 16 he had quelled a navy-led revolt.

There was no news about the whereabouts of President Perón tonight. Some reports had him in asylum at the Paraguayan Embassy in Buenos Aires. The embassy denied these.

Peron Statement Read

The low ceiling prevented any planes from leaving the city's army airport and seemed to cast doubt on other reports that the President had fled to Paraguay.

General Perón offered his resignation yesterday afternoon in a statement read for him over the state radio. He suggested that the Army take charge. He had made a somewhat similar offer to resign Aug. 31 but withdrew it after "protests" from his followers.

It was widely rumored that General Perón had committed suicide. There was no official announcement to this effect and well-informed diplomats doubted the report.

[A rebel radio broadcast from Bahia Blanca said the Argentine Confederation of Labor was planning a general strike for dawn Tuesday in an effort to restore General Perón to power, The Associated Press reported.]

The Government ordered troops that still remained loyal to it to cease fighting. It asked the rebels to do likewise to prevent further bloodshed after the Navy had shelled the seaside city of Mar del Plata and the rebels had shown other signs of strength throughout the country.

Large sections of the Buenos Aires population braved a light rain this afternoon to stage joyful demonstrations in the city's streets. The Plaza de Mayo, scene of many mass Peronist demonstrations in the past, had a small number of the President's supporters waiting for others to join them.

The occasional shouts of some supporters asserting that the Perón defeat was nothing but a lie were answered by jeers of other onlookers.

Two statues of Eva Perón, the President's late wife, at the city's railway station were toppled, roped to automobiles and dragged through the city's main street.

The Government's junta consisted of the Army Chief of Staff, Gen. Carlos Adolfo Wirth; Gen. Emilio Forcher, commander of the Forces of the Interior, and Gen. Angel Juan Manni, Chief of the Coordination Staff.

The junta became a four-man group when Gen. Jose Domingo Molina, Commander in Chief of the Army, was made its president.

A message reportedly read by Hugo de Prieto, secretary general of the Confederation of Labor, advised all its members "to maintain order and to follow the confederation's instructions."

In his statement, read for him by General Lucero, President Perón said, "I should not wish to die without having made a last effort for their [the people's] peace, their tranquility and their happiness."

He added that although his fighting spirit urged him to struggle, "my patriotism and my love for the people induces me toward every personal resignation" before the threat of bombing the nation's property "and its innocent people."

The Government junta offered to meet the rebel command last night at either the Cabildo, the capital's old City Halli, which is now a museum, or in the Palace of Justice. However, the rebels announced they were ready to meet only on the flagship of General Issac Rojas and on the understanding that the Government was ready to "surrender unconditionally."

The rebels' second demand was the recognition of a de facto Government of the Revolution "to be named by the triumphant forces."

Just before midnight it was announced that Admiral Rojas had asked the leader of the opposition forces in Cordoba, Gen. Eduardo Leonardi, to fly to the port and to join in any discussions aboard the cruiser.

Wording Unclear

General Lucero issued a statement offering to negotiate with the rebels, but the wording of his and General Perón's statements was unclear. President Perón referred to the fact that he had attempted to resign on Aug. 31. The next day the General Confederation of Labor staged a mass demonstration asking him to retract his offer and he did.

The President also said that he did not believe there was one man capable enough to rule the country, and this led him to think that it should be ruled by the army. If the army decided he should leave the Government he would do so, the statement implied.

These events were the climax of four days of fighting. This city and other areas dominated by loyal troops thus fell under the rule of the junta, which immediately confirmed Gen. Felix Robles was Chief of the Forces of Security. These forces were taking drastic steps to enforce order after curfew regulations became effective at 8 o'clock tonight.

The sudden turn in events was largely caused by the navy's shelling of Mar del Plata yesterday and its threat to take similar action against this capital.

Aided by the low ceiling which protected them from any important attack by planes, elements of the fleet lay a half-mile off the seaside resort and at 7:30 A. M. opened fire against the port and its installations.

Some of the shells struck the huge tanks of the Government's oil refinery and started large fires.

Although reports said that the damage caused was extensive, there were no details. Nor were there any casualty estimates.

Reports from Tres Arroyos in the northern part of Buenos Aires showed that the rebels had considerable air strength despite the Government's contention to the contrary. Loyal forces moving against a rebel force half way between that city and the town of Colonel Pringles were attacked by three bombers and four fighters Sunday.

Casualties among the Government troops were reported high.

In the Province of Mendoza the Commander in Chief of the revolutionary command, Gen. Julio Alberto Lagos, named Gen. Roberto Valentin Nazar the province's governor.

There were widespread reports that the provisional national government the rebels were planning to set up would include General Lagos, Admiral Rojas, Gen. Dalmiro Felix Videla Balaguer and three civilians. The latter were Maurico Yabarola, a Radical Deputy, Enrique Corominas Seguro, a Democrat, and Alfredo Paladios, a party leader.

Shops Close Quickly

Meanwhile, in Buenos Aires after word filtered to the population about the possible imminent bombardment, shops quickly closed. Most persons gathered around radios to keep abreast of developments.

President Perón's most ardent supporters, members of the Alianza Nacionalista, were armed with submachine guns and requisitioned trucks to add to their mobility. For a brief time they commanded the city's downtown streets, menacingly waving their guns at persons who failed to respond favorably to their cries of "Viva Perón."

Late in the afternoon a group of demonstrators cheering the rebel victory were fired upon by a group of Perón supporters.

Two tanks were brought up in front of the Alianza headquarters. Those inside were ordered to surrender. They left the building, were disarmed and got into waiting trucks. Not a shot was fired.

However, in other sections of the city and particularly the fashionable northern districts and suburbs, many shooting incidents, occurred between unidentifiable civilian groups.

The Confederation's headquarters were abandoned.

For the first time in more than a year the official radio carried a message by the Archbishop of Buenos Aires, Santiago Cardinal Luis Copello. He called upon all Argentines to adopt an attitude that would bring peace back to a nation that "once again has been sown with sorrow and death where there should only be happiness and concord."

General Strike Reported Set

BUENOS AIRES, Tuesday, Sept. 20 (AP)—Argentina's labor federation was reported preparing a general strike for dawn today in an effort to put General Perón back into power.

A rebel radio broadcast from Bahia Blanca said leaders of the 6,000,000-member General Federation of Labor, backbone of the ousted President's popularity following, had decided separately on the strike under General Perón's inspiration.

The federation used the same tactic successfully in 1945 to return General Perón to power after a military clique jailed him.

Warning for Rebel Leader

MONTEVIDEO, Uruguay, Tuesday, Sept. 20—A broadcast from the self-styled "Civilian Command of Buenos Aires," heard here, asked Admiral Rojas not to come into the capital but to let the junta "go to you." The broadcast said "another Oct. 17 is being prepared," a reference to the date on which General Perón was reinstated in 1945.

In another broadcast, the "Civilian Command" told Admiral Rojas that a column of tanks loyal to General Perón had reached Buenos Aires Province from Corrientes Province and was advancing on the Argentine capital.

* * *

October 24, 1955

DIEM WINS POLL IN SOUTH VIETNAM, OUSTING BAO DAI

Premier's Victory Confronts Big 4 at Geneva With Task of Implementing Truce

By HENRY R. LIEBERMAN
Special to The New York Times.

SAIGON, Vietnam, Oct. 23—Premier Ngo Dinh Diem replaced Bao Dai as South Vietnam's Chief of State today in a ballot-box revolution aimed at establishing a new republic.

It was the first national vote ever taken in South Vietnam. The vote involved a referendum on whether or not the people wanted Bao Dai removed and Mr. Diem to become Chief of State "with the task of organizing a republic."

Twenty-four hours or more may elapse before the official result is announced. By midnight tonight, however, the only question in Government quarters here was just how big Mr. Diem's victory vote would be. Vietnamese officials predicted Mr. Diem would get 80 to 90 per cent of the ballots.

The announced returns from Dalat, Bao Dai's former summer capital, gave Mr. Diem 98.7 per cent of 26,623 votes cast there. An unofficial tally showed Mr. Diem had 98.2 per cent of the 45,750 votes cast in the first of six Saigon-Cholon districts to report.

Some Ballots Invalid

In this district 519 ballots and at Dalat 231 ballots were declared invalid. The referendum was preceded by rumors here. Communists had been instructed to deface their ballots.

Bao Dai, who has been in France for more than a year, was installed by the French as Vietnamese Chief of State in 1949. He recently "dismissed" Mr. Diem as Premier, but the latter continued anyway with his plans for today's referendum.

Tons of thousands of South Vietnamese went to the polls in warm, clear weather to choose between Mr. Diem and the absent Bao Dai.

The results of the referendum confront the Big Four foreign ministers meeting later this week at Geneva with a fait accompli regarding the 1954 Geneva armistice agreement. The agreement, which split Vietnam in two at the Seventeenth Parallel, was signed by French and North Vietnamese representatives.

The declaration also projected general elections for all of Vietnam in July 1956. But South Vietnam did not sign the Geneva agreement and Mr. Diem has shown no disposition to accept it.

If there are to be general elections next year, the North Vietnamese Government will presumably have to deal with Mr.

Diem instead of with the French. For days now the Hanoi radio has been denouncing the South Vietnamese referendum as a "farce and swindle" designed to "sabotage the Geneva agreement" and "stifle the fighting spirit of the Vietnamese people."

Today's referendum has been interpreted by foreign observers as a preliminary step intended to activate the political life of South Vietnam. It is officially represented as a forerunner of moves to elect a National Assembly in the South and evolve a new Constitution.

A total of 5,335,688 men and women over the age of 18 were eligible to vote in the referendum.

Minor incidents were reported of Communist sympathizers trying to make speeches at polling places. But they were silenced quickly by small numbers of troops and white-uniformed policemen stationed at the voting centers to keep order.

In Cholon, Saigon's twin Chinese-populated city, the shopkeepers hung out the flag of the Chinese Nationalists along with the South Vietnamese banner.

The ballots, which were about six by six inches in size, consisted essentially of two pictures. One was a reddish-tinted photo of a smiling Mr. Diem among the people and the other was a greenish-tinted photo of a sullen-looking Bao Dai in court dress.

After having made their choice in curtained booths, the voters tore off the picture of the man they favored, put it in an envelope and placed the envelope in a sealed ballot box.

The 54-year-old Mr. Diem, a devout Roman Catholic and stubborn nationalist, began his political career as an official at the royal court in Hue. He was named Premier by Bao Dai in 1954 just as Vietnam was about to be partitioned at Geneva.

The 42-year-old Bao Dai, who abdicated as Emperor of Annam in 1945 and was restored by the French as Chief of State four years later, has been losing political influence here for some time.

* * *

November 21, 1955

BAGHDAD POWERS FORMING COUNCIL

Britain Joins Four Neighbors of Soviet in Pact Session— U. S. Observers Present

By The Associated Press

BAGHDAD, Iraq, Nov. 20—The premiers of four of the Soviet Union's southern neighbors and Britain's Foreign Secretary, Harold Macmillan, assembled in this ancient city today for the inaugural council meeting of the Baghdad Pact.

The pact links Turkey, Iraq, Iran, Pakistan and Britain in a mutual security system along the Soviet border from the Black Sea to the Himalayas.

It connects with the North Atlantic Treaty Organization to the west through Turkey and with the Southeast Asia Collective Defense Treaty grouping to the east through Pakistan.

The pact thus forms part of a non-Communist security chain virtually circling the globe.

The United States, which already backs some of the Baghdad Pact members with military aid, is sending observers to the council meetings, which open tomorrow.

Sixth Fleet's Chief at Hand

Waldemar J. Gallman, United States Ambassador to Iraq, and Admiral John H. Cassady, top United States naval officer in Europe and commander of the atomic-equipped Sixth Fleet in the Mediterranean, will be the observers.

Premier Adnan Menderes of Turkey and his delegation, a large one, arrived by plane three hours behind schedule.

Prime Minister Chaudry Mohammed Ali of Pakistan and his party and the Iranians, headed by Premier Hussein Ala, were here early in the day. The British party followed.

Premier Nuri as-Said of Iraq, his Foreign Secretary Burhanuddin Bashayan and Gen. Rafik Arif, chief of the Iraqi General Staff, raced from airport to railroad station and then back to the airport, greeting the officials as they reached here.

An audience with young King Faisal II of Iraq for the heads of delegations went on in the king's palace without awaiting Mr. Menderes' party.

The heads of delegations and military chiefs also laid wreaths on the grave of Faisal I, the first King of Iraq and grandfather of the present monarch.

When Mr. Menderes finally arrived with his delegation in two special planes, he, too, was welcomed by Premier as-Said who had been up since before dawn.

In a brief talk to newsmen at the airport, Mr. Macmillan called the newly formed pact "vitally important for peace and prosperity of all five countries working together."

"It is particularly important for Briatin to be represented here in the important work we are going to do together," he said.

Mr. Macmillan heads a six-member British delegation, including Gen. Sir Harold Templer, chief of the Imperial General Staff.

Reports had been circulating that Mr. Macmillan might return to London by way of Cairo or some other Arab capital in the Middle East, tense over the Arab-Israeli dispute. Mr. Macmillan ended these rumors with the statement that he would return directly to London, probably Wednesday.

In his brief speech, Mr. Macmillan said: "I am proud to be here as the representative of my country, to what will be an important occasion for better relations with other members of the Baghdad Pact."

Jordanian Comment on Israel

AMMAN, Jordan, Nov. 20 (Reuters)—A responsible Jordanian spokesman said today that Sir Anthony Eden's recent statement offering Britain's help in settling the Israeli-Arab dispute was "the first positive step to meet Arab claims and demands."

The British Prime Minister said at a London banquet earlier this month that, if an acceptable arrangement could be made about the boundaries of Israel and her Arab neighbors, Britain would be prepared to give a formal guarantee to both sides.

The Jordanian spokesman said no Arab state could solve the question alone; it must be solved by mutual understanding among the Arab countries.

The Iraqi Government has accepted a Syrian and Lebanese invitation to attend the Arab League Political Council meeting to be held in Beirut, Lebanon, early next month, Reuters reported. It is understood the council will discuss Prime Minister Eden's proposals. The United States has indicated reservations to Sir Anthony's proposals to the extent that they might require a "compromise" of Israel's boundaries.

* * *

March 16, 1956

SECRET KHRUSHCHEV TALK ON STALIN 'PHOBIA' RELATED

By HARRISON E. SALISBURY

According to diplomatic reports, Nikita S. Khrushchev, Soviet Communist party secretary, made a secret address to the recent Twentieth Congress of the Communist party explaining why Stalin was being desanctified.

Mr. Khrushchev's address, according to information reaching the United States from Moscow, was made at a closed session of the party congress on the evening of Feb. 24. Delegates from foreign communist parties were said to have been barred from this meeting.

Mr. Khrushchev was reported to have presented a sensational picture of events in the latter period of Stalin's regime. He touched on events surrounding the death of Lenin in January, 1924, and the party purges of the Nineteen Thirties.

It was understood Washington official quarters were aware of the reports about the Khrushchev speech and were giving them the closest study.

Mr. Khrushchev's address was said to have been comprehensive and forthright. It was said to make the speech in which Anastas I. Mikoyan, a leading party aide, criticized Stalin sound "like milk and water."

Stalin 'Not Himself'

The picture painted by Mr. Khrushchev, according to these reports, was of a Stalin who was "not himself" in his late years and who through his career had been subject to phobias about the supposed treachery of his associates.

Possibly the most sensational revelation that Mr. Khrushchev is said to have placed before his colleagues was a declaration that the case of treason in 1937 against Marshal Mikhail N. Tukhachevsky and other high ranking Red Army men had been a fabrication.

As Mr. Khrushchev is said to have described the inner Kremlin scene, many of Stalin's closest associates were unaware of the fate of intimate friends and collaborators. The full story of what happened during Stalin's long years, Mr.

Khrushchev was said to have indicated, became known only after Stalin's death.

According to the reports, Moscow, as Mr. Khrushchev described the atmosphere there in the late years of the Stalin regime, was a capital ridden by plots, counter-plots and intrigue, in which no one knew who might be the next victim.

Foreign diplomats in Moscow were said to be seeking official word on the precise contents of Mr. Khrushchev's address. The Moscow censorship has prevented foreign correspondents from cabling reports of rumors circulating in the Soviet capital.

It was established that Mr. Khrushchev's speech was designed to tell the Soviet party members why the leadership had found it necessary to destroy Stalin's reputation for infallibility, wisdom and good works.

Party delegates are now spreading by word-of-mouth around the country the essence of Mr. Khrushchev's remarks. Some experts suggested that after Soviet public opinion had been prepared for the full shock the whole case against Stalin might be made public.

The execution of Marshal Tukhachevsky and seven other high Red Army commanders was announced in June, 1937. It occurred, according to an official statement, after a one-day trial before a military tribunal that convicted the men of treason.

Mr. Krushchev told his colleagues, it was reported, that there was no foundation for the charge against the Red Army leadership. The case was a fabrication and a "terrible mistake" that, he was said to have declared, led the Soviet Union "to the brink of disaster" when Germany attacked in 1941. The Red Army, deprived of its leadership, almost was overwhelmed by the German attack, Mr. Khrushchev is said to have declared.

Army Influence Seen

It was believed by some specialists on Soviet affairs that the emphasis placed by Mr. Khrushchev on the Tukhachevsky case indicated strong Soviet Army influence in the present government, particularly that of Marshal Georgi K. Zhukov, Defense Minister.

Only one member of the tribunal that heard the Tukhachevsky case is known to survive. He is Marshal Semyon M. Budenny, an old associate of Stalin, who still is often seen in Moscow on official occasions.

Many of the announcements relative to Marshal Tukhachevsky and other cases involving Soviet defense forces at that time were made by Marshal Kliment E. Voroshilov, then People's Commissar for Defense and now the titular chief of state.

The official charge against Marshal Tukhachevsky and his associates was treason. There was never any explanation of the charges, but it was widely whispered that the Red Army chiefs had plotted with Germany and Japan to overthrow Stalin with the aid of foreign military assistance. These charges were accepted even in Western circles.

The picture that Mr. Khrushchev was said to have painted in his address was said to bear a startling resemblance to the picture of the Moscow scene presented by this correspondent in a series of articles written on his return from Moscow in 1954.

Mr. Khrushchev was said to have asserted that even the members of Stalin's Politburo were often kept in ignorance of what was happening. An example was the disappearance of Nikolai A. Voznesensky, a Politburo member and head of the State Planning Commission, in March, 1949.

Mr. Khrushchev, it was reported, declared that the Politburo members did not know what had happened to Mr. Voznesensky at the time. No explanation was made to them by Stalin. Only later, Mr. Khrushchev said, was it learned that Mr. Voznesensky was arrested in March, 1949, and shot sometime during the next twelve months.

It was reported that Mr. Khrushchev elucidated for the party members the details of the so-called Leningrad case, which has been frequently mentioned in Soviet circles.

The Leningrad case was first mentioned in December, 1954, at the time the execution of Victor S. Abakumov former Minister of State Security, was announced. Mr. Abakumov was said to have falsely fabricated this case.

It has long been suspected that there was a connection between Mr. Voznesensky's fate and the Leningrad case in which a number of former lieutenants of Andrei A. Zhdanov, a Politburo member who died in September, 1948, disappeared.

On the basis of Mr. Khrushchev's remarks it is now believed that these men, including Peter S. Popkov, former Mayor of Leningrad, A. A. Kuznetsov, a one-time Communist party secretary, Mikhail I. Rodionov, former Premier of the Russian Federated Republic, were all shot either in 1949, the year of their disappearance, or in 1950.

*   *   *

June 27, 1956

EXPOSE OF STALIN IS SAID TO IMPERIL KHRUSHCHEV ROLE

Washington Experts Predict Soviet Chief Must Retract or Go Into the Discard

EFFECT ABROAD SEVERE

Drive Held Out of Control—
But Others See Criticism as Part of Strategy

By JAMES RESTON
Special to The New York Times.

WASHINGTON, June 26—Experts on Soviet affairs are inclined to agree that Nikita S. Khrushchev's anti-Stalin crusade has got out of hand.

Indeed, some of them feel that Mr. Khrushchev has gone so far in loosening the reins on the Communist parties outside the Soviet Union that he will either have to reverse himself or follow Stalin into the discard.

This is not the unanimous opinion of the men here whose job it is to read the Soviet riddle. Some of them think the criticism of Moscow by the Communists in Rome, Paris, London and New York was planned that way.

These who favor this interpretation see the rash of anti-Khrushchev statements among non-Soviet Communists as part of Moscow's plan to dramatize the new Soviet line of independence for all national Communist parties.

This is not the general view of the experts here, however. The majority of them feel that the Communist criticism of Mr. Khrushchev has gone beyond anything Moscow expected and will have to be handled with great skill if the Communist alliance is not to be seriously weakened.

Party Demands Studied

It goes without saying that all this is sheer speculation. Nobody knows better than the men who have studied the Soviet Union all their lives how little they really know about the inner workings of the Communist sorcery.

Yet nothing that has happened in the Soviet world since the Khrushchev tirade against Stalin has intrigued officials here more than the outspoken demands by the Communist party leaders outside the Soviet Union for an explanation of what Khrushchev and company were doing while Stalin perpetrated the crimes reported to the Twentieth Communist Party Congress.

Palmiro Togliatti, Communist leader in Italy, was the first to demand "a Marxist explanation" of "how such errors could have crept into the evolution of socialistic society."

This same line was taken up by Maurice Thorez, Communist leader in France, but with this difference: While condemning Stalin and indirectly Mr. Khrushchev, the French line has continued seeking opportunities to praise Stalin's "achievements."

To most of the experts here this does not look like a carefully arranged, systematic plan of criticism outlined by Moscow to demonstrate the new independence of the national communist parties.

It is true that all the outside Communist leaders have criticized the way Mr. Khrushchev's speech was leaked first to the capitalist press in the West, and that some of them seemed to be concentrating their fire on Mr. Khrushchev in a way to deflect criticism from the Communist "system." But at the same time the system is being criticized and Mr. Khrushchev is being put definitely on the spot.

Mr. Khrushchev was able to ignore the publication of his speech in the West, and even the sharp criticism of Western leaders, particularly Secretary of State Dulles. But the feeling here is that he cannot very well ignore the waspish comments of Signor Togliatti, M. Thorez, Pietro Nenni, Italian Left-wing Socialist leader, and the others.

These men carried out Stalin's business for many years. By criticizing Mr. Khrushchev and asking "Where were you during all these Stalinist crimes?" they raise the same questions about themselves. This point has not been lost on the Communist rank-and-file members in Italy and France.

For Signor Togliatti and M. Thorez were themselves beneficiaries in their own countries of the "cult of personality" that they now criticize in relation to Stalin. The Italian and French Communists are demanding that there should be less of this, more freedom of discussion and more "collective leadership" in the future of the Italian and French Communist parties.

The main question being asked by the experts here is what the effect of all this will be, first, on the Communist movements all over the world, and second, on the future of Mr. Khrushchev and Soviet Premier Nikolai A. Bulganin and all the others closely identified with Stalin in the era of the officially confessed crimes.

One view here is that the Communists may very well succeed in making themselves more acceptable as political partners in their own countries by loosening their ties with Moscow. But by concentrating on the sins of Stalin they inevitably encourage criticism of themselves as partners in Stalin's barbarism.

Younger Leaders Discussed

Some of the best informed of the Soviet experts here therefore expect to see, in due course, either a reversal of the anti-Stalinist line or a weakening of the leadership of those who were closely identified with Stalin and his terror.

For the first time there was some talk here today about the Khrushchev-Bulganin team as a transitional regime pending the rise of new leaders in the Soviet Union who were not of Stalin's generation and not part of the inner circle that tolerated his policies.

Younger men in the Presidium of the Central Committee of the Communist party, such as Maxim Z. Saburov, chairman of the Planning Committee of that organ and Mikhail G. Pervukhin, a First Deputy Premier, were being mentioned, for example. Also there was considerable talk about the possible rise of Marshal Georgi K. Zhukov, Defense Minister, who was a friend of General Eisenhower when they were commanders in Berlin.

Some here feel that, in the next phase, the Soviet military leaders, who were so roundly criticized by Stalin, may emerge as the men to carry out the new line and that, in turn, the events of the last few months may well lead to the emergence of new Communist leaders to replace Signor Togliatti, M. Thorez and the others in the West.

French Reds Approach Tito

Special to The New York Times.

BUCHAREST, Rumania, June 26—French Communist leaders have asked for an invitation from President Tito of Yugoslavia to visit him in Belgrade, according to reports here. It is not certain, however, whether the Yugoslavs are yet ready to receive them.

Because of his heavy schedule in the Soviet Union and during his visit in Rumania, Marshal Tito has not seen the latest resolution of the French Communist Party criticizing the Soviet leadership.

He said he had not heard of the French Communists' request but would look into it on his arrival in Belgrade tomorrow.

It was clear that Yugoslav officials were not impressed with the previous French Communist Statement. When Marshal Tito visited Paris last month he turned down requests for interviews from the French Communist leaders Maurice Thorez and Jacques Duclos, it was disclosed here.

On the other hand, Yugoslav officials have been pleased with the recent statements of the Italian Communist leader, Palmiro Togliatti, who expressed sharp discontent with Moscow. Asked tonight what he thought of Signor Togliatti's latest speech, Marshal Tito nodded and said: "Very good. It was a very good speech."

The Yugoslavs do not consider that the attacks on the Soviet leadership weaken the position of Nikita S. Khrushchev. On the contrary, their view is that Mr. Khrushchev and Marshal Bulganin are faced with continued resistance to their new policies from loyal Stalinist elements in the middle ranks of the Soviet Communist party.

Belgians Confess Laxity

Special to The New York Times.

BRUSSELS, June 26—The Belgian Communist party admitted today it had failed to pay enough attention to the possibility of excesses in the Soviet Union during Stalin's regime.

The confession was printed in Le Drapeau Rouge, organ of the Belgian Communist party. It was part of a resolution adopted Sunday at a meeting of the party's Central Committee. This condemned as "inadmissible the violations of the way of life established by the [Russian] Revolution and of the rules of democratic socialism."

*   *   *

October 21, 1956

POLES REPORT FIRING ON RUSSIAN REGIMENT TO PREVENT ITS ENTRY FROM EAST GERMANY; GOMULKA DEFIES SOVIET, PLEDGES ELECTIONS

WITHDRAWAL ON

Peril of Moscow Coup Appears Waning but Debate Continues

By SYDNEY GRUSON
Special to The New York Times.

WARSAW, Sunday, Oct. 21—Soviet troops were reported to be drawing away from Warsaw today.

This developed, it was said, after Polish frontier forces had barred with gunfire the attempt of a Soviet regiment to move into Stettin (Sczeczin) from East Germany during Friday night.

A reliable Polish source said cryptically last night that the "military situation is better." But the political crisis over Polish demands for an independent course remained unsolved.

Soviet troops were said to be pulling back from Sochaczew, about thirty miles west of Warsaw, and from Siedlce, fifty five miles east of the capital.

Move From the East

The troops at Siedlce were believed to have crossed into Poland from the Soviet Union early Friday.

[State Department officials said in Washington that the reported clash between Soviet soldiers and Polish troops, if confirmed, would be the first between Soviet troops and those of a satellite.]

The net effect of the day's developments was to leave Polish officials in Warsaw considerably relieved. The danger of a Soviet military take-over appears to have ended, and what remains, though serious enough, apparently is going to be settled by negotiation rather than by force.

Nikita S. Khrushchev, the Soviet Communist party chief, who had rushed here Friday with three First Deputy Premiers to demand maintenance of direct Soviet influence in Poland returned to Moscow early yesterday. He and Vyacheslav M. Molotov, Anastas I. Mikoyan, and Lazar M. Kaganovich left by plane at 6:45 A. M.

Khrushchev's Demands

The demands Mr. Khrushchev had laid down kept the Central Committee of the Polish United Workers (Communist) party in lengthy session last night. Wladyslaw Gomulka, who has returned to power after surviving Stalin's purges, addressed the committee for two and a half hours.

The Stettin incident was the most serious of three involving the Soviet Army in Poland since the crisis flared openly. There were said to have been casualties in that skirmish.

The Russian soldiers first asked permission to enter Poland, it was reported, and then tried to cross by force when they were refused. Polish troops fired, and the Russians withdrew. No other information was available here.

Polish party members were the only sources of news on the military incidents, and even their information was sketchy.

The second incident involved "loyal" Polish troops and what was described as a "large concentration" of Soviet troops reported to have been in the area of Sochabeztycz, about sixty miles due west of Warsaw.

The third incident was said to have occurred in western Poland, presumably during Thursday night before the arrival of Mr. Khrushchev and his party gave public evidence of the extent of the crisis between the two countries.

Part of a Soviet armored force, moving in great haste toward Warsaw from the Poznan area, reportedly smashed through a grade crossing and rammed a train.

This armored force is believed to be the one referred to by Edward Ochab Friday at the start of the talks with the Russians. M. Ochab was the Polish party's First Secretary until the Politburo resigned at a meeting of the Central Committee that preceded the conference with the Russians.

At this meeting, M. Gomulka, former party leader who had been deposed on Stalin's orders in 1948 as a "Titoist" and imprisoned in 1951 for nearly four years, was re-elected to the Central Committee.

M. Ochab was quoted as having told Mr. Khrushchev:

"If you do not halt your troops immediately, we will walk out of here and break off all contact." Thereupon Mr. Khreschev gave the orders to halt the troops, it was reported.

Troop movements have been under way throughout the country for the last two days. With few exceptions it was not known whose leadership—Russian or Polish—the various forces on the move were following.

The Ministry of Defense, headed by Marshal Konstantin K. Rokossovsky, acknowledged the troop movements in a statement said to have been issued only to his own organization. The ministry described the movements as routine shifting of soldiers to assist in potato harvesting.

Debate Resumes Today

The meeting of the Polish party's Central Committee debating the political crisis was adjourned late last night. It will resume this morning.

Eighty speakers were listed to participate in the continuing debate. The committee decided to limit their time so that the crucial vote might be taken late tomorrow on whether Marshal Rokossovsky, the former Soviet Army soldier who became Poland's Defense Minister in 1949, would be retained in the Polish party's Politburo.

There was no way of knowing beforehand how the vote would go. But the few indications available to foreigners suggested that the majority of the Central Committee was behind M. Gomulka and the other Polish leaders standing firm against the Russians.

The Warsaw radio broadcast abroad excerpts of M. Gomulka's speech before the Central Committee. One part strengthened the belief that there had been no shift in the majority sentiment behind M. Gomulka.

According to the radio, he said the Polish people would "defend themselves with all means so that we may not be pushed off the road of democratization."

Poland has the right to be sovereign, and this sovereignty should be respected, he declared, adding, "I would say it begins to be so."

Technically, no Politburo or party secretariat existed early today. But for all intents and purposes, M. Gomulka, the rehabilitated "Titoist," was again leading the party.

Gomulka Goes to Airport

He had been proposed as the party's new First Secretary, replacing M. Ochab, at the Central Committee meeting Friday morning.

The proposed Politburo excluded Marshal Rokossovsky and all other members of what was known as the pro-Soviet faction of the old Politburo.

Despite the nastiness of some of Friday's scenes with the Russians, M. Gomulka went to the airport early yesterday to see Mr. Khrushchev and the other Soviet leaders off for Moscow.

M. Gomulka shook hands with each member of the Soviet group and finally turned to Mr. Khrushchev, saying:

The New York Times

FRICTION BEHIND THE IRON CURTAIN: Soviet troops moving into Poland from East Germany were reported to have been barred from Stettin (1) by Polish gunfire. Russian forces also were said to be withdrawing from Sochaczew (2) and Siedlce (3).

"Oh, Comrade Khrushchev. I almost forgot to say good-by to you."

Friday, Mr. Khrushchev had referred to M. Gomulka as a traitor during his diatribe against the entire Polish leadership.

The Russians originally had told the Poles that they were leaving at 3 A. M., about an hour after the final meeting of M. Gomulka, the old Polish Politburo and the Soviet leaders. What the Russians did between their scheduled take-off and the 6:45 A. M. departure was not disclosed.

The old Politburo and the Russians met for the second time Friday night between 11 o'clock and 2 A. M. today. Despite the Russians' tough attitude during the six-hour daytime session Friday, the Polish Central Committee had remained firm against Marshal Rokossovsky.

According to the Poles, the Soviet leaders finally agreed that the Polish list for the new Politburo was satisfactory, and the Poles agreed to go to Moscow for further discussions "soon." But it was not to be as simple as that.

When the Central Committee reconvened at 11 A. M. yesterday, Aleksander Zawadzki presented a motion to add Marshal Rokossovsky to the proposed list of members of the new Politburo.

On the original list were M. Gomulka, M. Ochab, Premier Jozef Cyrankiewiez, Foreign Minister Adam Rapacki, Stefan Jedrychowski, chairman of the Economic Planning Commission; Roman Zambrowski, Jerzy Morawski, Col. Ignacy Loga-Sowinski, who was re-elected yesterday with M. Gomulka and two others to the Central Committee, and M. Zawadzki, who also is chairman of the Council of State, which replaced the Polish Presidency in 1952.

As a member of the Central Committee, M. Zawadzki had every right to do so. He was the only one of the nine on the list considered close to the group being excluded, and the move, when it came, was no surprise to the other leaders.

The Russians' demands were listed under three main headings by Polish sources. First and most important was the retention of Marshal Rokossovsky in the Politburo. Second was for the Poles to halt anti-Soviet agitation, and third, to halt the process of "democratization" in Poland.

What had happened in Poland was not "democratization" but anarchy, Mr. Khrushchev was reported to have said.

The top-ranking military men who had accompanied Mr. Khrushchev to Warsaw Friday did not return with him yesterday. Their exact whereabouts here was not known. Nor was their identification certain.

Marshal Georgi K. Zhukov, Soviet Defense Minister, was reported among them Friday. But there were considerable doubts that he had come. There was agreement, however, that Marshal Ivan S. Konev, a First Deputy Defense Minister and commander of the Warsaw Pact forces, had made the trip.

A deceptive quiet hung over Warsaw last night. There did not seem to be any more soldiers than usual about. But either trusted troops or workers from the Warsaw factories, who have been in the vanguard of Polish liberalizing movements that upset the Russians were on guard at vital communication centers and the factories.

From the news coming out now it was clear that the security police troops, now commanded by Gen. Waclaw Komar, one of M. Gomulka's close friends, had been mobilized for two weeks. It was said Polish leaders had ordered this done quietly after they received word that the regular army under Marshal Rokossovsky had been put on a state of alert.

According to Polish sources, the regular Army officers were told that they might be needed to "defend" the party and Government against a coup. But if one was being prepared, most Poles believed it was the work of the men who had alerted the regular Army.

* * *

October 27, 1956

HUNGARIAN REVOLT SPREADS; NAGY TOTTERS; THOUSANDS IN ARMY FIGHT SOVIET TROOPS; U. S. CONSULTS ALLIES ON TAKING U. N. ACTION

NEW PEACE PLEA

Shake-Up of Regime and Revision of Tie to Moscow Vowed

By ELIE ABEL
Special to The New York Times.

VIENNA, Saturday Oct. 27—The battle of Budapest was still in doubt early today with Soviet Troops on one side and a fiercely hostile Hungarian populace on the other.

The insurrection had spread over a large part of the country. The desperate regime of Premier Imre Nagy was struggling to maintain itself in a few scarred Government buildings along the Pest embankment with the aid of Soviet tanks and artillery.

The bulk of the Hungarian Army had given up the fight, according to reports reaching Vienna, and thousands of officers and soldiers had joined the insurrection, now in its fifth day.

[The Budapest radio said at dawn Saturday that Soviet and Hungarian troops had launched new attacks throughout Hungary against the rebels, The Associated Press reported from Vienna. The broadcast said fighting must continue because rebel elements had defied an ultimatum to surrender. No further word had been received up to 4 A. M., New York time.]

A Rebel Government

Rebel forces controlling the industrial town of Gyor in West Hungary, proclaimed their town "independent Hungarian Government." Western reporters managed to establish contact with this group from the Austrian frontier.

The anti-Communist Hungarians said they were expecting an early attack on Gyor by Soviet Army forces. The rebels told newsmen they had a number of tanks, some of them captured and the rest surrendered voluntarily by Hungarian Army units.

The indication during the night was that Premier Nagy could count only on the support of the Hungarian Red Security Police and the Soviet Army. The weakness of his three-day-old Government was plain.

The Central Committee of the Hungarian Working People's (Communist) party made a fresh appeal for peace and order yesterday afternoon after an emergency meeting under the new First Secretary, Janos Kadar.

Communists' Program

The committee outlined a program virtually identical with that of the Polish United Workers (Communist) party led by Wladyslaw Gomulka. A new relationship with the Soviet Union will be worked out, the Hungarian committee promised, on the principles of "national independence, complete equality and non-interference."

The party leadership pledged that it would seek a withdrawal of Soviet forces from strong points as soon as order was restored, and offered an unconditional amnesty for all insurrectionists who laid down their arms by last night.

The Government under Premier Nagy would be reorganized on a broadly representative Popular Front platform, the Central Committee said, and the regime would undertake negotiations for a new military relationship with the Soviet Union "as the Polish Government had demanded."

The party leadership acknowledged that "hundreds" had lost their lives in the warfare of the last four days. It called for an end of the bloodshed and for a united attack on the wrongs of the old Matyas Rakosi regime.

Borrowing a leaf also from Yugoslav President Tito's book, the Hungarian Central Committee said it would establish workers' councils throughout industry with a voice in deciding wages and production.

But the fighting went on. At one stage it washed up to, but not over, the border of Austria.

A Hungarian ambulance appeared near the Austrian frontier village of Nickelsdorf and requested medical aid for injured rebel forces including blood plasma and other supplies.

Last midnight's communiqué by the Budapest radio asserted that "several groups of rebels" had surrendered but acknowledged that fighting was still in progress after the 10 P. M. deadline for clemency.

The people of the capital were warned once more to stay indoors. The broadcast said the curfew would be lifted between daybreak and 10 A. M. today so that food and other essentials could be purchased.

As the fighting continued early yesterday, the tone of the official pronouncements from Budapest became almost frantic. The regime's reiterated threats to shoot on sight anyone caught in the streets with firearms were obviously empty words.

In an effort to wring what persuasion it could out of concessions already made to the embattled rebels, the Budapest radio drew attention time and again to the removal of Erno Gero as party chief.

Radio Pleads With Soldiers

"Soldiers, remain loyal to your Government," the radio pleaded. "Please help us.

"Party members say to the insurgents: 'Your demands are being fulfilled. We have a new Government. All members of the new party leadership were in prison under Rakosi.'

"Hungarian youth, your wishes have been attained. Gero is gone. Nagy is back. He will create a new order. Why do you go on fighting?

"Workers, go back to your jobs. Help in clearing the ruins of our capital. Damage is increasing hour by hour.

"Old Communists, everything now depends on you, you old proven fighters."

The party organ Szabad Nep, appearing in Budapest for the first time since its plant was sacked by rioters Tuesday, joined the official chorus of condemnation for Mr. Gero.

"A new national government will be formed within the next few hours," the paper said. "The guilty man, Erno Gero, has been removed, and Janos Kadar, who under the Rakosi tyranny was imprisoned for many years, has taken over the leadership of the party.

"Kadar's program calls for an independent Socialist Hungary coalition of all national forces, the democratization of our national life, and raising of the living standards for our people."

The spread of the insurrection to the provinces was conceded by the official news agency M. T. I. Soviet army tanks were firing on Hungarian fighters in the cities of Gyor, Szeged, Pecs and Szolnok, according to the news agency.

In the streets of Budapest warfare between Hungarians and Russians was bitter and intense despite the Government's proclaimed determination to crush the revolt at all cost yesterday morning.

A Vienna business man who reached the Austrian border from the Hungarian capital Thursday evening said the worst battle since the beginning of the revolt was in progress at 11 A. M. He described the Stalin Bridge over the Danube as a no-man's land with Soviet troops holding one end and Hungarian soldiers the other.

Whenever Soviet tanks appeared in the streets, they were fired upon from windows and roofs by Hungarian patriots, the business man said. He added that Russian tank crews did not dare show their heads above the turrets.

Other travelers reported that except in the immediate border zone, all towns they passed through in western Hungary were controlled by rebel forces.

Along a 200-kilometer (124-mile) drive from the Hungarian capital to the Austrian frontier village of Nickelsdorf, the travelers passed hundreds of trucks loaded with civilians waving red-white-and-green Hungarian flags headed for Budapest.

A mass defection of Hungarian soldiers continued through the day. There was little evidence that Soviet forces were getting any help from the Hungarian Army in the struggle to put down the insurrection.

Yesterday afternoon, the Budapest radio addressed a specific appeal to "young soldiers" to lay down their arms. This was the bluntest indication from any official source that Army men were fighting on the side of the rebels against the Russians.

Several eyewitnesses who reached Vienna yesterday said they had seen Hungarian officers as well as enlisted men with rebel bands. It was apparent also that most of the equipment being used against the Russians had been turned over to the rebels voluntarily by Hungarian soldiers.

Three Belgian diplomats who reached the Austrian-Hungarian frontier at mid-afternoon said there was no question but that the battle for Budapest had become a matter of Hungarians against Russians. But confusion was complete in the Hungarian capital, they added, with shots being fired at random in all directions.

The confusion was compounded by broadcasts monitored fleetingly in Vienna from low-power transmitters in hands of rebels.

One calling itself Freedom Station of the Hungarian People proclaimed a general strike throughout the country. It called for the immediate release from imprisonment of Joseph Cardinal Mindszenty and his restoration as Roman Catholic primate of Hungary.

Another rebel transmitter, which identified itself as broadcasting from Pacs, put out instructions to resistance groups using the code names of Kinizi and Zrimyi.

A weak signal was also heard here from a rebel-controlled radio at Miscola, but its wavelength was so close to that of the Budapest radio that the message could not be distinguished clearly.

* * *

October 30, 1956

ISRAELIS THRUST INTO EGYPT AND NEAR SUEZ; U. S. GOES TO U. N. UNDER ANTI-AGGRESSION PACT

DEEP DRIVE MADE

Tel Aviv Declares Aim is to Smash Egyptian Commando Bases

By MOSHE BRILLIANT
Special to The New York Times.

TEL AVIV, Israel, Oct. 29—An Israeli military force thrust into the Sinai Peninsula of Egypt today. It was reported to have reached within twenty miles of the Suez Canal.

Army sources said the Israelis were west of the crossroads where the road to Kuntilla branches off from the Suez-Quseima highway.

The Israelis were said to have halted there and to have dug in.

A Foreign Ministry statement said the operation had been started "to eliminate the Egyptian fedayeen [commando squad] bases in the Sinai Peninsula."

Army sources said the Israelis had smashed the Egyptian position at Kuntilla and Ras el Naqb at the southern end of the international border. The forces then advanced more than seventy-five miles.

No fighting was reported on the northern end of the border or in the Gaza Strip, which is heavily populated.

"Too Big for a Reprisal"

Reports from the Sinai area described the fighting as too big for a reprisal and too small for a war." Details on the fighting were not available tonight but reliable sources said there had been no aerial bombardment of Egyptian positions.

It was not clear tonight whether the Israelis proposed to push on to the Suez Canal or withdraw to Israeli territory as they have done after reprisal raids. A high official said: "I do not know. It depends on developments."

Yesterday the Israeli Government attributed its decision to call up reserves to what it said was a renewal of commando activities, to the Egyptian-Jordanian-Syrian military alliance negotiated last Wednesday, to Arab declarations that "their principal concern is a war of destruction against Israel" and to the movement of Iraqi forces to Jordan's border.

According to information here, the Egyptians have a considerable part of their Army in the Sinai Peninsula. Their land forces are reported equipped with the latest Soviet Stalin tanks as well as British Centurions.

Israeli sources said an Egyptian destroyer, two minelayers and another warship were seen approaching the Israeli coast off Haifa late this morning, a few hours before the fighting started in the Sinai Desert.

News of the invasion was made public in a communiqué from Army General Headquarters. This said:

"Units of the Israeli defense forces have penetrated and attacked fedayeen bases in the Kuntilla and Ras el Naqb area and have taken up positions to the west of the Nakhl road junction toward the Suez Canal.

"This operation was necessitated by the continuous Egyptian military attacks on citizens and on Israel land and sea communications, the purpose of which was to cause destruction and to deprive the people of Israel of the possibility of peaceful existence."

French Ambassador Pierre Gilbert was reported to have been critical when he sought information in an interview with Foreign Minister Golda Meir tonight.

British Ambassador Sir John Nichols was reported to have taken a position not far from that of the Americans, who had sharply condemned the Israeli military build-up.

Premier David Ben-Gurion replied this afternoon to two notes of warning from President Eisenhower. Mr. Ben-Gurion's message was delivered to United States Ambassador Edward B. Lawson. The note was reported to have explained the great danger to Israel from fedayeen attacks and from the establishment of a unified Egyptian-Jordanian-Syrian command under Egyptian control. This development was said here to presage a wider scope of fedayeen operations.

U. S. Begins Evacuation

Foreign military attachés were notified of the development at 8 o'clock tonight (1 P. M. Eastern standard time), one hour before the statement was issued to the press by Maj. David Landor, a Government spokesman.

The Israelis believed the time was ripe for action against Egypt because threatened Soviet intervention was obviated by the Kremlin's troubles in Eastern Europe.

While the Israeli troops were moving, sixty wives and children of United States technical assistance officials were evacuated to Athens in a United States Army transport plane. Fifty more dependents of embassy personnel are being evacuated tomorrow.

Earlier today the United States embassy posted notices to 2,000 citizens registered with the consulate here. They were advised "to leave Israel without delay."

An embassy spokesman said commercial airlines and shipping companies had been approached about providing transportation facilities on a commercial basis.

The British and French embassies said they were not urging their nationals to evacuate.

Subterfuge Used

The decision to move into Egypt was taken at a Cabinet meeting this morning. As a subterfuge, it was officially stated after the session that the meeting had been inconclusive and that it would be resumed Wednesday. The vote to the Cabinet was not made public.

Earlier today an Army spokesman reported a well had been blown up between Erez and Nir Am north of the tip of the Gaza Strip. The spokesman reported encounters with fedayeen in the same area during the night.

Reports from the area said an Army patrol near Erez challenged Arab raiders in the darkness at 3 A. M. The Arabs opened fire and the Israelis shot back.

When the shooting subsided the Israelis captured two men and found two wounded Arabs in fields. They found a bloody trail of other men who appear to have been wounded and got away.

Israelis who interrogated the prisoners said one of them spoke in an Egyptian dialect. He refused to give his name. The others were dressed in uniforms of the fedayeen and were Palestinian Arabs. They said the first man, known to them as Yusuf, commanded the group. They said they crossed into Israel from the Gaza Strip at midnight.

Burns Cancels Trip to Syria

JERUSALEM, Oct. 29 (Reuters)—A spokesman at United Nations truce headquarters here said Maj. Gen. E. L. M. Burns, chief truce supervisor, had postponed his departure by air for Damascus, Syria, and would remain at his headquarters.

Asked whether General Burns had ordered more United Nations military observers to the Israeli-Arab borders, the spokesman said headquarters was functioning on a "normal" schedule.

* * *

November 2, 1956

SOVIET TANKS AGAIN RING BUDAPEST; NAGY IN APPEAL TO U. N.

Nagy Quits Warsaw Pact, Declares Hungary Neutral

By JOHN MacCORMAC
Special to The New York Times.

BUDAPEST, Hungary, Friday, Nov. 2—Budapest is ringed with Soviet steel once again.

With Soviet tanks guarding every exit from the city, Premier Imre Nagy has demanded the immediate withdrawal of reinforcements Moscow is said to be pouring back into Hungary.

Two Soviet tank divisions were reported advancing on Budapest this morning.

The Hungarian regime said last night that the Premier had told the Soviet Ambassador, Yuri V. Andropov, that his Government would immediately denounce the Warsaw Pact, declare Hungary's neutrality and ask the help of the United Nations and the four great powers.

The Premier also cabled Dag Hammarskjold, Secretary General of the United Nations, asking that Hungary's case be put before the "forthcoming General Assembly."

The Gyor radio in western Hungary said this morning that new fighting between Hungarian and Soviet forces was under way in the eastern part of the country. Miskolc and Debrecen were reported to be threatened by Soviet air attacks.

Ferenc Erdei, leader of the National Peasants party, who is a member of Premier Nagy's inner Cabinet, was quoted as having said that "dramatic events" had been taking place in Hungary since yesterday morning. Mr. Erdei was said to have announced that strong Soviet forces had entered across the eastern border and occupied a large part of the country.

Mr. Erdei appealed to Hungarian workers to go back to their jobs despite the presence of Soviet troops. The Gyor radio, however, warned the workers to continue their strike as long as Soviet forces were in Hungary.

At 11:30 last evening there was some cannonading in Budapest, apparently in the west, and a few bursts of machine-gun fire.

That Soviet reinforcements were coming back into Hungary was known yesterday. Russian, East German and Czech residents here embarked on a steamer for Bratislava. The next development was Soviet occupation of the Budapest airfield. It is now surrounded by 160 Soviet tanks.

It was announced last night that a Hungarian Socialist workers (Communist) party had been formed, apparently succeeding the Working People's (Communist) party.

It was said that the new party was not grounded on orthodox Marxist-Leninist principles but instead on nationalist principles.

[The Presidium of the new party includes Janos Kadar, Gyorgy Lukacs, Imre Nagy, Zoltan Szanto and Ferenc Donat, Reuters reported.]

The Christian People's party, those formation was announced Wednesday, issued a statement last night. The party, which appears to be under the patronage of Joseph Cardinal Mindszenty, said that as long as the Hungarian Cabinet consisted of members who had "compromised themselves" the party could not collaborate with the Government.

Cardinal Mindszenty himself went on the air. He said he would study the present situation. He added that he would make another statement two days from now in which he would try to show how Hungary could emerge from her present difficulties.

Cabinet in Day-long Meeting

The Hungarian Government's announcement last night came after a day-long Cabinet meeting. Apparently the Government had received reports that left no doubt of Moscow's intentions.

The question is whether Hungary will use her Army to defend her territory. Of some significance in this connection is the fact that Lieut. Col. Pal Maletar, who led the heroic defenders of a Budapest barracks in their five-day fight against Soviet tanks, has been appointed Deputy Minister of Defense.

The Government's announcement that the Russians were returning caused a panic in the streets of Budapest. People hurried home to join their families.

A diplomat who visited the Soviet Embassy reported that it was deserted by all of its staff except the Ambassador and a few secretaries, and that boxes and crates were stacked as if for removal.

Russians Ring Airfields

Special to The New York Times.

VIENNA, Friday, Nov. 2—Soviet tank forces have surrounded Hungarian airfields, according to the Budapest radio, to assure safe evacuation of Russian wounded.

Other reports said that a procession of Soviet Embassy cars under military escort had operated a shuttle service to Budapest Airport through the day.

These reports suggested the Russians were moving out not only their wounded but also wives and children of the Embassy staff as well as Hungarian Communist officials whose lives are threatened by the revolutionaries.

Intent of U. N. Note in Doubt

Special to The New York Times.

UNITED NATIONS, N. Y., Nov. 1—Premier Nagy, in his note to Mr. Hammarskjold, asked today that the Hungarian case be placed as an additional item on the agenda of the "forthcoming Assembly." It was not clear whether this referred to the regular General Assembly session opening Nov. 12, or to the emergency meeting tonight on the Suez crisis.

Whether the matter is taken up at the emergency or the regular Assembly session, United Nations spokesmen said tonight, acceptance would be conditional on a favorable vote by a two-thirds majority, or thirty-nine nations.

Twenty votes in support of the Hungarian request are now assured with the arrival of more communications supporting the move made Sunday by Britain, France and the United States to bring the intervention of foreign troops in Hungary before the Security Council.

TEXT OF HUNGARIAN NOTE

Reliable reports have reached the Government of the Hungarian People's Republic that further Soviet units are entering into Hungary. The President of the Council of Ministers in his capacity of Minister for Foreign Affairs summoned [Yuri V.] Andropov, Ambassador Extraordinary and Plenipotentiary of the Soviet Union to Hungary, and expressed his strongest protest against the entry of further Soviet troops into Hungary. He demanded the instant and immediate withdrawal of these Soviet forces.

He informed the Soviet Ambassador that the Hungarian Government immediately repudiates the Warsaw Treaty and, at the same time, declares Hungary's neutrality and turns to the United Nations and requests the help of the four great powers in defending the country's neutrality. The Government of the Hungarian People's Republic made the declaration of neutrality on Nov. 1, 1956. Therefore I request Your Excellency promptly to put on the agenda of the forthcoming General Assembly of the United Nations the question of Hungary's neutrality and the defense of this neutrality by the four great powers.

* * *

BRITISH AND FRENCH FLEETS CLOSE ON SUEZ

AIRFIELDS RAKED

*Warships Move From North and South—
Carriers in Attack*

By THOMAS P. RONAN
Special to The New York Times.

LONDON, Friday, Nov. 2—British and French warships were closing in on the Suez Canal last night after an all-day pounding of Egyptian airfields by planes of the two nations.

The French Defense Ministry said the Allied naval forces were approaching the canal from the north or Mediterranean side and from the south in the Gulf of Suez. It gave no hint of their size, but the belief was they were prepared to land troops in the canal zone. There was no indication when the landing could be expected. [No further report had been received up to 5 A. M. New York time.]

It seemed obvious the British and French were hoping to discourage the Egyptians from resisting or to win a quick victory with a minimum of fighting.

Planes on Ground Hit

After a brief overnight interval, Cyprus and Malta-based bombers were joined for the first time yesterday morning by planes from British and French aircraft carriers in an intensified assault on the airfields. The object was to destroy as many planes as possible on the ground and neutralize the fields in advance of the landing.

British-French headquarters in Cyprus said more than fifty Egyptian planes on the ground were believed destroyed and at least forty seriously damaged. It also reported that French naval aircraft had attacked and set on fire an Egyptian destroyer of the Soviet Skoryl class off Alexandria this morning.

The communiqué added that no Allied losses had been reported. It said Egyptian interceptor aircraft had been sighted but had failed to engage the raiding planes. The Cairo radio said six British aircraft had been shot down.

The operation was to implement the ultimatum Tuesday by Britain and France that they would occupy the key positions of Port Said, Ismailia and Suez if the Egyptians and Israelis did not cease hostilities and withdraw their forces ten miles from the zone.

The British Ministry of Defense said a blockship prepared by the Egyptians for sinking in the canal to stop traffic had been sunk in Lake Timsah about halfway down the canal.

Allied Strength Cited

Early reports still to be confirmed by aerial reconnaissance said the ship had gone down in the lake outside the canal, the Ministry said. But Egyptian General Headquarters in Cairo described the ship as an Egyptian naval frigate and said all transit through the waterway had been stopped as a result of the sinking.

Anthony Head, Minister of Defense, told the House of Commons yesterday that the operations so far carried out were aimed solely at one purpose, "to induce the Egyptian Government to accept the requirement put forward."

In Cyprus, Gen. Sir Charles Keightley, Commander in Chief of the joint operation, said the attacking forces were sufficiently strong "to deal severe blows." "Our only hope is that we shall not need to use them," he added.

How swiftly the operations would end depend on how quickly Egypt agrees to the British-French demands, the general said.

"Purely as a military commander I must say that the sooner Egypt sees reason and agrees to temporary international control of the Suez Canal, the less lives will be lost," he declared.

That there might be stubborn fighting was indicated by President General Abdel Nasser when he told his people in a radio broadcast that arms were available for every citizen "to defend the enemy against usurpation and aggression."

"We shall fight from village to village, from place to place," he said.

Mr. Head also told the Commons of reports that Egyptian armored units deployed west of Cairo had begun moving eastward Wednesday toward Suez and Ismailia.

The force included an armored brigade, armored regiments equipped with light and heavy anti-aircraft weapons and infantry in armored personnel carriers, he said.

While the victories that Israel is reported to have scored in the northern Sinai Peninsula may soften the Egyptian opposition, Britain has flatly denied that she is concerting military action with Israel.

A Foreign Office spokesman said that suggestions to this effect were entirely false. He was commenting on an Israeli Government demand to Egyptian forces in the Sinai area to lay down their arms because their air force was about to be put out of action by "Anglo-French-Israeli bombing."

The military aims of Britain and France are as stated Tuesday and therefore are quite distinct from the aims of Israel, the spokesman said.

Jordan, Libya Reassured

The Foreign Office also announced that Jordan and Libya had been assured British bases in their territory would not be used for operations against Egypt.

In yesterday's air attacks, nine Egyptian Air Force fields were bombed and strafed. These included Almaza and Inchass near Cairo and Abu Suweir and Kabrit, former Royal Air Force stations in the Suez zone, which were hit yesterday.

The others were Fayid, Kasfareet, a former Royal Air Force maintenance station, Kabul, Cairo West and one other not yet named. All five were in the delta and canal zone.

The medium-level bombing raids Wednesday night were followed from dawn to dusk by low-level attacks by fighter-bombers armed with rocket-projectiles and cannon. The pilots reported that in addition to aircraft, runways, hangars and servicing buildings were badly damaged.

The British said unusual precautions were taken to avoid casualties among civilians and others. In some cases, delayed action bombs were dropped to give personnel a chance to get away, it was said.

Meanwhile, the British are continuing to marshal their military forces. The aircraft carrier Ark Royal, the Navy's largest operational ship, was recommissioned at Devonport yesterday.

With a displacement of 36,800 tons, the vessel carried fifty aircraft in peacetime, but her wartime striking power can be much greater.

The transport Empire Fowey sailed yesterday for the Mediterranean loaded with troops. The troopships Asturias and Dilwara and the liner New Australia, chartered for troop-carrying, are to sail today.

Under an order signed by Queen Elizabeth II, the Government obtained power to impose gasoline rationing. But a spokesman for the Ministry of Fuel and Power said that it was precautionary measure and that no decision had been made to reintroduce the wartime rationing.

Sir Walter Monckton, the Paymaster-General and former Minister of Defense, was named by the Government to coordinate all its information services during the operations in Egypt. He was Director General of the Ministry of Information from 1939 to 1940 and Director General of the British Propaganda and Information Services at Cairo in 1941 and 1942.

There was no confirmation from Government sources of reported mention by a Labor member of Commons today that anti-aircraft measures had been taken at some civil airports here.

The Foreign Office said that it had received a report from its embassy in Cairo that three employes of British contracting concerns in the canal zone had been arrested but that the charge was not known. The contractors' employes had been instructed Tuesday to leave the zone, the Foreign Office said.

*   *   *

November 4, 1956

SOVIET ATTACKS HUNGARY, SEIZES NAGY; U. S. LEGATION IN BUDAPEST UNDER FIRE; MINDSZENTY IN REFUGE WITH AMERICANS

CAPITAL STORMED

Freedom Radios Fade From Air
as Russians Shell Key Centers

By PAUL HOFMANN
Special to The New York Times.

VIENNA, Sunday, Nov. 4—Soviet troops started attacking Budapest and other Hungarian cities, towns and key military installations at dawn today.

At 9 A. M. local time (3 A. M. Eastern standard time) four hours after Budapest had been awakened by Russian artillery fire, overpowering Soviet tanks and infantry forces had stormed the Parliament Building and made Premier Nagy and most members of his government prisoners.

Fighting in Budapest and many other parts of the country was continuing but the prospects for the free Hungarian Government forces were nearly hopeless in the face of crushing Soviet superiority.

The Budapest radio and other Hungarian freedom stations went off the air one after another.

Before going silent they directed desperate pleas to the West, especially to the United States and to the United Nations, for help to save the Hungarian people from annihilation.

Mindszenty in U. S. Legation

Joseph Cardinal Mindszenty, Roman Catholic primate of Hungary who had been freed from detention last week, and his secretary had taken refuge in the building of the United States Legation.

The United States legation near the Parliament Building was under fire at 9:30 A. M.

A fierce battle was raging in the immediate surroundings.

At 7 A. M. "several hundred" Soviet heavy tanks were reported attacking key Hungarian Army positions on the outskirts of Budapest and attempting to penetrate the city. The main thrust of the Soviet forces came apparently from the southeast.

Shortly before 7 A. M. the Budapest radio repeated Premier Nagy's announcement of the Soviet attack. It directed an appeal to Dag Hammarskjold, Secretary General of the United Nations. At the same time the M. T. I. Hungarian news agency reported:

"Russian troops have suddenly attacked Budapest and the entire country. They have opened fire on everyone in Hungary. It is a general attack.

"Janos Kadar [since Oct. 24 secretary of the Hungarian Communist party], Gyorgy Marosan and Sandor Ronai have formed a new Government and started crushing the counter-revolution. They are on the side of the Russians."

Other reports said the three men had proclaimed a pro-Soviet regime in opposition to the Nagy Government.

This report indicated that the Soviet authorities had carefully prepared today's all-out assault politically, as well as militarily. They had apparent assurance about Kadar, who has the reputation of being an old tough Communist, as head of the counter-government challenging the Nagy cabinet.

During the early morning Premier Nagy again went on the air and called dramatically for Maj. Gen. Pal Maleter and Maj. Gen. Istvan Kovacs to return to their posts. General Maleter was the Nagy regime's Defense Minister and General Kovacs was Chief of Staff.

Generals Maleter and Kovacs and other members of a Hungarian military mission had left Budapest last night to meet Soviet officers for preliminary discussion of the withdrawal of Russian troops from Hungary. This meeting appears to have been a trap for the Hungarians. The indication here is that Generals Maleter and Kovacs and their companions were made prisoners by Russians.

Blow Struck from South

Information reaching Vienna confirmed that the main attack of the Soviet forces on Budapest came from the South. The thunder of artillery from the hillside south of the Danube stirred the city at 5 A. M.

Immediately afterward Hungarian armored detachments and troop transports raced into the suburbs and reinforced the roadblocks on the approaches to the Danube bridges.

Other reports from the Hungarian provinces showed that the Russians had started attacking everywhere at dawn.

The M. T. I. agency said that Gyor, a town half way between Vienna and Budapest, was completely encircled by the Soviet forces. Communications between Budapest and Szekesfehervar, the old coronation city southwest of Budapest, had been cut.

Farther to the south Pecs near the Yugoslav border was believed to be the scene of heavy fights between Soviet and Hungarian troops.

Soviet forces had started attacking the uranium mines and airfields near Pecs as early as 2 A. M. After several hours of fierce combat the Russians were said to have taken Pecs while the Hungarians claimed to be holding highways that lead out of that city.

Later, Soviet aircraft including MIG jet fighters were reported to participate in operations at Budapest. After thorough artillery preparation had attempted to soften Hungarian resistance, the Russian tanks and infantry advanced on the center of Budapest and stormed public buildings.

Radio Budapest went silent shortly after 8 A. M.

Afterward only the faint voice of the Freedom Radio at Eger in Northeast Hungary was heard. It implored the West to give immediate help.

"UN comes too late," the Eger station said. "Only an American ultimatum could halt the Russians from annihilating our whole people."

Nagy's Broadcast

Following is the text of Mr. Nagy's announcement made over the Free Budapest Radio Kossuth shortly after 5 A. M. (11 P. M. Saturday, Eastern standard time):

"Early this morning Soviet troops attacked the Hungarian capital with the open purpose to overthrow the legal Government.

"The Hungarian troops are in combat and the Hungarian Government is on its post."

"This I announce to our people and to the world."

The announcement was repeated in English, French and German by excited-sounding speakers on the Budapest radio every five minutes. Between announcements the Hungarian National Anthem and other patriotic musical pieces was played.

The Russians seized the military delegation commissioned by Mr. Nagy to negotiate for the withdrawal of all Soviet troops from Hungary.

A late message from M.T.I. ended with the words: "Long live Hungary and Europe! We shall die for Hungary and Europe!"

A Budapest broadcast in the Russian language to Soviet troops was heard about 7:20. It said, "Russian soldiers, do not shoot at Hungarians. Avoid bloodshed. The Hungarians are your friends."

Nagy's Ousting Reported

VIENNA, Sunday, Nov. 4 (AP)—The Russians launched a massive early morning attack against Hungary today and apparently succeeded in ousting the Government of Premier Imre Nagy.

An informant in the Szabad Nep newspaper office in Budapest reported shortly before 9 A.M. that the Government had been taken over by Janos Kadar, first secretary of the Hungarian Communist party. This had been announced on the radio, said the informant.

Heavy firing had been reported at the parliament building in Budapest where the Nagy Government had been installed. Mr. Nagy's fate was not known immediately although it had been reported earlier that he had been taken to safety.

The Australian press agency said, without stating its source of information, that the Parliament Building had been occupied and Mr. Nagy taken prisoner along with other members of his Government. Many of the Government ministers had been living in the building.

Bela Kovacs, leader of the Small Landholders party, who had joined in attempting to set up a coalition Government with Premier Nagy, also was reported to have disappeared.

The first Russian bombers were reported over Budapest at about 9:15 A. M. There were about fifteen planes accompanied by fighters.

Kadar's Red Move

VIENNA, Sunday, Nov. 4 (UP)—The proclamation by Janos Kadar, Hungarian Red who went over to the Russians during the night, was broadcast in Szolnok, a city sixty miles east of Budapest. Mr. Kadar said he had asked the Russian troops for help.

World of the Soviet attack in Budapest and the proclamation from Szolnok apparently heralded a new bloodbath for Hungary.

As many as 15,000 persons were estimated to have died in the revolution that erupted the night of Tuesday, Oct. 23, and as late as yesterday had seemed to be leading the way to a free Hungary.

Early today the Soviet troops that had been pouring into the country from Russia, Czechoslovakia and Rumania began their new drive.

The M. T. I. Hungarian news agency said fighting was under way at Veszprem, fifty miles southwest of Budapest and in Jutas and Hajmasker. It said the "biggest and heaviest fight" was near Hajmasker.

The Szolnok radio, reporting on the Kadar announcement of a new pro-Soviet regime, said four persons dismissed from Premier Nagy's cabinet last Thursday when Mr. Nagy was liberalizing his government, had been installed as ministers in the Kadar Government.

They included former Interior Minister Ferenc Munich, who had been considered a Titoist; Imre Dogel, who had been a National Assembly President, Isvan Kossa, former Finance Minister, and Gyorgy Marosan, a Social Democrat who helped put his party under Communist control.

Nagy Regime Balked

By JOHN MacCORMAC
Special to The New York Times.

BUDAPEST, Hungary, Nov. 3—Zoltan Tildy announced on behalf of the Hungarian Government at a news conference today that a joint Hungarian-Soviet military commission now was discussing how Soviet troops could be withdrawn from the country.

Mr. Tildy, a non-Communist and leader of the Smallholders party, said the Russians had agreed "in principle" to the appointment of a political committee to discuss the same subject.

Any optimism was dissipated, however, when Mr. Tildy, after absenting himself some minutes declared on his return:

"The answers to our protests against the influx of Soviet reinforcements have been unsatisfactory. This Government from its first days had demanded the withdrawal of Soviet troops. With this any legal or political basis for their presence disappeared. We demanded their withdrawal in innumerable notes. We have never received a satisfactory reply.

"Neither the Soviet Government nor the military commanders have ever informed us what roads they want to use, what points they want to occupy, or the direction or purpose of their military movements."

His replies strengthened a belief widely entertained here that the Russians, in their customary fashion, were dragging out the negotiations for the withdrawal of their troops to gain time to widen their occupation.

* * *

November 7, 1956

EISENHOWER BY A LANDSLIDE

41 STATES TO G.O.P.

President Sweeps All the North and West, Scores in South

By JAMES RESTON

Dwight David Eisenhower won yesterday the most spectacular Presidential election victory since Franklin D. Roosevelt submerged Alfred M. Landon in 1936.

The smiling 66-year-old hero of the Normandy invasion, who was in a Denver hospital recuperating from a heart attack just a year ago today, thus became the first Republican in this century to win two successive Presidential elections. William McKinley did it in 1896 and 1900.

Adlai E. Stevenson of Illinois, who lost to Mr. Eisenhower four years ago, thirty-nine states to nine, conceded defeat at 1:25 this morning.

At 4:45 A. M. President Eisenhower had won forty-one states to seven for Mr. Stevenson. His electoral lead at that time was 457 to 74 for Stevenson, and his popular vote was 25,071,331 to 18,337,431—up 2 per cent over 1952. Two hundred and sixty-six electoral votes are needed for election.

Victory in All Areas

This was a national victory in every conceivable way. It started in Connecticut. It swept every state in New England. It took New York by a plurality of more than 1,500,000. It carried all the Middle Atlantic states, all the Midwest, all the Rocky Mountain states and everything beyond the Rockies.

More than that, the Republican tide swept along the border states and to the South, carried all the states won by the G.O.P. there in 1952—Virginia, Texas, Tennessee and Florida—and even took Louisiana for the first time since the Hayes-Tilden election of 1876.

For the President and his 43-year old Vice Presidential running mate, Richard M. Nixon of California, who carried much of the Republican campaign, it was a more impressive victory than for the Republican party.

So close were many races for both the House and the Senate that control of the national legislature was not expected to be decided until later in the day.

About the only consolation for the Democrats other than that it was all over, was that they picked up strength in the Governor races and thus improved their chances of rebuilding for the post-Eisenhower election of 1960.

Starting with the advantage of holding twenty-seven state governorships to twenty-one for the Republicans, the Democrats won the state capitals yesterday in Iowa, Kansas and Massachusetts. Of the twenty-nine governorships at issue, they won twelve to ten with seven in doubt at 3:40 this morning.

The Eisenhower-Nixon sweep not only broke the Roosevelt coalition of the large urban states of the North and the "Solid South," but also carried into almost every group in the nation that was supposed to be strong for Mr. Stevenson and his running mate, Senator Estes Kefauver of Tennessee.

It clearly gained momentum in the last days during the fighting in the Middle East and Eastern Europe. It established the President as the man the nation wanted to lead it through the difficult period of transition in the Allied, Communist and neutral worlds.

The farm "revolt" was there all right in the areas where drought and falling prices had created a hardship situation, but it was not strong enough to sweep the farmers away from their natural Republican moorings.

Mr. Stevenson not only lost in the areas where his foreign policy arguments were supposed to be the strongest, as in New York, but he also lost ground on the civil rights issue in many of the Negro wards in the North.

He lost, too, in the so-called "Polish wards" of the North, no doubt because of the anti-Communist uprisings in Eastern Europe just as he was preparing to concentrate on the argument that the Administration's foreign policy had failed.

The Chicago Story

The story of Chicago illustrates what happened yesterday. Chicago, in Cook County, is the home of one of the strongest Democrat Party machines in the New Deal days, actually went for Eisenhower by a projected margin of about 16,000.

The irony of this was that Mr. Stevenson had founded his hope on the assumption that the Democratic Party machine was his main hope. Yet it failed him there, and the same trend was present if not so marked through most of the populous cities from the Mississippi to New York, another Democratic "stronghold," which Mr. Stevenson carried by fewer than 100,000 votes.

Outside of a few states of the Old Confederacy, Mr. Stevenson's forces broke against the combination of the President's popularity, the prosperity of the nation, and the ominous international situation, which brought out a record number of voters in a serious frame of mind.

The steel workers of Lorain, Ohio, the Negroes of Ward 32 in Philadelphia and the so-called Polish voters of Ward 21 in Buffalo, all supposed to be strong for the Democrats, shifted the other way.

They didn't "go Republican" but they cut down their margins for the Democrats. And when that happens the coalition that kept the Democrats in power for a generation in the Nineteen Thirties and Forties is badly hurt.

What was particularly impressive was the strength of the President's vote in the Northern and border state cities. Four years ago, he took Bridgeport by 314 votes. Yesterday he carried it by 16,000. He took 55 per cent of the total vote yesterday in New Haven which gave Mr. Stevenson 54 per cent of that city's vote in 1952.

The President now has the opportunity to pursue the three objectives he gave in explanation of his decision to seek reelection: the maintenance of a just and stable peace in the world; the strengthening of what he has called "The New Republicanism"—that is, conservative in fiscal affairs and liberal in human affairs—and finally the liberalization of the Republican party.

One of the most remarkable aspects of the President's victory is that he apparently was inclined not to seek re-election until after his heart attack a year ago last September. Before then, he repeatedly urged his party not to count on him but to find younger men to carry on the job he had started.

For example, when he was asked after he announced his candidacy last February what his decision was before his heart attack, he said this was something would probably not be disclosed until twenty-five years after his death. However, his associates have said privately that he finally decided to run because, after his convalescence, he felt it was too late to build up a successor who could win and he was determined to do what he could to liberalize his party and complete the program he had started.

The general expectation was that he would make a start toward rebuilding his party in his second term by changing his Cabinet at some key posts. Secretary of State Dulles is now in Walter Reed Hospital in Washington recovering from an operation to remove a cancerous section of his large intestine. He is expected to be given a new post, probably as a foreign affairs adviser to the President.

There have also been reports that Secretary of Defense Charles E. Wilson has no intention of staying on at the Pentagon through a second Eisenhower term, and Attorney General Herbert Brownell Jr. has told friends he will retire before the President's second-term inauguration on Jan. 20, 1957.

Gov. Christian A. Herter of Massachusetts, who started his federal government career in the State Department, former Gov. Thomas E. Dewey of New York, former U. S. High Commissioner in Germany, John J. McCloy, and General Eisenhower's former Chief of Staff at the North Atlantic Treaty headquarters, Gen. Alfred Gruenther, have all been mentioned as possibilities for any vacancies that may occur in the top four posts in the State and Defense departments.

Meanwhile, Sherman Adams, the Assistant to the President, and Vice President Nixon, who carried the main brunt of the campaigning for the Republicans in the last six weeks, are expected to assume increasingly important roles in the second Eisenhower Administration. The President, who will be seventy at the end of his second term, is forbidden by an amendment to the Constitution from seeking re-election in 1960.

Accordingly, with both General Eisenhower and probably Mr. Stevenson out of the running for the 1960 Presidential election, both parties will be seeking new potential candidates before long. Mr. Nixon and Mr. Adams are expected to be high on the Republican list of G. O. P. possibilities.

The main issues of the campaign were as follows:

• Mr. Stevenson asserted that President Eisenhower was too old at 66 to meet the responsibilities of his office for another four years. He characterized him as a "part-time resident" who delegated his Presidential responsibilities to cabinet officials of inferior ability, and, despite two major illnesses in the last year, had chosen as his Vice-Presidential running mate a controversial politician. Mr. Nixon, he declared would divide the country if he ever succeeded to the Presidency. President Eisenhower dissented on all counts.

• The Republicans contended that President Eisenhower alone had the popular following at home, and the experience and influence abroad, to guide the nation safely through a period of revolutionary transition in the world. The Democrats charged that, ever since the death of Stalin,

the President had failed to understand or deal effectively with the new Soviet leaders, or the rising nationalism of the neutral nations, and had allowed the Atlantic Alliance to split wide open over the present crisis in the Middle East.

• On the home front, the Republicans said that they had freed the national economy from unnecessary controls and not only had ended United States participation in foreign wars but also had produced the greatest era of prosperity in the history of the Republic. The Democrats, in reply, said this prosperity, like the Eisenhower "peace," was an illusion. They charged that the Republican appointments policy, tax policy, and farm policy had produced a "farm depression," and hurt "small business."

There were many subsidiary issues, including attempts by Mr. Stevenson late in the campaign to persuade the electorate that the President was remiss 1) in continuing tests of the hydrogen bomb and 2) in rejecting suggestions that the military manpower draft could be continued. However, there was little evidence that these issues had impressed the voters when they went to the polls yesterday.

The voting took place once more under pressure of extraordinary events overseas. Not since the election of 1944, when the Second World War was reaching its decisive phase with the American armies deep in Germany, have the American people gone to the polls so preoccupied with alarming foreign policy developments.

Despite the more hopeful news from Egypt yesterday afternoon, the war scare, combined with good weather over most of the nation, brought out an unexpectedly large crush at the polls.

The President drove to his home in Gettysburg, Pa., early yesterday morning after a meeting with his aides on the foreign situation. He and Mrs. Eisenhower reached the polling place at 11:15 A. M. and were applauded by their neighbors as they left the building. The President then flew back to Washington, though he originally had planned to drive back to the Capital.

Mr. Stevenson cast his ballot at Half Day, Ill., near his Libertyville farm. With him was his son, Borden, a first-time voter. Incidentally, the Census Bureau showed that 7,500,000 Americans reached voting age between the last Presidential election and this.

The Democratic nominee was cheerful and optimistic. He bantered with a small crowd at the polling place and said he had been told that leaders in several cities had reported to him that there was "a very strong Democratic turnout."

The Democratic Vice-Presidential nominee, Senator Estes Kefauver of Tennessee, the "iron man" of the campaign, was the last to stop exhorting the voters. He was in Miami, Fla., shaking hands with everybody within reach. He finally quit campaigning late yesterday morning and flew home to Chattanooga to cast his vote. Vice President Nixon had sent his absentee ballot to his home town of Whittier, Calif., earlier. He was in Washington yesterday.

* * *

April 23, 1957

DULLES STRESSES PEACEFUL FREEING OF RED COUNTRIES

With President's Approval He Implies Policy Now Includes Soviet Itself

LINKS IT TO FOREIGN AID

Secretary Appeals for Public Support of Help in Talk to The Associated Press

By RUSSELL PORTER

Secretary of State Dulles, with President Eisenhower's blessing yesterday, revived the idea of peaceful liberation of captive peoples as a positive concept.

He extended it by implication to take in eventual liberation of the people of the Soviet Union itself as well as the satellite nations from Soviet despotism. He also linked it with the issue of foreign aid now under attack in Congress. He urged public support of foreign aid, both military and economic, as a means of some day bringing about liberation without war.

Mr. Dulles put forward the doctrine of liberation for the satellites in the 1952 Presidential campaign. It was widely criticized as provocative. Subsequently it was played down or mentioned in the most guarded way, as in Mr. Dulles' speech in Dallas last October. Since the Hungarian revolt last fall it apparently has acquired new significance.

President Approved Text

The Secretary of State delivered a major foreign policy address yesterday before 1,600 members and guests of The Associated Press at its annual luncheon in the Waldorf-Astoria Hotel. His text had been approved by the President. Titled "Dynamic Peace," the address solemnly set forth the basic concepts of the Eisenhower foreign policy. Mr. Dulles said the policy was founded on collective action for "peace, justice and liberty."

Mr. Dulles said the vast majority of peoples, living under communism hated its despotism and longed for freedom. The United States can take advantage of this situation, he went on, by following the example of the American Revolution. Americans just freed from colonial rule then created a climate, he said, in which liberating forces were stimulated throughout world.

Americans now, he held, can spread world-wide knowledge of the "blessings of liberty." He said the United States would let the captive and divided nations under Soviet rule know they were not forgotten, that the United States would never make any deals with the Communists at their expense, and that it would help them as they gained more freedom.

Mr. Dulles said the United States should also make it apparent to the Soviet rulers that it sought the liberation of captive nations, and the reuniting of divided countries, not to encircle the Soviet Union but for the sake of peace and freedom.

The New York Times (by Carl T. Gossett Jr.)

ASKS FOR DYNAMIC PEACE: Secretary of State Dulles sets forth Administration's foreign policy in a major address before the annual luncheon here of The Associated Press.

"We revere and honor those who as martyrs gave their blood for freedom," he said of the Hungarian freedom martyrs. "But we do not incite violent revolt. Rather we encourage an evolution to freedom."

The pressures of liberty are rising throughout the Soviet orbit, he went on, even in the Soviet Union itself. There, he said, the people are demanding more personal security, intellectual freedom and material well-being.

Mr. Dulles said military defense of the free world would eventually collapse unless the free nations also collaborated to "spread the blessings of liberty." The use of United States government funds to aid undeveloped countries economically, he held, is not a "giveaway."

"It assures that the free world will be a vigorous, hopeful community," he said. "That corresponds to our interests and our desires.

"There are some who, in a zeal to economize, would slash that part of our budget which is often called 'foreign aid'—as though it did not aid us," he said. "That would not be economy but extravagance."

He said it was the "considered judgment" of the President and his military advisers that the defense budget of the United States would have to be greatly expanded if foreign aid were discontinued.

Mr. Dulles urged Egypt and other formerly colonial nations in the Middle East and elsewhere not to abuse their newly won independence by "flouting other independent nations" such as Israel. He warned that that would be "suicidal sovereignty" and would expose them to absorption by Communist despotism.

He defended United States policy in the Middle East. If the United States had acquiesced in the British-French invasion of Egypt, he said, it would have been disloyal to its commitment under the United Nations Charter to renounce the use of force except against armed attack.

Defending the extent to which the Administration has relied on the United Nations, he said:

"That is no abdication of foreign policy. It is the exercise of foreign policy, in the way which presents the best hope for humanity."

Mr. Dulles asserted that recent Soviet threats would not cause the North Atlantic Treaty Organization and other free-world defense alliances to break up. He said the United States would stand by its alliances, and under the Eisenhower Doctrine might extend these treaties into the Middle East.

"Collective measures are here to stay," he said.

He rejected the idea that world war was inevitable and said it could be averted by "waging peace * * * patiently, resolutely and resourcefully."

The speech was Mr. Dulles' first in President Eisenhower's second term and the Secretary's first major statement on foreign policy since last October.

The luncheon was the main event at yesterday's annual meeting of The Associated Press, a world-wide cooperative newsgathering organization. The meeting itself was the first event of New York's annual Press Week. Today, tomorrow and Thursday the American Newspaper Publishers Association will hold its annual convention at the Waldorf-Astoria.

* * *

July 3, 1957

U. S. PROPOSES BAN ON NUCLEAR TESTS FOR TEN MONTHS

Will Agree to a Suspension If Soviet Approves Halt in Making Such Arms

ZORIN SEEMS GRATIFIED

Stassen Makes Offer After Western Powers Present a Broad-Scale Plan

By DREW MIDDLETON
Special to The New York Times.

LONDON, July 2—The United States formally proposed today a ten-month suspension of tests of nuclear weapons.

Harold E. Stassen told the United Nations. Disarmament Subcommittee that the United States would agree with the Soviet Union to halt the tests of nuclear weapons if the Soviet Union agreed with the United States to stop the manufacture of such weapons.

The United States suggestion of a ten-month suspension of tests advanced further a broad proposal for a suspension of tests put forward at the committee meeting by the representatives of Canada, France, the United States and Britain, the four Western members of the subcommittee.

Valerian A. Zorin, chief Soviet representative, expressed the satisfaction and gratification of the Soviet delegation at the four-power proposals, United States sources said. He also asked for a detailed clarification of the proposal and said the Soviet delegation would have to study it before replying.

Zorin to Consult Moscow

Western diplomats said Mr. Zorin would consult his superiors in Moscow, probably by telegraph, possibly in person before submitting the Soviet answer. The four-power proposal was submitted by Selwyn Lloyd, British Foreign Secretary. It made these principal points:

• Acceptance by the Soviet Union of the requirements for inspection posts to monitor nuclear arms testing was welcomed as an "essential requirement" for progress on the suspension of tests.

• The "temporary suspension" of tests consequently is possible provided there is "precise agreement" on its duration, timing and controls and on its relation to first cuts in armed forces and designated non-nuclear arms and the end of the production of fissionable materials for weapons under agreed conditions.

• A group of experts should meet on a date to be decided by the subcommittee under its direction to prepare an inspection system to certify the suspension of tests, and the five delegation chairmen should consider the relationship of the suspension of testing to other provisions of a first-stage disarmament agreement.

Mr. Stassen spoke for an hour elaborating this basic proposal. It is expected that three or four more meetings will be required to complete his detailed exposition of the Western plan.

After Mr. Lloyd had spoken in support of the Western plan, Mr. Zorin asked Mr. Stassen for a detailed explanation of it. This was natural since the Western plan, in essence, represented a decision taken by the United States Government last month, which Mr. Stassen brought back here after his trip to Washington.

Therefore Mr. Stassen was describing the ramifications of what is basically a United States plan now accepted by other Western powers.

The three other Western chairmen did not get an opportunity to speak in support of Mr. Stassen after he had concluded his presentation. But Western reaction to his explanations was generally favorable.

The United States Administration is convinced that the type of agreement the West proposes is in the national interest of all nations concerned, including the United States, Mr. Stassen said.

Stassen Cites Alternative

He asked that in studying the proposals they be considered not in relation to some unattainable standard of perfection but in relation to the alternative of failure. It is only when this alternative, with all its dire consequences for mankind, is fully understood that the merits of a first-step agreement on disarmament can be truly evaluated, he remarked.

From the United States view Soviet acceptance of inspection was the turning point of the disarmament talks, Mr. Stassen went on. After this was made known June 14, the Washington Administration decided it was willing to take the first step toward disarmament with a ten-month suspension of nuclear arms tests.

During this period test monitoring posts could be set up throughout the world and put into operation for that period and for a longer period that might be agreed upon should the system be accepted, Mr. Stassen explained. The Soviet Union already has proposed the establishment of such posts on its own national territory and in the United States, Britain and in the Pacific areas.

Mr. Stassen said ten months also would provide time for other nations now outside the subcommittee to sign a first-step disarmament treaty. The United States believes such additional signatures are necessary to assure the success of the treaty, he remarked.

Early Suspension Urged

The United States will insist that suspension of the nuclear arms tests begin immediately upon ratification of a first-step disarmament treaty, Mr. Stassen said. A proposal for the suspension would be written into the treaty and not included in the annex establishing terms of negotiation.

During the ten-month period, national attitudes, by which Mr. Stassen evidently meant the attitude of the Soviet Union, would decide whether the period was to be expanded to two or three years or whether the agreement was to be broken off and the tests resumed.

The ten-month period also would provide time for the establishment of an inspection system to check the end of the manufacture of fissionable materials for military use. The United States hopes such a system might be put into effect in late 1959 or even earlier.

For a number of political and scientific reasons the prohibition of the manufacture of fissionable materials for use in weapons cannot become operative when the tests are suspended, Mr. Stassen explained. But arrangements for inspection and control of their manufacture can be completed or at least well begun during the suspension period, he said.

What the United States envisages is a treaty providing for a suspension of tests and for negotiations for the control and inspection of nuclear arms production, the United States delegate went on. The two cannot become operative simultaneously because at present the exchange of nuclear information is forbidden by law in the United States, he said.

Moreover, although the detection and monitoring of nuclear weapons tests already is well advanced, the negotiation of an agreement for controlling the manufacture of such arms would necessarily be an involved and intricate matter in which the scientists of all interested nations would be involved, Mr. Stassen said.

United States sources emphasized there was no suggestion that international control teams should take over the atomic economy of the nations involved. Inspection, rather than control, is the goal.

Rather sharply Mr. Stassen reminded Mr. Zorin that although it was important to get scientists working together on the technical questions the Soviet delegate had raised, the United States did not intend to let scientists make decisions.

Scientists advise, governments decide, Mr. Stassen said.

In the United States view an inspection system for the maintenance of a suspension of nuclear arms tests can be established rapidly if cooperation is forthcoming from other nations. The system would involve various methods now in use, including seismographic, electronic, barometric and the registration of radioactive fall-out.

The United States evidently recognizes that a ten-month temporary suspension would be a test period for the success of the whole first-step disarmament plan. Consequently the United States Government does not desire now to spell out exactly what its conditions would be for an expansion of the suspension period or for deciding that the proposal had failed.

On the whole most members of the Western delegations felt the day's meeting had brought them appreciably closer to the final stage of negotiation of a first-step disarmament treaty. There was no tendency to discount the risks involved. But these were felt to be balanced by these primary advantages offered by a first-step treaty:

- The elimination of the dangers of a surprise attack.
- The prevention of a spread of nuclear armaments.
- Protection against incidents that might lead to war.
- Relief of the armaments burdens on governments and peoples.

*   *   *

July 24, 1957

BOOKS OF THE TIMES

By ORVILLE PRESCOTT

Nevil Shute, one of the most consistently popular novelists in the English-speaking world, has an old habit of writing with immense good cheer about the most dreadful disasters and the most horrible possibilities. In one his early books, "Ordeal," he imagined what the serial bombardment of urban centers would be like in the Second World War and did not make too bad a guess. In "Pied Piper" he wrote about children orphaned by the war, and in "Most Secret" about the fun and games which can be had with a flame thrower. In his new novel, his twentieth, "On the Beach,"* Mr. Shute has turned his benevolent and sentimental attention to the year 1963 when most of mankind had already perished from the radioactive dust of "the short war" of 1962.

"On the Beach" is science fiction of the purest ray serene. During the last decade dozens of science-fiction writers have produced their variation on its central theme. But few indeed have treated it at such length or with such smooth narrative facility.

That's one thing Mr. Shute can always be counted on to do: to tell a story briskly. And as a former aeronautical engineer he can also be counted on to write with authoritative assurance about technical matters. In "On the Beach" his descriptions of the radioactive dust, which had already exterminated all life in the Northern Hemisphere and was slowly creeping southward around the globe, are enough to chill one's blood stream.

Contemplation and Doubt

But while one flinches from the contemplation of such an imminent finis to the human race and recognizes its possibility, it is still difficult to take Mr. Shute's story seriously. The same shortcomings that deface all his work are here as usual: the clumsy structure and awkward writing, the superficial and inadequate characterization, the odd mixture of precise and convincing circumstantial details with improbable and unconvincing human behavior.

In 1963 four characters and the rest of the population of South Australia had about nine months to live, according to the best estimates of the scientists. Peter Holmes was delighted to get a chance to further his career in the Royal Australian Navy as a liaison officer on an American atomic submarine. His wife, Mary, was happy planning changes in her garden which wouldn't show for several years. Mary dreamed of a normal world and refused to believe in the terrible real world about her. She is pathetic and the best realized of Mr. Shute's characters.

Dwight Towers, captain of the submarine, recognized the fate that awaited him, but disguised it in his own mind by thinking of death as a reunion with his wife and children. And Moira Davidson, who loved Dwight in vain, drowned her fear in double brandies.

Cause and Effect

What happens to this quartet is not particularly interesting; but what does happen happens so fast that one keeps reading. And if one's interest in Mr. Shute's people is tepid at best, it still is a matter of considerable interest to consider his book as a prophecy of doom.

The Third World War began as an Israeli-Arab War, spread into a Russian-NATO war and finished as a Russian-Chinese war. Some 4,700 nuclear bombs were dropped, none in the Southern Hemisphere.

"It's mighty difficult to stop a war when all the statesmen have been killed," remarked one of Mr. Shute's calm commentators. "It wasn't the big countries that set off this thing. It was the little ones, the Irresponsibles."

A scientist spoke up. "The trouble is, the damn things got too cheap. The original uranium bomb only cost about 50,000 quid toward the end. Every little pip-squeak country like Albania could have a stockpile of them, and every little country that had that thought it could defeat the major countries in a surprise attack. That was the real trouble."

Areas untouched by bombs were made uninhabitable by radioactivity. In Melbourne public drunkenness increased, and as time got short services and shops were left unattended. But there was no orgy of immorality, no riots and looting of the haves by the have-nots, no mass religious revival. Most people tried to go on as usual, even planting trees, building fences and studying at the university. A few devoted themselves to alco-

hol, which was said to increase resistance to the sickness caused by radioactivity. Some went fishing (the trout season was opened a month earlier than usual). And some participated in automobile races with a reckless daring hitherto unequaled in the world. The Government distributed free cyanide pills to all who wished to shorten their suffering when the time came.

All these grim and gruesome matters, plus a submarine trip to the uninhabitable West Coast of the United States, are described in "On the Beach" with an altogether remarkable degree of cheerfulness. If Mr. Shute intended to shock his readers and to aid the good cause of preventing nuclear warfare, he certainly chose an odd tone of voice in which to express his warning.
*ON THE BEACH. By Nevil Shute. 320 pages. Morrow. $3.95.

* * *

July 26, 1957

SUPINE SURRENDER

By GERALD SYKES

ON THE BEACH. By Nevil Shute. 320 pp. New York: William Morrow & Co, $3.95.

If this atomic thriller is ever televised, there may be a wilder stampede than Orson Welles wrought two decades ago with his Martians. The time is 1963, a final war has been fought, some 4,000 cobalt bombs have been dropped, and the end of humanity has come in all but the extremities of the Southern Hemisphere. In Australia, the residents of Melbourne know that winds are inexorably bringing radiation sickness and death in a few months. At the last moment the Government will issue suicide pills.

Cars and planes lie about unused—no gasoline. An old man in his club drinks more port than before—too much of it. A young woman who once dreamed of seeing Paris and of having children now resigns herself to as many brandies as she can put away.

Romance promised to enter her life briefly when a nuclear-powered American submarine comes safe and uncontaminated into port, and its commander meets her on a week-end party. They are attracted to each other—but she does not succeed in destroying his conviction, despite all the evidence, that his wife and children are still alive in Connecticut. Even after he has made an undersea voyage to the Pacific Coast of the United States and discovered no life at all through his periscope (though the neon signs are still blazing) the most she can get out of him is a nasty kiss. The story ends with her washing fatal pills down with brandy, as he sinks his ship and all Melbourne takes docilely to bed.

The humdrumness of the characters is no doubt intentional, since it makes their story more convincing. This is the orderly, unimaginative way most people would probably behave at the last crump. Perhaps Australia and the U. S. Navy have been slandered, but their order-following "solidity" does make the reader more nervous, as he wonders why they don't even come up with a wind-machine. The book after all, is a disguised sermon shrewdly designed to drive home what the aftermath of atomic war would mean and merits the widest possible reading.

Unlike his predecessors in the British novel of dismal prophecy (Aldous Huxley in "Brave New World" and George Orwell in "1984"), the more middlebrow Nevil Shute, who has written eighteen other novels, makes no attempt to appeal to the moral imagination. Philosophic passion is inconceivable in this cast of drab conformists, who permit life to be taken away from them without any assertion of its meaning or dignity.

"He stood up and poured himself a drink. 'You know,' he said, 'I'd rather have it this way. We've all got to die some day, some sooner and some later. The trouble always has been that you're never really ready, because you don't know when it's coming. Well, now we do know, and there's nothing to be done about it. I kind of like that * * *'"

If humanity ever does surrender as supinely as Mr. Shute's dramatis personae (I for one don't believe it could)—it will only deserve what it gets.

*　*　*

October 5, 1957

SOVIET FIRES EARTH SATELLITE INTO SPACE; IT IS CIRCLING THE GLOBE AT 18,000 M. P. H.; SPHERE TRACKED IN 4 CROSSINGS OVER U. S.

560 MILES HIGH

Visible With Simple Binoculars, Moscow Statement Says

By WILLIAM J. JORDEN
Special to The New York Times.

MOSCOW, Saturday, Oct. 5—The Soviet Union announced this morning that it successfully launched a man-made earth satellite into space yesterday.

The Russians calculated the satellite's orbit at a maximum of 560 miles above the earth and its speed at 18,000 miles an hour.

The official Soviet news agency Tass said the artificial moon, with a diameter of twenty-two inches and a weight of 184 pounds, was circling the earth once every hour and thirty-five minutes. This means more than fifteen times a day.

Two radio transmitters, Tass said, are sending signals continuously on frequencies of 20.005 and 40.002 megacycles. These signals were said to be strong enough to be picked up by amateur radio operators. The trajectory of the satellite is being tracked by numerous scientific stations.

Due Over Moscow Today

Tass said the satellite was moving at an angle of 65 degrees to the equatorial plane and would pass over the Moscow area twice today.

"Its flight," the announcement added, "will be observed in the rays of the rising and setting sun with the aid of the simplest optical instruments, such as binoculars and spyglasses."

The Soviet Union said the world's first satellite was "successfully launched" yesterday. Thus it asserted that it had put a scientific instrument into space before the United States. Washington has disclosed plans to launch a satellite next spring, Oct. 4."

The Moscow announcement said the Soviet Union planned to send up more and bigger and heavier artificial satellites during the current International Geophysical Year, an eighteen-month period of study of the earth, its crust and the space surrounding it.

Five Miles a Second

The rocket that carried the satellite into space left the earth at a rate of five miles a second, the Tass announcement said. Nothing was revealed, however, concerning the material of which the man-made moon was constructed or the site in the Soviet Union where the sphere was launched.

The Soviet Union said its sphere circling the earth had opened the way to interplanetary travel.

It did not pass up the opportunity to use the launching for propaganda purposes. It said in its announcement that people now could see how "the new socialist society" had turned the boldest dreams of mankind into reality.

Moscow said the satellite was the result of years of study and research on the part of soviet scientists.

Several Years of Study

Tass said:

"For several years the research and experimental designing work has been under way in the Soviet Union to create artificial satellites of the earth. It has already been reported in the press that the launching of the earth satellites in the U. S. S. R. had been planned in accordance with the program of International Geophysical Year research.

"As a result of intensive work by the research institutes and design bureaus, the first artificial earth satellite in the world has now been created. This first satellite was successfully launched in the U. S. S. R. October four."

The Soviet announcement said that as a result of the tremendous speed at which the satellite was moving it would burn up as soon as it reached the denser layers of the atmosphere. It gave no indication how soon that would be.

Military experts have said that the satellites would have no practicable military application in the foreseeable future. They said, however, that study of such satellites could provide valuable information that might be applied to flight studies for intercontinental ballistic missiles.

The satellites could not be used to drop atomic or hydrogen bombs or anything else on the earth, scientists have said. Nor could they be used in connection with the proposed plan for aerial inspection of military forces around the world.

An Aid to Scientists

Their real significance would be in providing scientists with important new information concerning the nature of the sun, cosmic radiation, solar radio interference and static-producing phenomena radiating from the north and south magnetic poles. All this information would be of inestimable value for those who are working on the problem of sending missiles and eventually men into the vast reaches of the solar system.

Publicly, Soviet scientists have approached the launching of the satellite with modesty and caution. On the advent of the International Geophysical Year last June they specifically disclaimed a desire to "race" the United States into the atmosphere with the little sphere.

The scientists spoke understandingly of "difficulties" they had heard described by their American counterparts. They refused several invitations to give any details about their own problems in designing the satellite and gave even less information than had been generally published about their work in the Soviet press.

Hinted of Launching

Concerning the launching of their first satellite, they said only that it would come "before the end of the geophysical year"—by the end of 1958.

Several weeks earlier, however, in a guarded interview given only to the Soviet press, Alexander N. Nesmeyanov, head of the Soviet Academy of Science, dropped a hint that the first launching would occur "within the next few months."

But generally Soviet scientists consistently refused to boast about their project or to give the public or other scientists much information about their progress. Key essentials concerning the design of their satellites, their planned altitude, speed and instruments to be carried in the small sphere, were carefully guarded secrets.

* * *

April 1, 1958

SOVIET ANNOUNCES ATOM-TEST HALT WITH CONDITION; U. S. WANTS CHECK; WEST REQUESTS PRE-SUMMIT PARLEY

WARNING IS GIVEN

Moscow Says It Will Resume Explosions if Example Is Ignored

By WILLIAM J. JORDEN
Special to The New York Times.

MOSCOW, March 31—The Soviet Union declared today that it was halting tests of atomic and hydrogen bombs. It called on the other nuclear powers, the United States and Britain, to do the same.

No time limit was set for the unilateral Soviet suspension of nuclear testing. The Government said that if other coun-

tries ignored the Soviet lead and continued bomb tests the Soviet Union would resume its own explosions.

The dramatic Soviet move was the highlight of the final meeting of a session of the Soviet Union's newly elected parliament, the Supreme Soviet. The measure was announced by Foreign Minister Andrei A. Gromyko.

Tractor Plan Approved

Other developments in the final day's gathering were the acceptance of Nikita S. Khrushchev's plan for abolishing machine-and-tractor stations and selling farm machinery to collective farms, and the naming of Premier Khrushchev's Cabinet.

But it was the Gromyko speech and the decision to halt nuclear tests that occupied most of the time and attracted most of the attention. Foreign diplomats recognized that the carefully calculated Soviet move once again had given Moscow the initiative.

The Kremlin was evidently forcing the United States and Britain either to follow the Soviet lead or to try to justify their rejection of a plan that doubtless would meet with wide approval.

'Clean' Bomb Derided

In setting forth the Soviet proposal, Mr. Gromyko said continued testing of nuclear weapons was making the world situation worse and was increasing the danger of war.

"The purpose and meaning of those explosions," he said, "is to develop new, even more destructive and deadly weapons of mass extermination, and not to study conditions of the use of those weapons in specific military situations."

He derided talk of developing "clean" bombs. He asked whether people would find it any more pleasant to be killed by a "clean" bomb than by a "dirty" one.

The Foreign Minister assailed the idea that nuclear bombs were necessary as a "deterrent" against attack. He said this was the talk of those who sought to mislead people and who planned to plunge the world into war.

He said most people realized hydrogen bombs could destroy everything in even fairly large European countries and that such bombs could be delivered to any point on the globe "almost instantaneously."

"It requires no great flights of fancy," he said "to imagine what the world will come to if the perfection of nuclear weapons is to proceed."

Mr. Gromyko said no special inspection methods would be required to insure that nations were not testing nuclear weapons. He charged that the United States Atomic Energy Commission had withheld information proving this contention. He said talk of the impossibility of detecting tests had been "fully disproved by the experience and opinion of specialists in both the Soviet Union and the United States."

Pact Hold Urgent Now

The Soviet spokesman said it was urgent to reach agreement on halting nuclear tests while only three countries—the

Soviet Union, the United States and Britain—had them. As other countries developed them, he said, it would become more difficult to reach agreement.

Mr. Gromyko derided France for wanting to become a nuclear power. He asked: "How many Frenchmen seriously believe that the road to genuine security and prosperity for their country can be blazed by atomic and hydrogen bombs with the trade mark 'Made in France.'?' form of a decree. It said that nuclear tests were contaminating the atmosphere with radioactive elements that threatened present and future generations. In addition to its decree on halting nuclear tests here the Supreme Soviet also:

• Sent separate appeals to the United States Congress and the British Parliament urging them to take similar action.

• Addressed a strongly worded message to the West German Bundestag warning against the "suicidal course" of accepting atomic and rocket weapons from the United States.

• Ordered the chairmen of the two houses of the Supreme Soviet to send messages to the Governments of all countries that fought against Germany in World War II, asking them to support the Soviet Union's position.

Mr. Gromyko in his speech was particularly bitter about West Germany and its leaders. He charged that "the same forces that brought Hitler to power" now wielded power in Bonn. He said the action of West Germany in expressing its willingness to accept atomic and rocket weapons could only be taken as a challenge to West Germany's neighbors.

The Foreign Minister warned that if the Nazis had been wrong in trying to smash the Soviet Union "the calculations of those in charge of West Germany's policies today are a million times more short-sighted and adventurous." He said that in case of war launched from West Germany that country would be the first to be engulfed in the "scorching flame of rocket and atomic war."

Mr. Gromyko said that by accepting atomic arms the West Germans would be shutting off the only remaining road to the unification of Germany. It would be "the death knell for German unity and this is what every German must know," he said.

The Soviet Union is not afraid for itself, Mr. Gromyko said, because it is strong enough to repel any attack. But his bitter words and his warning to the West Germans was a gauge of the deep feelings about the danger of a strong and remilitarized German state that prevails here.

The Soviet action raised two questions in the minds of foreign observers here. The first was what the reaction would be from Washington and London. The second was how long the Soviet Union would be willing to forego nuclear testing.

The United States has already announced that it plans to conduct tests in the Marshall Islands area of the Pacific Ocean in April. It has defined a danger zone there to go into effect on April 5. The Soviet decree gave no hint of the answer the Soviet Union would make if those tests were carried out.

TEXT OF RESOLUTION

LONDON, March 31 (AP)—*The text of the Soviet resolution on the suspension of nuclear tests as broadcast today by the Moscow radio:*

Deputy A. Gromyko has tabled in the Supreme Soviet a draft resolution providing for the cessation of tests of all forms of atomic and hydrogen weapons in the Soviet Union.

The Supreme Soviet has charged the Council of Ministers with the task of taking the necessary steps for the implementation of this decision and has addressed an appeal to the governments of other states possessing atomic and hydrogen bombs to take similar steps to insure the termination of tests of atomic and hydrogen weapons everywhere and for all time.

If other powers possessing atomic and hydrogen weapons continue tests of these weapons, the U. S. S. R. will naturally be free to act in the question of the carrying out of atomic and hydrogen tests by the Soviet Union in accordance with the interests of its own security.

*   *   *

May 14, 1958

U. S. FLIES TROOPS TO CARIBBEAN AS MOBS ATTACK NIXON IN CARACAS; EISENHOWER DEMANDS HIS SAFETY

ROCKS SMASH CAR

Vice President Unhurt

As Furious Crowds Halt Reception

By TAD SZULC
Special to The New York Times.

CARACAS, Venezuela, May 13—Hundreds of fury-spouting demonstrators attacked Vice President Richard M. Nixon's car with rocks and heavy sticks on his arrival today from Bogota.

About ten minutes later another mob, described as being in "lynching mood," tried to assault Army and Navy attachés of the United States Embassy at the National Pantheon. The Americans were there to attend the laying of a wreath by Mr. Nixon.

The ceremony never took place and two companies of helmeted infantry with poised bayonets were necessary to escort the two officers to safety.

Rocks Shatter Car Windows

In the first attack, three windows in the Vice President's closed limousine were smashed by melon-size rocks and Mr. Nixon was covered with shattered glass. Venezuelan Foreign Minister Oscar Garcia Lutin, riding next to the Vice President, was struck in the eye by a piece of glass.

[Later in the day mob violence broke out at the Government Palace as members of Venezuela's ruling junta returned from a meeting with Mr. Nixon, The Associated Press reported. The Government leaders' cars were stoned and two windows of one were smashed. Soldiers fired into the air and used tear gas to disperse the mob.]

The Vice President canceled all his scheduled visits in Caracas and said he would be seeing as many persons as possible at the Embassy residence. That building was the center of an armed camp tonight as more than 400 soldiers and military and civil policemen guarded Mr. Nixon.

Nixon Sees Red Direction

The Communist-led demonstrations appeared tonight to be turning into general manifestations against the Venezuelan armed forces and the governing junta.

Mr. Nixon, in a news conference, acknowledged that "a great majority of those who participated in the riots were not Communists." But he said "those who organized it were subject to central direction and are without a doubt Communist-dominated."

The Vice President's recognition of the fact that the presence in the United States of Venezuela's former dictator, Marcos Peréz Jiménez, and his police chief, Pedro Estrada, is one of the main irritants underlined the seriousness of the anti-United States sentiment here three and a half months after the dictatorship was overthrown.

Mr. Nixon said that in the light of an extradition treaty with Venezuela, the United States would be glad to take proper action and turn over Gen. Peréz Jiménez and Estrada if Venezuelan courts requested it.

"I personally could not think less of any of them," Mr. Nixon said.

[Gen. Peréz Jiménez has bought a home at Miami Beach and is believed to be in New York.]

Speaking of the attack on him, Mr. Nixon said: "It is not easy to endure the kind of activity we went through today. It certainty is not pleasant to be covered from head to foot with spit and to have a man spit directly in the face of my wife.

"We have a situation where the Communists were able to gain great support from students in this country because of what has happened here over the last ten years. What we are seeing is a terrible legacy of the dictatorship of Peréz Jiménez."

Venezuela's Ministers of Interior and Education and the heads of the three principal political parties went on the air tonight to appeal to the population to remain calm.

The assault on the Vice President came about noon when the Nixon motorcade was brought to a standstill by heavy lunchtime traffic on the Avenida Sucre. The cars became sitting targets for a screaming enraged crowd.

As if by prearranged signal the mob, made up of students, teenagers and older men emerged from a side street. To newsmen watching from a truck about fifteen feet ahead, it seemed several times that the rioters were on the verge of breaking into the big black car and dragging the Vice President out.

The car's doors were locked from inside. When the windows were smashed, two United States Secret Service agents riding in the limousine pulled out revolvers, ready to fire at the attackers.

Mr. Nixon had been warned that violence against him was expected. Last night there was even a report of an assassination plot. But he insisted on going through with the visit. However, he agreed not to use an open car and this may have saved his live.

Mrs. Nixon was riding in the second car, which also was showered with rocks. With her were the wife of the Foreign Minister and Maj. Don Hughes, Air Force aide to the Vice President. Later Major Hughes said, "Mrs. Nixon was as brave as any man I have ever seen."

Mob Menaces U. S. Attachés

The mob outburst at the National Pantheon, a shrine to Simon Bolivar, occurred after Mr. Nixon's party had bypassed the scheduled ceremony there. A car carrying Lieut. Col. Gerald Dailey, Army attaché, and Capt. Robert Hughes, Navy attaché and three Venezuelan officers missed the turn and drove up to the Pantheon.

Immediately they were engulfed by a mob of demonstrators, who forced them up on the steps of the shrine. The demonstrators had pelted the binding with eggs and smeared the walls with "Go home, Nixon."

Colonel Dailey and Captain Hughes were rescued when two infantry companies on hand as an honor guard rushed up the steps and circled the officers. To escort them to safety at an Army barracks, three blocks away, the soldiers had to jostle the crowd with bayonets.

This was by far the biggest and most violent organized demonstration against Mr. Nixon since he began his eight-nation South American tour April 26.

Whereas in Lima, Peru, last Thursday the highlight of two student demonstrations against Mr. Nixon was the heaving of a handful of stones, oranges and bottles and one man's spitting on the Vice President, today so many rocks were hurled that count was lost.

Spitting at Mr. Nixon and his party became so intensive that hardly a person in the group escaped it. Later the Vice President remarked: "I was covered with glass and something that was not rain."

*   *   *

July 16, 1958

EISENHOWER SENDS MARINES INTO LEBANON; CALLS FOR A U. N. FORCE TO REPLACE THEM; SOVIET CHARGES MOVE THREATENS NEW WAR

RECOGNIZES RISKS

President Says More Troops Will Go if They Are Needed

By FELIX BELAIR Jr.
Special to The New York Times.

WASHINGTON, July 15—President Eisenhower dispatched more than 5,000 marines with supporting sea and air power to revolt-ridden Lebanon early today to protect American lives and help that Government defend its sovereignty and independence.

In a special message to Congress the President later gave a detailed explanation of his action, saying the initial commitment of United States forces would be "augmented as required" and "withdrawn as rapidly as circumstances permit"

General Eisenhower recognized that "serious consequences" might follow the United States response to the urgent appeal for military assistance he received yesterday from President Camille Chamoun of Lebanon.

But he stressed that this country "could not in honor stand idly by in this hour of Lebanon's grave peril."

Necessary Despite Risks

"I have come to the considered and sober conclusion," said the President, "that despite the risks involved, this action is required to support the principles of justice and international law upon which peace and a stable international order depend."

In his separate statements during the day the President was at some pains to stress that "we wish to withdraw our forces as soon as the United Nations has taken further effective steps designed to safeguard Lebanese independence."

Meanwhile, General Eisenhower insisted, "we might be prepared to meet the situation, whatever the consequences." There was more than a hint in the President's context that the United States and Lebanon would be the judges of what they would consider "effective steps" by the United Nations to maintain Lebanese sovereignty and territorial integrity.

The President's recitation of his reasons for committing United States forces in the Middle East failed to win unanimous bipartisan support in Congress. Titular leaders, Democratic and Republican, were agreed that the President had taken the only course open to him.

Among some Democratic members of the Senate Foreign Relations Committee, however, the reaction ranged from doubting reservations to alarmed opposition. These sentiments were expressed on the Senate floor despite a clear endorsement by Senator Lyndon Johnson, the majority leader.

There were no more than a dozen members in the Senate chamber during the reading of the President's message.

A PLEDGE: Henry Cabot Lodge (left) tells Security Council U. S. Marines will remain in Lebanon only until the U. N. can insure country's "continued independence." A PROTEST: Arkady A. Sobolev (right) of the Soviet Union calls on the United States to "cease its armed intervention" in the affairs of the peoples of the Arab states.

In the House a lone dissenting Democrat was politely but firmly cut off by Speaker Sam Rayburn who made one of his rare comments from the chair by observing that it would be far better to allow matters to develop than to talk about them on the floor of the House.

The President's message to Congress was but one of three statements he issued during the day in explanation of his action. The first was handed at 9:20 A. M. to White House newsmen who had been alerted to be on hand from 7 A. M. A third explanation was made before newsreel and television cameras after he sent the message to Congress.

All were substantially the same. Later he addressed the nation by radio and television.

The President stressed to the newsmen that Lebanon had been the victim of clear aggression from without. He drew a line between the strident policies of the United Arab Republic of Egypt and Syria, and the free world concept of government with the consent of the governed and nonintervention in the internal affairs of independent sovereign states.

The gravity with which all parts of the Government viewed the Middle East political picture was emphasized by these other developments.

• The departure for an undisclosed destination overseas of a striking force from the tactical aid command. A Defense Department announcement of the move gave no details.

• An order to all units of the Atlantic and Pacific Fleets to be in readiness to sail on four hours' notice. The bomber fleet of the Strategic Air Command was ordered to be prepared for instant readiness.

• A warning to United States citizens everywhere to avoid travel in the Middle East, particularly in Lebanon and Iraq, except for the most urgent reasons.

It was clear from the private explanations of officials that President Eisenhower had decided to commit American forces first and then to notify the United Nations and Congress lest Lebanon, Jordan and possibly Saudi Arabia fall with Iraq under the sway of the United Arab Republic while the United Nations was deciding what might be done to prevent it.

It was beyond doubt, the President said, that the purpose of these activities was to overthrow the legally constituted Lebanese Government "and to install by violence a government which would subordinate the independence of Lebanon to the policies of the United Arab Republic."

Evidently determined that the American public in particular should understand his reasons for sending United States forces to Lebanon, the President reserved for his filmed explanation the linking up of the aggressive policies of the United Arab Republic with the carefully laid plans of international communism as dictated from Moscow.

Drawing an analogy between the insurrection in Iraq and the Communist attempt to take over Greece in 1947 and the frustration of that effort by United States military aid under the Truman Doctrine, General Eisenhower recalled similar and more successful Communist aggressions in Czechoslovakia, China, Korea and Indochina.

"We had hoped," the President told his unseen audience, "that these threats to the peace and to the independence and integrity of small nations had come to an end. Unhappily, they now reappear, Lebanon was selected to become a victim."

Turning then to the possible serious consequences mentioned in his Congressional message, the President said:

"The United States is determined that history shall not now be repeated. We are hopeful that the action which we are taking will both preserve the independence of Lebanon and check international violations, which, if they succeeded, would endanger world peace."

Drawing upon history, General Eisenhower said in his television presentation that it was the failure of the League of Nations to put down direct and indirect aggression in Europe, Asia and Africa that had made World War II inevitable.

The President appeared to be bearing up well under the impact of the far-reaching commitment on which he alone had decided. In his one public appearance of the day, he seemed in a jovial mood and confident of Congressional and public acceptance of the wisdom of his action.

This appearance came just before the lunch hour when General Eisenhower walked from his office in the west wing of the White House to an improvised podium below the south portico of the executive mansion to talk informally to a thousand high school students from many foreign lands. The students are preparing to return to their own countries after a year in the United States on exchange scholarships.

In his Congressional message the President suggested that the United States could do no less than proceed under Article 51 of the United Nations Charter, which recognizes the right of collective self-defense by member nations in emergencies.

PART V

THE GREAT CRISES: BERLIN, CUBA AND ELSEWHERE

November 11, 1958

KHRUSHCHEV BIDS FOUR POWERS END BERLIN CONTROL

Says at Polish Fete Soviet
Is Ready to Yield Role to East Germany

POTSDAM PACT ASSAILED

Soviet Premier Charges the West Has Made Accord
Virtually Dead Letter

By MAX FRANKEL
Special to The New York Times.

MOSCOW, Nov. 10—Premier Nikita S. Khrushchev demanded today the end of the Big Four occupation of Berlin. He said the Soviet Union was ready to turn over its functions there to East Germany.

The Soviet Premier spoke at a meeting honoring a visiting Polish delegation led by Wladyslaw Gomulka, Polish Communist leader.

[Mr. Khrushchev's challenge to the Western presence in Berlin was denounced by State Department officials as propagandistic and legally baseless.]

The Soviet leader called the Potsdam agreement of 1945, providing for four-power control of Berlin, "out of date." By consistently breaking the agreement, he said, the Western powers abolished the legal basis on which their stay in Berlin rested.

East German Role Stressed

Mr. Khrushchev told the United States, Britain and France that their right to be in the Western half of Berlin and their right of access to it through East German territory would have to be negotiated with the East German Government. The three Western powers and West Germany do not recognize East Germany.

The Soviet Premier warned that any attack against East Germany as a result of the proposed Soviet move would be considered an attack on the Soviet Union.

Mr. Khrushchev made it plain that he thought the Western occupation force should withdraw from West Berlin. He charged that the West had created "a kind of state" within a state in Berlin and was using it for "subversive activity" against East Germany, the Soviet Union and other Eastern European Communist countries.

For Normal Atmosphere

He called on the West to "create a normal atmosphere in the capital of the German Democratic Republic." But he did not order the Western powers out. Instead, he said:

"The Soviet Union, for its part, will hand over those functions in Berlin which are still with Soviet organs to the sovereign German Democratic Republic. I think that this would be the right thing to do.

"Let the United States, France and Britain form their own relations with the G. D. R. and come to an agreement with it if they are interested in certain questions connected with Berlin."

Mr. Khrushehev left the clear implication that West Berlin, situated like an island in Communist territory 100 miles from West Germany, was part of East German territory. He said that the air lanes, rail lines and highways hitherto recognized as Western access routes to West Berlin belonged to East Germany.

By stressing East German control of these transport links, Mr. Krushchev has presented Western powers with a problem potentially far more difficult for them than the Berlin blockade of 1948-49. At that time the Western right to use the air lanes into Berlin remained undisputed and the United States and Britain staged a dramatic airlift that kept West Berlin supplied with food and fuel for ten and one-half months.

Mr. Krushchev gave his hard-hitting address here this afternoon at a friendship meeting honoring the Polish delegation led by M. Gomulka, First Secretary of the United Workers (Communist) party.

M. Gomulka, who has been denouncing the rearming of West Germany throughout his seventeen-day sojourn in the Soviet Union, followed Mr. Krushchev to the rostrum at the Sports Palace and supported "the revision of the status of Berlin planned by the Soviet Union" as "logical."

Both the Soviet Premier and the Polish leader also denounced the "revisionism" of orthodox Communist theory by Yugoslav Communists. M. Gomulka said the Poles had done everything possible to dissuade the Yugoslavs from their present course. But when they refused to be influenced, he said, the Polish Communists criticized them even before they knew what Moscow's attitude would be.

Mr. Krushchev's announcement about Berlin overshadowed all else at the meeting. His declarations on the subject were enthusiastically applauded by an audience of 10,000 persons.

He began his discussion of the German issue by warning West German "ruling circles" that an attack on East Germany would be "tantamount to death" for West Germany, which "will not live more than one day in case of war."

The Soviet Premier reiterated Moscow's position that the reunification was a question for the two Germanys to settle without the interference of the occupation powers.

Since the Western nations have drawn West Germany into the North Atlantic treaty, the Soviet leader said, the Communist nations have every right to approach the Berlin question from the interests of the Warsaw Treaty, the Communists nations' counterpart of the Atlantic alliance.

Mr. Krushchev warned the West not to resort to force in answer to the Soviet action. He said:

"If any aggressive forces attack the German Democratic Republic, which is an equal member of the Warsaw Treaty, we shall consider this as an attack against the Soviet Union, against all countries that belong to the Warsaw Treaty."

M. Gomulka and the members of his delegation, including President Aleksander Zawadzki and Premier Jozef Cyrankiewicz, were feted at a Kremlin party tonight and will leave for home tomorrow morning. A communiqué covering their talks with the Soviet leaders will be published in several days.

Before leaving, the Poles invited Mr. Krushchev and other Soviet officials to visit Poland soon.

* * *

January 2, 1959

BATISTA AND REGIME FLEE CUBA; CASTRO MOVING TO TAKE POWER; MOBS RIOT AND LOOT IN HAVANA

ARMY HALTS FIRE

Rebels Seize Santiago and Santa Clara—
March on Capital

By R. HART PHILLIPS
Special to The New York Times.

HAVANA, Friday, Jan. 2—Fulgencio Batista resigned as President of rebellion-torn Cuba yesterday and fled to exile in the Dominican Republic. The rebel forces of Fidel Castro moved swiftly to seize power throughout the island.

Dr. Manuel Urrutia, Señor Castro's own choice, appeared likely early this morning to become the provisional President. Col. Ramon Barquin, who had been imprisoned for conspiring against the Batista Government, was brought here by military plane from the Isle of Pines penitentiary and named chief of the joint staffs.

Colonel Barquin immediately sent out a call to Señor Castro to come to the capital with Dr. Urrutia and set up a new Government. The rebel leader and his forces had entered Santiago de Cuba late yesterday and had taken over the Moncado army post without firing a shot. About 5,000 soldiers there surrendered.

Key Cities Captured

Truckloads of soldiers moved into Havana last night to maintain order in conjunction with militia of Señor Castro's 26th of July Movement, who were also patrolling the streets armed with machine guns and rifles.

The rebel forces forged ahead throughout the island. While some insurgents spread out from Santa Clara, capital of Las Villas Province, which they had seized Wednesday, other groups announced the capture of Camaguey.

General Batista led an exodus from Cuba that has reached a total of perhaps 400 persons fleeing by ship and plane to the United States and the Dominican Republic. They included key political and military leaders and their families.

Piedra Is Rejected

Calling his military chiefs together early yesterday at Camp Columbia, army headquarters, General Batista, strong man of Cuban politics for most of the period since 1933, declared he was resigning "to prevent further bloodshed."

He left behind a junta headed by Gen. Eulogio Cantillo, recently the commander in Oriente province, the center of the Castro revolt. The junta immediately designated Dr. Carlos Piedra, the oldest judge of the Supreme Court, as provisional President in accordance with the Constitution of 1940.

General Cantillo took over as chief of staff of the army. Dr. Gustavo Pelayo was designated Premier.

But Señor Castro declared that his insurgents would remain on a "war footing" and refused to accept the designation of Justice Piedra as provisional President. The Supreme Court refused to administer the oath of office to the Justice.

The rebel leader called a general strike for today in protest against the Piedra regime. He demanded that Dr. Urrutia, former judge of the Urgency Court of Santiago de Cuba, be installed as the provisional President, as he had proposed a year ago.

The Cane Planters Association of Cuba, speaking for the island's pivotal sugar industry, last night issued a statement supporting Señor Castro and his movement.

General Cantillo, as army chief, issued a cease-fire order to troops throughout the island. Political prisoners were being freed in Havana and the interior. Yesterday afternoon several hundred in Principe Fortress in Havana were released.

Restaurants Barricaded

Since it was New Year's Day, commerce and industry were halted. Restaurants, cafes and grocery stores closed their doors as rioting began. Mobs broke windows and looted some stores. The police fired on the mobs and a number of persons have been killed and wounded.

A mob set fire to the plant of El Tiempo, a newspaper owned by Senator Rolando Masferrer. Senator Masferrer, an intimate friend of General Batista, had a private army of some 2,000 operating in Oriente Province. They were accused by the inhabitants of many killings and tortures. The office of Dr. Rafael Guas Inclan, elected Mayor of Havana in November, was burned.

As the news of the fall of the Government spread early yesterday, the public poured into the streets.

The black and red flag of the 26th of July Movement, headed by Señor Castro, appeared on automobiles and buildings. Cars raced through the streets with horns blowing.

Mob Destroys Gambling Casino

Firing broke out near the docks but details were not immediately available. A mob destroyed the new gambling casino in the Plaza Hotel.

Amleto Battista, owner of the Sevilla Biltmore Hotel and its casino and a Representative in Congress, took refuge in the Uruguayan Embassy.

Armed young rebels seized the radio stations. Broadcasts called on the people to remain calm and orderly.

Crowds also attacked the Banco de la Construccion in the Central Plaza.

Latin-American embassies were crowded with officials who had taken political asylum. Hundreds of others were hiding in the city.

In the afternoon the National Association of Newspapermen declared a strike until the situation was clarified. But several Havana newspapers had published extra editions.

Cruise Ships Leave Port

United States Ambassador Earl E. T. Smith warned American citizens to take "appropriate precautions." Two big cruise ships with many American tourists aboard, in Havana harbor for the New Year's holiday, left yesterday.

Many tourists were stranded here by the swift fall of the Government. Plane service was curtailed for a time and ships arriving at Havana were unable to dock owing to the strike. The United States Embassy said it was trying to arrange transportation for a large number of tourists and some students who had asked its assistance.

Later, it was announced that it was arranging for a ship to come from Key West today to pick up stranded citizens.

City Almost Deserted

Restaurants and other establishments that closed during the voting did not open because personnel heeded the strike call. However most hotels supplied their guests with meals.

The resistance movement told the public that the strike would not include telephones, broadcasting and power services.

At night Havana was almost a deserted city, the inhabitants remaining in their homes. Only a few automobiles moved on the streets. The mobs had disappeared.

In the luxurious Miramar residential section, a few of the homes of high officials were looted, including that of the chief of the national police, Pilar Garcia, who fled in the morning.

No Patrolmen Seen on Street

No policemen on foot were seen patrolling the streets of Havana. Some patrol cars drove about. The lack of display of force was in startling contrast with the number of armed forces that patrolled the city and guarded strategic posts heretofore.

Later last night, troops and militiamen took over the task of guarding the city.

Eusebio Mujal, secretary general of the Confederation of Cuban Workers, sought asylum in the Argentine Embassy. Señor Mujal and his labor leaders strongly supported the Batista regime.

* * *

May 25, 1959

JOHN FOSTER DULLES DIES; SPECIAL FUNERAL DECREED; GENEVA TALKS TO SUSPEND

RITES WEDNESDAY

Burial in Arlington for Secretary of State From '53 to '59

By DANA ADAMS SCHMIDT
Special to The New York Times.

WASHINGTON, May 24—John Foster Dulles died this morning.

The man who was Secretary of State shaped United States foreign policy for six years died in his sleep of cancer complicated by pneumonia at 7:00 o'clock at Walter Reed Army Hospital. He was 71 years old.

His wife Janet; his two sons, John and Avery; a sister, Eleanor, and his brother Allen, stood in the bedroom of the Executive suite as he died.

When his labored breathing stopped, Mrs. Dulles moved silently to the head of the bed. A moment later the others turned quietly and left her alone in the green-painted room where Mr. Dulles had been a patient since Feb. 5, except for a two-week visit to Florida.

President Writes Tribute

President Eisenhower, notified within minutes at his Gettysburg farm, cancelled plans to go to church and wrote in longhand a tribute to his former Secretary of State as one of the truly great men of our time.

From many parts of the world words of praise for Mr. Dulles poured into Washington. They included messages from former President Harry S. Truman, Sir Winston Churchill and Congressional leaders of both Republican and Democratic parties.

At Geneva, the conference of foreign ministers agreed to recess to permit the Western ministers to attend the funeral. There was some speculation that Andrei A. Gromyko, the Soviet Foreign Minister, might also fly to Washington for the funeral.

President Eisenhower, who drove back to Washington this afternoon, ordered an official funeral with military honors on Wednesday afternoon.

Flags at Half Staff

By order of the President, flags at the White House, State Department, all official buildings in the United States and at embassies, legations and consulates abroad, were lowered to half staff.

Officials of the State Department said that the official funeral directed by the President would be the first of its kind. Official funerals are somewhat smaller and differ slightly in ceremony from state funerals, which are reserved for Presidents, Presidents-elect, Vice Presidents and Vice-Presidents-elect.

The State Department issued the following statement:

"By direction of President Eisenhower, an official funeral for the late John Foster Dulles will take place on Wednesday, May 27, 1959.

"The remains will lie at Bethlehem Chapel, National Cathedral, from noon, May 26, until noon, May 27. An honor guard will be posted.

"Those wishing to pay their respects are invited to do so at the Bethlehem Chapel.

"Services will be held at the National Cathedral at 2 P. M. on May 27.

"Dr. Roswell P. Barnes of New York City, a Secretary of the World Council of Churches, will officiate along with Dr. Paul Wolfe of the Brick Presbyterian Church in New York and Dr. Edward L. R. Elson of the National Presbyterian Church in Washington.

"Mr. Dulles was himself a ruling elder of the Presbyterian Church and the son of a minister of that church.

"Services will be followed by interment at Arlington National Cemetery where military honors will be rendered."

Although Mr. Dulles was an elder of the Presbyterian Church, the funeral will be held in the National Cathedral, a Protestant Episcopal church, because it is the largest in the capital.

Cancer Surgery in '56

Mr. Dulles was first operated on for abdominal cancer on Nov. 3, 1956. The operation was reported a success. After a brief convalescence, the Secretary resumed his duties.

On Dec. 5, 1958, upon returning from Mexico, Mr. Dulles was hospitalized for a week at Walter Reed Hospital for what was described as an inflamed colon. He left the hospital on Dec. 12 and no cancer finding was reported.

He went immediately to Paris for a meeting of the North Atlantic Treaty Organization's foreign ministers. He returned Dec. 16.

The Secretary left for Europe on Feb. 2 to confer on building Allied unity in the face of Soviet threats over Berlin.

Eight days later he entered Walter Reed for a hernia operation. The surgery was undertaken Feb. 13. The next day

President Eisenhower announced that laboratory examinations had showed that Mr. Dulles had abdominal cancer.

The physicians decided against any further surgery and on Feb. 20 deep X-ray therapy treatments began at Walter Reed. This therapy ended on March 17 after eighteen such treatments and an injection of radioactive gold.

Mr. Dulles remained at Walter Reed until March 31, when he went to Hobe Sound, Fla., for "rest and recuperation."

Cut Short Vacation

Although he had expected to remain in the South for three weeks, Mr. Dulles flew back to Washington on April 12 and re-entered Walter Reed. He was suffering increasing discomfort in his lower neck.

The State Department announced on April 14 that the neck discomfort was feared to be "attributable to the presence of malignant tumor in the lower cervical vertebrae."

The next day President Eisenhower sadly announced Mr. Dulles' resignation as Secretary of State.

Mrs. Dulles spent each night at the hospital. His sister, Eleanor, an official of the State Department in charge of Berlin affairs, returned from a trip to Germany. His sons, John, a mining engineer in Mexico City, and Avery, a Jesuit priest, who had been studying at the Vatican, also flew to Washington.

A daughter, Mrs. Robert Hinshaw of New York, and two sisters; Mrs. Margaret Edwards of Rye, N. Y., and Mrs. Natalie Seymour of Utica, N. Y., were also summoned.

His brother, Allen, director of the Central Intelligence Agency, resides here.

*   *   *

July 25, 1959

NIXON AND KHRUSHCHEV ARGUE IN PUBLIC AS U.S. EXHIBIT OPENS; ACCUSE EACH OTHER OF THREATS

NO TEMPERS LOST

Both Express Hopes for Agreement in Geneva Talks

By HARRISON E. SALISBURY
Special to The New York Times.

MOSCOW, July 24—Vice President Richard M. Nixon and Premier Nikita S. Khrushchev debated in public today the merits of washing machines, capitalism, free exchange of ideas, summit meetings, rockets and ultimatums.

Mr. Nixon cut a symbolic red ribbon and formally opened the American National Exhibition. He said the fair was representative of the American way of life and called for peaceful competition, spiritual as well as material, between the United States and the Soviet Union.

Premier Khrushchev joined Mr. Nixon in expressing hope that the American exposition would promote understanding between the two countries. In a message read by Mr. Nixon, President Eisenhower extended his best wishes to the Soviet people and said he hoped one day to visit them.

"We should be glad if President Eisenhower found it possible to visit the Soviet Union," Mr. Khrushchev said.

Clashes Mark Day

But the day was highlighted by the sharp informal exchanges that took place between Mr. Nixon and Mr. Khrushchev.

The exchanges started in Mr. Khrushchev's quiet offices in the Presidium Building of the Kremlin. They reached a high point in an hour-long debate in the kitchen of a model house at the exhibition, and they wound up with laughs, finger-shakings and more argument at the formal opening of the exhibition.

In the course of the discussion, Mr. Khrushchev accused Mr. Nixon of trying indirectly to threaten the Soviet Union. Mr. Nixon rejoined that Mr. Khrushchev, by saying that the Soviet Union had better weapons than the United States, was also making an indirect threat.

But both agreed that each nation wants peace.

Mr. Nixon appealed to Mr. Khrushchev not to let the Big Four Geneva conference of foreign ministers on Germany end in failure. He said it was now stalemated and that a way must be found to get it moving toward a solution.

Mr. Khrushchev agreed.

Mr. Khrushchev and Mr. Nixon debated with strong words and forceful arguments. But their talk was straightforward and there was no hint of ill feeling in their fast and furious interchanges.

Nothing like the Nixon-Khrushchev exchange has occurred within the memory of the gray-haired member of the Moscow or Washington press corps. Most of the talk was conducted with dozens of photographers recording every gesture. Newsmen sat at the feet of the Vice President and the Premier taking down each word.

Even to correspondents familiar with Mr. Khrushchev's capacity for catch-as-catch-can conversation and Mr. Nixon's ability to field rhetorical line drives, the day seemed more like an event dreamed up by a Hollywood script writer than a confrontation of two of the world's leading statesmen.

The high point occurred after the two men, accompanied by most of the members of the Soviet Presidium, had started a hectic tour of inspection of the American Exhibition.

Mr. Nixon had started the frank talk with some remarks earlier in Mr. Khrushchev's offices. They had a further exchange before the color cameras of the television studio of the exposition.

Argument in the Kitchen

But the climax came when they went into the model American home—the home that Pravda had criticized as not representative and too expensive for the average American worker.

Associated Press Radiophoto

INSIDE STORY: Vice President Richard M. Nixon describes operation of an automatic washing machine at the U. S. fair in Moscow to Premier Nikita S. Khrushchev of the Soviet Union. Mr. Nixon acted as host during tour of the fair.

The two statesmen, a little exhausted after battling through hundreds of camera men, newsmen and Russian and American workers, were walking rather swiftly through the house when Mr. Nixon halted Mr. Khrushchev.

He drew him over to the model kitchen. Here Mr. Nixon said: "You had a very nice house in your exhibition in New York. My wife and I saw and enjoyed it very much. I want to show you this kitchen. It is like those of our houses in California."

Mr. Nixon showed Mr. Khrushchev a built-in panel washing machine.

"We have such things," Mr. Khrushchev said.

"This is the newest model," Mr. Nixon replied. "This is the kind which is built in thousands of units for direct installation in the houses."

Mr. Nixon added a word about the interest of Americans in making the life of their women easier. Mr. Khrushchev rejoined that in the Soviet Union they did not have what he called "the capitalist attitude toward women," apparently meaning that discrimination and exploitation of women did not occur under communism.

"I think that this attitude toward women is universal," Mr. Nixon said. "What we want to do is to make more easy the life of our housewives."

Housing Prices Discussed

Mr. Nixon explained that the model house could be built for $14,000 and that most United States veterans of World War II had bought houses in the bracket of $10,000 to $15,000.

"Let me give you an example you can appreciate," Mr. Nixon said. "Our steel workers, as you know, are now on strike. But any steel worker could buy this house. They earn $3 an hour. This house costs about $100 a month to buy on a contract running twenty-five to thirty years."

"We have steel workers and we have peasants who also can afford to spend $14,000 for a house," Mr. Khrushchev said.

He said American houses were built to last only twenty years, so that the builders could sell new houses at the end of that time.

"We build firmly," Mr. Krushchev said. "We build for our children and grandchildren."

Mr. Nixon said he thought American houses would last more than twenty years, but even so, after twenty years many Americans want a new house or a new kitchen. Their kitchen is obsolete by that time, he said. The American system is designed to take advantage of new inventions and new techniques, he explained.

"This theory does not hold water," Mr. Krushchev rejoined. He said some things never get out of date—houses, for instance, furniture and furnishings perhaps, but not houses.

Mr. Khrushchev said he had read much that Americans had written about their houses and did not think it was all strictly accurate.

Mr. Khrushchev said he hoped he had not offended Mr. Nixon.

"I have been insulted by experts," Mr. Nixon said, laughing. "Everything we say is in good humor. Always speak frankly."

Mr. Khrushchev said in reply:

"The Americans have created their own image of the Soviet man and think that he is as you want him to be. But he is not as you think. You think the Russian people will be dumfounded to see these things, but the fact is that newly built Russian houses have all this equipment right now."

Moreover, Mr. Khrushchev said, "In Russia all you have to do to get a house is to be born in the Soviet Union. You are entitled to housing." "I was born in the Soviet Union," he continued, "so I have a right to a house. In America, if you don't have a dollar you have the right to choose between sleeping in a house or on the pavement. Yet you say that we are the slave of communism."

"I appreciate that you are very articulate and energetic," Mr. Nixon said.

"Energetic is not the same as wise," Mr. Khrushchev said with a laugh.

"If you were in our Senate," the Vice President said, "we would call you a filibuster. You do all the talking and don't let anyone else talk."

Mr. Nixon said the American exhibition was designed not to astound but to interest—just as was the Soviet exhibition in New York.

"Diversity, the right to choose, the fact that we have 1,000 builders building 1,000 different houses is the most important thing," Mr. Nixon said.

"We don't have one decision made at the top by one government official. This is the difference."

"On political problems," the Soviet Premier said, "we will never agree with you. For instance, Mikoyan likes very peppery soup. I do not. But this does not mean that we do not get along."

"You can learn from us, and we can learn from you," Mr. Nixon said. "There must be a free exchange. Let the people choose the kind of house, the kind of soup, the kind of ideas that they want."

And so it went on the opening day of the American National Exhibition in Moscow.

* * *

September 19, 1959

KHRUSHCHEV, IN U.N., BIDS NATIONS DISARM DOWN TO POLICE UNITS WITHIN FOUR YEARS; WEST IS CRITICAL; U. S. STRESSES CONTROL

WAR PERIL CITED

Destruction of Arms and Abolition of All Forces Asked

By THOMAS J. HAMILTON
Special to The New York Times.

UNITED NATIONS, N. Y., Sept. 18—Premier Khrushchev proposed today that all the nations of the world abolish their weapons and armed forces within four years and turn to competition in the arts of peace.

The Soviet Premier, speaking to the General Assembly, warned that "a single spark" would be enough to start a nuclear war.

With "general and complete disarmament," he said, "there would remain no material possibilities for the pursuit by states of any other than a peaceful policy."

He proposed that only forces needed to maintain internal security be retained.

Mr. Khrushchev recalled that when Maxim M. Litvinov, the Soviet representative at the League of Nations, proposed total disarmament in 1927 and 1932, critics attributed it to the weakness of the Soviet Union. It would be "preposterous" to make such a statement now, Mr. Khrushchev emphasized.

Anticipates Objections

The Soviet Premier, anticipating Western objections that his proposal was impracticable, said that his Government would agree to partial disarmament if the Western powers did not accept total disarmament.

These partial measures, however, would call for the withdrawal of United States forces from Western Europe and the liquidation of United States bases overseas, and are unacceptable to the Western powers.

Secretary of State Christian A. Herter promised "very careful examination" of the proposals, but drew attention to the necessity of "control," because "up to now the previous proposals have foundered on the Soviet Government's refusal to agree to effective controls."

Other Western delegates were more critical, and expressed the belief that the speech, which said that some of the money, saved by disarmament should go to under-developed coun-

STATEMENT OF POLICY: Soviet Premier Khrushchev speaking yesterday at United Nations General Assembly.

tries, was a propaganda appeal to the peoples of Asia, Africa and Latin America.

Under the three-stage Soviet program, the armies, navies and air forces of the world would be abolished, and foreign bases would be liquidated.

All types of armaments, including nuclear, rocket, bacteriological and chemical weapons, would be destroyed, and the manufacture of replacements would be prohibited.

Nuclear energy and rockets would then be used solely for peaceful purposes, Mr. Khrushchev said, and no state would retain any type of military force beyond that required to maintain internal security.

He promised "strict" international control by an organization in which all states would have membership. He said that the control organization "may set up a system of aerial observation and air photography over the territories," thus reviving the proposal for the detection of surprise attacks made by President Eisenhower at the summit conference in 1955.

However, Mr. Khrushchev's program apparently would defer the establishment and operation of the control body until the third and final phase of total disarmament was reached.

Ceilings on Forces Asked

In addition, a Soviet "declaration" outlining the program said that the first stage would be confined to the establish-

ment of ceilings of 1,700,00 men on the armed forces of the Soviet Union, the United States and Communist China, and 650,000 for Britain and France.

Armed forces and bases on foreign countries would be abolished in the second stage. The prohibition of air forces, nuclear weapons and outer space missiles would take effect in the third stage.

"The essence of all proposals is that over a period of four years all states should effect complete disarmament and should no longer have any means of waging war," Mr. Khrushchev said. "This means that land armies, navies and air forces shall cease to exist; that general staffs and war ministries shall be abolished; that military educational establishments shall be closed. Dozens of millions of men shall return to peaceful creative labor."

The partial disarmament program, as Mr. Khrushchev noted, was based on the Soviet proposals of May 10, 1955, which for a time gave new life to the negotiations in the subcommittee of the United Nations Disarmament Commission.

The partial program is as follows:

The establishment of a control and inspection zone, with the reduction of foreign troops in the territories of the corresponding countries of Western Europe.

The establishment of a denuclearized zone in Central Europe.

The withdrawal of all foreign troops from the territories of European states and liquidation of military bases in foreign territories.

The conclusion of a nonaggression pact between the members of the North Atlantic Treaty Organization and the Warsaw Treaty states.

Agreement on the prevention of surprise attack by one state against another.

Plan Proposed by Pole

All these points have been championed by the Soviet Union in recent years, although it has given only sporadic support to the proposal of an atom-free zone. This was first advanced by Adam Rapacki, Foreign Minister of Poland, in a speech in the General Assembly in October, 1957.

The first point did not make clear whether the "reduction" of foreign troops in Western Europe would be matched by reductions in Soviet forces in the Soviet satellites. No machinery for inspection and control to determine compliance was suggested by Mr. Khrushchev.

The first half-hour of the Premier's seventy-two-minute speech repeated the arguments he had advanced in favor of peaceful coexistence since his arrival in the United States Tuesday. He took occasion to emphasize once again the advantages he hopes will result from his exchange of visits with President Eisenhower.

Mr. Khrushchev, who was the sole speaker at today's meeting, avoided the inflammatory language that a succession of Soviet representatives—Andrei A. Gromyko, Yakov A. Malik, the late Andre I. Vishinsky—have used in the past when presenting disarmament proposals to the Assembly.

He was applauded when he walked into the Assembly hall with Dr. Victor A. Belaunde of Peru, the Assembly President. But the only major applause during his speech was when he denounced the Nationalist Government of China as "a corpse," and said that the Assembly should "carry it out" and seat the representatives of Communist China.

The nine members of the Soviet bloc, together with some Asian delegates, applauded determinedly at this statement.

The ten seats allotted to Nationalist China were vacant. Dr. T. F. Tsiang, the permanent delegate, had announced in advance that the delegation would boycott Mr. Khrushchev's appearance in the belief that the special arrangements made for his appearance at the United Nations went too far.

There was a shorter round of applause when Mr. Khrushchev began to discuss the disarmament situation.

Indian and most Asian and African delegates applauded when the Premier finished speaking, but the United States and most Western delegations were silent.

The Assembly adjourned immediately afterward, and Mr. Khrushchev, accompanied by Foreign Minister Gromyko left with Secretary General Dag Hammarskjold on a tour of the United Nations headquarters.

Later Mr. Khrushchev had a short talk with Mr. Hammarskjold, and he returned tonight for a dinner given by the Secretary General in his honor.

Welcomes New Members

Mr. Khrushchev gave a warm welcome to the new members of the United Nations from Asia and Africa—he did not include Israel since the Soviet Union now backs the Arab states.

Aside from his disarmament program, the only comment he made on other United Nations problems was his insistence that the organization must not take decision except by unanimous vote. Both the Assembly and the Council of the League of Nations were required to take most decisions by unanimous vote, and this played a part in the failure of the predecessor of the United Nations.

Mr. Khrushchev's insistence upon the necessity of the veto seemed to be a comment on the recent decision of the Security Council that overrode the negative vote of the Soviet Union to establish a subcommittee inquiry into the situation in Laos.

However, the Soviet Premier did not mention Laos.

He appealed to the United States, Britain and France to agree to a settlement of the Berlin question, but did not elaborate on the Soviet position.

It was assumed that if Mr. Khrushchev has anything new to say on either Berlin or the prohibition of nuclear test explosions, he is saving it for his final talks with President Eisenhower. These will be held at Camp David in Maryland at the end of the Premier's visit to the United States.

Mr. Khrushchev's failure to offer an concessions on the test explosion question was perhaps the most disappointing feature of his speech.

Negotiations between the United States, Britain and the Soviet Union, which began in Geneva last October, are to be resumed in a few days.

The differences have been narrowed to the point where only a few mutual concessions could produce an agreement. The major unsettled point is believed to be the Soviet refusal to drop its opposition to a dependable inspection system.

Mr. Herter told reporters tonight that the Soviet disarmament proposals would be considered by the new ten-nation disarmament group that the Big Four has set up outside the United Nations. This will meet in Geneva early next year.

Mr. Herter said he was uncertain whether the Soviet proposals would be considered in the Assembly. this might mean that the Western majority will insist that the proposals be considered by the disarmament group rather than by the Assembly.

In any event, Mr. Khrushchev's proposal for total disarmament stands no better chance of acceptance than the proposal by Mr. Litvinov between the two world wars.

The League of Nations Disarmament Commission ended in failure, and Mr. Khrushchev pointed out today that the years of negotiations in the United Nations have produced no results.

Many delegates believe it to be unrealistic, in the existing state of international tension, to talk about total disarmament after the failure of earlier efforts. Their hopes are now concentrated on getting an agreement on such a peripheral question as the prohibition of nuclear test explosions.

*   *   *

September 20, 1959

KHRUSHCHEV THREATENS TO RETURN HOME; WARNS COAST AUDIENCE OF SOVIET ROCKETS; PUTS QUESTION OF WAR OR PEACE UP TO U. S.

PREMIER ANGERED

Flares Up as Mayor Cites 'Bury You' Gibe—Is Still Hopeful

By HARRISON E. SALISBURY
Special to The New York Times.

LOS ANGELES, Sept. 19—Nikita S. Khrushchev's trip to America took a critical turn late tonight that raised serious implications as to its outcome and its effect on relations between the two countries.

The Soviet Premier told a Los Angeles audience that he still had hope that he and President Eisenhower could find common ground. But he warned that the question as it stood today was one of "war or peace, life or death." He strongly implied that the choice must be made by the United States.

Mr. Khrushchev told a stunned audience that he had come to America in only twelve and a half hours by plane and that he could return in ten and a half. Calling out in the audience to A. A. Tupelov, son of the designer of the aircraft on which he arrived, he asked, "isn't that so?"

"Less than that," was Mr. Tupelov's laconic reply.

An Outburst of Temper

There was no mistaking the grave course that the Khrushchev trip had taken, arising originally in what had appeared to be a limited temper outburst by Mr. Khrushchev over the refusal of State Department and local authorities to set up security arrangements that would enable him to pay a visit to Disneyland.

A few hours later, however, he was warning his audience in terms of the greatest seriousness that if the United States really wanted to continue the "cold war" it was welcome to do so and that it would find in such a continuation that the Soviet Union was able to hold its own and then some.

"If you want to go on with the arms race, very well," Mr. Khrushchev said. "We accept that challenge. As for the output of rockets—well, they are on the assembly line. This is a most serious question. It is one of life or death, ladies and gentlemen. One of war and peace.

"If you don't understand—" a voice from the audience shouted in Russian "Panimiau" ("We understand").

Mr. Khrushchev's grave remarks were uttered after the close of a formal speech at a civic dinner at which he was the honored guest of the city of Los Angeles and the Los Angeles World Affairs Council. Mayor Norris Poulson had mentioned in his introductory re-remarks a phrase of Mr. Khrushchev once uttered, "We will bury you."

Mayor Poulson told Mr. Khrushhcev that Los Angeles was not interested in burying anyone, but that if challenged it was prepared to take up the challenge.

Mr. Khrushchev took this as his text and made it plain that he felt that he was being made the victim of a calculated campaign of needling.

He said "the unpleasant thought" had been creeping up on him that someone had thought that once Mr. Khrushchev had been brought to America that it would be a good idea to "rub him in your sauce" and show him the might and strength of the United States and that this might make him "a little shaky in his knees."

"Well," Mr. Khrushchev said, "it took me twelve and a half hours to get here and it will take me ten and a half hours to get home."

Seeks Common Ground

However, he then said that in spite of this he did feel that it would be possible to find a common language with the United States. He said that he was the first Russian Premier, and the first Soviet Premier as well, ever to visit the United States and that if his visit came to naught perhaps he would be the last Russian Prime Minister to visit the United States.

"You may say that you can live without such visits," Mr. Khrushchev said, "but it is much better to live in peace than to live with loaded pistols and guns aimed at objectives. It's much better to live in peace and be sure that your sleep will not be disturbed and that the peace will be eternal."

Mr. Khrushchev delivered his words in tones of the utmost gravity. He made it plain that he felt that he was being received in a manner that was light and frivolous.

He said that he had never before, in any of his speeches in the United States, mentioned rockets because he did not believe in using threats, but when he did this tonight he felt he had no other choice because he was being challenged to go ahead and continue the "cold war."

"But think what that means with modern weapons?" he said.

Stresses Disarmament Plea

In his prepared speech Mr. Khrushchev made a strong plea in behalf of the total disarmament proposals he submitted to the United Nations General Assembly yesterday.

"We have unvarying faith in the good aspirations of human beings and that human beings are not born to kill each other but to live in peace and friendship," he said. "You know that the First Commandment of the Christian religion says 'Thou shalt not kill.'"

Mr. Khrushchev said that he realized that the idea of disarmament has enemies in that not everyone will like his new proposals. Nevertheless he expressed hope that as a result of his talks with President Eisenhower the governments of the Soviet Union and the United States would arrive at better understanding of each other's positions.

Premier Khushchev indicated that he did not expect immediate acceptance of his "total disarmament" plan. But he said he would hope that it would lead to closer understanding between the United States and his country on the problem of controlling the arms race.

Speaking before a group of civic leaders, business men and public officials in this Southern California city, Mr. Khrushchev repeated most of his more familiar themes—peace, better understanding and ending of the "cold war."

Fresh from his barbed and impromptu exchange with Spyros P. Skouras, president of the Twentieth Century-Fox Film Corporation, at a movie industry luncheon, Mr. Khrushchev took a considerably softer and milder approach in his prepared talk. The Premier concentrated on the similarities he said existed between the Russian and American people.

At the luncheon, Mr. Skouras' sharp questions had provoked the Premier into recalling the intervention of United States troops in the Soviet Union after the Russian Revolution. Tonight Mr. Khrushchev quoted President Eisenhower, who once said that "our two countries have always been at peace."

The Premier's speech, made in the glittering main ballroom of the Ambassador Hotel, seemed almost deliberately designed to smooth the ruffled feelings that his luncheon appearance aroused. He spoke of close relations, better understanding and of the advantages to all people of a reduction in tensions of the "cold war."

About 1,000 persons attended the dinner.

Mr. Khrushchev sat at the head table between Walter Coombs, president of the World Affairs Council, and Mayor Norris Poulson. The guest of honor wore a black suit, a light gray tie and the familiar decorations on his lapels.

When he spoke of the plan to eliminate all armaments—nuclear as well as traditional—the Soviet Premier offered a broad hint that he expected no immediate acceptance. He realized, he said, that his proposal "will not be to everybody's liking."

He asserted that he hoped the response would be favorable in the United States, but he said it in a way that did not show any great expectation.

"We also hope," he added "that as a result of our talks with President Eisenhower, the Governments of the U. S. S. R. better understand each other's and the U. S. A. will be able to positions on the question of disarmament and then will join their efforts in solving the most complex, the most vital problem of our time."

At the same time, he attacked the one thing that the United States and its allies insist upon in discussing any disarmament plan: effective supervision and control.

Mr. Khrushchev referred to such control as "military intelligence." If there were no armies, he said, "such intelligence becomes meaningless."

The Premier likened Los Angeles famous smog to the "cold war." Both contain much "inflammable material," he said.

Premier Khrushchev expressed gratitude for the opportunity he had received in his tour "to acquaint ourselves with the life and achievement of the great American people."

*   *   *

September 25, 1959

KHRUSHCHEV OPENS TALKS WITH EISENHOWER TODAY; AN ATOMIC ACCORD LIKELY

TOUR OF U. S. ENDS

Reason, Not Force, Urged by Premier as Parley Basis

By HARRISON E. SALISBURY
Special to The New York Times.

WASHINGTON, Sept. 24—Premier Khrushchev returned to Washington tonight with a call for talks with President Eisenhower based on reason and not force.

Tomorrow he will begin three days of talks with the President.

Mr. Khrushchev arrived from Pittsburgh, where he had had a friendly reception from some of the largest crowds of his American tour. His plane landed at 5:29 P. M. The party drove directly to Blair House, the President's guest house.

Hopes for Agreement

Tonight, at a dinner attended by a small group of business leaders, Mr. Khrushchev was quoted as saying that he would begin his talks with the President with the impression that the United States wants agreement with the Soviet Union "to live in peace."

He was reported also to have said that he was convinced that the American people wanted peace, but that the Government had still to prove itself.

This seemed at variance with his statement in San Francisco Monday that he drew no distinction between the Government of the United States and the American people.

Mr. Khrushchev was represented as saying at the dinner, which was given at the Sheraton-Carlton Hotel by Eric Ridder, publisher of The Journal of Commerce, that disarmament and willingness to trade were the tests of whether the United States wanted war or peace.

Host at a Reception

Earlier, the Premier and Mme. Khrushchev were hosts at a diplomatic reception for more than 500 guests at the Soviet Embassy.

Tomorrow he will lunch with Secretary of State Christian A. Herter. He will leave late in the afternoon for the talks with the President in Camp David, Md. The other members of the Premier's family are expected to stay here until the departure of the entire party for Moscow Sunday night.

At a luncheon at the University of Pittsburgh, Mr. Khrushchev made a fervent appeal for a reasonable approach in the Camp David discussions.

"May God give us the strength," he said, "to solve matters by reason and not by force. That is what the people are expecting from us."

Mr. Khrushchev said the purpose of the talks was to seek "a reasonable solution." He said he hoped that neither he nor President Eisenhower would interpret the unity of public support that each commands in his own country in "an oversimplified way."

If either of them did, he said, the outcome of the conversations would not be "such a joyful one."

The talks, he suggested, would then become a kind of "bulls' contest."

It would, he said, become a competition to see "who was more stubborn, who had the stronger legs and the longer horns and who could shift the other from his position."

"You have strong legs," he said. "Ours don't bend either."

Mr. Khrushchev's remarks were touched off by a statement from Gov. David L. Lawrence of Pennsylvania who told him he would find Americans united, regardless of party, in support of Mr. Eisenhower's foreign policy.

'Mandate of Love' Seen

Mr. Khrushchev said he preferred to interpret Governor Lawrence's remarks as a "mandate of your confidence and your love for the President, and for that I take part in the search for a reasonable solution leading to the strengthening of friendship between our peoples and leading to world peace."

"I have come here with precisely such a confidence and support on the part of my people and these sentiments will guide me in my talks with your President," Mr. Khrushchev said. "If our two countries instead of distrusting each other establish relations of trust and pool their efforts in the struggle to strengthen peace for themselves and for all, we shall be supported by the peoples of the whole world."

Mr. Khrushchev said he wanted to bring the "cold war" to an end but "the political cold is coming from you and not from us."

"We are not afraid of the cold but we would like more favorable winds to blow," he said.

Mr. Khrushchev's call for reasonableness was in line with the tone of his day in Pittsburgh. He spent the morning touring the sprawling Mesta Machine Company works along the Monongahela River at near-by West Homestead. This is one of the few large plants in the area that have not been affected by the steel strike.

He had high praise for some of the techniques, but criticized several of the machines. In each case, the Mesta executives said Mr. Khrushchev's points were well taken.

At one point he suggested that a kind of gear would better be made by a rolling process. The Mesta men asked if the Russians had invented such a method. Mr. Khrushchev shrugged.

No Pickets Visible

In a morning of driving around Pittsburgh, he never saw a union picket, although he several times passed big mills on strike, including the famous United States Steel Corporation mill at Homestead. Only token picket lines are maintained at the mills.

Mr. Khrushchev did encounter large groups all along his line of march. Many schools turned out, and the youngsters cheered him shrilly. In the center of Pittsburgh, the Golden Triangle area, and around the Carlton House Hotel, where he halted briefly at noon, there were large crowds.

He was guest at a civic luncheon given him by the University of Pittsburgh, the city and the state, at the University.

Mr. Khrushchev began to deliver a prepared speech, but after reading a few paragraphs he turned it over to his interpreter to read to save time.

In his text Mr. Khrushchev called for outlawing the cold war "for all time, now and forever."

He said the purpose of his mission to America was to lay the groundwork for the United States and the Soviet Union to "live in the world like good neighbors." He said he felt a good start had been made through the agreement for the exchange of visits by himself and President Eisenhower.

"If we both have a will for this there will be a way," Mr. Khrushchev observed.

How happy the world would be, he said, if all the steel now used for war could be used for peace, if all the production of Pittsburgh could be devoted to peaceful rather than military purposes.

"Even if we had two lives," he said, "we should devote them both to this one task of establishing peace among our countries."

He said the people dreamed of the day when all arms would be sent to the open hearth furnaces to be melted down for peaceful uses, when the atom was used only for peace and when "the sword is beaten into ploughshares."

He said that at times there were gaps in the "gray skies" in international relations, and that such a time was present.

The alternative to outlawing war, said Mr. Khrushchev, is ashes and destruction.

"Peace not war," he said, "is the natural state of mankind."

He said some people had supposed that his purpose in coming to America was to divide up the world between the United States and the Soviet Union. This, he said, would be a highway robber's reasoning.

"We use our strength," the Premier said, "to serve peace and international security. The talks are useful not only to our countries but to others as well."

Mr. Khrushchev, as on many occasions in his American tour, had a few remarks about religion and prayer. He expressed his deep appreciation to the Roman Catholic Bishop of Pittsburgh, John Joseph Wright, who, he said he had been informed, had appealed to all to receive Mr. Khrushchev like good hosts.

He said his trip had shown him that the United States was a rich country and that the people were "living a good life."

He recalled that when the United States declared a week of prayer for the "slaves of Communism" he urged Americans to come to the Soviet Union and see how the slaves are living.

"I have come to see how the slaves of capitalism are living," he said. "I see that the way they live is not bad at all."

But, he added, the Soviet Union will catch up and overtake the United States. He said this would be achieved by creative effort. But even better than surpassing the United States, he said, "would be to march step in step with each other."

In any event, he said, in the competition of the two countries there "will be no bloodshed."

* * *

February 13, 1960

FRANCE EXPLODES HER FIRST A-BOMB IN A SAHARA TEST

Successful Shot Puts Paris With U. S., Soviet and Britain as Nuclear Power

DE GAULLE HAILS FEAT

Plutonium Device Is Used— Weather Reported Clear and Blast Area Safe

By W. GRANGER BLAIR
Special to The New York Times.

PARIS, Saturday, Feb. 13—France successfully exploded her first atomic bomb this morning in the Sahara.

The explosion took place at 7 A. M. [1 A. M. Eastern Standard time] at the atomic proving grounds near Reggan in southwestern Algeria. The weather was clear and the area had been checked for security.

The nuclear material used was plutonium and the bomb was exploded from a tower.

The explosion marked the entrance of France under President de Gaulle into the nuclear club of the United States, the Soviet Union and Britain.

Statement by de Gaulle

The announcement of the explosion was made in a statement released by the Elysee Palace, residence of President de Gaulle. The statement said:

"The President of the French Republic and Community makes known that on Feb. 13 at 0700 hours (7 A. M.), taking into account meteorological conditions, which were very favorable, the order was given to explode an atomic device in the Sahara Desert at Tanezrouf, southwest of Reggan. The explosion took place in the conditions of strength and security foreseen.

"The device was placed at the summit of a tower. The explosive utilized was plutonium.

"The security of the populations of the Sahara and of neighboring countries has been integrally assured.

"General de Gaulle expresses the gratitude of the nation toward the artisans of this success: ministers and scholars, officers and engineers, industrial workers and technicians. Thus France, because of her national effort, can reinforce her defensive potential, that of the community and that of the West.

"On the other hand, the French Republic is better placed to make its actions felt for the conclusion of agreements among the atomic powers with a view toward realizing nuclear disarmament."

Technicians at Hand

The only persons who witnessed the historic moment were several hundred French technicians and military personnel at the bomb site. No Cabinet Minister was present.

No technical information was given in this morning's official announcement of the Sahara blast. It was estimated, though, that the explosive force of the bomb was greater than the equivalent of 20,000 tons of TNT, which was approximately the force of the United States' first atomic bomb at Hiroshima in 1945.

It was understood that the nuclear device was exploded at the top of a steel tower about 300 feet high. More explosions, probably of a similar nature, are expected to be set off soon.

Work on the bomb test site commenced two years ago. Reggan is 750 miles south of Algiers and about 625 miles southeast of Casablanca, the two major cities nearest to the proving grounds.

More than 200 nuclear devices have been exploded since the atomic era opened on July 16, 1945, at Alamorgordo, N. M. This blast was quickly followed by those over Hiroshima and Nagasaki which brought Japan to her knees and ended World War II.

Other momentous steps in the growth of the world's atomic powers came on July 14, 1949, when the Soviets exploded their first atomic bomb, and on Oct. 3, 1952, when the British exploded their first atomic bomb.

Warning Issued to Airlines

Yesterday the French Government announced that it was putting into effect at 6:30 A. M. today tight security regulations against flights over the region of the Sahara that had been set apart for the atomic test. The announcement was directed to airlines concerned.

The Government issued a similar warning Jan. 21, only to rescind it several hours later.

The warning to the airlines, which are predominantly British and French, that normally fly over the Sahara was flashed at 3:45 P. M. This was in accordance with the Jan. 8 Government announcement that airlines would have at least twelve hours' notice to adjust their flight schedules.

Divided Into Zones

The flight-security region in the Sahara is divided into Central, Blue and Green Zones.

The central zone, known as Zone 42, covers 23,000 square miles and includes Reggan in its northern area. France has not permitted flights over this area since Oct. 15.

Around the central zone is a belt about thirty miles wide that is called the Blue Zone. Planes are forbidden to enter this zone at an altitude of less than 9,750 feet for six hours after "H" hour, or 6:30 A. M. tomorrow.

Surrounding the Central and Blue Zones is a vast area known as the Green Zone. This extends from Rio de Oro in the west to the Libyan frontier in the east and reaches south 1,000 miles from El Goléa in Algeria. For a twelve-hour period following "H" hour planes will not be allowed to fly over the Green Zone at an altitude above 9,750 feet.

The different regulations were established for the Green and Blue Zones because of usually prevailing wind conditions. Winds are expected to keep radioactive fall-out above 9,750 feet in the Green Zone and below that altitude in the Blue Zone.

* * *

May 6, 1960

SOVIET DOWNS AMERICAN PLANE; U.S. SAYS IT WAS WEATHER CRAFT; KHRUSHCHEV SEES SUMMIT BLOW

PREMIER IS BITTER

Assails 'Provocation Aimed at Wrecking' May 16 Parley

By OSGOOD CARUTHERS
Special to The New York Times.

MOSCOW, May 5—Premier Khrushchev said today that a United States plane on a mission of "aggressive provocation aimed at wrecking the summit conference" invaded Soviet territory May 1 and was shot down.

The Premier, in the most blistering speech against American policies he had made since his meetings with President Eisenhower last autumn, declared that the incursion, as well as declarations by United States policy makers, cast gloom on the prospects for the success of the summit meeting in Paris eleven days hence.

He expressed anger over the fact that President Eisenhower had supported declarations against Soviet foreign policies by Vice President Richard M. Nixon, Secretary of State Christian A. Herter, Under Secretary of State Douglas Dillon and others.

He Seems to Bar Nixon

He surmised, Mr. Khrushchev said, that General Eisenhower, while wanting peace, was a victim of tight restrictions by "imperialists and militarists" around him.

Mr. Khrushchev expressed regret that the President wanted to limit the summit meeting to one week and he virtually rejected a proposal to sit at the table with Mr. Nixon if the Vice President was delegated to take over for General Eisenhower in case the session went over the time limit.

The most sensational section of Mr. Khnushchev's three-and-a-half-hour speech, made before the opening session of the Supreme Soviet, the nation's version of a parliament, was that concerning the charges of United States violations of Soviet airspace.

Foreign Policy to Fore

Mr. Khrushchev actually had been called upon to open the Supreme Soviet session to deal exclusively with sweeping new domestic policies that will affect every Soviet worker: gradual abolition of income taxes by 1965 and by next year, reduction of the work day to seven hours and an upward revaluation of the ruble.

However, the Soviet leader seized the occasion to discuss foreign policy and the summit conference. He apparently had determined to tell the Soviet people that recent Western actions and statements had darkened his previous optimism.

The Premier predicted to foreign diplomats earlier this week that his talk on foreign and domestic policies would contain major surprises. Indeed, his report of the plane incident came as a shock to Westerners and Soviet citizens alike. The United States Ambassador, Llewellyn E. Thompson Jr., would make no comment on the development.

Mr. Khrushchev declared that actually there had been two incidents involving intrusions by United States military planes during the last month.

One plane, he said, flew from the direction of Afghanistan and was permitted to leave without military action or subsequent-diplomatic protest.

On May Day morning, he said with emotion, "when our people were celebrating their most beloved holiday," another plane crossed the southern borders and on quickly delivered orders from the highest authority in Moscow, was shot down.

The Premier gave no details as to the type of plane, which was said to bear no markings, or the fate of its crew.

[The United States said the plane was a U-2 weather-observation plane carrying a crew of one.]

He declared that it was presumed by the Kremlin that both planes had been based in either Turkey, Iran or Pakistan "which are linked with the United States in the aggressive" Central Treaty Organization.

Mr. Khrushchev said the Soviet Union intended not only to protest to the United States over the second incident but also to take the matter before the United Nations Security Council. His Government also will extend "serious warnings" to countries that permit the American planes to be based on their territory, he added.

These heated disclosures raised an explosive outcry of "bandits," "aggressors" and other angry expletives among the more than 1,300 deputies gathered from all over the Soviet Union to give quick and unanimous approval to Mr. Khrushchev's policies.

Foreign observers in the huge white hall of the Grand Kremlin Palace got the impression that these were expressions of genuine surprise and consternation.

Even before his address Mr. Khrushchev had let it be known that he was upset and, in fact, angered by a series of recent policy declarations from the United States and the North Atlantic alliance regarding the Western refusal to budge from the status quo on the German question.

It was his contention that his agreement with President Eisenhower during his meeting at Camp David last September had provided that on the question of Germany and West Berlin there would be no ultimatums but also no stalling on efforts to come to at least an interim agreement.

He spoke once again about a speech by Mr. Dillon, as he had last week in a surprisingly tough speech at the oil center of Baku, in Azerbaijan. Mr. Dillon's assertion that Mr. Khrushchev was walking on thin ice on the German issue particularly irked the Premier. His retort was:

"If one should speak of thin ice at all, then look, Mr. Dillon, what are you standing on? Your policy rests in large measure on the support of colonialism, the enslavement and the plundering of backward peoples and economically dependent countries."

Later Premier Khrushchev declared that recent statements by Messrs. Herter, Nixon and Dillon were "a bad sign."

"They are far from giving hope for a favorable conclusion of negotiations that open on May 16," he continued.

"Unfortunately, these speeches have been approved by the President of the United States himself, who stated at a press conference that they had set out the foreign policy of the United States Government. This makes things still worse."

Letter From Eisenhower

Mr. Khrushchev said he had received a letter from President Eisenhower in which the President had said he could stay in Paris only until May 23 and then would have to return home after a stop in Lisbon, Portugal.

The President also informed him, he said, that if the summit conference went beyond this date Vice President Nixon would be delegated to sit in for the United States.

"The intention of the United States President is to be regretted," Mr. Khrushchev asserted.

He said he had replied that the duration of the conference should be decided by all four participants after they had seen how the meeting was developing. He said it was his belief that there was no more important business at hand.

"And if a statesman intends to limit his attendance at the conference irrespective of the progress of the talks, this shows that the questions which are to be discussed at the summit meeting evidently are not given due attention by the United States Government.

"I do not doubt President Eisenhower's sincere desire for peace. But though the President is the highest authority in the United States, there are evidently circles which restrict him."

As far as sitting down with Mr. Nixon was concerned, Mr. Khrushchev said he had already met the Vice President on several occasions. The Premier added:

"I find it difficult to get rid of the impression that Mr. Nixon bothers about anything, but least of all about reaching agreement on disputes, liquidating the state of tension, ending the cold war and the arms race. May Mr. Nixon pardon me for my frankness, but I told him this when we met and I hope that he will not condemn me for stating this now in our Parliament.

"I am afraid that if Mr. Nixon is instructed to hold these negotiations, a situation might arise resembling the one of which the people: 'To leave the cabbage to the care of the goat.'"

Mr. Khrushchev said that recent negotiations in Geneva on disarmament and the banning of tests of nuclear weapons had not produced signs of a Western intention to come to agreement on these vital issues.

"Comrade Deputies," Mr. Khrushchev declared, reading from a prepared speech, in an emotion-laden voice, "the impression is being formed that the aggressive actions newly taken by the United States against the Soviet Union are a foretaste of the summit meeting.

"Are they taken in order to exert pressure on us and to attempt to frighten us with their military superiority in order to undermine our determination to work for easing tension, to eliminate the cold war and to put an end to the arms race?

"All these missions are sent in order to prevent any agreement on vexing questions, for we cannot say that this aircraft was a harbinger of peace; that it was on a goodwill mission. No it was a real bandit flight with aggressive intentions.

"We can say to those gentlemen who sent the aircraft that if they think they can bend our knees and our backs by means of such pressure, this will have no effect on us."

The Premier expressed gratitude to the military unit that had fulfilled the task of "securing the borders of our country with honor" by shooting down the plane on May Day. This gave him the opportunity to repeat a threat that the Soviet Union would retaliate with its new rocket force against any attack and that foreign bases from which such an attack was launched would also be destroyed.

Nevertheless, Mr. Khrushchev urged against an emotional reaction to his disclosures and said he still planned to go to the summit meeting "with a pure heart" and with the full intention to seek agreement with the West. He said he did not consider the intrusion as a reconnaissance in prelude to war.

The Premier added that he believed the American people, "except for certain imperialist, monopolist circles," wanted peace and friendship with the Soviet Union.

* * *

May 6, 1960

U. S. ASKS DETAILS OF PLANE INCIDENT

---

*Data Sought From Envoy in Moscow
as Washington Reacts With Restraint*

By WILLIAM J. JORDEN
Special to The New York Times.

WASHINGTON, May 5—Washington reacted with restraint today to Premier Krushchev's announcement that a United States plane had been shot down Sunday on Soviet territory.

There were some angry words on Capitol Hill—including a suggestion that President Eisenhower refuse to go to the summit meeting with Mr. Krushchev in Paris May 16. But the

Administration would say little more than that additional information was being sought from Moscow.

A message went to Ambassador Llewellyn E. Thompson Jr. in Moscow this afternoon instructing him to request more details from the Soviet authorities.

Text Made Available Late

The text of Mr. Krushchev's long speech to the Supreme Soviet became available to officials only late this afternoon. Their first reaction was that he seemed to be preparing the way for placing the blame for a summit failure on the Western powers.

He also seemed to be giving advance warning that the Allied leaders could expect little softness from him at the Paris meeting. The consensus was that the Krushchev address was the latest move in pre-summit maneuvering, but that it had not altered measurably the outlook for the summit meeting.

Mr. Krushchev said that the Governments of the United States, Britain and France did not seem to be looking forward to settlement of major East-West differences at the summit.

The State Department admitted the possibility that the plane, identified there as an unarmed U-2 weather reconnaissance craft of the National Aeronautics and Space Administration, might have crossed the Soviet frontier by accident.

The question was raised, however, why the weaponless craft had been shot down and not merely forced to land. Diplomats also questioned the propriety of the Soviet Premier's decision to announce the incident publicly before informing the United States.

The Premier's approach appeared to officials here to be an effort to incline the Western Governments to soften their own positions. He has given no sign of being prepared to modify his own demands, particularly on the vexed question of Berlin, officials said.

West Plans Berlin Firmness

It was noted that Mr. Khrushchev said nothing new today on any of the major problems that the governmental leaders will consider at Paris on disarmament, a nuclear test ban, or Berlin.

In this connection, it was thought here that Mr. Khrushchev's speech at Baku last month—in which he again threatened to sign a separate peace treaty with the East German Communist regime—had done more to dampen hopes for the summit than his speech to the Supreme Soviet.

Such a treaty, Mr. Khrushchev said, would end Allied rights in Berlin and would transfer controls over land, sea and air routes to the city to the East Germans.

The Western Governments have said they would not permit any lessening of their rights in Berlin. They have hoped to reach some interim agreement with Mr. Khrushchev on Berlin to end the diplomatic crisis.

Mr. Khrushchev's recent statements have reduced those hopes. It now seems that he is intent on pressing his stand on Berlin, counting on a weakening of Allied resolve.

It is believed by some influential officials here that heavy pressure from Mr. Khrushchev on the Berlin problem at the summit meeting might produce a cancellation of President Eisenhower's planned trip to Moscow in June. The plane incident might also influence that trip, it was believed.

The White House declined any comment on this problem this afternoon. James C. Hagerty, press secretary, refused to say anything about the downed aircraft or the President's plans.

There is a feeling among some Soviet experts that Premier Khrushchev has been under some pressure to adopt a tougher stand in foreign affairs. It is believed that some of the Premier's colleagues in the Soviet hierarchy have contended that too much talk of relaxing tensions and of peaceful coexistence with the West weakens internal discipline in parts of the Soviet bloc.

But it was recognized, of course, that tough talk now by Mr. Khrushchev would only enhance the impact of any concessions he might be prepared to make at Paris. It remains to be seen, officials here said, how much of the Baku and Supreme Soviet speeches are firm policy and how much was designed to lay the groundwork for the summit meeting.

Senator Styles Bridges, Republican of New Hampshire, said he thought President Eisenhower should refuse to go to the Paris meeting until he had a proper explanation of the Soviet action.

Senator Mike Mansfield, Democrat of Montana, said prospects for the summit were poor indeed "if the Russians are going to shoot first and complain later."

Controls Questioned

Senator Mansfield also said the plane incident raised the question of adequate controls over such flights. He said reports indicated that President Eisenhower had not been aware of the flight.

"Can any agency of this Government, without the knowledge of politically responsible officials, assume for itself the right to probe for scientific or whatever purposes along a dangerous border and, hence, endanger the policies of the President?" Senator Mansfield asked.

Senator E. L. Bartlett, Democrat of Alaska, said he thought the United States should proceed with the summit meeting despite "the crude, rude provocative remarks of Khrushchev."

* * *

May 8, 1960

U. S. CONCEDES FLIGHT OVER SOVIET, DEFENSE SEARCH FOR INTELLIGENCE; RUSSIANS HOLD DOWNED PILOT AS SPY

ACTION EXPLAINED

Officials Say Danger of Surprise Attack Forces Watch

By JAMES RESTON

Special to The New York Times.

WASHINGTON, May 7—The United States admitted tonight that one of this country's planes equipped for intelligence purposes had "probably" flown over Soviet territory.

An official statement stressed, however, that "there was no authorization for any such flight" from authorities in Washington.

As to who might have authorized the flight, officials refused to comment. If this particular flight of the U-2 was not authorized here, it could only be assumed that someone in the chain of command in the Middle East or Europe had given the order.

President Clears Statement

"It appears," said the statement, "that in endeavoring to obtain information now concealed behind the Iron Curtain, a flight over 'Soviet' territory was probably undertaken by an unarmed civilian U-2 plane."

The statement was issued by the State Department after clearance by President Eisenhower. It came at the end of a day of uneasy silence. All through the day the highest officials of the Government had worked on an answer to Premier Khrushchev's charges that the United States had been caught red-handed in an aerial-intelligence operation behind the Soviet borders.

The statement contained what was probably the first official admission that extensive intelligence activities were being conducted along the Soviet frontiers. It gave no assurance that these activities would be curbed in the future.

Soviet Activity Cited

But it justified this intelligence work on several grounds. "The Soviet Union," it pointed out, has not been lagging behind in this field." Furthermore, it said, the excessive secrecy practiced by the Russians and their refusal to accept a United States plan for mutual protection against surprise attack obliged the free world to take every precaution.

"It is in relation to the danger of surprise attack that planes of the type of the unarmed civilian U-2 aircraft have made flights along the frontiers of the free world for the past four years," the statement said.

It did not repeat the original explanation of the plane incident issued here Thursday by the National Aeronautical and Space Agency. According to this explanation, the Lockheed U-2 plane was engaged in tests of aerial turbulence and other weather phenomena at high altitudes. The agency said the American pilot had last reported difficulty with his oxygen supply and suggested that he might have strayed over the Soviet frontier by inadvertence.

Asked about the space agency's statement, officials replied with some embarrassment that "it was issued in complete good faith." They said, however, that they did not know whether the story of oxygen failure was true and that they did not know what officer or official outside Washington had authorized the flight.

Asked whether the pilot had been engaged on a mission for the space agency, as stated officially on Thursday, one official replied, "Obviously not."

Khrushchev Shatters Calm

Premier Khrushchev's sensational speech shattered the calm of this hesitant spring day in the capital. President Eisenhower was at his Gettysburg farm and he managed to play eighteen holes of golf, but high officials were on the phone to him at various times.

At the State Department, Secretary of State Christian A. Herter met with Under Secretary Douglas Dillon, Charles E. Bohlen, former Ambassador to the Soviet Union, and other high officials. Allen W. Dulles, director of the Central Intelligence Agency, and other officials from different Government departments were consulted from time to time.

The discussions led up to one vital issue: Should the United States admit that one of its planes had penetrated Soviet territory on an intelligence mission?

A determined argument was made by some high officials that the United States should concede nothing. It is the almost invariable custom for governments to refuse to own up to intelligence activity of any kind.

On the other hand, some officials were reported to have argued that it would be better to make some kind of avowal, to give a justification for what was being done and to state that the flight of the U-2 into Soviet territory had not been authorized in Washington.

By stressing this lack of authorization, it was apparently contended, the good faith of President Eisenhower would be safeguarded. This would keep things open for him to go to the summit conference in Paris on May 16 as scheduled.

Behind the charge in the official statement that the Russians themselves have not been shy about espionage lie some unpublicized facts gathered by United States intelligence services. The Russians are reported on reliable authority to have made many reconnaissance flights over United States and Allied air, naval and missile bases in Europe, Asia, the Middle East and Africa.

Premier Khrushchev's triumphant announcement that the Russians had captured the United States pilot together with damning evidence of espionage dispelled some of the rosy optimism about the summit conference that had pervaded the capital.

Air Chief's Visit Debated

Though this optimism had been somewhat shaken by Mr. Khrushchev's recent public statements, some reassurance

ACCUSES PILOT: Premier Khrushchev displaying before the Supreme Soviet in Moscow one of the views of Soviet territory he said had been obtained by United States flier.

was provided by two private messages that arrived here from Moscow earlier this week.

The first, sent Monday, indicated that the Soviet Union was going to cancel the visit to this country of the head of the Soviet Air Force, Marshal Konstantin A. Vershinin.

On Wednesday, however, even before Mr. Khrushchev disclosed the plane incident before the Supreme Soviet in Moscow, a second message arrived saying the visit would take place.

This at first led officials to hope that the Soviet leader was not going to make the crisis worse than it was early in the week. Later today, however, with the announcement that Mr. Khrushchev had added to his charges and threatened a trial of the United States flier, it appeared that Washington was the main target of a major propaganda offensive just before the summit meeting.

As a result it was widely believed here that Mr. Khrushchev had decided to try to bring the United States to the conference table in Paris under a serious psychological and diplomatic disadvantage.

That this was already having some effect was obvious today from the private reaction of Allied officials. They said nothing in public and were restrained in their private comments, but it was obvious that they were critical of Washington for getting involved in what many of them regarded as an unnecessary controversy.

Part of the difficulty within the Government and within the alliance was that Allied officials and even some prominent State Department officials did not feel confident that they knew the facts of what, if anything, other United States agencies were doing on and around the southern boundaries of the Soviet Union.

What they did know, however, was that this incident was being used by Mr. Khrushchev to support his suspicion that the United States was trying to put difficulties in the way of an East-West summit accommodation on Berlin and Germany.

For the last few weeks, Soviet officials here and in Moscow have been charging that Washington is breaking "the spirit of Camp David." This was a reference to last fall's meeting between President Eisenhower and Premier Khrushchev at Camp David, Md., where they agreed to try to work out a German settlement, not with a deadline but as soon as possible.

Since then, no progress has been made on any agreement, though President Eisenhower had agreed with Mr. Khrushchev at Camp David that the Berlin situation was "abnormal."

On April 4 in Chicago, Secretary Herter noted that Mr. Khrushchev had supported the principle of self-determination for peoples in Asia but that he was unwilling to do so for the peoples of East Berlin and East Germany.

Mr. Herter insisted that this principle be met in Germany and Berlin, and he criticized Mr. Khrushchev for the latter's attacks on Chancellor Adenauer of West Germany.

This insistence on supporting Dr. Adenauer produced some sharp criticism here by the Soviet Ambassador, Mikhail A. Menshikov, who complained in private that the United States seemed to be "reviving the cold war."

Shortly thereafter, Mr. Dillon made an even more critical speech on Soviet policy in Germany before an A. F. L.-C. I. O. gathering in New York on April 20.

In this speech, Mr. Dillon questioned the accuracy of Mr. Khrushchev's policy on Germany and discussed that policy in often scornful terms.

Speaking in Baku on April 25, Mr. Khrushchev complained that Mr. Dillion's speech "just reeks of the cold war spirit."

Blame for U. S. Expected

This was the mood of the Soviet leader even before the plane incident. The feeling in official quarters here was that he realized the United States was not going to agree to his proposals for Berlin at the summit and was, therefore, preparing to blame the United States for the breakdown of the Paris meeting.

Actually, the Eisenhower Administration has not changed its policy and was not trying to increase tension before the summit. It did want to make clear in advance that it was not prepared to accept the Soviet proposals for Germany, any more than it had been at the Geneva meeting of the foreign ministers last summer.

But with an election coming up, in which "peace and prosperity," as usual, are likely to be the issues, the last thing the Administration desired was a crisis that might throw doubt on the validity of the peace argument.

*   *   *

May 17, 1960

U.S.-SOVIET CLASS DISRUPTS SUMMIT TALKS; KHRUSHCHEV CANCELS EISENHOWER'S VISIT

HARSH EXCHANGE

Russian Asks Parley Be Postponed for 6 to 8 Months

By DREW MIDDLETON
Special to The New York Times.

PARIS, May 16—The summit conference suffered an apparently mortal blow at its opening session today when Premier Khrushchev and President Eisenhower exchanged charges that blighted hopes for an early relaxation of tension between East and West.

The Soviet Premier bluntly told the United States President that he would not be welcome if he went to the Soviet Union on his proposed visit next month.

The Soviet Government is convinced, Mr. Khrushchev continued, that the next United States Administration, or even the one after that will understand that there is no other course but peaceful coexistence with the Soviet Union.

'No Better Way Out'

There is "no better way out" of the dispute arising from United States Intelligence flights over Soviet territory, the Premier said, than to postpone the conference for six to eight months.

At the close of his blistering speech, the system of high-level consultation and negotiation seemed wrecked. The Big Four adjourned their closed sessions without setting a date for another meeting in Paris.

Mr. Khrushchev demanded that President Eisenhower fulfill three conditions if there were to be summit talks. His demands followed a tirade against the United States for having sent U-2 photo-reconnaisance planes over the Soviet Union. One such plane was shot down in the Urals May 1.

President Eisenhower met one demand only. He announced that the flights had been suspended after the recent incident "and are not to be resumed."

Move at U. N. Planned

The President also said he planned, in the event an accord with the Soviet Union on the subject proved impossible, to submit to the United Nations a proposal for "aerial surveillance to detect preparations for attack."

These moves failed to satisfy Mr. Khrushchev, who had demanded, first, condemnation of "inadmissible provocative actions" on the part of the United States Air Force; second, a ban on flights now and in the future and, finally, United States punishment of those "directly guilty" of "deliberate violation of the Soviet Union."

Prime ministers, presidents and diplomats worked long into the soft spring night trying to salvage something of the long-hoped-for meeting of heads of government.

"Long and serious" discussions between Mr. Khrushchev and Prime Minister Macmillan ended late tonight with prospects for the resumption of the conference slightly improved.

The three Western heads of government will meet tomorrow morning as a consequence of this discussion. There will be "continued contacts" with the Soviet Premier, British diplomats said. These are expected to take the form of yet another meeting between British and Soviet leaders after the western talks.

Mr. Macmillan will not relay any specific message from Mr. Khrushchev to General Eisenhower, it was emphasized. Nor did he take a message from the President when he saw Mr. Khrushchev tonight after he had concluded a brief conversation with the American.

The Soviet leader remarked at the end of the disastrous session that he would be "happy" to spend a day or two strolling under the chestnut trees. Mr. Macmillan and General de Gaulle hope to lure him from the boulevards into a small, closed session with General Eisenhower.

But Mr. Khrushchev still was demanding more than the President appeared willing to give. A high Soviet official declared his Government did not believe the President's statement to the conference had met Mr. Khrushchev's conditions.

'Waiting for a Reply'

Georghi A. Zhukov, head of the State Committee for Cultural Relations With Foreign Countries, said the Premier was "still waiting for a reply" to his demands. The Eisenhower statement ending espionage flights was "canceled out," Mr. Zhukov said, by a single line in the speech.

This was the President's remark that actual United States statements were not threats but only declarations "that go no further than to say that the United States will not shirk its responsibility to safeguard against surprise attack."

Mr. Khrushchev's speech was a devastating and explosive performance. His denunciation of the United States and his imposition of conditions were capped by his brutally frank announcement that in the circumstances General Eisenhower's visit must be postponed.

The Premier, who in the past had stressed his reliance on the President's desire for a relaxation of tension, obviously had abandoned his hopes for personal negotiations with his United States host of last year. His earliest date for another summit meeting is after the United States Presidential elections.

Aim to 'Wreck' Charged

President Eisenhower thought Premier Khrushchev's speech, as bitter as any made at the height of the "cold war," showed he had come to Paris intending to "wreck" the conference.

How far beyond Paris the wreckage from the Soviet explosion extends no one knows.

A Soviet spokesman reported that no action was contemplated on West Berlin or Germany—including conclusion of a separate peace treaty with Communist East Germany—for

the period that Mr. Khrushchev wants to elapse before the Big Four meet again.

The United States-British-Soviet conference in Geneva on a ban on tests of nuclear weapons held two "useful" meetings today, according to Sir Michael Wright, British representative, who arrived in Paris this evening.

Another Soviet spokesman said that the ten-power East-West disarmament conference in Geneva, now in recess, would not be affected by Mr. Khrushchev's statement, since the issues there "have nothing in common" with those contemplated here.

The entire Soviet diplomatic activity concentrated on the United States flights over the Soviet Union. President Eisenhower received from Moscow tonight the text of a new protest against them.

"The Soviet Government considers that the time has come for the Government of the United States to demonstrate its concern not in words but in deeds," the note said.

The summit conference, so long in the making, opened at 11 o'clock, an hour late. President de Gaulle made a speech of welcome and then Premier Khrushchev embarked on his tirade.

Macmillan Hails 'Old Friend'

President Eisenhower responded in what Prime Minister Macmillan described afterward as a "statesmanlike and restrained manner." The Prime Minister said he thought his "old friend" had "reacted with disregard for 'face' that one would not find in lesser men coming from lesser countries."

Mr. Macmillan told the conference session that the President had made it "absolutely clear" that flights over the Soviet Union were no longer United States policy. Consequently there is no question of the conference's meeting under the threat of such flights, the Briton added.

After the conferees' addresses, it developed, according to Charles E. Bohlen, State Department expert on Soviet affairs that Mr. Khrushchev did not regard the meeting as a summit conference. The Soviet leader made the admission, without precedent in Mr. Bohlen's long experience, that the issue of the United States flights was deeply involved with the internal policies of the Soviet Union.

This appeared to confirm persistent reports that the shooting down of the United States plane had exacerbated the opposition to Mr. Khrushchev's détente policy that had been developing in the army and among Communist party fundamentalists.

De Gaulle Bid Rebuffed

Some form of internal pressure may have compelled the Premier to come to Paris and explode his land mine under the conference, British diplomats said. To do this he thrust aside General de Gaulle's suggestion of an intimate private meeting.

Mr. Khrushchev also refused General Eisenhower's offer of direct talks on the flights over Soviet territory.

Later Mr. Khrushchev, responding to the suggestion that the Soviet Union also engaged in Espionage, raised his chubby arms and declaimed, "As God is my witness, my hands are clean and my soul is pure!"

The Soviet leader found his match in General de Gaulle. At one point he asked "what the devil pushed these people" to fly over the Soviet Union. The French President replied: "There are many devils in the world, and we are here precisely for the purpose of exorcising them."

General de Gaulle also tartly reminded Mr. Khrushchev that espionage flying, including the Soviet Union's newest sputnik, could be considered an element of great danger for international security. The Soviet satellite passes over France, he continued, and such devices have the capacity of photographing territory and "even to sow the means of terrible destruction."

The watchful Mr. Bohlen noted that Mr. Khrushchev seemed to pay a great deal of attention during the meeting to his two chief aides, Marshal Rodion Y. Malinovsky, Minister of Defense, and Andrei A. Gromyko Foreign Minister.

*   *   *

May 17, 1960

TEXTS OF KHRUSHCHEV AND EISENHOWER STATEMENTS

PARIS, May 16 (Reuters)—Following are the text, in unofficial translation, of a statement made by Premier Khrushchev at today's session of the summit conference and made public by the Soviet Union, and the text of a statement issued by President Eisenhower after the session:

KHRUSHCHEV STATEMENT

President de Gaulle.

Prime Minister Macmillan.

President Eisenhower.

Permit me to address you with the following statement:

A provocative act is known to have been committed recently with regard to the Soviet Union by the American Air Force. It consisted in the fact that on May 1 a United States military reconnaissance aircraft invaded the Soviet Union while executing a specific espionage mission to obtain information on military and industrial installations on the territory of the U. S. S. R. After the aggressive purpose of its flight became known, the aircraft was shot down by units of the Soviet rocket troops. Unfortunately, this was not the only case of aggressive and espionage actions by the United States Air Force against the Soviet Union.

Naturally, the Soviet Government was compelled to give appropriate qualification to these acts and show up their treacherous nature, which is incompatible with the elementary requirements of the maintenance of normal relations between states in time of peace, not to speak of its being in gross contradiction to the task of lessening international tension and creating the necessary conditions for the fruitful work of the summit conference. This was done both in my speeches at the session of the Supreme Soviet of the U. S. S. R. and in a special note of protest sent to the United States Government.

At first, the United States State Department launched the ridiculous version that the American plane had violated the borders of the U. S. S. R. by accident and had no espionage or sabotage assignments. When irrefutable facts clearly proved the falsity of this version, the United States State Department on May 7, and then the Secretary of State on May 9, stated on behalf of the United States Government that American aircraft made incursions into the Soviet Union with military espionage aims in accordance with a program endorsed by the United States Government and by the President personally.

Confirmed by President

Two days later, President Eisenhower himself confirmed that execution of flights of American aircraft over the territory of the Soviet Union had been and remained the calculated policy of the United States. The same was declared by the United States Government in a note to the Soviet Government on May 12. Thereby the United States Government is crudely flouting the universally accepted standards of international law and the lofty principles of the United Nations Charter, under which stands the signature of the United States of America also.

The Soviet Government and the entire people of the Soviet Union met these declarations of leading statesmen of the U. S. A. with indignation, as did every honest man and woman in the world who displays concern for the destinies of peace.

Now, at a time when the leaders of the Governments of the four powers are arriving in Paris to take part in the conference, the question arises of how is it possible productively to negotiate and examine the questions confronting the conference when the United States Government and the President himself have not only failed to condemn this provocative act—the intrusion of the American military aircraft into the Soviet Union—but, on the contrary, have declared that such actions will continue to be state policy of the U. S. A. with regard to the Soviet Union.

How can agreement be sought on the various issues that require a settlement with the purpose of easing tension and removing suspicion and mistrust among states when the Government of one of the great powers declares bluntly that its policy is intrusion into the territory of another great power with espionage and sabotage purposes and, consequently, the heightening of tension in relations among states?

It is clear that the declaration of such a policy, which can be pursued only when states are in a state of war dooms the summit conference to complete failure in advance.

We, naturally, take note of the declaration by the United States Government of such a policy and state that in the event of a repeated intrusion by American aircraft into the Soviet Union we shall shoot these planes down.

The Soviet Government reserves the right in all such cases to take the appropriate retaliatory measures against those who violate the state sovereignty of the U. S. S. R. and engage in such espionage and sabotage regarding the Soviet Union. The U. S. S. R. Government reiterates that, with regard to those states that, by making their territory available for American military bases, become accomplices in aggressive actions against the U. S. S. R., the appropriate measures will also be taken, not excluding a blow against these bases.

In this connection it is impossible to ignore the statement by President Eisenhower to the effect that under the threat of a peace treaty with the German Democratic Republic he could not take part in the summit conference, though what he called a threat was merely the declaration by the Soviet Government of its firm resolve to do away with the vestiges of war in Europe and conclude a peace, and thus to bring the situation—particularly in West Berlin—in line with the requirements of life and the interests of insuring the peace and security of the European nations.

How then can the Soviet Government take part in negotiations under conditions of an actual threat emanating from the United States Government which declared that it would continue to violate the U. S. S. R. borders and that American aircraft had flown and would continue to fly over the Soviet Union's territory? The United States Government has thereby declared its intention to continue unheard of and unprecedented actions directed against the sovereignty of the Soviet state, which constitutes a sacred and immutable principle in international relations.

'Overt and Honest Policy'

From all this it follows that for the success of the conference it is necessary that the Governments of all the powers represented at it pursue an overt and honest policy and solemnly declare that they will not undertake any actions against one another which amount to violation of the state sovereignty of the powers.

This means that if the United States Government is really ready to cooperate with the Governments of the other powers in the interests of maintaining peace and strengthening confidence between states it must, firstly, condemn the inadmissible provocative actions of the United States Air Force with regard to the Soviet Union and, secondly, refrain from continuing such actions and such a policy against the U. S. S. R. in the future.

It goes without saying that in this case the United States Government cannot fail to call to strict account those who are directly guilty of the deliberate violation by American aircraft of the state borders of the U. S. S. R.

Until this is done by the United States Government, the Soviet Government sees no possibility for productive negotiations with the United States Government at the summit conference. It cannot be among the participants in negotiations where one of them has made treachery the basis of his policy with regard to the Soviet Union.

If, under the obtaining conditions, the Soviet Government were to participate in negotiations clearly doomed to failure,

it would thereby become a party to the deception of the nations, which it has no intention of becoming.

It stands to reason that if the United States Government were to declare that in the future the United States will not violate the state borders of the U. S. S. R. with its aircraft, that it deplores the provocative actions undertaken in the past and will punish those directly guilty of such actions, which would assure the Soviet Union equal conditions with other powers, I, as head of the Soviet Government, would be ready to participate in the conference and exert all efforts to contribute to its success.

As a result of the provocative flights of American military aircraft and, above all, as a result of such provocative flights being declared national policy of the United States of America for the future in regard to the Socialist countries, new conditions have appeared in international relationships.

Naturally, under such conditions, we cannot work at the conference; we cannot because we see the positions from which it is intended to talk with us: under the threat of aggressive reconnaissance flights. Espionage flights are known to be undertaken with reconnaissance purposes with the object of starting a war. We, therefore, reject the conditions the United States of America is creating for us. We cannot participate in any negotiations and in the solution of even those questions which have already matured; we cannot because we see that the United States has no desire to reach a settlement.

'Deception' Is Ruled Out

It is considered to be a leader in the Western countries. Therefore, the conference would at present be a useless waste of time and a deception of the public opinion of all countries. I repeat, we cannot under the obtaining situation take part in the negotiations.

We want to participate in the talks only on an equal footing, with equal opportunities for both one and the other side.

We consider it necessary for all the peoples of all the countries of the world to understand us correctly. The Soviet Union is not renouncing efforts to achieve agreement. And we are sure that reasonable agreements are possible, but, evidently, not at this but at another time.

For this, however, it is necessary first of all that the United States admits that the provocative policy by a policy of "unrestricted" flights over our country is to be condemned and that it rejects it and admits that it has committed aggression and admits that it regrets it.

The Soviet Government is deeply convinced that if not this Government of the United States then another, if not another then the next one would understand that there is no other way out but peaceful coexistence of two systems, capitalist and Socialist. Either peaceful coexistence or war, which will result in a disaster for those who are pursuing an aggressive policy.

Peaceful Links Stressed

Therefore, we think that some time should be allowed to elapse so that the questions that have arisen should settle and so that those responsible for the determining of the policies of a country would analyze what kind of responsibility they placed upon themselves, having declared an aggressive course in their relations with the Soviet Union and other Socialist countries. Therefore, we would think that there is no better way out than to postpone the conference of the heads of government for approximately six to eight months.

The Soviet Union on its part will not lessen its effort to reach an agreement. I think that public opinion will correctly understand our position, will understand that we were deprived of the possibility to participate in these negotiations.

However, we firmly believe in the necessity of peaceful coexistence because to lose faith in peaceful coexistence would mean to doom mankind to war, would mean to agree with the inevitability of wars, and under the circumstances it is known what disasters would be brought by a war to all nations on our planet.

I wish to address the people of the United States of America. I was in the U.S.A and met there with various sections of the American people and I am deeply convinced that all the strata of the American people do not want war. An exception constitutes but a small frantic group in the Pentagon and, supporting it, militarist quarters that benefit from the armaments race, gaining huge profits, which disregard the interests of the American people and in general the interests of the peoples of all the countries, and which pursue an adventurous policy.

We express gratitude to President de Gaulle for the hospitality and rendering us the possibility to meet in Paris, the capital of France. We also appreciate the efforts of the government of Great Britain and Prime Minister Macmillan personally.

We regret that this meeting has been torpedoed by the reactionary circles of the United States of America by provocative flights of American military planes over the Soviet Union.

We regret that this meeting has not brought about the results expected by all nations of the world.

Let the disgrace and responsibility for this rest with those who have proclaimed a bandit policy toward the Soviet Union.

Issue of Eisenhower Visit

As is known, President Eisenhower and I have agreed to exchange visits. Last September, I made such a visit to the U. S. A. We were greatly gratified by that visit, the meetings and talks we had in the United States, and for all this we expressed our appreciation.

The President of the U. S. A. was to make a return visit to our country. Our agreement was that he would come to us on June 10. And we were preparing to accord a good welcome to the high guest.

Unfortunately, as a result of provocative and aggressive actions against the U. S. S. R., there have been created now such conditions when we have been deprived of a possibility to receive the President with the proper cordiality with which the Soviet people receive welcome guests. At present, we cannot express such cordiality to the President of the U. S. A.

since, as the result of provocative flights of American military planes with reconnaissance purposes, there are created conditions clearly unfavorable for this visit.

The Soviet people cannot and do not want to be sly. That is why we believe that at present the visit of the President of the U. S. A. to the Soviet Union should be postponed and agreement should be reached as to the time of the visit when the conditions for the visit would mature. Then the Soviet people will be able to express proper cordiality and hospitality toward the high guest representing the great power with which we sincerely want to live in peace and friendship.

I believe that both President Eisenhower and the American people will understand me correctly.

The Soviet Government states that on its part it will continue to do its utmost to facilitate the relaxation of international tension, to facilitate the solution of problems that still divide us today. In that we shall be guided by the interests of strengthening the great cause of peace on the basis of peaceful coexistence of states with different social systems.

EISENHOWER STATEMENT

Having been informed yesterday by General de Gaulle and Prime Minister Macmillan of the position which Mr. Khrushchev has taken in regard to this conference during his calls yesterday morning on them, I gave most careful thought as to how this matter should best be handled. having in mind the great importance of this conference and the hopes that the peoples of all the world have reposed in this meeting, I concluded that in the circumstances it was best to see if at today's private meeting any possibility existed through the exercise of reason and restraint to dispose of this matter of the overflights which would have permitted the conference to go forward.

I was under no illusion as to the probability of success of any such approach but I felt that in view of the great responsibility resting on me as President of the United States, this effort should be made.

In this I received the strongest support of my colleagues, President de Gaulle and Prime Minister Macmillan. Accordingly, at this morning's private session, despite the violence and inaccuracy of Mr. Khrushchev's statements, I replied to him on the following terms:

I had previously been informed of the sense of the statement just read by Premier Khrushchev.

In my statement of May 11 and in the statement of Secretary Herter of May 9, the position of the United States was made clear with respect to the distasteful necessity of espionage activities in a world where nations distrust each other's intentions. We pointed out that these activities had no aggressive intent but rather were to assure the safety of the United States and of the free world against surprise attack by a power which boasts of its ability to devastate the United States and other countries by missiles armed with atomic warheads. As is well known, not only the United States but most other countries are constantly the targets of elaborate and persistent espionage of the Soviet Union.

Misapprehension Discerned

There is in the Soviet statement an evident misapprehension on one key point. It alleges that the United State has, through official statements, threatened continued overflights. The importance of this alleged threat was emphasized and repeated by Mr. Khrushchev . The United States has made no such threat. Neither I or my government has intended any. The actual statements go no further than to say that the United States will not shirk its responsibility to safeguard against surprise attack.

In point of fact, these flights were suspended after the recent incident and are not to be resumed. Accordingly, this cannot be the issue.

I have come to Paris to seek agreements with the Soviet Union which would eliminate the necessity for all forms of espionage, including overflights. I see no reason to use this incident to disrupt the conference.

Should it prove impossible because of the Soviet attitude to come to grips here in Paris with this problem and the other vital issues threatening world peace, I am planning in the near future to submit to the Untied Nations a proposal for the creation of a United Nations aerial surveillance to detect preparations for attack.

This plan I had intended to place before this conference. This surveillance system would operate in the territories of all nations prepared to accept such inspection. For its part, the United States is prepared not only to accept United nations aerial surveillance but to do everything in its power to contribute to the rapid organization and successful operation of such international surveillance.

Bilateral Talks Suggested

We of the United States are here to consider in good faith the important problems before this conference. We are prepared either to carry this point no further, or to undertake bilateral conversations between the United States and the U. S. S. R. while the main conference proceeds.

My words were seconded and supported by my Western colleagues, who also urged Mr. Khrushchev to pursue the path of reason and common sense, and to forget propaganda. Such an attitude would have permitted the conference to proceed. Mr. Khrushchev was left in no doubt by me that his ultimatum would never be acceptable to the Untied States.

Mr. Khrushchev brushed aside all arguments of reason, and not only insisted upon this ultimatum but also insisted that he was going to publish his statement in full at the time of his own choosing.

It was thus made apparent that he was determined to wreck the Paris conference. In fact, the only conclusion that can be drawn from his behavior this morning was that he came all the way from Moscow to Paris with the sole intention of sabotaging this meeting on which so much of the hopes of the world have rested.

In spite of this serious and adverse development, I have no intention whatsoever to diminish my continuing efforts to promote progress toward a peace with justice. This applies to the remainder of my stay in Paris as well as thereafter.

* * *

November 9, 1960

KENNEDY IS APPARENT VICTOR; LEAD CUT IN TWO KEY STATES; DEMOCRATS RETAIN CONGRESS

MARGIN NARROW

California and Illinois Give a Setback to Senator's Outlook

By JAMES RESTON

Senator John F. Kennedy of Massachusetts, the cool young Democratic leader of a new generation of American politicians, appeared yesterday to have won election as the thirty-fifth President of the United States.

Vice President Nixon of California appeared on television at 3:20 o'clock this morning to say that "if the present trend continues, Senator Kennedy is going to be the next President of the United States."

However, after both the Vice President and Senator Kennnedy had about agreed with the television audience that it was all over and time to go to bed, the trend that had favored Senator Kennedy East of the Mississippi River began to veer toward the Vice President in the key Middle Western state of Illinois and in and beyond the Rockies.

In California, with half the voting districts uncounted, Senator Kennedy's lead was cut to just under 100,000 at 5 o'clock this morning. While the reports indicated that the Democratic nominee would retain his lead there, some of the officials in key voting districts stopped counting the votes until later in the day, throwing the thirty-two electoral votes of California in doubt until the count could be completed.

Victorious in East

The situation at 6:30 o'clock this morning was as follows:

Senator Kennedy was assured of 258 of the 269 necessary to win after scoring impressive victories in New York, Pennsylvania, Massachusetts and New Jersey. He was leading by a margin that had declined from more than 200,000 to less than 50,000 in Illinois, which has twenty-five electoral votes.

It was at this point, with only half the votes counted for California's thirty-two electoral votes, that many of the key electoral districts stopped counting. This created a critical element of doubt, for, even if the experts felt that Senator Kennedy's lead in California would not vanish, there was always a chance that it could drop as it did early this morning in Illinois.

Two considerations increased the element of doubt after important California voting districts stopped adding the totals.

One was the spectacular fact that, while Mr. Kennedy had seemed to be well on his way to an impressive victory on the basis of the electoral votes in the populous industrial Northern states east of the Mississippi, his nation-wide popular vote margin declined to 823,000 by 6 o'clock.

1916 Election Recalled

The second consideration was the memory in the minds of the politicians of the presidential election of 1916.

In that year, the election was decided, again after the candidates had gone to bed, by President Wilson's cliff-hanging victory in California. By winning that state, 466,289 to 462,516—a margin of 3,773—Wilson took the election, 277 electoral votes to 254.

Actually, between 5:30 and 6 o'clock this morning, Senator Kennedy picked up nearly 30,000 votes in Illnois and about 15,000 in California, but because the vote could not be completed in California, it was impossible to be aboslutely sure that he would pick up the electoral votes necessary to win.

What Mr. Kennedy needed at 6 o'clock this morning was only eleven electoral votes in addition to his sure 258 electoral votes to be certain of victory.

He could get those eleven by holding his lead in California (thirty-two electoral votes), Illinois, twenty-seven, or Minnesota, eleven.

What Vice President Nixon needed, however, was to hit the jackpot in all three states and then some. He was sure of 172 electoral votes. California, Illinois and Minnesota would add seventy, bringing his total to 242, still twenty-seven short of the 269 needed for victory.

Short of Majority

He could get 23 of these 27 if he won all of the other undecided states: New Mexico, 4 electoral votes, Hawaii, 3, and Washington, 9, in all of which he held slim margins; plus Alaska, 3 electoral votes, and Montana, 4, where he was slightly behind.

That would still leave him four votes short of the 269 majority necessary. However, there are fourteen electors from Mississippi and Alabama, who are feuding with the National Democratic party and have refused to promite that their votes would go to the Democratic ticket of Kennedy and Johnson.

Thus, in addition to winning everything still undecided—California, Illinois, Minnesota and all the rest—Vice President Nixon would still have to get four of the fourteen electors to go against the Southern Democratic tradition.

Thus, by a fantastic turn of events, Mr. Nixon still had a long-shot chance to win, and nobody could deny it to him for the simple reason that the votes could not be counted, and therefore nobody could count him out.

Odds Still on Kennedy

The odds, however were still on Senator Kennedy, just as they had been ever since the Democratic tide started running in New England early last night. But the tide ran into a blocked channel, which could not be opened until the officials started counting the votes again in California or the officials in the other close states completed their work.

When the Vice President appeared before the television cameras at the Ambassador Hotel in Los Angeles, he told his protesting supporters:

"While there are still some results to come in, if the present trend continues, Senator Kennedy is going to be the next President of the United States."

The Vice President, accompanied by his wife, who struggled hard to keep back the tears, was disarmingly cheerful.

Pledges Support

"I want Senator Kennedy to know and I want all of you to know," he said, "that certainly if this trend continues and he does become our next President, he will have my wholehearted support …"

Senator Kennedy did not take this as a concession, and went to bed at 3:45, saying he would have no statement until 10 o'clock this morning.

At 43, Senator Kennedy would be the youngest President ever elected in this country, although Theodore Roosevelt, the twenty-sixth President, was 42 years old when he succeeded to the Presidency after the assassination of President McKinley. Senator Kennedy would also be the first American President of the Roman Catholic faith.

Senators Kennedy and Johnson brought back to the Democratic party the minority groups in the Northern cities and just enough of the rebellious South to restore something like the old Roosevelt coalition that dominated the

An analysis of the votes indicated that the predominantly Catholic districts went 15–30 per cent more for Senator Kennedy than they did for Adlai E. Stevenson, the Democratic nominee in 1956; that Northern Negroes voted 10 per cent and Southern Negroes 30 per cent more for the Democratic candidate than four years ago, and that the Protestant farm areas went for the Vice President only slightly less than they did for President Eisenhower in 1956.

Religious Shifts Compared

Spot checks of districts around the country where religion was expected to be a factor in the voting indicated that Roman Catholics had switched more solidly to Mr. Kennedy than Protestants voted against him.

For example, the Forty-fourth Precinct of Chicago's Eighteenth Ward is a solidly Catholic area, which went to President Eisenhower in 1956. Yesterday's totals showed 306 for Kennedy, 98 for Nixon.

The Democratic plurality in the Sixteenth Ward in Pittsburgh's South side, an area that is 97 per cent Catholic, was double that for Mr. Stevenson in 1956.

In the Kennedy sweep in North Carolina, fundamentalist votes against the Senator were running behind the predictions. Anti-Catholicism showed in the Nixon plurality in Cabarras County, a normally Democratic area populated mainly by textile workers who are fundamentalists.

A check in a Swedish Lutheran township—Whitefield, Minn.,—indicated that Senator Kennedy had overcome religious feeling evidenced there during the campaign. He won, 162 to 100. In 1928, Alfred E. Smith, a Catholic and a Democrat, lost the township to Herbert Hoover, 46 to 143.

Similarly, with the Negro voting districts, the low-income Eleventh and Fourteenth Assembly Districts in Harlem gave Mr. Kennedy ratios of 4 to 1. President Eisenhower had gained about one-third of the vote in these districts in 1956. In the Eleventh Assembly District in Queens, New York, which contains many middle-income Negro voters, Mr. Kennedy carried Negro sections by 11 to 6, an improvement over 1956.

The strength shown by Senator Kennedy in major industrial centers brought immediate assertions by union leaders that labor had played a major role in the Democratic victory, although there was disappointment at the showing in Ohio, where labor had scored an impressive sweep two years ago in defeating a proposed state "right to work" law.

Senator Kennedy's appeal to the electorate in the campaign was that this country, growing at the rate of 3,000,000 persons a year, and confronted by the rising challenge of Soviet power in Asia and in the Caribbean and Latin America, had to use the power of the central government more effectively to increase to economic growth and military capacity of the nation.

Among Major Pledges

"I want America to move again," he cried over and over during his 75,000-mile tour of the states of the Union. Among his major pledges were the following:

• To have a "conservative" fiscal policy and a "sound dollar," but to put more Federal money into education, school construction and slum clearance.

• To end "high interest rates" so that small business could expand.

• To increase the rate of economic growth so that the nation could hope to reach a goal of 82,000,000 jobs by 1968.

• To put medical assistance to the aged under the Social Security System.

• In the foreign field, to ally the United States with the rising tide of nationalism in the under-developed nations, to assist the movement for land reform in Latin America, and improve the quality of United States diplomatic representation abroad.

G. O. P. Now Divided

The Republican party demonstrated yesterday that it was more of a national party than it was in the thirties and forties by increasing its popularity in the conservative South. But by losing control of the Executive, failing in its bid for the House of Representatives, and running well behind in the race for the governorships of the states, it now faces a bleak prospect as a minority opposition party split between the Conservative forces symbolized by Senator Barry Goldwater of Arizona and the liberal forces around Governor Rockefeller of New York.

Outside of the South, which has been dominated by more conservative Democrats for more than a generation, the main issue of the election was the Democratic party's effort to establish a more liberal, more powerful central government.

The pace rather than the direction of policy by the central government was in dispute. Vice President Nixon and most of the other Republicans seeking election were defending the domestic and foreign policies of the Eisenhower Administration or urging moderate extensions of this policy.

Senator Kennedy and most of the other Democratic candidates for national office had argued that the pace of the nation's economic growth, of its educational opportunities, and of its military growth were not adequate to the needs of an expanding population at home or of the "cold war" overseas.

In sum, neither party asked the electorate to repeal the social program introduced by Presidents Roosevelt and Truman and expanded by President Eisenhower. Nor was either party questioning America's economic or military efforts as a leading member of the non-Communist nations.

*   *   *

January 18, 1961

EISENHOWER'S FAREWELL SEES THREAT TO LIBERTIES IN VAST DEFENSE MACHINE

VIGILANCE URGED

Talk Bids 'Godspeed' to Kennedy— Voices Hopes for Peace

By FELIX BELAIR Jr.
Special to The New York Times.

WASHINGTON, Jan. 17—President Eisenhower cautioned the nation in a farewell address from the White House tonight to be vigilant against dangers to its liberties implicit in a vast military establishment and a permanent armaments industry unparalleled in peacetime.

In his speech, which brought down the curtain on fifty years of public service, the President also warned of a second threat—"the prospect of domination of the nation's scholars by Federal employment, project allocations and the power of money." He said this danger was "ever present and is gravely to be regarded."

The President concluded his televised speech with a prayer for the well-being of "all the peoples of the world."

Sees a 'Long Struggle'

He warned Americans that they faced a long struggle in the "cold war." He also cautioned the nation against being tempted by any "miraculous solution" to world problems.

President Eisenhower also spoke as an old soldier preparing to turn over the burdens of the Presidency to his much younger successor, President-elect John F. Kennedy. The two men will hold their second and final discussion of problems confronting the nation Thursday morning.

Foremost among these problems, the President listed the continuing Communist threat to the West and the need to combat it while striving for universal disarmament. It was "with a definite sense of disappointment" that he contemplated the failure to make greater progress toward a lasting peace.

Wishes Kennedy Well

He said that, with all Americans, "I wish the new President and all who will labor with him Godspeed" in working for solutions.

The President stressed the need to guard against "the acquisition of unwarranted influence, whether sought or unsought, by the military-industrial complex."

This warning against the political potential of the huge military-arms production apparatus by the President came as a surprise to many in the capital. A more sentimental leave taking had been expected from the old soldier.

He noted that the conjunction of an immense military establishment and a large arms industry—both essential to national and free world security—was something new in American experience.

"The total influence—economic, political, even spiritual, is felt in every city, every state house, every office of the Federal Government," the President said.

Stressing the need for constant vigilance against undue influence in the hands of the newly combined military and industrial sector, the President went on to say "The potential for the disastrous rise of misplaced power exists and will persist."

Closely related to this new development in the American system, President Eisenhower said, is the increasing centralization of research under Federal control or direction. This necessary evil has been part of the technological revolution of recent decades and its increasingly complex and costly nature, he continued.

"Partly because of the huge costs involved, the Government contract becomes virtually a substitute for intellectual curiosity," the President reflected. "For every old blackboard there are now hundreds of new electronic computers."

Sees a Real Danger

There is real danger of Federal domination of the nation's scholars in this way, the President said. While scientific research and discovery must be held in respect, he continued, "we must also be alert to the equal and opposite danger that public policy could itself become the captive of a scientific-technological elite."

It is the task of statesmanship to mold, balance and integrate these conflicting forces within the principle of the democratic system and toward the constant goals of a free society, the President said.

The address was an assessment of the nation's condition today and a frank effort to penetrate the uncertainties of the future.

The President said America today was "the strongest, the most influential and the most productive nation in the world"

even though it has been involved in three major wars during the first sixty years of this century.

There will always be crises ahead, foreign and domestic, he said, but the real dangers lie not in the exigencies themselves but in the means chosen for meeting them.

Then, apparently addressing himself to his successor' administration, he said:

"There is a recurring temptation to feel that some spectacular and costly action could become the miraculous solutions to all current difficulties. A huge increase in newer elements of our defense; development of unrealistic programs to cure every ill in agriculture; a dramatic expansion in basic and applied research—these and many other possibilities, each possibly promising in itself, may be suggested as the way to the road we wish to travel."

The great need in seeking to meet recurring crises, the President suggested, is to maintain balance between the private and public economies; between cost and hoped-for advantage; between the clearly necessary and the comfortably desirable and between essential requirements as a nation and the duties imposed by the nation on the individual.

Finally, President Eisenhower saw as the nation's "continuing imperative" the ultimate goal of disarmament with mutual honor and confidence.

"As one who has witnessed the horror and the lingering sadness of war—as one who knows that another war could utterly destroy this civilization which has been so slowly and painfully built over thousands of years—I wish I could say tonight that a lasting peace is in sight," the President said.

He noted that war had been averted and steady progress had been made toward the ultimate goal, but said that much remained to be done.

"As a private citizen I shall never cease to do what little I can to help the world advance along that road," he said.

*　*　*

January 18, 1961

TEXT OF EISENHOWER'S FAREWELL ADDRESS

Following is the text of President Eisenhower's farewell address to the nation last night from Washington as recorded by The New York Times:

Good evening, my fellow Americans:

First, I should like to express my gratitude to the radio and television networks for the opportunities they have given me over the years to bring reports and messages to our nation. My special thanks go to them for the opportunity of addressing you this evening.

Three days from now after half a century in the service of our country, I shall lay down the responsibilities of office as, in traditional and solemn ceremony, the authority of the Presidency is vested in my successor.

This evening I come to you with a message of leave-taking and farewell, and to share a few final thoughts with you, my countrymen.

Like every other citizen, I wish the new President, and all who will labor with him, Godspeed. I pray that the coming years will be blessed with peace and prosperity for all.

Our people expect their President and the Congress to find essential agreement on issues of great moment, the wise resolution of which will better shape the future of the nation.

My own relations with the Congress, which began on a remote and tenuous basis when, long ago, a member of the Senate appointed me to West Point, have since ranged to the intimate during the war and immediate post-war period, and finally to the mutually interdependent during these past eight years.

His Relations Good

In this final relationship, the Congress and the Administration have, on most vital issues, cooperated well, to serve the nation good rather than mere partisanship, and so have assured that the business of the nation should go forward. So my official relationship with the Congress ends in a feeling, on my part, of gratitude that we have been able to do so much together.

We now stand ten years past the midpoint of a century that has witnessed four major wars among great nations—three of these involved our own country.

Despite these holocausts America is today the strongest, the most influential and most productive nation in the world. Understandably proud of this pre-eminence, we yet realize that America's leadership and prestige depend not merely upon our unmatched material progress, riches and military strength, but on how we use our power in the interests of world peace and human betterment.

Throughout America's adventure in free government, our basic purposes have been to keep the peace; to foster progress in human achievement, and to enhance liberty, dignity and integrity among peoples and among nations.

To strive for less would be unworthy of a free and religious people.

Any failure traceable to arrogance or our lack of comprehension or readiness to sacrifice would inflict upon us grievous hurt, both at home and abroad.

Progress toward these noble goals is persistently threatened by the conflict now engulfing the world. It commands our whole attention, absorbs our very beings.

We face a hostile ideology—global in scope, atheistic in character, ruthless in purpose and insidious in method. Unhappily the danger it poses promises to be of indefinite duration. To meet it successfully there is called for, not so much the emotional and transitory sacrifices of crisis, but rather those which enable us to carry forward steadily, surely and without complaint the burdens of a prolonged and complex struggle—with liberty the stake.

Only thus shall we remain, despite every provocation, on our charted course toward permanent peace and human betterment.

Says Crises Will Continue

Crises there will continue to be. In meeting them, whether foreign or domestic, great or small, there is a recurring temptation to feel that some spectacular and costly action could become the miraculous solution to all current difficulties. A huge increase in newer elements of our defenses; development of unrealistic programs to cure every ill in agriculture; a dramatic expansion in basic and applied research—these and many other possibilities, each possibly promising in itself, may be suggested as the only way to the road we wish to travel.

But each proposal must be weighed in the light of a broader consideration; the need to maintain balance in and among national programs—balance between the private and the public economy, balance between the cost and hoped for advantages—balance between the clearly necessary and the comfortably desirable; balance between our essential requirements as a nation and the duties imposed by the nation upon the individual; balance between actions of the moment and the national welfare of the future. Good judgment seeks balance and progress; lack of it eventually finds imbalance and frustration.

The record of many decades stands as proof that our people and their Government have, in the main, understood these truths and have responded to them well in the face of threat and stress.

New Threats Cited

But threats, new in kind or degree, constantly arise. Of these I mention two only.

A vital element in keeping the peace is our military establishment. Our arms must be mighty, ready for instant action, so that no potential aggressor may be tempted to risk his own destruction.

Our military organization today bears little relation to that known of any of my predecessors in peacetime—or indeed, by the fighting men of World War II or Korea.

Until the latest of our world conflicts, the United States had no armaments industry. American makers of plowshares could, with time and as required, make swords as well.

But we can no longer risk emergency improvisation of national defense. We have been compelled to create a permanent armaments industry of vast proportions. Added to this, three and a half million men and women are directly engaged in the defense establishment. We annually spend on military security alone more than the net income of all United States corporations.

Now this conjunction of an immense military establishment and a large arms industry is new in the American experience. The total influence—economic, political, even spiritual—is felt in every city, every state house, every office of the Federal Government. We recognize the imperative need for this development. Yet we must not fail to comprehend its grave implications. Our toil, resources and livelihood are all involved, so is the very structure of our society.

Warning on Influence

In the councils of Government, we must guard against the acquisition of unwarranted influence, whether sought or unsought, by the military-industrial complex. The potential for the disastrous rise of misplaced power exists and will persist.

We must never let the weight of this combination endanger our liberties or democratic processes. We should take nothing for granted. Only an alert and knowledgeable citizenry can compel the proper meshing of the huge industrial and military machinery of defense with our peaceful methods and goals, so that security and liberty may prosper together.

Akin to and largely responsible for the sweeping changes in our industrial-military posture has been the technological revolution during recent decades.

In this revolution research has become central. It also becomes more formalized, complex and costly. A steadily increasing share is conducted for, by, or at the direction of the Federal Government.

Today the solitary inventor, tinkering in his shop, has been overshadowed by task forces of scientists, in laboratories and testing fields. In the same fashion, the free university, historically the fountainhead of free ideas and scientific discovery, has experienced a revolution in the conduct of research. Partly because of the huge costs involved a Government contract becomes virtually a substitute for intellectual curiosity.

For every old blackboard there are now hundreds of new electronic computers.

Prospect of Domination

The prospect of domination of the nation's scholars by Federal employment, project allocations and the power of money is ever present, and is ever present, and is gravely to be regarded.

Yet, in holding scientific research and discovery in respect, as we should, we must also be alert to the equal and opposite danger that public policy could itself become the captive of a scientific-technological elite.

It is the task of statesmanship to mold, to balance and to integrate these and other forces, new and old, within the principles of our democratic system—ever aiming toward the supreme goals of our free society.

Time Element Involved

Another factor in maintaining balance involves the element of time. As we peer into society's future, we—you and I, and our Government—must avoid the impulse to live only for today, plundering, for our own case and convenience, the precious resources of tomorrow.

We cannot mortgage the material assets of our grandchildren without risking the loss also of their political and spiritual heritage. We want democracy to survive for all generations to come, not to become the insolvent phantom of tomorrow.

During the long lane of the history yet to be written America knows that this world of ours, ever growing smaller, must avoid becoming a community of dreadful fear and hate, and be, instead, a proud confederation of mutual trust and respect.

Such a confederation must be one of equals. The weakest must come to the conference table with the same confidence as do we, protected as we are by our moral, economic and military strength. That table, though scarred by many past frustrations, cannot be abandoned for the certain agony of the battlefield.

Disarmament, with mutual honor and confidence, is a continuing imperative. Together we must learn how to compose differences—not with arms, but with intellect and decent purpose. Because this need is so sharp and apparent, I confess that I lay down my official responsibilities in this field with a definite sense of disappointment. As one who has witnessed the horror and the lingering sadness of war, as one who knows that another war could utterly destroy this civilization which has been so slowly and painfully built over thousands of years, I wish I could say tonight that a lasting peace is in sight.

Happily, I can say that war has been avoided. Steady progress toward our ultimate goal has been made. But so much remains to be done. As a private citizen, I shall never cease to do what little I can to help the world advance along that road.

'My Last Good Night'

So, in this, my last good night to you as your President, I thank you for the many opportunities you have given me for public service in war and in peace.

I trust in that you—that, in that service, you find some things worthy. As for the rest of it, I know you will find ways to improve performance in the future.

You and I—my fellow citizens—need to be strong in our faith that all nations, under God, will reach the goal of peace with justice. May we be ever unswerving in devotion to principle, confident but humble with power, diligent in pursuit of the nation's great goals.

To all the peoples of the world, I once more give expression to America's prayerful and continuing aspiration:

We pray that peoples of all faiths, all races, all nations, may have their great human needs satisfied; that those now denied opportunity shall come to enjoy it to the full; that all who yearn for freedom may experience its spiritual blessings, those who have freedom will understand, also, its heavy responsibility; that all who are insensitive to the needs of others, will learn charity, and that the sources—scourges of poverty, disease and ignorance will be made to disappear from the earth; and that in the goodness of time all peoples will come to live together in a peace guaranteed by the binding force of mutual respect and love.

Now, on Friday noon, I am to become a private citizen. I am proud to do so. I look forward to it.

Thank you, and good night.

* * *

January 21, 1961

KENNEDY SWORN IN, ASKS 'GLOBAL ALLIANCE' AGAINST TYRANNY, WANT, DISEASE AND WAR; REPUBLICANS AND DIPLOMATS HAIL ADDRESS

NATION EXHORTED

Inaugural Says U. S. Will 'Pay Any Price' to Keep Freedom

By W. H. LAWRENCE
Special to The New York Times.

WASHINGTON, Jan. 20—John Fitzgerald Kennedy assumed the Presidency today with a call for "a grand and global alliance" to combat tyranny, poverty, disease and war.

In his Inaugural Address, he served notice on the world that the United States was ready to "pay any price, bear any burden, meet any hardship, support any friend, oppose any foe to assure the survival and the success of liberty."

But the nation is also ready, he said, to resume negotiations with the Soviet Union to ease and, if possible, remove world tensions.

"Let us begin anew," Mr. Kennedy declared. "Let us never negotiate out of fear. But let us never fear to negotiate."

Asks Aid of Countrymen

He called on his fellow-citizens to join his Administration's endeavor:

"Ask not what your country can do for you—ask what you can do for your country."

At 12:51 P. M., he was sworn by Chief Justice Earl Warren as the nation's thirty-fifth President, the first Roman Catholic to hold the office.

Ten minutes earlier, Lyndon Baines Johnson of Texas took the oath as Vice President. It was administered by Sam Rayburn, Speaker of the House of Representatives.

At 43 years of age, the youngest man ever elected to the Presidency, Mr. Kennedy took over the power vested for eight years in Dwight D. Eisenhower, who, at 70, was the oldest White House occupant.

President Kennedy alluded to this change of generation in his Inaugural.

'Torch Has Passed'

He said:

"Let the word go forth from this time and place, to friend and foe alike, that the torch has been passed to a new generation of Americans—born in this century, tempered by war, disciplined by a hard and bitter peace, proud of our ancient heritage—and unwilling to witness or permit the slow undoing of those human rights to which this nation has always been committed, and to which we are committed today at home and around the world."

A blanket of 7.7 inches of newly fallen snow, bitter winds and a sub-freezing temperature of 22 degrees held down the crowds that watched the ceremonies in front of the newly renovated East Front of the Capitol.

But the crowds swelled under a cheering, if not warming, sun from a cloudless sky as the new President and his wife Jacqueline led the inaugural parade from the Capitol back to the White House shortly after 2 P. M. The police estimated that the crowds might have totaled 1,000,000, but this seemed excessive.

A crowd estimated at 20,000 persons saw the new President assume office.

From snow-mantled Capitol Hill, he led the big parade, with peaceful themes as well as displays of military might, down broad Constitution and Pennsylvania Avenues to the White House. With his wife he rode in the familiar "bubble-top" Presidential limousine.

Reviews Parade

At the White House, he mounted the canopied reviewing stand, where he stayed for the entire three-and-a-half-hour parade. Most of the time he was bareheaded and occasionally he sipped soup and coffee.

The retiring Republican leaders—Mr. Eisenhower and Richard M. Nixon—joined in the applause as the new President outlined in sober terms and a deliberate manner the general course of his Administration.

Mr. Nixon, defeated for the Presidency by Mr. Kennedy last Nov. 8 in the closest election of modern times, was the first after Chief Justice Warren to shake hands with President Kennedy after the oath-taking.

The Kennedy Inaugural, which was both firm and conciliatory in its approach to the Soviet-led Communist bloc, was well received by both Republicans and Democrats on Capitol Hill.

President Kennedy called on the Soviet Union for a new beginning. He asked a renewed effort to negotiate problems that he said threatened destruction of the world, but, if settled, could afford hope that all forms of human poverty might be abolished.

Warning that civility should not be mistaken for weakness and that sincerity was always subject to proof, Mr. Kennedy asked "both sides" to explore what problems "unite us instead of belaboring those problems which divide us."

"Let both sides, for the first time, formulate serious and precise proposals for the inspection and control of arms—and bring the absolute power to destroy other nations under the absolute control of all nations," he continued.

"Let both sides seek to invoke the wonders of science instead of its terrors," he went on. "Together let us explore the stars, conquer the deserts, eradicate disease, tap the ocean depths and encourage the arts and commerce."

Associated Press Wirephoto

NEW PRESIDENT TAKES THE OATH: John Fitzgerald Kennedy taking the oath of office yesterday. Administering it is Chief Justice Earl Warren, and holding the Bible is James R. Browning, Clerk of the Supreme Court. In the foreground, from left, are Mrs. Kennedy; Mrs. Warren; outgoing President Eisenhower; Mrs. R. Sargent Shriver, a sister of President Kennedy; Dean Rusk and, at right, Lyndon Baines Johnson, who was sworn in as Vice President. Partly hidden behind Mrs. Shriver is Adlai E. Stevenson.

'New World of Law'

If a beachhead of cooperation could "push back the jungles of suspicion," Mr. Kennedy said, both sides could then join in a new endeavor, not simply for a new balance of power, but rather "a new world of law, where the strong are just and the weak secure and the peace preserved."

With Mr. Eisenhower sitting about a yard away, President Kennedy emphasized some of the stands he will take on foreign policy.

He told the newly emerging nations of Africa he would not "always expect to find them supporting our view."

"But we shall always hope to find them strongly supporting their own freedom," he declared, "and to remember that, in the past, those who foolishly sought power riding the back of the tiger inevitably ended up inside."

He emphasized that he favored a stronger North Atlantic Treaty Organization, unqualified support of the United Nations, and helping the under-developed nations "break the bonds of mass misery."

"If a free society cannot help the many who are poor, it cannot save the few who are rich," he asserted.

In an apparent allusion to the regime of Premier Fidel Castro of Cuba, with which the Eisenhower Administration broke diplomatic relations earlier this month, the new President sounded a warning to the Russians not in interfere in the Western Hemisphere.

"Let all our neighbors know that we shall join with them to oppose aggression or subversion anywhere in the Americas," he said. "And let every other power know that this hemisphere intends to remain the master of its own house."

To the Latin-American nations generally, he offered "a special pledge" that good words would be converted "into good deeds" in an effort "to assist free men and free governments in casting off the chains of poverty."

Uses Family Bible

During his induction, President Kennedy's hand rested on a family Bible—a Douay version, the English translation made for Roman Catholics in the sixteenth century. He chose not to have it open to any particular passage, as has been the custom in some past inaugurations.

He took office with the prayers of four major faiths to bolster him in his pledges. The invocation was delivered by Richard Cardinal Cushing of Boston, a close friend of the Kennedy family.

The Protestant denomination to which Vice President Johnson belongs, Disciples of Christ, was represented by the Rev. Dr. John Barclay, pastor of the Central Christian Church of Austin, Tex. Archbishop Iakovos of New York, head of the Greek Orthodox Archdiocese of North and South America, also said prayers. Rabbi Nelson Glueck, president of the Hebrew Union College of Cincinnati, gave the benediction.

The ceremonies were presided over by Senator John J. Sparkman, Democrat of Alabama, chairman of the Joint Congressional Committee on Inaugural Arrangements.

They opened with "The Star-Spangled Banner," sung by Marian Anderson, the contralto.

Robert Frost, the New England poet, read his poem, "The Gift Outright," which President Kennedy had especially requested in inviting Mr. Frost to the Inaugural. He also sought to preface it with a verse he had written for the occasion to praise Mr. Kennedy for "summoning artists to participate." But the bright sun and wind combined to defeat him. He did not need to read "The Gift Outright."

Has 4 Hours of Sleep

In his day of triumph President Kennedy seemed unaffected and unfrightened as he approached the responsibilities of leadership.

With barely four hours' sleep after last night's Inaugural Concert and gala and a victory celebration thereafter, he was up at 8 A. M. He attended a mass in Holy Trinity Roman Catholic Church at 9 A. M.

Outside his Georgetown home at 3307 N. Street, N. W., he joked with reporters.

Recalling that President Eisenhower had broken with tradition eight years ago by decreeing black homburgs instead of tall silk top hats for inaugural wear, Mr. Kennedy was mockingly severe when he spotted a newsman in a homburg today.

"Didn't you get the word?" he asked. "Top hats are the rule this year."

Mr. Kennedy, who is usually hatless, seemed self-consciously uncomfortable in his topper. He wore it as briefly as possible in the trips back and forth from the White House to Capitol Hill. He also shed his coat frequently in the long day outdoors.

Bronzed by the Florida sun during his pre-inauguration holiday, with his brown hair neatly brushed, he looked the picture of health as he tackled the White House job.

He lost no time in getting to work: Minutes after he took the oath, he repaired to a Senate office to sign the official nominating papers for his ten Cabinet members and Adlai E. Stevenson as representative to the United Nations, a post with Cabinet status.

He also sent word to the White House staff to be on duty by 8:45 A. M. tomorrow, although tonight was a long night of celebration at five inaugural balls at the National Guard Armory and four Washington hotels.

He told the Inaugural crowd it could expect no swift miracles to solve the nation's problems or end the "cold war."

His Administration's aims, he said, could not be finished in "the first 100 days," the period for which the first Franklin D. Roosevelt Administration is remembered because of the speed with which Congress and the new Administration moved.

Indeed, Mr. Kennedy went on, the problems of this world would not be solved in the first 1,000 days, "nor even perhaps in our lifetime on this planet."

* * *

March 14, 1961

PRESIDENT GIVES 10-YEAR AID PLAN TO LATIN AMERICA

Pledges to Put New Vigor in 'Good Neighbor' Policy and Provide Help to All

WARNS OF FUTURE PERIL

Tells Envoys at White House Reception That Republics Must 'Do Their Part'

By W. H. LAWRENCE
Special to The New York Times.

WASHINGTON, March 13—President Kennedy set forth tonight a ten-point, ten-year economic and social development program for Latin America to meet the challenge of "a future full of peril, but bright with hope."

The President outlined his program in an unusual White House ceremony that combined a diplomatic reception with a major speech.

Mr. Kennedy told 250 persons, including diplomats from Latin America and leaders of Congress and their wives, that the United States was prepared to give financial aid "if the countries of Latin America are ready to do their part." His plan sought to help "all."

He spoke in the East Room after he and Mrs. Kennedy received their guests in the Red, Blue and Green Rooms.

Although the President does not speak Spanish, his twenty-minute speech contained several Spanish phrases. He spoke for twenty minutes while his audience sat on gilt chairs arranged in semicircles on both sides of the rostrum. Mr. Kennedy declared:

"Our motto is what it has always been—'Progress, yes! Tyranny, no!'—'Progreso, si! Tirania, no!'

He Lists Ten Points

The President reiterated his campaign pledge to put new life and vigor into the "good neighbor" policy of Franklin D. Roosevelt as he proposed this ten-point effort:

1. A ten-year plan to raise the living standards of all Americans, provide basic education, end hunger and place each nation on a basis of self-sustaining growth.

2. An early ministerial meeting of the Inter-American Economic and Social Council at which each nation will be expected to put forward long-range programs.
3. A request to Congress for the $500,000,000 in American aid promised in the Act of Bogota.
4. Support for all "economic integration which is a genuine step toward larger markets and greater competitive opportunity."
5. Cooperation by the United States in "serious, case-by-case examinations of commodity market problems."
6. A step-up now in the Food for Peace emergency program.
7. An invitation to Latin-American scientists to work with the United States.
8. Rapid expansion of training programs.
9. Reaffirmation of the United States pledge to go to the defense of an American nation whose independence is endangered.
10. An invitation to contribute to the enrichment of life and culture in the United States by providing teachers here and welcoming United States students to Latin American universities.

The President warned that the economic development program he advocated looked toward modification of "social patterns so that all, and not just a privileged few, share the fruits of growth."

Friendship to Cuban People

President Kennedy included in his talk an expression of "special friendship to the people of Cuba and the Dominican Republic—and the hope that they will soon rejoin the society of free men, uniting with us in our common effort."

The broad program he outlined today, to be explained in a special message to Congress tomorrow, bore no price tag other than the $500,000,000 commitment that was made by the Eisenhower Administration last year.

But Mr. Kennedy compared his plan with the Marshall Plan, which rebuilt the war-damaged economies of Western Europe. He said the United States should provide "resources of a scope and magnitude sufficient to make this bold development program a success."

The President noted Communist encroachment in Cuba. He warned of the perils faced by the Western Hemisphere and said the dream of progress, freedom and glory never had been in "greater danger" from the forces that "have imperiled America throughout its history—the alien forces which once again seek to impose the despotisms of the Old World on the people of the New.

Mr. Kennedy said that the revolution of freedom that began at Philadelphia in 1776, and at Caracas, Venezuela in 1811, was not finished and that the hemisphere's mission was not yet complete.

"For our unfulfilled task is to demonstrate to the entire world that man's unsatisfied aspiration for economic progress and social justice can best be achieved by free men working within a framework of democratic institutions," he declared.

The President's words were transmitted at once by the Voice of America in English, Spanish, Portuguese and French to the nations of the South. It was not broadcast live here, but was recorded and videotaped.

* * *

April 12, 1961

SOVIET ORBITS MAN AND RECOVERS HIM; SPACE PIONEER REPORTS: 'I FEEL WELL'; SENT MESSAGES WHILE CIRCLING EARTH

187-MILE HEIGHT

Yuri Gagarin, a Major, Makes the Flight in 5-Ton Vehicle

By United Press International

MOSCOW, Wednesday, April 12—The Soviet Union announced today it had won the race to put a man into space. The official press agency, Tass, said a man had orbited the earth in a spaceship and had been brought back alive and safe.

A brief announcement said the first reported spaceship had landed in what was described as the "prescribed area" of the Soviet Union after a historic flight.

A Moscow radio announcer broke into a program and said in emotional tones:

"Russia has successfully launched a man into space. His name is Yuri Gagarin. He was launched in a sputnik named Vostok, which means "East."

Reports on Landing

Tass said that on landing, Major Gagarin said: "Please report to the party and Government, and personally to Nikita Sergyevich Khrushchev, that the landing was normal, I feel well, have no injuries or bruises."

He landed at 10:55 A. M. Moscow time [2:55 A. M. New York time.]

Earlier, the major reported: "Flight is proceeding normally, I feel well."

After orbiting the earth, the major applied a braking device and the vehicle space landed in the Soviet Union, Tass said.

Major Gagarin, 27 years old, is an industrial technician, and married. He was reported to have received pre-flight training similar to that of the astronaut who will man the United States' first space ships.

Soared to 187 Miles

The announcer said the Sputnik reached a minimum altitude of 175 kilometers to (109½ miles) and a maximum altitude of 302 kilometers (187¾ miles).

He said the weight of the Sputnik was 10,395 pounds, or slightly over five tons.

The announcement of the launching came at 2 A. M. New York time.

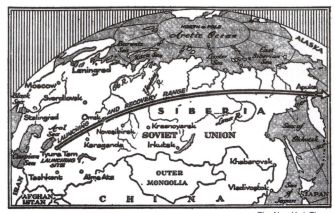

The New York Times

PROBABLE TRACK: Reported path of astronaut's flight from launch site at Tyura Tam.

It said everything functioned normally during the flight.

Constant radio contact was maintained between earth and the sputnik, the Moscow radio said.

The announcer said the direction of each revolution around the earth was 89.1 minutes.

The title of the announcement was "The First Human Flight into the Cosmos."

The radio, which was quoting a Tass press agency statement on the launching, said that Maj. Gagarin "is feeling well" and that "conditions in the cabin are normal."

As soon as the Moscow announcement was made, Russians began to telephone congratulations to each other.

The first astronaut is a major in the Soviet Air Force and is believed to be a test pilot.

The Tass announcement said that the launching of the multi-stage space rocket, which carried the Sputnik into orbit, was successful.

After attaining the first escape velocity, it said, and the separation of the last stage of the carrier rocket, the spaceship went into free flight on a round-the-earth orbit.

Reports of the launching of a Soviet space man had been reported repeatedly in Moscow for the last twenty-four hours.

The London Daily Worker and other sources had said the Soviet Union had sent a man into space last Friday and had brought him back alive.

Many persons in Moscow were convinced after today's announcement that another flight into space was attempted on Friday and there was speculation that something might have gone wrong.

The announcement of the first flight into space was repeated three times, after which the normal radio program of music was resumed.

The radio also broadcast patriotic songs.

The announcement said the condition of the navigator was being observed by means of radio telemetering devices and television.

Major Gagarin, the announcement went on, withstood satisfactorily the placing of the satellite ship into orbit.

He's 'You-Ree Gah-GAH-Rin'

The Soviet Union's man in space is Maj. Gagarin—pronounced You-ree Gah-GAH-Rin with the accent on the second syllable of his last name. The New York office of Tass, official Soviet news agency, gave the pronunciation of his name.

* * *

April 16, 1961

CASTRO FOES BOMB 3 AIR BASES; 2 OF RAIDERS FLEE TO FLORIDA; CUBA IS MOBILIZING, BLAMES U.S.

ARMS DEPOT HIT

Heavy Firing Follows Attack—7 Reported Killed at Havana

By R. HART PHILLIPS
Special to The New York Times.

HAVANA, April 15—Three Cuban military air bases were attacked almost simultaneously this morning by bombing planes.

[A statement issued by a pilot who said he had defected from the Cuban Air Force when he landed in Miami Saturday declared the attacks had been made by him and two other Cuban pilots in Cuban Air Force B-26's. A second plane landed at Key West, Fla.]

The planes, which the Government said were United States B-26's, bombed the airfield at Camp Libertad, on the outskirts of Havana, where an arms dump was hit; the San Antonio de los Baños air base, twenty-five miles from Havana, and the Antonio Maceo Airport at Santiago de Cuba, used by military and civilian planes.

Planes Fire Rockets

The planes, of a type purchased by Cuba from the United States during the Batista regime, also fired rockets. Seven militiamen were killed at Camp Libertad. At least forty-seven persons on the ground were reported wounded at the sites of the air raids.

Premier Fidel Castro ordered a general mobilization of the armed forces and civilian militia.

"If this air attack is a prelude to an invasion, the country, on a war basis, will resist and destroy with an iron hand any force which attempts to disembark on our soil," he said in a communiqué.

He also reported that the Cuban delegation to the United Nations had been given instructions to accuse the United States Government of being guilty of the attack.

Attack Termed 'Imperialistic'

"Our country has been the victim of a criminal imperialistic attack which violates all the norms of international law," the Premier declared.

President Osvaldo Dorticós Torrado denied later that the pilots had defected from the air force, as has been reported in the United States.

"No planes or pilots have taken off from Cuba," the President said. "We believe that these planes left from the United States and returned to bases there and that the United States supplied these planes with rockets and bombs."

President Dorticós called on United States news agencies to "report the truth" about the Cuban situation.

At the same time, Capt. Rolando Diaz Aztarain, Minister of the Treasury, said that two auxiliary fuel tanks had been recovered off the north coast, about twelve miles west of Havana, after the attack. He said this was proof that the planes had come from a distant point. He maintained that if they had taken off from Cuba they would not have needed such tanks.

However, an eyewitness said the attacking places did not carry auxiliary tanks.

At 6 A. M. the people of Havana were awakened by anti-aircraft and machine-gun fire. In Miramar, a suburb near the army airfield, early risers said they saw two planes making bombing runs. The bombs were said to have struck the ammunition dump, and flames shot skyward. Explosion after explosion followed.

The attack lasted about fifteen minutes, but the guns kept firing until 7 o'clock.

The administration building at Camp Libertad was struck by fragments and holes were blown in the runway. Five big trucks that were unloading ammunition were blown up.

Besides the seven men killed at Camp Libertad, thirty-nine militiamen were wounded at the facility, according to a Government announcement. Two residences were struck by rockets just outside the camp, wounding two children and a man.

Two soldiers were wounded and two planes on the ground were destroyed by the attack on the San Antonio air base, the army said tonight. It said the attack on the Antonio Maceo Airport resulted in the wounding of three soldiers and the destruction of four planes.

Attacker Reported Struck

A communiqué this morning by Premier Castro said one of the planes attacking the Camp Libertad airfield had been struck by anti-aircraft fire and was seen in flames.

At noon the entire foreign diplomatic corps in Havana was called to the Foreign Ministry. Dr. Carlos Olivares, acting Minister, who was dressed in a militia uniform, told the diplomats that Cuba had "proof" that the United States had "directed" the attack on Cuba.

Scorched fragments of what appeared to be rockets were displayed. Dr. Olivares said the fragments bore the inscription "U. S. A."

The accusation by Dr. Olivares against the United States did not greatly impress the majority of the diplomats of Western Europe and Latin America, according to the opinions expressed in diplomatic circles. The diplomats were inclined to reserve judgment on the accusation.

"Personally," one diplomat said, "I limited myself to transmitting Dr. Olivares' statement to my Government.

It was impossible to ascertain how the delegates of the Communist bloc and the neutralist nations regarded the Cuban charge. However, Cuba has received warm support from these countries in its fight against the United States.

A report that two of the planes that bombed the Santiago de Cuba airport had landed in the United States Guantanamo Naval Base, forty miles away, was denied tonight by Lieut. James Lloyd, the information officer of the base.

"No airplanes coming from Cuba have landed in this base," Lieutenant Lloyd said.

By mid-day guards had appeared at all strategic points in Havana and nationalized concerns had been reinforced. Armed militiamen walked the streets. Traffic was cut off from the Presidential Palace. Militiamen armed with Czechoslovak automatic weapons were posted on many roofs.

In Santiago de Cuba, Maj. Raul Castro, Minister of the Armed Forces and younger brother of the Premier, issued a statement accusing the United States of the attack. He called on the Cuban people to mobilize against their enemies.

Reports reaching Havana from Florida that two of the pilots had landed there and requested asylum caused considerable confusion.

However, Government television commentators immediately termed the reports a "trick of Yankee imperialism." The pilots who landed in Florida were undoubtedly Americans, these commentators said.

The atmosphere in Havana was tense tonight. Many Cubans feared a repetition of the bombings. Small groups gathered in street-corner discussions. This afternoon a number of small demonstrations were held throughout the city to protest the bombings and to accuse "Yankee imperialism," but there was no spontaneous mass demonstrating.

All theaters in Havana were closed tonight out of respect for the militia men and troops killed in the bombing of Camp Libertad. The bodies were moved from the municipal morgue to the University of Havana and will lie in state there until the funerals tomorrow.

The International Airport was closed to all commercial traffic tonight.

* * *

April 18, 1961

ANTI-CASTRO UNITS LAND IN CUBA; REPORT FIGHTING AT BEACHHEAD; RUSK SAYS U. S. WON'T INTERVENE

PREMIER DEFIANT

Says His Troops Battle Heroically to Repel Attacking Force

By TAD SZULC

Special to The New York Times.

MIAMI, Tuesday, April 18—Rebel troops opposed to Premier Fidel Castro landed before dawn yesterday on the swampy southern coast of Cuba in Las Villas Province.

The attack, which was supported from the air, was announced by the rebels and confirmed by the Cuban Government.

After fourteen hours of silence on the progress of the assault, the Government radio in Havana broadcast early today a terse communiqué signed by Premier Castro announcing only that "our armed forces are continuing to fight the enemy heroically."

The announcement, made shortly before 1 A. M., said that within the next few hours details of "our successes" would be given.

The communiqué came amid a wave of rebel assertions of victories, new landings and internal uprisings. The rebel spokesmen were acclaiming important progress in new landings in Oriente and Pinar del Rio Provinces, but none of these reports could be confirmed.

Government Reports Battle

The Government communiqué said a battle had been fought in the southeastern part of Las Villas Province, where yesterday morning's landings occurred.

Although the communiqué was signed by Premier Castro, the Cuban leader has not spoken to his nation since the attack began. An earlier communiqué, issued yesterday, reported the rebel landings.

In a communiqué issued last night, the Revolutionary Council, the top command of the rebel forces, said merely that military supplies and equipment were landed successfully on the marshy beachhead. The communiqué added that "some armed resistance" by supporters of Premier Castro had been overcome.

Premier Castro was reported to have escaped injury in an early-morning air raid yesterday near the beachhead.

The Revolutionary Council's announcement spoke of action in Matanzas Province, indicating that the rebels might have crossed the provincial border from Las Villas. The border is about ten miles north of the presumed landing spot.

The communiqué also said that "substantial amounts of food and ammunition" had reached the underground units in that region.

The Government accused the United States of having organized the attack.

Late last night unconfirmed reports from rebel leaders asserted that the attacking force had penetrated deep into Matanzas Province, reaching the central highway near the town of Colón.

An insistent spate of reports said that numerous landings also had occurred in Oriente Province, in the eastern part of Cuba, in the vicinity of Santiago de Cuba. But a complete blackout of direct news from Cuba made it impossible to assess the situation accurately.

In New York, the Revolutionary Council announced that "much of the militia in the countryside has already defected from Castro." The council predicted that "the principal battle" of the revolt would be fought along with a coordinated wave of sabotage before dawn.

President José Miró Cardona of the council in an earlier statement had called for Western Hemisphere peoples to support the revolt "morally and materially." The council has announced its aim to set up a "government in arms" as soon as it can get territory in Cuba and then to ask for foreign recognition and help.

[A dispatch said that the Cuban naval station at Veradero had reported a fleet of eight strange ships off Cardenas, north coast seaport about eighty-five miles east of Havana.]

National Alert Declared

The invaders, in undetermined numbers, are under the orders of the Revolutionary Council. In the words of its declaration, the Council seeks the overthrow of the Castro regime and the freeing of Cuba from "international communism's cruel oppression."

Premier Castro declared shortly before noon a state of national alert and called all his militia forces to their posts.

The Cuban official radio devoted most of its time yesterday to broadcasts of Dr. Castro's three proclamations and to vituperation against United States "imperialists."

The official Cuban radio announced last night the arrest of Havana's Auxiliary Bishop, Msgr. Eduardo Boza Masvidal, on charges of hiding United States currency and medicine for anti-Castro rebels.

The Government-controlled radio stations offered their normal music programs and soap operas. There were no further references to the landing.

An occasional announcement spoke of foreign support for Cuba, including a mention of volunteers from Czechoslovakia seeking to enlist to fight in Cuba.

According to official statements by both sides, the rebel forces went ashore during the night near the Bay of Cochinos as paratroop units were dropped farther inland to link up with underground fighters.

It was believed that the rebels landed near Playa Larga, on the eastern bank of the Cochinos Bay, which means the Bay of Pigs. This bay is wedged into the vast swamp of the Cienega de Zapata.

Report of Capture Unconfirmed

Persistent reports in exile circles that Raul Castro, Fidel's brother and Minister of the Revolutionary armed forces, had been captured somewhere near Santiago could not be confirmed.

One Cuban in close touch with Democratic Revolutionary Front activities here said the report was given credence by the fact that Dr. Castro had assumed the military role that for recent months he had turned over to his brother.

Dr. Castro charged that the invaders were "mercenaries" in the service of United States "imperialism." He pledged the Cubans to fight until death for the preservation of their "democratic and Socialist revolution."

The Revolutionary Council members were standing by, ready to move into Cuba and proclaim a "government in arms" as soon as the beachhead is firmly secured.

It was not known early last night how many troops had participated in the Las Villas landing. Whether this was to be the principal thrust against the Castro forces or the first of several such attacks also was not known.

The total strength of forces available to the rebels is estimated at somewhat over 5,000 men. Opposed to them is a military establishment of 400,000 of the regular army and the militia armed with the most modern Soviet bloc weapons.

The rebel command is known to believe that one or more major landings would set off internal uprisings and many desertions by soldiers and the militia.

Today it was too early to tell whether this optimism was justified.

The use by the rebels yesterday of planes and gunboats covering the landing indicated that it was an operation of major scope and not just another guerrilla foray of the type that has been occurring in the past.

It was believed here that the attacking forces came from the camps in Guatemala, where they have been trained for the last nine months. Some of the units may have come from a rebel camp in Louisiana.

Battle Area Strafed

It was believed, however, that the rebel troops left their camps a day or so ago and were staged for the jump-off at Caribbean islands somewhere between Central America and the Cienega de Zapata Peninsula of Las Villas Province.

A possible location of the staging area is the Swan Islands, where there is an anti-Castro radio station.

Capt. Manuel Artime, a 29-year-old former Castro officer, is reported to be the field commander of the operation. He was appointed last week by the Revolutionary Council as its "delegate to the armed forces."

Rebel aircraft bombed and strafed the battle area that extends into Matanzas Province.

About 7 o'clock in the morning, Premier Castro personally leading the defense operations, was reported to have found himself under an aerial bombardment in the small town of Boca de Laguna de Tesoro, about ten miles to the northeast of Cochinos Bay.

Cuban radio stations broadcast at 11:07 A. M. proclamations by Dr. Castro and President Osvaldo Dorticós Torrado acknowledging that Cuba had been attacked and declaring a state of national alert.

Up to then, radio stations had kept up normal musical programs, which beginning at 8 A. M. were interrupted by constant "urgent" calls from the general staff of the army ordering militiamen to report immediately to their battle stations.

The only report issued during the day by the Castro regime on the progress of the fighting came in the Premier's proclamation. He declared that "our troops are advancing against the enemy * * * in the certainty of victory."

Radio messages on the Government microwave—network monitored here—which gave a dramatic minute-by-minute account of the first hours of the landing—included appeals for reinforcements from additional militia battalions and a request for ambulances for the "many wounded."

It was a frantic conversation between Government radio operators in the invasion area that provided the news that Premier Castro was in the town being bombed.

The network ceased transmitting at 7:20 A. M.—except for the sudden call for the ambulances that came at 11 A. M.

Varona's Visit Cited

There were many indications that the mechanism of the invasion was set finally into motion Sunday when Dr. Manuel Antonio de Varona, a member of the Revolutionary Council and Minister of Defense in the Provisional Government, made a quick flight and visit to Miami.

Simultaneously, a large number of exile leaders here, including military figures, vanished early Sunday. They have not been seen since.

The climate for the invasion anticipated and promised by the Cuban rebels for many weeks was created to a large extent by events of last week.

Since last Thursday a major wave of sabotage swept Cuba. Saturday three B-26 aircraft bombed three air bases on the island. Beginning in the middle of last week informants in Cuban groups made it known confidentially that "important events" were to be expected over the week-end.

Final preparations for the move against the Castro regime started in earnest about three weeks ago after the Revolutionary Council was formed and a secret mobilization order went out to rebel volunteers.

For the last three weeks hundreds of volunteers had been leaving the Miami and New York areas for the camps in the training grounds in Guatamala.

Yesterday as word of the attack spread in Miami, additional hundreds of volunteers began appearing at the recruiting offices of several of the movements that make up the Revolutionary Council.

At least one sizable group of highly trained officers and men were still held back at a ranch on the outskirts of Miami.

In his proclamations, Dr. Castro appealed repeatedly for support by Latin-American nations. The Havana radio broadcast reports of Latin-American solidarity for the Cuban cause.

The Revolutionary Council also addressed itself to Latin America. Its dawn declaration stated that the rebels were convinced that "the freedom loving people of this hemisphere will make common cause with them and support them."

* * *

June 4, 1961

KENNEDY AND KHRUSHCHEV STRESS PROBLEM OF LAOS IN 4-HOUR TALK; DISCUSSION 'FRANK AND COURTEOUS'

PARLEY IS LIVELY

Soviet Veto Proposal a Topic in Vienna—More Talks Today

By JAMES RESTON
Special to The New York Times.

VIENNA, June 3—President Kennedy and Premier Khrushchev held today what was described as a "frank and courteous" four-hour discussion of the troubled world relationships between the United States and the Soviet Union.

A statement issued by the official spokesmen of the two countries at a joint news conference said special attention had been paid to the Southeast Asian country of Laos, whose Government is facing a Communist-backed rebellion.

It is understood that this produced some lively discussion of the recent Soviet insistence on a veto over the control of the present "cease-fire" in that country, but no agreement.

In fact, while the atmosphere of the conversations was apparently more cordial than had been expected afzter the rising controversies of the last few months, no agreements were expected or reached on any of the topics discussed.

Randolph Churchill 'Bored'

The leaders' discussions will be continued tomorrow.

At the end of the mammoth news conference this evening—broken up by Randolph Churchill, son of the former British Prime Minister, who forced his way out of the closed conference room because he was "bored"—it was not possible for the official spokesmen to agree on how to characterize the results of the day's talks.

Mikhail A. Kharlamov, chief of the press department of the Soviet Foreign Office, described the conversations as "fruitful." Pierre Salinger, White House press secretary, said he preferred to stand on his previous description of the meeting as "frank and courteous."

Fruitful or not, the meetings at least avoided both the false optimism of the first summit meeting of 1955 and the angry Soviet denunciations of the ill-fated U-2 summit meeting in Paris last year.

The unexpectedly small Soviet delegation arrived here by slow train yesterday complaining that the United States seemed determined to turn the Vienna meeting into a propaganda circus, but the President insisted personally today on precisely the opposite approach.

He greeted Mr. Khrushchev warmly at the beginning of the session at 12:45 P. M., running down the steps of the United States Embassy residence to meet him.

The President took the Premier into the building for a working session with their aides until 2 o'clock, entered into some good-natured bantering at lunch and then proposed that the afternoon sessions be held in private with only interpreters present.

President Kennedy started the afternoon talks during a ten-minute stroll through the garden with Mr. Khrushchev and they went on until 6:45 P. M., when the President, still pleasant, saw Mr. Khrushchev to his car to end what amounted to about four hours of tediously interpreted conversations.

Rusk and Gromyko Talk

The complex and sensitive topics of Germany and Berlin and the control of nuclear testing were not explored by the two leaders, though these topics will be on the agenda for the final meetings tomorrow.

It is understood, however, that they were discussed, without noticeable change in the positions of either side, by Secretary of State Dean Rusk and Andrei A. Gromyko, Soviet Foreign Minister, who conferred with their aides in another part of the embassy during the Kennedy-Khrushchev afternoon session.

On the basis of the limited information available tonight, it appeared that the only topic explored at length by the President and the Premier was Laos. Recently, efforts to establish a commission to maintain the cease-fire in that country have led to Soviet insistence that all decisions involving inspection of violations of the cease-fire be taken by "unanimous agreement."

Veto Principle Fought

The United States is strongly opposed to this, not only in the specific case of Laos but in principle. Ever since the United Nations intervened successfully to get the Soviet technicians and representatives out of the Congo, Moscow has been demanding that international action by the United Nations or any other international group be taken only when representatives of the Western world, the Communist world and the neutral world agree unanimously.

In the United States' view this not only would give the Communists a veto over international control of delicate disputes but would virtually paralyze the post-war movement toward the peaceful settlement and supervision of disputes by international organizations.

The present International Control Commission in Laos, for example, is made up of Canada, India and Poland. It takes action on violation of the 1954 truce agreement on a basis of majority rule except in those instances where a resumption of hostilities is threatened.

The future control commission, as envisaged by the Soviet Union in a unified, neutral Laos, could consist of the same members but all decisions would be by rule of unanimity. The Communist Polish member would thus have a veto on whether an alleged violation should be investigated or action taken after any investigation.

However, it is not Laos that is primarily at issue here, but defense of the principle that there are an increasing number of things in the world today that cannot be left to national control but must be subjected to the judgment of the international community.

This is one reason why the President is understood to have raised and pressed the Laos question this afternoon. But there is another reason, namely, that the President has become increasingly disturbed by Moscow's insistence that it has the right to intervene in disputes that it deems just, whereas the United States and even the United Nations should stay out of controversies that involve the national or even the ideological interests of the U. S. S. R.

Doctrine Troubles U. S.

One of the President's reasons for coming to Vienna was to try to get some clarification of a Khrushchev doctrine that has troubled Washington ever since it was delivered in a report by the Soviet Premier to representatives of Communist and workers parties in Moscow last Jan. 6.

In this report Mr. Khrushchev defined what has been called the "doctrine of three wars." He ruled out atomic and hydrogen "world wars" and also "limited" or local wars on the ground that both might lead to the death of hundreds of millions of people.

"Wars of national liberation," however, he said, were not only permissible but necessary and would have the support of the Communist peoples. He gave as examples of these the war in Algeria and Fidel Castro's war against Fulgencio Batista in Cuba.

"These are revolutionary wars," he said. "Such wars are not only admissible but inevitable * * * In these uprisings these people are fighting for the implementation of their right of self-determination, for independent social and national development. These are uprisings against rotten reactionary regimes, against the colonizers. The Communists fully support such just wars."

This has raised a number of fundamental questions among the President's advisers on Soviet affairs, who were discussing them before today's meeting between the President and the Premier.

According to this doctrine, which has become the basis of Communist activity all over the world, Dr. Castro's war against President Batista was a "just war," which would justify Communist support as a "war of liberation," but the recent uprising against Dr. Castro would be regarded as a counter-revolutionary war by a "rotten reactionary" regime backed by the American "colonizers."

Similarly, under this doctrine Communist aid to the rebels in Laos and Vietnam as "just," but United States aid to the legitimate Government of Laos is "imperialism."

Need for Clarification

The point being made to Premier Khrushchev and his aides here by the United States is that this is a fallacious and highly dangerous argument. The United States is insisting that, as "limited" or "local" wars might lead to the big nuclear war, so this attempt to back whatever the Communists think is a "just" uprising might also lead to the intervention of other states that have a different notion of justice.

In short, the "wars of liberation," like the limited wars, could also lead to a major nuclear war, and President Kennedy's point was that persistence in such a doctrine would inevitably produce precisely the kind of world tensions that Mr. Khrushchev says he wants to avoid.

No one on the American side expected Mr. Khrushchev to abandon the "just war" doctrine, or even to debate it at any length in the limited time available here, but nevertheless the point was being raised for a fundamental reason.

If the Russians merely mean to provide limited aid to those engaged on their side in such wars, Washington would feel that the situation, while awkward, might be controlled.

If, however, the Soviet Union decides to maintain its people at their present low standard of living and devote the rising Soviet production to such wars, then United States officials would be extremely gloomy about the outlook for peace.

This is why Washington was hoping to deter Mr. Khrushchev from the latter course.

More than a thousand reporters attempted to question Mr. Salinger and Mr. Kharlamov, but succeeded mainly in confusing each other.

This conference was held in the new palace, a wing of the Imperial Palace, which formerly housed Archduke Franz Ferdinand, the unfortunate nephew and heir of Franz Joseph, who was assassinated at Sarajevo in 1914.

Mr. Salinger refused to say whether any agreement had been reached on Laos, what the advisers to the two leaders had discussed or who said what in the toasts at lunch.

This agreement between the spokesmen to say nothing was what led to the incident with Mr. Churchill. Seeing that he was not likely to get an exhaustive account of what had happened, Mr. Churchill rose and went to the door. There his exit was blocked by a security agent, who apparently had orders not to let anyone out until the conference was over.

Mr. Churchill thereupon roared his insistence—the only angry voice reported all day. He demanded to know whether there was anything compulsory about news conferences, announced that he wanted to leave because he was "bored" with the briefing, and finally asked whether the agent thought he was in Russia.

This thought apparently startled a near-by Austrian security guard, who liberated Mr. Churchill, who thereupon held his own news conference and spoke more freely than anyone else had all day.

Tomorrow it is expected that the foreign ministers and their aides will continue their discussions, separate or with the leaders.

Those who attended the side conference today, along with the two foreign secretaries, were:

United States—Llewellyn E. Thompson Jr., Ambassador to the Soviet Union; Charles E. Bohlen, chief Soviet adviser to the Secretary of State; Foy D. Kohler, Assistant Secretary of State for European Affairs.

For the Soviet Union—Mikhail A. Menshikov, Ambassador to the United States, and Anatoly F. Dobrynin, head of the American Section of the Soviet Foreign Office.

* * *

June 5, 1961

KENNEDY AND KHRUSHCHEV FIND LIMITED LAOS ACCORD BUT SPLIT ON BERLIN AND KEY ARMS ISSUES

VIENNA TALKS END

Meeting Closes With Hard Controversy—Kennedy Solemn

By JAMES RESTON
Special to The New York Times.

VIENNA, June 4—President Kennedy and Premier Khrushchev ended their two-day conversation today with a limited agreement on Laos and a sharp three-hour disagreement on all questions concerning Germany and Berlin.

The conference, which started well yesterday, ended in hard controversy today. There were no ultimatums and few bitter or menacing exchanges. Indeed, Premier Khrushchev described the conference tonight as a "very good beginning," but the differences on Germany were nevertheless both wide and deep.

This was true as well of the two leaders' differences on the control of nuclear testing, on the Soviet demands for a veto over international control of other disputes, on the means of controlling disarmament and on Mr. Khrushchev's doctrine of what he regards as "just" wars of "national liberation."

Kennedy in Solemn Mood

Accordingly, President Kennedy flew off to London tonight in a solemn, although confident, mood. He had re-established high-level United States-Soviet diplomacy, which was broken off last year after the U-2 spy plane incident, and had agreed to maintain diplomatic contact at all levels, but on the big disputes between Washington and Moscow he had found absolutely no new grounds for encouragement.

In the hope, on both sides, that today's sharp disagreements might be modified after further conversations, the official statement on the meeting was vaguely incomplete.

It said merely that the two leaders had completed their "useful" meetings, had discussed Germany, nuclear tests and

Associated Press Radiophoto

A MEETING ENDED: President Kennedy and Premier Khrushchev after Vienna talks.

disarmament, had reaffirmed their support for a neutral and independent Laos and had agreed to continue contact on all questions of common interest.

Joint News Conference Held

Pierre Salinger, White House press secretary, and Mikhail A. Kharlamov, press officer of the Soviet Foreign Ministry, subsequently held a joint news conference at which they carefully avoided discussion of the disagreements.

They were obviously working under strict instructions not to get involved in the substance of the disputes. But the text of their remarks discloses the efforts of the two delegations to try to keep negotiations going forward.

This apparently satisfied the Communist representatives here, for they went away emphasizing how "useful" the talks had been, and talking about the importance of the agreement to continue trying to reach accommodations on the unsettled questions.

In line with this moderate and even hopeful Soviet approach, which has characterized the comments of Soviet officials and journalists ever since they reached this lovely city, Premier Khrushchev decided against holding a news conference tomorrow as he did in his tumultuous exit from the Paris summit meeting with President Eisenhower, President de Gaulle and Prime Minister Macmillan in May, 1960.

Indeed, the Communists scarcely mentioned the German part of the talks, though this was the main preoccupation of the day and was the point the Soviet Premier insisted upon discussing more than anything else.

One possible reason for the Soviet display of satisfaction may have been an ambiguity in the day's discussion about the critical question of the Allied rights and duties toward Berlin.

The former German capital, responsibility for which rests jointly with the victorious powers of World War II—the

United States, the Soviet Union, Britain and France—lies 110 miles inside Communist East Germany.

The Russians have been threatening to ignore the joint responsibility of the four powers for Berlin, to turn over the control of East Germany to the German Communist government of that state and thus to leave to the East Germans the power to check on the shipment of essential supplies to the military and civilian population of West Berlin.

Kennedy Takes Firm Stand

President Kennedy argued this whole legal and moral question, point for point, with the Soviet Premier for more than an hour.

He concluded his argument by reminding the Soviet leader that the United States had twice gone to war to prevent Western Europe from being overwhelmed, and he added that the United States regarded the freedom of West Germany as essential to the freedom of Western Europe.

This was not said provocatively but simply as an objective fact. But in the discussion that followed, the ambiguity arose.

The President placed his emphasis in this discussion not on the legal question whether the Soviet Union had any right to recognize Communist East Germany as a sovereign Government, but on the practical question of getting necessary supplies through the Communist territory to West Berlin.

He insisted that this was not only a right of the Western powers as a result of their conquest of Germany, but a duty to the 2,200,000 people of West Berlin, assumed not only by the United States, Britain and France but also by the Soviet Union.

This was interpreted by some Communists here as an indication that the President was concerned, not about recognition of East Germany by Moscow, but only about freedom of access to Berlin, regardless of who controlled the checkpoints on routes between West Germany and the former German capital.

It is true that the United States is more concerned about the freedom and the lives of the people of West Berlin than in the legal aspects of the question, but this does not mean that the United States has agreed to acquiesce in turning over sovereign power to the East Germans.

Envoys Sent to Bonn and Paris

President Kennedy came here with a careful understanding on the Berlin question with both President de Gaulle and Chancellor Adenauer. Accordingly, he sent Secretary of State Dean Rusk to Paris this evening to report on the Vienna talks to President de Gaulle and instructed Foy D. Kohler, Assistant Secretary of State for European Affairs, to go to Bonn to report to Chancellor Adenauer.

Mr. Rusk will also discuss the Vienna meetings with the members of the Council of the North Atlantic Treaty Organization in Paris tomorrow.

At no time during these long discussions, eventually made tedious by translation, did Premier Khrushchev depart from the past positions that have been rejected by the United States, Britain and France in two long foreign ministers' conferences in Geneva.

Finally, the President told the Soviet leader that the Soviet Government was asking the United States to accept Mr. Khrushchev's policy for Germany in detail or run the risk of war.

It was at this point that the President reminded the Premier that the United States had fought in two wars to defend Western Europe and that he regarded the freedom of West Germany as essential to the freedom of Western Europe today.

No Progress on Test Ban

The discussions on the possibility of reaching a controlled ban on nuclear testing were equally negative. As a matter of fact, Mr. Khrushchev indicated that he was not very interested in reaching a test ban agreement unless it was made part of a general disarmament agreement.

Accordingly, United States officials left here without much hope for the stalemated United States-British-Soviet discussions in Geneva on a nuclear test ban agreement, which had virtually stopped in the hope that President Kennedy and Premier Khrushchev could break the deadlock.

President Kennedy told the Soviet leader quite explicitly that he would not enter into any nuclear or disarmament agreement that involved a Soviet veto on the control of such an agreement.

Premier Khrushchev insisted in turn that the Soviet Union would not permit its interests to be determined by international bodies unless it agreed with the decisions of such international groups.

These discussions went on, with time out for a lavish lunch, for approximately six hours in the Soviet Embassy while crowds of curious Austrians stood outside. Mr. Rusk and Mr. Gromyko and their principal aides were present most of the time.

Cuba was mentioned only once during the discussions, when Mr. Khrushchev said that "Castro is no Communist."

This came up during a discussion of the Khrushchev doctrine of the "three wars."

This doctrine was laid down by the Soviet leader in a major report last Jan. 6.

In it he said that, while world wars must be ruled out and limited local wars should also be banned because they might lead to world war, "wars of national liberation," such as the nationalist rebellion in Algeria and Dr. Fidel Castro's struggle to overthrow the regime of Fulgencio Batista in Cuba not only were permissible but were "just" and should have the support of the Communist peoples.

President Kennedy said these wars of national liberation were also dangerous because, while limited wars such that in Korea could conceivably get out of control, so also could conflicts such as that in Laos, which Mr. Khrushchev regarded as "just." The President warned of the danger of miscalculation.

Khrushchev Objects

Mr. Khrushchev not only did not accept this argument, but added that he did not like the word "miscalculation," which he said was a misleading "Western word."

Once when the going got a little difficult, Mr. Khrushchev attacked the United States for defending a lot of "unrepresentative" governments. To this, the President replied that a free vote in the Eastern European countries might not return an overwhelming majority for the parties now in power.

This, however, merely led to charges that the President was attacking governments with which the United States had normal diplomatic relations—governments that were, Mr. Khrushchev added, truly representative of the people.

Most of this took place during a long morning session that lasted from shortly after 10 o'clock until shortly after 2, when the discussions broke up for lunch. Earlier in the morning 1 resident and Mrs. Kennedy went to church.

Despite the hard going during the talks, the atmosphere at lunch was jovial, with the usual toasts to peace, freedom and a safe journey home.

While this was going on in one part of the Soviet Embassy, another party for about twenty-five persons was going on in another section of the building. These were the Soviet, American and Austrian security and administrative officers who had helped organize the conference.

No detail of protocol, no personal courtesy was overlooked by the Russians. They not only saw to it that the security and administrative officers had the same food, drink and toasts, but were elaborately courteous and restrained in their demeanor here from beginning to end.

The whole Soviet approach to this first conference with President Kennedy has been interesting. Every time Premier Khrushchev has come west from the Soviet Union in the past, he has been preceded by weeks of fanfare in the press and radio.

This time Moscow has played it pianissimo. There was very little comment in the Soviet press ahead of time. Few Soviet journalists appeared in Vienna, and for the first time in the history of summitry the Russians held no separate briefings or news conferences, even after the meetings were over.

Now tonight, at the end, though there has been no change on any major problem, they profess to be not only satisfied but pleased.

Meanwhile, President Kennedy, if not pleased, has had his first major experience in "cold war" diplomacy and has come out of it very well. He did not expect much and he did not get much, but he went away from here more experienced and he now rates more highly in the estimation of the men who watched these exchanges than he has at any time since he entered the White House.

* * *

KENNEDY SAYS KHRUSHCHEV TALKS EASED DANGER OF A 'MISJUDGMENT'; U. S. BIDS SOVIET END LAOS FIGHTING

REPORT IS SOMBER

Nation Informed No Concessions Were Made in Vienna

By JOSEPH A. LOFTUS
Special to The New York Times.

WASHINGTON, June 6—President Kennedy reported to the nation tonight that his talks with Premier Khrushchev should at least have lessened chances of a "dangerous misjudgment" on either side.

The President saw some hope of resolving the conflict in Laos but conceded that in general "the gap between us was not, in such a short period, materially reduced."

His hopes for agreement on a nuclear test ban and slowing the arms race suffered a "serious blow," at Vienna, Mr. Kennedy acknowledged.

But the "most somber" subjects in his two-day meeting with the Soviet leader were Germany and Berlin, he said.

States U. S. Position

"I made it clear to Mr. Khrushchev," said the President, "that the security of Western Europe, and therefore our own security, are deeply involved in our presence and our access rights to West Berlin, that those rights are based on law and not on sufferance, and that we are determined to maintain those rights at any risk, and thus meet our obligation to the people of West Berlin, and their right to choose their own future."

"No spectacular progress was either achieved or pretended," the President said. "No advantage or concession was either gained or given."

Talks 'Immensely Useful'

Nevertheless, he said, he found the talks "immensely useful" because the channels of communication are now clearer. He declared:

"At least the chances of a dangerous misjudgment on either side should now be less, and at least the men on whose decisions the peace in part depends have agreed to remain in contact."

The President spoke for twenty-six minutes, starting at 7 P. M., over all major television and radio networks. It was his first public address from the White House.

The President's journey to Europe began May 30 and ended earlier today, when he received a bipartisan welcome home at Andrews Air Force Base, Md.

During his speech tonight, Mr. Kennedy appeared rested from his European travels. At times he seemed to be reading notes as well as a prepared text, and he finally pleaded for foreign aid support without resort to any written references.

Mr. Kennedy repeatedly used the word "somber" to describe his meeting with Mr. Khrushchev, a word that sometimes described his delivery. He has rarely spoken with such unbroken earnestness.

As he approached the close of his report, the President pleaded with extraordinary earnestness for support of his foreign aid program.

He said he was aware of a feeling that the United States had borne the burden for many years, but that it had an obligation, not merely on the ground of anti-communism, to go on trying to help the undeveloped nations to stand on their own feet and learn the values of freedom.

"If we're not prepared to assist them," he said, "then I believe the prospects for freedom in those areas are uncertain. * * *

"We must be patient, we must be determined, we must be courageous; we must accept both risks and burdens, but with the will and the work, freedom will prevail."

Pleased by de Gaulle

The President appeared to be immensely satisfied with his talks with President de Gaulle of France.

"No question, however sensitive, was avoided," Mr. Kennedy reported. "No area of interest was ignored, and the conclusions that we reached will be important for the future—in our agreement on defending Berlin, on working to improve the defenses of Europe, aiding the economic and political independence of the under-developed world, including Latin-America, on spurring European economic unity, on concluding successfully the conference on Laos, on closer consultations and solidarity in the Western alliance."

As he reported on the problem of Laos, the President saw this as "one area which afforded some immediate prospect of accord."

The immediate objective of the United States, in the current Geneva negotiations on Laos, is to achieve an effective cease-fire. The United States sees that as an essential basis for agreement on a neutral and independent Laos. The Russians, in the Geneva meeting, are much less concerned with the importance of an effective cease-fire as a first step.

In Vienna, said President Kennedy, "both sides recognized the importance of an effective cease-fire."

The President evidently regarded this as one test of the value of the talks and of Mr. Khrushchev's words.

"It is urgent," the President went on, "that this be translated into new attitudes at Geneva, enabling the International Control Commission [in Laos] to do its duty, to make certain that a cease-fire is enforced and maintained.

"I am hopeful that progress can be made on this matter in the coming days at Geneva, for that would greatly improve international atmospheres."

The President then reported grimly that he had found no such hope with respect to another Geneva conference, the two-and-one-half-year-old-meetings that seek a treaty to ban nuclear weapons tests.

"Mr. Khrushchev made it clear that there could not be a neutral administrator," the President reported. This referred to the United States proposal for an international commission with a neutral administrator. The Russians want a three-power commission that would act, unanimously or not at all, thereby building in a one-nation veto.

The President said Mr. Khrushchev believed that "no one was truly neutral, that a Soviet veto would have to apply to acts of enforcement, that inspection was only a subterfuge for espionage, in the absence of total disarmament, and that the present test-ban negotiations appeared futile."

"In short," the President said, "our hopes for an end to nuclear tests, for an end to the spread of nuclear weapons, and for some slowing down on the arms race have been struck a serious blow."

President Kennedy said, however, that he was determined not to abandon the United States proposals because "the stakes are too important."

The President reported that nobody lost his temper at Vienna and that there was no discourtesy, no threats, no ultimatums and "no concession was made or given." No future summit meetings are planned, he added, but the two men did agree to maintain contact with each other.

"I found this meeting with Mr. Khrushchev, somber as it was, immensely useful," the President reported. He said he had been told what manner of man the Soviet chief was but that it was his obligation to see for himself so that his decisions would be as informed as possible.

He wanted insight for himself, he said, and to make sure that Mr. Khrushchev knew the United States and its aims.

'Direct Give and Take'

"The direct give and take was of immeasurable value in making clear and precise what we consider vital," he said.

The President grimly observed that the Soviet people and the people of the United States were so far apart that they gave wholly different meanings to the same words, words such as war and peace. They have wholly different concepts of where the world is and where it is going, he said.

"Our views contrasted sharply, but at least we knew better at the end where we stood," the President asserted.

Citing these conflicts in goals and philosophies, the President said that no matter, how difficult it might seem to give an affirmative answer to the question of living in peace with an antagonistic philosophy, "I think we owe it to all mankind to make the effort."

In addition to his visits to Paris and Vienna, President Kennedy stopped off in London on the way home and conferred with Prime Minister Macmillan.

* * *

July 26, 1961

KENNEDY CALLS FOR 217,000 MEN AND 3.4 BILLION FUND TO MEET 'WORLD-WIDE' THREAT BY SOVIET

NO NEW TAX NOW

207 Million Is Sought for Civil Defense in Speech on Berlin

By TOM WICKER
Special to The New York Times.

WASHINGTON, July 25—President Kennedy asked tonight for an over-all increase in the nation's military preparedness to meet a Soviet threat he described as "world-wide."

The President proposed adding 217,000 men to the armed forces and increasing expenditures by $3,457,000,000, including $207,000,000 for civil defense.

Mr. Kennedy said that $1,800,000,000 of the total would be earmarked for non-nuclear weapons and ammunition and equipment.

The President spoke from his desk in the White House. His address, carried by all radio and television networks at 10 P. M., was firm in tone.

Offers to Negotiate

He held out an offer to negotiate on Berlin, however, and declared that if the Russians "seek genuine understanding—not concessions of our rights—we shall meet with them."

Mr. Kennedy said that the preparedness measures he was requesting would bring the expected budget deficit for this year to more than $5,000,000,000. Nonetheless, he said, he is requesting no new taxes at this time.

The President indicated, however, that new taxes might become necessary later.

"I intend to submit to the Congress in January a budget for the next fiscal year which will be strictly in balance," he said. "Nevertheless, should an increase in taxes be needed to achieve that balance in view of these or subsequent defense rises, those increased taxes will be requested."

Support of People Asked

There was no suggestion in the speech that Mr. Kennedy would declare a national emergency. In a personal note added at the end of his prepared text, however, Mr. Kennedy left no doubt how gravely he regarded the situation.

"We must look to long days ahead," he said. "In these coming months, I need your goodwill and your support—and above all, your prayers."

The President said that the "first steps" he was asking "will require sacrifice on the part of many citizens." He said further sacrifices might be needed in the future. "Courage and perseverance for many years to come," Mr. Kennedy said, will be required of all Americans, if the Communist challenge is to be met.

In addition to the money he said was needed, the President said he would ask for an increase in the Army's strength from 875,000 to 1,000,000 men, and increases of 29,000 and 63,000 men respectively for the Navy and the Air Force.

These manpower needs, Mr. Kennedy said, would be met by doubling and tripling draft calls in the coming months. In addition, he said he would ask Congress for authority to order active duty for some ready reserve units and individual reservists, and extended duty for others.

"We do not want to fight," he asserted, "but we have fought before."

With the increases sought by the President the total requested defense budget will become $47,500,000,000, or about $6,000,000,000 more than was sought in the budget submitted last January by former President Eisenhower.

Mr. Kennedy put heavy stress on the role of our allies in helping to maintain the West's position in Berlin and strengthen the West's hand elsewhere.

"A first need is to hasten progress toward the military goals which the North Atlantic allies have set for themselves," the President said. "We will put even greater resources into fulfilling those goals, and look to our allies to do the same."

Despite the military moves he outlined, the President said "our response to the Berlin crisis will not be merely military or negative."

"It will be more than merely standing firm," he said, "for we do not intend to leave it to others to choose and monopolize the forum and framework of discussion. We do not intend to abandon our duty to mankind to seek a peaceful solution."

Mr. Kennedy also insisted that Berlin did not present a black and white choice between "resistance and retreat, between atomic holocaust and surrender."

"We intend," he declared, "to have a wider choice than humiliation or all-out nuclear action."

The President made two proposals concerning the West's presence in Berlin.

One was a "free vote in Berlin, and if possible among all the German people" on the question whether the presence of the West is desired by the people of West Berlin, "compared to East German feelings about their regime."

The other proposal was the adjudication of the West's legal right to be in Berlin, if anyone doubted it. Mr. Kennedy did not say to what court or forum the issue would be submitted.

There was a hint, too, that Mr. Kennedy might be planning to carry the Berlin issue directly to Mr. Khrushchev.

The Soviet Premier, he said "may find that his invitation to other nations to join in a meaningless treaty may lead to their inviting him to join in the community of peaceful men in abandoning the use of force, and in respecting the sanctity of agreements."

This was viewed as a possible indication that the President was thinking of submitting the Berlin issue to the United Nations or perhaps to a multi-nation conference, at which the issue of self-determination might be raised against the puppet East German regime.

The President made it clear, however, that he was not reacting solely to Soviet prodding in Berlin.

"That isolated outpost is not an isolated problem," he said "The threat is world-wide. Our effort must be equally wide and strong, and not be obsessed by a single manufactured crisis."

He cited the Communist challenge in Southeast Asia, and another "in our own hemisphere"—an apparent reference to the Castro regime in Cuba.

This world-wide view was reflected in another specific request. Mr. Kennedy said he would order to active duty a number of air transport squadrons and Air National Guard tactical squadrons "to give us the airlift capacity and protection we may need."

The President plans to present details of all his requests to Congress in a series of messages, the first of which will be sent tomorrow. It is expected to detail his civil defense requests.

He made this pledge to his audience of millions:

"Everything essential to the security of freedom will be done; and if that should require more men, taxes, controls or other new powers, I shall not hesitate to request them."

The President laid down this doctrine for the crucial months to come:

"While we will not let panic shape our policy, neither will we permit timidity to direct our program."

He cautioned others against assuming that the West was too soft and selfish to defend its freedoms.

He repeated, however, that "we are willing to consider any arrangement for a treaty in Germany consistent with the maintenance of peace and freedom and with the legitimate security interests of all nations."

"We have previously indicated our readiness to remove any actual irritants in West Berlin," Mr. Kennedy said, "but the freedom of that city is not negotiable."

Recovery Is Seen

He said that the nation was recovering from last winter's recession, increasing its output but maintaining both wholesale and retail price stability. The nation's gold position is improving, he said, "and the dollar is more respected."

All this, Mr. Kennedy argued, would mean improved revenues and would make possible the balanced budget he envisioned for fiscal year 1963.

Mr. Kennedy closed his address with an appeal to the Russian people and a tribute to their bravery in World War II.

As for the people of the United States, the President vowed, "we seek peace but we shall not surrender."

Then Mr. Kennedy made an extemporaneous personal appeal. No one could realize, he said, the seriousness of the Communist challenge until he bore "the burdens of this office.

"I must tell you that there is no quick and easy solution," Mr. Kennedy warned. As he did so often in his campaign for the Presidency, he then asked for the help and advice of his hearers.

"All of us love our country, and we shall do our best to serve it," he concluded.

* * *

August 13, 1961

EAST GERMAN TROOPS SEAL BORDER WITH WEST BERLIN TO BLOCK REFUGEE ESCAPE

COMMUTING ENDED

Warsaw Pact States Say Allies' Routes Remain Open

By Reuters

BERLIN, Sunday, Aug. 13—East Germany closed the border early today between East and West Berlin.

East German troops stood guard at the Brandenburg Gate, main crossing point between the Eastern and Western sectors.

The East Berlin City Government banned its citizens from holding jobs in the Western part of the divided city. This will affect tomorrow the thousands of East Berliners who daily commute to work in the Western sector.

The Communists' orders do not affect the Western Allies' access routes to Berlin along the 110-mile passage from West Germany. Especially they do not affect Allied military trains, which are under Soviet jurisdiction.

Action Comes in Night

The quietness of East Berlin's deserted streets was shattered in the early hours of the morning by the screaming of police sirens as police cars, motorcycles and truckloads of police sped through the city.

The action came shortly after publication of a declaration by the Communist Warsaw Pact states that effective controls must be put into force on the borders of West Berlin because of a "perfidious agitation campaign" by the West.

The declaration made it clear these measures were directed at stopping the flow of refugees from East to West through West Berlin. The flow of refugees has recently been reaching 1,700 daily. From 4 P. M. Friday, to 6 P. M. yesterday, 2,662 new arrivals registered in West Berlin's reception camp.

Subways Are Closed

The East Berlin order barring commuters from reaching their jobs in West Berlin said that no East German could cross into the western sector of the city unless he had "a special certificate."

The orders would stand "as long as West Berlin is not changed into a neutral demilitarized free city," the East Germans said.

Elevated trains and subways between the two halves of the divided city were closed; a railroad policeman said he did not know how long the shutdown was for.

The Warsaw Pact declaration was published by the East German press agency A. D. N., but the East German radio, which was broadcasting a late night jazz program, did not immediately mention it.

The declaration admitted that the proposed measure would "create certain discomforts for the population," but said the blame for this rested squarely on the West.

"Naturally these measures will not affect the valid conditions for traffic and control on the connection routes between West Berlin and West Germany," it added.

The necessity for these "protective measures" would cease to exist as soon as a peace treaty with Germany was signed and "questions of strike resolved on this basis," the statement added.

The Warsaw Pact states are the Soviet Union, East Germany, Poland, Czechoslovakia, Rumania, Bulgaria, Hungary and Albania. A week ago, ending a meeting in Moscow, they issued a call for a German peace treaty soon. Shortly after 3 A. M., a Reuters reporter who tried to drive through the Brandenburg Gate from East Berlin was told by a policeman: "You are not allowed to go through—we received instructions to this effect about an hour ago."

The closing of the border came after East Berliners had waited nervously yesterday for the Iron Curtain to ring down on refugee escape routes to the West.

Warsaw Pact Statement

The Warsaw Pact powers' declaration accused the Western Powers and West Germany of "misusing the present traffic position on the West Berlin border to disrupt the economy of the (East) German Democratic Republic."

"In view of the aggressive efforts of the reactionary force of the (West German) Federal Republic and its NATO allies," the declaration said, "the Warsaw Pact states cannot avoid taking the necessary measures themselves to guarantee their safety and above all the safety of the German Democratic Republic.

"The Governments of the Warsaw Pact states appeal to the People's Chamber (Legislature) and Government of the German Democratic Republic to all workers of the G. D. R. with the proposal to introduce such an order on the West Berlin border that the way is stopped for the agitation campaign against the G. D. R. and a trustworthy guard and effective control be guaranteed around the whole territory of Western Berlin, including its borders with the G. D. R.

"Naturally these measures will not affect the valid conditions for traffic and control on the connection routes between West Berlin and West Germany.

"The Government of the Warsaw Pact states naturally understand that the taking of protective measures on the borders of West Berlin will create certain discomforts for the population. But in view of the existing position, the blame for this must be taken exclusively by the Western powers and above all by the Government of the (West German) Federal Republic."

* * *

August 13, 1961

SPACE RACE APPRAISED

United States Takes View That Outcome Is Not Yet Decided as It Strives to Overcome Soviet Lead

By JOHN W. FINNEY
Special to The New York Times.

WASHINGTON, Aug. 12—In the eyes of the world, the two great powers seem to be playing a space-age counterpart of that childhood game of "take the giant step." And as with children, different national interpretations are being made of how big a "giant step" really is and how many "baby steps" go to make up one "giant step."

By any definition—technical, historical or psychological—the twenty-five-hour space flight of Gherman S. Titov seventeen times around the earth this week was indeed a giant step in manned exploration of space.

Whether the flight was such giant step in establishing Soviet leadership in the space age is a matter of debate and interpretation. In a psychological context, the flight obviously enhanced the already commanding lead of the Soviet Union. But it could be argued, and was by United States officials this week, that the United States has taken a number of less spectacular baby steps in space equaling or surpassing the Soviet achievement in long-range practical and scientific significance.

Several Events

The difficulty of answering that popular question of "who is ahead in the space race" is that it is not a one-event race but rather more like a decathlon in which several events are being run to determine the winner.

In the most spectacular event—man-in-space—the Soviet Union obviously holds a commanding lead. It will be six months or so before the United States can match the first orbital flight of Maj. Yuri A. Gagarin and probably eighteen months before an American astronaut will equal the day-long flight of Major Titov.

Yet, paradoxically, this does not mean that in the period of three months the Soviet Union has broadened its lead by twelve months or is any closer than the United States to the ultimate objective of landing a man on the moon. In fact, it could be argued with considerable justification that in this three-months period the United States had finally begun to close the gap with the adoption of the Kennedy Administration's greatly accelerated space program.

The difficulties in determining the leader in the space race are illustrated by a few comparative ratios, some favoring the United States, some the Soviet Union.

U. S. Leads in Numbers

In terms of number of earth satellites launched, the United States has overcome an initial Soviet advantage to gain better than a 3-to-1 margin. The United States has orbited forty-five earth satellites, the Soviet Union thirteen. From its more numerous if smaller satellites the United States is believed to have gained far more scientific knowledge about space than the Soviet Union.

In terms of successful launchings, the two sides in the last few years have been having about the same ratio of failures to successes, indicating they are about on a par in the reliability of their rockets.

In terms of weight placed into space, the Soviet Union has placed about 120,000 pounds into orbit, the United States about 50,000.

Measured as of today, the United States is probably two years behind in rivaling and perhaps three years behind in surpassing Soviet weight-lifting capability. The Centaur, which has been having its developmental difficulties, should be ready for space missions by 1962-63. The immediate United States hopes of taking the lead in rocket power hinge on the Saturn, which clusters together eight rocket engines in the booster, or first stage, to produce a total of 1,500,000 pounds of thrust.

It is in rocket power that the Soviet Union has a decisive advantage. It is an advantage that also explains why the Soviet Union is ahead in man-in-space. With its less powerful rockets, the United States has been able to match and surpass the Soviet Union in scientific exploration through miniaturization of instruments. But one thing that cannot be miniaturized is man.

The Soviet Union now has rockets about twice as powerful as those of the United States. The Soviet rocket believed to have been used to launch the two five-ton space ships as well as most of the other heavy satellites has a take-off or booster thrust estimated at about 750,000 pounds. The most powerful United States rocket presently available—and the one that will be used at the end of the year to launch the one-ton Mercury capsule into orbit with an astronaut—is the Atlas missile, with 360,000 pounds of thrust.

But here again comparison can be deceptive. By combining the Atlas with high-energy, liquid hydrogen upper stages, as is now being done in the Centaur rocket, the United States can have a rocket with a weight-lifting capability near as great as the present Soviet multi-stage rocket.

The big unknown of course, in this rocket power equation is what progress the Soviet Union is making or will make in the next three years in developing ever larger, more powerful rockets. By the time the Saturn is developed, the Soviet Union may have a comparable sized rocket.

The United States lag in rocket power is attributable to a head start on the part of the Soviet Union and lack of foresight, indecision over the importance of space and budget skimping on the part of the United States. Immediately after World War II, the Soviet Union decided to develop an intercontinental ballistic missile. The only warhead then available was an extremely heavy fission bomb, with the result that the Soviet Union had to develop an extremely large rocket, which by fortuitous circumstances was to prove invaluable a decade later for space launchings.

The United States decided after World War II that an ICBM was impractical and infeasible and followed the manned bomber route. It was only after a significant breakthrough in 1952-53 in developing a compact, extremely powerful hydrogen bomb warhead that the United States decided to develop an intercontinental missile.

Even after undertaking development of intercontinental missiles, the United States failed to appreciate their significance for space exploration. Within the scientific community and the Administration, opinion was divided about the importance and usefulness of space research.

The indecision continued even after the launching of the first Soviet Sputnik, with its tangible demonstration of Soviet rocket power. Reflecting the indecision and disinterest, the Saturn rocket was starved for funds in its early stages in 1958-59, and the 1,500,000-pound-thrust F-1 rocket engine, which someday will be incorporated in the Nova, slipped six months in its developmental schedule because of budgetary cutbacks made a little more than a year ago.

U. S. Decides

If there has been a change in the outlook for the space race in recent months, it is because the Kennedy Administration, after some initial hesitation and indecision, has made that firm policy decision. This is that the United States should attempt to take a leading role in space achievements and strive as part of "a great new American enterprise" as the President put it in his speech May 25 to Congress, to be first in landing a man on the moon. This Presidential decision was affirmed by Congress this week in voting $1,671,755,000 in funds for the space agency, nearly all the President had requested as the first installment on an accelerated and costly space program over the next decade.

For the first time, therefore, the space program has a firm policy decision for leadership in space and adequate funds to start achieving this objective. The question now beginning to concern Government and industry officials is whether the Administration, and the space agency in particular, will supply the necessary third ingredient—decisive, clear-cut management.

In many quarters within and without the Government, worried grumblings are beginning to be voiced about whether the Government is yet properly organized to take on probably the most difficult, costly and complex exploration of all time. As yet no one person has been placed in charge of the lunar expedition.

With proper management, Administration officials believe the United States has a fifty-fifty chance of being first with a man to the moon. Without it, the odds are against the United States' winning the climactic and probably decisive event in the space decathlon.

*   *   *

August 15, 1961

REDS TIGHTEN SQUEEZE ON BERLIN, BAR WESTERN SECTOR'S VEHICLES; KENNEDY REVIEWING ALLIED STAND

CITY STILL UNEASY

Both Sides Clear Line to Avoid a Clash—Mail Curbed

By SYDNEY GRUSON
Special to The New York Times.

BERLIN, Tuesday, Aug. 15—The East German Communists, apparently emboldened by success, tightened their squeeze on West Berlin early today.

Shortly after 1 A. M. with an uneasy quiet prevailing on the intra-city border, the East German Interior Ministry announced that all West Berlin cars and other vehicles must have special permits to cross into East Berlin.

The announcement said the freedom of movement permitted the West Berliners after the border was closed early Sunday had been abused for espionage purposes. However, pedestrian traffic by West Berliners is still permitted at the twelve border crossings unclosed to them.

Aware of the danger of clashes on the border, the authorities on both sides acted separately but similarly yesterday to reduce the risks. They created a three-quarter-mile No Man's Land for civilians on both sides of the wide road running through the Brandenburg Gate, the most sensitive border point.

Brandenburg Gate Closed

The Communists closed the Brandenburg Gate, a huge multicolumn monument standing just inside their territory. The gate was one of thirteen crossing points between the two Berlins left open by the Saturday midnight decrees barring East Berliners and East Germans from going into West Berlin "without special permits."

Bit by bit the East Germans were isolating their people from both West Berlin and West Germany. They cut telephone communications from East Germany and East Berlin early yesterday. In Bonn, Richard Stuecklen, West German Minister of Posts, said postal and telegraph service between the two parts of Germany had also been interrupted.

The purpose of all this was not yet entirely clear. It also was not known how long the interruptions were to last. It was presumed that the communications would remain cut until the situation brought about by the closing of the border had been stabilized to the Communists' satisfaction.

The quiet along the border only barely hid the continuing danger of explosion.

For the moment at least the danger does not appear to be of an uprising of East Berliners and East Germans but of a clash on the border between Communist military forces and West Berliners. The latter are becoming increasingly bitter over the lack of Western reaction to the Communist restrictions.

The East Berliners, now barred from crossing to the West, went about their business with no apparent joy but also with no apparent will to test the overwhelming military strength brought in by the Communists.

It was confirmed that two Soviet divisions had ringed West Berlin, an enclave 110 miles from the West German border.

The restriction on vehicular traffic was the first of the new measures aimed directly at the West Berliners. The decrees on the border closing had specified that "peaceful" West Berliners could come and go as before.

Since last September, West Germans, as distinct from West Berliners, have had to get special permits to enter East Berlin or East Germany.

A West Berlin official commented on the lack of a prohibition on West Berliners crossing to the east by foot or on the elevated railway.

"It's another slide of the salami," he said, clearly reflecting the belief of the majority of West Berliners that one pretext or another would be found for further Communist restrictions.

Guards at Monument

At the Brandenburg Gate about 100 armed men of a factory fighting brigade, neat and tough-looking in gray uniforms, lined the front of the monument, tommy guns and rifles at the ready. Behind them were six water-gun trucks, which the Communists have been using to disperse unruly crowds, and six armored cars.

The Communists announced that the gate had to be closed because of "continuing provocations" instigated by Western officials among the West Berliners. At the time the latter were massed 5,000 strong behind rope barriers about 160 feet from the border.

The West Berliners jeered and whistled at the Communist troops. They had thrown rocks earlier and had drawn a vain burst of tear gas in return.

These "demonstrations," and broadcasts by West Berlin radio stations calling on the public "to violate forcibly the borders at the Brandenburg Gate," were responsible for yesterday's actions, the East German Interior Ministry said.

Reprisals Authorized

Shortly afterward the ministry announced that the troops on the border had been ordered to take "counter-measures" against any "hostile actions."

In the meantime Communist policemen cleared the road, Unter den Linden, on their side of the gate for about half a mile and closed all the side roads leading to the broad avenue.

The Interior Ministry announcement warned West Berliners to keep at least 100 yards from the Communist troops and "to avoid any unnecessary stay in their vicinity."

Meanwhile, West Berlin officials and the Allied commandants who have the final responsibility of the city's security conferred. Joachim Lipschitz, West Berlin Senator, or director of the Interior, announced that no demonstrations would be permitted on the border and that the police would disperse unauthorized gatherings.

West Berlin policemen then began moving the crowds about a quarter of a mile back along the street, named for the 17th of June, the day of the East Berlin and East German uprisings against the Communists in 1953. The crowd was pushed beyond the Soviet war memorial, with its two Russians on guard.

Brig. G. J. Hamilton, commander of the British Army's Infantry Brigade Group, confirmed that the two Soviet divisions had ringed Berlin, ready to act against an uprising.

"We know they alerted two motorized divisions as a precautionary measure around Potsdam," Brigadier Hamilton said. "Elements of one went north and elements of the other to the south. But they may have gone home now."

Refugees Swim Across

A few East Berliners swam the canals that form the border at some points, but the bulk of the 1,500 people registered at the West Berlin camp yesterday were in the city since Saturday, before the border was closed.

East Berlin barges were prohibited from using the waterways in West Berlin, presumably to prevent escape.

Yesterday had been considered a critical day, by both the Communists and Western officials here.

It was the first working day after the border closing. No one knew for sure how the East Berlin workers, who spearheaded the 1953 revolt, would react after they got into their factories and discussed the situation.

No one was sure either what would happen when the 53,000 East Berliners barred from their jobs in West Berlin were stopped at the new elevated railway terminal in East Berlin.

Lesson of 1953 Learned

Nothing happened. The Communists had learned the lesson of 1953 well. Then they tried to hold down the first flames of revolt with a minimum display of power, and not until Soviet tanks came into action did they regain control.

This time the tanks, Soviet-made World War II T-34's manned by East Germans, were there from the start, along with troops from outside Berlin who showed as little desire to fraternize with the people as the people to fraternize with them.

A few—very few—of the East Berliners who work in West Berlin were permitted to go to their jobs. These included at least seven employed at Templehof Airfield. The willingness of the Communists to let them over made the authorities in the West wonder why.

Some Economic Effect

West Berlin officials said there might be some dislocation of the city's economy through the loss of manpower, especially in small industries where the East Berliners held skilled jobs. But the dislocation would be minor, the officials predicted.

The bitterness of the West Berliners over the lack of Allied reaction was becoming more apparent. The feeling among ordinary people was that the Communists were "getting away with it," as one man put it, "without our lifting a finger."

About 5,000 West Berlin workers marched from their factories to the Rathaus Schoeneberg, or city hall, early yesterday carrying posters saying, "We demand counter measures."

The same demand was voiced by BZ, a mass-circulation tabloid newspaper and the only West Berlin paper that publishes on Monday. The newspaper said what the East Germans had done Saturday night was only the first blow of many to come. "The Western powers also know this," the article said. "It is up to them to react accordingly."

Mayor Willy Brandt, speaking briefly to the workers outside the city hall, hinted at the outlawing of the West Berlin branch of the East German Socialist Unity (Communist) party, which operates in the city under four-power agreement although it is banned in West Germany.

Mayor Brandt indicated also that permission might be refused for the 13,000 West Berliners who work in East Berlin to continue with their jobs there.

* * *

August 17, 1961

BRANDT NOTE TO KENNEDY URGES 'POLITICAL ACTION,' NOT JUST TALK, ON BERLIN

FEARS A 'MUNICH'

Mayor Tells Big Rally Reds Will Not Stop if West Fails Test

By SYDNEY GRUSON
Special to The New York Times.

BERLIN, Aug. 16 —Mayor Willy Brandt told President Kennedy in a personal letter today that West Berlin expected "not merely words but political action" against the Communists' closing of the city's border with East Berlin.

Announcing this at a West Berlin rally, Mayor Brandt warned that the existence of the entire non-Communist alliance was at stake in the Berlin crisis.

A crowd estimated at 250,000 attended the rally. It reflected the rising anger becoming apparent in the city.

The West Berliners are angry over what they consider the failure by the Allies and the city government to take effective counter-action against the Communists' measures.

Warns of 'New Munich'

Mayor Brandt compared the sealing off of East Berlin and East Germany to Hitler's occupation of the Rhineland in 1936.

"In the weeks and months that lie before us," he said, "the question at issue is that Berlin should not become a new Munich."

The allusion was to the meeting in 1938 where an agreement that led to Czechoslovakia's occupation by the Nazis was reached between Hitler, Mussolini, Prime Minister Neville Chamberlain of Britain and Premier Eduard Daladier of France.

Mayor Brandt promised that the West Berliners would be equal to the test, the sternest, he said, since the Soviet blockade of West Berlin in 1948.

"Woe to us," he went on, "if through indifference or moral weakness we do not pass this test. Then the Communists will not stop at the Brandenburg Gate. They will not stop at the zonal border. They will not stop on the Rhine."

Talk Matches Crowd's Mood

The Brandenburg Gate marks the border between East and West Berlin. The reference to the zonal border was to that between East and West Germany.

The Mayor's speech was geared to the mood of the crowd assembled in the square before the Schoeneberger Rathaus, or city hall. They cheered every reference to counter-measures, whistled derisively at another speaker's mention of the Allies protest to the Soviet Union and acknowledged with silence the grave warnings of the Mayor.

Mayor Brandt said the protest sent by the three Western commandants of West Berlin yesterday was "good," although he implied criticism over the delay in sending it. "And," he added, the Allies' reaction "must not stop at that."

There is evidently a serious difference of opinion between the Berlin leaders and the Allies, including West Germany, on how to react against the Communists. The West German Foreign Office issued a statement that Chancellor Adenauer had told the Soviet Ambassador that Born would do nothing to worsen relations with Moscow.

Mayor Brandt is known to have told visitors today that West Berlin's morale had received a serious blow and that the Allies were handling the situation in the wrong way.

He has not said exactly what he wants the Allies to do. But the three-day delay in sending the first note of protest astonished him and the West Berlin people.

In general Mayor Brandt wanted the Allies to react more quickly and to take some immediate steps to show that they could not be bullied, even if the steps were only the halting of travel by East German Communist officials to the West.

This was done last year in retaliation against a less serious event—partial restrictions on the movement of West Germans into East Germany and East Berlin.

The workers in the huge crowd at the rally had marched there from their factories, many carrying posters reflecting, as did the newspaper headlines and editorials, the bitter and uneasy mood in West Berlin.

One poster was on the Munich theme. Another advised the Western powers, "You can't stop tanks with paper." A third invited President Kennedy to come to Berlin.

A gesture to remind the West Berliners that the United States was as concerned as ever about their security was made today. Gen. Bruce C. Clarke, commander of United States forces in Europe, arrived to confer with the present United States commandant, Maj. Gen. Albert Watson 2d.

The two generals toured the sector border with Mayor Brandt and other officials. When the eight cars in the party drove up to the Brandenburg Gate, which was closed Monday by the Communists, the Communist police sent one of their armored water trucks to the barbed-wire barrier in front of the monument and aimed the high-pressure water gun at the generals and the Mayor.

As news of the inspection spread, the Communists reinforced their guards. Armed East German emergency policemen lined the Communist side of the route along the sector border in North Berlin.

Refugees Trickle Stops

The few holes in the barrier of barbed wire and guns set up by the Communists to halt those trying to flee to West Berlin seemed to have been plugged. There were no reports of new refugees reaching the city.

The Communists evidently expected that with East Berlin shut off East Germans would start trying to get into West Berlin from what is called here the "Soviet zone." It has always been difficult to reach the border through the woods and lakes there, and not many tried it before.

At the twelve crossing points on the border still open, the Communists threw up barriers to make it impossible for cars to speed through.

Western travelers on the so-called interzonal trains between East and West Germany reported that the Communist police were removing East Germans on westbound trains at the border between the two countries, even though their papers were in order.

This evidently was a move to take back East Germans who had received permission to travel to West Germany before the Communists began to seal off their country.

Meanwhile, the Soviet Union rejected an Allied protest of Aug. 3 against restrictions on East Berliners working in West Berlin. The Soviet Commandant in Berlin, Col. Andrei I. Solovyev, told the Allies their protest was an attempt to interfere in matters that were the exclusive concern of the East German Government.

In any case, events have overrun their exchange. The latest East German decrees barred East Berliners from working in West Berlin and the fifty-three East Berliners affected have not been coming across.

Western officials here received word that the Soviet troops who moved out of their barracks Sunday morning in a display of power were still in the field.

The Mayor disclosed that he had finally received the approval of the Allied commandants to halt the exchange of East marks earned by West Berliners working for the Communists in East Berlin.

About 13,000 West Berliners work in the Communist sector of the city. They have been entitled to exchange their East marks on a one-for-one basis, although on the free market of West Berlin the East mark is worth only one-fifth of a West mark.

*   *   *

August 20, 1961

JOHNSON HAILED IN WEST BERLIN AS HE RENEWS PLEDGE OF U.S. AID; SOVIET REJECTS ALLIES' PROTEST

300,000 APPLAUD

Vice President Tells Them Washington Will Not Forget

By SYDNEY GRUSON

Special to The New York Times.

BERLIN, Aug. 19—Vice President Johnson pledged to the people of West Berlin today that the United States would never forget its obligations to them.

This was the heart of three speeches the Vice President made shortly after arriving here on a mission for President Kennedy to reassure West Germany and West Berlin.

In an address at a special meeting of the West Berlin Parliament, the Vice President said:

"To the survival and to the creative future of this city we Americans have pledged, in effect, what our ancestors pledged in forming the United States: 'Our lives, our fortunes and our sacred honor.' "

These are the final words of the Declaration of Independence.

Mr. Johnson's presence and his words had an electric effect on the city. There were tears and cheers as he spoke to a crowd estimated at 300,000 persons massed in the square in front of the City Hall.

Cheers on 8-Mile Route

There was a near mob scene as he got out of his car on the ride to the City Hall from the airport to shake hands with a few of the 100,000 others who braved intermittent rain to cheer him along the eight-mile route.

The city was like a boxer who had thrown off a heavy punch and was gathering stamina for another round.

The punch was the Communists' closing of the border at midnight between East and West Berlin last Saturday and the long delay in Western reaction, a delay that was made doubly bitter when the first reaction was confined to a protest note.

The Vice President said nothing essentially new. That did not seem to matter. The West Berliners wanted the words said at this time in their city and, above all, they wanted his presence as a tangible expression of the link that sustains them.

Mr. Johnson flew here from Bonn, where he had talked with Chancellor Adenauer. A West German Government spokesman said the two men agreed that the non-Communist world must watch carefully for anything that could increase the danger of war.

They also agreed, the spokesman said, that a "satisfactory settlement" of the German and Berlin problems must be sought through negotiations with the Soviet Union.

The Vice President changed from the big jet plane that carried him across the ocean in the night to an Air Force Constellation for the eighty-minute flight from Bonn to Berlin. The plane, like all air traffic from the West, came through a twenty-mile-wide air corridor over Communist East Germany.

Seven tanks drawn up on Tempelhof Airfield fired a salute as the Vice President, the United States Ambassador to Bonn, Walter C. Dowling, and the city's leader, Mayor Willy Brandt inspected a guard of honor of American troops and West Berlin police.

Welcoming the Vice President at the airport, Mayor Brandt told him and the radio and television audience:

"It is a great day for Berlin * * *. We are deeply grateful that you came at just this moment."

Mr. Johnson said West Berlin had become an "inspiration to the entire free world."

"Divided, you have never been dismayed," he went on. "Threatened, you have never faltered. Challenged, you have never weakened. Today, in a new crisis, your courage brings hope to all who cherish freedom and is a massive and majestic barrier to the ambitions of tyrants.

"As the personal representative of President Kennedy and the American people I have come here to salute your courage, to honor your faith in freedom, and to assure you that your friends will never, never forget their obligations to you. Standing together and working together, you shall prevail.

"This city will continue to be the fortress of the free because it is the home of the brave."

Reinforcement Is Cited

Then he told the West Berliners of President Kennedy's order for 1,500 United States troops to move from West Germany to reinforce the West Berlin garrison.

As he spoke, the men of the First Battle Group, Eighteenth Infantry, were on their way from the Mannheim area of West Germany to their overnight encampment near Brunswick.

It is a symbolic increase raising the total of the American garrison to about 6,500 men. The British are sending in some additional armored and scout cars but are keeping the number of their troops at 3,000. France has announced that she will strengthen her 3,000-man garrison.

The Vice President said the suffering and heroism of the people in East Berlin, now sealed off behind barbed-wire and paving-brick barricades, would never be forgotten.

The Communists divided Berlin, but, Mr. Johnson went on, "they have united us even more strongly and we will be separated neither by Communist strength nor Communist threats."

Then, accompanied by Mayor Brandt, the Vice President drove to the City Hall. From the airfield, where the cement bridge-like design juts into the sky to commemorate the airlift that broke the Communists' 1948-49 blockade of West Berlin, they proceeded to the Potsdamer Platz.

There the Vice President's car stopped less than ten yards from the barbed-wire and cement barricade thrown up by the Communists.

Two Get Out and Walk

At the lower end of Dudenstrasse, Mr. Johnson and Herr Brandt got out of the car and walked for nearly three-quarters of a mile.

Men and women stretched out their arms to the Vice President. Some had tears in their eyes and many cried openly.

This was the second rally this week in front of the City Hall. The difference in mood between that of last Wednesday, when Mayor Brandt was still calling for "not merely words but political action" by the West, and today's welcome to the Vice Presidential party was like the difference between night and day.

The difference was all there to see in the Mayor's face. He had looked haggard and grim when he spoke Wednesday. The lines seemed to have lifted, and he grinned broadly as he introduced Mr. Johnson to an accompanying thunderous cheer.

Speaking briefly outside the City Hall, Mr. Johnson said that "freedom can prevail and peace endure."

Message for East Berlin

He addressed a message to the people of East Berlin: "Do not lose courage, for while tyranny may seem for the moment to prevail, its days are counted."

Then Mr. Johnson, Ambassador Dowling and General Clay signed the visitors' golden book. Mayor Brandt presented to members of the Vice Presidential party porcelain copies of the Freedom Bell, a gift from the American people after the blockade. The bell was tolling during the ceremony.

The Vice President will tour the city tomorrow morning with Mayor Brandt. He has decided not to go into East Berlin, a decision in line with his statement in Bonn that "we are not provocative."

Mr. Johnson will remain in Berlin tomorrow to welcome the reinforcement troops. He will fly back to Washington Monday morning instead of tomorrow afternoon as originally planned.

Tonight, in a toast at a dinner given him by the city, Mr. Johnson said:

"There is no easy solution, but a solution will come." He said the Germans would one day get self-determination.

* * *

August 24, 1961

WEST PUTS TANKS AND 1,000 TROOPS ON BERLIN BORDER

Allied Show of Force Replies to East Germans' Bid for Extension of Control

RED WARNING IGNORED

Citizens Congregate in Area Declared No-Entry Zone by Communist Regime

By SYDNEY GRUSON
Special to The New York Times.

BERLIN, Aug. 23—The Western powers deployed 1,000 troops of their West Berlin garrison, backed by ten forty-ton United States tanks, along the border with East Berlin today.

This was the swift Allied answer to the attempt by East German Communists to establish remote control over a 110-yard zone all along the West Berlin side of the twenty-five-mile border. The Communists have warned all persons to stay at least 110 yards away from both sides of the intracity border.

Late tonight three of the United States tanks were drawn up on main streets leading to the border running along Zimmerstrasse in the United States sector.

Two of the tanks were on Friedrichstrasse, one of them about forty yards behind ten American soldiers with a machine gun. The soldiers took up positions directly on the border line.

Citizens at Border

On Charlottenstrasse, the parallel street to the north, the third tank was about fifty yards from the border, its 90-mm gun pointing at the new Communist barricade there.

The drama of the night unfolded at Friedrichstrasse. The street is the only crossing point left open to foreigners, including members of the Allied forces, under the latest border restrictions, ordered by the Communists late last night.

Several hundred West Berliners milled about the two streets near the border. They walked around the tanks and went almost up to the border itself to talk to the West Berlin policemen on duty there with the troops. Under the streetlights, about fifty Communist policemen could be seen on the East Berlin side of Friedrichstrasse.

There was no sign of Communist armor on the Eastern side of Friedrichstrasse.

But behind the border barricade on Wilhelmstrasse, which parallels Friedrichstrasse to the south, the Communists were believed to have several tanks. The tanks were out of sight at ground level.

There was a curious atmosphere tonight on Friedrichstrasse. The situation looked dangerous but, with the crowds all around, it also looked a little like a movie set. The people seemed to be waiting for a director to come along and start the cameras rolling.

Ironically, a movie house on Friedrichstrasse near the border was showing "All Quiet on the Western Front," an anti-

Associated Press Radiophoto

BORDER PATROL: U.S. Army tank, its 90-millimeter gun facing east Berlin, is deployed at the Friedrichstrasse crossing point between city's western and eastern sectors.

war film based on a novel about World War I, even as the warlike preparations were being made outside.

The only incident of the day was reported from a border point in the American sector about five miles from Friedrichstrasse. The West Berlin police report made no mention of American soldiers having been involved.

The Communist police, according to the report, threw several canisters of tear gas into a crowd of about forty West Berliners on Elsenstrasse, one block from Wildenbruchstrasse, where an American tank had been posted earlier in the afternoon. A young man threw one of the canisters back at the police.

About 600 United States troops were involved under the field command of Col. Roy Murray of Berkeley, Calif. Two hundred British and 200 French troops completed the Allied force. The troops were to remain on duty throughout the night.

Show of Strength

The show of military strength was accompanied by a statement of the United States, British and French commandants condemning the Communists' latest restrictions on travel between East and West Berlin.

Last night, ten days after they sealed the East Berliners and East Germany behind barbed wire and guns, the Communists announced that they were reducing the number of crossing points on the intracity border to seven.

They left one open exclusively for foreigners, including members of the Western forces. Four were left open for West Berliners and two for West Germans.

In their statement the Western commandants elected to interpret the Communist warning for all persons to keep 110 yards away from the border as applying only to West Berliners. But the Allies had no doubts, according to reliable sources, that it was meant for Western forces as well.

The reaction to the new Communist challenge was swift. It was in vivid contrast to the three days of silence after the border was closed on Aug. 13.

The three commandants—Maj. Gen. Albert Watson 2d of the United States, Maj. Gen. Sir Rohan Delacombe of Britain and Maj. Gen. Jean Lacomme of France—met this morning and came to a quick agreement. Their decisions were not referred back to their Governments.

By 1 P. M. the troops were moving—the Americans along their sixteen-mile sector of the border from the center of the city to its southernmost point, the British along two miles in the center and the French along seven miles to the north.

The commandants dismissed the Communist warning as an "affrontery" and announced that they were "taking the necessary actions to insure the security and integrity of the sector borders."

Not long after the Allied troops were deployed, several thousand armed factory guards, hard-core Communists who have been out in force to support the police and army against any resistance to the border closing, staged a parade down Stalinallee in East Berlin.

Walter Ulbricht, the East German Communist leader, took their salute, a chorused cry of "Alert!"

In a brief speech Herr Ulbricht said: "We will succeed in maintaining peace although the imperialists again and again try to provoke us."

"If they continue to provoke us we will teach them a lesson," he added.

Soviet Army 'Alerted'

He said the Soviet Army in East Germany had been "alerted" since the border closings. Reports to West Berlin in the last ten days have told of Soviet Army units showing up in every town and city of East Germany Aug. 13, apparently to impress upon the East Germans the futility of resistance.

There was other talk from the Communists today. Otto Arndt, director of the East German railway, warned that continued "hooliganism" on the Communist-operated elevated line in West Berlin could affect railway service between the city and West Germany.

Herr Arndt said 102 elevated railway cars had been damaged by West Berliners since Aug. 13 and that the lives and health of passengers had been endangered. He noted that the elevated line, which West Berliners are boycotting, and the regular railway, were "closely linked."

He left little doubt of his meaning when he said:

"Railway traffic serves travel from West Berlin to various countries. At the same time a large proportion of supply goods to West Berlin is transported on the railway. The production of West Berlin industry is closely linked with the railway because of the need to supply industry with raw materials and shipping the finished products."

The railway is West Berlin's lifeline. Most of the goods that keep the city going economically come in by train from West Germany.

The Allies have said repeatedly that they would fight to maintain access between West Berlin and West Germany.

They have never specified that freight traffic to West Berlin was included in the access rights they would fight for, but this is understood by Allied officials here to be the case.

The purpose of the show of military strength was to make clear to the Communists that they could not impose orders involving the Western rights to be in West Berlin territory.

West Berlin's morale, which was badly shaken by the border closing and restored only by Vice President Johnson's visit and the reinforcement of the United States garrison by 1,500 troops last week-end, was a secondary factor.

The fear of Allied authorities here was that if the Communists got away with clearing the West Berlin side of the border, they would try to keep enlarging the zone on one pretext or another. This apparently was the major factor in the commandant's decision to enforce their rights up to the demarcation line.

All the troops—Americans, British and French—were ordered to patrol right up to the border. The British brought up an anti-tank gun and placed it in a park near the old Reichstag, the seat of pre-Nazi German Parliaments, which fronts on the border at the Brandenburg Gate.

* * *

September 2, 1961

SOVIET EXPLODES ATOMIC WEAPON OF INTERMEDIATE FORCE OVER ASIA; NASSER ASSAILS TEST RESUMPTION

ATMOSPHERE TEST

Long-Range Devices of U.S. Detect and Identify Blast

By TOM WICKER
Special to The New York Times.

WASHINGTON, Sept. 1—The White House announced today that the Soviet Union resumed the testing of nuclear weapons early this morning by exploding a device over Soviet Central Asia.

The announcement said the explosion took place "in the atmosphere" at Semipalatinsk, about 350 miles south of Novosibirsk.

Andrew Hatcher, the assistant White House press secretary, said the explosion was detected "early this morning, Western time" by what he described as "long-range detecting equipment." It was apparently the first nuclear test by the Soviet Union since its announcement Wednesday that it would resume testing.

Event Was Anticipated

Mr. Hatcher said that after the detection of the explosion was confirmed as a nuclear device, the news was given to President Kennedy at the White House at 3:15 P. M. He explained that the lag between detection and the report to the President was caused by the time required to check the information obtained by United States detection equipment.

"This has been anticipated," he said. "It didn't come as a surprise."

There was no precise estimate of the size of the nuclear device. The announcement said only that it had had "a substantial yield in the intermediate range." Mr. Hatcher said this yield meant that the Soviet device was larger than the "average atomic bomb" and larger than the bomb exploded over Hiroshima in 1945.

First Test Since Agreement

He further explained that the device was not in the range of a megaton, the equivalent explosive force of 1,000,000 tons of TNT. Rather, he described it as being in the kiloton range. This would mean an explosive force of hundreds of thousands of tons of TNT, perhaps between 100,000 and 500,000 tons. The Hiroshima bomb was twenty kilotons, or the equivalent of 20,000 tons of TNT.

The Soviet explosion was the first known nuclear test by one of the three nuclear powers—Britain, the Soviet Union and the United States—that agreed in the fall of 1958 to refrain from testing while trying to negotiate a test ban. France, however, has set off four nuclear devices since then, one of them this year.

Despite the moratorium on testing, the United States maintained its secret global system that has detected atomic explosions in the Soviet Union over the years.

Semipalatinsk is an industrial and transportation center near the Mongolian border, 560 miles northeast of Alma-Ata and 1,700 miles east of Moscow. The Russians are believed to have launched many of their missiles from there.

Its principal industries are meat-packing, flour milling, wool washing, and tanning.

The White House announcement came after the President conferred with Arthur H. Dean, the United States representative at the Geneva test ban conference, and John J. McCloy, the President's disarmament adviser. Shortly after the meeting the President left for a weekend with his family at Hyannis Port, Mass.

Earlier Mr. Dean had charged:

"The Soviet policy is the policy of overkill. But the Soviet Government underestimates the people of the world if it thinks they will capitulate to a strategy of blackmail and terror."

Speaking with the approval of the President, to whom he had reported this morning, Mr. Dean said, the Soviet announcement that it would resume testing showed a "determined Soviet purpose to rest its future policy on the terrorization of humanity."

Mr. Dean thus amplified the vigorous effort the Kennedy Administration is making to exploit world-wide indignation at the Soviet nuclear testing plan. He spoke from a brief text prepared at a White House meeting this morning with the President, Secretary of State Rusk and Mr. McCloy.

Mr. Dean and Mr. McCloy made it plain, however, that diplomatic contact with the Soviets is still being maintained on the issue of a nuclear test ban treaty, and the larger question of general disarmament.

"Now they want to lump it all back together," Mr. McCloy said. "It's kind of a shell game."

Belief Undermined

He added that many persons, "I suppose including me," had believed there was an "element of sincerity" in the expressed desire of the Soviets for an end to nuclear weapons testing. "This certainly undermines that," he said.

The statement approved by the President and read by Mr. Dean contained a caustic reference to Mr. Khrushchev's "boasting about a 100-megaton bomb, a weapon far too large for military objectives."

This referred to the announced Soviet intention to test a bomb with an explosive force of 100,000,000 tons of TNT. The device exploded early today by the Soviet Union was far below that level.

Mr. Dean bitterly denounced the intention to test so huge a weapon. Such a bomb, he said, is "not a military weapon" but a "weapon of mass terror."

He said it was impossible to direct a 100-megaton bomb with any degree of accuracy and "the use of it would be wanton and cruel in relation to the tremendous loss of human life."

By comparison, he said, a twenty-megaton bomb, which is regarded as a usable weapon, could destroy a 100-square-mile area, or roughly an area the size of the District of Columbia.

He explained his reference to "overkill" (a military word in vogue since the development of nuclear weapons) as meaning that a 700-megaton bomb "could only be used to kill human beings solely for the sake of killing them" and for "mass terror, intimidation, with no necessity for it."

Mr. Dean offered a personal view as to why the Soviets had announced their test resumption on the eve of the conference of noncommitted nations at Belgrade, Yugoslavia.

It was "coldly calculated," he said, "in the belief that someone there would beg the Soviets not to test if the United States would agree not to stand firm on its commitment in West Berlin."

Mr. McCloy said that the "strategy of blackmail and terror" attributed to the Soviets in the statement approved by Mr. Kennedy appeared aimed primarily at the neutrals rather than at the Western Allies.

Thus, both men seemed to believe that Premier Khrushchev had hoped to frighten the neutrals into supporting him on the Berlin issue. If so, the immediate testing of a 100-megaton bomb might be calculated to heighten the effect.

The use for the second consecutive day in an official statement of the term "blackmail," and the Administration's insistent hammering on the "terrorization of humanity" theme, showed, however, that officials here hope that exactly the opposite reaction will result.

The almost unanimous opinion here is that the United States will resume its own nuclear tests, but will do so in a manner carefully timed not to reduce the shock value of the Soviet action or to precipitate a final breaking off of diplomatic contact at Geneva or in the disarmament talks between Mr. McCloy and Valerian A. Zorin, the Soviet representative, in New York Wednesday.

Congressional leaders were informed at a White House meeting yesterday, it was understood, that the United States' nuclear arsenal is entirely sufficient at the present time and that, in any case, tests can be resumed here in a matter of a few days.

The assistant White House press secretary said there was no plan at present for President Kennedy to make a similar public report. This has been suggested by some of the Congressional figures who attended the White House meeting.

*   *   *

October 22, 1961

GILPATRIC WARNS U. S. CAN DESTROY ATOM AGGRESSOR

Puts Nuclear Arms in 'Tens of Thousands'—
Doubts Soviet Would Start War

By JOSEPH A. LOFTUS
Special to The New York Times.

HOT SPRINGS, Va. Oct. 21—The United States is so strong and its power so well deployed that an aggressor making a sneak nuclear attack would invite self-destruction, an Administration spokesman said tonight.

Roswell L. Gilpatric, Deputy Secretary of Defense, said the Government's confidence in its ability to deter Communist action or resist Communist blackmail was based on an appreciation of the military power of each side.

Mr. Gilpatric's remarks had been cleared at the highest level.

Although the Russians use rigid security as a military weapon, he said, "their Iron Curtain is not so impenetrable as to force us to accept at face value the Kremlin boasts."

Tells of Lethal Power

"The fact is that this nation has a nuclear retaliatory force of such lethal power that an enemy move which brought it into play would be an act of self-destruction on his part," he said.

At a news briefing related to the council meeting, Secretary of Treasury Douglas Dillon said economists expected a rise in business activity next year.

Mr. Gilpatric addressed a dinner meeting of the Business Council, an organization of the country's leading business men. He gave a summary of the Government's thinking and planning, saying the ultimate objective was peace.

"The United States has today hundreds of manned intercontinental bombers capable of reaching the Soviet Union, including 600 heavy bombers and many more medium bombers equally capable of intercontinental operations because of our highly developed in-flight refueling techniques and worldwide base structure," Mr. Gilpatric said.

Refers to Missiles

"The United States also has six Polaris submarines at sea carrying a total of ninety-six missiles, and dozens of intercontinental ballistic missiles.

"Our carrier strike forces and land-based theatre forces could deliver additional hundreds of megatons.

"The total number of our nuclear delivery vehicles, tactical as well as strategic, is in the tens of thousands; and of course, we have more than one warhead for each vehicle.

"Our forces are so deployed and protected that a sneak attack could not effectively disarm us. The destructive power which the United States could bring to bear, even after a Soviet surprise attack upon our forces, would be as great as, perhaps greater than, the total undamaged force which the enemy can threaten to launch against the United States in a first strike.

"In short, we have a second strike capability which is at least as extensive as what the Soviets can deliver by striking first. Therefore, we are confident that the Soviets will not provoke a major nuclear conflict."

Defense outlays for the current fiscal year totaling about $47,000,000,000, can be expected to rise year to year unless there are significant reductions in international tensions, he declared.

"If forceful interference with our rights and obligations should lead to violent conflict, as it well might, the United States does not intend to be defeated," he emphasized.

"As the President reminded the world at the United Nations last month, our country has both the will and the weapons to join free men in standing up to their responsibilities.

"We in the Defense Department believe that the proper exercise of our will and the development and management of our weapons will eventually force the Soviet Union to participate with us in a step-by-step program to guarantee the peace which so many nations earnestly desire."

He explained that the department was aiming for flexibility rather than rigidity.

"This requires a strengthening of conventional, non-nuclear arms," he went on. "It does not rule out the use of tactical nuclear weapons in a limited war if our interests should so require."

He said the chief purpose of the Soviet Union's announcement that it might explode a fifty-megaton thermonuclear device was terror.

United Stated scientists, he said, have considered the advisability of exploding such a device and decided against it. Such explosions are not necessary for development purposes, he added.

* * *

October 31, 1961

SOVIET EXPLODES BIGGEST A-BOMB, BUT 50-MEGATON FORCE IS DOUBTED; U. S. JOINS IN WORLD-WIDE PROTEST

TEST DENOUNCED

White House Asserts Purpose Is to Incite 'Fright and Panic'

By JOHN W. FINNEY
Special to The New York Times.

WASHINGTON, Oct. 30—The Soviet Union detonated the most powerful man-made explosion in history today by setting off a hydrogen bomb with a force of up to fifty megatons.

The White House, joining in world-wide indignation, denounced the test as a "political" act designed to incite "fright and panic in the cold war."

The explosion, which Premier Khrushchev had said would be the climax of an intensive series of Soviet atomic tests, took place at 3:30 A. M., E.S.T., in the vicinity of Novaya Zemlya Island, the Soviet proving ground above the Arctic Circle. It was confirmed by the White House about thirteen hours later.

Plan Might Have Failed

The White House announcement said preliminary evidence indicated that the magnitude of the explosion was "on the order of fifty megatons"—or the equivalent of 50,000,000 tons of TNT.

There were reliable indications, however, that the Soviet Union might have fallen short in its vaunted plan to test the fifty-megaton device as a trigger for a 100-megaton bomb.

The exact size of the explosion will not be known until there has been more opportunity to examine the detection information. Well-informed officials, however, reported that the explosion might have been as low as thirty-five megatons.

The Atomic Energy Commission revised downward today the size of the huge Soviet explosion a week ago from the original estimate of thirty to fifty megatons to twenty-five megatons.

A Bigger Test Possible

If the latest Soviet explosion reached only thirty-five megatons, it raises the possibility that the Soviet Union may explode a still bigger device before ending its test series. Premier Khrushchev told the Communist Party Congress on Oct. 17 that the Soviet Union would conclude the series at the end of October by "probably" exploding a bomb equal to 50,000,000 tons of TNT, and thus "test the device for triggering a 100-megaton bomb."

The explosion took place in the atmosphere at an altitude of about 12,000 feet. This is a relatively low altitude for so large an explosion. It raised the possibility that fairly heavy fall-out might descend on the Soviet Union downwind from Novaya Zemlya.

From the time when the explosion was first detected by seismic observatories in Sweden early in the day, confusion and speculation mounted about its size. Some estimates suggested that the test might have reached as high as 100 megatons.

The early speculation that the Soviet Union might have exceeded even the fifty-megaton level served only to kindle the protests and condemnations from the United Nations, Capitol Hill and foreign offices throughout the non-Communist world.

'Great Leap Backward'

The Soviet action was condemned as an act of terror against mankind and an immoral act of intimidation. It was in defiance of a "solemn appeal" passed only three days ago by the United Nations General Assembly for Russia not to test its fifty-megaton weapon.

In the United Nations, Chief Delegate Adlai E. Stevenson, acting on the basis of early speculation, said the Soviet test had sent the world on "a great leap backward toward anarchy and disaster."

The White House and Atomic Energy Commission withheld any announcement or comment until Government scientists could study the results of the United States detection network. These tend to be more accurate than the observations by the seismic observatories that first reported the tests.

President Kennedy learned of the explosion this morning at the ranch of Senator Robert S. Kerr near Poteau, Okla., where Mr. Kennedy had spent the night. Upon returning to the capital early in the afternoon, the President immediately went into a series of unannounced meetings with his staff and other Government officials.

Not until 4:30 P. M. were Government intelligence officials certain enough of their estimates of the size of the explosion for the United States to confirm the test and the White House to issue its strongly worded condemnation. White the statement was issued in the name of the White House, it had almost certainly been reviewed by the President.

'An Incitement to Fright'

The White House statement branded the Soviet action as "a political rather than a military act" and said the test had been conducted as "primarily an incitement to fright and panic in the cold war." The statement went on:

"Fear is the oldest weapon in history. Throughout the life of mankind, it has been the resort of those who could not hope to prevail by reason and persuasion. It will be repelled today, as it has been repelled in the past—not only the steadfastness of free men but by the power of the arms which men will use to defend their freedom."

The Soviet test, the statement said, "does not affect the basic balance of nuclear power."

From a technical standpoint the statement said there was no need for such a test.

From a military standpoint, it continued, the Soviet's new bomb would be "primarily a mass killer of people in war" and would "not add in effectiveness against military targets to nuclear weapons now available both to the Soviet Union and the United States."

20-Megaton Weapon

The largest device ever tested by the United States was a fifteen-megaton explosion on March 1, 1954. The largest warheads now in the United States arsenal are believed to have a power of around twenty megatons.

The White House statement noted that the Soviet test "will produce more radioactive fall-out than any previous explosion." In fact, in a split second, the Soviet Union added nearly 30 per cent to all the radioactive debris created since the start of nuclear testing in 1945.

Since it resumed atomic tests on Sept. 1, the Soviet Union has conducted twenty-six explosions announced by the United States and a few more that have been detected but not announced. Of these explosions, thirteen have been a megaton or larger in yield.

The effects of the Soviet test series will be to more than double the amount of radioactive debris created by testing by all the nuclear powers. Up until the 1958 moratorium, the three major nuclear powers had conducted explosions with a total force of 180 megatons. Of this, 130 megatons had been exploded by the United States and Britain.

In its latest series the Soviet Union is estimated to have exploded devices with a total force of about 700 megatons. Combined with its earlier tests producing around fifty megatons, the Soviet Union has now unleashed more nuclear power than Britain and the United States, although it has conducted only about half as many tests.

Much of the radioactive debris from the latest Soviet tests has gone into the stratosphere where it is expected to remain until spring. When this fall-out returns to earth, it is expected to concentrate in the temperate zone in the Northern Hemisphere and about double the level of strontium-90 on the ground.

Similarly, most of the radioactive material created in today's explosion is presumed to have been carried by the fireball into the stratosphere, with only a small percentage remaining in the lower atmosphere to descend in the immediate days and weeks ahead.

Could Fall on Soviet

There was a definite possibility, however, that a considerable proportion of the radioactive material could fall on the Soviet Union through a Soviet miscalculation in detonating the device. This possibility arises from the 12,000-foot altitude at which the explosion is estimated to have taken place.

At this altitude, the huge fireball may have touched or grazed the surface and drawn up heavy materials that would incorporate some of the radioactive debris and bring it quickly down to earth.

The Weather Bureau said the wind was blowing to the southeast from Novaya Zemlya at the time of the explosion. If the fireball did scoop up materials from the ground, this would mean there would be fairly intensive "local" fall-out several hundred miles downwind into the Ural Mountains region of the Soviet Union.

*   *   *

May 12, 1962

REDS WIDEN GAINS

Push to Thai Border Seen by Regime as Peril to Capitals

By The Associated Press

VIENTIANE, Laos, May 11—Pro-Communist battalions completed the occupation of Northwest Laos today in an advance that carried them more than 100 miles beyond the cease-fire line to the border of pro-Western Thailand.

Battered Royal Laotian troops were reported to have fled across the Mekong River into Thailand after having abandoned Houei Sai, the last Government outpost in the northwest.

The Laotian Government said it feared that the pro-Communist Pathet Lao rebels were ready to follow their push to the Thai border with a general offensive against the royal Laotian capital of Luang Prabang and against Vientiane, the administrative capital in the south.

The Vientiane Defense Ministry said Government troops had abandoned Houei Sai because they were weary from a five-day retreat from Nam Tha and were not in a position to defend the outpost.

Headquarters Shifted

A spokesman said a new headquarters had been set up south of Houei Sai.

The Defense Ministry said three to five Soviet-made Ilyushin transports had been unloading men and war equipment daily at two air bases in the rebels' newly won territory since the fall of Nam Tha five days ago. A communiqué also reported movement of a column equipped with artillery from rebel headquarters in the Plaine des Jarrez.

In Vientiane, King Savang Vathana appealed to Laotian leaders to try to solve the crisis peacefully. He did not name the leaders, but his remarks were clearly aimed at the rebel side.

In a speech from the throne to the National Assembly, the King lauded Royal Army troops who, he said, are sacrificing their lives to oppose foreign invasion—an apparent allusion to Communist Vietnamese and Communist Chinese units reported by the Royal Government to have participated in the latest thrusts.

An observer said six United States Military Aid Group personnel were still in Houei Sai early Friday. Two Americans on the staff of the Tom Dooley Foundation Hospital were said to have moved to Thailand with most of the hospital equipment.

Muong Sing, where the late Dr. Thomas A. Dooley founded a jungle hospital only five miles from Communist China's border, fell to rebel troops last week.

Retreat Is Disorderly

VIENTIANE, May 11 (UPI)—The Royal Laotian Government's last defenses in northwestern Laos crumbled today under a Communist-led rebel offensive. The Defense Ministry warned that the Laotian capitals of Vientiane and Luang Prabang were threatened.

Control of northwestern Laos gives neutralist forces and the pro-Communist Pathet Lao rebels control of most of the small kingdom. It reduces Government holdings to isolated Vientiane, Luang Prabang, a small strip paralleling the Thai border and a few pockets inside rebel territory.

Houei Sai was deserted by its civilian population, which joined deserting soldiers in swimming 150 yards across the Mekong River or paying 40 cents to be carried over to Thailand in canoes.

Reliable observers estimated the disorganized defenders of Houei Sai at roughly 1,000 men. They were the remnants of a 5,000-man garrison at Nam Tha, which covered 100 miles of jungle trails in 100 hours.

*   *   *

May 12, 1962

U.S., SHIFTING LAOS POLICY, WRITES OFF ROUTED ARMY; PLANS ASIAN FLEET MOVES

ACCORD IS SOUGHT

Kennedy Acts to Force Rightists to Join a 3-Faction Regime

By MAX FRANKEL
Special to The New York Times.

WASHINGTON, May 11—The United States has written off the Right-wing Laotian Army as useless against the pro-Communist forces and is therefore losing interest in supporting the army's leaders politically.

To fill the developing vacuum and in an effort to salvage a peaceful settlement, President Kennedy, it was reported today, will order a show of United States force in the Southeast Asian waters near landlocked Laos. The show of force will probably start this week-end.

The naval movements and coordinated diplomatic activity will seek to create a coalition Government of Rightists, neutralists and pro-Communists and make Laos a neutral buffer state.

To force the reluctant Right-wing leaders into the coalition, the United States is said to be threatening to disown the Rightist leaders, Prince Boun Oum, the Premier, and his strong man, Deputy Premier Maj. Gen. Phouml Nosavan.

No Political Value

With their army in virtual disarray after a Communist attack in northwestern Laos, the Rightists have no further independent political value, it is felt here.

The Pathet Lao forces were reported today to have driven the remnants of the Right-wing army out of northern Laos and across the border into Thailand, near Houei Sai. Their assault began last week-end with the capture of Nam Tha, about twenty miles from the border of Communist China.

The entire Laotian situation is still under extensive review in the Administration, with the emphasis on measures that would not lead to direct United States involvement in the fighting.

But the rout of the Right-wing forces in the north this week was taken as final evidence that no partial United States commitment of military advisers and equipment, as in neighboring South Vietnam, would do any good. President Kennedy and key State and Defense Department aides were said to have concluded at a White House meeting last night that only the credibility of United States power could now serve to uphold the West's bargaining position in the formation of a neutralist government for Laos.

The specific measures will not be ordered until tomorrow, after Secretary of State Dean Rusk and Secretary of Defense Robert S. McNamara have reviewed the problem with the President. Both Secretaries were returning tonight from Asia.

Moderate Moves Planned

The tentative plans, however, are said to call for some moderate naval and troop movements that would draw attention to United States power in Southeast Asia without implying a threat to join in the Laotian fighting.

The movement will be by sea, though Laos is cut off from the water by Thailand, Cambodia and South Vietnam. Aircraft carriers and assault ships carrying Marine contingents are a part of the Seventh Fleet.

The Administration has tried both in Moscow and Washington to get the Russians to restrain the advancing Pathet Lao pro-Communist guerrillas in northern Laos.

Although the Administration has revised its earlier opinion about the seriousness of this cease-fire violation, it still believes that the Right-wing forces share much of the blame for the deteriorating situation.

The Rightists' ignoring of repeated warnings from Washington against a build-up of their forces around Nam Tha is thought here to have provoked the Pathet Lao attack. Prince Boun Oum's refusal to join a coalition government through many months of negotiation is also thought to have contributed to the resumption of fighting.

Leftists to Fight On

The pro-Communist leaders have told members of the Laotian International Control Commission that they intend to continue fighting until there is some progress in the political negotiations.

In the United States pressure on the Rightists to join the coalition, monthly aid payments of $3,000,000 have been held up since February.

The fighting of the last week has persuaded officials here that the Right-wing army can no longer be counted upon to do anything effective, even if it were to get additional advisory or logistic support from the United States.

Prince's Return Sought

The United States is said to be pleading with Prince Souvanna Phouma, the Laotian neutralist leader, to return to his country from Europe. The big powers that agreed on a Laotian neutralist settlement at Geneva last year unanimously chose Prince Souvanna Phouma to head the proposed coalition Government.

The Rightists have refused to meet Prince Souvanna Phouma's demand that they surrender to him the ministries of Defense and Interior, involving control of the Laotian armed forces and police.

Thailand, which has faced Communist subversion in her northeastern section adjoining the Laotian frontier, has not yet expressed concern for her security. But some officials here said the expected show of force might involve other members of the Southeast Asia Treaty Organization of which Thailand is a member.

Among the ships in the United States Seventh Fleet that may be called upon to maneuver southward from their extended patrol duties in southwestern waters of the Pacific are three attack carriers, the Midway, Hancock and Coral Sea; an anti-submarine warfare cruiser, the Bennington, and the assault carrier Valley Forge carrying marines.

The Third Marine Division, based at Okinawa, has an 1,800-man battalion constantly afloat with the Seventh Fleet. A further dispatch of some of its troops was held out here as one possibility.

* * *

June 17, 1962

M'NAMARA WARNS AGAINST DIVIDING ATOM DETERRENT

Alluding to France, Secretary Asserts That West's Might Should Be 'Indivisible'

GIVES POLICY IN DETAIL

Says NATO Must Maintain Over-All Nuclear Strength to Avert Surprise Attack

By E. W. KENWORTHY
Special to The New York Times.

WASHINGTON, June 16—Secretary of Defense Robert S. McNamara made today the first full-dress, public explanation of the reasons why the United States was so strongly urging upon its allies that the nuclear deterrent of the West should be "indivisible."

In a commencement address at the University of Michigan in Ann Arbor, released here by the Defense Department, Mr. McNamara said that "relatively weak national nuclear forces" would not be "sufficient to perform even the function of deterrence."

On the other hand, Mr. McNamara said, in the event of war the use of such a force on military targets would have "a negligible effect on the outcome of the conflict," and would be "tantamount to suicide" if used against the cities of a major nuclear power such as the Soviet Union.

Disturbed by Stand

The Secretary did not mention France, but officials conceded that he had that nation in mind.

The Kennedy Administration, like the Eisenhower one, has not disguised its unhappiness over President de Gaulle's determination to create an independent French nuclear force. Nor has it made any secret of its unwillingness to seek modifications in the Atomic Energy Act to permit the sharing of information to help President de Gaulle achieve his objective more speedily and economically.

Until now, the stock public explanation of the Administration's policy has been the dangers attendant upon a proliferation of national nuclear forces.

Today Mr. McNamara did not underrate these dangers. But he went far beyond this obvious reason to explain that the Government's aversion to the creation of relatively weak nuclear forces was tied in with basic American strategy for deterrence of nuclear war and for waging it if necessary.

Mr. McNamara's argument today was substantially the same except for certain reinforcing details that are classified—as that he made to a secret meeting of Council of Ministers of the North Atlantic Treaty Organization last month in Athens.

The Administration has been weighing for some time the desirability of having a high official deliver publicly an extensive explanation of United States policy on nuclear weapons in the hope of making it better understood in Europe, and particularly in France.

Mr. McNamara's speech was put together after long consultations among the White House, the Defense and State Departments. It was intended to be a major pronouncement on United States policy and as such had President Kennedy's personal attention.

The three elements in United States nuclear strategy, as expounded by Mr. McNamara, are as follows:

First, the Western alliance must maintain over-all nuclear strength sufficient to deter surprise nuclear attack or resort to use of nuclear weapons "as an outgrowth of a limited engagement in Europe or elsewhere."

The Administration believes that the current balance of nuclear power, which it expects to maintain, makes either of these actions unlikely, simply because they would be irrational. However, nations do not always act rationally, and sometimes they act on the basis of misjudgment of the actual situation. Therefore, there is no guarantee that nuclear war will not occur.

Second, the United States has decided that if nuclear war should come its basic strategy—to the extent feasible—should be much the same as in past conventional warfare. That is, Mr. McNamara said, the principal objectives, following an attack upon the alliance, should be "the destruction of the enemy's military forces, not of his civilian population."

Third, if an enemy should launch a massive surprise attack on allied civilian centers, the alliance must have "sufficient reserve striking power to destroy an enemy society."

Essential to this strategy, Mr. NcNamara said, is unity of planning, concentration of executive authority and central direction in order that there may be a "controlled response" to an enemy move."

"We are convinced," he declared, "that a general nuclear war target system is indivisible, and there must not be competing and conflicting strategies to meet the contingency of nuclear war."

Essential, also, he said, is the economic ability to support a nuclear force large enough to promote deterrence and discourage an attack on civilian centers if war comes. In the coming fiscal year, Mr. McNamara disclosed for the first time, the United States plans to spend $15,000,000,000 on nuclear weapons "to assure their adequacy."

Mr. McNamara argued that an independent nuclear force of the kind that most of the United States allies could afford would not only jeopardize the strategy of controlled response but would also be unable to protect Europe.

"In short, then," he said, "Limited nuclear capabilities, operating independently, are dangerous, expensive, prone to obsolescence and lacking in credibility as a deterrent."

The United States has become more vulnerable to nuclear attack with the development of powerful Soviet rockets, and there has been some fear in Europe that this vulnerability would make the United States hesitate to come to the defense of Europe. This fear has been an argument for creation of independent nuclear forces. Mr. McNamara was at pains today to reaffirm United States pledges.

"Our own strategic retaliatory forces," he said, "are prepared to respond against these [enemy] forces, wherever they are and whatever their targets."

This mission is assigned, he declared, not only in fulfillment of treaty commitments but also because the nature of nuclear war compels it.

* * *

July 24, 1962

ACCORDS ON LAOS SIGNED IN GENEVA

Khrushchev and Kennedy Hail Neutrality Pacts

By SYDNEY GRUSON
Special to The New York Times.

GENEVA, July 23—In a casual twenty-five-minute ceremony, the representatives of fourteen countries signed agreements today guaranteeing the neutrality and independence of Laos.

The ceremony in the green and gold council chamber of the Palais des Nations, European headquarters of the United Nations, ended the fifteen-month conference designed to take the Southeastern Asian kingdom out of the power struggle between West and East.

Foreign Minister Andrei A. Gromyko of the Soviet Union presided over the ceremony. Secretary of State Dean Rusk and W. Averell Harriman, Assistant Secretary for Far Eastern Affairs, signed for the United States.

There were two documents. All fourteen members of the conference signed the protocol setting out the terms of reference for the International Control Commission that will oversee the withdrawal of foreign troops and other measures to establish Laotian neutrality.

The second document, signed by all except Laos, was a pledge to respect the kingdom's new status. This document incorporated the agreement among the three rival Laotian factions to cooperate in a Government of national unity under the neutralist Premier, Prince Souvanna Phouma.

Premier Khrushchev of the Soviet Union and Prime Minister Macmillan of Britain sent congratulatory messages to this morning's final gathering. Their countries had served as co-chairmen of the conference.

Mr. Macmillan expressed his assurance that the agreements "will afford the people of Laos the chance to pursue their own peace and prosperity to which all parties in Laos are devoted."

"The conference has been able to show the world that difficult international problems can be solved by discussion and mutual compromise," he said.

Khrushchev Hails Accord

This point was also made by Premier Khrushchev, who described the agreements as "of signal international importance" in removing a "dangerous hotbed of war" in Southeast Asia.

The first to sign today was the Laotian Foreign Minister, Quinim Pholsena. Then came the representatives of Poland, South Vietnam, Thailand, the United States, Burma, Cambodia, Canada, Communist China, North Vietnam, France, India, Britain and the Soviet Union.

At one point in the signing ceremony, as the delegates chatted across the table, the voice of the Earl of Home, Britain's Foreign Secretary, came clearly through a microphone accidentally left on.

"I always think the decorations on the walls of this place are rather depressing," he said.

The sepia and gold murals by José-Maria Sert, the Spanish artist, depict justice, strength, peace, law and intelligence.

An agitated aide rushed over to Lord Home, pointed at the press gallery and whispered something. The microphone went dead.

At 10:50 A. M. Central European time, Mr. Gromyko signed for the Soviet Union and the agreements went into effect.

* * *

October 21, 1962

CHINESE PUSH INDIANS BACK IN HEAVY BORDER FIGHTING; TAKE OUTPOSTS ON 2 FRONTS

CASUALTIES HIGH

Menon Vows Soldiers Will Take Big Toll of Enemy Forces

Special to The New York Times.

NEW DELHI, Oct. 20—Chinese Communist troops have overrun many Indian positions and shot down an Indian helicopter in a pitched battle that has been raging since early today on the western and eastern sectors of the disputed Himalayan frontier.

[In a dispatch from New Delhi, Reuters quoted V. K. Krishna Menon, Indian Defense Minister, as having said that casualties were heavy but that the Indian troops would take a heavy toll among the attackers.]

The fighting appeared to be the heaviest since the Chinese-Indian border clashes erupted three years ago.

India Loses Main Post

India lost her main Dhola post near the Tibetan border to a large force of Chinese troops. Another Indian main post, 10 miles east of Dhola, Khinzemane, also fell before noon.

The Chinese simultaneously opened an attack 900 miles to the northwest on Indian forward posts in Northern Ladakh. The Indians abandoned two of the posts and have taken "better defense positions," according to an official spokesman.

Rifle fire near Dhola shot down a helicopter while it was removing casualties. The pilot parachuted to safety and returned to his base, the spokesman said.

According to the Indian spokesman, the Chinese also attacked Indian supply planes in Ladakh, but the aircraft returned to their bases safely.

Combat Planes Grounded

China had warned India early this week that it would shoot down intruding Indian planes. India replied that the Indian planes had the right to fly over Indian territory under Chinese occupation and if the Chinese shot any planes an air offensive would be launched.

However, there were no combat planes in operation on either side today, the spokesman said.

He said the Chinese began an attack last night when they opened heavy mortar and machine gun fire on an auxiliary Indian post near Dhola.

The Chinese have crossed a 30-foot wide river, Namka Chu, between the Indian and Chinese military camps. "Fighting is now raging a little distance south of this river," a Government spokesman said.

According to the spokesman, the Chinese forces, "estimated at a division or more," were entrenched on a 15-square mile slope south of the Thag La Ridge on the McMahon Line and beyond it.

The Chinese were said to have a large supply of arms and ammunition and an advantageous plateau behind them at a much higher level. Thag La Ridge has an altitude of 14,500 feet and Dhola an altitude of about 12,500 feet.

The Namka Chu runs 12 miles east from the Dhola post and flows into another river, Namlang, which runs north to south. Khinzemane is at a crossing of the river and the Thag La Ridge, which slopes down to 9,000 feet at this point.

Fighting was reported still raging on a 12-mile stretch sloping upward south of the Namka Chu.

In Ladakh, Eastern Kashmir, the fighting is believed to be in Chip Chap River Valley area and the Galwan Valley area. Indian and Chinese troops have established several posts, with some encircling others.

Reports show that winter has set in in both sectors and snow has started. The Indians suffer from the handicap that they are less acclimatized to these conditions than are the Chinese.

Observers believe the battle will be over within a week, with the Indians retreating to safer positions. The Indian troops were said to have been taken by surprise by the sudden onslaught.

An Indian spokesman said the Chinese attacks were "premeditated and concerted and obviously undertaken after long preparation and deliberate planning."

Official and political circles in New Delhi are dismayed. The Indian forward posts had been thought impenetrable. Indian military men have said recently that they would be able to contain a Chinese advance effectively.

Defense experts, however, assert that this does not mean that the Indians are losing. They say the withdrawal has been to better positions.

Observers agree that Indians have failed in their attempt to oust the Chinese from Indian territory south of the McMahon Line before the onset of winter. The McMahon Line, drawn by Sir Henry McMahon, a British diplomat, in 1914, determined the border between Tibet and India. China and India disagree on the places situated within the line.

Lieut. Gen. Birj Mohan Kaul is believed to be at the front personally directing the Indian operations in the eastern sector. He took over recently as commander of a corps for defense against the Chinese.

Defense Minister V. K. Krishna Menon is reported to have said, "We do not want to sacrifice our soldiers unnecessarily."

Addressing a public meeting here today, he described the Chinese action as a "naked, large-scale aggression." He told the Indians that the "days to come might bring some hardships" and asked them to be prepared to undergo any "material sacrifice."

Chinese Attack in Waves

NEW DELHI, Oct. 20 (Reuters)—Indian troops were driven back today from defense posts by a massive two-pronged Chinese Communist attack on the Northeastern Frontier, the Government announced.

Successive waves of Chinese troops, armed with medium machine guns and backed by heavy mortars, were said to have swept over the MacMahon border line on India's North East Frontier agency.

An "overwhelming" Chines force, supported by "superior firepower," also spearheaded into the Ladakh area of Kasmir, more than a thousand miles from the North East Frontier agency.

The fighting has brought heavy casualties, but no firm figures are as yet available, the Indian Defense Ministry said.

So far the fighting has been restricted to the ground, but informed sources said Indian fighter planes had been placed on alert.

Reports on the fighting were disclosed by the Indian Defense Minister, V. K. Krishna Menon. Mr. Menon said Indian troops had fought "to the last round" before falling back in the face of "superior Chinese forces."

"Indians prefer to die on their feet than to live on their knees. For every man the Chines kill, we will kill more," Mr. Menon said.

In the North East Frontier area, Mr. Menon said the Chinese had advance four miles south of the border. He reported that the Chinese had stormed and captured Dhola, the chief Indian outpost on the Thag La Ridge.

The Chinese also captured the Northeastern post of Khinzeman, but not before Indian troops fought "to the last round" of their ammunition, the defense Minister said.

Mr. Menon charged that the two-pronged Chinese attack was "premeditated and concerted."

The North Eastern Frontier Agency fighting extended along a 20-mile front in a steep valley bordered by the 14,500-foot high Thag La Ridge, which India asserts marks the frontier in this area.

Under the direct administration of the Indian Foreign Minister, the Northeast Frontier Agency is a tribal area of more than 30,000 square miles.

The full-scale fighting followed and Indian threat earlier this week to drive the Chinese out of the Indian border area.

In some sectors the Chinese are alleged to have occupied thousands of square miles of Indian territory.

Thursday the Chinese charged that the Indians had started heavy shelling in the North East Frontier Agency area in what was considered a preliminary softening up of the Chinese position in preparation for an Indian attack.

The worst previous clash broke out 10 days ago when the Chinese were said to have suffered about 100 casualties in an attack along the Thag La Ridge.

Thousands of Troops Involved

NEW DELHI, Oct. 20 (AP)—Thousands of troops were engaged in the fighting that erupted early today along the Indian-Chinese border, the Defense Ministry indicated today.

The Defense Ministry said the Indian troops were facing "more than one division, perhaps two divisions."

Defense Minister Menon gave no casualty figures, but he said he had no doubt that the Chinese had lost four for "one of ours."

By Indian account, the battle flared at 5 A. M. (7:30 P. M Friday, New York time), when all the Chinese forces in the area opened mortar and machine gun fire on all Indian outposts in the area.

The Indians were forced to pull back from Khinzemane and a place called Tsangle, outposts at either end of a Chinese salient.

India was reported to have decided to ask Bhutan to allow Indian forces to enter that country to strengthen the Himalayan kingdom's defenses against China.

The fighting in the North East Frontier Agency is just east of Bhutan. While the little kingdom is building a modern army with the help of India, it has resisted such requests in the past.

A dispatch from Calcutta said the rising menace of the Chinese Reds might lead Bhutan to reverse her decision. Bhutan's premier, Jigme Dorji, is leaving for New Delhi tomorrow for high-level defense talks.

The Crown Prince of Sikkhim, an Indian protectorate to the west of Bhutan, will join in the New Delhi meeting, officials said.

* * *

October 23, 1962

U.S. IMPOSES ARMS BLOCKADE ON CUBA ON FINDING OFFENSIVE-MISSILE SITES; KENNEDY READY FOR SOVIET SHOWDOWN

PRESIDENT GRAVE

Asserts Russians Lied and Put Hemisphere in Great Danger

By ANTHONY LEWIS
Special to The New York Times.

WASHINGTON, Oct. 22—President Kennedy imposed a naval and air "quarantine" tonight on the shipment of offensive military equipment to Cuba.

In a speech of extraordinary gravity, he told the American people that the Soviet Union, contrary to promises, was building offensive missile and bomber bases in Cuba. He said the bases could handle missiles carrying nuclear warheads up to 2,000 miles.

Thus a critical moment in the cold war was at hand tonight. The President had decided on a direct confrontation with—and challenge to—the power of the Soviet Union.

Direct Thrust at Soviet

Two aspects of the speech were notable. One was its direct thrust at the Soviet Union as the party responsible for the crisis. Mr. Kennedy treated Cuba and the Government of Premier Fidel Castro as a mere pawn in Moscow's hands and drew the issue as one with the Soviet Government.

The President, in language of unusual bluntness, accused the Soviet leaders of deliberately "false statements about their intentions in Cuba."

The other aspect of the speech particularly noted by observers here was its flat commitment by the United States to act alone against the missile threat in Cuba.

Nation Ready to Act

The President made it clear that this country would not stop short of military action to end what he called a "clandestine, reckless and provocative threat to world peace."

Mr. Kennedy said the United States was asking for an emergency meeting of the United Nations Security Council to consider a resolution for "dismantling and withdrawal of all offensive weapons in Cuba."

He said the launching of a nuclear missile from Cuba against any nation in the Western Hemisphere would be regarded as an attack by the Soviet Union against the United States. It would be met, he said, by retaliation against the Soviet Union.

He called on Premier Krushchev to withdraw the missiles from Cuba and so "move the world back from the abyss of destruction."

All this the President recited in an 18-minute radio and television address of a grimness unparalleled in recent times. He read the words rapidly, with little emotion, until he came to the peroration—a warning to Americans of the dangers ahead.

"Let no one doubt that this is a difficult and dangerous effort on which we have set out," the President said. "No one can foresee precisely what course it will take or what costs or casualties will be incurred."

"The path we have chosen for the present is full of hazards, as all paths are—but it is the one most consistent with our character and courage as a nation and our commitments around the world," he added.

"The cost of freedom is always high—but Americans have always paid it. And one path we shall never choose is the path of surrender or submission.

"Our goal is not the victory of might but the vindication of right—not peace at the expense of freedom, but both peace and freedom, here in this hemisphere and, we hope, around the world. God willing, that goal will be achieved."

The President's speech did not actually start the naval blockade tonight. To meet the requirements of international law, the State Department will issue a formal proclamation late tomorrow, and that may delay the effectiveness of the action as long as another 24 hours.

Crisis Before Public

The speech laid before the American people a crisis that had gripped the highest officials here since last Tuesday, but had only began to leak out to the public over the weekend. The President said it was at 9 A.M. Tuesday that he got the first firm intelligence report about the missile sites on Cuba.

Last month, he said, the Soviet Government publicly stated that its military equipment for Cuba was "exclusively for defensive purposes" and that the Soviet did not need retaliatory missile bases outside its own territory.

"That statement was false," Mr. Kennedy said.

Just last Thursday, he continued, the Soviet foreign minister, Andrei A. Gromyko, told him in a call at the White House that the Soviet Union "would never become involved" in building any offensive military capacity in Cuba.

"That statement was also false," the President said.

Appeal to Khrushchev

He made a direct appeal to Premier Khrushchev to abandon the Communist "course of world domination." An hour before the President spoke, a personal letter from him to Mr. Khrushchev was delivered to the Soviet government in Moscow.

Mr. Kennedy disclosed that he was calling for an immediate meeting of the Organ of Consultation of the Organization of American States to consider the crisis.

The O.A.S. promptly scheduled an emergency session for 9 A.M. tomorrow. State Department officials said they were confident of receiving the necessary 14 votes out of the 29 nations represented.

The President said the United States was prepared also to discuss the situation "in any other meeting that could be useful." This was taken as an allusion to a possible summit conference with Mr. Khrushchev.

But the President emphasized that discussion in any of these forums would be undertaken "without limiting our freedom of action." This meant that the United States was determined on this course no matter what any international organization—or even the United States' allies—might say.

Support From Congress

Congressional leaders of both parties, who were summoned to Washington today to be advised by the President of the crisis and his decision, gave him unanimous backing.

Mr. Kennedy went into considerable detail in his speech in outlining the nature of the military threat in Cuba, and this country's response.

He said "confirmed" intelligence indicates that the Cuban missile sites are of two types.

One kind, which his words implied were already or nearly completed, would be capable of handling medium-range ballistic missiles. The President said such missiles could carry nuclear weapons more than 1,000 nautical miles—to Washington, the Panama Canal, Cape Canaveral or Mexico City.

The second category of sites would be for intermediate range ballistics missiles, with a range of more than 2,000 miles. The President said they could hit "most of the major cities in the Western hemisphere" from Lima, Peru, to Hudson's Bay in Canada.

Mr. Kennedy declared:

"This urgent transformation of Cuba into an important strategic base by the presence of these large, long-range and clearly offensive weapons of sudden mass destruction constitutes an explicit threat to the peace and security of all the Americas."

He said the Soviet Union's action was "in flagrant and deliberate defiance" of the Rio (Inter-American) Pact of 1947, the United Nations Charter, Congressional resolution and his own public warnings to the Soviet Union.

O.A.S Chiefs Back Kennedy

HOUSTON, Tex., Oct. 22 (AP)—Three high-ranking officials of the Organization of American States said here tonight that the O.A.S. would fully support President Kennedy's blockade of Cuba, even to the point of using arms.

The officials were Dr. José A. Mors, secretary general, Dr. Alberto Zulesa Angel, President and Gonzalo J. Facio, Costa Rican ambassador to the organization and to the United States.

*   *   *

October 24, 1962

SOVIET CHALLENGES U.S. RIGHT TO BLOCKADE; INTERCEPTION OF 25 RUSSIAN SHIPS ORDERED; CUBA QUARANTINE BACKED BY UNITED O. A. S.

MOSCOW REPLIES

It Warns Washington Action by Navy Risks Nuclear Conflict

By SEYMOUR TOPPING

Special to The New York Times.

MOSCOW, Oct. 23—The Soviet Union challenged today the right of the United States to impose a quarantine on the shipment of weapons of any type to Cuba. It asserted that the Castro regime could make whatever defense arrangements it pleased.

Warning the Kennedy Administration that its naval quarantine risked thermonuclear war, Moscow announced that the armed forces of the Soviet bloc were taking suitable measures to enhance their combat readiness.

The Defense Ministry was ordered to cancel all leaves of military personnel and to defer the discharge of senior age groups in the strategic rocket and antiaircraft forces and in the submarine fleet.

Council Meeting Asked

It was also announced that Marshal Andrei A. Grechko, Commander in Chief of the Warsaw Treaty forces, had conferred with his staff and issued instructions "to raise the military preparedness of the troops and fleets." The orders affect the aimed forces of the Soviet Union, Czechoslovakia, Poland, East Germany, Hungary and Rumania.

[The Moscow radio said the Soviet Union would not usc nuclear weapons against the United States "unless aggression is committed," according to United Press International.]

A Government statement said Moscow had asked the United Nations Security Council to convene immediately to discuss the "violation of the United Nations Charter and the threat to peace on the part of the United States."

Ambassadors Summoned

Foy D. Kohler, the United States Ambassador, was summoned to the Soviet Foreign Ministry and was handed a 2,500 word statement by Vasili V. Kuznetsov, a First Deputy Foreign Minister. It was described as a reply to the television speech made last night by President Kennedy.

Earlier the Cuban Ambassador, Carlos Olivares, called at the Foreign Ministry and Ambassadors of the Communist nations were summoned throughout the day to be informed of developments.

The Government statement addressed a "serious warning" to the United States, but it did not specify any forceful countermeasures to be taken to break the quarantine of Cuba.

The Soviet Government statement today indicated that Moscow would resist United States demands that the missile bases in Cuba be dismantled.

Insisting that the weapons provided by the Soviet Union were designed "solely for enhancing Cuba's defense potential," the Soviet statement asserted:

"The United States demands that military equipment Cuba needs for self-defense should be removed from Cuban territory, a demand which naturally no state which values its independence can meet."

Statement Termed Mild

Western diplomats considered the statement relatively mild, although it was replete with the warning phrases familiar to Soviet Government statements of that character. These officials said the statement indicated that Soviet leadership had not yet decided on a firm course of action.

It was believed that Moscow had braced before the President's speech for even more drastic measures by the United States in retaliation for the apparent establishment of Soviet ballistic missile bases in Cuba.

Soviet officials said privately that the tone of the statement had been kept moderate pending developments in the Security Council meeting that has been requested individually by the United States and Cuba as well as by the Soviet Union.

The complaint of President Kennedy that the Soviet Union was constructing offensive medium and intermediate range ballistic missile bases in Cuba and had provided the regime of Premier Fidel Castro with jet bombers was not mentioned in the Soviet Government's statement or in the news bulletins for the Soviet people.

Sept. 12 Note Recalled

In a statement of Sept. 12 the Soviet Government said that it was supplying Cuba with purely defensive weapons and that Soviet intercontinental missile capabilities had made the establishment of launching bases on foreign territory unnecessary.

It was obvious tonight that one of the cardinal points of difference between the United States and the Soviet Union in the Cuban dispute was the difference of what constituted an offensive or a defensive weapon.

In its Sept. 12 statement the Soviet Government warned the United States that any attack would mean war. Today's statement went only as far as to call the naval quarantine piracy. It added:

"The United States arrogates the right to demand that states report to it how they organize their defense and what they carry in their ships in the open seas.

"The Soviet Government resolutely rejects such claims. The arrogant actions of American imperialism could lead to disastrous consequences to all mankind," the statement warned.

Soviet newspapers and domestic radio broadcasts withheld news of the United States quarantine for 13 hours after President Kennedy made his speech.

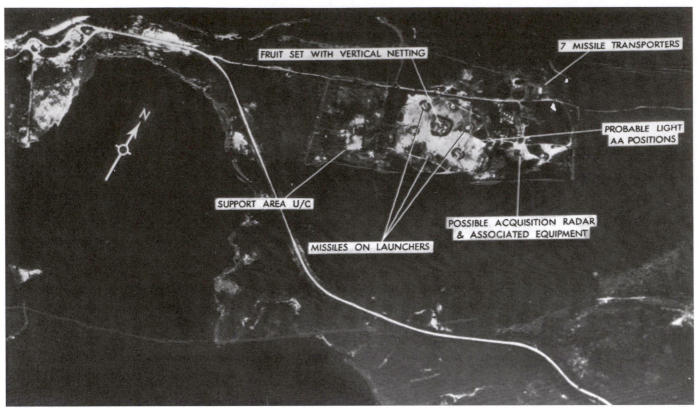

MISSLE SITE IN CUBA: This is a copy of a photo made public by U.S. Embassy in London and radioed to U.S. The Embassy said picture showed typical surface-to-air missile base in Cuba. Printed notes were not explained, but "Fruit set with vertical netting" may refer to camouflage, "Support area U/C" to facilities under construction and "AA positions" to antiaircraft weapons. "Acquisition radar" is of long-range type. Similar photographs were later released by the Defense Department in Washington.

At 3:30 P.M. Moscow time, 30 minutes after the United States Ambassador had been summoned to the Foreign Ministry, the Moscow radio broadcast a 300-word summary of the President's speech. It omitted the complaint against the Soviet Union and the charge that Moscow was guilty of deception in constructing the missile bases.

Thirty minutes after the broadcast began, the Moscow radio commentators began reading the text of the Soviet Government's statement. This was followed immediately by announcements of "spontaneous" meetings throughout the country protesting the United States action.

Atmosphere of Tension

There was an atmosphere of tension in the Soviet capital tonight, but not one of acute crisis.

Premier Khrushchev and other members of the ruling Presidium attended a performance tonight of the opera "Boris Godunov" at the Bolshoi Theater. They were hosts to Georghe Georghiu-Dej, Rumania's chief of state, and the Rumanian Premier, Georghe Maurer. The two are passing through Moscow en route home from a state visit to Indonesia.

The title role in the opera was sung by the United States bass Jerome Hines. Mr. Khrushchev, who seemed relaxed, led the ovations for Mr. Hines and later congratulated him backstage.

The treatment of the news of the Cuban developments reflected some apprehension on the part of the Soviet Government a possible adverse reaction from the Soviet people.

The omission from the domestic news bulletins of the President's references to Soviet missile bases was consistent with the Government's policy of minimizing the extent of its military involvement in Cuba. Soviet television and radio commentaries went to great lengths to explain why it had become necessary to supply arms to Cuba.

There have been persistent signs of uneasiness on the part of the Soviet people about any risky Soviet ventures in the distant Caribbean.

Any statement on the missile bases in Cuba might have compelled the Soviet Government to disclose that they were manned by Soviet personnel. It was regarded here as extremely unlikely that Moscow would give control of any long-range missiles to Cuban officers who might unilaterally provoke a rocket nuclear war between the United States and the Soviet Union.

The Soviet statement did not reply to the appeal by President Kennedy asking Premier Khrushchev to reverse his policy in Cuba and to enter into stable relations with the United States.

This appeal was contained in the President's speech and in a personal message to Mr. Khrushchev that was delivered here last night to the Soviet Foreign Ministry together with a copy of the speech.

The Soviet statement denounced the assertion by President Kennedy that the United States would retaliate against the Soviet Union if it was struck by a missile from Cuba. It said:

"This statement is permeated with hypocrisy because the Soviet Union already has repeatedly declared that not a single Soviet nuclear bomb would fall either on the United States or any other country unless an aggression is committed."

* * *

October 29, 1962

U.S. AND SOVIET REACH ACCORD ON CUBA; KENNEDY ACCEPTS KHRUSHCHEV PLEDGE TO REMOVE MISSILES UNDER U.N. WATCH

THANT SETS VISIT

He Will Go to Havana Tomorrow
to Seek Castro Consent

By THOMAS J. HAMILTON
Special to The New York Times.

UNITED NATIONS, N.Y., Oct. 28—U Thant, the Acting Secretary General, will fly to Cuba Tuesday with his top assistants to discuss arrangements for a United Nations check on the dismantling of Soviet missiles and the halting of the building of bases.

Mr. Thant plans to stay in Cuba only long enough to obtain Premier Fidel Castro's acceptance of the Thant plan to send observer teams to inspect and be sure Premier Khrushchev's agreement to dismantle the missiles is complied with.

According to reliable sources, once the Acting Secretary General makes these arrangements, he will return to obtain authorization from the Security Council for the inspection program.

Mahmoud Riad of the United Arab Republic, who on Thursday will take over the monthly presidency of the Security Council from the Soviet delegate, had a talk with Mr. Thant today. Mr. Riad said he saw no need for a Council meeting until Mr. Thant returned—perhaps Thursday or Friday.

Outcome Awaited

The Council suspended its debate Thursday night to await the outcome of messages exchanged by President Kennedy and Premier Khrushchev.

Premier Castro's consent will be necessary under the precedent set in the Suez crisis of 1956.

At that time the late Secretary General Dag Hammarskjold ruled that President Gamal Abdel Nasser would have to agree to all arrangements for stationing United Nations forces in the United Arab Republic, including which countries might supply the troops.

Premier Castro offered to provide a Cuban plane to transport the Acting Secretary General and his aides, who are expected to include Brig. Indar Jit Rikhye of the Indian Army, a military adviser.

Mr. Thant told Premier Castro, however, that he preferred to charter his own plane. An airline belonging to a country not involved in the Cuban dispute will be chosen.

According to plans worked out hurriedly today, 50 military officers will be needed as inspectors. These will come only from states that have diplomatic relations with Cuba.

Brazil and Mexico are thus the only Latin-American States now able to contribute to the teams.

Among the other states that are likely to be asked to participate are three neutrals—Ethiopia, Sweden and Switzerland, which is not a member of the United Nations.

Reliable sources said Mr. Thant would aim at wide geographical distribution, seeking observers from countries in Asia and other areas—in particular those not allied with either the United States or the Soviet Union.

Reliable sources said that Adlai E. Stevenson, the chief United States representative at the United Nations, and Mr. Thant discussed these and other possibilities this morning. Canada also has been mentioned.

Neutralist delegates, however, prefer that Mr. Thant recruit the observers from the eight "neutrals" who have been taking part in the Geneva disarmament negotiations.

In addition to Brazil and Mexico, Ethiopia and Sweden, the group at Geneva consists of Burma, India, Nigeria and the United Arab Republic.

The United States is expected to oppose observers from the eight "neutrals" because this would mean participation by military officers from the United Arab Republic and India, both of which have taken Cuba's side in the dispute.

The Soviet Union and Cuba are expected to express their views on countries that might furnish observers.

Gets Late Dispatch

Mr. Stevenson had had an appointment for 10 A.M. today to discuss developments with Mr. Thant. But he was handed a dispatch reporting Mr. Khrushchev's latest message as he left the delegation building for the United Nations.

As a result, Mr. Stevenson spent the hour with the Acting Secretary General discussing United States suggestions on the inspection arrangements.

During the morning Mr. Thant talked on the telephone to Mario Garcia-Inchaustegui of Cuba and Valerian A. Zorin of the Soviet Union.

Mr. Thant formally accepted Premier Castro's invitation to visit Cuba when he was with the Cuban representative at 3 P.M.

Mr. Thant received Mr. Zorin two hours later.

Mr. Stevenson had a second talk with Mr. Thant early tonight. Joseph V. Charyk, Under Secretary of the Air Force, accompanied him, leading to the supposition that United States aerial reconnaissance might supplement United Nations inspections.

Reliable sources said that Mr. Stevenson had given Mr. Thant a letter from President Kennedy that apparently answered a letter sent to the President by Mr. Thant earlier in the day. It was understood that the letters dealt with arrangements for the observation.

Although long negotiations are ahead, Mr. Thant's decision to visit Cuba to discuss arrangements was welcomed by delegates as a sign that the danger of a war over Cuba was ended. Only yesterday, many believed that an air attack on the missile bases was imminent.

The delegates were cheerful today despite the fact that Mr. Thant's inspection program does not yet provide for naval inspections to assure that no additional offensive weapons are sent to Cuba.

Castro Changes Stand

Premier Castro had previously followed the traditional Soviet-bloc position of refusal to permit United Nations observers. A major change in his position came yesterday, when he invited Mr. Thant to visit "with a view to direct discussions on the present crisis, prompted by our common purpose of freeing mankind from the dangers of war."

Further according to reliable sources, Mr. Garcia-Inchaustegui gave Mr. Thant an oral assurance yesterday that anyone the Acting Secretary General brought with him to Cuba would be welcome.

In addition to Brigadier Rikhye, Mr. Thant will take with him Omar Loufti of the United Arab Republic, Under Secretary for Special Political Affairs; and Hernane Tavares de Sá of Brazil, the ranking Latin-American official on the Secretariat, who is Under Secretary for Political Information.

Brigadier Rikhye and Mr. Loufti have been present at almost all the discussions between Mr. Thant and the United States, Soviet and Cuban representatives in the crisis.

Mr. Thant has not, according to reliable sources, decided whether there will be one committee or commission to direct the observers, or two. He is said to believe that the 50 or more neutralist members of the United Nations, who made the original request that he intervene, should be represented.

Mr. Thant's planning is believed to be based on the thought that no missiles experts will be needed because of Mr. Khrushchev's promise to dismantle the missiles and ship them back to the Soviet Union.

The task of verification would therefore be entrusted to officers from the rank of army captain up, who would inspect the sites.

Aerial photographs supplied by the United States will be used to find the missiles.

* * *

October 29, 1962

RUSSIAN ACCEDES

Tells President Work on Bases Is Halted—Invites Talks

By SEYMOUR TOPPING
Special to The New York Times.

MOSCOW, Oct. 28—Preier Khrushchev agreed today to end the construction of Soviet bases in Cuba and to dismantle Soviet rockets there, both under United Nations supervision.

In a message to Present Kennedy, the Soviet leader said that he already had issued instructions for this and for crating and returning the rockets to the Soviet Union.

This was said to have been done in return for the commitments offered in a letter sent to Mr. Khrushchev yesterday by President Kennedy. The letter expressed the United States' readiness to lift the naval quarantine of Cuba and join with other nations of the Western Hemisphere in providing assurances against an invasion of the island.

Offer of Talks Welcomed

Mr. Khrushchev's message, which was broadcast at 5 P. M. Moscow time, indicated unconditional acceptance of the measures stipulated by the President to bar offensive Soviet weapons from Cuba.

The Premier also welcomed the readiness of President Kennedy to discuss a détente, or relaxation of tension, between the nations of the North Atlantic Treaty Organization and its East European Communist counterpart, the Warsaw Pact organization.

The Russian leader insisted that Soviet weapons had been introduced in Cuba solely for the defense of the island. He added that, in view of the assurances of the President, "the motives which induced us to render assistance of such a kind to Cuba would disappear."

There was no mention in the Khrushchev message of the proposal made in the Premier's communication of yesterday to the President. Mr. Khrushchev then offered to withdraw Soviet weapons from Cuba, but in exchange for similar action by the United States in respect to Turkey, where a missile base of the North Atlantic Treaty Organization is maintained.

Western observers here believe that Mr. Khrushchev's letter represents a retreat on the Cuban issue that may have profound repercussions.

The manner in which this question has been handled, the clandestine installation of the missile bases to their withdrawal under United States pressure, was regarded as likely to damage Soviet prestige abroad and possibly affect the internal political position of the present Soviet leadership.

Premier Khrushchev and the other leading members of the Soviet Presidium appeared tonight at a performance of the touring Bulgarian Dramatic Theater. The Moscow broadcast at 10 P.M. (2 P. M. Eastern standard time) the text of President Kennedy's statement welcoming "Chairman Khrushchev's statesmanlike decision."

Mr. Khrushchev said in his letter that he had instructed Vasily V. Kuznetsov, the Deputy Foreign Minister, to proceed to New York to discuss the details of an agreement with U Thant, Acting Secretary General of the United Nations, and the delegates of the United States and Cuba.

Both Mr. Khrushchev and Mr. Kennedy have said that detailed arrangements of the agreement on Cuba should be settled in New York within a few days.

Air Intrusion Charged

Mr. Khrushchev complained in his letter that a United States reconnaissance plane violated Soviet territory today. He said that it had flown over the Chukchi peninsula in northeast Siberia opposite Alaska.

Reminding the President that the Soviet Union in the present situation was in a state of combat readiness, the Premier asked if it was not a fact that an intruding American plane could easily be mistaken for a nuclear bomber.

Mr. Khrushchev recalled the Soviet downing on May 1, 1960, of the U-2 reconnaissance plane piloted by Francis Gary Powers. He said that incident had wrecked the Paris summit conference.

The Premier called the President's attention to his statement upon assuming office that he would continue the ban on overflights imposed by the Eisenhower Administration after the original U-2 incident. Mr. Khrushchev then cited the flight by a U-2 last Aug. 31 over Sakhalin Island off Siberia, north of Japan.

Mr. Khrushchev cautioned Mr. Kennedy about the dangers involved in further overflights.

"I should ask you to correctly appraise this and to take appropriate measures to prevent this from becoming a provocation for touching off a war," he declared.

He also asked President Kennedy to halt the United States flights over Cuba.

Protest Considered Mild

Mr. Khrushchev's complaint about a new violation of Soviet airspace was mild in comparison with his angry denunciations of the United States in the earlier incidents. This was in keeping with the entire tone of his message to the President.

In urging that the present tense atmosphere be dispelled, Mr. Krushchev said, "We should also make sure that no other dangerous conflicts which could lead the world to nuclear catastrophe should arise."

This was interpreted here in the first instance as an allusion to the problem of Berlin, which Mr. Krushchev did not specifically mention in his message.

In welcoming Mr. Kennedy's interest in exchanges on an East-West détente, Mr. Khrushchev said, "We should like to continue the exchange of views on the prohibition of atomic and thermonuclear weapons on general disarmament and other problems relating to the relaxation of international tension."

Mr. Khrushchev did not give any hint as to the manner in which he would like to continue these exchanges with the President. There has been no reference in the Premier's public statement to a summit meeting since his message of Thursday to Bertrand Russell, the British pacifist leader. He said in that message that he thought a summit meeting would be useful.

Western officials here considered it possible that Mr. Khrushchev might elect to attend the United Nations General Assembly in late November or December and then meet with President Kennedy to discuss Berlin and other problems.

The ramifications of the events of the last week have been unfortunate for the Soviet Government in terms of foreign policy and in the ideological struggle to win over the non-aligned nations and has diminished the stature of the present leadership in the estimate of the Soviet people, observers here believe.

In terms of foreign policy, Western observers do not expect that much credence will be given to Mr. Khrushchev's assertion that the missile bases were established in Cuba solely for the defense of that island. The offensive weapons there included medium and intermediate missiles with ranges up to 2,000 miles and also jet bombers capable of carrying nuclear bombs.

President Kennedy in a statement on Sept. 4 and again on Sept. 13 declared that the United States would not take military action in respect to Cuba unless it was discovered that "significant offensive capability" was being supplied to the Castro regime by the Soviet Union. The President said this would be regarded as a threat to the security of the United States and the hemisphere.

The President announced on Monday that such offensive capability had been discovered in Cuba in the form of Soviet missile bases that were then in the process of hasty construction. In the view of Western diplomats here, the Soviet military preparations in Cuba had invited United States action against the island rather than serving to deter it.

Mr. Khrushchev's proposal yesterday to give up his bases in Cuba if the United States would withdraw its missiles from Turkey also indicated that they had been placed there for something more than the defense of the Caribbean island, these diplomats consider.

The abrupt manner in which the proposal about Turkey was dropped after it had been rejected by President Kennedy was regarded as humiliating for Moscow.

It was the opinion of senior Western diplomats here that the original decision to place missile bases in Cuba was taken in the hope of being able to use them as bargaining counters in an even more ambitious bid, possibly affecting Berlin.

It is not yet clear what Moscow may have to pay for its decision to withdraw in terms of its relations with the Castro regime. Mr. Khrushchev reiterated tonight Moscow's intention to continue economic assistance to Cuba and to defend the interests of the Castro regime.

However, Soviet news media did not distribute the part of Premier Castro's statement in which he demanded the evacuation of the United States Naval base at Guantanamo.

In his message to Mr. Kennedy yesterday, the Soviet Premier said that verification by United Nations inspection would have to be approved by the Cuban Government. It was believed here that the flying trip of Mr. Thant to Havana may be designed primarily to deal with this problem.

*   *   *

October 29, 1962

CAPITAL HOPEFUL

Plans to End Blockade as Soon as Moscow Lives Up to Vow

By E. W. KENWORTHY
Special to The New York Times.
WASHINGTON, Oct. 28—President Kennedy and Premier Khrushchev reached apparent agreement today on a formula to end the crisis over Cuba and to begin talks on easing tensions in other areas.

Premier Khrushchev pledged the Soviet Union to stop work on its missile sites in Cuba, to dismantle the weapons and to crate them and take them home. All this would be done under verification of United Nations representatives.

President Kennedy, for his part, pledged the lifting of the Cuban arms blockade when the United Nations had taken the "necessary measures," and that the United States would not invade Cuba.

U. S. Conditions Met

Essentially this formula meets the conditions that President Kennedy set for the beginning of talks. If it is carried out, it would achieve the objective of the President in establishing the blockade last week: the removal of the Soviet missile bases in Cuba.

While officials were gratified at the agreement reached on United States terms, there was no sense either of triumph or jubilation. The agreement, they realized, was only the beginning. The terms of it were not nailed down and Soviet negotiators were expected to arrive at the United Nations with a "bag full of fine print."

Although Mr. Khrushchev mentioned verification of the dismantling by United Nations observers in today's note, sources here do not consider it unlikely that the Russians may suggest that the observers be under the procedures of the Security Council.

This would make their findings subject to a veto by the Soviet Union as one of the 11 members of the Council.

No Big Gains Envisioned

United States officials did not expect a Cuban settlement, if it materialized, to lead to any great breakthroughs on such problems as inspection for a nuclear test ban and disarmament.

On the other hand, it was thought possible that a Cuban settlement might set a precedent for limited reciprocal concessions in some areas.

The break in the crisis came dramatically early this morning after a night of steadily mounting fears that events were running ahead of diplomatic efforts to control them.

The break came with the arrival of a letter from Premier Khrushchev in which the Soviet leader again changed his course.

Friday night Mr. Khrushchev had sent a lengthy private letter to the President. Deep in it was the suggestion that the Soviet Union could remove its missiles from Cuba under supervision and not replace them if the United States would lift the blockade and give assurances that United States and other Western Hemisphere nations would not invade Cuba.

The President found this proposal generally acceptable and yesterday morning his aides were preparing a private reply when the Moscow radio broadcast the text of another letter that was on its way.

The second letter proposed that the Soviet Union remove its missiles from Cuba in return for the dismantling of United States missiles in Turkey. This was advanced as an equitable exchange.

Fearing that it would be viewed in this light by many neutral nations, the White House immediately postponed a reply to the first letter and issued a statement on the second.

The White House said that the "first imperative" was the removal of the threat of Soviet missiles. The United States would not consider "any proposals" until work was stopped on the Cuban bases, the weapons were "rendered inoperable" and further shipments of them were halted.

Then White House aides turned back to drafting a reply to the first letter. They hoped to persuade Mr. Khrushchev to stand by his first offer.

The President accepted the first Khrushchev proposal as the basis for beginning talks but he planted in it two warnings which, the White House hoped, would not be lost upon Khrushchev.

Threat of Action Noted

First, he said the arrangement for putting into effect the Krushchev plan could be completed in—"a couple of days"—a warning that the United States could take action to halt the work on the missile bases if Mr. Khrushchev did not order it stopped.

Second, the President said that if the work continued or Mr. Khrushchev linked Cuba with broader questions of European security, the Cuban crisis would be intensified.

Just before 9 o'clock this morning the Moscow radio said there would be an important announcement on the hour. It turned out to be a reply to Mr. Kennedy's letter of the night before.

Mr. Khrushchev said that in order to "complete with greater speed the liquidation of the conflict dangerous to the cause of peace," the Soviet Government ordered work stopped on bases in Cuba and the dismantling, crating and return of the missiles.

Mr. Khrushchev said he trusted that, in return, "no attack will be made on Cuba—that no invasion will take place not only by the United States, but also by other countries of the Western Hemisphere."

Kuznetzov to Negotiate

Mr. Khrushchev said that he was sending Vassily V. Kuznetzov, a First Deputy Foreign Minister to the United Nations to conduct negotiations for the Soviet Union. He arrived in New York tonight.

Without waiting for the formal delivery of the letter, the President issued a statement at noon, saying he welcomed Chairman Khrushchev's statesmanlike "decision" as an important and constructive contribution to peace.

Shortly before the statement was issued, the President flew by helicopter to Glen Ora his country home in Middleburg, Va., to have lunch and he spent most of the afternoon with his wife and children.

All the communications this week between the two leaders—and there have been several more than have been made public—have been sent by the usual diplomatic route. First, they have been delivered to the Embassies, there translated, and send to the State Department or the Soviet Foreign office for delivery to Mr. Kennedy or Mr. Khrushchev.

Process Too Slow

This is a time-consuming process and late this afternoon, the last section of Mr. Khrushchev's letter had not yet arrived at the White House when it was decided to make the President's reply public and speed it on its way.

The President said that he welcomed Mr. Khrushchev's message because "developments were approaching a point where events could have become manageable."

Mr. Kennedy said:

"I think that you and I, with our heavy responsibilities for the maintenance of peace, were aware that developments were approaching a point where events could have become unmanageable. So I welcome this message and consider it an important contribution to peace."

He also stated that he regarded his letter of the night before and the Premier's reply as "firm undertakings" which both governments should carry out "promptly."

The President hoped that the "necessary measures" could be taken "at once" through the United Nations so that the quarantine could be removed on shipping.

All these matters, the President said, would be reported to memders of the Organization of American States, who "share a deep interest in a genuine peace in the Caribbean area."

And the President echoed Mr. Khrushchev's hope that the two nations could now turn their attention to disarmament, "as it relates to the whole world and also to critical areas."

The President by tonight had not named the negotiator for the United States, but it was reported by authoritative sources that Adlai E. Stevenson, the head of the United States delegation at the United Nations, would get the assignment. The talks are expected to begin soon, probably tomorrow.

A spokesman at the State Department said in reply to questions:

"The quarantine remains in effect but we don't anticipate any problems of interception since there are no ships moving into the quarantine area that appear to be carrying cargoes on the contraband list."

Fears About Castro

There was also some concern that Premier Fidel Castro, out of chagrin, might cause incidents over the United States surveillance flights.

Officials here believed that Dr. Castro was making a major effort to bring in extraneous issues, such as the evacuation of the United States base at Guantanamo, to salvage his prestige.

However, the United States was not prepared to deal over the base, and the feeling here was that no other matters except the President's guarantee not to invade could be discussed until the dismantling of the missiles had been verified.

Officials emphasized today, as they reflected on the events of the week, that at all times the White House was trying to keep things on the track. At no time, they insisted, was any ultimatum delivered to Mr. Khrushchev, although he was made to understand that the missiles would be destroyed unless they were removed in a short time.

*   *   *

November 2, 1962

CASTRO REFUSES ANY INSPECTIONS, SAYS ROCKETS ARE BEING REMOVED; THANT HAS A PLAN; MIKOYAN HERE

CUBAN HEAD FIRM

In Havana Broadcast, He Rejects Soviet's Compromise Plan

Special to The New York Times.

WASHINGTON, Nov. 1—Premier Fidel Castro announced tonight Cuba's rejection of any form of international inspection on the withdrawal of Soviet missiles.

In a radio and television speech to the Cuban people, monitored here, Dr. Castro specifically turned down a Soviet compromise proposal that the International Red Cross Committee carry out the inspection task.

But he said that "if we have any misunderstandings with the Soviets they must be discussed only among the principals and not before the world."

The original Soviet proposal, contained in Premier Khrushchev's message to President Kennedy last Sunday, was for United Nations inspection of the withdrawal.

He Emphasizes Trust

Despite his rejection of the first and then the subsequent Soviet proposals on inspection, Dr. Castro made a point of saying that "we trust the principles of the policy of the Soviet Union."

"Between the Soviet Union and Cuba there will never be a breach," he said near the end of his speech, which ran an hour and 22 minutes.

Dr. Castro also rejected an alternative proposal for United Nations aerial inspections to determine that the missile bases had been dismantled.

Further, Dr. Castro remarked that the missiles sent to Cuba were Moscow's and accordingly Moscow had the "right" to withdraw them.

Dr. Castro told his audience that U Thant, Acting Secretary General of the United Nations, presented the inspection proposal to him at their first meeting in Havana Tuesday.

Issue of Ship Inspections

Premier Castro said that, according to Mr. Thant, the Soviet Union had also offered to agree to United Nations inspection of Soviet ships on the high seas along with the inspection of such ships in Cuban ports by the Red Cross.

But, Dr. Castro said, if Moscow agreed to inspection of ships on the high seas, there should be no need for inspection in Cuban ports.

From the notes read rapidly by Premier Castro, it appeared that this Soviet proposal related to inspection of ships bound for Cuba rather than ships outbound from Cuba.

Premier Castro's remarks appeared to set the stage for the arrival in Havana tomorrow from New York of Anastas I. Mikoyan, a Soviet First Deputy Premier.

The Cuban leader said that "we respect the Soviet decision to withdraw their strategic weapons" and stressed that no obstacles were being placed against their removal. The missiles were "not our property" he remarked and, therefore "we have no reason to be discontented."

Under the applause of the audience, Premier Castro declared that Cubans were grateful "friends of the Soviet Union" and pledged that there "never will be a breach between Cuba and the Soviet Union."

It was the first time that such a possibility has been mentioned publicly in Cuba since Premier Khrushchev's proposal last Sunday that the missiles be withdrawn under United Nations inspection.

"We do not accept the inspection demands," Dr. Castro said, adding that Cubans would be humiliated by such a procedure.

Discussion With Thant

The Cuban Premier read on his broadcast the entire text of the conversation between him and Mr. Thant during their first conference Tuesday. He explained that he could not read the minutes of yesterday's second and final meeting because of certain "confidential matters" that the United Nations official had discussed with him.

The Premier added that he had informed the Acting Secretary General that the Soviet pledge on withdrawing the missiles "should be enough."

"We are not placing obstacles on the withdrawal of these arms," Dr. Castro disclosed. "The Soviet decision was serious and the arms are being withdrawn."

But he shouted that "if the United States also wants to humiliate us, it will not succeed."

"It cannot impose upon us conditions that are imposed on defeated nations," he said. "First, they will have to destroy us."

His Conditions to U.S.

Dr. Castro made clear that he was rejecting all the inspection demands outright and that he was not conditioning their acceptance on the approval by the United States of his "five points."

These points include the United States' evacuation of its naval base at Guantanamo Bay and a Washington pledge to discontinue all pressures on Cuba including the current air surveillance.

Throughout his talk with Mr. Thant, Dr. Castro insisted that it was impossible to separate the immediate problem of Cuba from long-range aspects.

These long-range aspects, he said, were the guarantees that Cuba would be left to live in peace.

Mr. Thant told Dr. Castro—according to the minutes of the meeting read by the Premier—that he had been authorized by the Security Council to discuss only the immediate problem of the withdrawal of the missiles.

Mr. Thant said, however, that he understood that the immediate and the long-range problems were linked.

According to Dr. Castro the explanation of the inspection procedure outlined by Mr. Thant called for its operation in a period of two or three weeks.

Thant's Proposals

Mr. Thant said that the United States was anxious to have assurances that the bases were being dismantled and the equipment shipped out.

He said that Monday night he had communicated with the headquarters of the International Red Cross Committee in Geneva and received its agreement to take over the inspection.

Mr. Thant stressed that the Soviet proposal for the Red Cross verification was conditioned on the Cuban acceptance of it and that he was putting it forth in the same manner.

In replying to Mr. Thant, Premier Castro asked, "What right has the United States to ask us to submit to inspection?"

Speaking of Mr. Thant's statement that the United States would make a "no invasion" pledge in the Security Council, after the inspection machinery was established, Dr. Castro said that the United States "has no right to invade Cuba and we cannot negotiate on the basis of a promise that crime will not be committed."

Dr. Castro made what amounted to an admission that the United States reconnaissance aircraft lost over Cuba last Saturday was shot down by Cuban defenses.

He said that Cuba would return the body of the pilot Maj. Rudolf Anderson Jr., who died while "making an illegal flight" over Cuba.

"The American had to die in our country in an action that was a violation of our rights," Dr. Castro said, "and I hope this will not be repeated."

The entire concluding section of Dr. Castro's speech was devoted to Cuba's relations with the Soviet Union and to his explanation that Moscow "had the right to take away the weapons that were theirs."

He said that Cubans were "Marxist-Leninists" and that "we are friends of the Soviet Union."

"We respect the Soviet decision to withdraw their strategic weapons," he said.

"There are those who say we are not in agreement any more with the Soviet," Dr. Castro said, "but if we have misunderstandings with the Soviets it must be discussed only among the principals.

"These international problems which are difficult and delicate cannot be discussed in public."

"There is time for ample discussion," he went on, "and the enemy must not gain by our impatience or lack of judgment. We must have firmness, confidence and faith.

"With these misunderstandings it is important to remember what the Soviet has done for us and we thank him [Premier Khrushchev] for it."

Dr. Castro said the Soviet Union had given Cuba arms "and did not charge us for it."

"Their military technicians taught us how to build a strong fighting force," he said.

"The missiles were not Cuba's. They were not our property. We have no reason to be discontented. We must remember their generosity!

"We must respect them, thank them, be grateful to them for all they have done for us," he said.

*　　*　　*

November 9, 1962

U.S. FINDS BASES IN CUBA STRIPPED, MISSILES ON SHIPS

Pentagon Says Photographs Show 'All Known' Sites Have Been Dismantled

SOME VESSELS DEPART

Navy Will Confirm Removal in 'Alongside Observation' With Soviet Approval

---

By MAX FRANKEL
Special to The New York Times.

WASHINGTON, Nov. 8—The United States announced this evening that "all known" offensive-missile bases in Cuba had been dismantled.

A statement issued through the Defense Department said the Government had photographic evidence that "significant" items of equipment from the bases had been moved to port areas, that a "substantial" number of missiles had been

Defense Department via Associated Press Wirephoto

The Defense Department identified this vessel, with two laden missile carriers on afterdeck, as the "Divnogorsk."

loaded onto the main decks of several Soviet cargo vessels and that some of these vessels had already left Cuban ports.

Additional confirmation that missile equipment is being removed from Cuba will become available within 24 hours, the department said, when Navy ships conduct "close alongside observation" of the outbound Soviet ships.

Russians to Cooperate

By agreement the statement added the Soviet vessel "will cooperate in this procedure."

The Pentagon also made public some photographs that it said showed Soviet ships loading missile equipment in Cuba and three ships bearing 18 medium-range missiles from Cuba.

Premier Khrushchev said yesterday the Soviet Union had sent 40 missiles to the island. United States experts are looking for the departure of a total of 42 or 43—all medium range weapons with a range estimated at 1,200 miles.

Both medium-range and intermediate-range missile sites have been dismantled, the Pentagon said. Government sources never said that any intermediate-range weapons, with ranges up to 2,500 miles, had reached Cuba before President Kennedy stopped the build-up with a naval blockade Oct. 24.

Bombers Not Mentioned

The Defense Department statement said nothing about removal of IL-28 jet bombers from Cuba. Thus far, sources explained, the Soviet Union has refused to accept United States contentions that these are "offensive weapons" of the type Premier Khrushchev agreed to remove.

At the same time, the Russians are believed to have worked hurriedly to turn over control of the bombers to Cuban authorities.

The Pentagon announcement came at the end of a day of considerable confusion about the state of negotiations with the Soviet Union on removal of the weapons and about the nature of the "verification" and "inspection" that the United States would demand before it canceled the blockade.

Ability to Get Evidence

The purpose of the Defense Department statement was to demonstrate that the United States was able to gather its own evidence on the disposition of Soviet weapons in Cuba. The President said last Friday that this evidence would be gathered "through a variety of means, including aerial surveillance."

In view of this evidence, officials here attached no major intelligence significance to the planned "observation" of departing Soviet vessels at sea. The Russians have agreed that they would cooperate with this until Monday, by which time sources here estimate all the Soviet missiles will have moved out of Cuban waters.

What other importance may be attached to the "observation" arrangement was more difficult to determine. As far as is known, it will involve tying a Soviet cargo ship to an American naval ship only briefly for a "count" of the missiles lying on deck under canvas.

This arrangement, officials said, was the only definitive one established so far by Soviet, Cuban and American negotiators.

They have been trying to find means to carry out Premier Khrushchev's promise to the President that all weapons that Mr. Kennedy regarded as offensive would be promptly taken out of Cuba with United Nations "verification" of the removal.

Premier Fidel Castro has thus far refused to permit any inspection of Cuba. Anastas I. Mikoyan, a Soviet First Deputy Premier, who has conferred with Dr. Castro in Havana for the last week, apparently has not been able or willing to obtain a change in the Cuban's attitude.

A growing impression here was that the Russians were now preparing to adopt a new negotiating position, possibly when Mr. Mikoyan returned from Havana in the next day or two.

It would be that Moscow has fulfilled its part of the bargain because, first, the United States had "counted out" and conceded the removal of all missiles from Cuba, and, secondly, that the bombers still in Cuba had been sold to the Castro Government.

Technicians Leaving

Some Soviet technicians and their families are also leaving Cuba and accompanying the missiles back to Russia.

But it could not be determined how many of the 5,000 Soviet military personnel who have reached the island in recent months were departing.

The Pentagon released today various photographs showing Soviet ships engaged in the transfer of missiles and missile-launching equipment back to the Soviet Union.

The photographs released by the Defense Department were in two sets. Some showed dock activity at the port of Mariel, west of Havana, on Nov. 1, 4 and 5, with missiles being loaded onto three Soviet cargo ships.

The other set showed various views of two of these vessels plus a third at sea. Four missile transporters—a kind of trailer—each with a canvas-covered missile were shown lashed to the deck of one of the vessels on Tuesday, a day after she sailed from Cuba.

Six missiles were shown aboard the Fizik Kurchatov on her day of sailing yesterday.

Eight missiles were photographed aboard the Anosov, which sailed Tuesday and was photographed yesterday.

One of the Soviet vessels was identified by the Defense Department as the Divnogorsk. Lloyd's Register does not list a Russian ship of that name but does list the Dvinogorsk, a Soviet ship of 6,900 gross tons.

Sailing of 400 Reported

HAVANA, Nov 8 (Reuters)—Diplomatic sources here reported today 400 Soviet technicians had sailed from Cuba recently. They also said they knew three days ago that Soviet equipment was being loaded at the port of Mariel, 20 miles west of Havana.

Meanwhile, a Government official announced that six foreign journalists, held incommunicado since their arrival here last week, would be expelled tomorrow.

*　*　*

December 7, 1962

U.S. MAY ABANDON SKYBOLT MISSILE

British Were to Have Used the Air-to-Ground Weapon—
Controversy Expected

By JACK RAYMOND
Special to The New York Times.

WASHINGTON, Dec. 6—The Kennedy Administration has decided that the Air Force does not need the Skybolt ballistic missile as a strategic weapon. The Air Force disagrees. Thus another major public controversy over a military weapon is in prospect.

The Skybolt was designed as a 1,000-mile, nuclear-tipped missile to be launched from high speed bombers against ground targets.

The Air Force has been told that the Skybolt is not needed because the land-based Minuteman intercontinental ballistic missile, soon to be declared ready for operation, can reach any Skybolt target from underground launching silos in the United States.

There was speculation that an announcement of the Minuteman's readiness would come tomorrow, during President Kennedy's tour of military bases.

The British Royal Air Force as well as the United States air arm had been counting on the Skybolt. Britain has a number of the missiles on order for delivery in 1964.

In fact, the British said in 1960 that they were abandoning their own Blue Streak land-based missile in favor of the United States-made Skybolt.

Secretary of Defense Robert S. McNamara is planning to fly to Britain Monday to discuss the future of the Skybolt, among other defense matters, with British Defense Minister Peter Thorneycroft.

Secretary McNamara will attend the semiannual ministers meeting of the North Atlantic treaty council in Paris Dec. 13-15.

His advance meeting with British officials probably would have been scheduled regardless of the latest Skybolt decision, qualified sources said.

Now, however, complicated arrangements may be required to protect the British interest in the weapon. Mr. McNamara is expected to suggest to Britain that it may have to take over the cost of the Skybolt program.

The United States has appropriated about $500,000,000 for the Skybolt, the total development and production cost of which has been estimated at $1,000,000,000.

Britain was reported recently to have agreed to spend $20,000,000 on the missile. She has established a training base of British military men, accompanied by their families, to carry out development tests at Eglin Air Force Base in Florida.

According to a qualified source, the Administration's budget to be presented to Congress next January will request no new appropriations for the missile.

Thus, while some further spending on research and development may be carried out with earlier appropriations, production of the weapon, originally scheduled for 1964, appears to be ruled out.

It was pointed out that by that time, the Polaris submarine-launched missile and intercontinental ballistics missiles would fulfill all requirements for long-range weapons.

May Seek a Reversal

Unless the Air Force can win a reversal of the decision that the Skybolt is not needed in the United States strategic arsenal, the weapon's future may be similar to that of the Thor and Jupiter intermediate-range ballistic missiles.

The liquid-fueled rockets were developed expressly for European sites, because their range of about 1,600 miles did not make them feasible as United States-based weapons.

The missiles were based in Britain, Italy and Turkey. The Thors in Britain are being withdrawn, however, in anticipation of the Skybolt deliveries.

The British Government recently has been questioned in the House of Commons about reports that the Skybolt program was in doubt.

British spokesmen insisted, however, that they must act on the assumption that United States-British agreements for deliveries of the Skybolt would be carried out.

Qualified sources here pointed out, nevertheless, that the elimination of the Skybolt from United States strategic requirements would put another light on the situation.

In addition to the Skybolt, Mr. McNamara is expected to discuss with the British their over-all contribution to Western defense. He is believed prepared to press the British hard to increase their military expenditures.

But he will not single out the British alone, it was noted here. He has prepared a broad demand for presentation at the Atlantic pact meeting for a greater defense effort on the part of all the allies, especially to build up ground forces in Europe.

Meanwhile, Air Force officials here are despondent over the decision on the Skybolt. The weapon was hailed in an official "fact sheet" as heralding "a new era of global mobility."

Air Force strategists pointed out it would enable bombers to hover out of range of enemy antiaircraft rockets, while launching nuclear-armed missiles to a target "over 1,000 miles away."

In addition, Air Force sources pointed out that the Skybolt was intended to extend the life of the country's jet bomber force, particularly the B-52s. Both the B-52 and B-58 assembly lines were shut down last summer and the follow-on aircraft, the RS-70, is now given a dim chance for final adoption.

Thus, it was pointed out, with no new bombers in production, the Skybolt was considered to be an important weapon strategically as well as technologically.

Officials and scientists of the Defense Department took another view however. According to an authoritative source, the Air Force was told that the Minuteman intercontinental ballistic missile could hit any of the targets that were being considered for the Skybolt.

The first Minuteman is expected to be declared ready for operation shortly. President Kennedy is scheduled to visit Strategic Air Command headquarters at Offut Air Force Base, Omaha, Neb., tomorrow.

It is believed possible that he may announce the operational status of the first 6,300-mile solid fuel Minuteman at Great Falls, Mont. In any event, the speculation indicated the imminence of the event.

The Douglas Aircraft Company is the prime contractor for the skybolt. It has been working on it since May 26, 1959, when it received the first development contract.

Army Drops Program

FORT HUACHUCA, Ariz., Dec. 6 (AP)—The Army announced today that it was dropping a program on which $86,000,000 already had been spent.

In a statement the Army said the action was being taken because production costs for the SD5 jet drone program would be more than had been anticipated. The SD5 contract was held by Fairchild Stratus Corporation of Hagerstown, Md.

* * *

December 19, 1962

KENNEDY CONFERS WITH MACMILLAN TO NARROW RIFTS

Skybolt Dispute and Congo Put at Top of Agenda in Nassau Talk Today

ISLAND HAILS LEADERS

President and Briton Plan to Review Post-Cuba Stance Toward Soviet Union

By WALLACE CARROLL
Special to The New York Times.

NASSAU, the Bahamas, Dec. 18—President Kennedy arrived here today for two days of intensive talks with an aroused British ally.

Prime Minister Macmillan, who arrived here from London last night, was at the airport to greet the President as he came down the ramp from his blue and silver jet.

The sun glinted on the bayonets of the color guard, the flags of the two nations snapped in the breeze and a delighted crowd of Bahamians and tourists cheered as the President and Prime Minister spoke warm familiar words of Anglo-American comradeship.

All this masked for a moment the sobering fact that because of the differences between the two nations over development of the Skybolt ballistic missile, the future of Britain as an independent nuclear power is at stake in the talks.

Many Issues Involved

So, too, is the future of the Anglo-American alliance, which has had a decisive influence on the course of world affairs during 20 years of war and uncertain peace.

Also involved, perhaps, are the political fortunes of Mr. Macmillan and the Conservative party for unless the Prime Minister can return home with a satisfactory assurance that the United States will continue to help Britain maintain a strong nuclear deterrent, the underpinnings of British foreign policy and strategy will be badly shaken.

Tonight, after a first informal meeting of the President and the Prime Minister, United States officials said that Skybolt and the threat of chaos in the Congo would be the first subjects for discussion tomorrow when two days of more formal meetings will begin.

This crisis in Anglo-American relations arises because of a decision by the Kennedy Administration that the Skybolt is not needed by the United States Air Force. If this decision is maintained, Britain would either have to pursue the development and production of the missile alone or abandon its plans for an airborne nuclear striking force that would keep Britain in the "nuclear club" until the early Nineteen-Seventies.

Failure in 5 Tests

The Skybolt, which is still under development in the United States, is a ballistic missile designed to be carried under the wings of jet bombers and fired at distances of 1,000 miles from the target.

The idea was that such a missile would prolong the effective life of the B-52 bombers, which otherwise could deliver their nuclear bombloads only by piercing the increasingly effective anti-aircraft defenses of the enemy country.

Britain wanted the Skybolt because it would similarly prolong the usefulness of the Vulcan bombers of the Royal Air Force. On the assumption that the Skybolt would be effective and ready for delivery in 1965, Mr. Macmillan's government abandoned plans for land-based and airborne missiles of British design. It did this in the face of warnings from the Labor party that Skybolt probably would not work and that the Americans would renege on delivery of the weapon.

Now, after the commitment of about $375,000,000 for research and development, five unsuccessful tests have been run on the Skybolt. At the same time, the Atlas and Minuteman intercontinental missiles have become operational from bases in the United States and increasing numbers of Polaris missiles have become available for firing from nuclear submarines.

President Kennedy and Secretary of Defense Robert S. McNamara have therefore decided that the Skybolt is no longer needed and that the money and technical skill that its perfection would require can best be spent on other weapons.

The British, however, were counting entirely on Skybolt as their strategic deterrent. In their dismay at the prospect that the United States would cancel its part in the program, some British spokesmen have been threatening to deprive the United States of its nuclear submarine base in Scotland and even predicting the collapse of the alliance.

United States officials pointed out today that the British were free to continue with the Skybolt program if they chose, taking advantage of the substantial expenditure already made by the United States.

These officials estimated that for about $200,000,000 the British might be able to complete the development of the missile. Several hundred million dollars more would then be required to buy 100 missiles to arm the Vulcan bombers.

Questions for Review

The difficulties over Skybolt and the worry over the Congo have complicated what was to have been a board review of three broad questions:

The future of Europe and particularly the difficulties Britain is encountering in her effort to gain admittance to the Common Market.

How to deal with the Soviet Union in view of the setback in Cuba and the difficulties with the Chinese Communists. Here, the two sides intended to discuss the negotiations with the Soviet Union for a nuclear test ban, the possibility of getting an agreement on measures to prevent surprise attacks, and whether to take an initiative on the Berlin question or wait for the Russians to press the issue.

The coordination of Anglo-American efforts to help India improve her defenses against further Chinese attacks.

The ceremony at the airport carried no hint of impending difficulty, even though the Nassau police band played between two renditions of the Star Spangled Banner and a tune called "Early in the Morning," which tells the story of a girl who is about to be deserted by her lover.

While this was going on, President Kennedy inspected the honor guard provided by the Nassau police.

The guard was composed entirely of Bahamian Negroes wearing white pith helmets with brass spokes, white tunics and black trousers with red stripes. All of them were as well attired as members of a British guards regiment. And they marched with the same swinging stride.

Welcomed by Premier

After the inspection, Mr. Macmillan made a short welcoming speech in which he recalled that this was his sixteenth meeting with an American President.

In response, Mr. Kennedy said that this was his sixth meeting with the Prime Minister. He went on to say that if the world was not the better for their five previous encounters, "I feel that at least, as President, I have been better off."

They then drove ten miles to the west end of the island of New Providence, past pink stucco villas under green palm trees, over roads flanked by walls over which pink and scarlet Bougainvillea tumbled in profusion.

At the end of their drive, they entered Lyford Cay, an isolated peninsula on which E. P. Taylor, a Canadian brewer, has developed a planned residential community of about 4,000 acres.

Mr. Kennedy is staying at the home of Mr. Taylor. Prime Minister Macmillan is staying next door at Bali Hai, the home of Mrs. Robert Holt of Montreal. Cabinet members of the two countries and other advisers are staying in Lyford Cay Club.

They include, for the United States, Under Secretary of State George Ball; Mr. McNamara; McGeorge Bundy, special assistant to the President for national security affairs; Llewellyn E. Thompson, former Ambassador to the Soviet Union and adviser on Soviet affairs, and David Bruce, Ambassador to London.

The British side includes the Foreign Secretary Lord Home, Secretary of Defense Peter Throneycroft, and Secretary of Commonwealth Affairs Duncan Sandys.

*   *   *

December 19, 1962

103 TORIES BID MACMILLAN PROTECT NUCLEAR STRENGTH

By DREW MIDDLETON
Special to The New York Times.

LONDON, Dec. 18—A Conservative attempt to put Prime Minister Macmillan on a spot much less pleasant than Nassau in the Bahamas gathered momentum today. A total of 103 conservative members of Parliament, nearly one-third of the

parliamentary body, now has signed a motion urging him to ensure in his talks with President Kennedy that Britain remains an independent nuclear power.

The motion says that "this house wishes the Prime Minister and his ministerial colleagues a successful outcome to their Nassau discussions with the President of the United States of America, with particular reference to this country's determination to retain its own nuclear deterrent within the Western alliance."

The inference drawn by politicians of all parties is that the important section of the Conservative party has told the Prime Minister it wants either the Skybolt missile, whose development the United States wants to discontinue, or a substitute that will enable the United Kingdom to remain a nuclear power in its own right.

Viewed As Important

Opinion in the House of Commons was that the Prime Minister would have to return from the Bahamas with something more tangible than an eloquent expression of trans-Atlantic solidarity if his supporters are to be appeased.

The motion was considered more important than anti-American motions that customarily emerge from the right of the Tory party in the House of Commons whenever there are serious differences of policy between Washington and London.

The first signature to the motion was that of Sir Arthur Vere Harvey, chairman of the powerful Backbenchers Defense Committee. Another was that of Harold Watkinson, who, as Minister of Defense, dealt with the United States Defense Department when research and development of Skybolt began.

Signatures included those of most right wing Tories. But a considerable number of members from the party's center and left also signed.

The prospect that the United States will drop Skybolt, whose possession would have extended Britain's role as a nuclear power, is the focus for general dissatisfaction in the party with the Prime Minister, his lieutenants and his leadership.

This began late last month when the party suffered reverses in five by-elections. It has snowballed in the wake of the dispute over Skybolt. For the first time Conservative politicians are openly discussing successors to Mr. Macmillan.

Sir Cyril Osborne, another Conservative Backbencher, has suggested that Ian MacLeod, the Conservatives' chief political strategist, be relieved of his duties as chairman of the party.

Hailsham Is Supported

A number of Backbenchers and some junior ministers are known to favor the reappointment to that post, equivalent to campaign manager in American politics, of Viscount Hailsham. He directed the party through the triumphant election campaign of 1959.

Rumblings of mutiny on the right have extended to other fields. Less than a week ago 47 Conservative members of Parliament signed another motion. This called on the government to recognize that it might have to break off negotiations with the European Economic Community if E.E.C. failed to meet its conditions. The motion asked an attitude of "proper firmness" by the government in talks with the six-nation community.

Although other cabinet ministers are getting their share of the blame, dissidents have fixed their sights on Mr. Macmillan himself. This is one consequence of his wholesale reshuffle of the cabinet in July, when several veterans were dropped.

Mr. Macmillan then was thought to have done all he could to revitalize the government. Politicians pointed out that in the present situation it was natural that Conservative dissatisfaction should be directed at the Prime Minister himself.

Labor Balks at Holiday

Labor's parliamentary tacticians, who know a favorable situation when they see it, did their utmost today to prevent the house from rising on Friday.

George Brown, deputy leader of the Opposition, complained the members of Parliament were being asked to depart not when there was only one issue, Skybolt, unresolved, but "when the executive is in a state of chaos over the whole field of its policies."

Government, he charged, has not "a single answer to these defense questions" and is in "a shambles." The country, Mr. Brown asserted, "is worried about where we are going to be in a month's time."

Politicians thought Mr. Brown's oratory wasted. They said it would take a more important issue than Skybolt to curtail the Christmas recess. As indeed was the case when the house voted 198 votes to 22 to adhere to the arrangements for a Christmas adjournment.

But in that recess, they believed, dissension in the Conservative party would grow as members of parliament received at first hand doubts and uncertainties of their constituents.

* * *

December 20, 1962

BRITAIN GIVES UP ON THE SKYBOLT, MAY GET POLARIS

Friendly Accord Reached by Kennedy and Macmillan in First Nassau Talk

PLEDGE ON NATO NOTED

U.S. Pegs Aid for London's Nuclear Force on Its Later Link to Allies

By WALLACE CARROLL
Special to The New York Times.

NASSAU, the Bahamas, Dec. 19—President Kennedy and Prime Minister Macmillan neared an agreement today to wash out the controversial Skybolt missile program and seek other ways of assuring the British a nuclear striking force of their own.

The price of continued American support for Britain's nuclear ambitions, according to officials of the two countries, was an understanding that the British would eventually integrate their nuclear power into a North American Treaty Organization nuclear force if such an international force can be brought into being.

Thus, after the first formal meeting between the President, the Prime Minister and their advisers, the sharp difference over the Skybolt project seemed about to be resolved in a friendly spirit.

Cost Put at 2.5 Billion

In place of the Skybolt, the British seemed likely to get the Polaris, a medium-range missile with which the United States has armed its nuclear submarines.

The Skybolt is a ballistic missile designed to be carried under the wings of jet bombers and fired at distances of a thousand miles from the target.

It is a $2,500,000,000 program in which the chief contractor is the Douglas Aircraft Company. The United States Air Force hoped to use the missile to prolong the life of its heavy bombers, which otherwise would be made obsolete by the improvements in anti-aircraft weapons.

The British similarly hoped to prolong the usefulness of their Vulcan jets into the early Nineteen-Seventies by using the Skybolt. Recently, however, after five unsuccessful tests, the Kennedy Administration decided that the United States Air Force did not need the missile.

Setting for Conference

The decision caused dismay and anger in Britain, which felt it could not delay on the expensive programs alone.

Thus, when President Kennedy and Prime Minister Macmillan opened their two days of formal meetings here today they were dealing with the future of Britain as an independent nuclear power and with a problem that threatened serious damage to Anglo-American relations.

The two sides met today on Lyford Cay, an isolated finger of land at the west end of New Providence Island about fifteen miles from Nassau. Their meeting place was the living room of the villa of Mrs. Robert Holt, of Montreal, in a framework of palm trees and flowering bougainvillea, with a sapphire and emerald sea in the distance.

Mr. Macmillan, it is understood, made it clear that Britain intends to remain an independent nuclear power with a striking force of its own. It hopes to do this, he is reported to have said, with continued United States cooperation.

If, however, this cooperation were denied, Britain would have to persist in its nuclear program relying entirely on its own resources.

The Prime Minister also indicated, according to one official, that he fully understood why the United States wants to cancel the Skybolt program.

The United States' argument is that, even if the technical difficulties now being encountered can be overcome, the weapon will not be ready until 1966 and it will then be outdated by other missiles on which the United States chooses to rely.

Mr. Macmillan, in accepting this argument, was said to have expressed willingness to consider alternatives to the Skybolt if the United States had any to offer.

Whether Mr. Kennedy took the occasion to restate United States misgivings about a proliferation of nuclear forces among the Western allies could not be immediately learned. The President and his advisers are uneasy about an independent striking force of this kind even in the hands of so trusted an ally as Britain.

Their misgivings increase when they think of an independent French nuclear force and they would be most concerned if West Germany ever asserted a right to have what the British and French have achieved for themselves.

Source of Reasoning

The reasoning behind this uneasiness is a belief that none of the allies except the United States has the wealth and resources to produce the kind and number of nuclear weapons that will really deter the Soviet Union from rash adventures.

Britain and France, in the United States view, may merely acquire enough nuclear weapons to set off a nuclear war but not to end it. Limited nuclear capabilities operating independently, said Secretary of Defense Robert S. McNamara last June, are dangerous, expensive, prone to obsolescence and lacking in credibility as a deterrent.

Because of these misgivings, the United States has told its allies in NATO that it would be willing to consider proposals for a joint nuclear force in which all the NATO countries would probably have a part.

In view of this, Mr. Kennedy presumably told the British that the United States would be willing to aid them if it could have some assurance that their independent nuclear power might eventually become part of such a NATO effort.

The two leaders and their two advisers then reviewed the alternatives to the Skybolt program to find which United States weapons might be suitable for British use.

According to one official, all the weapons in the United States nuclear arsenal were mentioned—the Polaris missile that can be fired from nuclear submarines; the Atlas, Minuteman and Titan intercontinental ballistic missiles, and the Hounddog, an air-breathing guided missile fired from low-flying airplanes.

The Polaris appeared to be the most likely choice for the British. In order to use it, they would have to build new nuclear submarines, or they could install it on surface ships.

Big Questions Ahead

Agreement on the weapons problem will permit the two leaders and their advisers to get down to work on the three big questions they originally hoped to review:
• How to deal with Soviet Union after the Soviet setback in Cuba and the recent signs of the Soviet and Chinese Communists.

• The difficulties Britain is encountering in her efforts to gain admission to the European Common Market.
• The joint Anglo-American program of military aid to India to enable her to ward off any further Chinese attacks.

American officials said yesterday that the threat of civil war in the Congo would also be discussed. Their assertion that this problem would be given high priority and taken up immediately after the Skybolt question apparently irritated the British, who have never shared American views as to what can be done to end the secession of Katanga province.

The likelihood now is that the Congo will be discussed but, in deference to the British, after most of the other questions have been reviewed.

* * *

December 22, 1962

U.S. AND BRITAIN PROPOSE JOINT NATO ATOM FORCE; ASK FRANCE TO TAKE PART

ACCORD REACHED

London Will Commit Polaris Weapons to West's Pool

By WALLACE CARROLL
Special to The New York Times.

NASSAU, Dec. 21—The United States and Britain called for the creation of an international nuclear force to protect the North Atlantic area and immediately invited France to join it as their partner.

After three days of hard negotiation in this island resort, President Kennedy and Prime Minister Macmillan announced that they had settled their differences over missiles for Britain with a plan for the establishment of a "multilateral NATO nuclear force."

These were the main elements of their agreement and proposals:
• The United Stated agreed to sell Britain the Polaris submarine-borne missile in place of the Skybolt airborne missile, which will now be abandoned. The British will equip the Polaris with their own warheads and will design and build their own nuclear submarines to carry the missile.
• Britain agreed that the Polaris missile systems acquired in this way will become part of a NATO nuclear force and will have their targets designated by the North Atlantic Treaty Organization. Only if "supreme national interests" were at stake would the British use them for any purpose other than the defense of the Western alliance.
• The United States guaranteed to match this British contribution to the proposed NATO nuclear force with "at least equal United States forces."
• President Kennedy offered to sell France Polaris equipment under the same conditions. That is, the French, who have already set off a nuclear "device," would fit their own warheads to the missiles and put them in their own subma-

rines. These missile systems would then be put under NATO command.

• The United States and Britain agreed that they would immediately contribute to NATO part of their existing nuclear forces including "allocations from United States strategic forces, from United Kingdom bomber command, and from tactical nuclear forces now held in Europe." At present, though, the United States has nuclear weapons in Europe but none are under NATO command. By far the greater part of American nuclear power, it is understood, would remain outside the pooling arrangements because of the worldwide commitments of the United States.

The American and British agreement on nuclear defense systems was expressed in a two-page typewritten statement.

American participants in the talks immediately called it the "Pact of Nassau."

The invitation to France was contained in separate letters from Mr. Kennedy and Mr. Macmillan to President de Gaulle.

They were delivered in Paris this morning and have been published.

The Anglo-American statement revealed in considerable detail how the President and Prime Minister converted their differences over the Skybolt into an imaginative defense agreement that would carry into the 1980's.

The basic cause of the differences was this:

The British Government was determined to maintain a nuclear striking force of its own but the Kennedy Administration opposes the maintenance of the independent nuclear forces by even its closest allies, considering such forces dangerous, ineffectual, and beyond the means of the countries that want them.

The immediate cause of the trouble was President Kennedy's decision that the United States would abandon the development and the production of the Skybolt for its own purposes. Britain had been counting on the Skybolt developed entirely at American expense to use with its jet bombers and thus give it an independent striking force until the early 1970's.

The joint statement showed that it was Mr. Macmillan who raised the question whether Britain could buy the Polaris in place of the Skybolt.

"After careful review," it then said, "the President and the Prime Minister agreed that a decision on Polaris must be considered in the widest context both of the future defense of the Atlantic alliance and of the safety of the whole free world."

It continued: "They reached the conclusion that this issue created an opportunity for the development of new and closer arrangements for the organization and control of strategic Western defense and that such arrangements in turn could make a major contribution to political cohesion among the nations of the alliance."

For the "immediate future," the statement went on, the two men agreed that a start could be made by "subscribing to NATO some part of the forces already in existence … such forces would be assigned as part of the NATO nuclear force and targeted in accordance with NATO plans."

Returning to the Polaris, the President and the Prime Minister agreed that the purpose of their two Governments with respect to the provision of the Polaris missiles must be the development of a multilateral NATO nuclear force in the closest consultation with other NATO allies, "they with use their best endeavors to this end."

Accordingly, the statement said, the United States would let the British have Polaris missiles and the British would assign their Polaris submarines to NATO and let the North Atlantic Command designate their targets in case of war.

"The Prime Minister made it clear," the statement said, "that except where Her Majesty's Government may decide that supreme national interests are at stake, these British forces will be used for the purpose of internal defense of the Western alliance in all circumstances."

American officials said that the exception for "supreme national interests" was one that any sovereign power would insist upon. Presumably, however, it would exclude the use of Polaris missiles in such a limited contingency as the British and French attack on Egypt in the Suez crisis of 1956.

American officials did not hesitate to call the agreement historic. The British, too, seemed pleased and privately said that it would enable Mr. Macmillan to return home with at least enough of an "independent nuclear force" to head off a political crisis in Britain.

The U.S. Objectives

The Americans said that the proposed arrangements would go a long way to meet three of the major objectives of the Kennedy Administration.

These objectives are:

1. Recognition among the allies that the nuclear war is "indivisible"—that is, that the use of even the relatively feeble nuclear forces of Britain or France would inevitably set off an all-out nuclear war.

2. Prevention of the spread of national nuclear forces and gradual integration of the existing forces into a coordinated allied effort.

3. Recognition that strategic nuclear forces—even those as powerful as the United States now possesses—are not an infallible deterrent to an aggressor. In other words, powerful conventional forces are needed to deal with all forms of political and military aggression.

The joint statement pleased the Americans with the heavy emphasis on the indivisibility theme.

"The President and the Prime Minister are convinced," it said, "that this new plan will strengthen the nuclear defense of the Western alliance.

"In strategic terms this defense is indivisible, and it is their conviction that in all ordinary circumstances of crisis of danger, it is this very unity which is the best protection of the West."

As for the prevention of the spread of nuclear forces, American officials made clear that participation in the proposed nuclear pool is limited to present powers among the allies.

This would restrict it to the United States, Britain and France. It would thus exclude West Germany. The possibility that the Germans might eventually claim the right to have nuclear weapons has been a source of uneasiness among the allies, and it would undoubtedly be considered especially "provocative" by the Soviets.

Though no American official would say so, President Kennedy and his advisers obviously hope that Britain and France will eventually decide to abandon their national nuclear efforts and put their entire nuclear forces in the proposed NATO pool. As for the other 12 NATO countries, it is hoped that the pool will give them the assurance they need that Europe will have a powerful voice in its own nuclear defense and will not be dependent entirely on the United States. If the non-nuclear members of NATO wish to participate in the proposed international force, they will be allowed to contribute men and money. The men would probably be put into crews with the Americans, British and French. American sources made clear, however, that no financial contributions would be accepted from any country if that country tried to use this to justify a cut in its conventional forces.

The Kennedy Administration has been pressing all the allies to increase the strength of their conventional forces. It has argued that this would give the alliance additional "options" to deal with lesser aggressions that would not seem to warrant the risks of nuclear war. In this connection, the final paragraph of the joint statement said:

"The President and the Prime Minister agreed that in addition to having a nuclear shield it is important to have a non-nuclear sword. From this purpose they agreed on the importance of increasing the effectiveness of their conventional forces on a world wide basis."

Though Britain and the United States are pledged to make an immediate contribution to a NATO nuclear force the success of their long-range project including the Polaris missiles depends to a great extent on President de Gaulle.

Some of the British officials here believe that the French leader will not like the idea of putting such an international force under NATO command.

He has never been enthusiastic about NATO nor contributed the French units that the NATO agreements called for.

On the other hand he has always been resentful of the special arrangements on nuclear matters between the United States and Britain.

The proposed nuclear pool, it is pointed out, would start the breakdown of these exclusive arrangements and give him a big voice in the nuclear defense of Western Europe.

American officials also hope that he may soon realize that the nuclear force he is creating will be obsolete before it is ready. By joining the proposed pool, he would have a stake and vote in an up-to-date nuclear deterrent.

In this connection, the Americans point out that the manned bomber will become obsolete by the end of this decade but the Polaris is expected to remain a useful weapon into the 1980's.

* * *

January 12, 1963

31 AFRICAN LANDS BACK U.N. ON CONGO

Group Gives Thant Support on His Moves in Katanga to Restore Unity

By SAM POPE BREWER
Special to The New York Times.

UNITED NATIONS, N. Y., Jan. 11—Thirty-one independent nations of Africa gave formal assurance today of their full support for the United Nations' efforts to unify the Congo.

After a meeting here, they sent a delegation of seven to announce to Thant their approval of the measures that had been taken against the secessionist province of Katanga.

Mohamed H. El-Zayyat of the United Arab Republic, as their spokesman, said they had "expressed the full support of the independent African states for the actions carried on."

Only Libya of the African group was not represented at the meeting, because there was no delegate available to attend.

The delegation to the Secretary General included representatives of Cameroon, Dahomey, Ghana, Guinea, the Sudan, Tanganyika and the United Arab Republic.

Mr. El-Zayyat said the meeting was suggested by Ethiopia and Guinea in an effort to help unify the Congo.

Secretary General U Thant devoted his morning to an intensive conference with Dr. Ralph J. Bunche, Under Secretary for Special Political Affairs, who returned yesterday from a one-week trouble-shooting visit to the Congo.

A United Nations spokesman said no statement would be made for the present on Dr. Bunche's report. Dr. Bunche himself said that as an international civil servant he must reserve his remarks for his chief.

United Nations forces in the Congo are marking time, according to a headquarters source, awaiting political developments as repair of bridges blown by dissident Katanga forces proceeds.

There is fear that if the advance toward the last major stronghold of the dissidents at Kolwezi is continued, mercenaries or undisciplined Katanga gendarmerie forces may blow up vital industrial installations.

Reliable sources said there were indications that President Moise Tshombe of Katanga might no longer have control of his forces. Mr. Tshombe himself was reported cooperating with United Nations forces. Sources here were still mindful of the fact that he had frequently reversed his policies in the past when things seemed to be going well.

Kolwezi is an important mining center about 150 miles northwest of Elisabethville, the capital of Katanga province. United Nations forces were reported today to be still halted at Jadotville about midway on the road.

Advance Not Pressed

A United Nations source said advance patrols were feeling out the situation on the road from Jadotville to Kolwezi but that no effort to advance was being made.

Mr. Tshombe's backers were said to have planted explosives in the installations of the Union Minière de Haut-Katanga at Kolwezi and in a big hydroelectric dam. What cannot be known here is whether Mr. Tshombe can prevent them from setting off the charges if he tries.

Meanwhile, United States and United Nations sources were reported trying to persuade the Central Government of the Congo to rescind its expulsion order against the Belgian and British consuls in Elisabethville. Edmund Guillion, United States Ambassador in Leopoldville, was said to be intervening with Premier Cyrille Adoula. The consuls were ordered yesterday to leave the country because of their contacts with Mr. Tshombe.

Reliable diplomatic sources here said that their activities in fact had been "extremely helpful" to the United Nations in making Mr. Tshombe listen to reason.

One diplomat said that especially Derek Dodson, the British consul, "did a particularly good job in keeping things from going to pieces a few days ago."

The Belgian consul, Frederik Vandewalle, also is credited with having helped to calm the situation.

It had not been made clear here up to today just why Mr. Adoula's Government objected to the activities of the two consuls.

*   *   *

January 15, 1963

DE GAULLE SAYS MARKET SHOULD KEEP BRITAIN OUT; BARS A NATO ATOM FORCE

CLASH FORESEEN

Majority in European Bloc Want London as Full Member

By ROBERT C. DOTY
Special to The New York Times.

PARIS, Jan. 14—President de Gaulle virtually wrote off today Britain's chances of winning membership in the European Economic Community. At the same time he turned down, in effect, a United States proposal for an integrated Atlantic nuclear force.

For Britain, which he described as too "insular and maritime" to become fully integrated to Europe, the French President suggested an "accord of association" with the six-nation continental economic grouping.

In response to President Kennedy's offer of Polaris missiles to be assigned under French control to a multilateral North Atlantic treaty force was a restatement of his determination to build and "employ in case of need" an independent French nuclear force.

General's Aims Discussed

These positions, outlined at one of the French President's rare news conferences, seemed likely to pose an explosive issue between France and her partner in both the Atlantic alliance and the continental Common Market.

A majority of both favor full British participation in European economic and political unity moves and some form of multi-national nuclear force. If France assumes full responsibility for blocking both of these goals, some observers foresee the possibility of a breakup of the economic community and severe stresses within the North Atlantic Treaty Organization.

[A three-nation committee within the North Atlantic Treaty Organization to consider emergency decisions on operations of the nuclear forces of the alliance were suggested Monday by Gen. Norstad, who recently retired as NATO commander.]

The over-all effect of President de Gaulle's long exposition of foreign and defense policy was to make crystal clear that his own "grand design" for France and Europe is sharply at odds with President Kennedy's Atlantic concept in the economic and strategic spheres.

The most striking impression of the French President's 82-minute lecture was, first, of French and then of continental European "nationalism." His basic motivation appeared to be to protect a nascent European entity from dilution in a "colossal Atlantic community under American dependence and direction."

Thus, it was because Britain was not "fully" European but, instead, linked to countries around the globe, General de Gaulle suggested, that she probably could not meet the qualifications for full membership. He forecast that sometime in the future, Britain might so "transform" herself as to win entry. But he made no effort to hide his fear that if Britain, and some or all of the countries in the British-sponsored European free trade association, were to enter the community on anything like their terms they would so transform it as to change its basic nature.

Contrasts and Conditions

He drew a contrast between the more or less similar traditions, economies and social organizations of the six present members and the radically different British equivalents.

"But the question [is] to know if Great Britain currently can place herself with the continent and like it inside a truly common tariff, can renounce all preference with regard to the Commonwealth, to cease to pretend that her agriculture should be privileged and to hold null and void the engagements she has taken with the countries that were part of her free trade zone," General de Gaulle said.

He made it clear that he did not think this could be done and that, therefore, Britain could not hope for full membership.

He sugar-coated the pill by paying tribute to Britain's single-handed defense of the destinies of the entire free world during part of World War II. But he also began his discussion with the statement that sentiment had no part in determination of such issues as British membership.

In his discussion of defense matters, President de Gaulle again implied that it was because the United States was not

European that France must continue to equip herself with an independent nuclear force, rather than rely on exclusively American nuclear protection, which might be wanting in a purely European showdown.

So long as the United States nuclear monopoly exists, he said, France and Europe can count on it to ward off Soviet aggression.

"One cannot too much appreciate the extent of the service, although it was happily a passive one, that the Americans have rendered in this way to the peace of the world in that period," General de Gaulle said.

But with the growth of a comparable Soviet nuclear power, he said, it became inevitable that in case of nuclear war there would be "frightful, perhaps mortal destructions in both countries."

"In these conditions no one in the world can say—no one in the world and, in particular, no one in America can say where, when, how and in what measure American nuclear arms would be employed to defend Europe," General de Gaulle said.

Sees French Force Vital

He acknowledged that those arms remained the essential guarantee of world peace and that President Kennedy's determination to use them if necessary in the Cuban crisis demonstrated this.

Nonetheless, France, he went on, finds it essential to continue building nuclear power even if this is of negligible size by comparison with the two atomic giants.

He complained mildly of the "multiple chorus of officers, specialists, American publicists" who strongly attack France's autonomous nuclear armaments, holding it to be a wastefully, ineffective duplication of American effort, a diffusion of Western strategy.

It was natural, he said, that in politics and in strategy, as in economics, "the monopoly appears to him who holds it to be the best possible system."

But he pointed out that in 1945 two bombs had been sufficient to end a war when the enemy could not reply in kind.

The French Capacity

"I do not want to evoke here the hypothesis in which Europe could be subjected to localized nuclear action from which the political and psychological consequences would be immense unless there was the certitude that a riposte of the same kind, of the same degree would be immediately unleashed," President de Gaulle said.

"I can only say the French atomic force, from the beginning of its organization, will have the sober and terrible capacity to destroy in a few instants millions and millions of men. That fact cannot fail to influence, at least a bit, the intentions of any eventual aggressor."

* * *

January 17, 1963

KHRUSHCHEV ASKS TRUCE WITH CHINA; BARS REDS' PARLEY

But in Berlin Address He Defends Coexistence Policy and Cuba Withdrawal

TONE IS CONCILIATORY

Premier Again Proposes U.N. Role in Berlin but Sets No Treaty Deadline

By SYDNEY GRUSON
Special to The New York Times.

BERLIN, Jan. 16—Premier Khrushchev today called for a truce in the public ideological battling between the Soviet Union and China for the sake of the "most holy cause" of Communist unity.

In a two and a half hour speech to the East German Communist party congress, he strongly defended his policy of peaceful coexistence with the West and particularly his withdrawal of Soviet missiles from Cuba.

But he did not, as many observers had expected, drive the bitter dispute with Communist China to the point of no return. Instead he said that time should be allowed to heal the wounds opened by the Chinese leaders' insistence that Communists should not draw back from using nuclear weapons to gain their ends.

Tone is Conciliatory

Mr. Khrushchev gave nothing of substance away to the Chinese but his tone was conciliatory. He seemed to suggest the reason for this in turning down the Chinese proposal for a formal conference of all Communist parties to discuss the differences.

Such a conference now, Mr. Khrushchev said, would "aggravate" the differences and "pose the danger of a split."

"Let time work for us," he went on. "Time will help us realize who is right and who is wrong. After a period we will be able to agree successfully."

There were no fireworks either in the relatively short part of his speech devoted to the Berlin and German problems.

On Berlin, he merely reiterated an old and previously rejected proposal for Western troops to remain in West Berlin "for a certain time" under the United Nations flag.

No Hint of Deadline

There was no hint of any future deadline for the long-threatened separate peace treaty with Communist East Germany and, in fact he seemed to imply that the Communists had already gained what could be achieved through a peace treaty:

The problem had changed in the four years since the Soviets proposed transforming West Berlin into a demilitarized free city, Mr. Khrushchev said. The building of the wall through Berlin in August, 1961, he asserted, had won for East Germany "the right to protect its borders and to assume soveign control over its roads."

But he warned the West not to think that the solution of the Cuba crisis automatically had solved the Berlin problem. And he linked progress in disarmament negotiations with the conclusion of a peace treaty that would "cut through the knot" of the Berlin problem.

In passages that clearly were aimed at the Chinese, Mr. Khrushchev warned of the terrible results of a nuclear war.

Quoting unidentified "foreign scientists" he said the United States had 40,000 atomic bombs and warheads. And, he added, "we have plenty of them too."

In the first blow of a nuclear war, he went on, between 700 and 800 million people would be killed and all the great cities of China as well as of other countries would be "devastated and swept from the face of the earth."

"These facts must be taken into account," Mr. Khrushchev said.

Then, telling the 4,500 delegates he was going to let them in on a secret, he said the Soviet Union had a 100-megaton bomb that his military advisers had warned could not be exploded over France or West Germany because "we could not save ourselves or you."

In denouncing the pro-Chinese Albanian Communists as "deviationists" and talkative "witch doctors," Mr. Khrushchev said "true heroism is not in dying beautifully. Many can do that. You need more qualities to live beautifully."

Mr. Khrushchev defended his policy in the Cuban crisis at length, calling the results a victory because the Soviet missiles there had prevented an invasion of the island.

Rejects Peking Thesis

Arguing directly against the Chinese thesis that Cuba was a "Munich" for the Communists and that the missiles should never have been placed there if they were to be withdrawn later, Mr. Khrushchev said:

"If we had put the missiles in Cuba to start a nuclear war on the United States and then had withdrawn them, it would look as if we had given up our aim. But in reality the Soviet Union never had such an aim. We wanted only to prevent an invasion of Cuba by the imperialists. Judging events from this point of view, then you will see that we have won."

"It was strange logic," he argued, to say that the Soviet Union had suffered a defeat in Cuba because "revolutionary Cuba exists and is being strengthened."

Those who contended the Soviet Union had retreated in Cuba, Mr. Khrushchev said, "cannot understand the complicated nature of the political struggle in our time."

The struggle, he added, demanded "flexibility and the ability to maneuver. It is true that we made a concession but it was in reply to a concession by the other side."

He said President Kennedy had "undertaken an obligation before the whole world" not to invade Cuba and to prevent the United States allies from trying to do so. This he contended was "a defect of the policy of aggressive imperialism and a victory for peaceful coexistence."

* * *

ERA OF CLOSE UNITY PLEDGED BY DE GAULLE AND ADENAUER

By DREW MIDDLETON
Special to The New York Times.

PARIS, Jan. 21—President de Gaulle and Chancellor Adenauer today concluded a treaty between France and West Germany aimed at a permanent reconciliation and an end of the historic rivalry between the two countries.

The two statesmen approved the text of a treaty for the closest Franco-German cooperation on foreign affairs, defense and cultural relations at a plenary session of the two delegations at Elysee Palace.

Intimate collaboration between the two Governments is provided for by an agreement that the two chiefs of state and of Government shall meet at least twice a year.

Claude Lebel, spokesman for the French Foreign Ministry, declared that the treaty was not directed against any third party but was "the first and indispensable measure leading to the unity of Europe which both sides desire."

The treaty, Mr. Lebel emphasized, is in the nature of association rather than integration. It will be based on contacts between high officials of the two Governments.

Nothing was said about the awkward difference that separates France and Germany on Britain's negotiations to enter the European Economic Community, to which the two newly associated states belong.

A German spokesman said that the Federal Republic still desired British entry into E.E.C. and believed that "an appropriate formula for British membership can be found in conformity with the Treaty of Rome."

General de Gaulle, however, wants Britain kept out of the community and its negotiations with the United Kingdom broken off at once.

The intransigence of the French position was emphasized in Luxembourg today, where the six members of the European Coal and Steel Community were to have met to discuss Britain's application for membership. The French delegation did not appear. The other five delegations from West Germany, Italy, the Netherlands, Belgium and Luxembourg continued their work.

Text of the accord between France and West Germany will be signed tomorrow or Wednesday and submitted for ratification to the French and West German National Assemblies. It is not yet certain whether General de Gaulle and Dr. Adenauer will themselves sign or leave this to their ministers.

Provisions of Treaty

The French Foreign Ministry disclosed the principal provisions of the treaty and the means by which they will be carried out.

Personal contacts between ministers play an important role. But there is no provision thus far for a permanent integrated organization of the two Governments.

In addition to meetings between the chiefs of state and of Government, the Foreign and Defense Ministers are to meet every three months. The chiefs of the two general staffs will confer every two months.

In the culture sphere, meetings will occur every three months. These are to take place between France's Minister of Education and a West German official with similar duties, who has not yet been designated, and between the French Commissioner for Youth and Sports and the West German Minister for Family and Youth.

The treaty provides for a monthly meeting of senior officials dealing with foreign affairs, defense, economic affairs and cultural affairs.

In the field of foreign affairs, the two Governments agreed that since circumstances are different in each country it would be impossible to bind the two states to a common policy.

Military Clauses

Military cooperation, however, is a good deal more extensive.

The clauses of treaty dealing with this provide:

1. The exchange of officers for training, organization of joint manuevers and disposition by each country of training areas for troops of the other.

2. Research, development and production of arms except for nuclear weapons.

3. Joint studies on strategic and tactical problems.

Agreement on these points seemed to some Allied diplomats to duplicate existing arrangements of the North Atlantic Alliance and its Supreme Command. Observers noted that General de Gaulle appeared to have gone a good deal further toward integration with West Germany than he has with the United States or Britain.

The exclusion of nuclear weapons from the agreement drew attention to another point of difference between the two Governments.

West Germany has accepted the United States proposal for a role in a multi-national nuclear force. France has rejected it and intends to build her own nuclear striking force.

Other Exchanges

Cultural, educational and scientific exchanges are provided lavishly in the treaty.

There will be an interchange of diplomas between the two countries, allowing graduates in one country to matriculate in the other, and an expansion of the present programs for the exchange of students and scholarships.

The development of study of German in French schools and French in German schools is to go forward as rapidly as possible.

Scientific research is to be coordinated, according to the treaty, especially in the field of basic, theoretical science.

The development of what was originally intended as a series of protocols and agreements into the treaty owes much to Dr. Adenauer's advocacy. The Chancellor sees the accord between the two old foes as a monument to his political career.

On the French side, however, there was an evident, and perhaps an unexpected, desire to impress that the treaty is not to be interpreted as being directed against any other party or as excluding anyone.

Progress Is Speedy

The conclusion of the treaty moved faster than expected because of the rapid progress made this morning in a series of meetings between the French and West German ministers.

These included conferences between Foreign Ministers Maurice Couve de Murville of France and Gerhard Schroeder of West Germany, Defense Ministers Pierre Messmer of France and Kai-Uwe von Hassel of West Germany and Bruno Heck, West German Minister of Family and Youth Affairs, and Maurice Herzog, High Commissioner in France for Youth and Sports.

Out of these meetings came detailed agreements which the two principals were able to approve when the plenary session met this afternoon.

The question of Britain's entry into the Common Market, and of differences between the two Governments on the issue, remains outstanding. It was discussed inconclusively when General de Gaulle and Dr. Adenauer met privately this morning.

* * *

April 6, 1963

RUSSIA APPROVES 'HOT LINE' TO U.S. TO CUT WAR PERIL

Accepts Proposal at Geneva for Communications Link to Guard Against Error

BOTH SIDES PRAISE PLAN

Soviet Sees 'Positive' Gain in Parley's First Accord— Details Await Talks

Special to The New York Times.

GENEVA, April 5—The Soviet Union accepted today the United States proposal for a direct "hot line" communications link between Moscow and Washington to reduce the threat of accidental war.

The acceptance marked the first practical achievement of the year-old disarmament conference.

Semyon K. Tsarapkin, the Soviet delegate, announced that Moscow was "ready to agree" to have a special telephone or teletype link with Washington without waiting for a disarmament accord.

Such a measure, Mr. Tsarapkin said, "may have certain positive results."

Charles C. Stelle of the United States said his delegation "welcomes warmly" the Soviet announcement. "We will want to consult with the Soviet delegation informally and privately to get progress on this important development," he added.

Moscow Asks Return

After the conference session Aleksei A. Roshchin, the Soviet delegation spokesman, stressed that Soviet acceptance of the United States proposal proved that Moscow "is not taking a completely negative position" at the conference, as had been charged.

On the other hand, he continued, the West "has not accepted a single Soviet proposal."

Mr. Tsarapkin explained to the conference that the Soviet Union agreed with the United States view that each of the two governments would be responsible for installing and maintaining the line on its territory.

As also suggested by the United States, he recalled, each government would also be responsible for the line's security on its territory and for arranging that messages received were transmitted to the proper government service.

Likewise, the Soviet delegate continued, the Soviet Union agreed with the United States that each Government would decide for itself where to locate its terminal point of the line. The United States has said it will install its end of the link at the National Command Center because the center maintains continuing contact with principal Government officials, including the President.

No Difficulty Expected

Mr. Tsarapkin said he foresaw no difficulty in reaching agreement with the United States on just where the link leading from the two capitals would join.

The "hot line" proposal was one of a series of so-called "collateral" measures the United States offered at the conference's outset for reducing the risk of war by accident, miscalculation, failure of communications or surprise attack.

Although not disarmament proposals in themselves, these measures are aimed at improving the chances for disarmament by reducing international tensions. The United States had often pressed for their consideration, but the Soviet Union had refused to have anything to do with them until today.

The Cuban crisis was often cited as having shown the need for guaranteeing quick communications between Moscow and Washington to stave off war. President Kennedy remarked at a news conference in December that the crisis had shown the need for such a link.

Although it was hoped that the Soviet Union also saw such a need, it continued to ignore appeals to discuss the problem.

Instead, Moscow insisted that its own "collateral" proposals were the only ones that would effectively reduce international tensions.

Announcement Is Delayed

Even today Mr. Tsarapkin held off the announcement of Moscow's agreement to the communications link until the end of a long speech in defense of the Soviet "collateral" measures.

These call for a ban on missiles, including Polaris submarines, from foreign bases and ports, and for a nonaggresion agreement between the member states of the West's North Atlantic Treaty Organization and the Communist Warsaw Pact.

The speech was mostly a repetition of Soviet charges that the proposed plan for a multilateral nuclear force armed with Polaris missiles under NATO would increase international tension by placing atomic weapons in the hands of West German "revanchists."

Mr. Tsarapkin used his speech to read into the record a communication that Dr. Lothar Bolz, Foreign Minister of the East German Communist regime, had addressed to the United States and the Soviet Union, the conferences co-chairmen.

Any participation of the West German Government and the "Hitlerite generals" in a NATO nuclear force would "undermine" the chances to end nuclear armament and make "disarmament from German soil" Dr. Bolz wrote.

The East German Foreign Minister declared his Government stood by its earlier proposals for a series of accords with Bonn "to open the way for disarmament from German soil."

Mr. Stelle said the United States had "no obligation" to sponsor the East German communication for consideration by the conference. The document, he commented, came from a "nongovernmental organization and should be treated accordingly." None of the Western powers recognizes East Germany.

* * *

April 21, 1963

NERVE CENTER FOR A NUCLEAR NIGHTMARE

By LEON MINOFF

LONDON—Chances are that Whitehall's recent decision to reshape itself along Pentagon lines—perhaps including a War Room—was not inspired by the odd construction on Stage A at Shepperton Studios, where Stanley Kubrick is guiding "Dr. Strangelove: Or How I Learned to Stop Worrying and Love the Bomb." One enters Mr. Kubrick's War Room as one enters a mosque. Felt overshoes must be donned to prevent scuffing 13,000 square feet of jet black laconite floor glittering like an eight ball caught in the rain. Once inside, however, a visitor is apt to regard his new footwear as the least strange thing about "Dr. Strangelove."

The War Room of the Pentagon is one of the principal sets of the nightmare comedy that deals with the possibility of nuclear annihilation by accident, which Kubrick is producing, directing and co-writing.

The fact that no one has ever publicly acknowledged a subterranean precinct in the real Pentagon, much less issued a photograph, did not faze the 34-year-old filmmaker or his art director, Ken Adam. "We've never seen an H-bomb, either,"

Kubrick said between rehearsals, "but two whoppers are being built right now on an adjacent stage."

Science Fiction

In the center of the War Room—conceived as a sort of vast lean-to bomb shelter—was a circular table 22 feet in diameter and covered in green baize like the playing fields of Las Vegas and Monte Carlo. Seated in 29 chairs and bathed in an eerie light were the Joint Chiefs of Staff, brain-trusters and State Department officials. The 30th place was conspicuously empty. But not for long.

On a hand signal from the director, a floor panel slid open and a chairborne Peter Sellers, unrecognizable in one of his four roles in the film, emerged on a hydraulic lift and bounced jerkily into his place at the table as Merkin Muffley, President of the United States. He then addressed himself to co-star George C. Scott, chairman of the Joint Chiefs, who was fingering a book entitled "World Targets in Megadeaths." "General Turgidson," said the President, "what is going on here?"

During a tea break, Kubrick explained what was going on. "A psychotic general, who believes that fluoridation of water is a Communist conspiracy to sap and pollute our precious bodily fluids, has unleashed his wing of H-bombers against Russia. That's why the President has been summoned to the War Room. It develops that for various and entirely credible reasons, the planes cannot be recalled, and the President is forced to cooperate with the Soviet Premier in a bizarre attempt to save the world."

The Bronx-born director, whose credits include "Paths of Glory," "Spartacus" and "Lolita," said he had wanted to make a film about the bomb for three years. He estimates he has read upward of 70 books on the subject and keeps a copious magazine and newspaper file. He's also spoken with such strategists as Herman Kahn and Thomas Schelling. But it was Alastair Buchan, director of London's Institute for Strategic Studies, who brought to his attention a suspense novel called "Two Hours to Doom."

Mr. Buchan thought it a rare fictional treatment of how nuclear war might start inadvertently. So did Kubrick. He bought the screen rights for $3,000 and set about adapting it in his Central Park West apartment with the novel's author, Peter George, a former Royal Air Force flight lieutenant. It was only then, Kubrick divulged, that he began to see the film as a grim comedy.

Multi-Faced

Scheduled for release by Columbia Pictures in early fall, "Dr. Strangelove" is being shot in England, it was explained, to accommodate Peter Sellers, who was unable to leave the country for domestic reasons. In addition to the President, the protean Sellers also plays the title role of a German scientist, a Texas pilot of an H-bomber headed inexorably for Russia, and an R.A.F. exchange officer. What roles are left are handled by Sterling Hayden, Keenan Wynn, Peter Bull, James Earl Jones, and Tracy Reed, Sir Carol Reed's daughter, who,

as the sole girl in the cast, is making her screen debut as a Pentagon secretary.

Background air sequences were shot over the Arctic. The sole other nonstudio location, Kubrick stated, was at International Business Machines in London, where Computer 7090—the same data processor that calculated where Astronaut John H. Glenn Jr. would descend into the ocean after his earth orbit—figured in sequences with Sellers.

The tea break over, the unit lined up for their felt slippers and padded back into the War Room. As cameras began to turn, 30 phones around the table were picked up simultaneously. The President was on the "hot line" to the Soviet Premier in the Kremlin (a full week, incidentally, before that headline-making announcement from Geneva). He spoke in the tones of a progressive nursery school teacher.

"Hello!... Hello, Dimitri.... Yes, this is Merkin. How are you?... Oh fine. Just fine. Look, Dimitri, you know how we've always talked about the possibility of something going wrong with the Bomb?... The Bomb? The HYDROGEN BOMB!... That's right. Well, I'll tell you what happened. One of our base commanders ..."

* * *

June 27, 1963

PRESIDENT HAILED BY OVER A MILLION IN VISIT TO BERLIN

He Salutes the Divided City
as Front Line in World's Struggle for Freedom

LOOKS OVER THE WALL

Says Berliners' Experience Shows Hazard
in Trying to Work With Communists

By ARTHUR J. OLSEN
Special to The New York Times.

BERLIN, June 26—President Kennedy, inspired by a tumultuous welcome from more than a million of the inhabitants of this isolated and divided city, declared today he was proud to be "a Berliner."

He said his claim to being a Berliner was based on the fact that "all free men, wherever they may live, are citizens of Berlin."

In a rousing speech to 150,000 West Berliners crowded before the City Hall, the President said anyone who thought "we can work with the Communists" should come to Berlin.

However, three hours later, in a less emotional setting, he reaffirmed his belief that the great powers must work together "to preserve the human race."

Warning on Communism

His earlier rejection of dealing with the Communists was a warning against trying to "ride the tiger" of popular fronts that unite democratic and Communist forces, Mr. Kennedy explained in an interpolation in a prepared speech.

The President's City Hall speech was the emotional high point of a spectacular welcome accorded the President by West Berlin. He saluted the city as the front line and shining example of humanity's struggle for freedom.

Those who profess not to understand the great issues between the free world and the Communist world or who think Communism is the wave of the future should come to Berlin, he said.

In his later speech, at the Free University of Berlin, President Kennedy returned firmly to the theme of his address at American University in Washington June 10 in which he called for an attempt to end the cold war.

'Wounds to Heal'

"When the possibilities of reconciliation appear, we in the West will make it clear that we are not hostile to any people or system, provided that they choose their own destiny without interfering with the free choice of others," he said.

"There will be wounds to heal and suspicions to be eased on both sides," he added. "The difference in living standards will have to be reduced—by leveling up, not down. Fair and effective agreements to end the arms race must be reached."

The changes might not come tomorrow, but "our efforts for a real settlement must continue," he said.

Then the President introduced an extemporaneous paragraph into his prepared text.

"As I said this morning, I am not impressed by the opportunities open to popular fronts throughout the world," he said. "I do not believe that any democrat can successfully ride that tiger. But I do believe in the necessity of great powers working together to preserve the human race."

Nuances of policy, however, were not the center of attention today in this city of at least 2,200,000 alert people. For them the only matter of importance was to give a heart-felt and spectacular welcome to the United States President and to see a youthful-looking smiling man obviously respond to their warmth.

Pierre Salinger, the President's press secretary, said the reception here was "the greatest he has had anywhere."

Along the route from Tegel airport to the United States mission headquarters in the southwest corner of Berlin, waving, cheering crowds lined every foot of the way.

Banners Hung at Gate

The crowds must have nearly equaled the population of the city, but many persons waved once and then sped ahead to greet Mr. Kennedy again.

Only once in a jammed eight hours, during which he was almost uninterruptedly on a television screen, did Mr. Kennedy fail to dominate the scene.

Shortly before noon he approached Brandenburg Gate where he caught his first view of the Communist-built wall that partitions Berlin.

The President had been scheduled to gaze over the wall through the gate onto Unter den Linden, once the main avenue of the German capital. However, the five arches of the gate were covered by huge red banners, blocking his view there of East Berlin.

The cloth barrier was put up by East Berlin officials last night.

Just across the wall from the podium where the President's party stood was a neatly lettered yellow sign in English. It cited the Allied pledges at the 1945 Yalta conference to uproot Nazism and militarism from Germany and to see it would never again endanger world peace.

Asserting that the pledges had been fulfilled in East Germany, the sign called on President Kennedy to see that they were fulfilled in West Germany and West Berlin.

The President appeared not to read the words, busying himself with a map indicating key points along the wall.

Sees East Berliners

At Checkpoint Charlie, the United States-controlled crossing point to East Berlin on the Friedrichstrasse, Mr. Kennedy had an unobstructed view several hundred yards into the eastern sector.

About 300 yards away, well beyond the 100-yard forbidden zone decreed by the Communists last week, he glimpsed a small group of East Berliners attracted by his presence. Though he could not hear them, they cheered.

In West Berlin there was no Communist attempt to embarrass the President. The problem for West Berlin's 13,500-man police force and the President's Secret Service guards was to restrain excited crowds from rushing to the President to shake his hand or hand him gifts.

On his arrival this morning at Tegel airport protocol went wrong when Mr. Kennedy first grasped the hand of Chancellor Adenauer instead of that of Gen. Eduard Toulouse, the French commandant in West Berlin. The airport is in the French sector, and technically under French sovereignty.

Brandt Gives Reassurance

Mayor Willy Brandt, greeting the President, said West Berliners did not expect constantly renewed assertions of allied guarantees "because we trust our friends."

The President responded by saying: "The legendary morale and spirit of the people of West Berlin has lit a fire throughout the world. I am glad to come to this city. It reassures us."

At the first of six stops on the tour—the modernistic Congress Hall where the West German construction workers union was in convention, Mr. Kennedy told the union delegates a free trade union movement was a guarantee and proof of democracy. He urged West German unions to help newly independent countries establish a strong free union movement.

The Presidential motorcade arrived 15 minutes behind schedule at Schöneberger Rathaus, West Berlin's city hall.

Mr. Kennedy's speech was emotional and the West Berliners responded in like manner. Several times they chanted "Kennedy! Kennedy!"

The only break in the day of speech-making and waving to the crowds was a luncheon in the city hall given by Mayor Brandt.

From there the President drove to the Free University, endowed in 1948 by the Ford Foundation, where Mr. Kennedy was made an honorary citizen of the university. This is a traditional form of honor, dating from the days when European universities enjoyed autonomous political rights.

The motorcade went next to Clay Allee, named after Gen. Lucius D. Clay, defender of West Berlin during the blockade 10 years ago and who, as a member of the Kennedy party, won especial cheers today. There, the United States community of 15,000 soldiers and diplomats and members of their families greeted the President.

"No beleaguered garrison serves in comparable conditions under conditions so dangerous and with adversaries so numerous," the President told the soldiers.

"Your role is to commit the United States. But you are more than hostages. You are in a sense a real force, for you represent the will and perseverance of your fellow Americans."

This was the final stop and the motorcade then sped back to the airport, where, after a brief farewell, the President took off for Ireland.

*   *   *

June 27, 1963

TEXT OF KENNEDY STATEMENTS IN BERLIN

Following are the texts of President Kennedy's statements in Berlin yesterday, as recorded by The New York Times through the facilities of the A.B.C. Radio Network:

AT TEGEL AIRPORT

I want to express my warm thanks to Mayor Brandt for his generous welcome. I am very proud to come here and meet the distinguished Chancellor and to be accompanied by an old veteran of this frontier, General [Lucius D.] Clay, who in good times and bad has been identified with the best in the life of this city.

I do not come here to reassure the people of West Berlin. Words are not so important but the record of the three powers, our French friends, whose hospitality we enjoy here, our British friends, and the people of the United States—their record is written in rock.

AT CITY HALL

I am proud to come to this city as the guest of your distinguished Mayor, who has symbolized throughout the world the fighting spirit of West Berlin.

And I am proud to visit the Federal Republic with your distinguished Chancellor, who for so many years has committed Germany to democracy and freedom and progress, and to come here in the company of my fellow American, General Clay, who has been in this city during its great moments of crisis and will come again if ever needed.

Two thousand years ago the proudest boast was "civis Romanus sum." Today in the world of freedom the proudest boast is "Ich bin ein Berliner."

I appreciate my interpreter translating my German.

There are many people in the world who really don't understand—or say they don't—what is the great issue between the free world and the Communist world. Let them come to Berlin.

There are some who say that Communism is the wave of the future. Let them come to Berlin.

And there are some who say in Europe and elsewhere "we can work with the Communists." Let them come to Berlin.

And there are even a few who say that it's true that Communism is an evil system but it permits us to make economic progress. Let them come to Berlin.

Freedom Needs No Wall

Freedom has many difficulties and democracy is not perfect. But we have never had to put a wall up to keep our people in, to prevent them from leaving us.

I want to say on behalf of my countrymen who live many miles away on the other side of the Atlantic, who are far distant from you, that they take the greatest pride that they have been able to share with you, even from a distance the story of the last 18 years.

I know of no town, no city that has been besieged for 18 years that still lives with the vitality and the force and the hope and the determination of the City of West Berlin.

While the wall is the most obvious and vivid demonstration of the failures of the Communist system, all the world can see we take no satisfaction in it, for it is, as your Mayor has said, an offense not only against history, but an offense against humanity, separating families, dividing husbands and wives and brothers and sisters and dividing a people who wish to be joined together.

What is true of this city is true of Germany. Real lasting peace in Europe can never be assured as long as one German out of four is denied the elementary right of free men, and that is to make a free choice.

Right to Be Free Earned

In 18 years of peace and good faith this generation of Germans has earned the right to be free, including the right to unite their families and their nation in lasting peace with goodwill to all people.

You live in a defended island of freedom, but your life is part of the main. So let me ask you as I close, to lift your eyes beyond the dangers of today to the hopes of tomorrow, beyond the freedom merely of this city of Berlin and all your country of Germany to the advance of freedom everywhere, beyond the wall to the day of peace with justice, beyond yourselves and ourselves to all mankind.

Freedom is indivisible and when one man is enslaved who are free? When all are free, then we can look forward to that day when this city will be joined as one and this country and this great continent of Europe in peaceful and hopeful globe.

When that day finally comes, as it will, the people of West Berlin can take sober satisfaction in the fact that they were in the front lines for almost two decades.

All free men, wherever they may live, are citizens of Berlin. And therefore, as a free man, I take pride in the words "Ich bin ein Berliner."

* * *

June 27, 1963

BERLINERS LIVE WITH REALITY OF COMMUNISTS' WALL IN CITY

Swift Construction of Barrier in 1961 Split Families and Hurt Economy by Blocking Workers From East

Special to The New York Times.

BERLIN, June 26—The Berlin wall, which President Kennedy viewed today, was put up Aug. 13, 1961, to halt the flow of refugees from Communist East Germany into West Berlin. It was also intended to seal off East Germans from Western influence.

Soviet tank divisions took up positions around Berlin as East German workmen, under military guard, began to build the concrete-block wall. Members of the Soviet-bloc's Warsaw Pact defense alliance were called upon to give their approval and a pledge of military support for the action.

The Western allies denounced the wall as an offense to humanity and a violation of the Four-Power agreements drawn up at the end of World War II. But they recoiled from using force to break it down.

Berliners, shocked at being cut off from their families by a wall of concrete slabs, steel girders and barbed wire, gradually began to recognize the reality of the wall and the fact that they had to live with it.

Flow of Refugees Halted

In their aim of halting the stream of refugees the Communists were successful. Several thousand crossed into West Berlin daily in the weeks before the wall was built. The movement now has been reduced to a handful of people who manage to scale the border fortifications or crawl under them.

But in the broader sense of blocking Western influence on the thinking, aspirations and convictions of the East German people, the Communist regime failed. Western experts, in assessing the situation in East Germany, are convinced that 90 per cent of the population remains hostile to the Communist regime.

West Berlin suffered economically from the wall by the loss of about 60,000 skilled workers who had commuted daily from their homes in East Berlin to their places of work in West Berlin.

An influx of almost 30,000 young workers from West Germany during the last year and a half has helped to overcome the city's labor shortage.

Wall Stretches 28 Miles

The wall stretches 28 miles along the entire length of the intracity border through former business and residential areas, now deserted, to fields, woods and lakes in the city's outskirts.

Seven East-West crossings are open, including Checkpoint Charlie, on the Friedrichstrasse, the only crossing point reserved for the Western allies and other non-Germans. The other six are for Germans.

Armed East German guards are stationed along the wall with orders to shoot anyone trying to escape. The majority of those who make their way to the West come through tunnels or swim across border lakes and canals.

Last week the East Germans restricted access to a border strip 100 meters wide in a new attempt to halt escapes.

* * *

July 2, 1963

BRITISH LINK EX-DIPLOMAT TO BURGESS-MACLEAN CASE

By SYDNEY GRUSON
Special to The New York Times.

LONDON, July 1—H. A. R. Philby, 51-year-old former British diplomat and newspaper correspondent, was named by the Government today as a Soviet agent and the "third man" in the Burgess-Maclean spy case of a decade ago.

Edward Heath, Lord Privy Seal, told the House of Commons that Mr. Philby, Middle East correspondent of The Observer of London until he disappeared from Beirut, Lebanon, last January, was believed to be behind the Iron Curtain.

It was Mr. Philby, Mr. Heath said, who warned Donald Maclean and Guy Burgess that the security services were about to move against them. This was in 1951, when the two men, then Foreign Office diplomats, vanished.

They later turned up in the Soviet Union, where they have lived since. In 1955 the Government said Burgess and Maclean were suspected of having been Soviet spies while employed in the Foreign Office.

History of Trio Reviewed

Mr. Heath reviewed some history involving the three men. On Nov. 7, 1955, Prime Minister Macmillan, then Foreign Secretary, told the Commons that Mr. Philby resigned from the foreign service by request in July, 1951, after his "Communist associations" had become known.

Mr. Macmillan also said that a "close investigation" had uncovered no evidence that Mr. Philby had warned Burgess and Maclean "or that he had betrayed the interests of this country."

Mr. Heath then continued:

"In fact, the security services have never closed their file on this case and now have further information.

"They are now aware, apparently as a result of an admission by Mr. Philby himself, that he worked for the Soviet authorities before 1946 and that in 1951 he, in fact, warned Maclean, through Burgess, that the security services were about to take action against him."

Mr. Heath said Mr. Philby had had no access to "any kind of official information" since he resigned. The minister noted that Mr. Philby had lived outside British legal jurisdiction for the last seven years.

Diligence Is Questioned

Until 1951, Mr. Heath said, Mr. Philby had "knowledge of certain information," which he had passed to Burgess and Maclean. Mr. Philby served as first secretary in the British Embassy in Washington from late 1949 to April, 1951.

Under sharp questioning by opposition Labor members, Mr. Heath refused to disclose to whom Mr. Philby had admitted his role in the Burgess-Maclean case.

The minister also rejected an implication by Patrick Gordon Walker, Labor's spokesman on foreign affairs, that "more diligent" investigations would have turned up Mr. Philby's Soviet connections in 1955.

During a Commons debate on Burgess and Maclean in November, 1955, Marcus Lipton, a Labor member, implied that Mr. Philby was the mysterious "third man" in the Burgess-Maclean case.

Mr. Philby, who was decorated for his counter-espionage work for the Foreign Office during World War II, challenged Mr. Lipton to repeat the charges outside Parliament. Mr. Lipton apologized and asked permission of the House to withdraw his remarks.

Today Mr. Lipton asked Mr. Heath: "Does that statement mean that Mr. Philby was, in fact, the third man they were talking about when Burgess and Maclean disappeared?"

"Yes sir," Mr. Heath replied with deliberation.

Shortly after Mr. Philby disappeared from Beirut, his American wife, Eleanor, said she had received word from him in Cairo. She described the reports of his disappearance as a "misunderstanding" and said that her husband had left "in a great hurry on a long assignment." Mrs. Philby now is in Britain.

More recently, Mr. Heath told the Commons, Mrs. Philby received messages from her husband "purporting to come from behind the Iron Curtain."

Philby Reported in Yemen

The minister noted, however, that the Soviet Government newspaper Izvestia reported on June 3 that Mr. Philby was working for the deposed Imam of Yemen. Mr. Philby's father, St. John Philby, was a famous explorer of Arabia.

The Earl of Dundee, Minister of State for Foreign Affairs, repeated Mr. Heath's statement to the House of Lords.

It drew from Lord Morrison the remark that newspapers, especially those mainly edited "by long-haired journalists," should exercise "reasonable care" about whom they employ. Lord Morrison, then Herbert Morrison, was the Labor Government's Foreign Secretary at the time of Mr. Philby's resignation.

Lord Morrison said he assumed that Mr. Philby would be liable to prosecution under the Official Secrets Act if he came within British jurisdiction. The former Foreign Secretary added:

"I do not see why these people guilty of treachery to the state should be able freely to draw money from this country to keep themselves going. I just do not understand it."

Lord Morrison was believed to be alluding to the fact that Burgess, for one, is believed to be drawing dividends from stocks and bonds he holds in Britain.

The Government gave no reason for the timing of its disclosures about Mr. Philby.

Starting with the Burgess-Maclean case, several security breaches involving Government officials or employes have been revealed. The most sensational of these has centered on John D. Profumo, the former Secretary of State for War.

He admitted, after first denying it, that he had had an affair with Christine Keeler in 1961 while the 21-year-old party girl was the mistress of a Soviet deputy naval attaché in London.

Defectors Deny Contact

Special to The New York Times.

MOSCOW, July 1—Guy Burgess and Donald Maclean declared in separate interviews here tonight that they did not know whether H. A. R. Philby was behind the Iron Curtain.

Burgess denied assertions that Mr. Philby, prior to their flight, had warned either him or Maclean of imminent arrest by the British counter-intelligence service.

Maclean declined to comment on the case beyond saying that he did not know Mr. Philby's whereabouts.

Burgess said it was not Mr. Philby but the Special Branch, the intelligence arm of Scotland Yard, that directed his and Maclean's attention to the imminent danger of arrest.

He said Maclean found that they were being shadowed when his cab was bumped accidentally in St. James Square, London, by a car of the Special Branch. After that it was easy for them to spot the agents who were keeping them under surveillance, he added.

"It was this and this alone that revealed to Maclean that he was being followed," Burgess said.

Burgess described Mr. Philby as one of his oldest and closest friends and said that if Mr. Philby was in Moscow he would certainly have got in touch with him. He added, "If I had heard he was in Prague or some place like that, I would have gone there to see him."

Burgess, who met Mr. Philby while the two were students at Cambridge, declared that to his knowledge Mr. Philby was not a member of the British Communist party at the university. He "joined the [British] Secret Service as my assistant," he said. Burgess is understood to have been a member of the Secret Service early in the war.

Burgess's stated position is that he is a Communist and was a member of the British Communist party, but that he never acted as a Soviet agent and since coming here has not joined the Soviet Communist party.

Burgess has occasional contact with newspaper correspondents and other Westerners. Maclean lives in almost comple seclusion.

Philby Known as Journalist

The son of St. John Philby, famed desert explorer and Arab scholar, Mr. Philby, known to his friends as Kim, has a reputation as a brilliant journalist, with a quick, incisive mind.

During World War II he served with Britain's security forces, where his acumen won him the Order of the British Empire for his work in analyzing foreign intelligence reports.

As a correspondent, Mr. Philby covered the Spanish Civil War for The Times of London. He spent the entire war with the Franco forces.

Mr. Philby has been married three times. His first marriage ended in divorce. His second wife died in 1957. His present wife, Eleanor, is the former wife of Sam Pope Brewer, a New York Times reporter. Mr. Philby has two sons and three daughters.

* * *

August 5, 1963

ANOTHER SUICIDE AROUSES VIETNAM

Young Priest Burns Himself to Death in Coastal Town in Protest Against Diem

---

Special to The New York Times.

SAIGON, Vietnam, Aug. 4—A Buddhist priest burned himself to death today in the center of the seacoast town of Phanthiet in protest against his country's religious policies.

A spokesman for the Government confirmed that there had been such a suicide, but said he had no details.

Buddhist sources said that the priest had left behind a testament explaining his action, but that it had not yet reached Saigon.

Phanthiet, on the South China Sea 100 miles east of Saigon, is a substantial fishing port, the capital of Binhthuat province. It has many fishing craft, a saltworks for fish-curing, and resort facilities.

Up to now Buddhist agitation has been more militant farther north.

Troops Take Away Body

Reliable sources said troops had been rushed to the scene and had tried to stop the suicide but had arrived too late. They carried away the charred body.

Buddhists in Saigon said they had been asked by the Phanthiet Buddhists to request the Government to hand over the body for Buddhist services.

They indicated that it would now be important to watch what the Government did with the body. If it was not given back, this could become another divisive issue.

Buddhist sources said the last name of the priest who killed himself was Le. The sources said he was in his 20's. It appears that he slipped quietly out of a pagoda, where he was among a group of fasters, to set himself on fire.

The informants in Saigon said Buddhists in Phanthiet had been fasting in groups, with each fast lasting for 48 hours, since the protest began last Tuesday. Buddhist leaders here said that they had asked the Phanthiet Buddhists to stage the demonstrations.

This new incident came as many observers felt the Buddhist protest in Saigon itself was losing some of its force, although its effect here was still considered extremely important.

Some observers feel that the Buddhist movement has slowed down in the last two weeks because the Government has been shrewder and less repressive in handling the Buddhists. They say much of the Buddhists' earlier strength stemmed from Government mishandling. They are now watching to see how well the new development is dealt with.

In a country where 70 per cent of the population belongs to sects that call themselves Buddhist, the protest pits Buddhist leaders against the family Government of President Ngo Dinh Diem. The family's members are Roman Catholics.

The protest dates from May 8 when troops fired into a crowd of Buddhist demonstrators in Hue and killed nine.

On June 11 a priest named Quang Duc burned himself to death publicly as a protest. On July 7 Vietnam's most famous writer, Nguyen Tuong Tam, killed himself by taking poison. His death was largely related to the current dispute, although he was also accused of complicity in an attempted coup.

Yesterday Mrs. Ngo Dinh Nhu, President Ngo Dinh Diem's sister-in-law and an extremely powerful figure in the country, referred to Buddhist leaders as murderers because of Quang Duc's suicide.

* * *

August 6, 1963

TEST BAN TREATY SIGNED IN MOSCOW; LEADERS REJOICE

Khrushchev and Ministers Join Glittering Reception After Solemn Ceremony

WARM SPIRIT PREVAILS

Thant and 70 U.S., Russian and British Officials Attend— 'First Step' Is Theme

---

By HENRY TANNER
Special to The New York Times.

MOSCOW, Aug. 5—The foreign ministers of the United States, Britain and the Soviet Union signed the test ban treaty today at a ceremony that was both solemn and joyous.

Then, led by Premier Khrushchev, they strode into one of the Kremlin's most glittering ballrooms for a reception as a Soviet band played Gershwin's "Love Walked In."

TREATY IS SIGNED IN MOSCOW: Seated at table at ceremony are, from left: Secretary of State Rusk, Andrei A. Gromyko and the Earl of Home, who signed triplicate copies of the pact for the U.S., Soviet Union and Britain, respectively. In the front row of those standing are, from left: Senators George D. Aiken, Republican of Vermont, and J.W. Fulbright, Democrat of Arkansas; Alexander Akalovsky, State Department interpreter; Senator Hubert H. Humphrey, Democrat of Minnesota; Adlai E. Stevenson, chief U.S. representative at United Nations; U Thant, U.N. Secretary General, and Premier Khrushchev. Behind Lord Home and his aide is Edward Heath, British Lord Privy Seal, and beside him, to left, is Valerian A. Zorin, an official of Soviet Foreign Ministry. The ceremony for the signing of the treaty was conducted yesterday in the Kremlin.

The song summed up the mood of the day. From the start of courtesy calls by the ministers at 9 A.M. to the end of the gala reception just before nightfall it was filled with firm East-West handshakes, warm smiles, friendly jokes and toasts to "peace and friendship" drunk in Soviet champagne.

Premier Poses With Clergy

One diplomat called it a "unique day" in East-West relations. "Peace—it's wonderful," said another, and meant it.

Premier Khrushchev, who insists he does not believe in religion, was moved by the spirit of conciliation to the point of posing for pictures with the elders of the Russian Orthodox Church.

The signing of the 1,500-word treaty banning nuclear tests in the atmosphere, in space and under water took only five minutes.

It was held in Catherine Hall, a vaulted, white marble chamber in the Kremlin's Great Palace.

Bathed in White Lights

Secretary of State Dean Rusk, Foreign Minister Andrei A. Gromyko and the Earl of Home, Britain's Foreign Secretary, sat in gold-trimmed chairs at an oblong table as they affixed their signatures to the three copies of the document.

Above their heads was a huge, glittering chandelier. They were bathed in the brilliance of the klieg lights set up for Soviet and Western television.

Standing behind them and watching the signing were about 70 Soviet, American and British dignitaries led by Premier Khrushchev. U Thant, the United Nations Secretary General, stood next to the Premier.

The Soviet group included Leonid I. Brezhnev, the Soviet chief of state, and almost all the key leaders of the Soviet Government with the exception of Anastas I. Mikoyan, a First Deputy Premier, who is ill.

British Groups Smaller

The large American delegation included Adlai E. Stevenson, Senators J. W. Fulbright, Democrat of Arkansas; George D. Aiken, Republican of Vermont; Leverett Saltonstall, Republican of Massachusetts; John J. Sparkman, Democrat of Alabama; Hubert H. Humphrey, Democrat of Minnesota, and John O. Pastore, Democrat of Rhode Island, and Ambassador Foy D. Kohler.

The smaller British group included Deputy Foreign Minister Edward Heath, Sir Harold Caccia, Permanent Secretary of the Foreign Office, and Sir Humphrey Trevelyan, the Ambassador to the Soviet Union.

After the signing, the foreign ministers made short statements.

Each stressed the theme that the treaty, in which the world's three most powerful Governments pledge to refrain from further contaminating the air and the oceans with nuclear tests, was merely a first step.

Each pledged that his government and his nation was intent on taking further steps toward easing world tension and creating the conditions for lasting peace.

After each declaration the assembly raised long-stemmed champagne glasses to drink to "peace and friendship," the toast proposed by Mr. Gromyko and seconded by Mr. Rusk.

Americans and Russians, Britons and Russians, and Americans and Britons in turn clinked glasses, smiled and nodded at each other and took a few sips as the television cameras whirred.

No one smiled more broadly and clinked glasses more eagerly or more often than Premier Khrushchev. He stood in the center of a group, wearing a gray suit and silver tie and a row of three medals hanging from red ribbons.

Although he did not speak, he obviously assumed the role of host, and, by implication, of chief architect of the treaty.

The three-power communiqué issued after the signing echoed the declarations of the foreign ministers.

'Important Initial Step'

It said their governments regarded the partial ban on testing as an "important initial step" and hoped that "further progress" toward peace would be achieved.

The communiqué expressed the hope that other states would join the treaty. It announced that the treaty would be available for signing in London, Moscow and Washington beginning Thursday.

Thirty-three states had served notice by early this afternoon that they wanted to sign the treaty now. Thirty additional governments have said that they plan to do so later.

In spite of the smiles and the champagne, the day was not all celebration.

There were moments when the statesmen showed their old wariness and engaged in some deft diplomatic fencing.

Secretary Rusk made a point in his statement of stressing some of the things the treaty did not do.

"It does not end the threat of nuclear war," he said. "It does not reduce nuclear stockpiles, it does not halt the production of nuclear weapons, it does not restrict their use in time of war."

The American delegation here regards the reference to the possible use of nuclear weapons in time of war as an important one.

There has been some concern among legal experts in the Administration that the language of the treaty is ambiguous on this point and that an attempt may be made later to interpret it as forbidding the use of nuclear weapons in time of war.

The concern prompted a clarifying statement from President Kennedy 10 days ago. Secretary Rusk seized the opportunity of today's formal ceremony to restate the American position.

Mr. Khrushchev, while not speaking at the signing ceremony, made a statement at the gala reception that followed it.

He stressed the long-standing Soviet request for conclusion of a nonaggression treaty to follow the test ban.

The Western representatives here have made it clear that they will listen to the Soviet argument, but cannot enter into negotiations on such a treaty because they have no mandate from the North Atlantic Treaty Organization to do so.

Russians Take Credit

The Russians also indicated that they regarded the treaty that was signed today as a Soviet initiative and that they meant to take primary credit for it.

Premier Khrushchev referred to it as a "Soviet proposal" to which the two Western powers had agreed.

This is not quite the way the West sees it. The American diplomats say the Russians were the first to propose an overall test ban treaty without inspection.

It was the West, these diplomats say, that broke the deadlock by proposing a treaty barring tests in the atmosphere, in space and under water where the issue of inspection does not arise. The Western proposal left the issue of underground tests, which involves inspection, for future negotiations.

Mr. Thant spoke at the signing ceremony. He called on the three powers to go beyond the present treaty and to heed United Nations proposals for prohibiting the further dissemination of nuclear weapons and for the reduction of the means of delivery of nuclear weapons.

He also urged prohibition of the use of nuclear weapons in time of war and asked for further consideration of proposals for the creation of "denuclearized zones" in Asia and Africa.

This morning the American and British delegations paid separate courtesy calls on Mr. Khrushchev and Mr. Gromyko at their offices.

The calls served to introduce the members of the delegations to the two Soviet leaders before the signing ceremony and the talks to be held tomorrow.

Premier Khrushchev will not participate in tomorrow's talks. He said now that the treaty had been signed he would fly to Gagra, a resort on the Black Sea coast, to start a long-delayed vacation.

Secretary Rusk is expected to visit him there Thursday or Friday after a quick visit to Leningrad Wednesday.

Fulbright Sees Ratification

MOSCOW, Aug. 5 (AP)—Senator Fulbright, chairman of the Senate Foreign Relations Committee, said at the Kremlin reception that after serving 21 years in the Senate he felt sure he could predict that his colleagues would back the nuclear test ban treaty.

"Lately the world has been moving toward catastrophe," he said. "The signed treaty halts this movement and we are beginning to move away from the catastrophe."

Senator Aiken described the treaty as a seed from which a fine tree could grow and "from which we can expect wonderful fruit."

Senator Humphrey called the ban an important step in improving East-West relations.

More Than 30 Nations Plan To Sign Test-Ban Accord

More than 30 nations have publicly announced that they intend to sign the test ban treaty. France and Communist China have refused. West Germany has announced it will not sign as of now.

The nations that have publicly announced they will sign are: Afghanistan, Australia, Belgium, Brazil, Britain, Bulgaria, Canada, Czechoslovakia, Denmark, East Germany, Ecuador, Ethiopia, Finland, India, Iran, Ireland, Israel, Italy, Jamaica, Japan, Laos, Liberia, Mexico, New Zealand, Norway, Outer Mongolia, Poland, Saudi Arabia, Senegal, Somalia, the Soviet Union, the United Arab Republic, the United States and Uruguay.

* * *

September 14, 1963

PEKING CHARGES SOVIET VIOLATION OF AMITY TREATY

Asserts Khrushchev Helped Foes of Mao—
Scores Incidents on Border

By HARRY SCHWARTZ

Communist China has accused the Soviet Union of "flagrant violation" of the 1950 Chinese-Soviet treaty of friendship and alliance.

Peking has also accused Premier Khrushchev of having supported opponents of Mao Tse-tung, head of the Chinese Communist party, and of an attempt in 1958 "to bring China under Soviet military control."

These and other charges are contained in the official Chinese reply to a statement by the Soviet Communist party, on July 14, attacking Peking's policies. The Chinese reply was published last week by the Peking organs Jenmin Jih Pao and Hung Chi.

The text of the reply was distributed in English by Hsinhua, the Chinese Communist press agency, and has just become available here.

Issue Raised in 1956

The Peking reply indicates that the Chinese, as early as 1956, demanded that the Soviet leaders acknowledge their own errors committed during Stalin's dictatorship instead of attributing all the misdeeds of the time to Stalin.

The Chinese statement is the first comprehensive account of the origin and development of the Chinese-Soviet ideological dispute. It describes in detail the behind-the-scenes events from 1956 to the present.

Both China and the Soviet Union make charges against each other that appear to amount to accusations of violation of the 1950 treaty.

The Chinese accuse the Russians of allying themselves with the United States against China, thus participating in an alliance prohibited under the treaty.

Sinkiang Plot Alleged

Peking also charges that Premier Khrushchev has shown sympathy for "anti-party elements" in the Chinese party and coerced and enticed tens of thousands of Chinese citizens to leave Sinkiang Province for the Soviet Union.

The Soviet Union, on the other hand, has charged the Chinese with interfering in Soviet internal affairs by illegally distributing literature assailing the Soviet Communist party's ideological position: this, too, can be construed as a treaty violation.

Similarly, a Soviet charge that the Chinese attacked India last year without having consulted the Soviet Union implies a Chinese violation of a treaty provision calling for consultations on important international matters affecting each side's interests.

In October, 1969, the Chinese say, Premier Khrushchev, in a conversation with the Chinese delegation to the Soviet party congress, "flatly turned down our criticism and advice and even expressed undisguised support for antiparty elements n the Chinese Communist party." The term "antiparty elements" alludes to Chinese Communists opposing Mao Tse-tung, chairman of the Central Committee of the Peking party, and his policy.

This statement makes it clear that the Russian-Chinese unity and friendship proclaimed in Moscow and Peking in the late nineteen-fifties and early sixties was a façade behind which there raged a bitter doctrinal and international struggle. A summary of the Chinese statement follows:

The dispute began in early 1956 when Premier Khrushchev at the 20th congress of the Soviet Communist party, made a secret speech denouncing Stalin and enunciated several new points of Communist doctrine. These included the idea of a peaceful victory by Communism over capitalism and a denial that war between capitalist and Communist nations was inevitable.

Main Points of Quarrel

Less than two months later Mr. Mao told a Soviet First Deputy Premier, Anastas I. Mikoyan, that he felt Premier Khrushchev had gone too far in his attack on Stalin.

In Moscow, in December, 1957, at the first comprehensive Communist international party meeting since World War II, the Chinese and Soviet leaders quarreled bitterly over the drafting of a statement that was intended as a platform for world Communism.

The quarrel centered on Soviet determination to mention only a peaceful transition from capitalism to Socialism and Soviet emphasis upon the importance of Communist winning a "majority in Parliament" to attain power.

The Chinese managed to have a final draft of the statement incorporate also endorsement of a "nonpeaceful transition" from Socialism to Communism, and identify "United States imperialism" as "the center of world reaction and the sworn enemy of the people."

In 1958, there existed a Chinese-Soviet treaty providing for Soviet aid to help the Chinese obtain nuclear weapons. The Chinese assert that at that time the Soviet Communist party "put forward unreasonable demands designed to bring China under Soviet military control."

A Surprise Assault

The Chinese statement then notes that after Chinese rejection of the Soviet demands, the Soviet Government abrogated the atomic aid agreement. The nature of the Soviet demands is not specified, but the implication appears to be that the Soviet leaders refused to give Peking nuclear weapons unless Moscow controlled use of the weapons.

In June, 1960, the Chinese charge, Premier Khrushchev carried out a "surprise assault" on the Chinese Communists at the Rumanian Communist party congress in Bucharest. The meeting there, the Chinese say, had been called nominally for an exchange of views. Instead, they say, Premier Khrushchev delivered a bitter anti-Chinese speech, calling them "madmen," "pure nationalists" and "Trotskyites."

The Chinese statement says "troubles on the Chinese-Soviet border" began in 1960. This indicates that the Soviet decision to give refuge to Moslems fleeing from China's Sinkiang Province last year had its roots in problems of a wider scope.

* * *

November 2, 1963

REBELS IN VIETNAM OUST DIEM, REPORT HIM AND NHU SUICIDES; SHARPER FIGHT ON REDS VOWED

PALACE BESIEGED

Army, Air Force and Marines Combine to Oust President

By HEDRICK SMITH
Special to The New York Times.

WASHINGTON, Saturday, Nov. 2—The South Vietnamese Government of President Ngo Dinh Diem has fallen in a swift military coup d'état.

The insurgents reported over the Saigon radio this morning that Ngo Dinh Diem and his powerful brother Ngo Dinh Nhu had committed suicide.

High officials here confirmed that President Ngo Dinh Diem surrendered to the rebels at 6:05 this morning, Saigon time (5:05 P.M. Friday, New York time), and that the brothers were arrested. There was no official confirmation of the suicide report, which was relayed by the United States Embassy in Saigon.

Anti-Red Drive Promised

All indications were that the military committee that staged the coup was firmly anti-Communist and pro-Western. It was viewed as eager to eliminate the repressive features of the Ngo Dinh Diem Government, which had so frustrated the United States recently.

The insurrectionists pledged to intensify the country's struggle against the Communist guerrillas—the cause that the United States feared might suffer from Ngo Dinh Diem's loss of popular support.

According to the Saigon radio, the brothers escaped the rebel forces after their surrender and sought asylum in a church. Then, the radio added, they were recaptured. The time of their suicide was given as 10:45 this morning (9:45 P.M., Friday, New York time).

Officials said that Vice President Nguyen Ngoc Tho, a Buddhist highly regarded in Washington, was expected to become Premier of a caretaker civilian government.

Discrimination Was Issue

Vu Van Mau, who resigned as South Vietnam's Foreign Minister last August, was also expected to play a prominent role. His resignation protested the Government's August 21 destruction of Buddhist pagodas, which intensified the religious crisis that led to the coup.

Since last May South Vietnam's Buddhists had been charging the Government of the Roman Catholic Ngo family with religious discrimination.

The military leaders were reported to have assured Ambassador Henry Cabot Lodge that they intended to turn over control of the Government to responsible civilian officials.

This made it likely that the United States would extend diplomatic recognition to the new Government within the next few days.

The end of the smoothly organized uprising was announced by the Voice of the Armed Forces in a broadcast from Saigon at 6:25 A.M. today, Saigon time (5:25 P.M. Friday, Eastern standard time).

The broadcast said that rebel forces had seized the Presidential Palace and that President Ngo Dinh Diem had "surrendered unconditionally" at 6:05 A.M. Saigon time.

High officials here, who had discounted earlier reports of President Ngo Dinh Diem's surrender as premature, confirmed that this time the claim of the rebels was correct.

In its early stages the revolt moved like clockwork. Elements of the Vietnamese army, air force and marines seized virtually every key point in Saigon but the presidential palace, where fighting raged late into Friday night.

The primary resistance came from some units of the Vietnamese navy, which fired at insurgent air force planes strafing loyal military headquarters, and from loyal Special Forces and Palace Guard troops.

The palace was the last outpost of the President and his brother. Late into last night they were defended by about

1,500 troops. Then, just before dawn, the State Department reported, there was a brief lull in the fighting.

As dawn broke the insurgents launched the decisive attack on the palace.

Kennedy Keeps Watch

President Kennedy and other top officials kept close watch on the lightning-like developments in Saigon. The President was awakened at 3 A.M. yesterday with early word of the coup and met with his top National Security Advisers at 10 A.M. for a full briefing.

Commercial communications links with Vietnam were closed and the Saigon airport was shut down by the insurgents. The best available information on the coup was relayed by radio or through the State Department, which kept continuous contact with its embassy in Saigon.

The August raids on pagodas and Mr. Lodge's persistent protests had a profound impact on the Kennedy Administration. Loath though it was to proceed down the always unpredictable path of stirring up political unrest in an already unstable nation, it concluded that the risks of inaction might be greater than the risks of cautious maneuvering.

While a year ago the slogan here was "Sink or swim with Diem," it became clear in September that Washington was prepared to consider alternatives to his leadership.

The open expressions of hostility and the suspension of economic aid were intended as signals to the opposition that Washington would not necessarily defend the Ngo Dinh Diem regime against domestic challengers.

Although the United States had helped create the climate for the coup with its sharp denunciations of the Government's repressive measures and recent cutbacks on economic aid, officials here were emphatic in denying that the United States had an active hand in the coup.

Coup Is Second Attempt

This was the second major attempt of a coup against the Government. One in November, 1960, failed at the last minute when President Ngo Dinh Diem rallied military forces to his support.

The present coup was triggered by a demonstration in Hue on May 8 when Government troops killed nine persons. Since then the Buddhist protests gained a political tenor and drew support from various elements of the Vietnamese population that opposed repressive aspects of the Diem Government.

The tension reached a peak August 21 when Government Special Forces units raided Buddhist pagodas and arrested scores of Buddhists and students who later demonstrated against the regime.

As a result, United States officials feared the regime had so severely lost popular support that it would impair the joint American-Vietnamese war effort against Communist guerrillas.

On Sept. 3, President Kennedy said in a television interview that he felt the Vietnamese Government could regain popular support "with changes in policy and perhaps with personnel."

At that time there were rumors of an impending military coup, but President Ngo Dinh Diem and his brother outmaneuvered any potential foes.

Officials here said the coup was led by a committee of 14 Vietnamese generals and 10 colonels, including the four commanders of Vietnam's main army corps.

A number of generals were known to have disagreed with President Ngo Dinh Diem's management of the war against the Communists. In their broadcasts over the Saigon radio they expressed discontent over humiliation of top Vietnamese officers by the palace leaders.

According to State Department sources, the coup began about 1:45 P.M. Friday, Saigon time, or about 12:45 A.M. here. First word of the revolt reached Washington about 1:20 A.M. through military communications channels.

The initiative in the revolt, officials said, came from insurgent army and marine units. The army immediately blocked off roads to Saigon's airport and overwhelmed Special Forces units there.

Vietnamese marine units camped outside Saigon were reported to have swept into the city. They quickly seized control of the Ministry of Interior communications center, naval headquarters, the police compound and the Ministry of Defense.

From there the insurgent forces wheeled toward the presidential palace, where they assaulted the barracks of the presidential guard. Light artillery and small-arms fire broke out around the palace.

Four air force fighter-bombers attacked the palace and loyal army headquarters in the first hours of the revolt, the reports said.

Naval vessels in the Saigon River, loyal to the President, opened fire on the aircraft and, according to an unconfirmed report, one of the planes was shot down.

While the city rocked with gunfire and tanks wheeled down the main streets, insurgent naval vessels were reported to have surrounded and quelled those loyal to the Government.

One of the first moves of the plotters was to arrest pro-Diem military leaders. Among the first arrested was Colonel Tung, who as head of the Special Forces was regarded as Ngo Dinh Nhu's military right arm.

According to reports reaching here, the insurgents also arrested the police commissioner, the air force chief of staff and the commander of Saigon's 150,000-man civil guard, all considered hostile to the group.

Martial Law Declared

At 4:45 P.M. Friday, Saigon time, three hours after the coup began, the military insurgents declared over the Saigon radio that the President had capitulated. But the report was false.

Two hours later, the "council of generals" broadcast its "military order No. 1," signed by General Duong Van Minh.

The order decreed martial law, established a curfew from 8 P.M. until 7 A.M. and banned all meetings or circulation of publications and leaflets "harmful to public security and order."

All organizations and individuals were ordered to turn over "hand weapons and ammunition, including sharp weapons," to the nearest military authorities.

In subsequent broadcasts the rebel leaders announced the release of Buddhists, teachers and students arrested by the Diem Government.

They also broadcast appeals for the general population to cooperate with the insurrection "with order and discipline in the struggle against the Communists."

The surrender was reported to have come in a telephone call from the President to General Duong Van Minh, the key military figure in the rebellion, after a fierce battle at the palace.

Officials said that an escort guard had gone to the palace to take the President and his brother into custody, but that no Americans had actually witnessed the arrest.

Although the rebellious military forces held complete control of the city by 7 A.M. Saturday, there were conflicting reports from Saigon about the final fate and whereabouts of President Ngo Dinh Diem and Dinh Nhu.

* * *

November 20, 1963

CONCERN IS RISING IN AUSTRALIA OVER INDONESIA'S EXPANSIONISM

By J. ANTHONY LUKAS
Special to The New York Times.

SYDNEY, Australia, Nov. 17—Australia's newspapers carried today an advertisement, sandwiched between reports of the political campaign, that showed an enchanting Japanese maiden in a flowered kimono, strumming a samisen by the shores of a still lagoon.

Such a scene is less than 13 hours away by jet, the advertisement said.

Australian readers may reflect that if Tokyo is only 13 hours away, then Peking is only 15 hours away by jet bomber and, perhaps more important, Indonesia, with a Soviet-equipped air force, is only two hours away.

Qántas, Australia's overseas airline, says that it brings the Orient as close as tomorrow, but for many Australians Asia's millions are already too close for comfort. This new awareness of the proximity to what Australia calls her near north gives defense and foreign policy issues unusual prominence in the campaign for the Nov. 30 elections.

This country's voters have traditionally shown little interest in events beyond their shores unless those events affected the price for wool or the cost of beer.

Rely on U. S. Deterrent

Isolated by miles of Pacific waters, they felt cut off from world politics until World War II, when they were protected by the British Navy. Since then they have relied on the United States nuclear deterrent.

However, recent events have given Australia a new sense of her vulnerability. Indonesia's takeover of Netherlands New Guinea, now West Irian, raised deep concern among those who do not like to share a boundary with President Sukarno's regime. Australia controls the eastern half of the island.

The threats that the Indonesian President has made toward the new federation of Malaysia have done nothing to ease those doubts. Australians fear that Mr. Sukarno may soon look longingly at the inviting open spaces of their own underdeveloped north.

"If your Yanks were worried by a couple of million Cubans and their Soviet missiles, you can understand why 10 million Australians are concerned by 90 million Indonesians with Russian arms just 300 miles away," one Australian official said this week.

Observers believe Australia's Prime Minister, Sir Robert G. Menzies, called elections one year earlier than required partly because he hoped to exploit this new concern about Indonesia and other threats from abroad.

Fight for Malaysia Backed

According to these sources, Sir Robert was strongly influenced by the results of a poll taken last August. Fifty-eight per cent of those polled said that Australia should fight to defend Malaysia if the federation were attacked by Indonesia. Twenty-two per cent said no and the rest were undecided.

The Prime Minister evidently hoped to use this support for a "hard line" foreign policy to rally Australians behind his Government, which for two years has had a precarious one-vote margin in Parliament.

When he dissolved Parliament Oct. 15, Sir Robert announced that he would fight the campaign on foreign policy and defense issues. He asked for a mandate to deal with the critical problems in "our near neighborhood."

Since then the opposition Labor party has advanced sweeping proposals for new Government programs in housing, education and social services. The governing Liberal party has been forced to reply in kind. Many observers now believe that the election will be decided on these traditional Australian bread-and-butter issues.

The Prime Minister depicts the Labor party, led by Arthur A. Calwell, as a dangerously left-wing force that does not recognize the Communist threat. However, it is difficult to find many significant differences between the parties' foreign and defense policies as outlined in the speeches of the two leaders.

Probably the greatest difference is over Labor's advocacy of a nuclear-free southern hemisphere.

Mr. Calwell contends that this is only an effort to achieve what President Kennedy has declared to be the first step toward general disarmament. Sir Robert has labeled it a suicidal proposal.

Sir Robert is also hitting hard on differences over the new communications station now being built for the United States Navy at Northwest Cape, an important link in the worldwide control network for submarines carrying Polaris missiles.

The Labor party demanded earlier this year that the treaty be renegotiated to provide for joint Australian-United States control over the station.

The Prime Minister contends that this attitude jeopardizes Australia's relations with the country's most important ally. However, Mr. Calwell has already assured the United States that a Labor government would never repudiate the treaty even if it were unable to negotiate joint control.

On Malaysia the line between the parties is also indistinct. The Government maintains a 1,500-man garrison in Malaya, the heartland of the federation, and has pledged to come to Malaysia's aid in the event of attack.

The Labor party has said it would seek to negotiate a treaty to cover the continued presence of Australian troops in Malaysia.

*   *   *

November 23, 1963

KENNEDY IS KILLED BY SNIPER AS HE RIDES IN CAR IN DALLAS; JOHNSON SWORN IN ON PLANE

GOV. CONNALLY SHOT; MRS. KENNEDY SAFE

President Is Struck Down by a Rifle Shot From Building on Motorcade Route—Johnson, Riding Behind, Is Unhurt

By TOM WICKER
Special to The New York Times.

DALLAS, Nov. 22—President John Fitzgerald Kennedy was shot and killed by an assassin today.

He died of a wound in the brain caused by a rifle bullet that was fired at him as he was riding through downtown Dallas in a motorcade.

Vice President Lyndon Baines Johnson, who was riding in the third car behind Mr. Kennedy's, was sworn in as the 36th President of the United States 99 minutes after Mr. Kennedy's death.

Mr. Johnson is 55 years old; Mr. Kennedy was 46.

Shortly after the assassination, Lee H. Oswald, who once defected to the Soviet Union and who has been active in the Fair Play for Cuba Committee, was arrested by the Dallas police. Tonight he was accused of the killing.

Suspect Captured After Scuffle

Oswald, 24 years old, was also accused of slaying a policeman who had approached him in the street. Oswald was subdued after a scuffle with a second policeman in a nearby theater.

President Kennedy was shot at 12:30 P.M., Central standard time (1:30 P.M., New York time). He was pronounced dead at 1 P.M. and Mr. Johnson was sworn in at 2:39 P.M.

Mr. Johnson, who was uninjured in the shooting, took his oath in the Presidential jet plane as it stood on the runway at Love Field. The body of Mr. Kennedy was aboard. Immediately after the oath-taking, the plane took off for Washington.

Standing beside the new President as Mr. Johnson took the oath of office was Mrs. John F. Kennedy. Her stockings were spattered with her husband's blood.

Gov. John B. Connally Jr. of Texas, who was riding in the same car with Mr. Kennedy, was severely wounded in the chest, ribs and arm. His condition was serious, but not critical.

The killer fired the rifle from a building just off the motorcade route. Mr. Kennedy, Governor Connally and Mr. Johnson had just received an enthusiastic welcome from a large crowd in downtown Dallas.

Mr. Kennedy apparently was hit by the first of what witnesses believed were three shots. He was driven at high speed to Dallas's Parkland Hospital. There, in an emergency operating room with only physicians and nurses in attendance, he died without regaining consciousness.

Mrs. Kennedy, Mrs. Connally and a Secret Service agent were in the car with Mr. Kennedy and Governor Connally. Two Secret Service agents flanked the car. Other than Mr. Connally, none of this group was injured in the shooting. Mrs. Kennedy cried, "Oh no!" immediately after her husband was struck.

Mrs. Kennedy was in the hospital near her husband when he died, but not in the operating room. When the body was taken from the hospital in a bronze coffin about 2 P.M., Mrs. Kennedy walked beside it.

Her face was sorrowful. She looked steadily at the floor. She still wore the raspberry-colored suit in which she had greeted welcoming crowds in Fort Worth and Dallas. But she had taken off the matching pillbox hat she wore earlier in the day, and her dark hair was windblown and tangled. Her hand rested lightly on her husband's coffin as it was taken to a waiting hearse.

Mrs. Kennedy climbed in beside the coffin. Then the ambulance drove to Love Field, and Mr. Kennedy's body was placed aboard the Presidential jet. Mrs. Kennedy then attended the swearing-in ceremony for Mr. Johnson.

As Mr. Kennedy's body left Parkland Hospital, a few stunned persons stood outside. Nurses and doctors, whispering among themselves, looked from the window. A larger crowd that had gathered earlier, before it was known that the President was dead, had been dispersed by Secret Service men and policemen.

Priests Administer Last Rites

Two priests administered last rites to Mr. Kennedy, a Roman Catholic. They were the Very Rev. Oscar Huber, the pastor of Holy Trinity Church in Dallas, and the Rev. James Thompson.

Mr. Johnson was sworn in as President by Federal Judge Sarah T. Hughes of the Northern District of Texas. She was appointed to the judgeship by Mr. Kennedy in October, 1961.

The ceremony, delayed about five minutes for Mrs. Kennedy's arrival, took place in the private Presidential cabin in the rear of the plane.

About 25 to 30 persons—members of the late President's staff, members of Congress who had been accompanying

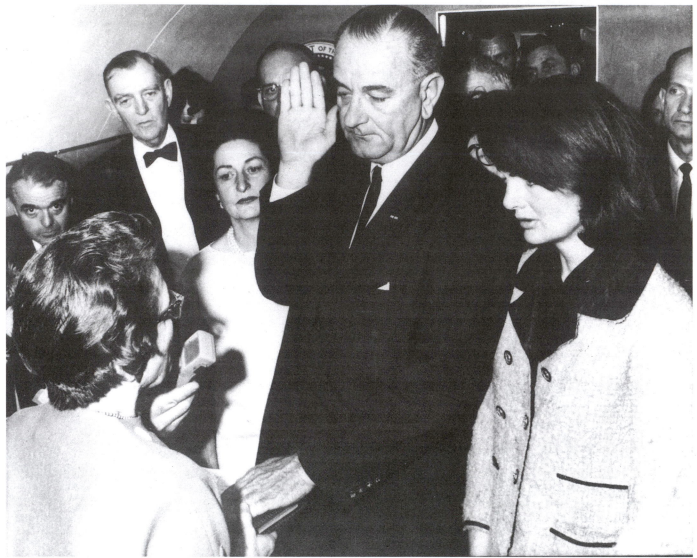

Capt. Cecil Stoughton via United Press International

THE NEW PRESIDENT: Lyndon B. Johnson takes oath before Judge Sarah T. Hughes in plane at Dallas. Mrs. Kennedy and Representative Jack Brooks are at right. To left are Mrs. Johnson and Representative Albert Thomas.

the President on a two-day tour of Texas cities and a few reporters—crowded into the little room.

No accurate listing of those present could be obtained. Mrs. Kennedy stood at the left of Mr. Johnson, her eyes and face showing the signs of weeping that had apparently shaken her since she left the hospital not long before.

Mrs. Johnson, wearing a beige dress, stood at her husband's right.

As Judge Hughes read the brief oath of office, her eyes, too, were red from weeping. Mr. Johnson's hands rested on a black, leather-bound Bible as Judge Hughes read and he repeated:

"I do solemnly swear that I will perform the duties of the President of the United States to the best of my ability and defend, protect and preserve the Constitution of the United States."

Those 34 words made Lyndon Baines Johnson, one-time farmboy and schoolteacher of Johnson City, the President.

Johnson Embraces Mrs. Kennedy

Mr. Johnson made no statement. He embraced Mrs. Kennedy and she held his hand for a long moment. He also embraced Mrs. Johnson and Mrs. Evelyn Lincoln, Mr. Kennedy's private secretary.

"O.K.," Mr. Johnson said. "Let's get this plane back to Washington."

At 2:46 P.M., seven minutes after he had become President, 106 minutes after Mr. Kennedy had become the fourth American President to succumb to an assassin's wounds, the white and red jet took off for Washington.

In the cabin when Mr. Johnson took the oath was Cecil Stoughton, an armed forces photographer assigned to the White House.

Mr. Kennedy's staff members appeared stunned and bewildered. Lawrence F. O'Brien, the Congressional liaison officer, and P. Kenneth O'Donnell, the appointment secretary, both long associates of Mr. Kennedy, showed evidences of weeping. None had anything to say.

Other staff members believed to be in the cabin for the swearing-in included David F. Powers, the White House receptionist; Miss Pamela Turnure, Mrs. Kennedy's press secretary, and Malcolm Kilduff, the assistant White House press secretary.

Mr. Kilduff announced the President's death, with choked voice and red-rimmed eyes, at about 1:36 P.M.

"President John F. Kennedy died at approximately 1 o'clock Central standard time today here in Dallas," Mr. Kilduff said at the hospital. "He died of a gunshot wound in the brain. I have no other details regarding the assassination of the President."

Mr. Kilduff also announced that Governor Connally had been hit by a bullet or bullets and that Mr. Johnson, who had not yet been sworn in, was safe in the protective custody of the Secret Service at an unannounced place, presumably the airplane at Love Field.

Mr. Kilduff indicated that the President had been shot once. Later medical reports raised the possibility that there had been two wounds. But the death was caused, as far as could be learned, by a massive wound in the brain.

Later in the afternoon, Dr. Malcolm Perry, an attending surgeon, and Dr. Kemp Clark, chief of neurosurgery at Parkland Hospital, gave more details.

Mr. Kennedy was hit by a bullet in the throat, just below the Adam's apple, they said. This wound had the appearance of a bullet's entry.

Mr. Kennedy also had a massive, gaping wound in the back and one on the right side of the head. However, the doctors said it was impossible to determine immediately whether the wounds had been caused by one bullet or two.

Resuscitation Attempted

Dr. Perry, the first physician to treat the President, said a number of resuscitative measures had been attempted, including oxygen, anesthesia, an indotracheal tube, a tracheotomy, blood and fluids. An electrocardiogram monitor was attached to measure Mr. Kennedy's heart beats.

Dr. Clark was summoned and arrived in a minute or two. By then, Dr. Perry said, Mr. Kennedy was "critically ill and moribund," or near death.

Dr. Clark said that on his first sight of the President, he had concluded immediately that Mr. Kennedy could not live.

"It was apparent that the President had sustained a lethal wound," he said. "A missile had gone in and out of the back of his head causing external lacerations and loss of brain tissue."

Shortly after he arrived, Dr. Clark said, "the President lost his heart action by the electrocardiogram." A closed-chest cardiograph massage was attempted, as were other emergency resuscitation measures.

Dr. Clark said these had produced "palpable pulses" for a short time, but all were "to no avail."

In Operating Room 40 Minutes

The President was on the emergency table at the hospital for about 40 minutes, the doctors said. At the end, perhaps eight physicians were in Operating Room No. 1, where Mr. Kennedy remained until his death. Dr. Clark said it was difficult to determine the exact moment of death, but the doctors said officially that it occurred at 1 P.M.

Later, there were unofficial reports that Mr. Kennedy had been killed instantly. The source of these reports, Dr. Tom Shires, chief surgeon at the hospital and professor of surgery at the University of Texas Southwest Medical School, issued this statement tonight:

"Medically, it was apparent the President was not alive when he was brought in. There was no spontaneous respiration. He had dilated fixed pupils. It was obvious he had a lethal head wound.

"Technically, however, by using vigorous resuscitation, intravenous tubes and all the usual supportive measures, we were able to raise a semblance of a heartbeat."

Dr. Shires said he was "positive it was impossible" that President Kennedy could have spoken after being shot. "I am absolutely sure he never knew what hit him," Dr. Shires said.

Dr. Shires was not present when Mr. Kennedy was being treated at Parkland Hospital. He issued his statement, however, after lengthy conferences with the doctors who had attended the President.

Mr. Johnson remained in the hospital about 30 minutes after Mr. Kennedy died.

The details of what happened when shots first rang out, as the President's car moved along at about 25 miles an hour, were sketchy. Secret Service agents, who might have given more details, were unavailable to the press at first, and then returned to Washington with President Johnson.

Kennedys Hailed at Breakfast

Mr. Kennedy had opened his day in Fort Worth, first with a speech in a parking lot and then at a Chamber of Commerce breakfast. The breakfast appearance was a particular triumph for Mrs. Kennedy, who entered late and was given an ovation.

Then the Presidential party, including Governor and Mrs. Connally, flew on to Dallas, an eight-minute flight. Mr. Johnson, as is customary, flew in a separate plane. The President and the Vice President do not travel together, out of fear of a double tragedy.

At Love Field, Mr. and Mrs. Kennedy lingered for 10 minutes, shaking hands with an enthusiastic group lining the fence. The group called itself "Grassroots Democrats."

Mr. Kennedy then entered his open Lincoln convertible at the head of the motorcade. He sat in the rear seat on the right-hand side. Mrs. Kennedy, who appeared to be enjoying one of the first political outings she had ever made with her husband, sat at his left.

In the "jump" seat, directly ahead of Mr. Kennedy, sat Governor Connally, with Mrs. Connally at his left in another "jump" seat. A Secret Service agent was driving and the two others ran alongside.

Behind the President's limousine was an open sedan carrying a number of Secret Service agents. Behind them, in an open convertible, rode Mr. and Mrs. Johnson and Texas's senior Senator, Ralph W. Yarborough, a Democrat.

The motorcade proceeded uneventfully along a 10-mile route through downtown Dallas, aiming for the Merchandise Mart. Mr. Kennedy was to address a group of the city's leading citizens at a luncheon in his honor.

In downtown Dallas, crowds were thick, enthusiastic and cheering. The turnout was somewhat unusual for this center of conservatism, where only a month ago Adlai E. Stevenson was attacked by a rightist crowd. It was also in Dallas, during the 1960 campaign, that Senator Lyndon B. Johnson and his wife were nearly mobbed in the lobby of the Baker Hotel.

As the motorcade neared its end and the President's car moved out of the thick crowds onto Stennonds Freeway near the Merchandise Mart, Mrs. Connally recalled later, "we were all very pleased with the reception in downtown Dallas."

Approaching 3-Street Underpass

Behind the three leading cars were a string of others carrying Texas and Dallas dignitaries, two buses of reporters, several open cars carrying photographers and other reporters, and a bus for White House staff members.

As Mrs. Connally recalled later, the President's car was almost ready to go underneath a "triple underpass" beneath three streets—Elm, Commerce and Main—when the first shot was fired.

That shot apparently struck Mr. Kennedy. Governor Connally turned in his seat at the sound and appeared immediately to be hit in the chest.

Mrs. Mary Norman of Dallas was standing at the curb and at that moment was aiming her camera at the President. She saw him slump forward, then slide down in the seat.

"My God," Mrs. Norman screamed, as she recalled it later, "he's shot!"

Mrs. Connally said that Mrs. Kennedy had reached and "grabbed" her husband. Mrs. Connally put her arms around the Governor. Mrs. Connally said that she and Mrs. Kennedy had then ducked low in the car as it sped off.

Mrs. Connally's recollections were reported by Julian Reade, an aide to the Governor.

Most reporters in the press buses were too far back to see the shootings, but they observed some quick scurrying by motor policemen accompanying the motorcade. It was noted that the President's car had picked up speed and raced away, but reporters were not aware that anything serious had occurred until they reached the Merchandise Mart two or three minutes later.

Rumors Spread at Trade Mart

Rumors of the shooting already were spreading through the luncheon crowd of hundreds, which was having the first course. No White House officials or Secret Service agents were present, but the reporters were taken quickly to Parkland Hospital on the strength of the rumors.

There they encountered Senator Yarborough, white, shaken and horrified.

The shots, he said, seemed to have come from the right and the rear of the car in which he was riding, the third in the motorcade. Another eyewitness, Mel Crouch, a Dallas television reporter, reported that as the shots rang out he saw a rifle extended and then withdrawn from a window on the "fifth or sixth floor" of the Texas Public School Book Depository. This is a leased state building on Elm Street, to the right of the motorcade route.

Senator Yarborough said there had been a slight pause between the first two shots and a longer pause between the second and third. A Secret Service man riding in the Senator's car, the Senator said, immediately ordered Mr. and Mrs. Johnson to get down below the level of the doors. They did so, and Senator Yarborough also got down.

The leading cars of the motorcade then pulled away at high speed toward Parkland Hospital, which was not far away, by the fast highway.

"We knew by the speed that something was terribly wrong," Senator Yarborough reported. When he put his head up, he said, he saw a Secret Service man in the car ahead beating his fists against the trunk deck of the car in which he was riding, apparently in frustration and anguish.

Mrs. Kennedy's Reaction

Only White House staff members spoke with Mrs. Kennedy. A Dallas medical student, David Edwards, saw her in Parkland Hospital while she was waiting for news of her husband. He gave this description:

"The look in her eyes was like an animal that had been trapped, like a little rabbit—brave, but fear was in the eyes."

Dr. Clark was reported to have informed Mrs. Kennedy of her husband's death.

No witnesses reported seeing or hearing any of the Secret Service agents or policemen fire back. One agent was seen to brandish a machine gun as the cars sped away. Mr. Crouch observed a policeman falling to the ground and pulling a weapon. But the events had occurred so quickly that there was apparently nothing for the men to shoot at.

Mr. Crouch said he saw two women, standing at a curb to watch the motorcade pass, fall to the ground when the shots rang out. He also saw a man snatch up his little girl and run along the road. Policemen, he said, immediately chased this man under the impression he had been involved in the shooting, but Mr. Crouch said he had been a fleeing spectator.

Mr. Kennedy's limousine—license No. GG300 under District of Columbia registry—pulled up at the emergency entrance of Parkland Hospital. Senator Yarborough said the President had been carried inside on a stretcher.

By the time reporters arrived at the hospital, the police were guarding the Presidential car closely. They would allow no one to approach it. A bucket of water stood by the car, suggesting that the back seat had been scrubbed out.

Robert Clark of the American Broadcasting Company, who had been riding near the front of the motorcade, said Mr. Kennedy was motionless when he was carried inside. There was a great amount of blood on Mr. Kennedy's suit and shirt-front and the front of his body, Mr. Clark said.

Mrs. Kennedy was leaning over her husband when the car stopped, Mr. Clark said, and walked beside the wheeled stretcher into the hospital. Mr. Connally sat with his hands holding his stomach, his head bent over. He, too, was moved into the hospital in a stretcher, with Mrs. Connally at his side.

Robert McNeill of the National Broadcasting Company, who also was in the reporters' pool car, jumped out at the scene of the shooting. He said the police had taken two eyewitnesses into custody—an 8-year-old Negro boy and a white man—for informational purposes.

Many of these reports could not be verified immediately.

Eyewitness Describes Shooting

An unidentified Dallas man, interviewed on television here, said he had been waving at the President when the shots were fired. His belief was that Mr. Kennedy had been struck twice—once, as Mrs. Norman recalled, when he slumped in his seat; again when he slid down in it.

"It seemed to just knock him down," the man said.

Governor Connally's condition was reported as "satisfactory" tonight after four hours in surgery at Parkland Hospital.

Dr. Robert R. Shaw, a thoracic surgeon, operated on the Governor to repair damage to his left chest.

Later, Dr. Shaw said Governor Connally had been hit in the back just below the shoulder blade, and that the bullet had gone completely through the Governor's chest, taking out part of the fifth rib.

After leaving the body, he said, the bullet struck the Governor's right wrist, causing a compound fracture. It then lodged in the left thigh.

The thigh wound, Dr. Shaw said, was trivial. He said the compound fracture would heal.

Dr. Shaw said it would be unwise for Governor Connally to be moved in the next 10 to 14 days. Mrs. Connally was remaining at his side tonight.

Tour by Mrs. Kennedy Unusual

Mrs. Kennedy's presence near her husband's bedside at his death resulted from somewhat unusual circumstances. She had rarely accompanied him on his trips about the country and had almost never made political trips with him.

The tour on which Mr. Kennedy was engaged yesterday and today was only quasi-political; the only open political activity was to have been a speech tonight to a fund-raising dinner at the state capitol in Austin.

In visiting Texas, Mr. Kennedy was seeking to improve his political fortunes in a pivotal state that he barely won in 1960. He was also hoping to patch a bitter internal dispute among Texas's Democrats.

At 8:45 A.M., when Mr. Kennedy left the Texas Hotel in Fort Worth, where he spent his last night, to address the parking lot crowd across the street, Mrs. Kennedy was not with him. There appeared to be some disappointment.

"Mrs. Kennedy is organizing herself," the President said good-naturedly. "It takes longer, but, of course, she looks better than we do when she does it."

Later, Mrs. Kennedy appeared late at the Chamber of Commerce breakfast in Fort Worth.

Again, Mr. Kennedy took note of her presence. "Two years ago," he said, "I introduced myself in Paris by saying that I was the man who had accompanied Mrs. Kennedy to Paris. I am getting somewhat that same sensation as I travel around Texas. Nobody wonders what Lyndon and I wear."

The speech Mr. Kennedy never delivered at the Merchandise Mart luncheon contained a passage commenting on a recent preoccupation of his, and a subject of much interest in this city, where right-wing conservatism is the rule rather than the exception.

Voices are being heard in the land, he said, "voices preaching doctrines wholly unrelated to reality, wholly unsuited to the sixties, doctrines which apparently assume that words will suffice without weapons, that vituperation is as good as victory and that peace is a sign of weakness."

The speech went on: "At a time when the national debt is steadily being reduced in terms of its burden on our economy, they see that debt as the greatest threat to our security. At a time when we are steadily reducing the number of Federal employees serving every thousand citizens, they fear those supposed hordes of civil servants far more than the actual hordes of opposing armies.

"We cannot expect that everyone, to use the phrase of a decade ago, will 'talk sense to the American people.' But we can hope that fewer people will listen to nonsense. And the notion that this nation is headed for defeat through deficit, or that strength is but a matter of slogans, is nothing but just plain nonsense."